TRADITIONS

AND

MEMORIES

OF

AMERICAN YACHTING

By

William P. Stephens

Reprinted from

MotorBoating

Hearst Magazines, Inc.
572 Madison Avenue
New York 22, N. Y.

MoToR BoatinG
Hearst Magazines, Inc.
New York 22, N. Y.

TRADITIONS AND MEMORIES OF AMERICAN YACHTING

Contents

PREFACE

In offering this book to my fellow yachtsmen I feel that a few words of explanation or excuse are necessary: first, for the absence of that formal style which is usually found in the recording of serious history; and, secondly, for the lack of chronological order.

Several years ago Mr. Chapman said to me "I hear you speak at yachting meetings telling yachtsmen of their fathers and grandfathers and the yachts which they owned; would you not like to write something of this kind for MoToR BoatinG?" The idea appealed to me and I started, perhaps too hastily, with no realization of the length to which the yarn would run, and with no definite plan for an extended history.

The method of narration which suggested itself as the most fitting is that pursued by yachtsmen about the fire in winter and afloat or on the club porch in the season—reminiscent, discursive, argumentative, often wandering from the immediate subject. While this may be open to criticism from a strictly literary point of view, the many comments which have come to me indicate that it has met the approval of readers.

Starting as a matter of course with the first yachting about New York, and the yacht America, a close study of old records became necessary; the further this was followed, the more fascinating it became. My own views of yachting have broadened materially; I have been led to live as far as possible in the past, and many periods and events which once seemed isolated and disconnected have revealed themselves as intimately related elements of a great whole. The complete field of yachting is so vast in extent that the story has outgrown the national limits of its title, but I believe that the yachtsman of today is interested not only in his own yacht and his own club, but in the sport in both its historical and technical aspects, and especially in those details of design and construction which were once sealed books to him.

W. P. Stephens

TRADITIONS AND MEMORIES OF AMERICAN YACHTING

Part One

By WILLIAM P. STEPHENS

THE GENESIS OF AMERICAN YACHTING

A recent photograph of W. P. Stephens actively at work computing areas with a planimeter

THE origin and early growth of American yachting date back to a period when the followers of the sport were few in number, widely scattered, and the sport itself so limited and inconspicuous as to receive little attention from the press. In view of such conditions it is a difficult matter to piece out a continuous and consecutive narrative, and much must be left to inference and conjecture. While a few exceptional events, such as the organization of the New York Yacht Club and the victory of the America, were exploited at length in the daily press, it was not until the end of the Rebellion that yachting began to share the publicity accorded to older and more generally popular sports.

The first official summary of yachting is found in a modest little booklet, Fox's Yachting Annual for 1872, published by Edward Fox, the first American yacht broker, at 83 Nassau Street, New York. The List of Yacht Clubs includes a total of 24, which (with those marked #, which were not listed) are as follows:—The clubs in the New York district are marked "N. Y."; those in the Boston district "B."

New York	N. Y.	1844	San Francisco		1867
#Southern		1859	Columbia	N. Y.	1867
Carolina, N. C.		1854	#Savannah, Ga.		1867
#Hoboken	N. Y.	1856	South Boston	B	1868
Brooklyn	N. Y.	1857	Lynn	B	1868
Jersey City	N. Y.	1858	Portland, Me.		1869
*Union, L. I.	N. Y.	1864	Oceanic	N. Y.	1869
Boston	B	1865	Bunker Hill	B	1869
#Ione	N. Y.	1865	#Pavonia	N. Y.	1869
Atlantic	N. Y.	1866	#Williamsburg	N. Y.	1869
Eastern	B	1870	#Madison, Wis.		1871
Dorchester	B	1870	Beverly	B	1872
Manhattan	N. Y.	1870	#St. Augustine, Fla.		1872
Stapleton	N. Y.	1870	Bayonne	N. Y.	187?
#Oshkosh, Wis.		1870	Crescent City, Miss.		18??
Seawanhaka	N. Y.	1871	Pensacola, Fla.		18??
New Jersey	N. Y.	1871			

Special mention should be made of the Royal Canadian Y. C., 1852, and the Royal Halifax Y. C., 1857.

* Changed to Long Island Y. C., 1872.

The process of organization of most of the small clubs seems to have followed this course: half a dozen or so owners of small yachts in the same locality sailing individually, met on the water, informal trials of speed followed as a matter of course, then set matches, backed by a small stake, were made between two rival owners;

ultimately all hands came together in a set meeting and a permanent organization was formed.

The origin of the New York Yacht Club is too well known to call for repetition; the formation of the second yacht club, in a remote locality, seems to have been a matter of chance. In 1849 The Stingaree Club, a social organization in New Orleans, purchased for the use of its members the cabin sloop Eliza Riddle, 32 feet; following a race of twelve yachts off Pass Christian on July 20, 1859 in which Eliza Riddle and Stingaree took part, the Southern Y. C. was organized. The Carolina Y. C., with only a slightly shorter record of longevity, has never figured prominently outside of its immediate locality.

The influence of the War of the Rebellion, beginning in 1861, and continuing to 1865, is plainly shown in the above list; the general organization of yacht clubs, begun by the Brooklyn, Jersey City and Hoboken clubs, was stopped abruptly; not to be resumed until the final year of the War, after which it proceeded rapidly.

A study of Mr. Fox's book, which is most interesting in containing the names of yacht builders, sailmakers and yachtsmen now almost forgotten by even the older generation, shows a total of 401 yachts listed, of which seven were steam craft. Taking 35 feet waterline as the dividing line between cabin and open yachts, there were 100 above this limit. A large proportion of these were the great schooners which made so much yachting history through trans-Atlantic passages and international races in the decade following 1865. The number of cabin cruising yachts of moderate size was small, and the yachtsmen of the day may be divided into two classes:—a small number of wealthy sportsmen who cruised and raced in large schooners, and a much larger number of men of modest means who sailed and raced a large fleet of open sandbag boats. The small fleet of cabin yachts of 35 to 45 feet (mainly sloops about New York) included East of Cape Cod many schooners and a large proportion of keel yachts; keel craft of deep body, and the schooner rig even on very small yachts, being popular; though unknown about New York and Long Island Sound.

Among the builders listed (the yacht designer was unknown in those days) we find names which indicate clearly the size and type of yacht:—David Kirby, J. B. Van Deusen, C. & R. Poillon, James Lennox, Samuel Pine, George Steers, C. H. Mallory, R. F. Loper and David Carll stand for the largest yachts; almost exclusively schooners. The names of J. B. Herreshoff of Bristol, Allan Hay of Lynn, and Pierce Bros. of South Boston are associated with much smaller craft; keel, keel-centerboard, many schooner-rigged. The names greatly in the majority are Smedley, McGiehan, Bates, Schmidt, Snellgrove, Force, Mumm and Wallin; the modellers and builders of a great fleet of sandbag boats from 16 to 32 feet; with a relatively small number of cabin yachts, all centerboard. Equally famous in both classes was Captain Bob Fish, modeller, builder, improver and skipper of some of the largest yachts; and at the same time equally expert as a modeller, builder and handler of sandbag craft.

W. P. Stephens, in the uniform of the New York Canoe Club, photographed in August, 1885

As to ownership, the major division of this primitive fleet rested with men of wealth and leisure who, as a class, were no more interested in yachting than in a wide range of sports. Following the return of peace came a period of wide-spread popular interest in sports, old and new. The turf claimed many, prominent in his day being John C. Stevens; hunting and trap-shooting were popular. Cricket was better known than today, and a new game, baseball, was played generally, not as a professional sport, but every little town and village had its diamond, with the leading men of the town as patrons if not participants. Rowing as an amateur sport, now extinct save in the colleges, was at the height of its popularity in the seventies; not beneath the participation of professional men of high standing. Athletic sports of all kinds were coming into fashion, especially pedestrianism, both amateur and professional; on the less strenuous side was croquet, recently imported from England and for some years enjoying wide-spread popularity. The owners of the large yachts, as a class, were interested in many of these sports, at least as spectators if not participants. Jim Bennett, an athlete in his early days, once walked on a wager from the old Herald office near the City Hall to Jerome Park. Devoted as they were to schooner racing, the Lorillards, the Osgoods, and Willie Douglass, owner of Sappho, had many other interests.

In the smaller and much more numerous division were no names to be found in the Social Register had one existed in those days. Both owners and crews of the sandbaggers were men of very moderate means, very often workers about the water, ship and yacht builders, or mechanics in less nautical trades but keenly interested in boat-sailing. As the rivalry was very keen, some wealthy men owned these boats just as they might a race horse, hiring a professional water-jockey to sail them and a paid crew to sling sandbags, while they looked on from the shore and made their bets.

Between these two distinct and widely separated classes of yachts and yachtsmen there was no middle ground for the man of moderate means who wished to own a yacht with one or two paid hands, aboard which he might cruise and indulge in an occasional race. As for the boy with limited pocket money and a nautical taste, there was no place for him. Save for an occasional berth as bilge-boy he was not wanted on a sandbagger, where only beef, brawn and muscle counted; and until the advent of the canoe, aptly termed the poor man's yacht, in the middle seventies, the individual ownership and command of anything other than a bateau or a Whitehall boat with a small sail was out of the question.

The dominating factor in the development of yacht design in other than the largest classes was the locale available to the yachtsman. For the large yacht with a full crew and an anchor watch the question of anchorage or mooring ground was of minor importance, there was deep water in plenty about New York and Boston for yachts in company with general shipping. With the small craft, however, it was a different matter; there were few clubs affording mooring and landing facilities. The waterfront of New York Harbor, however, provided space in plenty for free moorings on the miles of mud flats found within a wide range of the city proper. There were shoal coves on the North and East River fronts and the Harlem River, a large area at Hoboken, another at Communipaw just below Jersey City, and another still further down at Saltersville, later known as Pamrapo and now Bayonne. Even the higher shores of Staten Island offered shelter in small bays, and there was almost unlimited mud along the Brooklyn and Long Island shores even below the Narrows. These mud flats were but waste, of no use to anyone but the owner of a shoal yacht, who was free to moor where he pleased. Where a yacht of even five or six feet draft would have required a protected basin on deep water, the centerboard boat of but two feet draft was safe from traffic and fully provided for, even though she might lie on the mud for nearly half the time.

ALL that was now needed was a foothold on shore for a dinghy and a landing float, and these were provided by a waterside pub. This popular institution provided, in default of a yacht club, shore shelter, landing facilities and social intercourse, while mine host was at least an enthusiastic sailor if not a builder as well. Such was the Idle Hour at Saltersville; another Idle Hour at Factoryville now West Brighton, on the Staten Island shore of the Kill von Kull; Jake Schmidt's saloon at Tompkinsville on the East Shore of the Island, Garrison's Inn on Little Bay just West of Fort Totten at the entrance to Long Island Sound, Crocheron Inn around the corner and up Little Neck Bay, with many similar oases about New Rochelle on the North Shore of the Sound, and on Cow Bay, now more politely known as Manhasset Bay.

Most famous of all such localities was that known in the familiar parlance of the sixties and seventies as Foot-o'Court-Street, a no-man's-land on the lower Brooklyn shore. Here was Gowanus Bay, to yachtsmen the Gowanus Flats, an area of about a square mile, on to which debouched Gowanus Creek, a Stygian and unsavory stream, spanned at Hamilton Avenue, near its mouth, by a wooden bridge; one of the many Penny Bridges about New York. The presiding deity of this locality was Hen Smedley, who shared with Neef Willis on Cow Bay, Jake Schmidt at Tompkinsville and Pat McGiehan at Saltersville the honor of being the best modeller, builder, and handler of a sandbag boat. The Smedley boats were known far and wide as Penny Bridge boats.

On the still marshy but more solid ground along the mouth of Gowanus Creek, bordering the soft, oozy Flats, were saloons and boat houses; here was Smedley's shop and Frank Bates' shop and saloon, Dick Wallin also had a boatshop and John Mumm was located here at one time; he and Dick, the latter with his pardner migrating to Bay Ridge as the Flats were dredged and piers and warehouses erected. Perched on piles, with duckwalks leading to floats, were first the Brooklyn Yacht Club, later, after a division, the Atlantic Yacht Club, and the Union, later the Long Island Yacht Club.

While the shoal-draft sloop or catboat (the hull being identical under both rigs) is distinctly an American institution, it is impossible today to say when and how it originated, it is apparently a spontaneous growth called forth by certain needs and certain fixed conditions. The one fixed date in its history, and that not so remote, is 1853; when Earl Mount Charles, visiting Capt. Bob Fish's shop at Saltersville, saw and purchased a 16-foot catboat, which he named Una and shipped to England; thus introducing the type and giving it what has since become the generic name abroad, Una boat. It is probable that the type was first developed, for fishing and working use, as best adapted to the conditions found along the entire Atlantic seaboard; shoal waters both for sailing and mooring. As trials of speed were inevitable even among fishing and working boats, the adaptability of the type for racing was soon appreciated; the racing, at first accidental and informal, took more definite shape, and efforts were made to develop speed above all other qualities. At least a century ago a very fast craft had been developed, under the cat rig (a single mainsail) and the jib-'n' mainsail (sloop); and formal racing became popular even before the organization of yacht clubs.

FOR about a third of a century, from the fifties into the eighties, sandbag racing figured as one of the most popular branches of American yachting; the names of Bob Fish, Pat McGiehan, Hen Smedley, Jake Schmidt, Neef Willis and Buckshot Roahr as they were popularly known to their partizans being as well known as those of Burgess, Paine, Herreshoff, Nicholson and Fife are to the yachtsmen of today. Going further in the line of conjecture, it is probable that the establishment of yachting in a few isolated points in the South, New Orleans, Wilmington, N. C., Pensacola, Fla. and Charleston, was due less to an interest in the sport of itself than to the facts that the speed of the sandbag boats, many of the best being imported from the North at times, appealed to the sporting instincts of Southern yachtsmen; and the shoal draft was specially suited to local conditions.

The victory of the schooner America in 1851, while hailed widely as a triumph of Brother Johnathan over John Bull, had no influence at home in awakening public interest in a little-known sport; in the years immediately succeeding, the attention of the entire nation was centered first on the discussion of the slavery question and then on a bitterly fought war. The great ocean race of 1866, exciting as it proved to be, was after all a purely domestic affair; the outgrowth of a good dinner and good wine. Three years later the international side of yachting came to the fore through the challenge of an English yachtsman for the cup won by the America, resulting in two matches in which the defender was successful. In addition, each match was followed by a prolonged and acrimonious dispute, in which the challenger, in spite of his argumentative disposition, was by no means entirely in the wrong. For over two years, 1870-71, yachting received through the American press an amount of publicity far in excess of all previously known; and to this gratuitous advertising may be ascribed the activity shown in the organization of yacht clubs in the first half of the seventies.

The beginning of yachting in the larger classes was sporadic and irregular, depending entirely on individual effort. The first yacht of which there is any definite record was the sloop Jefferson, 22 tons, built in 1801 for George Crowninshield, of Salem, Mass. The Crowninshield family, merchant sailors engaged for generations in the East India trade, were wedded to the sea; the boys of each generation being sent to sea on the family ships at the age of twelve. George, born in 1766, thus served, working his way up at sea before taking his place ashore in the firm. The Jefferson was built for his use as a yacht, but in the War of 1812 she was commissioned as a privateer, and three years later was sold for fishing.

In her place was built a larger yacht, a brigantine of 191 tons, modelled after one of the Crowninshield trading ships, and bearing the unusual name of Cleopatra's Barge. In addition to being in every respect a seagoing vessel, she was most luxuriously equipped in furniture, china, glassware, as a fitting home for a wealthy sailor; and she was used as such for two years, Captain Crowninshield dying suddenly at the end of 1817. During this time he lived aboard her, whether wintering in Salem harbor or cruising in the Mediterranean; after his death she was converted to a merchant vessel. Interesting as is this incident, it had no effect in the promotion of yachting in America.

THE introduction of yachting about New York was due to the Stevens family, father and four sons, of Hoboken, N. J.; in no way associated with the sea, but notable as experimenters, inventors, and pioneers in transportation both by steamboat and rail. While Robert was closely associated with his father in many inventions, in the building of river steamboats and railroads and the Stevens Battery, an experimental warship; John, born in 1785, was the sportsman of the family, interested in horse racing, cricket and general field sports. Separated from the city by the Hudson River, with no public ferries, the Stevens boys relied on their own boats and own skill for visits to the metropolis; and John, above all the others, found his pleasure largely on the water. In 1809 he owned a 20-foot sailboat, Diver; in 1816 he built Trouble, a periagua 56 feet in length; in 1820 he built a catamaran, Double Trouble, apparently well named, as she was not a success. In 1832 he had built by Bell & Brown, New York shipbuilders, a schooner of 65-foot length, Wave; following her in 1839 by a schooner Onkahie, 91 feet waterline and 250 tons; and in 1844 by the schooner Gimcrack, 49 feet waterline, aboard which craft the New York Yacht Club was formally organized on July 30 of the same year.

Here is a continuous record of progressive yacht building, presumably the earliest; from about 1830 on a few other yachts were built for New York and Boston owners. As eight yachts were represented at the inaugural meeting, it is evident that the sport had made material progress in the decade immediately preceding. The early patrons were partly from old sea-going families, the Peabodys, Crowninshields and Forbes in Boston and the Grinnells, Minturns, Bells, Aspinwalls, Marshalls, Griswolds and Kingslands of New York; the Mallorys of Mystic, the Palmers of Stonington, and the Lopers of Stonington and Philadelphia. Another class not distinctly of the sea was well represented by John C. and Edwin A. Stevens, interested in yachting in its two phases, sailing for pleasure and the technical side of yacht architecture; added to these was a largely non-nautical element of society men. The growth of yachting in its early years may be gauged by the roll of the New York Y. C. fleet at the outbreak of the Rebellion: 21 schooners and 24 sloops.

TRADITIONS AND MEMORIES

OF

American Yachting

By WILLIAM P. STEPHENS

Part Two: AMERICA ON THE SEAS

A POINT of more than general interest, though it seems to have escaped the notice of the many who have written on American yachting history, is that its first growth, while still in its infancy, was not in home waters but in trans-Atlantic voyages and races. Accidental as this movement was, its results were highly beneficial—the prestige of American yachtsmen was greatly increased, both abroad and at home. Furthermore, the publicity given to these international events in the home newspapers did much to advertise and popularize a new and little-known sport.

Accepting the technical definition of a yacht as a vessel designed, built or adapted for pleasure use, as distinguished from commerce and war, it is still difficult to draw the line between vessels of the early days. From time immemorial vessels of state have been used for both the convenience and pleasure of rulers; such "jaghts" were used, both officially and privately, by the burgomasters of Holland in the sixteenth century, and it is probable that similar craft were used about Nieuw Amsterdam in its early days. The first purely pleasure craft mentioned in American history is the sloop Fancy, built in 1717 for Col. Lewis Morris, after whom Morrisania was named. After a gap of almost a century we come to the two Crowninshield yachts described last month; and those of the Stevens family. Apart from the yachts as owned by the two yachting members, John C. and Edwin A. Stevens, was Maria, a sloop of 92 feet l.w.l., built in 1844 by William H. Capes, of Hoboken, under the direction of Robert L. Stevens, the inventor and scientist of the family. She was a remarkable craft in many ways with a padding of lead outside her bottom planking, two centerbords, the larger forward one raised and lowered by chains at each end in place of the usual pin and tackle, a crosscut mainsail, a hollow boom, and a streamlined mast.

AMERICA

As a maker of yachting history, both national and international, a turning point in yacht design, and a stimulus to the sport on both sides of the Atlantic, the schooner America stands out prominently; even in comparison with the speedy, costly and useless toys identified today by the lubberly and meaningless term of "Jay Boats." No other yacht has been so studied and written of; and yet, while there was no attempt at secrecy, no locked doors and soaped windows, but everything open in her building and racing, she is today in many ways a mystery ship. All the salient points in her long history are known, and yet there are many important questions still unsolved.

The inspiration for her construction came in a letter suggesting that, as New York was famous for her pilot boats, a sample craft should be sent to England on the occasion of the first great World's Fair, the Crystal Palace of 1851. This letter has disappeared, its writer and recipient being both unknown. All that is known is that it came into the hands of George L. Schuyler, a member of the New York Y. C. and an intimate of the Stevens brothers who, with Mr. Schuyler and three associates, formed a syndicate to carry out the suggestion. The work of modelling and construction was entrusted to George Steers, an American by birth though the son

Reproduction of an illustration, 1851, showing the schooner America making a start ahead of competitors at Royal Yacht Squadron regatta at Cowes

Construction of the schooner America in a yard at 12th Street and East River, New York, 1851, under the direction of George Steers

The sloop Sylvie, built about the same time, which had an interesting career under several owners

of an English shipwright, who had been closely associated with John C. Stevens. While Steers had been in business for himself, the yacht was built in the yard of another builder, William H. Brown, who was the contractor. As Steers was the moving force in both design and actual building, we are left to conjecture as to their exact relations. The answer seems to be that Steers had been obliged to close his yard on account of financial troubles, and consequently could not make a contract under his own name.

Prior to 1849 the yachts of both America and England were modelled on the "cod's head and mackerel's tail" principle; the midship section, or point of greatest breadth, being about one-third the length from the stem; the entrance thus being very round and full, while the two-thirds of after-body or run gave a long, clean delivery. In that year George Steers modelled and built the pilot boat Mary Taylor (named after a favorite New York singer and actress) with a long, hollow entrance and a relatively short run; in marked contrast to all his previous practice. Why he thus went contrary to all established ideas on both sides of the Atlantic is another question to which there is no answer.

By way of conjecture we may turn to the close relationship in yachting between George Steers and the Stevens family. Col. John Stevens and his four sons were originators and inventors in many lines; railroads, steamships and yachts, and they were in close touch with technical progress abroad. The abstract investigations of John Scott Russell, the great scientist, in the flow of water around submerged bodies, carried out about 1840, were widely published. While John C. and Edwin A. Stevens were the sportsmen of the family, interested in horse racing and field sports as well as yachting, another brother, Robert L., worked with his father in developing both railroads and steamboats. It is quite probable that they knew of the experiments of John Scott Russell and were directly interested in them as affecting the modeling of steamboats. The design of the sloop Maria is attributed to Robert L. Stevens, following the general form of the North River trading sloops; full forward and fine aft. Built in 1845, she was lengthened in 1850 by an addition of 18 feet to her bow. It thus seems probable that this lengthening was due to the theories of Scott Russell and ultimately led to the change of form so noticeable in Mary Taylor and America.

The victory of America against the fleet of the Royal Yacht Squadron, though in reality a fluke over a notoriously unfair course, had its sensational side and turned the attention of British yachtsmen to her fine bow. Alterations along this line were made in the home fleet, new bows on old yachts and a radical change of model in new ones; just as, forty years later, ancient tubs were renovated with the Gloriana bow, even the Cape catboat, a distinct type, falling a victim to the craze.

Sold twice in England, America, under a new name, Camilla, was laid up at Pitcher's Yard, Northfleet, on the Thames, and neglected by her owner. She developed dry rot and was purchased by Pitcher, who took her apart, timber by timber, in times when work was slack, and rebuilt her with frames of English oak and planking of teak. As her masts were rotten in the step they were cut down, five and six feet. She was finally purchased by a Henry E. Decie (sometimes spelled Deasy) an Englishman of whom little is known. What is known is that he took her to Richmond and Savannah in the winter of 1860-61, and was in the latter city as the outbreak of the Rebellion neared, being entertained by prominent Southerners. When he sailed for home on May 25, 1861 he carried four passengers as guests, Lt. James H. North, U.S.N., and Capt. E. R. Anderson, U.S.A., who had just resigned to accept the ranks of captain and major respectively under the new Confederate Government. Captain North was accompanied by his wife and daughter. The mission of these two gentlemen was similar to that of Mason and Slidell, but technical rather than diplomatic—the inspection of arms, vessels and munitions for the new Confederate States. On August

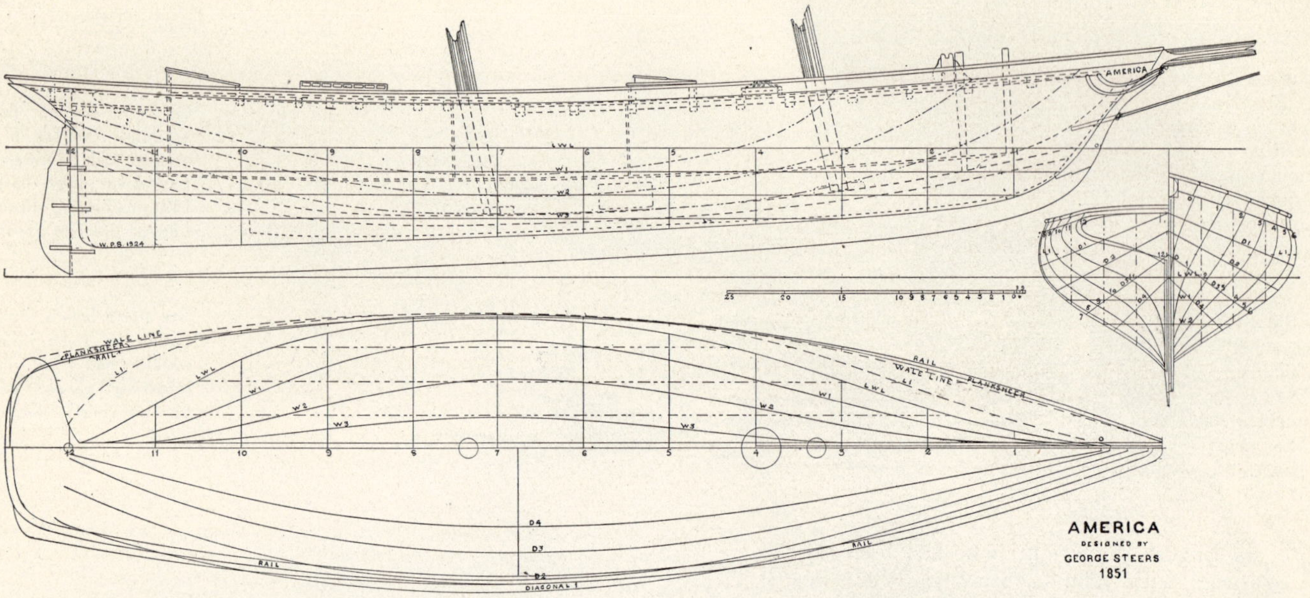

Lines of two early American yachts built about the same time. Above, America, which is well known; and, below, Sylvie, of the centerboard type, but with the same hollow bow as America, in contrast with all the earlier Steers sloops

17, 1861, Mr. Decie landed the Norths at Cherbourg and disappeared from the scene. A long and thorough search in recent years has failed to disclose anything more of his origin, identity, or his relations with the South—a mystery that may never be solved.

Here follows another blank, until March 13, 1862, when the yacht was discovered by Lt. S. H. Stevens, U.S.N., sunk in the St. Johns River 70 miles above Jacksonville, Florida, in three fathoms with only her port rail above water. After the failure of various efforts to raise her by mechanical means, a diver was sent down, three augur holes were plugged, she was pumped free and rose herself. Where she was, and what she did, between August 17, 1861 and March 13, 1862 is another unsolved riddle. She was turned over in some way by Mr. Decie to his Savannah friends; there is an unverified report that her name was changed from Camilla to Memphis. She was undoubtedly running the blockade, carrying despatches and medical stores, as she had no room for bulky cargo. The records of her various transfers, from the original syndicate to Sir John de Blaquière, from him to Lord Templetown, then to Henry Sotheby Pitcher and again to Henry E. Decie, are on file; the records of the U. S. and Confederate navies show nothing, and the story ends. On a summer night in Marblehead Harbor, nearly fifty years ago, sitting in the cockpit of the old yacht, I heard from General Benjamin F. Butler, in picturesque and highly characteristic language, the story of his "purchase" of the yacht from the U. S. Government, but he mentioned only one principal, Lucius Quintus Curtius Lamar, a resident of Savannah, prominent in the Rebellion; and in the General's phraseology, "thanks to the Amnesty Proclamation, washed until he was whiter than snow." Resting now in inglorious ease in her berth at Annapolis, the old yacht has back of her a history that may never be equalled in romance, variety and incident.

SYLVIE

In the winter of 1850-1 another yacht was built by William H. Brown in co-operation with George Steers; to all appearances, on speculation. She was a centerboard sloop, similar in general type to the other Steers yachts, except that in her he carried the hollow bow of Mary Taylor and America a step further, with a new extreme of breadth and of very light draft. This yacht, when launched in July 1851, was named Mayflower in her register, with William H. Brown as owner; but in April 1852 George L. and Robert Schuyler were recorded as owners, and the former as

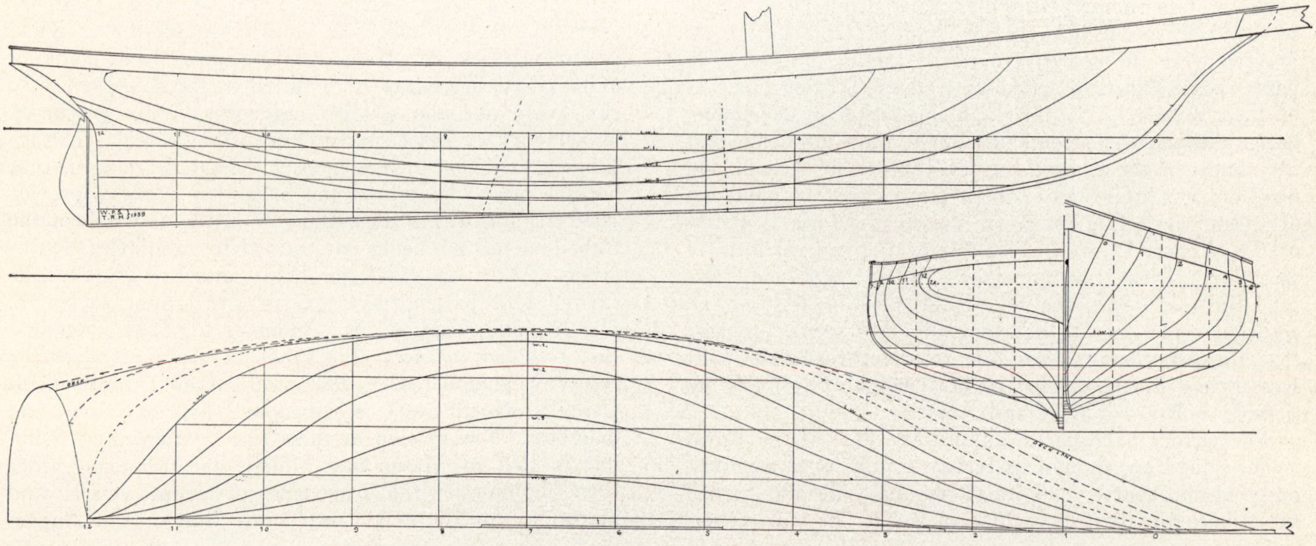

master. Here, again, we are all at sea, and must resort to conjecture as to the mutual relations of Steers, Brown, Schuyler and the Stevens brothers. It would seem that George Steers was intent on a further experiment in the application of the ideas embodied in the keel schooner America to a centerboard sloop of truly national type; and that in this he was backed by Brown, Schuyler, and possibly the Stevens brothers as well. There is no mention in the records of the New York Y. C. of the sloop Mayflower; she first appears, under the name of Sylvie, in the yearbook of 1853, under the ownership of Louis A. Depau. It is probable that the official record of the Schuylers as owners was made at this time in clearing up the title preparatory to the sale to Mr. Depau. His interest was, shortly after, transferred to Mortimer Livingston, a brother-in-law, not a yachtsman, the name of the yacht appearing as Silvie; though the original Mayflower was carried on the Government records until 1867.

The new owner, Louis Augustus Depau (sometimes spelled Depaw) was the son of Francis Depau, of New York; who married Sylvie, daughter of the French Admiral Count de Grasse, who figures in our Revolutionary history. In 1822 Francis Depau founded the first line of sailing packets between New York and Havre. One of his later vessels, the Sylvie De Grasse, was the third ship to round Cape Horn in 1848, at the beginning of the California gold rush. The family home was on Depau's Island, now Glen Island, off New Rochelle, the old mansion standing until destroyed by fire only a few years ago. The name appears in various forms: Sylvie, Silvie, Sylvia, Silvia and even Sylva. One of the original members of the club from its initial meeting in 1844, Louis Depau in 1846 owned the sloop Mist.

THE racing career of Sylvie began with her new ownership, her record in her first season being as follows; premising that the fleet of that era was small in numbers, and yachts of different rigs and classes raced together. The tonnage of the yachts mentioned in this narrative is usually omitted for the reason that it was computed in different ways at different times, and has no real meaning without special explanation. In the race of June 3, 1852, Sylvie, 68 tons, finished at 3:21:43; Ultra, slp., 72 tons, at 3:26:31; Una, slp., 54 tons, 3:36:48; Sport and Alpha, "far astern"; Cornelia, not timed. The race of June 4 failed for lack of wind; in that of June 7 Sylvie finished, Sport, Cornelia and Alpha not timed; on June 9 Sylvie was timed at 5:35:30, with Cornelia, Sport and Alpha not timed. As far as these races in very light weather show, Sylvie was a fast yacht.

In studying these old racing records one is apt to be confused by the contradictory rigs—sometimes sloop, sometimes schooner. In the days of the old hit-or-miss methods of the Rule-o'-Thumb modellers it happened only too frequently that a yacht built as a sloop proved so unsatisfactory on trial that alterations were made to her hull, and when these failed she was re-rigged as a schooner; being finally sold for fishing service or for a pilot boat. A conspicuous instance of this is found in the famous schooner Magic, originally the sloop Madgie (1) and finally ending as a fishing vessel in Florida; though in the long interval she made a great reputation as a fast schooner. Among the many thus converted for one reason or another were Madgie (2); Rebecca, Julia, Maria, Ray, Eva and Madeleine.

With the home record given above, Sylvie sailed from Depau Island on June 11, 1853, with Captain Peter H. Comstock, a New York pilot and yacht captain, in charge, her destination being Havre. There is some confusion of dates here, but she is generally credited with the exceptionally fast passage of 16 days, 12 hours. Mr. Depau made the passage on the steamer Humboldt and joined the yacht at Havre; where her racing spars, shipped by steamer, were set up, and she crossed to Cowes. On Friday, August 19, there was a race of the Royal Yacht Squadron, open to foreign yachts, the first prize being of the value of £100; Sylvie entered against Arrow, Aurora, Alarm, Osprey; a new Swedish schooner, Aurora Borealis; and Julia, a new cutter designed and built by Michael Ratsey. The course was from a start off Cowes to the eastward to the Nab Buoy, thence 18 miles to windward and return to the Nab. As in the case of America's race, the wind was variable and fluky and gave no fair test; Julia won, with Sylvia only 6 minutes 38 seconds astern. As a recognition of this performance the Squadron presented Sylvie with a special prize; a silver cup of the value of 50 guineas.

PREMISING that the many "Queen's Cups" presented by Queen Victoria from 1838 down were open only to yachts enrolled in the Royal Yacht Squadron or other British clubs, it may be noted that the special 100-Guinea Cup won by America in 1851 was for many years known in this country as a Queens Cup, this title being used almost exclusively in the numerous reports of the first matches of 1870-1. The subsequent history of the Sylvie Cup, romantic as it is, has no part in this story. The trophy, still in active competition, has recently been the subject of much exhaustive study by T. R. Hedegren, a Finnish yachtsman long resident in America, who has unearthed much that is new and important concerning the yacht and the Depau family.

Not satisfied with this one race, Mr. Depau made several efforts for other matches, but nothing came of them; and on September 6 he started on a cruise to the Baltic and the Gulf of Finland; on his return to Cowes the yacht was laid up at Croskey & Sons Yard, Southampton, where she rested until 1856, when she sailed back to New York; losing boom and bowspirit and almost losing her mast in a rough passage of 34 days. Shortly after this she was purchased by C. A. Stebbins, a member of the New York Y. C., who, in the following year, converted her to a schooner. Under the new rig and many successive owners she had a long and honorable career, being broken up in 1906.

MAYFLOWER—SYLVIE—SILVIE

THE lines reproduced have been drawn from the best information obtainable today. In the early days of yachting little attention was paid to dimensions, the universal unit being tonnage: "Old," "New," "Carpenters,'" etc., in this country and similarly different forms in Great Britain. It was not until 1872 that the New York Yacht club published the dimensions of yachts in its Year Book. Prior to 1887 "Manning's Yacht List" gave only the names of the builders, ignoring the designers, in all early records the term "modeller" was employed, that of designer being unknown.

Many of the old half-models were made to the outside of the frames and the inside of the planking, and it is often impossible to say which method was used. It was a common practice to make the lifts of models parallel with the bottom of the keel and not with the load waterline, the waterlines thus shown in the model being very different from the true waterlines shown in modern designs. These lines have been very carefully drawn with the above facts in view, and it is believed that they are practically correct. One of the spline weights used in this work was once the property of George Steers, and has his name stamped on the bottom.

The dimensions are: length over all, 80 feet; load waterline, 68 feet; breadth, 24 feet 6 inches; draft, 6 feet.

THE SILVIE CUP

THE prizes in the race of the Royal Yacht Squadron on August 19, 1853, were a cup of the value of 100 guineas, and one of the value of 50 guineas. The former was won by the British cutter Julia, the second prize going to the American sloop Silvie. Neither prize was a Queens Cup, and no American yacht has ever won a Queen's Cup. The trophy won by Silvie was brought to New York by Louis A. Depau and no trace of it is to be found until 1874, when it was presented by Joseph H. Godwin of New York through Commodore K. C. Barker of the International Yacht Club of Detroit as an international challenge cup, to be known as the Godwin Cup. In course of time the International Yacht Club was disbanded and the cup disappeared, not being found until 1898, when it was given to the South Shore Yacht Club of Milwaukee as a perpetual international challenge trophy for yachts of the Great Lakes.

The various hall marks on the cup show that it was made by R. & G. Garrard, London, makers of the America's Cup, and in 1847-8; or five or six years before it was won by Silvie. As shown in the cut, the cup bears the inscription Queen's Cup; when or by whom this marking was made is unknown, but it is certain that Silvie never won a Queen's Cup.

TRADITIONS AND MEMORIES OF AMERICAN YACHTING

Part Three

AMERICA ON THE SEAS

By *WILLIAM P. STEPHENS*

EARLY EXPLOITS—VISION—RED, WHITE AND BLUE

AMPLE proof has been given in recent years that size and seagoing qualities are in no way essential in trans-Atlantic passages, or even in the circumnavigation of the globe; provided the adventurer is sufficiently ignorant of the nature of the sea, its dangers, and what is required in a vessel which would combat them. Ventures of this kind are so frequent today as to have become commonplace, but some of the earliest are at least worthy of note. One of the first attempts recorded is that of the brigantine Vision, built by one John C. Donovan. She was 16 feet over all; 4 feet 10 inches breadth, and 2 feet 9 inches depth. On June 26, 1864, she sailed from the Battery in New York for Liverpool, Captain Donovan being accompanied by a friend and his dog, Toby. On July 5 she put in to Boston, leaking. After repairs she made a new start and never was heard of again.

Following Vision was the ship Red White and Blue, which sailed from New York on July 9, 1866, and arrived at Margate, England, on August 16 after a passage of 34 days to the chops of the Channel and 39 days to Margate. This vessel was an Ingersoll lifeboat, of galvanized iron; 26 feet over all, 6 feet 1 inch breadth of beam, 2 feet 8 inches depth of hold; 2.38 tons. The crew included Captain J. M. Hudson and a friend, Francis E. Fitch, with a dog, Fanny. The voyage was marked by continual bad weather, the decks leaked and spoiled the stores, the signal lamp was lost at the start, the chronometer (a common watch) stopped from rust; three times she was thrown on her beam-ends; and as a final tragedy, poor Fanny died as they were nearing Gravesend for a triumphant entry. Having been exhibited at the fair of the American Institute in New York in 1865, the object of the voyage was to exhibit at the Paris Exhibition of 1867. Another venture, of which the details are lacking, is that of a schooner 24 feet 6 inches over all, 7 feet breadth, and 2 feet 4 inches depth which sailed from Baltimore for Havre in 1867 and never was heard of again.

ALICE

A notable venture for its day was the voyage of the sloop Alice, of Boston, in European waters in 1866. Built in that year at Portsmouth, N. H., Alice, with a plumb stem, was 66 feet over all, 59 feet 9 inches waterline, 17 feet 6 inches breadth, 6 feet 3 inches depth of hold,

Above: The 16-foot brigantine Vision, Captain Donovan leaving New York for Liverpool, June 26, 1864. Left: Another miniature ship, Red, White and Blue, 1866.

and 6 feet 4 inches draft. Though always mentioned as a sloop, she had a double headrig, with the very high mast and short topmast of the old sloops. Her owner, Thomas G. Appleton, a wealthy Boston yachtsman, desired to cruise abroad, so the yacht was sent to Cowes under the command of Captain Arthur H. Clark, then in his twenty-fifth year. With him were Charles Appleton Longfellow, the son of the poet, and Harry Stanfield of New York. With a crew of

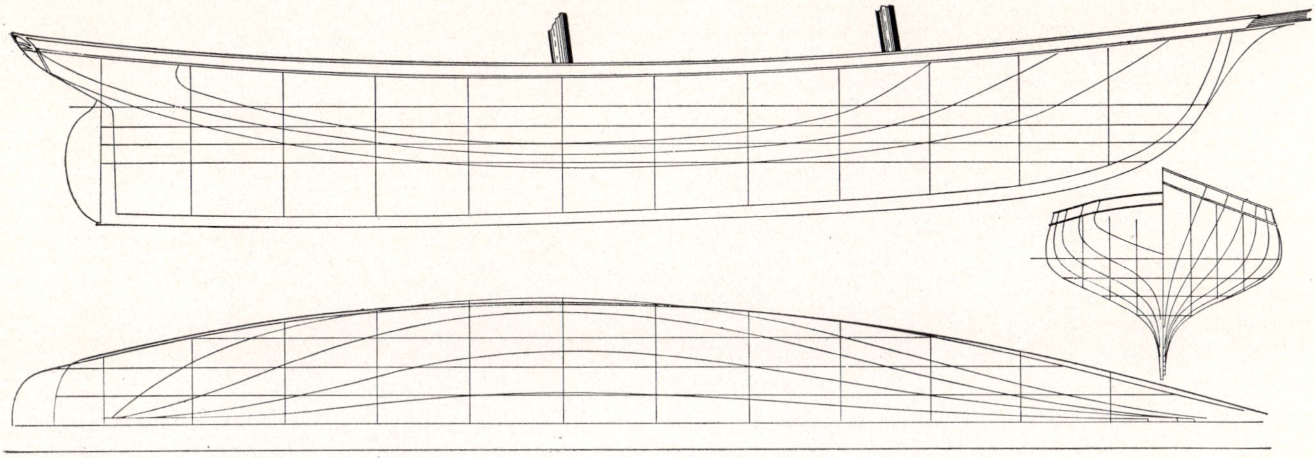

Lines of the schooner Sappho reproduced from some early records and drawings

three men she sailed from Boston on July 11, 1866, and arrived at Cowes on July 30—a passage of 19 days 6 hours and 20 minutes. Joining her at Cowes, Mr. Appleton cruised through the season and the yacht, still under Captain Clark's command, returned in July, 1867.

FLEETWING, VESTA AND HENRIETTA

The inauguration of the sport of ocean racing, since become so popular, was the outcome of a good dinner and perhaps a liberal portion of good wine. The principals were George A. Osgood, owner of the schooner Fleetwing, and Pierre Lorillard, Jr., owner of the schooner Vesta, both members of the New York Yacht Club. After a discussion of the speeds of their yachts, a proposal was made for a race outside. The course finally decided on was from Sandy Hook to the Isle of Wight, the start to be made in December and the stakes to be $30,000 per side.

"Original articles of agreement. New York, Oct. 27, 1866. George and Frank Osgood bet Pierre Lorillard, Jr., and others, thirty thousand dollars ($30,000) that the Fleetwing can beat the Vesta to the Needles, on the coast of England. The yachts to start from Sandy Hook on the second Tuesday in December, and to sail according to the rules of the New York Yacht Club, waiving allowance of time. The sails to be carried are mainsail, foresail, flying jib, jib topsail, fore and main gaff topsails, main topmast staysails, storm staysails and trysails."

When news of the match came to James Gorden Bennett, Jr., owner of the schooner Henrietta, he asked to be permitted to enter, and a supplementary clause was added:

"The yacht Henrietta enters the above race by paying $30,000 subscription by members of the New York Yacht Club. Any minor points not embraced in the above that cannot be settled by Messrs. Osgood, Lorillard and Bennett shall be decided as follows: Each shall choose an umpire, and the umpires chosen, in case of disagreement,

Outward bound on an ocean yacht race off the Hook

Sappho, modeled by William Townsend, built by C & R Poillon 1867, showing light canvas as carried in 1867

to choose two others; 20 percent of the money to be deposited with Leonard W. Jerome on Saturday, the 3d of November, the balance to be deposited on the first Tuesday of December—play or pay."

Signed J. G. Bennett, Jr.
Franklin Osgood
George A. Osgood
Pierre Lorillard, Jr.

December 3, 1866.

It was agreed later that no Channel pilot was to be taken from New York and that each might carry a square sail. It was further agreed that everything but ballast might be shifted, and that each might trim ship up to the hour of starting, disregarding the 48-hour rule of the club.

Vesta was a centerboard schooner of 201 tons; her sailing master was Captain George Dayton. George Lorillard, brother of the owner sailed aboard her, with Colonel S. M. Taylor as company. Fleetwing was a keel yacht of 212 tons, commanded by Captain Thomas of the steamship City of New York; with her owner were Robert Center and Ernest Staples, the former representing Vesta and the latter Henrietta. The steward was Neils Olsen. Henrietta was a keel yacht of 205 tons; during the Rebellion Mr. Bennett had placed her at the service of the Government, being in command with the rank of lieutenant. In this race she was under the command of Captain Samuel Samuels, with Martin J. Lyon, a New York pilot and yacht captain, as sailing master. In those days New York was noted for two classes of watermen, the pilots and the Battery boatmen who rowed the famous Whitehall boats all over the harbor and even outside Sandy Hook. With Mr. Bennett were Lawrence (Larry) W. Jerome, Melvin Knapp and S. R. Fisk.

Wire rigging and turnbuckles were still in the remote future, both shrouds and lanyards being of manilla or hemp. When the schooner Siren was built in 1874 for Dr. Clifford D. Morrough of New Brunswick, N. J., she was fitted with shrouds of iron wire rope, but at the foot of each was a cylinder of rubber to give elasticity. The tiller was in general use aboard yachts as well as pilot boats, but each of the contestants was refitted with new rigging. Screw steering with a wheel was installed, apparently an innovation.

The run was made quickly with only one mishap. On December 19, when running before a gale, Fleetwing was pooped and lost six men, washed out of her cockpit. The logs showed a run of 3,105 nautical miles in 13 days, 21 hours, 55 minutes by Henrietta; 3,135 miles in 14 days, 6 hours, 10 minutes by Fleetwing, and 3,144 miles in 14 days, 6 hours, 50 minutes by Vesta. The latter lost a commanding position by a blunder on the part of her navigator and another on the part of the Channel pilot.

After the race Mr. Bennett offered Henrietta to the Prince of Wales, but the offer was politely declined. Though recognized as a spirited yachtsman, there had been some feeling against Mr. Bennett as not being up to the social standing of the New York Yacht Club, but after sailing across and back aboard his yacht this disappeared and he was elected Vice Commodore, holding the office for four years and then being elected Commodore.

The effects of this race were twofold. It demonstrated to British yachtsmen the sporting spirit of their American cousins, and introduced the American type of schooner. At home it was publicly exploited throughout the nation, awakening a wider and keener interest in a sport which was, from its nature, confined to the seaboard.

SAPPHO

The fore-and-aft gaff schooner rig, if not originating in America, has been a favorite with American yachtsmen from the beginning of the sport; just as the cutter rig has been the more popular with British yachtsmen. Though declining in favor today, the American schooner for the past 75 years has scored as many great victories, both at home and abroad, as any other type of yacht. In this record one name stands out above all others, that of Sappho.

This yacht was built in 1867 by C. & R. Poillon at their yard in Greenpoint, Brooklyn. She was modeled by William Townsend, superintendent of the yard, who must also be credited with such large yachts as Coronet, Norseman, Clio, Agnes, Peerless, Dreadnaught and Viking—a man whose identity is lost in that of his employers. The yacht was built on speculation, originally entered in the New York Yacht Club under the ownership of Richard Poillon, a member of the club and her builder. A keel yacht, with both breadth and draft, a very hollow entrance, an excessive hollow in her floor, and a strong tumble-home, she was intended to represent the latest advance in American schooners. In her races at home in her first season she was not notably successful, but in 1868 she was sent abroad with the hope of selling her. She crossed to Cowes in 14 days, under the nominal ownership of E. A. Lawrence, a member of the club. The venture was not well managed and proved a failure, the yacht sailing home with nothing added to her previous reputation. Back in New York she was purchased by William P. Douglass, a spirited and wealthy young yachtsman, who placed her in the hands of Captain Bob Fish for alteration.

The principal place for docking yachts in Manhattan was the little screw-dock on South Street, a lifting dock of peculiar construction. Though I have been on it many times I am at a loss as to its details, the platform was lifted by a series of chains running over sheaves on each side and leading into a power house where they were drawn in by hydraulic cylinders or revolving sheaves. Sappho was hauled here, *the planking stripped from her sides about the waterline, and the frames were padded to the extent of seven inches on each side, after which the planking was replaced, the operation being known as hipping. With 14 inches more breadth and Captain Bob in command she started a new and most successful carreer. In 1869 she crossed from New York to Queenstown in 12 days, 9 hours, 36 minutes.

Later she defeated the British schooner Cambria in a series of three matches. In 1870 and 1872 she crossed again, and her sensational performances through a term of years under the ownership of Mr. Douglass and of the Italian Prince Sciarra, to whom she was sold in 1876, make her the most notable of a grand fleet of ocean cruising and racing yachts. As already stated, but little attention was paid in the early days to those dimensions and other elements of a yacht which are now considered of first importance. The measurements of Sappho are given differently from time to time, but the most correct appear to be as follows, the length over all being taken from the extreme forward point of the stem to the after side of the taffrail. The breadth is that after the hipping; she was probably about 14 inches narrower when built.

*From New York *Herald*, April 1, 1869:—"Sappho will be placed upon the balance dock this week." April 4.—"She will be hipped, and fitted with new masts (8 feet longer), sails and rigging."

Neils Olsen, known to three generations of yachtsmen during 35 years' service as superintendent of the New York Yacht Club

Length over all, 145 feet 6 inches, load waterline, 121 feet, breadth, 27 feet 4 inches, draft, 12 feet 9 inches.

THE work of the great American schooners in the first thirty years of the sport is well shown in the following table from The American Yacht List of 1874, the second American yacht register, compiled by that grand old Norse seadog Neils Olsen. Born in Christiansand, Norway, in 1835, Nels, as he was familiarly and effectionately known to three generations of yachtsmen, took to the sea at the age of 18. After cruises on many waters he jumped ship in New York and sailed aboard the schooner Norma, Alexander Major, owner, about 1860. Later he was in the crew of the schooner Widgeon, Franklin Osgood; in 1866 he was steward of Fleetwing. He was mate of Magic in the Cup Match of 1870 and of Columbia in the match of 1871. Shortly afterward he entered the service of the New York Yacht Club, continuing for 35 years as Superintendent, a factorum with no set limit to his multifarious duties. At one time a reporter of yachting, he started The American Yacht List in 1874, continuing it until 1887. Himself a walking Yacht List, a cyclopedia of yachting information, and an authority on yachting history, it was a privilege to know him and to benefit by his yarns of the past.

EARLY TRANS-ATLANTIC PASSAGES OF AMERICAN YACHTS

Year	*Rig.*	*Name*	*Owner*	*Tonnage*	*Ports*	*Time d.*	*h.*	*m.*	
1851	Schr.	AMERICA	Com. J. C. Stevens	170	New York to Havre	21	..	..	Sold in England
1853	Slp.	SILVIE	Louis Depau	105	Halifax to Havre	16	12	..	
1856	"	SILVIE	H. G. Stebbins	105	Southampton to N. Y.	34	..	..	
1857	"	CHARTER OAK	C. H. Webb	23	N. Y. to Liverpool				Sold in Europe
1858	"	CHRIS. COLUMBUS	C. H. Webb	45	N. Y. to Cowes	45	..	..	Sold in Europe
1863	Schr.	GIPSEY	A. W. Morse	135	N. Y. to Queenstown	19	..	..	Sold to T. N. Mather, Esq.
1866	Slp.	ALICE	Thos. G. Appleton	27	Boston to Cowes	19	..	..	
1867	"	ALICE	Thos. G. Appleton	27	Cowes to Boston	34	..	..	Returned July, 1867
1866	Schr.	HENRIETTA	J. G. Bennett, Jr.	205	Sandy Hook to Cowes	13	21	55	3,106 miles. Ocean Race, Dec. 11, 1866
1866	"	FLEETWING	Geo. A. Osgood	206	Sandy Hook to Cowes	14	6	10	3,135 miles. Dec. 11, 1866
1866	"	VESTA	Geo. L. Lorillard	201	Sandy Hook to Cowes	14	6	50	3,144 miles. Dec. 11, 1866
1867	"	VESTA	Geo. L. Lorillard	201	Cowes to N. Y.	34	..	..	
1867	"	HENRIETTA	J. G. Bennett, Jr.	205	Cowes to N. Y.	36	..	..	
1867	"	FLEETWING	Geo. A. Osgood	206	Cowes to New Bedford	42	6	..	
1868	"	SAPPHO	E. A. Lawrence	274	N. Y. to Cowes	14	..	..	
1868	"	SAPPHO	E. A. Lawrence	274	Cowes to N. Y.	32	..	..	
1869	"	SAPPHO	W. P. Douglass	310	N. Y. to Queenstown	12	9	36	
1869	"	DAUNTLESS	J. G. Bennett, Jr.	268	N. Y. to Queenstown	12	17	6	
1869	"	METEOR	Geo. L. Lorrillard	293	N. Y. to Cowes				Lost on Cape Bon, Coast of Africa, 1869
1870	"	DAUNTLESS	J. G. Bennett, Jr.	268	Queenstown to N. Y.	23	7	..	Ocean race with the *Cambria*
1870	"	SAPPHO	W. P. Douglass	310	Cowes to N. Y.	32	..	..	Returned Aug. 8, 1870
1871	"	ENCHANTRESS	Geo. L. Lorrillard	253	N. Y. to Gibraltar	..	..	..	
1871	"	ENCHANTRESS	Geo. L. Lorrillard	253	Cowes to Newport	34	..	..	
1872	"	SAPPHO	W. P. Douglass	310	N. Y. to Cowes	18	..	..	
1872	"	DAUNTLESS	J. G. Bennett, Jr.	268	N. Y. to Cowes	25	..	..	
1872	"	DAUNTLESS	J. G. Bennett, Jr.	268	Cowes to N. Y.	35	..	..	
1873	"	ENCHANTRESS	J. F. Loubat	253	N. Y. to Cowes	22	..	..	
1873	"	FAUSTINE	G. P. Russell	95	N. Y. to Cowes	18	..	..	
1874	"	VIKING	Mahlon Sands	157	N. Y. to Cowes	30	..	..	

Mattie, later named Protos, built by Pat McGiehan, 187—, 27 feet 4 inches, rounding a mark in Lower Bay. Old-time steamboats in attendance

TRADITIONS AND MEMORIES OF AMERICAN YACHTING

Part Four

By *WILLIAM P. STEPHENS*

SANDBAGS TO WINDWARD

ONCE the most popular type of small yacht in this country, the origin of the wide, shoal-draft sloop or catboat, the hull being the same under both rigs, is unknown. It is easy to trace the origin of other native types, the New Haven sharpie, the Block Island boat, the Staten Island oyster skiff, the Chesapeake Bay bugeye, the Massachusetts dory, the Barnegat sneakbox and the Connecticut River shadboat. Each is the outcome of some local need met by a regard for some specific purpose, for local conditions, and the employment of local materials. The need in this case was for a small vessel of very light draft, both for sailing in shoal water and for mooring on mud flats which were free to all. One purpose for such a craft was fishing at a distance too great for a rowboat, another, and perhaps more general one, was for the mere pleasure of sailing.

The "Report on the Ship-building Industry of the United States" compiled by Henry Hall, Special Agent, and published in 1884, is a very complete and comprehensive work, covering every class of commercial vessel. Unfortunately, it devotes little space to pleasure craft. Its description is as follows: "Down the Jersey coast the fishermen use a light-draught sailboat which, like the dory and sharpie, is an American invention and goes by the name of the cat-rigged boat. As a rule, these boats are built by regular carpenters. Nevertheless, in New Jersey, as in New England, amateur boatbuilders are numerous, and probably one-third of all the petty craft that sail in or out of the shallow harbors of this part of New Jersey, cruising with the guests at the beach hotels in the summer months, and diligently employed in gathering oysters in the fall and winter, are the products of those who build chiefly for themselves.

"The frames are cut from cedar roots. There is an abundance of material remaining in the woods (1884), and the roots being crooked, tough and light, are desirable for the purpose named. With axe and spade a young man will, in one day, provide himself with the material necessary to frame a 24-foot boat. He digs out the stumps, sends them to the sawmill, and has them cut into from three to eight slices, paying ten cents a cut. The stuff for the planking is bought from the nearest sawmill, and is usually cedar but sometimes it is oak. The keel and center work are of oak; the decking of pine. Cedar planking costs $35.00 per thousand board feet during the Census year, an average price; but during the war (1861-5) the price was $55.00. About 75 days' labor is consumed in building a 24-foot boat. . . In New Jersey it is the fashion, when an oysterboat has proved to be fast under sail, to enter it in the yacht races in New York Harbor in order to make a record for its benefit; and then, should the boat win, its value, which is only $250.00 for oystering, would at once rise to $400.00 or $600.00 for yachting, and its owner would promptly find a purchaser at a high price."

This description, if not entirely convincing, must be accepted in default of more detailed and reliable information. It is probably not far from the truth; but

Brooklyn, built by James Lennox, 1891, 27 feet 10 inches. Builder's model showing block glued up in lifts. Peabody Museum, Salem, Mass.

Susie S. (Bella) off the wind from a painting by Frederick S. Cozzens, Peabody Museum, Salem, Mass. Built by Pat McGiehan, 1869, 27-3 by 11-0 by 1-9. Slightly hollow floor. Deadrise, 19 degrees. Lines taken off by John Hyslop, 1888

the type was by no means limited to the Jersey coast. It seems, like Topsy, to have "just growed up" wherever a man wished to sail, both on the North and South seaboard and the inland lakes. Just when, in a more perfected form, it found its place in yaching, is another question — presumably back in the forties? As to the building of racing craft, whether under cat or sloop rig, this was an established industry in Bayonne, N. J., prior to the fifties. With club books and yacht registers still far in the future, it is not possible to fix a definite date for the beginning of the sport, but we know from the exportation of the little Una from Bayonne to England in 1852 that the building of such craft was not in its in fancy.

By the second half of the sixties the racing sandbagger, sometimes cat-rigged but more frequently jib-n'-mainsail, had captured the fancy of many New York yachtsmen, growing in favor through the seventies and middle eighties, then gradually declining until extinguished by various changes in yachting methods. While it lasted it was the most sensational and exciting form of yacht racing. From a puiely sporting standpoint but little can be said of its ethics and its practices. It was largely professional in its personnel, the racing was for substantial money prizes, and there was much incidental betting, with the inevitable disputes. While it cannot be said that it did anything to advance the study of naval architecture, it is, nevertheless, well worthy of study, both as to the yachts themselves, their owners, their builders, and the men who served them as skippers and crews.

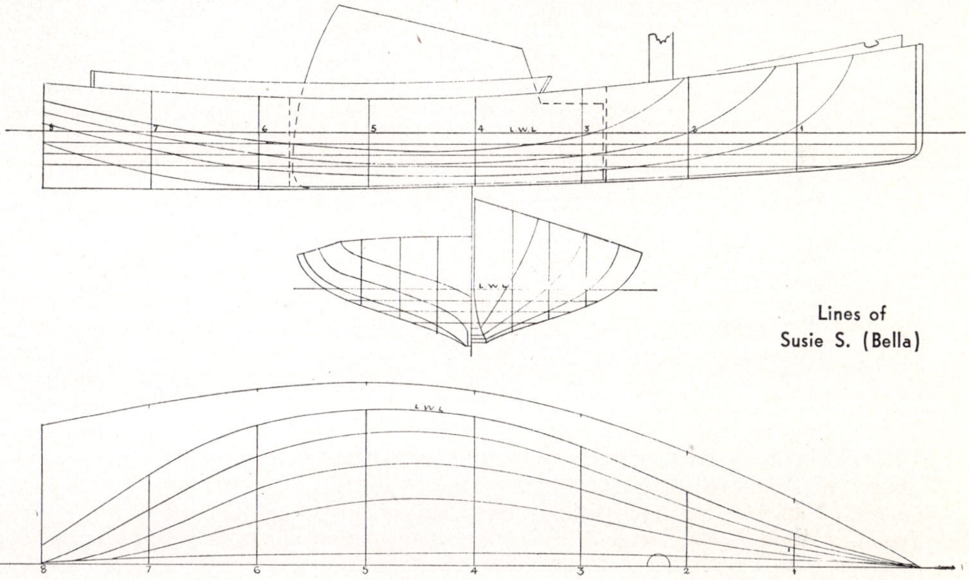

Lines of Susie S. (Bella)

Below: Una, built by Capt. Bob Fish, 1852. Shipped to Cowes, 16-6 by 6-6 by 0-9. Rounding bottom

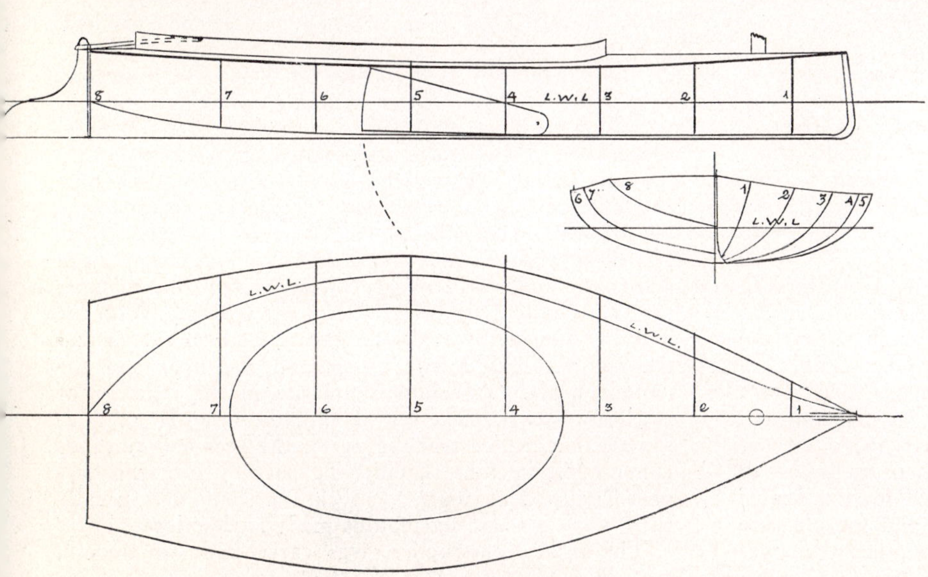

LOCALE

The center of the building and the sailing of the sandbagger was New York Harbor, with its great population devoted to the water and its miles of mud flats free to all who cared to moor on them. Mention has been made in the opening article,

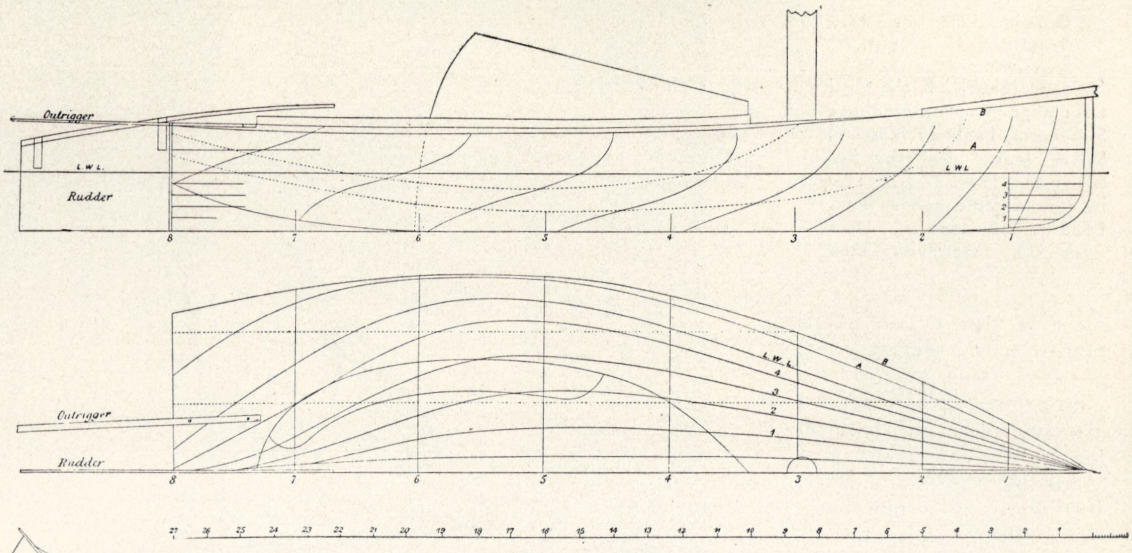

Parole, built by Jake Schmidt, 1875. Lines drawn from model (without plank) by W. P. Stephens, May, 1882. 27-0 by 11-3 by 1-8. Deadrise, 16 degrees. Sail plan: Mast, deck to truck, 36 feet; bowsprit, outboard, 22 feet 6 inches; outrigger, outboard, 10 feet; boom, 39 feet; gaff, 20 feet 6 inches; luff of mainsail, 29 feet 6 inches; tack of jib to boom end, 70 feet; mainsail area, 1034; jib area, 540; total, 1574 square feet

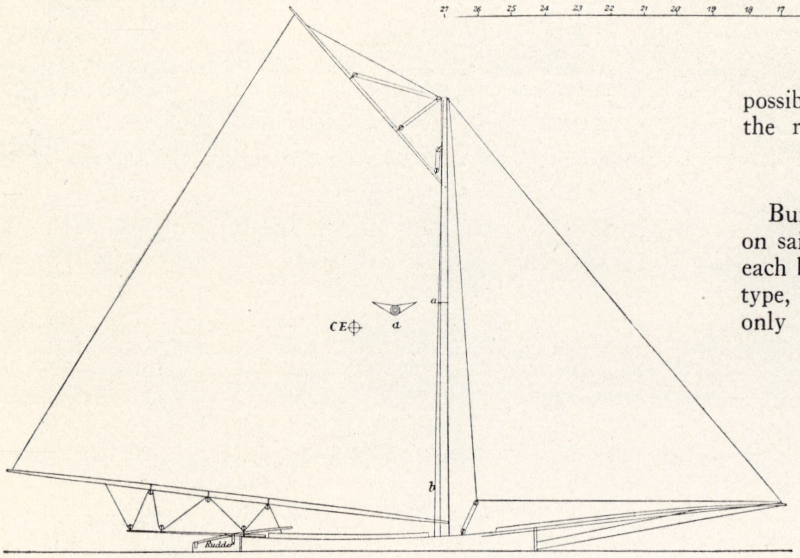

of the Foot-o'-Court Street, the mouth of Gowanus Creek in Brooklyn, where land was of little value, and a great colony of boat and yacht builders had established itself. While yachts of some size were built by such men as John F. Mumm, James Lennox, A. M. Witman and R. B. Wallin, it was the Penny-Bridge boats of Hen Smedley which made the place famous. Across New York Bay on what was once Bergen Neck but is now the city of Bayonne, was another vast expanse of flats, and on the shore a settlement known as Pamrapo or Palmipaw, with another, Saltersville. Here a large number of boats was turned out by such builders as Cap'n Bob Fish and Pat McGiehan, both for local yachtsmen, for the Western lakes, and for exportation abroad. About the shores of Staten Island, on Raritan Bay, on the Harlem River, and on Long Island Sound, were local builders and general, if unorganized, racing. On the Sound was New Rochelle, Cow Bay (now Manhasset Bay), Norwalk and Bridgeport, each boasting local builders and a local fleet.

More open and nearer to the sea, with much deep water at its doors, Boston at the same time had its shoal bays where the type flourished, though not to the extent of New York. Philadelphia, Charleston, Savannah and New Orleans had their fleets. Apart from racing, every waterside estate or farm on the Hudson, the Delaware and the Connecticut rivers had a catboat of the type of Una and up to 25 feet length made fast to a little pier or anchored nearby, and used for the double purpose of a vehicle for transportation and for pleasure sailing. On the shoal inland lakes no other type was possible until the comparatively recent introduction of the racing scow.

THE BOATS

Built under one restriction, of length, with no limit on sail, the yachts were all of one general model, though each builder had his own ideas as to detail of form. The type, at least, was standardized to an extent seen today only in the one-design classes; plumb stem and sternpost, a breadth of about 36 percent of the length, a draft of about 7 percent, the midship section about 66 percent of the total length from the bow. Classed generally as "open boats," there was a large oval cockpit, with wide sidedecks for the ballast bags. The rig included but two sails, mainsail and jib; the latter being boomed out with a setting-out pole. In a few cases a topsail was carried, the topmast being rigged as in a cutter, to raise and house. Such a sail was carried on Bella about New York, but it was mainly used about New Orleans; the extra gear involved kept it from general use. The crude construction described in the Hall report was not followed in yachting practice. The frames were of white oak, steamed and bent over a timber-block, the fastenings were largely wrought boat nails of soft iron, galvanized. These would hold when merely driven *into* oak, but in many cases copper nails were used, *through* planking and frame, and riveted inside over burrs.

The construction started with the glueing-up of a block of soft white pine, a wood no longer to be had. The block was in lifts of about a half-inch thickness. At times mahogany or black walnut were used in alternation with the pine. After standing for several months to season the block was carved to the desired form, using spokeshave, gouges, rasps and sandpaper, working mainly by eye. When completed, the elevation and deck plan could be drawn on paper and sections at certain points were taken off by means of a strip of lead and transferred to paper. In some cases saw cuts were made across the model, cardboard was inserted and marked, then cut out to give the outline of the section. With the drawing thus completed, the offsets were measured and the sections laid down full-size on the floor and the moulds made. A common practice in the building of rowboats was to make one mould, the dead-flat or midship section, which was set up on the keel and ribbands run around it, thus shaping the boat by eye; this was occasionally done with a catboat or sloop, but usually there were at least six moulds made as described.

The usual construction was carvel-built or smooth,

Cruiser, built by Neet Willis, 1868; a birthday present for Grenville Kane (still living). Lines drawn by W. P. Stephens, 1886. 20-8 by 9-9 by 1-5. Deadrise, 15 degrees. Sailed under both cat and sloop rig

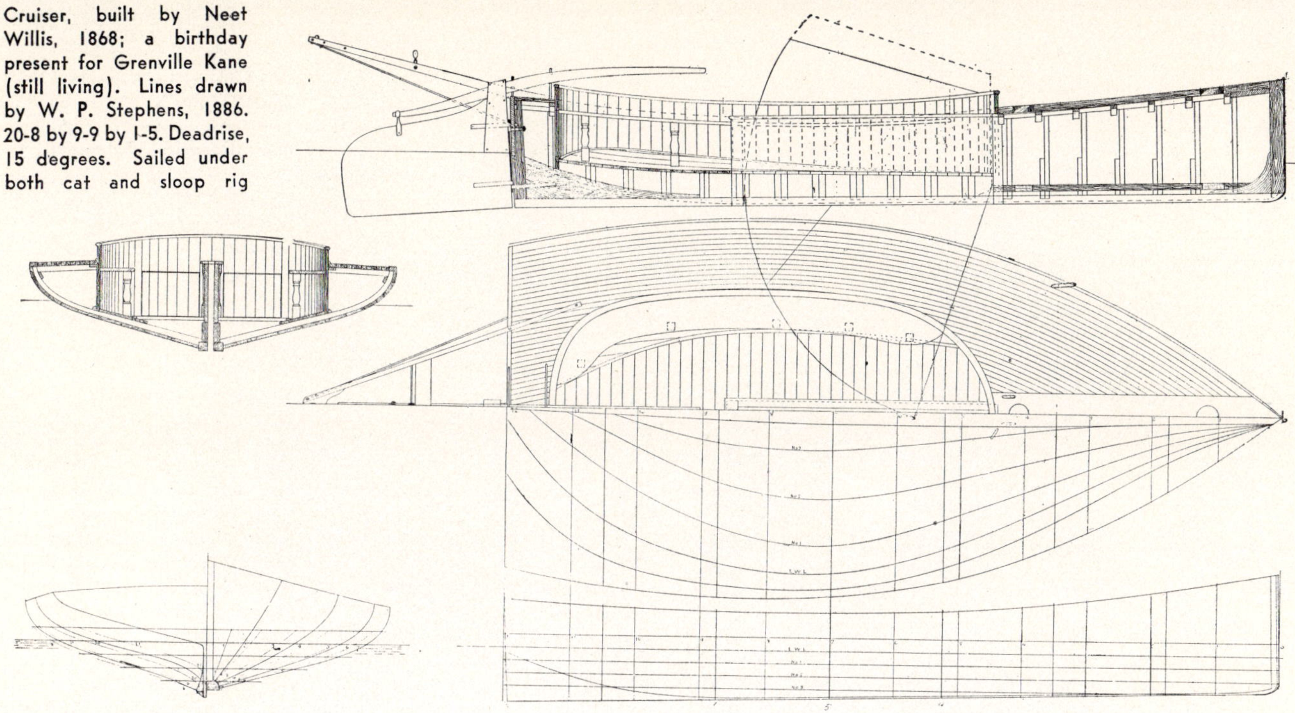

the lapstrake or clinker being lighter but more liable to wring under the strain of sails and ballast. Crude as it would seem in these days of double planking, bronze screws and straps, these boats, costing about $1,000 for a 28-footer, stood the strain of hard racing for years. The fleet was divided into four classes, 26 to 30 feet, 23 to 26 feet, 20 to 23 feet, and under 20 feet. This classification was varied at times in different clubs and localities. The boats were always raced on pot-lead (graphite or plumbago). This was sometimes mixed with stale beer as a vehicle, but the proper method was to lay a coat of spar varnish and when it was tacky (nearly hard) to dust in the graphite, a fine black powder. After this coat was hard the whole bottom up to the planksheer was polished with rags or brushes and more of the dry powder.

BALLAST

Though the stability of these boats depended entirely on the weight piled on the weather deck, each carried iron or lead to the weight of 600 or 700 pounds stowed as low as possible, to keep her upright when at anchor. The ballast bags were made of heavy canvas, the roping forming handles, and contained from 50 to 60 pounds, gravel being preferred to sand as being heavier and less liable to rot the bags. At times potato sacks were used, filled with 100 pounds of gravel and tied at both ends; these were not in general use, as they were all that two strong men could handle. The bags were piled along the planksheer, not touching, but piled some distance apart so that the second layer rested not on but partly between the first, and the third in the same manner on the second, with other bags inside. A general rule was that all ballast must be brought home, but this was one cause of discussion in making a match, and in some cases it was permissible to dump ballast after turning the weather mark. Where this was not permitted it might happen that some bags slipped overboard, while a knife in a potato sack served the same end. The extreme of this ballasting was seen at times, mainly about New Orleans, in the use of a folding frame or outrigger—three arms about three feet long pivoted to the deck with a crosspiece at their outer ends. Working like a parallel ruler, the arms could be swung out, a board placed across their outer ends, and sandbags piled on this shelf. As in the case of the topmast and topsail, the device was too cumbersome.

OWNERS

The ownership of the class was in itself exceptional in yaching; it embraced a number of wealthy yachtsmen, owning

Dare Devil, built by Jake Schmidt, 1878, for C. Oliver Iselin, 27 feet 4 inches. Note club on foot of jib, barn-door rudder, and sandbags. The bags are not piled as described in article. From model in Peabody Institute, Salem, Mass.

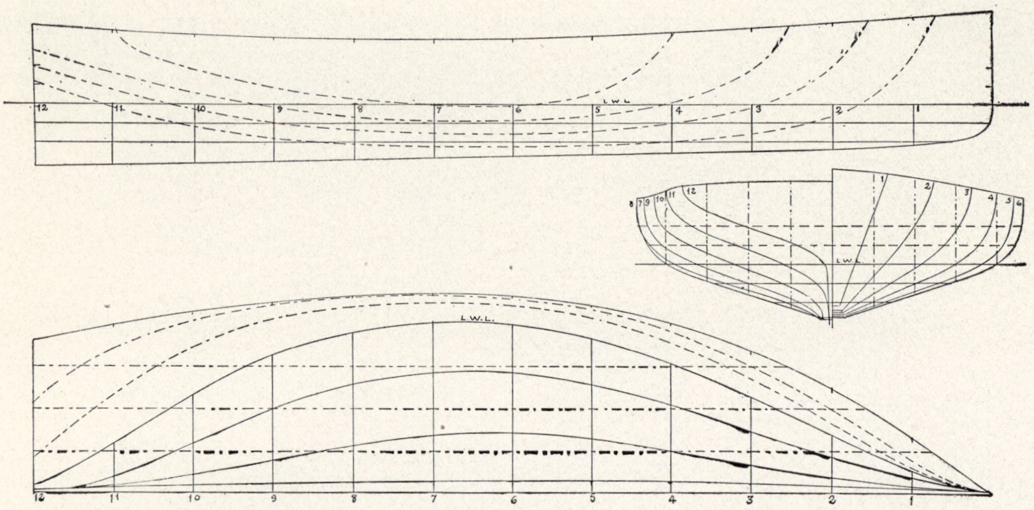

W. T. Lee, built by Hen Smedley, 1871, 28-0 by 11-4 by 1-9. Straight floor. Deadrise, 17 degrees

and racing larger craft, who found their pleasure in the small catboats and sloops either for mere sailing or for racing. The spectacular nature of the racing and the high stakes appealed to many as a sporting proposition, and wealthy men enjoyed the mere ownership of a sandbagger in which they did not sail, but backed freely, watched from a steamboat, and cheered their paid captains and crews. Many were owned by men who sailed their own boats and enjoyed the excitement of a race; apart from Corinthian yachtsmen were many working men employed about the water who owned and raced their boats for love of the sport. The gambling element, however, predominated; and exercised a controlling influence over both building and racing.

BUILDERS

THE creators of the class, call them builders, modelers or designers, were in themselves an anomaly in yachting. Some of the boats, but by no means the fastest, were built by established yacht builders, David Kirby at Rye, N. Y., D. O. Richmond at Mystic, Conn., John Mumm, Dick Wallin and James Lennox at Gowanus, Johnnie Driscoll at Greenpoint, L. I., Billy Force at Keyport, N. J., and James Snellgrove in Jersey City. These men had the technical training of the day, and were conversant with all details of the modeling and building of large vessels. The honors of the class, however, went to men of an entirely different type; amateurs with no knowledge of the technique of modeling and building, who were not able to define such terms as center of buoyancy, center of effort and range of stability, much less to calculate those elements now considered as the prime essentials of a design. They were self-instructed, working solely by an innate sense of form which, all theory to the contrary, produced results. They drifted into this work by chance, *con amore.* Such was Pat McGiehan, Jake Schmidt and Neef Willis. It may be noted here that honors were easy in those days, and prefixes and titles at a discount, familiar nicknames being in universal use: "Pat" McGiehan, "Hen" Smedley, "Buckshot" Roahr, "Jake" Schmidt, "Neet" Willis, "Dave" Snedecor, "Cap'n Joe" Elsworth, "Cap'n Phip" Elsworth, and "Watty" Elsworth.

One of the most unique and original characters in early yachting was "Cap'n Bob" Fish, already mentioned as the builder of Una in 1852, at which time he had a boatshop in Pamrapo. Originally a boatbuilder, his activities embraced most lines of yachting work. Following Una he built other small catboats and sloops and in 1861 the sloop Annie, 45 feet 6 inches waterline, a very successful craft. In 1865 he modeled the schooner Eva, in 1868 the schooner Sea Witch, in 1869 the the schooner Oriole and the steam yacht Emily, in 1870 the schooner Enchantress. Other yachts modeled by him were the schooners Cornelia, Fearless, Wanderer, the sloops Vision, Vixen, Coming, Whitecap, the steamers Lurline, Mariquita, Skylark and Lookout. A skillful handler in sandbag boats, he also served as master of many large yachts; his work in hipping Sappho has already been mentioned, he sailed her to England and raced her there, and he also took across Enchantress, making many changes on her.

Born in Ballindrate, County Donegal, Ireland, on March 17, 1828, Patrick McGiehan, the son of a carpenter, after leaving school served his three years as an apprentice in his father's shop. At the age of sixteen he built the altar and sacristy in a local church, for which work he was well paid, this enabling him to visit the United States. Arriving in 1845, he settled in Jersey City, continuing at the carpenter's trade for a couple of years and then turning to the millwright's trade and building several mills in Jersey City and the Eagle Mills in New York. As his business had prospered but his health had suffered from this heavy work, he abandoned it for a time, and in the winter of 1851-2 started to build a small sailing boat for his own use, working in the shop of Daniel Crane, a boatbuilder and grandfather of his wife. This boat, Wave, 18 feet long, found a purchaser as soon as she was finished, as did several others which followed, and Mr. McGiehan was soon fairly launched in a new occupation. An order for

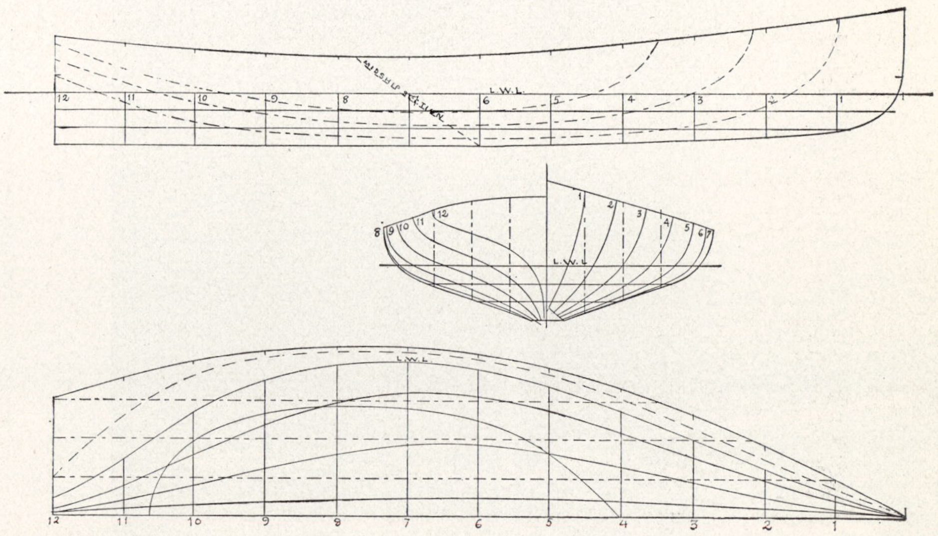

George B. Deane, built by George Roahr, 1872 21-11 by 8-2 by 1-4. Deadrise, 18 degrees. The raking midship section, characteristic of all boats of this type, is shown by the dotted line on the sheer plan; starting from the deck down, the widest point of each level line is further forward than in the one immediately above

a racing boat, the 24-foot Colleen Bawn, led him to specialize in the sandbag class, in which his great success lay, though he built such notable craft as the sloops Meta, Cora and Kaiser Wilhelm.

TWO names stand out prominently in the history of sandbag racing: Bella and Susie S., both carried by the same boat. As Bella she was built by Mr. McGiehan in 1869, for Nicholas W. Duryea, a member and in 1871 commodore of the Bayonne Yacht Club. She was 28 feet long, 10 feet 6 inches breadth and drew 2 feet; the type has been described as "all deadrise and no bilge," and this applies to her, as she lacked the power of later boats, but she was very fast in light winds and soon made a reputation. In 1876 she was sold to Cap'n Ira Smith, who re-named her Susie S.; in 1880 she was re-sold to Alexander Brewster, of New Orleans, who changed her name to Albertine, after his daughter; later Cap'n Smith took to New Orleans a new boat, Silence, built by James Lennox, traded her for Albertine and raced her about New York again under the name of Susie S.

There is no complete list of the McGiehan yachts, but he built upward of one hundred from 18 to 76 feet. Some of the most noted of the sandbaggers were Addie Taylor, Molly Bawn, Annie E., Only Son, Only Daughter, Mark Twain, Emma Sophia, Idle Hour, Annie Mack, Jeannette, Mystery, Lily R., and Joseph Jefferson.

Skilled in carpentry and millwork, Mr. McGiehan lacked practical training in boatbuilding. He paid no attention to the conventional methods of the craft, but used his knowledge of woodworking in devising a system of his own. The custom in both boat and yacht building is to make the stempiece a unit, a knee of oak or hackmatack with a rabbet cut to receive the hood ends of the planking; the seam between stem and hood ends being caulked from the outside. In the McGiehan method that part of the stem forward and outside of the planking was a separate piece, bolted on after the hull was otherwise completed. The face of the stem being the planking fastened to it was planed flush, all the seams were caulked and made tight independently of the outer stem. In the not infrequent event of a collision the outer stem might be wrenched off and yet the inner caulking would keep tight. In place of a knee at the after end, the deadwoods were built up, bread-and-butter fashion, of two-inch stuff, preferably chestnut, well caulked and stop-watered.

Born in 1838 and dying at the age of 42 after two years of lingering illness, "Buckshot" Roahr (christened George), crowded many activities into a comparatively short life. In his early years he was prominent in rowing, handling both oar and sculls and also taking the lines as coxswain. His principal occupation was the building of racing shells, with Tom Fearon of Yonkers and "Judge" Charlie Elliott of Greenpoint he shared the honors of building the best shells of the day. When canoeing was introduced in New York about 1870 he built some of the first of the New York Canoe Club fleet. In the sandbaggers he built such noted boats as Commodore, George B. Deane, George E. Sherman, Little Dean, Annie B. and Arrow, their reputation being due in no small degree to his personal work at the stick.

A hatter by trade, Jake Schmidt began by sailing in racing boats on the Brooklyn shore. After proving his skill at the stick he started to build, with no training in the trade. One of his fastest boats, Dare Devil, 1878, was built in a lumber yard on Clason Avenue, Brooklyn; 27 feet 4 inches by 10 feet 6 inches. She carried 80 sandbags of 75 pounds each, with the largest rig of her class. His most famous boats were Parole and Pluck and Luck. About 1879 he established himself in a boatshop at Tompkinsville, Staten Island, in partnership with Adolph Panick, with the "Good Success Anchorage," a dispensary of liquid refreshment, as a side issue. He had as a constant companion a big mastiff with an engraved plate on his collar, "Touch me not, but let me jog, for I am Jake Schmidt's dog: Sailor." There was a story afloat of a race in which the crew was limited; when a count was made Jake was told that he had one too many. He protested that Sailor could not handle a handbag, but the answer was "He is the first up to windward," and Sailor had to walk the plank. For many years Jake sailed out a markboat for the starting line of the New York, Seawanhaka and other clubs, a conspicuous figure with Sailor beside him.

BAPTIZED with the scriptural name of Epenetus, Willis of Cow Bay was known wherever these boats were raced as "Neef" or "Neet." The many who knew him well recognized no other name. He built many fast boats, notably Cruiser, Thomas Paine, Lizzie R., Nahli and Lorna; one of his fast boats, Jennie A. Willis, was built and used for oystering. His one large yacht was Eclipse, 54 feet over all, built in 1881 and quite fast. She was recognizable from a distance by the peculiar bar iron channels for her shrouds, counterparts of Fanny's "sheepwalks" for the same purpose. Hen Smedley, with his brother Saul, were boatbuilders as well as skilful handlers, but there is no record of how they came into the sport; between 1858 and 1883 they built many yachts, mostly sandbaggers, but a few larger cabin craft. The most famous Smedley boats were William T. Lee, Dodo, Fidget, Kate, Mary Emma, General Tweed, W. R. Brown and Mollie. The owner of W. T. Lee, a Corinthian, was very badly crippled, his legs being undeveloped and twisted under his body. In spite of this handicap he sailed his own boat, with the aid of a wheel, lashed to the deck outside the cockpit coaming.

Combining business with pleasure, Frank Bates was the proprietor of the Short Branch House, at the foot of 37th Street in the Gowanus district, at one time commodore of the Union Yacht Club, later the Long Island Yacht Club, and builder, owner and handler of fast boats, though his various activities prevented the building of many. The fastest were Dart, M. C. Campbell and Frank. In later years after the passing of the sandbag era he had a yard of second-hand boats derisively known as the Morgue, where youthful sailors who had saved a few dollars during the winter sought for bargains in the spring. "Judge" Charlie Elliott, though a builder of racing shells, tried his hand on Mistake, a lapstrake 27-foot boat sailed with shotbags instead of sandbags. Apart from the professional builders, many boats, and some of them fast, were built by the amateur owners who sailed them.

TRADITIONS AND MEMORIES OF

AMERICAN YACHTING

Part Five

SANDBAGS TO WINDWARD

By WILLIAM P. STEPHENS

Annie, built by D. O. Richmond, Mystic, Conn., about 1880. 29-0 by 12-6 by 2-0. Mast 36-6; Bowsprit 20-0; Boom 42; Gaff 18-0. Tack of jib to clew of mainsail 68 feet. Hull now preserved by Marine Historical Association of Mystic

Photographs by Henry C. White

THE manning of the great fleet of sand-baggers called for skilled hands; first, the boat handler, captain of the yacht and also holding the long tiller with which all were steered. He was in a class of his own, similar to that occupied today by the heroes of the diamond and the prize ring. First on this list comes Cap'n Ira Smith, a pilot on one of the Brooklyn ferries, but always in demand for a match. A master of the sandbag boat, as of all larger yachts, was Cap'n Joe Elsworth; others were Dave Snedecor, Sam Greenwood, Jim Sweeny, Joe Morris, Charlie Thatford, Jake Schmidt, Frank Bates, George Roahr, and, in his early days, A. Cary Smith. Next to the skipper was the jib-sheet tender, stationed near the shrouds where he could keep the sheets clear and handle them quickly. On him, perhaps, more than any other of the crew, depended the safety from those capsizes which were at times inevitable.

The main sheet man was aft, near the captain, ready to ship the sheet into the snatchblock as she came on the wind, and to call on the crew for beef. In the cockpit were, on a 28-foot boat, nine or ten huskies under the leadership of one who might be called second mate, as his duties were to direct the others; two or three pulling the bags from the weather deck as the time came for a tack, while two or three more passed them over and stacked them on the other deck as she filled away. The time from tack to tack was short, much had to be done, and fights were not unknown in the hurry and bustle. The responsibility for rapid, orderly work fell on this man. One bilge-boy was carried, to man the pump or the bailing scoop.

Prior to the eighties the opportunities for sailing were limited to those who owned large yachts, and their friends; for the average man of nautical tastes there was nothing but the sandbagger, and crews were easily found. The Gowanus district provided an ample supply of volunteers, but hardly to

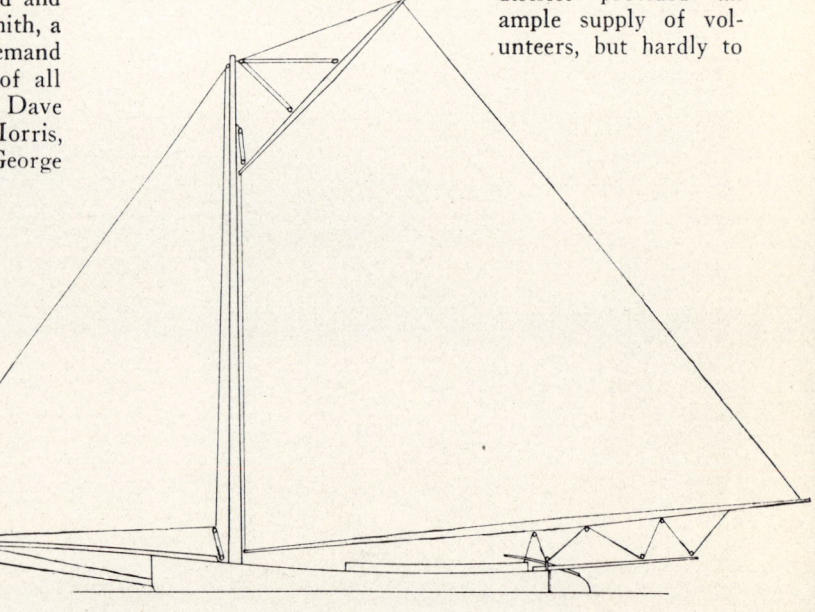

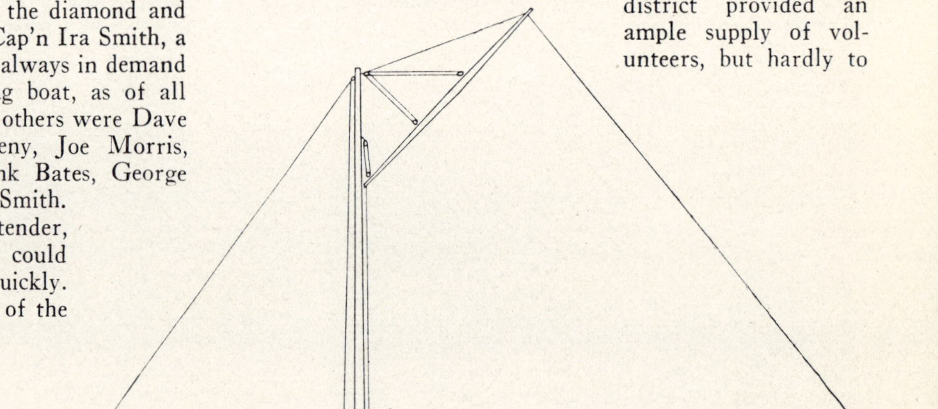

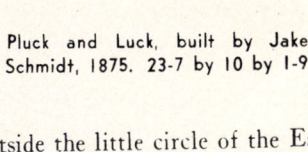

Pluck and Luck, built by Jake Schmidt, 1875. 23-7 by 10 by 1-9

compare with the opposite side of New York Bay, the Pamrapo, Saltersville and Greenville section. This was the stronghold of the Elsworth tribe, the patriarch, Cap'n Joe, originally coming from Tuckerton, on the Jersey coast, but for many years a resident of Pamrapo or Bayonne. Brought up to fish New York waters from boyhood, casting nets about the Narrows, one of the leaders in the oyster business of the city, he piloted his oyster sloops up and down the Harbor in all seasons and all weathers, perforce studying tides, currents and winds until he was better posted than even the professional pilots and Whitehall boatmen. He was at home equally at the wheel of a large yacht and the tiller of an oyster sloop or sandbagger, and his services were in demand in every big match in either class. In selecting with rare good judgement the quarterdeck crew of Puritan for the defense of the America's Cup in 1885 General Paine went outside the little circle of the Eastern Yacht Club and invited Cap'n Joe as honorary pilot. It was due to his advice that in the final race, at the end of the run, Puritan stopped and permitted Genesta to turn ahead of her while she housed her topmast for the 20-mile beat home against a hard norwester, winning by 1 minute, 38 seconds.

A brother, Philip, always known as "Cap'n Phip," was noted as a modeller of such fast schooners as Montauk and Grayling and many fast cabin sloops. Other brothers were "Cap'n Bill," "John H" and "Watty" (J. Watson Elsworth). The next generation was a large one, with a most confusing assemblage of Christian names: — "Joe's Bill," "Bill's Bill," "Joe's Mary" and "Phil's Mary." Allied by marriage was the Van Buskirk family with more boys, all born to the water, plus a few Vreelands. With such a group at hand, three junior McGiehans as well, there was no difficulty in manning all the yachts which Bob Fish, "Phip" Elsworth and Pat McGiehan could turn out; and few of these suffered from poor handling either at the stick or about the deck.

Close on the sidelines of the game was one conspicuous figure, John M. Sawyer, a sailmaker, who shared the canvassing of the New York yachts with Gilbert M. Wilson, another interesting character. While the firm

Undine, owned by C. E. Willis, one of the founders of the Seawanhaka Corinthian Yacht Club. Built 1866 by W. Latham, Oyster Bay, L. I. 31-0 overall; 27-6 waterline; 13-0 breadth; 2-0 draft

Dare Devil, built by Jake Schmidt. On the day of the capsize of the schooner Mohawk, July 19, 1876, the sloop, Mary Emma, was defeated by Pluck and Luck. C. Oliver Iselin, owner of Mary Emma, at once placed an order with Jake Schmidt for a new yacht, Dare Devil, a very successful boat under his ownership, and some years later under the ownership of Commodore W. H. Dilworth, New Jersey Yacht Club

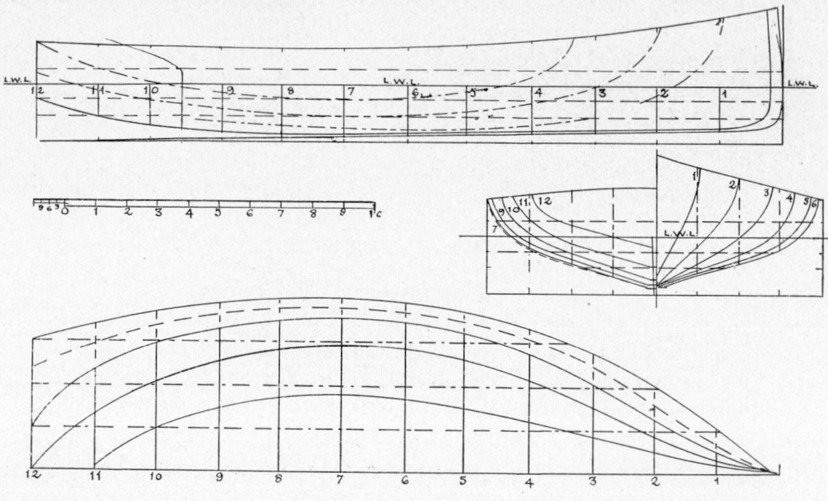

Right: Truant, built by William Kyle, 1882. 24-2 by 10-9 by 1-9. Lines taken off by John Hyslop, 1883. Deadrise 16 degrees

of Wilson & Griffin made most of the sails for the great schooners and other large yachts, John Sawyer had practically a monopoly of the sandbag boats. Genial, jovial, everybody's friend, he enjoyed the confidence of all parties, even in those days of heated controversy, and was always in demand as judge, referee or stake-holder.

There was a time in little old New York when a well cooked and well served French or German lunch could be had for fifty cents, with a waiter who would have fallen in a faint if he had been offered a dime instead of a nickel as a tip. There was a place of this description on Fulton Street between Broadway and Nassau (just opposite Mouquin's of delightful memory) much frequented in the nineties by a group of yachtsmen.

At this time Sawyer had practically retired, going about with a pocketful of bankbooks for the computation of interest, and his time was his own. I was not so fortunately situated as to time (or money), but hours with him were never wasted as he sipped his ordinaire, reflectively smoked his cigar, and drew upon an inexhaustible fund of recollections. One thing which he told me was that after a match, before the decision had been announced, he was smuggled into a hack and hurried to the railway station, the cry of the defeated always being "kill the umpire."

There is an old story which I never have been able to substantiate, of a yachtsman afterwards

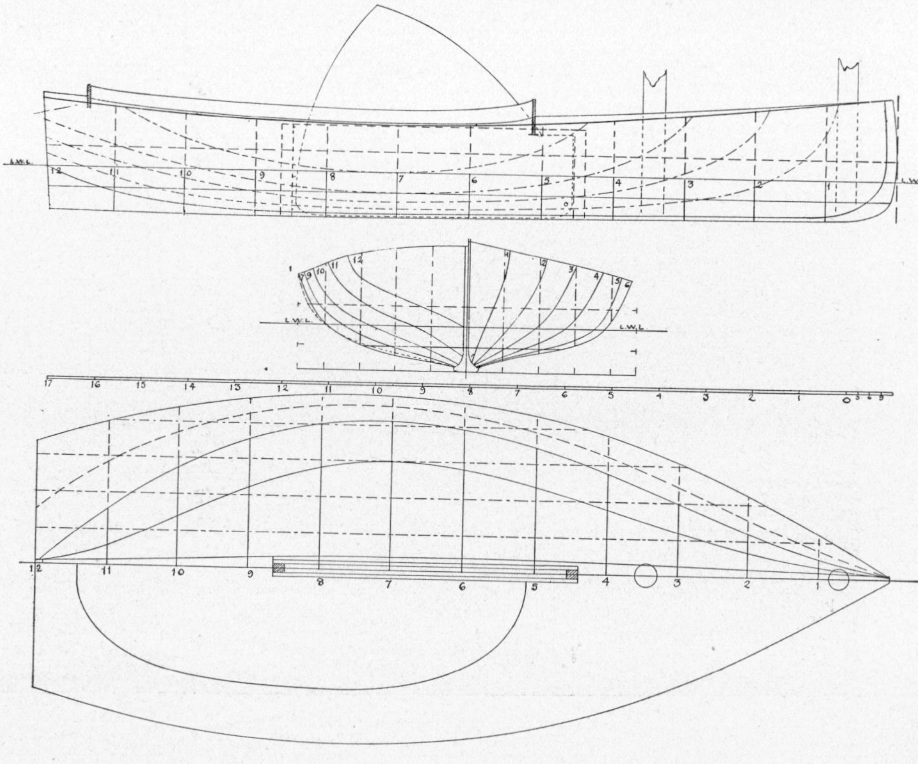

Comet, built by A. Cary Smith, 1862. 18-2 by 7-3 by 11 inches. Deadrise 13 degrees. Built over a single midship mould and battens. As the result of this system of building the lines were very difficult to fair in making the drawing. Sailed as both catboat and sloop.

very prominent in Cup defense who began his career in sandbaggers. After a race at Cow Bay all went ashore to hear who had won. The prize was on a table; the discussion was long and heated. Suddenly this man jumped up, seized the prize, ran down the dock and dove off, swimming to his boat and sailing away; a nautical Young Lochinvar.

A race of ten miles and back might be sailed in three hours or might run well into the night, so the provisioning was an important matter. The sandwiches made by Mrs. McGiehan, for instance, would not have fitted in an afternoon tea; slabs of bread, probably home-made from stoneground and un-doctored flour, a quarter of an inch of butter, a great slice of beef or ham, and mustard enough to bring tears to the eyes of even a sandbag tosser. The rule was that the grub box was not to be broken out until the first mark was turned. The liquor, if carried, was under the same limitation. The main reason for the inclusion of pie in this menu was once given by A. Cary Smith. The pieplates were not of cardboard, nor even, in those pre-McKinley days, of poor American steel with a wash of tin, but of honest Welsh iron with two coats of hand-rubbed tin, a substantial and lasting material. Going home in the twilight after a drifting match, six or eight of these discs wielded silently but skilfully along the lee side might mean the winning of a race.

The sandbaggers, whether catboats or sloops, were technically yachts, duly entered in organized yacht clubs, but in the vernacular of the day they were known as boats:—catboats and jib-'n-mainsail boats; while the captain was the boat-handler. The pleasures of sandbag sailing were thus set forth in an article by Tom Cringle in *The Aquatic Monthly* of November 1872:—"Many a time and oft' have I perched on the weather washboard, half in and half out of the cockpit, with the jib sheet brought up from the lee cleat, easing it off now and then in the heavy puffs; and well do I know how difficult it was to get back the few inches when the workers have nearly as much as they can do to keep inboard. Nor has the helmsman any easier post; he must watch his canvas sharply, with an occasional rapid glance to windward, to judge the weight of the squall, while his strength is often hardly tasked with the strong weather helm carried by these vessels, and the difficulty of exerting the required amount of strength when the yacht is pressed and heeled over. This is good fun for an hour or two, but when it is kept up for several hours on a stretch, with accompaniment of showers of spray, it is apt to become unpleasantly like work, and very hard work, too. ***** A man must be a sailor to handle these small vessels in a breeze; he can't stand a minute or two scanning the clouds and his canvas, speculating as to whether or not he must reef, as one may do in large yachts. In his case action must be simultaneous with the change which necessitates it, he must work as much by instinct as by thought or knowledge; and if the amateur sailor, in his tyro days, does not find that this faculty is his by nature or comes by practice, he had better buy a big boat and become a passenger in her cabin, or join the go-ahead-and-back-her fraternity, and scud along the coast with the aid of a tea-kettle."

Before the advent of elevated railways, bridges, subways and tunnels, New York Harbor boasted of a fine fleet of sidewheel steamboats carrying not only the local traffic, as between the Battery and Harlem, but joining Manhattan Island to the New Jersey, Staten Island, Brooklyn and Long Island shores. Some of these ran on established routes, as the Sylvan Dell, Sylvan Grove and Sylvan Stream, running to Harlem; Red Jacket and Kill von Kull running to Bergen Point and Elizabethport in connection with the Central Railroad of New Jersey before that road was extended to Communipaw; to the North Shore and the South Shore of Staten Island, to Keyport, Norwalk and Bridgeport.

Outside the established lines were many steamboats used for excursions:—Pomona, Magenta, Thomas P. Way (the boys called her the P-Way) Pope Catlin, Osseo, D. R. Martin (the boys called her Doctor Martin) conspicuous with double hogframes, Thomas Collyer, John H. Starin, Myndert Starin, and General Sedgewick, with a steam calliope which rent the air with perversions of popular and patriotic tunes. All of these were painted white, in marked contrast to Virginia Seymour and William Fletcher, black with their names in big white letters on the paddleboxes. Each of these was known to every boy alongshore by her whistle. How many are there today who can recall the once-familiar names? One or more of this fleet was seen at every sandbag match, and the entire fleet was mustered on the occasion of such an event as the Cup races of 1870-1.

BELLA—TIGER

OF the innumerable races sailed while the sport was most popular it is possible to mention only a few; the match between

Duster, owned by T. P. Christie, 1865, 24-7 by 10-4 by 2-4, and Adele racing at Knickerbocker Yacht Club, 1887

Photograph by Thomas I. Miller

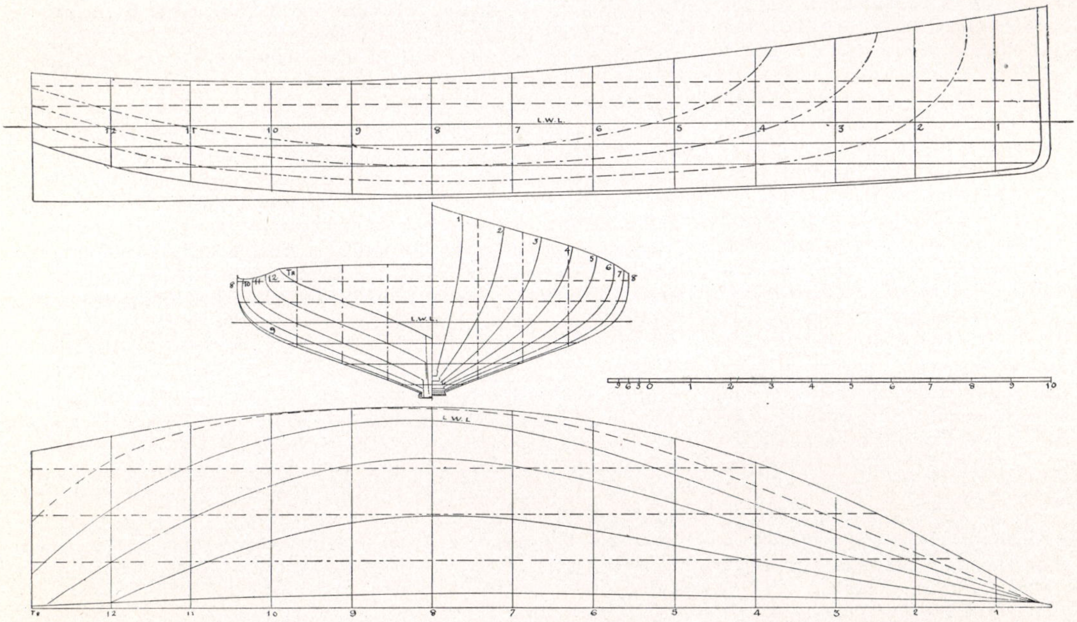

Jennie A. Willis, built by Neef Willis for oystering. Sailed in races of Larchmont Yacht Club for working boats. 25-5 by 9-8 by 1-10. Deadrise 18 degrees. Lines taken from model (unplanked) by John Hyslop

Bella and Tiger, the latter owned by Francis Bradbury, being one of the fastest of the Bridgeport fleet, was sailed on June 22, 1870; the conditions being ten miles to windward and return, $1,000 per side. Tiger, of local build, was 27 feet 10 inches over all, or two inches more than Bella, thus allowing 45 seconds. The odds before the start were 100 to 80 on Bella, and it was estimated that over $50,000 was placed in outside bets.

The steamboat Sylvan Grove carried a large party from New York and took aboard much of the population of Bridgeport; the town was *en fete*, with the Bridgeport band, flags flown everywhere ashore, and not only yachts but working vessels displaying all the bunting they could muster. The wind was SW., enough to call for a start with single reefs, though they were shaken out later. After the start the odds were 25 to 5; later they shifted to 105 to 40. As they neared the turn the bets were $20 to $10 that Bella would lead, but Tiger overtook her and turned at 12:46:34, with a lead of 31 seconds. On the run Bella regained her lead and the finish was timed:—Bella, 2:07:15 Tiger, 2:07:54. The elapsed time was 2:35:45.

BELLA—METEOR

A MATCH which aroused much feeling was sailed on August 3, 1872 between Bella and Meteor, the course being from a stakeboat off Bay Ridge around Buoy 5 off the point of Sandy Hook. The original owner of Bella, one Nicholas W. Duryea, was one of the notorious characters of the times, but his social and financial standing at one time was such as to make him eligible for membership in the Bayonne Yacht Club, of which he was commodore in 1871. He was part owner of a tugboat named after him which figured in some of the races. The Virginia Seymour carried a party from New York and Bayonne, while the Brooklyn contingent was aboard the J. Birkbeck. Mr. Duryea followed the race aboard his tug.

As a decidedly light-weather boat Bella was at a disadvantage against a fresh head wind and foul tide. When nearing the Hook she was seen to turn a channel buoy and head for home. The Seymour ran up to Buoy 5 and A. C. Bush, the owner of Meteor, had it identified as the proper turning mark. Bella finished at 5:17:30 and Meteor at 5:27, the former claiming the race. The matter was taken up by the Bayonne Yacht Club, the boat-handler of Bella testified that he was ordered by Mr. Duryea from his tug to turn the lower buoy, and ultimately Mr. Duryea was expelled from the Club. Later on he sold the yacht to Cap'n Ira Smith. His career was ended after a dispute with a business partner, one Simmons, who shot him.

METEOR—JEANETTE

IN this match, sailed on July 15, 1872, Meteor, being the longer of these two McGiehan boats, allowed two minutes over the course from Pamrapo to a mark off Fort Lafayette, two rounds, making 32 miles. This course was decided on only after much argument. The skipper of Jeannette was Cap'n Bill Elsworth, with one of his brothers in the crew. Meteor was handled by Cap'n Bob, with a fourth of the family in his crew, each boat being limited to ten men. With a flying start Meteor gave a half minute at the line. They beat down against a flood tide, and at the turn Meteor led by four minutes, which was made into eight at the end of the round.

When nearing the Narrows on the second round a heavy squall struck in, with fog. The schooner Josephine, 87 feet l.w.l., sailing about the Bay with a party of guests, capsized and sank, but all hands were rescued. Meteor finished at 3:23:34, Jeannette at 6:50:30. The judges were John M. Sawyer, Hiram Van Buskirk and Pat McGiehan. Two days later, in the annual regatta of the Bayonne Yacht Club, over the course, Bella won handily from Meteor, Maud, and Jeannette. The usual summer squall in the late afternoon capsized W. T. Lee. Following the custom of the day, the two Elsworth working sloops, Captain and Watson, sailed in the same classes as the cabin yachts, the former winning the Union prize and the Flag Officers' prize, the latter the similar prizes in her class.

MAUD—W. F. DAVIDS

THIS match, sailed on August 27, 1872, was for stakes of $1,000 per side, the referee being Thomas Thorn and the judges John M. Sawyer and Stephen Van Nostrand. Starting off New Rochelle with a fresh NW breeze, it was not possible to lay a straight ten-mile course, so after some argument it was decided to start off New Rochelle and round the judges' steamer, the Virginia Seymour, lying off Glen Cove dock; two rounds. The W. F. Davids, owned and sailed by her builder, T. R. Kissam, and named in honor of her backer, had sailed originally as a catboat, this being her first trial under mainsail and jib; each carried 11 or 12 men.

The Davids led by a minute over the line, both wung out, with jibs poled out to port; they ran very evenly to the turn, but while the Davids cleared the steamboat, Maud ran into her, one of Maud's crew climbing to the deck of the Seymour, fending off and running aft until he could jump aboard his boat from the stern. On the wind Maud did better work and led by 1 minute 45 seconds at the end of the round.

The wind freshened on the second round until both lowered mainsails and ran under jibs, the Davids being at one time under bare poles. Both started home under reefed mainsails only, but the Davids could not carry hers, and both were knocked down, the Davids losing thirty ballast bags. They were timed with Maud 33 minutes in the lead and then the fun began. It was estimated that between $12,000 and $15,000 was laid in outside bets, many of the bettors being aboard the Seymour. The final decision of the judges was that Maud had won, and the stakes were paid over to her owner. There was so much feeling between the owner of Maud and W. F. Davids that they could not agree upon another race, but finally Cap'n Ira Smith and Mr. Kissam agreed on two races for the same stakes; and on September 17 the flotilla was again off New Rochelle, with the Virginia Seymour, the tug P. C. Schultz, and attendant yachts. The first preliminary was measurement, Maud proving the longer by 4½ inches. Then came the question of the referee. The judges, Frank Walsh and Stephen Van Nostrand, could not agree, so after nearly an hour of argument they decided to toss; Mr. Walsh won and named Lawrence D. Huntington, of New Rochelle. Maud was handled by Cap'n Ira Smith and W. F. Davids by Jim Starkins. There was little wind and after a slow drifting match Maud won by 17 minutes.

The second race was sailed on September 23, the flotilla including the Fletcher with Grafulla's Band, one of the popular musical organizations of the day, the Pope Catlin, and the tug P. C. Schultz, with the usual fleet of yachts and working boats. All conditions were the same, Maud allowing 45 seconds and the Davids leading over the line by 20 seconds. At the turn Maud led by five seconds, but at the finish she was four seconds astern:—W. F. Davids, 4:40:10, Maud, 4:40:14. Cap'n Smith claimed that Maud's mainsail had been touched by the Davids' boom at the turn, but his protest was disallowed. A third race was sailed on October 5, in which the Davids won by 1 minute 3 seconds, this ending the series.

THESE few races are characteristic of the many in which both the stakes and the outside betting were heavy. In addition, there were many private matches in which sport figured more prominently than money. The repetition of conventional names, Frolic, Fidget, Spray, Ripple etc., with such changes of name as that from Bella to Susie S., then to Albertine and back to Susie S., makes it a very difficult matter to clear up the old records.

Throughout the first half of the nineteenth century American yachting flowed in a smooth and placid course. Measurement was mainly by length, with no limit on sail. The centerboard was in the ascendant and keel yachts in the minority. There was no limit on breadth or ballast, so the great schooners grew wider and more shoal with added sail spread, and the small craft carried these features to an even more dangerous extreme. With the beginning of the last quarter century a change became manifest. There were protests against extreme breadth and shoal body, against shifting ballast, a demand for a limitation on sail, objections to the anchor start and the flying start, a crusade for Corinthian sailing, proposals for small keel cruising yachts, even going so far as to advocate the British cutter.

There was in the yachting and daily press a growing discussion of these and similar subjects, and, at the same time, an increase in the popular interest in yachting, especially in the smaller classes. Many whose original interest had been in watching from a steamboat or following the reports of the schooner and sandbag races, were desirous of owning and sailing their own craft, however small and unpretentious. The many capsizes of all sizes of yachts from the schooners Mohawk, Josephine, Grayling and Agnes down to small cruising yachts did much to stimulate interest in deeper and narrower craft with fixed ballast. From about 1880 this form of sport declined rapidly, fewer matches for big money, more yachts sailed with fixed ballast, more manned by Corinthian crews.

THE Seawanhaka Yacht Club, established in 1871, started with a fleet of sandbaggers, the only two cabin yachts being Glance and Salus. The club grew rapidly, both in membership and yachts, and in its first Sailing Regulations, appearing in the club book for 1878, Rule V reads: "Yachts in Corinthian races must be manned by amateurs exclusively." Rule VI continuing: "Every yacht, before starting in a Corinthian race, must have filed with the Regatta Committee a list of names composing her crew, with the occupation and address of each." To add to this, Rule VII began: "Every yacht winning a prize in any regatta of this Club shall deposit with the Secretary her lines, accurately taken off and drawn upon paper by the Measurer of the Club, or approved and certified by him."

These restrictions, though not directly designed as such, constituted a fatal blow to sandbag racing should they be generally adopted. The filing of the crew certificate was specially objectionable; in one case of a crew from the Bayonne shore all hands were entered as "agriculturists," though their farming was limited to tending oyster beds in Raritan Bay. The demand for the lines of winning yachts was resented as an attempt to steal the brains of the modeller. Its wisdom, however, is fully recognized today when such records as remain of some of the most famous yachts of the seventies and eighties are those in the possession of the Club; for instance, Bella, whose model was destroyed in the burning of the McGiehan shop.

The search for a satisfactory rule of measurement continued for forty years after the organization of the New York Yacht Club, innumerable plans being advanced, and many tested only to be rejected. The basic idea in most of them was to tax length and leave sail free. In 1882 the Seawanhaka Yacht Club adopted a system in which both sail and length were taxed, and in the following year embodied the idea in a new formula known as the length-and-sail-area rule—the load water line added to the square root of the sail area and the sum divided by two. Another change at this time was the introduction of the one-gun start in place of the anchor start and the flying start. All such changes as they were generally adopted acted to hasten the disappearance of the sandbagger, but it must be said that while a new class established today at a cost of some thousand dollars for a small half-decked yacht in a one-design class has a life of but five or six years, the sandbagger can boast a life of a full generation, from at least 1850 to 1885 or later. It served a purpose in a day of experiment and development, it bred a host of bold, hardy and skillful sailors, and its history deserves a prominent place in the records of American yachting.

THE following appeared in "Forest and Stream" on December 26, 1896, as comment on a meeting of the Yacht Racing Union of Long Island Sound at which the old length rule was replaced by the length and sail area rule:

"Shortly before midnight on December 18, 1896, in one of the parlors of the Fifth Avenue Hotel, New York, there passed away quietly and peacefully an historic feature of American yachting. Though the end was in no way sudden or unexpected, no friend was near to cheer the final moments; and alone among a heartless and indifferent throng the American sandbagger dumped its sandbags overboard for the last time, and gave up a struggle that has long been hopeless.

"Among the number present, probably every one of whom learned his yachting on the weather rail with his lap full of sandbags, not one raised his voice in behalf of his old ally; and the motion to amend the rule was passed as a matter of course by a unanimous vote.

"We no not propose to write the obituary of the sandbagger, we have in the past written too many obituaries of its victims. Granted that it was at one time a necessity, and that those who survived to graduate from its severe curriculum have been a credit to it as a teacher of sailormen, the harm that has been done to American yachting by the long and close adherence to sandbag models and sandbag methods, to say nothing of the direct loss of life, is even yet felt in yachting.

"The least we can say by way of epitaph is to quote the words of the "noble High Executioner":—"It *never* will be missed."

Cambria. Madgie. Phantom. Light-Ship. Silvie. America. Dauntless. Idler. Magic. Tidal Wave.

THE RACE FOR THE QUEEN'S CUP—ROUNDING THE LIGHT-SHIP.—Drawn by Charles Parsons, from a Sketch made on Board A. S. Hatch's Yacht "Calypso."

First race for the America's Cup. Note title, "Queen's Cup", from *Harper's Weekly*, August 27, 1870

TRADITIONS AND MEMORIES OF AMERICAN YACHTING

Part Six

THE DAY OF THE GREAT SCHOONERS

•

By WILLIAM P. STEPHENS

EVEN if we disregard the somewhat apochryphal origin ascribed to the term "schooner," it must be admitted that this rig, fore-and-aft, gaff-rigged, two-masted, is distinctively an American institution. In British yachting the schooner rig was not only second in numbers and popularity to the cutter, but it had as competitors the topsail schooner, the yawl and the ketch. While in America the sloop rig shared in popular favor with the schooner, the two had the field to themselves until the introduction of the cutter and the yawl in the late seventies, and the ketch some years later. The rig itself, and the form of hull best suited to carry it, attained their highest development on this side of the Atlantic. That in the early days of yachting it was no less popular than the simpler sloop rig with but two lower sails was due, possibly, to the influence of the pilot boats; all schooners, and noted for their seaworthy qualities.

The growth of American yachting, slow as it was in its early years, was abruptly stopped in 1861 by the outbreak of the Rebellion; not only did all building cease, but some of the larger yachts were turned over to the Government, as was the case with Henrietta, given by James Gordon Bennett, Jr., who entered the Navy in command of her. The end of the war brought a quick reaction from four years of tension; much progress had been made along technical lines, business was good, and men turned to all forms of sport with an interest never before known in America. With the ocean at its doors and water on all sides, New York had always been a maritime city; it boasted of great shipyards with expert mechanics in all branches of shipbuilding, many of its merchants were shipowners, and others owed their fortunes to the shipping trade; when time and means came for sport it came almost as a matter of course that many turned to the water. The fleet of the New York Yacht Club in 1860 numbered 21 schooners with a total tonnage of 1,511, and 25 sloops with a tonnage of 1,361; three years after the close of the war the schooners numbered 28, with a total tonnage of 3,604; the sloops 13, with a tonnage of 752.

The reason for this great disparity lies in the fact that yachting was then more fashionable than generally popular; it found its support in a rich leisure class which included many who regarded it merely as a society sport. Built of wood after the manner of great ships, in an era of low wages and cheap materials (our oak, spruce, cedar and pine forest had not been cut off), an outlay of ten to thirty thousand

Cambria's typical English rig of 1870. Pole bowsprit fitted to run in. Yard topsails. From *Harper's Weekly*, August 27, 1870. Lines of Cambria, first challenger for the America's Cup. Designed and built by Michael Ratsey, Cowes, 1868, for James Ashbury. Typical English schooner. L.o.a., 120 feet; l.w.l., 101 feet; breadth, 21 feet 2 inches; draft, 12 feet

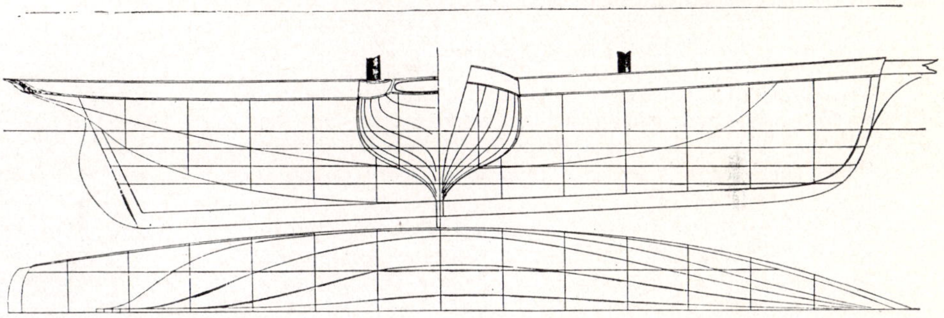

dollars provided the largest and best yacht which a man might desire; the cost of the entire New York fleet of that day was less than that of building and running a Jay-Boat (what a lubberly term) in this year of grace.

As noted in a previous article, the field of American sports in the post-war period was very limited: rowing, both barge and shell, was popular, as was walking (pedestrian matches); baseball was a mild form of amateur sport instead of a great professional industry; a very small group played a little imported cricket; croquet, another foreign importation, was rapidly growing in favor; a few French velocipedes were seen in the larger cities, football was unknown, as was polo, and golf existed only in the pages of "The Arabian Nights." The turf and the prize-ring, long-established favorites with betting men both in and out of society, had a wide appeal; and the racing of large schooners, as both spectacular and exciting, attracted many in the same way.

Prospero, keel cruising schooner designed by A. Cary Smith for C. H. Contoit in 1873. Bowsprit in a single piece, with no jib-boom. This innovation was generally condemned at the time. Staysail, jib and large jibtopsail. Balloon jib, yard topsails and maintopmast staysail

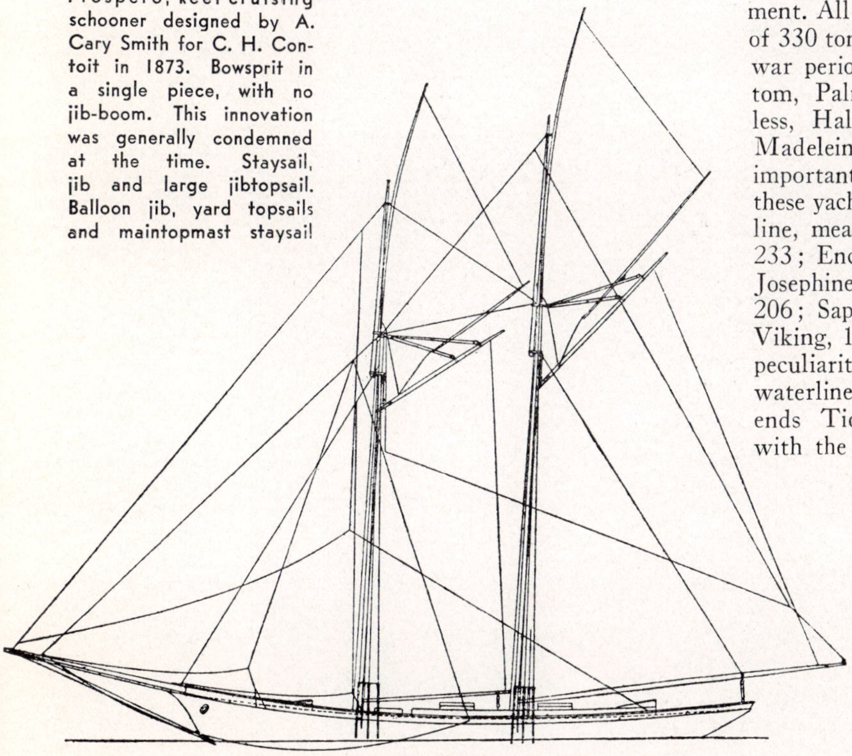

SCHOONER "PROSPERO"—1873.

The Growth of the Yacht Fleet

A REFERENCE to "Olsen's American Yacht List" for 1875 shows the growth of the schooner fleet in the ten years immediately following the end of the war; some sixty yachts of a total of 6,000 tons, Old Measurement. All of these, with the exception of the great Mohawk of 330 tons, were built prior to 1875. Those closest to the war period were:—Eva, Fleetwing, Fleur de Lis, Phantom, Palmer, Josephine, Idler, Juniata; 1865; Dauntless, Halcyon and Vesta, 1866; Sappho, Alice, 1867; Madeleine, 1868, Magic, 1869. From 1870 to 1874 important additions were made to the fleet. Many of these yachts were of great size, Dauntless, 116 feet waterline, measured 268 tons; Columbia, 183; Dreadnaught, 233; Enchantress, 253; Fleetwing, 206; Halcyon, 121; Josephine, 143; Palmer, 195; Rambler, 233; Resolute, 206; Sappho, 310; Tarolanta, 204; Tidal Wave, 233; Viking, 157; Vesta, 201; Wanderer, 208. Owing to the peculiarity of her model, with a breadth of 25 feet on a waterline of 100 feet; a full middle body with very fine ends Tidal Wave was familiarly known as "the snake with the toad in her belly."

The ownership of this fleet may well be divided into two classes: yachtsmen and yachtowners. In the first class were many who, young and enthusiastic, sailed their own craft—"Willie" Douglass, "Jim" Bennett, Lloyd Phoenix, "Watch Tackle Bob" Center, Rutherfurd Stuyvesant, William E. Iselin, Henry S. Hovey, J. Rogers Maxwell, Anson and Ludlow Livingston, Henry G. and Charles H. Stebbins, T. Denny Boardman, John S. Dickinson, Franklin and George A. Osgood and Pierre and George A. Lorillard;

all active sailing men throughout their lives. James Gordon Bennett, Jr., was born in New York about 1840, but educated in Paris; elected to the New York Y. C. in 1857, he bought the sloop Rebecca and sailed her in the famous race around Long Island, in which she was disqualified for passing through Plum Gut instead of the Race; Mr. Bennett claiming that the instructions were not definite. As a young man and "the son of his father," the senior Bennett then proprietor and editor of *The New York Herald,* he could not claim the social standing of some of the older members, and he was not popular. This mishap earned him the sobriquet of "Plum Gut Bennett. On the outbreak of the Rebellion he offered his schooner Henrietta to the Government and was in command of her at the capture of Fernandina, and of Fort Clinch and Fort Marian. His ownership of yachts, the last being the great steam yacht Lysistrata, was continuous to his death in 1918. William E. Iselin, elected in 1872, bought the schooner Meta in 1875 and sold his last schooner Enchantress in 1924, a half century of practically unbroken schooner ownership. Not a few, however, of these early yachtsmen looked on their craft as merely necessary adjuncts of their social position; leaving all technical details to their employees.

Matches for High Stakes

MENTION has been made in a previous chapter of both Silvie and Sappho; another notable craft was the schooner Magic, the first defender of the America's Cup. The genesis of this yacht, a remarkable story in itself, must be left for a future chapter; in brief, she was originally a sloop of very crude amateur design, so frequently and radically altered that the process might be compared to building a barrel with only the bunghole as a pattern.

A notable feature of this era was the sailing of private matches for high stakes. Some of the more famous of these may be summarized as follows: interesting as they are, the details are too voluminous for this story. In 1859, Rebecca, slp. vs. Restless, schr., Brenton's Reef to Throgg's Neck, $500:—in each case the sum mentioned is per side, Favorite vs. Haze, schrs., 24 miles, off New London; Gipsy, Favorite and Zinga, Hart's Island around buoy of Eaton's Neck, $50. In 1860, Julia vs. Rebecca, slps., from Sandy Hook Lightship 20 miles to windward and return, $250; in 1865, Magic vs. Josephine, schrs., from Lightship 15 miles to windward and return, no time allowance, no limit to crew or sails, each yacht to tack every thirty minutes, $1,000. Henrietta vs. Fleetwing, Sandy Hook Lightship to Cape May. Henrietta vs. Palmer, $500. Henrietta vs. Restless, Sands Point to Bartlett Reef, $500. In 1866, Widgeon vs. Vesta, Fort

James Gordon Bennett, Jr., elected to New York Yacht Club, August 12, 1857; Vice-Commodore, 1867-8-9-70; Commodore, 1871-2-3-4. Yacht owner for 60 years

Private match, Mohawk and Dauntless, October 25, 1875. From *Harper's Weekly*, November 13, 1875

Adams around Block Island, $1,000. Henrietta vs. Vesta, Sandy Hook to Cape May and return, $500. Halcyon vs. Vesta, Sands Point to Bartlett Reef, $500. L. Hirondelle vs. Vesta, Lightship 20 miles to windward and return. Vesta, Fleetwing and Henrietta, Sandy Hook to Isle of Wight, $30,000. Sappho vs. Palmer, Brenton's Reef around Block Island. In 1868 Magic vs. Pauline, around Sandy Hook Lightship, $3,000 on Magic to $2,500 on Pauline. In 1869, Rambler vs. Magic, N.Y.Y.C. course, Rambler, $1,000 to $500 on Magic. In 1872, Meta vs. Gracie, slps., 20 miles to windward and return. In 1873, Mera vs. Vision, slps., 20 miles to leeward and return, $500. Brooklyn vs. William T. Lee, jib-and-mainsail boats, $1,000. In 1874, Comet vs. Magic, for the Bennett Challenge Cup, outside wagers estimated at $100,000. It was said that his winnings in this race induced and enabled Mr. Garner to build Mohawk.

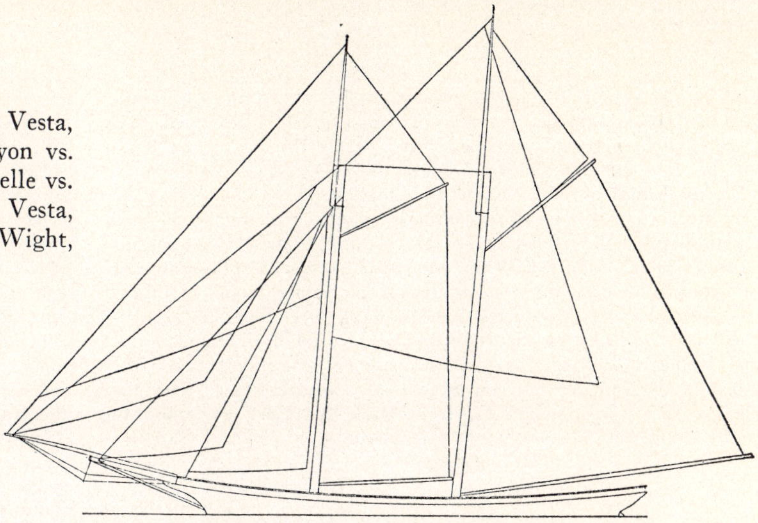

SCHOONER "COLUMBIA"—1875.

Columbia, typical schooner rig of 1870. Built-in bowsprit with jib-boom. Staysail, jib, outer jib and jib-topsail. Gaff topsails and maintopmast staysail

An editorial in *The New York Times* of September 21, 1875, by an unknown writer (I wonder whether it could have been my old friend W. L. Alden, the founder of canoeing in America and then an editorial writer, and also known as the funny man of *The Times* from his absurd stories) in which the centerboard was denounced as suitable only for small sailboats, aroused a heated controversy in yachting circles and resulted in several challenges. Vice Commodore Garner wrote:—

Editor of New York Times:—

Observing the remarks concerning the Mohawk in your editorial upon yachting in this morning's issue, and with a view of ascertaining if the yachting fraternity coincide with the opinions therein expressed, I will, during the next month, upon any day when an eight-knot breeze or upward is

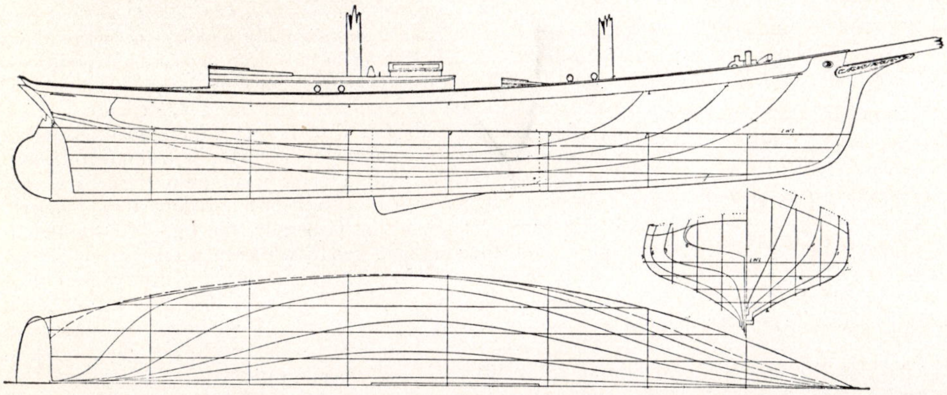

Magic, first defender of the America's Cup. Built in 1857 as sloop Madgie (1) from model by R. F. Loper. Lengthened and rebuilt as a schooner, 1869. L.o.a., 90 feet; l.w.l., 80 feet; breadth, 21 feet; draft, 7 feet 1 inch

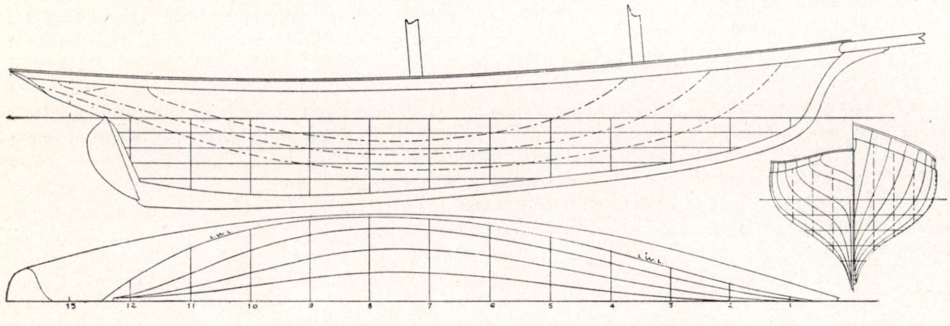

Fortuna, designed by A. Cary Smith for Henry S. Hovey, built by Poillon Bros. in 1883. L.o.a., 117 feet 8 inches; l.w.l., 94 feet 10 inches; breadth, 22 feet 9 inches; draft, 11 feet 10 inches. Typical then-modern cruising schooner

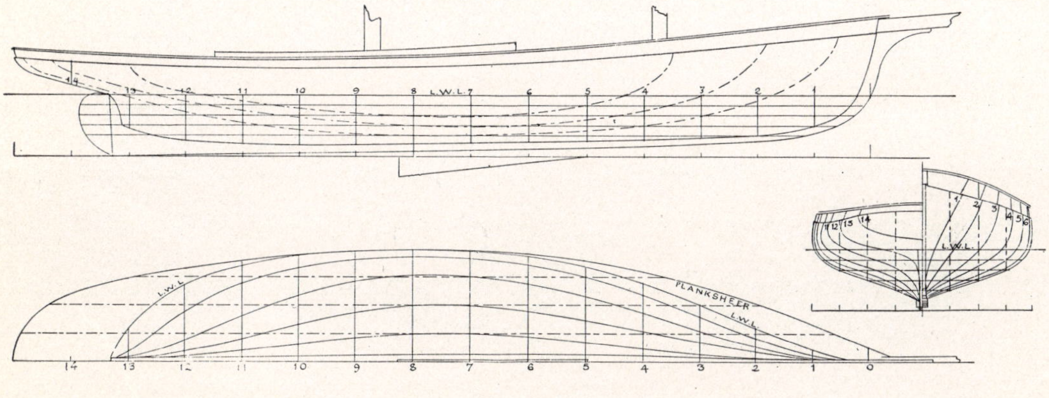

Halcyon, modeled and built by J. J. Harris, Port Jefferson, L. I., 1866. Typical centerboard schooner of her day. L.o.a., 82 feet; l.w.l., 79 feet 6 inches; breadth, 23 feet; draft, 6 feet. There is no record of lengthening, but in later years the l.o.a. is given as 96 feet, as in the drawing. For some years prior to the building of Puritan in 1885, Halcyon was owned and raced by Gen. Charles J. Paine, head of the Puritan Syndicate; these lines were owned and probably taken off by Edward Burgess. The challenger of 1885, Genesta, was 81 feet waterline; the New York defender, Priscilla, was designed to a waterline of 85 feet, thus giving time to Genesta; but Puritan was designed to 80-foot waterline

blowing, sail any yacht,—keel or centerboard—twenty miles to windward and back, outside of Sandy Hook Lightship, provided that notice shall be given to your newspaper before the 1st of October." This brought out an immediate answer:—

"To the Editor of 'The New York Times':—

In answer to Commodore Garner's manly challenge published in your paper today, I beg to say that I am prepared to accept his challenge in accordance with his letter, to sail the Dauntless against the Mohawk twenty miles to windward of Sandy Hook Lightship and return, on any day during the last week in October, in accordance with the Rules of the New York Y.C., for a thousand dollar cup. I am also willing to sail the Mohawk at any time between the 10th. and the 25th. of November next, also in accordance with the rules of the New York Y.C., from Brenton's Reef Lightship to Sandy Hook, for five or ten thousand dollars.

(signed)

James G. Bennett.

Resolute, then under charter to "Uncle Rufus" Hatch, was named by him as ready to sail any schooner in any day in October with an 8-knot breeze, over the Club course or from the Lightship to Cape May and return. This offer was taken up by Dauntless as a friendly match with no stakes; by Comet, W. H. Langley, for a $500 cup over the Club course; by James D. Smith over the Club course, and by Vesta, J. M. Mills, and Dreadnaught, C. J. Osborn, over the Cape May course; the stakes in the last three being dinners for twenty covers.

These matches were typical of the New York society of the day; some, no doubt, were inspired by a keen love of yacht racing and pride in one's yacht, some by the same spirit of gambling which is found on the turf. In those days society in the little old city was a more closely knit unit than today; yacht owners met to dine at the Yacht Club, at the Union Club, and at Delmonico's; after a good dinner with good wine came boasts of the speed of their respective yachts, and then followed challenges and the posting of stakes.

While the national type, the shoal, wide, centerboard model, predominated, some of the leading yachts were of the keel type:—Sappho, Dreadnaught, Alarm, Enchantress, Rambler, Wivern, Tarolinta, Faustine, Nettie, Tempest, Dauntless, Restless, Fleetwing and Fleur de Lis.

Early International Contests

THE visits of early American yachts to British waters were important factors in the development both of yachting and of the class of large schooners; the racing of Sappho in England in 1868 and again in 1869 included a series of three races with the schooner Cambria, owned by James Ashbury, a wealthy English yachtsman. Having defeated Sappho on her first visit, and prior to her hipping, in the fall of 1868 he wrote to the New York Y.C. proposing that the Club should send the best vessel of its fleet to England in 1869 for series of races, after which he would race his yacht Cambria to New York against the American visitor, and later would race for the America's Cup. As this proposition was not accepted, in the fall of 1869 he issued a formal challenge for the Cup; and in July 1870 Cambria started from Gaunt, Ireland, for Sandy Hook, with the American Dauntless as a competitor; Cambria winning by one hour and 17 minutes. When it came to the question of defending the Cup, the New York Yacht Club decided to throw the defense open to the entire Club fleet of schooners.

Two beliefs were immovably fixed in American minds for many years;—one that the great international trophy was a "Queen's Cup"· the other that, in as much as the Cup was won from a fleet, it was perfectly fair to defend it with a fleet. In answer to these beliefs it may be said in brief that no American yacht has ever won a "Queen's Cup," as such prizes are given only for yachts of a royal yacht club. On the second point, the conditions under which the Cup was originally won were those of an open race in which 19 yachts competed on equal terms, the winner to take and hold the trophy. In the race in defense of the Cup not one of the 23 defending yachts was racing *for* a prize, but solely to prevent one other yacht from winning it; the odds being 23 to 1.

This race, and the series of three races against Mr. Ashbury's Livonia in the following year, aroused a deep interest even in parts remote from the coast and where yachting was unknown; it was America against England, and the spirit aroused was one of patriotism rather than sport. On the coast, and wherever yachts were sailed, these races, widely exploited in the papers, did much to increase the national interest in the growing sport.

The winner of the race of 1870, the little Magic, came in for most extravagant praise, as per this technical description from a New York daily:—"Of her model every builder and seaman speaks in praise; she has convexity forward, but her bows are fine, and the greatest breadth of beam is forward of the mainmast. She draws 6 feet 6 inches of water aft and 4 feet forward. In her cockpit she has a large manhole for descent into the large sailroom abaft; she has no wheel, but steers with a tiller. A glance at her booms and gaffs shows that her sails are secured along the head and foot by lacings to wooden jackstays, and along the luffs by ordinary masthoops. *Her frame is double througout, firmly knit, and able to combat the strongest waves.* She stands up admirably and has no more than eight tons of ballast. Let the reader reflect upon what conditions bring such desirable stiffness without stowing large quantities of pig iron? She is sharp at both ends and has a flat counter, drags no water; she is hung with precision, and with these qualities and a fine sailing master she has achieved victories now known everywhere in yachting circles. In a brisk wind sailing free she can crowd all sail; but, as with other schooners, judgment is required in reducing canvas closehauled. Generally, the light sails will not draw on a wind, though some good yachtsmen persist in spreading every stitch of canvas aloft. The result has frequently been that yachts following this practice have often lost a race; too much sail is a retarding factor." Then follows "sofas in red velvet, carved and gilded mahogany, *verde antique* bronze cupids, fine china marked M, icebox 15 by 10, and similar important details.

A number of the more important yachts of the schooner division started life as sloops, later being converted, usually with very radical alterations. Among these were Maria, Silvie, Rebecca, Meta, Madgie I (Magic), Julia, Ray and Madeleine The last, built in 1868 by David Kirby, was re-built as a schooner by J. E. Smith of Nyack in 1871-3 and 5; being lengthened 17 feet aft, and raised 14 inches. The famous Dauntless was modelled and built in 1866 as L'Hirondelle by Forsyth & Morgan at Mystic Bridge, Conn.; in 1870 she was re-built by J. B. Van Deusen. In this operation 38 feet of her forebody was cut away and re-built with a lengthing of her waterline from 107 to 116 feet 5 inches; her tonnage being increased from 260 to 286.

AMERICAN YACHTING

Part Seven

THE DAY OF THE GREAT SCHOONERS

By **WILLIAM P. STEPHENS**

THE high point of the schooner development was attained in the building of Mohawk in 1875 and Ambassadress (nicknamed "The Astor House") two years later; the underlying motive in each case seemingly being the great American idea of "the biggest thing on earth" and "licking all creation." Mohawk was 150 feet from knightheads to taffrail; 121 feet waterline; 30 feet 4 inches breadth; 9 feet 4 inches depth of hold; and but 6 feet draft; the total draft with centerboard being 31 feet 6 inches. Her bowsprit was 42 feet long; 30 feet outboard with jib-boom 24 feet outboard. Her mainmast was 96 feet; main topmast 60 feet; foremast 94 feet; fore topmast 55 feet; main boom 90 feet; main gaff 41 feet 6 inches; fore boom 39 feet; fore gaff 39 feet; squaresail yard 63 feet.

In a highly eulogistic description *The New York Herald* said: "The spars will be as long as it is possible to procure sticks, reaching 100 feet if they can be procured." It was further stated that *if* a bridge should be built between New York and Brooklyn it would be necessary to house both topmasts in order to pass under it. Below was a main saloon 28 feet square, with paintings by De Haas, a noted marine painter; the owner's stateroom was 18 by 13 feet. The furnishings included hot and cold running water, steam heating, and an electric call bell; all novelties in that day. The rigging was of steel wire specially manufactured in England; special cranks (winches) were built for sails and centerboard, and the ballast (what there was of it) was lead, and not the then universal pig iron. Launched from Van Deusen's yard in Williamsburgh on the Long Island shore on June 9, 1875, she raced through the season, and in the early races of 1876.

It is not possible to draw a distinct line between cruising and racing yachts; the fleet which took part in all the races of the New York Y. C. was to be found between races cruising about Sandy Hook, along the Sound, and to the eastward. While Mohawk

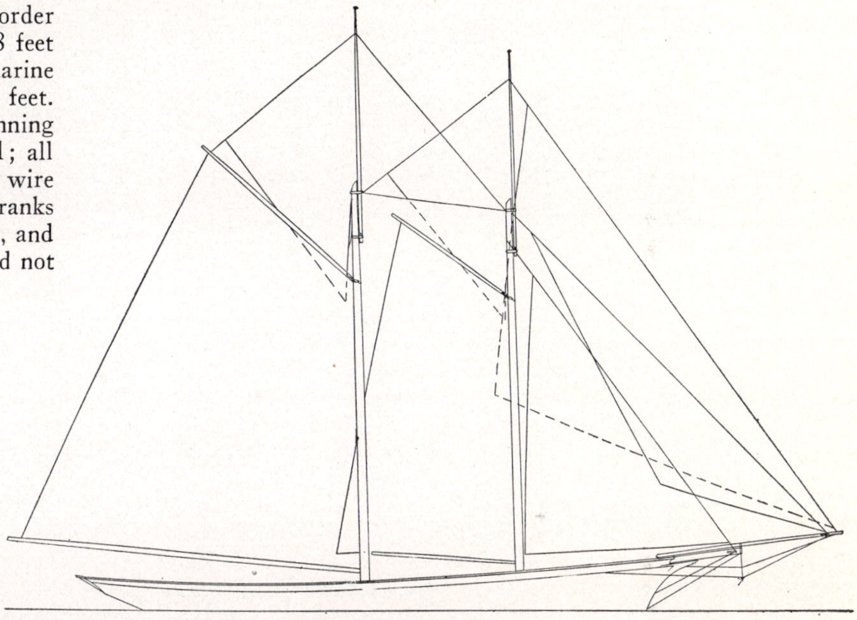

Fortuna Sail Plan, showing built-in bowsprit and jib-boom; as used prior to the introduction of the pole bowsprit

Ambassadress, modelled and built for William Astor by David Carll, City Island, N. Y., 1877. L.o.a. 146 feet 2 inches; l.w.l. 130 feet 6 inches; breadth 28 feet 2 inches; draft 11 feet. Centerboard yacht altered to keel, with draft increased to 12 feet 8 inches in 1881

THE YACHT "MOHAWK."—[Drawn by Charles R. Parsons.]

was built for this double purpose, Ambassadress was built solely for cruising; in her first season she made two cruises to Jacksonville, one to Newport, and one to New London. She was a centerboard craft, flush-decked; but in 1881 she was converted to keel, with an addition of 1 foot 8 inches to her draft. Her dimensions were: over-all 146 feet 2 inches; waterline, 130 feet 6 inches; breadth, 28 feet 2 inches; draft, 11 feet. Her mainmast was 93 feet; foremast, 91 feet; mastheads, 11 feet. Main topmast, 61 feet; fore topmast, 58 feet. Bowsprit outboard, 28 feet; jib-boom, 54 feet 3 inches, heel to cap. Height from water to main truck, 142 feet; length from end of jib-boom to end of main boom, 235 feet.

As was the custom, much of the technical description is devoted to the furnishings: "main saloon 24 by 22 feet, headroom 7 feet 4 inches, finished in walnut, maple, mahogany and cherry—elegant bronze chandelier—sofas, lounges, chairs, sideboard, etc., in blue upholstery—mainmast panelled with mirrors—owner's stateroom 17 by 14 —hot and cold water, fresh and salt—the judgment exhibited in the furnishing is most excellent; nothing violating the standard of good taste." Her standing rigging was of American hemp, her headstays of English steel; she steered with a wheel and screw gear, and her ballast was of kentledge; iron cast to fit the frame spaces, 140 tons.

When elected to the New York Y. C. on July 20, 1871, at the age of 31, William T. Garner had no yachting background; the owner of the Harmony Print Mills at Cohoes, N. Y., and of other similar mills, his fortune was estimated in fabulous figures of millions. His yachting began in 1874, when he purchased Magic from "Uncle Rufus" Hatch, and at once matched her against the older generation of yachting men. In the fall of that year he placed an order for a new yacht. Joseph B. Van Deusen was a native of the Mohawk Valley, born in 1832, of Dutch descent; coming to New York he worked under George Steers and William H. Webb. His first yacht was Gipsy, built in 1857, later he built Narragansett and Alarm; in 1865 with his brother he had a yard at the foot of 16th Street, New York, and built Rambler, Fleetwing, Fleur de Lis, and Phantom; the last, for Henry G. Stebbins, said to have been based on Silvie, lengthened 10 feet. Later at the foot of North 7th Street, Williamsburgh, he built two steamships. In addition to Columbia and a steam yacht, Ideal, he built the fleet of gunboats for the Spanish Government which nearly caused international complications in 1869. He was in no sense a rule-o'-thumb modeller, but an expert shipwright according to the standards of the day. How far he was personally responsible for the model of Mohawk is an open question; but the underlying objects in her building seem

Grayling Sail Plan after alteration of 1887

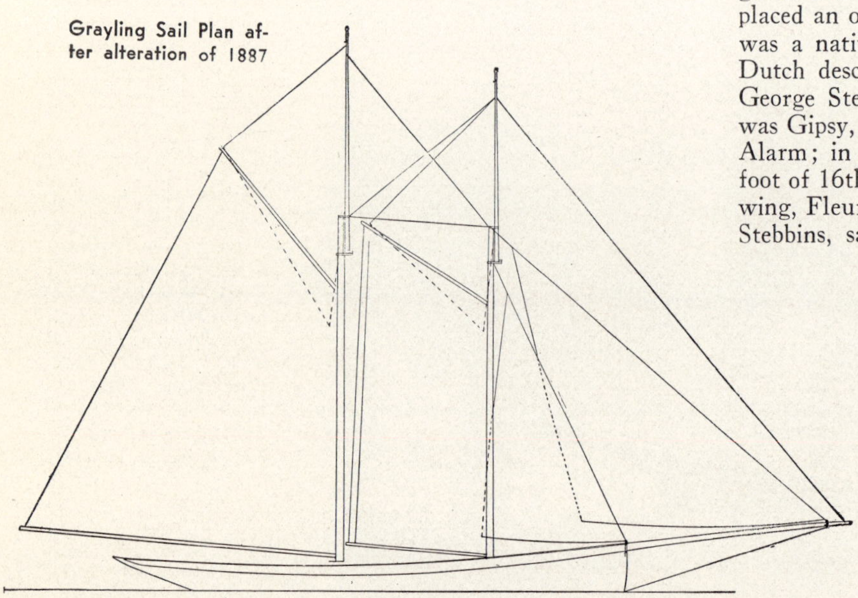

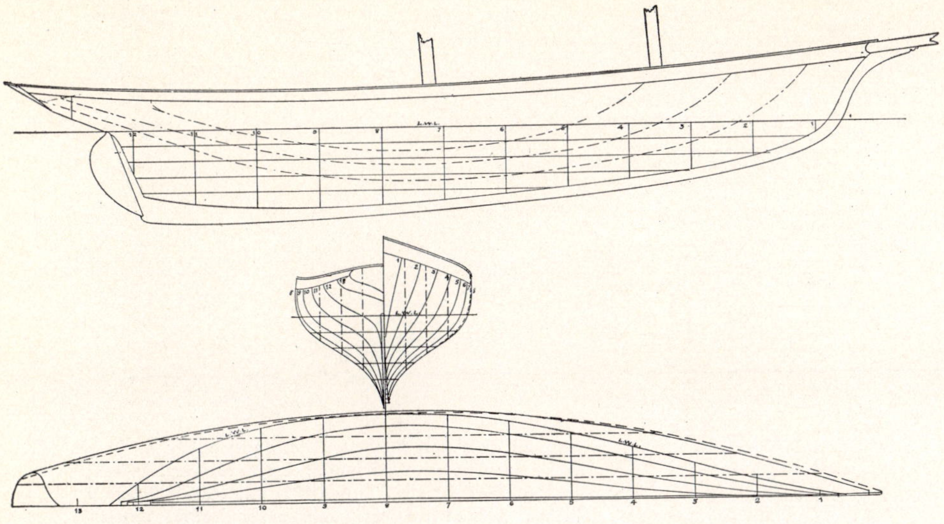

Fortuna, designed by A. Cary Smith for Henry S. Hovey, and built beside Grayling in Poillon's Yard, 1883, was a distinct advance in schooner design; a keel yacht intended for general racing and cruising. Her dimensions were: L.o.a. 109 feet; l.w.l. 95 feet; breadth 22 feet 6 inches; draft 12 feet; outside ballast 11 tons.

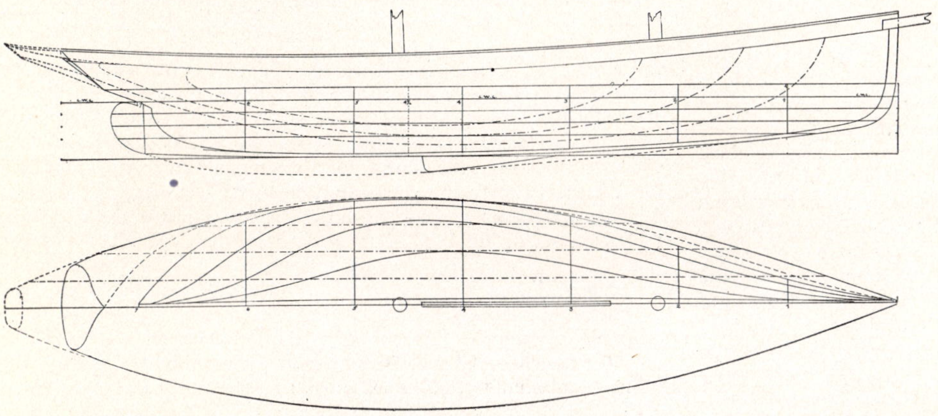

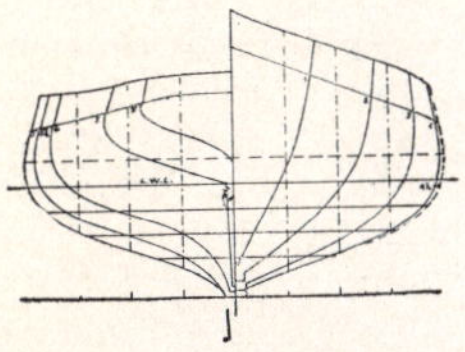

Grayling, modelled by Philip Elsworth, built by C. & R. Poillon, for Latham A. Fish, 1883. L.o.a. 91 feet; l.w.l. 81 feet; breadth 23 feet; draft 5 feet 9 inches. Grayling was the last of her type of capsizable centerboard schooners; the measurement of "over-all length" which produced the sandbaggers was replaced about 1880 by "mean length," the length over all added to the length on waterline divided by two. Grayling, in 1887, was placed in the hands of Edward Burgess for modernization; her after overhang was extended six feet, a keel, including 15 tons of lead, increased her draft to 8 feet 6 inches; her lower masts were cut 10 and 11 feet, and her headrig was changed by the shipping of a pole bowsprit

to have been size, speed, and the utmost extreme in elegance of furnishings. As a matter of detail, her model seems to have been based primarily on the size of her main saloon.

On July 20, 1876, Mohawk lay at anchor with the fleet off the New York Y. C. Station at Stapleton, Staten Island; there was a party aboard for an afternoon sail on a fair summer day; in addition to Mr. and Mrs. Garner were Miss Adele Hunter, Miss Edith Sybil May, Col. Schuyler Crosby, Gardner Howland, Louis B. Montant and Frost Thorne. Her mainsail, foresail and both topsails were set and the crew were forward ready to heave short, but before the anchor was off the ground a puff struck her and heeled her until her port rail was under water; before she could recover a heavier blow from the Staten Island hills capsized her. The captain and crew on deck were thrown into the water and picked up by boats from other yachts, Countess of Dufferin, Phantom, Dreadnaught and others; most of the party were below, and not only the ballast but the unsecured furniture fell to leeward and pinned them down. Mr. Garner died in the attempt to rescue his wife, Miss Hunter and Frost Thorne died with them, and also a cabin boy.

The summer home of Mr. Garner was on the North Shore of Staten Island and he had an interest in the North Shore Ferry; the superintendent of the ferry, Annin Smith, took charge of the salving operations.

The yacht was towed by tugs to the flats inside Constable's Hook on the New Jersey shore, and as the tide fell she righted and a diver was sent down after nightfall, but he was unable to do anything on account of the furniture and ballast jammed on one side. Next morning the body of Mrs. Garner was found, then that of the cabin boy, and later those of Miss Hunter and Mr. Garner. After midnight on July 22 the wrecking steamer Lackawanna placed a pipe aboard and soon cleared the yacht of water; at 5 A.M. the body of Mr. Thorne was discovered in an angle between the cabin bulkhead and a pile of furniture. The sailing master, Captain Oliver P. Rowland, asserted that he had cast off the main sheet and that it had jammed after two-thirds had run out; when examined it was found hauled flat aft, with two turns around the upper and one around the lower part of the bitts, the helm being hard up; Captain Smith had the turns lashed as evidence.

There was much feeling against Captain Rowland and he was arrested on a charge of criminal negligence; on July 21 a jury was empanelled including such yachtsmen as William Krebs and James O. Proudfit, with prominent neighbors of Mr. Garner at West Brighton. After hearing the testimony of Messrs. Montant, Crosby and Howland, the captain, quartermaster and other officers, the jury acquitted Captain Rowland, but with the mild statement "that the evidence shows that, with the approaching squall, *it was not prudent* to get the yacht under way, particularly with the topsails set." As a matter of fact, she was not under way when struck, her anchor being on the ground.

The capsize of Mohawk, the greatest catastrophe in American yachting, marked the slack point of the tide, just before it turned against what was the national type, and in favor of narrower, deeper and better ballasted yachts. The defenders of the centerboard type credited the capsize to an act of Providence, a so-called twister from the Staten Island hills; this view was expressed by Captain Coffin, a thorough sailor, the leading yachting writer of his day; but an offensive partisan of the sloop. "In point of fact, the Mohawk was as safe a vessel as ever floated. She was lost through the grossest carelessness, and in consequence of the over-confidence felt in her stabil-

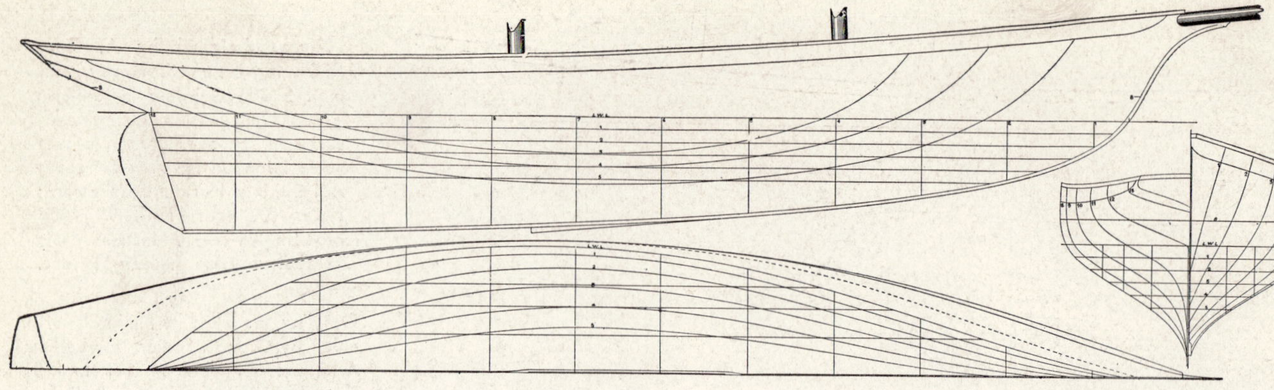

ity. There has been no vessel yet built in this world that cannot be wrecked by careless handling, and that the Mohawk upset was in no wise due to any defect of model. Properly handled, she was more than ordinarily safe."

Throughout the period of her building much had been said of her great size, elegance and expected speed, and a very lively controversy was carried on in the daily press and in such publications as *The Spirit of the Times* and *The Aquatic Monthly*. On the side of the defense were "Handy Billy," "Enthusiast," "Hard-a-lee," "Anchor," "Devoted Yachtsman" and the valiant Col. S.M.T. The opposition was a minority of little more than one, the irrepressible "Big Topmast" (C. P. Kunhardt) for years a voice crying aloud in the wilderness. One correspondent, "Cutty Hunk," in criticizing the model made the suggestion "Take two feet from Mohawk's beam and add it to her draft." After her initial trial her sternpost was moved seven feet aft to improve her steering, changes were made in her ballast, which varied from 30 to 50 tons, much of it, with her chain, being stowed aft. It was stated that with a designed displacement of 200 tons she was ballasted to 260 tons, with her draft increased to 6 feet 9 inches. Her brief career as a yacht thus ended, she was sold to the Government, her rig cut down, and a keel added; and under the name of Eagre she was used for many years in the Coast and Geodetic Survey.

THERE was at that time no general knowledge on the part of modellers, builders, professional yacht hands or yacht owners, of the difference between *initial stability*, the first resistance of a vessel to the heeling power of the wind, and the *range of stability*, the ultimate point to which a vessel may be forced before capsizing. This subject was treated exhaustively by "Big Topmast" in *The Aquatic Monthly* of October 1875, with diagrams and geometrical demonstrations, but it is doubtful whether it was studied or even read by those who might have profited by it; or whether it would have meant anything to them had they read it.

The year 1876 was a most active one in yachting, the racing spirit was very keen among the schooners, there was the Centennial Exhibition, with the Centennial Regattas for all classes; and the third match for the America's Cup. The challenger in this case came from Canada, the schooner Countess of Dufferin, easily defeated by Madeleine; this match marking the exit of the schooner rig from the Cup competition.

MENTION has been made in an earlier article of the capsize of the schooner Josephine on July 15, 1872, in the Upper Bay on a clear summer day with a party of ladies aboard watching a sandbag race. This yacht, built in 1865 and re-built in 1870, was 87 feet 6 inches on the waterline, 21 feet 6 inches in breadth, and drew 8 feet 3 inches; her owner, Lloyd Phoenix, a Navy man, was an experienced sailor. Fortunately, no one was drowned, and two years later Mr. Phoenix took Josephine on a cruise through the islands of the West Indies. What a centerboard yacht might do was proved by the winter passage of Vesta in the race of 1866; a yacht of 100 feet waterline, 25 feet breadth, and but 7 feet 6 inches draft. Such performances, however, presented no conclusive answer to the growing storm of criticism of the type as dangerous in the extreme.

One of the most successful exponents of the rule-o'thumb school was "Capt'n Phip" Elsworth of Bayonne, in business with his brothers in the oyster fishery, but modelling some of the fastest yachts of the day. Among the sloops were Fanita, Anaconda, Elephant, Kangaroo, Crocodile, Middy, Sasqua, Eurybia, Gleam, Arab, Penguin and Gertrude. In addition were two steam yachts, Fedalma

Iroquois, originally built as Julia, designed by A. Cary Smith for Chester W. Chapin. L.o.a. 96 feet 3 inches; l.w.l. 80 feet 6 inches; breadth 21 feet; draft 9 feet 9 inches. Built of steel, this yacht marks a radical departure in her deep body with both keel and centerboard; the forerunner of the modern "compromise" type

and Cora. Mr. Elsworth's work was limited to the carving of the half-model, he made no calculations and did no building; his models, generally with straight plumb stems and very short after overhangs, were characterized by beautifully moulded forebody with an easy entrance, perhaps at the expense of a clean run. In 1874 he modelled for W. H. Langley the schooner Comet, 82 feet over all; 73 feet 4 inches waterline; 22 feet breadth and 4 feet 7 inches draft; a very successful yacht. In 1882 he modelled for Samuel R. Platt a larger schooner, Montauk, 103 feet 10 inches over all; 94 feet 8 inches waterline; 25 feet 4 inches breadth and 7 feet 4 inches draft; she repeating in a larger class the success of Comet. In 1882 he modelled for Latham A. Fish the schooner Grayling, 91 feet over all; 81 feet waterline; 23 feet breadth and 5 feet 9 inches draft. She was like Montauk, well constructed by Poillon Bros.

BY this time the battle of the types had reached an acute stage, with the new cult of "Cutter-Cranks" loudly denouncing the old national type and ready to gloat over every fresh capsize. Charles P. Kunhardt was above all a fatalist, with a firm conviction —realized, alas, too late—that he would "make his pile." While engaged for some years in the editorship of the Yachting Department of *Forest & Stream*, he broke away at intervals on wild mining ventures which were to make his fortune. In the early winter of 1882 he went to North Carolina to mine mica, but the venture proved as unsuccessful as other previous and later ones, and he arrived in New York on May 14, 1883. During the winter I had built for my old friend Henry W. Eaton a yawl, Aneto, of 21 feet waterline, from his own design; on May 12 we started from the Seawanhaka Basin at Tompkinsville and ran down to the Horseshoe for a trial trip. We sailed back on Sunday, a bright clear day, and when abreast of Hoffman Island sighted the masts of a schooner, the tops just clear of the water and the crew working there to unbend the topsails. They paid no attention to our very foolish question as to the name of the yacht, but the answer came in Monday's papers in headlines announcing the trial trip and capsize of the new Grayling. By the irony of fate, Kunhardt was on the spot, with his virile and caustic pen to chronicle the event in *Forest & Stream* of the following Thursday. Fortunately no one was lost, so his comments were unrestricted. As in the case of Mohawk, the event was attributed to Nature, another twister; the only comment which Captain Coffin had to make was:—"the principal result of the accident being to bring into prominence the indomitable pluck and perseverance of the owner; who, in eighteen days from the time she sank, had her ready to start in the Decoration Day sail of the Club (the Atlantic)." Considering that hull and spars were uninjured, and that she was quickly raised and pumped out, there was little remarkable in her reconditioning.

A similar disaster on a much smaller scale than that of Mohawk occurred on June 15, 1888, a little higher up the Bay, off the Corinthian Y.C. Station at Tompkinsville; the little schooner Agnes was at anchor at night, with sails stowed, when a squall hit her and rolled her over, only three of her crew of four escaping. Modelled by E. Harvey and built by the Poillons in 1871, she was altered in her first season and again in 1881, with a new counter

(*Continued on page* 40)

CUTTER YACHT "MARIA"
In Her Trial of Speed with the Clipper Yacht America in New York Bay, 1851
To John C. Stevens, Esq., Commodore of the New York Yacht Club this print is with permission respectfully dedicated

TRADITIONS AND MEMORIES OF American Yachting

Part Eight: THE BIG SLOOPS

By WILLIAM P. STEPHENS

From a painting by J. E. Butterworth, 1852. The caption of this lithograph is The Cutter Maria; it is not clear why the term cutter was used, as the yacht was distinctly a sloop, cutters being unknown in America

THE size, and imposing appearance of their hulls, together with the acres of billowing canvas, account in a measure for the popularity of the big schooners; especially among the wealthier yachtsmen. At the same time, the sloop, an importation from Holland in the early days of Nieuw Amsterdam, later localized in the trade of the North River, exerted a powerful influence on the early yachts.

A search for the origin of the term "sloop" carries us far back in maritime history; its early form in Holland was "sloepe," while the French form was "chaloupe," in English, "shallop." The first sloops were ship's boats, a size larger than the "pinnace"; that eminent antiquarian and historian, my old friend Captain Arthur H. Clark, to whom I owe so much for my knowledge of old craft, described a "sloepe" of 1675, but traced the term even further back, to 1599. In size about 32 by 9, manned by one in command, probably a boatswain, who held the helm, with five oarsmen, its work was to carry cargo, to carry out and lift anchors, and heavier work in general than the "pinnace"; while the smallest boat, the "gig," carried only officers and passengers. Both the "sloepe" and the "pinnace" carried masts and sails, to be stepped and set when the wind was favorable.

The first boats of this type in the new colonies were probably left by visiting ships, and used for fishing, trading, and general water transport; gradually increasing in size, and with permanent instead of emergency rigs. By the end of the seventeenth century sloops of 30 to 50 tons were used on the North River, in coastal trading, and even in voyages to the West Indies. While the sails were limited to a mainsail, one big jib, and working topsail, some of the sea-going sloops carried a square topsail.

One of the first ventures in yachting of the Stevens family was the building of the sloop Maria, named after the wife of Commodore Stevens, in 1845; her planning being ascribed to Robert Livingston Stevens, brother of John C. and Edwin A., and chiefly noted as the assistant of his father, Col. John Stevens, in the building of the Camden & Amboy Railroad, the steamboat Princeton, and the development of both rail and water transportation. The illustration of Maria is a print by N. Currier, 1852, from a painting by J. E. Butterworth; which not only shows the yacht, but gives many details; the title is interesting, "Cutter Yacht Maria, in her trials with the

Sloop Alice, built by Townsend, Portsmouth, N. H., 1866, for Thomas G. Appleton, of Boston. Elected to N. Y. Y. C., July 12, 1866. Sailed from Boston to Cowes under command of Capt. Arthur H. Clark, in July 1866. 19 days, 6 hours, 20 minutes. Right: Old New York Working Sloop from an etching by R. J. Pattison, 1889

Clipper Yacht America in New York Bay, 1851." The details are thus given: Tonnage by displacement, 137. Length on deck, 110 feet. Breadth of Beam, 26½ feet. Depth of Hold, 8 feet 8 inches (the draft, not given, is said to have been 5 feet 2 inches). Mast, 91 feet. Boom, 95 feet. Gaff, 50 feet. Jib-boom, 70 feet. Bowsprit, outboard, 27 feet; in the partners 24 inches. It is stated that the mast was hollow, bored like a pump-log; the boom was built up of staves, like a barrel, the hoops being visible in the picture; it was trussed internally by iron rods. The topmast, as in all sloops of this era, was very short, and not fitted to house. The two forward shrouds led to the hounds, the two after ones to the cap; the chainplates were in pairs, each two connected by diagonal braces. The sails were cross-cut, with a bonnet in the jib; the sails of America, seen in the background, have vertical cloths; she also has lanyards, not discernible in Maria. The deck was flush, with a small trunk over the companion. The rowboat shown in the foreground is pre-

Bianca, built by Fish & Clark, 1854, for Charles Macalaster, Jr., of Philadelphia. Elected to N. Y. Y. C., May, 1852. Said to have been modeled by R. L. Stevens. Length on deck, 44 feet; length on keel, 42 feet; mast, 54 feet; bowsprit, 25 feet; outboard, 19 feet; boom, 44 feet; gaff, 23 feet; hoist of mainsail, 45 feet; foot of jib, 30 feet

sumably a Whitehall boat as they existed ninety years ago.

There were two centerboards, the smaller in the after deadwoods; the larger was of 7 tons weight (as reported), of iron and loaded with lead; it did not swing on a pin, but both ends were lowered and raised together by chains from a horizontal shaft over the trunk. With a small sheave on the forward end and a larger one on the after end, the after end of the board dropped more rapidly than the fore end. At one time a part of her lead ballast was transferred to the outside of the planking in a layer from 5 inches thick next the keel to 2 inches at the outer edge. There is a vague story that this lead was poured from inside, through holes cut in the planking, but this would bear much corroboration; though there apparently was no limit to Robert Stevens' daring and originality.

Prior to 1865 the regular course of the New York Y. C. was from a line between the Club House at Hoboken (now the Glen Cove Station of the Club) to a flagboat moored across the river. The yachts were anchored head-to-wind on the north side of this line in the following order of position: the third class abreast the stakeboat, 80 yards apart on a line due east; the second class, 90 yards apart, on a line parallel with the same, 200 yards to the north; the first class, 100 yards apart on a similar line 200 yards to the north of the latter; the schooners anchored to the eastward of the second and first class lines in the same order. The yachts to pass to the north and west of a flagboat stationed off Robbins Reef Lighthouse; thence easterly to a flagboat stationed off Owl's Head, Long Island, passing it to the north and east; thence around the buoy off the South West Spit, passing it from north and east. Returning, first pass the flagboat off Owl's Head, passing it to the south and east; thence to the flagboat off Robbins Reef Light, passing it to the south and west; thence to a flagboat off Castle Garden, passing it to the south and east; thence to the flagboat off the Club House, passing it to the westward. In going and returning all buoys on the West Bank, namely, Nos. 11, 13 and 15, must be passed to the eastward. Before starting yachts were allowed to have mainsails, foresails and gaff-topsails set. Such a course as this, especially in the southwest winds which prevailed throughout our old summers, placed a premium on the longest yacht, and the one with the best reaching qualities; and may account in part for Maria's reputation for extreme speed. If her trials with America were sailed over this course it is no wonder that the newer and more modern yacht was defeated. She was altered at various times, lengthened, reballasted, and finally converted to schooner rig. While interesting as an evidence of the comprehensiveness of the Stevens genius, and as an experiment, she had little effect on the development of yacht design.

The typical working sloop in use about New York and the west end of Long Island Sound about the middle of the nineteenth century is well shown in an old lithograph without caption or date. Crude as she is, this craft was the progenitor of the sloop yacht. The open hold indicates an oyster boat, but with the usual deck she could carry a cargo, in the hold or on deck. The model is of extreme "Cod's-head" type, with very bluff bows. The rig has all the characteristics of the sloop yacht: mast set well forward and very high; topmast, short, and not fitted to house; bowsprit a heavy balk of timber, square in the knightheads, outboard eight-square, tapering into a round; with a heavy bar bobstay. The shrouds, set up with deadeyes and lanyards which are concealed by the chafing gear, are rattled down. The jib is fitted with lazyjacks fast to a toggle which hoists up on the jib-stay. The environment is one familiar to all the old boys who may have sailed canoes or catboats two generations ago about Raritan Bay, Staten Island Sound, or the numerous small creeks debouching into the west end of Long Island Sound. A muddy creek beween salt marshes, in the background a meadow with a farm house and orchards; today this scene is probably marred by a modern steel bridge across the creek and a motor speedway through the farm. Certainly Kipling was right when he wrote "An' there ain't no 'busses runnin' from the Bank to Mandalay."

AS late as the seventies oyster sloops and working boats of this class were admitted with the yachts in the races of some clubs; still later the Larchmont Y. C. had a special class for working boats. Enrolled in the fleet of the Brooklyn Y. C. were the working sloops Admiral and Commodore, owned by Cap'n Joe Elsworth and used regularly in his oystering operations in the Lower Bay and Raritan Bay, but racing in the regular yacht classes of the Club. Admiral was of 29 tons, 60 feet l.o.a., built by L. H. Hoagland of New Brunswick, N. J., a yacht builder, in 1872. Commodore, 25 tons, was built by Lon Smith at Islip, L. I., in 1873; she was 45 feet l.o.a.; 41 feet 4 inches l.w.l.; 12 feet 6 inches breadth.

The sloop division grew gradually from 1851 (the building of Silvie has been described in an earlier chapter). George Steers also contributed to the class Ray, 1853, and Julia, 1854; Rebecca, 1855, was modeled and built by William Tooker, a brother-in-law of Steers.

Unfortunately, there is little reliable data now available on these early yachts; many were built, more or less by eye, from the half-model; and few of these models are left. There were very few drawings such as are made today, and these few have disappeared. The once-universal standard of size was Custom House tonnage, Old or New Measurement, both meaningless today; dimensions were seldom made public, yacht registers were unknown, and the few club books published gave such measurements as cubic contents; or the product of the length and breadth on the waterline.

In the first regattas of the New York Y. C. the time allowance was based on tons, at first by Custom House Measurement, but later apparently by displacement obtained by actual weighing; though there is no record of how this was done. The fleet was small, and divided into two classes of schooners and three of sloops. In the sixties the basis of measurement was the circumscribing rectangle of the load waterline plane; later the Cubic Contents Rule was adopted. Under this peculiar rule the actual bulk below and above water, from the rabbet of the keel to a horizontal plane tangent to the lowest point of the sheer, and not including overhangs, was calculated in cubic feet. As new clubs were formed other systems of measurement were adopted; bringing new class groupings as the yachts sailed under different burgees. By 1880 the fleet of the New York Y. C. had increased to 65 sailing yachts, with two classes of schooners and two of sloops racing under the Cubic Contents Rule; in 1883, with a fleet of 85 yachts, of which 33 were sloops, the Club adopted the Length-and-Sail-Area Rule, but with waterline length as the basis for classification. As these various changes progressed the fleet increased in numbers, the yachts became segregated in more classes with less difference in size within each class. In the smaller class were such yachts as Wave, Schemer, Kaiser, Genia, Whitecap, Kelpie, Rover, Madcap, Volante and Lizzie L.; in the next larger were Vision, Vixen, Eclipse, Regina, Addie, Fanita, Wizard, Coming and Viola; while in the largest (not over 70 feet waterline), Julia, Gracie, Fanny, Hildegard, Arrow, Pocahontas and Mischief raced together under the popular name of "The Big Sloops."

(*Continued from page* 36)

in 1887. She was 53 feet 11 inches waterline; 16 feet 9 inches breadth, and 6 feet draft; later increased to 6 feet 6 inches. Her owner, J. Norton Winslow, was very careful to explain to me that she did not *capsize,* but only *cut under;* a distinction without a difference.

These major disasters were multiplied almost innumerably in the capsizes not only of half-decked racing craft, but of cabin cruisers of all sizes; matters of almost weekly occurrence throughout the yachting season. "The principal result," to quote Captain Coffin's comment on the Grayling capsize, was to arouse a wide-spread sentiment in favor of less breadth, greater depth of body and draft, and outside lead as ballast. Not only were the true keel cutters growing in favor, but there came in a new type of "compromise sloop"; very different in dimensions and form from the yachts of the seventies and early eighties; with a centerboard working through an outside lead keel, and a rig of the proportions of the cutter, whether with one or two headsails.

Changing conditions of business and social life, with the growing interest in the single-stick rig created by the battle of the sloops and cutters, dimmed the popularity of the schooner rig for racing. After the match of 1876—Countess of Dufferin and Madeleine—the America's Cup matches were sailed by cutters and sloops; another blow at the schooners. The rig, however, retained its popularity for cruising and general sailing; many very fine craft of up-to-date design being built. The three Cup defenders of 1885-6-7, Puritan, Mayflower and Volunteer, originally compromise centerboard cutters, were in turn converted to schooners as being more easily handled and more economical to run; this process continuing until recent years. Ocean races were sailed at times by schooners, as that between Coronet and Dauntless in 1887; and many long cruises were made in schooners specially designed for sea-going; the rig being deservedly popular for the largest size of cruising yachts today.

The cup won by the American sloop Sylvie in August, 1853. The engraving "Queen's Cup" was added later and is incorrect

TRADITIONS AND MEMORIES OF American Yachting

By WILLIAM P. STEPHENS

Part Nine: THE BIG SLOOPS

(Continued)

THE invasion of American waters by the British cutter in 1880 inaugurated a merry war which waged furiously for five years, dividing yachtsmen into two hostile camps, breaking up old friendships, and completely revolutionizing both design and construction. As this movement began in the class of which we are writing, it is necessary, before taking up the yachts themselves and their creators, to consider yacht construction as it had existed from the beginning of the sport.

Throughout its first half-century yachtbuilding was only shipbuilding in miniature; the same materials and the same methods. The material was abundant and cheap: white oak for keel, stempiece, sternpost, keelsons, frames and part of planking; hard pine for the longitudinal members such as stringers, clamps, ceiling, waterways and planking, hackmatac, with its crooked roots giving knees and its straight trunk deck beams and similar members; white pine for decks and spars, white cedar for planking of small vessels, especially yachts; locust for bitts, stanchions, kevels, cleats; and, in particular, treenails; and spruce and pine for spars.

All of this material was worked by hand with axe, adze, saw, auger, maul and beetle. The shipbuilder, who put in his ten hours of heavy labor for a wage of $1.50 to $2.00 (even as late as 1880), was originally an all-around worker; felling the trees, hewing and sawing them to shape, carrying the timbers about the yard in erecting the frame, "squaring off" with the adze the frames for the faying of the planking, boring for and driving bolts, dumps and treenails, "squaring down" the planking, caulking, and finally laying down the ways, wedging up, and cutting out the keel blocks before the order "Down dogshore" sent her on her way. Even after this was the shipping of the spars which he had shaped. By degrees the work was divided and specialized, with gangs for each division. As timber became less plentiful in the vicinity of such centers as Boston and New York, special gangs felled the trees in distant forests and loaded them on vessels for transportation.

In the earliest phase of American shipbuilding the moulds for all members were taken into the woods, and as the trees were felled they were cut to the required shapes for stem, frames, knees, etc.; mainly with axe and adze. The sawing into long timbers, such as keel, clamps, ceiling and planking, was done by placing the log on trestles over the "sawpit," dug in the ground, in which the "pitman" pulled the saw down, while the "top-sawyer" pulled it up.

The fastenings were bolts or "dumps" (spikes cast in composition); copper, though more costly, was used in preference to iron owing to the rusting of the latter through the tannic acid in oak; and to the corrosion through galvanic action in the case of a coppered vessel. In small craft sweet gum was preferred to oak for the keel, as this wood had no effect on iron. With the metal bolts, treenails (pronounced trunnels) were used; round pins of oak or locust, driven through planking, frames and ceiling. While white oak was preferred in large ships, locust, once abundant about New York and Long Island, was generally used in yachts. Strong, hard and tough, with a very straight grain, the butt of the tree was sawn into lengths of about two feet, and split into pieces roughly over an inch square. The trunnel maker sat astride of a bench (such as was also used for getting out barrel hoops) with a swinging vertical arm projecting below and above. There was a rest for the foot on the lower end, and a projection on each side of the upper end. A pressure on the foot acted to grip the locust

Arrow, modeled and built by David Kirby, 1874. L.o.a., 66 feet 8 inches; l.w.l., 61 feet 3 inches; breadth, 20 feet 2 inches; depth, 6 feet 8 inches; draft, 5 feet 6 inches

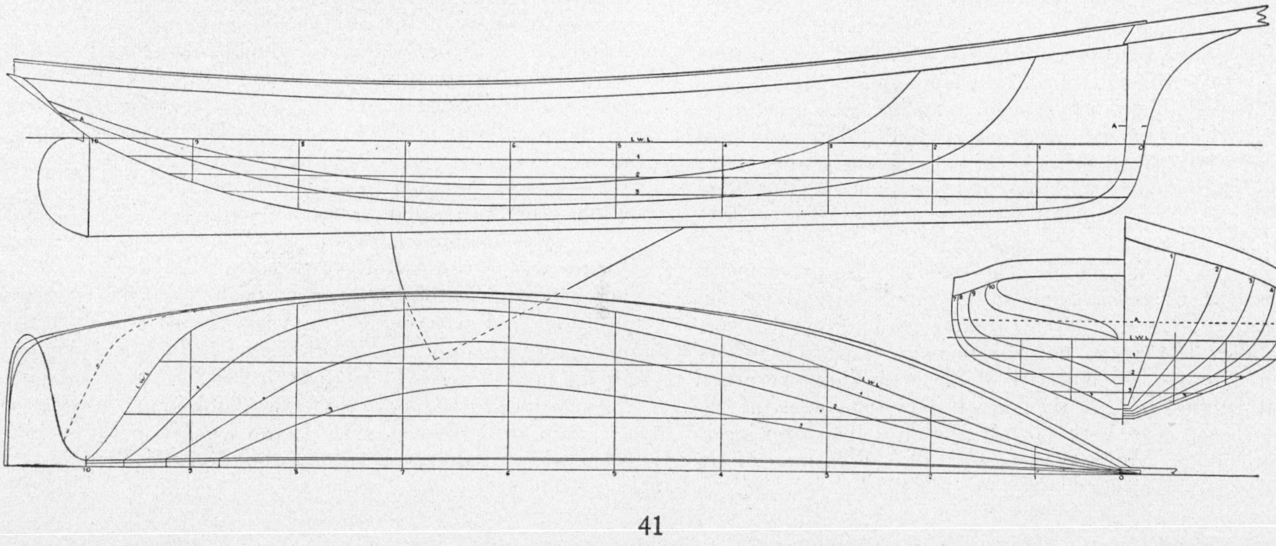

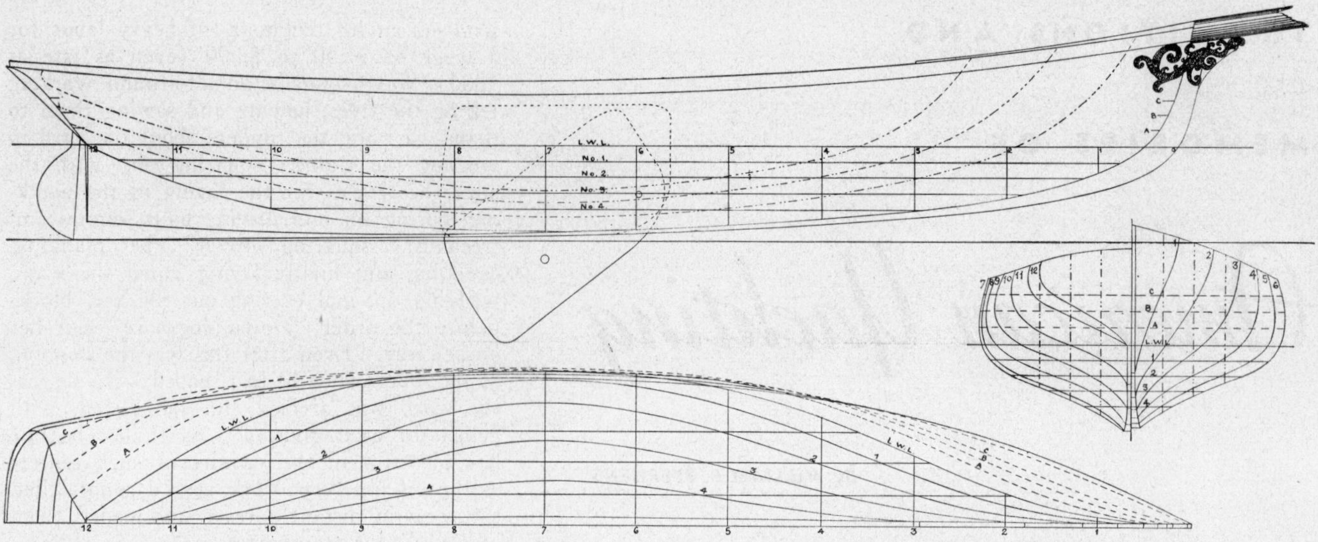

Sloop Julia, modeled and built by George Steers, 1854. L.o.a., 81 feet; l.w.l., 71 feet 2 inches; breadth, 20 feet; depth, 6 feet 6 inches; draft, 6 feet 3 inches

within reach of a drawknife in the hands of the operator; who, turning it constantly, soon shaped it into "eight-square" or "six-square" (eight or six-sided), with a taper. These trunnels were made up in advance and allowed ample time to dry out and season. The hole for the trunnel was bored with an auger, the trunnel was greased and driven with an iron maul, or, preferably, a wooden beetle; the projecting ends were cut off flush with planking and ceiling, both ends were wedged, and the outer end caulked as well. In planking of such width as was used in yachts there was a bolt or "dump" and a trunnel in each frame; each alternately on the upper and lower edge. The trunnel made a very secure fastening, lasting as long as the wood through which it passed.

The general specifications for a yacht of 70 feet waterline would call for a frame of oak, chestnut, hackmatac and black walnut, 8 by 9 inches at keel and spaced 24 inches between centers; bolted with 3/4 inch iron. Keel sided 17 inches and about two feet deep; stem and apron of white oak, of natural crook with long scarph to keel. Sternpost of oak. Deck framing of chestnut, 6 by 9 inches, spaced 3 feet; with carlins between and double-kneed throughout, fastened with 3/4 inch iron. Garboards and upper strakes of 2½ inch oak, other plank of 2½ inch yellow pine. Planksheer of 3 inch oak, and rail of 2½ inch oak. The deck will be laid with 2½ inch square white pine; and ceiling of 1½ inch yellow pine. Sides of centerboard trunk 6 inches thick below; 5 inches in middle, and 4 inches at topsides; bolted with 3/4 and 7/8 iron. The board to be 21 feet long, 9 feet wide, and 4 inches thick; bolted with 7/8 inch iron. Rudder stock of toughest white oak; the head being 9 inches in diameter.

The system of construction here described was entirely satisfactory when applied to packet ships, clippers and war vessels; but when applied to yachts on a greatly reduced scale it did not work out so well. This was most apparent in the fastenings: with a ship's frame of 12 inches siding (the thickness in a fore-and-aft direction) a hole of 1 or 1½ inches for bolt, or 1¼ for a trunnel, did not reduce the strength materially, but with the frame of a yacht sided 4 inches a hole of 5/8 or 3/4 inches for a bolt, or an inch hole for a trunnel meant a serious reduction of area. While centerboard vessels of considerable size were not uncommon, especially in the United States, the majority of the great ships were keel craft; almost all of the yachts, however, were of the centerboard type, with slots of a fifth of the waterline in length in the center of the keel. This weakening of the backbone of the structure, with the vertical stiffness, the depth of girder, cut to a minimum by the limited depth of hold, necessarily resulted in a weak hull.

A material advance was made by that great American shipbuilder Donald McKay (born in Shelburne, Nova Scotia in 1810) in the years about 1850 in the replacement of hand power by machinery. His most important invention was the power saw; not only for vertical cuts, but capable of being changed while in operation from one angle to another, thus cutting the varying bevel on frames. For the cutting of metal bolts, round iron or copper up to 1½ inches diameter, previously done with chisel and hammer, he invented power shears; while for making the trunnels he invented a lathe which turned them out not only more rapidly but more accurately. Another important invention was the derrick, for raising frames formerly erected by hand.

Turning now to the men who produced the early yachts, first on the list comes George Steers; a shipwright, with all that the term implies, by birth and training: the modeller and builder of war vessels, sailing ships, pilot boats and yachts. Associated with him at one time was William H. Brown, another shipbuilder; their yard or yards being in New York, on the East River, at or about 12th Street.

The lines of Arrow and Gracie are typical of the yachts of the seventies, a very hollow entrance with an exaggerated fullness of the after body, as shown in the load waterline; it is interesting to compare these two yachts with Julia, of twenty years earlier date; her clean run and beautifully balanced fore and after bodies. Julia, by the way, built in 1854, ended her days, of course after many alterations and rebuildings, when she grounded (as the schooner Nirvana) on the Isle of Pines in October 1906, after 52 years of service.

A very notable character who appears in the early forties was "Capt'n Bob" Fish; originally a boatbuilder and a skillful handler of sandbag boats, probably engaged in fishing and oystering at times; later noted as a modeller of yachts, a builder, and a very clever professional skipper in the largest yachts. As early as 1845 he built a sloop, Newburgh, for Henry Robertson, following her with Ultra in 1848, Bianca in 1851, and Luckey in 1855. His shop was at Saltersville or Pamrapo, on the New Jersey

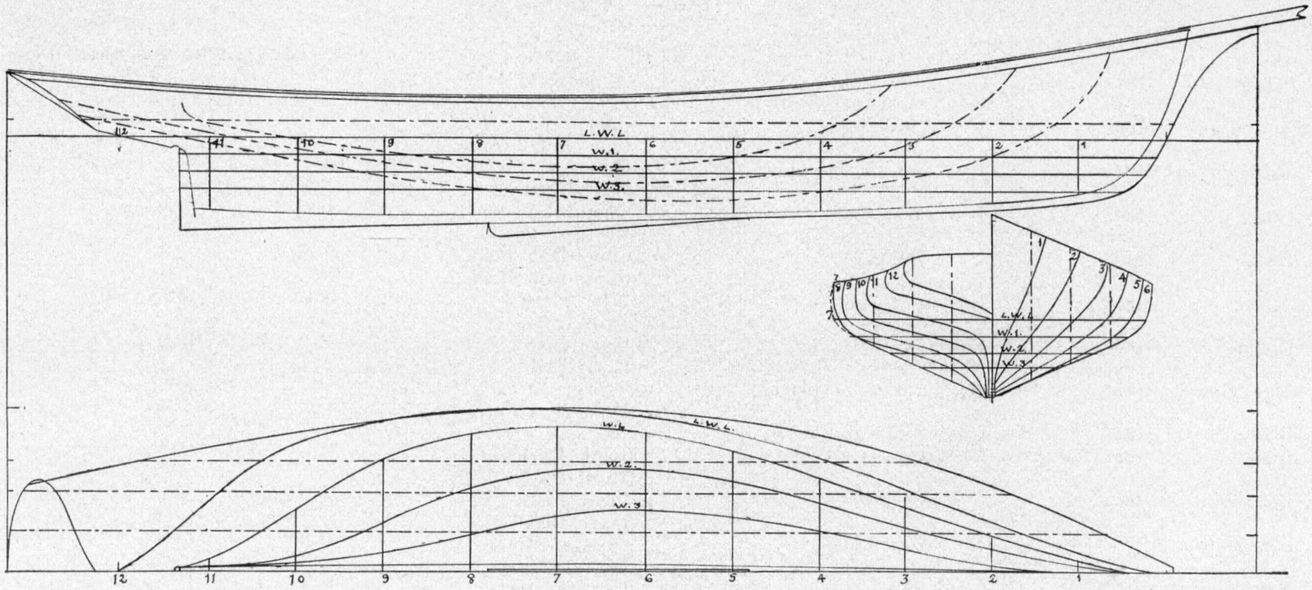

Gracie, modeled by Abraham A. Scank, built by A. G. Polhamus, 1868. Lines as taken from yacht by John Hyslop, 1882. L.o.a., 82 feet 6 inches; l.w.l., 70 feet 8 inches; breadth, 21 feet 6 inches; depth, 6 feet 6 inches; draft, 6 feet 3 inches

shore. At one time he was in partnership with Charles F. Morton, of Hudson, N. Y., for whom Luckey, of sharpie model, was built; Mr. Morton made his journeys from Hudson to New York aboard the yacht. There was also an Isaac Fish, who built the sloop Gertrude in 1852 and Undine in 1850, of whom little is known.

The recognized yacht builders at this date were very few, most of the yachts being built as a side line by shipbuilders. There were two concerns in Philadelphia, Theodore Byerly & Son, afterwards Byerly, Hillman & Streaker, and Albertson Bros., who built several yachts for R. F. Loper; John Letts built some yachts in New York, and J. B. Voris, at Nyack, N. Y., also built some, One of the first established yacht yards about New York was that of David Kirby, at Rye, N. Y. There were in the fifties two cousins of the same name, one on Milton Point and the other at the old mill back of Manursing Island; the former was a yacht and boatbuilder, but the latter was known only as a clever boathandler in sandbag craft. He moved across the Sound to Roslyn, L. I., and consequently was known as "Long Island Dave" to distinguish him from his cousin. There were five members of the Kingsland family in the New York Yacht Club, and in 1854 Kirby modelled and built the sloop Mary for D. C. & W. L. Kingsland. In 1868 he built the sloop Madeleine; he built many sandbag boats, but his greatest success was the sloop Arrow, built in 1874. In 1881 he was called on by a syndicate of the New York Yacht Club to model and build an improved Arrow for the defense of the America's Cup against the Canadian challenger Atalanta. The new yacht, Pocahontas, proved a failure; but the question of Mr. Kirby's responsibility is still an open one.

Other builders were James E. Smith, at Nyack, N. Y.; W. L. Force, at Keyport, N. J., and "Lon" Smith, at Islip, L. I. The correct name of the latter was Alonzo E., but by the custom of the time the more familiar abbreviation was in common use. When first apprenticed to Bob Fish, and later when engaged in yacht portraiture, Archibald Cary Smith was known to his friends as "Archie", but later, when designing yachts, to avoid the confusion of A. E. and A. C., he signed himself A. Cary Smith. C. & R. Poillon, on the Brooklyn shore of the East River, and James M. Bayles, at Port Jefferson, Long Island, were shipbuilders, but did much yacht work; the modelling for the Poillons was done by their superintendent, William Townsend.

Well outside the New York district, at the extreme easterly end of Long Island Sound, is the little town of Mystic, Conn., at the mouth of the Mystic River; at one time a center of both ship and yachtbuilding. This was the home of the Mallory family, allied to the sea for generations; Charles H. Mallory, grandfather of the Mallorys now so prominent in yachting, having been an able seaman aboard the brig Appalachicola at the age of 17, and in command of the same vessel two years later. For many years head of the Mallory Line, first sailing ships and then steamships, Mr. Mallory throughout a long life was interested in everything relating to ship and yacht construction. Many of his vessels were built at Mystic, and canvassed in the Mallory sail loft. Closely associated with him for many years was a builder, David O. Richmond. Just how the two worked in the production of many vessels is not known; the method of the day, as far back as the forties, was through the cut model, and this was undoubtedly followed by Richmond. At one time he was in the employ of Mr. Mallory, but about 1865 he purchased the Mallory Yard and carried on business for himself. While Mr. Mallory claimed no such title as naval architect, and presumably knew little of designing as carried on today, he was thoroughly familiar with every class of vessel, and brought to bear this knowledge in collaborating with Richmond in the discussion of the model.

In 1855 Richmond built a sloop which her owner chose to name after him; she was launched on August 10, and four days later entered, as an outside yacht, the regatta of the New York Yacht Club on Narragansett Bay, winning from Ripple, Sachem and L'Esperance in her own class, and finishing in elapsed time ahead of five larger sloops. Richmond is described as having been built in 27 days, she was double-planked on the bottom, the spaces between her frames were filled with 120 bushels of cork; her cost was $3,000. Elected to the New York Yacht Club in May, 1856, Mr. Mallory sailed Richmond with success in many of the regattas of the Club; in 1858 he replaced her with a larger sloop, Haswell, selling her after one season to Henry and Charles Butler, of New York. In 1860 he built the schooner Zouave, and in 1864 the sloop Kate. In later yachts, the steam yacht Kate, the schooner Waterwitch, and some built by Richmond for other owners; the credit must be divided between

EARLY AMERICAN SLOOPS

1840 — 1868

Yacht	Year	Owner	Modeller Builder	L.o.a.	L.w.l.	Breadth	Hold	Draft
Petrel	1840	George B. Rollins	"Cole, et al"	...	...	...	...	...
Mist	1843	Lewis A. Depau	....	...	...	...	...	...
Newburgh	1845	Henry Robertson	Capt. Bob Fish Capt. Bob Fish	...	...	...	...	...
Maria	1846	J. C. & E. A. Stevens	Robert L. Stevens William Capes	94-0	88-0	26-6	8-8	5-2
Una	1847	J. M. Waterbury	George Steers George Steers	60-0	...	17-8	6-3	6-3
Ultra	1848	C. B. Miller	Capt. Bob Fish Capt. Bob Fish	...	...	...	...	...
Alpha	1850	Richard R. Morris	John Letts John Letts	42-0	37-0	13-8	4-10	3-9
Undine	1850	Henry C. Babcock	Isaac Fish Isaac Fish	58-0	57-5	18-0	5-6	5-0
May Flower	1851	Geo. L. & R. Schuyler	George Steers Wm. H. Brown	80-0	74-4	24-6	7-0	6-6
Bianca	1851	Charles Macalaster, Jr.	....	44-0	42-0	...	...	...
Irene	1852	Thomas B. Hawkins	J. M. Bayles J. M. Bayles	70-0	65-0	18-5	5-8	5-6
Gertrude	1852	J. G. Pendelton	Isaac Fish Isaac Fish	70-0	65-0	22-0	7-6	7-6
L'Esperance	1853	Woodbury Langdon	George Steers George Steers	42-0	38-0	12-8	5-3	4-6
Ray	1853	F. M. Ray	George Steers George Steers	48-4	45-1	15-0	5-4	5-9
America	1853	Richard F. Loper	R. F. Loper Byerly, H. & S.	62-0	57-0	20-6	4-4	5-6
Julia	1854	James M. Waterbury	George Steers George Steers	78-8	70-0	20-2	6-8	6-4
Ripple	....	A. C. Kingsland	Capt. Bob Fish Capt. Bob Fish	...	...	...	...	...
Mary	1954	D. C. & W. M. Kingsland	David Kirby David Kirby	43-0	39-0	15-0	3-3	2-6
Ceres	1855	Thomas P. Ives	Benj. Appleton Benj. Appleton	40-0	36-6	15-0	4-6	4-0
Widgeon	1855	William Edgar	George Steers George Steers	80-0	75-0	20-0	7-6	6-8
Prima Donna	1855	D. D. Westervelt	D. D. Westervelt D. D. Westervelt	...	...	...	...	...
Richmond	1855	Charles H. Mallory	D. O. Richmond D. O. Richmond	43-0	40-6	18-0	4-6	3-0
Stella	1855	W. A. Stebbins	H. Nettleton H. Nettleton	56-0	...	21-0	6-6	4-0
Lucky	1855	Charles F. Morton	Capt. Bob Fish Fish & Morton	51-0	48-6	13-0	3-0	2-10
Rebecca	1855	J. J. Van Pelt	William Tooker William Tooker	72-6	65-0	19-2	5-8	6-3
Island Fawn	1856	Charles T. Cromwell	David Kirby David Kirby	44-8	40-0	14-8	3-3	2-0
Edgar	1856	H. A. Dennison	David Kirby David Kirby	43-3	40-0	14-9	3-4	2-0
Mystic	1856	J. H. Dayton	D. D. Mallory D. D. Mallory	49-0	...	17-0	5-0	...
Minnie	1857	W. H. Thomas	J. V. Voris J. V. Voris	60-0	54-0	20-0	5-6	5-6
Madgie	1857	Richard F. Loper	R. F. Loper T. Byerly & Son	...	...	...	...	...
Haswell	1858	Charles H. Mallory	D. O. Richmond D. O. Richmond	63-0	58-0	18-6	5-6	4-6
Manursing	1858	Charles T. Cromwell	David Kirby David Kirby	58-0	54-4	18-1	4-0	4-0
Flying Cloud	1858	L. B. Senat	D. D. Mallory D. D. Mallory	50-1	49-6	14-7	4-0	...
White Wings	1859	Charles P. Williams	Robert Palmer Robert Palmer	...	...	...	...	...
Bonita	1860	Robert Center	D. O. Richmond D. O. Richmond	60-0	55-0	18-0	6-0	4-2
Annie	1861	Anson Livingston	Capt. Bob Fish Albertson Bros.	53-0	45-6	18-0	4-2	3-6
Kate	1864	Charles H. Mallory	D. O. Richmond D. O. Richmond	52-9	47-10	19-0	4-6	4-3
Jessie	1864	Effingham A. Lawrence	....	51-5	50-2	13-5	5-0	...
Eva	1865	George L. Lorillard	Capt. Bob Fish C. & R. Poillon	74-9	69-0	22-0	6-6	5-0
Sadie	1866	John B. Herreshoff	J. B. Herreshoff J. B. Herreshoff	50-0	46-0	16-2	6-3	5-3
Addie V.	1867	William Voorhis	James E. Smith James E. Smith	64-2	56-6	17-1	5-1	4-0
Coming	1868	W. B. Nichols	Capt. Bob Fish C. & R. Poillon	62-0	57-0	20-3	5-5	5-0
Madeleine	1868	Jacob Voorhis	James E. Smith James E. Smith	70-0	65-1	21-0	6-6	6-6
Gracie	1868	William Voorhis	A. A. Schank A. G. Polhamus	72-6	65-0	21-3	6-6	6-3

patron and builder for that close and harmonious collaboration which produced such results.

THE basic particulars of a yacht, as published today, include the length over all, from tip of stemhead to after side of taffrail, the length on waterline, the extreme breadth, the depth of hold, as shown in the ship's papers, and the extreme draft. These measurements were considered of no importance in the days of the cut model, usually made to the inside of the plank, and they are not to be found today. Where length is given it is presumably "between perpendiculars," or "length for tonnage" as taken by the Custom House surveyors; neither of these mean anything today. The load waterline was not considered, in fact it changed with every shift of ballast, and it was frequently altered by lengthening. The breadth where given is usually correct; to the outside of planking at the widest part. The depth of hold may be assumed to be correct, being taken from the ship's papers, but it is largely a structural measurement and means little. It was not until 1872 that the New York Yacht Club included in its yearbook the five measurements mentioned. Few of the dimensions given in the above table may be relied on as actually correct, and of the date of build prior to alteration; they give merely the approximate figures. They show, as a whole, the extreme breadth in comparison with the load waterline, the limited depth of hull, and the limited draft; and account for the capsizes which were of such frequent occurrence.

In the first yachts all dimensions are lacking, the dimensions given for Maria are presumably the original ones, prior to the lengthening. Those who have read the first part of this story will recognize May Flower as the yacht universally known as Silvie; though there is no possible question that she was originally named May Flower and under this name sold to Lewis Augustus Depau in 1852. There is a tradition, which cannot be verified, that the sloop Jessie was built by Effingham A. Lawrence from timber cut on his estate at Bayside, on Little Neck Bay; no record is to be found of her dimensions.

The table shows the growth of the sloop class from its beginning; all were centerboard craft, with a very tall mast stepped well forward, and a mere stump of a topmast; the bowsprit was a heavy baulk of timber built in immovably. One large jib set on a stay was carried. It will be noticed that there are a number of about the length of Richmond; 40 feet waterline; above this were scattered lengths of 55 to 65 feet. Racing in different clubs, and under different rules of measurement, there were no fixed classes; but by degrees a thousand different theories as to the factors of yacht measurement were rejected in favor of two:—length on waterline and sail area. In 1882 the Seawanhaka Corinthian Yacht Club adopted a rule embodying these two factors with a resulting unit of "sail tons," in conformity with the still general use of "tons" in yachting; but in the following year it adopted what has since been known as the "Seawanhaka Rule":—length on waterline plus square root of sail area, divided by two. At the same time the New York Yacht Club adopted the same rule in principle, but the feeling in the Club against a tax on sail was so strong that the rule took the form of twice the length plus the sail area with three as a divisor.

AT the same time definite class limits were established:—for schooners, 100 feet and over, less than 100 feet and not less than 80 feet, and all under 80 feet. For sloops and cutters:—all of 55 feet and over, all less than 55 feet and not under 45 feet, and all under 45 feet. Under this classification there soon developed a large fleet under the two rigs; the actual beginning of systematic building to class and class racing. The very mixed fleet of sloops, to which was now added a fleet of keel cutters imported from England or built in America, started a new era in yacht racing.

One of the most prominent of her day was the sloop Arrow, modelled and built by David Kirby; as launched in April 1874 her dimensions were given as:—l.o.a., 66 feet 8 inches; l.w.l., 61 feet 3 inches; breadth, 20 feet 2 inches; depth, 6 feet 8 inches; draft, 5 feet 6 inches. Mast, 77 feet, topmast, 28 feet, bowsprit 31 feet, boom 63 feet, gaff 33 feet. Built for Daniel Edgar, she was sold out of New York Y. C. in 1877 to Ross R. Winans, who did not race her; but in 1884 she was sold to that keen racing man, W. P. Douglass.

While Arrow was in her day one of the most famous of her class, her racing career was rather brief; at least, compared to that of Gracie, from 1868 to 1910. It is worthy of note that while alterations of rig and name were the rule rather than the exception, both Arrow and Gracie were unchanged in either detail throughout their long lives. The origin of Gracie is somewhat obscure; she was built for William Voorhis, of a well known yachting family, in the yard of James E. Smith, at Nyack, N. Y., in 1868. Her original model is ascribed to Abraham A. Schank, who ran a paint store in Nyack and also painted some portraits of yachts; her builder was A. G. Polhamus; the modelling and building of Tidal Wave, also for Mr. Voorhis, in 1872, is ascribed to the same men. Their relations with James E. Smith are unknown; she was built in the Smith yard, and taken back there frequently for alterations. Her first recorded dimensions were:—l.w.l., 58 feet 3 inches; breadth, 16 feet 4 inches; draft, 4 feet 8 inches. She came into Smith's hands in 1869, 1874 and 1877 for rebuilding and alterations; being raised, hipped, and lengthened 7 feet aft in 1874.

MR. VOORHIS soon sold her to William Krebs and H. W. Johnson, who raced her, selling her in 1872 to J. S. Colgate, who in turn sold her in 1873 to John R. Waller; after other changes of ownership Mr. Waller again raced her in 1877-8-9, then selling her to Charles R. Flint who, in partnership with Joseph P. Earle, raced her for many years. Her dimensions changed constantly, the final ones being:—l.o.a., 81 feet; l.w.l., 72 feet; breadth, 21 feet 6 inches; depth, 6 feet 6 inches; draft, 5 feet 8 inches. The lines shown were taken from the yacht by John Hyslop in 1882; but four years later she was hauled out at the Piepgrass Yard at Greenpoint on the Brooklyn shore for further improvement under the direction of J. Fred Tams, the Corinthian who sailed her for many years in both Corinthian and open races. To quote a report of the day "Her sides will be raised one foot amidships, reducing the sheer; as the height at the bow will remain unchanged and the height aft will be increased but little. The stern will be narrowed in and altered in shape to conform more nearly with modern ideas; and a new deck and cabin house will be added. Sister keelsons will be worked along the keel, jogged down over the heels of the floor timbers, as this part of the boat has been weak ever since the alterations to her centerboard trunk. The new trunk, a large one put in a few years since, will be cut down two feet on the after end, the board being shortened to correspond. The interior will be refitted throughout; the rig will not be materially changed." This continued process of rebuilding and alteration was characteristic of the custom of the day; in common with most of her type Gracie had a pair of "hinge-joints," one at each end of the centerboard trunk. After defending the sloop cause valiantly for many years, Gracie as well as Fanny became nominally cutters in rejecting the typical sloop headrig of one large jib and substituting the jib and forestaysail of the cutter.

It was not until 1910 that Gracie's papers were turned in and she was sold to the old Kirby Shipyard; her rig was removed, a gasoline engine was installed, and she started a new career carrying freight between Milton Point and New York; she did not pay and as a sheer hulk she was sold to the American Yacht Club as a floating bath-house. As she would not float even in this service the hulk was sold and towed away to disintegrate on distant mud flats.

Mischief leading Atalanta (challenger) in fourth match for the America's cup. First race, November 9, 1881

TRADITIONS AND MEMORIES OF AMERICAN YACHTING

Part Ten: THE BIG SLOOPS (Continued)

By WILLIAM P. STEPHENS

THE capsize of the great schooner Mohawk, on July 20, 1876, marks a turning point in American yachting. Prior to this date yachtsmen were committed, almost unreservedly, to the wide, shoal-bodied centerboard type of hull; much as was made of the exploits of America and other large keel schooners, the great majority of yachts were centerboard, and of standardized proportions. While the trans-Atlantic passages of such yachts as Silvie and Vesta, backed by the performance of large centerboard commercial vessels, gave proof of the seaworthiness of properly designed centerboard craft, it was beyond all dispute that the general type, with its dangerously low range of stability, and its growing record of fatal capsizes, was faulty in the extreme.

In the early seventies, however, the pride and self-satisfaction of American yachtsmen were shocked by criticisms, at first few in number but rapidly increasing, of the national type. These appeared in *Forest and Stream,* a weekly established in 1871, and in the *Aquatic Monthly,* established in the following year; both devoted to sports in general, but giving much attention to yachting. The pioneer in this campaign was

Gracie, under double head rig, with topmast housed, on way to start of races in June, 1884

Charles P. Kunhardt, an American, writing over the nom de plume of "Big Topmast" in the *Aquatic Monthly* and later Yachting Editor of *Forest and Stream.* With him were a few other wise and far-sighted yachtsmen who joined in condemning the standard proportions of the day, and in advocating a reduction of breadth, an increase of depth of body, lower and better ballast, and changes above deck. While mention was made at times of the British cutter, coupled with a plea for the keel type for seagoing, the main demand at first was for a deeper study of the principles of ship designing, and its application to the improvement of centerboard yachts.

This attack on the national type was deeply resented; the dangers of the type were minimized, and its virtues in point of speed widely extolled. As the controversy became more heated there came into existence under the leadership of Mr. Kunhardt a clique of extremists who were soon known as "cutter-cranks"; advocating boldly the rejection of the centerboard sloop and the adoption in toto of the British cutter. It is a mere coincidence, but about this period there was a growing interest in things English, and a disposition to imitate them; the great American public being divided. The "Anglo-maniacs," so-called, were the subjects of much ridicule, as instanced by the song "The queer things you see, and the queer things you do, are English, you know, quite English, you know." This feeling entered strongly into what should have been a purely technical discussion of physical facts.

What the Cutter Was

The typical cutter at this time was of moderate breadth and depth, each about one-fourth of the length on waterline; with all ballast inside this gave a hull which was fast, able, seaworthy, and absolutely non-capsizable. With it was a rig which, though heavy and clumsy to American eyes, was eminently practicable for sea-going, and had much to recommend it in its mechanical details. Between 1870 and 1876 a great change took place, the racing was very keen, a new class of young naval architects appeared, intent on the development of speed, and there began the transfer of ballast from within the hull to a position beneath the keel; coupled with an increase of displacement. As the old stability of form was replaced by stability due to weight, the evil influence of the old "Thames Tonnage" rule, hitherto latent, came into full effect. It was soon discovered that by placing the ballast under the keel the breadth might be materially reduced, thus making it possible to build a much longer yacht on the same nominal tonnage. The four-beam cutter of the seventies was displaced by the five-beam cutter of the eighties, and then followed rapidly the six-beam Genesta and Clara of 1884-5. Still further extremes, up to seven and eight beams, were tried experimentally, but with no success.

The schooner Prospero with pole bowsprit as rigged in 1873, British fashion

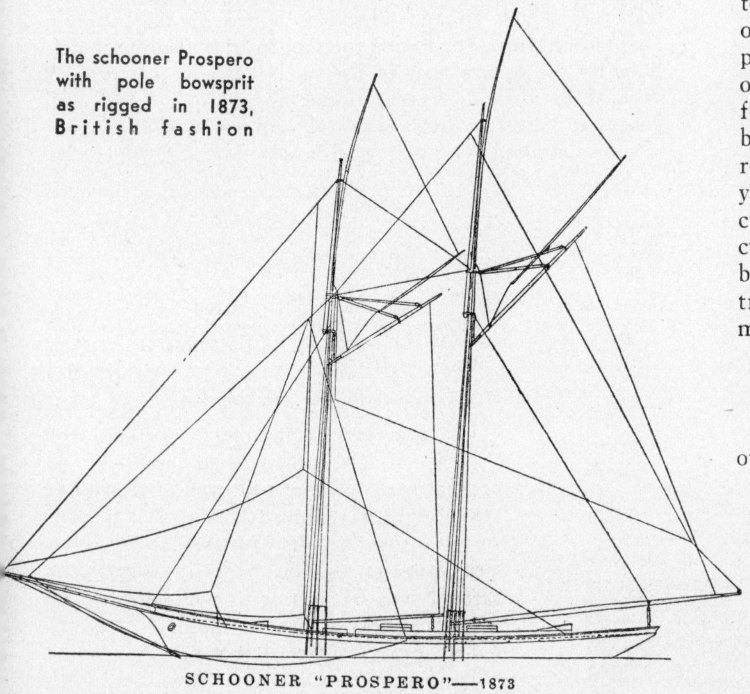

SCHOONER "PROSPERO"—1873

Enter the Yacht Designer

In thus dipping into history we have gone far wide of our course; now to get back to the "Big Sloops." Having mastered the modelling, building and sailing of small centerboard boats under the capable tuition of Cap'n Bob Fish, A. Cary Smith abandoned the bench for the easel, and devoted himself with much success to the portraiture of yachts in oils. About 1870 he established himself in the Studio Building, 51 West 10th Street, then tenanted by the leading New York artists. About 1868 he was called on by his life-long friend Robert Center for aid in designing a yacht on paper, without first recourse to the model. A drafting board was installed beside his easel and together he and Mr. Center started the study of what may be called scientific designing in the planning of the cutter Vindex. By degrees the easel was set aside for the drafting board, in 1873 he designed the schooner Prospero for C. H. Contoit; in 1875 the centerboard sloop Madcap for Joseph R. Busk; and in 1878 the schooner Intrepid for Lloyd Phoenix, all being successful in holding their own against the many rule-o'-thumb craft with which they raced.

In the fall of 1877, having built my second canoe and made my second cruise, knowing that Mr. Smith was measurer of the New York Canoe Club, I ventured to intrude on him, and met with a characteristically gracious reception. He showed me the new *Yacht Designing* recently published by Dixon Kemp, with the lines of a Nautilus canoe; and told me about the canoes of the New York Canoe Club. I was so bold as to tell him I wished to become a yacht designer, but his reply, told with that stutter which was a life-long affliction to him, was hardly encouraging: "My b-b-boy, you had better g-g-get a j-j-job on a p-p-peanut stand, it will p-p-pay you b-b-better in the end." How many bambinos, then chasing butterflies in sunny Italy, have rolled up fortunes in bananas and peanuts in little old New York since that time 63 years ago? In 1879 he was called on by Joseph R. Busk to replace Madcap with a sloop in the largest class.

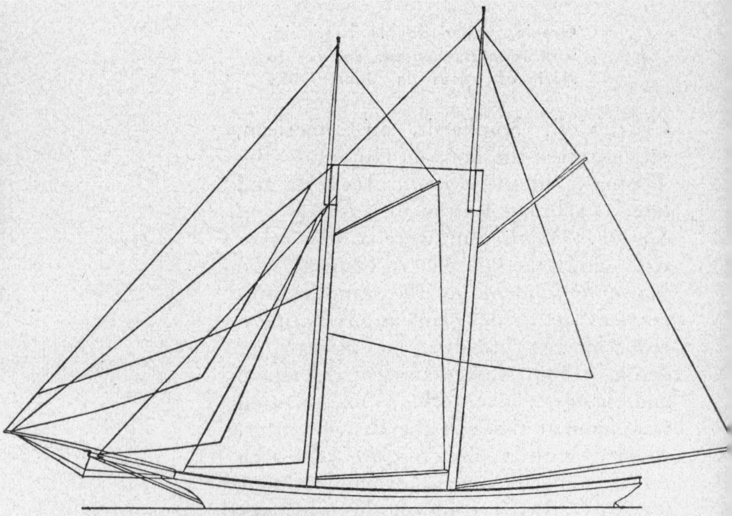

SCHOONER "COLUMBIA"—1875

Experiments in Yacht Measurement

In its early races the New York Yacht Club tried various methods of measurement: displacement computed from the hull, displacement ascertained by actual weighing, sail area, and tons by Custom House measurement, the simplest and most easily ascertainable. In 1856 a sail area rule was adopted, but in 1859 it was replaced by a rule based on "the product of the multiplication of the extreme length, on or under the waterline from fore side of stem to aft side of sternpost, by the extreme breadth, wherever found." What relation this circumscribing parallelogram had to the speed factors of a vessel it is hard to understand. This rule was followed in 1870 by a crude form of displacement rule, the areas of three sections "from the waterline to the intersection of the outer planking with keel" were measured, and computed by Simpson's Rule. In the Club book of 1872 there appears the following: "Note—The Club having abolished the Measurements and Allowances adopted in 1871, and not having, at the date of this issue, decided positively upon those under which the June Regatta of this year shall be sailed, rules for Measurements and Allowances are omitted." The "Cubic Contents" rule made its debut in the Club book of 1873, calling for the measurement of five cross-sections at equal points of division of the waterline, "from the rabbet line of the keel to the line of the lowest point of the top of the planksheer" the areas being computed by Chapman's Rule. This included the bulk of the hull, above as well as below the water, from the rabbet to a horizontal plane tangent to the lowest point of the freeboard. This rule was the law of the Club at the time of printing the 1883 book; to which an appendix was added giving the rule adopted on June 4: Twice the length of waterline multiplied by the square root of the sail area, and the product divided by three. It was under the "Cubic Contents" rule that the sloop division was developed; how the larger sloops compared is shown as follows:

	L. W. L.	Cubic Feet	L. x S. .A.
Gracie	#	4693	71.6
Arrow	61 ft. 5 ins.	3487	...
Fanny	66 " 0 "	4561	69.7
Pocahontas	65 " 0 "	4586	...
Atalanta	64 " 0 "	3568	...
Hildegard	60 " 6 "	3535	64.2
Mischief	61 " 0 "	3932	65.2
Vision	60 " 2 "	3921	...

#In the course of her long career the waterline of Gracie grew from 58 feet 3 inches to 70 feet. it is impossible to give her exact waterline length at any one stage of her career.

Above: Schooner Columbia with conventional American head rig, bowsprit and flying jib-boom. Left: Conventional sloop rig on Fanny

Mischief, the Iron Pot

The practice of planning every detail of a yacht in conformity to a fixed rule of measurement was not followed at this time; how closely Mr. Smith endeavored to conform to the "Cubic Contents" rule is an open question. The waterline which he selected was 61 feet with a breadth of 19 feet 8 inches; depth of hold, 5 feet 11 inches; draft, 5 feet 4 inches. All of the existing yachts were of wood, and with

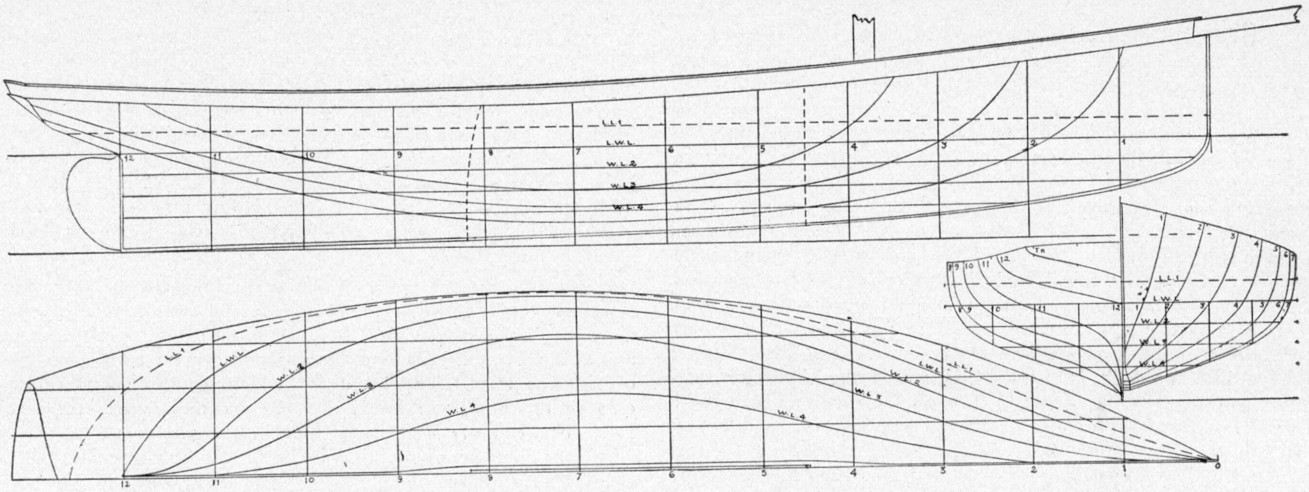

Mischief, center-board sloop designed by A. Cary Smith for Joseph R. Busk in 1879

long clipper bows carrying trailboards and figureheads; following Vindex, it was decided to build her of iron, with a plumb stem and no forward overhang nor ornamentation.

The knightheads were very important members in the structure of the old ships, oak planks in an approximately vertical position in the angle between the stem and the forward ends of the planking. The name was derived from the fact that in ancient ships these members projected above the rail, the extensions being carved into heads of knights. In French they are known as "apostles," and in German as the "Judas ear," or the "ear timber," being pierced for a line to run through. In addition to filling the triangular space between the stem and the planking, and supporting the forward ends of the bulwarks, the knightheads played an important part in taking the side thrust of the bowsprit. This same heavy construction was found in yachts down to the Arrow period; in these yachts the bowsprit was a square baulk of timber, in Arrow 14 by 14½ inches in the knightheads and diminishing aft until it butted against the bitts; outboard it was worked six-square, tapering to the end. In the schooners, and even in some sloops, this bowsprit carried another spar, the flying jib boom. When once in place the bowsprit was as much a permanent part of the structure as the stem itself.

In the British yachts of the period a very different method of construction was followed: the bowsprit was a round spar, square only on the heel, which was shipped between the bitts. In the old cutters the stemhead was carried as high as the rail, and the bowsprit was shipped on one side of this stemhead, which carried the gammon iron, the ring holding the bowsprit. With this plan the bowsprit could be run in (housed) the heel clearing the mast; and this was done regularly in bad weather, a smaller jib being set as the outboard end was shortened. If necessary the bowsprit could be taken in and stowed on deck. The arrangement was simpler and lighter than the American plan, but it had one serious objection in the case of the long bowsprit of a racing rig. I remember one race about 1883-4 when the joke was on the "cutter-cranks"; three of the cutters, I think Bedouin, Wenonah and Ileen, came in to the Stapleton anchorage after a hard race without their bowsprits—some wag on the Committee Boat said, "Why didn't they house 'em?" In designing Prospero in 1873 Mr. Smith fitted her with this headgear, the single round bowsprit and no flying jib boom; the rig was soon condemned by the professional sailormen and the old gear shipped. When Puritan came out with this rig in 1885 it was hailed as a great advance in rigging.

Mischief carried this plain spar over her plumb stem; on it she swung one big jib, never changing it throughout her racing career; though Gracie, Fanny and other sloops gradually shifted to the double headrig of the cutter. Another innovation was a horizontal steering wheel. In a day when sanitary plumbing was little more than an experiment even in private houses the conditions in yachting were still more crude; for the accommodation of the crew there was an institution known as the Josephine, a toilet seat hinged to the rail and supported by brackets with a canvas hood over and partly around it. Mischief had her mooring just off the site of the present ferry slip on Staten Island, in front of Mr. Busk's house; a most conspicuous detail of her anatomy was the Josephine projecting over her starboard bow. She carried no spinnaker boom but, instead, a "booming-out pole," by means of which the jib was set out when before the wind. With a moderate and well proportioned rig, ironwork made to the designer's plans, and always well handled, she soon took her place near the head of the class.

The First Sloop Match

The first three challengers for the America's Cup named schooners, but in May, 1881, there came a challenge from the Bay of Quinté Yacht Club, of Belleville, Canada, naming as its representative the sloop Atalanta. The moving spirit in this case was Captain Alexander Cuthbert, of Cobourg, Canada, who had modelled, built and sailed the schooner Countess of Dufferin in the match of 1876. Captain Cuthbert was a genius in his way, the modeller and builder of some very fast yachts, all of the American centerboard type: he was a skillful skipper of racing yachts. His countrymen had sufficient confidence in him to back him in a second venture in spite of the lamentable failure of the first. There was, as before, insufficient money subscribed for the campaign, the time was short, and the result was as disappointing as in 1876.

When the question of defense came up the first thought was of Arrow; but she was no longer available, having been sold out of the Club in 1877 to Ross Winans, of Baltimore, who did not race her, but kept her at Newport. Brief as her career had been, it had given her a reputation as the fastest of American sloops, and it was decided that she was the yacht to oppose Atalanta. It was proposed to buy her back, but Mr. Winans was in Europe; and the idea was abandoned when Mr. Kirby came forward with an offer to build an improved boat. A syndicate was formed by the Flag Officers, Commodore John R. Waller, Vice Commodore James D. Smith, and Rear Commodore Herman Oelrichs, and the contract was made with Mr. Kirby.

The work progressed slowly, and it was not until August 9 that Pocahontas, as she was named, was launched. Her dimensions were given as 71 feet 6 inches on deck; 65 feet l.w.l.; 21 feet breadth; 7 feet 10 inches depth; and 6 feet 6 inches draft. She had a big rig, mainsail 62 feet on foot, 55 feet hoist, 32 feet head and 84 feet luff; jib 46 feet 6 inches on foot. After the launching trouble began, it is impossible at this late date to guage the details, even after reading the heated controversy in print, but there was much friction between builder and owners. After trial the rig was cut down and ballast shipped, to the total of 32 tons. Her first performances were very unsatisfactory, and she entered the trial races in November in a very poor condition. In the first race the corrected times were: Mischief, 5:22:29; Hildegard, 5:28:01; Gracie, 5:55:00; Pocahontas, 6:04:50. With no masthead runners the new boat could not hold the luff of her big jib. Both Pocahontas and Gracie lost their topmasts. The second race was timed: Gracie, 5:14:46; Mischief, 5:18:35; Pocahontas, 5:32:03. In the third race both Mischief and Pocahontas housed topmasts; the new boat pulled out the chain plates of her bowsprit shrouds and withdrew. Mischief's time was 6:05:10; Gracie's 6:05:24, a difference of but 14 seconds. Mischief was chosen to defend the Cup, giving rise to much ill-feeling on the part of the adherents of Gracie. In these races no spinnakers were carried, the jibs and jib topsails being boomed out as shown in the illustration of Mischief.

BEFORE the races I saw Mischief out on Jones' Railway at Elm Park, Staten Island. It is, of course, impossible to get a racing bottom on an iron yacht in her first season on account of the scale on her plates. In a lecture on yacht construction before the Seawanhaka Corinthian Yacht Club Mr. Smith once stated that this scale was caused by the profanity of the boatyarders (platers, riveters and caulkers). I cannot vouch for this, though I have heard some pretty hard language at times in a shipyard. By this time Mischief had been afloat for three seasons, her bottom had rusted and been scaled down to the bare iron and painted. Under the motherly care of old Cap'n Than Clock she had, on this occasion, been scaled with scrapers and steel brushes, painted with red lead, and given a final coat of potlead rubbed in hard and polished with stove brushes until it shone like a mirror. A few days later I visited a little drydock in Jersey City where the challenger was out for painting after a hard trip through the canals; her breadth was greater than that of the locks, and she had been heeled by ballast in the bilge until she could be pulled through by a tug. Her wooden sides, none too smooth at best, had been scored deeply by spikes in the sides of the locks. When it came to the racing there were the usual troubles attendant on the building of a challenger on a shoestring; and all of Captain Cuthbert's pluck and skill went for nothing in the final sacrifice.

The aftermath of the trial races was a quarrel between owners and builders, and partisans on both sides; Mr. Kirby claiming that he was inadequately paid; that he was not permitted to have his own way; that he was not responsible for the faulty ironwork, etc. All of these charges were denied by the other side; Pokey, as she was derisively called, remained under the joint ownership of Messrs. Smith and Oelrichs for several years, but did nothing to retrieve her reputation.

Mr. Kirby, though of the rule-o'thumb school, seems to have been a man of more than ordinary intelligence; an expert according to the methods of the day. In self defence he wrote two long letters to *Forest and Stream* setting forth his views on yacht form, very sensible in some points; though he was insistent that the friction and resistance on a yacht's keel of say ten feet depth was very much greater than near the surface owing to the weight of the water. The failure of Pocahontas was a crushing blow to him, just as the capsize of Mohawk had been to her modeler. As illustrating his theories he sent in to *Forest and Stream* in the fall of 1881 a model of a proposed sloop of the size of Arrow and Pocahontas showing very fair lines, only moderately fine entrance, and a very easy curve to the after waterline as compared with the rump on Arrow.

ONE of the most successful of the rule-o'-thumb modellers was "Cap'n Phip" Elsworth, especially in the smaller sloop classes, his Kangaroo, Elephant, Crocodile, Amazon, Arab and the larger Fanita, being notably fast. Two of his largest yachts, the schooners Montauk, 1882, and Grayling, 1883, were very successful; but his most ambitious venture, the 85-foot compromise sloop, Atlantic, 1886, proved a complete failure in the Trial Races of that year. With the success of Mischief and the failure of Pocahontas and Atlantic the modeller passed aside and gave way to the professional naval architect.

It was the fate of many of the early sloops to be converted to schooners very early in their career; the reason for this is not apparent, but in many cases they had proved failures with one mast, and as a part of lengthening, hipping and other alterations a change of rig was tried. The yachts of which we are now treating all escaped this fate, and ended their long careers under the original rig. The end of Gracie was told in the previous chapter, Mischief was sold out of yachting in 1901; still sound in hull, she was used as an oil barge about Boston until 1929, when she was offered for sale as junk. In this emergency that sentimentalist "Boston Bill" Swan stepped into the breach, collecting from yachtsmen enough money to buy the hulk and scuttle it decently. Fanny continued in yachting service until she was sold into trade about 1903; Hildegard shared the same fate about the same time. Arrow was owned in the Knickerbocker Yacht Club as late as 1899; Pocahontas was used as a yacht, but with no racing record, until about 1908, when she was sold for trading use. Here were useful careers in yachting, much of the time in racing, of from 25 to 40 years; compared with the few brief years of a 20th Century Cup yacht built at a cost greater than that of this whole fleet.

To the yachtsman of today these old craft, with their many crudities of form and rig, would compare as does a model T Ford with a new V-8; but it must be remembered that this famous "70-Ft. Class" was the backbone of American yachting for over twenty years; in it was worked out an important course of development; its owners stood high in the estimation of all yachtsmen; its skippers were all known by name, Cap'n Hank Haff, Cap'n Than Clock, Cap'n Sam Gibson, Cap'n George Cooley, Cap'n Jim Berry; famous in their day. The competition was keen and well sustained, and while not one of the many-times altered models was ever towed in a tank, and the times per mile might not compare with the speeds of today, there was sport in plenty for owners, friends, and the great yachting public.

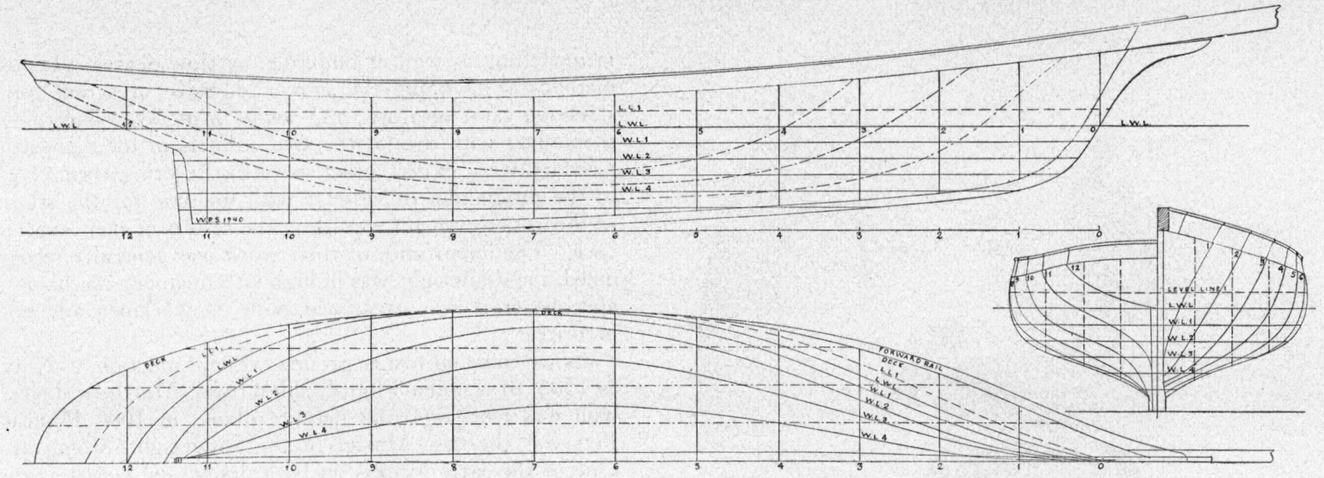

TRADITIONS AND MEMORIES OF AMERICAN YACHTING

Part Eleven

FROM THE BENCH TO THE DRAFTING BOARD

By WILLIAM P. STEPHENS

Above: Hildegard, centerboard sloop, modelled and built by Lon Smith, Islip, L. I., 1876. Originally Niantic, re-named Hildegard by Herman Oelrichs (after his sister) in 1880. Competitor in Trial Races of 1881. From lines taken off by John Mumm, about 1886. Length overall, 76 feet; L. W. L., 62 feet; breadth, 19 feet; draft, 6 feet 5 inches. The round stern is characteristic of all of Lon Smith's yachts

THE development of navigation from its beginning, when man first attempted to make progress in the water by means of bundles of reeds under the arms, logs, rafts, and framework covered by skins, is comparatively easy to trace; many of the crudest of these methods have survived in remote localities even until today. When, however, this development progressed from the rivers and seacoast into open waters, the mast and sail displacing paddle and oar, we are left in doubt. The history of the origin of the construction of anything large enough to be classed as a ship is still a closed book. While ships of such size and strength as to venture on open waters were common prior to the thirteenth century, the introduction of the magnetic compass into Europe about this date, making it possible to depart from the land with a certainty of returning to it, created a demand for a new and larger type of vessel, and a more substantial construction.

In the absence of definite records of this era we must rely on what we know was the recognized practice of a much later date. The first step was the selection of a stick for the keel; this, when shaped, was laid level on blocks resting on the ground. The stem and sternpost were then got out from such timber as was most easily obtainable; then the "midship bend," the largest frame in the vessel, was shaped by eye, built up, and placed in position on the keel. The position of this frame, also known as the "dead-flat," was marked on the keel by a symbol, cross within a circle. The form of the hull was then outlined by means of ribbands or "harpens," long flexible strips of wood, fastened to stem, sternpost and midship frame, and braced or shored to a shape conceived by the builder; the moulds for the remaining frames being

Below: Fanny, centerboard sloop. Modelled and built by D. O. Richmond, Mystic, Conn., 1874, for Charles H. Mallory. L. O. A., 78 feet; L. W. L., 65 feet 4 inches; breadth, 21 feet 9 inches; draft, 5 feet 3 inches. In spite of the forward position of the mast, channels were the exception on the old sloops. As previously mentioned, Eclipse had channels of bar iron. Those of Fanny were built out of solid wood, almost in the form of a half-model, and were familiarly known as her sheep-walks

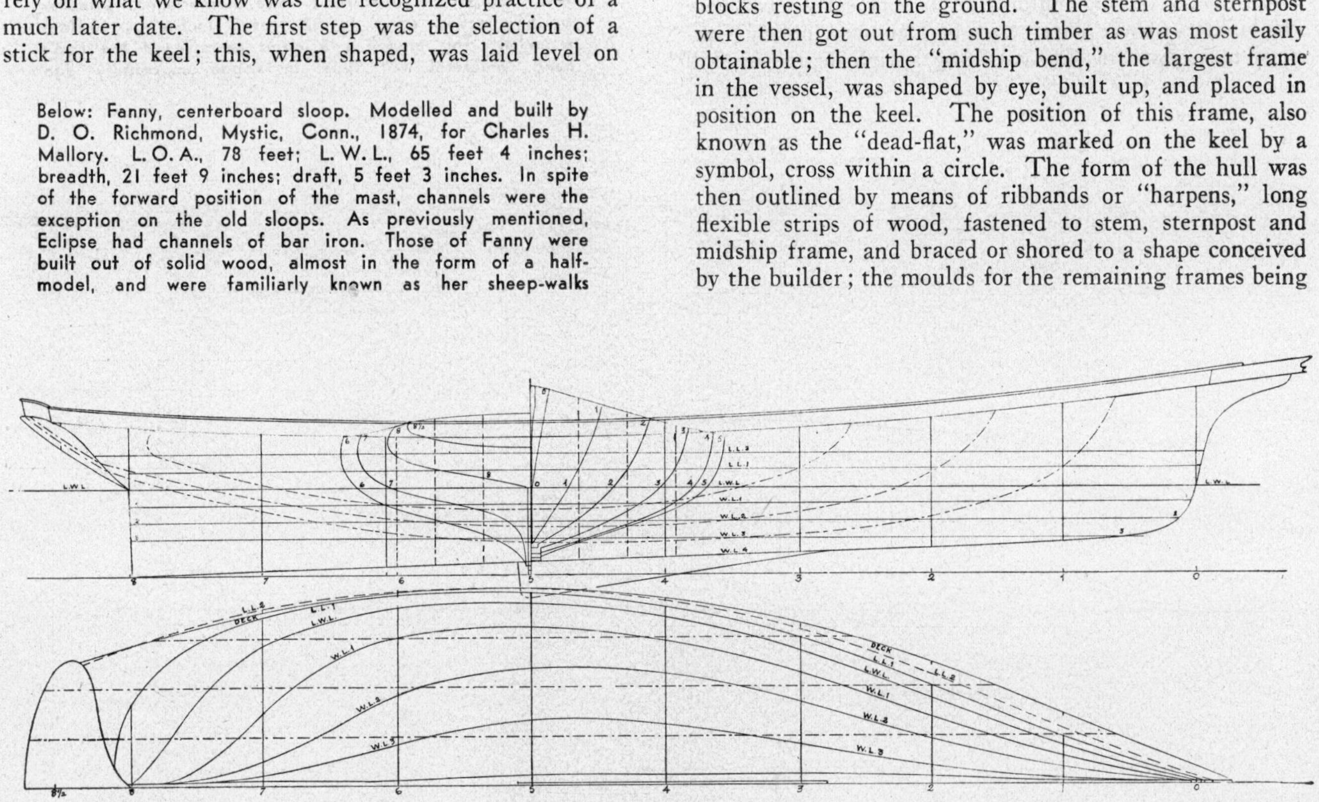

Pat McGiehan, born March 17, 1828, deceased December 9, 1901. Successful exponent of the system of modelling in the sloops Cora, Ina, Meta and Kaiser Wilhelm, and in many fast sandbag boats

made to fit the harpens. This method has survived in boat building to the present day. In Stalkartt's treatise on ship building, 1781, a method is outlined, described by him as "whole-moulding," by which the form of the main body of the vessel is obtained by moving the "midship bend" forward and aft, cutting off the head and heel of the mould as it goes from the middle.

The art of navigation had not progressed far before the demand came for vessels of war, rather than for exploration or trade, and we find that the leaders in the art and mystery of ship building from very early days were the builders of war ships. Such builders were purely practical men, some in time attaining a high degree of skill in modelling as well as building; by slow degrees various methods of planning the ship in advance of actual construction came into use; and while in no way concerning themselves with theory, the ship builders of the Sixteenth Century were expert practical men, devoting themselves to the production of vessels; with no time for the study of theory, or even for recording the results of their experience. The importance of their work was generally recognized, the shipwright was in high esteem among mechanics, and the craft was organized with its workmen and apprentices.

As we come on firmer ground we find mention, as early as 1586, of a noted English shipwright, Matthew Baker, who was working from definite plans; in 1606 Phineas Pett was the first Master of the Shipwrights Company. One of the early writers on both design and construction as he understood them was William Sunderland, an English "Shipwright and Mariner," as he describes himself; who, in 1711, published "The Ship-builders Assistant, or Some Essays Towards Compleating the Art of Marine Architecture." The preface sets forth that:—"The great Usefulness of the Art of Ship-building is so well known to all that to say anything of it here would be wholly unnecessary; and those who have any acquaintance with it must be sensible that neither the Theory nor Practice has hitherto been so far advanced but that both are yet capable of very great Improvements." One of the most important chapters is entitled "OEconomy," dealing with the conversion of woods to the best advantage; rather than with the form best suited to the intended uses of the vessel. In this chapter the writer lays emphasis on conversion in the woods where the timber is felled, to save cost of transportation. In one chapter he makes an interesting allusion, as follows:—"In 1612 it was observed that many Abuses and Frauds had been committed, which were then amended, and 44 Rules and Ordinances were added to the Shipwrights' Charter; agreeable to the Statute of Henry the Seventh. One

Old lift half-model of unknown date and origin. Made to inside of planking and showing nothing of stem, keel, sternpost or deadwood. Size of model, 31⅜ inches by 5⅜ inches, equal to 62 feet 3 inches by 10 feet 6 inches. This model is a good example of the cod's head, mackerel tail type in vogue a century ago

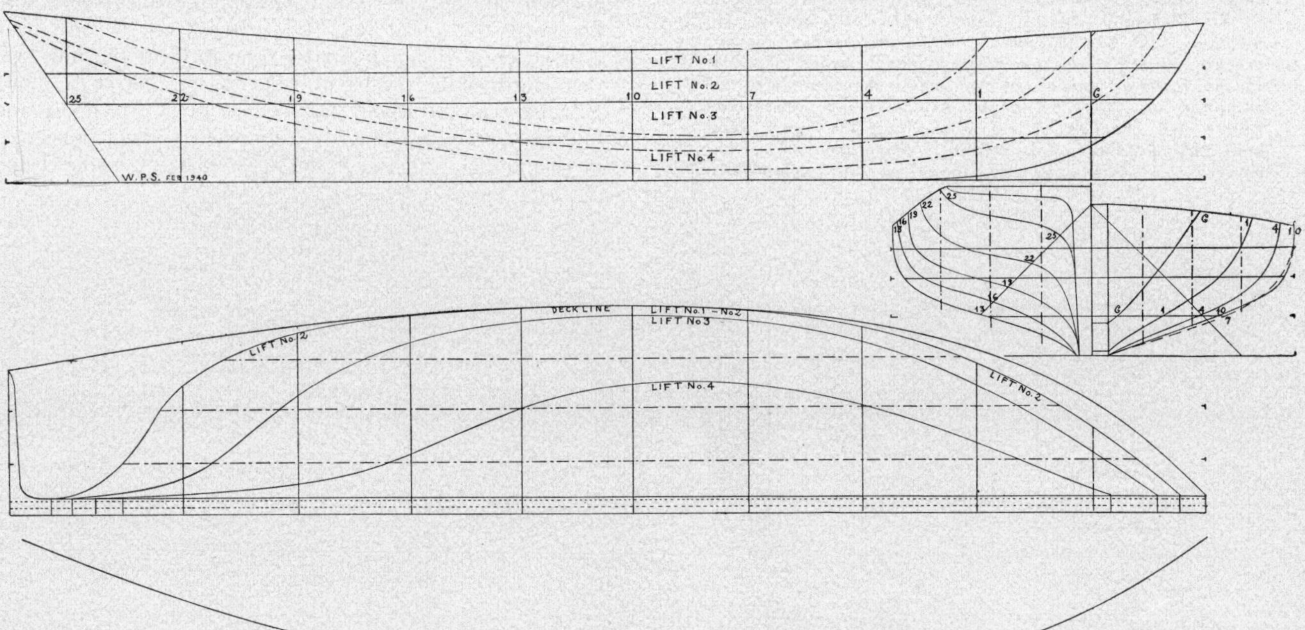

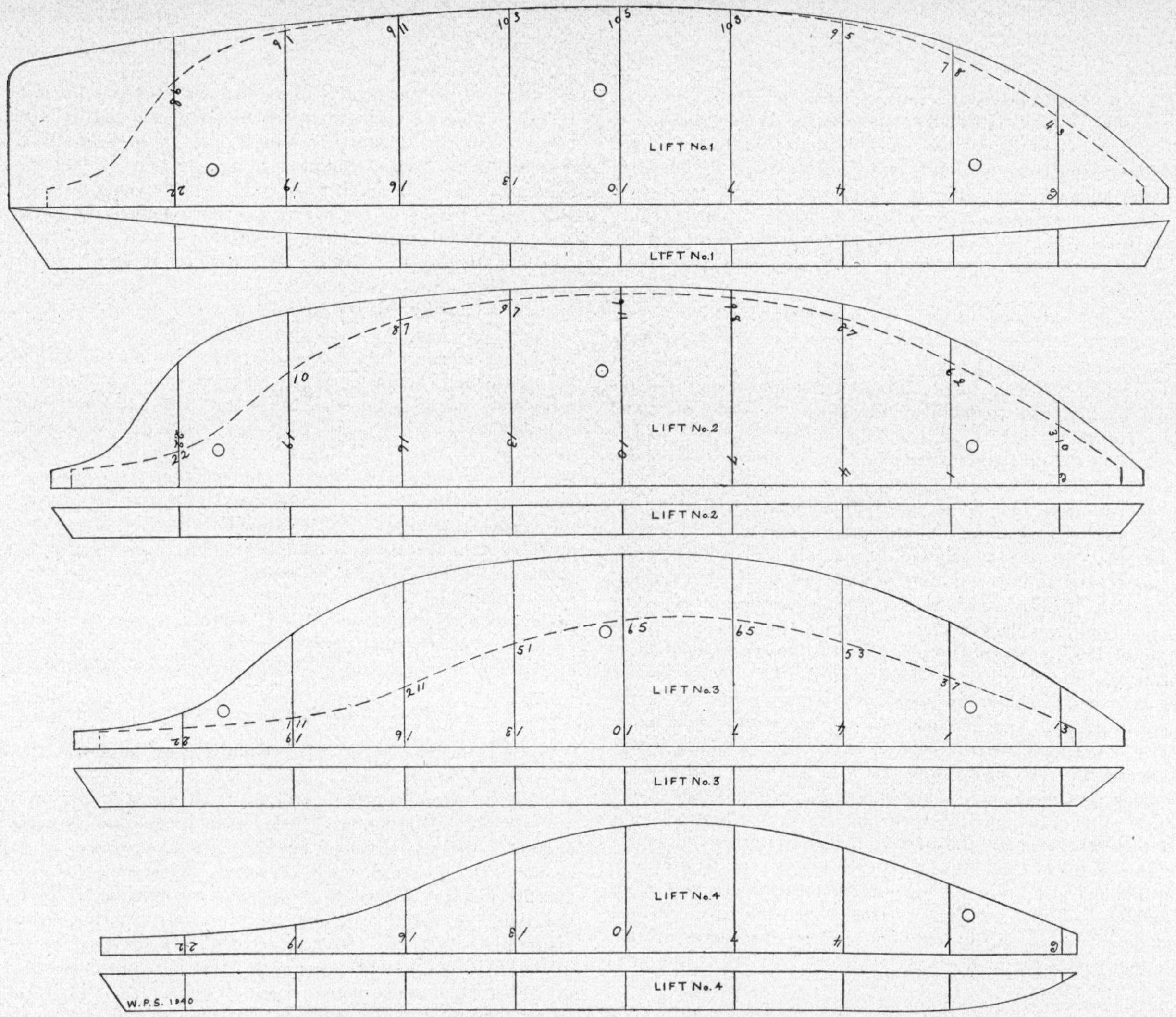

Separate lifts of model, showing dowel holes and numbering of stations, with offsets marked in inches and eighths from which lines were laid down on floor

of them being for a Nursery to increase the Number of able Shipwrights; and to incourage that sort of people was always accounted a thing very requisite." Here is a suggestion of an attempt, probably the first, at the systematic training of the ship builder.

The early study of the theoretic side of naval architecture was made by scientists, or others not associated with actual ship construction; about the end of the Sixteenth Century we find Sir Walter Raleigh and Samuel Pepys, both associated with the British Navy, and Sir Isaac Newton, the great scientist, writing on the general subject of naval design. In 1749 Leonhard Euler wrote a treatise, largely theoretical, on the resistance of a vessel at sea; and in 1761 a namesake, Johann Albrecht Euler, wrote of the abstract qualities of a vessel. Still earlier, in 1677, Sieur Dessié, a French writer, wrote a book on naval architecture (in French) containing the manner of construction of "Ships, Galeases and Chaloupes."

The Day of the Half Model

THE origin of the half-model as the basis of the design has been treated very fully by the late Dr. Charles K. Stillman in one of the publications of the Marine Historical Association of Mystic, Conn. Concerning the use of the half-model in America he says:—"It has been stated that the builder's half-hull waterline model was an invention of the 1790's, and the names of Enos Briggs and Orlando Merrill of Newburyport are the earliest ones to be coupled with it. * * * * Rather than run risks in assuming that the building of half-models was an unknown art before some particular date in the Colonial period prior to 1800, it seems better simply to admit that we have no evidence of earlier half-models building." There seems little doubt that the half-model, in lifts, was in general use in America at an earlier date than in England; and that such models as were in use in England were of the skeleton type, thwartship sections representing the frames being mounted on a backboard, and ribbands run around them. There is one such model, of an English cutter, in the New York Yacht Club; said to have been brought to New York in 1851 by Commodore Stevens on his return from the America trip.

That the half-model was not unknown in England is proved by the following, from a curious book by William Annersley, published in 1818, describing a method of construction devised by him. As to the model, he says:—"Place the semi-model in a trough or cutting box (mitre-box?) fitting it exactly; having a perpendicular cut or slit in the center, and square athwart. By moving the model along the box until the divisions come in line of the cut, and running the semi-model through with a fine saw, the sections will be all perfectly perpendicular and square from the base of the bottom." This method is occasionally employed in America, fine saw-cuts being made partly through the model, and the sections drawn on cardboard. The book also describes a method of towing very small models in a very small tank by means of vertical weights and lines running over pulleys.

The half-model is found in two widely different forms; the ornamental and the useful. The first is the office model, for exhibition purposes; such models were common in the offices of builders and shipping men; there is a very fine collection of the William H. Webb models in the Webb Institute of Naval Architecture, in New York; and a similar collection of the C. H. Mallory models in the office of C. D. Mallory, also in New York. These models, in lengths up to six feet, are cut from solid glued-up blocks of woods of different colors, highly finished. Some models are painted to represent the original coloring of the vessel; models of this kind being found in the homes of old ship masters, or aboard their ships.

The second type of model, usually of smaller size, was cut by the builder to put in concrete and workable form his mental conception of the proposed ship or yacht. In some cases the block was glued up and left to season before being carved into shape, but the more usual method was to build up the block of layers of wood, lifts, put together in such a way as to be easily separable. The favorite wood in the past was white pine, now no longer obtainable, a wood very easily worked; the best of the so-called white pines of today are gummy, and do not yield to the knife. The present generation can know nothing of whittling of white pine with a sharp knife just for the pleasure of it; in old caricatures Uncle Sam was portrayed as thus whittling a stick just to see and feel the chips come off. In many cases woods of constrasting colors, white pine and mahogany or black walnut, were used, showing clearly the different level lines. At times each separate lift was glued up of two contrasting woods, giving a checkerboard effect to the model. The lifts were held together by screws, by round dowels, as in the model here illustrated, and in some very old models by rectangular dowels with a taper on one edge and a mortice at the top, a wedge through the mortice serving to draw the lifts together. After shaping the block by means of spokeshave, gouges, rasps and sandpaper, lines were drawn on the back and top at the stations; the lifts were then separated and the outline of each was drawn on paper; or, dispensing with this, the breadth on each lift at every station was measured and marked. From these measurements there was made out the "table of offsets"; dimensions from which the enlarged lines were laid down on the mould-loft floor. These measurements are shown on the lifts of the model.

The Model vs. the Draught

AN important figure in American ship building through much of the past century was John Willis Griffiths, the son of John Griffiths, a shipwright; born in 1809 and living an active life until 1882. Apprenticed as a boy to his father's trade, at the age of 19 he laid down the lines of the frigate Macedonian. A practical shipwright, he was also a modeller, a designer, and a lifelong writer on the subjects of ship design and construction. Thoroughly familiar with both subjects, and deeply interested in the development of American shipping, it must be confessed that in his writings he was inclined to be verbose and tautological. As to his practical work, in 1845 he modelled the clipper ship Rainbow, one of the first of the type; following her in 1846 with Sea Witch, another fast clipper. In 1836 he published in Portsmouth, Va., "The Advocate," a small periodical devoted to naval architecture; in 1842 he lectured on the subject and opened a free school. In 1850 he published "A Treatise on Marine and Naval Architecture, of Theory and Practice Blended in Ship Building"; in 1856-58 he was part owner and editor of the "Nautical Magazine and Naval Journal"; later he published "The Ship Builder's Manual," and, in 1874 when editor of "The Nautical Gazette," he published "The Progressive Ship Builder." His whole career gives value to his opinions, narrow and erroneous as they may seem to be in the light of modern practice.

While his writings show him as familiar with the accepted method of ship draughting, he gives first place in planning to the cut half-model; as follows: —"Few, if any, of those who have the reputation of being skilled in draughting vessels can by any power of conception form a correct idea of the form of the vessel drawn in its rotundity; or, if they possess this rare endowment, it is impossible to convey in language the same to a second or third party. In Europe the ship owners as well as builders have found it necessary to learn and practice drawing, that they might be able to acquire a proper conception of the form of vessels from the same, and with the aid of a work on naval architecture many have become proficient in the art; while they really know much less of shape in its rotundity than the operative mechanic in the United States, who, in obedience to his own notions, has whittled out his first model. It will at once be apparent to the thinking man that it is impossible to represent two curves in a single line, or to delineate the shape of a line in two ways without making two lines; the most profound mathematician will admit this; and, still further, it is difficult to retain two shapes in the eye at the same time in all their relative proportions . . . thus it will be perceived that the draught alone does not furnish an index to the rotundity in ships; and, although useful, and in many respects far more convenient, yet for the single purpose of delineating the form of a vessel by the eye, the model is incomparably superior; and to its invention are we measurably indebted for much of our success in preserving an equilibrium against the conflicting interests which surround us. That the model is completely adapted to our wants must be admitted even by the casual observer when he discovers that every part of a vessel may be exhibited, all the proportionate lengths, breadths and depths, every line may be seen in its appropriate place; it exhibits not only the form, but a ready mode of obtaining tables for the loft; and is, for the purposes delineated, to the draught what statuary is to a written description of the physical man; the latter a shadow, the former the substance." This strong statement is a strange line of argument from a man who was familiar with modern methods; the preliminary calculations of displacement and stability, center of buoyancy and center of effort, the disposition of the lateral plane, and the draughting of sheer, load waterline, and other essential elements."

CONTINUING, Mr. Griffiths gives in detail the method of constructing the model: "The model, as we have said, is a proud emblem of American skill, and to it we are indebted for much of our success. Models have been made in Europe as early as the middle of the last century; but they are what would be recognized as the skeleton model, made of pieces representing the half-frames, and are neither adapted to the purpose of building, or of exhibiting the lines of flotation. The invention of waterline models, like many others, was the result of accident. In the Eastern states, and in the British provinces, men who were unacquainted with the art of construction upon paper, made from a block the form of the vessel they intended to build, which was cut into several transverse sections; those sections, representing the frames, were then expanded from the scale upon which the model was made to the size of the vessel; and frames were worked out to which harpens were attached, and the remaining parts, or intermediate spaces, filled in by moulds to these harpens. In making one of those block models the block was found to be too small to give the required depth, to which a piece was added, and when finished it was discovered that the longitudinal form of the vessel was shown by the line uniting the two pieces together. The question at once arose, if one seam was an advantage, two would be still greater; and as early as 1790 waterline models were made for building purposes. The author has seen the model of a ketch, called the Eliza, 190 tons burden, which was launched in the middle of June 1794; this model was made in three pieces, by a scale of one quarter of an inch to the foot; 84 feet keel; 24 feet beam; and 9 feet hold; and may be seen in the rooms of the East India Marine Society of Salem, Mass. This model has been preserved on account of the remarkable qualities the vessel possessed for sailing fast; she was built by Mr. Briggs, the same builder who built the brig Essex at Salem. The first model made in this city (New York) was by David Seabury, which was soon followed by others. The Ohio, 74, built for the Government from a model made by Stephen Smith of this city, then an apprentice to Mr. Eckford, was among the first vessels built from the model in the immediate vicinity of New York; its advantages were soon appreciated, and the draught was laid aside and has at length grown obsolete."

"BEFORE entering upon the responsible duties of delineating the construction of models, we shall render our readers a service by furnishing them with materials for reflection. From the framework of 30 years experience in building ships, by one whose opinion we have had occasion to notice in the first chapter. To an inquiry made of several builders of this city the author received but one reply, viz, the eye is the textbook for modelling vessels. The following letter we have deemed worthy not only of a place in this work, but of an inscription on the tablet of memory of all such ship owners or others as may suppose they know all that is worth knowing about building and masting ships:

New York, January 20, 1850.

Mr. J. W. Griffiths:

Dear Sir:

I am truly gratified to know of your intention of publishing a treatise on the subject of Naval Architecture. * * * I suppose there is no class of mechanics in the world who have labored at such disadvantages in the practice of their profession as ship builders. Although ship building as a practical art has been in existence for thousands of years, yet as a matter of science little or nothing has been done in its favor until quite lately. It is still true that, with the exception of those conflicting rules of tonnage, and that ill-advised dictation of owners, by which he is hampered and vexed rather than assisted, each individual modeller has little else besides his own taste and eye to guide him. In addition to all this, she is often required to be previously modelled in accordance with the fancy of some conceited owner, who, having made perhaps, a single voyage in a ship—and perhaps not even that—thinks he knows more than all the builders in the world. It is not ship merchants, nor is it always ship captains, that are possessed of that cultivation of the eye which is necessary in order to pass judgement at a glance upon the merits of any particular model.

Yours,

(*signed*) DAVID BROWN

Mr. Brown was one of the leading New York ship builders in a day when ship building in wood and sail flourished as it never has done since.

Mr. Griffiths continues to give details of the actual construction of a model: "In our exposition of the readiest mode of making models we shall assume that the eye alone is our textbook with regard to form; if the ordinary mode is adopted, of making alternate sections of cedar and pine, the lowest piece should be of cedar, because it presents to the action of the file the largest surface, and is more easily made fair than pine. It is to be regretted that so many mechanics regard the model of a ship as a mere block of wood, like the casual observer who looks upon the marble in the quarry, without being able to discover the statue of the statesman or philosopher. The only way to drive work successfully on a ship is to begin at the model; one day spent there is worth a week on the ship."

Writing thirty years later, in his "Progressive Ship Builder," Mr. Griffiths treats at great length of what we would call scientific design; but still refers to the "rotundity" of the vessel as something which cannot be grasped from the projections on paper.

Model Making in Practice

ONE of the most noted yachts of the 19th Century, second only to America in the esteem of yachtsmen, was the little schooner Magic; winner of the first race in defense of the America's Cup in 1870. By a mere chance, a dispute over the modelling of another yacht, the story of her origin is told in detail. Born in Stonington, Conn., in 1800, Richard Fanning Loper was of a Philadelphia family, but connected with the Fanning family of Stonington, long associated with shipping. Going to sea as a boy, at the age of 19 he was second mate of the sloop Hero, commanded by Captain Nathaniel F. Palmer, on a sealing voyage to the Arctic in which Palmer's Land was discovered. In the early 30's he established a line of sailing packets between Philadelphia, New York and Hartford; replacing them by steamers as the new power came into use. In 1844 he invented the Loper screw propeller, one of 13 marine patents taken out in a lifetime of 80 years. In 1846, at the time of the Mexican war, a fleet of 150 surf boats was called for to land General Scott's expedition, the estimated time of construction being 90 days; Mr. Loper turned them out in 30 days, and General Scott landed his force at Vera Cruz 60 days later. He built more than 400 vessels, sail and steam, prior to 1860; when, on the outbreak of the Rebellion, land transportation between Washington and the Delaware River was threatened, he assembled a fleet of steamboats at Trenton to transport New Jersey troops to the Capital. In 1845 he patented a system of composite construction for vessels, and he was associated with the Cramp shipyard in Philadelphia and that of Harlan & Hollingsworth in Wilmington, Del. Joining the New York Yacht Club in 1855, continuing his membership until 1876, owning many yachts, both sail and steam, and mostly of his own design, the method of working of a man of such wide nautical experience is of more than ordinary interest. Through a mere chance, a dispute with a yacht builder over the credit for a model, we are told in detail of the method which he employed.

THE yacht Madgie, mentioned in the letter which follows, was built as a sloop in 1857, it is said, to defeat the sloop Julia built by George Steers; in 1859 she was lengthened by the stern, and later given a new bow, being converted to a schooner; in 1864 she was sold to William H. McVickar, who re-named her Magic; again in 1869 she was re-built by David Carll, at City Island; with another re-building in 1873. In 1868 Mr. Loper modelled and had built a second Madgie, also a sloop; but altered to a schooner in the following year, being lengthened from 70 to 78.9 feet tonnage length; in 1870 she was again lengthened to 96.9 feet; in 1871 her foremast was shifted aft and certain iron plates were removed from her keel. In 1873 she was sold to Capt. Graham H. Lester, of Key West, Fla., for use as a pilot boat off that port. It is an interesting coincidence that a quarter of a century later her older sister, the original Madgie, found her way to Key West for similar service as a supply boat for the sponge-fishing fleet. This history of alterations, enlargements, and final sale for commercial use, is characteristic of the general practice of the day.

New York, October 23, 1865

To the Editor of The Herald:

In the Herald of the 17th instant I find the following: "Mr. John A. Forsyth modelled and built at Stonington the yacht Josephine," this is not so. Will you please make the following corrections.

The yacht Josephine was built from the moulds taken from the yacht Madgie; allow me to explain. I modelled and had built by Messrs. Theodore Byerly & Son, of Philadelphia, the sloop Madgie. After using her for two years as a sloop I put a false stern on her, ten feet in length on the keel, and fifteen feet of false bow. I altered her rig to a schooner. The false stern was put on in Philadelphia and the bow in Stonington by Mr. Stanton Sheffield. I made the model for the false bow and sent it to Mr. Sheffield at Stonington. The model of the bow is now and has been with Mr. James G. Bennett, Jr., for the past two years. After having used the Madgie as a schooner for four years I sold her to Commodore McVickar, with the privilege of keeping her for thirty days for the purpose of taking her moulds, the original model being completely destroyed by the additions to her bow and stern. I made arrangements with Mr. Stanton Sheffield, ship carpenter, to haul out the Madgie (now known by the name of Magic) to take her moulds and make a model from them. Mr. John A. Forsyth was employed to assist Mr. Sheffield in taking the moulds. After they were taken I added ten feet in the middle of the model from the moulds of the Madgie, and it was brought to my office, Pier 12, North River, New York, by Mr. Forsyth for my approval. I altered the model so made by taking off the full place above the waterline abreast the fore chains, which is now in the Madgie and not in the Josephine.

I then made arrangements with Mr. Sheffield and Mr. Forsyth to build me a vessel by the day's work, after the model so made. I also furnished Mr. Sheffield with a specification for building the vessel now called the Josephine, now owned by Mr. Daniel Devlin. I gave him (Sheffield) the dimensions of the keel, stem, sternpost, bedpieces, keelson, and size and location of centerboard and well and masts; the exact size of all her frame timbers, deck beams and knees, the thickness and quality of her planking from her keel to her deck, and also all her deck planks in thickness and width, dimensions of her fore and main masts, and each and every spar belonging to or used aboard the yacht Josephine. I further certify that I agreed with Mr. S. Sheffield, ship builder of Stonington, and Mr. Forsyth, to build the yacht Josephine now owned by Mr. Devlin, by the day, according to the above statement, and I furnished the materials necessary for the construction of the said yacht Josephine. I positively say there is no difference between the Madgie (now called the Magic) and the Josephine, except what was made under my sole directions. For the correctness of this statement I refer to Mr. Stanton Sheffield, of Stonington, the partner of Mr. John A. Forsyth while the yacht was being built.

Respectfully,

(*signed*) R. F. LOPER.

The above statement, made by R. F. Loper, Esq., is correct.

(*signed*) S. SHEFFIELD.

As regards Palmer, I designed her from stem to stern; she was built under contract with me by Byerly, Hillman & Streaker, of Philadelphia. She is the model of the Josephine with the exception of being ten feet longer in the middle of the vessel; is wider in order to make the lines run fair over the new part added, as in the Josephine, and the top timbers are a little longer than in the Madgie or the Josephine, in order to increase the depth of hold. There is no difference between the Madgie, or Magic, Josephine or Palmer, except that which was directed and approved by me.

(*signed*) R. F. LOPER.

THUS is set forth in detail the method by which yachts were produced by a man of exceptional experience and training in many branches of nautical work; in the case of the average boat and yacht builder who drifted into the business through a liking for the work, even less might be expected. A pertinent comment on this cut-and-try system of modelling is found in a newspaper of 1876 in which a yacht is mentioned as being lengthened and otherwise re-modelled; "the changes being so extensive it reminds us of building a barrel having only the bung-hole as a pattern." There is now in the Model Room of the New York Yacht Club a model marked "Madgie, 1857," and believed to be that of the yacht in question, though it will be noted that Mr. Loper distinctly states that the original model was destroyed through alterations; this model is perhaps the most crude in form of the entire great collection. The mention of the model of the altered bow being in the possession of James Gordon Bennett, Jr., is interesting in view of the fact that when Mr. Bennett bought the schooner L'Hirondelle, in 1869, he sent her to Stonington for a similar alteration of the fore-body in converting her into the schooner Dauntless.

In spite of the strong plea for the cut model made by John W. Griffiths, the faults of the system—if it may be thus called—far outweigh its merits. In the first place, it was purely individualistic; model cutting was not learned from others, it was a case of inspiration; and it was not taught to others in turn. In spite of the talent and skill of some individual modellers, as attested in the success of their yachts; it did nothing to advance the development of yacht design, or to promote a wider knowledge of the subject. As a record of progress it was almost worthless, the comparatively few models still in existence teaching us very little. The half-model was made to the inside of the planking, with no indication of the form of stem, keel, sternpost, deadwoods and rudder; no position of centerboard and spars. It disclosed nothing of the displacement, trim, center of lateral plane, or other essential elements. In many cases, as in that of the model here illustrated, all means of identification are missing. If in this and the majority of other cases the maker had written his name, the date, and the name of the vessel, the value of the model would have been increased by fifty per cent. As to permanent records of progress, both boat shops and mould lofts carried heavy fire risks; a fire in the mould loft of William H. Webb destroyed many of his models; the models of Pat McGiehan were destroyed when his shop was burned; some time after the death of Jake Schmidt his models were in the cellar of Mrs. Schmidt's home; it is easy to guess their end as well dried kindling wood. While, on the other hand, there is a wealth of material for the antiquarian and student in existing drawings and specifications, there is comparatively little to be learned from such half-models as are known today.

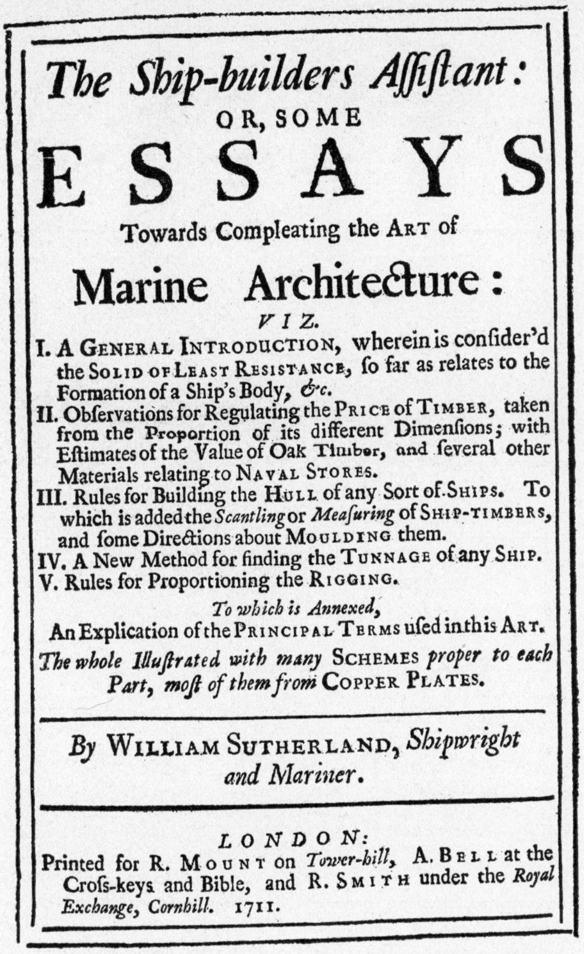

The Ship-builders Assistant:
OR, SOME
ESSAYS
Towards Compleating the ART of
Marine Architecture:
VIZ.

I. A GENERAL INTRODUCTION, wherein is consider'd the SOLID OF LEAST RESISTANCE, so far as relates to the Formation of a Ship's Body, *&c.*
II. Observations for Regulating the PRICE of TIMBER, taken from the Proportion of its different Dimensions; with Estimates of the Value of Oak Timber, and several other Materials relating to NAVAL STORES.
III. Rules for Building the HULL of any Sort of SHIPS. To which is added the *Scantling* or *Measuring* of SHIP-TIMBERS, and some Directions about MOULDING them.
IV. A New Method for finding the TUNNAGE of any SHIP.
V. Rules for Proportioning the RIGGING.

To which is Annexed,
An Explication of the PRINCIPAL TERMS used in this ART.
The whole Illustrated with many SCHEMES *proper to each Part, most of them from* COPPER PLATES.

By WILLIAM SUTHERLAND, *Shipwright and Mariner.*

LONDON:
Printed for R. MOUNT on *Tower-hill*, A. BELL at the Cross-keys and Bible, and R. SMITH under the *Royal Exchange, Cornhill.* 1711.

TRADITIONS AND MEMORIES OF

AMERICAN YACHTING

Part Twelve

FROM THE BENCH TO THE DRAFTING BOARD

(Continued)

By WILLIAM P. STEPHENS

TURNING for the time from the practical side of ship construction, we find the development of the technical side of naval architecture to be no less important and interesting. By the beginning of the seventeenth century the practical side of ship building had been brought to a very high degree of perfection. The shipwrights of the day were educated in a hard school of apprenticeship in a royal dockyard or a private yard, beginning with the roughest forms of work, with no technical instruction, and gradually advancing to master workmen; some in time to positions at the head of the yard. They had no time for study, even if the opportunity had existed. Their work, however, mainly on naval vessels, stood the test of practical sea-going and hard sea fighting.

One of the first to take up the pen in the interest of naval architecture was Sir Walter Raleigh (1562-1618). In his "Discourse on the Royal Navy and Sea Service" he says, in brief: "We find by experience that the greatest ships are lesse serviceable, goe very deep to water, and of marvellous charge and fearefull cumber; our channells decaying every year. Besides, they are lesse nimble, lesse mineable, and very seldom imployed. . . . And, in the building of all ships, these six things are principally required. 1 First, that she be strong built; 2 Secondly, that she be swift; 3 Thirdly, that she be stout-sided; 4 Fourthly, that she carry out her guns in all weathers; 5 Fifthly, that she †hull and *try well, which we call a good ship; 6 Sixthly, that she stay well when bourding and turning on a wind is required."

The specifications necessary to the attainment of these ends are too lengthy to be quoted in full: "1, To make her strong consisteth in the truth of the workmen and

†A-Hull: Driving under bare poles.
*A-Try: "A ship is said to try when she hath not more sails abroad but her Main Course, when the Tacks are close aboard, the Bowlings are set up, and the Sheets hauled close aft, or when the Helm or Steering Wheel is so fastened as to prevent their having any Power of the Tiller, so as she is let lie by the Sea; and sometimes when it blows so hard that she cannot bear her Main Course, they make her lie a-Try under Mizon only." From "A Naval Expositor," Thomas Riley Blanckley, London, 1750.

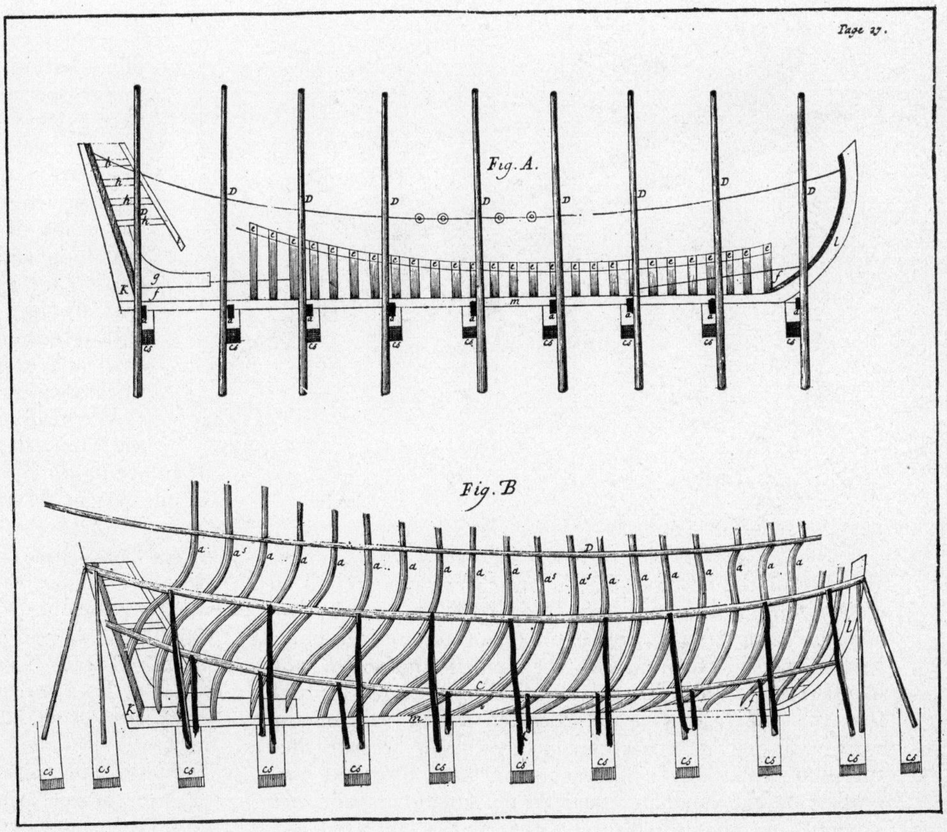

Above: Title page of "The Shipbuilder's Assistant," an early text on naval architecture. Right: Vessel in frame. Fig. A, keel, stem, sternpost, fashion timbers, floors. Fig. B. Showing bents or frames, ribbands, or harpens, and shores to support frame during construction. From "The Ship-Builder's Assistant"

Pl. XXXI.

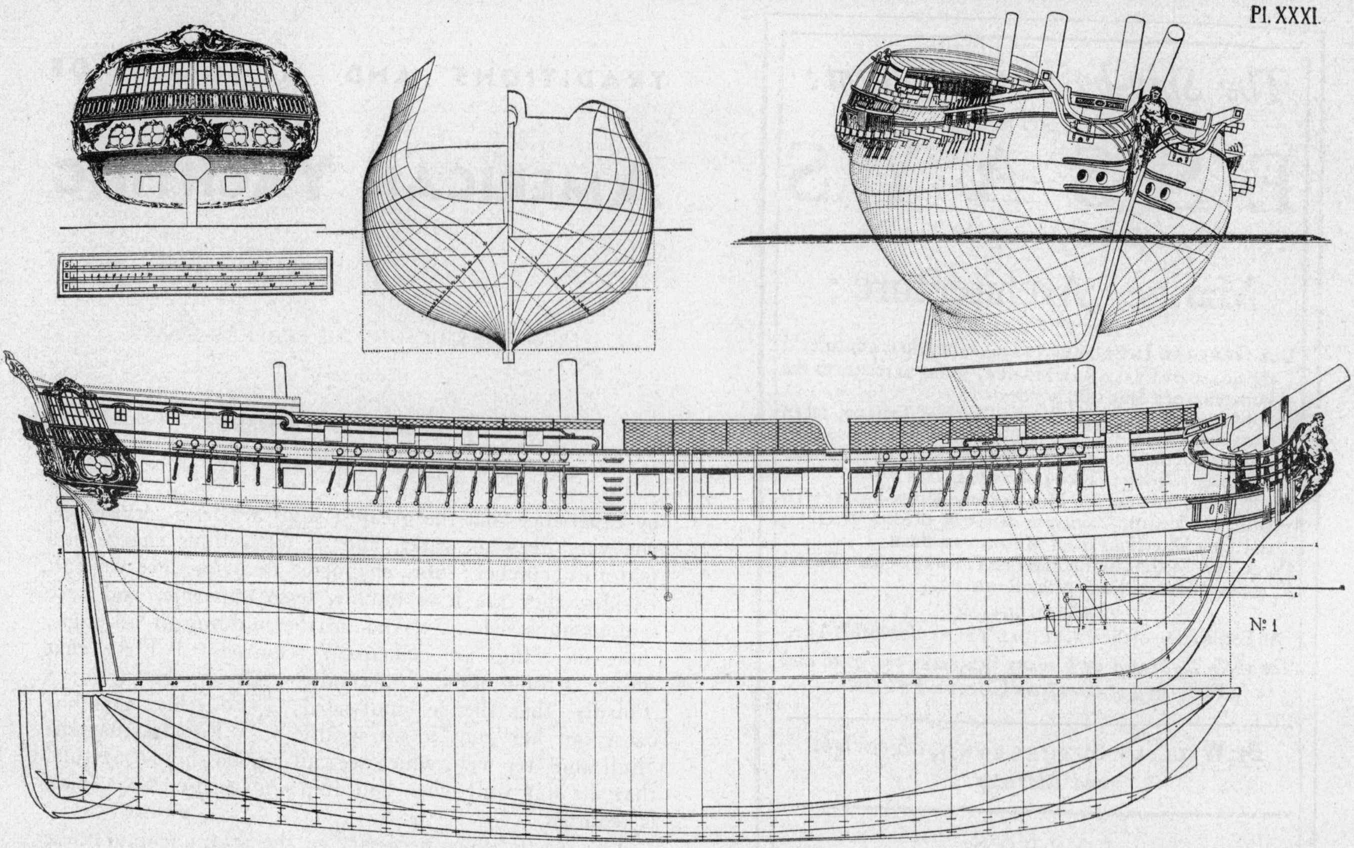

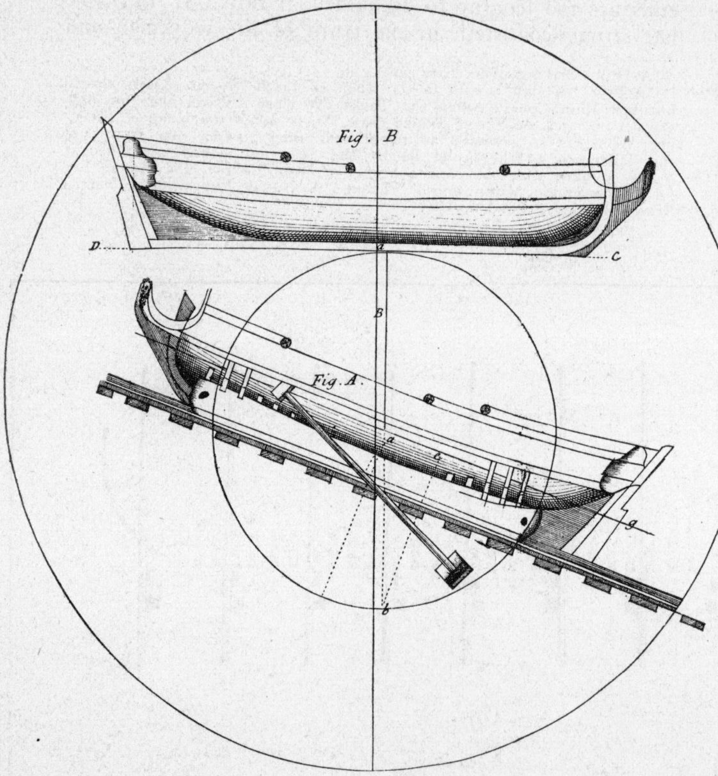

Left: Vessel on ways, ready for launching, showing blocking, groundways, bilgeways, cradle, and dog-shore holding vessel. The final order in launching was "down dog-shore," a man on each side knocking down the dog-shore with a maul. From "The Ship-Builder's Assistant"

Above: Example of the old-time art of ship draftsmanship; artistic ornamentation of the lines; and the hulls shown in elaborate perspective. From "Architectura Navalis Mercatoria," 1768, by Frederik H. Chapman

the care of the officers. 2, To make her sayle well is to give a long run forward, and so aftwards done by art and just proportion. For, as in laying out of her bows before and quarters behind, she neither sinck into nor hang in the water, but lye cleare of and above it; and that the shipwrights be not deceived herein (as for the most part they have ever been), they must be sure that the ship will sinck no deeper than they promise; for, otherwise, the bow and quarter will utterly spoile her sayling. 3, That she be stout, the same is provided and performed by a longe bearing floore. 4, To carry her ordnance all weather, this long bearing floore is a chief cause. . . . 5, To make her a good sea ship, that is, to hull and trye well, there are two things specially to be observed; the one that she have a good draught of water; the other, that she be not overcharged, which commonly the King's ships are. 6, The hindrance to stay well is the extreme length of a ship, especially if she be floaty, and want of sharpness forward . . . one hundred foot long and five and thirty broad is a good proportion for a great ship. It is a special observation that all ships sharp before, that want a long floore, will fall roughly into the sea and take water over head and ears. So will all narrow-quartered ships sinck after the tayle."

We read of the organization, in April 1606, of the Shipwrights Company, the charter, granted in 1612, being to "The Master Warden and Commonalty of the Art or Mystery of Shipwrights"; the first Master being Phineas Pitt (1570-1647); a man of most exceptional antecedents. Of an old shipbuilding family, he was a graduate of Cambridge, and not of a dockyard; with his brother Christopher and his son Peter (1610-1670) he played an important part in the building up of the British Navy. The time was most propitious as Charles II, after his return from exile in Holland, had a deep interest in all that related to the sea, from yachts to battleships; and a much deeper knowledge of technical matters than possessed by most sovereigns, even those of a more serious turn of mind than the "Merry Monarch." To Peter Pett is ascribed the credit for the first frigate,

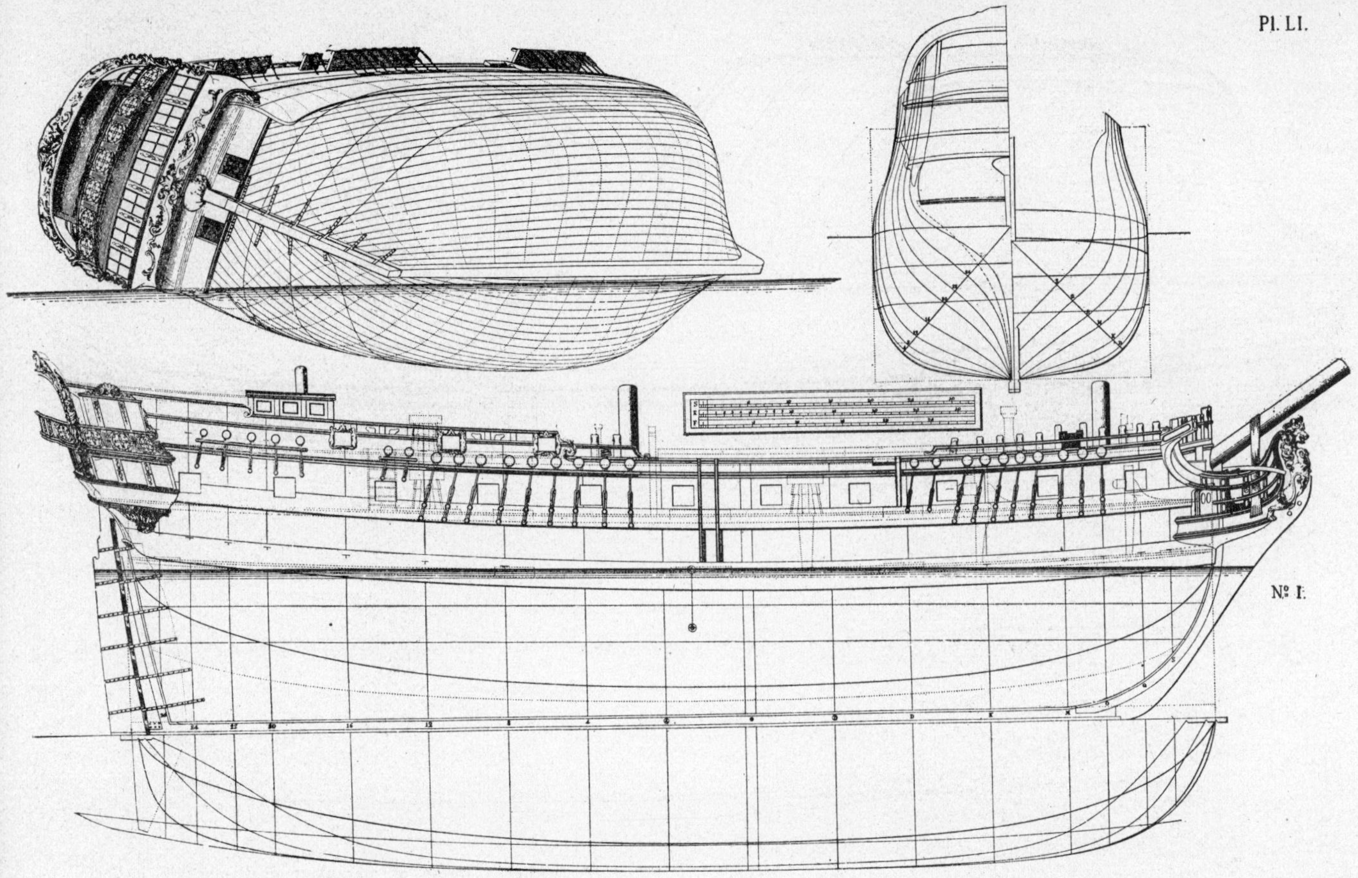

the Constant Warwick, built in 1646; nine years previously he had built the Sovereign of the Seas, the first three-decker built in England. Following the Petts came Sir Anthony Deane (1638-1721), who began life as an apprentice in Woolwich Dockyard, followed the sea as a "mariner," and finally rose to the leadership in construction. He built a number of yachts for the royal family; but his chief claim to fame is as the first naval architect to calculate the displacement of a vessel from the draught. To quote Pepys' Diary, "And then he fell to explain to me his manner of casting the draught of water which a ship will draw beforehand, which is a secret the King and all admire in him; and he is the first that hath come to any certainty beforehand of foretelling the draught of water of a ship before she be launched." We are fortunate today in that the reign of Charles II could boast of two writers, Samuel Pepys (1633-1703) Clerk of the Acts, and later Secretary to the Admiralty, and John Evelyn (1620-1706); intimate friends, and both diarists by habit. What they told us of the manners of the day, and more particularly, of naval matters, is of inestimable value.

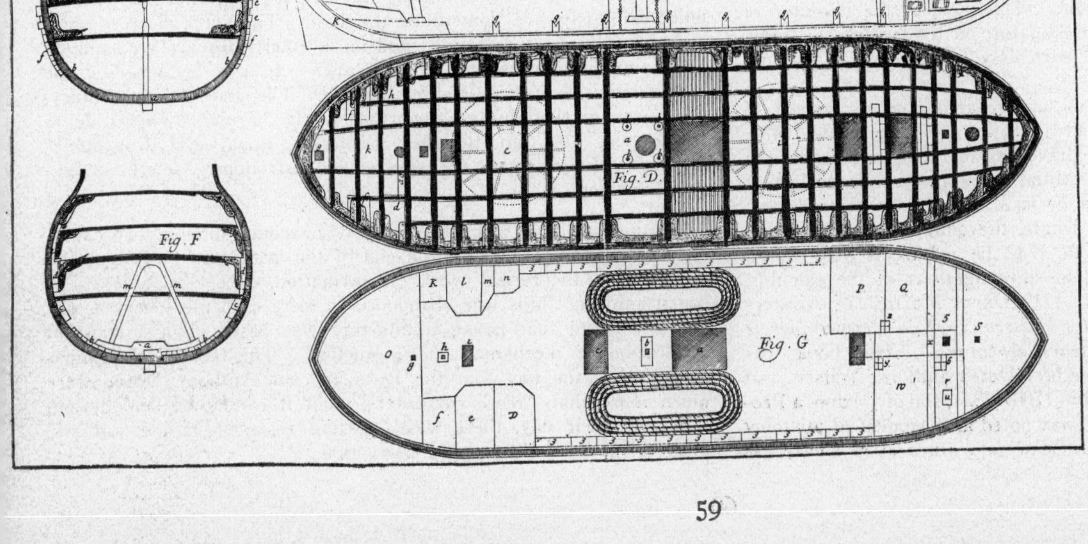

Above: Another beautiful example of the art of the ship draftsman with a complicated perspective drawing, from Architectura Navalis Mercatoria, by Frederik H. Chapman, 1768

Left: Elevation, sections, deck framing plan, storage plan of warship. From "The Ship-Builder's Assistant"

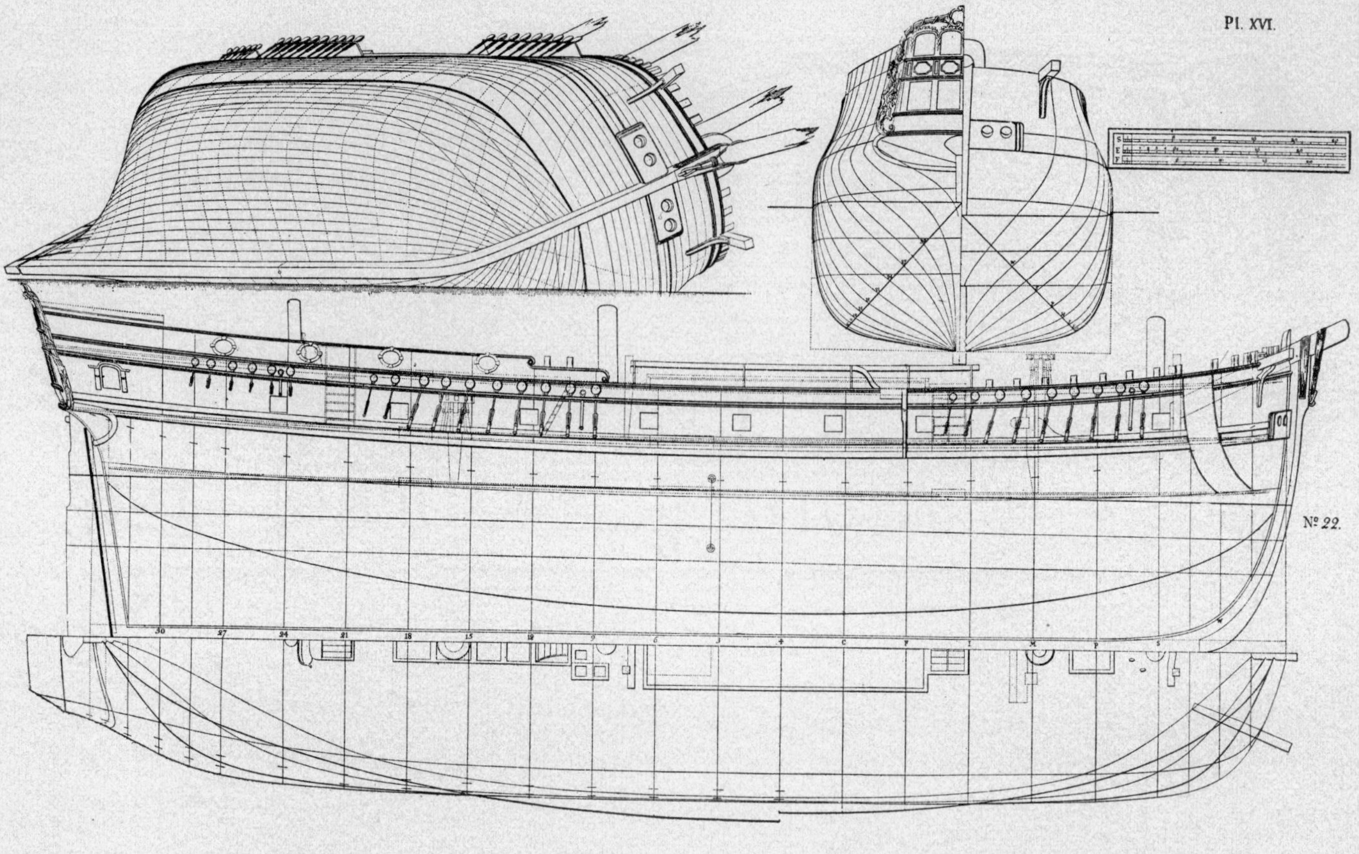

A further example of marvelous draftsmanship in a complex system of lines, from Architectura Navalis Mercatoria, by Frederik H. Chapman, 1768

The Science of Ship Design

While Sir Walter Raleigh seems, from a more extended study of his writings, to have had an interest in theory as well as practice, the first purely theoretical studies were made by scientists entirely separated from all branches of the shipping industry. The appeal, in the case of these men, was that of an abstract problem in physics; involving wind, water, and a body floating freely; these independent studies marking the last quarter of the seventeenth century. In *"La Statique, ou la Science des Formes Mouvantes,"* published in 1673, Father Ignace Gaston Pardies investigated the behavior of a ship under the influence of a side wind; in 1677 Le Sieur Dassie followed him with *"L'Architecture Navale"* treating of the manner of construction of *"Navires, Galeres & Chaloupes"*; and the definition of several other varieties of vessels, the book being in French. In 1681 a conference was held in Paris at which the ship was considered as a geometric body or bodies, sphere and cone; from the standpoint of pure rather than applied mathematics. One of the participants, Chevalier Renaud, published in 1689 *"Le Théorie de la Manoeuvre des Vaisseaux."* His theories and conclusions were actively disputed by one of the leading scientists, Christopher Huyghens (1629-1695); famous not from any association with the sea, but as an astronomer, a maker of telescopes, the inventor of the pendulum clock, and an investigator of the nature of light. Others became involved in the controversy, which lasted well into the eighteenth century.

The family of Bernoulli figures largely among the scientists of this day; James (1654-1705), had a brother, Johann (1657-1748), Professor of Mathematics at the University of Basle, noted specially for his investigation of the exponential calculus, but the author of an *"Essai d'une Nouvelle Théorie de la Manoeuvre des Vaisseaux,"* 1714; in which he discussed at length the action of wind on the sails, and water on the hull. In 1742 he published his *"Opera Omnia,"* in which were included his investigations of the calculus, light, trigonometry and ships. In 1719 David Mortier, of Amsterdam, published *"L'Art de Batir les Vaisseaux, et en Perfectioner le Construction et les Garnir de leurs Apparaux."* This book was described as being drawn from the best Dutch authors; Witsen, van Eyck, Allard, etc. Daniel Bernoulli (1700-1782), son of Johann, a Professor of the University of Basle, was noted as a student of anatomy and botany, but in 1751 he wrote *"Sur le Nature et la Cause des Courans, et les Meilleure Manière de les Determiner."* Two years later he followed with the comprehensive title: *"Recherches sur le Manière le plus Avantageuses de Suppleer l'Action du vent sur les Grandes Vaisseaux; soit en y Applicant les Rames, soit en y employant quelque autre Moyen que ce puisse etre; fondées sur une Nouvelle Théorie de l'Economie des Forces et des Effets."* This paper, which took into consideration the use of oars and all other possible auxiliary powers, so essential for warships in combat in calms, and also his previous paper, won prizes awarded by the Société Royal des Sciences of France. Be it noted that both father and son were natives of Switzerland, a nation without a sea coast or a navy.

Turning back in a necessarily devious course, an important advance was made by Father Paul Hoste, a Jesuit priest, Professor of Mathematics at Toulon, writing first in 1692 and again in 1697. In his *Théorie de la Construction des Vaisseaux"* he says "The best constructors build the two principal parts of a ship—the bow and stern—almost entirely by eye. . . . It cannot be denied that the art of constructing ships, which is so necessary to the State, is the least perfect of all arts. . . . Chance has so much to do with construction that the ships which are built with the greatest care are commonly the worst; and those which are built carelessly are sometimes the best. Thus, the largest ships are often the most defective; and more good ships are seen among merchantmen than in the Royal Navy." In this he endorsed the older criticism of Sir Walter Raleigh. The end of this century, 1698, was marked by an important work, *"Traité Complet de la Navigation,"* by Jan Bouguet, Professor Royal d'Hydrographie; dealing with geometry, the sphere, and astronomy; solely navigational subjects.

Writing in 1763, a French author, Leveque, summarized conditions as follows: "Toward the end of the last century Europe had not a single theoretical work on navigation, except pilotage. The construction of ships was abandoned to mere carpenters, and it was not considered that naval architecture was based upon a constant application of mechanics and goemetry." This severe condemnation ignores the fact that the Petts and Sir Anthony Deane were much more than "mere carpenters"; but it cannot be denied that, following their day, there was a serious recession in the "art and mystery" of naval design and construction.

Science and Theory in Design

THE second half of the eighteenth century was marked by a wide-spread interest in subjects relating to the sea and ships; but many of the studies were of an abstract nature. In 1749 Leonard Euler (1707-1783) Swiss by birth but a Professor of the Universities of Berlin and St. Petersburg, brought out his "Scientia Navalis," a work in two quarto volumes with 65 folding plates, in which he discusses from a mathematical standpoint the resistance encountered by a vessel in its movements in water. This work was translated from the original Latin into French; and, again, in 1776, from French into English by Col. Henry Watson, under the title of "Compleat Theory of the Construction and Properties of Vessels; with Practical Conclusions for the Management of Ships." In 1752 Euler supplemented the original work, shortly before he had translated it into French, by a *"Memoire sur la Manière le plus Avantageuses de supplier a l'Action du Vent sur les grands Vaisseaux"*; dealing with the use of sweeps and oars on ships. This work, written in Latin in spite of its French title, won the prize of the Société Royal des Sciences. In commenting on Euler's theories Col. Watson included this work in his translation of the earlier one. In his dedication Euler says "Although forty years have elapsed since mathematicians have labored with some success, yet their discoveries are so much enveloped in profound calculations that "marineres" have scarce been able to derive any benefit from them." In 1761 another Euler, Johann Albrect, published *"Recherches sur l'Arrimages des Vaisseaux, et quelles bon Qualitiés on en Procurer a un Vaisseau"*; apparently dealing with stowage capacity.

In 1763-7 a navy captain, Chevalier de Borde, conducted experiments on resistance; and similar work was done by Abbe Bossut in 1775; in 1787 M. Romme, Professor of Navigation at Rochelle, published *"L'Art de la Marine,"* covering construction, armament, maneuvering and navigation; and in 1796 an Englishman, George Atwood, of Trinity College, Cambridge, wrote on "The Construction and Analysis of Geometrical Propositions determining the Position of Homogeneal Bodies which Float freely and at rest on a Fluid's Surface; also determining the Stability of Ships, and of other Floating Bodies." Two years later he added "A Disquisition on the Stability of Ships." In 1771 an important contribution was made by a Spaniard, Don Juan d'Ulloa, in his *"Examen Maritime,"* treating of resistance and, secondarily, of stability; a subject which had not yet received the attention which it deserved, save from one author. In 1755 a French naval constructor, Cauchot, won a prize of the Société Royal des Sciences by a paper *"Sur les Mouvements de Roulis et de Tangage des Vaisseaux du Roy"*; treating of the rolling and pitching movements of a vessel.

THE most important work of this era was that of Pierre Bouguet, son of Jan Bouguet, *"Le Traité du Naviere, de sa Construction et de sa Mouvements,"* first published in 1746. Though eminent as a scientist rather than as associated with the sea, his interest was awakened by a voyage of seven years to South America for scientific observations. In addition to a general treatment of the details of a ship, he devotes himself to a deep study of stability; defining and naming the metacentre; thus bringing to the fore one of the most vital elements of naval architecture; heretofore neglected as compared with propulsion and resistance. His opinion as a scientist of the practical ship builder was the reverse of complimentary: "It always happens that they (the builders) think differently from each other; and yet each alleges, with equal confidence in his favor, his own practice; or a tedious list of ships which he has already constructed. As it is impossible to reconcile them, because they have no means of doing it, neither common principle of agreement from which they can set out, nor rule, nor even index to discern the truth by, or to bring them acquainted with it, they are reduced to a continual repetition of the same assertion in place of truth." Among other scientists thus interested it is not strange to find Sir Isaac Newton (1642-1727) contributing his part.

Early Works on Construction

RETURNING to the practical side, we note the interest and knowledge of Sir Walter Raleigh in the ship as a prime element in the protection and growth of the British Empire; the three Petts were far ahead of their time, and did good work; Sir Anthony Deane left a place that was unfilled for at least a generation. One of the early works on the practical side was: "The Ship-Builders Assistant," by William Sutherland; the first edition appearing in 1711, and continuing in successive editions to 1794. The nature and scope of the work may be judged from the accompanying title page.

The dedication is "To the Right Honourable Lords Commissioners for Executing the Office of Lord High Admiral of Great Britain and Ireland, &c. May it please Your Worships, This small Treatise of Marine Architecture approaches Your Lordships with the greatest Sense of both Duty and Respect. And as both the subject itself, and the Circumstances of its Author, make it Your Lordships by a kind of Right, I am incouraged to hope that it will meet with a favorable Reception. . . . And, 'twill likewise be an Incouragement to hope it may find a candid Reception with all Ingenuous Persons, and Lovers of Art who have their Country's Interest truly at Heart; Improvements of this Kind being so very Serviceable to our Successes by Sea. Which, as they have hitherto been very great since the Accession of our Most Gracious Queen to the Throne; so that they may not only still continue, but constantly increase under Your Lordships Wise and Prudent Administration is the sincere and hearty Desire of,

May it please Your Lordships,
Your Lordships most Humble and most Obedient Servant
W. SUTHERLAND.

Following this most humble peroration, the Preface deals at some length with a great variety of points; it states: "'tis the product of 32 years study and experience; for 'tis very well known that I have been so long imployed in Her Majesty's service, and of that of her Royal predecessors; so that I may say that I was in a manner born a seaman, as most of my ancestors were. My grandfather was foreman to the shipwrights in Her Majesty's Yard at Deptford 30 years; my uncle, Mr. Bagwell, died master builder at Her Majesty's Yard at Portsmouth, my father and several of my relations were master carpenters in the Royal Navy, and I myself have had the honour to act as master carpenter of three of Her Majesty's ships; and for 15 years past have served Her Majesty in the inspection and direction of the work done by part of the shipwrights at Portsmouth and Deptford Yards. During which time I have made it my study to forward youth, and make them experts in the art of shipbuilding."

AFTER the preface come some general statements: "Plato examined the cutting of a sphere or globe, and reduced the dividing of it into five regular bodies. . . . The first shipwright that was ever publicly observed to inquire into the regular forming of a ship was Sir Phin Petts, one of our former Master Builders; who, being assisted by that famous mathematician, Dr. Wallis, composed a solid which he called conocuneous,* being ½ cone and ½ wedge; called by some the shipwright's circular wedge, which was allowed to be a very good foundation for the art of shipbuilding. . . . The incomparable Sir Isaac Newton has indeed demonstrated a solid which he calls the solid of least resistance, and finds that it may be very useful in building ships. . . . In Mr. Hayes' fluxions is investigated the center of gravity of divers solid bodies. And altho' variety of considerations will be requisite in pitching on the centers of gravity of a ship or such a moving machine; yet such considerations ought to be, before the direct center of the masts' place can be exactly known." Following this preamble is a short description of the lines of a ship, with the explanation: "since the body of any ship regularly formed is no other than a hanging conoid, those lines will be reciprocal to such a figure." The remainder of this chapter is devoted to the conversion and disposition of timber, the same subject being the basis of the next chapter: "an essay towards regulating the price of several valuable materials relating to naval stores."

The chapter "An Essay upon Marine Architecture" begins: "Architecture is a branch of mathematics founded upon geometrical precepts, and is three-fold: edification, or the art of building houses; gnomonics, or dialing; and machination, or the forming of machines or engines." Following a dissertation along this line come instructions for the laying of the groundways, blocks and keel, the erection of the stempiece and sternpost; the laying of the floors and other members. A chapter on "OEconomy" deals again with the conversion of timber; a chapter on "Disposition, or Habitude" is followed by one on "Conveniency," beginning: "To construe the cavity of a ship that it may admit of a due ranging and disposing of everything therein contained to the best advantage, is called Conveniency."

*Cono-cuneus: or the Shipwright's Circular Wedge, geometrically considered" by John Wallis, D.D., F.R.S., Savilian Professor of Geometry, Oxford, 1684.

This is a very long and discursive treatment of arrangement, details of construction, placing of gun ports, and many unrelated items. Much attention is given to "Tunnage": "The measure of a ship may be considered in three several ways; first, what the cavity will hold; secondly, what superficial or solid inches are contained in her; thirdly, what will she bear, or carry safely from one port to another without damnifying the goods so transported. And which of these three may most properly be taken to adjust the tunnage of a ship was never yet determined." Apart from the generous philosophizing, the practical operations of ship construction are given at length, with special attention to the rig; of a total of 162 pages no less than 50 are devoted to rig alone. The work as a whole is a curiosity; not only his training and experience, as set forth in the preface, indicate a man thoroughly familiar with all branches of ship design and construction, but with the practical handling of ships at sea; without questioning his skill with broad axe and adze, or at the tiller, he lacked the ability to describe clearly and succinctly the operations with which he was familiar. As the work passed through a number of editions, down to 1794, it must have met with favor throughout the craft.

The Union of Theory and Practice

WE have watched the course of two streams of naval architecture, practical and theoretical, for over a century as they ran side by side, sometimes uniting in the brain of one individual, but more frequently independent and separated; it is gratifying to know that we may place positively their final union in the brain and hand of one man. Born in Yorkshire, England, in 1679, and brought up to the sea, Thomas Chapman went to Sweden in 1715 and was appointed a captain in the Swedish Navy; he married an English lady, a member of the Colson family, long associated with British shipbuilding; a son, Frederik Hendrik, was born in 1721, at Gothenburg. The boy grew up as a shipbuilder, and is credited with having built a merchant vessel when but 19; a year later he was at work in the Deptford Dockyard, and in 1744 he started his own yard at Gothenburg. This practical work was followed by a study of naval architecture in Stockholm, and then in both study and practical work in the shipyards of France, England and Holland. In 1757 he was appointed assistant constructor of the Swedish Navy, in 1764 he was chief constructor at Stockholm, retiring on full pay in 1793, and his active work continuing until three years before his death; at Karlskrona in 1808. His services to Sweden were recognized by a title of nobility, Knight of the Royal Order of the Sword.

THE work of Frederik Hendrik Chapman as a practical designer and builder of all classes of vessels is second to his services in the advancement of a knowledge of naval architecture; both as a life-long student and a very able writer. As a part of his studies he built and used a tank for the testing of models by means of a system of weights. Chapman's writings include his *"Architectura Navalis Mercatoria,"* 1768, a series of most artistically executed ship plans; "A Treatise on Ship Building," 1775; a treatise on determining the sails, 1793; a treatise on the handling of ships; an account of model experiments made in 1794, and a work on warships, 1804. Even when we consider his long life, 87 years, we are filled with wonder at his achievements in so many and such varied lines of naval work; and at his mastery of design, construction, seamanship, and naval tactics. It is due to him that naval architecture was systematized, and given its proper place among the sciences; and that the independent and dis-associated labors of so many for nearly two centuries were put into orderly and compact form for the benefit of future generations.

FOLLOWING Chapman, in 1781 Marmaduke Stalkartt published his "Naval Architecture, or the Rudiments and Rules of Shipbuilding," written in English and published in London; the text, a large folio, is supplemented by 14 large plates, designs of ships, beautifully and ornately drawn. The method of designing is set forth clearly in all its technical details. The plates in the works of these two writers stand out today in advance of everything which has since been produced; high class steel engravings. Apart from the artistic quality of the conventional three plans of projection; with their florid ornamentation of the period the projections of hulls in perspective, at different angles of heel and of fore-and-aft trim, would puzzle an expert ship draftsman today. A modern designer, though fully competent to design a yacht fast enough to challenge for or defend the America's Cup, would hesitate before the task of making such a perspective of his design as would compare with similar work in either Chapman's or Stalkartt's books. It is possible that these elaborate perspective drawings were used in part to give that idea of "rotundity" on which John W. Griffiths lays such stress; and some of the drawings indicate, from the combined angles of heeling and scending, that they may have been the basis of paintings of vessels under stress of heavy weather. A feature of these works is the title page, most elaborately decorated, and usually with a dedication to royalty.

THE third author of this era was John Charnock (1756-1807) the son of a London barrister; his interest in naval affairs led him to writing, in 1794-8, the *"Biographia Navalis,"* and in 1801-2 he followed with a "History of Marine Architecture"; a monumental work in three quarto volumes with 100 plates. As items of interest pertaining to this period of development may be mentioned the numerous attempts, with very crude apparatus, at towing experiments; perhaps the most important being those of Col. Beaufoy, in 1793-8. In 1739 a school of naval design was established in Paris by one Duchamel; in 1741 the title *"Maitre de Charpenterie"* was replaced by that of *"Constructeur."*

Looking backward over a period of more than two centuries, we find that the majority of thinkers and writers were scientists, physicists, mathematicians and philosophers, with no association with the sea or ships. With many the attraction lay in the abstract problem involving three factors: a body floating freely in a fluid under the influences of wind and wave. Some extended their studies to ship forms, some still further to construction; while a few attempted to cover the entire field of theory of design, construction, masting and rigging, even down to stowage; with the inclusion of seamanship, navigation, pilotage, and maneuvering in war. A comparatively small number were content to deal only with design and construction; and still fewer estimated the vital problem of stability at its true value.

Progress on the theoretical side was almost entirely Continental; France leading, while England played a subordinate part. The discussions were often general and diffuse, covering many points only remotely related to the main issues; war vessels took precedence over commercial craft; the rights of Royalty were fully recognized in most humble if not fulsome dedications. As to material progress throughout the Seventeenth century, while ships increased in size, many naval battles were fought, many voyages of discovery made, and a growing volume of commerce carried, the advance in actual construction was less notable than that in the science of design.

TRADITIONS AND MEMORIES

OF

AMERICAN YACHTING

Part Thirteen

FROM THE BENCH TO THE DRAFTING BOARD

(Continued)

By *WILLIAM P. STEPHENS*

Captain Arthur Hamilton Clark
1841-1922
Seaman, Master Mariner,
Yachtsman, Antiquarian,
Historian

THE nautical world owes much to those men who possessed both the will and the ability to set down what they knew, whether technical or historical, for the benefit of future generations. To those writers of the past already mentioned may be added the names of Captain Arthur H. Clark, Montague Guest and William B. Boulton, of our own day. The preceding chapter, bringing us down to the end of the 18th Century, of necessity dealt only with the larger vessels of war and commerce; entering the 19th Century, we find a new type of craft: the yacht. The development of the yacht of today from the "Jaght" or "Jaght-Schip" of the 16th Century is well told in the works of these authors: "The History of Yachting, 1600-1900," by Captain Clark, and "The Memorials of the Royal Yacht Squadron, 1815-1900," by Messrs. Guest and Boulton.

Of Boston and Puritan origin, Benjamin C. Clark was a ship owner, with a line of sailing vessels engaged in the West India coffee trade and the Mediterranean fruit and wine trade between 1830 and 1850. He was a yachtsman, owning first Mermaid, one of the early decked yachts built about Boston; and later Raven, which in 1845 won the first yacht regatta sailed on Massachusetts Bay. The son, Arthur Hamilton Clark, was born in 1841, naturally growing up about the waterfront; at the age of 16, when a student at the old Boston Latin School, he rowed as one of the six-oared shell, Volante, which defeated the Harvard boat, Huron. It was decided that he should be apprenticed to Donald McKay, the noted ship builder; but his choice was the sea, and in January 1858 he shipped aboard the ship Black Prince. A voyage of two years took him around Cape Horn to San Francisco, Manila, Hong Kong, San Francisco again, Hong Kong, Shanghai, and back to New York by way of the Cape of Good Hope. After six months of study ashore, and rowing three successful races in single lapstrake wherries, he shipped aboard the Northern Light as second officer for a voyage to San Francisco; successfully dodging Confederate privateers on the return voyage. Failing in obtaining an appointment to the Navy, he shipped again aboard the Black Prince, now as first officer, making two trips carrying troops to Port Royal and Ship Island, and then sailing for Shanghai. By 1863 he was in command of his own ship, and the next ten years were spent in the China Seas. Back in New York in 1863, he took command of the steamship Indiana, of the American Line, between New York and Liverpool. In 1876 he abandoned the sea to become the London representative of New York, Boston and Philadelphia underwriters; continuing this business for 13 years. During this period he represented the United States as one of the Commission on the Alabama Claims, and he made the estimates and specifications for the Mackay-Bennett Atlantic Cable. In returning to the States in 1890 aboard the William R. Grace the ship was wrecked on Cape May, all hands being taken off by the local lifesavers.

Again in Boston as a maritime agent, he went to Chicago as head of the Marine Transportation Department of the World's Fair in 1893; but after three months established himself as a maritime agent in Chicago. Back in New York in 1895, he served as agent for the underwriting branch of Lloyd's of London until his retirement in 1920; the last two years of his life being spent in Newburyport, Mass. In 1865 he made a tour of Europe and Egypt, and in the following year took command of the sloop Alice, owned by Thomas G. Appleton of Boston, making the passage to Cowes in 19 days; in the same year he joined the New York Yacht Club, being No. 3 on the seniority list at the time of his death. In 1894 he brought the small steam yacht Sylvia to New York by way of Madeira and Bermuda, Mrs. Clark accompanying him. While living in England he owned the cutter Margery Daw; in New York, from 1900 to 1907 he owned the noted 40 foot Minerva.

With such a background, such world-wide experience, and such a love of everything associated with the sea, Captain Clark brought together the wonderful collection which is now in the Pratt School of Naval Architecture of the Massachutts Institute of Technology; some 2,500 items in number, pictures and models. In addition to his history of yachting he wrote "The Clipper Ship Era,

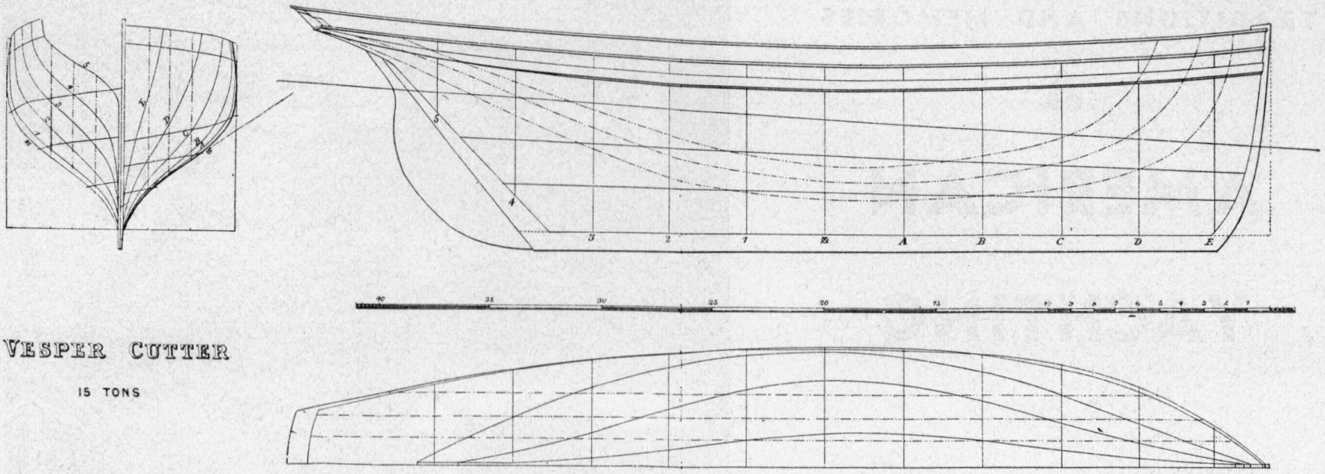

Cutter Yacht, Vesper. Designed by P. R. Marett (amateur) as illustrative of the method of designing about 1855, and type then in vogue. L. W. L., 37 feet; breadth, 9 feet 11 inches; draft, 4 feet 10 inches

1843-1869." As Librarian of the Royal Yacht Squadron for many years Montague Guest enjoyed exceptional opportunities for the study of yachting at its birthplace; his associate, William B. Boulton, shared his antiquarian tastes and is known also as the author of "The Amusements of Old London." Without quoting these authorities directly, it may be said that much of the information immediately following is drawn from the two books named.

The Yacht Is Born

The modern word "Yacht" is derived by various transitions from the Old Dutch "jaght"; Captain Clark quotes from a Dutch dictionary published in Antwerp in 1599 the verb "jaghen," to hunt or chase, with an implication of speed; with a supplementary meaning of towing with horses, as was customary on the canals of Holland. The noun occurs in various forms, jaght, jaghte and jaght-schip. In an English book, "Collection of Voyages and Travels," published in 1642, it is recorded that in 1598 the Holland East India Company despatched to India "six great ships and two yachts"; marking the incorporation of the word in the English language. While the use of certain vessels, usually of small size, for purely pleasure purposes dates back to the beginning of history, all such craft may be discarded as having no relation to the private yacht as it has existed for little more than two centuries. Such "yachts" were practically miniatures of the war vessels of their day; modelled and built by ship builders. The early royal yachts are described in detail by Captain Clark, a most interesting history; but, without presuming to differ with such an authority, a very careful study of the subject today leads to the conclusion that they had no material influence on the development of the craft in which we are interested.

Will Fife II
1822-1902
Yacht Builder

One of the earliest records of the sailing of small craft for mere pleasure is the statement that when stopping in the Channel Islands in 1646 the prince who was later King Charles II amused himself by such sailing. Later, after the Restoration made him a king in 1660, he continued the sport in company with his brother, the Duke of York, and a few friends, by sailing and racing such small craft as the width of the Thames permitted "above Bridge" abreast the city of London.

Physical conditions in Holland, a land divided by numerous watercourses, compelled the use of boats for the ordinary purposes of transportation and travel. While many of these "jaghts" were only miniature ships, fitted for sea-going, there was also a very large fleet of smaller craft. Built originally for service rather than pleasure, in the course of a natural evolution competition arose, and more and more of the craft were used exclusively for pleasure, thus warranting the designation of "yacht." Where to draw the line, both as to date and size, is a matter of doubt. The "yacht" on which Charles returned to England in May 1660 was merely a large vessel of state, one of a fleet; the king, always popular with the Dutch, expressed a wish for a similar craft, and one named Mary was presented to him by the Dutch Government. This vessel was 52 feet on the keel, 19 feet breadth, 7 feet 7 inches depth, and

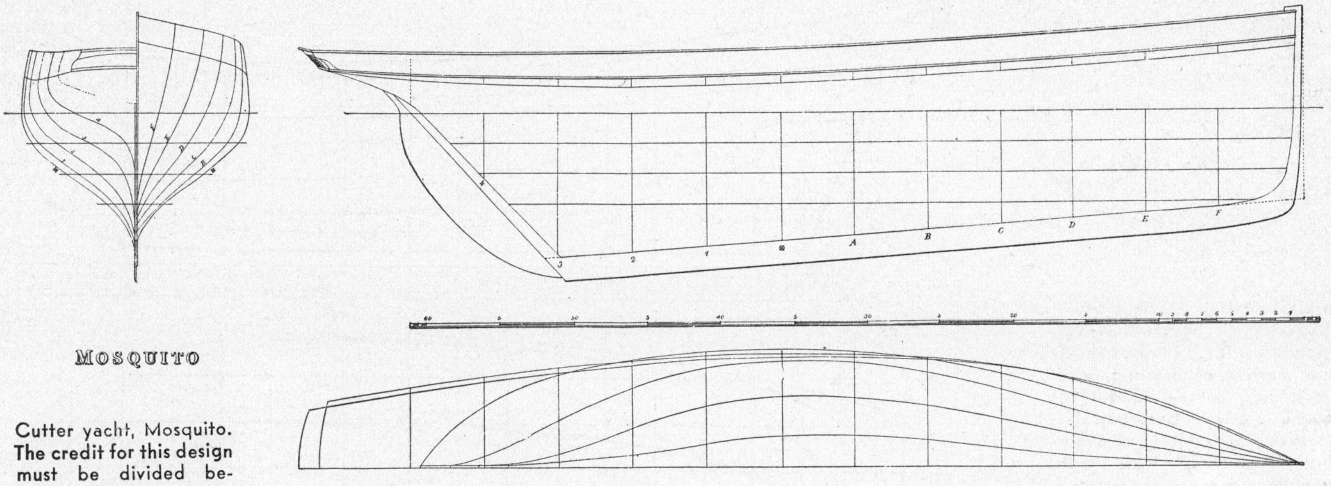

Cutter yacht, Mosquito. The credit for this design must be divided between three amateurs, Messrs. Mare, Ditchburn and Waterman. L. W. L., 60 feet; breadth, 15 feet 3 inches; draft, 11 feet 6 inches

10 feet draft, carrying eight guns. We find in that interesting book, the diary of John Evelyn, the following entry under date of October 1, 1661. "I sailed this morning with His Majesty in one of his yachts (or pleasure boats), vessells not known among us till the Dutch E. India Company presented that curious piece to the King; being very excellent sailing vessells. It was on a wager between his other new pleasure boat, built frigate-like, and one of the Duke of York's; the wager 100£; the race from Greenwich to Gravesend and back. The King lost in going, the wind being contrary, but saved stakes in returning. There were divers noble persons and lords on board, his Majesty sometimes steering himselfe. His barge and kitchen boate attended. I broke fast this morning with the King at return in his smaller vessell, he being pleased to take me and only four more, who were noblemen, with him; but din'd in his Yacht, where we all eate together with his Majesty."

Without attempting to draw a fixed line between the state vessels and the pleasure yacht; what with Charles' love of sailing in small boats, his knowledge of and interest in larger craft, we may well name him as the first English yachtsman; and his era as the introduction of the sport of yachting. Under the direction of the Petts, previously mentioned, and Sir Anthony Deane, ship building in all its branches flourished through the quarter century of Charles' reign; but yachting as a national sport was far from a permanent foundation.

While the English have always been considered as a sporting nation, this idea is very far from correct; as a matter of fact, prior to the 19th Century the leisure class had no interest in active physical sport, being well content with such amusements as the town afforded. As spectators the bucks of the day stood elbow to elbow with Tom and Jerry at boxing matches, badger-baiting and cockfighting; but they had no inclination to bestride a horse and follow the hounds, or to chance rough hands and a wet jacket aboard even a large yacht. It was not until the peace which followed the Battle of Waterloo that the more active branches of sport, including yachting, came into general favor.

The Birth of Yachting on the Thames

The impetus imparted to yachting by Charles soon died out, and a century later we find Henry Fielding, in his celebrated "Voyage to Lisbon," lamenting "on the deplorable lack of taste in our enjoyments which we show by almost totally neglecting the pursuit of what seems to me the highest degree of amusement. This is the sailing ourselves in little vessels of our own, contrived only for our ease and accommodation, to which situation our villas, as I have recommended, would be convenient and even necessary. * * * The truth is, I believe, that sailing in the manner I have mentioned is a pleasure rather unknown or unthought of than rejected by those who have experienced it." That yachting continued in a way is shown by a race from Greenwich to the Nore and return sailed in 1749; in June of that year, to celebrate his twelfth birthday, Prince George, later King

Cutter yacht, Cygnet, built by Wanhill, of Polle, 1846. L. W. L., 58 feet; breadth, 12 feet 6 inches; draft, 9 feet

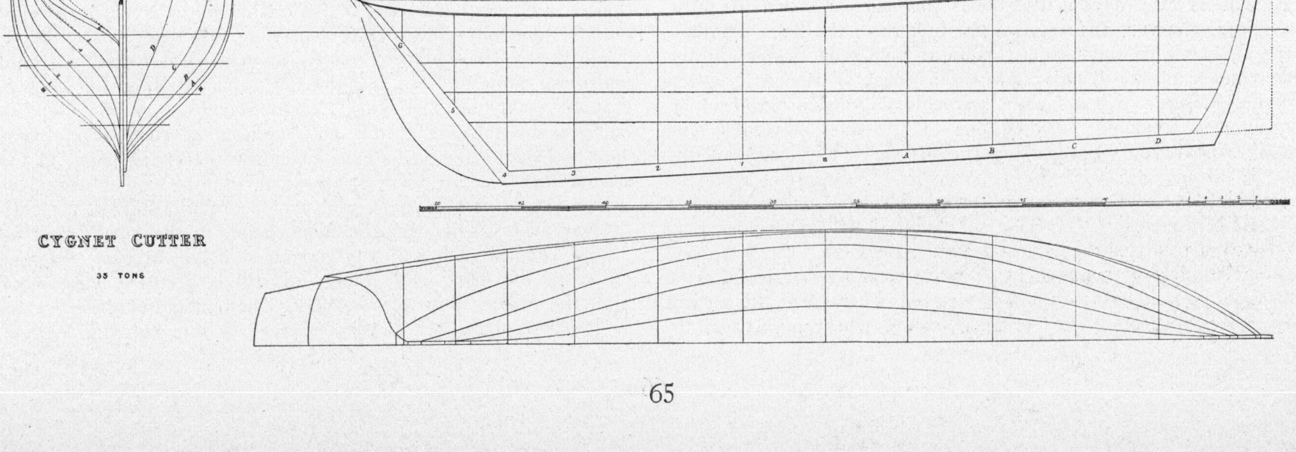

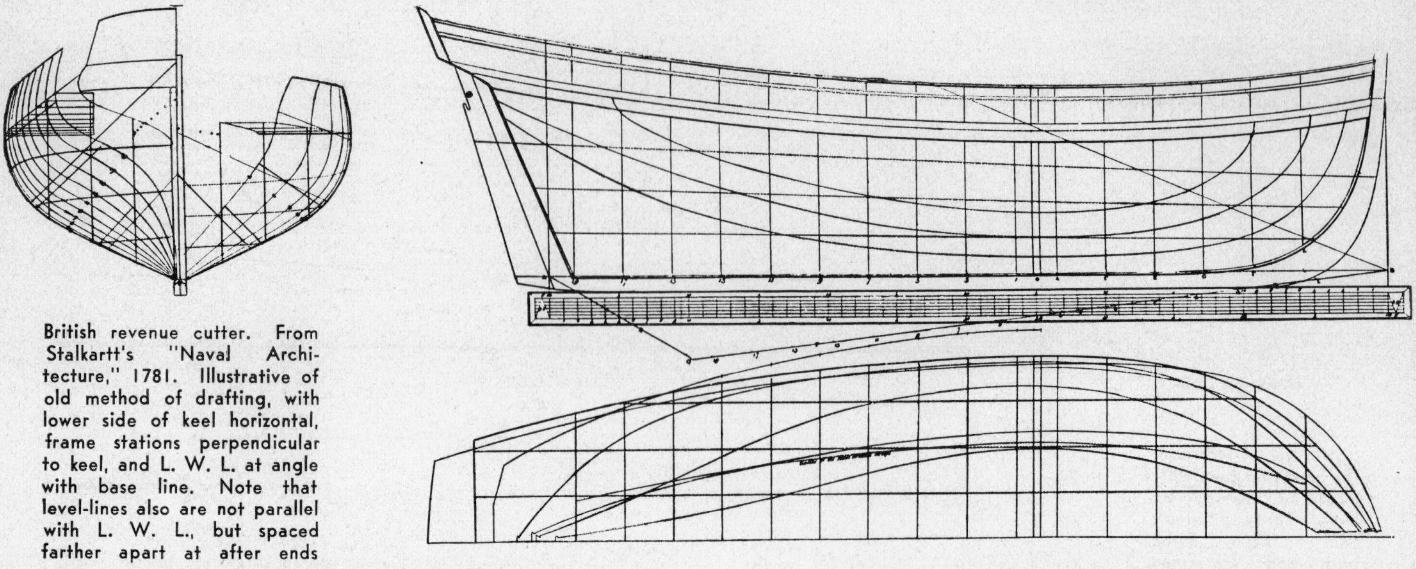

British revenue cutter. From Stalkartt's "Naval Architecture," 1781. Illustrative of old method of drafting, with lower side of keel horizontal, frame stations perpendicular to keel, and L. W. L. at angle with base line. Note that level-lines also are not parallel with L. W. L., but spaced farther apart at after ends

George III, gave a cup valued at 25 guineas for a rowing race from Whitehall to Putney, followed it a month later by a cup for a sailing race in which twelve yachts competed. As the yachts finished, in a very light breeze, "the Prince of Wales, with five or six attendants in his Chinese barge, and the rowers in Chinese habits, drove gently before" the fleet.

The beginning of permanent sailing on the Thames dates from 1775, when the Cumberland Fleet, or the Cumberland Sailing Society, was organized by the owners of existing sailing craft. The first rowing regatta in England was held on the Thames on June 23 of that year; prior to the regatta a meeting was held of "several very respectable gentlemen, proprietors of sailing vessels and pleasure boats on the River, at which it was decided that they should form in line off Ranelagh Gardens, clear of the course, to watch the race." Following this maneuvre, His Royal Highness, the Duke of Cumberland, offered a silver cup to be sailed for "By pleasure sailing boats from two to five tons burthen, and constantly lying above London Bridge," the course to be from Westminster Bridge to Putney Bridge and back; the entry to be limited to boats "which were never let out to hire," and "the gentlemen, about 18 or 20 in number, who sail for the prize, have come to a resolution to be dressed in aquatic uniforms." From this small beginning the Club grew, until, in 1823, the organization became the Thames Yacht Club, now the Royal Thames Yacht Club. The yachts of the fleet were small lapstrake craft, about 20 feet by 10 feet, keel boats drawing 4 to 5 feet; of cod's-head, mackerel-tail model. There is no record of their builders; probably local boat builders; and not, as in the larger yachts, ship builders.

Turning back to the beginning of the 18th Century, we find a curious development of yachting, sporadic and isolated, in the Water Club of Cork Harbor; an organization of unknown origin, but in active operation as early as 1720. Quoting from "A Tour Through Ireland," printed in 1748: "I shall now acquaint your Lordships with a ceremony they have at Cork; it is somewhat like that of the Doge of Venice wedding the Sea. A set of worthy gentlemen, who have formed themselves into a body which they call the 'Water Club,' proceed a few leagues out to sea once a year in a number of small vessels, which, for painting and gilding exceed the King's yacht at Greenwich and Deptford. Their Admiral, who is elected annually, hoists his flag on board his little vessel, leads the van, and receives the honors of the flag. The rest of the fleet fall in their proper stations and keep in line in the same manner as the King's ships. This fleet is attended with a prodigious number of boats with their colors flying, drums beating, and trumpets sounding, forming one of the most agreeable and splendid sights your Lordship can conceive." The rules of the Club, 21 in number, were most unusual: "I, Ordered, That the Water Club be held once every spring tide in April to the last of September, inclusive. II, That no Admiral do bring more than two dishes of meat for the entertainment of the Club. III, Resolved, That no Admiral presume to bring more than two dozen of wine to his treat; for it has always been deemed a breach of the ancient Rules and Constitution of the Club, except when my Lords, the Judges, are invited. IX, Ordered, That no long-tail wigs, large sleeves or ruffles be worn by any member at the Club. XIII, Resolved, That twenty-five be the whole number of members that this Club may consist of. XIV, Resolved, That such members of the Club, or others as shall talk of sailing after dinner shall be fined a bumper." The station of the Club was on Haulbowline Island, close to the shore at Queenstown, its course being outside Cork Harbor. Old pictures, still in the possession of the Royal Cork Y. C., show that the yachts were cutters of considerable size. After some forty years the Club activities ceased, to be resumed at intervals under other names until taking a new term of life about 1828 in the present Royal Cork Y. C. Its whole history seems apart from and systematic development of yachting in the Kingdom.

Cowes and the Solent

The end of the 18th Century was marked by a new movement in English society; away from the fashionable inland resorts such as Bath and Cheltenham, and to the seaside towns, hitherto comparatively neglected. The reason for this is not apparent, but does not concern us; only the fact itself is of importance here. Among the ports thus brought into prominence were Weymouth, Brighton, Torquay and, in the North, Scarborough. It is in no way strange that in this movement the Isle of Wight came into deserved prominence; both from its location and natural characteristics of climate and extent of sea front. In the first decade of the 19th Century the Island took on new life, with this invasion of a new element. It had been for years a center of maritime activities, its ship yards turned out vessels for the Royal Navy, its local fleet included fishermen, pilot boats, packet boats to the Hampshire shore as well as to France, smuggling luggers, and a nondescript fleet of pleasure craft, either privately owned or for the accommodation of "trippers." Competition existed among all of these craft, impromtu races between pilot boats and fishermen, revenue cutters and smugglers, similar trials of speed between rival party-boats.

In the troublous years preceding Waterloo and Trafalgar the waters of the Solent and the Channel were alive with larger craft, warships and privateers, some of the latter being yachts commanded by their owners. In such a nautical atmosphere as this the organization of individual elements into a yacht club was inevitable sooner or later, and on June 1, 1815, a meeting was held at The Thatched Tavern, St. James Street, London, at which was formally organized under the name of "The Yacht Club" what has been known for the past 107 years as The Royal Yacht Squadron. While there is no doubt as to the date of this first meeting, it would seem from the date of 1812 on the seal of the Squadron that some union of Cowes sailing men existed three years prior to this formal organization.

The yachts of the young club had no relationship to the class of "Royal yachts," nor, on the other hand, to the small craft sailed on the Thames. The majority resembled in type and size the revenue cutter of the day; while others of still larger size were modelled after the smaller ships of the Navy. The builders of these craft were in the first place men already engaged in ship building, largely for the Navy. There was a rapid growth of yachting between 1820 and 1830, bringing into the business a new class of men devoted exclusively to yacht construction; one of the first being Camper (now Camper & Nicholson) founded in 1833 at Gosport, on the Hampshire shore. One of the oldest families on the Island was that of Thomas White, born at Broadstairs in 1773, the grandson of a noted builder of warships who moved to Cowes, the first of a family of yacht builders, a son, Jospeh, was noted as a builder of clincher-built cutters for the Government. The Ratsey family, known the world over today as sailmakers, dates back to Lynn Ratsey who, in 1807, built the cutter Leopard at Cowes; his grandson, Michael Ratsey, being one of the leading yacht builders of the sixties and seventies. Of the builders unknown today were C. Miller of Cowes; List of Wooton Bridge, and Rubie of Southampton, originally a builder of fishing boats. Others who came into the business of later years were Inman of Lymington; Stow of Shoreham; Wanhill of Poole; and Hatcher of Southampton, the last known among yachtsmen as "King Dan" from the exceptional success of his yachts. In Scotland the firm of Robert Steele & Co. was building revenue cutters as early as 1807; in more recent years being noted for its large steel and iron steam yachts.

Notable in this catalogue of British builders is the name of Fife: "Fife of Fairlie," to give it the popular designation. This famous yacht yard was established about the beginning of the 18th Century by Will Fife, a wheelwright by trade and a builder of fishing boats and later larger craft; in 1814 he built the Industry, a river steamer which ran until she was the oldest steamer afloat. His son, the second Will, born in 1822, was apprenticed in his father's yard at the age of 13; by which time the yard was specializing in yacht work. In this line it soon became famous, the younger taking full charge before he was more than out of his teens. Following the cutter Stella in 1848 came a long line of successful yachts: Cymba, Fiona, Cythera, Cookoo, Bloodhound, Foxhound, Condor and Neptune. Cymba was remarkable in having an outside keel of three tons in 1852. While he lived until January 13, 1902, in 1881 he turned over the management of the yard, in particular the designing, to the third Will Fife; today the oldest of British designers. The most conspicuous success of the yard was Fiona, a cutter of 80 tons, launched in 1865; known to her partisans as "The Fawn o' Fairlie"; not merely a winner in her day, but the winner of the Helgoland race 35 years later and, in the following year, taking first prize in the Dover to Ostend race.

One of the most noted English yards was that of Harvey, at Wivenhoe, on the East coast; but as John Harvey, the last of the family, figures largely as one of the new school of professional designers, this story must follow later.

New Theories of Design

Turning now to the theoretical side, about 1830 a British scientist, John Scott Russell, inaugurated a series of experiments on form, resistance and skin friction, giving to the maritime world a new theory of "wave lines," so-called, as the correct level-lines for all vessels. The "wave line" developed by Mr. Russell was made up of a curve of versed sines for the entrance and a trochoid for the run. His work was published in two large volumes of text and plates, and awakened a wide interest in the subject of form. One of his adherents, Stephenson, designed and built the iron schooner Titania with a pure wave form, but she was not successful. She was, by the way, the only yacht which accepted the challenge of Commodore Stevens for a private match with his America; in which she was defeated. This crusade of Mr. Russell, though later proved wanting in its conclusions, served a good purpose in promoting a discussion of an important subject.

In 1853 appeared "Naval Architecture, A Treatise on Shipbuilding and the Rig of Clippers, with Suggestions for a new Method of Laying Down Vessels," by Lord Robert Montague, A.M.; dealing with the elements of a vessel, stability, calculations, and a method of design (or more properly practical drafting) by means of what the author called "dividing lines," a form of diagonals. Yachts were treated in a separate chapter under the headings: "Rigging and management, masts, sails and ballasting." On November 18 of the same year a naval architect, T. Ditchburn, lectured before the Prince of Wales Yacht Club in London on "The Elements of Naval Construction, and the Knowledge of the Nature and Laws of Elastic and Non-Elastic Fluids"; the first of a series. This seems to be the first official display of interest on the part of a yacht club in the vital subject of design.

On April 1, 1887, a paper was read before the Institution of Naval Architects, in London, by an American, Professor Robert H. Thurston, on "Forms of Fish and Ships," transverse sections of different fishes being taken from plaster casts and the curves of areas plotted. So far from this being a new idea, the same subject was treated in the Report of the Royal Cornwall Polytechnic Society, published in 1854; a paper by John S. Enys, F.G.S. The same method of investigation was followed, and similar plottings of fish forms and curves of areas are given.

A Call to Yachtsmen

Mention has been made of the work of Frederik Hendrik Chapman in the inauguration of a new order in ship design; some sixty years later a similar task was undertaken in British yachting. The writer in this case was one Philip R. Marrett, an Englishman of whom very little is known; who failed to receive the credit due him from his contemporaries, and who is today forgotten. As the author of the first book on yacht design which came into my possession I have always felt an interest in him, but a rather careful inquiry some ten years ago failed to disclose anything more than that he was of Norman extraction, resident in the Channel Islands, but with a branch at Southampton. Mr. Marett, whose home was at West Quay, Southampton, was apparently a barrister by profession, but deeply interested in yachting. In 1855 there appeared in "Bell's Life in London," one of the leading sports journals of the day, a series of articles on yacht designing; which, in June 1856, were re-published in book form under the title of "Yachts and Yacht Building, being a Treatise on the Construction of Yachts, and Matters Related to Yachting."

The reason for the book is stated in the preface: "The great want of scientific principle in the construction of yachts must be evident to everyone who has given the subject any consideration; and it is on account of this want that so few yachts are built which answer the expectations of the builder or owner. The deficiency may be traced to two principal causes; first, to the imperfect knowledge of the theory of Naval Architecture which the generality of our yacht builders possess; and secondly, to the very slight inducement to any improvement given by the yacht clubs. Although the builders are undoubtedly men of great experience, still the very nature of their employment prevents that careful study of the scientific part of their business which can alone produce a competent naval architect; in fact, Naval Architecture is with them of secondary importance, instead of demanding the greater share of their attention. In other constructive arts there are two distinct branches; the architect, to whom is entrusted the design, and the builder, whose business it is to carry out the design; and whenever these separate branches of a trade have been united, mediocrity has invariably resulted, because the time and attention requisite to produce proficiency in either branch prevents more than a partial knowledge of both. In yacht building the separation is even more necessary than in other constructive arts, for the designer should not only be a scientific constructor, but an experienced yacht sailor; otherwise, he can form no correct estimate of the probable effect of the combinations in his design. . . . The yacht clubs have hitherto done little to improve the construction of vessels; their prizes are offered for speed only, and that speed must be measured by an arbitrary standard which has not only ceased to be a correct measure, but is found to engender a very bad form of yacht. * * * In the way of improving the scientific construction and ensuring that a yacht shall answer the expectations of her constructor, the yacht clubs may accomplish much by insisting upon a proper drawing of every yacht entered for a race being deposited in their custody, to be used as club property.* Yacht owners should endeavor to force the builders into paying more attention to the construction of their vessels by making them furnish proper and correct designs of any yacht to be built. At present there seems no prospect that a class of scientific yacht constructors will arise; and the only improvement now likely to take place is that yacht owners should learn to construct their own vessels; or, at all events, to understand the drawings and calculations, and thus be able to control the construction. * * * The builders have an objection to supply any drawings for the purpose of publication, preferring to maintain a mysterious secrecy about their pro-

*A similar rule adopted by the Seawanhaka-Corinthian Yacht Club in 1878, under which no prize was delivered until the lines of the yacht were in the possession of the Club, is responsible for the preservation of many valuable designs which otherwise would have been lost.

ceedings. * * * Now this system of model making has had a most pernicious influence in yacht building; no correct idea can be formed of the properties or qualities of a vessel from a model, unless it be made from the drawing; and, if so, then it is useless except as a toy."

Following this confession of faith, the writer proceeds to explain the three projections of a vessel, and to describe the manner of making them; naming the necessary instruments and their uses, and discussing displacement, length, depth, breadth, drag, raking sternpost and stem; form, area and position of the midship section, and other elements. Extensive tables of dimensions and elements of successful yachts were given; with a design for a schooner of 80 feet waterline fully worked out, with all calculations. The twelve plates include America, the New York pilot boat Mary Taylor, and such typical yachts as Mosquito, Cygnet, Thought and Flying Cloud. That which is perhaps the most interesting of these designs is Vesper, a cutter of 15 tons; 37 feet l.w.l., 9 feet 11 inches breadth, and 4 feet 10 inches draft, made by the author. With this book as a guide, any man of fair average intelligence and a working knowledge of arithmetic would be able to turn out a design that, while not inevitably a winner, would compare favorably with the work of the modeller.

TRADITIONS AND MEMORIES OF AMERICAN YACHTING

Part Fourteen

FROM THE BENCH TO THE DRAFTING BOARD

(Continued)

By WILLIAM P. STEPHENS

THE decade from 1870 to 1880, especially the second half, was marked by radical changes in many details of British yachting. In the first place, shifting ballast having been abolished in 1856, another change was made in the transfer of all ballast from the inside to the outside of the hull below the keel. This, in turn, introduced a keel very wide amidships and tapering to the normal siding of stem and sternpost. This change in ballasting made it possible, under the existing Tonnage rule, to increase the length and decrease the breadth, thus introducing a radically new form of hull. It is a mere coincidence that just at this time the old generation, which included in one person both modeller and builder, was displaced by a new class of scientific yacht designers; young men specially trained in Naval Architecture, and most of them in no way associated with yacht building. In the later years of this period the subject of the measurement rule, then the ancient Tonnage rule, came to the fore in a long and animated discussion in the yachting journals and among yachtsmen at large. While the immediate result was only a change in the details of the rule, the way was opened for its complete rejection a few years later. Another change was in the establishment of new and fixed classes, notably the 3-Ton, 5-Ton and 10-Ton.

The condition of yacht architecture at the beginning of this period was summarized in a paper read before the Institution of Naval Architects at the meeting of March 22, 1872 in London by Henry Higgins, an Associate. "Up to the present time the designs of yachts have been made by gentlemen who carry out the construction, working magnificently well; but who so completely guide themselves by the rule of thumb, and not by scientific knowledge, that it is really all a chance how the vessels turn out. The present arrangement, of combining the skill of the designer and the work of the builder in one person, tends greatly to check orders, and to retard the development of a trade that might be made, if more certain of success, of greater importance to the nation at large as a field for the improvement of the science of naval architecture generally."

It is impossible after the lapse of well on to a century to estimate the result of the Marett crusade, but that it was far from successful is indicated by another voice crying in the wilderness twenty-two years later; that of Dixon Kemp, one of the most noted of English yachting writers. In his book, "Yacht and Boat Sailing," published in 1878, in a chapter on building a yacht, after covering the more technical details he says: "A curious feature in connection with yacht construction is that naval architects should have had so little to do with the designing of yachts. Yacht builders as a rule keep draughtsmen who are instructed as to design, and thus the builder becomes his own architect. That this plan has succeeded there can be no doubt, and it might even be questioned whether an architect could at present compete with the builder if the latter bestowed so much time on a design as he ought. But, as a rule, builders are too much occupied with the

Sketch design for naval training ship, showing draftsmanship of John Harvey

that yacht designing is gradually gaining recognition as a profession; and if improvement is to be made in the form of yachts we must look for it from the hands of the professional yacht designers."

If any one man may be named as the connecting link between the old and new he is John Harvey, designer and builder; the story of the origin of the Harvey Yard appealed to me when I first read it in *The Field* of February 15, 1879; it seems still of sufficient interest to warrant its exhumation from the dust of six decades. Mention has been made of the close relationship between the fast smuggling cutters, the Revenue cutters which chased them, and the yachts of similar size and model, with the muzzles of guns projecting through the portholes in their high bulwarks, which did service at times as privateers. The story is as follows:

"This record was made by a Customs officer about 1860.

"It is more than fifty years since Philip John Sainty built the first yacht, named Emerald, for the Marquis of Anglesea; it was during the French war, and when he left England to join the Duke of Wellington in the Peninsula he made the Prince of Wales a present of it. It was in 1814 that I came into the Excise, and was ordered to Colchester (Bonaparte had been sent to Elba and the short peace that took place led many to go abroad). There was in Colchester at that time a man by the name of Brown, a whip-maker by trade, he left Colchester and went over to Holland, and took with him a vast number of counterfeit guineas, and after a while he was detected. I, with many others, watched the newspapers every day, expecting to see a notice of his death for his crime. At that time Sainty used to sail backward and forward to Holland, and did a vast deal of trade in contraband goods; he had a vessel with false sides. Sainty had great influence in Holland, and through this he got Brown off and brought him home in his

Verve I, 10 tons. First professional design of George L. Watson, 1877. Built for Robert Wylie, Glasgow. L.O.A., 42 feet; L.W.L., 37 feet; Breadth, 7 feet 7 inches; Draft, 7 feet. Showing typical cutter overhang of that date. Sold to Toronto in 1881 when replaced by Verve II, the latter sold to Chicago. In their American careers they were known as Toronto Verve and Chicago Verve. Photo taken on railway at Port Dalhousie, Canada, 1884. Broken up in 1892, parts used in construction of cutter Zelma

George Lennox Watson, 1851-1904

cares of their business to devote much time to the mathematical considerations of design; and it is only their experience, and a prudent purpose not to depart in any radical way from a model which practice has proved to be possessed of undeniable good qualities, that keep them from blundering into failure. * * * So builders were compelled to do their own designing because the profession of a naval architect would simply have been starvation. But if builders as a matter of necessity did their own designing fifty years ago, it can scarcely be said that a similar necessity exists now, although the custom does. During the last ten years there have been on the average fifty vessels of all rigs and sizes built every year; and it might be assumed that emoluments from designing those would have kept a goodly number of naval architects in the necessaries of life. The few who have made yacht naval architecture a study and a profession have undoubtedly succeeded well enough to lead to the conclusion that, with more opportunities, they would make a very considerable advancement in yacht design. * * * It is, therefore, satisfactory to note

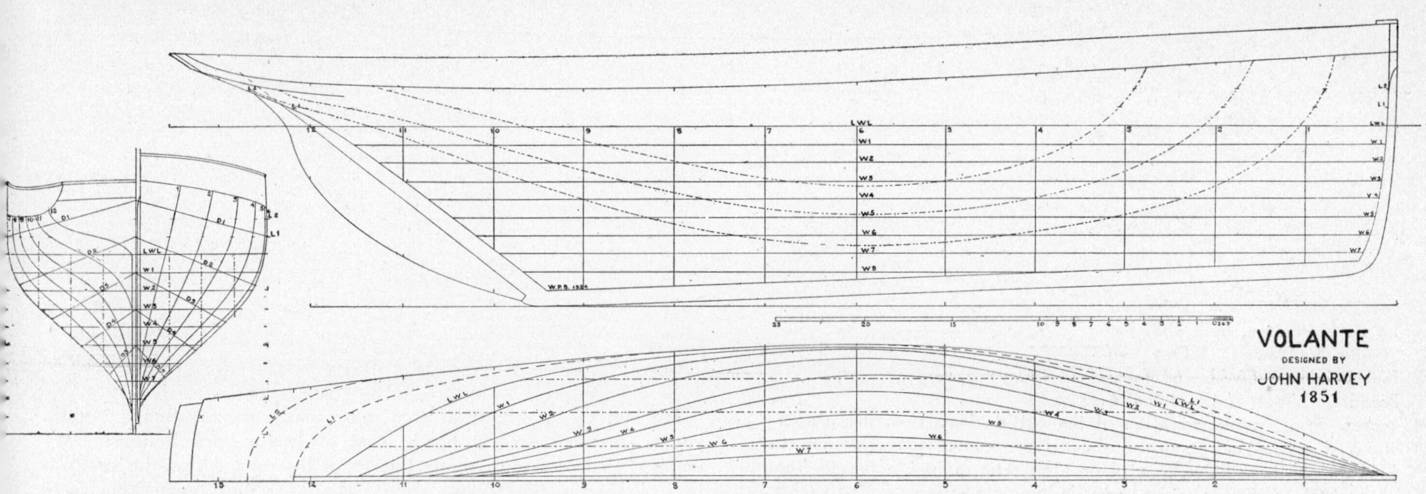

VOLANTE
DESIGNED BY
JOHN HARVEY
1851

Volante, cutter, 60 tons. Designed and built by John Harvey, 1851. Typical racing cutter of the day, with plumb stem, straight keel, and strongly raked sternpost. L.O.A., 69 feet, 6 inches; L.W.L., 61 feet, 6 inches; Breadth, 15 feet; Draft, 10 feet; Rake of sternpost, 37 degrees. Sailed against America in R.Y.S. race of 1851, at one time leading the fleet

vessel. As soon as they landed Brown went and informed against Sainty, and told where the smuggled goods were to be found. It was supposed that Brown got a vast sum of money for his information, as he came to Colchester and took a public house in Barrack Street, I have several times been in it and seen him; but he did not prosper long, he had to leave it and went to his trade again, but could not do, and I forget now what became of him. Sainty's vessel was condemned and Sainty, his son and his brother were sent to Chelmsford Gaol (it was stated, for life). In 1815 Bonaparte made his return to France, and soon after the Marquis of Anglesea lost one of his legs at the battle of Waterloo. After the war was over (it was in 1816 or 1817, I cannot say the year exactly); the Marquis came to Colchester to inquire about John Sainty, and they told him that he was in Chelmsford Gaol for life; and I heard the report that the Marquis said that if he were in Hell he would have him out. The Marquis went out and saw Sainty and asked him if he were the man who built him a yacht some years ago. He said he had. He then asked Sainty if he could build him one that could beat that one? He said that he could, and one that no other could beat. In consequence, the Marquis either went or wrote to the Prince Regent, and an order was sent down to the Governor to liberate John Sainty. Old Sainty knew what he was about; and, his son's name being John, let him get out. When the Marquis saw him he found that they had let the son out instead of the father. He then wrote for the father's liberation, which soon took place; and when he saw the Marquis he told him he had a brother in Gaol that he could not do without, and in a few days all were in Colchester. In a little while the yacht was commenced, about a mile out of Colchester, and during its building there were shipbuilders from all parts came to see its progress. One, Mr. Dotrell, a glazier, furnished the ballast for it, which were all cast-iron balls; and they were all behind the mast. The cabin had

Surf, cruising cutter designed by John Harvey for T. C. Zerega and R. W. Rathborne, New York, 1883. Showing peculiar sections, with no hollow near keel. L.O.A., 42 feet 10 inches; L.W.L., 35 feet 3 inches; Breadth, 7 feet 7 inches; Draft, 7 feet 4 inches

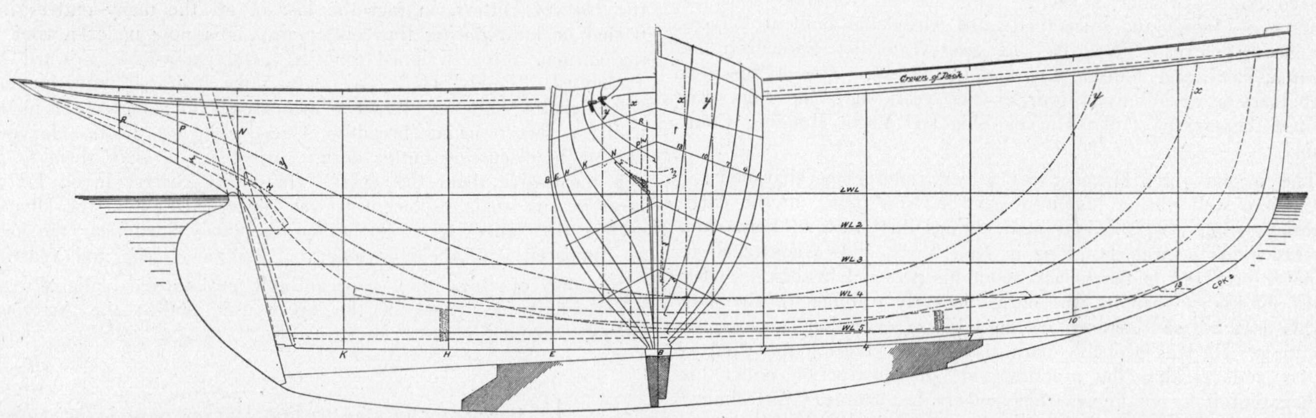

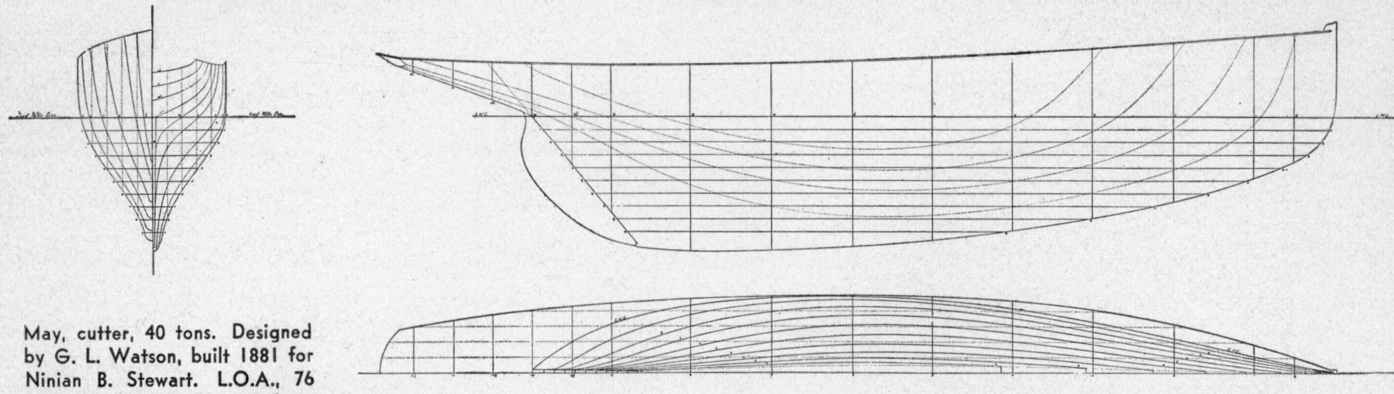

May, cutter, 40 tons. Designed by G. L. Watson, built 1881 for Ninian B. Stewart. L.O.A., 76 feet 6 inches; L.W.L., 64 feet; Breadth, 12 feet; Draft 11 feet 6 inches. Prior to the adoption of the outside lead keel, the proportions of racing cutters were about four-to-one; load waterline to breadth, the term being Four-beam. This ratio rapidly increased from about 1875 to 1885 to seven beams in the more extreme racing yachts. The highest point of the narrow cutter development was reached in such yachts as May, of five beams to length. In her first season she divided honors of a very active racing class with the Fife Annasona, May's record being 27 starts, 12 firsts, 4 seconds, and a total of £610 cash

three large frames,* one eight feet long and four feet wide; the Marquis having ordered the frames to be caned. The day came when the vessel was to be tried, and she surpassed all expectations. After the Marquis' first trip in her she came again to Colchester, and he ordered the large frame to be made shorter and narrower. After this the Marquis settled £100 a year on Sainty, on condition that he did not build a vessel for any other person; but after a time he broke his contract, and when I left Colchester in 1831 he was a large ship builder at Wivenhoe, four miles from Colchester."

Thus ends the story of the Exciseman. *The Field* continues: —"This craft which John Philip Sainty built for the Marquis of Anglesea was the Pearl, which is still in existence (1879) cruising in the Mediterranean. She was launched in 1819, and her Register, according to Lloyd's, bears date 1820. Mr. Sainty became, after the success of the Pearl, the fashion; and the retainer of £100 a year could not keep him from accepting tempting offers from other patrons. Among the vessels he built were the fine cutters Swallow and Arundel for the Duke of Norfolk, and Flower of Yarrow for the Duke of Buccleugh. In later years he built Gipsy, Gazelle, Corsair, Ruby and others. During the latter years of his life he was supported by the Marquis of Anglesea, the Duke of Norfolk, and one or two others; going under hatches at last in 1844 at the age of 93. His widow, now 92, lives in Wivenhoe and is supported by her son." When Mr. Sainty resigned business it was taken up by the father of the present John Harvey; and the new firm was employed by a son of the Marquis of Anglesea—Lord Alfred Paget—to build a yacht. This was the Resolute, some 27 years ago (1857), and since then Lord Alfred has built at Wivenhoe many yachts—Snowdrop, Yankee, Waterlily, Snowdrop II, Xantha, yawl, and Xantha, s.y., and Cecile, s.y. The premises of Mr. Harvey were burned four or five years ago, and then was formed the present "John Harvey Ship and Yacht Building Company."

The second John Harvey was a very interesting character; I knew him well during his first years in New York, in the early eighties; while we talked of many things, his work at home, the cutters which he was designing in New York, and of construction, it never occurred to me to ask about his personal history. Today I do not know when he was born, his early training, or the date of his death; a sad commentary on a life of exceptional activity in yachting. He was probably born about 1830, entering the yard as a boy and learning the practical side of construction under his father; but it is not known today where he obtained his technical training. It is certain, however, that as early as the sixties he was following the accepted methods of yacht designing. At the 19th session of the Institution of Naval Architects, held in London on April 12, 1878, he read a paper on "The Construction and Building of Yachts," which, in spite of its peculiar and inept title, actually treated of design rather than construction.

*These frames were cabin bulkheads, thus built to save weight.

He had to his credit at that time many successful and notable yachts, the more recent being Rose of Devon, Sea Belle and Midanda. In addition to these, purely of his own design, he stood as foster-father to the famous yawl, Jullanar. This remarkable yacht was designed in 1874 by an amateur, E. H. Bentall, a manufacturer of agricultural implements at Maldon, near Wivenhoe. Mr. Bentall's part went no further than to sketch out the general dimensions and novel features; the finished design, including alterations to the midship section, all calculations, and the adjustment of centers, being done by Mr. Harvey. The old Wivenhoe model now hangs in my hall, a treasured relic.

THE Harvey theory of design was, to say the least, peculiar; he first calculated the center of gravity of the load water plane, and of each successive plane below it, then the centers of gravity of the fore and aft halves of each of these planes. Vertical curves were then drawn on the sheer plan through the centers of gravity of the entire planes, and then through the centers of the forward and after sections. From the contours of these three curves he assumed to predict the performance of the yacht under different points of sailing, free, on the wind or reaching. It is not necessary to discuss this curious theory; all that we are concerned with is the evidence which it gives that its author was familiar, even as early as 1875, with all the calculations used by naval architects.

The Wivenhoe Yard, the firm being now Harvey & Pryer, was in financial difficulties shortly after this time. In 1881 Mr. Harvey visited New York in connection with the construction of the cutters, Oriva, Bedouin and Wenonah, designed by him, and he spent much of his later life on this side. His personal characteristics included a strong East-Anglian accent; his expression of assent was "Iss, Iss, Iss" (Yes, yes, yes) uttered very rapidly, or "Quite so, quite so, quite so" at the same speed. He was personally a very fine draftsman. The product of the Harvey Yard from about 1840 to 1880 included a very large number of yachts of all sizes and classes, successful alike in racing and cruising. The last of the Harvey cutters, in fact the last of all the many cutters imported or built during the "cutter-craze," is now under a roof in my garden, a toy designed for that good yachtsman, Edward M. Padelford. "Paddy" Henn, of Galatea fame, had a pet name for him, "Paddlebox." She is 14 feet 9 inches over all; 11 feet 11 inches l.w.l.; 3 feet 6 inches breadth; 3 feet 4 inches draft. Harvey's dictum, in discussing cutter design, was "If you want them to go you must give them the guts." This was correct in so far as large versus small displacement was concerned; but in the Harvey cutters the "guts" were in the wrong place, down near the keel, as compared with the contemporary designs of Fife and Watron.

In spite of this, his American-built cutters did valiant work in the first few years of the great war against the American sloops.

IN the matter of construction Harvey must be recognized as a master, developing new and lighter methods; his double-skin yachts were framed on wood, sawn alternating with bent; giving both lightness and strength. While he moved slowly in the adoption of the outside lead keel, he was fully aware of the advantage of low ballast. In Sea Belle, as early as 1874, the floors were of the size and shape of the usual wood knees, but cast of lead with heavy bent angle iron in the center. The bilge stringers and keelsons were of lead with angle iron centers.† His broad interest in yachting was shown in a letter to Dixon Kemp in November 1876, in part, as follows: "'Lloyd's Register of British and Foreign-Built Ships' bears now, and has enjoyed for many years past, such world-wide reputation for integrity that one feels as safe in the purchase of a vessel or in the insurance or underwriting of her, according to her standing on the list, as if every timber and fastening were open to inspection. Seeing that the general public are thus guardianed, we ask ourselves the question why any gentleman who is about to purchase or to build a yacht should not have similar protection? Some agree that it would be better to build yachts in accordance with the directions given in Lloyd's book, but there are reasonable objections to this, as an unnecessarily heavy and costly structure would be produced; and thus seeing and admitting that the unsatisfactory system of building yachts under no special survey, I submit that the state of things points to the necessity of framing a set of rules to be observed in the building of yachts such as Lloyd's have framed for the construction of merchant vessels." This letter resulted in the appointment of a committee to put the plan into operation, but after the first preliminary steps Lloyd's became interested and took over the matter, organizing its Yacht Department with a special staff of surveyors and, in 1878, publishing its "Register of Yachts" and rules for building. A charter member of the Institution of Naval Architects, organized in 1860, he was also active in the formation of the Yacht Racing Association, in 1875.

After the building of the Harvey cutters in New York he continued to reside there for a time, acting as Yachting Editor of *Forest & Stream* for a short period during the absence of Mr. Kunhardt on one of his many mining ventures. Later he was employed by William Gardner as a draftsman. Returning to England in 1898, he found no employment, and in *The Field* of May 5 there appeared a letter from George L. Watson suggesting a memorial fund to care for him; his many services to yachting being recounted and the writer heading the list with a personal subscription of 50 guineas. His death is not recorded in any of the yachting journals, a careful search through the three following years failing to disclose any mention of his name; even in *The Field,* which recorded the deaths of many less prominent in yachting.

It is beyond question that there is in yachting work a fascination which draws men into it; but those whose love of boats and sailing tempts them to choose as a career yacht designing, technical writing, or general writing and race reporting will do well to study the prospect of adequate financial return for a life work in a line which is not likely to prove "all beer and skittles." Two years before the death of Dixon Kemp a similar movement was started in his behalf, the sum of £307 being realized. The leading race reporter and general yachting writer in England from 1840 to his death in 1899 was Harry Horn; after his death a public subscription was started for his family.

The First Yacht Designer?

INTERESTING as it would be to know the first use of the term "yacht designer," the question is still in doubt. Down to 1886 no distinction was made between builder and designer in "Hunt's Universal Yacht List"; in Olsen's "American Yacht List" the distinction between builder and *modeller* appears in 1875; "Manning's" of the same year names only the builder. It was not until 1884 that "Lloyd's Yacht Register" (British) entered both designers and builders.

From such evidence as is available today it would seem that one of the first to use the term was Dixon Kemp; himself a designer, though better known as the author of standard books on design, as well as the Yachting Editor of *The Field* for many years. In 1876 he published his first book, "Yacht Designing," with the sub title "A Treatise on the Practical Application of the Scientific Principles upon which is based the Art of Designing Yachts." The preface began: "This work has been compiled with the main object of presenting in a complete form an explanation of the scientific principles which govern Yacht Designing. The discoveries which have been made during the last few years with regard to the laws of resistance of fluids have completely revolutionized preconceived theories based upon what were considered fundamental principles. These discoveries will, no doubt, prove of great assistance in the designing of yachts; and it is hoped that their value has been explained in such a manner as to render them of practical use to the designer. The accomplished naval architect will probably find nothing in the work with which he is unacquainted; but others who are not equally well informed will, it is believed, receive instruction from a study of its pages." This book, under the broader title of "Yacht Architecture," for later editions is still in general use. Born at Ryde, Isle of Wight, in 1839, the son of Edward Kemp, architect, he was destined for the same profession, but

Dixon Kemp, 1839-1899

a love for boat-sailing, and the opportunities afforded about his home, kept him afloat in his youth; and he drifted into reporting yacht races for *The Isle of Wight Observer* while still in his "teens." After some time as editor of this paper, in 1862 he was asked by *The Field* to act as its local reporter, and in the following year he went to London to assume the editorship of the yachting pages of that paper. He visited New York in both 1870-71 as the guest of Mr. Asbury aboard Cambria and Livonia; in 1875 he took the leading part in the organization of the "Yacht Racing Association," of which he was Secretary for many years. A second book, "A Manual of Yacht and Boat Sailing," followed in 1878; this with his "An Exposition of Racing Rules," 1898, is still a standard of reference. Apart from his writings on subjects of design and construction, he designed many yachts, both sail and steam. His death occurred in November 1899 after two years of illness.

In a letter to the writer dated December 7 1891 Mr. Kemp says: "I do not know when first† St. Clair Byrne started as a naval architect making yachts a specialty, but I think that it was about the year 1868; just when the rage for 10-Tonners began to be manifested. I began to study the subject of yacht design in 1870, mainly by taking off the lines of every yacht I could get permission so to treat, and subjected the lines to every process of examination I could think of. Many of the results were published. My first design was an 18-foot boat, Boojum, in 1871; and I believe she was broken up 9 or 10 years ago after quite a long service of coast work. In February 1873 I designed Oivana, 30 Tons, and in the following February I published the designs for two 5-Tonners, and in this year I started to compile "Yacht Designing" published in March 1876.".*****"I think that the yacht designer could not have existed prior to the time when yacht owners had been educated to appreciate his services."

†The plan mentioned as shown before the Institute of Naval Architects, now in my possession, is 10 feet 6 inches long and 2 feet 6 inches wide, elaborately drawn; it shows a vertical longitudinal section with entire arrangement and furnishing, including a special heating plant below the cabin floor with hot water pipes to the cabins. While always progressive, Harvey moved slowly in the transfer to all weight to the outside of a vessel; in Miranda, as the drawing shows, blocks of lead cast to shape were hung by iron straps to the bilge keelsons, thus distributing the weight over the entire bottom structure.

†About 1870 two young shipyard draftsmen, St Clair J. Byrne and Alfred H. Brown, turned to yacht designing, at first with small sailing yachts, but both later becoming eminent in the designing of steam yachts.

From Amateur to Professional

ONE of the first young men to adopt the new profession was George Lennox Watson, born in Glasgow in 1851, the son of a physician; in 1867 he started as a draftsman in the shipyard of R. Napier & Son, his brother, T. Malcolm Watson, choosing house architecture as his profession. In 1871, when employed by A. & J. Inglis, shipbuilders, he made his first design, a small keel sloop of supposedly American type, a somewhat grotesque creation, wide, shoal, with a rambow and a strong tumblehome. Built by her designer, she was not a success. His next venture, in 1875, was the 5-Tonner Clothilde, designed only; this class was very active, the leading yacht being the Fife Pearl. His next attempt, in 1876, was more ambitious, as he not only designed but built and raced a new 5-Tonner, Vril. The building was done in a corner of the Henderson Yard, his associates being J. B. Hilliard and John Lawrence, young amateurs, with the aid of two ship carpenters. Sailed through three seasons by her young builders, Mr. Lawrence being the owner, she was almost uniformly successful; only falling to second place in 1880 before the new Fife Cyprus. Mr. Watson's first professional venture was a 10-Tonner for his friend, Robert Wylie, built in 1877, Verve. For two seasons she repeated the success of Vril, but in 1879 the board was swept by a new Watson 10, Madge; whose home victories in two seasons were emphasized by her wonderful success in 1881 in American waters. After a career which included the designing of nearly 300 yachts, including some of the largest sailing and steam yachts, he died at the age of 53. While exceptionally successful in racing yachts, Watson never sacrificed beauty of line; even when working under the cramping influence of the old "Thames Tonnage Rule."

Galatea, Sixth Challenger for the America's Cup, 1886. Designed by J. Beavor-Webb for Lt. William Henn, R.N., Ret. L.o.a. 100 feet; L.w.l. 86 feet; Breadth 15 feet; Draft 13 feet 6 inches

TRADITIONS AND MEMORIES OF

AMERICAN YACHTING

By WILLIAM P. STEPHENS

Part Fifteen

FROM THE BENCH TO THE DRAFTING BOARD

(Continued)

FOR obvious reasons the development of the purely technical side of ship construction began earlier and proceeded much more rapidly in the ship yards engaged in large work than in the yards devoted exclusively to yacht construction. The construction of war and commercial vessels of great size and cost called for deliberate planning on paper by a permanent staff of draftsmen and estimators; which such an establishment could well afford. In the yacht yards of the same period such a course was neither necessary nor financially possible. Both planning and construction were carried out personally by the head of the yard. The introduction of new methods in yacht design came about gradually by infiltration from the ship yards; the younger generation, as in the Fife and Payne families, falling into line in competition with the recruits from outside the business. Young men, for better or worse, succumbed to the undeniable fascination of a career of yacht designing.

John Beavor-Webb

Born near the Old Head of Kinsale, in Ireland, in August 1849, John Beavor Webb graduated from Trinity College, Dublin, with the intention of becoming a civil engineer. Later, in professional life, he signed himself Beavor-Webb, with the hyphen. His early experience in small boats off the Irish coast made him an expert, and developed a love of yachts and racing which led to a different career. In 1867 he owned a 30-foot sloop Truant, in 1868 the 48-foot Esle, in 1871 the 45-foot schooner Nada, which he raced at Kingstown. Migrating to that center of yacht racing, the Solent, he sailed

WILL FIFE III

J. M. SOPER

ALEXANDER RICHARDSON

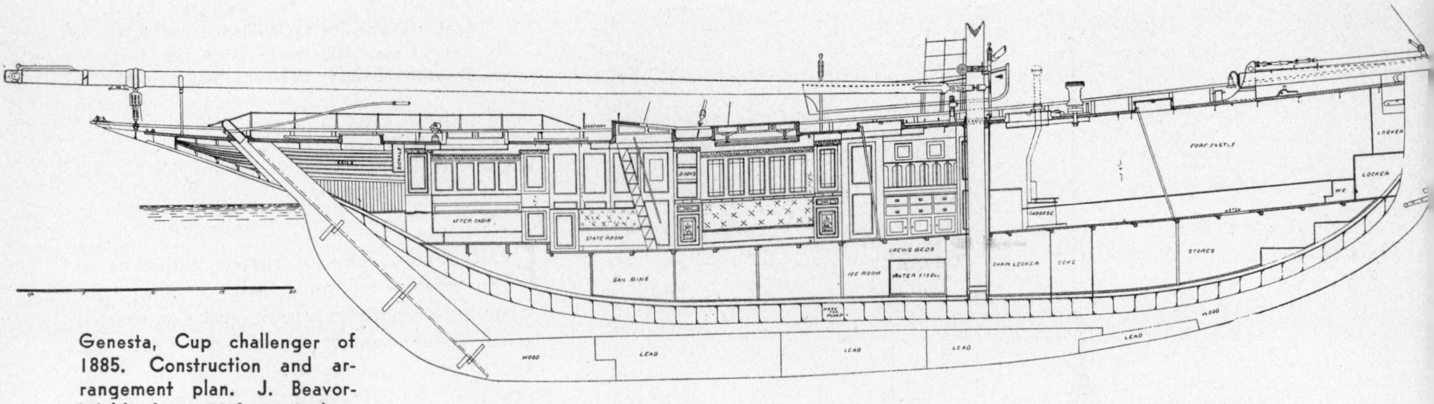

Genesta, Cup challenger of 1885. Construction and arrangement plan. J. Beavor-Webb. L.o.a. 96 feet 6 inches; L.w.l. 81 feet; Breadth 15 feet; Draft 13 feet; Ballast 72 tons, all outside. Ratio of ballast to displacement, .510

with success in 1871 the 25-foot Itchen boat, Israfel, winning ten firsts in twelve starts. When the 5-Ton Freda was built by Dan Hatcher for Thomas Gordon Freke, in 1876, Beavor-Webb had supervision of the work, living at Burlesdon, a short distance away, and being in the yard every day. He told me that while "King Dan"* was credited with the design, she was actually built from the offsets of Hatcher's famous 20-Tonner Vanessa, reduced and laid down on the mould-loft floor under the joint direction of Hatcher and himself. When the lines of Freda were first published, in 1880, they appealed to me so strongly that I made a full model to the scale of one inch to the foot. This model now stands on the mantel shelf in my living room, still in its original priming of lead color; I hope some day to have time to finish it. The mantel shelf, by the way, is a teak locker lid from the steam yacht Golden Fleece (1877), broken up a few years ago in a nearby ship yard. In her first season, with Beavor-Webb in command and at the stick, Freda won 13 firsts and 1 second, with a sum of £123; being somewhat less successful in the next two years.

As a designer Beavor-Webb's first important commission came in 1879, when he was asked by Freda's owner to design a yacht for the 20-Ton Class; under his helmsmanship this second Freda, in 1880, made 33 starts; bringing in 16 firsts and 5 seconds, with cash to the amount of £385. Her nearest rival, the new Louise, made 35 starts, with 8 firsts and 6 seconds. The third new yacht in the class, Euterpe, built by Hatcher, won but 3 firsts and 5 seconds, and never proved successful in her later career.

There is a note of tragedy in the fate of the great King Dan, who, like Edward Burgess 11 years later, died without knowing of the failure of his latest effort. He died in May 1880, in his 63d year, after two years of struggle with gout and dropsy, he was not in the yard after November, and was unable to direct the building of Euterpe. Quoting from *The Field* of May 15:—"For more than a quarter of a century the name of Dan Hatcher has been identified with the building of

J. BEAVOR-WEBB

All the comforts of home. Saloon of Galatea. When racing some of the draperies and rugs were stowed below

*Among yachtsmen Dan Hatcher was popularly known as "King Dan" in recognition of his high position as a builder.

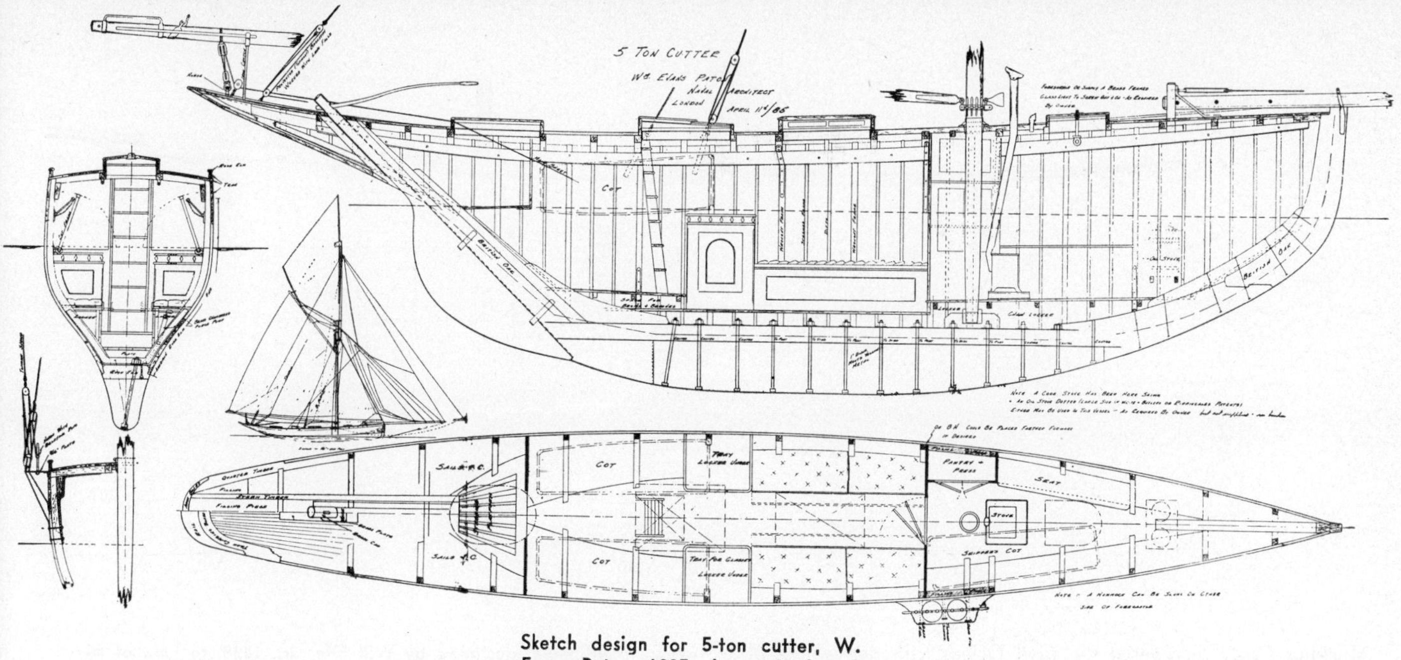

Sketch design for 5-ton cutter, W. Evans Paton, 1885. L.o.a. 40 feet 9 inches; L.w.l. 32 feet; Breadth 5 feet 11 inches; Draft 6 feet 3 inches. Typical construction, arrangement and deck fittings of that date

yachts; and it is hardly too much to say that no builder ever achieved a greater success than he did in the construction of racing yachts. He was not a scientific builder, and probably the displacement of no yacht which he built was calculated before she was laid down. In modelling he relied on a practiced eye and an almost unerring judgment of the causes of success or failure; and, whilst he fashioned many craft of wonderful achievements, he rarely was the author of a mistake. He began his career just at the time when the long bow had become a recognized advantage; and was always a believer in weight, depth and length against small displacement and beam. Beyond being a model maker of almost unexampled success, he was a most accomplished yacht sailer; and many thought that his vessels never sailed better than when he was aboard, either supervising the trimming of the sails or handling the tiller-lines. Without troubling himself about centers of buoyancy, metacenters and centers of effort, he was enthusiastic in discussing the forms of bows and runs; but what showed his keen enjoyment and love of yacht racing most was the fervent manner in which he took to yacht sailing and learned all about the capabilities and peculiarities of the vessels he built by sailing them himself whenever he got the opportunity."

Luffing up for the moment, how it came about that the second Freda was built by her designer instead of by Hatcher is an interesting story. In the last days of his life, when confined to his room, I saw a good deal of Beavor-Webb; to listen to him was both interesting and instructive. When Sir Thomas Freke decided to replace the 5-Tonner by a larger yacht, the order for the design was given to Beavor-Webb. When the design was completed Beavor-Webb took it to Hatcher for an estimate; the first question was "How much lead will you put in the keel? When he heard the reply, "All," he said, "I will not build her." At that time there was much vacant land in Battersea, a suburb of London "above Bridge" later made famous by "The little brown dog of Battersea"; part of it owned by the Prince Consort and part by Sir Thomas Gordon Freke; a piece on the shore was fenced in, men were hired, and Beavor-Webb started in to build the yacht himself.

CHARLES P. CLAYTON

ARTHUR E. PAYNE

One of the most enthusiastic partisans of the New Deal inaugurated by Kunhardt and "Robo" Schuyler in the first cutter crusade of 1879 was a young boy, Francis Peabody Magoun; of a Boston family, but then living in New York. He spread the cutter doctrine broadly, roaming about the yacht yards and deliberately picking arguments with yacht skippers and other sloop men. In 1880 he visited England with his cousin, Francis E. Peabody, who had built the compromise cutter Enterprise, in Boston in 1878. Under the pilotage of George Wilson, the yacht outfitter, they visited the yacht yards and sailed down Thames in Mr. Wilson's yacht Favorite; and in

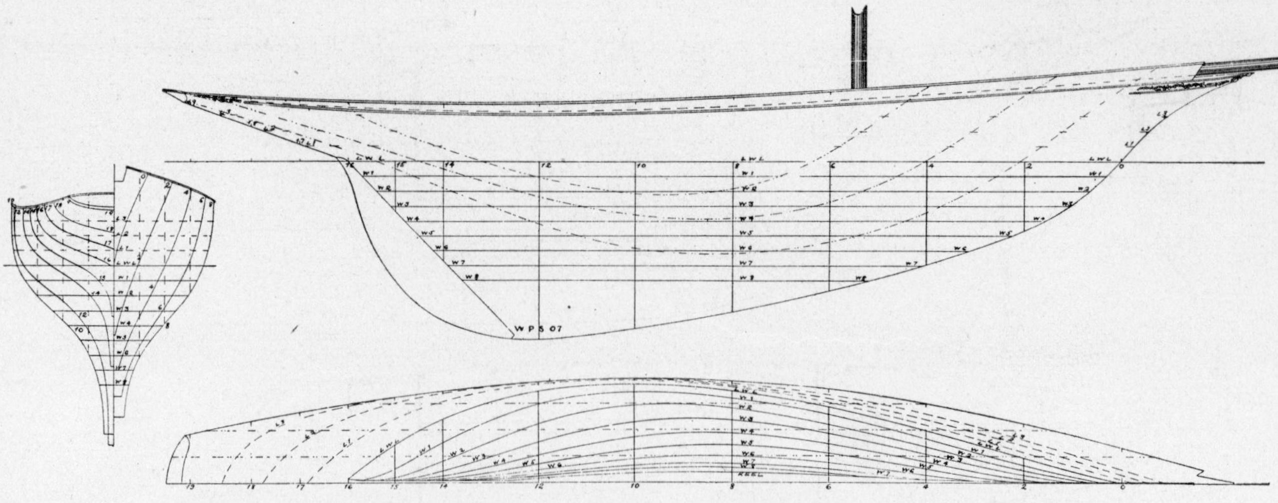

Mucking Creek discovered the yawl Orion, with her owner, R. T. McMullen, of "How I Sailed Alone" fame, aboard. He received them hospitably and showed them over the yacht. Inside each closet door and each drawer was posted a list of the contents. While he volunteered much information, if they ventured to ask questions he justified the reputation which he had of irritability and a quick temper, and showed annoyance. A few years ago Francis told me of a walk which he took by chance along the Chelsea shore, on which he spied on the opposite shore a yacht with flags flying, evidently ready for launching; making his way over Battersea Bridge, he came to a gate where all Mayfair in spring array was trooping in. He was stopped by the Bobbie on guard, who demanded his invitation. On the spur of the moment he said that he was invited by Mr. Wilson, the gentleman who had furnished the fittings for the yacht; and on this bluff he was permitted to enter. Beavor-Webb sat in the cockpit, and as the yacht struck the water the tiller swung over and hit him, he raised his leg and rubbed his ankle. When I told this incident to Beavor-Webb 40 years later he said: "That is true, we had to tow to Gravesend, under the bridges, to step the mast, we could not put chocks on the rudder, we were late and afraid of losing the tide, so we lashed the tiller. As she struck the water she swung and parted the tiller lashings, the tiller hit me a hard blow, and I raised my leg and rubbed my ankle." Incidentally, the rank sheer twisted the rudderstock and it was necessary to beach her and ship a new rudder.

Minerva, designed by Will Fife, Jr., 1888, to limit of 40-foot L.w.l. L.o.a. 55 feet 6 inches; L.w.l. 40 feet; Breadth 10 feet 3 inches; Draft 9 feet. Displacement 21 tons. Ballast 12.4 tons. Ratio of ballast to displacement .590

THE success of Freda started a long and successful career for her designer, both in sail and steam; coming to New York with Genesta in 1885, he made his home here, marrying an American lady and building up a good designing business. He designed the second and third Corsairs for J. Pierpont Morgan, among the largest steam yachts of their day, and the second and third Intrepids, both auxiliaries, for Lloyd Phoenix. His death occurred in 1927. In this country he is best known as the designer of two Cup challengers, both unsuccessful.

Genesta was built in 1884, to the largest class then racing in England, a composite cutter of 81 feet 8 inches l.w.l. and 15 feet breadth (just under 5½ beams). In her first season she did a little better than the Richardson Irex, also a new yacht. The Cup match, with Puritan as defender, was for two out of three races, the weather was light and fluky and strongly in favor of the defender. On three days the yachts were unable to finish, the first race, in light and fluky weather, was won by Puritan; in the next race Genesta was fouled by Puritan just at the start, losing her bowsprit; the defender was disqualified and the race awarded to the challenger. In the one real race, 20 miles to leeward in a freshening breeze, outside Sandy Hook, with a hard beat home, Genesta led by over 2 minutes on the run and was beaten by 1 minute 38 seconds at the finish.

In the following year the challenger was Galatea, also designed by Beavor-Webb, a steel cutter five feet longer on the waterline than Genesta and with the same breadth. Her owner, Lt. William Henn, R. N., had made a reputation as a young midshipman in chasing slavers on the Zanzibar coast. Retiring from the Navy he spent the

Freda, 5-ton cutter. Modelled and built by Dan Hatcher, 1876. L.o.a. 35 feet 9 inches; L.w.l. 30 feet 4 inches; Breadth 6 feet 1 inches; Draft 5 feet 6 inches. Ratio of ballast to displacement .605

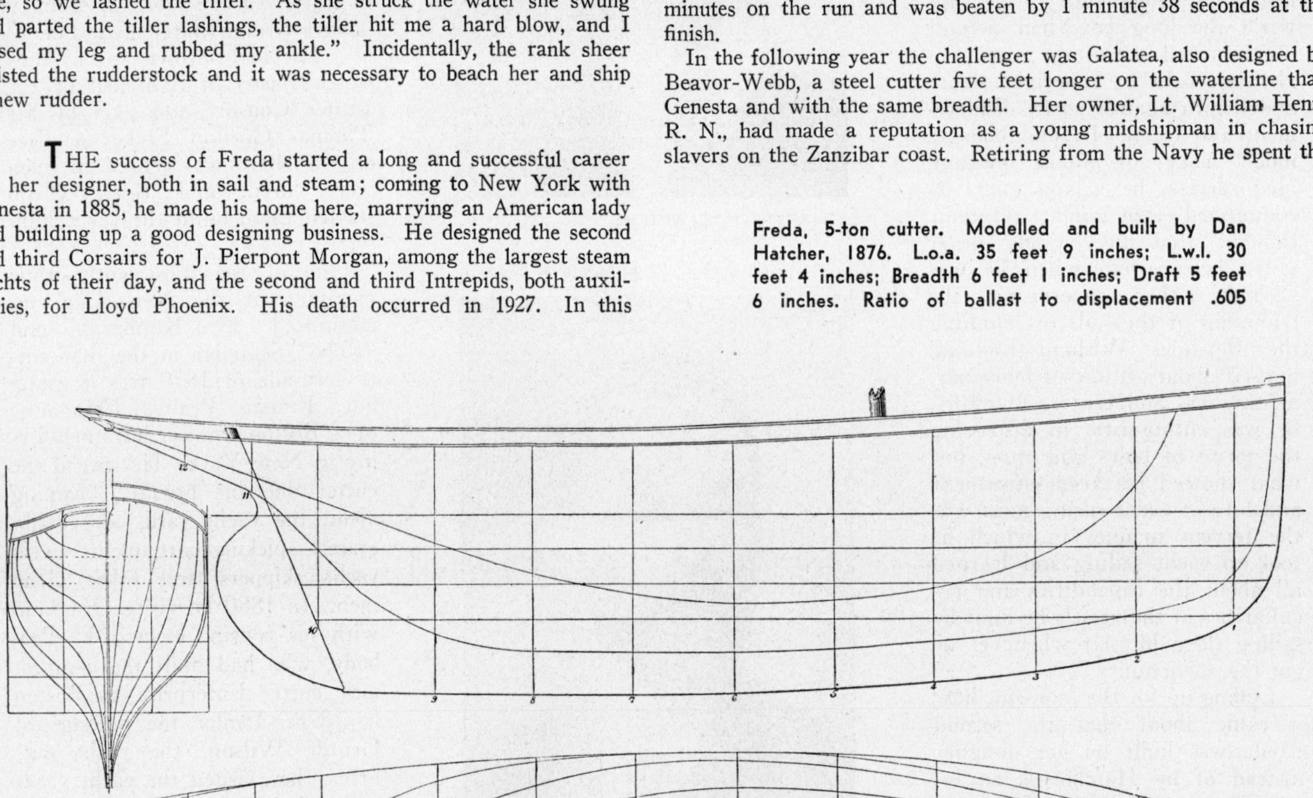

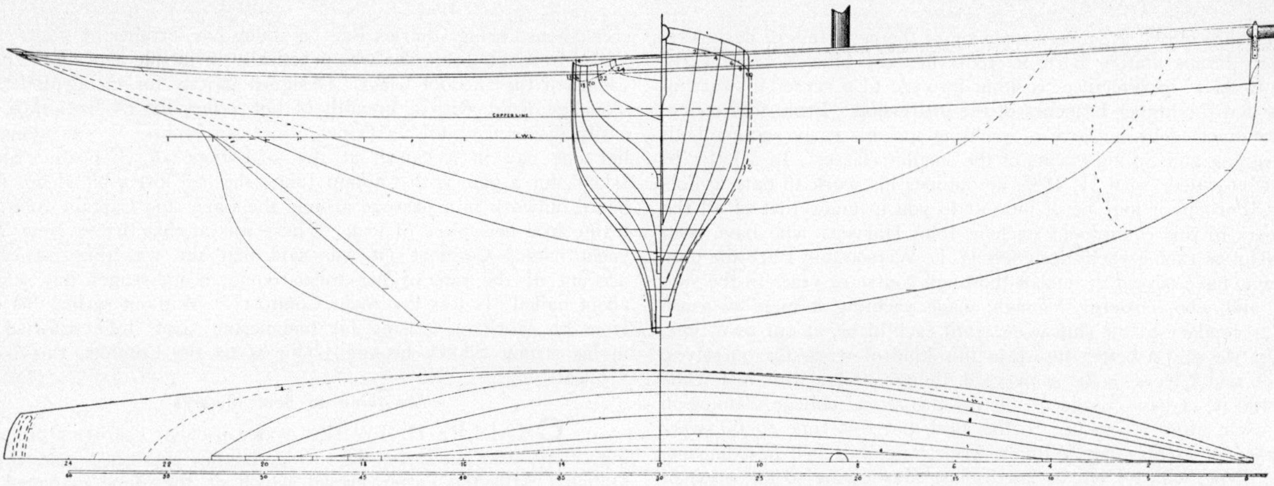

rest of his life in yacht cruising. The name was that of a vessel in which he had served. He spent much time in the Mediterranean in the Payne yawl Gertrude, 80 tons. Meeting a Miss Bartholemew, cruising with her brother in a yacht of 10 tons, he married her, and they spent many years together in cruising. Lt. Henn was a good sailor and a good sportsman, but in no sense a racing man, though he did race Gertrude in some mixed races in the Mediterranean; he told me of an incident in one race in which after Gertrude turned a markboat ahead of her competitors, the men in the boat weighed anchor and rowed toward the next yacht approaching the turn. A genial, jovial Irishman, one of his estates was on Paradise Hill, County Clare; and he was known to his intimates as "Paddy Henn, the Bird of Paradise." Save in that he was in every way a sailorman and a yachtsman, he was no more qualified to challenge for the America's Cup than his compatriots, Lord Dunraven and Sir Thomas Lipton, both landlubbers. Galatea, aboard which her owners crossed the Atlantic, was fitted up literally with all the comforts of a home; an elegantly fitted main saloon, the furnishings being left almost intact on racing days; her skipper, Capt. Dan Bradford, was strictly a cruising man, and in the races The Missus was aboard with her dogs and even a pet monkey. Racing against Mayflower, with General Paine and his picked crew, both Corinthian and professional, and hull stripped down to bare floors and ceiling, the merits of the design never were tested.

AT the risk of wasting paper and boring the reader, I am tempted to tell of an incident which testified to the spirit of Lt. Henn. He felt that the yacht had suffered by the weather in the Cup races, and laid her up in New York for the Winter. Fitting out in 1887, he took her to Marblehead for the annual regatta of the Eastern Yacht Club, and I had the privilege of sailing with him. There was a fresh S.W. breeze, the condition for which Galatea had waited; the first leg of the 30-mile triangle was to windward, and her adversary, Mayflower, at the line. Starting on the wind, Lt. Henn was nervous and anxious, walking about the deck; it did not take long to show, that while Galatea was doing good work, she had no business alongside Mayflower. As soon as this fact was evident Lt. Henn sat down on the rail, took out his pipe and lit it, and resumed his customary composure. He had the chance which he had missed in the Cup races, he recognized the superior speed of Mayflower, and he accepted the situation gracefully and philosophically.

The rounding of the first mark was a picture still distinct before me, as the jib topsail was broken out the yacht heeled as only a cutter could; the topsail yards were lashed along the port side of the companion and skylights, the weather side as it happened; and I stood on them, looking down over the rail into a deep gulf below the weather quarter. Looking inboard, far below me stood Captain Dan, on the bulwarks rather than on the deck, the water swirling up to his knees, the tiller, a 15-foot steel tube, was high above him, near where I stood, and as he looked up he hauled hard on the relieving tackle to bring her into the wind. Later there were calms and drifting, Mayflower winning by a quarter of an hour.

Alexander Richardson

ON May 29, 1875, the Royal Alfred Yacht Club, of Kingstown, Ireland, sailed a race for the 10-ton Class under very strict Corinthian regulations: All yachts to be bona fide property of and steered by members of the Club; and if any person not a member touch the tiller, or in any way assist in steering, the vessel to be disqualified. No paid men allowed, all on board to be members of the Club, their sons, or members of a Royal, foreign, or recognized yachting club having its headquarters at least 50 miles from Kingstown. . . . All persons except those immediately engaged in the match to leave immediately the first gun fires; and the helm to be given up to a helmsman duly qualified to steer her in the match." Making her debut was a new yacht, Lily, owned by James Leitch and designed by his son-in-law, Alexander Richardson, an amateur who had designed Naiad, of the same tonnage, five years previously. The crew of Dicky Sams (to quote from *Hunt's Yachting Magazine*) included Mr. Richardson at the tiller, with his brothers-in-law, James, Jr., and Robert Leitch, A. Anderson, and T. A. R. Littledale, all of Liverpool. Opposed to them aboard Queta of Kingstown were John Jameson, W. G. Jameson, Arthur Jameson, C. H. Fox and P. Haynes. The first of these was famous for many later years as the owner of the great cutters Samoena, Irex and Iverna; while the second, his cousin, was the famous Willy Jameson who, backed by Captain Billy O'Neill, made the reputations of these noted yachts. Lily won, thus beginning a most successful career and her designer took his place in the professional ranks, turning out such yachts as Silver Star, Amathea, Petronilla, Stranger, in addition to the more noted Irex and Iverna.

Clara, 20-ton class, 1884. Designed by Will Fife, Jr. L.o.a. 63 feet 9 inches; L.w.l. 52 feet 9 inches; Breadth 9 feet; Draft 9 feet 8 inches. Displacement 36.5 tons. Ballast 21.9 tons. Ratio of ballast to displacement .600

J. M. Soper

BORN in Southampton in 1857, J. M. Soper began life as a clerk in a timber merchant's office, and later in the office of Fay & Son, yacht builders, Northam, Southampton. Here his interest in the work going on about him led to a study of naval architecture, and a position as second draftsman. When the Company was reorganized, in 1889, Mr. Soper was appointed manager and designer. Of his many yachts, the most noted was Satanita, a cutter in the largest class, launched in 1893. With a waterline length of 97 feet 8 inches she exceeded by 10 feet the others of her class, with a proportionately smaller sail area; a difference so great as to make any fair comparison of model out of the question. Another self-taught designer was Charles P. Clayton, who began life in ship yards in Birkenhead, going later to the Millwall Iron Works, on the Thames; his work was mainly in the smaller classes, and he was noted as a skillful racing man.

William Evans Paton

NO better example may be found of the fine old crusted conservatism with which the British nation is credited than the obstinate adherence of British yachtsmen to a rule long proved obsolete and detrimental. In spite of the weight of evidence accumulating year by year, the rule was not abandoned until it had taken as a sacrifice one of the most promising of the new class of designers. William Evans Paton, born in 1861, devoted himself from early youth to naval architecture; looking forward to a career in warship design and the higher branches of the profession. From this course he was diverted by his love of yachting and his early success both in designing and sailing yachts of the smaller classes. In a letter to the writer dated April 15, 1885, he outlines his work to date as follows: "Perhaps it may be of interest to you to know that of all the designers in this country (I exclude John Harvey) who have been successful as racing yacht designers G. L. Watson and I are the only ones who have passed through a thorough course of years in the ship yard; and who, curiously enough, made yachting a mere pleasure study, secondary to the ship work, until each of us, at our own time, thought we saw a better future in this kind of work for ourselves. Watson and I were in the same yard, though he had just left when I entered it. I have to add to this my theoretical college training in Greenwich, after I returned to the yard, but this time to the warship yard of Messrs. Sir William Armstrong, Mitchell & Company, on the Tyne, which I left as late as last May owing to the press of evening work at designing small yachts; and also with the view of having the summer free to race the boats which I designed to the best advantage, and to pick up wrinkles for future designs. I have had a rather long apprenticeship in the small classes; I designed Trident, 5 Tons, six years ago for myself, and raced her for five years; and have had wonderful success throughout, which is very difficult to keep up year after year." Trident proved a very successful yacht, as did the other 5-Tonners, Olga and Luath; the 3-Tonner Currytush made 22 starts in her first season, scoring 16 firsts and 3 other prizes, with £93 in money.

Animated by the same spirit which works so much harm to yachting today, in 1886 Mr. Paton attempted to crowd five years of development into a single season in the most extreme cutter yet planned. With a waterline of 34 feet the new Oona had a breadth of 5 feet 6 inches (6 beams), with a draft of 8 feet. On a total displacement of 12.5 tons her lead keel weighed 9.6 tons. Her construction was more detailed and elaborate than anything previously attempted; double-skin planking on light steel frames. Strains and stresses were fully calculated for even the most unimportant elements of the light hull, and detailed plans were made by Mr. Paton personally for every part. The construction was carried out under his daily supervision. It is doubtful whether any yacht of other than great size was ever planned with such care and study. On May 4, 1886, the yacht sailed from Southampton for the Clyde, with her owner, her designer, an experienced professional skipper, and a crew of two, calling at Kingstown on the following day; continuing, she met a very heavy gale. When seeking shelter on the Irish coast she was apparently embayed off Malahide, driven ashore, and the light hull torn from the keel. All hands were drowned, the hull was driven ashore, but the keel sunk in the sand and never was found. This tragic occurrence, followed later by the successive defeats of Genesta and Galatea in America, dissolved the last opposition to the abolishment of the Tonnage Rule.

Will Fife, Jr.

TURNING now to the established builders, mention has been made of the Fife family of Fairlie, Scotland; the third of the name, born in 1857, began his career in the family yard, but with a realization of changing conditions entered the yard of J. Fullerton & Co., ship builders, at Paisley, after which he assumed the management of a yacht yard conducted for a time by the Marquis of Ailsa on his estate at Culzean, North Britain. Here in 1884 he designed and built the 20-Ton Clara, of composite construction. In her first season, in British waters, Clara topped her Class with a record of 20 starts, 17 firsts and a total of £340 in prize money. Early in 1885 she was sold to Charles Sweet, an English lawyer, and Charles H. Tweed, a Boston lawyer, both being associated in some railroad litigation which brought Mr. Sweet to New York for several years. While her regular skipper, Captain John Barr, crossed by steamer, Clara was sailed across by one of those professional crews which sail anything anywhere, the only one of her regular crew aboard being Charles Barr, a young boy, brother of Capt. John. Sailed by Capt. John, she was practically invincible against the home yachts of the 55-Foot Class. Designed strictly for racing under the Tonnage Rule, with a breadth of but 9 feet for 54 feet l.w.l., she easily disposed of all the wider American yachts. I was alongside her one day in a canoe, at the anchorage off Stapleton, Staten Island, for a gam with Captain John; she had lost a bit of her starboard bulwark in a passage around the Cape, and Captain John was fitting in a new piece of teak. There was at that time a New York yacht named Comfort (it was said that she was thus named on account of the size of her toilet-room), a messenger boy rowing about hailed "Is this the yacht Comfort?" Without raising his eyes from his work or ceasing his hammering Capt. John drawled out in his strong Scotch brogue, "This is na the Comfort, this is the torment."

"Anything to Beat Minerva"

CHARLES H. TWEED was a peculiar character in yachting, in no way interested in racing, but an enthusiast, and closely affiliated with the cutter crowd which at that time managed the Corinthian Yacht Club, a secession from the Seawanhaka Corinthian Yacht Club, the original partisan of the cutter. After the return of Mr. Sweet to England Clara was sold, and Mr. Tweed imported the 5-Ton cutter Shona; in 1888 he placed an order with Fife for a cutter of 40-feet l.w.l.; several yachts of this length being built about Boston. Left to his own judgment, Mr. Fife turned out a yacht of moderate displacement and low power; a keel craft of greater breadth than the older British boats. During his two years in the forecastle of Clara, and a year aboard other yachts, young Charles Barr occupied his time to good advantage in the study of his profession, and when the new Minerva was ready he went across and took command of her, acting as navigator with a crew of three. They made the passage from Fairlie to Marblehead in 28 days. Mr. Tweed used the yacht about Marblehead, and when in the spring of 1889 he was elected Admiral of the Corinthian Yacht Club, he sent her to the station at Staten Island. By the merest chance, the dismasting of Liris, of the new 40-Foot Class, Minerva was borrowed for the annual regatta of the Seawanhaka Corinthian Y. C.; sailed by a Corinthian crew new to the boat, she scored such a decisive victory over the Burgess and Gardner boats that it would have been foolish to have kept her out of the racing. For two seasons, 1889-90, she led the 40-Foot Class in spite of the agonized cry of "Anything to beat Minerva."

The list of yachts turned out by the Fairlie Yard in something less than a century and a half runs into the hundreds, large and small, mainly sail; but space permits of the mention of no more than these two of international fame. Will Fife still heads the Yard, though giving up active work to Robert Fife, a nephew.

Arthur E. Payne

"LITTLE ARTHUR," as he was affectionately known to many yachtsmen, Arthur E. Payne was born in 1858, and received his early training in the old yard of his father, Alfred Payne, in Southampton; adding a technical course to this practical work. While turning out some very successful yachts in the larger racing classes, as well as many cruising craft, his fame rests chiefly on the large number of small racing yachts which are found about the Solent. His career was cut short by death in September, 1903, after two years of very painful illness.

The yachts of Fife, Watson and Payne, not only under the old Tonnage Rule with which all were at first familiar, but under the various rules which followed on both sides of the Atlantic, show no sacrifice of fairness of line or beauty of form, even in the most extreme racing types. While some successful designers pay no attention to the artistic side, and some even go further in violating all accepted canons; the work of these three men has an artistic quality that appeals to the eye of every sailor.

The men here named this month and last were the pioneers of yacht designing in Great Britain; and while the America's Cup still rests in Tiffany's vault on Fifth Avenue, New York, each of them has to his credit a long list of yachts successful either in cruising or in racing both in home waters and abroad.

TRADITIONS AND MEMORIES OF

AMERICAN YACHTING

By WILLIAM P. STEPHENS

Part Sixteen

FROM THE BENCH TO THE DRAFTING BOARD

(Continued)

A. Cary Smith, collaborator with Robert Center in the first design on paper made in America

EIGHTEEN hundred and sixty-seven, perhaps the highest point of French history? *"L'Empire, C'est La Paix."* Such was the pronouncement of Napoleon III, he of the waxed mustachios and goatee; "Napoleon Le Petit," and "The Nephew of his Uncle," as he was nicknamed by his loving subjects. In blissful ignorance of the future, and in calm indifference, he was sitting on a bombshell with a lighted fuse—only four years before Sedan. Imperial France had opened her doors to the world with her great Exposition, bringing all the crowned heads of Europe to the capital. Of this gathering none was more widely known or more popular than Her Highness, Hortense Schneider, La Grande Duchesse de Gerolstein, holding her head high and kicking her heels still higher night by night at the Varieties Theatre as she sung to a delighted audience *"Voici le Sabre de Mon Pere,"* and told of the bibulous exploits of her ancestors in *"Il Etait un de Mes Aieulx"*; all to the music of an expatriated German Jew, Jacques Offenbach.

Prominent among the mechanical novelties of the Exposition was the velocipede, since famous the world over as the bicycle. This was not entirely a new invention, but the product of a series of crude experiments extending over a century. The earliest mentioned was a machine somewhat like a child's hobbyhorse on wheels, credited to two Frenchmen, Blanchard and Magurier, about 1780; but this merely served to excite the ridicule of Parisians. In 1817 the idea re-appeared in Germany, Baron Drais von Sauerbron, of Mannheim, building a frame with two wheels, one in front of the other, with a seat between. The rider sitting on this seat tried to propel the machine by kicking with his feet on the ground. This "drasine" was impracticable and short-lived, but in 1839 it was revided in the "dandy-horse" built by Kirkpatrick MacMillian, of Courthill in Dumfrieshire, Scotland. This machine introduced the principle of a movable front wheel for steering. In 1846 another Scotchman, Galvin Dalzell, made further improvements. The first practicable vehicle of this type was produced in Paris in 1865, by M. Michaux, a carriage maker; who, aided by one of his workmen, Pierre Lallement, discarded the side levers and treadles of the Scotch machines and substituted foot cranks on the ends of the front axle. Minus the modern refinements of wire wheels, pneumatic tires and springs, this was essentially the bicycle of today.

The new vehicle met with instant recognition from Parisians. Following *"La Grande Duchesse"* there was revived another of Offenbach's works, *"La Belle Helene,"* produced in 1864; a triangular love story similar in some points to "Tristan and Isolde"; when King Menelaus is ordered by the Oracle on a pilgrimage to Crete to plead for his people, in this case he was sent off, in royal robes and crown, on a Michaux velocipede, with an old-fashioned carpetbag lashed on one side and a red umbrella on the other.

There was in Paris that summer an American boy of ten, Hugh L. Willoughby; hearing of the new vehicle his father took him to the Michaux works, where the first ten machines were just on sale. Mr. Willoughby agreed to buy one if Hugh were taught to ride, and a little later he was navigating a velocipede on the boulevards and avenues of Paris. On his death in 1939 Hugh L. Willoughby had been No. 1 on the roll of the New York Yacht Club since the death of William E. Iselin in 1936; he joined the Club in 1875, getting in under the age limit through the kindly offices of his father's friend, Samuel J. Colgate, owner of the schooner Idler. At the same time there was built for him by Lon Smith of Islip the sloop Windward, 46 feet L.w.l. He raced her for four seasons but sold her when he took up land in Florida where he spent much of his later life, summering in another home in Newport.

My acquaintance with him began in 1883 when, as a member of the American Canoe Association, he ordered a decked sailing canoe which he named Windward. In the following year I designed and built for him, for use about Newport, a single-hand yawl of 18 feet l.w.l. When ordered to paint Windward on her archboard, with my deep-seated detestation of the stencil habit which afflicts so many yachtsmen I suggested Leeward as a change, but the proposal was voted down. Though giving up racing with the sale of the first Windward, his life was devoted to the water in various craft. He did much for the development of Florida, and he was one of the pioneers in aviation. In my last talk with him on the occasion of the Cup match of 1937 in his Newport home (he had been confined to an invalid chair for several years through a broken thigh) he told me the story of his Michaux velocipede.

Robert Center

The son of a New York merchant, himself a member of the New York Yacht Club, Robert Center was born in 1840. He was educated in Switzerland and, inheriting ample means from his father, devoted himself to a life of sport. Joining the New York Yacht Club in 1862, he first owned the sloops Ariel and Bonita. Then he joined The Seawanhaka Yacht Club of Oyster Bay in 1874. While yachting held the first place throughout his life, he was prominent in many lines of sport. In 1866 he was one of the founders of the American Jockey Club, one of the governors and active as long as the Club existed.

In 1877 he was one of the founders of the Queens County Hounds, being one of the first to import a hunting pack. Later he joined the Genessee Valley Hunt. In rowing he was an officer of the New York Rowing Club, sculling a single shell and acting as coxswain. He was foremost in the Seawanhaka fight for Corinthianism, and presented the Center Cup in 1876 for a Corinthian race around Cape May Lightship. He held many high positions in both the New York and Seawanhaka clubs, and he was one of the leaders in establishing a cup for the defending yachts of the America's Cup Class in 1886.

In society life he was equally active. He joined the Union Club in 1862, and was one of the founders of the Knickerbocker Club in 1871. His interest in sport was most unselfish. He worked not only for the broad interests of all organizations with which he was connected, but for the individual members as well, while preaching the doctrines of fair play and generous sportsmanship. A cultivated musician as well as linguist, he had a thorough technical knowledge of music. He was one of the founders of the Orpheus Glee Club, and always active in its support. It was said of him that the mere mention of the nickname Bob spoken in the circles of sport, music or society about New York, needed no surname for full identification.

The quarterdeck crew of the schooner Fleetwing in the ocean race of 1866 included two young New York yachtsmen, Robert Center and Ernest Staples. My recollection is that each of the three yachts carried as guests a representative of each of her competitors. With money and time, Robert Center made the grand tour, including the Paris Exposition, and on his return to New York brought a Michaux velocipede. I remember, in the summer of 1867, my father on returning from business told of seeing two men riding down Broadway on odd machines, one wheel in front of the other. I would like very much to know whether either was my friend of later days. My only conception of anything of the kind was derived from the child's toy tricycle, of wood, with a horse's head in front, and propelled by side levers. I had no conception of the principle of balance, and from my father's description pictured a vehicle with wheels at least eight inches wide. The Michaux velocipede had wheels identical with those of a buggy,

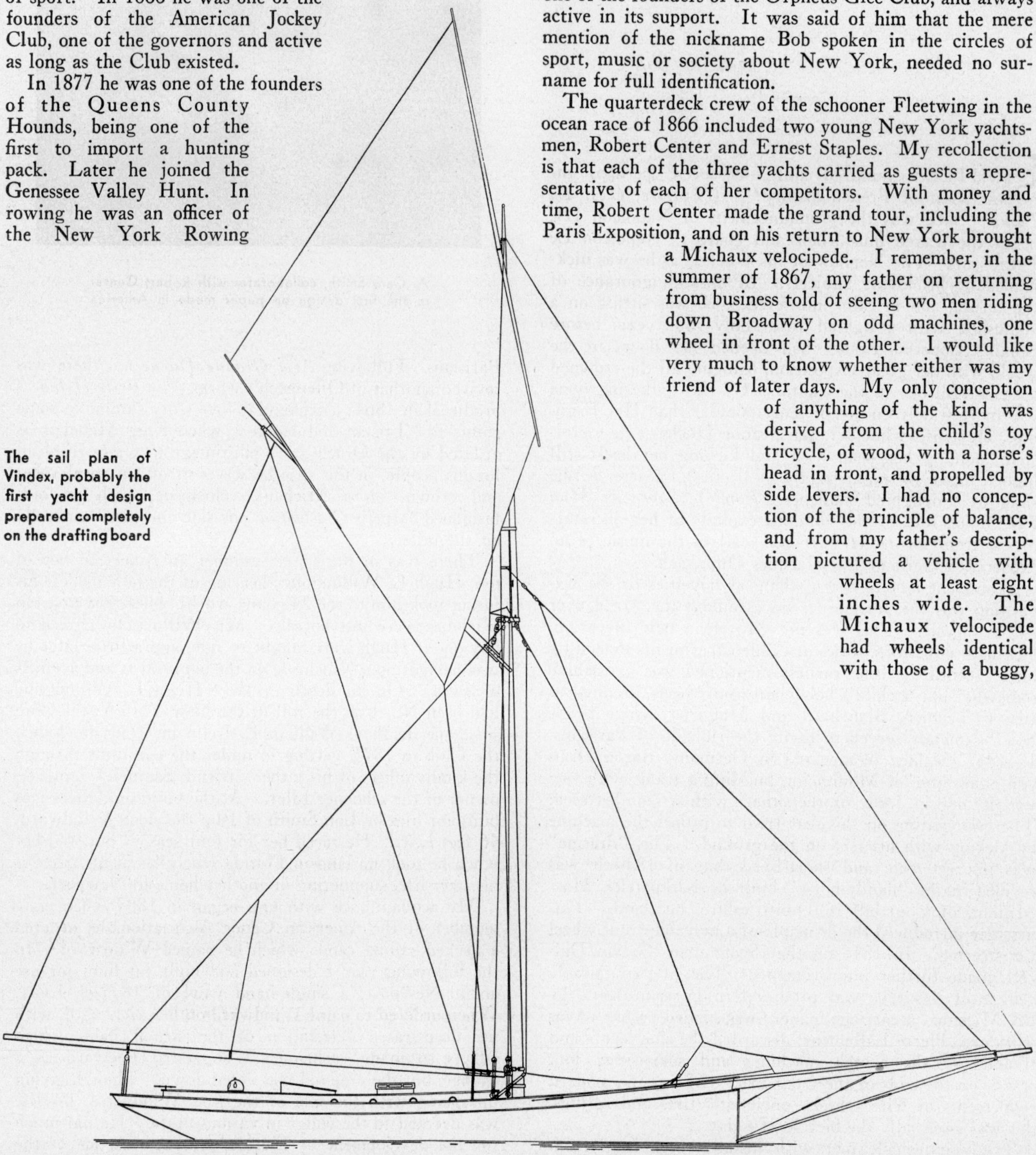

The sail plan of Vindex, probably the first yacht design prepared completely on the drafting board

but not dished; wood hub, spokes and rim, with a flat iron tire 1/8 by 7/8 inches. Even with the seat suspended on a spring they well deserved the nickname of "bone-shaker"; much more so did the imitations later put out by two of New York's leading carriage makers, with no spring and a solid backbone of 7/8-inch square iron.

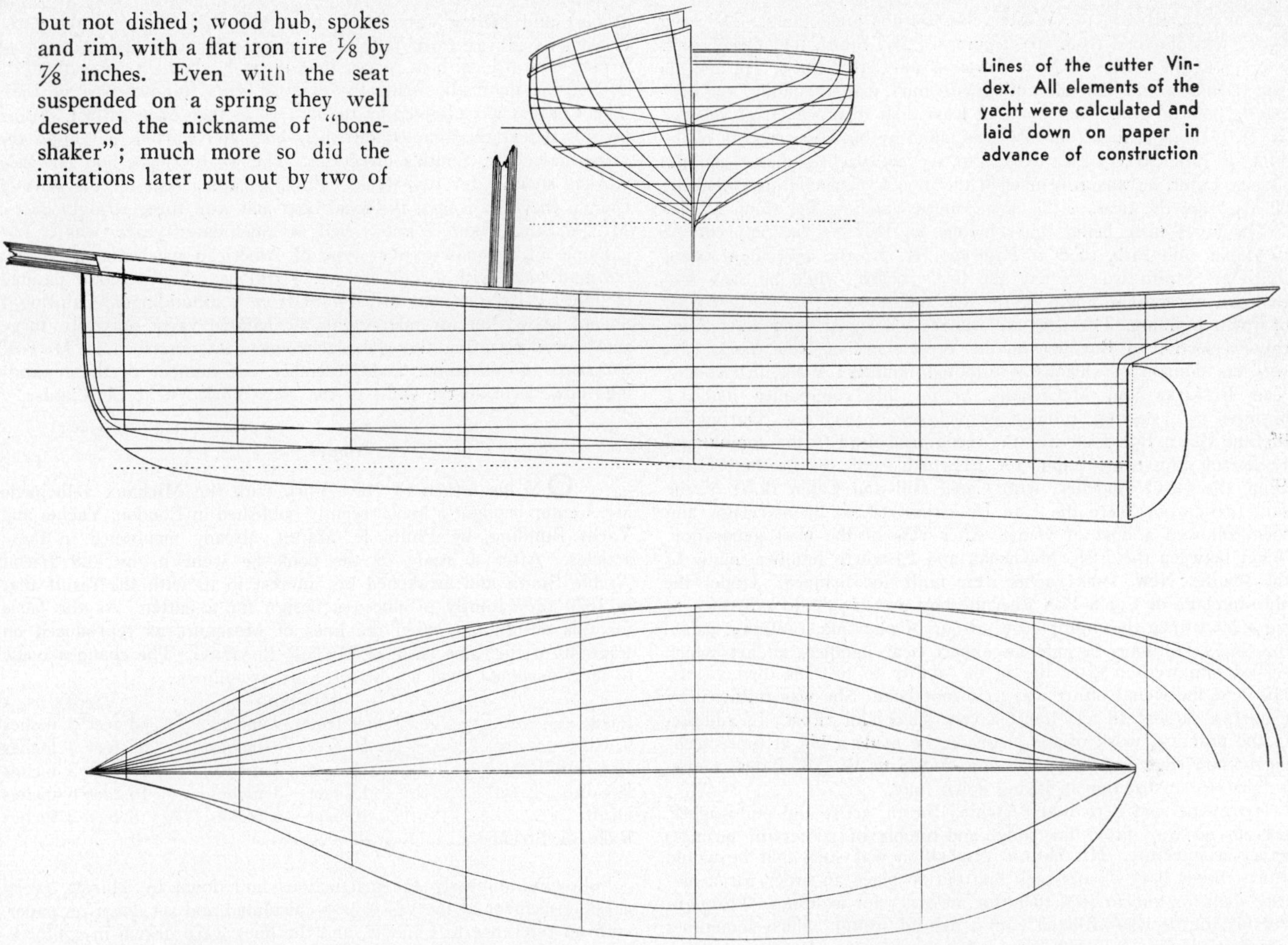

Lines of the cutter Vindex. All elements of the yacht were calculated and laid down on paper in advance of construction

It was by a strange freak of fate that Robert Center lost his life through the vehicle which he was one of the first to introduce to New York; the "safety" or low wheel which in turn succeeded the "high wheel" of the eighties, successor to the Michaux. A regular rider of the bicycle, on the evening of April 17, 1895, he was returning from a ride on the Boulevard, one of a party of wheelmen riding behind a street car bound down town. All turned out to the right to pass the car, Mr. Center, on the inside of the party, met a loaded coal truck passing around the car on the wrong side; a shaft knocked him from his wheel and the wheels of the heavy truck passed over his head and chest. The mishap occurred just in front of the Colonial Club, and was witnessed by some of his friends. He died three hours later in the hospital.

By way of personal tribute I can do no better than to quote what I wrote 45 years ago: "As a gentleman sportsman, the character in which he was most widely known, he stood alone in his thorough and enthusiastic devotion to all manly sports for sport's sake; the gambling side had no charm for him, nor was he even willing to take the passive part of an interested looker-on, but his enjoyment of sport was purely personal; he loved it, and desired to excel in all its branches and, above all, he desired that others should love it and enjoy it as he did."

Always a consistent advocate of the British cutter, he never went to the extreme, and denounced most forcibly the doctrines of "Robo" Schuyler and his followers. In 1886 he bought the cutter Medusa, designed by Beavor-Webb and built by Lawley for Franklin Dexter of the Eastern Yacht Club, a cruising yacht of the very moderate proportion of but 4½ beams. Aboard her he cruised extensively. He was a man of under medium height, of slight physique, but with muscles well developed. On a November day he was sailing Medusa in a strong N.W. breeze up and down the Upper Bay, with a party of ladies aboard. He never employed a professional skipper; in this case his mate or boat-keeper, Petersen, a big Norwegian, was below with all the crew. The relieving line slipped from the tiller and little Bob went overboard, under the lee quarter, the yacht continuing her course. It was some time before the frightened women could summon help from below, but he was finally parbuckled and hoisted aboard. They found him with the tiller line wound around his wrist and his teeth clinched on it.

A. Cary Smith

Turning back a full century, to the day when the little town of New York extended barely above Canal Street, there was on the West side a remote suburb, Chelsea Village, between Broadway and the North River and nearer to the latter; the center of the Village being from 20th to 23rd streets as numbered today. Here in 1837 was born Archibald Cary Smith, son of Rev. Edward Dunlap Smith, pastor of St. Peter's Episcopal Church, on the corner of Ninth Avenue and 20th Street. Whence the boy derived a taste for the water does not appear, but the East shore of the Hudson was then close at hand as a playground, then in a state of Nature. On the opposite Hoboken shore was moored the fleet of the young New York Yacht Club; and a walk across to the East River brought one to the great shipyards of William H. Webb,

William H. Brown, the Westervelts, Berghs and others. Drinking water was obtained from street pumps. Mr. Smith told me of such a pump at the corner of Ninth Avenue and 20th Street. He and his boy friends would dam the gutter with mud, man the pump, and provide a pool in which they could at least float their self-made models. In 1851, the boy, then fourteen, was taken by his father across to the foot of 12th Street, East River, to see the yacht America on the stocks. Later, he was a member of the model yacht club in Hoboken; he also saw the trial of the new America against the sloop Maria.

The boy's taste being thus obvious, in 1855 he was apprenticed to Cap'n Bob Fish, then at Pamrapo, N. J.; the agreement being that Mr. Smith was to pay the boy's board, while he was free to learn all that he could of the art and mystery, as it then was, of yacht building. The new atmosphere was most congenial. Pamrapo, a section of Bayonne on the West shore of New York Bay, was the domain of various web-footed families: Fishs, Elsworths, Van Buskirks and McGiehans. While this community made a business of oystering, it found its pleasure in yachting. During his lifetime Cap'n Bob Fish was the recognized head of the community. Following him came Cap'n Joe Elsworth, with his brother, Cap'n Phip, the yacht modeller, with Cap'n Bill and Cap'n Bob; of the same generation were the Van Buskirks, related by marriage, and then followed a host of young water rats of the next generation. What between the Fish, McGiehan and Elsworth families, many of the smaller New York yachts were built and manned. Under the able tutelage of Cap'n Bob Fish the boy was taught to sail, then to rig a boat, then the multiple operations of planking, caulking, painting, etc. He soon became an expert boat handler, an art which served him well in after life in the ability to test his own yachts. His first individual effort was a 16-foot boat. She was followed by Comet, a catboat 18 feet long; a very successful effort. In addition to the practical work of the boatshop, he made a bid at more technical knowledge in paying the sum of $25 to W. W. Bates, a ship builder, for instruction in laying down lines.

It may be said here that "Archie" Smith, artist and philosopher, was in no way fitted for rough-and-tumble of successful business naval architecture. His natural disposition was such that he would much rather have clients seek him out to place an order for a picture than for him to seek them for an order for a design. Throughout his life he was afflicted with a painful stutter, which sometimes added emphasis to his odd sayings, but was a serious handicap in business. With all his modesty, he was bold and outspoken in his opinion when the occasion required; no backing and filling. With a kindly heart and a ready wit, he had a hatred of all sham and pretense, and a sharp and caustic tongue on occasion. It will do no injustice to the memory of my dear old friend to quote a saying which gives evidence of his ready wit and quick repartee. While throughout a great part of his life he was an active and respected member of the Episcopal Church of Pamrapo, in his early sandbag days he acquired a full racing vocabulary and a taste for the native wine of the country—Jersey applejack. One Sunday morning a friend met him in the classic haunts of the "Foot-O'-Court Street" and hailed him: "Hello, Smith, what are you doing here?" The reply was: "My father is over in New York preaching Heaven and Salvation, and I've been over in Gowanus raising Hell and Damnation."

In the Comet days Mr. Smith was intimate with the Center boys, Robert and Henry. The latter bought an old boat and the three cruised as far as Port Jefferson, where they were induced to sail a race with a local boat owned by Gilbert H. Wilson, the sailmaker, son of the man who made the original sails for America in 1851. The Yorkers were hooted by the natives as they came in last. Stung by this defeat they hauled out their boat and started to rebuild the stern under Mr. Smith's directions. The weather was hot, but they worked steadily for two weeks. Finally, having sent for the sails of Comet, they challenged the local boat and won three straight races. Mr. Wilson, whom I knew well in much later years, was a fine example of the now-extinct type of American mechanic, a courtly old gentleman with a flair for art. I still have a watercolor painted by him. What diverted Mr. Smith from boatbuilding to painting I do not know, but for many years he painted yacht portraits, large canvases illustrating the great schooner fleet described in MoToR BoatinG of November and December. A number of these paintings now decorate the walls of the New York Yacht Club house.

An early photograph showing a deck view of the cutter, Vindex, the first yacht built from a prepared design

Vindex

ON his return to New York with the Michaux velocipede Mr. Center brought a book recently published in London, Yachts and Yacht Building, by Philip R. Marett, already mentioned in these articles. After a study of the book he went to his old friend Archie Smith and awakened his interest in it, with the result that in 1870 they jointly produced a design for a cutter. As the basis for this design they used the lines of Mosquito, as reproduced on Page 40 of the June issue of MoToR BoatinG. The changes made to meet assumed local conditions were as follows:

	Mosquito	Vindex
L.o.a.	69 feet 9 inches	63 feet 3 inches
L.w.l.	59 feet 6 inches	55 feet 3 inches
Breadth, Extreme	15 feet 3 inches	17 feet 3 inches
Breadth, L.w.l.	15 feet 3 inches	16 feet 6 inches
Draft	10 feet 6 inches	8 feet 2 inches
Rake of Sternpost	47 degrees	0

Following minutely the instructions laid down by Marett, every possible element of the vessel was calculated and set down on paper, with no reference to a model, and the lines were drawn in conformity with the calculated elements. Many years ago Mr. Smith promised to give me the original design, but he was unable to find it. With every probability that this was the first design made in America, it would be of great interest today. The lines here reproduced are from the delicately and carefully made tracings of Bob Center, who was as meticulously careful in his drafting as in everything else that he undertook. With a reduction in size there was made an increase in breadth and decrease in draft, while the after overhang was entirely changed. There was much of the old shipwright's art in the counters of such cutters as Mosquito,, Cygnet and Vesper, but this was discarded and replaced by the pie-plate type of elliptical counter characteristic of the yachts of Lon Smith.

Following the construction of Mosquito, Mr. Center determined to build of iron. The keel was an inch plate, three feet deep, one foot being inside. The garboards were of heavy plate; the body of the plating was 3/16 inch. Much of the hull weight was at the lowest possible point, while the use of angle iron in place of bulky wooden frames and floors permitted a very low stowage of ballast; 14½ tons of lead stowed within a length of 10 feet amidships. Fitted at first with a wood bowsprit weighing 1,260 pounds, this was replaced by an iron one weighing but 800. She was fitted with a tiller and also with a horizontal wheel and quadrant gear for use if preferred. Iron yacht construction was then unknown in America. In 1856 Robert B. Forbes built two sister yachts; one, the well known schooner Azalea, of wood, and the other, Edith, of iron. After using Edith personally for two years he sent her to the Argentine; making the run, of course under sail, in 47 days. After using her for a year in trading he sold her for use as a pilot boat.

Boring a Hollow Spar

THE consternation of the yachting world over the news of the construction of a cutter was heightened when it was known that she was to be built of iron, and dire predictions were made that she would not float. The construction was awarded to the firm of Reaney, Son & Archbold, of Chester, Pa.; the yard later better known as that of John Roach & Son. When employed in this yard in 1878-9 one of my intimate friends was an apprentice in the machine shop (I was a "boat-yarder"). He was the son of a pump and block maker in Wilmington, and I sometimes spent the week-end with the family. Mr. Taylor told me of an experience which he had in trying to make a hollow mast for Vindex. The old wooden pumps were made from long logs bored through by a "pod" or "pump" auger, a tool similar in shape to a spoon, and without the spiral point of a modern auger. These pump augers varied in diameter from 2 to 5 inches, or even larger, and for a mast the boring at the heel would be started with the larger size, smaller and smaller ones being used as the bore rose upward. The log to be bored was lined up as straight as possible on trestles in a long shed, then the auger, mounted on a rod perhaps a dozen feet long, was started, extra lengths of rod being screwed on as the bore progressed. The absence of the spiral point was supposed to prevent diversion from the center of the log, but in this case it failed. The mast was 15 inches diameter at the heel and 56 feet heel to hounds. After much industrious turning of the handle the auger emerged from one side of the mast, near the hounds. I can imagine the dear little man, with his quick and explosive temper and his command of sea language, shaking both fists and jumping up and down with blazing eyes.

This invasion of foreign ideas was met in no friendly spirit. It was predicted that not only would Vindex not float, but she would not sail. After sailing the season with fair success against the home centerboards, Mr. Center cruised up and down the coast in winter, and kept her outside Sandy Hook in company with the pilotboats. With hemp shrouds set up by lanyards, and tackles on bowsprit shrouds and bobstay, there was a constant stretching of rigging, and her skipper (he had no professional captain) earned among his friends the soubriquet of "Watch tackle Bob" as he trudged about the deck with a handy billy over his shoulder sweating up. While a success for the purpose for which she was designed, in ordinary racing she was described by Mr. Smith as a Dr. Jeckyl and a Mr. Hyde. She was least successful with the home fleet on Long Island Sound, but East of Newport she was generally respected, especially by those who saw her under reefed mainsail, No. 2 jib, and housed topmast. In later years Mr. Smith ascribed her faults to the extreme concentration of her ballast.

From Canvas to Paper

THIS experience with Vindex opened a new era for Mr. Smith. Introduced to the methods of the professional naval architect, he gradually abandoned the easel. In 1873 a commission came from Charles H. Contoit of New York, but not a member of a yacht club, for a cruising schooner of 72 feet l.w.l. She was described at the time as having a "hollow floor, is very sharp forward and aft, and has a graceful bow and stern. The Prospero was built from the paper plans and drawings of A. Cary Smith, the talented marine artist and designer." As he became more prominent in yachting A. C. Smith was frequently confused with A. E. (Lon) Smith, the builder, of Islip. To avoid this he signed his name A. Cary Smith, though always Archie to his early associates. In March 1872 he joined the New York Yacht Club, continuing his membership until his death. He served the Club as Measurer through 1872-82 inclusive, also on the Library Committee, and throughout his membership took an important part in all measurement legislation. Following Prospero came, in 1875, Madcap, a 42-foot sloop designed for an old friend, Ludlow Livingston. In 1878 came an order for a large cruising schooner, the first Intrepid, for Lloyd Phoenix, a retired naval officer who spent much of his life in cruising.

The Seawanhaka Yacht Club of Oyster Bay and the New York Canoe Club were organized at the same time, 1871, and by much the same party of young men interested alike in the yacht and the canoe. Though never a canoeist, Mr. Smith was a member and Measurer of the New York Canoe Club. My early environment was entirely apart from both yachts and canoes. I built my first and second canoes alone, and used them alone, my second cruise being the length of Long Island Sound. Knowing that Mr. Smith was Measurer of the Canoe Club, I ventured to intrude on him in his sanctum in the Studio Building, 51 West 10th Street. On one of the hottest of the hot days at the end of last month I made a pilgrimage to both Chelsea and Greenwich villages; finding St. Peter's Church, now a part of the Episcopal Seminary covering the block from 9th to 10th Avenues and from 20th to 21st Streets.

Built in 1857, the Studio Building still stands as I first knew it in 1877, old-fashioned and out of date in this era of skyscrapers. I hoped to find some record of when Mr. Smith's tenancy began, as that may have marked his entry into professional life as a painter, but no records have been preserved; it was at least as early as 1870. Though but one of the many strangers who intruded on similar missions, my reception was most gracious; he examined my plans and took down the new quarto, Yacht Designing, by Dixon Kemp, and showed me designs of canoes. When I ventured to say that I would like to be a yacht designer he replied: "My-y-y b-b-boy, you had b-b-better g-g-get a j-j-job on a peanut stand; it will p-p-pay you b-b-better in the end." Perhaps he was right. How many bambinos then rolling on the earth in sunny Italy have since then reaped riches and honors through peanuts and bananas, to say nothing of the humble hurdy gurdy?

Joining the New York Yacht Club in 1869, Joseph R. Busk was an Englishman, and typically English in appearance, tall and heavily built, with florid features, and very positive in his beliefs. I do not know his early yachting connections, but in New York, and as a member of the New York Yacht Club, he was American to the backbone, a staunch adherent of the sloop. After owning Madcap he built from Mr. Smith's design the sloop Mischief. At a gathering of yachtsmen, I think, on one of the cruises, Admiral Harmony, U.S.N., was telling the story of a chase of a blockade runner during the Rebellion, and he ended with: "And, Sir, the damned rascal got away." A voice in the background piped up "Admiral, I was the damned rascal." This came from Frank W. J. Hurst, a young Englishman who in his early twenties was purser aboard an English blockade-runner; after the war ended he came to New York, married the daughter of a New York merchant, and became a thorough American in his yachting. Joining the New York Yacht Club in 1874, in the following year he had built by Billy Force of Keyport, N. J., a centerboard sloop of 50 feet l.w.l. Though distinctly of the home type, Active was sometimes called a cutter. I think that she had a plumb stem, unusual at that time, and she did have the broad counter of a cutter. In nearly 30 years' membership he served the Club well, as Treasurer and on committees; but his sympathies, as with Mr. Busk, were on the side of the defender in all matches for the Cup.

In Cup Defense

WHEN the challenge of Genesta was received, early in 1885, the question of type at once came to the fore. In 1879 Mr. Smith designed for Mr. Busk the centerboard sloop Mischief, of but 61 feet l.w.l., though designed to race against the older sloops, Gracie, Fanny, Arrow and Hildegard, of 65 to 70 feet. Though essentially of the national type, the "iron pot" was superior in form to the older yachts; of the iron construction, which gave her the nickname, and a good modern rig; with Cap'n "Than" Clock at her wheel (which, by the way, was horizontal, like Vindex) she soon demonstrated her superiority in the class races, and in 1881 was chosen and successfully defended the Cup. In spite of his quiet and retiring manner Cary Smith was always very wideawake. He knew the cutter men; he sailed with them and argued with them, and he was fully alive to the defects of the American type. Here comes to mind a story, long forgotten, which he once told me with great glee. The trial trip of "Robo" Schuyler's cutter, Yolande, which he had designed for himself, was made on a breezy day in 1880, starting out from Piepgrass' Yard at Pottery Beach, on the East River, and up and down against a strong wind and tide. As the party stepped ashore someone on the pier asked: "How did she go 'Robo?'" The answer came: "Dry as a bone, not a drop on deck," as "Robo" walked up the pier with rivers running down from his clothing and spouting out of his shoes.

In 1881 Mr. Smith had designed Valkyr, a "compromise cutter" as the term then went, with an outside lead keel through which dropped a centerboard, and a moderate cutter rig. In 1884 he designed Rajah, a smart little cruising cutter of 3¾ beams and a lead keel. He knew that the bell had long since rung for the national type, and he was prepared to defend the Cup against Genesta with a thoroughly modern even though a centerboard yacht. The syndicate formed by Commodore Bennett was represented by a special America's Cup Committee, of which Mr. Busk and some equally conservative Americans were members. Coming home on the New Jersey Central ferry on February 26, 1885, I met Mr. Smith, as I frequently did. He had just left a meeting of the Cup Committee at which the final decision had been made. We took our usual station, just inside the chain on the bow of the ferryboat, facing a bitter N. W. wind. With tears in his voice, if not in his eyes, and the expression of a man led out to be hanged, he said: "Well, my b-b-boy, I've g-g-got to b-b-build a damned steel s-s-scow."

The "damned steel scow" was Priscilla. In the course of my

duties I went to Mr. Busk for such details as might be given out for publication, and I was told by him that it was no business of the public whether her garboards were 5 inches or 5/8 inch thick. She was built at Wilmington, Delaware, launched on May 19, and towed at once to New York. I was at Poillon's Yard, and on her deck as soon as the lines were made fast. I went over her from stem to gudgeon and published every detail I could measure. Poillon's had about finished two wood launches, to be fitted with Herreshoff engines, and my old friend John B., the "blind man," was looking after the job. He said to me, "How can I get down to the floors? I want to see the construction." He always used the word "see" though totally blind from early youth. I assured him that I was on the same errand, but the matched flooring was as yet uncut, not even the hole for the mast. When I was over a few days later he said, "I got down and saw what I wanted." John B. had made a practice for many years of visiting New York in Regatta Week with some new wonder, a fast yacht, a catamaran, or a new launch. Neils Olsen told me of a time when he came down with a new sloop. I have forgotten whether he won or lost, but after the race he went aboard the other boat, lay down on the deck forward, and passed his arm from planksheer to the water, feeling the form. Then he hitched aft a few feet and repeated the process, for the entire length of the yacht. In the case of Priscilla he went below and at the stem reached up to the shelf and passed his hand over a frame down to the floor. Then, stepping aft about three frames, he repeated the process, going to the transom. After he had got below the cabin floor and snooped about the bilge he knew all that he wanted. When Priscilla's mast was stepped I was one who threw a dime in the mast step for luck. A short time later, following her trial trip, I saw the mast unstepped in order that five feet might be cut off the heel. A failure in the trial races, she was later converted to a schooner, and with some alterations of her keel by Mr. Smith served a long and useful career. The experience was a bitter one for him. Had he been left free, I am confident, from what I know of his ideas, and of his previous and subsequent work, that he would have designed a yacht very similar to Puritan, with positive lead keel as well as a centerboard.

Pleasure Gives Way to Trade

N 1885 there came to the Studio Building a gentleman who was not a yachtsman but a capitalist, interested, among other enterprises, in passenger service on Long Island Sound. He explained to Mr. Smith what he wanted; a schooner of sufficiently light draft for Florida waters, but capable of making the coasting voyage down and back. The answer was Whim, of 55 feet l.w.l. and 2 feet 8 inchs light draft. Leaving New York with a load of stores for the winter, she drew over 3 feet; once, unloaded, she cruised the keys and the shoal waters around them. Joining the New York Yacht Club in 1886, Mr. Chapin was in the game for life. In this year he came back for a larger schooner for coastal work, Julia, later Iroquois. The lines of this beautiful combination of a deep keel and centerboard were given in MoToR BoATinG for December. She, in turn, was succeeded by the still larger Yampa, 110 feet l.w.l., for offshore cruising.

Following his experience with yachts, Mr. Chapin came back with the proposition that Mr. Smith should design a passenger steamer for Long Island Sound, but was met by the positive statement that he knew nothing about such work. Persisting in his demand, Mr. Chapin, a very determined and successful business man, overcame these doubts. The lines of one of the old wooden steamers were taken off and submitted to Mr. Smith. As he disavowed all knowledge of marine engineering, specialists were retained for this part of the work. Leaving the retirement of his old studio, Mr. Smith established a new and large organization, including engineers and other specialists in the many lines outside of hull design and construction. The marked success of the first steamer, the Richard Peck, led to larger vessels, the City of Lowell and the Chester W. Chapin, these displacing all the old type of Sound steamers. In still another line he turned out the steam pilotboat New Yorker. At the time when he first started work on the Richard Peck, Mr. Smith took into his service a young boy who, with few opportunities for serious study of naval architecture, had worked as a draftsman for several designers. Greedy in his desire for knowledge, and tireless and indefatigable in his devotion to his work and to his employer, he in time took over the heavy work of running such an establishment, carrying on the business of Cary Smith & Ferris after his superior's death, on December 8, 1911, following a long illness at his home in Pamrapo. In a career of 56 years A. Cary Smith had produced almost every type of yacht from the most diminutive sandbagger to the largest sailing cruiser, and in addition had revolutionized the type for which this country has long been famous, the large inland passenger steamer.

TRADITIONS AND MEMORIES OF AMERICAN YACHTING

By WILLIAM P. STEPHENS

Part Seventeen

EDWARD BURGESS AND HIS WORK

IN the years prior to 1880 the Boston yachtsmen who were later to contest the supremacy of New York, and to place The Hub firmly and permanently on the yachting map were mainly young men just out of or just entering Harvard; their yachts were small catboats and sloops, some keel and some centerboard, but the latter of less extreme type than the New York sandbaggers. Prominent in this group were the Bryant boys, Dr. John and Henry; the Burgess boys, and the Adams boys, George Caspar and Charles Francis Adams 3d. For many years prior to 1883 Benjamin Franklin Burgess had been one of the leading merchants of New England, owning sugar plantations in Cuba and a fleet of vessels for carrying sugar to the States. In addition to a handsome home in Boston he had a summer home at Sandwich, on Cape Cod. His seven children were: Thomas, Benjamin Franklin, Edward, Walter and Arthur (twins), Sidney W. and Edith. From early youth all of the boys sailed small sloops and catboats off Sandwich.

Edward, born on June 30, 1848, took to the water with his brothers, but his chief interest was in natural history, especially entomology; he was known to his intimates as a "bugologist." He graduated from Harvard in 1871, but continued at first for a year as instructor in the Bussey Institute, devoted to entomology, finally holding this office for 15 years. In 1877 he married Miss Caroline Louisa Sullivant, daughter of General William Starling Sullivant of Columbus, Ohio; and two sons were born, William Starling and Charles Paine Burgess.

In 1883 the family visited England and spent the summer in Torquay and on the Isle of Wight; in the very center of English yachting.

Fortune Changes

On their return to Boston the family were faced with the failure of the elder Burgess, and Sidney and Edward

Edward Burgess, 1848 - 1891

Puritan photographed in 1885 by N. L. Stebbins

opened an office as yacht brokers, acting also as agents for A. Cary Smith in New York. In an obituary published in *The Field* on the death of Edward, Dixon Kemp wrote: "He frequently corresponded with the writer of this notice, and in 1880 he wrote 'I am glad that you are publishing a new edition of *Yacht and Boat Sailing;* I have greatly enjoyed your books, and have used them until the binding is about gone.' He was at this time greatly impressed with the value of depth of hull and draft of water for sailing yachts, combined with moderate breadth; and in 1880 he got Cary Smith to adapt the lines of the Itchen boat, Wild Rose, for a 27-foot waterline boat with a counter. At this time he sent the writer a tracing which he had made himself of Cary Smith's design, and it showed that at this period he possessed considerable

Right: Launching of Mayflower, Lawley's Yard, South Boston, May 5, 1886

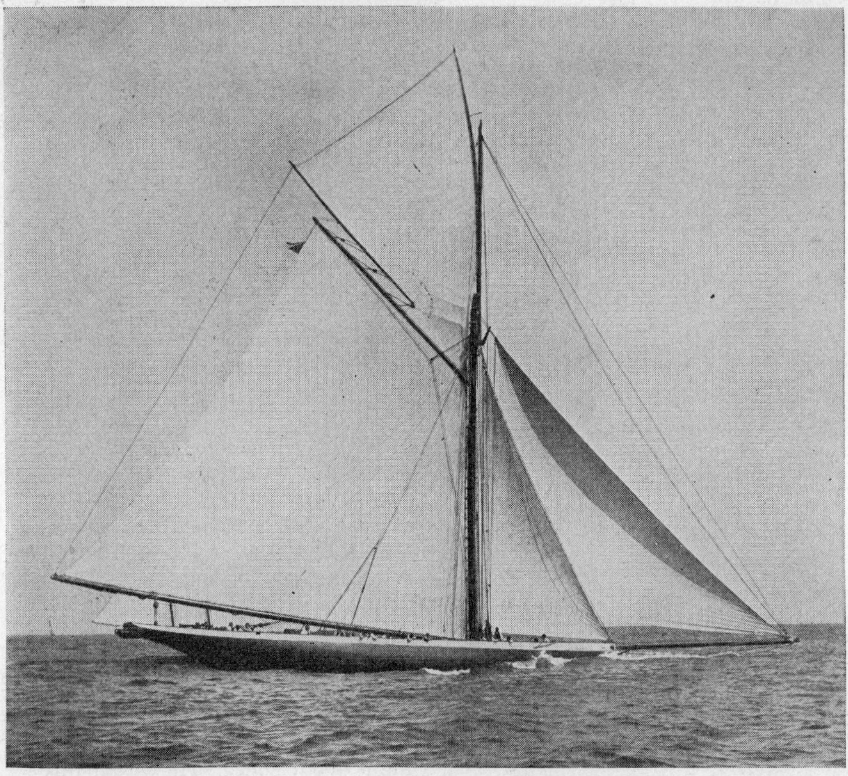

Below: Mayflower. All of the Paine-Burgess defenders were painted white; but Mayflower was potleaded in the races of 1886

skill as a draftsman. In 1882 when the Itchen boats were undergoing a sort of transformation by reason of their heavy lead keels, long overhangs and enormous sail spreads, as evidenced in Keepsake and Bonina, he commissioned the writer to make him a design for a 36-foot waterline yacht. This yacht was built for J. Malcolm Forbes, and named Lapwing; subsequently he had other designs from England, and his letters of instruction at this period showed that he had a perfect knowledge of the subject."

As little business came to the new firm, Sidney, who was possessed of some small means, became discouraged and went to England, leaving Edward to carry on alone. His first order came from Dr. W. F. Whitney, of the Eastern Y. C., for a cruising cutter, Rondina, 36 feet 4 inches l.o.a.; 30 feet l.w.l.; 8 feet 2 inches breadth and 6 feet 6 inches draft; of 12.74 tons displacement, 987 square feet of sail, and an iron keel of 6 tons. As a long-time frequenter of the boat yards about City Point, Mr. Burgess was well acquainted with the Lawleys. Old George and George F., father and son; and they built Rondina in 1884.

Boston Comes to the Defense

General Charles J. Paine—he won his title in the Rebellion as a commander of Volunteers—was a general in every sense of the term, able alike in picking his associates, in fitting each to his task, and in the direction of their work. A lawyer by profession, though he did not practice, with large interests in Western railroads, and of ample means, he was interested in yachting. He had owned and raced the schooner Halcyon from 1878, the date on which he joined the Eastern Y. C., and he had joined the New York Y. C. in 1880. As a loyal member of the Eastern Y. C. he must have appreciated the secondary position which it held, and when the opportunity came through a challenge for the America's Cup and the decision of the New York Y. C. to defend it with a conventional sloop he was quick to grasp it. Quoting from *The Eastern Y. C. Ditty Box,* by C. H. W. Foster: "In 1885, the challenge

Papoose, designed by Edward Burgess, 1887

of Genesta having been received, a number of gentlemen met in the office of J. Malcolm Forbes to discuss Eastern Y. C. matters. They were Vice Commodore Forbes, William Gray, Jr., Francis H. Peabody, General C. J. Paine and Edward Burgess. Allusion to the challenge of Genesta was made and, after a discusion of the relative types of English and American yachts it was agreed that none of the latter possessed the speed necessary to defend the challenge successfully. The suggestion was made that an Eastern yacht be built which would combine all the recent ideas in American yachting. The suggestion met with hearty approval and plans were then made to secure the co-operation of other yachtsmen. Messrs. Forbes, Gray and Paine were made a committee, and they at once sought the advice of Mr. Burgess." The final decision was quickly made and the designing of the yacht was entrusted to Mr. Burgess.

In approaching this task he was free from all allegiance to the national type; even in his centerboard boats he was accustomed to narrower and deeper yachts than those of New York, he had owned many small keel sloops and cutters, and he was fully alive to the advantage of outside ballast. His summer in England had made him thoroughly familiar with the racing cutter as it then was, of less than five beams. At the same time, he lacked the long experience of Cary Smith in both design and construction of large yachts, and the experience of the Herreshoffs, dating back to 1864, in designing and building; in the course of which they had developed in their steam yachts a system of exceptionally light construction with bent frames and double planking.

The Problem of Type

Conditions South and North of Cape Cod were radically different; the battle of the types, with its strong national side, was at its height; and New York was firmly committed to the defense of the centerboard sloop of its daddies. Boston, on the other hand, though the majority of its yachts were centerboard craft, had a number of keel boats, and some with outside ballast. While

Nymph, designed by Edward Burgess for the 40-foot Class, 1888. Owned by F. W. Flint. Compromise type of keel-centerboard

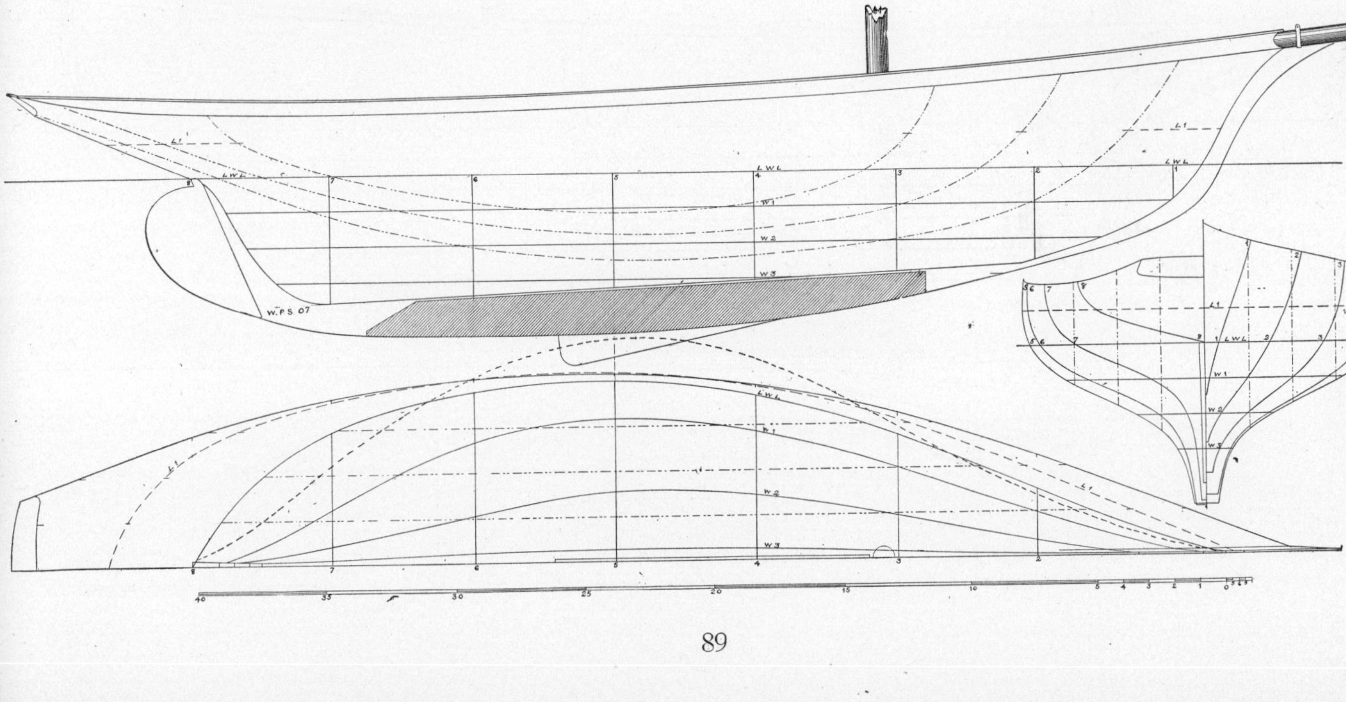

the adoption of modern ideas in a compromise type would have been a complete surrender on the part of New York, Boston not only had stood aloof thus far in the battle, but actually favored many of the features of the cutter; large displacement, moderate breadth, greater depth, and an outside metal keel.

The first notice of a challenge came in the form of a personal letter from J. Beavor-Webb, designer of Genesta and Galatea, dated December 6, 1884. Though the formal challenge was not sent until February 1885, there was sufficient certainty of the match to justify immediate action on the part of the New York Y. C. On December 26 a meeting of the Club was held, at which the subject was discussed in very broad terms by J. Frederic Tams:—"One type to be considered is the deep, sharp centerboard cutter, the so-called compromise. This type, in my opinion, is destined to become the national type of vessel, and combines, without claiming more for it, the qualities of safety and sea-going ability and a moderate rig, which the other two types mentioned do not possess; and an adaptability to the peculiarities of our coasts and harbors which the deep keel does not possess. In schooners this type stands pre-eminent, as illustrated in the Idler and Palmer and in the smaller Magic, once already a winner in a contest for the America's Cup. Another type is the large displacement, taunt rig type, which might be called half-way between the last mentioned and the beamy-shallow boats, and which has sprung up within the last few years, and is distinguished by the very high rig and great spread of canvas it is compelled to carry, and it has shown great speed in average weather and particularly in very light winds.

"We finally come to the regular, acceptedly national type of beamy-shallow centerboard vessels, our long-time friend; it is needless to describe them. From the Silvie, Maria, Eva and Scud among the large ones, down to the Fannies, Gracies, Mischiefs, Madcaps and Vixens, we know them well, and what they have done; but what such a type can do no man knows, for no vessel of the type has yet been constructed exclusively for racing, as is done in Great Britain. And this is also true of the other types mentioned. This type (beamy-shallow) also carries a large rig, but not so large as the previously mentioned one, not having to force as much boat through the water on account of her smaller displacement. In my opinion one of the boats to meet the English challengers should undoubtedly be of this type; and the other of one or the other of the two previously mentioned types. There will not be the slightest difficulty in rigging or constructing such a vessel of the requisite size. We talk about our sloops of the present day being too large; our predecessors of twenty years back and thereabouts would have considered them moderate in size, and in those days the appliances and material entering into rig and construction were comparatively primitive; but, notwithstanding, we find the Silvie crossing the Atlantic and cruising along the coasts of Norway and other European countries and returning safely; and, I am informed, comparatively comfortable under one big jib, at that.

"Given the strains, and science can always provide the required strength, and if it was deemed necessary to build at all, I would build a vessel of the Vixen, Mischief, Gracie, Fanny type, say 80 to 85 feet in length, with a flush deck, no house; and, when being designed and constructed, provision could be made for her ultimate conversion into a schooner. This type could be constructed of wood, with light frames and double planking, so as to combine lightness with strength, as her stability is principally due to her form, and there is not the same necessity for having her ballast at the lowest possible point; but she should be constructed of the lightest possible material, whether of wood or metal. Perhaps a steel frame and centerboard trunk, with wooden planking, would be preferable (the so-called composite construction), or she might be built of all steel or iron, whichever proved the lightest and strongest, (simple calculations by an expert would decide these questions), or she could be built of steel, with light sheathing of wood over the steel plating, so that in all cases she could be coppered if necessary. These conditions apply to all the variations of this type; or, in the large displacement, taunt rig type, but the compromise type must be built with steel or iron frame, as it is of paramount importance that ballast should be placed as low as possible. All three of these vessels should have a double head-rig to consist of No. 1 and 2 jibs, the former full size and of lighter stuff, and also the ordinary staysail and balloon staysail and gaff storm trysail."

Diversity of Counsel

No sooner was it assured that there would be a match than the New York Y. C. was deluged with a multiplicity of projects for the defense; not only every yacht builder, even from as far

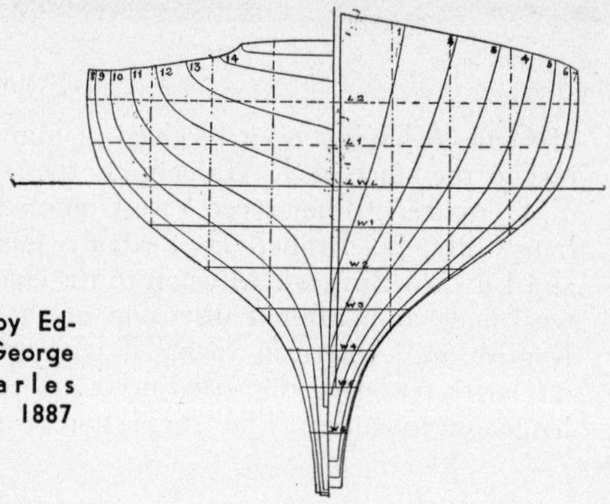

Papoose, designed by Edward Burgess for George Caspar and Charles Francis Adams III, 1887

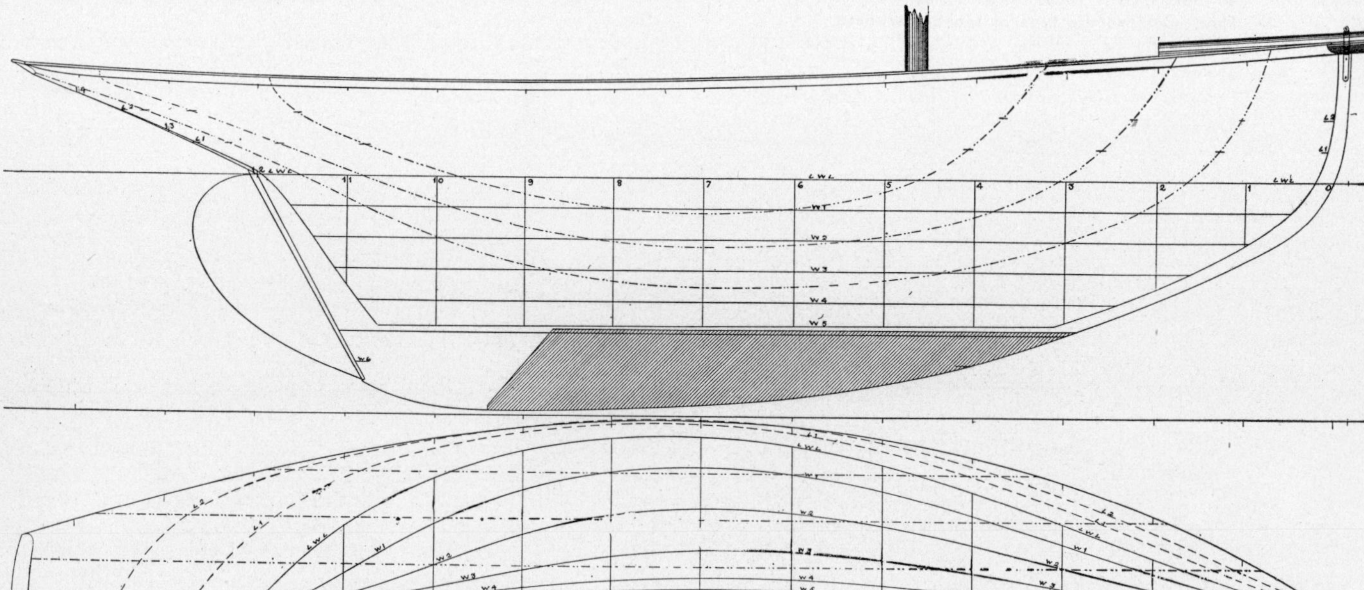

inland as Chicago, came to the fore with a model, but even the boat builders vied in planning yachts of 90 feet length. The always irrepressible Thomas Clapham proposed a 90-foot sharpie, fin-keel with a hollow fin of boilerplate in which any desired amount of lead might be stowed. David Kirby, modeller and builder of the unfortunate Pocahontas, suggested a modernized sloop of more depth and displacement. It was also suggested that the old Una of George Steers be modernized; and that such tried and tested schooners as Comet and Grayling (the latter had capsized on her trial trip) be altered to the sloop rig. Bold Ben Butler, then owner of the original America, wrote to the Club, of which he was not a member, offering the yacht and suggesting that whatever the result of the formal races, no challenger should be allowed to take the "Queen's Cup" as he always persisted in calling it, until she had also defeated the original winner. As illustrative of popular opinion of the day, Edward A. Willard, a member of the New York Y. C. and a sailing companion of General Paine, had owned the 49-foot l. w. l. sloop Eclipse, one of the few large yachts modelled and built by Neet Willis; she was notable from her channels; her mast being well forward, these were built out of bar iron and plate to give spread to her shrouds. When it was proposed to build to meet Galatea in 1886 Mr. Willard had cut by Willis a model for a sloop of 90-feet l. w. l. which he proposed to turn over to Mr. Burgess for further perfection by modern methods; the idea being to combine the supposed intuitive talent of the old modeller with the education of the new naval architect. Cavalier, as it was proposed to call her, never was built. The old Bourbon element prevailed, the beamy-shallow type suggested by Mr. Tams was selected, and the order was given to Cary Smith for the "damned steel scow" mentioned in the preceding chapter.

Puritan

THE challenge of 1885 was a double one; first, from Genesta and then, in the event of her defeat, from Galatea, a new and untried yacht. The latter, newly launched, was unsuccessful in her first season; built of steel with a trough keel, too many cold pigs were stowed before the hot lead was poured, resulting in a lawsuit and the cutting-out and re-pouring of the lead. As Galatea was the longer, 86 feet l. w. l. as compared with 81 feet for Genesta, the New York defender was designed to a waterline of 85 feet. General Paine, after owning Halcyon for six years, was thoroughly familiar with her; just how much she was used as the basis for the proposed design is not known, but it is interesting to compare their dimensions:

	l. o. a.	l. w. l.	breadth	draft
Halcyon	82-0	79-9	23-9	6-0
Puritan	94-0	81-1	22-7	8-8

The sheer plan of Puritan was that of a cutter, plumb stem and long counter, the excess of draft over Halcyon was made up of an S section at the garboards and a deep outside keel of 30 tons. Both she and Priscilla carried the double head-rig of the cutter, but the mainsails were laced to the boom, as became an American yacht.

At that time the designer contented himself with the form and general construction of the hull, and the proportioning of the sail plan. Such a proceeding as calculating strains and stresses was not even dreamed of, and the sparring, rigging and sail-making were entrusted to practical men. Thorburn in New York made the spars for Priscilla, J. F. Byers got out her rigging, and Wilson & Griffin made her sails. In Boston the rigging of Puritan was got out by Charles Billman & Son, the spars by H. Pigeon & Sons and the sails were made by J. H. McManus & Son. The construction was given over to George Lawley & Son, and may be characterized as light-heavy; the conventional wood frames and single planking, but with an effort to save weight. The feeling on the part of many New York yachtsmen over this attempt of Boston to butt in was very well expressed by Captain Cornelius McKay, a writer for *The Evening Telegram,* a Bennett paper, to the effect that it was a good thing that Boston was to build a Cup candidate, as after the trial races she could be used for carrying brick on the Hudson River.

The meeting of the rival defenders in club races, on the New York Y. C. cruise, and finally in the trial races, proved that Puritan was, beyond question, the faster, especially to windward; and her selection followed as a matter of course. An important factor in her success was the make-up of her Corinthian crew; all personal friends of General Paine and Mr. Burgess, and experienced handlers of their own yachts. J. Malcolm Forbes, Dr. John Bryant, Henry Bryant (a very clever amateur designer), George H. Richards and Charles A. Welch, Jr. Her professional captain was Aubrey Crocker, who had sailed Shadow for many years for the Bryants. In the Cup races Captain Joe Elsworth was invited to serve as honorary pilot; he was noted as not only one of the best yacht handlers about New York, but his long experience in handling his fleet of oyster sloops in all weathers gave him an unequalled store of local knowledge of the tides and currents of New York Harbor and the outlying ocean. Taken all in all, it is safe to say that the talent aboard Puritan out-matched that aboard her opponent.

Mayflower and Volunteer

THE victory over the British yacht was hailed as a national triumph, even in the far West and among persons unfamiliar with and not interested in yachting; Mr. Burgess became famous over night, and orders came in from all quarters. To meet Galatea in 1886 it was decided to build a yacht of her length; and General Paine assumed the construction of Mayflower. A longer and deeper Puritan, built of wood, it is a question as to how much superior she was; as the new challenger was in no way in the class with Genesta, and the victory was a hollow one. In the following year, 1887, came a challenge from Scotland, backed by the Royal Clyde Y. C.; the yacht, designed by George L. Watson for a syndicate of Glasgow yachtsmen, being named Thistle. To meet her General Paine again came forward with Volunteer, of 87 feet l. w. l., built of steel with a deeper hull and a trough keel. The name gave a chance for a wisecrack (I think, from one of the Adams boys) to the effect that she should have been named Pensioner as all volunteers were pensioners now (1887), and this thirty years before the Bonus scandal of the World war.

By this time, with a greatly enlarged office and a staff of assistants, Mr. Burgess was deluged with orders; not merely for yachts, but for other types of craft. In 1887 he was approached by Charles Francis Adams 3d whose previous sailing had been in small catboats with his brother George, for a keel cabin yacht for both cruising and racing. The answer was Papoose, spelled with one p omitted to give seven letters and two ciphers for luck. She was not built to class, but in the following year a movement was started for a class to the limit of 40 feet l. w. l. This was one of the first classes built to a fixed limit. It gained instant popularity, and in 1889 had 19 yachts. Of these Mr. Burgess designed 11, of different types from the deep keel to the shoal and wide centerboard; Cary Smith had two, William Fife and William Gardner each one. In power the fleet ranged from 3600 square feet of sail on Liris, the Gardner boat, down to 2700 square feet on Minerva, the Fife boat. The accidental entry of Minerva to the class races demonstrated her invincibility; in 1888 Messrs. Adams had replaced Papoose by Babboon, with an extra b added; and in 1889 she gave way to Gossoon; a series of ten races with Minerva, now in her second season, resulted in a draw.

In 1892 Papoose was sold to John T. Mott, of the Oswego Y. C., who prized her not only as the work of Mr. Burgess, but as having been owned by the Adams boys. It is the fate of many yachts on Lake Ontario when condemned for pleasure use to be degraded to some mere freighting service. Mr. Mott would have none of this, and when the yacht was no longer fit for his use in 1927 he had her hauled out, broken up, and the fragments decently cremated. The rudder stock was cut from the blade by his skipper, Phil, packed like a piece of fine furniture, and shipped to Bayside, where it now serves as a newel post to my stairway, a memorial of more than one old friend. By one of those unreasonable impulses so common among yachtsmen this fine class was suddenly abandoned, to be replaced by a similar class of keel and centerboard yachts of 46 feet waterline; Mr. Burgess contributing five out of the ten new yachts of 1891. This time the honors again went to a dark horse, the one Herreshoff entry, Gloriana; she like Minerva in the 40-foot Class, sweeping the field with no second.

The End

THE work of Mr. Burgess by this time had grown beyond the endurance of any one man, even with able assistants. With no natural inclination for mathematics he was obliged to study the mathematics of naval architecture: in addition, it was necessary for him to inform himself fully on steel construction; and as his practice expanded to include steam craft, both yachts and commercial vessels, on steam engineering as well. In a period of but seven years his work included the designing of 137 vessels, mostly yachts, both sail and steam, but also pilot boats, fishermen and commercial craft. Among the many unusual tasks he was commissioned by General Butler in 1886 to modernize the old America; this work including the replacing of a part of the old wooden keel by a wider one to carry a lead keel of 30 tons, and an entirely new rig with shorter lower masts and pole bowsprit. Apart from his Cup defenders, two notable successes were the single stick Titania in the 70-foot Class and the 65-foot centerboard schooner Quickstep, a remarkable little yacht of most convenient size on a limited draft. When the new White Fleet was under consideration about 1887 he was chosen by William F. Whitney, Secretary of the Navy, as one of a special board which selected the designs of the Maine and Texas for construction. As the result of this labor he was taken ill with typhoid fever and died on July 31, 1891; Mrs. Burgess surviving him by only five months.

The saying that republics are ungrateful was discredited in this case, as not only the yachting world but the entire nation praised him as the thrice savior of the treasured Cup. Honors of all kinds were heaped on him; early in 1888 the sum of $12,000 was raised, from which was purchased at a cost of $1,200 a silver salver for General Paine, and a $500 cup for Mr. Burgess; the balance of the fund being presented to him in cash. A cup costing $700 was presented to him by the St. Augustine Y. C. Specially notable was the reception tendered to him and General Paine in Boston on October 7, 1887. At this time the sum of $11,500 was presented through subscriptions of New England yachtsmen, while New York contributed $10,172. In addition to a bronze group to General Paine, the Atlantic Y. C. of Brooklyn presented a small silver tankard with lid, containing $1,000 in twenty-dollar gold pieces. After his death a beautifully worded memorial, written by the Secretary, J. V. S. Oddie, embossed on vellum, was presented by the New York Y. C. to Mrs. Burgess.

The Designer

THE following is from the notebook mentioned below; apparently begun at the time that the firm of Burgess Brothers was started.

List of Boats Built by Burgess Brothers

1 Kitty Pierce Bros. 1879	11 Beetle Lawley & Son 1882
2 Hoiden Pierce Bros. 1879	12 Rondina Lawley & Son 1884
3 Scorpion Pierce Bros. 1880	13 Harbinger Lawley & Son 1884
4 Mavis Lawley & Son 1881	14 Herald and Telegram Lawley & Son 1884
5 Moya Lawley & Son 1881	15 Columbine Lawley & Son 1883
6 Playmate D. J. Lawlor 1881	16 Fad Lawley & Son 1884
7 Hornet Hutchins & Pryor 1883	17 Binney
8 Whitewing Lawley & Son 1883	18 Catboat J. M. F.
9 Medusa Lawley & Son 1883	19 80-Foot Design
10 Lapwing Lawley & Son 1882	

The list is not in chronological order, it may be divided into three classes; yachts built for the Burgess boys, yachts built for others under the superintendence of Edward Burgess, and yachts designed by him. The latter are but three in all; Columbine was a very shapely little keel sloop, apparently the first design made by Edward, and built for his own use. Rondina was his first professional commission, and the 80-Foot Design was Puritan. Kitty was built for himself, a keel sloop of 23 feet l. w. l., 10 feet 6 inches breadth and 5 feet draft, with 1250 pounds of iron on her keel. Hoiden was built for Sidney, a 20-foot l. w. l. catboat which he raced successfully for several years; his brother Arthur at the same time racing Fanchon, 26-foot keel sloop built by the Herreshoffs in 1866. Scorpion was a 23-foot l. w. l. cutter for Dr. W. F. Whitney. Mavis and Moya were 27-foot l. w. l. keel sloops, built from the design mentioned by Dixon Kemp; the first for J. Malcolm Forbes, the second for Edward. Playmate and Hornet were both built for Sidney; Whitewing was originally Butterfly, a cutter of 32 feet 6 inches l. w. l., designed by Beavor-Webb and built for Edward. Lapwing is also mentioned by Dixon Kemp. The cutter Medusa, later owned by Robert Center, was designed by Beavor Webb; Edward superintended her construction, as he did that of Harbinger, designed by A. Cary Smith, and the two launches Herald and Telegram, designed by Beavor-Webb and built for harbor service of the two papers about New York. Fad was designed by her owner, George A. Goddard, an amateur, an odd little yawl of 24 feet l. w. l. and 6 feet breadth, her cabin was designed by Edward. The Binney design was not built; nothing is known of the Forbes catboat. The list gives an idea of the technical training of Edward Burgess prior to the designing of Puritan. His first knowledge of designing was gained from the book *Yacht Designing,* published in 1875; always interested in sailing, from this time on he devoted more and more time to construction and later to designing. Mayflower is numbered 25 and Volunteer 60.

In attempting to evaluate the work of Edward Burgess many things must be taken into account; though generally proclaimed a genius in naval architecture, he would be the first to repudiate such a title. All of his tastes and his early training lay in a different direction from naval architecture; he had no interest in mathematics or mechanics, and he lacked the technical training considered essential today for success in designing. What he accomplished when confronted suddenly with a new and difficult task was only through natural intelligence and hard Yankee commonsense. His first and greatest effort, Puritan, was built on deductions as simple and logical as those which produced The One-Horse Shay. Rejecting from the start the British cutter, even of moderate breadth, he narrowed somewhat and deepened more the national model. In displacement he took a mean between the two types; while retaining the centerboard he added a deep and heavy keel through which it dropped. Save for the laced foot to the mainsail, the rig was that of the cutter, with short lower mast and long topmast and pole bowsprit. In form Puritan was of the conventional type of the day, with very hollow bow; and this general form was retained to the end; he introduced no new feature of design, such as was seen in Gloriana.

As a draftsman he was most particular; his designs were made on linen-backed paper prepared by himself, mounted with paste made by Mrs. Burgess. When thoroughly dry the surface was finished with very fine sandpaper. All of his lines were faired to a degree which it was not possible to reproduce on the floor.

The Man

WITH other treasured relics I have a little notebook used by him in the early days of his new profession; one of the first entries is an extract from an article by our mutual friend John Hyslop, published in *The Country* of May 4, 1878: "Put midship section 55 per cent of waterline from stem. The bulk of the boat under water at any point of its length must be related to the size (area) of the midship section as the ordinates of the waveline curve at corresponding points are related to the length of the longest ordinate." Then follows the conventional diagram showing the construction of the curve of versed sines for the forebody and the trochoid for the afterbody, with explanatory notes. Then, "After drawing below-water sections up to l. w. l. continue curve fairly to height as on shearplan; which will give the point for the deckline." Then follows: "To lay out a deck beam a la Smith," with diagram. "Smith said his l. w. l. forward was nearly a wave curve less one-fourth its length." It must be remembered that he was entirely self-taught, first taking up yacht designing merely as an interesting study, with no thought of practical application, and then, under new conditions, applying himself to it assiduously as a means of livelihood.

What are of far more importance than these technical notes as an index of the inner mind of this truly noble man are the following interspersed with them: "Praise undeserved is satire in disguise." Pope. "Wear your learning like your watch, in a private pocket; do not pull it out and strike it merely to show you have one. If you are asked what o'clock it is, tell it; but do not proclaim it hourly like a watchman." Chesterfield.

"We left behind the painted buoy that tosses at the harbour mouth;
And madly danced our hearts with joy, as fast we fleeted to the South:
How fresh was every sight and sound, on open main or winding shore;
We knew the merry world was round, and we might sail forever more."

Tennyson "The Voyage."

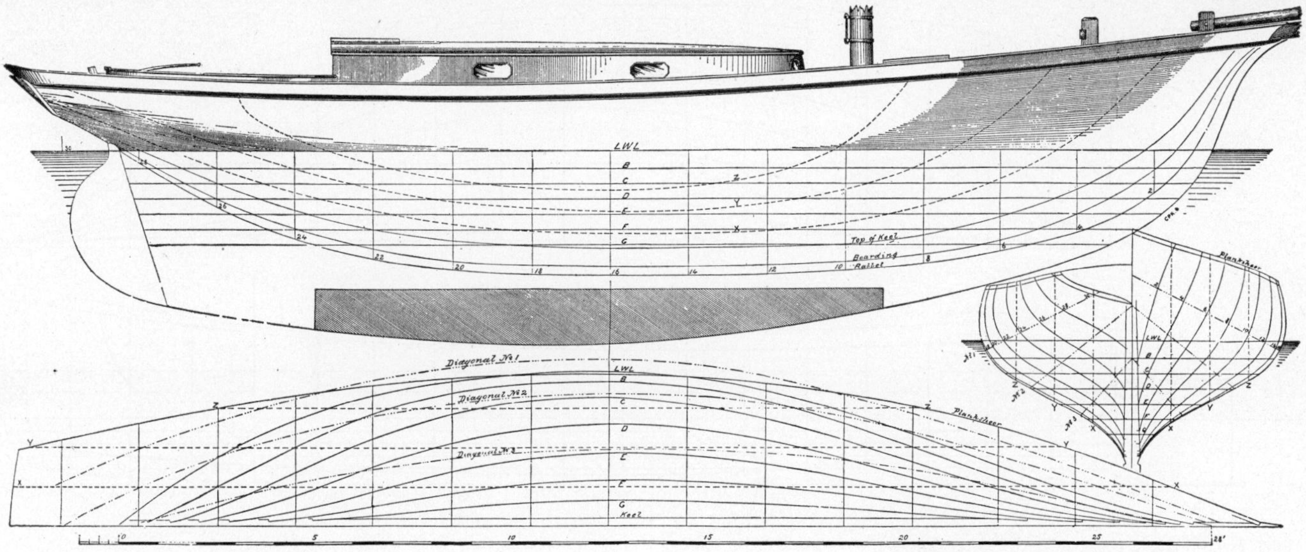

Petrel, designed by John Hyslop in 1875. Her sail plan at the left

TRADITIONS

AND MEMORIES OF

AMERICAN YACHTING

By WILLIAM P. STEPHENS

Part Eighteen

THE WAVE LINE AND WAVE FORM THEORIES

THOUGH carried today to an extreme never dreamed of in the past, the search for speed has always held a foremost place in the efforts of the shipbuilder. From the earliest day of the commercial vessel the quick carriage of cargoes has been an important consideration; and no matter how low the average speed of the fleet might be, the first ship to drop her anchor or pass her lines to a pier was rated as fast. With the introduction of yachts for pleasure service and steam in passenger service there arose a demand for absolute speeds far exceeding those of the old sailing ships, and the attention of builders was directed to the "form of least Resistance." One of the pioneers in this search a full century ago was John Scott Russell.

Born in the Vale of Clyde in 1808, the eldest son of Rev. David Russell, in a life of 74 years he established himself as one of the most noted scientists of the 19th Century; his work covering a wide range from practical mechanics to abstract investigation and ethics. His early education included studies at the universities of Edinburgh, St. Andrews and Glasgow, graduating from the latter at the age of 16. His father intended him for the pulpit, his tastes for mechanical work led him into a machine shop; but his general studies were so extensive that in 1832 he was appointed Professor of Natural Philosophy in the University of Edinburgh, in which position he delivered a noted course of lectures on the subject in which he specialized.

Returning to mechanical work, he built small steam canal boats and also steam carriages running on the highways, at one time he was manager of a canal; affording ample opportunities for his experiments. Later he had charge of one of the largest shipbuilding and engineering establishments on the Clyde, and as a part of this work he is credited with the introduction of in-and-out plating. During this period he was deeply interested in the subject of the waves created by a moving vessel; his experiments are said to have reached the total of 20,000, and included tests of full-sized vessels in canals as well as models in tanks. In the course of this work he built a yacht, Wave, in 1835, followed by the steamboats Scott Russell, Flambeau and Fire King in 1839; all designed on what he termed the wave line principle. In 1837 he read a memoir on the subject of waves before the Royal

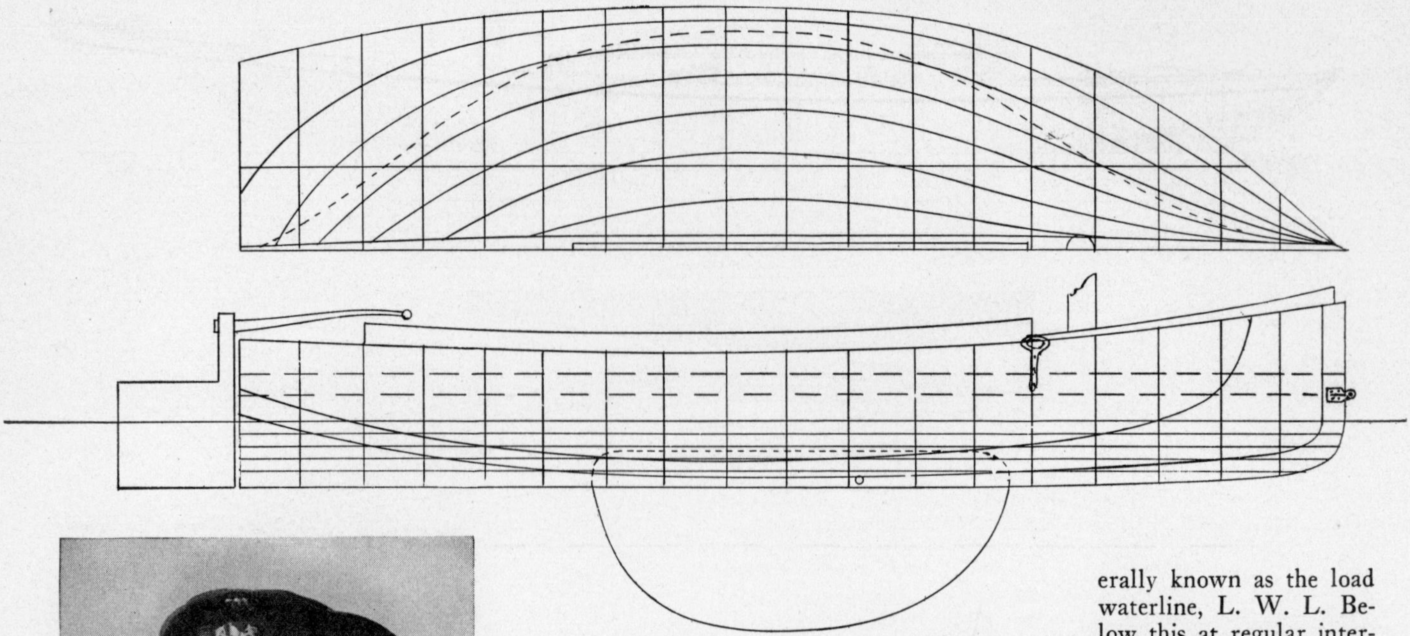

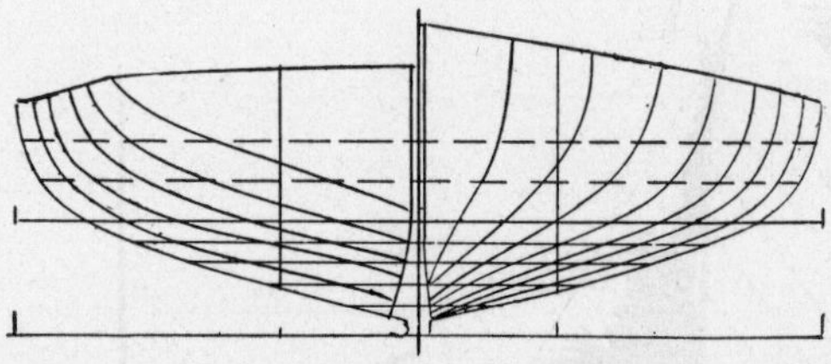

Boz, a sandbag type of sloop designed and built by John Hyslop

John Hyslop
1834 - 1919

Society of Edinburgh for which he was rewarded by the gold medal of the Society, election to a fellowship, and a place on the Council. In 1844 he removed to London and devoted himself more closely to naval architecture and marine engineering; he was associated with the great engineer Isambard Brunel in the building of the then monster steamship Great Eastern, the design being based on the wave line theory. He was also concerned in the designing of the noted Warrior class of ironclad warships. His practical work in other lines included car ferries for the Boden Sea, and a dome in Vienna with a diameter of 360 feet and no columns. He was one of the promoters of the World's Fair in London in 1851, and one of the founders of the Institute of Naval Architects in 1860. In an entirely different line he proposed, in 1871, "The New Social Alliance," a plan for the co-operation of the legislative and the working classes for the improvement of the working man.

The Wave Line Theory

There is a marked lack of exactness in the definition and use on the part of all writers on naval architecture of the term "waterline"; *the* waterline is easily understood, the intersection of the surface of smooth water with the hull; generally known as the load waterline, L. W. L. Below this at regular intervals down to the rabbet are similar lines, also known as waterlines. Above, to the planksheer, are similar lines which are more properly air lines, but are still known as waterlines. In shipbuilding as it was carried on more than a century ago, with the straight keel laid level on blocks on the ground, all similar horizontal lines parallel to the keel from rabbet to planksheer were known as level lines, to distinguish them from the true line of flotation L.W.L. and the lines parallel to it. It would be more simple and logical today if all the lines parallel to the L.W.L. both above and below it were known as level lines.

The wave line theory was, in brief, that all the level lines of a vessel from the load waterline down should take the form in the fore body of a curve of versed sines, and in the after body of a trochoid. This theory was based on the study of the waves created by a vessel in moving

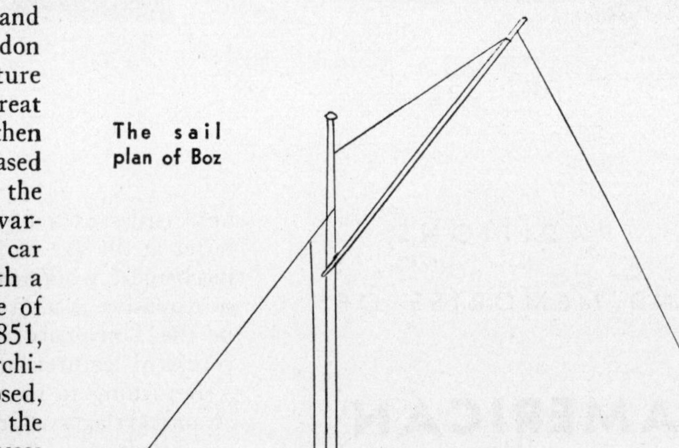

The sail plan of Boz

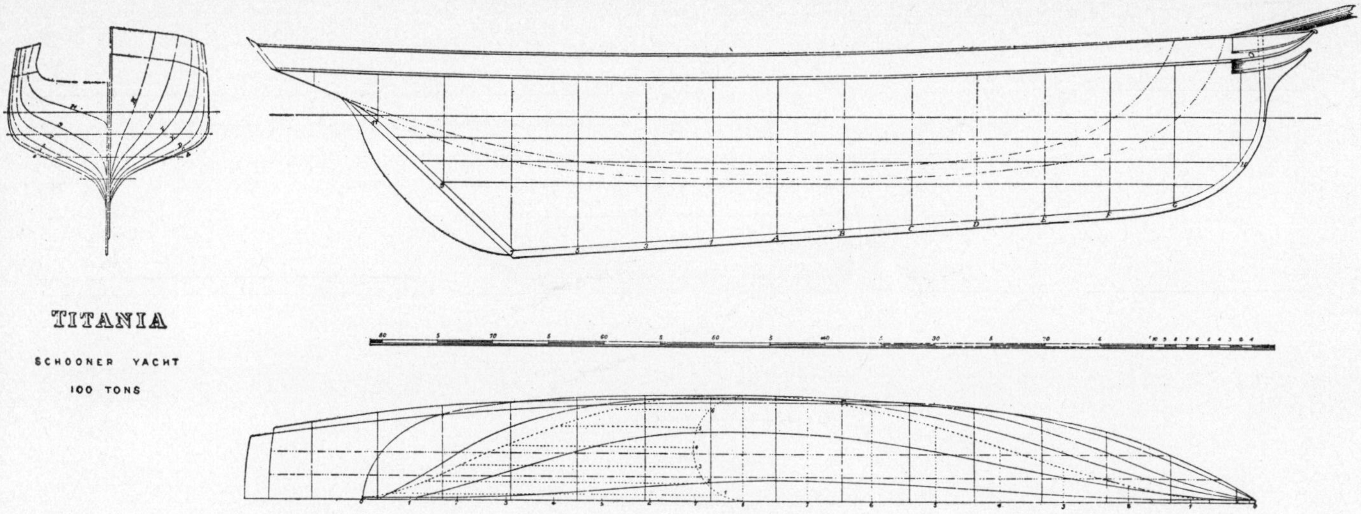

Titania, an iron schooner designed by John Scott Russell on his wave line system, 1851

through the water; the opening creating the "wave of translation," while the gap was filled by the "wave of oscillation." As the result of his studies Mr. Russell determined that the outline of the first wave was a curve of versed sines, and that of the second a trochoid.

In 1864-5 he published The Modern System of Naval Architecture, possibly the largest book ever printed. The volume of text is 21 by 27 inches and 3½ inches thick, weighing over 50 pounds, printed in large type on heavy paper, with a 3-inch margin. It is not only most inconvenient for reference, but when stored in a vertical position on a shelf the weight of the pages tears them from the cover. With this text are two volumes of the same width and height containing 165 large folding plates. One must admire both the physical strength and the courage of men like Colin Archer and John Hyslop who penetrated and mastered this storehouse of naval knowledge. Apart from his own early experiments the only yacht designed by him and on this system was the iron schooner Titania, built for Robert Stephenson in 1851; he was the only British yachtsman who accepted the challenge of Commodore Stevens for a match with America; in which Titania was decisively defeated. A long and useful life terminated at Ventnor, Isle of Wight, on June 8, 1882.

Dissenters from the Theory

As the interest in yacht designing increased the wave line theory was studied by many; among others by Colin Archer, a shipbuilder and naval architect of Laurvig, Norway. His first criticism was that Scott Russell gave too much prominence to the level lines, to the exclusion of all others such as buttock lines and diagonals which he esteemed of much greater importance; as the level lines are really only the framework on which the design is constructed, and in no way represent the course of the water around the hull as do the diagonals and still more the "dividing lines" advocated by Lord Robert Montagu. Mr. Archer inaugurated a series of experiments, first with a model with the Russell level lines, involving an excessively hollow entrance and a deep fore foot; then with entirely different forms, notably, a spindle with convex level lines and no fore foot. As the result of these experiments he reached the conclusion that the true point of the Russell theory was not that the level lines, but the progression and diminution of bulk, should conform to the two governing curves. This new theory was set forth at considerable length in The Field (London) in the issues between September and December 1877. At the 19th meeting of the Institution of Naval Architects on April 13, 1878 he read a paper entitled, On the Wave Principle Applied to the Longitudinal Disposition of Immersed Volume.

John Hyslop

There is a fascination about the science of naval design which has enlisted the interest of many from a purely amateur standpoint; among those who have placed yachting under a heavy debt none is more notable than John Hyslop, a native of Wigan, a small town in Lancashire, where he was born in 1834. At the age of 13 he shipped aboard the barque Mary and spent 20 months at sea. Living in Liverpool and engaged in commercial pursuits in 1858-9 he became acquainted with a set of young men deeply interested in model yacht sailing; all of them being employed in the shipyards of the Mersey. A pond in Parliament Field, a park, afforded a course for their tests, and the long hours of summer twilight in that high

Construction of wave form curve of areas

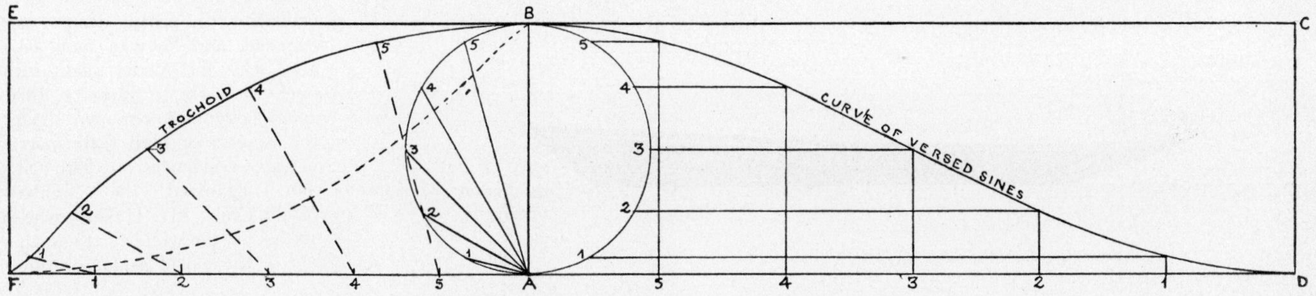

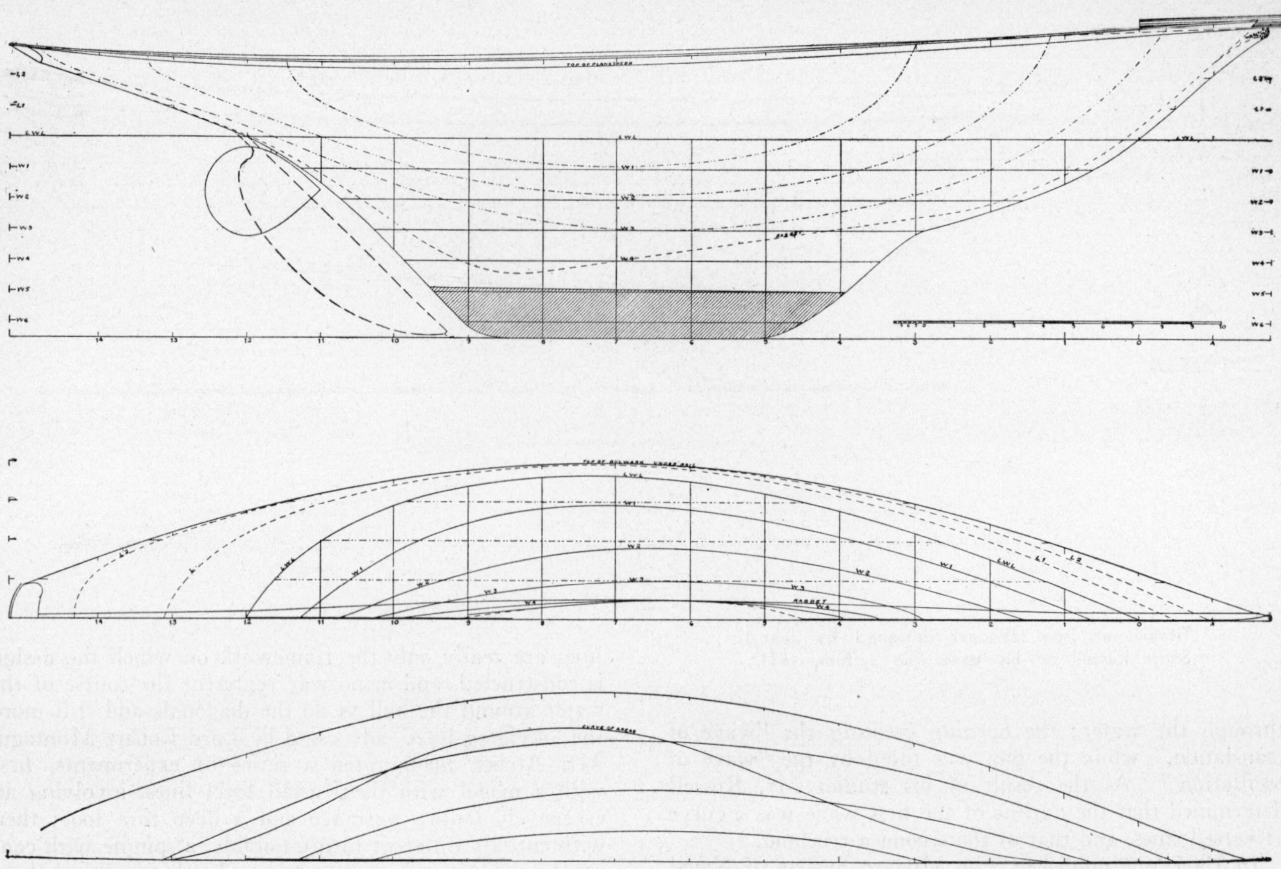

Audax, designed by John Hyslop in 1893. The broken lines show conventional stern-post and rudder which replaced the balanced rudder in 1902. The sail plan below

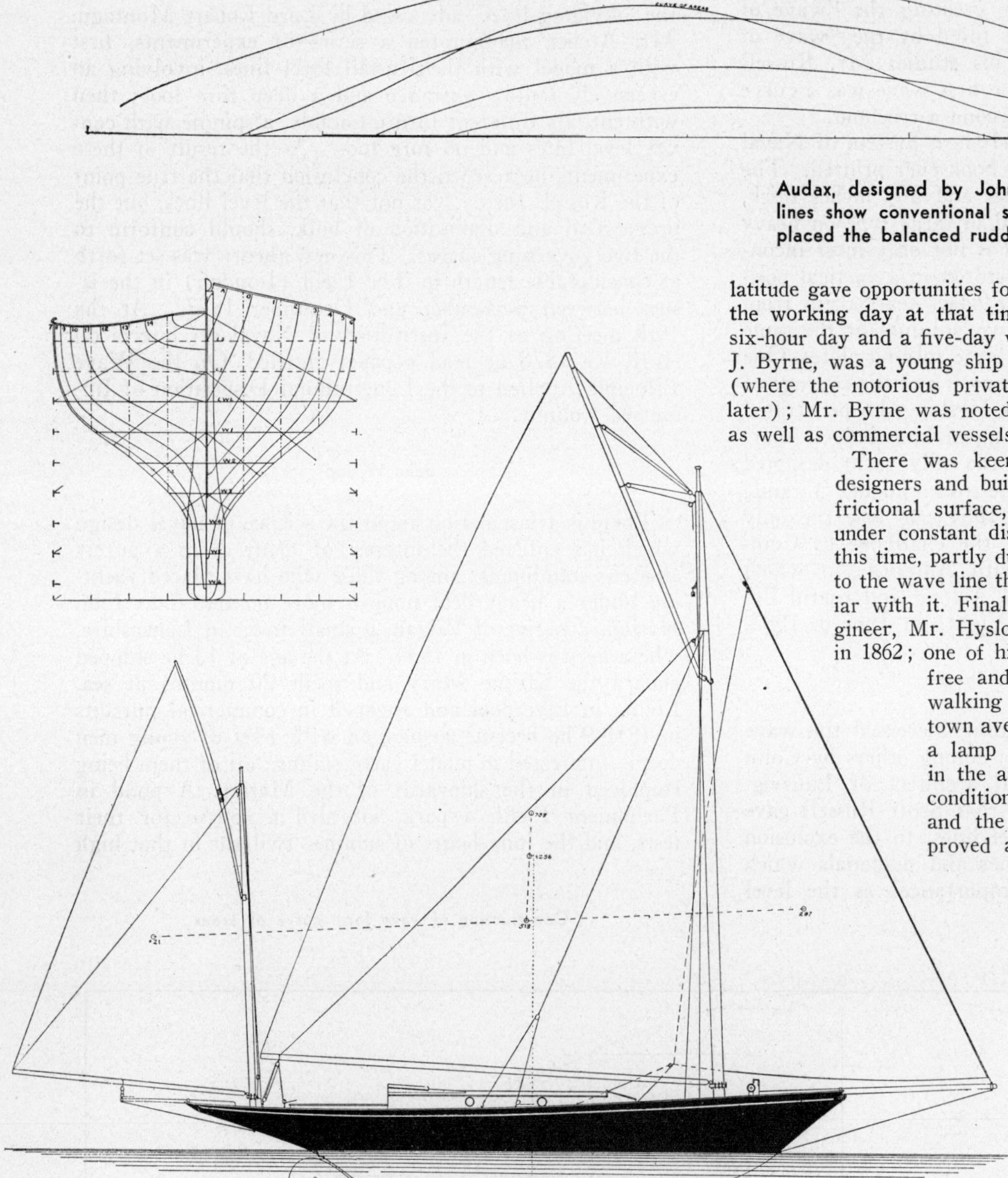

latitude gave opportunities for sailing in spite of the great length of the working day at that time, years before anyone dreamed of a six-hour day and a five-day week. One of his competitors, St. Clare J. Byrne, was a young ship draftsman from the great Laird Yard (where the notorious privateer, Alabama, was built a few years later); Mr. Byrne was noted in later life as the designer of yachts as well as commercial vessels.

There was keen competition between these amateur designers and builders, and such subjects as hull form, frictional surface, and material and cut of sails, were under constant discussion. Much publicity was given at this time, partly due to the building of the Great Eastern, to the wave line theory, and these young men were familiar with it. Finally settling in life as a ventilating engineer, Mr. Hyslop came to New York with his family in 1862; one of his early experiences in this land of the free and the home of the brave being, while walking with his little son on one of the uptown avenues, the sight of a negro hanging from a lamp post, dead with a fire under his feet, in the anti-draft riots of 1863. The term "air-conditioning" was then a half century distant, and the task of building up a new business proved a difficult one, by way of introducing himself and his work he installed ventilating systems in the Stock Exchange, several churches and other buildings without charge. In spite of this, the interest in the problems of naval design never lessened, and he was soon associated with the model yacht sailers of New York. In January, 1870, a small body of yachtsmen living in the vicinity of Hell Gate met at a private residence on 98th Street and organized the Manhattan Yacht Club; Mr. Hyslop, who had settled in the vicinity, then almost out of the world as far as the city proper was concerned, joined the Club on May 31 and continued a member for many years; in the fall he was elected secretary. The yachts owned in the Club were small sandbag boats, and some of the members were also interested in model sailing. His first venture was an open ship's boat, 17 feet long, with a centerboard on one side of the keel (presumably a conversion) and a sloop rig, which he named May Bird. She was bought on lower South Street, and on a cold day in March he started to sail up the East River, his home then being on 105th Street. The boat leaked and his one companion started to bail, but as he found the plug in the way of the bailer he pulled it out; in spite of this they finally reached a boathouse on a creek at 106th Street which ran through marshes back as far as Second Avenue. The keeper of the boathouse, one Sandy Gibson, lived on Mill Rock, in Hell Gate. In 1870, as mentioned later, he built a boat from his own design.

The Wave Form Theory

In January, 1878, a series of five lectures was delivered before the Seawanhaka Corinthian Y. C. by A. Cary Smith, on the subject of yacht designing. Mr. Hyslop attended these lectures, joining the Club on March 5 of the same year. At one he met William M. Tileson, editor of *The Country,* a weekly devoted to all forms of outdoor sport (as I remember, he met his death a few years later through the fall of a wall in Madison Square Garden where he was attending a dog show). On mentioning to Mr. Tileson his views on Scott Russell's work he was informed that a series of articles on the subject had been published in *The Field* only a short time previously. Sending for the copies of *The Field,* he found the name of the author, Colin Archer, and opened what proved to be quite a lengthy correspondence with him. A comparison of their views proved them to be in complete agreement on all essential points, differing only on some of the immaterial details of the practical application of what has since been known as the wave form theory.

Both of these men, be it noted, were sincere and ardent admirers of Scott Russell, both gave him full credit for the discoveries which he had made as to the nature of waves; but both criticized the wave line system as not capable of practical application in the designing of a vessel. In the paper read before the Institution of Naval Architecture in London, previously mentioned, Mr. Archer comments: "There probably does not, up to the present time, exist a more complete and elaborate exposition of the wonders of wave phenomena, at the time of its publication comparatively little understood, than we find in Mr. Russell's work. Nevertheless, it must be confessed that the working system of naval construction deduced from these phenomena, and elaborated with great ingenuity and skill in the most minute detail, has not succeeded in gaining the confidence of the practical shipbuilder. The eminent author seems not to have succeeded in devising the best means for transferring the wave properties to his solid structure." As to the practical application, Mr. Archer criticizes the method of operation, by waterlines, noting that waterlines only in one way approximate the course of water around a hull; as do, in a great measure the diagonals and dividing lines. The method is hampered by a rigid adherence to a mechanical set of lines; and, further, that pure wave lines cannot possibly be employed in many types of vessels, particularly those of great carrying capacity.

In a similar strain, Mr. Hyslop writes: "It is impossible for anyone to have given attention to the writings of J. Scott Russell without being impressed with a feeling of respect for this earnest labor and study, and for the reasoning with which he supports the theory, and his claims to have discovered the form of least resistance. Mr. Russell claims for his principle that it is not arbitrary—that it is eminently practicable; but the reverse of this seems to be the fact, for when he proceeds to carry the theory out, and to furnish examples, we find him adopting 'compromised,' 'corrected,' 'reconciled' and 'modified' lines." Mr. Hyslop was so fascinated by Scott Russell's work at one time that he enlarged the design of Titania in Marett's book and made a model of the yacht. Like much of my own work, it never was finished, today, after sixty years in overheated houses, but little is left. It was intended to be a whole, not half model, the block was glued up with half inch lifts of alternate white pine and black walnut, and hollowed to a thickness of barely ⅛ inch; the frames ⅛ inch square were sawn from oak, made up with beams and floors, but never fitted in the hull.

Model Experiments

The experiments of both Archer and Hyslop were carried out in the same manner, models of varying form were towed against a standard model of pure wave form. The only "yachts" available for study by Mr. Hyslop more than seventy years ago were the sandbaggers described in MoToR BoatinG of September and October, 1939; their lines were taken off, the immersed area of every section measured, and plotted as an ordinate of a curve of displacement; where this curve did not agree with the theoretic curve, the difference was noted. Other measurements such as the angle of entrance and the rise of floor were taken, but proved to be useless as a basis of comparison, so a series of model tests of the wave line and wave form were taken up. The guide was a little book, Ships and Boats, by William Bland, an Englishman; published early in the sixties in Weale's Elementary Series, a very extensive library of technical handbooks published at a low price, this particular book selling for a shilling and sixpence. The method described involved the use of a balance rod with a model attached to each end, the rod towed by a line so attached as to be readily shifted. The first model was strictly in accordance with Scott Russell, all level lines were of wave form; this being the unit by which all the others were tested. The models (I still have ten of them) were about 10 inches long, with three holes bored in the top of each

Tern, designed by John Hyslop in 1901

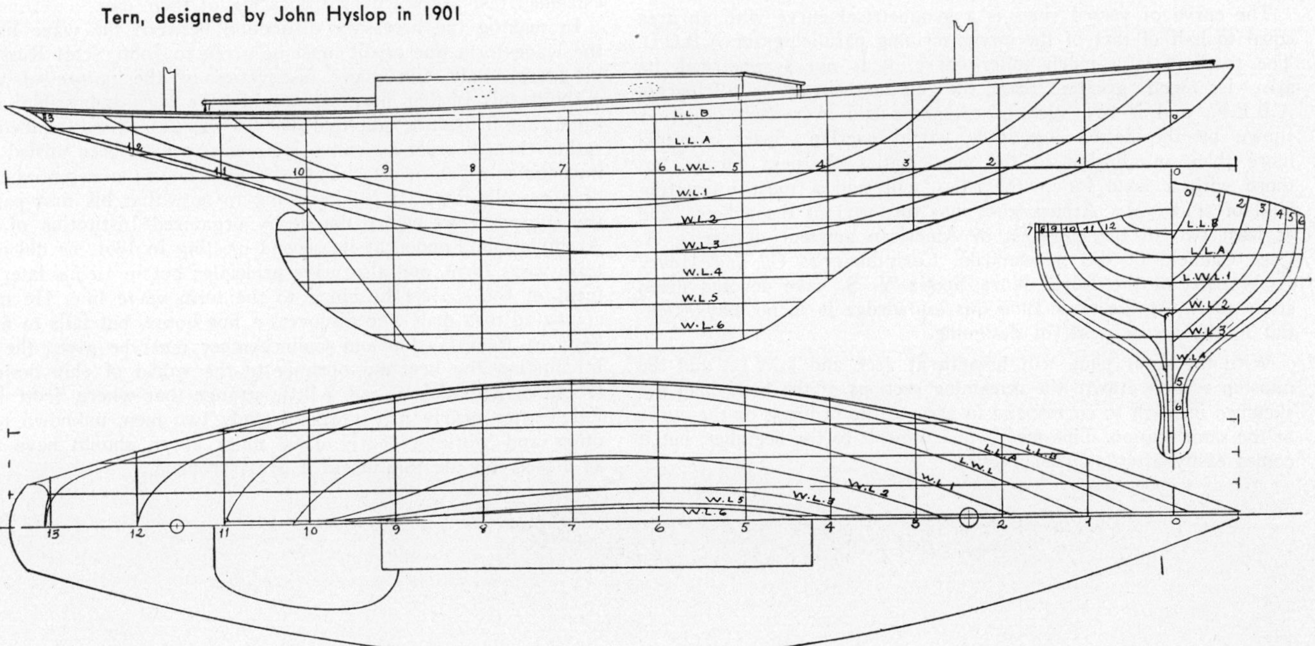

for shot by which they were ballasted and trimmed, after which the holes were stopped by cork. At that time, before the rocks in Hell Gate were blown up by Gen. Newton, there were patches of slack water where it was possible to row a boat with a balance beam and models astern.

The other models were more or less of spindle form, with rounded instead of rectangular sections and rockered keel, with no draft at bow and stern; their L.W.L. and level lines were convex, as in modern yachts, and bore no resemblance to the curve of versed sines or the trochoid. As the result of many expriments there came the important discovery that in the models showing least resistance, as measured by the relative lengths of the two portions of the balance rod, the areas of the cross sections were in direct proportion to the ordinates of the Scott Russell curves. This opened a new field of experiment, the lines of larger yachts were taken off, the areas of cross sections measured, and plotted as ordinates. It was soon evident that those vessels which were generally recognized as the fastest conformed most closely to the standard curve. In his articles in *The Country,* Mr. Hyslop gives the curve of areas of a dozen yachts, both English and American, varying from America and Sappho down to the sandbagger Pluck and Luck; following this he lays down a complete method of designing by this system of the wave form. His work met with immediate recognition; the new system was adopted by A. Cary Smith, mention was made last month of the quotations from *The Country* and the diagram of the curve of areas in the notebook of Edward Burgess; and, as expounded by Colin Archer, John Hyslop and by Dixon Kemp in his several books on designing, the system came into general use on both sides of the Atlantic.

Its Practical Application

THE first step is the laying off a baseline equal to the L.W.L.; it may be noted here that a small part of the fore end of the curve is cut off to allow for the fact that the stem is not actually a knife edge. One great service that Scott Russell did was to demonstrate that the entrance should be about 60 per cent of the total length, instead of nearly the reverse in the bluff-bowed hookers of old; and in accordance with this a perpendicular is erected at the point of the midship section, usually about 55 per cent from the stem. On this line is described a circle whose diameter is the area selected for the midship section; and each half of this circle is divided into six equal parts. For the curve of versed sines of the fore body lines parallel to the base line are now drawn, each to intersect the vertical through its corresponding station, giving a series of points through which a perfectly fair curve may be drawn. For the trochoid of the after body are drawn from Station 1 a line parallel to A-1, from Station 2 a line parallel to A-2, etc.

The curve of versed sines is a symmetrical curve with an area equal to half of that of the circumscribing parallelogram A.B.C.D. The trochoid is a much fuller curve, it is not symmetrical, its area is much greater than the circumscribing parallelogram A.B.E.F., and if two such curves were laid over each other, as shown by the dotted line, they would overlap. Space prevents more than an allusion to the mathematics of these curves, but those with a taste for mathematics will find a most interesting field of study. Mr. Archer goes into this part of the subject, and at least two of the cleverest of American amateur designers, A. Cass Canfield of the Seawanhaka Corinthian Y. C., and Henry C. McLeod of the Royal Nova Scotia Y. S. have devoted much study to it. At the same time this knowledge is in no way essential in the actual work of designing.

With the sheer plan, half breadth at deck and L.W.L., and the midship section drawn, the remaining sections of the body plan are sketched in, each to correspond in area to the ordinate of the curve at the same station. This may sound difficult to the beginner, but it comes easily after a little practice.

The Result

THE best proof of the merits of John Hyslop's theory is to be found in the many yachts which he designed, as an amateur, for his friends and himself. His first effort at designing other than a sailing model was the little Boz, built in 1870 by himself and a friend; a sandbag sloop (in spring and fall she was sailed as a cat), 18 feet l.o.a.; 7 feet 9 inches breadth and 1 foot draft. She sailed in the races of the Manhattan Y. C. about the turbulent waters of Hell Gate, on one occasion capsizing. In her pleasure sailing, apart from racing, the sandbags were handled by the Hyslop children. Her longest cruise was to Oyster Bay, in the course of which she met one of the conventional Nor'easters of Long Island Sound. After her second season she was altered, her sail plan increased, and she evidently raced under a new name, Zephyr. In the fall of 1875 he designed for himself the cutter Petrel, 32 feet l.o.a.; 28 feet l.w.l.; 8 feet breadth and 5 feet draft. With a displacement of 7½ tons, she carried 2,526 pounds of lead inside and 5,474 in an outside keel; her sail area being 800 square feet. She ante-dated by a short time the advent of the "cutter-craze" which for ten years divided the yachtsmen of New York into two bitterly hostile camps. She was built by W. T. Johnson at Elm Park, Staten Island, on the Kill van Kull. The news of the then novel craft brought many to inspect her, among others Captain Philip Elsworth, who told her builder to advise the owner not to put lead on her keel, as it would make her logy; a somewhat indefinite term which later figured largely in the sloop-cutter controversy. She carried a hollow mast, but this may have been fitted at a later date.

In 1882 he designed for a friend, Henry W. Eaton, the yawl Audax, 42 feet l.o.a.; 30 feet l.w.l.; 10 feet 4 inches breadth and 6 feet 6 inches draft. Following the fashion of the day, she carried what the late C. P. Clayton once characterized as the "nasty rudder," then recently introduced by the Herreshoffs. This was later replaced by the conventional stern-post and rudder. Though designed primarily for cruising on Long Island Sound, she was very successful in a class of similar yawls which raced for some seasons and made good sport. For his own use in 1901 he designed the yawl Tern, of similar type but a little larger; 48 feet l.o.a.; 33 feet 8 inches l.w.l.; 10 feet 5 inches breadth and 6 feet 6 inches draft. Aboard her he sailed for 18 years, handling her with one paid hand in both cruising and racing, and disposing of her only in his 85th year. He was elected measurer of the Seawanhaka Corinthian Y. C. in 1883, New York Y. C. in 1886, and Larchmont Y. C. in 1890; in many years of service in these three clubs, as well as in several others, he probably measured more yachts than any other holding a similar position.

Petrel, 1875, Audax, 1893, and Tern, 1901, were all designed strictly in accord with the wave form theory; in judging them in this year of Grace 1940, they must be compared with the average yachts of their day, and not with the modern creations of elaborate tank tests. While designed primarily for cruising, the three were esteemed fast as shown by the racing of their day.

In making the necessary distinction between the wave line and the wave form due credit must be given to John Scott Russell for his deep study and many discoveries of the nature of waves; without this further progress would have been impossible. At the same time it must be admitted that his work alone was of theoretical rather than of practical value. He seems to have been misled by the importance which he attached to the wave line as an essential element of a vessel's form. It is interesting to note that his first paper on the subject, read before the newly organized Institution of Naval Architects in London at its second meeting in 1861, he did use the term wave form, and also wave principle; but in all his later treatment of the subject he clung to the term wave line. He may be compared to a man who discovers a fine house, but fails to find the key; to John Hyslop and Colin Archer must be given the credit for finding the key and opening to the world of ship design the treasures within. It is not a little strange that where Scott Russell failed after nearly fifty years of study two men, unknown to each other and working nearly 3,000 miles apart, should have agreed so closely on the solution of a great problem.

TRADITIONS AND MEMORIES OF

Part Nineteen

American Yachting

TONNAGE

By WILLIAM P. STEPHENS

TONNAGE—that *bete noir* of naval architecture; of doubtful parentage and nurtured on conservatism and conventionality. For at least six centuries it exerted the most powerful and most evil influence over every detail of shipping:—modelling, construction, cost and operation. As a measure of both external and internal capacity it acted against the interests of the United States in the days of the cotton trade when British ships were built of iron, with only cargo battens inside of thin plates and frames, as compared with the bulky outside planking, deep wood frames and thick ceiling of American ships. Its varying formulae, but all with a heavy tax on breadth, compelled the building of excessively narrow and consequently deep ships and yachts, and impeded the progress of naval design for centuries. In seeking to trace its origin and development one is impressed by the fact that the lexicographers and encyclopedists seem to have evaded an obscure and difficult subject.

In the most remote times and countries, prior to all authentic history, the ship seems to have appealed to the governing powers as most admirably adapted for purposes of taxation; in both China and India some form of hull measurement was thus used. One early standard in England was the tun, a barrel in which wine was stored and shipped. It contained "not less than 252 gallons"; the number of tuns carried giving the "tunnage." The bulk of this tun was 40.32 cubic feet, or about 42 cubic feet for the barrel; the weight was about 12 per cent over 2,240 pounds. As units of tonnage in later days we find "freight tonnage," sometimes used as a measure of capacity, with a weight of 40 cubic feet allowed to the ton of 2240 pounds.

Tons and Tuns

The word was originally spelled in two ways, and with a great variety of meanings, ton and tun. The ton seems to have been originally a measure of weight, but later of space or bulk, and still later of the cost of construction; also a controlling factor in scantling and equipment, and the basis of numerous taxes in the forms of port charges, light dues and pilotage. The tun, as already mentioned, was a wooden container for spirituous liquors; a huge circular tank for mash or brew, and a barrel for storage and shipment.

Tonnage measurements and calculations for a vessel of 1700. From the Shipbuilder's Assistant

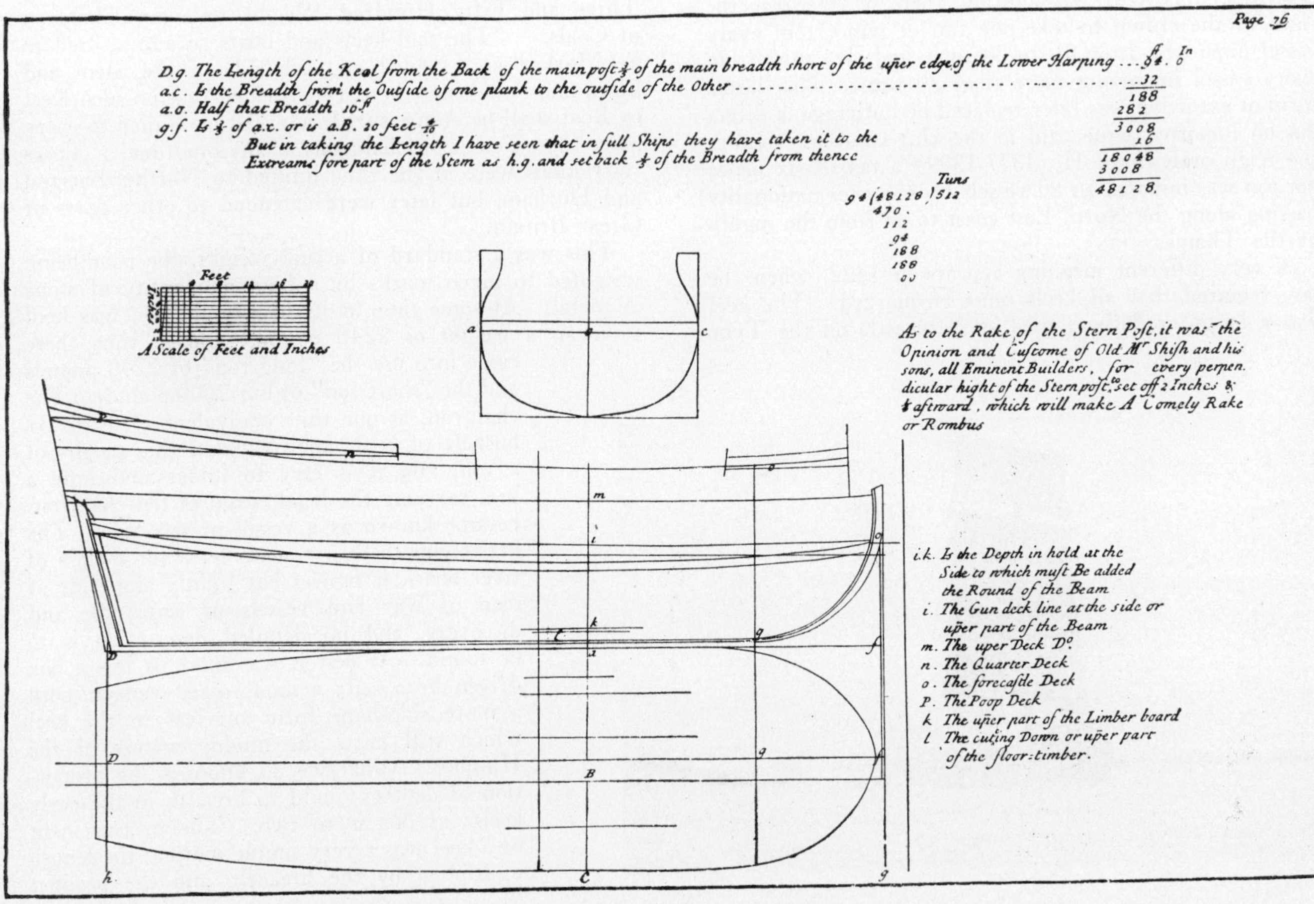

PLATE A.

Construction Draught of a Yacht of Thirty-six Tons Measurement by Old Rule for Tonnage.

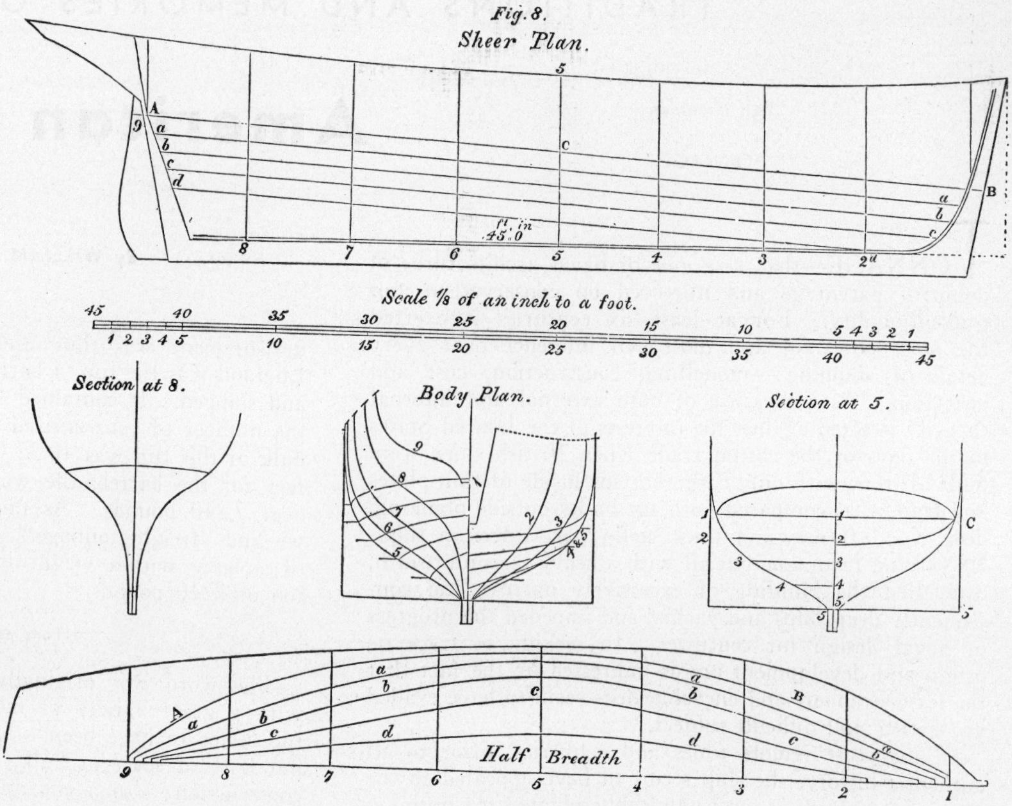

PRINCIPAL DIMENSIONS.

	Ft.	in.
Length for Tonnage	45	0
Keel for Tonnage	36	$10\frac{3}{4}$
Breadth for Tonnage	13	6
Burthen in Tons	35	$0\frac{72}{94}$

A B.—Load Water Line.

aa, bb, cc, dd } Lines parallel to A B at the distance of ·92 foot apart.

DRAUGHT OF WATER.

	Ft.	in.
Afore	4	6
Abaft	7	6

Above: Tonnage measurements of a yacht of about 1830. Below: A Keel, a type still in use on the river Humber. Square sail, square topsail and leeboards. From etching by G. F. Holmes

As a starting point in history we find as early as 1302, under Edward I, mention of tonnage and poundage; the former being a direct duty of two shillings per tun on all wines imported, the latter being a subsidy of three pence per pound exacted by the crown on all goods exported or imported. In addition, there was prisage, the right of the crown to take one tun of wine from every vessel importing from 10 to 20 tuns, and two tuns from every vessel importing more than 20 tuns. This latter form of extortion was later replaced by butlerage, a direct tax on imported wine paid to the king's butler. Under the reign of Richard II (1377-1399) a tax of six pence per ton was imposed on all vessels of whatever nationality passing along the North East coast to or from the mouth of the Thames.

A very different meaning appears in 1422, when the law required that all keels must be marked. The keel was a barge or flatboat used at Newcastle on the Tyne to carry coal from the shore to ships in the offing. Coming further down the years, in the reign of William and Mary, 1694, the law reads: "Such Admeasurement shall be by Dead Weight of Lead or Iron, or otherwise as shall seem meet to the said Commissioners, allowing Three and Fifty Hundred Weight to every Chaldron of Coals." "The said keels and boats so admeasured to be Marked and Nailed on each side of the Stem and Stern and Amidships thereof—provided that no such Keel or Boat shall be Admeasured, Marked or Nailed to carry more than Ten such Chaldrons at any one time." These restrictions were at the time limited to Northumberland and Durham, but later were extended to other ports of Great Britain.

This was a standard of actual weight, the boat being weighted to given marks by a known quantity of stone or metal. At some time in its history the ton was held to mean a weight of 2240 pounds, and in time there came into use the "long ton" of 2240 pounds and the "short ton" of but 2000 pounds. The chaldron, at one time equivalent to 36 to 37 bushels of coal, approximated the weight of a ton, and it is easy to understand how a keel carrying the legal cargo of ten chaldrons became known as a vessel of ten tons. The keel seems to be a generic term for a class of river boats, it figures but lightly alongside of men of war and vessels of commerce and discovery, and no detailed description is to be found. At best it was more or less a box driven by a sail; a modernized version with a more shipshape form survives in the keel which still parts the muddy waters of the Humber. What we do know is the proportion of depth of hold to breadth in the early keels; as one is to two. The measurement of a keel was a very simple matter; the length multiplied by the breadth, and the product

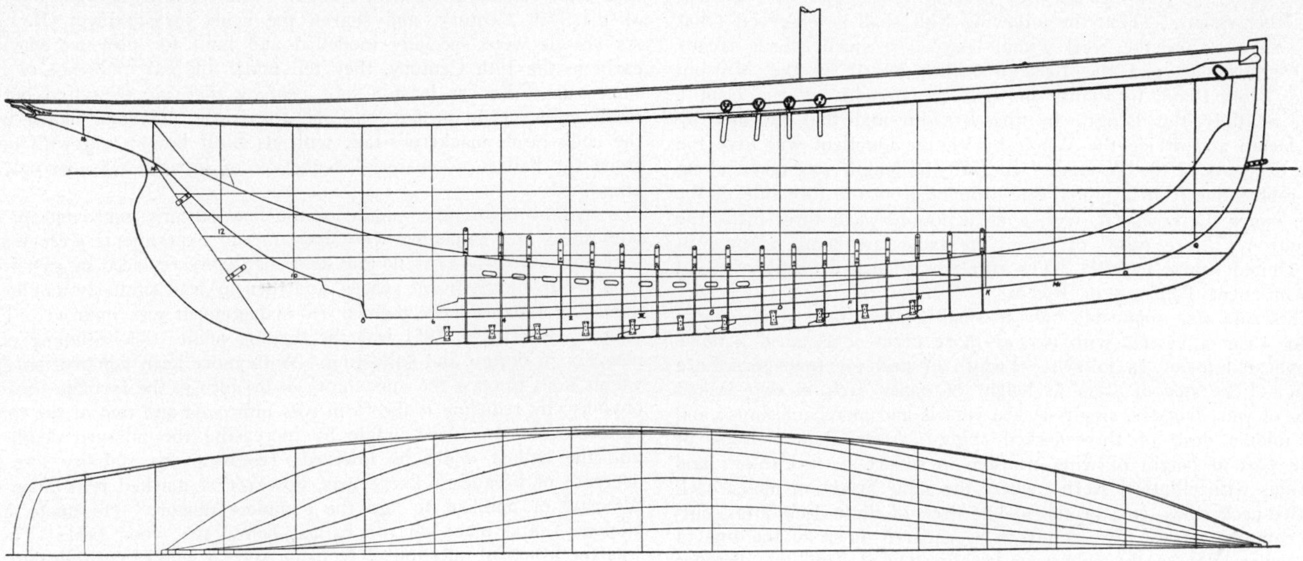

Kriemhilda, cutter designed and built by Michael Ratsey, Cowes, 1872. Tons, Thames Measurement, 104 80/94. L.O.A., 90 feet; L.W.L., 78 feet 4 inches; Breadth, 17 feet 6 inches; Draft, 12 feet

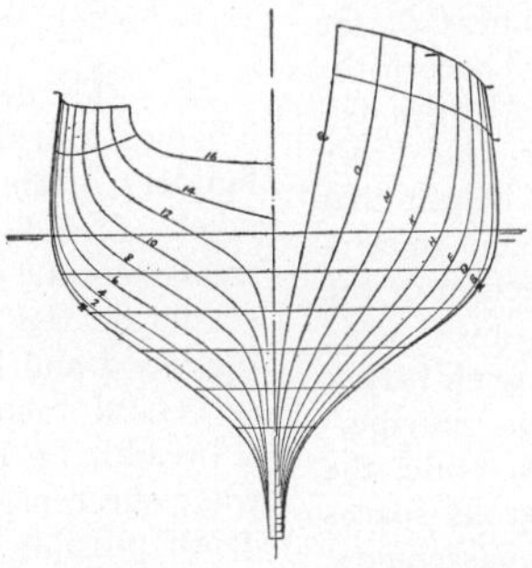

by the depth; as in the case of a box; the problem came in the case of a loaded keel, as it was not possible to measure the depth. The solution of this problem was an easy one, as in all cases the depth was just half of the breadth the formula became $L \times B \times \frac{B}{2}$. In the same year, 1694, an Act of Parliament was passed by which duties were levied on both coasting and sea-going ships, the formula being $\frac{L \times B \times D}{94}$; this law was repealed in 1696 as far as duties were concerned; but a new law was passed calling for the registry of all vessels. In the reign of Queen Elizabeth (1558-1603), a proud era in British naval history, it was found necessary to supplement the Navy proper with merchant ships chartered under a system of "Deadweight of Ton and Tonnage." The tonnage rule then used by the Royal Navy was $\frac{L \times B \times D}{100}$ the "Tons Burthen" thus obtained were increased by 25 to 33 per cent to give the "Deadweight of Ton and Tonnage" by which the ship owner was paid.

The Genesis of the Tonnage Rule

In that interesting work, The Shipbuilder's Assistant, by William Sutherland, first edition, 1711, much space is devoted to the subject of "tunnage"; what is called "The Shipwrights Hall Rule" being given; before quoting this in full it will be worth while to lay to for a moment to quote a comment of the author on the social standing of the shipwright at the time. "Besides, the proper Business of a Shipwright is counted a very vulgar Imploy, and which a Man of very indifferent Qualifications may be master of. Many have as mean an Opinion of it as a certain Gentleman who told one of our former Master Builders that he had a Blockhead of a Son, uncapable to attain any other Trade unless that of a "Ship-carpenter, for which he designed him."

The writer prefaces the Rule by the following comments: "The Measure of a Ship may be considered in three several Ways. First, What the Cavity will hold? Secondly, What superficial or solid Inches are contained in her? Thirdly, What will she bear or carry safely from one Port to another without damnifying the Goods so transported? And which of these three may most properly be taken to adjust the Tonnage of a ship was never yet determined? But, in my Opinion, the last ought principally to be considered in measuring either Ship, Bark or Boat."

"Shipwright's Hall Rule.* Take the Length of the Keel measured from the Back of the Main Post to the fore-side of the Stem at the upper Edge of the lower Harping, by a Perpendicular made from thence to the upper or lower Edge of the Keel, only three fifths of the main Breadth from the outside of the Plank of one side to the outside of the Plank of the other Side at the broadest Place of the Ship, being set backward or aftward from the Right Angle made by such a Perpendicular and the Base. Observing also that as several Ships and Vessels have no false Post, in such a case there ought to be allowed one third of the Main Post from the after part of such a Stern-Post. Then, to take the extreme Breadth, as aforesaid, and in case the Ship heels much to use a large Square and a long straight Staff that will reach from one side of the Ship to the other, taking the Perpendiculars and parallels very exactly. The half Breadth is made use of instead of the Depth in the Hold, which was formerly used; but then the Ships Depth in Hold and Half Breadth were nearly equal; and now it is general to take the largest. But, not to enter upon Disputes, the Length as aforesaid is multiplied by the Breadth, and again by half that Breadth, and the Sum being divided by 94, the Quotient is the Tunnage of the Ship; for either sharp or full Ships, Merchant-Men or Men of War." It will be noticed that in his discussions the author used the spelling "tun," and applies it to both weight and bulk.

The smuggling of wines and brandies from France, Spain and Portugal was a very active industry in the early years of the 18th Century; much of this illicit trade was carried on in the smaller classes of vessels, which were relatively much faster and much more easily maneuverable than the larger revenue cutters which chased them. To meet this condition in 1720, sixth year

*See diagram on first page of article.

of George I, it was enacted "for preventing disputes over brandy and other spirits," "That the following Rule shall be observed (that is to say): Take the Keel within board (so much as she trends on the ground) and the Breadth within Board by the Midship Beam, from Plank to Plank, and half the Breadth for the Depth; then multiply the Length by the Breadth and that product by the Depth and divide the Whole by 94, the Quotient will give the true Contents of the Tonnage." In 1773 the length was taken along the rabbet line from a plumb line dropped from the fore side of the stem under the bowsprit, with a deduction forward three-fifths the breadth for "fore rake" of stem; the same law being adopted in the United States in 1792. The rule was known as Builder's Old Measurement Tonnage, or B.O.M.

This rule was applicable only to small craft with a single deck; in the case of vessels with two or more decks it assumed a more complicated form; as follows. Length of keel for tonnage. Fore point:—Fore side of stem at height of upper deck in two-decked ships of war, frigates, single-decked vessels and merchant ships; and the middle deck of three-decked ships. After Point:—Back of main post at height of wing transom in square-sterned ships; and in ships with elliptical sterns, where the same height of upper deck of two-deck ships, etc., or the middle deck of three-deck ships, cuts the counter. These two points to be squared down to the line of the lower edge of the rabbet of keel prolonged; and the distance between these two intersections to be the "length between perpendiculars for tonnage." Breadth:—The extreme breadth of the ship at the height of the wales; less the excess in thickness of the wales over the bottom plank. Stem and fore rake:—Three-fifths of the breadth for tonnage shall be deducted from the "length between perpendiculars for tonnage" to compensate for the "fore rake" of stem. Rake of stern post:—For every foot of height that the upper side of the wing transom at the middle line in square-sterned ships; or in ships with elliptical sterns, the intersection of the counter-line with the back of the main post, is above the lower edge of the rabbet of keel, a deduction of 2½ inches per foot of such height shall be made from the "length between perpendiculars for tonnage." With the "gross tonnage" thus calculated by the B.O.M. Rule, the "net tonnage" was obtained by the deduction of the numerous spaces not available for cargo; the quarters for officers, crew, passengers, ship's stores, sails, cables and many other details of equipment. With the introduction of steam in navigation an allowance for machinery and space and bunkers became necessary, and this was made in 1819.

The Fight for Reform

BUILDER'S Old Measurement spoke for itself in the narrow and deep vessels produced by it; in many cases unseaworthy, and at best deficient in most desirable qualities. At the same time the methods involved were open to criticism from a practical standpoint. It was not until 1821, however, that a movement for its abolition was inaugurated; the British Admiralty being requested to appoint a commission of inquiry. This body favored as a basis the dead weight which a vessel could carry, but decided that a measure of internal capacity was more practicable; however, nothing came of the movement. In 1833 a similar commission was appointed, which recommended internal capacity, to include all parts of a vessel available for cargo. Again the movement failed and the subject rested until 1849, when a third commission recommended an external measurement of the hull, with many deductions. It was not until 1854 that a "New Measurement" law was actually placed on the books; the gross tonnage including the entire internal capacity of the hull, with provision for its accurate measurement, and a comprehensive system of deductions for all space not available for cargo. The divisor in this rule, 100, established a unit of 100 cubic feet of cargo space as a ton. A similar rule was adopted by the United States in 1864, and the tonnage rules of all nations today embody the same principles. The building of the Suez, Panama and other canals, on which certain charges are necessary, has resulted in various forms of special rules.

Tonnage Rules in Yachting

THE preceding is a mere brief outline of a subject so vast that even the many pages of this publication would not suffice to print in full the present tonnage laws of Great Britain and the United States, to say nothing of other nations and the volumes of discussion in many languages. As the subject in which we are directly interested is yachting, all that is necessary is to show the relations between the vessels of war and commerce and those of the pleasure navy. As a matter of course, the early yachts of Holland and England were closely allied to the naval, commercial and fishing vessels of the 17th Century, and shared the same measurement, B.O.M. As vessels were specially modelled and built for pleasure service, early in the 19th Century, they fell under the evil influence of the same rule. For at least a half century the rule exercised but a small influence on proportions and form; the universal model was the cod's-head, mackerel's-tail, with its bluff bows; and with only stone for ballast no material reduction of breadth was desired or attempted.

Sometime before the middle of the last century improvements in both form and ballasting were introduced; experiments were made with the hollow bow, stone and kentledge were replaced by cast iron moulded to fit the frame spaces, and then by lead similarly moulded; as racing became more popular its management was improved. The visit of America in 1851 was the turning point; the beginning of a new era in design and ballasting. With more keen competition and yachts built to class the importance of breadth in the formula became obvious; by reducing it the form was improved and two of the three factors were decreased, while by increasing the untaxed depth of hull the ballast might be lowered; restoring the stability lost by decrease of breadth. There was, however, a marked reluctance on the part of builders to "go the complete unicorn" (to quote Mr. Bouncer) and place all the ballast below the wood keel. There was the practical question of securing such a weight entirely outside the wood structure, and also of the strains on the hull by this outside weight.

The Growth of the Lead Keel

IN designing and building the cutter Kriemhilda, 106 Tons, Thames measurement, in 1872, Michael Ratsey, one of the leading builders of the day, dared to go no further than to place a small layer of lead beneath the narrow keel; and this was cast in five small pieces. By way of fastenings, in addition to through-bolts set up on top of the iron floors, there were dovetail plates let into the wood and lead and well through-bolted. Kriemhilda was a very successful racing yacht; with a waterline of 78 feet 6 inches and a breadth of 17 feet 6 inches making her 4½ beams, as the term was; she represents the extreme of minimum breadth and maximum depth possible with practically all inside ballast. It has been told in MoToR BoatinG for July how John Harvey, skillful and progressive as he was, in building Sea Belle as late as 1874, ventured to place less than seven tons, a tenth of the total ballast, outside the wood keel, adopting a costly and complicated system of angle iron floors and stringers cast inside of lead floor knees and stringers as the lowest possible inside ballast. In designing Jullanar in 1875 Mr. Bentall, progressive and unconventional as he was, dared to place only six tons of her total 80 tons of lead in the keel. Florinda, yawl, built by Nicholson in 1873, had originally but 3½ tons out of a total of 52 tons on her keel. As more and more weight was placed outside by her competitors an effort was made to modernize her; her wood keel was very narrow, but a lead keel of double its width was cast and bolted beneath it. Slabs of lead, in depth from the top of this lead to the garboards, were cast, one on each side, and through-bolted.

The transfer of lead from above to below the keel progressed much more rapidly in the small than in the large classes; with proportionate decrease of breadth and increase of draft; in MoToR BoatinG for July it is told how J. Beavor-Webb, in designing the 20-ton Freda in 1880, placed all of her ballast in the lead keel. From this time on all British designers were in hot competition to cut down breadth and to increase draft, displacement, and the ratio of ballast to displacement. The extreme was reached in the small classes of 3 and 5 tons, with a ratio of length to breadth of 7 to 1; and a ratio of lead keel to total displacement of nearly 70 percent. Among the most successful of the large yachts of this era were May, of 5 beams, and Genesta, of 5.4 beams; both with practically all lead on the keel. In 1854 the Royal London Y. C. abandoned the length on keel and substituted length on deck from stem to sternpost; as this placed a heavy penalty on yachts with extreme rake of sternpost, the full breadth, in place of three-fifths breadth, was deducted from the new length. This rule, known from that time as the Thames Rule, was adopted by the Yacht Racing Association in 1875.

The Bubble Bursts

THOUGH growing steadily year by year, the agitation against the rule which produced such extremes had no effect for a long time on the ruling power, the Yacht Racing Association; the defeat of Genesta by the American Puritan in 1885, followed by the defeat of the still narrower Galatea in 1886, made a bad breach in the defense; but it was the tragic loss of the five-tonner Oona in the latter year which capped the climax, and in the winter of 1886-7 the Y.R.A. adopted a different type of rule based on length and sail area, the two factors previously introduced in America.

In 1881 a weak and ineffectual attempt had been made to improve the Thames Rule by what was known as the "1730 Rule," in effect in 1882. Length and breadth were added together and the sum squared, this product was multiplied by the breadth, and the final product divided by an arbitrary figure, 1730. The result, in nominal tons, was not widely different from the Thames Rule. The discussions and arguments attending the adoption of this change are most voluminous in volume and would be of no interest today; the essential fact is that the tendency to narrower and deeper yachts was in no way checked.

With that fine old crusted conservatism for which the British are noted, that antique fetish, B.O.M. is still worshipped even today in the form of the "Thames Rule." In the numerous accounts of cruises in small yachts in the English yachting magazines, and in the equally numerous and very interesting designs of "tabloid" cruisers, one reads regularly of yachts of 3, 5, 7 and 10 tons. Just what size of yacht is thus designated is difficult for an American to conceive, as such a unit gives no idea of the length over all, length on waterline, breadth, draft, sail area or displacement. The only explanation is that if one reads, for instance, of a yacht of seven tons he may recall a yacht of the same tonnage with which he is familiar; but with no certainty that the two are alike in any detail.

The same custom is still followed in the British edition of Lloyd's Yacht Register, the Thames Tonnage, with its length and breadth, being given for both small and large yachts, in addition to the modern Registered Tonnage.

Part Twenty

Measurement and Classification

Great Britain

THE nominal function of yacht measurement is the equalization of what, for lack of a better term, we may call "size"; the true standard of "size" being still an open question after well over a century of heated discussion. It is safe to say that more words have been spoken and written on this subject than on the far more vital subjects of naval architecture in general, yacht design in particular, yacht construction and handling. It is most fortunate for those interested at the present day that the origin of yachting has been cared for by such competent and reliable historians as our American Captain Arthur H. Clark in his book, *The History of Yachting,* 1600 *to* 1815; and Montague Guest, once Librarian of the Royal Yacht Squadron, and his associate, W. B. Boulton, in their *Memorials of the Royal Yacht Squadron,* 1815 *to* 1900. Much of the information in the early part of this chapter is drawn from these two sources. It must be noted that while the nominal fuction of measurement is the equalization of size, its most important effect has been as a mischievous and retarding influence on yacht design.

Passing over the first "yachts" as vessels of state in the service of royalty, dispatch boats, and the smaller naval craft, due credit as the first yachtsman must be given to the "Merry• Monarch", Charles II of England. In his youth in the Channel Islands he learned to sail small boats, and as king in 1660 he was presented by the Dutch Government with a vessel of 100 tons, Mary; 52 feet on keel, 19 feet breadth, 7 feet 7 inches depth, and 10 feet draft. This vessel was sailed for his pleasure by the King himself, and later in the same year he had an estimate from Peter Pett, a naval constructor, for a yacht of 80 tons; while in the following year another was built for his brother, William, Duke of York. There is on record an order for "New sails and four tons of musket shot required for ballast for the King's new yacht." In addition to the first two, Mary and Catherine, in 1661 he built a third, Bezan; and there is a record of a race in October 1661 for stakes of £100, between the King's Catherine and his brother's Anne. The first private yacht on record was Charlotte, built in 1663 for Sir William Batten, of the Admiralty.

Tons	Diff. of Time.	h.	m.	s.	Tons.	Diff. of Time	h.	m.	s.
Under 1	75	10	28	45	Under 16	60	10	46	15
2	seconds	...	30	0	17	seconds	...	47	15
3	per ton	...	31	15	18	per ton	...	48	15
4		...	32	30	19		...	49	15
5		...	33	45	20		...	50	15
6	70	...	35	0	21	55	...	51	15
7		...	36	10	22		...	52	10
8		...	37	20	23		...	53	5
9		...	38	30	24		...	54	0
10		...	39	40	25		...	54	55
11	65	...	40	50	26	50	...	55	50
12		...	41	55	27		...	56	40
13		...	43	0	28		...	57	30
14		...	44	5	29		...	58	20
15		...	45	10	30		...	59	10

Right above: This picture, from the collection of Captain Arthur H. Clark, is believed to represent the yacht Mary, presented to King Charles II by the Dutch Government. Above: Acker's Scale, the first table of Time Allowance, prepared by George Holland Ackers, 1843. The basis of all subsequent tables of allowance

Yachting as a Recognized Sport

This early yachting was limited to the Thames; and, for an unknown period, to Royalty and the nobility; very gradually attracting more general interest. One of the first open sailing matches is recorded in the summer of 1749; the course being down river from Greenwich to the Nore and return; the prize being a silver cup put up by the young prince who afterwards was King George III. What is described as the first "Regatta" was held on June 28, 1775; a rowing contest patterned after the water sports of the Venetian boatmen. On this occasion, to quote a newspaper, "several very respectable

American Yachting

By WILLIAM P. STEPHENS

gentlemen, proprietors of sailing vessels and pleasure boats on the river, agreed at their annual meeting at Battersea to draw up their boats in line off Ranelagh Gardens in order that they might be able to witness the rowing matches without interfering with them." The term "Regatta", thus introduced, has continued in general use as applied to yacht racing on both sides of the Atlantic until a very recent date. As at first applied, to an all-day festival on the water, it was fully justified. So, in more recent years, when the "Regatta" of the New York Y. C., with similar events of the Brooklyn, Atlantic and Seawanhaka C. Y. C., brought out great fleets of racing yachts attended by a spectator fleet of excursion steamboats, sail and steam yachts and working craft. Today, when the annual races of even the largest yacht clubs awaken less public interest than a game of baseball or football, the term has largely disappeared.

In this same year, on July 6, there appeared in The Public Advertiser, a London newspaper, the following notice: "A silver•cup, the gift of His Royal Highness, the Duke of Cumberland, is to be sailed for on Tuesday, the 11th Instant, from Westminster Bridge to Putney Bridge and back, by Pleasure Sailing Boats from Two to Five Tons burthen, and constantly lying above London Bridge. Any gentleman inclined to enter his Boat may be informed of particulars by applying to Mr. Roberts, Boatbuilder, Lambeth, at any time before Saturday Noon Next." The yachts of King Charles and his associates were comparatively large craft, kept "below Bridge" and sailing down the broad estuary of the Thames; here we find much smaller craft, kept and sailed in and above the city. In this same summer was organized the first yacht club, the Cumberland Fleet, or Cumberland Sailing Society; to quote from the Memorials of the Royal Yacht Squadron: "The boats of the Society were all anchored in line, flying the white flag with the St. George's cross. The captains waited in skiffs, and only boarded their boats when the Duke appeared in his gilded barge and proceeded to the boat of the commodore of the fleet. The victorious captain was then summoned to that vessel and introduced to the Duke, who filled the cup with claret and drank the health of the winner, to whom he presented the cup. The winner then pledged the health of His Royal Highness and his Duchess, and the whole squadron sailed to Mr. Smith's tea gardens at the Surrey end of Vauxhall Bridge, then a pleasant spot, the groves and arbors of which are today (1902) supplanted by an ugly set of gasworks." It is believed that Mr. Smith was the first commodore of the Fleet, but in 1779 he was succeeded by Thomas Taylor, owner of the yacht Cumberland. Under his administration the Club prospered, it continued under the original name until 1823, when, as the result of a dispute within the Club, a part of the membership seceded and formed the Thames Yacht Club; by virtue of a royal warrant in 1835 the Royal Thames Y. C.

Thus having traced yacht racing to its cradle, we find the yachts described as from two to 100 tons, and the fleet divided into two classes; those yachts "below Bridge" being of such size and build as to navigate the turbulent waters of the Thames Estuary and the English Channel, while "above Bridge" were small open sailing boats. The tabernacle, an institution little known in America but in use from very remote days in England, Holland and adjoining countries, was built of two stout planks, one on each side of the mast, bolted to the maststep and projecting some distance above deck. The mast was so pivoted between these planks that it could be lowered, the heel sometimes heavily weighted to ease the operation. This mechanism survives today in the Thames barges and the Humber keels, the latter passing under many bridges in their voyages to the upper reaches of the Trent and Ouse. Such of the larger yachts as were thus fitted were able to pass under the Thames bridges; but the young pleasure fleet as a whole was thus divided as to locality and size.

The transference of the center of English yachting

M. Rosenfeld

The six-meter yacht Goose, owned by George Nichols, New York Yacht Club, latest product of the present International Rule

RATING FORMULA

$$\frac{L + 2d + \sqrt{S} - F}{2.37}$$

MEASUREMENT OF SAIL AREA

MARCONI

TRIANGULAR MAINSAILS—The sail shall be set and the area shall be—

(a) LUFF. Measured from top of boom, where in its lowest position it cuts mast, to the top of the sheave, or black band at the after side of the mast. The lowest position of the boom must be indicated by a black band on the mast.

(b) DIAGONAL. Measured from pin of out haul, or slide extended, or black band at outer end of boom, to the nearest point on mast.

In yachts 12 metres and under:—

$$\text{Area} = \frac{a \times b}{2}$$

Height from the deck to where the line of luff of foremost head sail cuts the mast or topmast	31.67 feet.
Fore-side mast to where the line of luff of foremost head sail cuts the bow-sprit of hull	8.84 feet.
Main boom extreme	17.07 feet.
Main boom from aft side of mast to the inner edge of black band at boom end	17.03 feet.
(a) Luff of triangular mainsail	37.17 feet.
(b) Diagonal of triangular mainsail	17.05 feet.
Length of spinnaker boom over all, including gooseneck, from centre fore and aft line of mast	8.84 feet.

AREAS OF SAILS

Mainsail =	333.9
Foretriangle Total = ;	
" Total × 0.85 =	119.0
Topsail =	
Sail Area for Rating = S =	452.9
$\sqrt{S}$ =	21.28

MEASUREMENTS

Overall Length		36,38	
Add { Overhang Forward to L_1	4,08		
Add { Overhang Aft to L_1	6,73		
Subtract Total Overhang		10,81	
Measured Length		25,57	
Subtract { Girth at Bow	2,72		
Subtract { Twice Vertical Height at Bow	1,97		
O. at Bow	,75		
Add 1½ O. at Bow		1,12	
Subtract { Girth at Stern	6,70		
Subtract { Twice Vertical Height at Stern	3,88		
O. at Stern	2,82		
Add ⅓ O. at Stern		,94	
CORRECT LENGTH, L.			27,63
Subtract { Skin d to d_1 Port	5,81		
Subtract { Chain d to d_1 Port	5,78		
d Port		,03	
Subtract { Skin d to d_1 Starboard	5,82		
Subtract { Chain d to d_1 Starboard	5,79		
d Starboard		,03	
Add *d*		,06	
2*d*			,12
$\sqrt{S}$			21,28
Add to find sum of Measurements			49,03
Add { Mean Freeboard Bow O	2,74		
Add { Mean Freeboard Midship d	2,32		
Add { Mean Freeboard Stern O	2,23		
Sum of Freeboards	7,29		
Subtract (⅓ sum) FREEBOARD, F			2,39
Total of Measurements			46,64
Divide by 2.37 = Rating =		19,68	

OTHER MEASUREMENTS TO BE RECORDED BY MEASURER

Overall Length		36,38
Add { Overhang Forward to L.	5,02	
Add { Overhang Aft to L.	7,78	
Subtract Total Overhang		
Water Line Length		23,58
Beam Extreme		6,58
Tumble Home		0,11
Actual displacement by weighing		--------
Approximate weight of, and fore and aft position of ballast inside		50# on bow
Remarks on condition of water when marks were tested. State Fresh or Salt		Salt
Remarks on cabin fittings. Stating whether they comply with Schedule		Yes
Has Designer's Declaration (para. 4, Section I) been furnished to Measurer?		Yes

Measurement certificate of a typical six-meter yacht under the International Rule 1940

from London to Cowes was a slow course of evolution; in the early part of the 19th Century all traffic between the Isle of Wight, even then a popular summer resort, was carried on by means of sailing craft; while the fleet of fishing and pilot boats, racing among themselves at times, also served as party boats for the pleasure of visitors. The formal recognition came about on June 1, 1815, in the organization by 42 gentlemen, prominent among whom were the Marquis of Anglesea, the Earl of Yarborough, Joseph and James Weld and Thomas Assheton Smith, of the Yacht Club, later the Royal Yacht Club, and today the Royal Yacht Squadron. The first Queen's Cup was presented by Queen Victoria to the Squadron in 1838, a year after her accession to the throne, and was raced for by yachts of from 48 up to 217 tons; the allowance, given at the start, being three minutes per ton.

Classification and Time Allowance

In 1831 the yachts of the Squadron visited Cherbourg for a union regatta, the fleet being divided into classes of not more than five tons to a class, with an allowance of 1¼ minutes per ton, at the start. As the start took nearly two hours, the race was not understood by the French; before it was over they were asking when it was to start. In a race in 1841 there was an allowance of one second per ton per mile, figured at the finish. Two years later we find a division of the fleet on the basis of rig, one class for schooners and one for cutters; the original sloop rig derived from Holland having been replaced by the national cutter rig of the old revenue cutters and similar working craft. The cutters were divided into classes: 30 to 50 tons, 50 to 75, 75 to 105, and over 105. The allowance was according to the Graduated Time Tables, better known as "Ackers' Scale," devised in 1843 by George Holland Ackers, owner of two of the largest topsail schooners; also known as the originator of a yacht signal code. The "Graduated Time Tables by G. H. Ackers, Esq." began with an "Explanation. In the annexed scale the first column contains the tonnage of cutter yachts; the second, the difference of time allowed for each ton; the third, the hour; the fourth, the minutes; the fifth, the seconds; shewing the time of starting for each. Corresponding scales for Fore-and-Aft Schooner Yachts, and for all other Square Rigged Yachts, are placed alongside the first part of the Cutters' Scale, with the intention of matching them with Cutters as impartially as possible, and endeavoring to create more sport in the Regattas. Considering the difference in rig, it is quite impossible that any vessel can compete with a Cutter when *closehauled;* and it appears impossible for any Schooner or Square Rigged Vessel to make up in running the distance she must lose while closehauled; therefor, the annexed scale is formed from observations made upon many former matches, with the hope of placing all Yachts, handicapped, on as equal terms as possible, taking the difference in tonnage as a guide for the Scale. It has been said that Cutters can give 45 seconds per ton, which appears to be a good proportion for the smaller classes, but in larger classes above 60 or 80 tons the Yachts cannot give near so much per ton; therefore, the time allowed in the Scale decreases in proportion as the tonnage increases. If all Yachts entered for a prize are started together, which appears to afford the most amusement, it will be easily seen which Yacht is the winner by observing the exact time at which each Yacht passes the winning station vessel, and by referring to the Scale; or, if the Yachts are started by classes successively, so as to bring them to the winning station as near together as possible, each class may be started at the time placed opposite the smallest Yacht of each class. The Scale is suitable for all sorts of Yachts sailing together, or for Cutters only, or for Schooners and Square Rigged Yachts together or separately." A page of the Scale as printed in *Hunt's Universal Yacht List* for 1871 appears on first page of this chapter. As compared with the makeshift allowances previously quoted, it represents an earnest attempt at a logical and comprehensive treatment of the subject; it was the basis of various later scales, including that of the Yacht Racing Association.

Mid-Century Conditions

From the middle of the 19th Century British yachting grew rapidly in the number of clubs, the size of the fleet, and the number of races; but, at the same time, general conditions were far from satisfactory. There was a lack of union and co-operation among the clubs which resulted in local variations of the racing conditions; in the issue of *Hunt's Yachting Magazine* for January, 1856, the whole subject is treated editorially, the following instances of the defects of the measurement rule being given:—"The Phantom measures but 25 tons under the old system, or that adopted by the Welsh and other northern clubs; by the Thames Club New Measurement she is 27 tons, and by the London Club 31 tons. The Kitten under the old measurement is of but ten tons; but by the new measurement of the Prince of Wales Club she is twelve tons, and by the London Club 14. The Vampire, a 15-ton yacht under the old method of measurement, by the new system of the Thames Yacht Club she is 18 tons, and by the London Yacht Club 20 tons."

As a remedy for this state of affairs the magazine offers a suggestion; first, a prize of one hundred guineas for the "best and most approved method of yacht-racing tonnage admeasurement," the prize not to be awarded unless the system suggested shall be considered worthy of general adoption in every yacht club offering prizes for competition by yachts of any other club. A second proposition was for a public meeting in London by members of the different clubs, for the discussion of the subject of measurement, and the appointment of a committee to carry out the proposed plan. In speaking of a similar agitation two years previously in *Bell's Life,* the great sporting journal of the period, *Hunt's* makes a comparison of the course of yachting with the difficulties experienced in the use of the magnetic compass in the first iron vessels. "A remedy has been found for the latter by a talented engineer, Thomas Alan of Edinburgh, who points out the cause of error and lays before the world the result of a simple but ingenious invention whereby the compass needle may be adjusted with the same degree of certainty aboard an iron vessel as a wooden one. To suggest an improved system of yacht measurement is far more simple and far less open to obstacles than was the apparently uncontrollable difficulty of the compass needle." The old B.O.M. Rule, as given in MoToR BoatinG for December, was then quoted in full.

Shotbags as Shifting Ballast

ABOUT 1826 a limit was placed on light sails, with the result that yachts were grossly over-canvassed in their nominally working sails. This led to the introduction of shifting ballast in the form of shotbags stowed high up on shelves back of the cabin transoms. Under the influence of the tax on breadth yachts gradually became longer and narrower, calling for the shifting of tons of ballast on each tack. How this was done is told in *Hunt's* for April 1856:—"This yacht was fitted for trimming operations in the following manner. The sofa lockers were made of strong plank, about 1½ inches thick, securely kneed to the vessel's side. The ornamental front to these lockers was fastened to them by means of large brass thumbscrews from the inside. The buffets fitted on the locker boards and were fastened to them and to the vessel's side with screws. By this arrangement all the fancy work could be removed in a few minutes, and the shotbags thrown from locker to locker without damage to the elegant paint of the cabin. Without some such preparation much injury must be done to the sofas and buffets of a cabin by trimming ballast, and so far the practice is one which should be discountenanced."

How the handling of several tons of shotbags was done was told in subsequent issues of the same year:—In a vessel which can stay quickly four men are supposed to be able to trim a ton and a half of shot, but I never knew more than half this weight to be thrown over before the vessel was round, the consequence is that she falls over, stays sluggishly, and hangs sometime before she gets good way on again. The last twenty bags or so are terribly heavy, and go over but slowly, consequently, when working with very short tacks, the vessel does not acquire her full speed before 'Bout Ho, over with ballast' is the cry; once more she turns sluggishly, falls over, and just steadies herself in time to go through the same ceremony. If, instead of 30 cwt., half a ton only were shifted and the remaining ton placed amidships, the vessel will work quicker and sail better."

The First Yacht Racing Association

IN MOST fields of sport history will show that a popular movement for union and co-operation in the line of national action for better rules and conditions encounters at the outset serious opposition from some "premier" organization which considers that its prestige will be impaired by association with the younger and smaller bodies. Such was the case when the American Canoe Association was organized in 1880; the same thing happened on the attempt to organize the Yacht Racing Association of Long Island Sound in 1894; and it was not until 1926 that the dreams and aspirations of many American yachtsmen in the previous forty years were realized in the organization of a national yachting union. After many attempts at a national union of British yachtsmen, in 1875 there was formed the Yacht Racing Association; with a membership of individual yachtsmen, with its authority recognized by twenty clubs; only the Royal Yacht Squadron, the Royal Thames Y.C., and the New Thames Y.C. remaining aloof.

The new organization started off with uniform racing rules, a measurement rule and table of allowances; and under the Marquis of Exeter as President and Dixon Kemp as Secretary it was successful from the start. The breach with the Squadron continued, however, until in 1881 the yacht owners of the Y.R.A. refused to enter the Squadron races. The five days of racing brought out only three old schooners, one yawl, and several cutters. In this year the Prince of Wales, later King Edward VII, was not only Commodore of the Squadron and the Royal London Y.C., but President of the Y.R.A. as well, and through his characteristic diplomacy the two recalcitrant clubs were brought into line, accepting the Y.R.A. rules.

The measurement of length under the rule was a hotly disputed point for many years, the original measurements, beginning with the length of keel, were given in the previous chapter. In 1854 the Royal London Y.C. adopted the length on deck to the after side of the sternpost; this measurement introducing new forms of evasion. With this added length the deduction for fore rake was increased by the Royal Thames Y.C. from 3/5 of the breadth to the whole breadth, to keep the yachts as nearly as possible in their former classes.

As all subsequent measurement legislation has been under the control of the Yacht Racing Association, its course is easily traced; the first meeting was held at Willis's Rooms, in London, on November 17, 1875, attended by owners of yachts of and above 10 tons. The existing Thames Rule was adopted, with the Table of Allowances adopted by the Royal Yacht Squadron in 1866. The following rule was adopted: "No bags of shot shall be onboard, and all ballast shall be properly stowed under the platform or in lockers, and shall not be shifted or trimmed in any way whatever during a race." In the matter of classification the Y.R.A. adopted classes of maximum limits of 5, 10, 15, 20, 40, 80 tons and over 80 tons. The rule of the Royal Thames Y.C. provided that all fractions of a ton should count as a full ton in this classification, but the Y.R.A. version of the rule provided that only fractions of 47/94 should count as a ton, all under being disregarded. This point was the subject of much heated discussion. In 1878 the measurement of length was changed from the deck to the load waterline.

The Buttercup Bow

UNDER all previous rules the straight plumb stem, so characteristic of the British cutter, was compulsory, but with waterline as the limit of length the designer was free to adopt any extreme of overhang, forward as well as aft. In 1876 Mr. Bentall, while flaunting conventionality in other ways, matched the whaleboat counter of Jullanar with a short clipper stem which increased her measurement; though it was offset by an immersed counter and the forward position of the sternpost. In 1880, two years after the adoption of the waterline measurement, another English yachtsman, Robert Hewitt, astonished the sailing fraternity by a clipper stem and billethead on a new 10-tonner, Buttercup; the "Buttercup bow" creating as much of a sensation as the "Gloriana bow" of 11 years later. Under all forms of the old tonnage rule the designer had been compelled to work within the limits of a box, which changed each year only in growing longer, narrower and deeper; at the bow he was limited to the straight plumb stem, and on the sides the breadth on deck could barely exceed that on the waterline, the necessity for low ballast made compulsory a long, straight and level keel. Under the new ruling he was free to add as much overhang forward as his taste suggested, matching it by as much or more aft by way of balance.

In 1881 a weak effort was made to break away from the old tonnage rule, the new version reading:—"add the breadth to the length and multiply the sum thus obtained by itself and by the breadth, then divide the product by 1730, and the quotient shall be the tonnage, in tons and hundredths of a ton." In commenting on this rule, known as the "1730 Rule," under date of February 12, 1882 Dixon Kemp wrote:—"The Rule just adopted is a mere contrivance which will answer its purpose, but will not endure." So far from answering its purpose of curbing the building of longer and narrower yachts, the rule proved a failure; under it were built such yachts as *May, †Clara, Irex and †Genesta. The agitation for a radical change of rule continued with renewed force; the subject was hotly discussed in *The Field,* and through the efforts of its editor, Dixon Kemp, in 1886 a new formula was adopted experimentally; this was first proposed in *The Field* of January 10, 1880, being printed in the Appendix to the Y.R.A. book of that year. In this rule a new factor, sail area, was introduced; the formula being $\frac{L. \times S.A.}{6000}$ British yachting was not yet prepared to sacrifice the sacred fetish of tonnage, so the unit of the rule was termed "sail tons" with the added term "linear rating." This rule was adopted in 1882 by the Seawanhaka Corinthian Y.C. in New York, using the divisor first proposed by Mr. Kemp, 7000.

The End of All Tonnage Rules

THE successive defeats of two challengers for the America's Cup in 1886-7 put a quietus on the Thames Rule in the adoption of the 1730 Rule for all races; this ended the day of the narrow cutter and introduced a new type, such as †Minerva. The designers were freed from the cramping effect of the old rule and left free as to overhangs both fore and aft, and breadth in the topsides. The deck area was greatly increased, giving greater spread for the shrouds without channels, and much more space for deck work, both in the bows and on the counter. The rule was adopted for a period of seven years, beginning in 1887. In 1886 a new class of three tons was adopted, and also new supplementary classes based on waterline length:—21 feet, 21 to 25, 25 to 30.

In 1891 the yachting world was startled by a new type of hull, the fin-keel; practically a canoe-shaped hull which derived its stability from a deep fin of bronze plate carrying a cigar-shaped bulb of lead on its lower edge. The sensation aroused was as great as that attending the catamaran of the same designer, N. G. Herreshoff, in 1876, but more lasting. In 1891 two of the new type, Wenonah of 2½ rating and Wee Win, of ½ rating, invaded British waters; followed in 1895 by Niagara, a 20-Rater. All three proved successful in racing against the normal keel type. To meet this invasion a new rule was adopted in 1896, the formula being:— $\frac{L + B + .75G + .5\sqrt{S.A.}}{2}$ The new factor, G, represented the girth of the hull, including all keel, from waterline to waterline, at a point .6 of the waterline from the stem. This measurement, termed "skin girth," was taken by a tapeline in actual contact with the entire immersed surface of the hull; the yacht necessarily being docked for measurement. The unit was termed "linear rating" and new classes were 18, 24, 30, 36, 42, 52, 65 and over 65 feet, by the rule. In 1897 it was ruled that centerboards should be measured for girth when lowered as fixed keels.

In 1901 the girth measurement was changed, the upper points of measurement, at .55 of the waterline, being moved up to the planksheer. In addition to the "skin girth" the "chain girth" was measured by a chain passed under the keel, this being subtracted from the "skin girth" and giving the "girth difference (d), which was multiplied by 4 and added to .75 G. With this change, taking effect after 1902, the divisor was increased to 2.1. The centerboard, always a shining mark in trans-Atlantic measurement legislation, came in for another blow:—"Movable keels of any kind to be treated as fixed keels, and measured in the position which will give the maximum measurement."

The International Rule

IN MARCH, 1905 a movement was inaugurated for an international conference on the subject of uniform racing rules; being held in London in January, 1906. There were present 16 representatives of Great Britain and the continental countries, including Switzerland; the United States, though invited, declining to send representatives. After a conference lasting four days the Y.R.A. Rule was changed in several details; the waterline length was increased by the addition of penalties on flat, wide bows and sterns of the scow type; the girth multiplier was reduced from .75 to .50, and the multiplier of the factor d reduced to 3. The sail factor was reduced to ⅓. The position of the girth station was changed; and the freeboard as measured at both ends of the waterline and at the middle girth station was added as a minus quantity at the end of the formula:—$L + B + \frac{1}{2} G + 3d + \frac{1}{3}\sqrt{S.A.} — F.$ This rule was enacted to go into operation on January 1, 1908, and to stand until December 31, 1917. The measurements were to be taken in feet or meters, in actual practice the continental measurement being universally used; with classes of 5, 6, 7, 8, 9, 10, 12, 14, 17, 20 and over 20 meters. At a subsequent international conference further changes were made to go into effect on January 1, 1920 and stand for six years. The formula now was $\frac{L + \frac{1}{4} G + 2d + \sqrt{S.A.} — F}{2.5}$; centerboards being prohibited. In October, 1933 further changes were made to take effect after January 1, 1936, the formula being:—

$$\frac{L + 2d + \sqrt{S.A.} — F}{2.37}$$

*MoToR BoatinG, July, 1940. †MoToR BoatinG, August, 1940.

TRADITIONS AND MEMORIES OF American Yachting

Part Twenty-one

Measurement and classfication in America

By WILLIAM P. STEPHENS

IN studying the history of measurement and classification it is necessary in the first place to consider the three forms of modern yacht racing. The first and by far the most important is racing under a fixed rule of measurement and in an established class. The second is the racing of a mixed fleet under a system of arbitrary handicapping. The third is the racing of a monotype fleet built as nearly alike as is possible. Under the first method the skill of the designer is called on to produce the fastest possible craft within certain limitations of hull dimensions, sail area, displacement, or other assumed factors of speed. All advance, whether in the line of legitimate development or, as has too often been the case, over-development, is found in this class. The second method, racing a mixed fleet of existing yachts under what is admittedly a mere guess as to their relative capabilities, is a very old and popular form of sport, the parent of our modern per-cent handicapping. The origin of the term handicap is ascribed to an old English custom of writing on papers to be drawn from a cap, the odds on horse racing, dog racing, badger-drawing, bull-baiting and other forms of sport. Handicap racing has always been popular in Great Britain, and when conducted by an expert who has the confidence of yachtsmen the result is generally satisfactory. In 1898 the Thames United Sailing Club inaugurated a system for the revision of handicaps on the basis of actual performance; in 1902 the subject was brought up for discussion in *The Field* by Dixon Kemp, his proposal being to base the handicap on a varying percentage of the yacht's Y.R.A. measurement, using the regular time scale. The Per-Cent Handicap Class of Long Island Sound was organized in 1906 by George P. Granbery, of the New Rochelle Y. C., who is still sailing in the Class, and Harry A. Jackson. While the initial handicap for a yacht on entering the Class is still a guess, this is revised after every race on the basis of actual performance. This system, which originated about forty years ago with Louis M. Clark of the Boston Yacht Club, has stood the test of time and provided good racing for a very large fleet.

This boat races in the handicap class, as indicated by the % symbol on her sail. This includes a fleet of varying dimensions to race in one group

M. Rosenfeld

One of the first, if not the first, of the one-design classes was the Waterwag, designed in 1887 by Thomas B. Middleton, of Dublin, for racing at Kingstown, Ireland. The design showed a double-ended open boat 13 feet long, with a small lug sail; built at a cost of fifteen to twenty pounds. The idea proved successful and other classes followed in the same locality; soon extending to foreign countries. The strong points of the system were low cost through the elimination of the designer's fee and mass production; with the result of a race depending solely on the upkeep and handling of the owner. From this point of view it has been a boon to yachting; but only when limited to comparatively small craft. When extended to include yachts of 50, 65 and 70 feet waterline, and in classes of but three or four yachts, there enters an element of economy coupled with exclusiveness which are not conducive to the higher interests of the sport of yacht racing.

In both the handicap and one-design systems there is no incentive to the improvement of design, no encouragement to the yacht designer, and largely no question of absolute speed; some of the most popular of the one-design classes have been in no way absolutely fast.

It is beyond dispute that the backbone of yacht racing in all sizes of over thirty feet waterline is in the open racing of individually designed yachts under a measurement rule; today there is but one such class (12-Metre) about the great yachting centers of New York and Boston. If and when the war is over, the first question to be met by the larger clubs will be that of the creation of at least one open class under our Universal (Herreshoff) Rule.

The Tonnage Rule in America

Passing back over the years for almost a century (the first race of the New York Yacht Club was sailed in

1845) the historian is faced with the lack of reliable records; those of the Club are very imperfect, and the New York Custom House has nothing back of 1870. We know that in the first races the time allowance was based on tonnage; a tonnage certificate of that day would be most interesting, but a diligent search has failed to disclose one. Such little light as we have is found in an article on Measurements by A. Cary Smith in Manning's Yachting Annual for 1875. It is in the form of a letter to Thomas Manning, Esq., and begins: "A simple method of measurement has long been needed by yachting men, and the plain instructions here submitted will enable any owner of a Yacht to make his own measurements. The length for tonnage is from the wood-ends to the after side of the sternpost at deck. The breadth is found by dropping a plummet at each side at the greatest beam. The depth of hold is the distance from the top of the deck beam at the forward end of the cabin to the ceiling at the side of the keelson. O. M. is the Old Custom Measurement; from the length on deck from the wood-end to the after side of sternpost subtract 3/5 of the breadth; multiply the remainder by the breadth, and this product by the depth; divide by 95 and the quotient is the tonnage." This differs from all the British forms of B. O. M. in two respects; the actual depth of hold is taken, instead of half the breadth, for the second multiplicand; and the divisor is 95 instead of 94. How this form of the ancient rule originated in America is unknown, but it is far superior to the parent rule in that it imposes no accumulative tax on breadth with its mischievous influence on design.

Going back to the best known yacht of the early days, the schooner America, we find a half dozen sets of lines, each vouched for as correct, and no two alike; and an equal variety of tonnages, American and British. In a sea of conjectures and contradictions we find a little solid ground in the original builder's certificate: "Register 290, June 17, 1851. William H. Brown, master, builder and sole owner of the yacht schooner America. Built in New York in 1851. Length, 93 feet six inches; breadth, 22 feet six inches; depth, 9 feet; measurement 170 50/95 tons"; within a small fraction of the figure generally accepted as her American tonnage. Thus this rule may be accepted as the one in use in New York at the date of the founding of the Club. Though the great race was sailed without time allowance, the entry of America quoted this figure, 170 tons.

While there is mention in an old book of "the original drawings of the America by Steers" as in the original club house in Hoboken, no such drawings exist today. To what extent she was built from a design on paper is a matter of doubt, as George Steers is credited with a method of his own, changing the lines on the mould loft floor and even making further changes when in frame prior to planking. What appear to be the most reliable and detailed are lines taken off at Pitcher's Yard, Northfleet, England, in 1859; when the yacht, then under the ownership of Viscount Templetown and named Camilla, was laid up. The measurements marked on this plan are "Length between Perpendiculars, 96 feet 3 inches; Length of Keel for Tonnage, 82 feet 8 inches; Breadth for Tonnage, 22 feet 8 inches; Hold, 9 feet 7 inches; Tonnage, 225 61/94." These measurements applied to the original B. O. M. Rule, as previously quoted, fail to give exact results. Other lines give the British tonnage as 208.

Captain Roland Folger Coffin

It is most unfortunate that our American historian Captain Arthur H. Clark did not continue his work to include this side of the Atlantic, but there still exist the writings of one of his contemporaries, Captain Roland Folger Coffin. Born in Brooklyn, N. Y., in 1826, the son of a sea captain; the family, originally English Quakers, had settled on Nantucket Island in the 17th Century. The boy was educated in the Brooklyn schools and began his work behind the counter of a drygoods store. This life being distasteful, his father consented in 1846 to a sea career, and he signed before the mast aboard the ship Yorktown, plying between New York and Liverpool. After several voyages, being in port at the same time as his father, he was told that his captain was coddling him too much, and that he never would make a sailor; the result being that he was taken aboard his father's ship

Rosenfeld

The Stars are typical of the smaller craft which today race in one of the many one-design classes. They are 22 feet 7 inches overall, 15 feet 6 inches on the waterline, 5 feet 8 inches beam, and carry 280 square feet of sail

Senator. Voyaging to all parts of the world, by successive rises he commanded his own ships. During the Rebellion he was in the Navy, being present to witness the battle of the Monitor and the Merrimac, later he commanded the U. S. ship Ericsson, later returning to the merchant service.

While at sea he had studied shorthand, back in Brooklyn in 1869 he perfected himself by practice with his three sisters reading to him, and in 1870 joined the staff of *The New York World* as a reporter. One of his first assignments was on the arrival of the schooner Cambria as the first challenger for the America's Cup; he made a journalistic scoop in being the first to meet her and report her arrival, and then wrote the report of the one and only race of Cambria against the defending fleet. His knowledge of the sea, his extensive acquaintance among yachtsmen, and his experience and memory, made him the leading American yachting writer. In addition to general and yachting reporting for *The World,* he wrote for the weekly *Spirit of The Times,* for magazines, and, as "The Old Sailor's Yarns of The World," a series of quaint and wittty stories of seagoing life; "Archibald, the Cat," "Fighting Fire on a Cotton Ship," and others worthy of reproduction today. For many years he sat in a pew in Plymouth Church every Sunday and took down in shorthand the sermons of Henry Ward Beecher. Always deeply interested in yachting, his work in the seventies, when the first three challenges for the Cup aroused a more than local interest in yachting throughout the nation, did much to popularize the sport.

An ardent advocate of the national type, the wide, shoal centerboard sloop, he was its leading partisan in the war of sloop and cutter; while I admired him and esteemed his friendship in our frequent meetings at races, when busy with our pens we were mortal enemies; argument, contradiction, and even abuse passed freely in this merry war between my predecessor, C. P. Kunhardt, and myself as editors of *Forest and Stream* (Captain Coffin termed it contemptuously the Bust and Puddle) and the daily *World* and weekly *Spirit of the Times.* His death was as fitting as it was sudden, as usual he accompanied the annual cruise of the Atlantic Y. C. in 1888; on July 17 the fleet arrived at Shelter Harbor after a run from New London, Captain Coffin had written en route the fight between his old favorite, the sloop Fanny and the new compromise Katrina and Shamrock. Landing with the Committee, he walked up the beach to the telegraph office; the day was very hot, in reply to a comment on the heat he said: "Pretty tough on an old fellow, this, the doctor says one valve of my heart is out of order, but, pshaw, that doesn't amount to anything." Completing the first part of his story, he stepped to the operator to file it and fell dead. It is to him that we owe most of what is known today of yachting from 1840 to 1880.

The First Regatta

ORGANIZED in 1844, the first regatta of the New York Yacht Club was sailed on July 16, 1845; the conditions being: First, Tonnage by Custom House measurement; second, 45 seconds per ton *allowed at the start;* third, a cup of the value of the entrance money to the winning yacht. The starters were: Cygnet, 45 tons; Sybil, 42; Spray, 37; La Coquille, 27; Minna, 30; Gimcrack, 25; Newburg, 33; Ada, 17; Lancet, 20. What is historically entered as "the first annual regatta," though actually the second, was sailed on July 17, 1846, with 14 starters, 12 schooners and 2 sloops classed together, under the same conditions and with a $200 piece of silver as a prize. A second race was sailed on the following day, with three working boats competing with the yachts.

In commenting on the race of 1845 Captain Coffin, writing in 1887, says: "The regatta was a great event, and was witnessed by thousands of people; all New York who could get there being on the water. Now-a-days (1887) an ordinary club regatta attracts few besides club members; and old yachtsmen shake their heads gloomily and lament the decadence of American yachting, saying that all interest in the sport is dying out." What would he say in the year of Grace, 1940? In the regatta of June 2, 1847, a division was made into two classes, but on the basis of size, not rig; the allowance in the first class being 35 seconds per ton, in the second class 45 seconds, and for craft outside the Club 40 seconds. In the regatta of June 6, 1848, the same conditions were maintained, but the tonnage was displacement. There is no record of the manner in which yachts were weighed, but this would be possible on a floating or balance dock, two of which existed in New York. By measuring the amount of water pumped out from the time that the keel first grounded on the blocks until it was clear of the level of the water outside, the volume and consequently the weight of water could be ascertained. The competing yachts were: First Class, Siren, 60 tons; Cornelia, 75; Maria, 118; Second Class, Lancet, 19; La Coquille, 21; Dream, 28¾; Spray, 34; Cygnet, 39.

In describing this race, in which Maria was entered and, by the way, dismasted, Captain Coffin writes: "The Maria seems to have been constantly shrinking in size, for at this regatta she is entered at 118 tons, quite a drop from 160 at which she sailed her first race." Careful historian as he was, the Captain missed the fact that the larger measurement was the Custom House tonnage, while the smaller was the actual weight (displacement) in tons. In this race first and second prizes were given in each class. Throughout this period there had been other races of the Club, two of them Corinthian, some private matches, and more interest was awakened in the conditions governing racing. One result was seen in a Corinthian race of October 26, 1848, in which, for the first time, the fleet was divided on the basis of rig, schooners and sloops.

Considering the general conditions of racing, Article 26 of the Constitution as printed in the 1852 Year Book reads: "A mode to ascertain the actual displacement at different drafts of water, after the yacht has been weighed shall be prepared under the direction of a competent person, to be selected by the Club, which shall be the standard used to determine the tonnage of any yacht." One of the "competent persons" was Charles H. Haswell, the eminent engineer of whom New York is so proud; joining the Club in 1854, he was a member of the Regatta Committee from 1855 to 1864, and also Measurer for the same period.

In the 1853 book we find: "The measurement for tonnage shall be ascertained by the actual displacement; and the owners of all yachts entering for the regattas shall, at least three days previously thereto, give notice in writing to the Committee of Arrangements of the tonnage of their respective vessels, after which notice no alteration of any description shall be made in the vessels. The model of each yacht shall be deposited with the Recording Secretary before she can enter for the annual regatta. Each yacht to be allowed to carry one man for every four tons. No member shall be interested in more than one yacht entered for any regatta. All yachts sailing for prizes are limited to the following sails, viz, schooners, jib, foresail and mainsail; sloops, jib and mainsail; cutters, jib, foresail, mainsail, jib topsail and gaff topsail. (This mention of cutters is quite exceptional.) First Class, one man for four tons; Second Class, one man for 3½ tons; Third Class, one man for three tons."

In 1857 the displacement rule was abandoned in favor of sail area; the mainsail and jib of sloops; mainsail, foresail and jib of schooners, and any other duly measured sails actually set during a race. The classes were: 1st, 3,300 sq. ft. and upwards; 2nd, 2,300 sq. ft. and upwards, but less than 3,300 sq. ft.; 3rd, less than 2,300 sq. ft. The allowances were: 1st Class, 1 second per sq. ft.; 2nd Class, 1¼ seconds; 3rd Class, 1½ seconds. In 1856 the suggestion was made by the Regatta Committee that certificates of measurement be submitted by owners; and that all yachts proposing to start be on station for inspection on the afternoon before a race.

The Load Waterline Area Rule

IN 1858 a new rule was adopted, the greatest length from fore side of stem to after side of sternpost, on or below the waterline, being multiplied by the extreme breadth. There is no record of the reasons for the adoption of such an extraordinary rule; we can only conjecture that it may be based upon the current assumption that length gives speed, and that breadth may be taxed as a measure of stability. The "load waterline area" as employed in this rule was not the area of the load waterline plane, but of its circumscribing parallelogram. The limit of schooners in Class 1 was over 1,500 sq. ft.; Class 2, 1,500 sq. ft. and under; sloops, Class 1, over 1,300 sq. ft.; Class 2, 1,300 to 800 sq. ft.; Class 3, under 800 sq. ft.

There was at this time a very keen interest in the question of the measurement rule, as proved by a number of papers, by good fortune, still preserved in the Club. These, written in the fine old clerical hand which preceded the day of the typewriter, include most elaborate and involved calculations of speed, times and distances, with arguments pro and con. There existed two schools of thought, one upholding the waterline area system and the other the taxation of sail area. It would appear that a "Mr. Rutherfurd" was one of the leading advocates of the sail area plan; there were at the time four Rutherfurds in the Club; the one involved in this controversy was presumably Lewis M., owner of the sloop Ray. The discussions of this vexed question in the course of the past century would fill all the volumes of a modern encyclopedia, and can be touched on but briefly in this history; but the following, as embodying the ideas of the day, seems worthy of quotation; the author is unknown.

"The plan proposed by Mr. Rutherfurd for matching yachts appears to me objectionable on the following grounds, viz, That in considering yachts merely in the light of bodies to be propelled through the water at the highest rate of speed with the least amount of power he has totally disregarded the most essential requisites; viz, internal accommodation and seaworthy qualities. Of two vessels to be propelled by the same quantity of canvas, that one will excel in speed which has least resistance and least weight. The skimming dish, therefore, which has but little draught of water and is put together as lightly as possible for purposes of a single race, would be the victor. This is then giving a premium for the introduction into the Club of the most worthless type of vessels. The plan of allowance by canvas is also incorrect for the following reasons. It disregards the first and most important requirement, *stability*, or capability of carrying canvas, by requiring her to pay for it if she possess it in a greater degree than her adversary. Further, the proper canvasing of a vessel, both for disposition and quantity, is as much one of the component parts of a fast vessel as the form of the hull; and therefore no restriction should be put upon it. It is in the discretion of the master to set or shorten sail according to the requirements of his vessel; and we might, with as much justice, allow time between yachts for the difference in skill of their pilots as for the sail carried by them."

"A further objection to this plan is that the required measurements would be both troublesome, expensive, and liable to error. That the calculation would vary materially with any change in immersion, and would give rise to frequent protests and re-measurements. This plan, from the greater amount of canvas allowed to a deep vessel, would, in fact, act as a premium for such; as one of less draught must allow time or cripple herself by reducing her canvas below her capabilities."

On the other hand, Length and Beam appear to me the only index of size or power so far as matching vessels is concerned. This plan leaves each free to build such a vessel as best suits his purposes. Where different kinds of vessels are matched together, and also under different circumstances as regards weather, the advantage of the one at one time would be against her at another. The light draft vessel which may have the advantage in River sailing and light winds may find her long-legged competitor too much in outside work and a stiff breeze. The argument that it is useless to change the present system until we can get perfection seems to me a very weak one. In everything our aim should be to improve; even although we cannot put on our 7-league boots and arrive at perfection in one stride. In conclusion, it is not claimed that the plan proposed is the result of any abstruse calculations or high scientific attainments, it is merely the result of observation, and comparisons of yachts and yacht sailing; nor do I assert that I *know* it to be the *only correct one;* but merely offer it in the hope that, if not entirely perfect, it may still prove more correct than the very objectionable one under which we are now suffering."

Unsigned and undated, this protest against the use of sail area evidently dates from 1857-8, when the change to waterline was made. In a later communication the same writer replies to Mr. Rutherfurd, instancing the success of Luckey, a yacht of the sharpie type with small sail area.

Enter the Mathematicians

IN view of the allusion to "abstruse calculations" it is amusing to read other papers of this collection; column after column of theoretical calculations, and page after page of comparative race records. Among the first we find the following: "If a wind of No. 4 propels a vessel at 6 miles per hour with a resistance of 500, the wind No. 6 propels the same vessel 9 miles per hour with a resistance of 1125. Or, in proportion to the square of the velocity of the wind; or, 4 square is to 6 square as 500 is to 1125. As the resistance to the vessel also increases with the square of her velocity, we have 500 is to 1125 as 4 square is to 6 square. If the velocity of the vessel were in proportion to the force exerted by the wind, we should have 4 square is to 6 square as 6 is to 13.5, instead of to 9." Accompanying this proposition are pages of tables with speeds varying by quarter hours from 3½ miles to 8 miles, and areas varying from 2000 sq. ft. to 3200 sq. ft.

The practical effect of these tables in a comparison of the sail area rule with the then proposed waterline area rule is shown in the following; a part of the record of the regatta of June 4, 1857.

Name	Actual Time	Time by Sails	Time by W.L.	W.L. Area	Actual Order	Order by Sails	Order by W.L. Area
FIRST CLASS 1¾ SECONDS							
Julia	4-57-47	4-10-03	4-56-57	1421	1	1	1
Madgie .	5-11-29	4-55-32	5-10-26	1385	2	2	2
SECOND CLASS 2¼ SECONDS							
Minnie ..	5-09-13	4-59-42	5-10-26	1251	2	3	4
Una	5-06-14	4-56-36	5-04-37	1208	1	2	2
Irene ...	5-11-40	5-02-24	5-09-23	1190	6	5	6
Undine ..	5-22-34	5-07-16	5-14-25	1032	6	5	6
Rowena .	5-17-45	4-53-04	5-07-51	987	5	1	3
Escort ..	5-14-50	5-14-50	5-00-44	875	4	6	1

The table continued with five more yachts in the third class sloops; five in the first class; and three in the second class schooners.

In the First Class sloops the winner would be the same under both rules; in the Second Class the first yacht by the sail area rule would be the third by waterline area; the sixth yacht by sail area would be first by waterline area. This is but one of the many similar tabulations of races from 1856 until 1866, when the scattered opposition to the rule crystalized into a positive demand for a change.

In the application of this rule the following table was employed.

"Table of Allowance of Time for a Yacht under 2,000 sq. ft. Area, reduced to an Area of 2,000 sq. ft. and based upon a Race of Forty Miles.

Area		Seconds per Foot
2,000 to	1,900.1	1.25
1,900	1,800.1	1.29
1,800	1,700.1	1.32
1,700	1,600.1	1.36
1,600	1,500.1	1.40
1,500	1,400.1	1.44
1,400	1,300.1	1.49
1,300	1,200.1	1.54
1,200	1,100.1	1.60
1,100	1,000.1	1.67
1,100	900.1	1.74
900	800.1	1.83
800	700.1	1.93
700	600.1	2.04
600	500.1	2.19

To find the nett times of a yacht from the Table, subtract her area from 2,000 and multiply the remainder by the allowance in seconds per foot corresponding with her area, and subtract the allowance thus found from her actual time."

A supplementary table was given for yachts of over 2,000 sq. ft. area; the allowance to be added, instead of subtracted. This was necessary only in the case of a few large schooners: Fleetwing, 2208; Henrietta, 2233; Maria, 3068; Zinga, 2181; Palmer, 2371; L'Hirondelle, 2662; Vesta, 2512; Clara Clarita, 2754.

Prior to 1865 the Year Book gave only the waterline area and the tonnage, in that year a column was added giving the allowance of time for a course of 40 miles. Down to 1864 the Racing Rules formed a part of the Constitution, but in the 1865 book the Constitution is supplemented by the By-laws and the Sailing Regulations.

In spite of the revolt against the Rule in 1867, it was not abolished until 1871.

TRADITIONS AND MEMORIES OF American Yachting

Part Twenty-two

Measurement and Classification in America, Continued

Yachting Journals and Yacht Registers

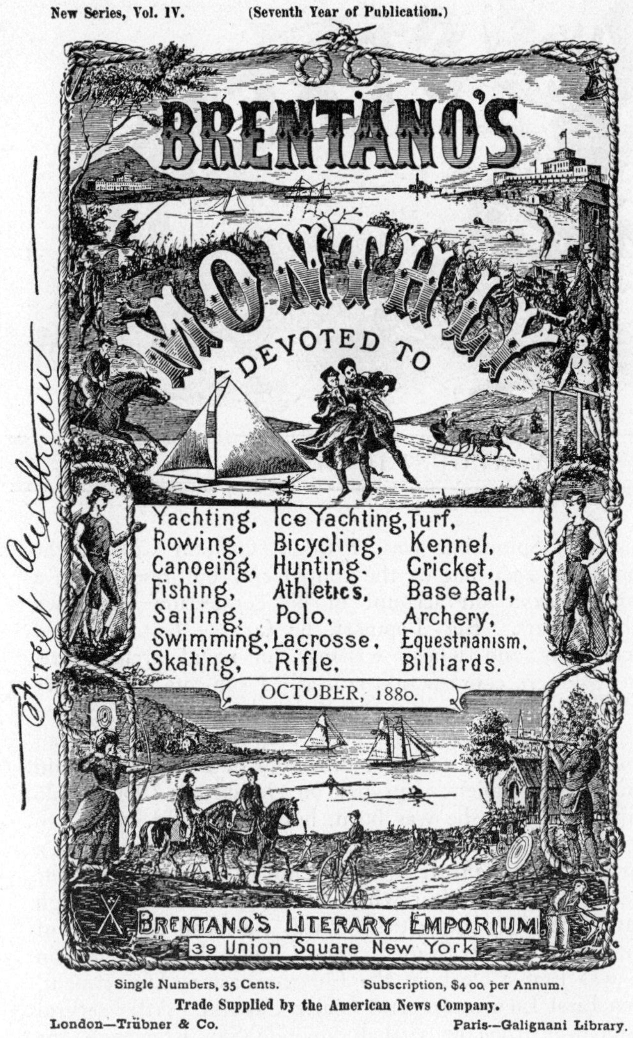

By WILLIAM P. STEPHENS

THE two matches for the trophy won by the schooner America at Cowes in 1851, popularly but improperly known as "The Queen's Cup," that of Cambria in 1870 and Livonia in 1871, did much to take yachting out of the local category and to give it a place as a national sport. Throughout the nation the news of two successive victories over England on the seas was hailed in much the same spirit as attended the battles of the Constitution and Guerriere and that of the Chesapeake and Shannon; the interest in the sport was no longer limited to New York and Boston, but covered the whole country. Marking a new development were the establishment of yachting journals and yacht registers.

As far as publicity was concerned, yachting had been compelled to take its chance in the daily press with older and more popular sports, prize fighting with bare knuckles; live pigeon shooting, not yet prohibited by law; rowing, the most popular aquatic sport; and baseball, then new and popular as an amateur sport. As a yacht owner and racing yachtsman "Young Jim" Bennett gave space in *The New York Herald,* and his competitors were obliged to follow him, so these two great matches were adequately reported. The one sporting weekly *The Spirit of the Times* long established, gave prominence to yachting through the writings of Captain Coffin; in June, 1872, there appeared a new publication *The Aquatic Monthly and Nautical Review, devoted to the interests of the Yachting and Rowing Community.* This was published by Cushing, Bardua & Co., the editor being Charles A. Peverelly, an old New York oarsman. Shell rowing, both civil and collegiate, and both amateur and professional, was then near the peak of its popularity; a fine form of sport which has succumbed to the automobile. While his personal interest was in rowing, Mr. Peverelly gave much attention to yachting. The cover design showed the start of the ocean race of 1886 and the Atalanta Boat Club crew in its last pull prior to sailing to England to row the London Rowing Club. The frontispiece of the first issue was a woodcut reproduction of a painting by A. Cary Smith of Sappho rounding the South West Spit in her last race with Livonia; the frontispiece of the July issue was a photograph of the noted McGiehan sloop Kaiser Wilhelm; the extent of the original circulation may be imagined from the use of photographs, continued for several years.

A marked feature of the magazine through its early years was the volume of letters from volunteer correspondents, most of whom endeavored to conceal their

Above: Elaborate wood engraving as used on the early Monthly. Right: Masthead of the Spirit of the Times, a weekly

Right: Masthead for Forest and Stream, for many years a leading yachting periodical. Below: Cover of The American Aquatic Magazine

identity under a *nom-de-plume,* and whose contributions served to fill a large part of each issue. Among these were: Tom Cringle, Long Tom, Big Topmast, Podgers, Mop Halliards, Handy Billy, Ballast, Skimming Dish, Binnacle, Devoted Yachtsman, Blue Jacket, Whitecap, Spinnaker, Hard-a-Lee, Waterwitch and Mast Rope. It would be interesting to know the identity of these too-modest writers, but few are to be recognized today. Devoted Yachtsman, who wrote at great length, was supposed to be Edgar H. Holley, engaged in the insurance business; Spinnaker was, I think, Captain Coffin, who could not keep out of the controversy but resorted to a *nom-de-plume* on account of his connection with two other papers. Big Topmast, by far the best informed technically and whose writings on naval architecture, yacht design, construction and allied subjects would have filled a large volume, was C. P. Kunhardt, then employed in the drafting room of the Cramp Shipyard. I recall with pleasure and regret my memory of Podgers, Captain Richard L. Ogden; who died on October 3, 1900. I do not know when he was born, but he was old enough to have had a hand in the Mexican War, presumably as a part of this adventure visiting Chili to purchase flour for the U. S. Army; after which he made a journey through Patagonia. In the fifties he was the head of a line of ships between San Francisco and China. In the Rebellion he was first a clerk in the Quartermasters Department, then First Lieutenant, and finally Captain. After several visits to Europe he settled down in San Francisco; the San Francisco Yacht Club being organized in his office in 1867. He was an expert in all lines of sport, hunting, fishing, yachting, and a ready writer on many topics. I knew him in New York in the early eighties. As he was a staunch defender of the national type, we wasted much time in ardent but fruitless attempts to convert each other in the cutter-sloop controversy which I might have employed much more profitably in listening to the story of his travels.

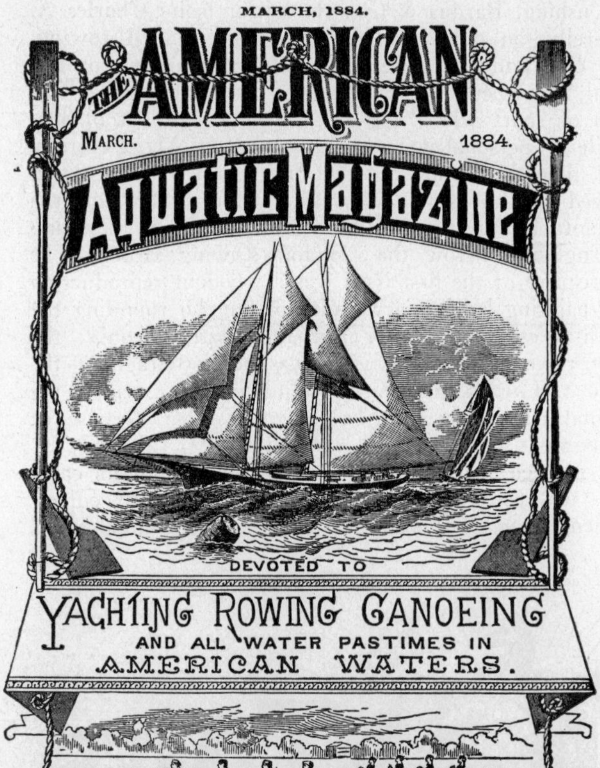

There were also contributors over their own names, Robert B. Forbes, the veteran shipmaster and yachtsman, J. W. Norcross, a naval architect; Oscar F. Burton and Col. Stuart M. Taylor, both yachtsmen. The reports of races and the descriptions of new yachts were well written; and the volumes represent a valuable contribution to yachting history. After the second year the publication was taken over by August Brentano, the founder of the present Brentano firm. The original Brentano store, on the West side of Union Square, down three steps below the sidewalk level, was a rendezvous for New York yachtsmen.

Three Score Years Backward

THE first letter of Tom Cringle, in the opening number, is interesting as a fair statement of the condition of yachting in 1872. "I learn with much satisfaction that the yachting and rowing communities are to have an organ specially devoted to their pursuits; and I feel certain that the *Aquatic Monthly,* if properly supported and conducted, will greatly promote the interests and well-being of the manly recreations it proposes to advocate. It is to be

The American Yacht List, 1875.					42
	101. CLYDE.	**102. CLYTIE.**	**103. COAST GUARD.**	**104. COLUMBIA.**	**105. COLUMBIA.**
OWNERS	Thomas Lutted.	A. A. H. Meredith.	J. B. Alley.	E. H. Osborn.	Lester Wallack.
MODELERS	Prior.	J. B. Herreshoff.	—	—	J. B. Van Deusen.
BUILDERS	"	"	—	—	"
SAILMAKERS	—	Brewer & Wheeler.	—	—	N. F. Wilson's Son.
RIG	Keel Sloop.	C. B. Sloop.	Keel Schooner	C. B. Sloop.	C. B. Schooner.
TONNAGE	Old 7—New 4.	Old 18—New 12.60.	—	Old 2—New 1.	Old 183.65—N. 106.35
CLUBS	*10*	*2, 4*	*21.*	*12.*	*1, 2*
PORTS	Boston.	Boston.	Lynn, Mass.	New York.	New York.
LENGTH OVER ALL	26 feet 6 inches.	37 feet.	27 feet.	1· feet 6 inches.	107 feet 10 inches.
LENGTH WATER-LINE	24 " 6 "	33 " 5 inches.	—	17 " 3 "	96 " 5 "
BEAM	9 " 8 "	12 " 5 "	11 " 6 inches.	8 " 6 "	25 " 6 "
DEPTH	—	5 " 2 "	—	2 "	8 " 1 "
DRAFT	4 " 4 "	4 " 4 "	—	1 "	5 " 11 "
DRAFT WITH C. B.	—	10 "	—	4 "	22 "
NUMBER OF MEN	—	Five.	—	Four.	Twelve.
BUILT OR ALTERED	Built 1870—Alt. 1874.	Built 1868.	—	Built 1871.	Built 1871.
WHERE BUILT	Portsmouth, N. H.	Bristol, R. I.	—	New Haven, Ct.	Chester, Pa.
	106. COLUMBIA.	**107. COME.**	**108. COMET.**	**109. COMING.**	**110. COMMODORE.**
OWNERS	Merrill, *et al.*	Holbrook & Bibber.	W. H. Langley.	H. H. Fay	C. H. McLellan.
MODELERS	R. W. Ribber.	" "	P. Elsworth.	R. Fish.	U. S. Gov.
BUILDERS	"	" "	Alonzo E. Smith.	Poillon Brothers.	"
SAILMAKERS	Brewer & Wheeler.	—	J M. Sawyer.	Cousins & Pratt.	Limbard & Clifford.
RIG	C. B. Cat.	C. B. Sloop.	C. B. Schooner.	C. B. Sloop.	Keel Schooner.
TONNAGE	—	—	Old 83.8.	Old 53—New 28.61.	Old 28—New 12.50.
CLUBS	*10.*	*10.*	*1, 3, 14.*	*2.*	*7.*
PORTS	Manchester.	Boston.	New York.	Boston.	Bath, Me.
LENGTH OVER ALL	24 feet 6 inches.	20 feet.	82 feet.	62 feet.	45 feet.
LENGTH WATER-LINE	19 " 9 "	18 " 9 inches.	72 " 4 inches.	57 "	41 " 4 inches.
BEAM	8 " 9 "	7 " 8 "	22 "	20 " 3 inches.	12 " 6 "
DEPTH	—	4 " 3 "	6 "	5 " 5 "	5 " 2 "
DRAFT	1 " 11 "	1 " 10 "	5 " 4 "	5 "	7 "
DRAFT WITH C. B.	7 "	—	18 "	15 "	—
NUMBER OF MEN	—	—	Five.	Four.	—
BUILT OR ALTERED	Built 1873.	—	Built 1874.	Built 1869.	Built 1869.
WHERE BUILT	South Boston.	South Boston, Mass.	Islip, L. I., N. Y.	Brooklyn, N. Y.	Charlestown, Mass.

Reproduction of a typical page from the American Yacht List of 1875

hoped we will now have such reports of races and regattas as will be intelligible to those interested. Every yachting man has been annoyed by reading accounts of regattas in which the direction of the wind, the state of the tide, and half a dozen other things equally necessary to a clear understanding of the events narrated are totally ignored. Even when the reports are comprehensible they are usually padded to an inordinate extent with long-winded descriptions of the company in the steamer, the number of flirtations, and amount of champagne consumed; which, we trust, will be omitted. We sadly need good and intelligent descriptions of new yachts and alterations of old ones. Elaborate descriptions of upholstery and mahogany fittings are all very well, but we want to learn the peculiarities of the yacht, whether in model or rig, height and position of spars, area of canvas, weight of ballast; and other information which will readily suggest itself to anyone conversant with the subject. I venture to express the hope that those who wish to exchange and ventilate their ideas on yachting and rowing will make the *Aquatic Monthly* their medium. Many interesting and instructive letters have from time to time appeared in various ephemeral publications, which, if gathered together, would be of considerable value; but they could only be retained by keeping an immense amount of other matter, or in the unsatisfactory shape of a scrapbook.

"Yacht owners and builders are usually very chary of making public the lines of the vessels they construct; but, if this prejudice could be overcome, the yachting community would be the gainers; as a proper understanding of the principles of naval architecture would be more generally diffused, models would be discussed, and we should rarely find such downright abortions as every season produces. The important questions of measurement and time allowance are yet in a most unsatisfactory condition, and discussion is one means whereby we may hope for an amendment. I venture to prophesy that the system just adopted by the N. Y. Y. C. will not survive the present season.

"After all, nothing appears so fair as length—the best yacht is the fastest of her length, and the builder may make her wide or narrow, shallow or deep as he prefers. I have said nothing about rowing for the very simple reason that I know little about it; although I have a love for every kind of outdoor sport, I am not able to get up much sympathy for those who work so hard and so uncomfortably for their fun when Heaven has been good enough to send wind to sail with.

"Success to *The Aquatic Monthly,* may it live long and prosper."

Tom Cringle.

How many today can place the last four words quoted above; Joseph Jefferson was then in the middle of a long run in his famous part of Rip van Winkle, and his drunken toast was: "Here's to the good health of you and your family; may you *live long and prosper.*"

IN August, 1873, another journal, the weekly *Forest and Stream,* made its debut under the editorship of Charles Hallock; its purport being to cover the entire field of outdoor sport, not excluding horse racing, military matters, and Art and Drama. The introductory editorial states: "Yachting and boating will be encouraged, and yachting news will be made an especial feature of the paper." As it happened, however, for several years this "feature" amounted to little more than a column of odd notes each week, and these largely on rowing. It was not until 1878 that the yachting department took definite form under a specially appointed Editor, Charles P. Kunhardt; with a fixed and aggressive policy in favor of a national yachting association, of Corinthian handling; and, by degrees, the adoption of the British keel cutter in place of the American centerboard sloop. This final move is suggested in the captions of different articles in 1878: "Can the racing cutter cruise?", "Is the sloop seaworthy?"; "Cutter and Sloop." From this time on for many years *Forest and Stream* was the most active force in the regeneration of American yachting. About the same time another New York weekly, *The Country,* devoted to all outdoor sports, took up the subject of yachting, publishing the series of lectures on naval architecture and yacht designing delivered by A. Cary Smith before the Seawanhaka Yacht Club; and the series of articles on the Wave-Line theory by John Hyslop described in MoToR BoatinG for November.

Yachting owes much to two enthusiasts, both writing largely without compensation through their devotion to the sport: Rouge-Croix, F. C. Sumicrast, a member and long secretary of the Royal Nova Scotia Yacht Squadron, of Halifax, N. S.; and Blue-with-Gold-Castle, Walter Lloyd Jeffries, of the Beverly Yacht Club. In December, 1879, Rouge-Croix contributed to *Forest and Stream* a most comprehensive review of the year's yachting, in four chapters. We quote briefly from his conclusions at the end of the series: "To give full value to an account of a yacht race the following points should be carefully attended to: 1. Locality of race. 2. Description and length—actual not estimated—of course. 3. Names of starting yachts, with tonnage or waterline length, rig, and names of owners and builders. 4. Amount and nature of prizes. 5. Weather and direction and force of wind. At present it is exceedingly difficult to trace the records of yachts owing to the absence of owners and builders' names, lengths, and the awful confusion and multiplicity of classes. It would greatly facilitate matters if we had an American Yacht List, published annually, containing full particulars, etc. I am well aware that attempts have been made to supply this want, and I have *The Commodore's Signal Book and Vade Mecum of* 1874, the *Yachting Annual* of 1875, both published by Thomas Manning; and the issues of 1874-5 of Neils Olsen's *American Yacht*

Fox's Yachting Annual of 1872, first of its kind, gave information on yachts as reproduced below

No.	NAME.	RIG.	OWNER.	LATE OWNER.	PORT.	TONNAGE. Old.	TONNAGE. New.	CLUB.	Length on Water Line.
70	COMMODORE,	K'l Sch.	C. H. McLELLAN,	....	Bath,	....	....	7,	41 4
71	COMMODORE,	C. B. Sl.	G. E. SHERMAN,	....	Jersey City,	....	....	16,	33 6
72	COMMODORE,	"	W. VAN DEUSER,	....	"	....	....	15,	18
73	CONFIDENCE,	"	CH. KEENEY,	..	"	....	....	15,	26
74	COQUETTE,	C. B. Cat	E. A. BOARDMAN,	Peabody,	Beverly,	....	....	21,	21
75	COQUETTE,	C. B. Sl.	R. B. EVERETT,	...	Boston,	....	....	9,	19
76	CORSAIR,	"	J. V. BLEASE,	....	Jersey City,	....	....	16,	19 6
77	CRAFTSMAN,	"	R. V. FREEMAN,	McKinnin,	New York,	....	....	12,	18 6
78	CREAMER, T. G.,	"	A. HARTMAN,	....	"	....	....	10,	....
79	CYGNUS,	"	J. MELLEN,	....	Stapleton, S. I.	....	....	20,	18 6
80	DAISY,	K'l Sl.	W. C. OTIS,	....	Boston,	12.34	5.89	2,	28 4
81	DAPHNE,	C. B. Sl.	E. T. WOOD,	R. Maxwell,	Brooklyn,	24.00	....	3, 5,	42
82	DART,	K'l Sch.	C. H. HATCH,	....	Charlestown,	....	....	19,	25
83	DAUNTLESS,	"	J. G. BENNETT	D. Bradford,	New York,	267.9	126.4	1, 2, 3,	116 5
84	DAWN,	C. B. Sch.	P. S. SHELTON,	G. Griswold,	Boston,	41.8	23.33	2,	54 8
85	DOLPHIN,	C. B. Sl.	J. KELLUM,	...	New York,	23.31	....	1,	....
86	DOLPHIN,	"	J. A. WEEKS,	....	Oyster Bay,	....	....	17,	28
87	DOLPHIN,	K'l Sl.	R. BROWN,	....	Charlestown,	....	..	19,	25
88	DREADNAUGHT,	K'l Sch.	S. SAMUELS,	....	New York,	176.50	...	1, 3,	103 2
89	DREAM,	C. B. Sch.	S. S. CURTIS,	....	Manchester,	26.76	....	2,	41
90	DREAM,	K'l Sl.	S. T. DOWNS,	....	Lynn,	....	....	18,	17 4
91	DUDLEY,	C. B. Sl.	J. L. GLADWIN,	....	Brooklyn,	32.00	....	5,	41
92	EARLY BIRD,	"	R. S. RUSSELL,	J. P. Gardiner,	Beverly,	....	....	21,	21

— 10 —

No.	Beam.	Draught	Prizes Won	Year Built.	Year Altered	No. of Men.	CAPTAIN.	BUILDER.	SAILMAKER.	PRIVATE SIGNAL.
70	12 6	7 -		1867	.	8	"		...	
71	12 6	2 6		1871		5	"	G. Roahr,	Chester & Keefe,	Red C, white diamond, blue field.
72	7 6	1 3		1872		3	"	S. Fowler,	Chester & Keefe,	
73	10	2	.	1872		4	"	....	Chester & Keefe,	
74	9	1 8	.	1869		3	"	....	I. Foster,	
75	9	2 2	..	1868		3	"		....	
76	8 6	1 6		1870		3	Moulds,	J. Snellgrove,	Chester & Keefe,	Red scull, white diamond, blue field.
77	7	1 6	1	1869		3	Owner,	W. H. Cornel,	Chester & Keefe,	Star on red and white field.
78	..	...				..	"	...	....	
79	8	1 3	..	1871	..	4	"	Gilroy,	Arents,	
80	11 6	4 5	.	1867	..	3	F. Brookins,	Prior,	....	White daisy on blue field.
81	14 2	3 10	..	1868	.	5	Owner,	J. Munn,	J. M. Sawyer,	
82	9	3 6	..	1867		3	"	....	...	
83	24 8	12	2	1867	1870	35	M. J. Lyons,	Mystic,	....	Blue diamond on white field, red triangle at back.
84	16	6 5	3	1856	1865	5	Kendrick.	....	Palfray & Pratt,	Blue and white squares, red & w't tails.
85	....	...	..	1871	..	4	....	....	J. M. Sawyer,	
86	10	2 2	..	..	..	..	Owner,	...	....	
87	9	3 6	..	1868	.	3	"	Waite,	Lyons,	
88	24 5	12 6	..	1871	..	29	"	Poillon Bro.	....	
89	16 5	3 5	2	1867	1872	5	"	....	....	D on a red field.
90	8	3	..	1870	..	3	"	....	....	White pipe on red field, blue tail.
91	14	3.	..	..	..	5	"	....	J. M. Sawyer,	
92	9	1 10	.	1870	..	5	"	....	....	

List before me as I write. I am also well aware that neither of these publications lived, chiefly for lack of support. I very much regret that Mr. Olsen's venture was not continued. Of the desirability of adopting a uniform system of classification I have already written; and I hope before long to see something done in this respect. Classification hinges on measurement, and this has been a constant source of trouble; as nearly every club has its own rule and system of time allowance. We want a uniform rule here also: a rule which shall, as far as possible, leave owners and builders unfettered and untrammeled, and yet which shall give a fair idea of the size of a vessel. I am not going, inviting though the subject may be, to enter upon the vexed question of cutter vs. sloop. Personally I prefer the cutter to the sloop for its rig, which I believe to be the better for outside work; at the same time, I do not want to cram my belief down any man's throat, or to say that the sloop is worthless. Dear fellow yachtsman, let us write and talk cutter, sloop, schooner and yawl all winter; when spring comes let us amicably fit out and race and cruise together to the greater glory of that noble sport whose welfare and progress we all have at heart." It would have been well for yachting had there been more men of such enthusiasm, such breadth of vision, and such broad-minded spirit to write and speak in the war which was then impending.

The Early Yacht Registers

THE mention above of the Manning and Olsen ventures brings us chronologically to a new detail of yachting. The first Yacht Register, as they are now commonly known, was *Fox's Yachting Annual,* 1872, a booklet of 60 pages containing the particulars of 401 yachts and 24 yacht clubs. The nature of the information is shown on the accompanying page reproduction; there was no color printing, but the private signals were described in type. The publisher, Edward Fox, was a reporter of yachting for *The Spirit of the Times,* and proprietor of Fox's Yachting Agency, at 83 Nassau Street, presumably the first American yacht broker. The few advertisements are interesting: Brooks Brothers sold clothing on the corner of Catherine and Cherry Streets, in the heart of the old shipping district. Captain Bob Fish had a boat yard at Bayonne, N. J., and an "Office and Model Room" on the corner of Front and Roosevelt Streets; C. & R. Poillon had their yard at the foot of Bridge Street, Brooklyn, and an office at 224 South Street, New York. Annin & Co. made yacht flags on the corner of Fulton and William Streets, P. McGiehan, "Builders of the famous sloop yachts Meta, Kaiser Wilhelm, Meteor and other well known racers" was at Pamrapo, N. J.; David Carll was at City Island, Joseph Van Deusen "Naval Architect and Yacht Builder" was in Brooklyn, Samuel H. Pine "Ship, Yacht and Pilot Boat Builder" was at Greenpoint, L. I.; Frank Bates was at Short Branch House, Gowanus Bay. The preface was both explanatory and apologetic: "The growth of Yachting in the United States during the past few years has called for a handbook of Yachting statistics, which the undersigned hopes to supply in the following Annual. The first edition of a work of this kind will necessarily contain many errors in the measurements and particulars of the different yachts; but it will open the way to a more perfect edition in 1873." The expectation of a second edition apparently was not realized, as no copies are to be found today.

In 1874, as stated by Rouge-Croix, Thomas Manning issued his *Commodore's Signal Book and Yachtsman's Vade Mecum;* and in the following year *Manning's Yachting Annual, Compiled from original sources by Thomas Manning. Officially Recognized.* "Tom" Manning was one of a coterie of men well known to yachtsmen, and usually by a nickname: "Bill" Bishop, the yacht plumber; "Sam" Pine, the yacht builder; with "Sammy" Ayers of the same trade; John Sawyer, the sailmaker; "Bob" Brown and "Jim" Knight, the shipsmiths; "Dave" Clark, the yacht painter. These men were representatives of a class of American mechanics which flourished in those ante-New Deal days and left a permanent mark on American yachting. An Englishman by birth, Manning was in business in Boston in the sixties, joining the Boston Y. C. in 1866 and being Vice Commodore in 1868 as part owner of the schooner Juniata. Moving to New York, in 1873 he established a yacht agency, at first in partnership with his brother. In the following year he published *The Commodore's Signal Book,* and a year later his *Yacht List.* He claimed, and probably with truth, that these publications entailed an annual loss which he wrote off as an advertising expense for the brokerage business. The *Yacht List* was arranged on the basis of clubs and club fleets, 36 yacht clubs in addition to several ice-yacht clubs and the young New York Canoe Club. The particulars of each yacht included the hull dimensions, tonnage, O. M. and N. M., cubic contents, the builders being indicated by numbers. The flags were poorly printed, the whole arrangement was inconvenient for reference, and the book was very poorly bound. In these two years Manning had a competitor in *The American Yacht List* published by Neils Olsen, Steward of the New York Y. C.; in much more convenient form, with all yachts in alphabetical order; 505 yachts being listed in 1874 and 667 in 1875. The second book contained lithographed plates of club burgees and private signals; nearly all of the latter being of swallow-tail instead of rectangular shape. Both of these men were well fitted for their work by their wide personal knowledge of all of the larger yachts listed, but their ventures proved unsuccessful and were discontinued; in 1881 Olsen revived his *Yacht List,* continuing it until 1887, when he sold out to Manning who continued it in larger size each year until his death in 1900; it was continued by his successors until 1903; in which year was established the present *Lloyd's Register of American Yachts.*

The Cubic Contents Rule

THIS rule, while nominally based on displacement, was very crude in form; the limits of measurement were from the load waterline to the rabbet of the keel; near enough in the case of a centerboard yacht, but ignoring a material bulk of keel in the case of the large keel yachts. The Rule read: "The areas of three sections, from the waterline to the intersection of outer planking with keel in the case of each yacht, one taken amidships, another equidistant therefrom to the stem, and the third equidistant therefrom to the stern, shall be measured and determined in square feet. The cubical contents of the immersion shall be calculated by multiplying the sum of the areas of the three sections by one-fourth of the length on waterline in feet and decimals; which shall, for the purpose of this measurement, be deemed the displacement of the yacht. The cube roots of the displacements shall be deemed the basis of comparative allowances of time. In order to apply the bases of measurement as above to the sliding scale of allowances, graduated according to time of making race, hitherto in use by the Club (but for no other purpose) the cube roots of the displacements shall in all cases be multiplied by one hundred; this forming the apportionments as given in the annexed tables." The Club Book for 1872 contained a very brief announcement: "Rule of Measurement for Time Allowances. Note—The Club having abolished the Measurements and Allowances adopted in 1871, and not having, at the date of this issue, decided positively upon those under which the June Regatta of this year shall be sailed, Rules of Measurement and Allowances are omitted."

Just what the allowances were is not plain, but the general dissatisfaction is proved by the action of James D. Smith, who refused to start his schooner Halcyon under them. The start was made in the Narrows, and this time flying, instead of from anchors.

In 1873 a new form of the same rule was tried, the sections, at each end of the waterline, in the middle and at two intermediate points, being measured from the rabbet to a horizontal plane tangent to the lowest point of the planksheer; the five sections thus obtained being computed by Chapman's Rule; thus giving a close approximation to the actual bulk of the hull from the keel to the level of planksheer, excluding overhangs. The theory of this Rule is hard to fathom, it was far from satisfactory, and the pages of *The Aquatic Monthly* were filled with long discussions of its demerits. Perhaps the best explanation of what was termed the "Lump of Putty" theory was that given me by Charles P. Kunhardt when I first made his acquaintance about 1880. You and I each take a lump of putty, five pounds, for instance, and having agreed on a scale and length of waterline, each moulds his lump into the shape which best pleases him; yours may be wide and shoal, mine narrow and deep; both racing together on even terms.

The discussion continued year by year, within the Club and in the *Aquatic Monthly* and *The Spirit of The Times;* as a whole it was very weak on the technical side, it abounded in personalities, and was largely a matter of personal preference for the yachts of one modeller and dislike of those of another. While it helped to keep alive the interest in yachting, it contributed in no way to the advancement of design or the improvement of racing.

WE have followed thus far the course of measurement legislation within the New York Y. C. as being eminently the leader in American yachting; the smaller clubs blundered on from year to year with no better results. Among many fruitless experiments was that of "mean length"; well named, as it meant nothing and did nothing to improve design. This rule included all or part of the length over all plus the length on waterline divided by two. In its early years the Seawanhaka Y. C. used "mean length" multiplied by breadth; many other clubs used "mean length" only. The crude and childish ideas of yacht measurement entertained by intelligent and educated yachtsmen even as late as 1878 are shown in the form of "mean length" rule published in the Atlantic Y. C. book in that year; a modification of a rule used by the Boston Y. C. "The overall measurements of the Yachts of this Club shall be taken from a point on deck perpendicular with that point on the forward point of the stem or cutwater where the waterline intersects to the point of extreme length of the Yacht on deck aft, irrespective of the rail. The principles on which this allowance is made: 1. Size is an advantage in respect to speed. 2. The elements of size are length, breadth and depth. Length is adopted as the element of measurement because: 1. It gives easier lines, which is an advantage. 2. It is easily measured. 3. It is easily verified. Note: As a yacht does not always sail on even keel, her length on waterline is not her actual sailing length if, as in some models, the bow extends forward and the stern runs out aft. Therefore, in measuring for allowance, we add the length on waterline to that over all and divide the product (sum?) by two to get the 'allowance length.'"

The era of trans-Atlantic ocean racing inaugurated by America in 1851 reached its climax in the race from New York to Cowes in 1866, and practically ended with the visits of Dauntless in 1872 and Enchantress in 1873; a few hardy sailormen like Lloyd Phoenix continued to sail blue water, but the majority of American yachtsmen built their yachts for coastal cruising, the Sound, and racing in and outside of New York Harbor. As racing became more popular greater attention was given to the measurement rule as owners began to realize that winning or losing depended almost entirely on utilizing the full possibilities of the rule.

The additions to the fleet in yachts above 50 feet waterline in the decade ending in 1883 were of a mixed nature; in the racing division there were but four sloops, Arrow, 1874; Fanny, 1876; Mischief, 1879, and Pocahontas, 1881. The schooner fleet of some forty yachts included some, such as the first Intrepid, Lloyd Phoenix, and Fortuna, Henry S. Hovey, keel schooners designed for offshore cruising; and a number, mainly centerboard, for Sound use and occasional cruising alongshore. A few, notably Ambassadress, William Astor, and Mohawk, William T. Garner, were built, just as were the great residences on Fifth Avenue, merely to uphold the social positions of their owners.

While many of these yachts had adequate freeboard, the influence of the Cubic Contents Rule on those specially built for racing could have but one effect: the reduction of freeboard below the danger-point. The heavy penalty on out-of-water bulk necessitated a low freeboard with a limited range of stability. It was not through essential qualities of design, but through a general recognition of the danger of capsize, and the skill of the men entrusted with the handling of the larger yachts that there were not more such disasters as the capsizes of Mohawk and Grayling in fair weather and smooth water.

TRADITIONS AND MEMORIES OF

AMERICAN YACHTING

By WILLIAM P. STEPHENS

THE year 1882 was a crucial one in American yachting, the beginning of a revolution which resulted in a radical change of the national type. The victories of the little Scotch cutter Madge in New York in the previous year, followed by the building and racing of the cutters Bedouin, Wenonah and Oriva, had changed the cutter proposition from an abstract idea to a material fact. The feeling that an owner should be more than a mere passenger aboard his own yacht, independent of both builder and professional skipper, was growing rapidly; with an accompanying interest in questions of design, measurement and racing rules. The Seawanhaka Yacht Club of Oyster Bay, founded eleven years before with a small fleet of sandbag boats and only two small cabin yachts, had taken a prominent position in New York yachting, and in addition to its proclaimed advocacy of the cutter, at a meeting on March 3, 1882 had incorporated the term "Corinthian" in its title; thereby subjecting itself to much ridicule on the grounds of snobbery and aping English ideas. It was in this year that the yawl rig, previously almost unknown in America, was introduced through a vigorous campaign in its behalf by C. P. Kunhardt; together with a plea for single-hand sailing. In defense of the old type the sloop Julia, built by George Steers in 1854 but for years sailing as a keel schooner, was bought by Rear Com. Edward M. Brown, N.Y.Y.C., and restored to her original rig as a centerboard sloop; the expectation that she would hold her own with the more modern yachts was very far from realization.

The racing in 1881 was very unsatisfactory and there were more and more complaints against the various rules; the matches of the cutter Madge with the American sloops gave new impetus to the question, and following these races at the

●

Part Twenty-three

Measurement and Classification in America, Continued

●

Above: Clara, a cat-yawl built in 1887 by N. G. Herreshoff for his personal use. L.O.A., 35'4"; L.W.L., 29'4"; breadth, 9'10"; draft, 5'5". Right: Katrina

end of the season came the Cup match of Atalanta and Mischief. The discussion in print became more voluminous and, if possible, more pointless, with no end in sight. As the yachts were laid up the paper war took on new strength; most of the combatants favored length in some form, waterline or "mean"; Kunhardt, though almost alone, still stood to his guns in defense of his "lump of putty" rule.

In *Forest & Stream* of December 29, 1881, there appeared a letter from Edward Burgess, recently returned from a summer on the South coast of England where he had every opportunity to study British yachts; it began, "In the first place, let me announce myself as a 'cutter man' and so no fondness for skimming-dishes influences my belief that length on the load waterline is the fairest standard for racing measurement. Of all systems, except perhaps a displacement one, a bulk rule seems to me the very worst."

Having outgrown its original suburban environment, the Seawanhaka Yacht Club was now established on New York Bay, with a club house at Edgewater, Staten Island, and numbered many of the larger yachts in its fleet. The crude rules which had served for its small yachts were useless; and, acting on a report of a committee including Dr. H. G. Piffard, A. Cary Smith and John Hyslop, on March 3 adopted a rule proposed several years previously by Dixon Kemp; the two factors being length and sail area, as follows.

Below: Lines of Wenonah, fin-keel, N. G. Herreshoff, 1892. L.O.A., 37'6"; L.W.L., 25'; Breadth, 7'2"; Draft, 6'2"

Above: Titania. Below: Ballast fin invented by General I. Garrard, Frontenac, Mich., 1881. Cast iron; length, 8'; depth, 3'; weight, 1,280 pounds. First fiitted to 22-foot sandbag boat

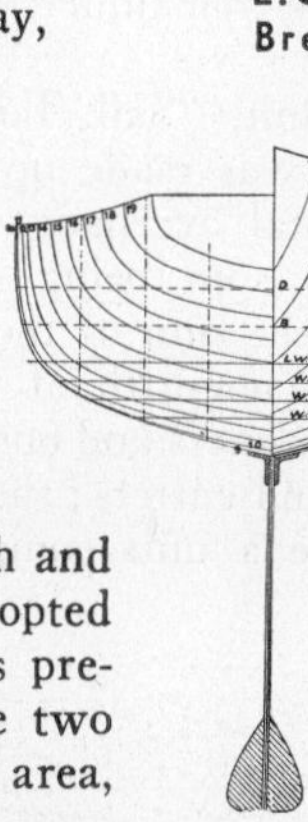

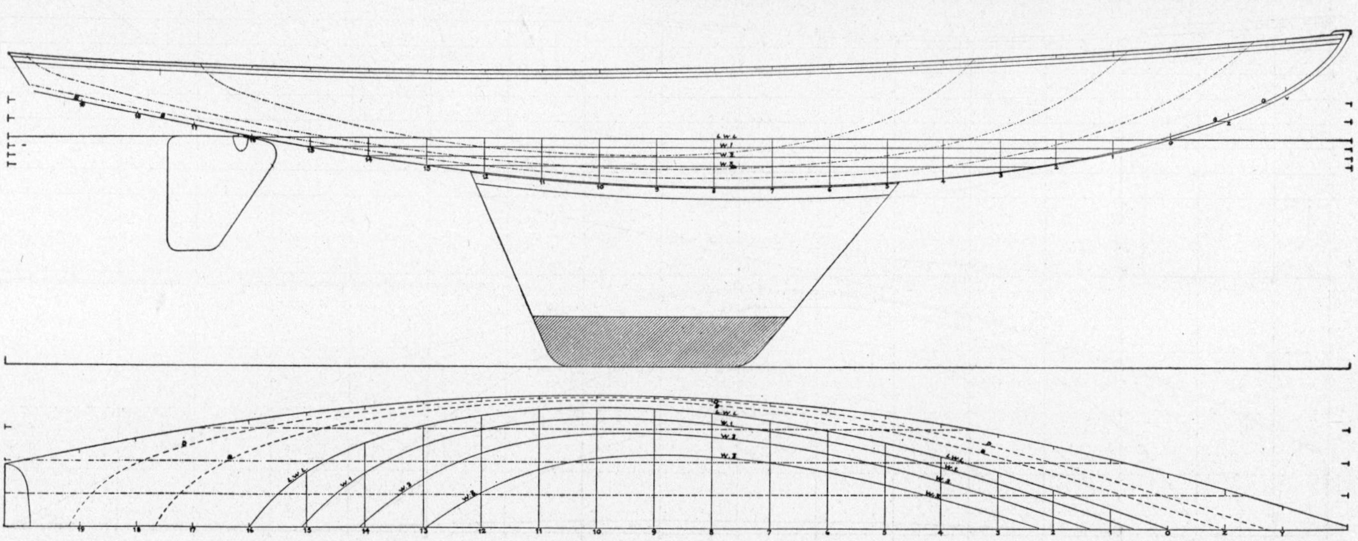

Left: Gloriana, designed in 1891 by N. G. Herreshoff for the 46-Foot Class. L.O.A., 70'; L.W.L., 45'4"; Breadth, 12'7"; Draft, 10'; sail area, 4,137 square feet. Ratio of square root of sail area to waterline, 1.41 per cent

Rules for Measurement

FIRST—The rule for the measurement of cabin yachts of this Club shall be as follows:

$$\frac{\text{Length} \times \text{Sail Area}}{4000} = \text{S.Y.C. tons,}$$

with the following definitions and restrictions:

In determining sail area, sails shall be divided into lower and upper sails. For one-masted vessels the sails to be measured shall be: Lower sails: Mainsail, staysail and jib. Upper sails: Topsails. For two masted vessels: Lower sails: Mainsail, foresail, staysail, jib and flying jib. Upper sails: Main topsail and fore topsail.

The sails shall be measured in the following manner, and the result expressed in square feet. Mainsail from tack to throat along the mast; from tack to clew along the boom; from throat to end of sail along the gaff. Diagonals will be taken from tack to peak and from clew to throat. Main sheet to be hauled hard down. This will apply also to foresails of schooners. Jibs will be measured from tack to head along the stay; from tack to clew along the foot; from clew to head along the leech. Topsails will be measured from jaws of gaff on mast to sheave on topmast; from jaws of gaff to after side of sheave on gaff.

The area of lower and upper sails having been determined as above, 20 per cent of the area of the main and foresails is deducted, if possible, from the area of the topsails, and the remainder, if any, shall alone be taxable as topsails.

The final unit, "Sail Tons," had as its main factor length, which was made up of load waterline plus one-fifth of the total overhang, both forward and aft; nine tenths of this sum being employed. This figure was multiplied by the sum of the areas of the lower sails and topsails, minus one-fifth of the area of the mainsail and headsails in schooners and one-fifth of the area of the mainsail in sloops and cutters; the final result being divided by 4,000 to make a unit comparable with the tonnage of

Below: Lines of Hit or Miss, Cape catboat, built by Herbert F. Crosby, 1893. Conventional plum stem and square stern replaced by after overhang and Gloriana bow, the point being presumed to add to the speed

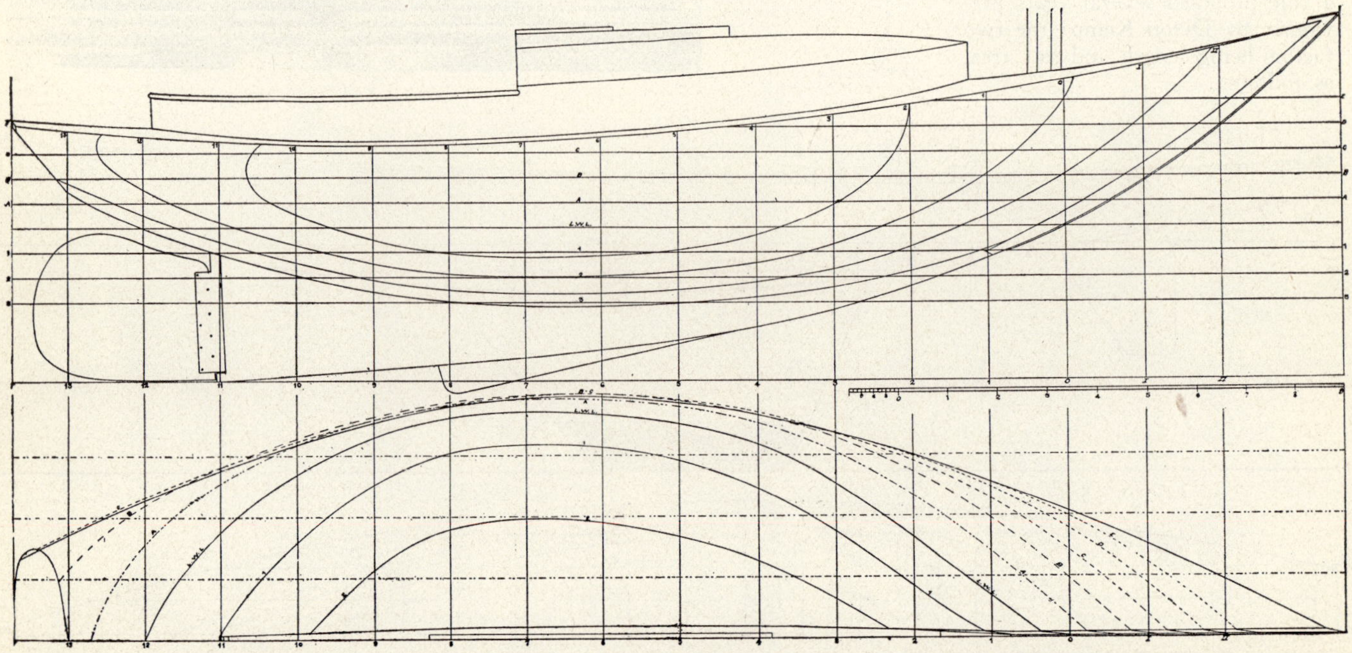

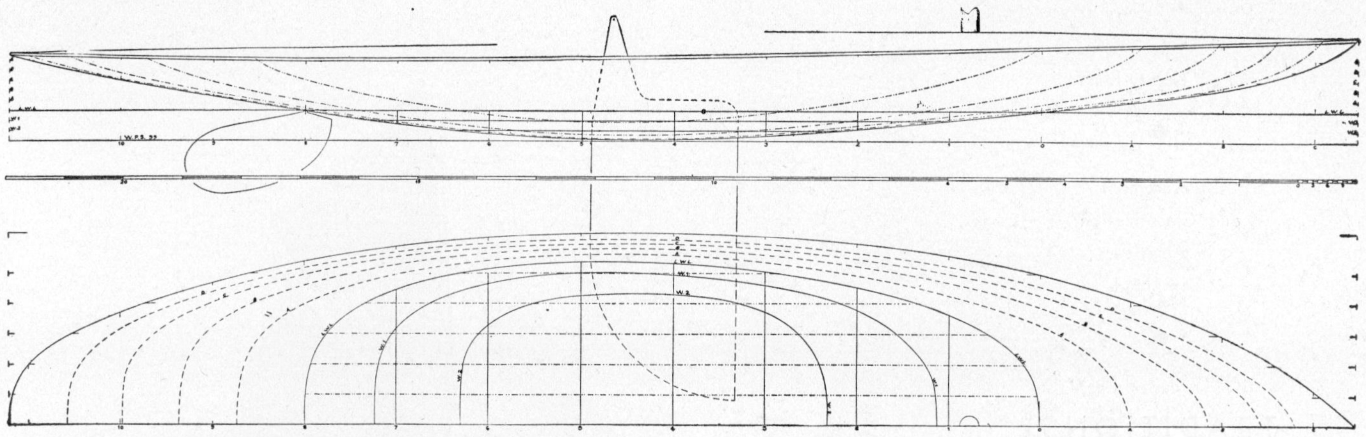

the yacht. Expressed in the usual manner, with the use of letters and mathematical symbols, this formula approaches the limit of length and complication.

It will be noticed that the virus of "mean length" was still working actively in the minds of the committee; while the formula as a whole was lengthy and complicated.

Speaking of this rule while under consideration, Forest & Stream of January 5 said: "One piece of patchwork, empyrical and unfair, will give way to another somewhat more acceptable, and so on; until, step by step, every agitation helps to clear away the cobwebs, and drives selfish interests to the wall. Finally, after essaying everything under the sun but the right thing, a bulk rule will receive a majority vote from sheer desperation as the *dernier resort*. We venture to believe that bulk measurement will be the upshort of it all in time."

The dire predictions of Kunhardt, of E. M. Brandt, in *The Herald,* Capt. Cornelius McKay in *The Telegram,* W. E. Simmons in *The Times,* and Captain Coffin in *The World* and *The Spirit of the Times* were not realized. The new rule worked well in practice in the races of 1882, though the form, with its unit of "Sail Tons," was not in accordance with American ideas and its measurement of canvas proved difficult of application.

At a meeting of the club on March 3, 1883, a special committee, Robert Center, C. Smith Lee and John Hyslop, was appointed to consider a revision of the rule, and also to confer with the New York Y. C. and other clubs with a view to uniting on a common rule of measurement and uniform classification. At this meeting a suggestion was made by Anson Phelps Stokes that a spar measurement should be adopted in place of measurement of canvas. The committee, after working with a similar committee of the New York Y. C., made its report at a meeting of the club on May 24, proposing a new formula, length on waterline added to the square root of the sail area, with a divisor of two; the sail area to be based upon the measurement of the spars. What was henceforth known as the "Seawanhaka Rule" was thus adopted.

Under this rule, which became the governing influence in yacht design in America for the ensuing twenty years, was built up the finest fleet of racing yachts ever floated; in type a compromise between American and British principles, with ample but not excessive rigs, fitted for racing and coastwise cruising. All of the great Burgess fleet were designed to it; Puritan, Mayflower, Volunteer, Titania, Sachem. A. Cary Smith designed a similarly large fleet of both racing and cruising yachts. The rule was at once adopted by the Eastern Y. C., the Knickerbocker Y. C. and the Toronto Y. C. The year book of the New York Y. C. for 1883 contained the regular cubic contents rule in its usual place in the Sailing Regulations, but across the page was printed in red "See Appendix." This read: "The alterations in the Measurement for Time Allowance, and the following amendments to the By-laws and Sailing Regulations, were adopted and went into effect on the 4th day of June, 1883, too late to be incorporated in the body of the Club Book for this year." The new rule was identical in factors with the "Seawanhaka Rule," but with one important exception: the length was multiplied by two, added to the sail area, and three was taken as the divisor.

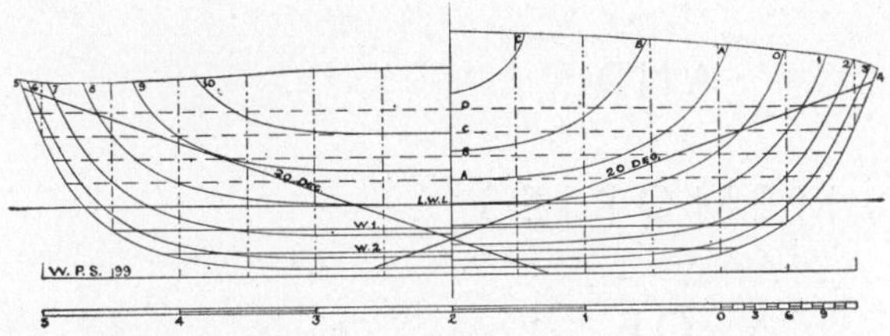

Lines of Glencairn, Half-Rating Class. Designed by G. Herrick Duggan, Royal St. Lawrence Y. C. (amateur), as the first challenger for the Seawanhaka Cup, 1896. Original of the Skow type. L.O.A., 23'; L.W.L., 12'6"; Breadth (extreme), 6'4"; Draft, 5". Breadth on waterline when upright, 5'5"; when heeled to 20 degrees (best sailing angle), 4'. Waterline when upright for measurement, 12'6"; when heeled, 15'

On March 27 Kunhardt wrote the obituary of the Cubic Contents Rule as follows: "A gentleman writes us he is sorry we have given up bulk measurement. We have not given it up, but recognize that with the prevailing want of knowledge it is no use trying to push what the people are not yet able to contemplate from a philosophical point; and that the best way to have a bad law repealed is to enforce it." This was his valedictory; a few weeks later he resigned as Yachting Editor and I took his place. My close association with such men as Robert Center, A. Cary Smith and John Hyslop, all older and much more experienced, naturally led me to share their views; and thenceforward all of my influence as a writer was centered on the extension of the new rule.

The feeling in favor of length measurement in its various forms was still very strong, while the New York Y. C. refused to place waterline on an equal footing with sail area, the Atlantic, Larchmont and other large clubs as well as the majority of the smaller ones retained the waterline with a tax on a part of the after overhang. An amusing incident, characteristic of the popular feeling of the day, occurred on January 31, 1889, when a number of yachtsmen representing the smaller clubs about New York met at the Gilsey House to organize what became the New York Yacht Racing Association. After the organization was decided on, the question of a rule was taken up; the Seawanhaka Rule was proposed, but actively opposed by one of the oldest and most experienced of New York sailing men.

Part Twenty-four

Measurement and Classification in America, Continued

TRADITIONS AND MEMORIES OF AMERICAN YACHTING

By WILLIAM P. STEPHENS

Katrina, compromise cutter or sloop, 1888. Mast stepped well amidships; relatively short with long topmast. Pole bowsprit with single bobstay. Double head-rig. Foot of mainsail laced to boom

THE controversy was carried on with much feeling, not all of it of a friendly nature, on both sides; the following letter from A. Cary Smith is characteristic of the "airy persiflage" in which he was wont to indulge:

Dear Mr. Stephens:

I am glad to see that you are working at the Measurement racket, and now is the time to pound; as the views held on this subject are appalling. I met a prominent man who had been called on to give his views before the New Rochelle Yacht Club, and he informed me that length plus one-half overhang was the best measurement, for then you could make your boat what you liked. I thought that I had gone back on the deal of Time, and grown ten years younger; about the time when Mr. K. (naming a well known yachtsman) said that we (the N.Y.Y.C.) were trying to beat a smart boat by measurement. And the peculiar part of it is that each man has a personal motive, and cannot be made to understand that it is for the good of the sport.

Events have proved that we—you, I, and other Cranks—are right, but "Jordan is a hard road to trabble" when you want to do right, and D—— few give much credit for this latter idea. Now, can you not put in some more like this week's, and put a picture—that is what killed

Below: Lines of Katrina, designed by A. Cary Smith and closely similar to Titania

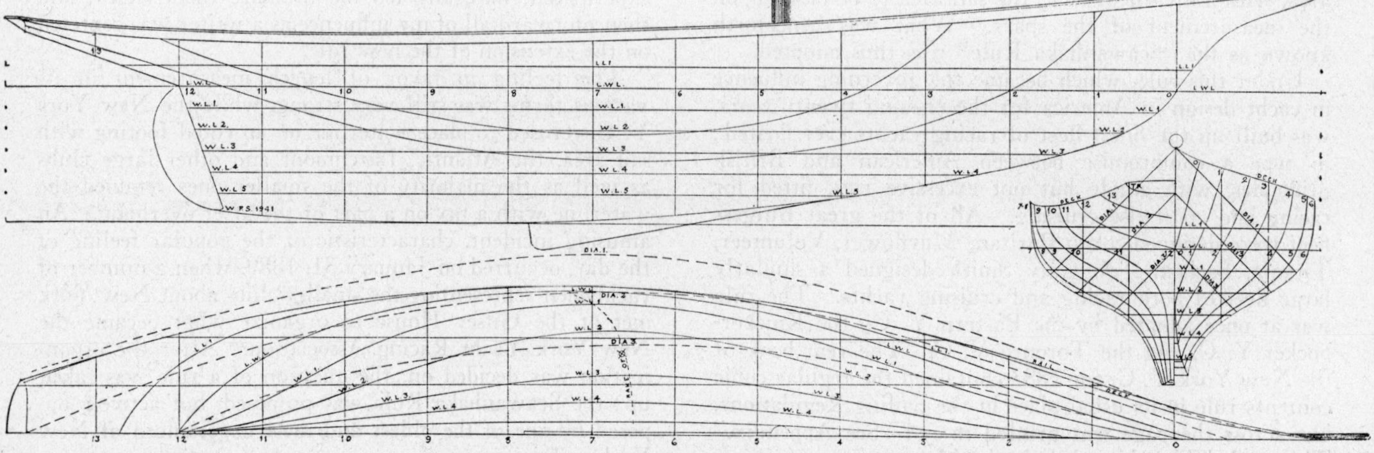

Titania on the stocks at Piepgrass' yard, City Island. Photograph by Thomas I. Miller, May, 1887

Tweed, pictures—what does length plus one-half overhang lead to, thusly? (here a crude sketch)

Yours truly

(signed) A. Cary Smith.

An amusing incident, characteristic of the popular feeling of the day, occurred when a number of yachtsmen representing the smaller clubs about New York met at the Gilsey House to organize what became the New York Yacht Racing Association. After the organization was decided on the question of a rule was taken up; the Seawanhaka Rule was proposed, but vigorously opposed by one of the oldest and most experienced of New York sailing men. He said, most sarcastically: "Length on waterline *plus* square root of the sail area; who knows what plus is? I don't know what *plus* is. You take the length of the waterline and add it to the length overall, and divide by two; then you have a plain and simple rule *with no plus in it.*" This convincing argument carried the day and the "plain and simple" mean-length rule was unanimously adopted.

In re-arranging the classes in 1883 the Seawanhaka C. Y. C. as well as the New York Y. C. adopted "correct length" in the one case and "measurement for time allowance" in the other, the two being synonymous, as the basis for classification. Why this was done is not clear; nor why, after two years, it was rejected and waterline substituted. Though by this time the New York Y. C. had agreed to meet a challenger with but one yacht, it would not agree on any limitation of waterline; Priscilla, the representative of the club in 1885, was designed to a waterline of 85 feet, to meet the 81 feet of Genesta. General Paine, who was the backbone of the defense in 1885-6-7, was a believer in the Scriptural doctrine that it is more blessed to give than to receive, and under the existing rule and an allowance table of but 40 percent he wished to be free to select the load waterline and to pile on sail, paying for it the light tax imposed by the rule. It was largely in view of probable challengers for the Cup that the New York Y. C. refused to accept the equal values for the two factors and taxed length twice to but once for sail; waiting until 1890 before falling into line with the Seawanhaka rule.

In the older and larger schooners the square root of the sail area was from 90 to 100 per cent of the waterline; in the leading racing yachts of the seventies and early eighties, including such cutters as Genesta and Galatea, it was little more than equal. The new Katrina of 1888 had 84.15 as the square root of her sail area on a waterline of 69.38 feet, a ratio of 1.21 percent; her leading rival, Titania, on the same waterline had a ratio of but 1.18 per cent. As the interest in racing increased there came a keener competition among designers and their patrons which disclosed a weak point in the rule, in the light direct tax on sail coupled with the classification by waterline and the 40 percent allowance table. The first extreme step in over-canvassing was made by the young American designer, William Gardner, in 1889 in his initial efforts, Liris, in the 40-foot and Kathleen in the 30-foot Class; on a waterline of 40 feet Liris had 3603 square feet of sail, the square root of this figure being 60.03, or 1.51 percent of the waterline. While yachtsman realized the evil as it increased from year to year, no steps were taken for its correction.

The yachts designed under the Seawanhaka Rule between 1883 and 1900 represent the high point of designing in America; the demand of owners was for craft that, while giving good sport in racing, were still adapted for cruising and general use; the designers, on their part, were content with a construction that, while light compared with the past, was still adequate for a long use after being out-classed in racing. Designing to recognized

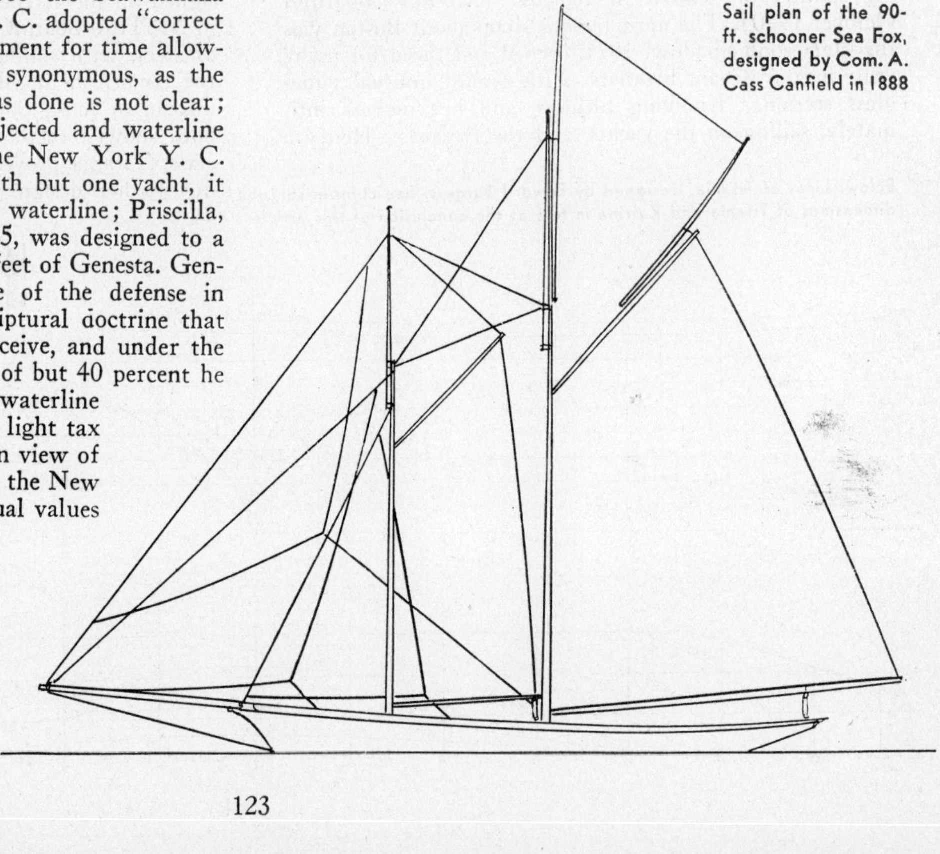

Sail plan of the 90-ft. schooner Sea Fox, designed by Com. A. Cass Canfield in 1888

Fanny, Old Time Sloop, 1874. Showing typical sloop rig. Long lower mast, stepped well forward, short topmast. Built-in bowsprit with multiple bobstays. In common with sloops of her era, Fanny originally carried a single large jib; when rebuilt in 1883 this was replaced by small jib and fore staysail

class limits had displaced the chance selection of length as in Gracie, 59-70; Hildegard, 61; Fanny, 66; Mischief, 61; all now racing in the new 70-ft. waterline class. Typical examples of this are found in this Class in Titania, 1887, and Katrina, 1888.

Mr. Burgess, a self-taught amateur, such an institution as a school of naval architecture being unthought of sixty years ago, was in his fifth year as a professional naval architect, having to his credit the already famous Puritan and Mayflower; while on his drafting boards with Titania were a third Cup defender, Volunteer, and Papoose. Mr. Smith, also a self-taught amateur, had practiced the profession of yacht designing for 17 years, his work including everything from the largest cruising schooners to small sloops and catboats. The lines of these two yachts afford a most interesting basis of comparison; their dimensions and elements being shown at the conclusion of this article.

In all of his early designs Mr. Burgess followed the cutter type of sheer plan; the plumb stem and long tapering counter, as shown in Papoose (MoToR BoatinG October 1940). The most famous sloop about Boston was the Herreshoff Shadow, 1871, owned and raced for many years by the Bryant brothers; with a most unusual wineglass section. Knowing Shadow and her owners intimately, sailing on the yachts, and the Bryants—Henry a clever amateur designer—being in the crew of Puritan, Mr. Burgess followed this section in both Papoose and Titania. The difference in the sections of the two yachts is plainly evident. Some of the most notable of the Smith yachts were large schooners such as Prospero, Intrepid and Fortuna, these showing the then fashionable "clipper stem"; this he used in Katrina. Both yachts were designed on the Archer-Hyslop wave-form system described in MoToR BoatinG of November 1940; both were built of steel, with similar scantlings. The rigs were similar, the American modification of the cutter, but with laced instead of loose-footed mainsails. In their racing, while both showed their superiority to the older yachts of the class, Titania proved the faster. How much of this was due to her design, and how much to the ownership of

Below: Lines of Titania, designed by Edward Burgess. See comparison of dimensions of Titania and Katrina in text at the conclusion of this article

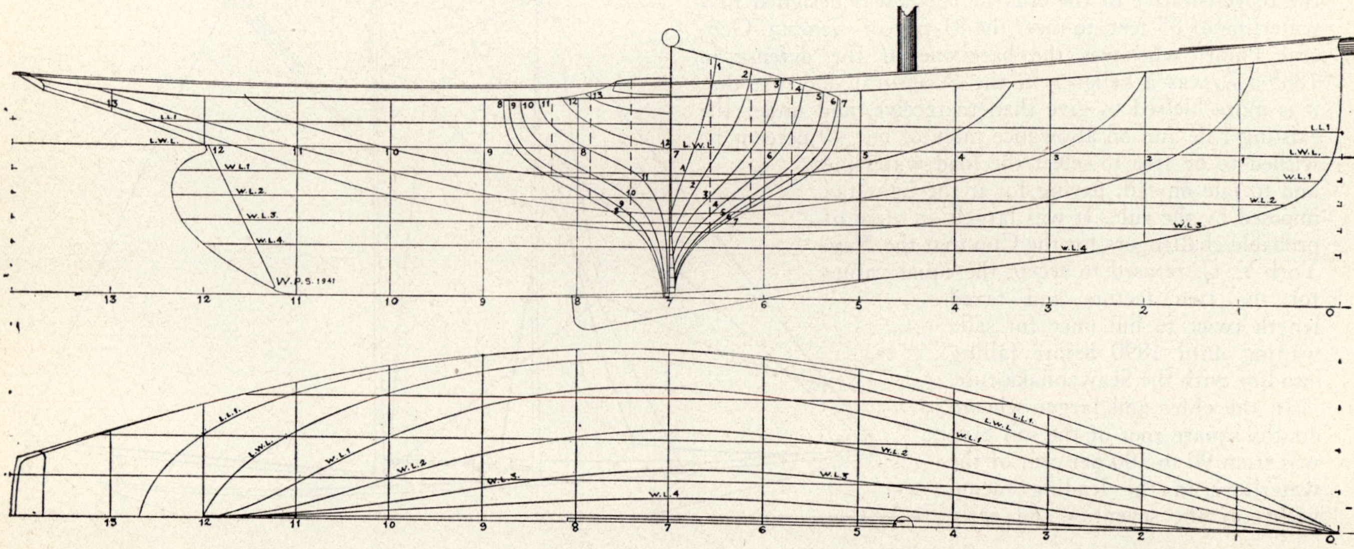

C. Oliver Iselin, one of the keenest and most skilful yachtsmen of his generation, backed by Cap'n Hank Haff at the wheel as opposed to Cap'n Jim Berry aboard Katrina, is still an open question.

In the schooner division at the same time, 1888, were two craft notable as the work of amateurs, Sea Fox, designed by Com. A. Cass Canfield, Seawanhaka C.Y.C., and Alert, designed by Henry Bryant, Eastern Y.C. Born in Detroit in 1853 and, graduating from Princeton in 1874, after a post-graduate course at Columbia Mr. Canfield made his home in New York and became interested in yachting; joining the Seawanhaka C.Y.C. in 1883 as owner of an old 47-foot centerboard sloop, Rosalie. Becoming interested in the cutter controversy, he took up the study of design, and in 1884 had built from his own design the cutter Isis, 51 feet l.w.l. by 13 feet breadth. In 1886 he bought the unsuccessful Cup defender Priscilla; in 1888 he designed the schooner Sea Fox, for the 90-foot Class; sailing her successfully for several seasons. Built of iron, not steel, after a long career in yachting she was sold in 1934 for freighting service to the West Indies. She has recently been restored to yachting, with the addition of a diesel engine and starts a new career in her 53d year.

In 1884 Henry Bryant designed a yacht of 64 feet l.w.l. of what was then called the "compromise type," a wide centerboard cutter, which proved quite successful as an experiment in a new line. In 1888 he had built from his own design the wooden schooner Alert, 107 feet l.o.a.; 90 feet l.w.l.; 23 feet 5 inches breadth and 13 feet draft; a sturdy keel cruising schooner; doing little racing. Like Thetis she had a plumb stem, with a high freeboard, a very able yacht. These four craft were typical of the advance of yachting to that date.

Comparison Between the Yachts Titania and Katrina

	Titania	Katrina
Designer	Edward Burgess	A. Cary Smith
Builder	Henry Piepgrass	Henry Piepgrass
Built at	City Island, N. Y., 1887	City Island, N. Y. 1888
Length Overall	82 ft. 6 ins.	91 ft. 3 ins.
L.W.L.	70 ft. 3 ins.	69 ft. 2 ins.
Breadth Extreme	21 ft.	21 ft. 6 ins.
L.W.L.	19 ft. 10 ins.	20 ft. 2 ins.
Draft	9 feet	9 ft. 3 ins.
Freeboard Bow	6 ft. 2 ins.	6 ft. 9 ins.
Least	2 ft. 10 ins.	3 ft.
Transom	4 ft.	4 ft. 6 ins.
Rake of Sternpost	116 Degrees	110 Degrees
Displacement	79 Long Tons	83 Long Tons
Ballast	33.50 Long Tons	35 Long Tons
Mast from Station O.	26 ft. 3 ins.	27 ft. 3 ins.
Mast Deck to Hounds	71 ft. 6 ins.	71 ft. 3 ins.
Topmast	40 ft.	45 ft.
Bowsprit Outside Sta.	34 ft. 6 ins.	34 ft.
Boom	72 ft.	70 ft. 6 ins.
Gaff	45 ft.	45 ft. 6 ins.
Mainsail Hoist	42 ft. 6 ins.	46 ft.
Sail Area by Rule	6844 sq. ft.	7082 sq. ft.
Square Root	82.73	84.15
Ratio S.A. to L.W.L.	1.18	1.21
Centerboard Length	20 ft.	17 ft.

TRADITIONS AND MEMORIES OF

American Yachting

Part Twenty-five

By WILLIAM P. STEPHENS

Measurement and Classification in America, Continued

AMONG the many orders which came to Edward Burgess after his two successive victories in the Cup contests were one from two young men popularly known about Boston as "The Adams Boys," George Casper Adams, born in 1863, and Charles Francis, born three years later. The ancestral Adams home was at Quincy, Mass., with a summer home on the water at Cohasset; the "Boys" grew up on the water, in 1879 George was sailing a small catboat, Bat, with Charles as crew; in the following year came Dandelion, an 18-foot catboat, and in 1886 Cricket, a jib-and-mainsail boat. Their next step is told by Charles Francis in the Eastern Y. C. *Ditty Box,* as follows:—"Edward Burgess was just approaching the period when everything of importance in the racing fleet came from his designing board, when my timid and youthful steps took me to the simple establishment where, nearly alone, he was working out the lines of some one of his triumphs. Being a sympathetic soul, he was soon busy in explaining what he could do to produce that long-sought product, the perfect combination of a race boat and a cruiser. Though it never had been done, he thought he could build a keel boat of approximately the speed of the well-tried centerboard type of the time, and hoped to produce something faster than the Shadow, the best product of Herreshoff's earlier period, which, for perhaps twenty years, had represented the perfection of racing speed possible on a 34-foot waterline. We chose 36 feet L. W. L. as the smallest boat that could combine a cabin, and stateroom aft."

My own comments, of course, from the cutter angle, after seeing her on the stocks, were:—"The beam (12 feet 6 inches) is great compared to the length (36 feet), but at the same time the boat is relatively deep, drawing 7 feet 6 inches. The bilge is kept light and the topsides flare, while the shapes of hull and lead keel merge fairly into each other, unlike the class of keel sloops once so common about Boston in which the body was wide but shoal, the draft being made up by a deep fin. In the matter of deck room the new boat has plenty to spare, and below she is equally roomy; but her great beam gives a lot of waste space above the lockers that only goes into extra width in the berths. She has good headroom, 5 feet 9 inches, and good room between the lockers, but both of these she might have had with less beam. While the cramped companions and narrow passages of the extreme cutters are absent owing to the increased beam, it certainly seems as though the economic limit had been exceeded in the other direction, and that more beam had been taken than was really necessary for the best average of interior accommodation and driving power." The lines of Papoose will be found in MoToR BoatinG for October 1940.

The first race, the 100th Regatta of the Dorchester Y.C. on June 17, 1887, sailed in a light air, settled finally two important questions, the elapsed times being:—Second-Class Keels, Papoose, 4:10:27; Aglaia, 4:20:50; Shona, 4:32:15. Second-Class Centerboards, Shadow, 4:10:50; Magic, 4:46:18; Violet, 4:52:14. Shadow, for 15 years the champion of the centerboard type, had been defeated by the new keel; Shona was a 5-ton cutter, 32 feet 1 inch by 5 feet 9 inches; Aglaia was one of the old type Boston keels, and Magic and Violet were good representatives of the centerboard type of the seventies.

Liris under full sail

There being no uniformity of classification, the selection of the waterline of Papoose was a matter of chance; in the following year there began a movement for a class of yachts, both centerboard and keel, of not over 40 feet L.W.L. "The Adams Boys" replaced Papoose by Babboon, of course designed by Burgess. In naming the former a "p" was dropped to give seven letters and two ciphers, for luck; in naming Babboon a "b" was added for the same reason, the series continuing with Gossoon, Harpoon, Raccoon and many others.

Before parting with Papoose a word is pertinent as to her subsequent history; in 1891 she was sold to Lake Erie, and shortly after to John T. Mott, of Oswego, N. Y., who later changed her to a yawl. In 1913 she was partially re-built; but as the years told on both yacht and owner she was reluctantly given up. Commodore Mott entertained a sentimental regard for her on account of both her designer and her original owners, and he held her worthy of a better fate than befell so many of the Lake yachts, carrying stone, or blowing about as partial wrecks under the ownership of boys. She was hauled out and broken up by her skipper, Phil, and the wood carted away and decently cremated. The rudder stock, with its bronze cap, was packed by Phil as carefully as a piece of fine furniture, and shipped to Bayside, where it now serves as the newel post in my stairway, close to the rudder stock of Madge which I retrieved many years ago from a swamp at Charlotte, N. Y., where she ended her days.

Papoose, and the now growing class of 40-Footers, with the yachts described last month, represented an honest attempt to combine speed with other qualities then considered desirable in a yacht; adaptability for general use, and a long life after being outbuilt. The leading professional designers were A. Cary Smith and Edward Burgess, with a few of lesser note, and a growing number of amateurs; in 1889 appeared the first of a class of professionals specially prepared for their work by a long course of technical training.

Reaper, Herreshoff fin-keel built in 1892. L.o.a., 31'; breadth, 6'-9". Showing canoe-like hull with pendulum bronze fin and lead bulb

William Gardner

Born in Oswego, N. Y., on May 10, 1859, William Gardner enjoyed from early life such advantages as are seldom afforded to those who choose the thorny path of yacht architecture. His acquaintance with the sea began when, as a boy of eleven, he accompanied his mother and sister on a voyage by sea to Panama, crossing the Isthmus by train and mule teams, and con-

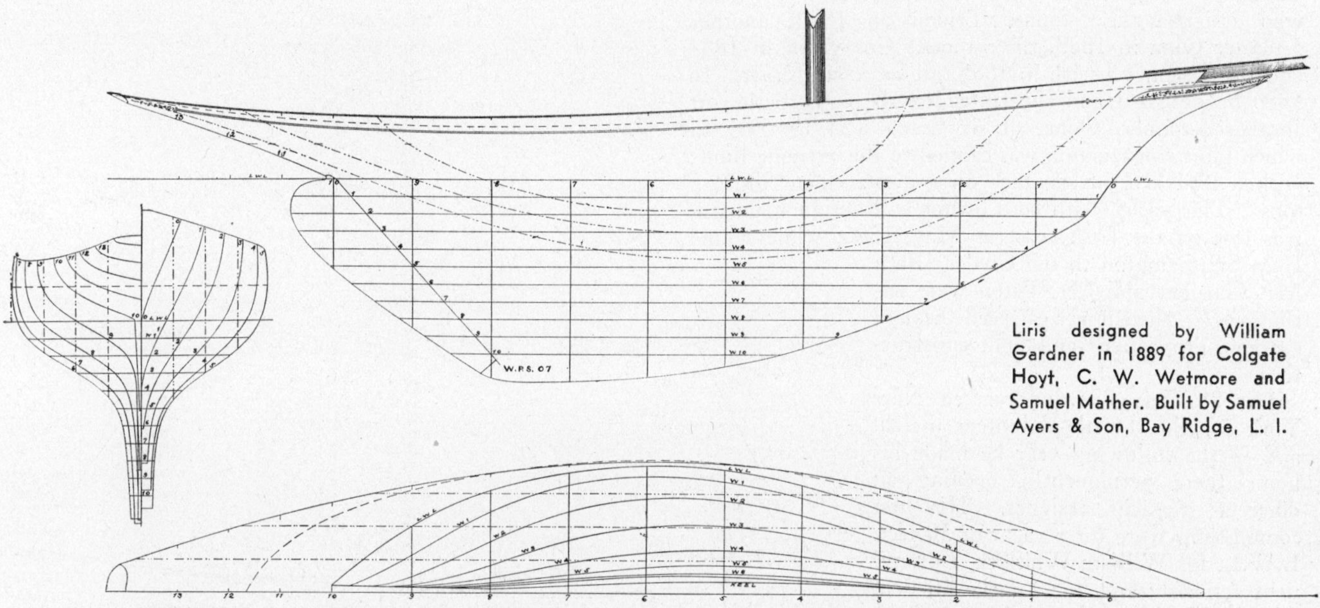

Liris designed by William Gardner in 1889 for Colgate Hoyt, C. W. Wetmore and Samuel Mather. Built by Samuel Ayers & Son, Bay Ridge, L. I.

Herreshoff Works, Bristol, R. I. South Shop in 1891; steam yacht Vamoose, designed and built for William Randolph Hearst, under construction

tinuing by sea to San Francisco. Two years later he returned to the East on one of the first trains of the Union Pacific Railroad. He prepared at Syracuse for Cornell University, from which he graduated in 1880. He was for a time in the Roach Shipyard at Chester, Pa., engaged in the practical work of the shops and mould loft, but in 1884 he obtained admission to the Royal Naval College at Greenwich, England, then the leading institution of the kind. The privilege of foreign entry was jealously guarded, being extended to but few Americans, graduates of Annapolis; the late Admirals Bowles, Capps and Woodward and Lewis Nixon. Mr. Gardner was able to exert some special influence which secured his entry, and he covered the full course, spending his vacations in visiting the leading British shipyards. While his studies covered the entire field of naval design, including warships, his interest in yachting led him to specialize in that subject, and during his residence in England he had every opportunity to familiarize himself with the latest developments of the narrow cutter. Among his intimates at Greenwich was a young Englishman, William Evans Paton, whose principal interest was also in yachts, and who designed the 5-tonner Trident in 1879; another 5-tonner Olga in 1883, the 3-tonner Currytush in 1884 and the 5-tonner Luath in 1885, all successful craft. In 1886 he designed and superintended the construction of another 5-tonner, Oona, of six beams (34 by 5-6) in which light construction was carried to the extreme limit; with a lead keel of 9.6 tons on a displacement of 12.5 tons. This yacht, with both owner and designer aboard, was lost on the Irish coast in May, 1886, while bound from Southampton to the Clyde. Both Mr. Gardner and Mr. Paton were enthusiasts on the subject of speed through extreme proportions and light construction.

In 1887 Mr. Gardner visited New York for the Thistle-Volunteer match, and in the following year he made his home there permanently, opening an office as a yacht designer. His first commissions were for a yacht of 30 feet, L.W.L. for William Whitlock, a prominent canoeist; and one for the 40-Foot Class. The latter commission was from Colgate Hoyt and Charles W. Wetmore, New York yachtsmen, who had owned for three years the 33-foot sloop, formerly Romeyn, built by John Mumm in 1883, using her for cruising about the Sound with a little racing throw in. With them was associated in the new venture Samuel Mather, a Cleveland yachtsman. The yacht, launched as Liris, was intended for general use, as well as for racing in the Class as it then existed.

An American Itchen Boat

While 98 per cent of the racing in Great Britain was done under the Thames Rule with its restriction on breadth, there was in the eighties a popular local class with no limitation save waterline length, the "Itchen boat." These boats were originally small fishing craft, used on the Itchen River, near Southampton; open, with plumb stem and transom; in the course of many years being developed into larger decked boats acceptable to yachtsmen. For racing they were found in three classes, 21-, 25- and 30-feet; and by 1882 they appeared as wide, deep craft, of heavy displacement, with lead keels, and overhangs both forward and aft. Familiar with the type, Mr. Gardner adopted it as best fitted for racing on a fixed waterline. With a waterline of 40 feet and a forward overhang of 8 feet 3 inches plus an after overhang of 11 feet 8 inches, the over-all length was barely under 60 feet. The extreme breadth was 13 feet 4 inches, and at the waterline 12 feet 9 inches, with a draft of 10 feet 2 inches; her lead keel weighing about 16 tons. The baseline of her sail plan was 95.55 feet, with a hoist of 71.15 feet from deck to topsail halyard block; from deck to tip of club topsail yard, 85 feet.

The oak keel was 10 by 18½ inches, the frames were

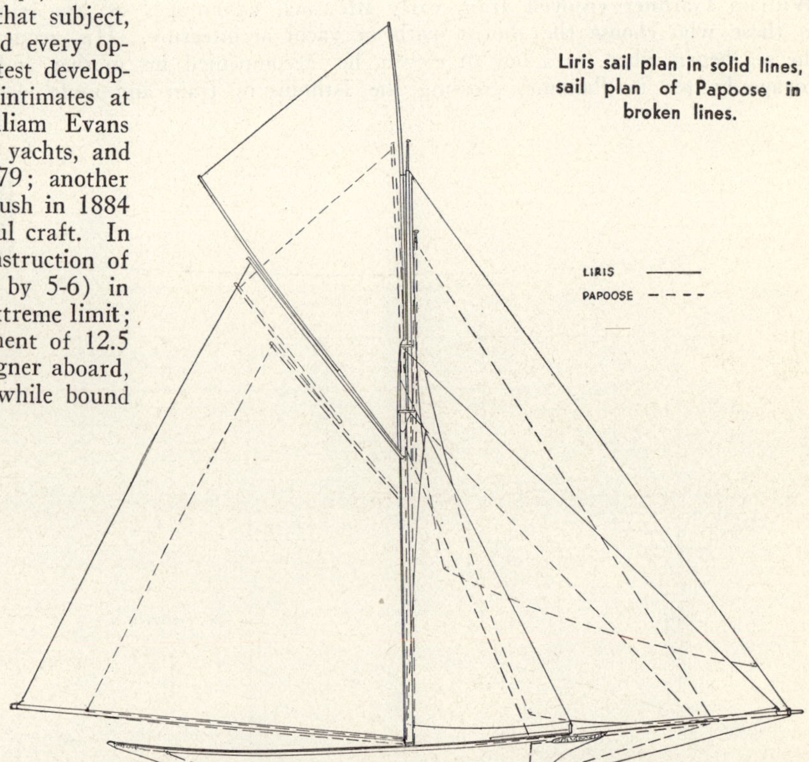

Liris sail plan in solid lines, sail plan of Papoose in broken lines.

of steel angles with bent oak between, the planking was double, the outer skin of mahogany, and the deck was also double. All spars were hollow, and the light sails were of the new "Union silk." The deck capstan was imported from London. Below she was fully fitted for the cruising which the owners proposed and actually did, with main saloon, after stateroom, and a large forecastle. Yacht plumbing was still in a primitive stage; a yacht was fortunate with one toilet, but Liris had two. Among the mixed fleet of old and new yachts which made up the Class in 1889 some were used solely for racing, and were stripped accordingly; some had tenders and no pretense was made of living aboard. The owners of Liris not only wished to live aboard, but to live comfortably even when racing. The mahogany table, large enough to seat eight, was of massive construction, and of course, swinging; the two weights which made the pendulum were of lead, about 8 inches diameter and 2 to 3 inches thick. Our only tender was a somewhat antique "naphtha launch". After breakfast on a race day all spare stuff, companion ladder, mahogany skylights, boom crotch, etc., were tumbled into the launch and taken ashore. The table was the *piece de resistance,* to be unscrewed from the floor, dissected, the weights removed with as little damage to the fingers as possible, up the companion and over the side into the launch. After the finish this process was reversed, and it was often late in the evening before we sat down to a four-course meal prepared by Earl, the colored chef.

In spite of the fact that she lost every spar, including a second mast, in the eleven races of her first season, Liris came through with a record of 3 firsts, 4 seconds, 3 thirds and 1 fourth; not so bad in a fleet of 12 yachts in which Minerva proved herself to be the fastest beyond all question. The development of the Class in two years is shown by the comparative sailplans of Liris and Papoose; 3,603 square feet against 2,334 square feet. The newer Burgess and Smith boats in the Class ran from 3,000 to 3,300 square feet. When the topmast of Liris carried away and with the 37-foot topsail yard fell across her gaff there was work for all hands in clearing away; when the mast went with the big club topsail set, it was still worse. The chaotic conditions existing in American yachting are shown by the measurements of Liris: under the Seawanhaka Rule, 49.86; when measured for the New York Y. C., 46.47; and for the Larchmont Y. C., 42.75

Space does not permit even a catalogue of the craft, yachts of all sizes, sail and power, and commercial vessels, which came from William Gardner's board between 1888 and 1930, when failing eyesight obliged him to retire. John Harvey, with whom he was associated in the early part of his career, when drafting at night used a number of wax candles disposed about the board. Working in the same way under the early electric lights, not moderated as they are today, caused premature blindness.

Herreshoff Turns to Sail

THE first ventures of John B. Herreshoff, and later the Herreshoff Manufacturing Company, were sailing craft, notably fast yachts and the catamarans which had a sensational career in the middle seventies. About 1878 they began to experiment with a small compound two-cyclinder engine and a coil boiler, building some small launches, and by 1882 they were building steam yachts up to 100 feet length. The demand for power yachts was increasing rapidly, and the company concentrated on this work to the exclusion of sailing craft. In 1883 N. G. Herreshoff built for himself a keel yacht, Consuelo, 28 feet 6 inches waterline, rigged as a cat-yawl; in 1887 he built a slightly larger yacht, Clara, for his own use. The steering gear of both included a vertical shaft carrying on its upper end a horizontal bar about 18 inches long with a vertical handle on each end, somewhat similar to the control of a trolley car. Consuelo had a hood of oiled canvas on bows, similar to a buggy top, which could be raised to protect the helmsman or folded flat on deck. In 1890, after a sail aboard Consuelo, E. D. Morgan ordered a sloop of 26 feet 6 inches, Pelican, for his brother-in-law, Mr. Moran, and in the following year he ordered a similar yacht, Gannet, for himself.

After this experimenting in yacht forms N. G. Herreshoff was prepared to return to the sailing field; and when in 1891, after the deliberate murder of the 40-foot Class the next larger, 46-foot Class was started, he prepared a design for a young yachtsman, Royal Phelps Carroll. As Mr. Carroll was about to commit matrimony, he decided to forego the yacht, and the order was turned over to Mr. Morgan. The new yacht, Gloriana, from the start easily outsailing the other new yachts of the class, placed her designer at the head of his profession and presented a new problem to the yachting world. An amusing incident associated with her debut was the comment of another designer when it was reported that the Herreshoffs were preparing to build for the new class: "The Herreshoffs are all right on steam yachts, but . . ." There were no ifs, buts nor ands about the triumph of Gloriana; it recalled the old fable of America's victory: "Your Majesty, there ain't no second."

For over forty years, from the days of Mary Taylor and America, the accepted form of fore body had been based on a very fine entrance, a hollow line such as is seen in almost all of the many designs published in MoToR BoatinG within the past two years. This form was common alike to American and British designers; accepted as correct by all from George Steers to Watson, Fife, Cary Smith, Burgess and Gardner. In entering permanently the field of sailing design Mr. Herreshoff, with his originality and disregard of convention, made a bold cut at what we now recognize as simply useless deadwood and detrimental wetted surface. Starting at the billethead of the conventional "clipper bow," he cut away the fine entering wedge shown in the level and waterlines in the figure; thus eliminating the "forefoot" long deemed essential. The conventional hollow entrance is shown in the solid lines, the new keel contour and the full load waterline being shown by the broken lines. While breaking the water when in an upright position with seemingly blunt and convex waterlines, the diagonals, the true index of form when a yacht is heeled, are quite as easy and fair as in the old form. The great majority of those who, after the first few races of Gloriana, attempted to discuss the novel form, simply went into hysterics over the "Wizard of Bristol" and the "Gloriana bow"; seeing nothing more than the shark-like snout above water, where it could have no effect, bad or good.

The craze for the Gloriana bow led to old yachts being rebuilt and even the full-bodied Cape Catboat, with its plumb stem and plumb square transom being re-designed to fit the fashion.

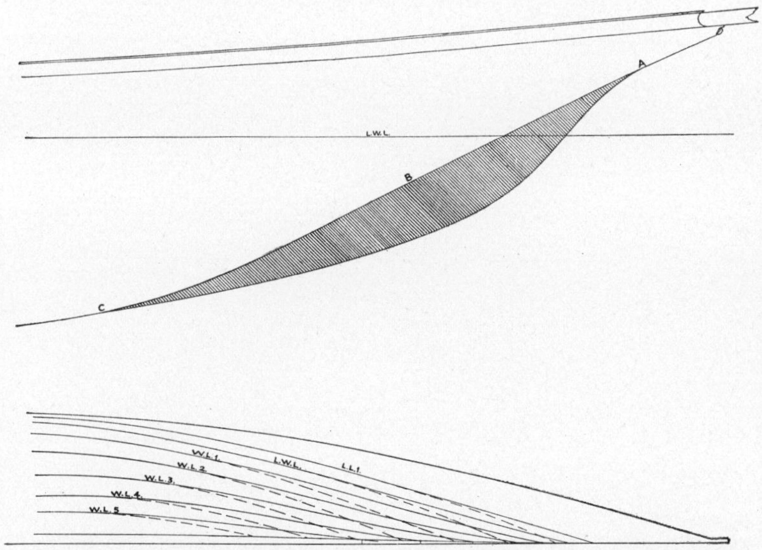

The evolution of Gloriana the conventional clipper bow, as designed by Watson, Fife, Burgess and Cary Smith prior to 1891, is shown by the line outside the shaded portion, and by the full lines in the half-breadth plan. The bow of Gloriana is represented by the line A, B, C, and the broken lines in the half breadth plan. The shaded portion, cut away, represents only unnecessary forefoot and detrimental wetted surface

The Machine Age in Yachting

NOT content with the triumph of Gloriana, in the fall of the same year N. G. Herreshoff brought out Dilemma, a canoe-shaped hull with a bronze plate fin carrying a cigar-shaped bulb of lead on its lower edge. Orders poured in to Bristol, not only for small racing craft, but for a 20-Rater, Niagara, also bulb-fin, which was successfully raced in British waters. As is usually the case, there came a claim of priority of invention by a General I. Garrard of Frontenac, Michigan, alleging that he had invented and used a similar device in 1881. This claim, while apparently correct, in no way detracted from the credit due to N. G. Herreshoff, as the Garrard fin was never known outside of its immediate birthplace.

While Gloriana with her full forward waterlines, and Dilemma with a similar fullness of entrance, her minimum displacement and ballast fin gave indisputable proof of the failure of load waterline as a factor of measurement, the end was not yet. In 1896 the yachting world received a new shock in the Canadian challenger for the new Seawanhaka Cup, Glencairn; the first of what was soon to be famous as the Skow type. This yacht, the creation of G. Herrick Duggan of the Royal St. Lawrence Y. C., an amateur yacht designer but famous for his great bridges, set at defiance all existing rules. On a measured waterline of 12 feet 6 inches when upright she showed when heeled to her best sailing angle an increase of at least 20 percent of effective sailing length, with a proportionate decrease of breadth on the loadwater plane. The Skow created a furore similar to that of the Herreshoff catamaran in 1876, Gloriana in 1891 and Dilemma in the same year; extending upward even into large yachts; while the fin-keel found its way into the Cup class in Jubilee, designed by an amateur, John B. Paine, son of General Paine, for the defending fleet of 1893. As the result of these developments the Seawanhaka Rule was evidently obsolete, and a change became imperatively necessary.

The five years, from 1886 to 1891 mark a period of change and confusion in yachting; the defeat of Galatea in the former year led to the abandonment of the tonnage rules and of the narrow cutters fostered by them; the development of the 40-foot Class from 1887 to 1890 produced the "brute" type, so-called, with extreme hull and spar dimensions, great displacement and ballast, and at the same time witnessed the defeat of this type by the tiny Minerva; in 1891 came Gloriana, a large yacht on a short waterline, and the fin-keel Dilemma; five years later came the Duggan skow, defying all previous evaluation of the load waterline. The racing world was in such a state of confusion as had never before existed; and the rule-makers were faced with a new and difficult problem.

American Yachting

By WILLIAM P. STEPHENS

Part Twenty-six

Measurement and Classification in America, Continued

OUR story, as it has run for some time past, deals with measurement and classification, two inter-related and complicated subjects; thus far nothing has been said about classification as it was practically non-existent; now it finds its place in chronological order. It may be divided into three parts; the basis of classification, the actual class limits, and the amount of time allowance between the yachts in any one class.

The basis of classification is one or the other of those units of that vague size which has included, as we have seen, waterline length, "mean length," sail area, "cubic contents," displacement, tonnage, etc. Following the adoption of various forms of the length-and-sail-area rule, there ensued a long dispute over the question of classifying by load waterline alone or by "corrected length" by which the final allowance was calculated. The second point, the class limits, may be deferred until we have considered the time allowance between the yachts in a class.

This allowance is based on tables prepared at various times on the basis of observations of the speeds actually made in racing; one of the earliest efforts in this direction was the "Ackers Scale," tabulated in 1843 by George Holland Ackers, owner of the schooner Brilliant, for the use of the Royal Yacht Squadron; this table being based on the B.O.M. tonnage. In his early days as a machinist in the Corliss Works N. G. Herreshoff was sufficiently interested in yacht racing to prepare an allowance table based on various forms of "mean length" which was generally used for many years. There seems no clue to the author of the table long used by the New York and other large clubs.

Though the entire subject of measurement and classification is obviously a technical one, to the great detriment of the sport it has long been treated solely from a political standpoint:—the defense of the America's Cup. In spite of sporadic experiments with other factors, American yachtsmen had long favored a length measurement for both time allowance and classification; the defenders of the Cup have adhered strictly to this idea, and have guarded jealously the right to decide on the length of all defenders, and to canvas them at will; paying the very light tax imposed by the early rules. As a part of this policy they have stood for length only as a basis of classification.

General Charles J. Paine, thrice defender of the America's cup. Served in the Union Army and became Major General. Joined Eastern Y.C. 1878. Deceased 1916. Leading proponent of waterline measurement with a minimum tax on sail

The Theory of Allowance Tables

All tables of time allowance are based on the theory that the speeds of vessels of a similar nature vary as the square roots of their lengths. The assumed speed is that which would be attained under perfect conditions; a uniformly steady wind of great force. As races are actually sailed under varying and often most unsatisfactory conditions, from a mere drift in smooth water to rough seas and strong winds which permit but a minimum of canvas, it has always been customary to use some percentage of the theoretic speed. We are fortunate in having for purposes of illustration two yachts recognized as the best of the 70-foot Class as it existed at this time, 1883. Gracie, built in 1868 with a waterline of 68 feet, had now grown to 71; Mischief, built in 1879, now measured 61 feet; both were centerboard boats of similar type.

The rule was:—"Subtract the time opposite the length of the larger yacht from the time opposite the length of the smaller yacht, and multiply the remainder by the length of course; the result is the allowance in seconds." The following supplementary instructions were added:—"The time taken as a basis is one hour, or 3,600 seconds; but it has been found in practice that this would make the allowance too large; and four tenths of 3,600 seconds, which is 1,440 seconds, has been taken." This percentage, while highly satisfactory to the majority of voting members, owners of the largest yachts which demanded a strong breeze, was grossly unfair to yachts of medium size, and much more so to the smaller yachts which reached more nearly their maximum speed in average summer racing weather. The calculation would be:—Gracie, 71 ft. l.w.l, square root $= 8.43$. Mischief, 61 ft. square root $= 7.81$. $G : M :: 8.43 : 7.81$ or $3{,}600 : X :: 8.43 : 7.81$ $X = 3.335$. $40\% = 1334 \times 40$ (miles) $= 533.6$ seconds $= 8$ min. 53 sec. Of course in practical application this calculation is avoided by taking from the table the figures 58.04 for Mischief and 44.56 for Gracie and subtracting the smaller.

As the larger schooners dropped from the racing fleet and the sloop division grew, especially on the smaller end, the injustice of the 40% allowance became more and more apparent, but the Old Guard still stood valiantly

S. Nicholson Kane. Graduate of U. S. Naval Academy 1866. Elected to New York Y. C. 1874. Rear Commodore, 1875; Vice Commodore, 1876; Commodore, 1877-8-9; Member of Regatta Committee, 1889-1896, 1898-1904

to its guns. It was not until 1887 that a slight breach was made in a change to 46%, three years later this was changed to 50%, and in 1897 to 60%. In 1901 it was raised to an extreme (80%) which proved too high, and in 1905 it was reduced to 70%. In 1909 it was further lowered to 60% and has thus continued to the present time; apparently to the satisfaction of all. Similar changes were made from time to time in other clubs.

The Basis of Classification

The rules committee of 1883 included A. Cary Smith, Anson Phelps Stokes, Charles Warren Lippitt, C. Smith Lee and J. Frederic Tams; while accepting the length-and-sail-area rule in principle, the Club would go no further than to place a double tax on waterline as compared with sail; the formula being $\frac{2L + \sqrt{SA}}{3}$. In adopting the same factors the Seawanhaka C.Y.C. gave both an equal value; and both clubs adopted the new measurements as the basis for classification. As told in MoToR BoatinG for May, after two years both went back to the waterline as the class basis.

This, as it proved, was a very important factor in the over-development of sail such as was noted previously in the case of Liris. With no limit but l.w.l., and a 40% allowance table, there was every inducement to expand the sail plan; and this was generally successful until Minerva taught a different lesson. The Cup defenders built under the N.Y.Y.C. rules were conspicuous examples of this, as in Reliance with 16,160 sq. ft. of sail on a waterline of 90 ft.

In the long battle for the improvement of racing conditions the recognized leader was John Hyslop (MoToR BoatinG, November 1940). Though his time was nominally occupied in the management of a manufacturing business, a great part of a long life was devoted to yachting:—the study of design, practical designing for himself and his friends, in the taking-off and study of the lines of noted yachts, as the official Measurer for several clubs, and in a vigorous crusade for a better rule of measurement and system of classification. A minor subject in which he was deeply interested was the percentage of the theoretic allowance, he fought long and earnestly for the increase from 40 to 60 per cent.

"The Classification of Racing Yachts"

The first gun in this battle was an article in *Forest & Stream* of February 10, 1887, under this heading, as follows:—

"With a large number of small organizations engaged in the same object, working for the same ends with the same means, and with all interests in common, it would seem the most natural thing possible for all to combine in a union that would join them closely together, rather than that they should continue to stumble along in a helpless independence of each other. The former course has been followed by many of the clubs connected with outdoor sports in this country, such as the League of American Wheelmen, the National Association of Amateur Oarsmen, and the American Canoe Association, in all of these cases with the best results; but while the necessity for such union of yachtsmen is just as apparent,

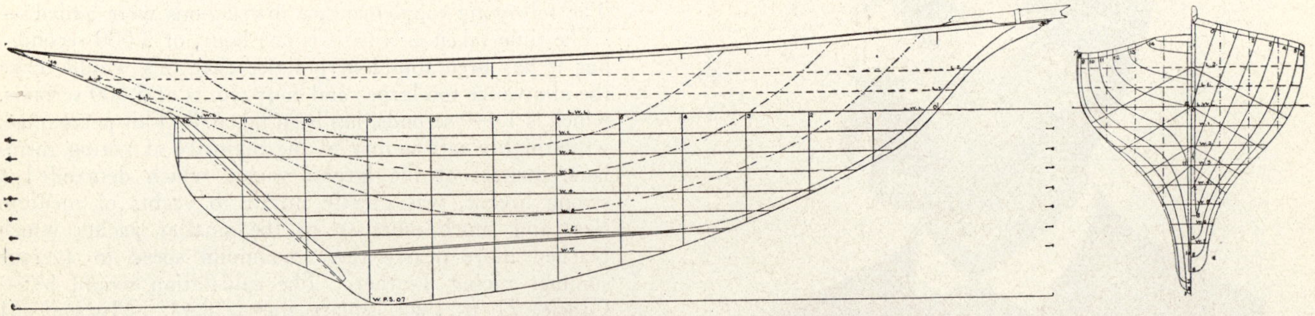

Gossoon, designed 1890 by Edward Burgess to demonstrate the value of power in 40-foot Class. Owned and sailed by Charles F. and Geo. Caspar Adams

the many attempts which have been made toward one have all resulted in failure. The reasons for these failures it is not necessary to consider here, as we do not propose now to inaugurate another attempt." . . .

"One of the most pressing questions now before the clubs, one in fact in which prompt action is necessary if much confusion and trouble in the immediate future is to be avoided, is that of a uniform and systematic classification of the racing fleet. That it is needed for the promotion of the races of this year and next for immediate use, is shown by an inspection of the classes of the leading clubs of the "Atlantic system," if we may coin a term, in which is included the bulk of American yacht racing. We take only the cabin sloops, cutters and yawls, as what is true of them is also true of the schooners, while the classification of the smaller open boats is not only under different conditions but is much less important than the larger sloops and cutters.

"The classes in the five larger clubs are as follows, the waterline length being taken in the New York, Seawanhaka and Eastern, while the Atlantic and Larchmont use the corrected length for classification as well as for time allowance. Before going further it may be well to state that we have not the slightest intention of reviving a discussion of the measurement question; most yachtsmen realize by this time that measurement and time allowance is one thing, while the classification of yachts is another and very different matter.". . .

TABLE I.—RACING CLASSES

New York—Class I., over 70 ft.; Class II., 55 and under 70 ft.; Class III., 45 and under 55 ft.; Class IV., under 45 ft.

Seawanhaka—First Class, 71 ft. and over; Second Class, 55 and under 71 ft.; Third Class, 45 and under 55 ft.; Fourth Class, 35 and under 45 ft.; Fifth Class, under 35 ft.

Larchmont—Class C, 55 ft. and over; Class I., 42 and under 55 ft.; Class II., 33 and under 42 ft.; Class III., 25 and under 33 ft.; Class IV., under 25 ft.

Atlantic—Class C, 60 ft. and over; Class D, 50 and under 60 ft.; Class E, 42 and under 50 ft.; Class F, 35 and under 42 ft.; Class G, 30 and under 35 ft.; Class H, 26 and under 30 ft.; Class I, under 26 ft.

Eastern—First Class, 75 ft. and over; Second Class, 55 and under 75 ft.; Third Class, 40 and under 55 ft.; Fourth Class, 30 and under 35 ft.

The racing fleet of the day in the sloop and cutter classes was tabulated as follows; as found in the existing classes and as redivided under the proposed new system.

TABLE II.—RACING YACHTS.

Existing Classes.		Ft. In.	Proposed Classes.
	Mayflower	85.00	
	Priscilla	85.00	Class I.
	Atlantic	82.01	
	Puritan	80.00	
E. First Class, 75. S. First Class, 71 and over.			—75
N. Y. Class I., over 70	Bedouin	70.1¼	
	Gracie	69.04	Class II.
	Iselin Boat	69.09	
	Shamrock	70.00	—65
	Fanny	65.09	
	Ileen	65.04	
	Stranger	65.00	
	Thetis	64.02	Class III.
	Huron	63.00	
	Hildegarde	61.06	
	Mischief	61.00	
	Wenonah	60.09	
A. Class C, 60 and over. N. Y. Class. II S. 2d Cl. 55 L. Class C. E. 2d Cl.	Clara	53.07	—55
	Whileway	53.00	
	Cinderella	52.00	
	Isis	51.05	
	Athlon	51.02	
	Oriva	50.11	
	Thistle	50.09	Class IV.
	Active	50.02	
	Eclipse	50.1½	
A. Class D, 50	Gaviota	50.00	
	Bertie	49.00	
	Roamer	48.10	
	Valkyr	47.04	—47
	Regina	47.03	
	Daphne	46.03	
	Hesper	45.10	
	Fanita*	45.05	
N. Y. Class III. S. 3d class. 45	Bayadere	45.00	
	Rover	44.08	
	Maggie	44.07	Class V.
	Adelaide	44.06	
	Vixen	44.01	
	Penguin	44.00	
A. Class E. L. Class I. 42	Ulidia	42.06	
	Imperia	41.10	
	Espirito	40.10	
	Muriel	40.06	
E. 3d Class	Crocodile	39.11	—40
	Madge	38.09	
	Rival	38.03	
	Hope	38.00	Class VI.
	Mona	36.06	
	Schemer	36.04	
	Lapwing	36.06	
	Polly	36.00	
S. 4th Class. A. Class F. 35	Surf	35.04	—35
	Hera	34.11	
	Mariota	34.00	
	Elephant	34.00	
	Shadow	33.08	
	Iseult	33.04	
	Ægir	33.00	Class VII.
	Shona	33.00	
L. Class II., 33	Wacondah	33.00	
	Daisy	32.09	
	Delvin	32.00	
	Culprit Fay	31.00	
	Ilderan	30.02	
N. Y. E. lower limit Cl. IV., 30	Magic	30.02	—30
	Arab	28.09	
	Aria	27.04	
	Iolanthe	27.00	
	Yolande	26.06	
	Vivien	26.03	Class VIII.
A. Class H., 26	Nora	26.01	
	Merlin	25.06	
	Stranger	25.03	
	Fad	25.02	
L. Class III., 25	Gem	25.02	—25
S. 5th Class, all under 35			Class IX., 21.
L. Class IV., all under 25			Class X., 18.
A. Class I., all under 26			

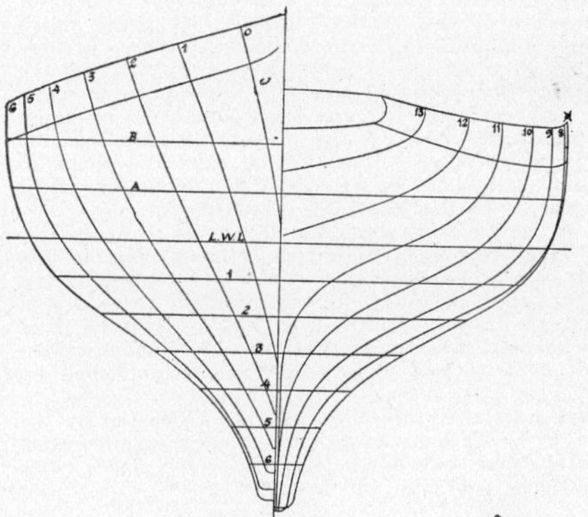

Lines of Sea Fox, 90-foot schooner class. Designed by Com. A. Cass Canfield, Seawanhaka C.Y.C. (amateur), 1888. L.O.A., 115'; L.W.L., 89'5"; Breadth, 23'10"; Draft, 11' (with board, 20')

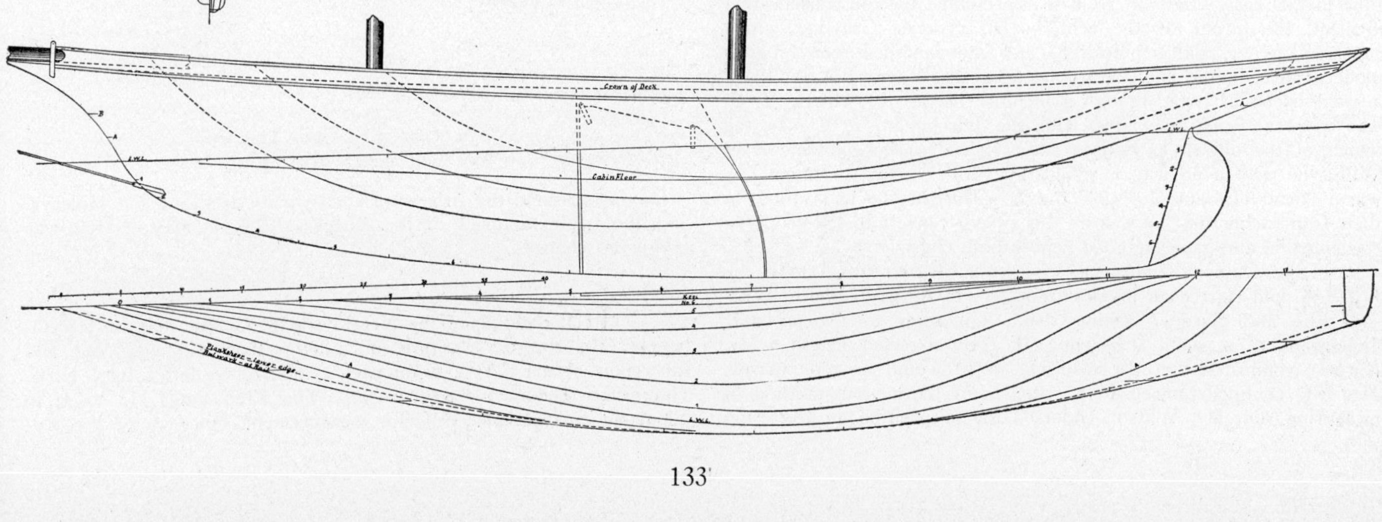

The subject was discussed in detail and at some length, giving consideration to many individual cases of existing yachts which would be affected advantageously or the reverse; a little appeasement being necessary here to avoid opposition on merely personal grounds. This first division of classes went too far in this direction in that the lower intervals were uniformly five feet; at a meeting on March 14, 1888, the Atlantic Y. C., in endorsing the general proposition, made a much more scientific division by graduated intervals; 4 feet at the lower limit from 26 to 30, increasing to ten feet at the top, from 65 to 70 feet.

It happened that this first attempt was made at a most inauspicious time; the Scotch challenger Thistle was then building in a locked shop; the mystery as to her form, her American debut and racing, made first-page news throughout the season, to the exclusion of all other matters. The subject was brought up a year later in a strong editorial in *Forest & Stream,* but the interest of yachtsmen was now centered on the building and racing of the new 40-foot Class; the details of the yachts and the records of the races monopolizing all the space which the various journals could devote to yachting, so the matter lay dormant.

The New Crusade

THERE was often a time, between Cup years, after the yachts were laid up and the results of the season tabulated and commented upon, when news was scarce and it was necessary to manufacture an issue. By 1889 the question of type was about worked out, and in looking for a subject for discussion that of classification seems the most important. The subject had been treated editorially in the interval, but this marked the beginning of the actual campaign. The question of the measurement rule was still to the fore, in spite of Minerva's victories it was predicted that the new 40-Footers of 1890 might run to 11 feet draft, with sail plans eclipsing that of Liris, and several of the clubs (of course, independently) were working on the revision of the rule. In *Forest & Stream* of October 24, 1889, the subject was treated at great length, the table published in 1887 being extended to include the entire racing fleet, from Dauntless down to sloops of 25 feet l.w.l., to a total of 102 yachts. In each case there was given the length on waterline, the sail area and its square root, the ratio of the latter figure to the waterline, and the corrected length by both New York and Seawanhaka rules. The single-stick yachts in this table were plotted on an elaborate diagram, the baseline representing the lengths on waterline and the vertical the ratio of square root of sail to waterline, the position of each yacht being plotted and a series of curves drawn, representing the class limits and showing the class in which each would fall. Supplementary tables gave the elements of measurement and classification:—length, square root of sail area, ratio, full measured area, and the proposed corrected length by both rules for every existing class. Still another table gave a comparison of possible classes by corrected length as applied to the existing 40-foot Class. The preparation of these tables and the plotting of the diagram, with the necessary explanation and consequent argument involved weeks of work.

In April the Seawanhaka C.Y.C. had appointed a committee to study the measurement rule throughout the season:—John Hyslop, A. Cary Smith, and W. P. Stephens. On October 24 the New York Y. C. appointed a similar committee:—Latham A. Fish, Edward A. Willard, John Hyslop and A. Cary Smith. The progress of civilization during the past half century has added some new terms to our vocabulary:—"under-cover," "boring from within" and "fifth column," the methods thus indicated, however, are much older than their names would indicate, and had been employed for some time in this case. Latham A. Fish represented the old conservative element, the owner of the centerboard schooner Grayling which capsized on her trial trip in 1883 and had conceded something to modern ideas in the addition of a lead shoe. Edward A. Willard, a good friend of mine, though a member of the New York Y. C. was more actively associated with the Larchmont Y. C.; as the owner of the old sloop Eclipse and a friend of her builder, Neef Willis, he was in no way in sympathy with the cutter element. A warm friend of General Paine and Mr. Burgess, he had sailed on their Cup yachts; but he was by this time a convert to the proposed classification and gave me good help in both clubs.

On Lake Ontario, under the leadership of Aemilius Jarvis, the L.Y.R.A. had started an inquiry by letters to Burgess, Smith, Watson, Fife and Gardner asking their opinion as to the probable dimensions of a yacht measuring 48 feet corrected length. Mr. Burgess suggested that the resulting yacht would be too narrow, Mr. Fife confined himself to a criticism of the current method of measuring sail, Mr. Watson endorsed the proposition as promising "fine, wholesome vessels," and Mr. Gardner endorsed the proposal for use on the Lakes. He added:—"My experience this year has been that large rigs pay from a racing point of view. The difficulty has been that we have tried to make too rapid strides; we have tried to kill the goose and get all the eggs. Because we have not put five years advance in one, a great many say the goose is no good, after all." The consensus of opinion over a wide circle was that even a heavier tax on sail would not operate to any material effect, but that classification by corrected length would be more effective than any other measure.

THE New York Y. C. Committee recommended the new classification, but with the retention of the two to one ratio of length to sail; the Seawanhaka Committee, as a matter of course, recommended the retention of its formula for measurement and its adoption for classification. Touching on the subject of the allowance table, the N.Y.Y.C. Committee recommended a percentage of 50 in place of the 46 then in use. The report of the special committee of the Eastern Y. C., read at the meeting of December 4, 1889, was the most brief and to the point of the three; no words were wasted on mere technical arguments or columns of figures. A young Boston yachtsman, George A. Stewart, whom death cut short after a brief career, was at that time associated with Mr. Burgess; we were warm personal friends, but that did not prevent some exchange of personalities in the heated argument. In the *Boston Globe* he described a revised sail plan of Babboon, made by Mr. Burgess under the proposed classification, in which it was claimed that by moving the mast forward and some other juggling permitted by the rule the sail area could be increased, with no increase of measurement but with a less effective plan. One objection made to this imaginary plan was that it would *shorten the base and increase the height* of the rig. The report was as follows:—

To the Eastern Yacht Club:

The undersigned committee of the club, appointed to report on any changes which may seem desirable in the sailing regulations, begs to call your attention to the changes of measurement and classification now under the consideration of the New York and Seawanhaka Y. C.'s.

Reports by special committees have been made to these clubs advocating the adoption of a classification based on racing measurement instead of the present classes limited by waterline length. It is also proposed that the New York Y. C. shall adopt the Seawanhaka formula for rating in place of its present formula.

It is, of course, of the greatest importance for the development of yacht racing in this country that the leading clubs should have similar rules of measurement and classification, so that yachts built by members of one club may not be practically debarred from racing under the rules of another club. Your committee supposes that the object sought by American yachtsmen in wishing to impose a greater tax on sail is simply to prevent the production of enormous rigs, such as we have seen in some recent boats in the smaller classes, and not to radically change the type of American yachts; but your committee holds the opinion that the classification proposed by the New York committees taxes sail so severely that its general adoption would produce a racing yacht comparatively long and narrow, and would lead either to the total extinction of centerboard racing yachts, or else the development of a dangerous and undesirable craft of the "canoe" type, thus going much further than what we have above supposed to be the wish of American yachtsmen.

In addition to this objection that the proposed rule will develop an undesirable type of hull, there is also the objection that any such severe tax on sail—at least as sail area is computed and valued by any present or proposed rule for its measurement—will be an irresistible temptation to spoil the shape of good rigs in order to obtain such sail plans as will yield the maximum effect with the least sail, or, still worse, with the least sail measurement.

If, however, a classification on racing measurements under the present New York Y. C. formula should be adopted, your committee believes there is less reason to fear that the tax on sail would be severe enough to confine racing to long and low-powered yachts, and, although the objection on the score of danger of badly-shaped rigs is not entirely removed, it will at least be diminished, and your committee believes it quite clear that the object above stated—preventing the production of over-sparred yachts—will be accomplished by such a classification.

Your committee, therefore, suggests that the following vote be passed by the club: Voted, That the Eastern Y. C. is prepared to adopt, in conjunction with our other leading clubs, a classification based on the formula which places twice the value on waterline length that it does on sail area.

C. J. Paine,
Augustus Hemenway,
C. H. Joy,
G. H. Richard,
Edward Burgess.

Again we hear the old refrain:—

"The Cup, The Cup, The Cup,
We will never give it up."

Having in mind the success of such yachts as Clara and Minerva, and the triple victories of the Burgess "Big sloops," Boston was taking no chances.

THE meeting of the New York Y. C. was held on December 13, Mr. Burgess was present, a letter from him was read, and the report of the E.Y.C. Committee as above. A letter from N. G. Herreshoff endorsed the proposal. The Club voted, 12 to 4, to adopt the Seawanhaka Rule for measurement, but rejected the proposal to class by it; the same Committee being continued. "The Noes have it," the battle was lost with not even a negotiated peace: the matter was forgotten and in a short time yachtsmen were busy with speculation as to what the 40-foot Class might show in 1890. When the 46-foot Class came in a year later General Paine, still true to his conviction as to the value of great power on a limited waterline built from a design by his son John B, then a young amateur, who later designed the bulb-fin Jubilee. The dimensions of Alborak were:—l.o.a., 63-2; l.w.l., 44-9; breadth, 14-2; draft, 10-3. She was conspicuous only as a failure, both structurally and in point of speed, even when subsequently rebuilt at heavy expense.

The bogie being thus laid to rest, there followed five years of notable development:—the revival of racing for the Cup, with the construction of two remarkable yachts, the very wide Vigilant with aluminum topsides and heavily weighted board, and the tobin bronze Defender; the advent of Gloriana and the fin-keel; the increase of exaggerated rigs, and of hulls with a minimum of displacement. All of these new issues served to monopolize the interest of the yachting world on both sides of the Atlantic. In its report of February 4, 1892, the New York Committee, while emphasizing its belief in the proposed classification, stressed the point that its adoption should be by a majority of the clubs, and not by one or two only; recommending the appointment of a conference committee to this end. Such a "Committee on Measurement and Conference," John Hyslop, A. Cass Canfield, William E. Iselin, Harold Sanderson and Edward A. Willard, was appointed. In reporting on January 21, 1893, it discussed existing conditions at length, including the bulb-fin, and reiterated its endorsement of classification by racing length. Two years later another committee, including A. Cass Canfield, W. Butler Duncan, Jr., John Hyslop, S. Nicholson Kane and J. Frederic Tams, in its report of January 29, 1895, repeated this recommendation; with the result that it was adopted by the New York Y. C. in common with all the leading clubs. This Committee included two of the old conservatives, S. Nicholson Kane, the author of "The Song of the Cup," Rear Commodore in 1875, elected in 1874; Vice Commodore in 1876, Commodore in 77-8-9, Chairman of the Regatta Committee for eight years. Mr. Tams, elected in 1872, was one of the noted Corinthian helmsmen in his early years; he served the Club in many offices for a period of 56 years. As typical representatives of the old order, the ready consent of these gentleman marked the passing of ancient ideas and the beginning of a new era of progressive legislation and mutual cooperation among American yacht clubs.

TRADITIONS AND MEMORIES OF

American Yachting

By *WILLIAM P. STEPHENS*

Part Twenty-seven

Measurement and Classification in America, Continued

Columbia, Defender of America's Cup against Shamrock I, 1899, and Shamrock II, 1901. L. O. A.; 132.00'; L. W. L., 89.77'; Breadth, 23.75'; Draft, 19.58'; Forward Overhang, 20.33'; After Overhang, 21.92'; Bowsprit to boom end, 182.87'; Boom to topsail halyard block, 134.74'; Sail area, 13,211.00 square feet; Square root of sail area, 114.94'; Racing length, 102.35'

SECONDARY to the subjects of the basis of classification and the class limits, is the naming of the classes. Throughout British yachting the custom has been to name the classes by the unit of classification, tons of one form or another; and the history of British yachting is based on the old yachts of 60, 80 and 100 tons, with the later 3-ton, 5-ton, 10, 20, 40, 60 and 80-ton classes; still later by the numerals denoting the measurement under the Rating Rule. In the early days of American yachting the classes were known by abstract numbers; in the New York Y. C. First and Second Class Schooners, and First and Second Class Sloops, there being only these two rigs. Later this was extended to take in smaller classes as they developed. In 1897 the New York Y. C. adopted the system of alphabetical designations: Schooners, Class A, all over 95 feet racing length, Class B, over 85 and not over 95 feet, Class C, over 75 and not over 85 feet, etc. For "Single-masted vessels and Yawls," Class G, all over 70 feet racing length, Class H, over 60 and not over 70 feet, down to Class M, not over 36 feet racing length. Down to 1889 the Seawanhaka C. Y. C. had designated its classes by Roman numerals, Class I, Class II, etc., but in that year it dropped the numerals and named each class by its upper unit of measurement: 30-ft. Class, 35-ft., 40-ft., 46-ft. and upward.

About the end of the century the custom came in of prefixing a letter to the numerical limit of each class; and also of placing designating marks on mainsails, at first both class letter and measurement being used. By degrees the measurement was dropped and the letter retained, with the result that each class was known by an arbitrary and meaningless symbol which might as well have been taken from a tea chest as from the alphabet. Following this usage came in the terms "R-Boat," "Q-Boat," "P-Boat," etc., up to the crowning atrocity of

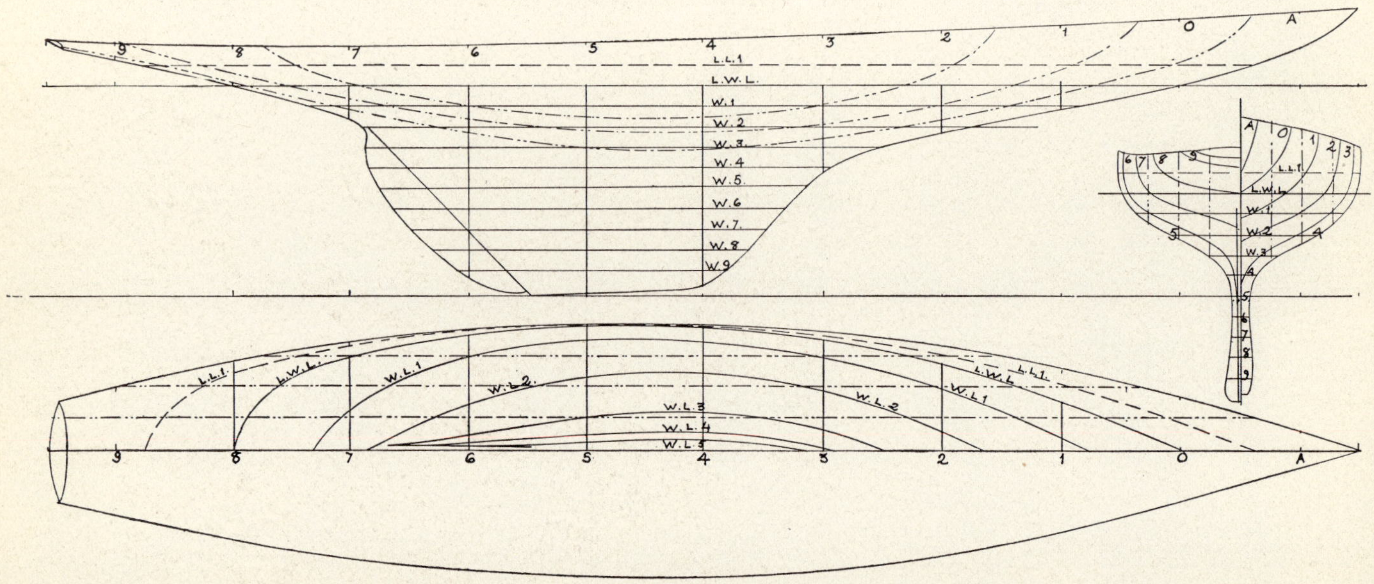

"Jayboat" for the largest, speediest, most spectacular and expensive yachts ever floated. This lubberly and confusing terminology is bad enough when limited to one locality, but it is much worse when used indiscriminately; a "P-Boat" on Long Island Sound or at Marblehead is one thing, on Great South Bay it denotes an entirely different size and type; and on the inland lakes again something different. The present is a dead period in yachting, of unknown duration, all classes under the Universal Rule are dead, with no hope of a speedy revival; this offers an opportunity for the clubs to drop all letters from their lists of classes and, when the time comes, return to the old custom of class names by the racing measurement; this, at least, would be to the advantage of yachting history, if not for the general good of the sport. The existing British system is so simple that it is well known to all American yachtsmen: the terms "6-Meter," "8-Meter," "12-Meter," etc., convey exact and definite ideas of the size and type in each class; with the class numeral above and the individual class number below it on the sails.

Back With the Rule-Makers

The course of measurement legislation in Great Britain was traced in MoToR BOATING for January, 1941, the formula of the International Rule including length, girth, freeboard and square root of sail area; the values of these factors were slightly changed in 1936 and the Rule in its present form is given in the Year Book of the North American Yacht Racing Union. In June we left American yachtsmen wondering, in Congressional parlance, "where they were at." On the one hand was Gloriana with her evasion of the measurement of load waterline, then the fin-keel with practically no displacement, and finally the skow going even further than Gloriana in the evasion of length and with almost no displacement. This broad subject was discussed informally in the club rooms, more formally and technically in committee rooms, and in the form of papers by recognized experts read before the Society of Naval Architects and Marine Engineers. Letters were sent to leading designers on both sides of the Atlantic, full replies being received. While all agreed on the necessity for belling the cat, no one came forward with a generally acceptable remedy. It was proposed to measure length at the quarter breadth, and also at a point above the waterline plane; another proposal called for the

Reliance, Defender of America's Cup against Shamrock III, 1903. L. O. A., 143'; L. W. L., 89.66'; Breadth, 25.83'; Draft, 19.58'; Forward overhang, 27.63'; After overhang, 26.40'; Bowsprit to boom end, 201.76'; Boom to topsail halyard block, 149.68'; Sail area, 16,159.00 square feet; Square root of sail area, 127.12; Racing length, 108.39'

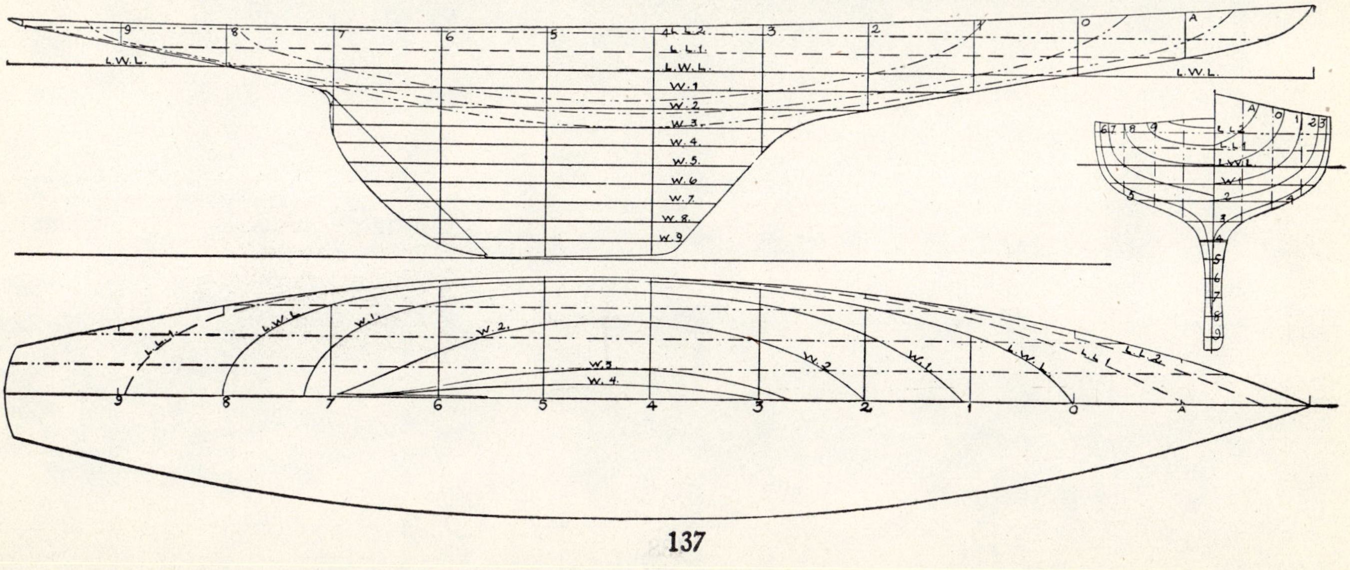

measurement of the waterline plane at the middle and at certain distances from each end; the inclusion of displacement as a factor in the form of a divisor was an obvious bar to the fin-keel type, but it was opposed by many.

The Disease and the Doctor

MEANWHILE, international competition continued. In 1899 there came the first of a fleet of Shamrocks, only to be defeated by the new Herreshoff Columbia, a fairly normal vessel. To meet the second Shamrock in 1901 the Bristol shops turned out Constitution, in no way extreme in form or construction. Whether her defeat by the older Columbia in the trial races was due to the yacht or her management is a question which never will be decided. When in 1903, the bold Sir Thomas came back for his third defeat in Shamrock III, he was met by Reliance, again from the Herreshoff shops, marking the extreme point of development in Cup defense. In tracing the full curves of this famous yacht, and running additional lines for fairing, there came to mind the remark made to me on February 26, 1885, by A. Cary Smith, as quoted in MoToR BoatinG, September: "My boy, I've got to build a damned steel scow," Priscilla. Here nearly two decades later was the greatest genius of all yacht designers deliberately building a "damned bronze scow" to defend the America's Cup; marking the advance of yacht designing in that period.

A move for a new formula was made by the Seawanhaka C. Y. C. in 1902, following a long series of special committees of the New York, Larchmont and other clubs. The standing Seawanhaka Rule was bolstered up by an added factor "L," which included three breadths on the waterline, a penalty on draft, and a premium on area of midship section; this lasted but one season. Of the many proposals advanced, in fact one of the really practicable ones, was that of the designer of Reliance: length multiplied by the square root of the sail area and the product divided by 5.5 cube root of displacement. Adopted by the New York Y. C. in 1903 and by the Seawanhaka C. Y. C. in the following year, and gradually by other clubs, it is now in general use in America under the title of the "Universal Rule." With its numerous details and instructions for measurers it now covers 25 pages in the Year Book of the N. A. Y. R. U., as compared with 49 pages for the foreign "International Rule"; a long way from the "plain and simple rule with no plus in it" advocated forty years ago.

Conferences, Home and Foreign

WHILE still opposed to the idea of a national union, the New York Y. C. in October, 1904 invited the leaders among the larger clubs to a conference looking to the general adoption of the new rule; the initial meeting of what was to be known as the "Atlantic Coast Conference" being held on October 27 at the clubhouse. This organization, though loosely knit and possessing little authority, continued for some years and did good work in furthering uniformity in the measurement rule, racing rules and scantling restrictions. A still more important move was made in the holding of an international conference in London in 1906; at which was adopted the present "International Rule." The idea for this conference originated in Germany in 1904, the original plan including only the continental nations and Great Britain. As the movement assumed definite shape it was decided to invite the participation of American clubs, and in May, 1905, a formal invitation was sent to the New York Y. C. to be present at the conference which finally opened in London on January 15, 1906.

The isolationists of that day were no less ingenious in methods of delay and in framing unconvincing excuses than those who are now with us; again, as in the so-called "revision" of the Deed of Gift in 1887, all considerations of mere sport were set aside, and the LAW was called in to find an excuse for the declination of the invitation. The reply, which came nominally from the Atlantic Coast Conference, was dated January 11, or only four days before the Conference opened in London, reaching there after its close. This very long and legalistic letter was boiled down to the following cablegram, received on the day of the opening of the Conference: "The Conference of American Clubs feels compelled to the conclusion that they could not take part in the movement for an international rule without serious injury to the sport here, because it would practically amount to re-opening for our clubs the whole question of measurement, which we have just succeeded after years of effort in settling. Your courteous invitation is highly appreciated, and we much regret our inability to avail ourselves of it. Letter mailed you by the direction of the Conference explains fully." The letter explained nothing except the fear of "foreign entanglements"; the argument, if such it can be called, was puerile.

So far as the Conference was concerned, the proposal was warmly accepted and two delegates, Henry A. Morss of the Eastern Y. C. and Stuyvesant Wainwright of the New York Y. C. had been appointed and were about to sail. On January 4 a call was issued for a special meeting of the Conference on the following day, it was proposed that no delegates should be sent, and the motion was carried by a vote of 7 to 6; Messrs. Morss and Wainwright cancelling their passages and unpacking their bags. The points of the long letter, summarized briefly, were that it would not be courteous for Americans to attend the Conference merely to urge the adoption of their own rule, no other rule could be accepted by America, and even if the Universal Rule were adopted by the Conference, the American clubs could not bind themselves to adhere to it. This masterpiece of the legal mind, as set forth at length in the letter and condensed in the cablegram, may be aptly summarized in one word "baloney."

The London Conference included some 20 delegates from 16 nations, among them many practical racing yachtsmen, eminent naval architects and yacht designers, and men noted for their attainments in various sciences associated with naval architecture. Through the successive victories of Vigilant, Defender, Navahoe, Columbia, Reliance and the smaller yachts built to foreign orders N. G. Herreshoff was well and favorably known to all. Had the American delegates been permitted to go, with him as technical adviser, they would at least have been assured of courteous consideration, and it is very probable that the Universal Rule would have been adopted. As matters stand today, there are nominally two rival rules in existence, but the Universal Rule is dead and the only rule known in America is the International.

TRADITIONS AND MEMORIES OF

American Yachting

Part Twenty-eight

Measurement and Classification in America, Concluded

By ***WILLIAM P. STEPHENS***

APART from the fact that there were two rival and conflicting rules, the result of the long agitation of the measurement question must be considered satisfactory. The International Rule has operated successfully in Great Britain and on the Continent, the yachts designed under it being popular with racing men and providing good sport. On this side the Universal Rule has worked similarly, as interpreted by such designers as N. G. Herreshoff, William Gardner, Charles D. Mower, John G. Alden, Prof. George Owen, L. Francis Herreshoff, Henry J. Gielow, Clinton H. Crane, Starling Burgess, Frank C. Paine, C. Sherman Hoyt and F. M. Hoyt.

Passing by the America's Cup Class, which follows no regular course of development, being dependent on the chance of a challenge, the M-Class included such craft as Medora, Prestige, Valiant, Windward, Avatar, Istalena and Simba. The P-Class was less popular, one of its most noted boats being Josephine, an amateur design by the late A. G. Hanan, Valiant and others of less note. The Q-Class boasted of such yachts as Spindrift, Tartar, Hope, Norn, Nor'-Easter IV, Lenore. The R-Class numbered Ardelle, Ardette, Gamecock, Bob-Kat, Yankee, Live Yankee, Doress, Tycoon, Astrild, Manhasset, Robin and Barbara. The schooner division, still prominent in racing, was similarly built up.

Why this great fleet is unknown today, and why such racing as has been done in recent years is in yachts designed under the International Rule, is a question which the writer is at a loss to solve, but one which demands the serious consideration of all interested in match sailing on this side of the Atlantic. A part of the blame for this condition undoubtedly lies with the promoters

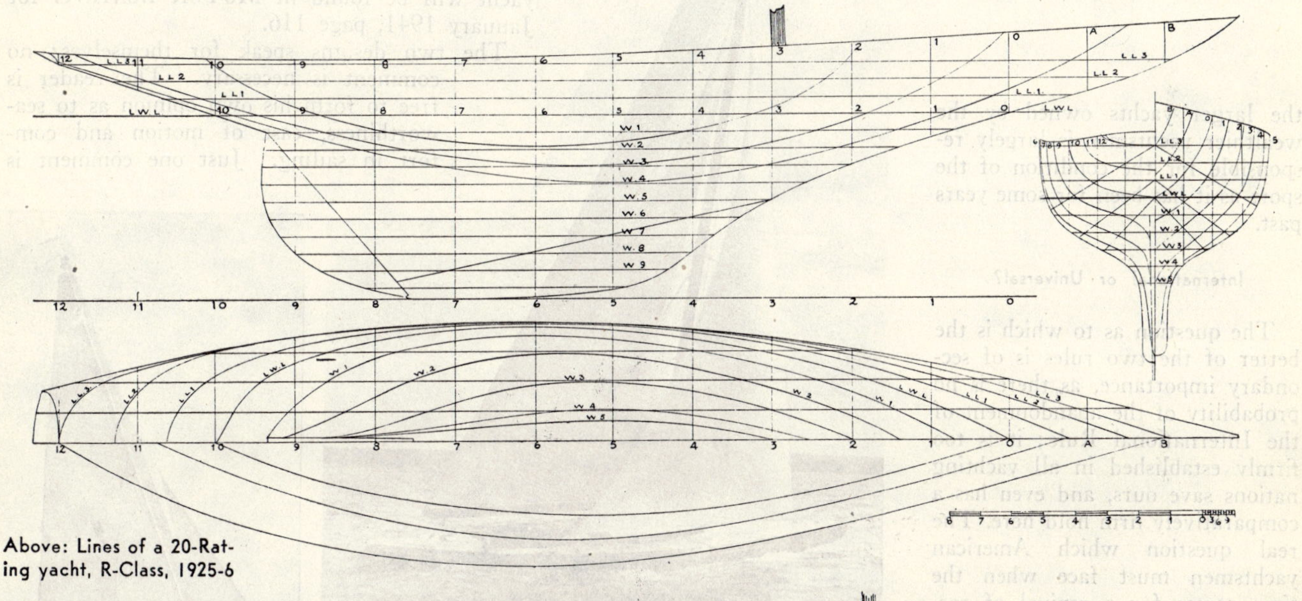

Above: Lines of a 20-Rating yacht, R-Class, 1925-6

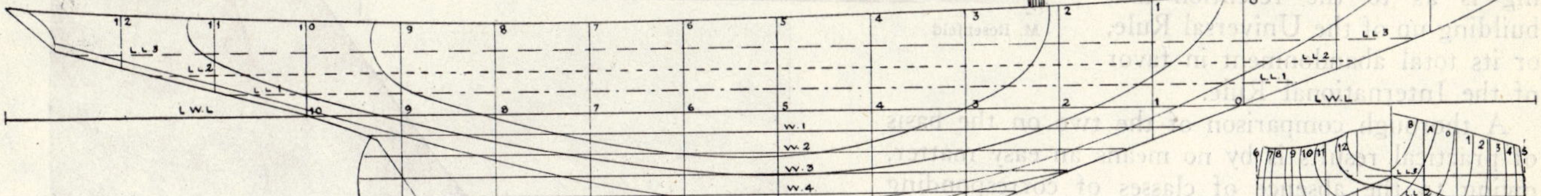

Above: Lines of a 6-Metre yacht, 1925-6, for comparison with the 20-Rater at top

of one-design classes, the New York Thirties, Forties, Fifties and Seventies, the Larchmont O Class, the Sound Schooners,*and others. Whatever the individual merit of some particular class may have been, the net result on yachting was to hinder progress in designing and to kill the business of the designers. In fostering this movement the designers merely worked to destroy the individual ownership and designing on which their livelihood depended. Whatever may be said for the one-design principle in many of the small classes, its extension to the larger yachts owned by the wealthier yachtsmen is largely responsible for the condition of the sport as it has been for some years past.

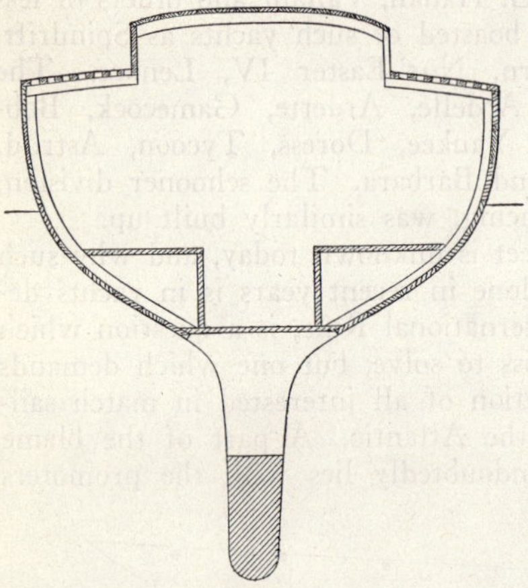

Left: Section through the cabin of an R-Class yacht. Below: One of the R-Class boats under sail. At bottom: An M-boat (46-Rating).

M. Rosenfeld

International or Universal?

The question as to which is the better of the two rules is of secondary importance, as there is no probability of the abandonment of the International Rule; it is too firmly established in all yachting nations save ours, and even has a comparatively firm hold here. The real question which American yachtsmen must face when the time comes for a revival of racing is as to the retention and building up of the Universal Rule, or its total abandonment in favor of the International Rule.

A thorough comparison of the two on the basis of practical results is by no means an easy matter, owing to the absence of classes of corresponding size. The Cup yachts, challengers as well as defenders, must be designed to the American rule; there is no foreign equivalent of the M-Class, and no American class similar to the 12-Metre. The best basis of comparison is in the R-Class and the 6-Metre Class; both offering many more examples than any of the larger classes. As the R-Class is now extinct, it is necessary to go back about fifteen years, when both classes were equally popular.

Fashions change in yachts as in articles of apparel such as ladies' hats and bathing suits, though less rapidly. As in the case of the latter, streamlining becomes more popular each year, though the effort of the yacht designer is to reduce and not to increase the amount of exposed wetted surface. Though the design here shown would differ from the most recent 6-Metres, the esential points of the two rules are unchanged.

The average load waterline of the 6-Metre Class is about 23 feet, that of the R-Class is about 25 feet. In order to make a closer comparison the R-Boat has been reduced to a load line of 23 feet, all other dimensions in proportion. The scales of the two sail plans are identical. The leading dimensions compare as follows:

	6-Metre	Class R	
		Reduced Scale	True Scale
Length Over All........	37-6	34-1	38-0
L.W.L.	23-0	23-0	25-0
Overhang, Bow..........	7-2	6-8	7-3
Counter	7-4	5-3	5-9
Breadth, Deck..........	6-3	6-10	7-4
Extreme	6-6	6-10	7-4
L.W.L.	6-3	6-5	7-0
Draft	5-4	5-3	5-9
Freeboard, Bow	3-1	1-11	2-10
Least	2-3	1-7	1-9
Transom	2-7	1-9	1-11
Mast, From L.W.L.......	5-0	6-5	7-0
L.W.L. to Truck.......	43-3	44-10	48-9
Boom	20-3	20-3	22-0
Sail Area, Square Feet..	455	504	595

The Measurement Certificate of a 6-meter yacht will be found in MoToR BoatinG for January 1941, page 116.

The two designs speak for themselves; no comment is necessary. The reader is free to form his own opinion as to seaworthiness, ease of motion and comfort in sailing. Just one comment is permissible, from the standpoint of the draftsman and designer: the easy flowing lines of the R-Boat, her slightly flaring sides as compared with the tumblehome of the 6-Metre, and the much easier curves of the body plan must appeal to any draftsman who attemps to copy the two designs. Furthermore, the 6-Metre is a half-decked racing boat, with no pretense of accommodation; the R-Boat is a cabin yacht with accommodation which gives added comfort and convenience in match sailing and also makes her when finally out-built a veritable yacht of which any young sailors might be proud.

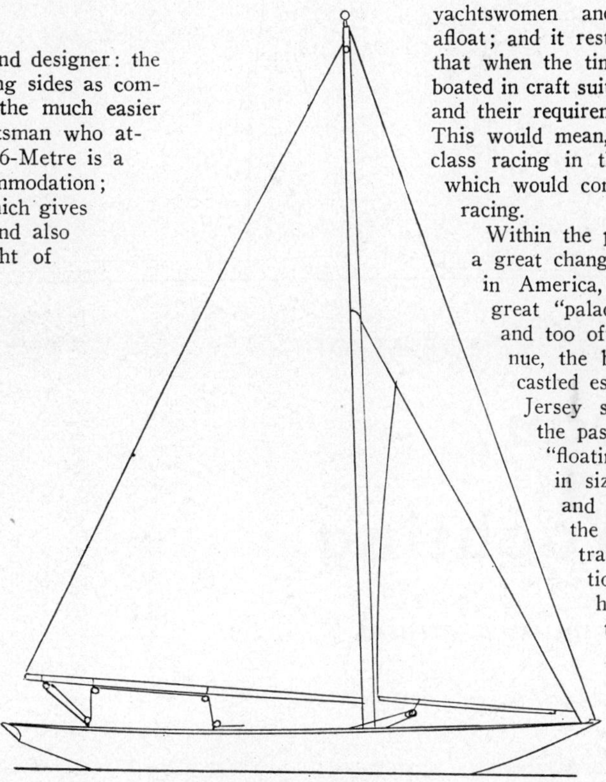

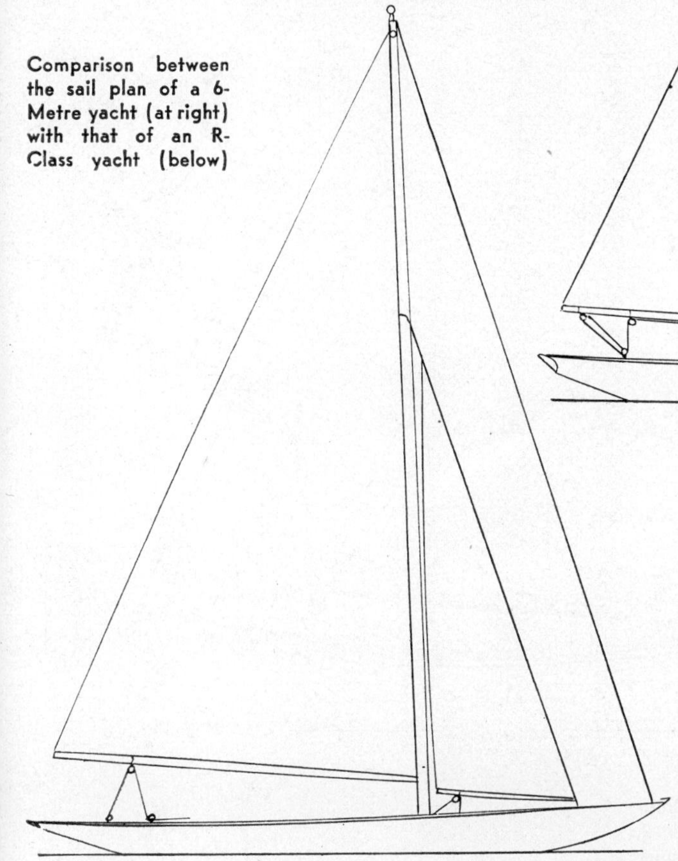

Comparison between the sail plan of a 6-Metre yacht (at right) with that of an R-Class yacht (below)

Certain points of yachts designed to the International Rule which might be considered disadvantageous show up more conspicuously in the 6-Metre Class than in the 10-Metre and larger sizes with full headroom in an enclosed cabin; but the premium on freeboard and the penalty on breadth tend to make vessels approaching the old cutters in deck plan and out-of-water profile.

In the important matter of cost, about 1925-6 the 6-Metre yacht and the 20-Rater (R) would each cost about $7,500; an 8-Metre in 1929 cost $15,000; a 12-Metre in 1935 $25,000, and a yacht of the 46-Rating Class (M) in 1929 $50,000. These prices were for the highest class work of New York and Boston yards, and represent the maximum.

The condition of yachting in recent years, apart from wars and rumors of wars, may be described as one of innocuous desuetude, in more nautical parlance, "in the doldrums," drifting without a rudder, with torn sails, and no helmsman. What the future may bring is beyond conjecture, but no devotee of yacht racing will believe that match sailing in open classes under a measurement rule and in individually designed and owned yachts, has passed forever.

Whatever there is of hope just now lies in the development of the midget classes, the junior organizations sponsored by the elders, the schools of instruction for girls and boys alike, the club and inter-club competitions, and the thousands of small craft available in all localities and at small cost.

A dozen years from now there will be the greatest fleet of young yachtswomen and yachtsmen ever seen afloat; and it rests with their elders to see that when the time comes all are properly boated in craft suited to their financial means and their requirements as to type and size. This would mean, first, the building up of class racing in the smallest classes, after which would come the question of major racing.

Within the past dozen or more years a great change has made itself evident in America, the destruction of the great "palaces" which once adorned and too often disfigured Fifth Avenue, the breaking up of the great castled estates on Long Island, the Jersey shore and Newport, and the passing of the great fleet of "floating palaces" which rivalled in size and surpassed in speed and over-elaborate furnishings the "ocean greyhounds" of the trans-Atlantic lines a generation ago. With these too have gone the "Jay-Boats," typical of the same era of over-display and lavish expenditure.

Until recently there have been in England a comparatively small number of racing yachtsmen with sufficient means to support the 23-Metre Class, the British equivalent of our J-Class, including the two Endeavours, but the largest yachts raced last year were the 12-Metres. It is unlikely that after the war there will be seen anything larger than these. As long as the minimum limit of 65 feet loadline is retained as the smallest Cup challenger there need be no fear of another British invasion such as those of 1930, '37 and '39 in the 23-Metre Class.

The question of the most desirable size for the largest class of single-stick racing yachts is an old one, dating back to the building of the so-called 90-foot Class: Puritan, 81 feet, 1885; Mayflower, 86 feet, 1886; and Volunteer, 87 feet, 1887. As long ago as the last year I argued it with Edward Burgess, my position being that the existing 70-foot L.W.L. Class was the largest which could be maintained permanently. On the other side Burgess claimed that the wealthier yachtsmen would not be content to sail such yachts as Titania and Katrina while their associates were sailing the faster and more imposing 90-footers.

History has given the answer. Every yacht of the Cup defense fleet since built down to 1930 has been converted to the schooner rig, for reasons of economy and easier handling, as soon as the match which called her into being was over; a little later she was relegated to the cruising division. The ultimate result of this policy is seen today in the disappearance of all smaller classes and the sale of Ranger to a junkman for ten thousand dollars.

The finest racing class which this country has ever known was the 46-Rating (M-Boats); single-stick yachts of about 54 feet l.w.l., 83 feet over all; 14 to 15 feet breadth and just over 10 feet draft; craft such as Windward, Istalena, Prestige, Avatar, Medora, Valiant and Simba. These yachts were large enough and fast enough to give good racing, and even at possible post-war prices they will cost enough to make the class exclusive and cause wealthy supporters of racing to think twice before placing an order. The requirement that a challenger for the Cup must cross the Atlantic on her own bottom has been made ridiculous by the repeated ocean passages of boats little more than decked dinghies and the form and construction of the modern racing yacht; it has also been effectually abrogated by the permission to tow across. A challenge from a yacht of this class would be the greatest boon which we may hope for when yachting revives, and the effect would be equally beneficial abroad.

Today is the time for thought if not for action on the part of all friends of match sailing to work out carefully and deliberately the problem of its future. As a minor detail now, while we are drifting in dead backwater, is the opportunity for the North American

(*Continued on page* 146)

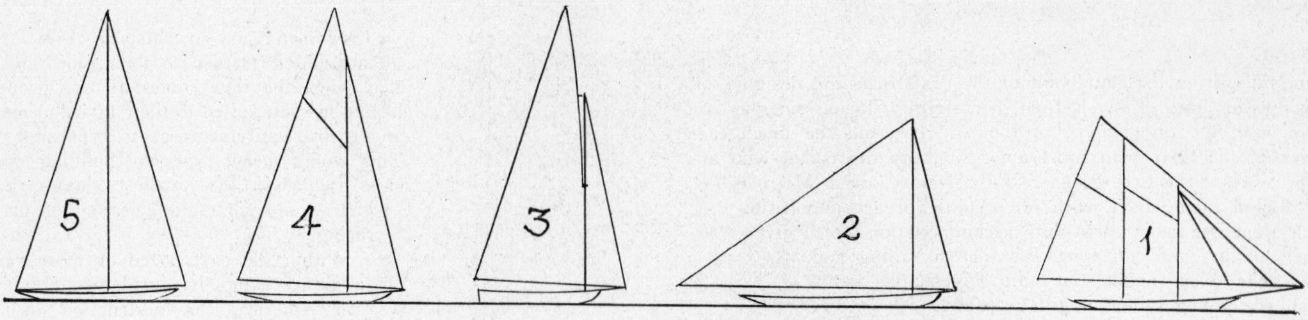

The Eternal Triangle: 1, Schooner, 1880; 2, One-Rater, 1890; 3, Gunter Sloop, 1900; 4, Shamrock, 1910; 5, Meter Class, 1930

TRADITIONS AND MEMORIES OF

American Yachting

By WILLIAM P. STEPHENS

Part Twenty-nine: The Rig

MAN'S triumph over the air, a victory which has wrought untold misery to humanity, and has made possible the destruction of human life and property on a scale never even dreamed of by the most ruthless vandals of the past, is of such recent date that its history is known to every boy who builds a model airplane. Man's victory over the water—waves and winds—on the other hand is of such remote origin that we may rely only on imagination and reasoning for its history. We can conceive that man's first attempt to cross a river was made by pushing a log from the beach, holding on with his hands as he floated, and kicking with his legs. The next step, presumably, was astride of the log and propelling it by paddling with his hands, or using a pole if in shoal water. The log possessed buoyancy, but no stability, later two or more logs were lashed together, giving stability in addition to added buoyancy; but, as the arms would no longer reach the water, a crude paddle was devised. As more logs were added and more passengers carried the paddle was made much longer and swung from a fixed support, thus becoming an oar. In course of time came the canoe, a log, perhaps a fallen one with the heart rotted by age, later roughly shaped with stone hatchets and hollowed largely by burning; this greatly increased the radius of navigation, encouraged exploration and trading, and with a large canoe manned by many paddlers long voyages were possible.

The origin of the sail is as much a mystery as the origin of the ship, but it was inevitable that eventually some one of these primitive canoeists, finding the wind astern, would stand up and hold out a paddle or a mat. The next step would be the erection of a pole on which some fabric, presumably a mat, was hung from a horizontal stick; and there was the squaresail. A further development would produce a fixed mast with stays, and a halyard for hoisting and lowering, with a sheet from each corner of the sail; the paddles becoming largely auxiliary.

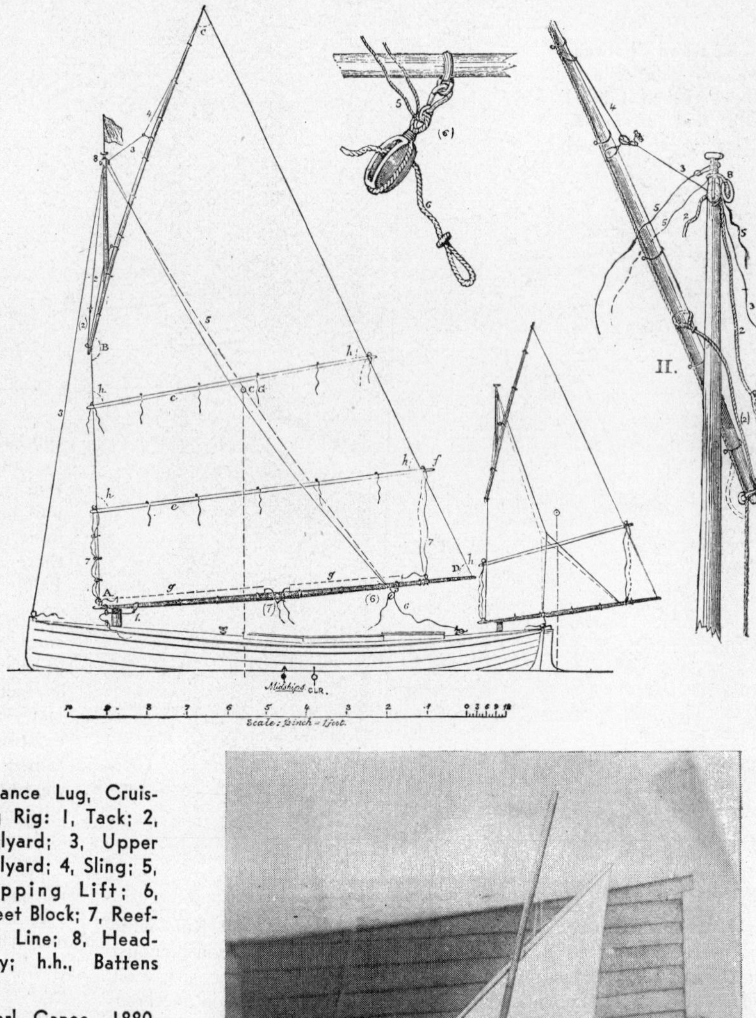

Balance Lug, Cruising Rig: 1, Tack; 2, Halyard; 3, Upper Halyard; 4, Sling; 5, Topping Lift; 6, Sheet Block; 7, Reefing Line; 8, Headstay; h.h., Battens

Pearl Canoe, 1880. E. B. Tredwen. Sailing position, reclining in cockpit. Side flap of deck open to permit sitting to windward. Chain with buffer spring for 56-pound centerplate. Roller mizzen, reefed from cockpit position

Right: Group of American canoes showing various rigs, 1884
Below: C. Bowyer Vaux, New York Canoe Club. Pioneer in canoe racing in America
Center: Bat sail plan, 1890. Lowering and reefing
Bottom: Evolution from Balance Lug to "Bafter" rig, 1890

There is good reason to believe that extensive voyages, of course, always before the wind, were made in vessels of this description. Progress to windward was out of the question, but one day an unknown genius, as the wind hauled and headed him, was seized with an idea. Swinging his yard fore and aft, he brought the forward corner down to the lee gunwale and made it fast, thus peaking up the yard, and led the other sheet aft, thus having a fore and aft sail with which he could reach. The original squaresail was thus converted to a standing lug, still quadrilateral; as this sail was perfected, and probably leeboards added, windward work was made possible.

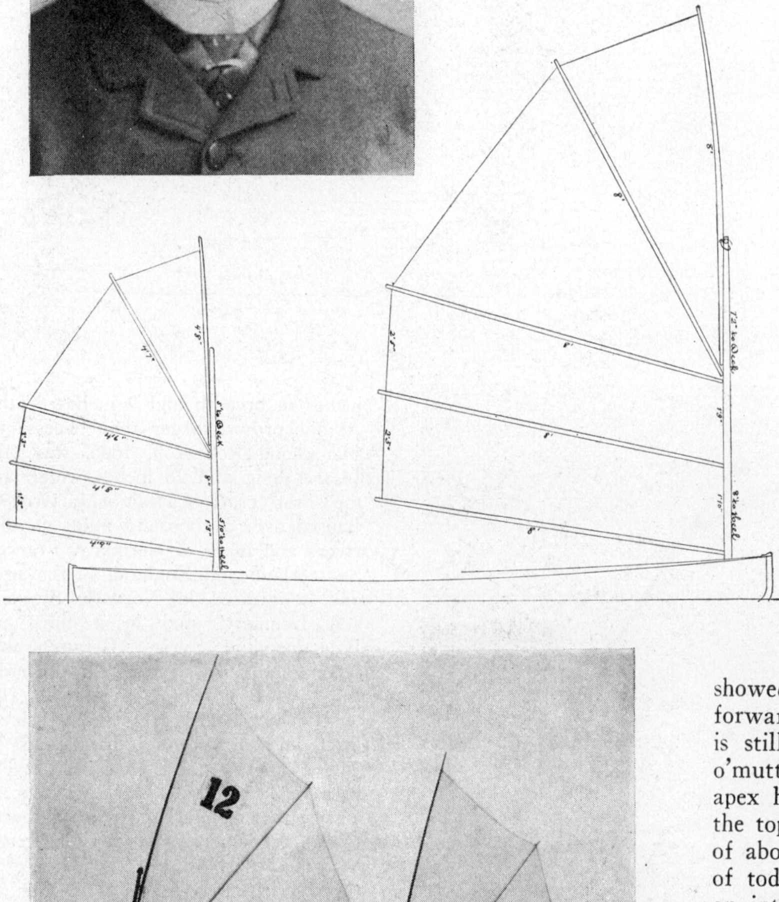

The history of sail has interested many writers, but the most which may be proved is that sails were used as early as 2600 B.C. in the eastern Mediterranean and Egypt, and by 600 B.C. in Mesopotamia; the squaresail with yard. The triangular sail, the lateen, was used by the Arabs about 900 A.D. The quadrilateral sail in the form of the lug is found the world over today, sharing its popularity with the triangular or leg-o'mutton sail. In course of time, as a matter of convenience and safety, the big leg-o'mutton sail was divided, the lower part quadrilateral, set with boom and gaff, and the upper part the triangular topsail. At this point all improvement stopped.

The Rig in Modern Days

Under the title The Eternal Triangle a writer, Cuthbert Grasemann, in The Yachting Monthly for June, points out that the majority of sail plans of yachts show an isosceles triangle, but in varying positions. The schooner rig of 1880 showed the triangle with one side down and the apex forward; in the small raters of ten years later the triangle is still on its side, but the apex is aft. In the leg-o'mutton rig of 1900 the triangle stands on its base, with apex high in air, the same arrangement (if we include the topsail) being found in the large boom-and-gaff rigs of about 1910, and in the yachts, both large and small of today. The details of this change of position offer an interesting study.

It must be admitted that in the matter of rig the yachtsman has shown himself among the most conventional and conservative of bipeds; he starts in a groove plowed for him by his father or grandfather and runs along in it until forced out of it by some exceptional accident. While the leg-o'mutton rig has been developed to a high degree of perfection by working sailors the world over, the yachtsman has clung to the boom-and-gaff rig for both racing and cruising. In Great Britain this rig was universal on schooners, cutters and yawls; in America on schooners and sloops, and catboats as well. The British cutter, with its short mast well amidships, its

Left: Standing Rig. Leg-O'-Mutton with leech extended by battens. Below: Pecowsic standing rig

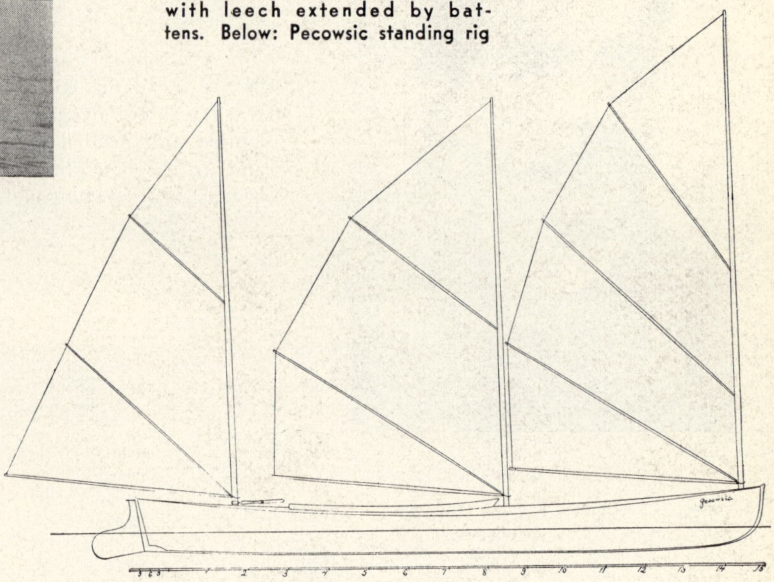

long topmast fitted to house in bad weather, its long bowsprit also fitted to house, its loose-footed mainsail, its jib set flying and its foresail hanked to a stay, was beyond question well fitted for the work of chasing smugglers in all weathers in the Channel and the North Sea. The sloop in its original form in Dutch waters, wide and shoal, with tall mast set well forward, a mere broomstick of a topmast, a huge baulk of timber built in permanently as a bowsprit, its mainsail laced to the boom and one big jib permanently hanked to a stay to the bowsprit end, served a good purpose on the canals and inland waterways of its native Holland, and also in the great carrying trade of the Hudson River prior to the construction of railroads. Just over a century ago British yachtsmen started in a groove in adopting the revenue cutter as the model for their pleasure craft; about the same time New York yachtsmen modelled their yachts after the local working sloops; each continuing in its rut, contently and complacently, until forced out of it a half century later by the clash of the two types in international racing.

The assimilation and improvement of the two rigs came about in 1885 in the construction of the compromise cutter Puritan, designed by Edward Burgess for the defense of the America's Cup. For the ensuing thirty years the larger yachts of America and Britain carried this rig with no change in its essential details; that it has virtually disappeared today is due not to the yachting fraternity, but to the enterprise and ingenuity of the canoeing world.

Pearl, as raced in New York

The Poor Man's Yacht

THIS was the title applied to an old-new type of craft which made its appearance in 1865; when Captain John MacGregor, a retired officer of the British Army, invalided by a railway accident which barred participation in the more strenuous sports planned his first canoe, he little realized that he was starting a sequence of events which would revolutionize the rigs of the yachts of all great yachting nations. The connection between his tiny cockleshell propelled by a short double-bladed paddle, and the costly and majestic craft which compete today for the America's Cup, is so remote as to seem incredible; and yet the two are joined by links as closely welded as those of a chain.

The first Rob Roy canoe, built of oak, lapstrake, was an adaptation of the eskimo kayak, a craft of unknown origin, just large enough to float one man, a frame of walrus bones over which sealskin was stretched and sewn, it was fully decked except for an oval cockpit in which the man sat, laced in by an apron of sealskin up to his armpits. These kayaks, propelled by a long double paddle, were used on the open sea in hunting walrus and seal; one exploit of the hunter was to capsize his craft until his head was downward, then to recover the upright position by making a complete revolution. The first Rob Roy was 15 feet long, the length being determined by the space available in German railway carriages, 28 inches in breadth and 9 inches depth. As she proved larger than necessary, the second Rob Roy, 1866, was but 14 feet long and 26 inches wide. In the first craft Captain MacGregor cruised over a thousand miles on the rivers and lakes of Germany, France, Switzerland and England, in the second he cruised in Norway, Sweden and Denmark, and in a third in Palestine and Syria. Between the second and third, in 1867, he had built the yawl Rob Roy, 21 feet over all, practically the first of what have since been known as single-hand yachts. The cruises of these four craft, each in a book by itself, were written in a style that is fresh and readable even today, and which made many converts to the novel sport.

On July 26, 1865, at a meeting at the Star and Garter Inn called by Captain MacGregor, the Royal Canoe Club was organized; by December the Club had 31 members, by June, 1868, the membership had risen to 178, with branches on the Humber, the Mersey and at Oxford. One of the early converts was a young Admiralty Lawyer, Warrington Baden-Powell, a brother of the founder of the Boy Scouts; in 1869, in company with a friend, each in a Rob Roy canoe, he went by steamer to Gothenburg and made a long cruise through Denmark and Sweden. The first canoes were fitted with a standing lug mainsail and a very small jib, the mainsail was 4 feet on the boom and 4 feet on the yard; I still have the sail which my mother sewed for my

Rob Roy in 1876; the material was a new yacht duck, just put out by Boyle, a dealer in canvas, on Fulton Street. Of this rig Baden-Powell says, and I can endorse him: "I had found the standing lug rig awkward to handle in sudden squalls; without a traveller, on letting go the halyard it was apt to bag out to leeward, then bang about in a most disorderly manner, and finally fall into the water. With a traveller it would often refuse the duty of coming down at all. Of course these little eccentricities could nearly always be nipped in the bud, but still it was not quite the style of rig for a long cruise." In his book, "Canoe Travelling," 1871, he goes into the question of rig in detail, describing the lateen, settee, Chinese lug, dipping lug, revolving lug, split lug, spritsail and sliding gunter, the last being his choice.

The Canoe as a Racing Craft

WHILE canoe cruising enjoyed great popularity for a time, with the canoes of the Royal Canoe Club berthed in a permanent home on the Thames racing followed as a matter of course; with a rapid development in both model and rig. The leaders were Baden-Powell and E. B. Tredwen; as both were addicts of the vicious habit of stenciling, the former with the name Nautilus and the latter with the name Pearl, it is difficult today to trace the exact development of their many craft, usually one each year. Each designed his own canoes, Baden-Powell's being built by professionals while Tredwen built his, assisted by his father. Baden-Powell, a skilled amateur designer, tried his skill on larger craft than canoes, a yachtsman and expert sailor, at one time by odd chance he owned the old cutter Pearl, built in 1820.

Nautilus II was largely a replica of No. I, but No. III was "intended to be used mainly for traveling, to fit a man weighing 11 stone, 10 pounds; height, 5 feet 8 inches; breadth of shoulders, 1 foot 10 inches, and stern, 1 foot 4 inches, with his baggage and his dog, was 14 feet long, breadth 2 feet 4 inches, depth, 10½ inches." With but one inch of keel, no centerboard, and but a very inefficient leeboard, windward work was out of the question, but as racing became more popular there was a great change in both hull and rig. While the length was unchanged, both breadth and depth were greatly increased, with added displacement and sail area. Metal centerboards, up to 56 pounds, were installed, supplemented by shot bags inside the hull, with many complicated fittings. The racing was on the Thames and Hendon Lake a small body of water near London, both surrounded by trees which cut off the wind, and about 1878 the balance lug in an exaggerated form was adopted. This sail originated on the rivers and canals of China where similar conditions of tree-sheltered waters prevailed; the sail was narrow and very lofty, with a considerable portion forward of the mast, whence the term "balance." Mast, boom and yard were of bamboo, and the sail was crossed by a series of light bamboo battens, from luff to leach, each held to the mast by a loop, "parrel," each with its reefline, and each with an individual sheet which united with the others in a single main sheet. In its ingenuity, complication, and adaptation to a special purpose the outfit was characteristically Chinese. As used by British canoeists most of these features were retained, the canoeist lying in the well could slack off the halyard and haul down one, two or three reefs in a moment.

The Canoe in America

MODERN canoeing was introduced in America by a half dozen enthusiasts led by William L. Alden, an editorial writer on The New York Times, and M. Roosevelt Schuyler, later prominent as a leader of the "Cutter Cranks," who organized the New York Canoe Club in 1871. The Club grew rapidly after its first few years, and in 1879 was installed in a house of its own on the N.E. tip of Staten Island, just where the St. George ferryhouse now stands. While canoe traveling and cruising was still very popular, the convenient location, the fine sailing waters of New York Bay, and the long American summer afforded every facility for sailing and racing. The first canoes, Rob Roy and Nautilus models, were imported from England and copied by American builders, but under the impetus of amateur designers and builders as well as professional, new models were introduced. All of the sails enumerated by Baden-Powell, beginning with the standing lug, were used in competition.

With the organization of the American Canoe Association, in 1880, canoeing assumed a national rather than a local phase, and canoe clubs were formed throughout the States and Canada; canoeists meeting each August at some central camp. Experimentation in rigs ran wild, and each gathering, local or national, saw new ideas, most of them impracticable. The English racing was watched closely by Americans, who, as well as the English, were deluded by the idea that the heavily ballasted and over-rigged Pearl and Nautilus were actually fast. In 1881 I built, from a design of the No. 3 Pearl, given me by Tredwen, a canoe, Queen Mab, for Dr. E. B. Bronson, fitting her with two balance lugs with multiple battens and reefing gear; but she made a very poor showing against the unballasted canoes of the Club. The rig, however, was imitated on many canoes in the States and Canada.

The Machine Age in Canoeing

IN all early sailing American canoeists followed the English practice of sitting as low as possible, on the floor, and merely bending the body to one side in balancing; the steering being done by the feet on a crossbar. The first to abandon this practice was C. B. Vaux, a lightly built but agile young man, who took his seat on the weather side of the canoe, steering by means of a deck tiller. The practice was soon generally adopted, the extreme in this hiking being reached by Dr. A. E. Heighway of the Cincinnati C. C., a tall powerful athlete. He sailed a 26-inch Rob Roy canoe, with two large lateen sails such as she never was designed to carry, with his toes under the lee deck, his calves on the coaming and weather deck, his body extended and his head touching the water as she heeled under squalls of Lake George.

The deck position was supplemented by a seat, of the width of the canoe, now 30 inches, removable at will, on which the canoeist might sit in comparative comfort and hike to better advantage. In 1886 there came to the Meet a young man from Lowell, Mass., Paul Butler, son of the famous old war general, B.F. His interest in canoeing was entirely on the side of racing; so far as I am aware he never cruised. His first canoe was a crude affair, but he was a born sailor and racing expert. Small in stature and even a cripple, a hunchback, he was sadly handicapped against the agility of sailors like Vaux and athletes like Dr. Heighway and W. G. MacKendrick. One day shortly after the opening of the 1886 Meet there was a rush from all parts of the camp to the point of Grindstone Island, off which Butler was sailing with a slide running on his fixed seat; rising just before the end of a tack, the slide fell to leeward of its own weight; as she filled away Butler was on the end of the slide, his body entirely outside the hull. The original slide was of the length of the fixed seat, 30 inches, but at the present time slides of 7 to 10 feet, elaborately trussed, are used on canoes of 30 inches breadth.

The Nations Meet

IN October 1885 the New York C.C. offered a trophy for perpetual international competition, and shortly after the Association established a similar trophy; challenges were at once received from Tredwen and Baden-Powell. New canoes were built, the Pearl being similar to her predecessors, but the new Nautilus was designed for competition with the lighter American craft. When the time came for his departure for America Mr. Tredwen was obliged to abandon the trip owing to the illness of his father, but the new Pearl was brought out by a young canoeist, Walter Stewart, a comparative novice but a skillful sailor; Baden-Powell accompanying his Nautilus. Both of the canoes were fully fitted for the lying-down position, with feet on the steering bar below deck, and the body thrown to windward as far as the side-flap would permit; but being familiar with the American method, Baden-Powell had provided a deck tiller, to be used at will. While he held to the lying-down position off the wind, he soon found his way to the deck when working to windward. Both canoeists attended the A.C.A. Meet at the Thousand Islands, taking part in the racing. In the Trophy race, 7½ miles, Nautilus was eighth, ten minutes astern of the winner, Pearl being a minute later. Owing to her very light construction Pearl was almost a wreck by the time the Meet was over, and a newer boat was sent out for the New York C.C. trophy. In the match on New York Bay both of the visitors made a better showing, Nautilus winning one of the three races. As the result of this American visit British canoeists at once discarded their 56 pound centerboards and 300 pounds of shotbags and cut down the displacement of their models to the American standard.

Evolution in Rig

BY 1885 the balance lug, with its battens and reef gear, had gone out of fashion, and canoe sails approximated the leg-o'mutton, but still with the leach extended in a curve by one or more sprit battens. Many, even of the racing men, still kept up the custom of cruising in part to the Meets, their rigs being fitted to lower and reef; one of the first proceedings on making camp being to display some new camp equipment or change in rig. As stated, Paul Butler's interest was solely in racing, and with him was Everett H. Barney of the Springfield C.C., maker of the Barney & Berry skate; a man much older than his competitors, but as deeply interested in competitive sailing. As in Butler's case, his first canoe was very crude in model and construction, but both soon found builders who turned out the highest class of work, Butler designing all of his canoes.

First shifted bodily abaft the mast, the balance lug found itself with its yard vertical and its battens gradually disappearing; one stage of this change is shown in the sail plan of Bat. This change continued until both Butler and Barney came to the simplest form of sail, a leg-o'mutton laced permanently to both mast and boom. By this time the forward mast was stepped as close as possible to the stem and the mizzenmast just abaft midships, the two mast tubes being of the same size. The racing outfit of both included five sails of varying sizes, and two, or even three on the Barney canoes, might be shipped at the last minute before leaving the float. Butler was accompanied to camp by an old colored man, a body servant of the General, whose duty it was to look after the sails; these stood in a rack and could be shipped instantly. This proceeding was strongly opposed by those who cruised with lowering and reefing rigs, and a very hot discussion ensued in print over the "standing rig"; but, as usual, the conservatives were defeated and the radicals won the day. What with the unlimited sliding seat and the unlimited standing rig, the canoe became one of the extreme of racing machines.

MEASUREMENT AND CLASSIFICATION

(*Continued from page* 141)

Yacht Racing Union, the Yacht Racing Association of Long Island Sound and the major yacht clubs to overhaul their club books and delete the whole system of class letters, restoring the correct terminology of 20-Rating Class, 25-Rating, and up to 76-Rating. The alphabetical designations have been used throughout this article as the correct terms would not be understood by most readers, but as the legal and official language of the rules they should be familiar to all racing men. With this reform it would be well to give the deep six to the word "Marconi," a bastard term which has found its way into yachting without legal warrant as a substitute for the "Bermudian" or "Leg-o-mutton" which properly designate the now universal pole-masted rig.

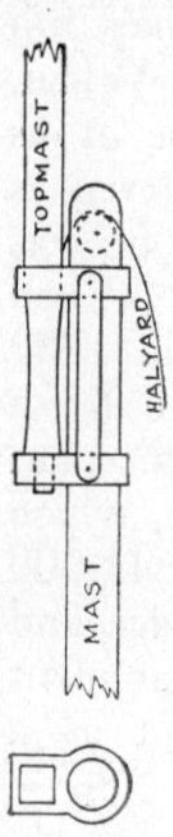

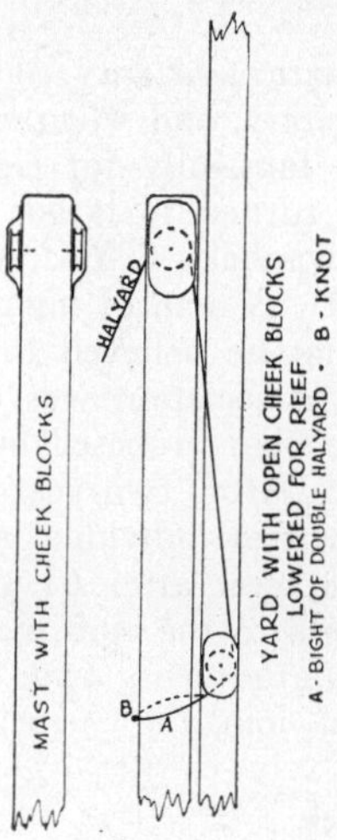

Left: Gunter Iron. Right: Details of Vagabond's rig. Below: Sliding Gunter rig on canoe Vagabond

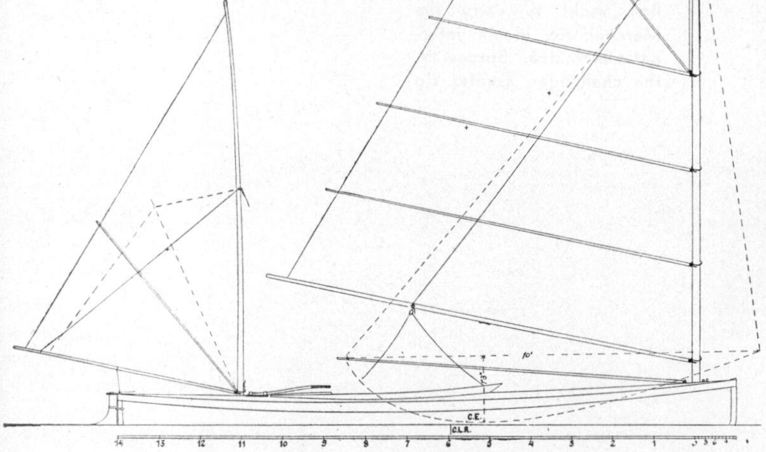

TRADITIONS AND MEMORIES OF AMERICAN YACHTING

By WILLIAM P. STEPHENS

Part Thirty: The Rig (Continued)

THE sliding gunter rig is very old, and of unknown origin, rarely mentioned in print, and yet it has many good features and is very widely used. Its essentials are a relatively short mast and a very long yard so rigged as to retain its vertical position when lowered for reefing. The short mast may be readily shipped or unshipped, an advantage in lifeboats, ship's boats and fishing boats, while the long yard carries a large sail which may be quickly reefed or lowered. The rig is specially adapted to inland waters such as the Thames, the Humber and in the Low Countries where the numerous bridges make a pole mast out of the question. In one of the older forms a "gunter iron" is used, two members each similar to the masthead cap of a yacht, joined by side bars. Each member has a ring on one side which slides on the mast and a square band on the other in which the heel of the yard, which really becomes a topmast, is stepped. The rings sliding on the mast are leathered and unless well greased are apt to jam.

In another form the yard is fitted with some form of jaw on the heel, with a sling on the upper part; there are two halyards, one fast to the heel and one ending in a bullseye running on the sling. In hoisting both are set up, but in reefing the heel halyard is slacked off, thus lowering the sail, while the yard is held in a vertical position by the sling. Various other methods are used, one being shown in the accompanying figure, the halyard is double, the hauling parts leading through a double block at the masthead while the bight leads through a block on the yard and another fast to a mast ring. A tail line from this block to the heel of the yard throws most of the weight on the bight, to jam the yard close to the mast even when lowered for a third reef. In a rig once popular with canoeists the halyard was double, with two cheek-blocks on the masthead and two on the yard, with a knot in the bight. In hoisting the strain was on one halyard, through the knot, but when the yard was up the second halyard was set up; when lowered for reefing the weight of the yard acted to hold it vertical. Some early experiments were made with pole masts, but all involved the use of mast-rings, which inevitably jammed.

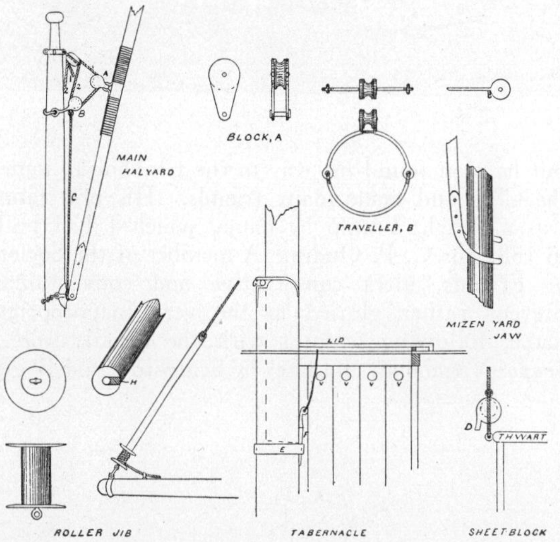

Details of English rigging. A, block on yard. B, mast traveller and block; C, heel rope. 1-1, 2-2, parts of double halyard. Details of roller jib and tabernacle. Left: Vagabond with Gunter rig

Born in London in 1856, Charles J. Stevens came to New York in 1880 as the representative of a firm of cement manufacturers; practically alone in a strange city, he found a home in a boarding house in New Brighton, Staten Island, then a center of yachting and canoeing and one of the most delightful suburbs of Manhattan. He was near to the house of the New York Canoe Club. On evenings and week-ends the whole fleet of the Club was visible from the shore and from the ferryboats. So far as I am aware Stevens had done no boating in England,

but he soon found his way to the Clubhouse, joined the Club and made many friends. His first canoe was a Pearl, Tramp by name, which I had built in 1882 for C. P. Oudin. A member of the Society of Friends, ultra conservative and conventional, Stevens rather gloried in the very inappropriate name, following it later with the equally *mal a propos* Vagabond, and later by Scarecrow and Bogie.

Methodical, systematic and very conscientious, he was an ideal man for secretary, and when elected by the Club in 1886 he served it faithfully for eight years. When, in 1892, his interest turned to larger craft, some of us put him into the Seawanhaka C.Y.C. which he served as Secretary in 1897-8-9. A man of high principles, he was most obstinate in what he believed to be right. When the American Canoe Association was organized in 1880 by N. H. Bishop the plan proposed by him called for a membership of clubs. After two years of trial this plan was abandoned in favor of individual membership, which has worked well, the total after 61 years being 11,000 members. Stevens held to the club membership idea and in the course of many arguments made the rash statement that he never would join the Association except as a

Seawanhaka Cup Match, 1896. Glencairn, challenger, under Gunter rig. Below: Seawanhaka Cup Match, 1895. Ethelwynn, defender, first yacht to carry the Marconi rig in an international match. Spruce IV, the challenger, Gunter rig

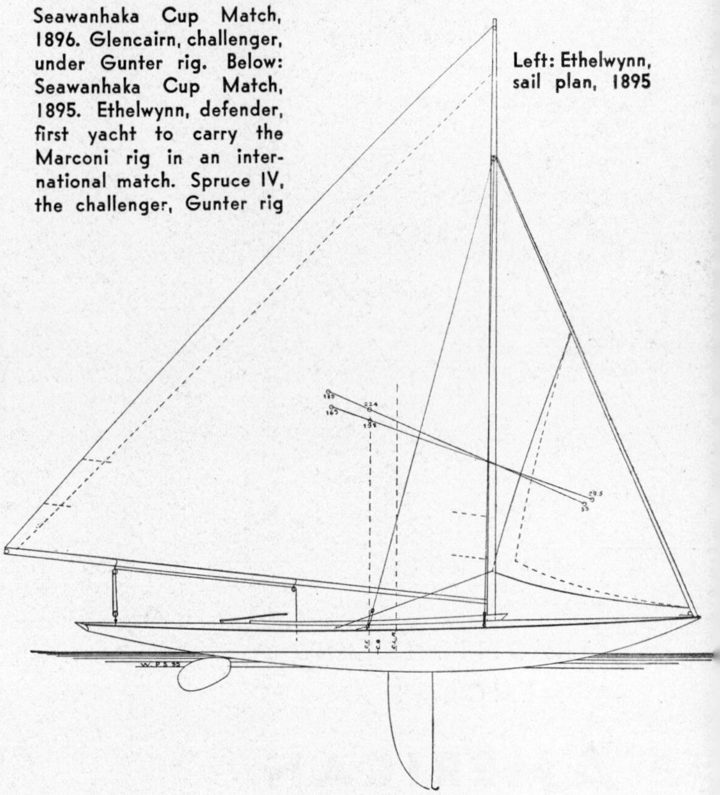

Left: Ethelwynn, sail plan, 1895

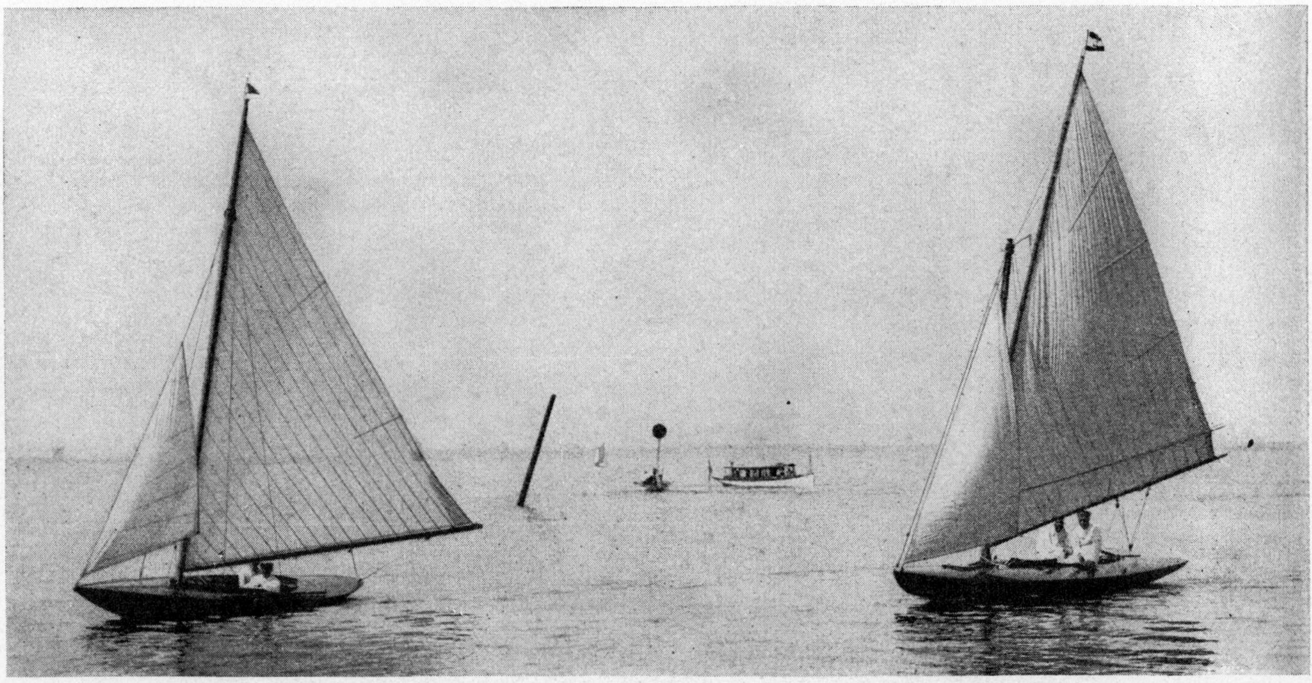

Scarecrow. Original sail plans by C. J. Stevens. Broken lines, Gunter rig, 1892. Solid lines, pole-masted rig, 1894

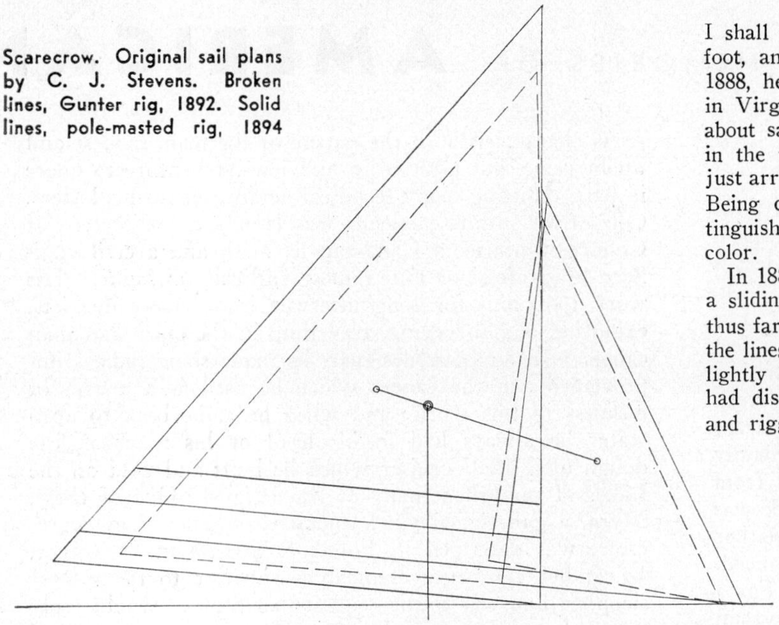

I shall use only one halyard, passing through a block 7 feet from foot, and one tack." In a letter dated New York November 2, 1888, he says:—"I leave here tomorrow evening to spend a week in Virginia, I want to have a chat with you when I come back about sails. My ideas are taking a radical direction, not so much in the form of sail as in its disposition. My new spinaker has just arrived, it is a beauty; it is in the office, do you want to see it?" Being color-blind, he was handicapped in not being able to distinguish a red flag from a green one, or to pick up buoys by their color.

In 1887, discarding the balance lugs on Tramp, he fitted her with a sliding gunter mainsail and pole-masted mizzen; the lightest rig thus far seen on a canoe. In 1888 I put on paper under his direction the lines of a racing canoe, Vagabond, 15 feet by 29 inches, the hull lightly built and the rig perfect in every detail. By this time he had discarded battens; the mainsail of 65 square feet, with spars and rigging, weighed but 9 pounds. Sailed by her owner she was good for fourth or fifth place, but when sailed by C. B. Vaux she was not far astern of Elipse and Fly, the outstanding canoes of the year. In 1891 we again collaborated in a radical design, Kismet, a keel-centerboard canoe which was not a success. In this year of Grace, 1941, when racing canoeists are turning to the sloop rig—leg-o'mutton mainsail and jib—it is interesting to know that 53 years ago Stevens planned the same rig for Vagabond, but discarded it for the reason that the long low-hung boom then in general use would not clear the body of the sailor. It now seems possible that this rig may displace the main-and-mizzen rig so long in universal use.

member of the New York C.C. When in each August the rest of us loaded our canoes on a train for the St. Lawrence River he was left alone to sail about New York Bay, and no amount of argument or persuasion would induce him to repudiate the thoughtless remark.

Deeply interested in the sport, he made an intensive study of the canoe and its fittings; he made no pretension to a knowledge of designing, and all work of this kind fell to me, to carry out his ideas. The subject of rig interested him deeply. We both were intimate with Gilbert H. Wilson, a courtly old gentleman of the family which made the sails for America; and he gladly gave his aid. The best of English cordage and fittings were imported. A stair-builder of Bridgeport, and a sandbag sailor, L. K. Young, was just coming into prominence as the maker of hollow spars, and he was enlisted in Stevens' service; he had for builders Samuel Ayers and W. F. Stevens, and his personal clerk (Stevens always pronounced it clark) was a clever amateur mechanic and made the patterns for special fittings. He had more leisure time and more money than most of us, and in every detail of construction, spars, sails and fittings his canoes were as nearly perfect as any in the fleet, but he had not the knack of winning races. Successful sailing men are born to the game; most canoe sailors, Vaux, Butler, Gibson, Ford Jones in particular, started with canoes crude in model, build and rig, and though they progressed to better craft, they depended largely on professional help; while Stevens gave his personal attention to every detail.

Bogie, Pole-masted rig, 1896

HIS business involved much travelling through the West and South, and apparently the time was beguiled by a study of sails and allied problems; as I was in regular receipt of letters from distant points, all on the same subject. In one dated Cincinnati December 21, 1887, he writes:—"My object in bringing the yard so low down is to avoid length in mast and get a light yard which, being held to the mast at the lower end by a jaw, will get good leverage; and, aided by the roach, will give a good tight leach.

IN 1892 I designed, under Stevens' personal direction, a fin-keel sailing boat, Scarecrow, of 18 feet l.w.l., not intended for racing but only for sailing about between Governor's Island and Sandy Hook carrying a tent and cooking equipment as was then done by canoes. The Tobin bronze fin was fitted in a trunk coming up to the floor of the watertight cockpit; the trunk being made 8 inches longer than the fin to permit of a fore-and-aft adjustment for either trim or sail balance. A pair of sheer legs was carried with a light chain hoist by means of which the fin of 247 pounds and the bulb of 400 pounds might be hoisted up when in shoal water. The mainsail was identical with that of Vagabond, the sliding gunter without battens, these having been discarded by Stevens several years previously; the yard was set with the double halyard. The sail area was 296 square feet, but as she carried it easily it was increased in 1894 to 381 square feet, and at the same time the yard was discarded and a pole mast substituted. In place of the jaws and mast hoops of the old rig the sail was attached to the mast by means of a track and toggles strung on the luffrope before it was sewn to the sail. In place of the rolled stock track now used there were two strips of sheet brass screwed to the mast about 3/8 inch apart; the toggles were slotted on the side to slide between the brass strips. The spars, made by Young, were hollow, he also made the blocks, a spring gooseneck, and other special fittings. The shrouds were of bronze wire rope with special turnbuckles.

In canoes of 29 to 31 inches breadth the first question was stability, and to this end the center of gravity of the rig and also the center of effort were kept as low as possible, the triangle having a base much longer than the hoist.

Part Thirty-one: The Rig (Continued)

IN changing to a pole mast on Scarecrow, a short bowsprit was added, as shown on Bogie in the previous part. In all its essential features and down to the minor details this rig was, with the exception of ratio of base to hoist, identical with that in use the world over today. The design was published to two scales, 18 feet and 15 feet l.w.l. and widely built to, both with the fin and with a centerboard; many, however, refused to adopt the freak rig and used the old boom and gaff. The stock hardware sold by ship chandlers a half century ago was made, mainly of malleable cast iron, for heavily rigged yachts of from 20 to 35 feet; from the latter size up the ironwork was made specially for each yacht by the yard smith, either working on his own or, more and more as time advanced, from detailed plans by the designer of the yacht. For a craft as small as Scarecrow there was little more than malleable iron awning blocks and similar crudities. Those who wished anything light and of good design had to make it for themselves; I still have a large box of patterns for rudder heads, turnbuckles, mast bands, etc., of that era.

As characteristic of the nature of the man, modest and unobtrusive, but positive in his views, I venture to quote in part, omitting many technical details, one of his letters. One of my intimate friends was Henry K. Wicksteed of Coburg, Ontario, a Canadian by birth and a civil engineer by profession, but a most enthusiastic sailor. His work took him for long intervals into remote districts, exploring and surveying, travelling in the open Canadian canoe. An amateur designer, he made some radical improvements in the canoes which he used as a matter of business in this work; and when he came back to open water he always had in his head or his notebook the design of a small cruiser which he built and used on the Lake. I published many of his designs. One of these, Myra, a gaff-rigged yawl somewhat smaller than Scarecrow, was described in Forest & Stream in December, 1892; her rig being claimed as superior to the gunter sloop. In answer to my request that Stevens would reply to this I received the following:

On Virginia Midland train, Southbound
Jan. 10, 1893.

My dear Stephens:

I have thought over your request that I should write out my views on the question of rig, more especially for such boats as Myra and Scarecrow, and have decided to do so; but not for publication. If you consider for a moment I think you will approve my objections to appearing in public because I have practically no experience with anything larger than a canoe, whilst Wicksteed has experience in larger classes. He should, therefore, know a great deal more about the needs of such craft than one who is, at the best, but a theoretical experimenter. Mr. Wicksteed has tried and abandoned the leg-o'mutton rig which I propose to put on Scarecrow; still, I intend using it because I believe it to be the best. I send you herewith a leg-o'mutton sail plan for Myra. I have used the jib-and-mainsail in preference to yawl, I think that the question of which is the better is one for each man to settle for himself. The former should be faster, whilst the latter is the better in bad weather; the former is the simpler rig while the latter is the easier to handle. In designing a leg-o'mutton rig my idea is to use the longest possible boom so as to get the lowest center of effort. . . . I am now running between Saulsbury up the mountain to Asheville, have left the snow behind, the sun is beautifully bright and the weather pleasant, I expect to be back in N. Y. about Feb. 1.

Yours truly,
(signed) C. J. Stevens.

The First Match for the Seawanhaka Cup

When, in 1895, I was called on to design a yacht, Ethelwynn, for the defense of the newy established Seawanhaka International Trophy for Small Yachts, I concerned myself solely with the hull, leaving all de-

Istria, 15-meter class. Designed by Charles E. Nicholson for Sir Charles Allom, 1912, pole mast and jib-headed jackyard topsail. Courtesy of Ernest A. Ratsey

 By WILLIAM P. STEPHENS

tails of rig to Stevens. These differed in no way from those already tested on Scarecrow; the hollow spars were made by Young, the sails by Gilbert H. and R. H. Wilson. No stock fittings were used, the spring gooseneck, toggles, blocks and other small parts being made by Young. The standing rigging was of phosphor bronze wire rope, lanyards being used instead of turnbuckles; and the running rigging of imported Italian hemp, as then used by canoeists. As it proved, we were astray on our balance, the original jib of 50 square feet proved too large and was replaced by one of but 35 square feet, which did wonderful work to windward and was an important factor in the final result.

The trial races brought out seven boats, two by Herreshoff, six with boom and gaff rigs; in each of the three races Ethelwynn was first with the Herreshoff beat, Olita, sailed by Vaux and Buchrard, expert canoe sailors, second. The English challenger, Spruce IV—her owner, J. Arthur Brand, was another stencil addict—carried the sliding gunter rig, but in spite of the weight and skill of her owner-skipper and a husky young professional she was badly beaten.

The rig of Ethelwynn, so radically different from the other six yachts, came in for general comment, largely unfavorable, the most severe being that of a recognized expert, Thomas Fleming Day, in *The Rudder*:—"I don't like Ethelwynn's sail plan. It may be prejudice, but to my mind there is no sail like a gaff-headed one; all others are makeshifts. A good jib-headed mainsail is better than a poor gaff-sail, but I would, for all-around work, much prefer the latter. The type of sail carried by this boat has been evolved by a slow process of getting rid of the bad points of the old English balance lug. Inch by inch the yard has been topped up until at last it paralleled the mast; and, then being useless, was done away with. No form of sail will send a boat to windward like a gaff-sail, and any man who will take the trouble to closely watch a yacht with a well cut sail, when on the wind, will soon note the reason why. Ethelwynn's rigging was devised by C. J. Stevens, and in lightness, strength and general adaptability to purpose, shows a remarkable knowledge of small-boat seamanship. The standing rigging is of phosphor bronze wire rope, set up with lanyards in place of turnbuckles, which is a return to sound principles. The spars are hollow, and the sail runs up the back (after side?) of the mast on a railway, which is another good point."

Small as the craft were, this international match awakened a nation-wide interest in the new class; Half-Rating by the British Rule and 15-Foot by the Seawanhaka Rule, and it was built to in large numbers. When, in 1897, the challenge came in a larger class—One rating or 20 Foot, many of this size were built. In spite of what seemed the indisputable superiority of the Ethelwynn rig, it failed to meet with popular favor. I had my share of the designing in both the 15-Foot and the 20-Foot classes, using the rig wherever possible, but many of my clients insisted on the boom-and-gaff rig. The Canadian challenger of 1896, Glencairn, carried a gunter rig, but in several succeeding years Mr. Duggan carried the boom-and-gaff rig. As for owners of larger yachts, they consistently ignored the lesson of the midgets and held to the old mast, topmast, boom and gaff.

Stevens' end was quite tragic, the firm for which he had worked for some twenty years abandoned its American business and early in 1900 he took a position as resident manager of the New York & Boston Dyewoods Co. in Haiti. With characteristic independence, not to say obstinacy, he refused to recognize the difference between a temperate and a tropical climate; he rode about the Island bare-headed, as he had sailed on New York Bay, when wet in a shower he dried out in the sun, with the result that on June 17 he died in Port dePaix of typhoid fever. Though his service to yachting is not known nor recognized today, he left many friends to mourn him in the clubs which he had served so faithfully.

The rig of Ethelwynn was very generally publicized in contrast with that of Spruce IV, and was used on a number of the half-decked sailing boats, centerboard and fin-kneel, which were built largely as the result of this

Britannia, typical cutter of 1893, modernized from Genesta and Irex of 1884. L.w.l., 87'10"; sail area, 10,328 square feet. Shows long topmast with doublings, jackyard (club) topsail with club on head and jackyard on foot. Broad low sail plan with long gaff

Akista, designed by George Hill, 1897. Cabin yacht with C. J. Stevens rig. Fin keel, l.o.a., 50'; l.w.l., 30'; breadth, 10'; draft, 6'6"; ballast, 3 tons; sail area, 1250 sq. ft.

international match. The only test of the rig in a decked yacht was in the fin-keel Akista, of 30 feet l.w.l., designed in 1897 by George Hill, an amateur, a full-bodied craft with full accommodation; it contributed materially to her success in racing with gaff-rigged yachts. Those interested in the larger craft, owners and designers alike, ignored the rig and clung to the time-honored gaff and the housing topmast. The match of 1895 for the America's Cup, between Valkyrie III as challenger and Defender as her opponent cast the small craft in the shade, but still the victory of Ethelwynn, with pictures of the two contestants, appeared in the English yachting journals without arousing comment on the rig.

The close relationship between Great Britain and Bermuda, a British colony, served to make the "Bermuda rig" familiar to British yachtsmen as the exponent of the pole mast and triangular sail; though it is in no way different in principle from the "bugeye" or "buckeye" of the Chesapeake, the "sharpie rig" of New Haven, Conn., the "Block Island" boats, or other local varieties of almost the oldest and the most crude and simple of rigs known to sailing men. In the discussions which filled the pages of British yachting journals from 1912 onward the term "Bermudian" is applied indiscriminately to the original Bermuda rig, to the leg-o'mutton sail on a pole mast, and to the same sail set on a gunter yard.

The distinctive features of the lug sail are that it is four-sided, and the *yard crosses the mast.* In the evolution of the lug on small British racing craft the yard was gradually hoisted to a vertical position, the heel swinging free so that it had to be shifted to leeward of the mast in tacking; later a jaw was added on the heel to hold the yard permanently abaft the mast and in a vertical position. In this case the sail was no longer a lug, but the distinction is not recognized in Britain, as in the term "Solent lug," which is the gunter rig shown on pages 36 and 37, November. The very loose use of the terms "Bermudian," "lug," "gunter lug" and "Marconi" adds greatly to the difficulty of research in a very complicated development.

The First Step for Improvement

The subject of the rigs of racing yachts came to the fore in England in 1912; in July of that year, in *The Yachting Monthly,* the editor, that talented naval architect and writer, the late Herbert L. Reiach, under his nom de plume of "M.I.N.A. (Member of Institute of Naval Architects) commented on the "soaring sails" then coming into fashion. "Today (1912) every sail tends to grow in a vertical direction, the headsails are steep, and low-footed jibs and foresails are no longer seen.—Even with main booms well inboard, the gaff is hard to hold." He mentions Satanita, 99 feet l.w.l., in her second season, 1894, having 3 feet off her boom, 5 feet off her bowsprit and 5 feet added to her gaff, and yet her ratio of total hoist to waterline was but 1.2; that of the big yawl Vanduara being 1.11. In the course of his comments he alludes to aeroplane designers, air pressure, and "apteroid aspect" and "pterygoid aspect"; terms belonging to the new science of aerodynamics.

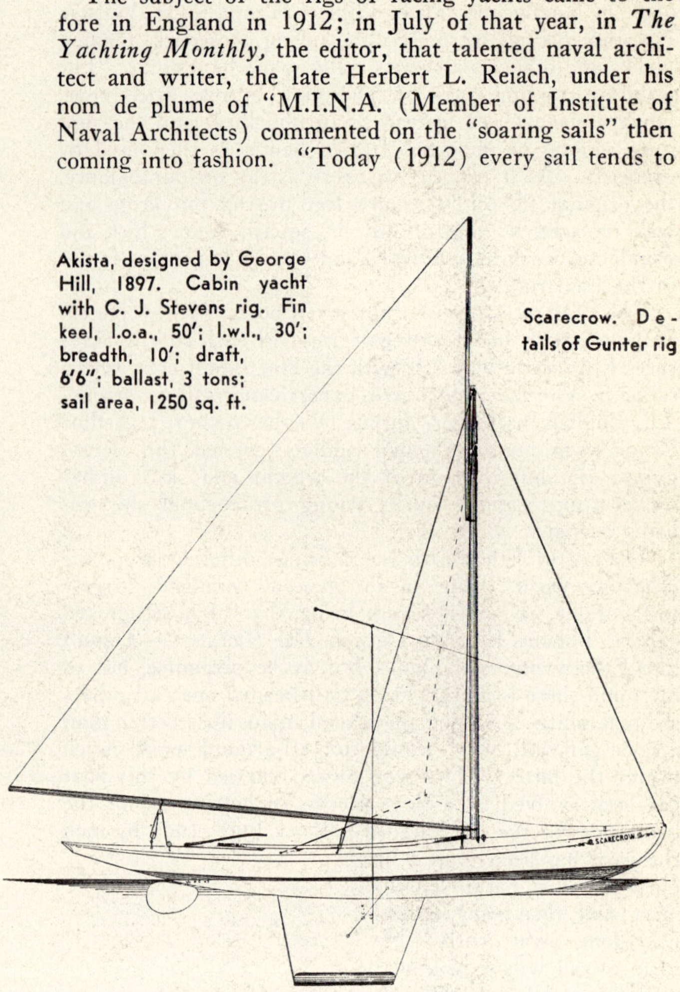

Scarecrow. Details of Gunter rig

On the opening of the racing in 1912 *The Field* commented as follows on the growing height of the sail plans:—"The most remarkable change that has taken place in the contour of British racing yachts in the past 20 years is in the shape of the sail plan. Nineteen years ago, when Britannia came out, she measured about 157 feet from the tip of the bowsprit to the end of the main boom. Her waterline was 87.8 feet. The modern cutter Shamrock is 12 feet shorter on the waterline and about 14 feet shorter from boom end to bowsprit end. We believe the Britannia in her best trim was 115 feet from deck to top of her topmast, and when she first came out her topmast was longer and her height as much as 120 feet. Now the modern 23-Meter cutter is several feet higher than was ever reached by Britannia. The way we have increased the height of our sail plans in proportion to the base is wonderful. The gradual growth of height is largely due to a great reduction in the weight of spars and gear. Britannia may have had a hollow main boom, but no other spar was hollow; today a racing cutter has a hollow topmast, topsail yard, jackyard, gaff, boom and, sometimes, a hollow bowsprit. The hollow mast is, of course, prohibited. This is the first time in history in which it may be said that it is the tendency of yachts built for Y.R.A. rules to carry more sail than yachts built for the N.Y.Y.C. rules. Today in the first class racing fleet English yachts net more canvas per foot of waterline length than American yachts."

The handling of the jackyard topsail, with a long and heavy club on its head and another heavy spar, the jackyard, on its foot, has always been a difficult business, the difficulty being aggravated by the increase of sail and again by the added heights of the rigs. The sail was hard to hoist, owing to the weight of its solid spars, and still more difficult to lower; as the halyard was slacked off and the yard came down its heel was apt to slip to the wrong side of the peak halyards.

The first attempt at a change was made by Charles E. Nicholson, of Gosport, England, designed of so many famous yachts down to the last two challengers for the Cup. In 1912 he brought out Istria, in the 15-Meter, then one of the most popular racing classes, with what may be described as a "fish-pole" mast. The lower mast, solid and of the usual type, was fitted at its head with a socket in which shipped the "topmast"; in this, in turn, was shipped what was described as "a hollow topsail yard socketed into the topmast." The largest topsail was jib-headed, but with the old jackyard on the foot, set over a gaff mainsail. The luff of the topsail ran on a track on the "hollow topsail yard." Incidentally, in this notable yacht, the dinghy was built to fit into a sunken cockpit, the helmsman sitting with his feet in the dinghy. In her first season Istria scored 23 firsts to 36 starts in a class in which the competition was most keen. In 1913 Mr. Nicholson added two yachts similarly rigged in the 15-Meter Class, Pamela and Paula III, and also fitted the new rig to the 19-Meter Norada, designed by him in 1911; Will Fife tried the new rig in the 15-Meter Maudrey and also fitted the new topmast in the 19-Meter Mariquita, designed by him in 1911.

From Naval Architecture to Engineering

In the small yachts of C. J. Stevens, with a broad base and low hoist to the sail plan, no engineering was necessary, the ordinary shrouds were sufficient; but with the tall masts of the 15-Meter Class the designer was called on to go outside the domain of pure naval architecture and to take lessons from bridge builders and other experts in structural design. Mr. Nicholson met the problem ably; while there were breakdowns on every hand, Maudrey losing her mast in one of the early races and the owner of Norada reverting to the old rig in the middle of the season, Istria carried all of her spars through two seasons, only losing her "hollow topsail yard" in a hard blow off Harwich in the opening of the season of 1914.

There was a rapid growth of racing in the smaller classes following the adoption of the Linear Rating rule in 1887, the most successful designer of this period being Linton Hope, who lost his life in 1920 through his exertions during the great war. An expert boatsailer as well as designer, he had a knowledge of engineering which helped greatly to place him at the head in the small classes. His first success with the new rig was in Scotia IV, in the 6-Meter Class, the first of the rig on the Solent in 1913; but he confessed to have made experiments with the "Bermuda rig" in 1895 but abandoning it; incidentally, Mr. Nicholson pleaded guilty to having tried and abandoned a "jackyard topsail on a railway" in Vigorna, 20 tons, at about the same time. Mr. Hope, in 1912, contributed to *The Field* a series of important articles on the rigging of yachts. Passing over some years, it may be noted here that much of the credit for the development and perfection of the rig is due to Johann Anker, of Oslo, whose death was announced only a few months ago. Personally an expert boathandler, he turned out many fast hulls in all classes up to and including the 12-Meter, and he was very successful in rigging them in the modern fashion.

Objections of British Yachtsmen

IT was inevitable that such a revolution would arouse much comment and criticism. *The Field* spoke as follows: "For want of a better term, this form of mast will probably be generally known by all yachtsmen as the Marconi mast. We do not know who it was that first gave this name to Istria's novel contrivance, but it was possibly some wit aboard the club steamer in one of the early matches of 1912. Yachting people of the future will find themselves speaking of Marconi masts just as their parents spoke of the spinaker in 1866. We gather that in practice the chief advantage of the Marconi mast is that the jackyard topsail can be more easily lowered during a race. It is often an advantage to be able to get the jackyarder on deck in a hurry and set a jib-header.—The saving in time in setting and lowering appears to be the chief advantage in the Marconi gear." It must be noted that the rig here described as Marconi was very far from that of a few years later—in brief, it was merely a pole mast carrying a gaff mainsail, and a jib-headed jackyard topsail on a track, the mainsail having the conventional mast hoops. The comment of an old tar is quoted in *The Field's* report of the regatta at Lowestoff in May, 1913, "Well, John, what do you think of the outfit?", was asked of a hardy old seaman. "If I was at the top o' one o' them", indicating with the stem of his pipe Pamela's topmast, "I should reckon I was a long way from home." As indicating the great change in all details of rig, there is a note at this time of the moving of the main gooseneck further from the deck with a dropping of the outer end of the main boom, a reversal of the practice of generations. To one brought up with the old rig there is a never-ceasing source of wonder in the booms of today, not only high in the air on the mast, but pitching downward instead of upward from that point.

In April, 1914, *The Field* commented as follows: "The use to which this piece of nautical slang has now been put is absurd. We hear of 6-meter yachts and Redwings with Marconi masts and Marconi rigs. These boats formerly carried the standing lug with vertical yard, or gunter sail. They now carry a leg-o'mutton sail on a long, slender mast; the mast is raked to a curve. It is a pretty rig, and highly efficient. Surely, however, there was no need for any slang term for this rig."

In November, 1920, Mr. Nicholson, speaking for his offspring, protested against its nickname, suggesting that it should be discarded as incorrect and meaningless and jib-header be substituted. His suggestion met with popular approval, Marconi was dropped in England, and the term Bermudian or Mudian substituted as in use today.

TRADITIONS AND MEMORIES OF

American Yachting

By WILLIAM P. STEPHENS

Part Thirty-Two

The Rig (Concluded)

●

Varuna, a Larchmont O Class sloop designed by William Gardner in 1917 and fitted with a Marconi rig as an experiment

Yachting and the Great War

On August 1, 1914, British yachting was brought to a sudden halt by the outbreak of the Great War, to lie dormant for six years. Meanwhile a new navigation, that of the air, was growing day by day under the stimulus of war needs. The new science of aviation has passed beyond its initial stage—*The Field* had already added a department of aeronautics to its many others, the sail was forgotten, and all experiment, invention and investigation was centered on wings. When yachting was revived in 1920, one of the first steps was to discard the gaff, matshoops and jackyard, to run the track down from topmast to gooseneck, and to replace the time-honored quadrilateral mainsail by the triangular leg-o'mutton. The British racing fleet had suffered sorely throughout the war, many of the best yachts being sold to the Scandinavian countries. Nyria, 15-meters, had been converted to a yawl with a diesel engine. She was taken in hand by her designer, Charles Nicholson, and fitted with a pole mast, track and leg-o'mutton mainsail and topsails. Britannia was brought out by King George V and Alfred Mylne was summoned from Glasgow to Cowes to modernize her rig. He was told very plainly that there should be "no

Marconi nonsense." A new topmast was spliced to her old lower mast, but she still swung her gaff and topsail yard. It was not until 1931, when in her 38th year, that she was re-rigged with a full pole mast and triangular mainsail. This famous yacht has been regarded in Britain with the same reverence which attends the schooner America on this side of the Atlantic. When she was thus converted, no further ground was left for opposition to the new rig.

On the outbreak of the war, Shamrock IV was in New York, in readiness to meet either Vanitie or Resolute a few weeks later. She was at once laid up at City Island, where she lay idle until 1920. Some of her spars were burned in a fire in the yard. New spars were made to replace them, and many changes made in both hull and rig; a new stream-lined topmast was shipped and a petticoat fitted around the mast for the full length of the luff, to ease the flow of air over the angle between spar and sail.

Two-Piece or One-Piece Masts?

The housing of topmast and bowsprit in bad weather meant much to the old cutters, a gain in both top weight and windage even at the expense of weight and complication of housing gear. The housing of the topmast in American sloops prior to the seventies was the exception rather than the rule; the lowering of the small topmast aloft on a very high mast would have been of little benefit, even if it had been practicable, which it frequently was not. In the fifteen matches for the America's Cup, there is one instance and, I think, only one, in which a topmast was housed. On September 16, 1885, when after starting the 20-mile beat to the finish, Puritan luffed up to house hers, while Genesta, with topmast aloft and a working topsail waving like a pennant, was finally defeated by 1 minute 38 seconds. While in succeeding matches every effort was made to improve form of hull, build and rig, it occurred to no one to cut out the useless weight and tophamper involved in the doublings and housing gear. The first move in this direction came in 1901 when, in designing Shamrock II, George Watson used a steel mast with the wooden topmast socketed in the head, this same idea being used by B. B. Crowinshield in his Independence. In Constitution, Mr. Herreshoff went still further, the wooden topmast being fitted to house inside the steel mast. These changes introduced the pole mast in the largest class. Throughout the entire period from 1912 to 1925, designers were experimenting, more or less in the dark, with innumerable breakdowns, with solid and hollow wooden masts and spars and steel spars.

The Marconi Rig in America

The late Addison G. Hanan, of the Indian Harbor Yacht Club was not only one of the ablest amateur skippers of his day, but a student of hull design and rig. Though not a designer in the accepted sense of the term, relying on others for the drafting and calculations, he was personally responsible for both model and rig of most of the yachts which he sailed. In some of them, while complying strictly with the letter of the rule, he exercised much ingenuity in utilizing the last fraction of an inch permissible. The stoppage of yachting was not carried as far on this side of the Atlantic, and though the Cup match was suspended, racing was maintained in many classes, the 31-foot being very popular about Boston and on Long Island Sound. In 1916, Mr. Hanan brought out Nahma, sailing her in the somewhat strenuous series of inter-city races between New York and Boston for the Manhasset Bay cup. Knowing of the success of the leg-o'-mutton rig in England, he sent for a sail plan for the new yacht and tried her under it, but in order to avoid any question of its eligibility he carried the gaff rig in these important races. In the following season he used the new rig successfully.

When in 1917 the so-called Larchmont O Class of five yachts of 38-feet l.w.l. was designed by William Gardner, four were fitted with the gaff rig, and one, Varuna, owned by Commodore James B. Ford of the Larchmont Yacht Club, was fitted with the Marconi rig by way of experiment. From this time on, the rig has made steady progress until it is in almost universal use on racing yachts. Its introduction into the Star Class is typical of the general sentiment of doubt and uncertainty as to its merits which prevailed for so long throughout the yachting world. This famous class was established in 1908 under the gunter rig, the same as then carried on small British yachts. In 1918 the new rig was tested on Long Island Sound, the birthplace of the Class, with a curved and raking mast and heavy wooden spreaders, but was soon discarded. In 1921, it was again tested with solid masts on several boats. In the following year it was generally adopted, and since then it has been perfected and refined to a point where it is a question in each race whether a boat will come in first or second or break down and withdraw.

Photographs by M. Rosenfeld

The J-Class sloop Ranger was to some extent responsible for some new terms in yachting terminology

One result of the Great War was the advancement of the science as well as the practice of aviation, the knowledge thus gained being applied on the return of peace to the rigs of yachts. In 1914 a wind tunnel was established at the Massachusetts Institute of Technology under the direction of Professor Cecil H. Peabody. In the following year a series of experiments on yacht sails was made by Professor H. A. Everett, the results being summarized in a paper read by him before the Society of Naval Architects and Marine Engineers. These experiments, and similar work abroad, removed the subject of wind and its action on sails from the domain of more or less rule-o'-thumb

practice to that of theoretical study. Nothing more is possible here than a mere mention of this work as conducted by Manfred Curry and others, but it has been a material factor in the great revolution in the rigs of yachts.

Marconi! What? Who? Why?

Though quickly abandoned in England, the term Marconi was welcomed in America, and is still in universal use. The rig is, in its essentials, the age-old leg-o'-mutton sail set to raise, lower and reef on a pole mast by means of a track on the mast and toggles on the sail. As secondary details, the mast is hollow, it is stayed by a complicated system of shrouds, fore and backstays and spreaders, the standing rigging is of high-tension steel in the form of wire rope or rods, the specially designed fittings are of the strongest bronze alloys, and every possible refinement is employed to reduce weight and windage without regard to expense.

Signor Guglielmo Marconi, born in Bologna in 1874, was a talented Italian scientist whose genius and industry gave to the world the system of wireless communication. He was a landlubber, knowing nothing and caring less

Above: Nahma, brought out in 1916 by Addison G. Hanan, with the English leg-o'-mutton rig. Left: The Star class was established in 1908 wtih the gunter rig. The Marconi rig used today was adopted in 1921

about yachts and sails, but in the course of his experiments in wireless telegraphy he erected very tall poles, so lofty as to require a complicated system of shrouds and guys.

Why was his name thus honored by yachtsmen? Merely through the carelessness and slovenliness which prevails in all matters of yachting terminology, as shown in such modern terms as Ginny Jib, Greta Garbo, Mae West, as are used to describe the overgrown and unmeasured headsails, and in the Jay-Boat applied to all Cup yachts. When the cutter Sphynx, in 1866, set a triangular running sail on the other side from her mainsail, the average paid hand who pronounced her name Spinx transformed the word into Spinxer, whence the present spinnaker, a useful word, but most of the terms added to the yachting vocabulary of recent years serve only to debase it. If credit for the mere erection of a pole with wires on it is to be given to any landlubber, then why not to our own Samuel F. B. Morse who strung a wire on poles and sent the first telegraph message from Washington to Baltimore?

It is difficult to trace any relationship between the true Bermuda rig with its heavily raked solid mast supported by two shrouds, its mainsail with a headboard and a boom extending several feet ahead of the mast and set up with a tackle, and the masterpiece of refined spar making, sail making and rigging which bears the name today. The forces of habit and usage are so strong that it is not likely that the British yachtsman will give up his pet Bermudian and gunter lug, incorrect and misleading as both terms are or, on the other hand, that the American yachtsman will abandon his Marconi. In the interest of technical accuracy and correct nautical terminology, however, it would be much better if both parties would agree on a term which would meet modern conditions. The subject is now open for discussion and suggestion.

American Yachting

By WILLIAM P. STEPHENS

Part Thirty-Three

East of the Cape

Robert Bennett Forbes

THE prominence of New York as the great center of American yachting is beyond dispute, the birthplace of the first Yacht Club, the home port of a great fleet of schooners, leaders in international racing, the winner and successful defender for nearly a century of the premier yachting trophy of the world. All this has acted to eclipse the achievements of other localities; notably that section of which Boston is The Hub, and which may broadly be described as East of the Cape.

Much as we owe to the men of New York who established the sport on such a broad and firm basis, it is interesting to note that they were not, as a class, bred to the sea; but, rather, business men taking up with enthusiasm a new sport. The recognized leaders, the three Stevens brothers, were wealthy landowners, men of broad culture and prominent in many lines of progress.

Though the fortunes of this great family were in part founded on shipping in the beginning of the 18th century, the generation in which we are interested were landsmen, active in social life, in all forms of sport, and in many lines of mechanical progress. They were leaders in the development of transportation, first by stages, then by rail, building the first locomotive to run on tracks, the Camden & Amboy Railroad (for which they imported the locomotive John Bull), the river steamer Princeton, the Stevens Battery, presented to the United States Government; to them is due the foundation of the Stevens Institute of Technology, now housed in the old family mansion at Castle Point, Hoboken. Robert was the mechanical genius and he is also credited with the modelling of the great sloop Maria; while John was the sportsman of the family and the leader in yachting.

Looking at the personnel of New York yachting, the first city directories, almost contemporary with the Club, show a variety of occupations: Alexander Major, merchant; C. H. P. Babcock, importer; E. H. White, merchant; L. M. Rutherfurd, lawyer; James M. and Lawrence Waterbury, rope; Francis Skiddy, broker; D. S. Appleton, books; John S. Dick-

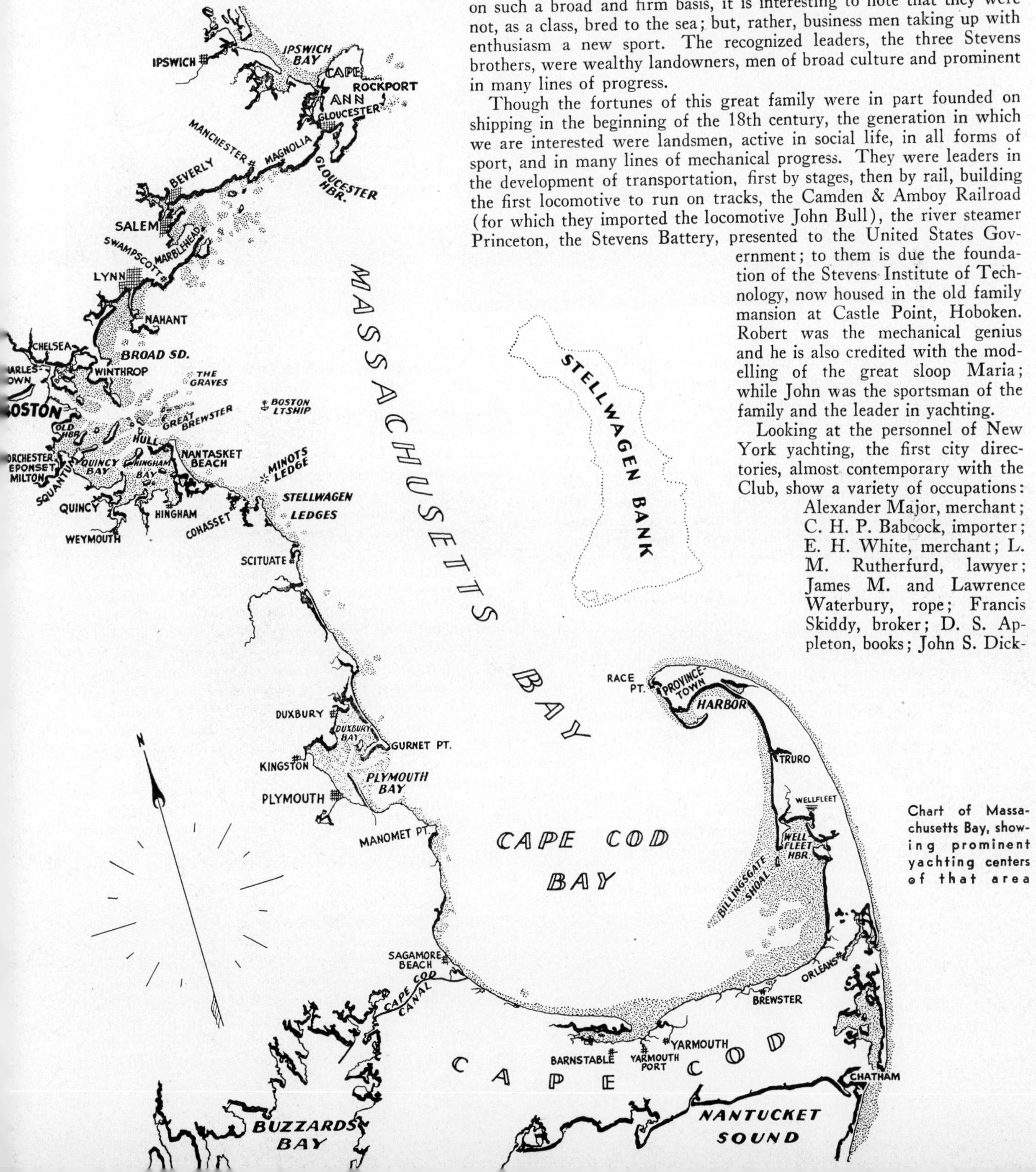

Chart of Massachusetts Bay, showing prominent yachting centers of that area

The schooner Raven built for Benjamin C. Clark in 1836

erson, importer; A. F. Craven, engineer; S. L. M. Barlow, lawyer; A. Belmont, banker; George L. Schuyler, civil engineer; W. H. McVickar, broker; Gilbert L. Haight, bank clerk; S. D. Babcock, importer; Charles T. Cromwell, lawyer; Hamilton Morton, lawyer; R. T. Hartshorn, glasses; J. H. A. Bell, paints; W. A. Stebbins, lawyer; N. P. Husack, auctioneer; R. B. Roosevelt, lawyer; Daniel Devlin, clothing; Henry Belknap, hardware; Edward Dodge, broker; I. & T. Barker, lawyers; G. R. J. Bowdoin, lawyer; the Lorillards, George L., Louis L. and Pierre, Jr., tobacco and snuff; T. C. Durant, forwarding; Samuel Fox, merchant; R. & E. C. Center, merchants; James Gordon Bennett, Jr., publisher.

Many early members were men of leisure whose occupations were not given. These names and occupations are representative of the membership of the Club in the first dozen years of its existence. On the ship-owning side were the Kingslands, the Howlands, Grinnels, Aspinwalls, Livingstons, Minturns and Griswolds. The firm of L. N. & G. Griswold was known by the nickname of "No Loss & Great Gain Griswold." With these exceptions, the personnel was made up almost entirely of men engaged in occupations closely associated with the land; it is worthy of note that they took up with enthusiasm a new and unknown form of sport. It must be said that they were most liberal and spirited in its support, both in building large yachts and in racing them at sea for high stakes.

Manhattan and Its Waters

The locale was such that few lived near the water. The Stevens had the ancestral estate in Hoboken on which the first house of the Club was built, and also city houses. The Livingstons lived on Staten Island on the Kill von Kull shore, and a few others lived on the East shore, where the second station of the Club was established. The majority, however, lived on the lower end of Manhattan Island, from the Battery up to about Grand Street, making necessary a long journey to the anchorage. The racing courses in the early years were from off the Elysian Field, Hoboken, down the North River, back and forth across the Upper Bay, and out as far as South West Spit.

The environment of New York neither encouraged nor permitted the use of yachts. The city occupied only the point of a large island; a short portion of the waterfront on both the North and the East Rivers boasted of piers for the accommodation of ships; both shores were high and rocky in some places, with shelving beaches of mud or sand in others; there were no mooring grounds for small yachts, and no inlets nor creeks offering protected harbors. Passage from the island to the New Jersey, Brooklyn and Staten Island shores was originally by rowboats for individuals and the "periagua," a flat-bottomed scow with two masts, boom-and-gaff sails and no jib, with space amidship for a couple of carriages and their teams. Gradually these were replaced by steam ferries.

The great glory of New York was in its fleet of large schooners racing along the coast, across and on the other side of the Atlantic, and making long and venturous cruises. Of the sloops there were some of moderate size, but very few small cabin yachts, and these scattered about the Bay and the Sound, all shoal in body and draft; except in the largest schooners the keel was unknown, all being of the centerboard type. The one class of small yacht which was popular from Nyack to the Narrows and about New Rochelle and Cow Bay (Port Washington) was the open sandbag sloop described in MoToR

Boating for September and October 1939; a dangerous craft and used largely as a betting proposition.

Thus the development of yachting about New York was largely influenced by exceptional conditions. The broad Hudson or North River was famous for its great trading sloops modelled after old Dutch craft. The famous Maria, though a yacht, was of this type and it largely influenced the design of the New York sloop as a class. The lower reaches of the River, and the Upper Bay, offered fine sailing waters for the early yachts of the Club, from 40 to 60 tons, and many races were sailed between Hoboken and the Narrows; while just outside was the ocean for longer contests. The pilot boats of New York were known far and wide and they furnished the model for the early yachts, notably the America.

Captain Arthur H. Clark

Long Island Sound, an ideal stretch of water for yachts of moderate size as well as small craft, was separated from New York Bay by the East River, a long and tortuous strait, and did not figure prominently in local yachting until the blowing up of Flood Rock and Mill Rock in Hell Gate in 1885. Prior to the founding of the Seawanhaka Yacht Club on Oyster Bay in 1871, there was no yacht club between Fort Totten and Fort Schuyler on the west and Block Island on the east. A few yachts were found about the older cities, New Rochelle, New Haven, New London, Stonington and Mystic, but the many cities which now house yacht clubs were not even dreamed of.

Within the Arm of Cape Cod

Turning now to the eastward, we find conditions radically different in Massachusetts Bay, a body of water opening directly on the sea from within the protecting arms of an irregular crescent with Cape Ann on its northwest point and Cape Cod on its southeast point. The inner rim of this crescent was lined with innumerable small harbors, each opening on deep water, with many islands and remote points of the mainland accessible only by water. Fish were plentiful in the Bay, the local fishery far exceeding that of New York. From colonial days these small harbors housed a fleet of small but able craft used both for fishing and for traffic about the Bay.

Dr. John Jeffries in flying costume, first aeronaut to cross the English Channel in 1784 in a balloon

The islands and outlying points about the Bay were the homes, at least in summer, of many families prominent at first in shipping and later in yachting: at Milton the Forbes family, who also owned the beautiful island of Naushon at the mouth of Buzzards Bay, at Beverly, John Heard, J. P. Gardner, J. P. Cushing, the Burgess family, F. Gordon Dexter, Dudley M. Pickman; at Nahant, Benjamin C. Clark and his family, Thomas G. Appleton, Thomas H. Perkins, Charles A. Longfellow, the Bacon and Amory families and the Paines; At Manchester, the Boardmans and Abbotts; at East Boston (Jeffries Point) the Jeffries family; at Swampscott, C. W. Galloupe and P. S. Shelton; at Salem, the Crowninshields, Appletons and Bensons; at Cohasset, the Bryants and Bigelows.

In the sober New England of colonial days, when the business of life was esteemed too serious for indulgence in mere sport, all conditions about Massachusetts Bay were conducive to the regular use of small craft, first for transit, fishing and other practical purposes; the youth of the communities along the shore were used to sailing from their earliest years. No fixed date may be set for the evolution of the yacht proper in this course of development but the main factor was the rapid increase of wealth and leisure which followed the expansion of the commerce of Boston in the far East.

The Hub as Shipping Center

The prominence of the port of Boston in everything associated with shipping—financing, building and handling—is shown in the long list of names first known in shipping before they were prominent in yachting: Forbes, Weld, Crowninshield, Sears, Heard, Jeffries, Frothingham, Pickman, Amory, Bacon, Hovey, Peabody, Tucker, Stevenson, Burgess, Thayer, Bryant, Russell, Appleton, Hemenway, Dexter, McQuesten and Curtis. Long before they found their way into club books and yacht registers there were flown on house flags in all ports of the world such familiar devices as the black horse of the Welds, the red crown on white shield of the Crowninshields, the blue chevron with white and blue triangles of the Forbes (the house flag of Russell & Company), the Heard white diamond on red, the blue field with red cross of the Atkinsons, the stripes, red, white and blue, of the Sears, the red cross on blue of the Uptons, the white chevron on red of the Dexters, the red bars with blue and white triangles of the Cabots.

Starting at Gloucester on Cape Ann, and following to Provincetown on Cape Cod, there was a chain of towns and villages: Manchester, Salem, Beverly, Marblehead, Swampscott, Lynn, Nahant, Winthrop, East Boston, Boston, Chelsea, Dorchester, Neponset, Squantum, Quincy, Weymouth, Hingham, Hull, Cohasset, Scituate, Duxbury, Kingston, Plymouth, Barnstable. Today every one is the home of one or more yacht clubs, to the total of fifty.

Out of the Ditty Box

THE growth of yachting in this district was slow, and in no way sensational, with little calling for official record. What we know today is largely through the writings of Robert Bennet Forbes two generations ago, and the recently published *Eastern Yacht Club Ditty Box* compiled by C. H. W. Foster, a member of the Club for over 60 years and a yacht owner for a still longer period. Much of the information in this and the following chapters is derived from this source.

The first suggestion of the use of a vessel for pleasure only is found in the following permit:

By Samuel Graves Esq., Vice Admiral of the White and Commander in Chief, etc.

The bearer, Dr. Jeffries, has my permission to fish and shoot in this Harbor. This pass to remain with him.

Given under my hand at Boston, the 10th October 1775

(signed) Samuel Graves.

To the Captains and Commanders of His Majesty's ships and vessels at Boston.

A sympathizer with the Crown, Dr. John Jeffries served with the British blockading fleet in the Revolution. After the peace he went to London and married an English lady and on his return he established a home for his family on Jeffries Point, East Boston.

One of his adventures is described as follows: "The first crossing of the English Channel by air was accomplished by Jean Pierre Francois Blanchard, the balloonist, on January 7, 1785, under the patronage of the distinguished American physician, Dr. John Jeffries, who accompanied the French aeronaut on this momentous trip. Dr. Jeffries signalized this extraordinary incident by writing and dropping from the air while the balloon was in motion a card addressed to a friend bearing the name of Thayer and resident in America, thus fairly earning the title of the founder of the aerial post."

A descendant, John Jeffries, Jr., owned the schooner yacht Mystery about the middle of the last century. His son, in turn, under the same name, was one of the founders of the Eastern Y.C. His brothers, William A. and Walter Lloyd Jeffries, were among the founders of the Beverly Y. C. The latter, a valued friend nearly 60 years ago, was one of those little known enthusiasts to whom yachting owes so much. Second only to his work for the Beverly Y.C. was his interest in the sport at large, writing over the *nom de plume* of "Blue-with-Gold-Castle," the family device.

THE outstanding personality in everything associated with the development of both shipping and yachting in New England was Robert Bennet Forbes, the patriarch of a great yachting family. Of Scotch descent, but for two generations American, he was born at Jamaica Plain, Boston, on September 18, 1804. In the course of a life which ended on November 23, 1889, he experienced adventures in storms and shipwrecks, encounters with pirates and slavers, which equal those of the heroes of Marryat, Michael Scott and Smollett. In 1811 his father was in business as a merchant in Marseilles, and on January 17 of that year his mother, with him and his elder brother Thomas, embarked on a small topsail schooner, Midas, to join him.

The vessel, with a cargo of salted fish, was in every way unfitted for such a voyage. When only a few days out she was hove down for 48 hours, almost under water, bulwarks and deck fittings washed away, flooded below, and chickens and pigs drowned. Following this came calms and more heavy weather until they reached Gibraltar on February 26. This was only the beginning of their troubles. They were held up by the British fleet, taken aboard a British man of war, and did not reach Marseilles until April.

After schooling in France, the family sailed for America in 1813 and were soon in the midst of a fight with British vessels in which their schooner was captured. After many adventures they arrived at Boston in August. In 1816 the boy started on a mercantile career as "sweeper" in a store run by the Cabots and Perkins, his duties being to open and sweep out the store, catch the rats which infested the place, make the fire, copy letters and do any other odd jobs. Disgusted with mercantile life, the boy of 13 shipped before the mast aboard the Canton Packet, sailing on October 17 and arriving at Canton on March 13, 1818.

This was the beginning of a long life of sea-faring, and of business on land in China and Boston, where he ultimately settled in business as a ship owner and merchant, largely in the China trade. In his autobiography he gives a list of 69 vessels with which he was associated between 1830 and 1866, including seven yachts. While making no claims as a modeller, designer or naval architect, he was the leading spirit in the construction of many vessels, selecting the builder, consulting with him on the design, and superintending the construction. Some were for himself and many for friends.

His long practical experience at sea led to many improvements in both hulls and rigs, notably the Forbes double topsails. In 1861 he superintended the construction of nine gunboats for the Government. In 1857 he had built by D. J. Lawlor from a model made by the builder the schooner Azalea, for his brother John M. Forbes. She was of wood, 71 feet l.o.a., 60 feet 6 inches l.w.l., 17 feet 8 inches breadth, and 5 feet 8 inches draft.

An Experiment in Iron

AT the same time he had built for himself the schooner Edith, using the same moulds but building in iron; by Otis Tufts of East Boston. The original tonnage of Azalea is given as 43 gross and that of Edith 36, the difference being due to the depth of hold. Edith had a double bottom, forming four water tanks, one forward and one abaft the centerboard trunk and one on each side. The four were piped by means of a four-way cock to a centrifugal pump by which water might be transferred from one tank to another.

In their trials Edith proved the faster, which was attributed by Captain Forbes to this shifting of ballast. In 1858 Edith was loaded with stores and sailed for the River La Plata, Captain Forbes following her in another vessel and cruising for some time on the La Plata. Later she was sold for use as a pilot boat.

In 1834 Mr. Forbes was "Commodore" of a boat club at Boston, with several rowboats. This lasted for only a year when he and a dozen friends purchased the schooner Dream, and organized the first yacht club east of the Cape. This little schooner, 46 feet over all and of 28-68/95 tons, was built in New York in 1832 and purchased in 1834 by Thomas H. Perkins, Jr., a relative of Captain Forbes. In 1835 she was purchased on a co-operative basis by twenty yachtsmen who contributed $200 each. They used her together for cruising, each carrying his own provisions, the annual assessment being about $27 each. In spite of its very loose organization and the lack of a formal title, this may be considered the first Boston yacht club. It lasted for two years, expiring in the panic of 1837.

Captain Forbes' experiences covered most of the globe, largely by sail, though he was one of the first to foresee that steam was the motive power of the future. His autobiography tells of many sports, fox-hunting at Pau, deer shooting on Naushon, rowing and sailing races in China. On another side, he was active in the Humane Society of Massachusetts in 1841, one of the founders of the Snug Harbor of Quincy in 1852, interested in the National Sailors' Home of Quincy, and also in the Coast Guard. During the Irish famine of 1846 he obtained from the Government the U.S. ship Jamestown, which he loaded with food at Boston and sailed to Ireland.

Nahant and the Clarks

TWO others prominent in early yachting were the Clarks, father and son. One of the first settlers on Nahant over a century ago was Benjamin Cutler Clark, a native of Boston, who, in 1830, owned a half-decked boat, Mary. Two years later he replaced her with a larger craft, and in 1836 by the schooner Raven, of 12 tons. One of his nine children was Arthur H. Clark, born in Boston in 1841. When a schoolboy of 16 he rowed in the crew of a six-oared shell which defeated a Harvard crew. In January 1858 he shipped as an apprentice aboard the Black Prince on a two-year voyage around the world, returning as third mate. After six months ashore, at school and rowing, he sailed as second officer aboard the Northern Light. At 22 he was master of a vessel and spent ten years, mainly in the China trade. Between 1873 and 1876 he was in command of the steamship Indiana, of the American Line.

His career after this was ashore, as the London representative of American underwriters and later, for 25 years, as Lloyd's Agent for the Port of New York. An incident of his early life was the crossing of the Atlantic in the sloop Alice in 19 days from Boston to Cowes. In the course of his extensive travels and long residence abroad he brought together a marvelous collection of marine pictures and books. He was widely recognized as an authority on the history of both shipping and yachting, and he has left valuable works on both subjects. His last days afloat were as owner of the Fife cutter Minerva. When too old for active work, he retired to Newburyport, ending his life in the quiet of an old New England seaport.

The first serious attempt at the organization of a yacht club was made in 1865, the Boston Y.C. Following this came the South Boston and the Lynn in 1868, the Bunker Hill in 1869, the Dorchester in 1870 and the Eastern in 1871. The organization of the Beverly Y.C. came about by chance. At the outset the Eastern Y.C. declined to recognize the small yachts owned by some of its members. In the fall of 1871 Walter Burgess, then a Harvard senior, and two friends, Franklin Dexter and William F. Whitney, were horseback riding along the Beverly shore near the Burgess home, and in discussing this subject the proposal was made that a local club should be formed for the small yachts. As the result of this chance conversation a meeting was held at the Burgess home on February 24, 1872 at which the Beverly Y.C. was formally launched.

The triumph of Puritan, a yacht designed, built and manned by Boston, in the international match of 1885, opened a new era in New England yachting and many clubs were formed. This victory, repeated by Mayflower in 1886 and Volunteer in 1887, gave an added impulse to a movement which never has ceased.

Northern Light, designed and built by Louis Winde for Col. W. P. Winchester, 1839. From a painting

TRADITIONS AND MEMORIES OF

American Yachting

By WILLIAM P. STEPHENS

Part Thirty-four: East of the Cape (Continued)

THE student of yachting history is faced with many difficulties in exploring those early days of the sport when no attention was given to such details and dimensions as are now considered indispensable. There was, of course, no systematic recording in club books and yacht registers, and we find little other than casual news in the daily papers. The most important dimension, the length on load waterline, was generally ignored; when "length" was given it was "on deck," which might mean over all as now used, but was more likely to mean some form of "length for tonnage," such as from the "hood ends" (the fore rabbet under the planksheer) to the after side of the sternpost on deck. The extreme breadth was usually correctly recorded, but the depth might mean anything or nothing; from the upper side of the main beam to an indefinite point about the floor or keelson. The draft was usually ignored.

The measurement most in use was the tonnage, which might be New Measurement, Old Measurement, Thames Tonnage, an American variation of the latter, and either Gross or Net tons. The search for such particulars from various sources, and the attempt to reconcile them when found, is far more exciting to the antiquarian than the most complicated form of crossword puzzle. In most cases the builder was also the modeler, and all that was necessary was to record his name; where the model was cut by another this important fact was usually overlooked.

The early models were commonly based on some fisherman or pilot boat with a reputation for speed. Most of the yachts thus built proved unsatisfactory in their first or second year and were altered; frequently a longer and finer bow, sometimes a new middle body—Azalea, 1857, was cut in two amidships and ten feet of middle body added—the masts were shifted, the rig changed from schooner to sloop and, more frequently about Boston, from sloop to schooner. After three or four years the yacht was sold for fishing or pilot service, thus returning to her ancestors. This change of condition was usually due to one of two causes. Most frequently she had proved unsatisfactory as a yacht, but in some cases she had made a reputation for speed and general good qualities which made her worth more to a pilot than to her original owner. As the three classes were largely identical in model, ballasting—all inside ballast of stone or kentledge—and in rig—with only plain working sails and no spinnakers, "genoas" nor "May Wests"—they were almost on even terms as to speed. The uses to which these "yachts" were put served to add to the confusion. In their early trials of speed they raced with fishermen and pilot boats, and it is often difficult to tell one from the other. In time of war they were privateers, a comprehensive term whose lower limit might be close to piracy. They were also used as revenue cutters and dispatch boats.

Prior to about 1880 the particulars given in the books of even the larger clubs were most inadequate, limited to some one item of length, sail area, the product of waterline length by breadth, or "mean length." The first register, *Fox's Yachting Annual* of 1872, was well planned, but in this initial effort it was impossible to gather complete data. No color plates were included, the private signals were described as "blue C on white ground, no border," or "red star, white field, blue edge." The book contained a form requesting for the following year these particulars:—Name, Owner, Late Owner, Port, Clubs, Captain, Builder, Sailmaker, Distinguishing Flag, Rig, Waterline, Beam, Draft, Tonnage, Prizes won, No. of Men, Year built, Year altered, and Price for sale. Mr. Fox seems to have been the first New York yacht broker, which accounts for the last query. No mention is made of the modeler, nor is the length over all requested. Unfortunately, the book did not survive its first season; but even as it stands it is a most valuable source of information.

Above: Caroline, later Bohemian, designed by Dennison J. Lawlor, built by W. L. Dolheare. Below: Lines of the schooner Northern Light. L.O.A. 63 feet, L.W.L. 57 feet 9 inches, breadth 17 feet 6 inches, tonnage 69-68/95

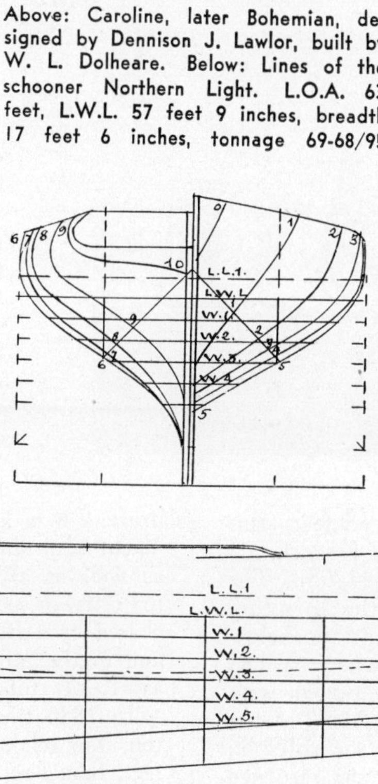

Captain Forbes and His Memories

For most of what we know of the earliest Boston yachts we are indebted to Captain Robert Bennet Forbes, whose intimate knowledge of the yachts, his deep interest in them, and his lifelong habit of writing of all manner of craft, have preserved many important facts in his *Discursive Sketch of Yachting Forty Years Ago*—1888. The first yacht mentioned is the sloop Jefferson, 22-15/95 tons, built by Christopher Turner of Salem for Captain George Crowninshield and launched in March 1801. The dimensions are taken from her papers, 35 feet 10 inches length for tonnage, 12 feet 4 inches breadth, 6 feet depth of hold.

The use to which she was put proves indubitably that she was built as a yacht, and she was thus used until the War of 1812, when Captain Crowninshield obtained a commission as a privateer; the second New England vessel thus authorized. Originally a sloop, she was converted to a schooner. As a privateer she was credited with a crew of thirty, and brought in the second prize

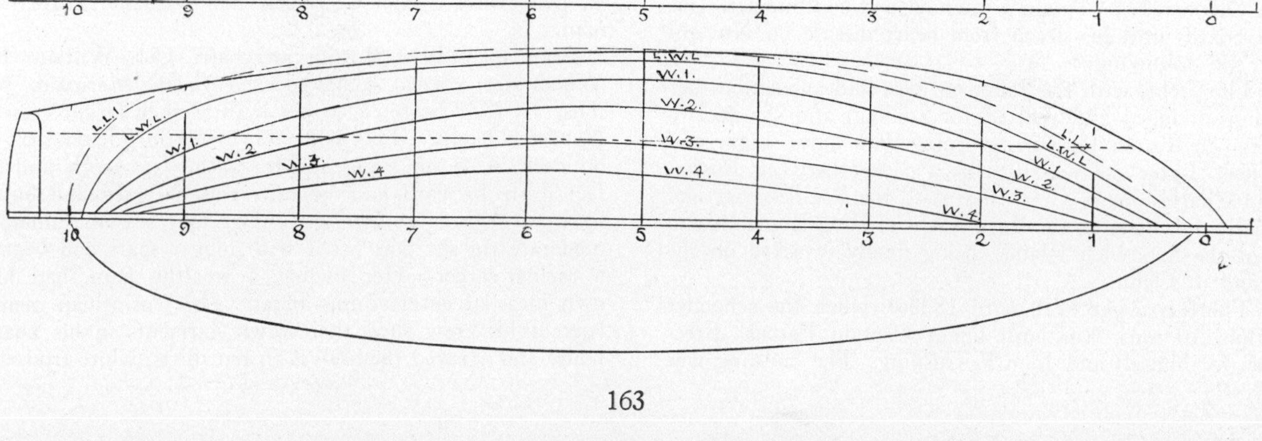

taken, the schooner Nymph. Sold after her owner's death, she ended her days as a fisherman. Mere casual mention is made under the date of 1816-7 of "a nice sloop or cutter about the harbor (Boston) of 20 tons, owned by Thomas Doubleday."

The next in chronological order is a yacht of exceptional size and remarkable in every way; though the model was cut and the yacht built by Retire Becket (his townsmen knew him familiarly as "Tyrey"), the leading builder of Salem, every detail was planned by the owner, Captain Crowninshield. His originality, not to say, oddity, was shown in the name, Cleopatra's Barge, finally selected after a first choice, Car of Concordia, was rejected. The outside of the ship was painted with horizontal stripes of brilliant colors on the starboard side and a herring-bone pattern in many colors on the port side. The furniture, decorations, and furnishing such as plate and glassware, were specially planned by the owner and such as would be fitting in a city mansion.

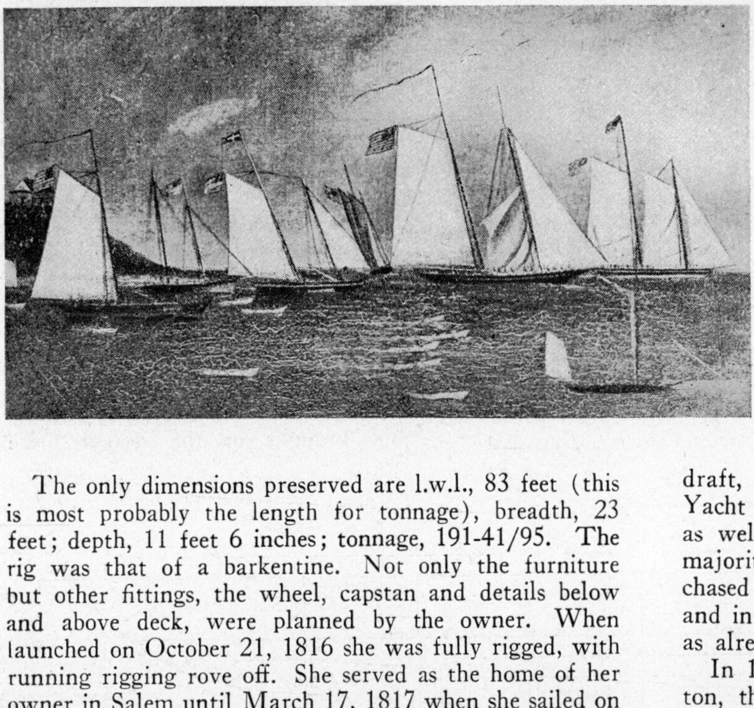

Above: Mist, a typical New England schooner, about 20 tons, built in Boston 1877. Left: Nahant Regatta, July 19, 1845

The only dimensions preserved are l.w.l., 83 feet (this is most probably the length for tonnage), breadth, 23 feet; depth, 11 feet 6 inches; tonnage, 191-41/95. The rig was that of a barkentine. Not only the furniture but other fittings, the wheel, capstan and details below and above deck, were planned by the owner. When launched on October 21, 1816 she was fully rigged, with running rigging rove off. She served as the home of her owner in Salem until March 17, 1817 when she sailed on a cruise to the Mediterranean from which she returned on October 17; Captain Crowninshield continued to live on board until his death from heart disease on November 26 following.

The yacht, with the Jefferson, was sold at auction, her cabins stripped and refitted for trading, and she took a cargo to Rio de Janiero, returning with hides, sugar and coffee. Later she was used as a packet between Boston and Charleston, S. C., then sent to the Pacific coast and finally purchased as the Royal yacht of King Kamehameha I of the Sandwich Islands, being finally wrecked on the island of Oahu.

There is a gap here until 1833-4, when the schooner Sylph, 10 tons, was built under Captain Forbes' direction for himself and John P. Cushing. The building was done by Wetmore & Holbrook of Boston, but in her second year she was hauled out at Medford and her bow lengthened seven feet, "like an English cutter"—probably a plumb stem. In a cruise to the westward she fell in, off Tarpaulin Cove, with the schooner Wave, Commodore John C. Stevens, and some inconclusive racing resulted. She was finally sold to a pilot.

Mention was made in the preceding chapter of the schooner Dream, built by Webb & Allen in New York in 1833; length, 46-4, breadth, 14-5, depth, 5-0, draft, 7-6, a keel yacht. Her models in the New York Yacht Club show a fairly lined vessel, rather fine forward as well as aft, and of a very different type from the majority of early Boston yachts. In 1834 she was purchased by a Boston yachtsman, Thomas H. Perkins, Jr., and in the following year was sold to the Dream Club, as already told.

In 1836 there was built by Holbrook & Dillon, Boston, the schooner Breeze, length, 51 feet, breadth, 15 feet, 8 inches, depth, 6 feet 4 inches. Her owners were R. B. Forbes, Daniel C. Bacon and William H. Boardman.

Prior to 1839 a Boston merchant, Col. William P. Winchester, owned a half-decked yacht, Mermaid, 12 tons. In 1839 he replaced her with a much larger vessel, Northern Light. This schooner, of 69-68/95 tons; 62-6 on deck, 47-6 on keel, 17-6 breadth, 7-3 depth and 5 feet draft forward and 9-6 aft, was designed and built by Louis Winde at Chelsea. After four seasons under a moderate rig she was fitted with longer spars and began a racing career. Her owner, a wealthy man, had his own ideas of entertaining afloat. The Corinthian members of his crew shed their town garments in his boathouse and arrayed themselves in red shirts, white trousers and straw hats with red silk bands with long flowing ends and the yacht's name in gold letters. The standard menu included a variety of strong drink known as Bimbo.

The First Inter-City Racing

IN 1844 the infant New York Yacht Club under the leadership of Commodore Stevens aboard the flagship Gimcrack made its first cruise to Newport. Col. Winchester took Northern Light around the Cape in company with a small schooner, Lancet, and Captain Forbes aboard Belle, chartered for the cruise. As a matter of course there were challenges, much talk, many disputes in the forms of letters to the press and newspaper comments, and a little inconclusive sailing. In the course of the heated press war, while the New York yachts were admitted to be "fine-looking boats, and essentially different from anything seen on the other (East) side of Cape Cod, the centerboard was denounced as "a machine which, in my judgment, entirely alters the character of the vessel; and which should not be tolerated in any boat that pretends to sail blue water."

In June, 1846, Northern Light and Coquette visited New York and sailed in the second annual regatta of the Club, later joining the fleet at Newport for the cruise. There followed more talk and writing and a little sailing, with very little satisfaction to either side. On her return from this cruise Northern Light was offered for sale and purchased for use as a packet between Boston and Plymouth. The enterprise was not successful and she was repurchased by Col. Winchester in 1848, but sold the following year to parties who proposed to sail her to California. On March 15, 1850, she was driven ashore in the Straits of Magellan and totally wrecked, her crew and passengers, including the wife and daughter of one of her owners, being saved. This brief outline does not do justice to a notable yacht, but her history has been written in full by my fellow antiquarian Winfield M. Thompson.

Continuing in chronological order, largely from Captain Forbes' *Sketch,* in 1840 was built Avon, 11 tons, a schooner, and in 1841 Ariel, a topsail schooner of 100 tons, for Captain Forbes. In 1842 he owned and used as a yacht the pilot boat Belle, 72 tons, length 66-6, depth 6-9, draft forward 6 feet, aft 8 feet; built by Samuel Hall of Salem. In the same year was built by Hall for Captain Forbes the schooner Gazelle, 116 tons, length 76-10, breadth 20-9, depth 8-2. She was sent to China and sold to English owners who used her in the opium trade.

THE schooner Nautilus, built in 1842 by Stephen Lowell at Newburyport for C. B. Pierce and others, is typical of the smaller yachts of the day. She is described as follows in *The Boston Post* of July 10, 1845:—"On the keel she is 23 feet 3 inches long; on the deck 32 feet; is 10 feet 2 inches beam, and 5 feet draft; she measures about 18 tons. She has about 18 inches deadrise and 18 inches sheer, draws 4 feet of water forward and 6 feet 6 inches aft. Her bow is quite sharp, her run clean, and her counter light and high. The stem rakes 4 feet 4 inches forward and the sternpost 1 foot 4 inches aft; her lines are slightly rounded, almost straight. She is built of oak and copper-fastened; is black outside and the paint work is green inside. On deck she has a trunk about 14 inches high over the cabin, and standing room aft similar to a pilot boat; her bulwarks fore and aft are double, and about 10 inches high. The cabin is painted and grained, has settees and lockers on both sides, and contains four large berths. The forecastle is furnished with cooking apparatus and several convenient lockers. She is rigged like a pilot boat and the dimensions of her spars and sails are nearly the same as those of other yachts of her size which we have already described. Her owners, who, of course, know all about her, say that no vessel of her size can outsail her in smooth water and a stiff breeze." Noting that this keel schooner is only about 28 feet waterline, in the lack of such lines and complete dimensions as are published today of many yachts, we can fully visualize the typical small Boston yacht of a century ago.

In 1843 a small schooner, Petrel, sailed for Australia; in 1845 the schooner Fawn was built by Stephen Lowell, also for C. B. Pierce and others. She was similar to Nautilus, of 12 tons, and "pilot boat rigged." "The after part of her inside is open, fitted with seats convenient for a fishing party. Forward she is decked over and has two berths. Those who wish to secure the use of this beautiful and capacious craft for a fishing excursion are informed that she may be found at Wales' Wharf, South End".

COQUETTE, "pilot boat schooner", was built in 1846 by Winde & Clinkard for James H. Perkins; 80 tons; 66 feet length; 19 feet beam; 7 feet depth; and 6 feet 10 inches draft. She was considered very fast. Mystery, schooner, 55 by 15, was built at Salem in 1849. Olata, 100 tons, was built about this time by Dennis J. Lawlor and sold for a pilot boat. In 1851 Young America, 52 tons, was built by Winde & Clinkard as a party boat and finally sold to Savannah pilots. Humming Bird, keel, 40 by 13, was built by Lewis of Salem for Captain Forbes and soon sold to a powder company. Volante, 53 tons, was built by Winde & Clinkard in 1855.

Among other yachts listed by Captain Forbes are Whip, "considered fast", by Brown & Lovell; Zephyr, 150 tons, built by Sam Hall for Daniel Burns of Canton, China; Foam, 25 tons, built to carry fishing parties, and the sloops Witch, 25 tons; Shearwater, 42 tons; Whisper, 10 tons; Whelp, 10 tons and Wench, 10 tons. These suggest a primitive one-design class. Joshua Brown of Salem built the sloop Clitheroe in 1866 for Benjamin Dean of the Boston Y.C. She was a centerboard craft 28 feet over all; 25 feet 6 inches waterline; 10 feet breadth and but 2 feet 10 inches draft.

The first regatta in Eastern waters was sailed off Nahant on July 19, 1845, "free for all, open to yachts of 50 to 10 tons; allowance, 30 seconds per ton; first prize, cup costing $50; second prize, set of colors." The starters were:—Nautilus, 11 tons; Avon, 11 tons; Neptune, 11 tons; Raven, 12 tons; Pathfinder, 12 tons; Naiad Queen, 15 tons; Gypsey, 21 tons; Alert, 22 tons; Vision, 24 tons; Odd Fellow, 30 tons; Cygnet, 31 tons; Susan, 18 tons; Brenda, 30 tons; Cloud, 22 tons. Raven won first prize and Vision second.

Contrasting Types

FRAGMENTARY and incomplete as these records are, they enable us to make a fair comparison between the yachting of Boston and New York. The New York fleet numbered many schooners of a size not known in Boston, some keel and some centerboard; its sloops, practically all centerboard, were larger than those of the Boston fleet. In the smaller classes the keel was almost unknown, and the majority of the centerboard boats were of the skimming dish type and sailed with shifting ballast. The Boston fleet was made up of yachts from small to moderate size, the keel type being strongly in the majority.

The very large number of small deep harbors ensured safe and convenient mooring grounds for keel boats, and when once clear of a harbor they were likely to encounter conditions of wind and wave unsuited to shoal bodies. At the same time there were many little harbors which dried out at low water, making the use of a keel yacht impossible. In such localities it was necessary to stay ashore or to adopt the centerboard. Under these conditions there grew up a very large fleet of small centerboard yachts. Many of these (locally known as "splashers") were of the sandbag type described in MoToR BoatinG of September, 1939, but less extreme in proportions and sailed with fixed ballast. As to rig, even down to the smallest classes excepting the "splashers" the keel was in the majority.

The following table, from Forest & Stream of April 23, 1874, shows the proportions of hull type and rig.

Clubs	Schooners		Sloops	
	Keel	Centerboard	Keel	Centerboard
Beverly	1	—	7	32
Boston	12	6	13	24
Bunker Hill	6	—	6	6
Dorchester	8	1	15	47
Eastern	11	16	5	9
Lynn	2	—	4	47
South Boston	9	—	12	15

Ten years previously the disparity would have been much greater in favor of the keel schooner. In the South Boston Y.C. the schooners ranged from 21 to 31 feet l.w.l; the keel sloops from 16 to 35 feet, and the centerboard sloops from 18 to 26 feet. In the Hull Y.C. as late as 1882 the fleet numbered 20 keel and 2 centerboard schooners; 26 keel and 23 centerboard sloops; and 3 keel and 45 centerboard catboats.

These divisions called for a number of classes in the races; in the Boston City Regatta of July 4, 1874 the fleet was divided as follows:—1st Class sloops, 3; 1st Class schooners, 3; 2d Class centerboard sloops, 8; 2d Class keel sloops, 7; 2d Class schooners, 3; Centerboard boats, 15; Fishing boats, 16.

In model the Eastern keel yachts were most interesting. In body they possessed the great breadth of the New York type, but much greater depth of immersed body; below this hull proper was deep fin of wood; the shape of the lateral plane, with its raking sternpost, heavy draft at heel, and little more than half this draft forward, giving good lateral resistance and superior maneuverability. In some cases, as shown in Northern Light, there was a very sharp deadrise and hollow of floor, a "wine-glass" section, permitting a low stowage of ballast. About the sixties the section was more like a T-square; a broad hull with very little deadrise above a deep wooden fin. The ballast was stowed entirely inside and at best of kentledge, if not of stone. A notable exception was the schooner Brenda, 30 tons, built by Louis Winde about 1845 for David Sears; her ballast was lead stowed amidships instead of being "wung out" as was necessary with a lighter material.

The Battle of the Types

THE victory of Puritan in the international match of 1885, followed by that of Mayflower in 1886, led to the abandonment by the Yacht Racing Association at the end of the latter year of the Thames Rule which had hampered yacht design in Britain for a generation. At the same time, with the building of another challenger, Thistle, with no limitation on breadth; and the recognition by both sides of a new "compromise" type, it ended a war which had raged for a decade, dividing even life-long friends into the two camps of the sloop men and the "cutter-cranks", also involving the issue of Corinthianism.

It is interesting today to find the genesis of this war in the earliest period of organized yachting. The Boston yachts as a class represented the keel, of at least moderate depth and displacement with fixed ballast which insured against a capsize. The New York yachts were mostly centerboard, of limited displacement and depth, and liable to capsize at any moment. In the smaller classes the unrestricted use of shifting ballast made a capsize an incident to be expected rather than feared. The question of shifting ballast is discussed at length from the Boston point of view in Forest & Stream of July 2, 1874, as follows:

"At a special meeting of the Dorchester Yacht Club held on June 19 at the Club House, Commercial Point, the rule restricting shifting ballast was stricken out of the Sailing Regulations by a very close vote. This action is very much regretted by many of the most influential and most thorough yachtsmen in the Club; and it is feared that some of the best yachts will be withdrawn on this account. Already four yacht owners have intimated that their resignations would be sent in at an early date. Hitherto the Dorchester Yacht Club has enjoyed an uninterrupted flood of prosperity; its regattas and cruises have always had large numbers of yachts in attendance; but for the future the prospect is not so encouraging. However, it is to be hoped that, seeing the error of their ways, recreant ballast-heavers will reconsider their rash movement; and that the Club will once again take its place in the foremost ranks of those that encourage the best interests of yachting.

"It is worthy of note that in the regatta of the 20th instant the yacht owned by one of the most prominent advocates of sandbags was badly beaten by a smaller boat that under the old regime was scarcely able to come to the front, and many yachtsmen are curious to know how such a result comes about; for of course if under the old rule neither of the boats shifted ballast, they now sail on the same equality as before?

"It would seem that in respect to the ballast question we should be safe in following the example of the English clubs; they have tried shifting ballast much longer than we, and finally gave it up. When the English yachts, with their extreme narrowness and consequent want of initial stability, decide to abolish shifting ballast, it is obvious that we, with our yachts of extreme beam and enormous natural stability, cannot want shifting ballast on the score of safety.

"It is only the 'Jockey interest' in the clubs, that desires to reduce the sport to the level of professional horse-racing, boating or baseball, that advocates this pernicious method of sailing. This 'Jockey-interest' is also opposed to owners sailing their own boats, and insists upon the privilege of hiring professional skippers, being determined to win the prize at any cost (of money and hired brains) caring nothing for the advancement of the true interests of yachting, or the encouragement of skill on the part of yacht owners."

MOST of the Eastern yachts were modeled and built by shipbuilders accustomed to large vessels and the heavy construction of fishermen and pilot boats; while those of New York were built by men who were more or less specialists in this lighter line of work:—Captain Bob Fish, J. B. Van Deusen, J. O. Voris, David Carll, David Kirby, Pat McGiehan, A. M. Witman, Poillon Bros., D. O. Richmond of Mystic and William Smith of Stonington. The yachts built by Smith seem to have been better known in the East than about New York; Captain Arthur Clark says of him:—"The boats built by Smith of Stonington may fairly be considered to have made great changes in the ideas of the yachtsmen of Massachusetts Bay; as, up to the time when the James Ingersoll Day came to Boston, there appeared to have been very little difference in the type between yachts, pilot boats and fishermen; they were almost all schooners, the few sloops being of the type of sloops used for trading purposes; but the James Ingersoll Day was a boat of an entirely different kind. Some time afterwards boats built by the Herreshoffs came to Boston and had a great effect upon the ideas of yachtsmen, as they were quite different from anything which had been produced in Boston."

Little is on record of this yacht with a peculiar name. She is mentioned by Captain Forbes as being a centerboard boat, half-decked and with only a lower mast mainsail and jib, and it would seem that she was more fisherman than yacht. Purchased by Samuel Hall of Salem, he added a full deck or cabin trunk and a topmast, re-named her Tartar, and she was for many years considered a fast yacht. It is to be regretted that more of her particulars were not preserved.

The Herreshoffs of Bristol—J. B. Herreshoff, Herreshoff & Stone, and the Herreshoff Manufacturing Company of modern days—were yacht builders from the start, distinguished by originality of design and construction. Their work was known in Boston at least as early as 1866, when they built quite a fleet of small yachts, catboats and sloops, for "the Burgess boys". From 1870 on, the number of their yachts, practically all of the centerboard type, increased rapidly about Boston; under this influence, while the keel type still held in favor for years, by degrees the fisherman and pilot boat type gave way to the modern centerboard yacht.

Thelga

TRADITIONS AND MEMORIES OF

American Yachting

By WILLIAM P. STEPHENS

East of the Cape

Part Thirty-five (Continued)

THE "cutter-craze", which was epidemic about New York from the late seventies, found few adherents East of the Cape. As we have seen, this locality strongly favored the keel yacht, with more displacement and deeper body than about New York, with shifting ballast strictly prohibited, and the fixed ballast, though still inside the hull, disposed of at the lowest possible point. The arguments of the "cutter-cranks" fell on deaf ears, even when they went no further than the "four-beam cutter"—a breadth of 10 feet on a waterline of 40 feet—much less as they advanced to the final extreme of "7-beam", or a breadth of 6 feet on a waterline of 42 feet. With both depth and low ballast, the latter by slow degrees transferred below the keel, the Eastern yachtsmen clung to breadth. As the keel craft developed as a distinct type, with no relationship to working craft, it assumed a very poor form—wide and shoal. In default of lines, we can only quote the dimensions of what was considered a fast yacht in her day, the sloop Quimper, modelled and built by two little known parties, S. W. Sampson and B. F. Bragdon & Co., for Henry T. Wheeler of the Bunker Hill Y. C. Her original dimensions were:—l.o.a., 28 feet; l.w.l., 26 feet; breadth, 11 feet 7 inches, depth, 3 feet 3 inches. Her original draft as a centerboard boat is not given, but in 1875 she was changed to a keel by the addition of a thin wood fin carrying an iron shoe, making her draft 3 feet 9 inches. The ratio of waterline to breadth—2¼ beams—seems to have been about the proportion of most yachts below 40 feet waterline.

The general characteristics of the yachts of the middle seventies are shown in Fig. 1, an unidentified sloop. On an overall length of 24 feet

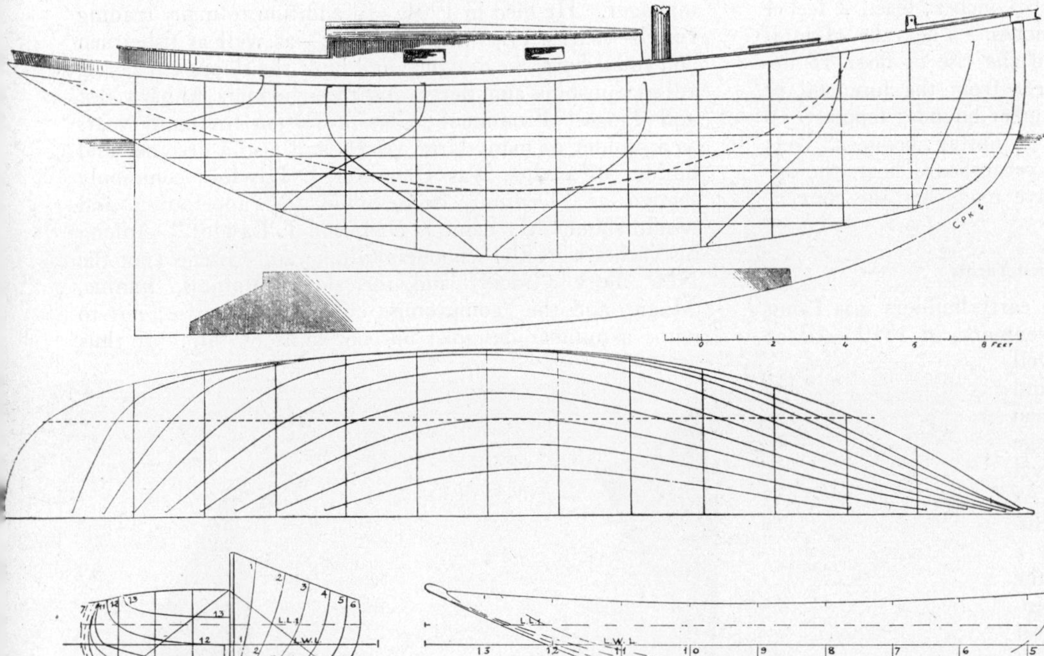

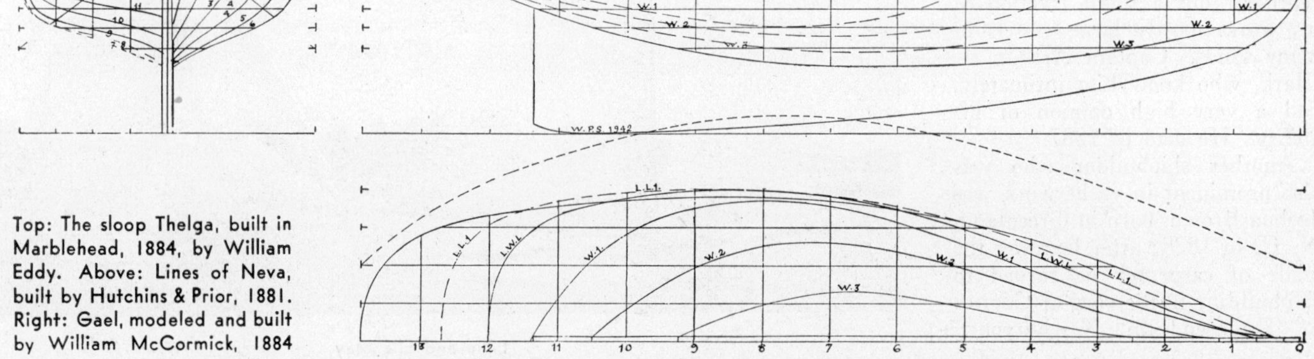

Top: The sloop Thelga, built in Marblehead, 1884, by William Eddy. Above: Lines of Neva, built by Hutchins & Prior, 1881. Right: Gael, modeled and built by William McCormick, 1884

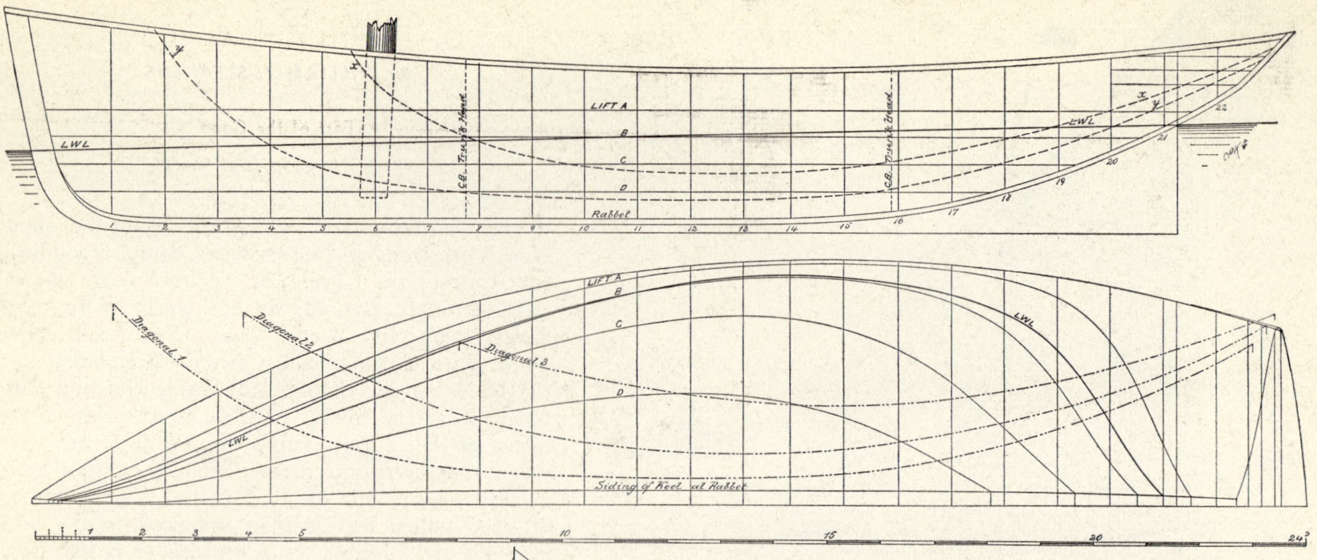

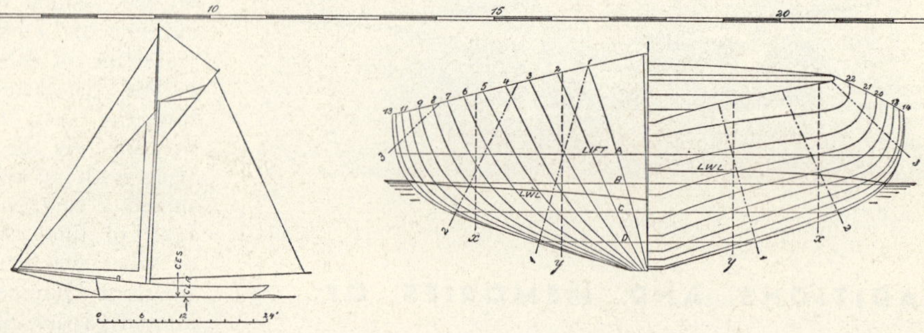

Fig. 1, right: An unidentified sloop of 24 feet overall length which is typical of the yachts of the middle seventies. Below: Lillie, a centerboard altered to keel, 1880, and Ella May, built by George Lawley & Son, 1884

her waterline was 21 feet 8 inches—2.4 beams—the entrance, very straight with only a slight hollow at the fore end, was 67 per cent of the waterline. The draft was 4 feet; freeboard at bow, 5 feet 3 inches; least, 2 feet 4 inches; at transom, 3 feet 3 inches. The rake of midship section was 57 degrees and the rise of floor 18 degrees. The mast, stepped 7 feet from the fore end of waterline, was 25 feet deck to upper hounds; topmast, 10 feet; bowsprit, 12 feet outboard to jibstay; boom, 23 feet; gaff, 14 feet. While she was a centerboard boat, the addition of a plank fin would have made her the conventional keel boat of her day.

Builders of the First Yachts

THE most noted of the early builders was Louis Winde, born in Helsingfors, Denmark, in 1810. All of the Scandinavian nations were well advanced in both the theory and practice of shipbuilding, and when he arrived in Boston at the age of 22 Louis Winde was a naval architect as well as builder. At one time he taught naval architecture, and in 1859 imported a set of Copenhagen curves for the use of his pupils. The yachts mentioned in the preceding chapter represent but a small fraction of his work, mostly large vessels of many kinds. Captain Arthur H. Clark, who knew him intimately, had a very high opinion of his ability. He died in 1887.

Another shipbuilder who was also prominent in yacht work was Joshua Brown, born in Greenland, N. H. in 1828; after learning the trade of carpenter he turned to shipbuilding in the yard of Currier & Townsend in Newburyport, moving to Salem in the early fifties. He was associated with the firms of Lewis, Turner & Brown; Lewis & Brown; and Turner & Brown as naval architect and manager. He died in 1901. In addition to many trading vessels—barks, brigs and schooners—as well as fishermen and small boats, he designed and built the sloops Clitheroe, Idler, Sunshine and Betty, and the schooners Anna, Crest and Tioga. Prominent in his profession for many years as a builder of many large vessels and also a designer and builder of yachts, was Dennison J. Lawlor; commonly known as "Dennis", he resented this appellation and would shout "My name is *Dennison* J. Lawlor." Among his yachts were the schooners Gitana and Gracie (not the New York Gracie) and the sloops Vanitas, Fannie, Magic, and the "compromise cutter" Enterprise; not to name a number designed but not built by him. It thus

Lillie and Ella May

appears that all of the early yachts were built by men mainly engaged in larger work, and were of ship rather than of yacht build.

Somewhere about the middle sixties yachts of medium and small size became generally popular, and to meet the new demand there sprung up all around the Cape a large number of small shops specializing in yachts. At Salem was A. J. Frisbie; at Marblehead, William Eddy and J. H. Keating; at Lynn, Allan Hay, Britt Bros., and Snow & Chapman; at Cambridge, W. B. Dinsmore; at Jeffries Wood Bros., and Ambrose A. Martin; at East Boston, S. W. Sampson; at South Boston, Pierce Bros., E. Harris, Bibber & Holbrook, and Hutchings & Pryor; at Dorchester, Charles A. Borden, and Coultier; at Quincy, W. B. Smith, W. F. Mayberry, Embree Bros., A. A. Lelois, and C C. Hanley; at Scituate, George Lawley & Son; at Kingston, George W. Shiverick; at Osterville, the Crosby family; at Provincetown, John Whitcomb. These firms were not all contemporary, nor always continued in the places named; but this list covers quite thoroughly the birth and early growth of what in time became a great industry.

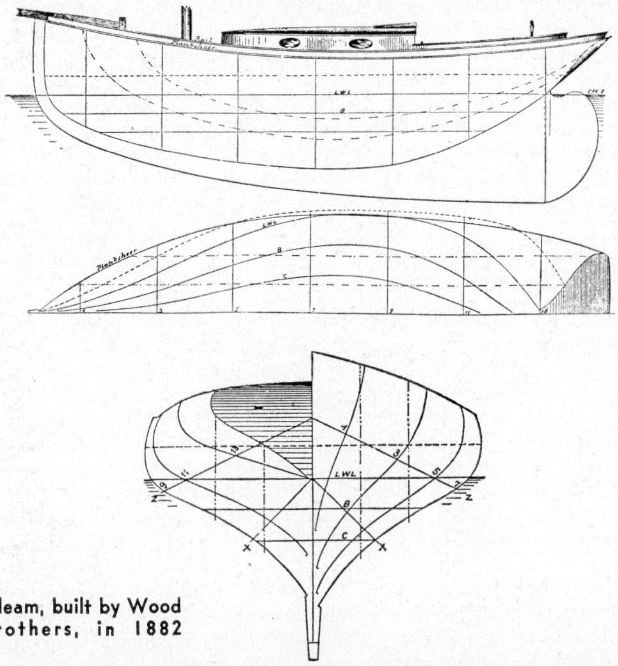

Gleam, built by Wood Brothers, in 1882

Born in London in 1823, George Lawley came to Boston in 1851 and started business as a boatbuilder; in 1865 he moved to Scituate and built his first small yacht. With his son George F. he founded the firm of Lawley & Son, and as their work progressed from catboats and small sloops in 1874 they moved to City Point, Boston. By 1880 they were building yachts of some size, and when called on five years later for a Cup defender they met the demand with Puritan; their knowledge of practical construction supplementing the comparatively limited experience of Edward Burgess. From that time on, with Mayflower, the steel Volunteer, and other metal yachts they worked upward to such craft as Independence and Yankee in the modern Cup Class.

The firm of Wood Bros., at Jeffries Point, with "Mil" Wood as the designer, was responsible for a large number of yachts through the seventies and eighties, mainly sloops under 40 feet;—Gleam, Lena, Clara, Gem, Actress, Cricket I, Cricket II, Dutchess, Maud, Caprice and Skylark; the steam yacht Aurora; and, by way of larger work, several ferryboats for the City of Boston. Most of their sloops were keel boats, and they had a prominent part in the development noted later. Starting with small craft at Quincy, W. B. Smith later moved to Boston and in 1883 built the "compromise cutter" Huron 53 feet 6 inches l. w. l., and in the following year another "compromise", Thetis, of 64 feet l. w. l. Further down on the Cape the Crosby family was building small fishing boats from which were finally to evolve the famous "Cape cats". In this era of experiment a numbei of yachts were built by non-professionals, men engaged about the water and interested in sailing, workmen in the boatyards, sailing masters, and men employed by sailmakers and ship chandlers. Quite a number of small cats and sloops were built by Captain Aubrey Crocker, for many years sailing master for the Bryants in Shadow, Thetis and Alert.

The Course of Development

IN all of these early keel yachts American ideas predominated; they were essentially centerboard hulls, somewhat deeper than their New York sisters, with a deep oak fin; all ballast being inside. The sloop Gael, in spite of her exceptional features, is a good example; she was built by her owner, William McCormick, of the East Boston and South Boston yacht clubs, a gentleman engaged in the shipping business; with him was associated another amateur, John F. Lovejoy, in later years prominent as a Corinthian skipper about New York. The design presumably is the work of Mr. McCormick, who hired yacht builders to do the work under his supervision. The hollow of the entrance and the rake of the midship section—43 degrees—are extreme, and there is no accounting for the tumble-home of the stem unless for some evasion of measurement, and this is hardly probable with such an excessively long after overhang.

Her appendage was entirely of wood, and when she was launched, in 1874, all ballast was inside; in her second season an iron shoe of 1,500 pounds was added, and a year later this was replaced by lead. Gael was one of a number of Eastern yachts of this keel type which by degrees found their way to New York, and it is only through the fact that she won a race in the Seawanhaka Corinthian Y. C. on June 17, 1882, defeating the centerboards Amazon and Vivien, that her lines, as taken off by A. Cary Smith for the Club, are in existence today. In writing of her now there comes to mind the story that about this time she dropped her lead keel in the Seawanhaka Basin at Edgewater, Staten Island, owing to the corrosion of the iron bolts. Her dimensions were:—l. o. a., 32 feet 6 inches; l. w. l., 28 feet 4 inches; breadth, 10 feet 4 inches; draft, 4 feet 11 inches; freeboard, at bow, 3 feet 3 inches; least, 1 foot 6 inches; at transom, 2 feet. Rise of floor, 22 degrees; displacement, 7.82 tons.

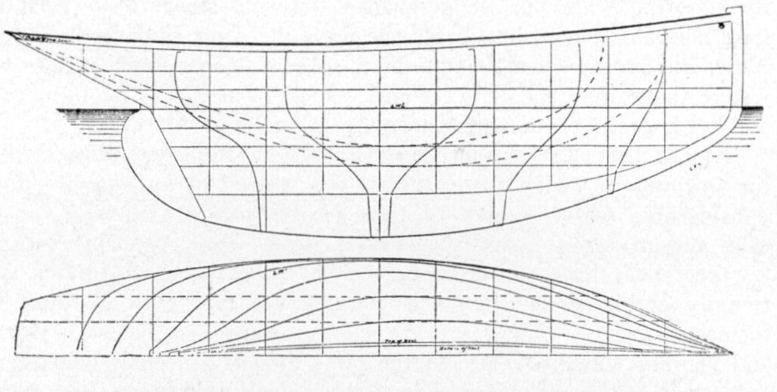

Vayu, designed by George F. Lawley in 1882

The most noted sloop in Eastern waters was Shadow, built by J. B. Herreshoff in 1871, a deep centerboard boat with a very heavy hollow in her midship section; in 1873 she was taken to Boston and dominated her class for many years. Though successful from the start, her model had little immediate effect on local design; though the deadrise was gradually increased, the distinct angle between garboard and keel was retained until about 1880. It is seen in Gem, a successful sloop designed by "Mil" Wood in that year, and to a lesser degree in his Neva, 1881, and Gleam, 1882; while in Vayu, designed by George F. Lawley in the same year, it has practically disappeared. From this date on the curve of the midship section was a fair and unbroken sweep from planksheer to lower edge of keel.

Neva was modelled and built in 1881 by Hutchings & Prior for George G. Branger:—her dimensions were l. o. a., 29 feet 2 inches; l. w. l., 25 feet; breadth, 9 feet 3 inches; draft, 5 feet 5½ inches. She was launched with an iron shoe of 1,100 pounds, but in the following year this was replaced by 3,050 pounds of lead; her deadrise was 36 degrees Gleam, known later in New York as Nyssa, was built by Wood Bros. in 1882; her dimensions were, l. o. a., 30 feet 4 inches; l. w. l., 26 feet 9 inches; breadth, 10 feet draft, 5 feet 11 inches; average deadrise, 46 degrees; lead on keel, 2,500 pounds. In the same year was built Vayu, for C. A. Welch, Jr., then Rear Commodore of the Boston Y. C. She was designed by George F. Lawley and built by the firm. Her dimensions were: l. o. a. 39 feet; l. w. l., 31 feet; breadth, 10 feet; draft, 7 feet. She carried 8.5 tons of ballast on a displacement of 14.8 tons, her iron keel weighing 6.5 tons. Her average rise of floor was 46 degrees.

Vayu marked a radical departure in that while all or nearly all of her predecessors had the same siding of keel as the siding of stem and sternpost, her keel was sided 16 inches; fairing into the iron with a hardly noticeable break at the rabbet. From this time on the placing of the bulk of the ballast below the wood keel, and shaping it as an integral part of the hull became the accepted practice.

Keel or Centerboard?

IN Forest & Stream of January 2, 1880 a correspondent, "Kedge", writes:—"A new Cutter 25 feet waterline is also to be built for Boston parties with 1,000 pounds of iron on keel. Centerboards have gone out of fashion, and keels with low ballast are fast displacing all others. They prove to be the best seaboats, and Viking last season showed them to be fast, as well." The issue of inside or outside ballast was disposed of, but there remained another of equal importance, the respective merits of keel and centerboard. This question was by no means settled by the obituary of "Kedge"; it continued for another six years before being settled in a manner which no one anticipated.

A Boston yachtsman, C. Fred Gorman, was sufficiently interested in the sport to take an active part in the discussion of such questions in print, and he was not ashamed to do so under his real name; he wrote as follows in Forest & Stream of December 10, 1874. "Most of the yachtsmen of the present day agree that the center-board yachts of the present day are faster than keels. This I admit to be true, but when they say a center-board is superior sailing before the wind I cannot agree with them for various reasons. If a keel boat cannot out-sail a center-board with sheets started, of what use is she for speed? In the first place, philosophy teaches that the object which makes the least resistance in passing through the water is wedge-shaped, offering much less resistance than a flat or round-bottomed one with the same bulk under water. Now, the average keel boat is built so as to come much nearer this wedge-shape than the center-board, which is, as a rule, of light draft and with great beam and a large 'seat' in the water."

"Again, there is another disadvantage in the center-board boat, the opening in which the center-board works up and down admits considerable water, which of course rises to its own level in the case and makes a heavy dead-water drag. But, it may be urged, the keel boat has a disadvantage in a heavy piece of timber continually acting as a drawback; but of the two evils I think the former is greater. But there are a great many keel boats in Boston and vicinity which are almost the same models as center-boards, the only perceptible difference being the substituting of a keel for a center-board. I am by no means certain that my argument would then hold good; but I think the records justify me in saying that keel boats as a class, are faster off the wind than center-boards. For racing, however, I would much prefer a center-board model. For working to windward this model is much to be preferred, and there is much less danger in miss-staying. But, for seagoing qualities and rough weather, commend me to the old-fashioned keel model smacking somewhat of the Deal lugger style. I am sorry to see these old styles fading away, to be replaced by the shallow 'skimdish' of the present day."

(signed) C. F. Gorman

NO partisan of the centerboard would admit Mr. Gorman's contention as to the drag of the water within the centerboard case; and his conclusions seem to have been based not on the average keel yacht as it existed in Boston at the time, but on a much heavier type of working craft.

A different view of the same question appeared in the same journal under date of January 7, 1875:—"A few weeks since, in an article on keels and center-boards, a correspondent has stated that center-board boats are faster than keels. Now, as an admirer of keel boats, I protest against any decision being made in the question of speed until all the facts are impartially stated. Of what does our fleet of keel boats consist? When a center-board boat gets old or leaky, or is too slow to obtain a reputation for speed, her owner begins to think of comfort, has his center-board and case removed, and a keel put on. By this change a much greater amount of room is obtained. In boatbuilding as in everything else practice makes perfect. From his experience in building center-boards a builder learns to improve his model and attain greater speed. So few keel boats are built, however, that the art remains almost at a standstill."

"A few second-hand center-board boats, and an occasional keel boat, make poor representatives from which to obtain an idea of the speed of a model. A disposition to return to keels seems to be gaining ground among our yachtsmen. When as much attention is given to the building of keels as to that of center-boards, a much fairer estimate of their relative speed can be made. The superior seagoing qualities of the keel boats are unquestioned. It is hardly fair to argue from a single instance, but the following case might be made an exception; in the Fourth of July Regatta of 1873 the White Cap a victor for many years, Shadow and many others, forming perhaps the fastest fleet of center-boards ever assembled in this harbor, were all beaten by a keel boat—Esperance. This one race shows that a keel boat can have a great amount of speed."

Respectfully,

Sheet Anchor

IN these early days Boston could boast of two institutions unknown to New York; in the early seventies the city maintained a free school of naval architecture in East Boston, the instructor being John L. Frisbee, cousin of A. J. Frisbee, the yacht builder of Salem. This school was later moved to the old City Hall building in Charlestown. There was another, the John Hawes Fund School, in the vestry of the Hawes Memorial Church in South Boston. Mr. Frisbee taught in both schools on different nights, with Albert Green as an assistant and successor. Among the pupils at different times were George F. Lawley and his sons, Capt. Jim Brown, Capt. Dicky Sherlock, Tom McManus, Capt. Charlton L. Smith, "Mel" Mclain, Tom Hibbard, Dr. E. C. Hebbard, McLellan, the sail maker and some of "Ad" Wilson's sailmakers, and "Dolly" McVey. It is impossible to over-estimate the value of this missionary work in a new field, at a time when it was greatly needed.

The other institution was the office of the fish store of Captain Thomas F. McManus, a general clearing house for all news of fishing and yachting. Here were to be met the captains of fishing vessels, Maurice Powers, John Cannon, Tom McLaughlin, among the yacht skippers were Capt. "Aub" Crocker, Capt. "Jim" Reid, of America when owned by Gen. Butler and, in later years, Capt. John Barr and his brother Capt. Charles. Among other notables in their day were D. J. Lawlor, Arthur Story, "Mil" Wood, "Nels" Sibley, John McPhail; and, of course, "Dolly" McVey of the *Boston Herald,* George A. Stewart, of the *Boston Globe,* and Jimmy McNally. In this gathering of the *cognoscente* of yachting was discussed from the date of which we are writing down through the years of international racing all the technical questions we are considering, with innumerable stories of races lost and won, and why.

No such center of friendly intercourse existed about New York; skippers might meet and pass the time of day in the sail lofts of Gilbert Wilson and Jack Sawyer, in Brooks Bros. clothing store on the corner of Catherine and Cherry Streets (many a long mile in distance and time from Madison Avenue at 44th Street) in Bill Bishop's plumbing shop, Dave Clark's paint shop and Jim Knight's blacksmith shop; and in Brooklyn at Krombach's saloon at Bay Ridge, but none of these compared in any way with the atmosphere of Tom McManus' private office.

TRADITIONS AND MEMORIES OF

American Yachting

By WILLIAM P. STEPHENS

Part Thirty-six

East of the Cape

(Continued)

THE years immediately adjacent to 1880 constitute the most important era in the history of American yachting; a period of investigation, experiment, argument and often heated controversy. A new interest was evident in the technical side of yachting, in design, in Corinthian sailing, all fostered by new publications devoted to the sport. After learning the trade of boatbuilding and the art of boatsailing from Cap'n Bob Fish in the fifties, A. Cary Smith abandoned the bench for the easel and painted some of the finest yacht portraits, great canvasses of the famous schooners. In the seventies he turned from the easel to the drafting board, advertising as a yacht designer, then a new profession, and designing a number of very successful yachts. In the first three months of 1878 he delivered a series of lectures on yacht designing before the Seawanhaka Corinthian Y. C. which were published in *The Country,* a competitor of *Forest & Stream* in the field of outdoor sports. In April 1878 there appeared in *Forest & Stream* the first of a series of articles on boat and yacht building by an anonymous writer, Nauticus.

In March 1878 *The Country* started a series of articles by John Hyslop describing in detail the series of experiments which he had conducted for several years in formulating his wave-form theory of design, a theory which exerted a very strong influence on design for many years. In 1879 David Kirby took part in a general discussion of type, giving his views of the correct principles of yacht design as applied to the sloop. In *The Country, The Aquatic Monthly,* in *Forest & Stream* and the daily papers there waged heated discussions by mainly anonymous writers, I Bolt, G M, Martin Gale, Bobstay, Open Sea, Big Topmast, and the many mentioned in MoToR BoatinG of March 1941.

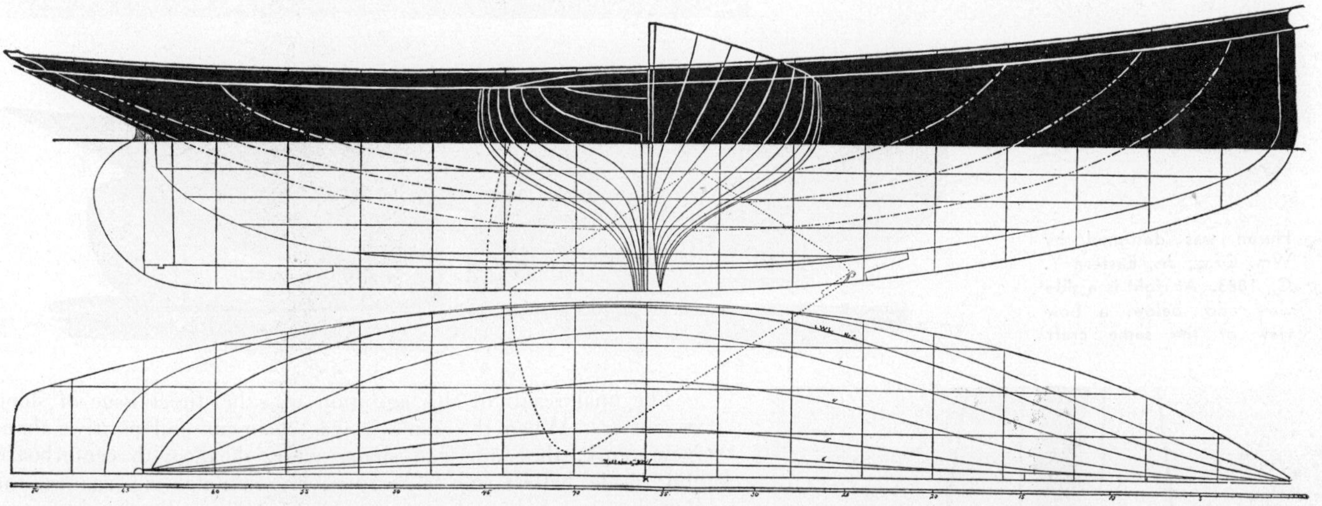

Above: The lines of Thetis, a compromise sloop or cutter. She was designed by Henry Bryant, Eastern Y. C., in 1884. At left she is shown under sail

Over the nom de plume of Rouge Croix, F. C. Sumichrast wrote regularly in reporting races as they were sailed, and ended the season with a long and critical review.

In this wide-spread discussion, which included every type and size from 20-foot sharpies to the largest sea-going schooners, even the short-lived freak, the catamaran, found a place. Following the introduction of the racing catamaran by the Herreshoffs in 1876, a member of the New York Y.C., Anson Phelps Stokes, owner of the schooner Clytie, had built under his personal direction a cruising catamaran, Nereid, originally with two hulls but with a third central hull interposed later. Though this weird craft, nicknamed by his fellow members Stokes' Folly, proved a complete failure, for a time it threw terror into the hearts of the owners of large and costly yachts, as they saw their treasured craft thus consigned to the junk yard.

The agitation was used by Rouge Croix as the occasion for a fling at the sloop:—"Some people admire these craft, I do not wonder at it, for with us the attainment of speed has always been a primary consideration, and so long as we get that we are content to sacrifice every other quality. That is why I like the catamaran, it is the *ne plus ultra* of our national model, it is the *reductio ad absurdum* of the sloop, it is the antithesis of the sea boat, and the more it exhibits its great speed under certain conditions of wind and sea, and its total lack of accommodation and comfort under all circumstances, the better I am pleased; as it leads me to hope the principles on which, along with the sloop, it is based, will be condemned." On behalf of the sharpie, the irrepressible Thomas Clapham seized on every letter, whether praising sloop or cutter, to advertise his improved model; even going so far as to challenge Robert Center to an ocean race in the fall between Vindex and a sharpie with the condition that each be sailed by her owner and one hand.

Huron was designed by Wm. Gray, Jr., Eastern Y. C., 1883. At right is a side view and, below, a bow view of the same craft

The final result of this agitation was the direct issue of sloop vs. cutter. When this came it was clean-cut and positive about New York, the American sloop, wide, shoal, with centerboard and inside ballast and a distinctively national rig against the British cutter hull with its national rig. About Boston, however, the issues were less cleanly defined; the East was largely partial to the keel yacht, with a small but increasing amount of metal under the keel, and a rig which in many cases included two headsails in place of the single jib. While distinctly opposed to the narrow doctrines of the extreme cutter-cranks, Boston yachtsmen experimented widely with types in their way.

The drift of opinion is noted in the journals of the day. Writing in *Forest & Stream* of March 27, 1879 under the disguise of Wanderer, a correspondent says:—"The Corinthian spirit runs higher than ever in Boston, and this summer will see more men sailing and navigating their own vessels than in years gone by. Cutters are rather growing in favor among the 'level-headed'—no disparagement intended to those who do not believe in them, however. The feeling seems to tend toward the cutter rig for vessels over 50 feet, but not under."

In the same issue an un-named correspondent writes under the heading Boston Takes to Keels and Lead:—"I notice in your columns that there is considerable discussion as regards the merits of the cutter, centerboard boats and sharpies, but very little is said about our keel boats. I think them not only the most comfortable boats of their size, but in a breeze and a jump of a sea they are the smartest boats we have in our waters, and for aught we know can equal if not beat the English cutter. In our keel boats we gain ability in rough water and cabin accommodations that cannot be had in either of the above-named boats—two qualities alone that the Boston yachtsman dislikes to do away with. We have here but one genuine cutter, that was brought over from England with great expectations, although there is now less faith to be placed in her as regards speed. But when it comes to comfort I cannot see where it is to be found, the cutter being so very deep and narrow that if a person wishes berths he is obliged to sacrifice transoms and narrow his floor.—The cutter enthusiast might say there is comfort in the feeling that the boat is uncapsizable; I agree with him on that point, but this comfort is also had in our keel boat, as we carry heavy iron or lead keels.—As for the centerboards, they are a class of boats that are fast going out of use in and around Boston—i.e., boats from 20 feet upward—as it has been and still is being shown that a keel boat in a breeze is the smarter of the two.—It might be said that the centerboard has beam, and makes up the room she lacks in depth; to this I can say that more than one-half the keel boats we have here have a beam equal to that of the centerboards; also, that a number of centerboards have been changed to keels and are now taking prizes and beating centerboard boats who took prizes from them before they were changed."

The "very deep and narrow" cutter mentioned above was the first of the type seen in Boston; Kitten, designed and built by John Harvey at Wivenhoe, England, in 1852. Her dimensions were: l.o.a., 43 feet; l.w.l., 37 feet 4 inches; breadth, 8 feet 9 inches; draft, 6 feet 8 inches. With a ratio of 4¼ beams to length she could not be classed as extreme. She was brought from England in 1870 by George F. Clarke of the Dorchester Y.C.; re-christened Saxon, but her original name was restored later. In 1878 Frank E. Peabody had built by D. J. Lawlor, from the latter's design, what was called the cutter Enterprise; l.o.a., 50 feet 6 inches; l.w.l., 43 feet 9 inches; breadth, 15 feet 8 inches; draft, 7 feet 3 inches. With a proportion of 2¾ beams she had much the same profile as Gael, and the same semicircular transom. In 1880 T. W. Merrill, of the Eastern Y.C., imported a design by Michael Ratsey from which D. J. Lawlor built Edith, with yawl instead of cutter rig; l.o.a., 49 feet; l.w.l., 40 feet 8 inches; breadth, 10 feet; draft, 7 feet 3 inches. In 1883 Edward Burgess had built by Lawley & Son, from a design by J. Beavor Webb, the cutter Butterfly, l.o.a., 39 feet; l.w.l., 32 feet 6 inches; breadth, 8 feet 6 inches; draft, 6 feet 9 inches. At the same time Lawley & Son built for F. Gordon Dexter, from a design by J. Beavor Webb, the cutter Medusa, l.o.a., 63 feet; l.w.l., 54 feet; breadth, 12 feet 4 inches; draft, 9 feet 6 inches.

With the Amateur Designers

THE interest in yacht design was growing rapidly among owners. In 1883 William Gray, Jr., of the Eastern Y.C., designed the cutter Huron, l.o.a., 63 feet; l.w.l., 55 feet 6 inches; breadth, 15 feet 9 inches; draft, 8 feet. She was very well built by W. B. Smith, all her frames steam-bent, then an unusual construction; she carried 10 tons of iron under her keel. As her early performances were not satisfactory, Mr. Gray had her taken apart in 1885, the keel lengthened 9 feet, and the frames replaced. In 1884 another member of the Eastern Y.C., Henry Bryant, owner of Shadow, designed and had built by Smith the "compromise" sloop Thetis: l.o.a., 71 feet 9 inches; l.w.l., 64 feet; breadth, 19 feet; draft, 8 feet 3 inches; with board, 17 feet. As she sailed at times with a single jib and again with double headrig, she may be classed as either cutter or sloop. Her displacement was 59 tons, with 22 tons of ballast, of which 18 tons was in her lead keel. She was designed for general use rather than for racing, partly as an experiment in type, very strongly built; and though she made no notable record in racing she was a very creditable amateur effort.

In 1888 Mr. Bryant replaced her with a schooner, Alert, of 90 feet l.w.l., also of his own design, a very able cruising yacht. In 1885 J. Malcolm Forbes had built in Scotland from a design by Watson the cutter Bayadere (nicknamed by his friends Bayardthayer after a fellow member of the Eastern Y.C.) l.o.a., 54 feet 3 inches; l.w.l., 45 feet; breadth, 9 feet 11 inches; draft, 8 feet. The cutter thus gradually worked its way into Boston yachting; all of these yachts were of the cruising type, sturdily built, and in proportions not under four beams, as compared with the six beams then found in British racing cutters and even in some of New York.

The fourth challenge for the Cup, in 1881, came from Lake Ontario, Canada, and was in the 70-foot Sloop Class, the strongest racing class in New York. However, it was considered necessary

Kitten, later Saxon, 1852

to build, in addition to the existing boats. The outstanding yacht of the Class had been Arrow, modelled and built by David Kirby in 1874, but she had been sold away from New York. The most recent addition to the Class was the iron sloop Mischief, designed by A. Cary Smith in 1879, of but 61 feet l.w.l. as compared with 70 feet for the largest of the Class. Under the existing time scale of 40 per cent this was almost a prohibitive handicap, but Mischief under the able handling of Cap'n Than Clock soon made her way to the head of the Class.

In this connection it is interesting to quote an anonymous writer in *Forest & Stream* of January 16, 1879:—"We question the utility or advantage of iron for sailing yachts of the sloop type, and think Mr. Busk may find more trouble in keeping his sloop bottom in racing condition than he expects. For cutters of deep draft and high freeboard iron, no doubt, presents the advantages of light topsides and heavy keel and garboards, but in the ordinary sloop these elements of success disappear to a great extent, and smooth skin is lost by the use of iron, even though kept well painted. Up to five knots in short, wide craft friction is the main and almost only cause of resistance; and, as light weather is the sloop's congeniality, iron is hardly to be regarded as favorable to her best weather"

There is no question as to the detrimental effect of scale on a newly rolled plate. Cary Smith once made the statement that this scale is due to the profanity of the "boat-yarders," and my experience in a shipyard of this era leads me to believe that he was correct. However, if he had seen Mischief as I saw her on the ways just previous to her races with Atalanta, the critic would have changed his opinion. What with three seasons of rusting, scaling, painting and polishing, the bare surface of the iron had a polish like the blade of a saw; over this was paint, and then potlead polished with shoe brushes until a fly could not have found a foothold. No possible amount of labor and care could put such a bottom on a wooden hull.

The order for the new "Flag Officers' sloop" was naturally given to Kirby, but Pocahontas proved a complete failure in the trial races. Mischief was chosen and won the match with ease. This practically ended the long battle between modeller and designer.

With the next challenge, that of Genesta, of 81 feet l.w.l., in 1885, the way was cleared for a practicable compromise between extreme theories and practices, but again the Cup Committee ordered a centerboard sloop; an enlarged Mischief with no material difference save in size. We have seen how different conditions acted to produce different types on the two sides of Cape Cod; while New York was faithful to its old love, Boston, profiting by a wider range of experiment, came to the front with the more modern Puritan and won.

have here but one genuine cutter, that was brought over from England with great expectations, although there is now less faith to be placed in her as regards speed. But when it comes to comfort I cannot see where it is to be found, the cutter being so very deep and narrow that if a person wishes berths he is obliged to sacrifice transoms, and narrow his floor. The cutter enthusiast might say there is comfort in the feeling that the boat is uncapsizable; I agree with him on that point, but this comfort is also had in our keel boats, as we carry heavy iron or lead keels.—As for the centerboards, they are a class of boats that are fast going out of use in and around Boston—i.e., boats from 20 feet upward—as it has been, and still is being shown that a keel boat in a breeze is the smarter of the two. It might be said that the centerboard has beam, and makes up the room she lacks in depth; to this I can say that more than one-half the keel boats we have here have a beam equal to that of the centerboards; also, that a number of centerboards have been changed to keels and are now taking prizes and beating centerboard boats who took prizes from them before they were changed."

The "very deep and narrow" cutter mentioned above was the first of the type seen in Boston; Kitten, designed and built by John Harvey at Wivenhoe, England, in 1852. Her dimensions were: l.o.a., 43 feet; l.w.l., 37 feet 4 inches; breadth, 8 feet 9 inches; draft, 6 feet 8 inches. With a ratio of 4¼ beams to length she could not be classed as extreme. She was brought from England in 1870 by George F. Clarke of the Dorchester Y.C.; re-christened Saxon, but her original name was restored later. In 1878 Frank E. Peabody had built by D. J. Lawlor, from the latter's design, what was called the cutter Enterprise: l.o.a., 50 feet 0 inches; l.w.l., 43 feet 9 inches; breadth, 15 feet 8 inches; draft, 7 feet 3 inches. With a proportion of 2¾ beams she had much the same profile as Cad, and the same semicircular transom. In 1880 T. W. Merrill, of the Eastern Y.C., imported a design by Michael Ratsey from which D. J. Lawlor built Edith, with yawl instead of cutter rig: l.o.a., 49 feet; l.w.l., 40 feet 8 inches; breadth, 10 feet; draft, 7 feet 3 inches. In 1883 Edward Burgess had built by Lawley & Son, from a design by J. Beavor Webb, the cutter Butterfly, l.o.a., 39 feet; l.w.l., 32 feet 6 inches; breadth, 8 feet 6 inches; draft, 6 feet 9 inches. At the same time Lawley & Son built for F. Gordon Dexter, from a design by J. Beavor Webb, the cutter Medusa, l.o.a., 63 feet; l.w.l., 54 feet; breadth, 12 feet 4 inches; draft, 9 feet 6 inches.

With the Amateur Designers

THE interest in yacht design was growing rapidly among owners. In 1883 William Gray, Jr., of the Eastern Y.C., designed the cutter Huron, l.o.a., 63 feet; l.w.l., 55 feet 6 inches; breadth, 15 feet 9 inches; draft, 8 feet. She was very well built by W. B. Smith, all her frames steam-bent, then an unusual construction; she carried 10 tons of iron under her keel. As her early performances were not satisfactory, Mr. Gray had her taken apart in 1885, the keel lengthened 9 feet, and the frames replaced. In 1884 another member of the Eastern Y.C., Henry Bryant, owner of Shadow, designed and had built by Smith the "compromise" sloop Thetis: l.o.a., 71 feet 9 inches; l.w.l., 64 feet; breadth, 19 feet; draft, 8 feet 3 inches; with board, 17 feet. As she sailed at times with a single jib and again with double headrig, she may be classed as either cutter or sloop. Her displacement was 59 tons, with 22 tons of ballast, of which 18 tons was in her lead keel. She was designed for general use rather than for racing, partly as an experiment in type, very strongly built; and though she made no notable record in racing she was a very creditable amateur effort.

In 1888 Mr. Bryant replaced her with a schooner, Alert, of 90 feet l.w.l., also of his own design, a very able cruising yacht. In 1883 J. Malcolm Forbes had built in Scotland from a design by Watson the cutter Bayadere (nicknamed by his friends Bayard-thayer after a fellow member of the Eastern Y.C.) l.o.a., 54 feet 3 inches; l.w.l., 45 feet; breadth, 9 feet 11 inches; draft, 8 feet. The cutter thus gradually worked its way into Boston yachting; all of these yachts were of the cruising type, sturdily built, and in proportions not under four beams, as compared with the six beams then found in British racing cutters and even in some of New York.

The fourth challenge for the Cup, in 1881, came from Lake Ontario, Canada, and was in the 70-foot Sloop Class, the strongest racing class in New York. However, it was considered necessary

Kitten, later Saxon, 1852

to build, in addition to the existing boats. The outstanding yacht of the Class had been Arrow, modelled and built by David Kirby in 1874, but she had been sold away from New York. The most recent addition to the Class was the iron sloop Mischief, designed by A. Cary Smith in 1879, of but 61 feet l.w.l. as compared with 70 feet for the largest of the Class. Under the existing time scale of 20 per cent this was almost a prohibitive handicap, but Mischief under the able handling of Cap'n Than Clock soon made her way to the head of the Class.

In this connection it is interesting to quote an anonymous writer in *Forest & Stream* of January 16, 1879:—"We question the utility or advantage of iron for sailing yachts of the sloop type, and think Mr. Busk may find more trouble in keeping his sloop bottom in racing condition than he expects. For cutters of deep draft and high freeboard iron, no doubt, presents the advantages of light top-sides and heavy keel and garboards, but in the ordinary sloop these elements of success disappear to a great extent, and smooth skin is lost by the use of iron, even though kept well painted. Up to five knots in short, wide craft friction is the main and almost only cause of resistance; and, as light weather is the sloop's congeniality, iron is hardly to be regarded as favorable to her best weather."

There is no question as to the detrimental effect of scale on a newly rolled plate. Cary Smith once made the statement that this scale is due to the profanity of the "boat-yarders," and my experience in a shipyard of this era leads me to believe that he was correct. However, if he had seen Mischief as I saw her on the ways just previous to her races with Atalanta, the critic would have changed his opinion. What with three seasons of rusting, scaling, painting and polishing, the bare surface of the iron had a polish like the blade of a saw; over this was paint, and then potlead polished with shoe brushes until a fly could not have found a foothold. No possible amount of labor and care could put such a bottom on a wooden hull.

The order for the new "Flag Officers' sloop" was naturally given to Kirby, but Pocahontas proved a complete failure in the trial races. Mischief was chosen and won the match with ease. This practically ended the long battle between modeller and designer.

With the next challenge, that of Genesta, of 81 feet l.w.l., in 1885, the way was cleared for a practicable compromise between extreme theories and practices, but again the Cup Committee ordered a centerboard sloop; an enlarged Mischief with no material difference save in size. We have seen how different conditions acted to produce different types on the two sides of Cape Cod; while New York was faithful to its old love, Boston, profiting by a wider range of experiment, came to the front with the more modern Puritan and won.

TRADITIONS AND MEMORIES OF

American Yachting

By WILLIAM P. STEPHENS

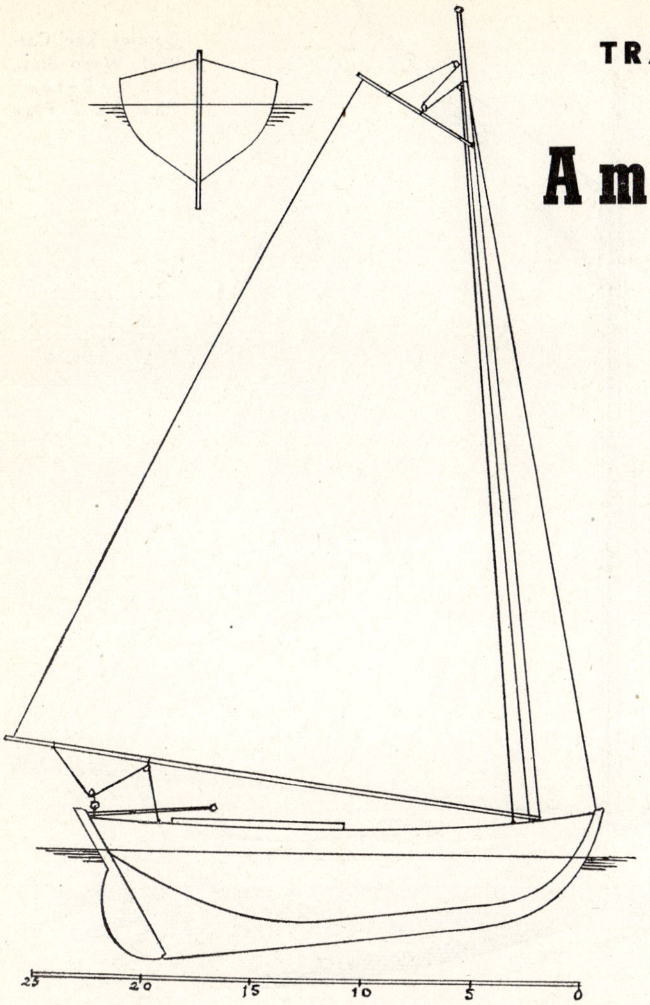

Part Thirty-seven

East of the Cape

(Continued)

Above: The "Newport Boat," 1836.
Right: Egeria, Half-Decked Catboat with Cuddy, C. C. Hanley, 1890

THE catboat is unquestionably an American craft. When one was sent to Cowes in 1852 by William Butler Duncan as a gift to the Marquis of Connyngham she was at once recognized as an American novelty; and her name, Una, was adopted and is still in use in England to describe the type. The catboat is essentially a half-decked sailboat of from 15 to 30 feet in length, of extreme breadth and limited draft, fitted with a centerboard, and with one mast—carrying a boom-and-gaff mainsail—stepped as close as possible to the stem. The origin of the type is unknown, it seems to have grown up spontaneously in different parts of the country, as it is peculiar to no one locality. The construction is simple, a plumb stem, a broad upright transom, usually carvel built on grown frames. In such localities as South Jersey, where white cedar once was plentiful, any fisherman or hunter could find material in the cedar swamps, the roots furnishing the frames and the trunks almost the finest planking known for boats and yachts of medium size. With an ax and saw and the aid of a neighboring sawmill the material was ready at small cost, and no great amount of skill was required in the construction.

One great advantage of the type was the limited draft, eked out by a centerboard; but keel catboats are found in a few localities, the most noted being known locally not as a catboat, but as a "Newport boat," and, sometimes, as a "Point boat" and the "Newport rig." The type and names are limited to Narragansett Bay and the vicinity of Newport, R. I. The type is described in the following letter:

Baltimore, Md., Sept. 28, 1887

Forest & Stream Publishing Co.,

Gentlemen:—

In Forest & Stream of July 28, 1887, there is a cut of the Shadow, which you speak of as a deep boat; as

a schoolboy in 1836-8 I spent a good deal of time in Newport, R. I., and at that period the boats in general use were deep keels, and I cannot remember to have seen a single centerboard boat in Newport Harbor. I enclose a sketch drawn from memory of a "Newport boat" of the period of which I write. The ballast, several tons of iron or iron-stone (ore?), was stored under the floor, a boat of 20 feet waterline had a keel usually 12 to 14 inches deep, and such a boat drew from 4½ to 5 feet of water. These boats were reported to sail within 3½ points of the wind. As the Shadow was built at Bristol, R. I., it would seem natural that her designer should produce a deep boat.

Yours respectfully,

(Signed) MORTON TOULMIN

Assuming that the writer's sketch is approximately correct, this ancient craft is suggestive of the British cutters of a century ago: just under three beams, a very similar profile and midship section; with her draft and drag she should be weatherly and readily maneuverable. Her dimensions were: l.o.a., 23 feet 6 inches, l.w.l., 22 feet; breadth, 7 feet 9 inches; draft, 4 feet 9 inches. The rig seems large, mast 36 feet 6 inches, deck to hound; boom, 24 feet; gaff, 6 feet; sail area, 445 square feet.

This letter carries the origin of the "Newport boat" back to a very early date; with Narragansett Bay studded with small islands, each with one or more farms, and other farms on points of the main land, a sail boat was as essential as a carriage and team to a farmer in a dry country; and these boats, by the way, all of lapstrake construction, were built to meet a practical need. That in time racing should have developed follows as a matter of course, and in *The Spirit of The Times* of 1853 we find an account of a race sailed off Bristol on October 3 of that year. There were 16 starters, in four classes, and among the five starters in the third class was the catboat Julia. The dimensions of the yachts and the names of the owners are not given, but Julian Herreshoff, father of John B. and Nathaniel G., owned four boats of this name; and, as Julia II was not built until 1864, this was probably Julia I. In 1885 Mr. Herreshoff showed me Julia IV, and pointed with pride to what I understood was a device of his own; two rails about a foot apart laid thwartship from bilge to bilge amidships, on which ran a small car carrying 550 pounds of iron; this was first fitted aboard Julia II. In a breeze this car was locked to windward, when about to tack a catch was tripped and it ran to the lee bilge, locking itself as the boat heeled in the opposite direction on her new tack. A similar car carrying 1,000 pounds of iron was fitted by John B. Herreshoff aboard Kelpie I, of 25 feet l.w.l., but it proved impracticable. While fixed ballast below the floor was used in ordinary service about Narragansett Bay, and when employed as "party-boats," in racing a part of this ballast was sent ashore, being replaced by sandbags to be shifted to windward.

In what is intended to be a technical comment on the "Newport boat," in *The Scientific American* in 1876, the model is described as follows: "The marked feature of these craft is the broad shoulders, this name being technically given to the part of the vessel just at the waterline; which, as the boat rolls, is above or below water as the case may be. By adding to the shoulders of a vessel the builder makes use of the *fluidity of the water* as a substitute for the deadweight of ballast, and thus gains greatly in stability. The bottom of the boat is always the upsetting, and the shoulders the righting power, so that on the predominance of one over the other the craft is stable or crank."

Caprice, Keel Catboat, Wood Bros., 1881. Below: The Sail Plan

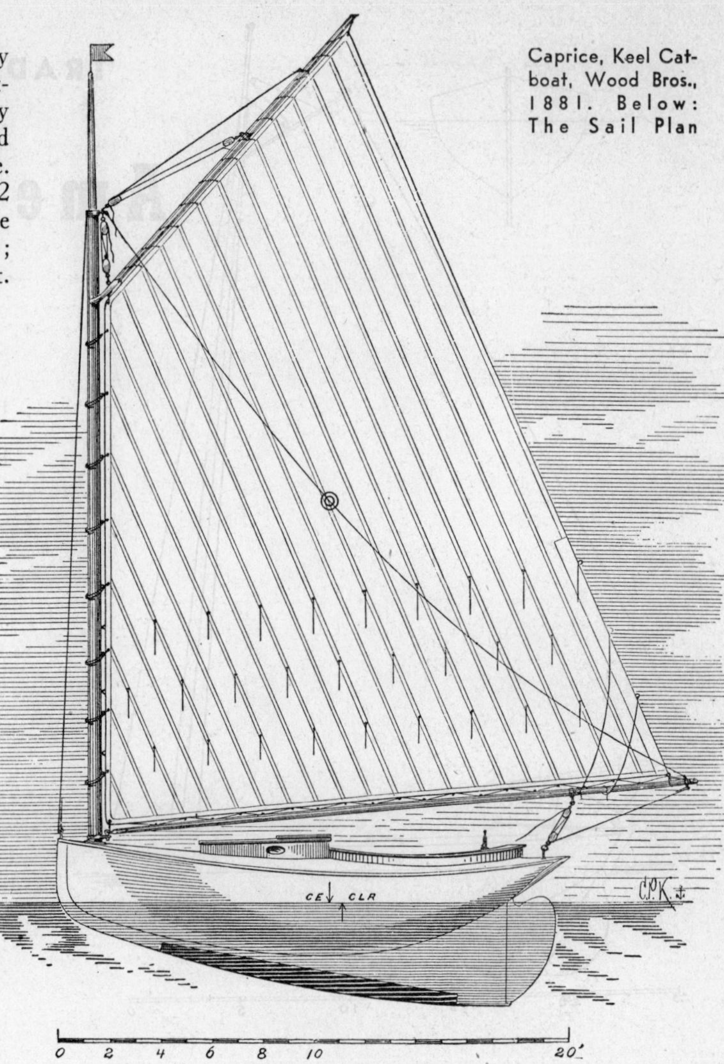

CAPRICE—SAIL PLAN.

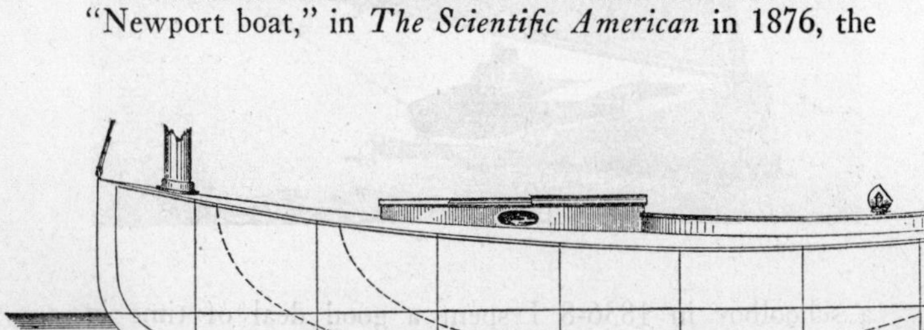

The Catboat in Massachusetts Bay

Interesting as it was in itself, the "Newport boat" was "another breed of cats" from those of the North side of the Cape; nearly all centerboard, of a different model, and carvel-built. The keel type, however, was not entirely unknown, and a very good example is found in Caprice, designed and built by Wood Bros. in 1881. Her dimensions were: l.o.a, 20 feet; l.w.l., 17 feet 6 inches; breadth, 8 feet 5 inches; draft, 4 feet. The sail area was 415 square feet; the least freeboard 1 foot 1 inch; the displacement 5,750 pounds; ballast, 1,856 pounds. The keel was of iron, 856 pounds, with 1,000 pounds of lead inside. The hull, with an average deadrise of 30 degrees, was similar to the centerboard hulls of the period; the profile was the same as the larger keel yachts built by the Woods. As to the suitability of the rig in open waters, the following letter appeared in *Forest & Stream* of October 4, 1883: "Concerning the rig of catboats spoken of in your last issue, my experience in such boats leads me to the belief that the heavy spar in the eyes of the boat is a disadvantage which it would be well to do away with for outside work and cruising in rough, open water such as we have about Massachusetts Bay. But the position of the mast cannot be

Mab, Half-Decked Catboat, Herreshoff, 1891

helped in a catboat, as it is a necessary evil of the rig. For sailing such as we have between Boston and Marblehead, just let some of your centerboard fellows follow my keel cat before the wind in a heavy sea, when the rollers look as though they were coming into the standing-room. That is when an iron shoe and deep keel aft tell."

(Signed) "CATBOAT."

From a theoretical standpoint this reasoning seems correct, but it was contradicted, even at that day, by the actual work—fishing in rough water and all weather—which the Crosby catboats were doing; with a heavy solid mast stepped as close to the apron as structural limitations would permit.

While keel boats were strictly in the minority, Hutchings & Pryor built a number for their own use, for hire; Prima Donna and Ianthe with V-sterns, and Undine, Racine, Molly and Millie with square transoms. The keel cat Charlotte, 20 feet 3 inches, l.w.l., was built by her owner, George G. Garraway, in 1881. He was perhaps the only colored yachtsman in Boston, and was known as "Nigger" Garraway by his associates in the Hull Y. C. When, in 1884, A. Bryan Alley of the Seawanhaka C.Y.C. took his sandbagger Cruiser to Boston to race the local boats, a few real sandbaggers were built locally, though, as already told, shifting ballast was generally prohibited. "Nigger" Garraway built Thrasher, of similar model, in 1885; but the extreme craft like Thrasher and M.L.I., the latter 19 by 10, never became popular.

The centerboard catboats, of which there were many, ran in length from 16 to 21 feet l.w.l., with about 2 feet greater length over all for the smaller and 3 feet for the larger. The "Burgess boys" experimented with every type of yacht, in 1882 Sydney had a Clapham sharpie. Caper, 15 feet l.w.l., in the same year he had built Teal or Tomboy, 18 feet l.w.l., a Mersey canoe-yawl, from a design by Dixon Kemp; in 1875 Edward had the Herreshoff sloop Nimbus, 33 feet 6 inches l.w.l.; in the same year Arthur had the Herreshoff sloop Fanchon, 25 feet 6 inches l.w.l.; in 1881 Edward had the keel sloop or cutter Moya, 26 feet 6 inches l.w.l., designed by A. Cary Smith; and Sydney had the sloop Playmate, 27 feet l.w.l. In 1882 Edward had the cutter Columbine, 20 feet l.w.l.; and in 1883 he had built by Lawley, from a design by J. Beavor Webb, the cutter, Butterfly, 32 feet, 6 inches l.w.l. Most of the boats of the family, however, were cats, and from the Bristol shop; in 1872 Edward owned Blue Bell, 15 feet; Walter owned Pansy, 21 feet and Pink, 12 feet; Sydney owned Rose, 14 feet; and Arthur owned Tulip, 16 feet. In 1875 Walter owned Tulip and Sydney owned Peri, 18 feet. Most of the early sailing and racing of the family was done in these and similar small catboats. It was this early sailing in a variety of types and sizes of yachts which, in default of the long technical training now deemed necessary, laid the foundation for the success of Edward Burgess as a naval architect.

Small as most of the Boston catboats were, they were used for general sailing about Massachusetts Bay, for passages to and from

Mabel, Half-Decked Catboat

the various clubs, and regularly for racing at these clubs, the competition being very keen from about 1880 on. In Olsen's *Yacht List* for 1875 no less than 70 of these boats are entered, and the number increased with the general growth of yachting. In 1885 there were 53 catboats enrolled in the Hull Y. C. fleet, only 5 keel, and in length from 15 to 21 feet l.w.l. The racing was well maintained among the smaller clubs through the eighties, but in the early nineties fashion's changes were evident; there came into existence new types, the 21-foot restricted sloops, the knockabout and the raceabout classes, various sizes of fin-keels, dories, and a number of one-design classes, the small open catboat gradually losing favor. A powerful factor in the eclipse of the type was the advent in yachting of the "Cape cat," a development so extensive and important as to demand a separate chapter. The Herreshoff shop turned out perhaps a majority of the catboats sailed on Massachusetts Bay from 1870 to 1890, one of the most noted being the little Mab, built for John Shaw, a keen racing man most closely identified with the Quincy and Hull Yacht Clubs. She was 18 feet 10 inches over all; 15 feet 10 inches l.w.l.; 7 feet 6 inches breadth and 1 foot 6 inches draft. Launched in 1891, she soon demonstrated her superiority over the older boats, and held first place for some years.

TRADITIONS AND MEMORIES OF AMERICAN YACHTING

By WILLIAM P. STEPHENS

Part Thirty-eight

East of the Cape

(Continued)

IN considering the term catboat the question of yachting terminology again comes up; whatever its origin, the term first applied to a definite type of hull with an equally definite rig: the hull very wide and shoal, with a centerboard, the rig a single mast with a boom-and-gaff sail. In course of time these meanings were expanded and confused, and we find in the second stage of the Cape cat a veritable sloop which could not sail without her jib; later the cat-yawl, with mast stepped in the eyes and a small mizzen aft; still later, with the after mast stepped nearly amidships and a large mizzen, the "double-cat," so called in the West.

The Cape Cod catboat or, more briefly, the "Cape Cat," is a type distinctly original, which has played an important part in American yachting, especially in the years immediately preceding and following the end of the last century. It will be noted that in the effort to discover the origin of most craft there is little to guide save conjecture and tradition, but we are more fortunate in the case of the Cape cat, as its birthplace and origin seem to be positively settled; while most of the vital points of its history are matters of positive record. Some time prior to 1850 Andrew Crosby, a ship carpenter, had settled at West Bay, Osterville on the South side of the Cape on Nantucket Sound, and about seven miles southwest of Barnstable on the North side of the Cape and on Massachusetts bay. He and his wife, "Aunt Theresa," had two sons, Worthington and Horace. When Andrew died, about 1850, the sons were about twenty years old.

Much of the fishing about Cape Cod was done from small double-ended boats called pinkies, a Dutch term; the two ends similar and the after ends of the planking being housed in a rabbet in the sternpost just as the fore ends were housed in the stem. The Block Island boats, from 20 to 23 feet over all, were examples of the earlier form. Later the stem was extended and the after ends of the bulwarks carried abaft the sternpost, meeting in a V transom similar to a dory and forming a seat for a man and a rest for the boom when lowered. This form of pinkie and the Block Island boats were rather narrow, they would not carry a full fare of fish, and they were slow.

Acting under the inspiration of their mother, who was a Spiritualist, after the death of their father the boys started to build a boat of an entirely new type; very wide, with plumb stem and plumb square transom and one mast stepped as far forward as possible; the first boat was but 14 feet long. The launching brought fisher folk from all along the coast, some by land and many in their pinkies to test her speed; the comment was that such a stern never would negotiate Chatham Bar. With the large mainsail set, Horace took the tiller and very soon out-sailed the older boats. Larger boats followed, and with their large open cockpits for fishing and their hold capacity they soon outclassed the pinkies.

The crucial question of Chatham Bar was settled about 1860 when Captain Nickerson of Chatham placed an order on the promise of Horace that he need not pay for her if she were not successful. She proved not only faster than the old boats, carrying a larger fare of fish, but able

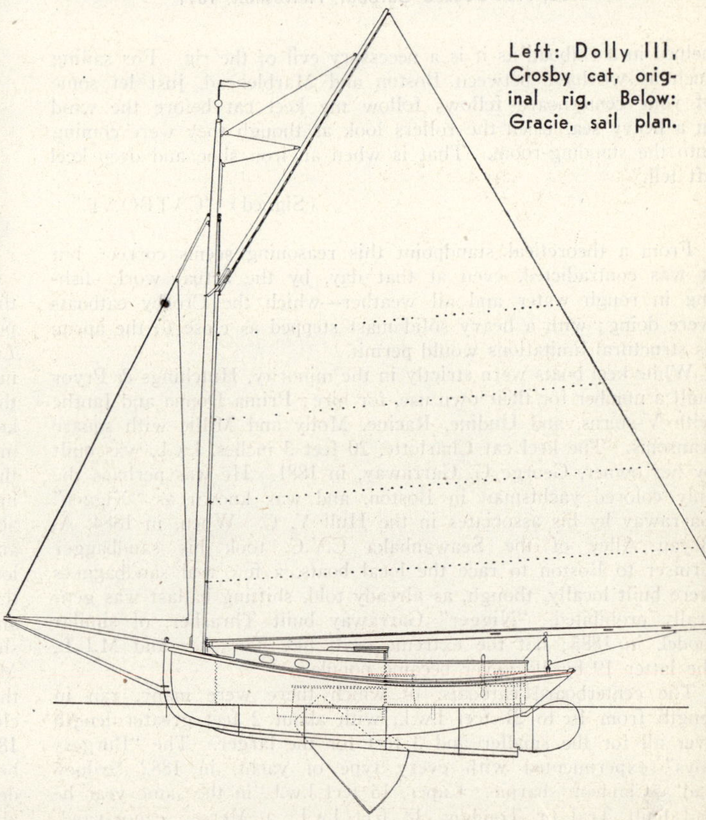

Left: Dolly III, Crosby cat, original rig. Below: Gracie, sail plan.

and seaworthy in the rough waters of the Bar. As orders came in from fishermen and many boats were built and tested, improvements followed, over one hundred boats being built as the new catboat displaced the two older types. A boat was built for a brother of Captain Nickerson, but later the two decided to build together a catboat of 48 feet which they named "The Big Nickerson." The partnership was soon dissolved and the boat sold to Captain Robinson, who sailed her for many years on fishing trips to George's Banks for cod, her seaworthiness being proved by the heavy weather which she encountered on this turbulent course.

The early Cape cats were built much like their sisters of South Jersey, from the native forests with only an ax, a handsaw and a local sawmill. The keel and stem were of oak, the frames were hewn and sawn from the native pitch pine trees, and the planking of native white cedar. The Cape Cod men claimed, and probably justly, that the pitch pine would outlast even the oak. All work was done with hand tools except the sawing of logs, which was done in the old tidal sawmills which once existed in every part of the Atlantic coast. What could be more restful and fascinating than the slow forward movement of the great carriage on which the log was dogged as it hitched its way along, inch by inch while the great saw, some eight inches or more in width with teeth two inches long, stretched tight in its vertical frame, moved slowly up and down, eating its way through the log? Such sawmills as these were my chosen playgrounds in my youth; two pieces from one of the long boards of clear white pine made the sides for my first bateau. Today on the North West coast similar work is done by steam-driven bandsaws sixteen inches wide, with teeth on both edges, a slab being thrown off as the carriage moves swiftly one way, and another on the reverse. A staff of experts is maintained to "peen" the middle of each saw after a certain amount of use in order that it shall run true on the upper and lower drums. It was not until 1892, when the business was growing, that a steam power saw was installed in the shop of H. Manley Crosby, and he was the first to use steam-bent oak frames in place of the grown pitch pine.

The Cape Cat in New York Waters

My first acquaintance with the Cape cat is best told in the following letter from one of my most intimate yachting associates of sixty years ago.

Pass-a-Grille, Fla., February 17, 1942

"I bought Gracie through a young Yankee yacht broker who gave me a list of boats for sale on the Cape during the winter of 1887-8; Leslie Burritt and I went to Barnstable, put up at a little inn, and the next day looked at Gracie and several other boats laid up on the beach, after which we hired a rig and drove over to Osterville, where Gracie had been built the previous winter by Herbert F. Crosby. We looked at several other boats and had the history of Gracie from her builder. She was built for two lobstermen who did not agree and wished to sell her; Crosby assured us that she was less than a year old and as well built as he knew how, and from the appearance of the other boats in his shop this was satisfactory to us. One of the things which interested me most was the construction of the keel and trunk, a slit was sawn in the center of the keel about twenty inches longer at each end than the length of the slot, the two sides of the keel were wedged far enough apart to take the headledges, and the spaces fore and aft were filled with triangular blocks of oak. We noted the heavy stem construction, the 8-inch hexagonal mast coming within 16 inches of the fore side of the stem. Gracie—as she was re-named by Mr. Serrell after his daughter—was the best bargain we saw, and considerably cheaper than Crosby would build a new boat. My only objection was that the cabin was only

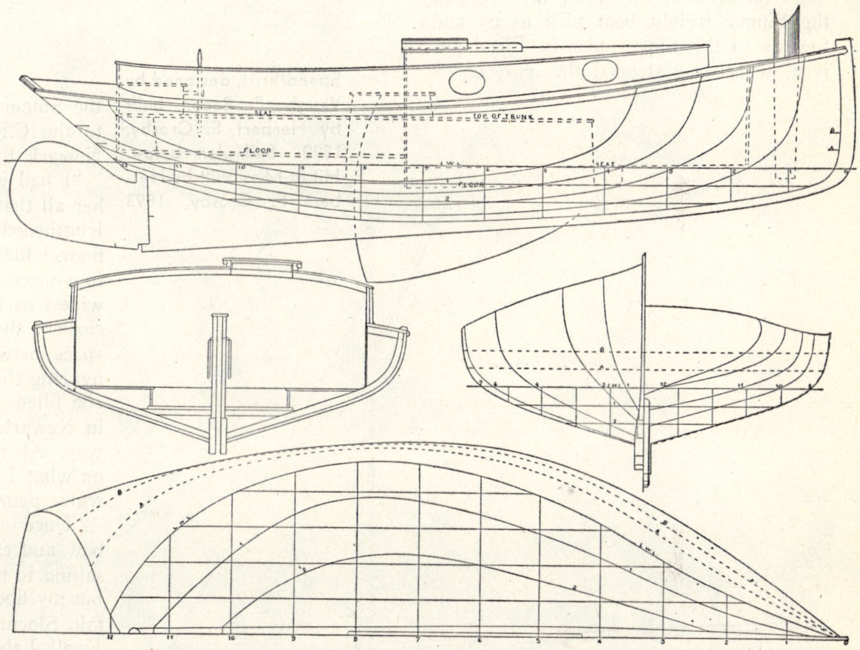

Gracie, owned by J. A. Serrell. Cape cat built by Herbert F. Crosby, 1887

a cubby hole about six feet long; and the cockpit, over nine feet long, was not self-draining.

"We made a bargain with the broker to deliver the boat early in the spring at the Boston pier of the Boston and New York freight steamer, and on the day agreed on she came sailing in from Barnstable and tied up alongside the steamer. We turned to and stripped her, the deck crane pulled her mast out and then landed her on the fore deck. We gave the head stevedore a dollar to get rid of the half ton of cobble stones with which she had been ballasted, but when we met the boat in New York we found that some kind soul had carefully put them aboard the steamer, and we had to hand out another dollar to get rid of them. The New York end of the line delivered her with her spars on deck in the water and we had the Singer freight boat pick us up and tow us to the Singer pier in Elizabethport, where we stepped the mast under

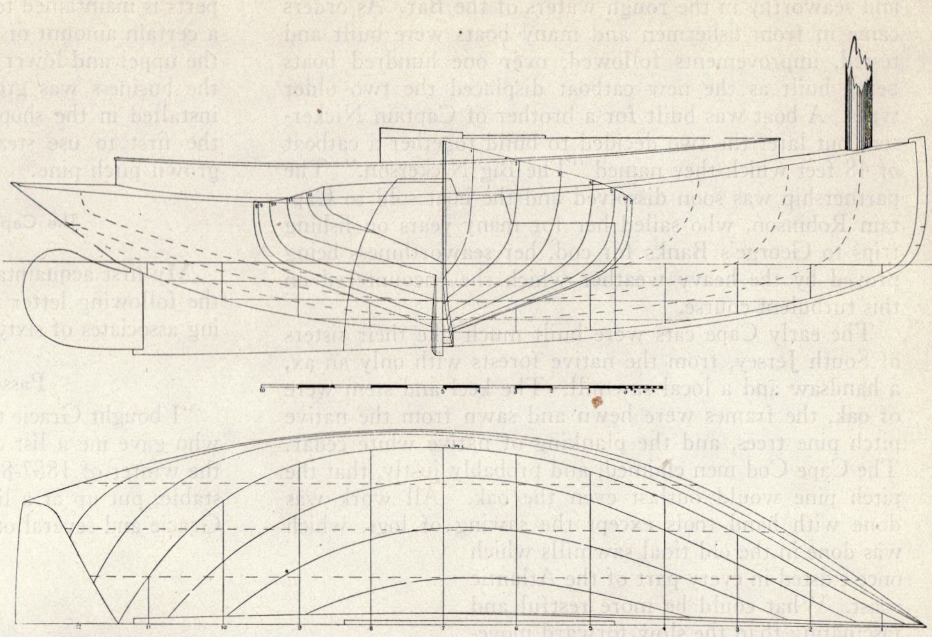

Spendthrift, designed by Vaughn D. Bacon, built by Herbert F. Crosby, 1890. Sail plan, below. Hit or Miss built by Herbert F. Crosby, 1893

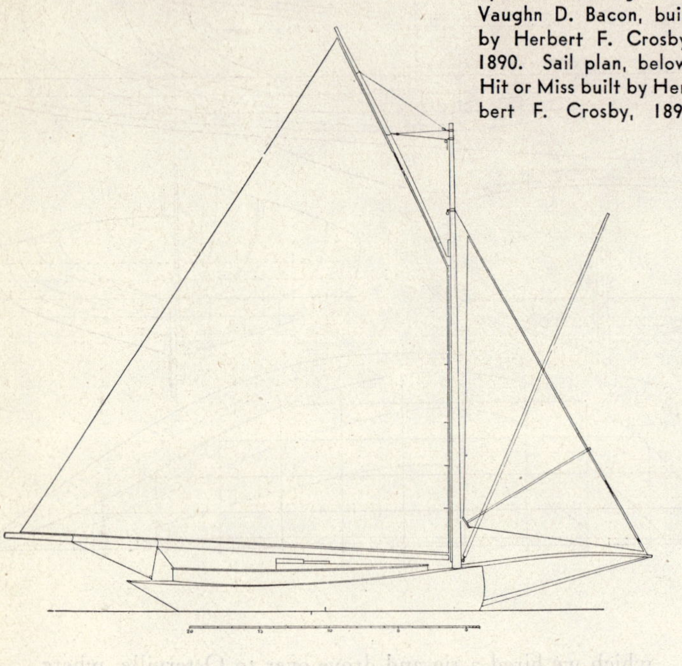

the Singer crane, bent the sails, and sailed a very tender boat dowr to the C.R.R. drawbridge over Newark Bay and then up to the Newark Bay Boat Club at Bayonne, N. J.

"I had iron ballast cast at a little foundry near home, and sailed her all that summer with it and the small cuddy. The next winter I lengthened the cabin house about three feet and put in a cockpi floor which was self-draining (if not crowded too hard), fitted a four-piece iron keel about three inches deep and seven inches at the widest part, and made up the ballast with inside lead moulded to fit close to the keel. I also bought a bale of cork and fitted it into the space between the cockpit coaming and the skin under the deck figuring that this, with the wood in the hull, would keep her afloat if she filled. I had one opportunity to test my theory, one calm day in Newark Bay a "twister" came along as we lay without steerage way. All that I could do was to put the helm hard down and sit up on what I knew would be the high side, as I watched the barrels o water pour over the high coaming before she came into the wind.

"Once or twice we had a barrel—or a hogshead—of water over the bow and cabintop in that strong chop near Swinburne Island wher sailing to the Highlands in a strong southerly wind with an ebb tide but my floor took that all right. One day we had a brush with Captain Slocum in his Spray, we were in the Lower Bay, near Flynn's Knoll, I think, when she crossed our bow, so we started to chase her She freed off for Keyport and we chased her for a half hour bu could not get by on a free wind so gave up the chase and headed for

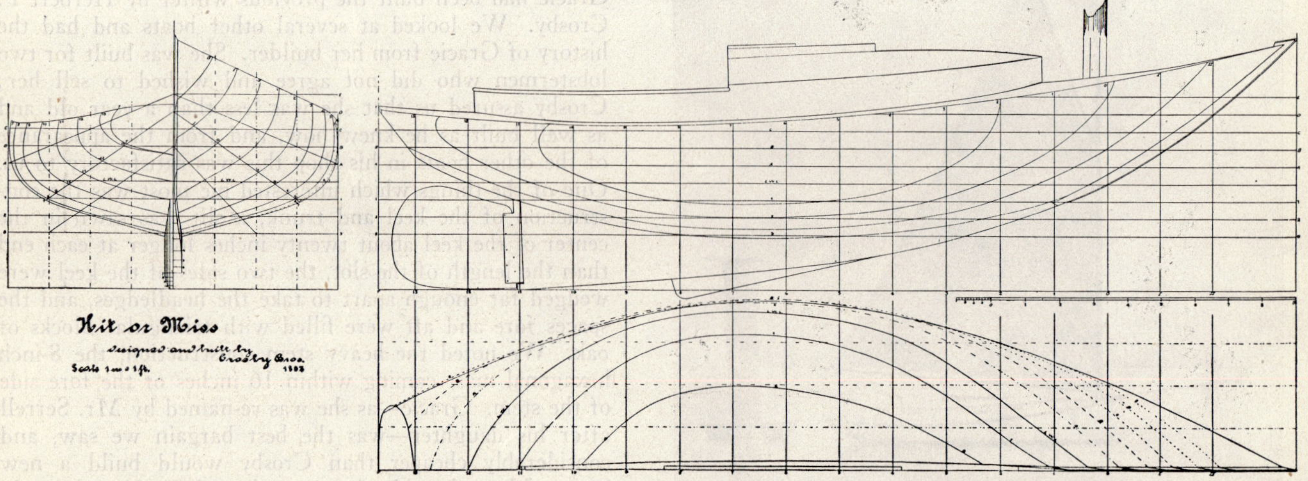

the Highlands. I believe that Gracie was the first Cape cat in New York Harbor, I kept her until I built Thermo in 1900; the last I heard of her she was somewhere up the Hudson and defiled with a gasoline engine."

(*signed*) J. A. SERRELL.

In spite of the fling at the gasoline engine, Thermo, designed by Mr. Serrell, was probably the first attempt at what is now so popular as the "motor-sailer" or "fifty-fifty"; a sailing man's effort to enjoy the pleasure of sailing in spite of limited time, calms and adverse tides. Powered with a gasoline engine, she was rigged as a schooner with an effective sail area. When she was fitted out in her second season, I think, at Billy Force's yard at Keyport, new mast wedges were put in and neatly cut off, the chisel cuts penetrating into the mast. When a man went aloft to set up the triatic stay the mast snapped where it had been cut. I fell heir to the wreck, a piece of strong tough spruce, and since 1901 it has done duty as mainmast of my Snikersnee. In 1903 Mr. Serrell designed a larger yacht of the same type, Rampant, a motor cruser of 56 feet waterline with raised deck, central pilot house and control, and a schooner rig which was really efficient; in her he cruised between New York and Florida and she was still in service within the past two years.

Sloop or Catboat?

THE sail plan of Gracie, her original rig, shows a very long bowsprit and a big jib, which she carried in common with all the catboats of her and a later generation. Just how this change of rig came about does not appear; the plain fact is that for fifty years the "Cape catboat" has been a sloop. Her dimensions were: L.o.a., 24 feet 4 inches; l.w.l., 21 feet 5 inches; breadth, extreme, 10 feet 11 inches, breadth at l.w.l., 9 feet 9 inches; draft, 2 feet 6 inches; freeboard, bow, 2 feet 5 inches, least, 1 feet 7 inches, stern, 2 feet. The mast, an 8-inch octagon in the partners, fore side 1 foot 6 inches abaft the stem, was 30 feet 10 inches deck to truck, bowsprit 9 feet 9 inches outboard; boom, 22 feet 4 inches; gaff, 19 feet; spinnaker boom, 23 feet 6 inches. Though a part of the original rig, the bowsprit has all the appearance of a jury rig or after thought; it is fitted by a mortice over the stemhead, the inboard end held down by a cleat on the mast. The area of the mainsail was 657 square feet; jib, 104 square feet; total, 751 square feet.

A similar yacht, Spendthrift, was built by Herbert F. Crosby, from a design by her owner, Vaughn D. Bacon, of Barnstable, an amateur designer; she was over all 25 feet 5 inches; l.w.l, 21 feet 10 inches; breadth, extreme, 10 feet 6 inches; on l.w.l 9 feet 6 inches; draft, 2 feet 6 inches; freeboard, 3 feet 8 inches and 2 feet. Mast 9 inches in diameter, stepped 1 foot 6 inches abaft stem; deck to truck, 31 feet; bowsprit outboard, 12 feet 3 inches; boom, 32 feet, gaff, 18 feet; spinnaker boom, 26 feet; mainsail, 632 square feet; jib, 134 square feet; total, 766 square feet.

FASHIONS change in yachts as in dress, and after the advent of Gloriana in 1891 the "Gloriana bow" was found on all types of yachts regardless of general form of hull; in 1893 Herbert F. Crosby built for Frank M. Randall of the Pavonia Y. C., one of his best customers, the yacht Hit or Miss, her dimensions being: L.o.a., 27 feet 1 inch; l.w.l., 18 feet 10 inches; breadth, extreme, 9 feet 9 inches; l.w.l., 9 feet; draft, 3 feet; freeboard, 4 feet, 1 foot 8 inches, 2 feet 3 inches. The rudder construction was unusual and not to be recommended, the stock was of cast iron, 2 inches in diameter, with two flanges on the lower part between which the blade, of 1½-inch oak, was fitted and bolted. Nearly sixty years ago an ingenious mechanic and boat sailer of Fall River, Babbitt, put out a special line of yacht fittings, blocks with skeleton shells of cast brass or iron and wheels in metallic bearings; and, in particular, the "Babbitt hoist," a mast track of wood with a V-groove on each side and a slide for both boom and gaff, all of these fittings were generally used on the Crosby and other local boats and proved successful.

It is safe to say that if the naval architect of today, unfamiliar with this type, were given the dimensions of Gracie and told to produce a safe, seaworthy and useful boat he would decline the task as impossible; but against such theory there is nearly a century of successful operation in many lines. Originally built as a working fishing boat, the Cape cat with its large open cockpit is well adapted for the ordinary fishing party, while the sturdy seaworthy hull, with its small angle of heel, was well suited to the average "tripper," and the type was largely used as a party boat from New London to Gloucester. As the use of the type extended to New York and Massachusetts Bay waters it was taken up by racing men and developed by the Crosbys and their rival, C. C. Hanley, of Monument Beach on the Cape, solely for racing.

Only a genealogist could trace the many decendants of the original Andrew Crosby, all engaged in building in the vicinity of Osterville and Barnstable; D. & C. H. Crosby, Herbert F., Wilton, and H. Manley; today the Crosby Yacht Building and Storage Co. carries on a large business at the old port, Osterville, specializing in the traditional type first developed by the family and in a large line of small sloops and catboats for junior sailors.

TRADITIONS AND MEMORIES OF

American Yachting

Part Thirty-nine

East of the Cape

(Continued)

By WILLIAM P. STEPHENS

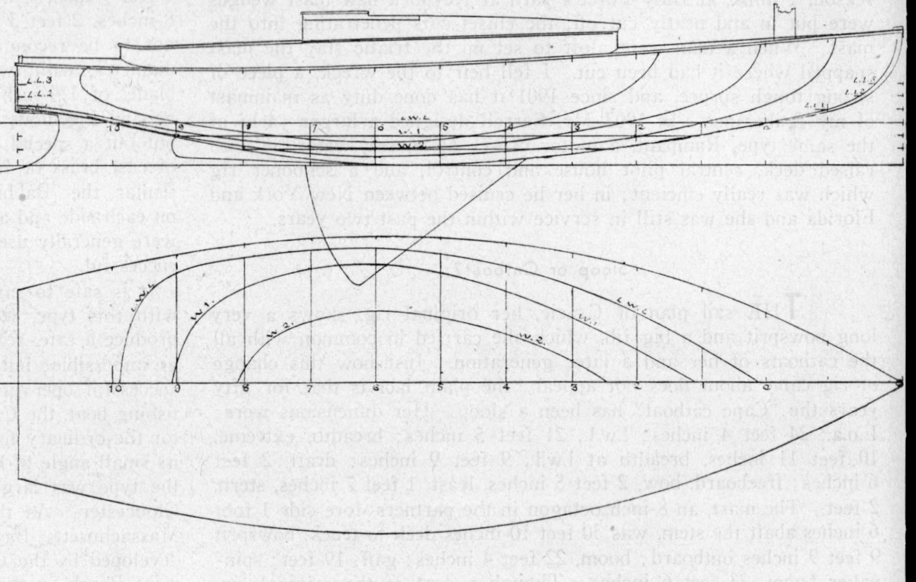

As the Cape Cat increased in numbers and popularity it was diverted from its original use as a fishing boat and later a party boat, and began a new career as a racing yacht. The original builders, the Crosbys, found a dangerous rival in C. C. Hanley, of Monument Beach on the lower part of the Cape, who was perhaps the first to realize the full possibilities of the type for racing. In 1888 he built for himself a catboat, Mucilage, which he raced successfully in local races about Buzzard's Bay.

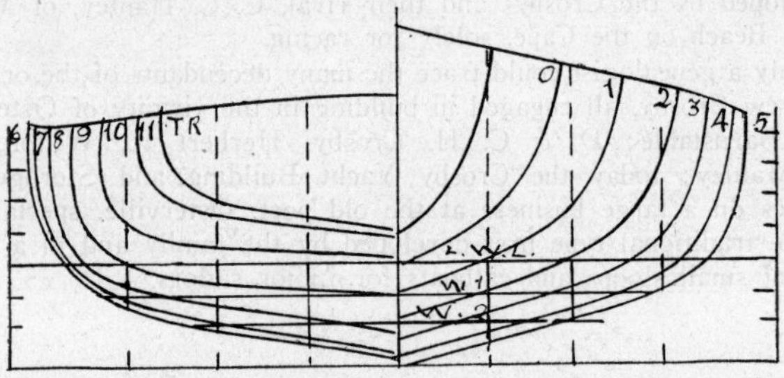

Lines of Step Lively, designed and built by H. Manley Crosby in 1896

On July 4 of the following year a special race for catboats was scheduled to be sailed off Newport. E. D. Morgan, of the New York Y. C., was anxious to take part in it and, knowing of the reputation of Mucilage, bought her and won the race. He had no further use for her and shortly after sold to Commodore Elbridge T. Gerry, who re-named her Iris and gave her to his sons to sail about Newport. They soon tired of her and she was stored away and forgotten.

When the racing of the class was at its height, about 1906, Commodore Frank Fessenden Crane, of the Quincy Y. C., recalled the old boat, bought her, and started her on a new career of racing; her record for 31 starts being 14 firsts, 3 seconds, 3 thirds, 8 fourths, 2 fifths and 1 seventh.

Apropos of her original name, suggestive of anything other than speed, most of the owners of racing catboats kept clear of the conventionally stencilled Sallys, Teals, Gypseys and Vagrants and sought names which were original and distinctive, though sometimes absurd for racing craft: Mucilage, Creep and Crawl. The long record of catboat racing is made up of many original names, Mucilage, Mudjekeewis, Moondyne, Almira, Dartwell, Arawak, Savitar, Step Lively and Hustler.

There was very keen rivalry in 1889 between the cutter Saracen, designed by Burgess for William P. Fowle of the Corinthian Y. C. of Marblehead, and Kathleen, designed by William Gardner, then almost unknown, for William Whitlock of the Seawanhaka C. Y. C.; the two of similar type and both in the new 30-foot class. Saracen visited New York and sailed several races with Kathleen and the latter, in turn, visited Massachusetts Bay.

On July 15, 1889 the Eastern Y. C. held a race off Marblehead for the two and an unknown yacht, the Cape Cat Harbinger, was allowed to enter. To the surprise of all, the unknown, though nearly two feet shorter, won by 20 minutes from the cutters. This race, apparently won on merit, followed by another shortly after, carried the fame of the Cape Cat far beyond all local limits, and served further to advertise Hanley. The rivalry of Saracen and Kathleen, Burgess against Gardner and Boston against New York, was watched with keen interest by yachtsmen far and wide, and when both were defeated by an unknown craft the interest shifted to the new type.

The accompanying sketch, made at the time in Mr. Burgess' office, shows the cutter and cat sail plans. Elf, a new addition to the 30-foot class, designed by George F. Lawley, was chosen as nearer to the length of Harbinger. With an over-all length of 35 feet 6 inches, her waterline was 28 feet 6 inches; breadth, 11 feet; draft, 6 feet 8 inches. Harbinger was 28 feet 10 inches over all; 27 feet 10 inches waterline; 13 feet breadth and 2 feet 6 inches draft. With mainsail, jib, fore staysail and working topsail Elf carried 1,397 square feet compared with 1,362 square feet in Harbinger's mainsail and jib. Off the wind, each carrying a 28-foot spinnaker boom, Elf had 1,681 square feet in mainsail, working topsail and spinnaker, while Harbinger carried 1,551 square feet in mainsail and spinnaker. Under the old Seawanhaka Rule, Elf measured 1,704 square feet and Harbinger 1,550 square feet. Harbinger was built for Joseph R. Hooper, of the Hull Y. C. who raced her successfully for four years, but discarded her in 1892 for the latest novelty in yachting, the Herreshoff fin-keel Handsel: in later years this same devotion to the

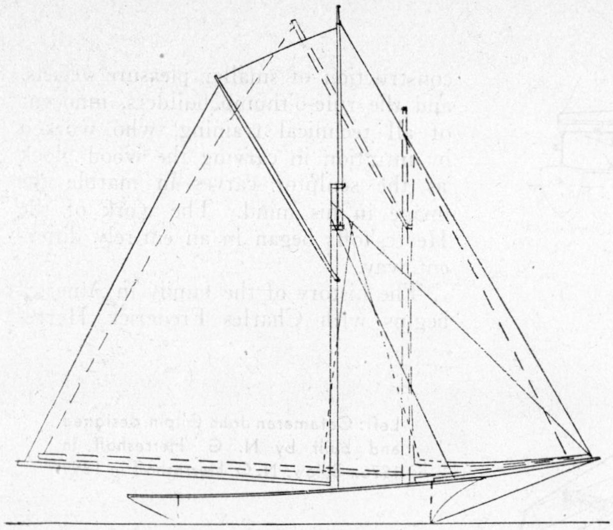

Harbinger, designed and built by C. C. Hanley in 1888. Above, a comparison of sail plans, cutter and catboat

demands of fashion acted to break up the Class as Raters, Sonderboats and other new types were introduced.

The Crosbys soon adapted themselves to the racing game and the contest between them and Hanley continued for some years. While their models were fined down and the construction somewhat lightened, the Crosby cats were true to their lineage, always sturdy and powerful. Coming into the game in its racing stage, Hanley as a rule built lighter boats. He was an artist in the building of this size of yacht, laying all the plank himself.

The popularity of the Class about New York was due mainly to the efforts of one man, Frank M. Randall, of the Pavonia Y. C. of Bayonne and later of the Atlantic Y. C. Just how many Crosby boats he bought or had built it is impossible to say, but he owned many and raced them on Upper New York Bay and about the West end of Long Island Sound. In 1896 he was instrumental in organizing the Crosby Catboat and Yacht Building Company at Bay Ridge, Long Island, with H. Manley Crosby, who is still alive, at its head. Step Lively, built for Mr. Randall, represents the extreme development of the Class under the stimulus of keen racing, with a reverse at each end of the waterline and no outside keel or deadwood. Her dimensions were: L.o.a., 34 feet 9 inches;

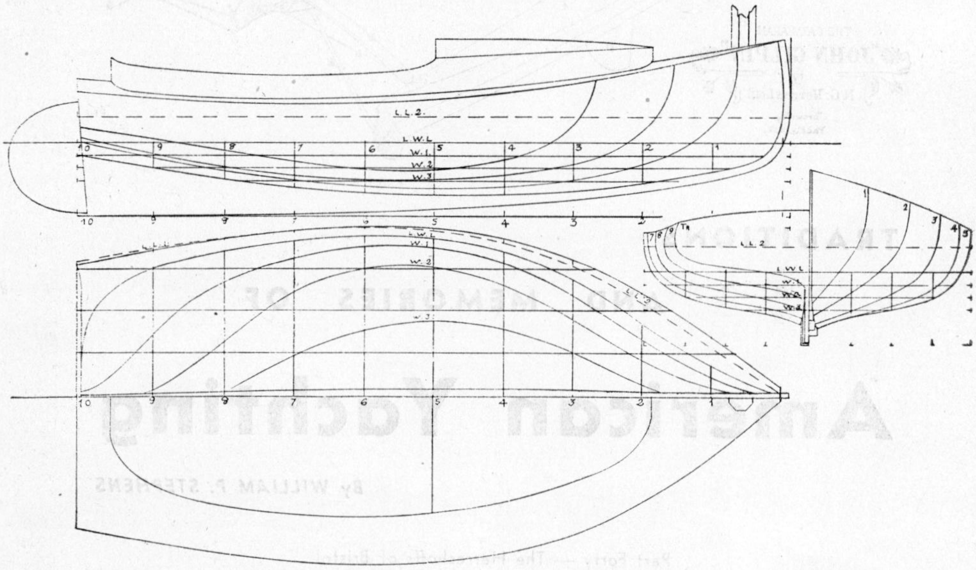

l.w.l., 25 feet 6 inches; breadth, 11 feet 3 inches; draft, 1 foot 9 inches; area of mainsail, 1,050 square feet.

Launched on May 30, 1896, she was second in a race of the Atlantic Y. C. On June 6 and 13 she was first in races in the same Club. On June 15 she won a race of the Brooklyn Y. C. and next day was first in a race of the Atlantic Y. C. In the Larchmont Y. C. race of June 30 she sailed a wrong course when leading the fleet. In preparation for the Atlantic Y. C. cruise, all stores were aboard and she was fitted with bowsprit, jib, balloon jib and spinnaker, but a very tempting offer accompanied by a check induced Mr. Randall to sell her. Under a new owner and name she did nothing of note.

The rivalry between the Crosbys and Hanley did much to keep alive the interest in the Class for some years through the last decade of the nineteenth century and the first of the present; it was specially strong in the Quincy, Winthrop, and Hull clubs under the patronage of Herbert W. Robbins, owner of Emeline; W. P. Whitmarsh, owner of Mudjekeewis; Ira M. Whittemore, owner of

(*Continued on page* 189)

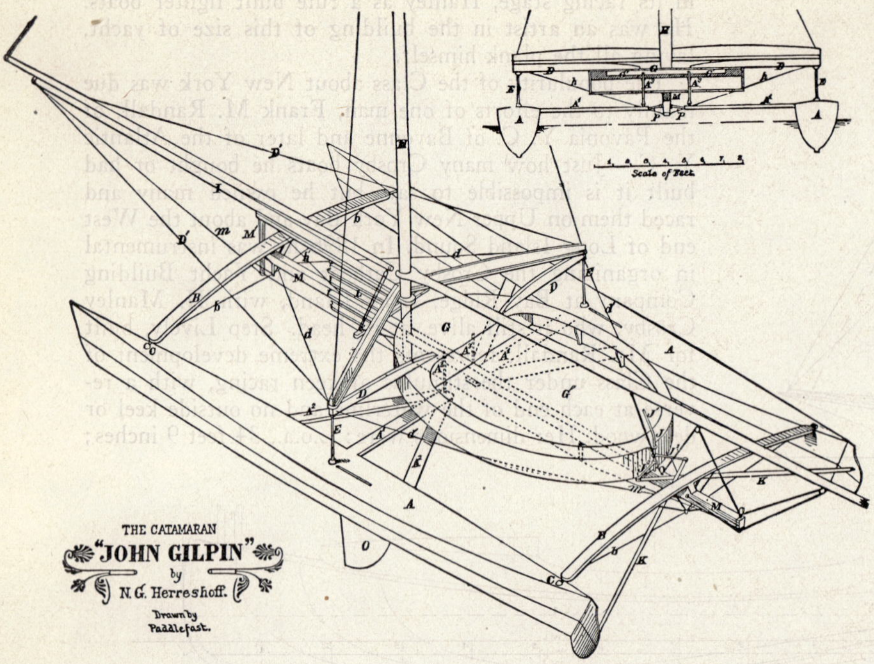

TRADITIONS AND MEMORIES OF American Yachting

By WILLIAM P. STEPHENS

Part Forty — The Herreshoffs of Bristol

RANKING near if not at the top of all the great yacht-building organizations of the world, the Herreshoff Manufacturing Company is unique in every respect, beginning with a name in no way descriptive of its purpose. Its origin is unusual, its methods original, and its scope far transcends the conventional field of yachtbuilding.

As already told, the production of yachts from the earliest days of the sport was in the hands of two distinct classes; the shipbuilders, trained in all technical details of larger work but at times devoting themselves to the construction of smaller pleasure vessels, and the rule-o'thumb builders, innocent of all technical training, who worked by intuition in carving the wood block as the sculptor carves in marble the image in his mind. The work of the Herreshoffs began in an entirely different way.

The history of the family in America begins with Charles Frederick Herreshoff, Prussian, rated as an engineer, a rather indefinite term in itself. He came to New York about 1790; by some lucky chance he resisted the lures of the metropolis and settled in a remote section of Rhode Island. Opinions may differ as to the merits of the many different yachting localities along the Atlantic Coast, New York Bay and the Hudson, the Sound, the Chesapeake and Massachusetts Bay, but as the home of the smaller yachts Narragansett Bay, though little known, has much in its favor. Its deep water, its many small snug harbors, its islands and its jutting peninsulas offer attractive home sites and open sailing water in plenty.

The young immigrant settled on a most favorable location, Popasquash Point, a little peninsula a half mile distant from Bristol, on a larger peninsula. Small as it was, Bristol had figured as an active shipping center. Many of the dwellers

Left: Catamaran John Gilpin, designed and built by N. G. Herreshoff in 1876. Below: N. G. Herreshoff in 1899

© M. Rosenfeld

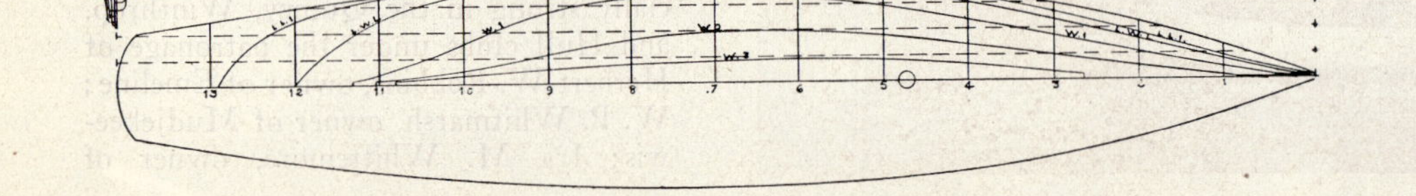

Lines of Madge, designed by George L. Watson, 1879

along the shores of Narragansett Bay were associated with shipping and familiar with the water. The use of a sail boat of some kind was essential for intercourse among the islands and access to the isolated peninsulas. Though its history never has been written, yacht racing of a primitive and informal kind existed on the Bay long before the organization of yacht clubs in the larger centers.

The type of sailing boat peculiar to Narragansett Bay was the "Newport Boat," sometimes called a "Pointer," a keel catboat of lapstrake build with high, narrow boom-and-gaff rigs, as described in MoToR BoatinG for last June. Other outside craft found their way to the Bay, among them craft from 28 to 30 feet long, flat-bottomed, and with centerboards and "periagua" rig. This name, which properly belongs to the rig but was applied locally to various forms of hull, swung two boom-and-gaff sails on masts stepped one as close as possible to the bow, the other amidships.

A Famous Genealogy

In 1801 Charles Frederick Herreshoff married Sarah, the daughter of John Brown, a ship owner of Providence, and in 1809 was born a son to whom the father's name was given. In 1835 the second Charles Frederick Herreshoff married Julia Ann Lewis, of Boston, also the daughter of a sea captain. The children of this pair were:—James Brown Herreshoff, 1834; Caroline Louise, 1837; Charles Frederick, 1839; John Brown, 1841; Lewis, 1844; Sally Brown, 1845; Nathaniel Greene, 1848; John Brown Francis, 1850 and Julian Lewis, 1854. A taint of hereditary blindness which ran through the family seems to have interfered but slightly with its activities and achievements.

James Brown Herreshoff was a chemist, the inventor of baking powder, of a thread tension for sewing machines, apparatus for measuring the specific heat of gases, and the coil boiler so closely identified with the family. He built a motorcycle operated by a naphtha engine, a sliding seat for rowboats, made a mercurial anti-fouling paint, and experimented with the fin-keel.

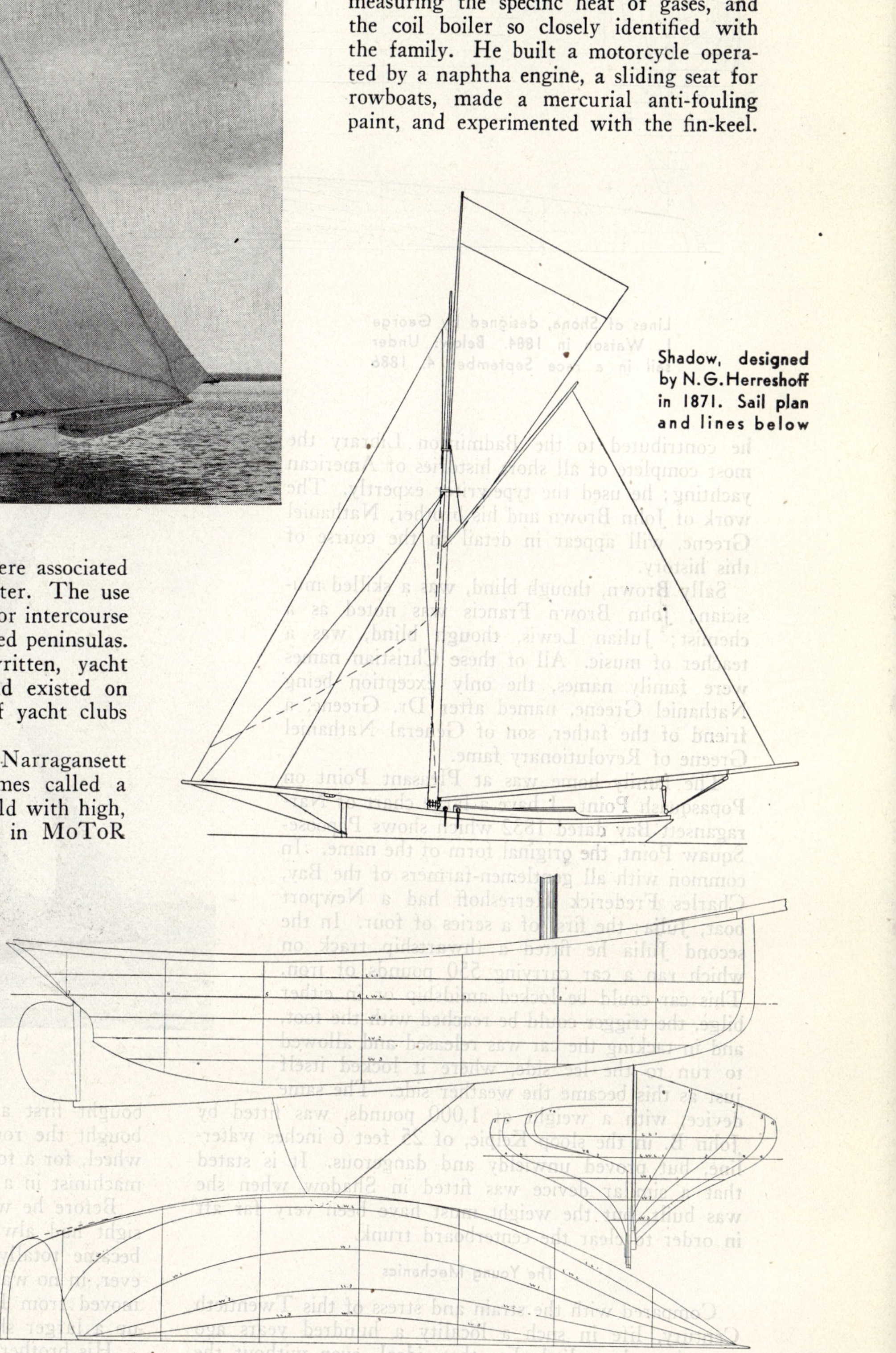

Shadow, designed by N.G.Herreshoff in 1871. Sail plan and lines below

Much of his life was spent in Europe.

Caroline Louise was married to a Mr. Chesebrough. Their son, Albert S. Chesebrough, was known in his day as a yacht designer. Charles Frederick chose the quiet life of a farmer, while Lewis, who was blind, was interested in the management of real estate. In 1894

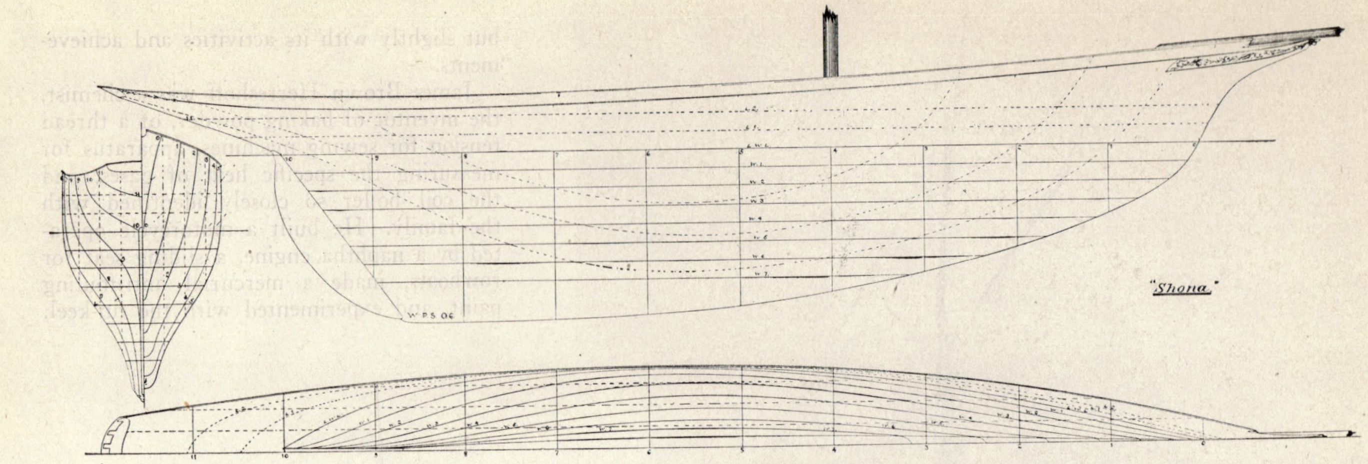

Lines of Shona, designed by George L. Watson in 1884. Below: Under sail in a race September 4, 1886

he contributed to the Badminton Library the most complete of all short histories of American yachting; he used the typewriter expertly. The work of John Brown and his brother, Nathaniel Greene, will appear in detail in the course of this history.

Sally Brown, though blind, was a skilled musician; John Brown Francis was noted as a chemist; Julian Lewis, though blind, was a teacher of music. All of these Christian names were family names, the only exception being Nathaniel Greene, named after Dr. Greene, a friend of the father, son of General Nathaniel Greene of Revolutionary fame.

The family home was at Pleasant Point on Popasquash Point. I have a large chart of Narragansett Bay dated 1832 which shows Papoose-Squaw Point, the original form of the name. In common with all gentlemen-farmers of the Bay, Charles Frederick Herreshoff had a Newport boat, Julia; the first of a series of four. In the second Julia he fitted a thwartship track on which ran a car carrying 550 pounds of iron. This car could be locked amidship or in either bilge, the trigger could be reached with the foot, and in tacking the car was released and allowed to run to the lee side, where it locked itself just as this became the weather side. The same device, with a weight of 1,000 pounds, was fitted by John B. in the sloop Kelpie, of 25 feet 6 inches waterline, but proved unwieldy and dangerous. It is stated that a similar device was fitted in Shadow when she was built, but the weight must have been very far aft in order to clear the centerboard trunk.

The Young Mechanics

Compared with the strain and stress of this Twentieth Century, life in such a locality a hundred years ago must have been little less than ideal, even without the telephone, the radio and jazz and swing, but cold hard cash was none too plentiful in this large family, all aiming at an education.

Born on the family farm, John B. started a small garden at the age of 11, selling the peas, corn and potatoes which he raised. As an old shipping town Bristol had a ropewalk; from seeing it John built one with three spindles alongside his garden and laid up cotton rope which he sold. With the money this earned he bought first a set of good carpenter's tools; later he bought the rough castings, headstock, tailstock and flywheel, for a foot lathe, fitting them up with the aid of a machinist in a local cottonmill.

Before he was 15, John started to build a boat. His sight had always been defective and in April 1856 he became totally blind through an accident. This, however, in no way discouraged him. At this time the family moved from Popasquash Point to Bristol, and he fitted up a larger shop.

His brother Nat, though but 8 years old, now became his guide and assistant in both play and work. In sailing, Nat acted as pilot, John was a skillful helmsman, and Nat profited by his instruction. In working at the lathe Nat guided the tool while John worked the treadle and held the tool.

With the help of the town blacksmith John became expert in forging and tempering steel and made all his tools, flat drills, turning and threading tools for the lathes and later taps and dies.

A small machine shop was fitted up in an adjoining room with the original lathe, a good engine lathe loaned by a friend in Providence, and a high speed dentist's lathe for polishing. The "manufacturing" of the firm of Herreshoff brothers was expanded to the turning of tool handles for sale, and later to articles in metal. By his tenth year Nat had learned to temper lathe tools, drills, taps and dies.

Shortly before he lost his sight John started, with his father's help, to build a 12-foot boat, Meteor; when finished he sailed constantly with Nat as pilot. Several other boats were later built and sold. In 1859 John, with his father's help, started a larger boat, Sprite. The model was made and young Nat, not yet in his twelfth year, was taught to take off the sections and make out a table of offsets.

Sprite was launched on June 28, 1860, the day the famous steamship Great Eastern arrived in New York. A month later the Herreshoffs made a cruise to New York to visit her. The party, aboard Sprite and the third Julia, 21 feet 6 inches, left Bristol about sunset one Monday, lay all night in Newport, and started out in a dense fog and light air. Progress was slow to Bartlett's Reef Light Vessel, but at sunset a fresh Northwest breeze came up and at 10 A.M. on Wednesday the flotilla passed down the East River. After ten days in the great city they left a pier in the East River off Blackwell's Island at 6 A.M. on Saturday and, with the aid of a fresh southerly, were home at 8 A.M. on Sunday.

Sprite proved fast in the many local races. She now rests in the Ford Museum at Dearborn, Michigan. Sprite was built in a vacant building, the Old Tannery. In the winter of 1862-3 John attempted a larger yacht, the sloop Kelpie, 27 feet 6 inches l.o.a.; 25 feet l.w.l. In this work he was assisted by Joe Southwick, a boatbuilder from Newport.

Yacht Building as a Business

IN 1863 the Herreshoffs cruised to the Camp Meeting at Vineyard Haven and there met Thomas Clapham, a young Englishman from the Housatonic River cruising in a sloop, Qui Vive, with several college friends. A discussion of the speed of their yachts let to a challenge and a race. The late Rutherfurd Stuyvesant was in the harbor with his sloop White Wings, and he agreed to act as Regatta Committee, laying the course, starting and timing the yachts. Kelpie won very easily and a second race resulted in the same way.

Clapham was much disappointed but eventually gave John an order for a yacht, also stencilled Qui Vive, thus starting him definitely in business as a yacht builder at the age of 22, totally blind. He did much work with his own hands, but had to rely on Nat's eyes for all drafting, laying down and writing, as well as work on models. The second Qui Vive was a sloop, 44 feet 11 inches l.o.a; 39 feet 9 inches l.w.l.; 14 feet 4 inches breadth and 3 feet 3 inches draft; with board, 10 feet 6 inches. She was raced successfully, Thomas Clapham at that time being a man of substantial means. After business reverses he removed to Roslyn, Long Island, and devoted himself to the development of the New Haven sharpie as a yacht.

The perceptions of John B. Herreshoff were little less than marvelous, his hands taking the place of eyes. As the business progressed he made it a practice to visit New York for the early races of the different clubs, usually with something fast enough to win when handled by himself and his brother. Niels Olson once told me of an incident after a race when John went aboard an opponent, laid down on the deck by the bitts and passed his arm down the side as far as it would reach, then hitched aft a few feet and repeated the process until he had felt the whole side of the yacht. In 1887 I showed him through the model room of the Seawanhaka-Corinthian Y. C., then in New York, and he repeated this process by passing his hand over the models, with a criticism of each.

When the order for the proposed Cup defender Priscilla, called by her designer a "damned steel scow," was given in the fall of 1884, I went to Joseph R. Busk, Chairman of the America's Cup Committee, and asked for some information for publication. He flatly refused, saying that it was no business of the public "whether her garboards were 5/8 inch or 5 inches thick."

I did not see the yacht under construction, but I was on the stringpiece at Poillon's Yard in Brooklyn when she came in tow from Wilmington in the following spring.

As it happened, John Herreshoff was at the yard for a few days, installing the engines in two launches built there. We met below and he went into the eyes of the empty hull, reaching up to the shelf and passing his hand over the first frame from deck to floor. Then he stepped aft and repeated the process, going the length of the 85-foot hull and feeling every third frame. Then he said to me "How do you get under the floor? I want to *see* the floor construction. He invariably used the word "see." I assured him that I was as anxious as he was, but there was no opening in the tightly laid matched flooring. I meet him again a few days later after a hole had been cut for the mast and a section of the flooring taken up. Said he, "I got down and *saw* everything."

While the early Herreshoff yachts followed the accepted method of the day, heavy sawn timbers, at the same time special care was taken in the selection of material and the proportioning of all members, with the result that they were decidedly lighter than those built about New York and Boston by professional shipwrights, and on the other hand were no such baskets as were set afloat by another class of builders.

In addition to yacht building John set up a sawmill with a gang saw for planking, circular saws and planer. In 1865 he took in a partner, Dexter S. Stone, the firm being Herreshoff & Stone, but this arrangement lasted only two years. The largest yacht built in this era was the schooner Triton, for George A. Thayer; 70 feet l.o.a.; 62 feet l.w.l.; 19 feet breadth; 6 feet draft; with board 12 feet. In designing her sail plan Nat gave her a jib and fore staysail, but this did not meet with the approval of the "talent" and she was soon fitted with a single big jib.

A novel feature of her construction was the employment of cast iron bed pieces for her centerboard trunk as a part of her inside ballast. The "Burgess boys" were quick to appreciate the Bristol work and owned many yachts, mainly small catboats. The sloop Nimbus, built for Edward Burgess in 1868, of 33 feet 6 inches l.w.l., was a noted boat for many years. It is unfortunate that the lines of few of these yachts have been preserved. Fifty years ago I knew many of them and could at least have taken the main measurements.

Nathaniel and His Work

IN 1866 Nathaniel entered the Massachusetts Institute of Technology for a short course in mechanical engineering, instruction in naval architecture being unknown in this country at the time. In the fall of 1869 he entered the drafting room of the Corliss Steam Engine Company of Providence, remaining with the company for nine years. During this time his evenings were devoted largely to drafting and similar work for his brother.

One of the wonders of the great Centennial Exposition in Philadelphia in 1876 was the Corliss beam engine which provided all power for Machinery Hall. N. G. Herreshoff had a part in designing this engine and had charge of it when the time came for starting. The actual turning-on of steam was done by two small gold cranks, one handled by President Grant and one by Dom Pedro, Emperor of Brazil. As soon as the engine was in operation Mr. Corliss slipped off both cranks and presented one to President Grant and one to the Emperor. Later on, when the engine was not operating satisfactorily, Mr. Herreshoff was sent to make the final adjustment of the valve gears.

The catamaran is one of the oldest and most crude vehicles of navigation, essentially two long narrow hulls, often mere logs, carrying a platform, the three units being rigidly connected. This Will-o'-the-Wisp of Naval architecture has long been the fond dream of ignorant inventors from its claims of unlimited stability, great deckroom, and assumed marvelous speed. The idea crops up at intervals in the form of racing craft, cruisers, freighters, steam passenger vessels, all doomed to failure.

By way of recreation from more serious work Nathaniel in 1876 took up the catamaran and made of it a wonderful sailing machine. In his hands the three elements, two hulls and a platform, were joined by a system of hinged joints, equalizing levers and springs so as to work freely in adapting the craft to the waves. The hulls were light pontoons and the deck was merely an oval platform for the two or three men of the crew.

AMARYLLIS, as the first was named, turned up in New York on the occasion of the open Centennial Regatta, easily outsailing the fleet, which included the fastest of the sandbaggers. The owners of the larger yachts were thrown into a panic as they foresaw their costly craft destined to extinction by this vicious machine, and steps were immediately taken to outlaw it as not a yacht. The idea was taken up by other builders and the type, including Tarantella, Centennial, Duplex, Jessie and Nonpariel, had a brief popularity.

Taking a holiday from the Corliss drafting room and taking out a patent, Nat went to Bristol, hired men and worked with them, building a number of catamarans which sold for $750.00, but the venture did not pay and he returned to Corliss; one, Tarantella, which he built for himself, and a later, Lodona, he sailed for some years. The situation was similar to the advent of the fin-keel from the Bristol shops fifteen years later, but the craze soon exhausted itself and calm reigned again in the bosoms of yacht owners.

A leading New York yachtsman, Anson Phelps Stokes, owner of the 78-foot schooner Clytie, was so impressed with the idea that he designed and had built by Capt. Lou Tonns, skipper of the schooner Triton, the catamaran Nereid, nicknamed by his friends "Stokes' Folly." The hulls were 32 feet long, with owner's quarters in one and crew's quarters in the other; she was finally abandoned on the beach, an utter failure.

Prior to the adoption of the length and sail area rule by the Seawanhaka C. Y. C. in 1882 the most popular basis of measurement was "mean length." In 1866 when a student at M.I.T., a boy of 18, N. G. Herreshoff calculated an allowance table for the Boston Y. C. based on waterline plus a fraction of the after overhang; this system being in general use for many years. Thirty-six years later he gave to yachting the Universal Rule now in use.

Shadow

IT would be a difficult matter to pick out any one yacht of the hundreds launched from the Bristol shops as the most notable or the most successful, but if there is one name which cannot be omitted it is Shadow. This sloop was built in 1871 to the order of Dr. E. R. Sisson, of New Bedford, who sailed a few races, but in the following year she was sold to C. S. Randall, of the Eastern Y. C., who sailed her against the sloop Coming, built by Capt. Bob Fish, 23 feet longer. While second in this race she defeated another Fish yacht, White Cap, of her own size. In 1873-4-5 she was owned by Caspar Crowninshield, also of the Eastern Y. C., but there is no record of her racing. In 1876 she was owned by Tucker Deland who sold her in the following year to Dr. John Bryant, who had just joined the Eastern Y. C. His bother Henry joined a year later, their membership continuing for nearly thirty years. Their summer home was at Cohasset and their skipper in Shadow, Thetis and Alert was Capt. Aubrey Crocker, long one of the best known of New England professionals. In the hands of the Bryants and their Corinthian friends, with Capt. Crocker, Shadow was one of the best kept-up and best handled yachts on Massachusetts Bay, and practically invincible.

In the fall of 1886 I wrote to Dr. Bryant for the lines of Shadow for publication. He replied that he had no lines, but that I was at liberty to take them off. This was not possible at the time, but early in the spring I heard from him stating that Shadow would be on her railway at a certain date, ready for launching. In May, in company with John Hyslop, I visited Cohasset, met Capt. Crocker, and assisted Mr. Hyslop in taking off the lines, later plotting them as the basis for the drawing here shown. On a fine spring day, the yacht shining in fresh paint and shored up plumb on her private railway and cradle, we had every opportunity for accurate work.

The form of Shadow is not only unusual in itself but it is different from all other Herreshoff yachts which preceded and followed it. The hollow in the midship section is so extreme that after all the sections were taken off by measuring out and plumbing I placed a straightedge from the rabbet to the bilge and made an independent measurement of the distance, seven inches. While the two brothers worked together on most models, John taking a leading part, Shadow is believed to be the individual work of the younger.

Shadow and Madge

WHEN the Scotch cutter Madge visited New York in 1881 she merely played with the shoal local sloops, Schemer, Wave and Mistral, winning all four races. She then went to Newport for a match with Shadow, the latter coming down from Boston.

Madge's speed in light weather was due largely to her big club topsail. In her first sailing about the Upper Bay while making matches this sail was not set, but as soon as she was racing it was sent aloft, to the astonishment and dismay of her opponents.

Without this sail in light weather she was like Samson with his hair cut. In the first race, on October 14, the course was ten miles to leeward and return. Shadow was sailed by her owners and captain, but Madge had to make up her crew by shipping two local hands, unfamiliar with her rig.

On the run Shadow led by a minute, Madge had trouble with her spinnaker and the new hands topped the boom with a run, carrying away one of the long spreaders supporting her topmast. Thus disabled she limped home, in danger of losing her topmast, and was timed 12 minutes 31 seconds astern of Shadow. The second race was over a triangle of ten-mile sides, Madge leading by 45 seconds at the first mark, by 6 minutes 30 seconds at the second, and 6 minutes 4 seconds at the finish. In the controversy which ensued each side based its claims on one of these two races, ignoring the other.

Shadow continued her successful career against the best of the Boston fleet until 1887 when Edward Burgess brought out the keel Papoose for the "Adams boys," then just graduating from smaller centerboard yachts. The two met on June 17, 1887, in a race of the Dorchester Y. C., Papoose winning by 9 minutes 32 seconds in light weather. They met again on August 23 in a race of the Beverly Y. C., in fluky weather, Papoose winning by 30 minutes 34 seconds.

The 5-ton Shona, a younger sister of Madge, sailed with Shadow in the open race of the Beverly Y. C. on September 4, 1886, in a strong east wind and defeated her by over three minutes; but in the annual regatta of the Eastern Y. C. in June following, ten miles to windward and return out in Massachusetts Bay with housed topmasts and reefed sails the little cutter was beaten by nearly 14 minutes.

It is impossible to find a common denominator for the racing of such craft as Shadow, Papoose, Madge and Shona, so radically different in type and leading dimensions; but the performances of these yachts played an important part in the controversy which changed the course of American yachting.

	Shadow		Papoose		Madge		Shona	
	Ft.	Ins.	Ft.	Ins.	Ft.	Ins.	Ft.	Ins.
Length, over all	37	1	44	3	46		43	9
waterline	34	2	36		39	9	32	10
Breadth, extreme	14	4	12	3	7	9	5	8
waterline	13		11	2	7	8	5	7
Draft, extreme	5	4	7	6	7	8	5	11
with board	12							
Displacement, long tons	13.9				16.5			
Ballast, total long tons	4.9				10.0			
Mast from stem	10		14		15	4	12	
deck to hounds	34	6	34		28			
Topmast fid to sheave	18		25		25			
Bowsprit, outboard	18		20	9	20			
Boom	40		39	8	36	2		
Gaff	22	6	24	6	25			
Topsail Club	27		25		24	6		
Sail Area								
Mainsail, sq. ft.	984							
Jib	358							
Foresail	..							
Working topsail	162							
Club topsail	342							

To return to her designer, Nathaniel never possessed the sturdy physique which distinguished most members of the family. His double work in the Corliss shops by day and drafting and writing at home by night told on him and, in 1874, in company with his brother Lewis and a cousin, he was sent to the South of France for a rest. Just how much he rested is a question. Lewis and the cousin built a 17-foot boat of the sharpie type and Nathaniel built a boat about 13 feet long with a small leg-o'-mutton sail. These boats, with a Rob Roy canoe owned by an Englishman, were carted to the upper waters of the river Var, the party cruising down to the mouth and then along the coast to Nice, some six miles, encountering rough water at the mouth of the Var and on landing at Nice.

They also built a boat, Riviera, 20 feet long, in which they cruised along the mediterranean coast and up the Rhone to Arles, shipped her by rail to the canal from the Rhone to the Rhine and

(*Continued on page* 189)

TRADITIONS AND MEMORIES OF American Yachting

By **WILLIAM P. STEPHENS**

Part Forty-one

The Herreshoffs of Bristol—Continued

Herreshoff Launch Engine. Designed by N. G. Herreshoff. Below: Stiletto Yacht—Torpedoboat, 1885

ONE idiosyncracy of this very peculiar family is seen in the Christian name of the male members of the generation with which we are now concerned:—the partiality for the letter J, the recurrence of John twice, of Lewis twice and Francis twice among the seven brothers; Brown, Lewis and Francis being family surnames. The various combinations of these names add to the troubles of the historian.

One important factor in the success of the Herreshoff steam yachts has been the coil boiler, one of the many inventions of James Brown Herreshoff, dating from 1874. This boiler is made in two forms, with a single and a double coil of iron pipe; the former being used where there is no limit to height. When vertical space has to be considered the double coil is used. The feed water is pumped into the upper coils *A* in which the heating begins; thence it passes to the top of the main coil *B* from which it enters the bottom of the outer coil *C*. From coil *C* it passes by the pipe *E* into the separator *D*, the end of *E* being so curved as to throw the current of water with a whirling motion against the side of cylinder *D*. The water and all impurities fall to the bottom of *D*, while the steam passes through the pipe *F* into the upper coil *G* in which it is superheated before passing to the cylinders. The coils are placed on a foundation of firebrick and enclosed by a casing of sheet metal. The light weight, compact form and rapid steaming qualities of the boiler make it superior for launch and yacht work to the conventional tubular land boiler.

With the experience gained by years of work under that master engineer George H. Corliss, Nathanael, working at home in the evenings, designed the engine which has made the brothers famous; the first being a vertical compound two-cylinder of light weight; due to simple design, skillful planning, and the use of the best materials. This careful selection of materials characterized all of the Herreshoff work from the start. When John B. built his second boat Sprite, in 1859, he and Nat sailed to the Warren shipyard in the 12-foot Meteor, bringing home a deckload of oak with more in tow.

The boys then sailed to Fall River for cedar, taking it part way to New Bedford to be sawn. For the frames, shells of blocks and mast hoops two trips were made in a larger borrowed boat to Wickford for the fine oak for which that town was noted. In the fall of 1876 Nat modelled a catboat, Gleam, for George and Frederick Allen Gower, of Providence, the agreement being that they were not to accept the boat if she failed to defeat the catboat Wanderer, of the same length, 25 feet, owned by Harvey Flint of Providence. This she did in two races, with Nat at the tiller. F. A. Gower went to England on business, taking Gleam with him, and she was in existence down to 1907. Mr. Gower was the first husband of our great American soprano, Lillian Nordica. He was interested in ballooning and lost his life in a balloon over the English Channel.

In planning Gleam, Nat adopted an original method of construction, a solid mould of two thicknesses of one-inch board was made for every frame, spaced about one foot apart. The two members of the frame were steamed and bent on the mould and held by dogs, their heels being united by a floor. With these moulds set up solidly on the keel the planking was done more rapidly and more accurately than by the conventional method of frames bent to skeleton moulds and ribbands. Sprite presumably was set up with the keel on blocks and the moulds on the keel, but later this method was reversed, the moulds being made with the top edge as the baseline and set up directly on the floor upside down, the keel being laid on top of the moulds. In time the floor knees and deck knees were made of malleable iron.

When it came to the construction of steam yachts an important member was a heavy sheer strake of moulded

Now Then, built for Norman L. Munro, 1887

oak, supplemented by an oak rubbing strake a little distance below; in a steam yacht of 90 feet l.w.l. built in 1887 the garboards were of 2½ inch oak, the inner planking ¾ inch yellow pine and the outer planking ¾ inch white pine, the deck of two thicknesses of ½ inch white pine. The inner planking was fastened to the frames by brass screws, the outer planking was fastened by still longer screws, and the two skins were fastened between the frames by galvanized screws from the inside. Though notable for its lightness, this construction has stood the test of time in many old Herreshoff yachts still afloat.

Organization

JOHN B. was a poor business man, interested primarily in the mechanical side of building, in a sawmill, and other side issues, and at one time he was in financial difficulty. As the business increased, however, in 1878 Nat left the Corliss company and became a partner in the Herreshoff Manufacturing Company. The rules he laid down for the conduct of the business were to attend strictly and fully to the business of yacht and engine building, to improve in every way the quality of the products, not to borrow money for capital, not to spend money on the plant until it had been earned, and to let the products of the plant be its advertisement.

The following partial list will show the growth and progress of the plant in its early years. In 1868 the small steam yacht Annie Morse, in 1870 the fishing steamer Seven Brothers; the machinery for the first was purchased, but that for the second, and the launch Anemone, 38 by 6-6, were designed by Nat. In 1871 was built the steam launch Actinia, 42 by 7, for Alexander Agassiz. In 1874 the torpedo launch Lightning was built for the U. S. Government; in 1876 the launch Speedwell, 45 feet l.o.a., with engine 3½ and 6 by 7 inches.

In 1877 a mysterious order was placed for a seagoing launch of 120 feet and 16 knots speed, the owner being unknown. Taking a leave of two months from the Corliss company, Nat worked in Bristol on the model, the hull being built by Terry at Fall River; and on the design for a two-cylinder compound engine, the patterns being made and the engine built by the Rhode Island Locomotive Works, while the boiler was built by John B. When Estelle was ready for a trial the U. S. Revenue Cutter Dexter turned up at Bristol and stood guard. Only after intervention at Washington was she permitted to make a trial trip, with officers of the Dexter aboard, showing the required 16 knots in a run of twelve hours. The final payment was no sooner made than the vessel was seized by the U. S. Government, as it was by this time known that her owners were the insurgents in Cuba. A little later an order for a similar vessel 135 feet long was placed by the Spanish Government for service in Cuba.

From Sail to Steam

THE plant had been enlarged gradually, taking in the old Burnside Rifle Factory and later the Old Tan-

Right: Magnolia, built for Fairman Rogers, 1883. Coast cruising yacht. Below: Clara, built for Charles Kellogg, 1887. Lower right: Ballymena, built for Alexander Brown, 1888

Top: Herreshoff Shop. Typical steam yacht stern. Lower: Stern view of Vamoose, bow of sailing yacht Pelican at left

nery. Prior to 1878 the Company's work was mainly in sail; many small catboats, some catboats and sloops of medium size, and a few large schooners. In 1878 was built the launch Puck, a duplicate of Speedwell, followed in 1879 by the 60-foot Idle Hour, the 42-foot Sinbad and Dolphin.

Then came the first really important order, a torpedo launch for the British Government; 59 feet 6 inches by 7 feet 6 inches with a draft of 1 foot 3 inches. The hull was of composite construction, wood planking on steel frames, and the topsides were of 1/16 inch sheet steel. The two cylinders were 6 and 10½ inches in diameter and 10 inches stroke. The coil boiler was 4 feet in diameter with about 300 feet of 3-inch pipe, with a working pressure up to 160 pounds; forced draft was supplied by a Sturtevant blower driven by an engine of 2½ h.p. The weight of hull and machinery was 6 tons; with a crew of four, stores, fuel and two torpedoes, 7½ tons.

The launch was given its first test on the Thames, from Erith down Long Reach, under a working pressure of 80 pounds giving 350 r.p.m. but she showed the same speed astern as ahead, turned in a circle of about three times her length, and stopped dead from full speed in little more than her length. In a later test before the First Lord of the Admiralty, Chief Constructor Barnaby and other naval officials she was lifted from the water by a crane, with crew and stores aboard, then lowered into the water, and steam was blowing off within five minutes of the lighting of the fire. On the run which followed she made the guaranteed speed of 16 knots.

The year 1880 saw the practical abandonment of sail yacht construction in favor of steam, with a new shop specially designed for the work. Quoting from a description in Forest & Stream after a visit in 1885:—"The building itself is 140 feet long and 36 feet wide, and equivalent to three stories in height. The floor is of wood, the middle portion being made in small sections. When these are removed a pit is disclosed, running down the center and into the water. This pit is lined with cement and fitted up with a railway for hauling and launching; the water end of the house being composed of large doors opening to the roof. A second floor is laid at the height of the eaves, on which are stored all the moulds on which the vessels are built. Long windows running up almost to the roof give ample light, six steam radiators keep the building warm in all seasons, and everything is fitted to give convenience for rapid, economical and

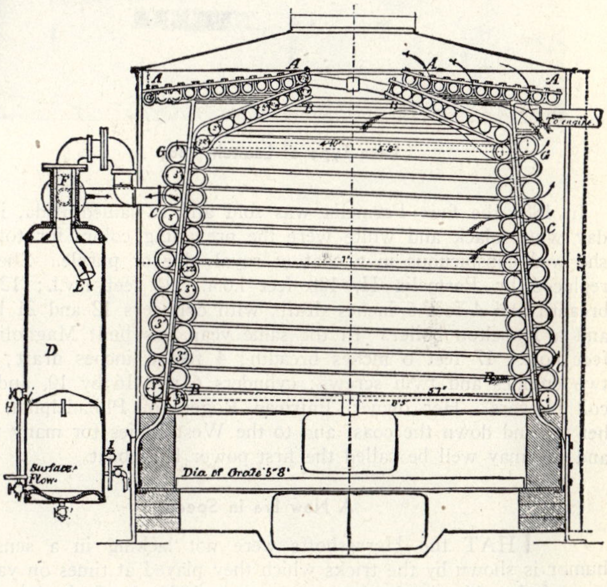

Coil boiler invented by James Brown Herreshoff, 1874. Below: Torpedoboat built for British Government, 1879

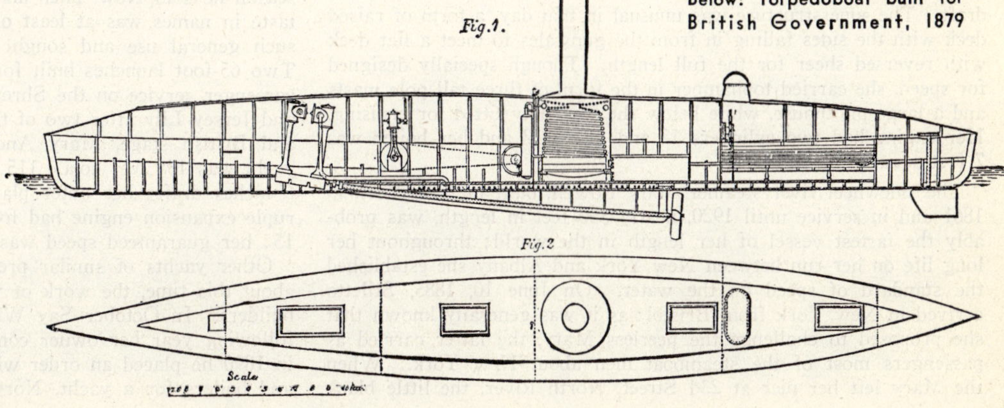

norough work. Overhead, running on railways on the plates of the walls, are two traveling cranes, each lifting up to seven tons. On the main floor are work-benches along the walls and on each side is a gallery giving additional room for woodwork or getting out rigging. Outside the shiphouse are two wharves, one fitted with a powerful steam crane by which a yacht may be lifted bodily on to the dock." All this may seem commonplace today, but it was then very different from the best to be found in the leading yards of Boston and New York 57 years ago.

In this new shop was built Gleam, 120 feet l.o.a.; 110 feet l.w.l.; 16 feet breadth; 5 feet 8 inches draft; a cruising yacht for T. H. Garrett of Baltimore. Her engine was 2-cyl., 10½ and 18 by 18, with boiler 5 feet 6 inches diameter. For William Woodward, Jr., of New York was built the cabin launch Edith, 60 feet l.o.a.; 55 feet l.w.l.; 9 feet 2 inches breadth; 3 feet 5 inches draft; 2 cyl., 6 and 10½ by 10; also Sport, a launch 45 feet l.o.a., for Messrs. Flint and Earle, as a tender for the sloop Gracie, one of the first launches specially used for this purpose; also a 42-foot launch Lucy. In 1881 was built Leila, 100 feet l.o.a., for Lake Michigan; in 1882 Siesta, 98 feet, for H. H. Warner of Rochester; Permelia I, 95 feet, with engine 8 and 14 by 14; for Mark Hopkins of Port Huron, Mich.; Orienta, 125 feet, with engine 16 and 28 by 16 for Jabez A. Bostwick of New York; and Nereid, 76 feet, for Jay C. Smith of New York. All of these were of composite construction and the Company was now known nationally as veritable manufacturers of steam yachts and launches.

Lake Type of Launch, 1880

In 1883 the first Permelia was sold and re-named Aida, in the day when black and white were the prevailing colors for topsides she was conspicuous in a coat of royal blue or purple. She was replaced by Permelia II, 100 feet l.o.a.; 94 feet l.w.l.; 12 feet breadth and 4 feet 6 inches draft; with cylinders 12 and 21 by 12 and a Hazelton boiler. In the same year was built Magnolia, 99 feet l.o.a.; 17 feet 6 inches breadth; 4 feet 3 inches draft; with two engines and twin screws; cylinders 6 and 16 by 10, and two coil blowers. Her owner, Fairman Rogers of Philadelphia, used her up and down the coast and to the West Indies for many years and she may well be called the first power houseboat.

A New Era in Speed

THAT the Herreshoffs were not lacking in a sense of humor is shown by the tricks which they played at times on yachtsmen of the old school; the catamaran in 1876, the fin-keel in 1891. In 1885 John B. built for himself the steam yacht Stiletto, 94 feet l.o.a.; 90 feet l.w.l.; 11 feet 6 inches breadth and 4 feet 6 inches draft. The superstructure was unusual in that day, a form of raised deck with the sides falling in from the gunwales to meet a flat deck with reversed sheer for the full length. Though specially designed for speed, she carried tophamper in the form of three tall pole masts and a large pilothouse, while below she was fully fitted for cruising. Her engine had two cylinders 12 and 21 by 12 and her boiler was 7 feet square.

The sidewheel river steamer Mary Powell, built in New York in 1861 and in service until 1920, nearly 300 feet in length, was probably the fastest vessel of her length in the world; throughout her long life on her run between New York and Albany she established the standard of speed on the water. On June 10, 1885, Stiletto arrived in New York from Bristol; as it was generally known that she proposed to challenge the peerless Mary, the latter carried as passengers most of the steamboat men about New York. When the Mary left her pier at 23d Street, North River, the little black and white nondescript was close at hand, starting as she did, at first abreast the Powell's stern. The steamboat adherents were in high glee, if the yacht could do no better at the start she never could hold her steam for the course; the 30 miles to Sing Sing. Holding her own at first, slowly the yacht crept up until those in her pilot house could look into her fireroom; she hung there for a short time until one of her party in the pilothouse said "Good afternoon, gentlemen" her jingle rang, and she was off in the lead. She was timed at Sing Sing at 4:31, 1 hour 15 minutes for the 30 miles with the steamboat five minutes later; the running time for express trains was 1 hour 2 minutes.

ON July 16 she entered a race of the American Y. C. over a course of 92 miles, starting off Larchmont and finishing off New London. Her elapsed time was 4 hours 49 minutes 54 seconds, as compared with the second yacht Atalanta 228 feet l.w.l. 4 hours 53 minutes 50 seconds. As this was under 20 m.p.h. it would seem that Stiletto, whose final record was 26½ miles per hour in an 8-hour run, was merely playing with Atalanta and the rest of the fleet. Jay Gould, owner of Atalanta, protested Stiletto, on the ground that she had cut the buoy on Sarah's Ledge, the protest was sustained, and an interchange of challenges ensued.

The owner of Stiletto challenged for a race on the Hudson, the loser to pay for a $500 cup; the owner of Atalanta declined on the ground that the river was too shoal to permit full speed for his yacht, at the same time proposing a race from New York to Newfoundland for $25,000 a side, which was declined on the ground that Stiletto was not fitted for the open sea. Her owner issued a counter challenge for a race in the following year from New York to Newport, and here the matter ended. Stiletto was sold in 1887 to the U. S. Government for use as a torpedoboat.

In 1885 the Herreshoffs built a 48-foot launch, Henrietta, for Norman L. Munro of New York, publisher of a sensational story paper and novels, in which he performed various stunts in running against fast steamboats such as the Monmouth and Sandy Hook, running between New York and Sandy Hook. In 1887 he placed an order with the Company for a high-speed yacht which he proposed to name Now Then. Prior to this the larger Herreshoff yachts had an after overhang of moderate length such as is shown in the views of the shops; in the new yacht a novel form was introduced, with the reverse of an after overhang, a flat run, and a form which may be compared to a duck's bill; the object being to prevent squatting at very high speeds. The dimensions of Now Then were: l.o.a., 85 feet; l.w.l., 81 feet; breadth, 10 feet; draft, 2 feet 6 inches. The limit of draft was imposed as Mr. Munro's home was on the Shrewsbury River. The cylinders were 7½, 12 and 19 by 10½, the shaft was of 3¼-inch steel and the four-bladed wheel was 36 inches in diameter. Before the yacht was completed her owner offered to race any steam yacht in America without allowance, giving a start of 10 miles. On her initial run from Bristol to New York, on July 12, she covered the 130 miles in 7 hours 4 minutes.

High Speed on the Water and in Type

THE interest in high-speed steam yachts had been growing for some years, and in 1883 the American Yacht Club was organized, with the backing of one of the larger builders, for the promotion of steam yacht racing; establishing itself at Milton Point on Long Island Sound. Meanwhile, in default of set races, the growing fleet contented themselves with such informal proofs of speed as that of Stiletto against the Mary Powell, and similar runs down New York Bay against the Sandy Hook and Monmouth. At the end of the season he sold Now Then and placed an order for Say When; his taste in names was at least original, as he discarded the stencil in such general use and sought a name which identified the vessel. Two 65-foot launches built for him by the Herreshoffs in 1888 for passenger service on the Shrewsbury River were named Our Mary and Jersey Lily after two of the reigning favorites of the American and British stage, Mary Anderson and Lily Langtry. The new yacht was 138 feet l.o.a.; 115 feet l.w.l.; 14 feet breadth and 4 feet 6 inches draft; her outer planking was of mahogany. Her quadruple expansion engine had five cylinders, 11, 16 and three 22½ by 15; her guaranteed speed was 25 miles.

Other yachts of similar pretensions of extreme speed were built about this time, the work of various designers, builders and engine builders. In October Say When was sold for $46,000 and for the following year her owner contented himself with his launches, but in 1890 he placed an order with a young designer of hulls, engines and boilers for a yacht, Norwood, which was built in secret in a locked shop at Amesbury, Mass. When completed the new craft, guaranteed to make 30 m.p.h., made her trials over a mile course on the Merrimac River, the distance being measured by a wire floated on corks by which the buoys were placed. Later she had an informal race with the Monmouth.

In 1891 two orders were placed with the Herreshoffs, one from William R. Hearst for Vamoose and one from E. D. Morgan for Javelin. The former was 112 feet 6 inches l.o.a.; 100 feet 4 inches l.w.l.; 12 feet 4 inches breadth and 6 feet 11 inches draft; her engines being the same as those of Say When. Javelin was 98 feet l.o.a.; 94 feet l.w.l.; 10 feet 2 inches breadth and 4 feet 9 inches draft; with cylinders 9, 14, 22½ by 12; her guaranteed speed being 23 miles. In September of that year Vamoose steamed around the Mary Powell on her regular run on the Hudson.

THESE informal scraps with the Mary Powell, Sandy Hook and Monmouth proved nothing as to the actual maximum speed, but resulted in much free advertising for the owners. In September the American Y. C. announced a race to be run on the 22d for a prize of $500, the course to be from Race Rock, at the eastern end of Long Island Sound, to the Club station, 90 miles. Invitations were sent to the U. S. torpedoboat Cushing, Stiletto, Javelin, Now Then, Norwood, Vamoose and Yankee Doodle. The Navy Department forbid the participation of the Cushing and Stiletto, Mr. Morgan failed to enter Javelin, and only Vamoose, Norwood and Yankee Doodle entered. On the day of the race only Vamoose, with that wild Indian Captain Theodore Heilbron in charge, was at the start. Yankee Doodle did not appear, and Norwood was detained by a most unfortunate accident. On her way from New York, in charge of a licensed pilot and in broad daylight, she ran on the well known Penfield Reef and lost her shaft, strut and wheel. Under such conditions, which reflected little credit on the over-boastful owners of these alleged flyers, the race was called off.

On October 12, Vamoose made four trial runs over a mile course laid off with the wire used for Norwood; on the first run, against tide, she scored 2 minutes 50 seconds, on the second, with tide, 2 minutes 30 seconds, on the third, against tide, 2 minutes 30 seconds. On the fourth, with tide, she blew out a stuffingbox on her steering gear and was obliged to ship a tiller with tackles, her time being 2 minutes 35 seconds; 24 knots or 27.03 m.p.h. Again came excuses, explanations, challenges and counter challenges, but the much advertised race never came off. After some years as the patron of the high-speed steam yacht the American Yacht Club settled down to the more prosaic but practical position which it has long occupied as a member of the Yacht Racing Association of Long Island Sound and a partner in the regular circuit of sailing races.

THE following contract, entered into with the Navy Department in 1888, shows the requirements then existing. The craft was a torpedoboat 138 feet l.o.a.; 134 feet l.w.l.; 15 feet breadth and 4 feet 8 inches draft; estimated displacement, 100 tons, estimated H.P. 1,000; engine, five cylinder; cost, $82,750. If the speed exceeded 22 knots a bonus would be paid of $1,500 for each ¼ knot over 23, and $2,000 for each ¼ knot over 24. If the speed were under 22 knots a penalty of $4,000 would be imposed; and if under 20 knots the Navy Department had the right to reject the vessel.

In 1887 Commander W. B. Hoff, U.S.N., of the U. S. S. Ossippee, made a disparaging comparison between the working Navy launches as draft horses, and the Herreshoff Navy launches as race horses. This challenge was taken up by Captain Bruce, U.S.N., of the U. S. S. Atlanta when at Bristol, using the Herreshoff launch of the Atlanta and the Navy launch of the Ossippee. The two launches were joined by a hawser over their sterns and both started. The Herreshoff launch first stopped the Navy launch and then towed her stern-first faster than Captain Bruce in a Navy launch could keep up with them.

The product of the plant during this steam yacht era may be judged from the following partial list: 1888, Ballymena, 148 feet l.o.a.; 1889, Augusta, 131 feet; 1890, Katrina I, 73 feet; Judy, 102 feet, Reposo, 72 feet; 1892, Truant, 132 feet, Tranquilo, 80 feet; 1893, Louisa, 102 feet, Kalolah, 92 feet; 1894, Eugenia I, 75 feet, Neckan, 100 feet; 1895, Eugenia II, 86 feet; 1896, Vacuna, 84 feet; 1897, Katrina II, 100 feet, Nina, 99 feet; 1900, Florence, 98 feet; Mirage, 81 feet, Scout, 80 feet; 1901, Niagara III, 81 feet, Tramp, 82 feet; 1902, Quickstep, 124 feet, Parthenia, 131 feet, Roamer, 94 feet; 1903, Eugenia III, 112 feet, Wana, 132 feet. This list is merely typical of the later work of the Company; with these and many other large yachts were built torpedoboats, Navy launches, yacht tenders (both davit boats and such craft as Mirage and Scout). The three Eugenias were built by John B. for his personal use; in 1912 Nat built for himself Helianthus I, 64 feet, and in 1921 Helianthus II, 62 feet, in 1902 Roamer, 94 feet.

In addition to yachts and Government craft, engines and special machinery for the works, and for outside customers were built. Meanwhile certain new conditions were leading to a radically new development in the business.

EAST OF THE CAPE, PART 39

(*Continued from page* 179)

Almira; Henry C. Nickerson, owner of Arawak, and Dr. F. E. Dawees, owner of Stranger. In 1904 the Cape Catboat Association was organized, mainly within the Quincy Y. C., with special rules for the government of the Class. From about 1910 the Class declined, though the Cape Catboat is still doing good service in many ports along the original lines of fishing and pleasure sailing.

The reader may form his own conclusions as to when a Cape Catboat is a sloop; the writer is unable to enlighten him further. The reason for the jib, as given by those most closely associated with the Class, is that it was found necessary when the boats were used for racing and the mainsail increased in area; calling for headsail to balance it. As opposed to this statement there is Gracie, as described in MoToR BoatinG for July; in model, construction and arrangement a typical Crosby fishing boat of a half century ago, with bowsprit and jib as part of her original rig.

THE HERRESHOFFS OF BRISTOL, PART 40

(*Continued from page* 184)

down the Rhine to Rotterdam. Crossing by steamer to London, they cruised on the Thames, shipped to Liverpool by rail, boarded the City of Brussels and lashed the boat on a deckhouse. On arriving in New York they launched her and sailed home to Bristol. Riviera was treasured by Mr. Herreshoff all his life; she was finally destroyed in the recent hurricane. In this boatbuilding only very crude tools were to be had, but the native workmen employed were skilled mechanics.

Shadow was used for years as a fisherman. She was finally left on the shore at Chelsea and her hulk was burned in the big fire a few years ago. Papoose, soft and punky in her 41st year, was cut up and decently cremated by John T. Mott of Oswego, who sailed her for many years. Her rudderstock now forms the newelpost in my home. Madge's bones were left to rot in a swamp at Charlotte, N. Y. Years ago I retrieved her rudderpost and it also hangs in my home. I wish that I had a part of Shadow to keep them company.

In 1868 John B. Herreshoff built the hull of a steam yacht, Annie Morse, for Samuel Shove, of Pawtucket, R. I., the engine and boiler being built elsewhere. Two years later he made a second venture in steam in Seven Brothers, built for Church Brothers, fishermen of Tiverton, R. I., the machinery for this and a smaller launch Anemone being designed by Nathaniel. From this time on the efforts of the new Herreshoff Manufacturing Company were diverted from sail and centered on the improvement of the hulls and machinery of steam craft.

TRADITIONS AND MEMORIES OF

AMERICAN YACHTING

By WILLIAM P. STEPHENS

Part Forty-two

The Herreshoffs of Bristol—Continued

BEGINNING about 1870, the steam yacht and steam launch, in lengths from 100 feet down to 20 feet, grew rapidly in favor, and were found on every lake and river East of the Mississippi and along the coast. It was used for cruising and fishing, for mere pleasure afloat, it was cheap to run, but had one serious objection—the laws of the United States made compulsory the employment of both a licensed engineer and fireman. The Herreshoff Manufacturing Company, as we have seen, while in no way possessing a monopoly, enjoyed through the excellence of its products a very generous share of this business. Though no one suspected it at the time, the climax of the steam yacht building came about 1885, the first hint of its decline being a short item in *Forest & Stream* of December 31, 1885.

"A New Gas Engine. The N. Y. Petroleum Gas Engine Co. have erected a two-story factory at Brown Place, mouth of the Kills, Harlem River, adjoining William Kyle's boatshop. They will manufacture engines for steam launches under a patent covering many novelties. Briefly described, the machinery for a 17-foot launch just completed is as follows:—at the bow of the boat is a tank containing eight gallons of benzine or naphtha. This tank is connected by two pipes with the engine, which is in the stern; all the working parts of the engine are enclosed in a small iron chest. There are three cylinders, one used to

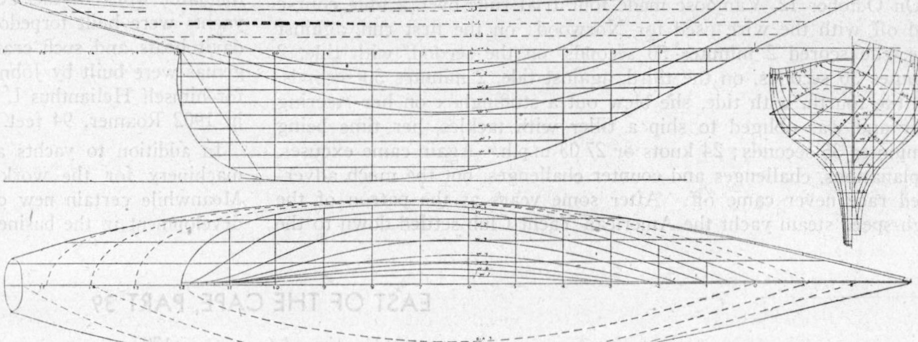

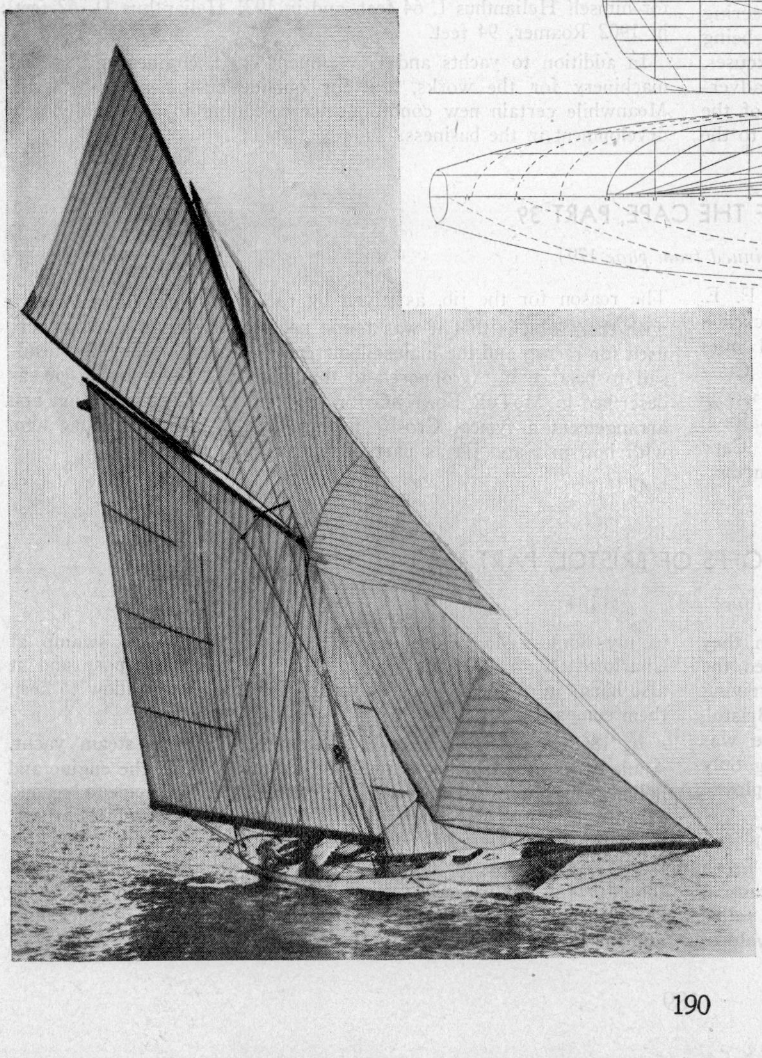

Above: Etcetera, auxiliary cruising Naphtha launch. L.o.a., 30 feet; l.w.l., 27 feet; breadth, 7 feet 6 inches; draft 3 feet. Designed and built by the Gas Engine and Power Company, 1889, for Louis Q. Jones, Hartford Canoe Club. Cruised from Portsmouth, Va., to Florida, in winter of 1889. Shows typical brass stack of the Naphtha engine. Left: Gloriana, 46-foot class, 1891. Designed by N. G. Herreshoff; built for Edwin D. Morgan

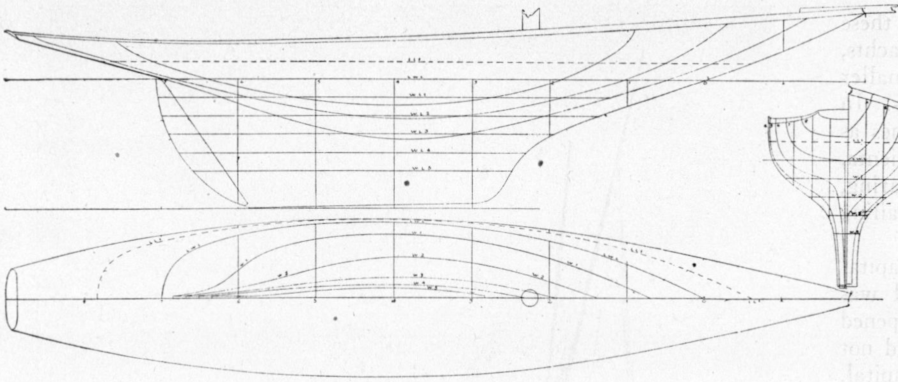

Wasp, 40-foot class, 1892. Designed by N. G. Herreshoff. Built for Archibald Roger-

New York; he found a backer in Jabez A. Bostwick, owner of the steam yacht Orienta, built by the Herreshoffs, a wealthy man associated with the Standard Oil. The Gas Engine & Power Company was thus established, with the works at 131st Street and Brook Avenue, Clement A. Gould, a relative of Mr. Bostwick, being installed as manager; as his assistant was a young man, his nephew, John J. Amory. Incidentally, the name "Gas Engine & Power Company," was originally chosen for a proposed organization for the manufacture of gas engines for land use.

After a short time the Company was building its own hulls and turning out small launches which found a ready sale in new fields. They were far lighter than the smallest steam launches, they cost less, the whole center of the hull was open for passengers, there were no coal dust, ashes nor smoke; and, what was of most importance, only one man was needed to run the engine, and he was not required to be licensed. A few of the first launches found their way into *Manning's Yacht Register* of 1886:—Sans Souci, 25 feet by 4 feet 10 inches; Secret, 21 by 5-6; Tax Payer, 40 feet. The steam davit launch, found only on the few large steam yachts, was costly, very heavy, the center was monopolized by engine, boiler and bunker, with attendant heat and dirt; and at least one licensed man, an engineer, if not a fireman as

pump the benzine from the tank, and two to operate the propeller shaft. Above the chest is a small stack, wherein is a coil of pipe containing benzine, which is vaporized and used in the cylinders, after which it is condensed and returned to the tank. To start the engine it is only necessary to pump a few drops of benzine on a suitable mechanism at the bottom of the stack, apply a match, and in one and one half minutes enough power is obtained to start the yacht. The whole thing is so simple that anyone can run it after ten minutes explanation. There is no dirt from coal or oil about the machinery. It is extremely light, and occupies only the two ends of the boat, thus leaving the middle body entirely clear for passengers. The hulls of the boats will be built by Mr. William Kyle. For small cruisers, yawls for yachts, it is likely these yachts will become very popular."

This unit, which soon became famous as the "naphtha engine" was the invention of a clever German, F. W. Ofeldt, located in

Above: Drusilla, 35 feet l.w.l. Designed by N. G. Herreshoff, 1892. Built for Edwin D. Morgan. At left: Wasp

well, was compulsory. Not only were these launches soon displaced from the large yachts, but the naphtha launch was carried on smaller steam yachts and also on sailing yachts. In 1887 the Company advertised its launches as in use on Lagonda, Corsair, Tillie, Orienta, Viking, Talisman, Norma, Nereid, Daring, Reva, Radha and Narwhal, and the sailing yachts Dauntless, Helen and Tarpon.

The combination of Genius and Capital was short-lived, it may be that Capital was unfair to Genius—such things have happened —but it is more likely that Genius could not adapt itself to the necessary routine of Capital. In any event, Mr. Ofeldt left the Company and started a new power plant, the "Alco-Vapor" engine. This was similar in its mechanical features, but in place of naphtha in the tank it used water with a merely nominal amount of alcohol; assuming to run on "alco-vapor" and thus being exempt from the Government regulations on steam. The new organization was backed by another capitalist, E. C. Benedict, owner of the steam yacht Oneida. After a time Mr. Ofeldt withdrew and with his sons started in South Brooklyn, building an engine running on kerosene. About the same time other concerns in different parts of the country started to manufacture small steam launch engines using a liquid fuel under the boiler. The Gas Engine & Power Company continued to expand, building yachts up to 100 feet or larger. In course of time Charles L. Seabury, who had been building steam yachts at Nyack, came to Morris Heights and combined with the older organization. About the beginning of the present century a new motive power, the internal combustion engine, was introduced by Dr. Otto, and still later came the Diesel engine, giving still higher powers; these two ending the era of steam in yacht propulsion.

Virginia, New York Y. C. 70-foot One Design Class, 1900

Bristol Goes Back to Sail

While still deeply involved in the problem of the steam yacht N. G. Herreshoff never lost his fondness for sail; in 1883 he designed for his personal use a keel yacht, Consuelo, 32 feet l. o. a.; 28 feet 6 inches l. w. l.; 8 feet 8 inches breadth and 5 feet 9 inches draft. The rig was a novelty, a "cat-yawl," the mainmast stepped well forward with a small mizzen. Both sails carried battens, after the fashion of the canoe sails of the day, each was hoisted by a single halyard, and the peak was held by a diagonal batten, with no gaff. The foot of each sail was laced to the boom, and in the case of the mizzen the boom was prevented from lifting by a sprit from its outer end to the mast, some distance above the gooseneck, and spanning the mast with jaws. The steering gear was original and unconventional, a vertical shaft carrying a pinion on its lower end gearing with the quadrant on the rudder stock, and carrying on its upper end a crossbar with two vertical handles similar to the control on a trolley car. A hood of oiled canvas on wood bows, similar to a buggy top, folded on deck when not needed but could be swung up to protect the helmsman from sun or rain. While most practical and effective, the whole arrangement was most unshipshape as compared with a gracefully curved tiller and a seat on the weather rail, even with a relieving tackle. In 1887 Consuelo was replaced by Clara, 35 feet l. o. a.; 29 feet 5 inches l. w. l.; 9 feet 10 inches breadth and 5 feet 5 inches draft.*

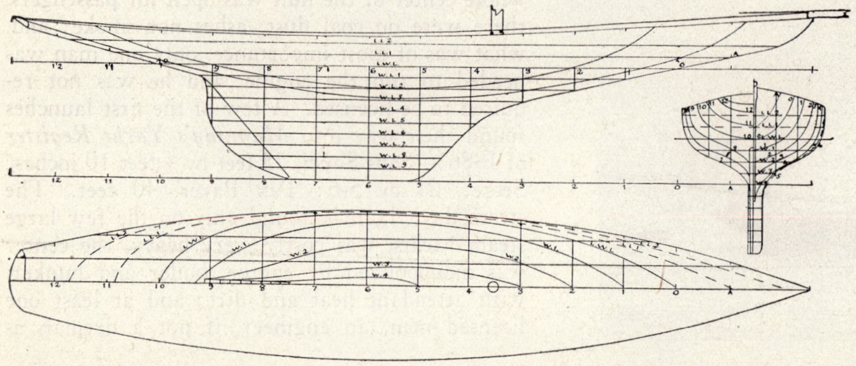

New York Y. C. 70-foot One Design Class, 1900. Rainbow, Yankee, Virginia, Mineola II

One of the outstanding personalities in American yachting was Edwin D. Morgan, Jr., nephew and namesake of a man noted as the "War

*See illustration page 118.

governor" of New York State in the Rebellion; while his innate modesty kept him out of the public eye, he was a moving power in yachting for 55 years. Joining the Sewanhaka Corinthian Y. C. in 1879, he owned Dudley, formerly Alpha, built in 1850; an old-time sloop 42 feet l.o.a.; 40 feet 6 inches l.w.l.; 13 feet breadth and 4 feet 6 inches draft; the last figure excessive for her type. As I remember her about Staten Island nearly sixty years ago, her breadth was carried well aft, almost to the very short transom, which was a long narrow oval. In 1881, Mr. Morgan bought the big schooner Wanderer and joined the Eastern Y. C. A year later he joined the New York Y. C. He was Rear Commodore of this Club in 1887-88; Vice -Commodore in 1891-92, and Commodore in 1893-94. His ownership included yachts of every size and type, from a steam yacht of 200 feet to a small catboat.

"Alty" Morgan, as he was known to his intimates, thought no more of buying a yacht than the average man does of picking up a paper as he passes a news-stand. In 1889 he built from a Burgess design the keel Tomahawk, in the new 40-foot Class, an iron yacht which was not a success; in 1890 he tried again in the Class with the Burgess Moccasin, a centerboard-keel compromise. In the summer of the latter year he sailed to Bristol in Moccasin and was shown over the shops by N. G. Herreshoff; when about to leave Mr. Herreshoff suggested that he should sail down the Bay aboard Clara, later shifting to his own yacht. Taking the helm of Clara, Mr. Morgan was surprised at the way in which, on the wind, she held his yacht, of ten feet greater waterline. Returning to Bristol later, he ordered a 27-foot steam launch and also a 27-foot cat-yawl, Pelican, for his brother-in-law, Percy F. Moran; the latter to have a fish well; still later he ordered a similar yawl, Gannet, for himself. Clara was kept afloat until both the launch and Pelican were completed, on November 11th. Pelican, with her fish-well corked, was tried against Clara and held her to Mr. Morgan's satisfaction.

In 1886 a young Baltimorean, Royal Phelps Carroll, came into yachting, purchasing the old schooner Nokomis, formerly Nettie, from Commodore W. A. W. Stewart and used her for cruising. In 1889 he built into the new 40-foot Class, Gorilla, from a design by A. Cary Smith, racing her with moderate success and selling her in the following year. In the fall of this year Mr. Morgan met Mr. Carroll on a train and learned that he proposed to build in the new 40-foot Class; he was advised to go to the Herreshoffs, and a contract was soon made. The design was completed and work was about to begin when a letter came from Mr. Carroll saying that he was contemplating matrimony and was doubtful about indulging in two such luxuries as a wife and a yacht. He asked to be released from his contract and to be advised of the cost of the cancellation. The reply congratulated him on his coming marriage and released him from the contract without charge. The design was laid aside until the beginning of February when Mr. Morgan visited the works, looked over the model and plans, and assumed the contract.

Gloriana

FORTUNATELY for yachting history, Mr. Morgan kept clear of the stencil-plate and chose an original name, Gloriana, the heroine of Spencer's poem *"The Faerie Queene."* There was a Gloriana in British yachting, the 90-foot schooner built by Michael Ratsey in 1852, but the name was new on this side and stands out as marking a new era in yacht design. While steel angles were gradually replacing wood frames at this period, they were used in a crude way, without strapping, gussets and floors; much trouble was experienced in some of the 46-footers built in Boston with a single planking of partly seasoned yellow pine on steel frames, the yachts leaking badly. Gloriana's frames, 1¾ by 1¾ spaced 16 inches, were strapped diagonally, as was her deck; her garboards were of oak and she had the regular heavy oak strakes below her planksheer; below the water she was planked with 1⅜-inch yellow pine, single, but above with ½-inch white cedar and ⅞-inch yellow pine, held to the frames by bronze bolts and with brass screws through the two layers. The deck was of 1⅛-inch matched and glued white pine, canvassed. The bulwark was of 1¼-inch oak, very plain, with no cap. The deck joiner work was very simple, in marked contrast to the many yachts then coming from the Fife Yard at Fairlie. At the same time nothing was sacrificed in the way of efficiency, all deck fittings being of special design. As one novel item, the main boom gooseneck and spinnaker boom cup were fitted on a ring which revolved around the mast.

Victorious in all her early races, Gloriana sailed but eight in all; having proven her superiority, Mr. Morgan was content to leave the field to the others of the Class to fight it out for second honors. Various statements to the effect that she had an initial advantage in early preparation brought out the following letter:—

Editor, *Forest & Stream*:

Referring to your article on Gloriana in *Forest & Stream* of April 28th, 1892, I wish to say that previous to her first race Gloriana went sailing but five times, inclusive of her trip to New York. There was no tuning-up attempted, as it would have been nearly impossible under the conditions, at one time with a large party of ladies, on another for but an hour, etc. I thought that you would wish to know this, as all previous reports have been misleading.

(signed) E. D. Morgan

Wheatley, Westbury Station, L. I.
April 30th, 1892

IN the issue of Forest & Stream referred to, and the following one, an attempt was made to discuss the qualities of the yacht from a purely technical standpoint, an imaginary design being prepared from such data as was obtainable. Not excepting America in England and the so-called "Queen's Cup," more sheer "baloney" has been written about Gloriana than any yacht which has ever floated. She has been described as out-sailing her Class by a half hour instead of by minutes, N. G. Herreshoff was hailed as "The Wizard of Bristol" and by some she was described as the sole effort of a man who was totally blind. Such comment as assumed to be technical was directed solely at her overhangs, especially the long pointed bow, it was stated that through these overhangs, while she measured less than 46 feet l.w.l. when at rest, as she moved she grew to a length of 65 feet. The following quotation is from *The New York Herald* of June, 1891:

"The Gloriana is simply a boat that measures a shade less than 46 feet on an even keel, but is so shaped as to her overhang, fore and aft, that for every foot she heels she extends her waterline immensely, and when fairly close-hauled she measures about 65 feet on her actual waterline. As she never sails practically on an even keel, she is constantly exceeding 46 feet on her actual waterline; and the greater the pressure on the canvas the more her resistance to it increases. The resultant force must be expended in making more arrowy her flight through the water. On an even keel a small craft can carry the canvas of a man-of-war, but, feeling the wind, would turn over. The Gloriana, with her 46-feet measured length, can carry the sail area of a 65-footer because she is built to sail on her side."

In Mary Taylor in 1849 and in America in 1854 George Steers revolutionized yacht design by discarding the round apple bows of the day in favor of a long hollow entrance; forty years later N. G. Herreshoff brought about another revolution by discarding the hollow bow and replacing it by a convex curve; contradictory and inconsistent as this may seem, a little serious study will reconcile the two statements. Again, after the single victory of America, British yachtsmen sought to apply the lesson by building new bows on ancient hulls and by lacing full-cut sails to booms; similarly in the case of Gloriana, new bows were built on old hulls and new yachts were designed with the "Gloriana bow," but no other change from conventional models.

MEANWHILE other events were on the carpet. On October 9, 1891, Mr. Herreshoff launched a boat built for his personal use, Dilemma; startling the yachting world with a new sensation, the "fin-keel."* Gloriana was placed on the sale list, being sold in the following spring to Dr. W. Barton Hopkins, a racing man. In October, Gannet was sold to Arthur B. Emmons of Newport, and in December Mr. Morgan placed an order for a fin-keel of 35 feet l.w.l., which he named Drusilla. At the annual meeting of the New York Y. C. in the following January he was elected commodore, with nothing larger than Drusilla for his flagship. In April Captain Harry Craven, Commodore Morgan's skipper for many years, sailed on an unknown mission to England, returning in July aboard the smart little steam yacht Ituna, designed by George L. Watson in that blessed era of the steam yacht in which style was not sacrificed to size. Small as she was, only 150 feet l.o.a., she was an ornament to the steam fleet for many years.

Going back to October, 1891, an order for another 46-foot yacht, Wasp, was placed by Archibald Rogers, one of the pestiferous "cutter-cranks" who had entered yachting in 1881 when he built

*See illustration on page 119.

the cutter Bedouin of 70 feet l.w.l. He was so much impressed by the performance of the 45-foot Gloriana against his larger yacht that he determined to build a similar yacht.

From this time on the work of the Bristol shops was gradually diverted from steam to sail; orders came in from both sides of the Atlantic:—for racing yachts of large size, for sailing cruisers, for fin-keels, small and large, for shoal-draft yachts for Barnegat and Chesapeake Bays, and for many types of small craft. Again the Company may be said to have been "manufacturing" on a scale of mass production.

The One-Design or Monotype Yacht

IN 1887 some residents of Shanklin, county Dublin, near Kingstown, Ireland, desirous of racing, were faced by hard conditions. The shelving beach was open to the seas of Dublin Bay; there was no anchorage, making it necessary to haul out the boats, thus limiting size and weight; and it was necessary to keep down the cost. The Water Wag Association was organized and a design was made by Thomas B. Middletown from which thirteen boats, all identical in every respect, were built. This appears to be the first record of a one-design class. The boats, pointed at both ends, were 13 feet over all with 4 feet 10 inches breadth, and carried one sail, a standing lug of 75 square feet with a spinaker of 60 square feet. The cost of the first boats ran from 13 to 15 pounds; the sail, made by Ratsey, cost 2 pounds 10 shillings if of cotton and 2 pounds 15 shillings if of silk. In racing the boats were sailed without ballast and a crew of two. From this insignificant beginning the one-design principle has gone round the world, with incalculable good so far as the sailing of small craft is concerned. We see today thousands of Stars, Snipes, Comets and innumerable other classes, of such low cost as to place them within the reach of children and many of them of amateur build. The principles of boat handling and racing tactics are acquired almost insensibly in this infant class of yachting, while many seniors profit from the sport thus afforded at small expense. It will be noticed that yacht racing at the present time, and probably "for the duration," is limited to the one-design classes.

The good that has thus been accomplished for yachting is beyond computation; and yet, if carried to an extreme, the principle has its evil side. In classes of not over 30 feet waterline as a maximum, well built to and with sustained competition, it has proved a boon to senior yachting; but when it is taken up by millionaires, in yachts of large size, and in classes of but three, four or five yachts, the result is distinctly detrimental. True, it is economical, the designer's fee, divided into three, four or five fractions, is absorbed in the builder's price; and, by "mass construction," even on the same three, four or five scale, this price is well below that of individual yachts built in different yards. As far as progress in naval architecture, improvement in yacht design and construction, and encouragement to designers, are involved, the one-design principle has proved an utter failure. There is, it is true, a certain distinction attending the ownership in the leading class of the year, but this, again, in no way advances the broad interests of the sport.

The Problem of Today

THE condition of yachting in America prior to the war, and its future when peace again reigns, offer a problem which demands early and serious consideration by all interested in the sport. Match sailing of the first class is now governed by two rival rules:—the International, generally in use on the other side of the Atlantic, and the Universal (the Herreshoff Rule) in nominal use on this side. While both were framed with the same end in view, they differ materially in their factors and the resulting models. Naturally, opinions differ as to the relative merits; but, leaving aside all national prejudice, there are good reasons for the belief that the American Rule produces a better yacht than the European. The condition existing in this country for some years prior to the war was that only two Rule classes, the 12-Meter and the 6-Meter, were racing; with no classes under the Universal Rule. Whether this condition was due in a greater or lesser degree to the prevalence, for the past forty years, of small classes of large one-design yachts is an open question. The issue today is whether it will be possible to build up a few racing classes under the Universal Rule.

One of the early one-design classes was built by the Herreshoffs in 1896, half-decked fin-keels limited to not over 30 feet waterline:—Hera, Ralph N. Ellis; Wawa, James A. Stillwell; Esperanza, A. S. Van Wickle, Jr.; Puck, E. D. Morgan; Asahi, Bayard Thayer; Mai, C. E. Jennings; Vaquero II, Hermanus B. Duryea; Carolina, Pembroke Jones. All of these owners were members of the New York Y. C., the Class did much of its racing about Newport and the boats were popularly known as the "Newport Thirties," but it was in part an open class of 30-feet waterline, with several yachts by Gardner, Wintringham and others. The boats were fast, smart and lively and furnished very good racing for several years. In 1900 a one-design class of 70-feet waterline was started, the four yachts being built at Bristol:—Rainbow, Cornelius Vanderbilt; Yankee, H. P. Whitney and H. B. Duryea; Virginia, W. K. Vanderbilt, Jr.; Mineola II, August Belmont (the name stencilled from his 46-foot Mineola I. The Class made good racing and held together for some years. In 1902 Yankee was sold to J. Rogers Maxwell and in 1904 Mineola II was sold to W. Ross Proctor.

TRADITIONS AND MEMORIES OF

AMERICAN YACHTING

By WILLIAM P. STEPHENS

Part Forty-Three

The Herreshoffs of Bristol—Continued

MENTION has been made of the one-design class built in 1896 and known popularly as the "Newport Thirties," much of their racing being done off that port. While proving satisfactory for the immediate purpose (racing), they did not entitle their owners to representation in the New York Y. C., the By-laws calling for "thirty feet load waterline length, if single-masted, and

that she is a full-decked vessel, reasonable cockpit excepted; and, further, by her design and construction she is well suited to accompany the Squadron on a cruise."

Late in 1904 a movement was started for a class of small yachts which would meet these requirements, and at a meeting in October the following resolution was adopted:—"That the Chair appoint a committee of three for the purpose of interesting members of the Club in the building of yachts in one-design or restricted classes, and of sizes either entitled to representation or not entitled to representation, with power to procure from naval architects designs and estimates, and to submit the same to the members who may contemplate building in such classes."

The Committee, W. Butler Duncan, Jr., Addison G. Hanan and Newbury D. Lawton, sent out the following circular:—

"A proposition having been made by a number of members of the New York Y. C. for the building of restricted or one-design class, and a committee having been appointed to take up the matter and put it in shape for consideration by such members as may be interested; following out the views of those who have originated the idea, the committee have prepared the following suggestions, as to the details for the class:

"Type.—The boat to be of a type intended to be promoted by the present rule of measurement of the New York Y. C., a wholesome seaworthy craft free from freak features.

"Size.—A keel boat, about 30ft. waterline, short overhangs and of moderate beam and draft.

"Plan.—Cabin house not less than 10ft. 6in. in length, about 4ft. wide, having straight sides with glass transom lights, toilet room with closet and basin, berth for man, forward, cockpit not less than 6ft. long with rail set outside to form seat on deck.

"Fittings.—Complete but simple outfit for cruising; transom cushions; stove, ice-box; tank.

"Sails and Rigging.—Sail area about 1,000 sq. ft.; jib and mainsail rig; spinnaker and balloon jib allowed; solid spars.

"Selection.—Boats when completed to be drawn by lot.

"Regulation.—Yachts to be steered by a member or amateur. Two paid hands allowed. Crew all told limited to four persons. Entire cruising outfit to be carried.

"Special specifications to be agreed upon for sizes, weights and details of outfit.

"Preliminary plans, specifications and estimates have been obtained.

"The committee would be glad to learn if you are interested in building in this

Left: Tobasco, a New York Thirty, 1905, showing the long square cabin trunk.

Below: A Thirty well heeled over in a stiff breeze

class and if you desire to have notice of the meetings of the committee.

"The committee wish also to state that, should the members so desire, they are prepared to take up the question of a class or classes, either larger or smaller than the one that has been outlined, and they would be glad to receive any suggestions as to such class or classes."

The Rule alluded to was the Universal Rule, just adopted by the Club, as formulated by N. G. Herreshoff.

Designs and estimates were received from several designers, but those of the Herreshoff Mfg. Co. received the first consideration, the position of this Company as both designers and builders giving it a great advantage over designers who had to rely on outside builders for estimates. At a special meeting of proposed owners in the Class held on November 10, 1904, the Herreshoff design and bid was submitted:—not less than 14 orders, the price to be $4,000 delivered at Bristol, payments to be $1,000 on signing the contract, $1,500 when hull was completed, and $1,500 on delivery; the yachts to be planked with yellow pine, single below the turn of the bilge, and double above, with an inner planking of cypress and outer of yellow pine; Herreshoff anti-fouling paint to be used on the bottom.

The first yacht was completed by January 5, 1905, and was tried by Mr. Lawton, representing the Committee; although the trial was made in very light air, it was declared satisfactory, and work went ahead on eighteen hulls. When completed the ownership was decided by lot, the names of the yachts and their owners being:—Minx, Howard Willets; Pintail, August Belmont; Maid of Meudon, W. D. Guthrie; Neola II, George M. Pynchon; Phryne, Henry L. Maxwell; Cara Mia, Stuyvesant Wainwright; Alera, A. H. and James W. Alker; Atair, Cord Meyer; Linnet, Amos T. French; Nautilus, Addison G. Hanan; Adelaide II, George A. and Philip H. Adee; Anemone, J. Murray Mitchell, Jr.; Tobasco, Henry F. Lippett; Banzai, Newbury D. Lawton; Ibis, O'Donnell Iselin; Dahinda, W. Butler Duncan, Jr.; Oriole, Lyman Delano; Carlita, Oliver Harriman.

The equipment furnished with each yacht was most complete, including no less than 88 separate items, among them one 47-pound gooseneck anchor; one 47-pound straight stock anchor; 300 feet 2¼ inch manilla cable; 50 feet 2-inch mooring line; 180 feet 1¾-inch manilla warp; 1 sounding lead and line; one 10 quart galvanized pail; 1 scrub brush; 2 pipe berths with mattresses; 2 blankets; 2 pillows; 8 sheets; 1 butcher knife; 1 can-opener; 1 coffee pot; 6 plates; 3 soup plates; 1 broom; 6 teaspoons; 6 dessert spoons; 1 doz. towels; 1 mainsail; 1 No. 1 jib, 1 No. 2 jib, 1 spinnaker, 9 sail stops. Judging by these samples from the long list, the outfit was the most complete ever furnished by a builder. All the yachts were painted white on delivery, but after a few races Phryne was painted black. Of recent years, in conformity with modern fashion, the fleet has shown a variety of colors.

The following rules were adopted on November 27, 1905, for the government of the Class:—

Outfit: Everything delivered with the boat, as per specifications, shall be on board in every race, except one anchor and cable, which need not be carried. Articles lost shall be replaced.

Crew: The crew shall not exceed five men, two of

Right: Raccoon, a Newport Thirty, 1896, half decked with shelter roof. Below: A fleet of Newport Thirties in a race, 1896

whom may be paid hands. The helmsman shall be an amateur.

Hauling out: The boats shall not be hauled out, or put on the beach, more than once in two weeks; and when hauled out shall not remain more than three days. In case of accident the Committee may waive this Rule.

Sails: Not more than two new suits of sails shall be used when racing in any one season on any boat. In case of an accident to a sail the Committee may waive this Rule. Balloon jibs shall be barred except when racing against boats not in the Class. A black band shall be painted around the mast at a point whose distance above deck shall be determined by the designer, above which the jaws of the gaff shall not be hoisted.

Length of spars shall not exceed:—boom, 32 feet; gaff, 19 feet; spinnaker boom, 19 feet 6 inches. The size of the mainsail and jib shall not be limited except that the length of boom, gaff, hoist or fore triangle shall not be altered. Spinnaker shall be of the same size as originally furnished. Bowsprits two feet longer than originals shall be fitted under supervision of designers. (Note: The boats proved hard-headed on a reach, and the original bowsprits were replaced by new ones two feet longer.)

Ballast or spars shall not be altered in any way. Pot-leading shall not be allowed. Only solid spars shall be carried. Each boat shall carry a special number above the reef points. Spinnaker sheets shall not be carried forward of or around the fore stay.

Prize money to professionals shall not exceed the following schedule:—$1.00 for start, $4.00 for first place, $3.00 for second place, $2.00 for third place. Questions arising under these Rules shall be decided by the Committee elected for the season by the owners, whose decision shall be final.

Newbury D. Lawton
W. B. Duncan, Jr. } Committee elected for 1906.
A. G. Hanan

These Rules shall be printed and a copy posted on each boat and in the Club House.

It must be admitted, that the original Committee, as above, handled the matter most ably from start to finish; the Class, large in numbers, was probably the most completely equipped from the start of any one-design class; and under the Rules the racing was keen and well sustained for many years. The boats measured 27.7 by the Universal Rule when racing outside the Class; in the first season the leading boat was Phryne, making a percentage of .780 in 20 starts; next came Cara Mia, with a percentage of .762 for 36 starts. Very close to her was Nautilus, with .726 for 35 starts; then Carlita, .682 for 16 starts.

A number of the boats were regarded with special affection by their owners, who held them for many years; but there were numberless changes of both ownership and names, and it is impossible today to determine the fate of some which have disappeared from club books and Lloyd's Register. There is no record in the 1942 Lloyd's of Phryne, Cara Mia, Atair, Adelaide II, Linnet, Nautilus, Anemone, Ibis and Oriole. In some cases the name has been changed six or seven times; only two, Alera and Banzai, retain their original names. One of the Class is now owned in Buffalo, one in Philadelphia, and one in Detroit. More than a half dozen have had engines installed. In its history of 38 years the Thirty-Foot Class has proved a credit to the yachtsmen who created it and the genius who was quick to realize the possibilities of the idea and to do his part to make it a success.

Top of page: Istalena, 65-foot One Design Class

Right: Lines for the New York Yacht Club 50-foot class, 1913

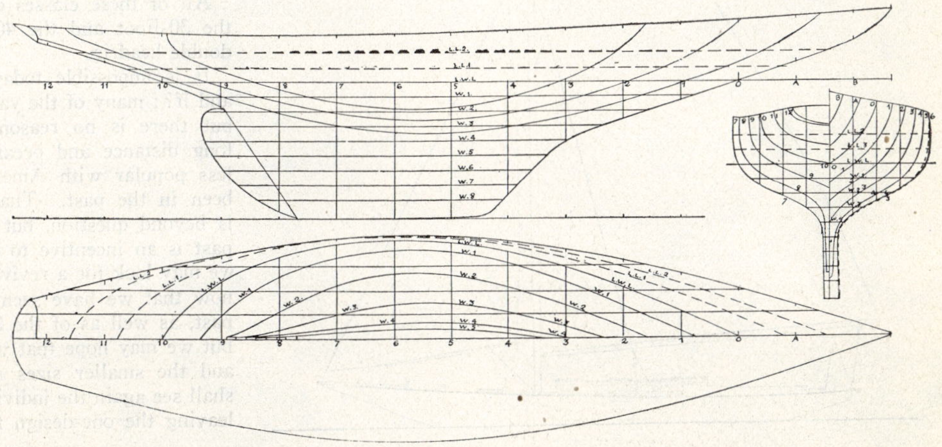

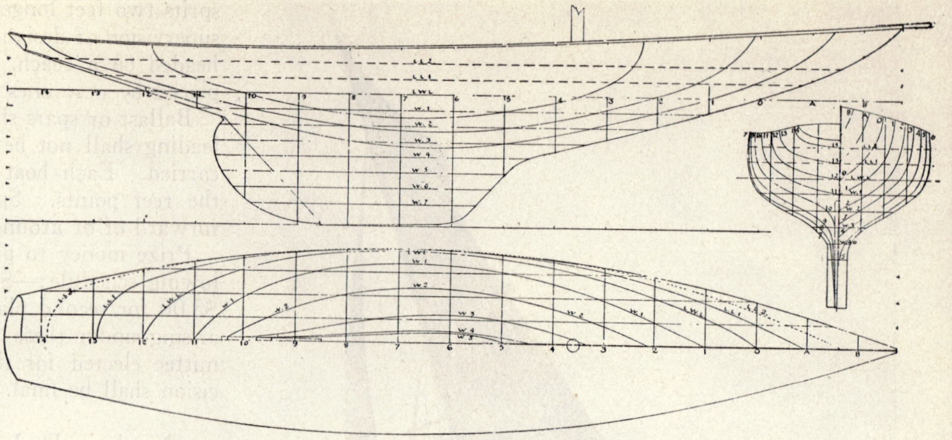

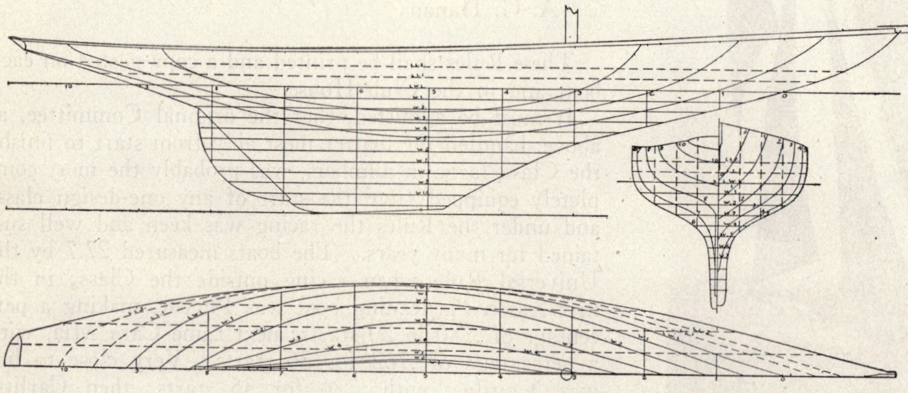

Above: Lines for the New York Yacht Club 30-foot class, 1905, and, at right, the New York Yacht Club 65-foot class, 1907

The 65-, 50-, and 40-Foot Classes

As much cannot be said of the next, the 65-Ft. Class, so called, a select and semi-private affair limited to three yachts. Built in 1907, it numbered only Aurora, Cornelius Vanderbilt; Istalena, George M. Pynchon; and Winsome, Henry F. Lippett. Their dimensions were: l.o.a., 85 feet 3 inches; l.w.l., 65 feet; breadth, 16 feet 7 inches; draft, 10 feet 10 inches. As the lines show, they were good boats, with no freak features, and they made good racing for their owners, but they did nothing for the broad interests of the sport.

Sail plan of the New York Yacht Club 30-foot class, with lengthened bowsprit

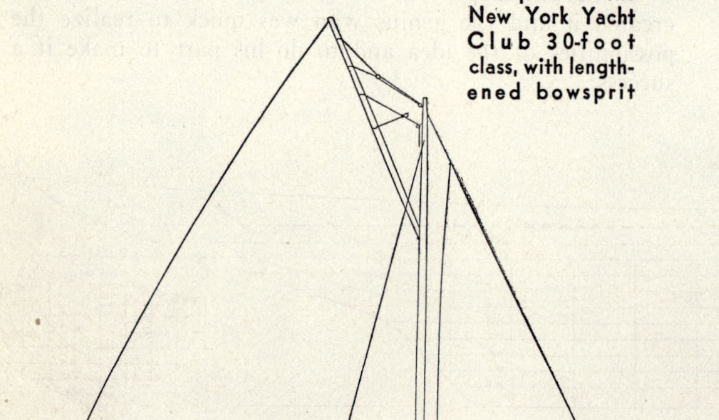

Following in 1913 came a large fleet, the 50-Foot Class: Grayling, J. P. Morgan; Acushla, G. M. Heckscher; Barbara, Harry Payne Whitney; Carolina II, Pembroke Jones; Iroquois II, Ralph N. Ellis; Peerless, Henry L. and Howard W. Maxwell; Samuri, W. Earl Dodge; Spartan, Edmund Randolph; Ventura, George F. Baker, Jr. The dimensions were: l.o.a., 72 feet; l.w.l., 50 feet; breadth, 14 feet 6 inches; draft, 9 feet 3 inches. As a racing class it proved very satisfactory and gave good sport for some years.

The last of these classes was the 40-Foot, built in 1916: Shawara, Harold Wesson; Black Duck, Arthur K. Bourne; Rowdy, Holland S. Duell; Zilph, James E. Hayes; Jessica, Wilson Marshall; Maisie, Morton F. Plant; Mistral, George M. Pynchon; Pampero, Dr. James Bishop; Pauline, Oliver G. Jennings; Dolly Bowen, Alexander S. Cochran; Katherine, Arthur F. Luke; Squaw, John S. Lawrence. The dimensions were: l.o.a., 59 feet; l.w.l., 40 feet; breadth, 14 feet 5 inches; draft, 8 feet. They were big, bulky boats, less graceful above water than their larger sisters of the 70-Foot, 65-Foot and 50-Foot Classes, but they gave good racing for many years and are still doing good work of another kind; the original rig has been changed to cutter, yawl or schooner, and in most cases auxiliary power installed.

All of these classes carried the conventional boom and gaff rig, the 30-Foot and the 40-Foot with single jib and the others with double headrig.

It is impossible today to predict the course of yachting when? and if?; many of the yacht clubs are in a very precarious condition; but there is no reason to believe that the sport of cruising, of long distance and ocean racing and of match sailing will be any less popular with Americans under normal conditions than it has been in the past. That its up-building will take time and effort is beyond question, but the spirit is still alive, the memory of the past is an incentive to new exertion, and with the return of peace we may look for a revival of all branches of sailing. It seems likely now that we have seen the last of the great racing cutters of the past, as well as of the big "floating palaces" in the power division; but we may hope that with the building of racing yachts of medium and the smaller sizes syndicate ownership will disappear and we shall see again the individual owner in consultation with his designer, leaving the one-design field to yachts not larger than the Thirties.

TRADITIONS AND MEMORIES OF

American Yachting

By WILLIAM P. STEPHENS

Part Forty-Four

Vigilant, left, and Valkyrie II ready for the start, showing attendant fleet

ON the evening of the final race between Thistle and Volunteer a preliminary challenge from the Royal Clyde Y. C. was delivered to the New York Y. C. at its house, 60 Madison Avenue, where all hands were celebrating the defeat of the Scotchmen. This challenge was ignored and steps were taken immediately to write a new Deed of Gift for the America's Cup. This "New Deed," which proved to be distinctly detrimental to all interests of a challenger, was generally denounced by all foreign clubs, and ended the racing for an indefinite time. In the autumn of 1892 a challenge was received on behalf of the Earl of Dunraven, a newcomer in yachting and ignorant of both the history and the technique of the sport. The challenge being finally accepted after a long series of negotiations, the holders of the Cup were faced with the question of a designer.

The career of Edward Burgess is probably the most unusual in the history of yacht designing. With ample means and leisure the Burgess brothers grew up on the water, owning racing and cruising in yachts by the leading builders of the day. Edward spent some time abroad and was personally familiar with British yachts and racing. While thus fitted in many ways, at the age of 36 he was only a tyro in yacht designing, self-taught and inexperienced. Much of the inside history of this day never has been written, but there is good reason for the belief that General Paine, a very shrewd and spirited yachtsman, a member of the New York Y. C. though more closely affiliated with the Eastern Y. C. and Boston yachting, racing his schooner Halcyon in both clubs, had in mind for some time the idea of placing Boston more prominently in the sport in which New York was then supreme. Whatever the cause, the fact was that a Boston syndicate was formed for the building of a defender and Edward Burgess was selected as the designer.

His first yacht, Puritan, though modern in every sense, followed closely the dimensions of the older Halcyon. In the planning of the design he was aided by General Paine, whose long experience and Yankee common sense offset in part his lack of technical knowledge of designing, and by Henry Bryant, another self-taught but skillful designer, as testified by his compromise Thetis. In a career of but seven years, terminated by his sudden death from over-work in 1891, Mr. Burgess had created three successful Cup defenders and a fleet of cutters, yawls and schooners, small and large, in addition to steam yachts and work of various kinds for the U. S. Government.

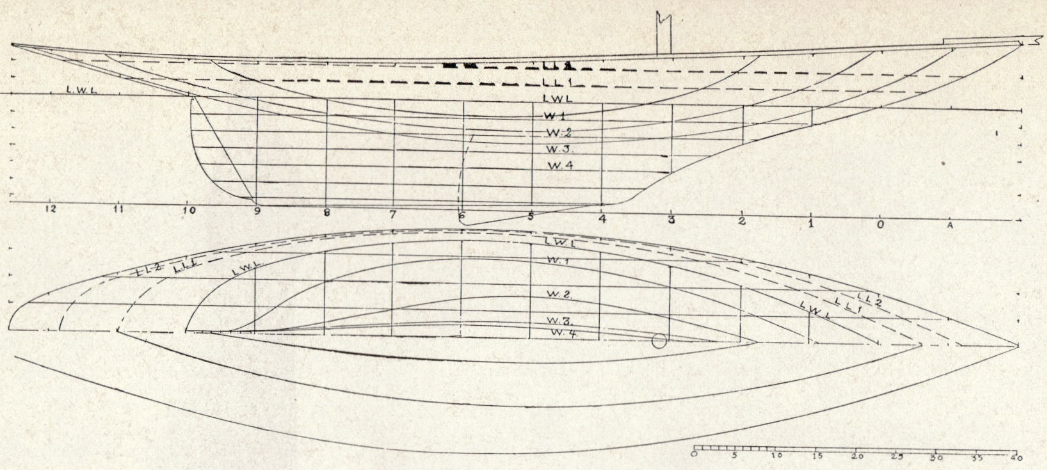

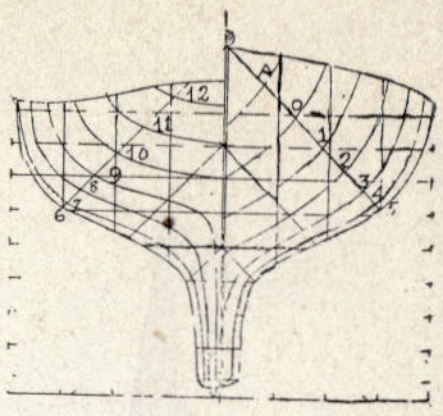

Lines of Vigilant, defender of the America's Cup, 1893. Center: "Me and Hattie," Vigilant and her chaperone, 1893. Bottom: Vigilant before the start, showing crew

Bristol Builds Its First Cup Defender

When the challenge of Lord Dunraven was accepted there were only two American designers, A. Cary Smith, who had to his credit the successful sloop Mischief of 1881, but against her record was the unsuccessful—through no fault of her designer—Priscilla of 1885. The other, William Gardner, was a young American with all the advantages of a modern scientific education at home and in Europe, but only three years of actual practice in yachts of 40 to 50 feet. The syndicate organized for the construction of a defender was headed by Archibald Rogers, with W. K. Vanderbilt, Frederick W. Vanderbilt, J. Pierpont Morgan, F. Augustus Schermerhorn and John E. Brooks as his associates. The Herreshoff plant had on the stocks at the time a steel centerboard cutter of 83 feet l.w.l., Navahoe, for Royal Phelps Carroll, who planned to race her in British waters. The experience of Mr. Rogers with Wasp, and the proof that the company was now equipped for large work in metal, led him to place the contract for both design and construction. His choice was for a keel yacht, Colonia, and the dimensions selected were: l.o.a., 126 feet; l.w.l., 85 feet 6 inches; breadth, 24 feet; draft, 14 feet; all that the depth of water over the ways would permit. The hull was of steel, in-and-out plated.

The hollow spar, though in use at this time in small yachts, was really no novelty, the sloop Maria in 1849 hav-

Hansen, formerly in command of the schooner Sachem for Jesse Metcalf, and in no way prominent as a racing skipper, was placed in command. Captain Hank Haff was engaged to sail Colonia.

The breadths of the six great cutters built in 1893 were as follows: Valkyrie II, 22 feet 6 inches; Jubilee, 22 feet 6 inches; Navahoe, 23 feet; Pilgrim, 23 feet; Colonia, 24 feet; Vigilant, 26 feet 6 inches. The number of men required to work one of these yachts was about 45, the only limit on number of crew being that of useless weight. Vigilant was designed to carry a crew of 70, an estimated weight of at least 4½ tons excess on the weather rail. As the yachts were measured without crew aboard, the 70 men aboard Vigilant compared with 40 aboard Valkyrie II gave the defender an advantage of about one foot of unmeasured waterline.

Above: Vigilant as a cruising yawl, 1901. Below: Colonia, built for Cup defense, 1893

ing a hollow boom 95 feet long, built of staves, like a barrel; in 1870 the challenger, Cambria, had bored spars. A hollow boom was built for Colonia at the yard of C. & R. Poillon, in Brooklyn under the supervision of John J. Driscoll, a skilled yacht builder of the old school. A form was set up with circular bulkheads of wood at intervals, over which were run staves of Oregon pine, in as long strakes as possible, each 1½ inches thick, hollowed inside and rounded on the outside, and screwed to the bulkheads. Over them a second similar layer was laid, breaking joints. The many excellent waterproof glues in use today are of recent origin. Nothing of the kind was known sixty years ago, but there was an old-world recipe, introduced as I remember by Henry Piepgrass, a Dane, a mixture of lime and pot cheese which forms a good cement, supposed to be waterproof. This was used between the joints of the staves and between the two layers; the spar was finally served at intervals with wire rope.

America Holds to the Centerboard

Whether or no the older element in the Club resented or mistrusted the selection of the keel type does not appear, but a second syndicate was soon organized by Edwin D. Morgan, then slated as the next commodore of the Club. The members were: E. D. Morgan, August Belmont, Oliver H. P. Belmont, Cornelius Vanderbilt, Charles R. Flint, Chester W. Chapin, George C. Clark, Henry Astor Carey and Dr. W. Barton Hopkins. On completion, Vigilant, as she was named, was turned over to C. Oliver Iselin as "managing owner," Commodore Morgan retiring from the picture; Captain William

The form of the yacht and the use of this live ballast aroused a general discussion which continued through the season; one view appeared in *Forest & Stream* of November 25, 1893. "Assuming the right of Vigilant, in default of any express prohibition, to avail herself of this kind and amount of ballast, there is still the nice question of ethics; whether such a course is to be considered fair and sportsmanlike. This much may safely be said, that had it been Valkyrie instead of Vigilant that thus took advantage of a plain defect in the rules, there would have been a greater clamor than was raised over the alleged over-length of Thistle in 1887; and, further, that it is one of those tricks which can be played just once." The subject was also discussed at much length from a technical standpoint, Dixon Kemp, an expert naval architect, taking the ground in the London *Field* that the excess weight to windward was a negligible factor. His contention was strongly opposed on this side, involving long letters with elaborate diagrams and lengthy calculations.

It frequently happens that the dimensions of important yachts as given to the press and even as published in club books are "cooked", with intent to deceive, and many of such published dimensions are unreliable. The following dimensions were taken from Vigilant by John Hyslop in 1896 with a 100-ft. tapeline (which, by the way, I still have); they are to the waterline with the crew. L.o.a., 126 feet; l.w.l., 86 feet 10 inches; breadth, 26 feet 6 inches, draft, 13 feet 2 inches; with board, about 22 feet. The construction was novel in the extreme, the frame and the topsides of steel, the hull below water of Tobin bronze, an alloy recently invented by Lt. John A. Tobin, U.S.N.; the centerboard frame, the sternpost and the rudder frame of cast brass. The Tobin bronze plating gave a hard smooth surface resisting all marine growth; the plating was in-and-out.

The centerboard, 16 feet 6 inches long, was plated on the sides with 7/32 Tobin bronze fastened with countersunk tapbolts to the brass frame; its thickness was 3½ inches and the bottom was filled with melted lead, over which was broken coke with fluid cement poured to fill all interstices, the weight was 7,750 pounds. The fore end was hung on a cast bronze hook with a plate base riveted to the keel plate, this attachment gave much trouble later in her career. A geared winch of special design was made by the Yale & Towne Company, capable of lifting six tons, but calling for much care in its use, the chain being paid out only as fast as the board could take it. The sternpost was a casting of special design, shaped to fit the rudder on its after side, and with ribs similar to a channel bar, to which the plates could be riveted, on the fore side. The brass rudder stock and frame, in one casting, was plated with Tobin bronze. As a matter of course, she steered with a wheel.

The original design of Vigilant called for inside lead in the ballast trough of the keel, as in Navahoe. On trial the latter proved tender, and her inside lead was removed in part and re-cast in such size pieces as could be conveniently handled, and bolted under the keel plate. In view of this it was proposed to put an 8-inch lead keel under Vigilant, but this was later changed to 16 inches. Though nominally fitted below in conventional fashion, with saloon, owner's and crews' quarters and galley, Vigilant was very lightly fitted up and though her crew lived aboard Valkyrie there was very little weight wasted on her; George Watson being credited with the remark that the furnishings of both amounted to little more than a coat of paint.

Again Boston came to the fore with two candidates for the defense, Pilgrim, an extreme bulb-fin keel designed by Stewart & Binney, successors to Edward Burgess, and Jubilee, designed by John B., son of General Paine, a combination of keel, centerboard and bulb. Though financed by the General, he openly disclaimed all responsibility for the design, speaking of her as "my son John's boat."

A Chaperone for a Cup Defender

BOTH Genesta and Galatea sailed across the Atlantic in ordinary cruising fashion, and when in New York the usual daily routine went on throughout the morning of a race, all hands piped to grub, decks swabbed and other work continued until it was time to take the covers off the sails and get ready for the race. Thistle also sailed across and her crew lived aboard her during the races. Colonia was handled in the same way, but with her large crew Vigilant set a new fashion. As a mother ship and tender the Hattie Palmer, an old sailing schooner refitted with a steam engine and a big deck house and used for carrying freight between New Rochelle and New York, was chartered for the season and the crew berthed and boarded aboard her, while she also did towing duty.

This innovation aroused some comment among conventional yachtsmen. The picture here shown was snapped for *Forest & Stream* and published over the caption, "Me and Hattie." There was current in New York a recent German engraving showing a nude boy seated on a branch over a brook, his back showing, while beside him sat a big dog with his tail hanging down, the caption being "Me and Jack"; this suggested the idea. Far from disapproving of it, Mr. Iselin borrowed the negative.

The engineering of the rigs of these great yachts was crude, experimental and empirical in the extreme; spars were sprung or broken, the sheaves of blocks crushed, and there were many other break-downs; in one trial race the jaws of Jubilee's gaff gave way before the start, but General Paine held on and sailed the race with the fore end of the gaff forward of the mast, as in a lug sail. On trial Colonia proved lacking in both stability and lateral resistance. She was hauled out in Brooklyn and two pieces of lead each shaped like a cigar halved on its long axis were cast and bolted on the sides of the keel. While this improved her stability it still left her weak to windward. The trial races served merely to show that Vigilant was the only one of the four fit to face the challenger.

Three Out of Five Races

WITH almost the same length of measured waterline Vigilant, with 11,272 square feet of sail, allowed Valkyrie, with 10,042 square feet, 1 minute 48 seconds. The first race failed through lack of wind, with Valkyrie in the lead when it was called. The second was to leeward and return, 30 nautical miles, in moderate weather, Vigilant winning by nearly 6 minuntes. The next race was over a triangle, in a working breeze, Vigilant winning by 10 minutes 35 seconds. The morning of the third race opened with a report from the Weather Bureau of a gale coming up the coast, at the start there was a 15-knot breeze and a tumble of sea; later the wind increased to 25 knots. Before the start a throat halyard sheave crushed aboard Valkyrie and she was allowed time for repairs.

A little later Mr. Herreshoff, at the wheel of Vigilant, was summoned below. The man in charge of the centerboard winch had released the brake and let things go with a run, so that the board and chain were jammed in the slot. A tackle was rigged in an effort to clear the board, but it could be forced only half way down, and when off the wind it could not be fully housed in the trunk. After a hard beat of 15 miles in a strengthening wind Valkyrie rounded two minutes ahead of Vigilant.

While Valkyrie had started with a half reef, Vigilant turned in a full reef and set a working topsail; after rounding she set her spinnaker in American fashion, in stops, with sheet and tack slack and sail bellying forward; then she set her balloon jib topsail. With the latter the halyard jammed in the block and a man was sent down the stay to clear things. Valkyrie, of course, followed the English practice of setting her spinnaker flying; by ill luck the foot was slightly torn in getting out the sail. The tear extended until the sail was in ribbons; it was taken in and her light-weather spinnaker of fine linen was set, this fouling the bitts before it was up, and blowing across the topmast stay, where it fouled a hook of the jib topsail. As a last resort the "bowsprit spinnaker," the equivalent of our balloon jib topsail, was set.

I had had my glasses on the boats from the time that the Committee tug reached the line. I had witnessed some thrilling Cup and trial races, but none like this. Now, as they ran off before the rising gale, I noticed a man suspended from a halyard and hauled by an outhaul along Vigilant's boom, cutting the stops as he went. At the topmast head was a second man, one at the end of the gaff, and a fourth whom I could not see at the masthead. The head of the working topsail was lashed and the halyard sent down, the clew of the sail lashed to the gaff end and the sheet sent down, and when all was ready the reef was shaken out, the whole mainsail spread, and immediately the second club topsail was sent up to windward of the working topsail. The fight for the last three miles was an inspiring one, perhaps more so than the last half hour of the final Genesta-Puritan race, Vigilant gaining foot by foot and winning by a margin of 2 minutes 13 seconds actual time.

Valkyrie II was one of the best yachts which ever came for the Cup. She was well sailed by Captain William Cranfield, but she came late in the season, there was not time for adequate preparation, and some ill-advised changes were made in the amount and disposition of her lead. After the race, in talking with young William Cranfield, I said, "Why did you not do as Vigilant did? His reply was, "If we had, the mast might have gone and we would have killed some men." I said, "We do not race that way on this side, if Vigilant's mast had gone it would have killed twice as many men as you would have lost." Altogether, it was a fine piece of work, creditable alike to Mr. Iselin and his crew.

It was in this match, which, by the way, for the first time was extended to three out of five races, that the attendant fleet of excursion boats, from fishing smacks to the largest Sound and Hudson River steamboats, became not only a nuisance but a menace, giving the yachts no space in which to maneuver, and killing with its deadwash the yacht which chanced to be astern. In these races, too, the one-gun start was used for the first time.

Braving the Lion in Its Den

DURING the winter Vigilant was sold to George J. and Howard Gould, who at once made arrangements to race in British waters in the following season. Captain Hank Haff was engaged as racing skipper, with Captain Leander Jeffrey as mate and young Clayton Haff as second mate. Mr. Herreshoff was invited to make the trip, and steered her in a number of the races. Gilbert Wilson, of Wilson & Griffin, sail makers, was another guest of Messrs. Gould; they with Captain Haff accompanying their hosts aboard the steam yacht Atalanta, while Captain Jeffrey was in command of Vigilant on the voyage.

The yacht was made ready at Erie Basin, Brooklyn, her hull was strengthened by T bars fore and aft under the deck beams and along the floor, these being joined by diagonal braces of steel angles; the braces being removed in Glasgow. A jury boom and gaff were shipped and a small mizzenmast was set up with a leg-o-mutton sail, which, when a few days out, was replaced by a gaff sail. Spars were run fore and aft along the deck, supported on horses, to act as bulwarks, and additional life lines were rigged. When I was aboard her shortly before she sailed I noted the cabin "joiner-work," the bulkheads light frames of wood with canvas panels. In her racing abroad she carried a crew of but 49, all hands being berthed aboard. She sailed from Brooklyn on June first and made Gourock on June sixteenth after an uneventful passage.

Vigilant's first start was in the regatta of the Mudhook Y. C., on the Clyde, on July fifth; Valkyrie II had been refitted and was ready for a long season of hot racing with an international flavor against the new Britannia, Satanita, Vigilant and Iverna. At the start Satanita, the giant of the racing fleet with a waterline of 98 feet, in coming for the line just before the gun, found her way blocked by a small boat in which were four men. She luffed to avoid them, but was unable to bear away, and her long sharp bow cut into Valkyrie, down below the waterline and six feet into her deck. While Lord Dunraven and his guests and crew were saved, the yacht sank rapily. She was later raised and broken up.

THIS race and ten others were won by Britannia, with five for Vigilant down to August sixth. One striking feature of Vigilant was her long straight keel, which made her slow in turning; a matter of comparatively small moment in her home races, but very serious on the Scotch and English courses, three or four short legs sailed two, three or four rounds. She had for the season an English skipper, Captain Tom Diaper, better known as "Tommy Dutch," one of a famous sailing family of the East Coast, at one time in New York as skipper of the cutter Ileen. On August 18 while passing near The Needles with her board down, she struck a rock, the board lifted and dropped suddenly, jamming the chain in the trunk.

It was believed at first that the board had dropped out, but such was not the case; however, she was out of the racing for some time for extensive and costly repairs. Again, on September 18, while sailing from Portland to Cowes to start in the race for the Cape May Cup against Britannia, the same disaster was repeated. Britannia had been withdrawn from the racing owing to a boat accident in which two of her crew were drowned, but the Prince of Wales had prepared to meet Vigilant in this cross-Channel race. Captain Diaper, who was conning her from the bow as she sailed among known rocks, claimed that Captain Jeffrey did not hear or heed his "Lee, Ho," but it is quite possible that her slow turning was responsible.

She struck heavily, the board jumped up and fell, stripping the gears from the winch in the saloon and finally breaking the chain and falling to the bottom. The table in the saloon was broken by fragments thrown by the rapidly revolving winch, Howard Gould and a friend narrowly escaping injury. Four tons of lead were shipped inside to compensate for the weight of the lost board, and her owners offered to sail her in that condition, but the Prince of Wales declined to race against a disabled boat.

THE performance of Vigilant abroad was a great disappointment to her many admirers at home, some very contemptible criticism of the Goulds appeared in American dailies, and there was similar idle gossip in some English circles. I was told by Gilbert Wilson after his return that there were no real grounds for complaint against the treatment which was accorded them in England, and it would seem that in their many meetings the owners of Britannia and Vigilant acted as gentlemen and sportsmen.

The following, from *The Field*, seems to cover the situation very fairly: "The result of the 17 encounters between Vigilant and Britannia leaves their relative merits rather indistinctly defined, but, judged by the bare records, Britannia is the superior sort of craft for match sailing. She cannot, it appears, be driven as fast through the water in a strong blow of wind as Vigilant can; on the other hand, she is a more certain and reliable performer in moderate breezes. Perhaps it would be just to say, putting the record on one side, that the two yachts are of equal merit, or that neither nation can claim superiority." In 1896 Vigilant was sold to Percy Chubb, of the New York Y. C., who raced her for several years, altering her to a yawl in 1901; in 1903 he sold her to F. Lothrop Ames, of the Eastern Y. C.; in 1904 she was owned by Stephen Peabody of the New York Y. C., and from 1904 to 1909 she was used for cruising by William E. Iselin, dropping out of yachting in 1910.

TRADITIONS AND MEMORIES OF

AMERICAN YACHTING

By WILLIAM P. STEPHENS

Part Forty-five . . . The Herreshoffs of Bristol

THE ninth match for the America's Cup brought about a new deal in yacht racing, with an increase of speed. But the student of the history of this era must draw his own conclusions as to the benefit to the science of yacht design, the maintenance of a high standard of sportsmanship, and the advancement of the sport of yacht racing. As our story is theoretically technical, as little as possible will be said of certain occurrences which may not be completely ignored, but which may well be forgotten as reflecting no credit on the participants.

As told last month, Vigilant represented an advance in the practically empty racing shell with crew berthed on an attendant steamboat; she also marked the replacement of steel by new and costly alloys. In the ninth match the challenger followed suit in the adoption of a steam tender, and the defender represented a new advance in greater extremes of model, in the employment of alloys, in lighter and more expensive construction, in larger rigs and less reliable spars, lighter canvas and larger kites.

The first challenger, in 1870-71, James Ashbury, was something of a sea lawyer, though with mitigating circumstances, but his performance was far exceeded by the quarrels, quibbles, rumors, gossip, fouls, protests, letters, cablegrams, trials and recriminations which attend this most unsavory era in international yachting. To put the matter in as few words as possible, when the new deed of gift was made public in November 1887 it was generally denounced by foreign clubs as unfair and illegal; many, including the Royal Yacht Squadron, declaring that they never would challenge under it. For eleven years there was no challenge, but when building Valkyrie I, Lord Dunraven, stating that he had no knowledge of the controversy and had no opinion on it, attempted to break the deadlock in a manner peculiarly his own. His proposition to the New York Yacht Club was that if it would grant him what he considered fair terms—three out of five races, courses outside Sandy Hook, starts made to windward, and certain details of measurement, he on his side would secure an agreement on the part of the Royal Yacht Squadron to hold the Cup, if won, according to the letter of the new deed. Though he eventually obtained the terms he desired, he failed completely in coercing the Royal Yacht Squadron.

Wyndham Thomas Wyndham Quin, Fourth Earl of Dunraven and Mount Earl of Dunraven Castle, Bridgend, Glamorgan, born in 1841 only a few months before his friend Albert, Prince of Wales, after graduating from Oxford was a war correspondent for the Daily Telegraph in Abbysinia in 1867 and later in the Franco-German war. Abandoning journalism for politics, he was Under Secretary of State for the Col-

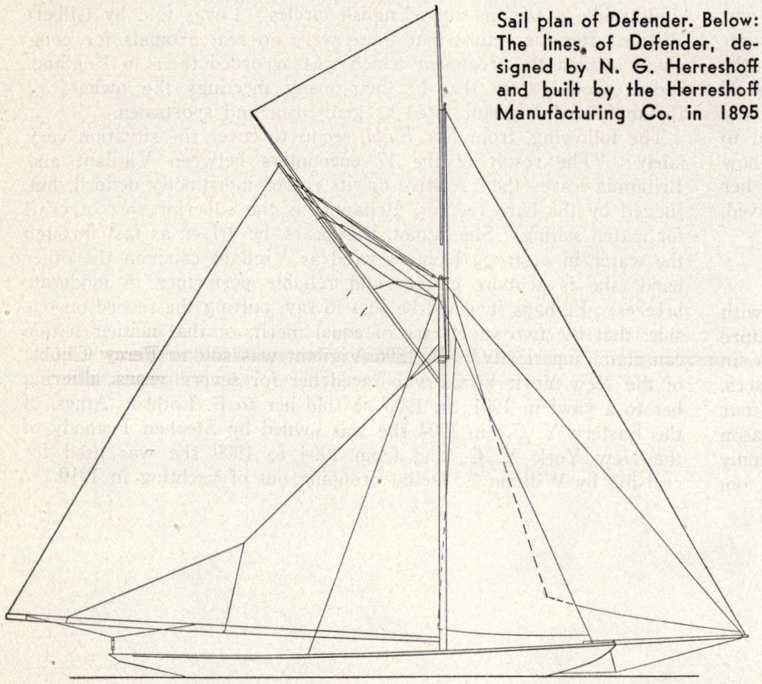

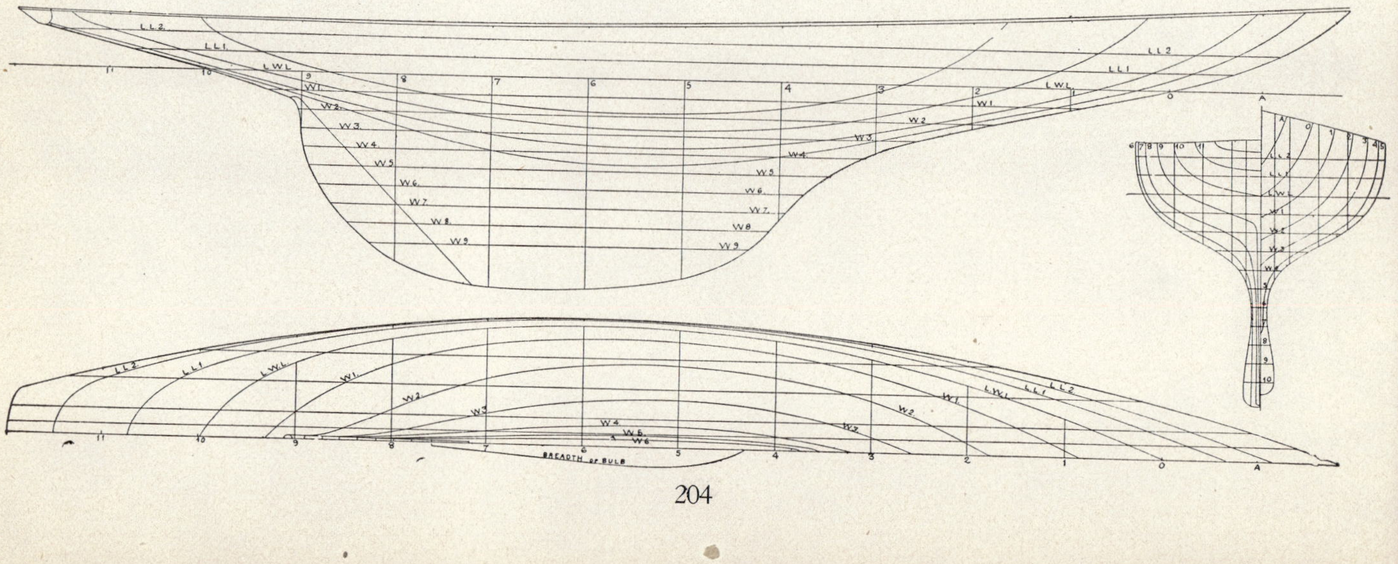

Sail plan of Defender. Below: The lines, of Defender, designed by N. G. Herreshoff and built by the Herreshoff Manufacturing Co. in 1895

onies, but resigned in 1887. He was accustomed to small sailing boats from boyhood, but never had shown any interest in yachting until he abandoned politics, when he sailed in some of the small rating classes. His first venture in a real yacht was in 1888 when he built the cutter Petronilla, 56 Rating, from a design by Alexander Richardson, racing her consistently with but moderate success; five firsts and four other prizes for 28 starts.

The Royal Yacht Squadron Challenges

Like his successor, Sir Thomas Lipton, another Irishman, Lord Dunraven was obsessed by the idea that the America's Cup might be won by the mere expenditure of money, with no experience in yacht racing and no knowledge of the history and technique of the sport. Together with Sir Thomas, he was a victim of the stencil craze; and, having once chosen a name, was content to stencil it on each succeeding yacht which he built. While, in the long history of the America's Cup, only once has a name been repeated on a defender, yachting history is confused by a series of three Valkyries and five Shamrocks. Evidently what George Bernard Shaw called "a perfect Wagnerite," Lord Dunraven chose a name of ill omen, the Valkyrs being the messengers of fate who carried tidings of death to those doomed to fall in battle. It is only fair to say that while Sir Thomas remained a landlubber down to his last proposed Shamrock VI, Lord Dunraven ultimately devoted himself to the study of yacht design and turned out the 20-Rater Audrey. In designing this yacht he first tried drafting the lines, but gave up and resorted to cardboard moulds and model. A failure in her first season, after being rebuilt and a metal fin substituted for one of wood she took second place to the Herreshoff Niagara. He also wrote a book on navigation.

On March 19, 1889, a challenge was sent by the Royal Yacht Squadron on behalf of Lord Dunraven, naming his yacht Valkyrie (I), designed by Watson, of 70 feet l.w.l. and 76 Rating. This challenge was eagerly greeted by the holders and accepted April 11th, a special committee being appointed to perfect the details. The negotiations finally ended with the following letter from the special committee of the Squadron:—"We are unable to confirm the challenge with the condition attached, that if the cup is won by the club challenging, it shall be held under and subject to the full terms of the new deed; the acceptance of which we consider would preclude the renewal of that friendly competition which it is so desirable to encourage and maintain, and for which the cup appears to have been originally conveyed to the New York Yacht Club." Sailing in the home races of 1889 Valkyrie made 34 starts, winning 14 firsts and 9 other prizes.

Undeterred by this failure, Lord Dunraven continued his efforts through personal correspondence with yachtsmen on both sides, with the result that in December, 1892, a long letter from the Secretary of the Squadron was accepted as a challenge, and the match between the Valkyrie II and Vigilant resulted, as already told. In all this correspondence the basic question of the full recognition of the new deed was left in abeyance.

The sinking of Valkyrie I in the opening race of the season of 1894 left Lord Dunraven without a yacht; while he amused

Top: The cup yacht Defender and, below, Valkyrie III on the Clyde. Photograph by Adamson, Gourock, Scotland

satisfactory to me, with the following modifications.

First: As by length on the L.W.L. is obviously meant length on which a vessel sails, I think yachts should be measured with all the weights on board, dead or alive, which they intend to carry during a race, and should be marked; that no alteration should be made in the amount of those weights, and no ballast trimmed without notice given to the Sailing Committee not less than 24 hours before a race; that the Committee should be entitled to take any steps they may think fit to ascertain that the vessels do not, when racing, exceed their measured length; and that a limit—and a generous one—to the number of persons on board should be fixed according to L.W.L. length or Rating.

Secondly: That all dead to-windward and leeward matches should be started to windward.

The superiority of a sailing length (rating) limit over a length on the L.W.L. limit had been advocated, I notice, both in the United States and here. If, in the opinion of the New York Yacht Club, a fairer test of the relative merits of yachts can be so obtained, the sailing length according to your rule, instead of the L.W.L. length to be furnished by the challenger.

I do not think it possible to find a naturally better place for sailing the matches than the outer Bay of New York; but it is open to two disadvantages. First, the distance from the Port, and, secondly, the over-crowding, and for those reasons I should prefer Marblehead. The superiority of Marblehead in the first respect is, I believe, undoubted. To what extent it possesses advantages over New York in the second respect it is difficult for me to say. Obviously, the N.Y.Y.C., or any committee appointed by them, will be more capable of judging. I hope

Top: Valkyrie III on the ways. Photograph by Adamson, Gourock, Scotland. Center: Defender stuck on the ways in launching. Right: Defender as she crossed the line at the finish of the last race

himself with the modeling and building of Audrey, his mind was still fixed on the America's Cup, and in October he sent the following letter, a purely personal one, to the Secretary of the New York Y. C.

Dunraven Castle, Bridgend, Glamorgan.
Oct. 25, 1894.

Dear Mr. Oddie:

I should have written you before now on the subject of challenging for the "America Cup," but that I was anxious before doing so to ascertain what alterations, if any, were to be made in our Y.R.A. rating rule? However, as time is running on, it would be well, I think, if certain preliminaries should be discussed without committing myself definitely to a challenge.

The terms and conditions governing the Vigilant-Valkyrie matches would be quite you will clearly understand that I attribute no *animus* whatever to the steamers, but I am sure the members of the late Committee will agree with me as to the extreme difficulty experienced in trying to keep a clear Course last year. It is of the utmost importance that the elements of uncertainty derived from a crowded Course should be as far as possible eliminated, and if there is even a probability of reducing it by sailing at Marblehead I hope the New York Yacht Club will consent to do so.

It appears to me somewhat unfair theoretically that a Challenging Club should be confined to one vessel while the Challenged Club can select a champion from an indefinite number. In practice, if a challenger should be inferior to another vessel of his nationality, a contest for the America Cup would have no interest or importance as an international test. I would therefore suggest that both parties should have equal rights of selection.

Will you kindly submit this to the New York Yacht Club at the earliest opportunity; and as, in the event of challenging, it is desirable that I should have a speedy answer to the question whether L.W.L. length or sailing length should be given, I should be greatly obliged if you would cable me "Length" or "Rating" according to the decision of the Club.

I remain, dear Mr. Oddie,

Yours very truly,

(signed) Dunraven.

THIS lengthy peroration is a mixture of sense and nonsense, the term "match" is used as synonymous with "race," a wide departure from accepted usage; the suggestion as to the limitation of crew obviously applies to the unlimited crew of Vigilant in the previous year; as to ballast and measurement, these points were already covered by the rules. The movement for "corrected length" instead of waterline length was started by Forest & Stream shortly before this, but was actively opposed by many in the New York Y. C. and there was no possibility of the adoption of the former. In the match of 1893 Valkyrie I and Vigilant were started not in the "outer" (Lower) Bay of New York, but from the Sandy Hook or Scotland lightships, on the open sea. The crowding of the spectator fleet was a serious evil, for a time beyond the control of the Club; but Marblehead was only a night's run for such coasting steamers as the Yorktown, and there would have been as many of them, with even more small craft, at Marblehead.

This epistle inaugurated a course of correspondence and discussion covering a period of three months and finally resulting in an agreement for a match. Some of the challenger's suggestions were accepted, more were summarily rejected; while most of the points related only to the details of the racing, the one vital issue was whether the Royal Yacht Squadron, in the event of winning the match, would swallow the new deed, body bones and breeches; and this was still left open. Meanwhile the building of the challenger was actually under way, lines and model being submitted by Mr. Watson. With Lord Dunraven in sharing the expense were Lord Lonsdale, Lord Wolverton and Captain Harry McCalmont, M.P., owner of the steam yacht Giralda of 1664 tons.

The Challenging Sloop and Defending Cutter

IN his third trial for the Cup Mr. Watson evidently gave careful study to American conditions and, possibly influenced by Vigilant, adopted a wide, shoal form of hull with a deep thin keel; the breadth and low lead being designed to carry a very large rig. The construction was composite, the builders, D. & W. Henderson of Partick, a suburb of Glasgow, turning out a very fine job. The sails, of course, were made by Ratsey & Lapthorn.

In the defense Mr. Iselin, again in charge as managing owner, had as his associates J. Pierpont Morgan and William K. Vanderbilt; the contract going to the Herreshoffs. In the selection of type and dimensions Mr. Herreshoff went as far afield in one direction as Mr. Watson had in the other; a keel craft of comparatively narrow breadth, only 23 feet 4 inches, a close approach to a fin-keel. In the selection of a name a contest was started, the prize being won by a girl of six years. The name, Defender, was criticized as being generic rather than specific, and the abandonment of the national type, the centerboard, was condemned by some as unpatriotic and a concession to British ideas.

The construction was as original as most of the Herreshoff work; the foundation was the heavy bulbed lead keel, on top of which was a cast brass keel plate in three sections joined by bronze bolts through flanges on the upper side; this keel plate was fastened by bronze lagscrews to the lead keel. The stem and sternpost were of cast bronze, as was the frame of the rudder. The plating, down from a little above the water was of manganese bronze; the garboards, each riveted at its middle to the flanges of the keel plate, extended downward for half its breadth over the lead keel, to which it was fastened by tapbolts, thus supplementing the lagscrews. The topsides were of aluminum, with a 4 per cent alloy of nickel, 5/16 and 3/8 inch thick, with a steel plate in the wake of the chainplates; the rivets were of bronze. The frames were of steel, in the form of bulb angles, and the deck beams were of aluminum. The spars were of wood with the exception of a steel boom, all the blocks were of special design with aluminum sheaves, the lightest ever placed on a yacht. While one suit of sails was ordered from Wilson & Silsby, of Boston, the Herreshoffs rented a vacant rubber factory near the works and started a sail loft of their own, turning out a suit which included a cross-cut mainsail. The deck was of conventional white pine; while the interior was well braced by aluminum angle bars, all cabin fittings were reduced to the minimum; the crew being berthed for the season on the Hattie Palmer.

THE veteran Captain Hank Haff was selected to command the new yacht and a very radical departure was made in the selection of the crew; Captain Haff in March visiting Deer Island, Maine, and picking a crew of fishermen. The manning of the yacht fleet from its early days was mainly in the hands of Scandinavian seamen; derisively called "skowegians" or "square-heads," but nevertheless competent and reliable. The change was commented on as follows in Forest & Stream.

"While the idea of manning the defending yacht with an American-born crew is likely to have no practical result in leading to the general employment of American seamen in place of Scandinavian, the idea is one that appeals to Americans as particularly appropriate under the circumstances. At the same time we confess to a feeling of sympathy for the Nielsens, Jansens, Hansens, Petersens and Andersen who are sitting idly on the stringpiece waiting for a berth afloat. These men, though some of them, it is true, were guilty of the crime of being beaten last year in Vigilant, have been the backbone of the yacht fleet for many years, and on the whole they have done their work well. As a class they have proved themselves honest, temperate, capable and willing; they pulled and hauled on Mischief, Puritan, Mayflower, and Volunteer, and, above all, on Vigilant in 1893; and until the latter vessel was defeated in 1894 no complaint was made against them. That they should now feel that they have not been treated quite fairly is natural.

"The petting and patting on the back which they once enjoyed at the hands of the press has been transferred to the men from Deer Island; and to an extent that is likely to make the experiment of Mr. Iselin of little value. From all appearances the Maine fishermen are good representatives of the best class of American seamen; but they must be more than human if their heads are not enlarged by the undue attention paid to them by some newspapers."

Following the loss of her centerboard Vigilant had been laid up at Southampton. In the early spring a new centerboard, a cast bronze frame with plated sides and lead filling was made at Bristol. With her slot blocked Vigilant, under yawl rig, with Capt. Charles Barr in command, sailed from Southampton on April 11 and made New York on April 29, being immediately refitted for racing. Two fin-keels had been built at Bristol during the winter for racing in England in the 20-Rating Class under the new Y.R.A. Rule, Niagara for Howard Gould and Isolde for Baron von Zedtwitz, a German yachtsman; and George Gould was now sole owner of the yacht. He placed her in the charge of Edward A. Willard, an experienced yachtsman, who, as a friend of C. Oliver Iselin, had sailed aboard Vigilant in 1893; the two friends were now rivals in the coming trial races. Volunteer, for several years under schooner rig, was changed back to cutter by J. Malcolm Forbes; she had been lengthened to 90 feet, and Jubilee, now 6 feet longer, was ready for the trial races.

Though not a member of the New York Y. C., George Gould spent money freely in putting Vigilant in the best possible form as a trial boat; about 20 tons of her inside lead was re-cast and bolted under her keel, the work being done under the direction of Henry C. Wintringham and Lewis G. Nixon at the shipyard of the latter at Elizabethport, N. J. New bolts of 1 1/4 inch Tobin bronze, some seventy in all, were run through the new and old lead, the brass keelplate and special steel angles with long arms riveted to the floor plates. The draft was increased about 6 to 9 inches and the fore end of the keel was rounded off as much as possible. With "Charlie" Barr was "Lem" Miller as mate; now in his old age growing fine flowers as an amusement at his home on Long Island.

The Trials of Trial Racing

THE first trial race was sailed on July 20, 15 miles to windward in a light breeze, Defender winning by only 2 minutes 45 seconds, though as the following boat, Vigilant, was badly served by the wash of the big spectator fleet. The second race was sailed on July 22 over a triangle of 10-mile sides in a light wind, Defender winning by 9 minutes 17 seconds. Just after the start a protest flag was set aboard Vigilant, and after the race Mr. Willard handed in a formal protest on the ground that Defender, when off the wind, had borne down on Vigilant. As the two were to meet on the New York Y. C. cruise, Mr. Willard requested that the Regatta Committee should withhold its decision until after the cruise.

On the opening day of the cruise on July 29 Defender beat Vigilant by less than two minutes; on the first run Defender's steering gear heated and jammed and she towed in; on the run from New London to Newport the elapsed times were:—Defender, 4:06:10; Vigilant, 4:18:12; Volunteer, 4:30:15. In the Goelet Cup race on August 2 Defender, when leading, broke her gaff in the middle and withdrew; Vigilant defeating Jubilee by 8 minutes and Volunteer by 26 minutes. The run from Newport to Vineyard Haven was timed:—Defender, 3:11:34; Vigilant, 3:17:58; Volunteer, 3:33:02. On the run back to Newport next day the times were:—Defender, 4:09:00; Vigilant, 4:18:09; Jubilee, 4:28:58. In a special race for the Drexel Cup Defender beat Vigilant by 6 minutes 10 seconds; and in the race for the Newport Cup Defender beat Jubilee by over 9 minutes.

In the last race Mr. Willard declined to start, as he claimed that on the previous day Defender had forced Vigilant off her course just prior to the starting gun. He did not protest, as two protests, if sustained, would have barred Defender from racing for the rest of the season. The first protest was finally decided against Vigilant, and the Regatta Committee declared that Vigilant was wrong in the second case. While much hard feeling was engendered on both sides, matters were patched up for the formal trial races; the first, for a cup given by Col. John Jacob Astor, on August 20, 10 miles to windward and return. Defender was obliged to withdraw owing to the slipping of her masthead band under the strain of the shrouds. Repairs were made at Bristol and they met again on August 29 for a second Astor Cup, Defender winning by 16 minutes 34 seconds. The third race was won by Defender by 3 minutes 58 seconds and she was chosen to meet Valkyrie III.

Sailing from Greenock on July 27 with Captain William Cranfield in command and Captain Edward Sycamore, another skilful racing skipper, to help him, Valkyrie III reached Sandy Hook on Augst 18, covering 2770 nautical miles in 21 days 9 hours; she crossed under ketch rig, all her racing spars and gear being shipped by steamer. The double outfit included a steel boom built in eight segments with the edges of each turned outward as flanges for riveting. The measurements of the two yachts by John Hyslop give the following figures:—

	Valkyrie III	Defender
L.O.A.	129.00	123.00
L.W.L.	88.85	88.45
Breadth	26.20	23.33
Draft	20.00	19.06
Racing Length	101.49	100.36
Mast Deck to Hounds	77.00	72.00
Topmast	55.98	57.42
Boom	105.00	106.00
Gaff	59.50	64.36
Spinaker Boom	78.94	73.36
Boom to Topmast Block	129.80	125.48
Sail Area, Square Feet	13,027.93	12,602.30
Ballast Approx.	77 tons	85 tons

It may be noted here that the utmost secrecy was observed during construction in the case of both yachts; no figure being given out by the designers.

The Amenities of International Racing

THE signing of the immediate conditions by Lord Dunraven and James D. Smith, Chairman of the America's Cup Committee on behalf of the Club took place on September 4; they called for a series of three out of five races, starting off Sandy Hook or Scotland Lightship; the courses to be thirty nautical miles, the first leg to windward when possible; the first, third and fifth races to be to windward and leeward, the second and fourth over a triangle. The starting signals were to be a preparatory at 10:50, start at 11, and final at 11:02; the start to be postponed in the event of a change of starting point, fog, or an agreed postponement. The time limit for all races was 6 hours; all excess of 89 feet l.w.l. to count double in the computation of racing length, yachts to be measured with all weights carried in a race on board, restrictions as to bulkheads, doors, floors, watertanks and anchors being waived. Time to be allowed for repairs in case of accidents. There was also a supplementary agreement as to re-measurement in case of any alteration of ballast, trim or rig.

On September 6 his Lordship sent the following letter to the Committee:—"It is obvious that alterations in the waterline length of a vessel may, under present conditions, be made without the owner's knowledge and without possibility of detection. It is, of course, impossible to guard absolutely against such an occurrence. But these contests cannot be compared with ordinary races, and in the interest of the public and of the owners who have to do their best to see that rules are obeyed, it is surely right and necessary that the Committee should take every precaution to insure that the vessels sail on their waterline lengths." Acting on this letter the Club appointed A. Cass Canfield and Archibald Rogers a special committee to mark the load lines; but as Valkyrie III had already left Erie Basin this was not possible prior to the first race. To anticipate, the various measurements of the two, as taken by John Hyslop, were:—Defender, August 17, with 48 men aboard, 88.85; September 6, Defender, 50 persons on board, 88.45; Valkyrie III with 60 persons on board, 88.85; September 8, Defender with 50 persons on board, 88.445; Valkyrie III with 60 persons on board, 88.86. September 11 load waterlines and spars marked on both yachts.

THE first race was sailed as scheduled on Saturday, September 7, in light easterly weather with a roll of old sea. About the Sandy Hook Lightship were the big passenger steamers City of Lowell, Richard Peck and Yorktown, with smaller steamers all loaded to the guards, the steam yacht Valhalla, owned by another "perfect Wagnerite" J. F. Laycock, a friend of Lord Dunraven, and innumerable steam and sailing craft. A steamer of the Postal Telegraph Co. was anchored in readiness to send the news abroad by cable. With the wind East by South a windward leg was out of the question and the start was shifted to a point off Seabright on the Jersey beach. With the preparatory at 12:10 and the start at 12:20 Valkyrie III, moving fast in the light breeze, with Captain Sycamore at the stick, crossed 46 seconds after the gun, with Defender 4 seconds later.

The wind freed at times, freshened a little, and there were showers and sunshine. In the roll of sea, slight as it was, one was reminded of the good old days of the cutter war when, under similar conditions, the cutters Bedouin, Wenonah, Oriva and Ileen, heeled gently, went to sleep, and made headway, while the sloops, Gracie, Fanny, Hildegard and Arrow, stood up straight and bobbed up and down. In this case the defender was the cutter and the challenger the sloop. The conditions were not such as to afford a fair trial, Defender finished at 5:21:14; Valkyrie III at 5:29:30; the defender winning by 8 minutes 49 seconds corrected time.

It was not known publicly until some time after the race that Lord Dunraven had stated to Latham A. Fish, the representative of the Club aboard Valkyrie III, that in his opinion Defender sailed with between three and four feet of her measured waterline immersed, at the same time requesting a re-measurement. On Sunday both yachts were towed to the Erie Basin and in still water Mr. Hyslop verified the load lines, with the results already given. Mr. Watson, in a bathing suit, went overboard and marked both ends of Valkyrie III's waterline, while Mr. Herreshoff performed the same office for Defender, working from a rowboat.

THE second race was sailed on September 10, in clear weather with a light breeze which freshened later. The start was made off the Sandy Hook Lightship, with a smaller attendant fleet than on Saturday, but the big steamer Yorktown was again present, taking a position very close to the starting line. The first leg of the triangle was South; in the final maneuvering Valkyrie III passed to windward of the Yorktown while Defender passed to leeward, the two converging as they cleared the bows of the steamer. Captain Sycamore again held the long tiller of Valkyrie III, he was ahead of the gun and bore off to clear the Committee tug; Defender holding her course on the wind. Seeing that a collision was imminent, Captain Sycamore swung his tiller to port and turned his yacht quickly on her heel, but too late; an eye on the end of her 105 foot boom fouled the starboard topmast shroud of Defender and broke off the end of the spreader. The defender bore off quickly as her topmast bent like a whipstock under her club topsail and jib topsail; a protest flag went aloft at once and was acknowledged by a gun from the Committee boat. Valkyrie III was timed 13 seconds after the gun, Defender 1 minute 2 seconds astern of her. The challenger continued her course, while those aboard Defender attempted to lash the topmast shroud to the broken end of the spreader, but this was impossible and she doused her jib topsail as she continued the race, turning the first mark with a loss of 2 minutes 50 seconds. With more wind on the second leg Valkyrie set her balloon jib topsail while Defender could carry but a working sail on the topmast stay; on the third leg the disabled spreader was to leeward and she did better, losing by only 1 minute 16 seconds actual and 47 seconds corrected time.

The following protest was sent immediately after the race:—

September 10th 1895 Onboard Defender

To the Regatta Committee,
New York Yacht Club.

Dear Sirs:

It is with much regret that I hereby protest the Valkyrie in the race today. I shaped my course for the line (which course, according to my orders, was not altered in the slightest degree) on starboard tack with sheets trimmed down, when Valkyrie bore down on us with wide sheets and, in luffing, fouled our starboard main rigging with her main boom, carrying away our spreader and springing our topmast.

Respectfully yours,
(signed) C. Oliver Iselin

The claim of Lord Dunraven, that Defender luffed into Valkyrie III, was contradicted, in addition to other evidence, by the many photos taken of the start, including some by West of Gosport, the leading British yacht photographer. The Regatta Committee sustained Mr. Iselin's protest and awarded the race to Defender. What was at least a contributory cause of the foul was the fact that Captain Sycamore, a skillful and experienced skipper, had been sailing 40-raters and other yachts built under the length and sail area rule of the Y.R.A., yachts with limited sail area and booms barely projecting beyond the taffrail; he had handled Valkyrie III in only a few starts, and he did not realize how long a tail his cat had. A maneuver which would have been perfectly safe in a fleet of 40-Raters was both dangerous and impossible with such rigs as the Cup yachts of 1895 carried.

THE decision of the Committee was followed by discussion, disputes and correspondence not worth recording in detail today, the net result being that when the third race was called on September 12, in clear weather, smooth water, and a light working breeze, Valkyrie III's weather; with the spectator fleet now at a safe distance; with Defender fully canvassed, Valkyrie III came to the line under mainsail and jib only, her topsail not even bent to its spars. Defender crossed 24 seconds after the gun, Valkyrie III crossed nearly two minutes later, luffed under the stern of the Lightship, broke out the New York Y.C. burgee at her masthead (Lord Dunraven had been made an honorary member) and took a line from her tug. Following the instructions of the Regatta Committee Defender sailed the course and was duly timed at 4:43:43 corrected time and awarded the race. This withdrawal was most unfair to Mr. Watson, as the conditions were those for which he had planned.

The twin subjects of ballast and measurement were very much to the fore at this time, and many idle rumors had been rife before and during this match as to shipping and un-shipping lead, trimming fore and aft, and allied illegal practices. Some of these had reached the ears of Lord Dunraven before his second visit to New York, and he evidently suspected some trickery. His claim that, as observed by him, Defender was sailing on three or four feet of un-measured waterline was preposterous, and disproved by the public re-measurement. On his return to England he made the public accusation that the ballast of Defender had been tampered with and that she had sailed the race of September 7 below her measured line. This charge aroused great indignation in New York, and a special committee was appointed including J. Pierpont Morgan, William C. Whitney, George L. Rives, Captain Alfred T. Mahan, U.S.N. and Edward J. Phelps. This committee met at the New York Y.C. house, then at 67 Madison Avenue, Lord Dunraven and his counsel, G. R. Asquith, having come from London; Mr. Iselin was present with Joseph H. Choate as counsel. The trial ran from December 27 to December 31, much testimony was taken.

The most which was brought out in the line of evidence was that on the night of September 6 the two yachts with their tenders lay at anchor inside the Horseshoe at Sandy Hook; some loose lead in pigs was taken from the hold of Defender to the Hattie Palmer, cut into smaller pieces for more compact stowage and then replaced. Whether this, though in no way illegal, was a wise proceeding under existing circumstances is an open question; but the complainants were unable to produce any evidence other than the appearance of Defender that she was in any way below her lines. The verdict of the committee was a complete vindication of Mr. Iselin. The complete report of the trial as published by the Club made an octavo volume of 554 pages.

In view of the possible value of aluminum in naval construction a very thorough study of its qualities was made by the Navy Department, Assistant Naval Constructor Richmond P. Hobson being detailed to make an investigation of its use in several vessels. He gave special attention to Defender, examining her in New Rochelle in July when just from the shop and finding the topsides in bad condition, with the paint peeling and corrosion visible at the juncture of the aluminum and bronze. In spite of a special paint prepared by a local painter after the usual yacht paints had failed it was difficult to maintain a satisfactory surface. In January 1896 she was found to be corroded all over, even under paint which had adhered. In June she showed more serious corrosion and the heads of many bronze rivets had fallen off; evidently due to the swelling of aluminum when exposed to salt water. The cast fittings about the deck were so corroded that many might be broken by the hand. The very voluminous report was conclusive as to the use of aluminum in union with steel or bronze when exposed to salt water.

This venture practically ended the racing career of Lord Dunraven, he owned Valkyrie III without using her until she was broken up in 1901, Defender being scrapped in the same year.

Columbia, built in 1899 to defend the America's Cup against the challenge of Sir Thomas Lipton. © J. S. Johnston

TRADITIONS AND MEMORIES

OF

American Yachting

By WILLIAM P. STEPHENS Part Forty-Six

THE Dunraven fiasco at the end of 1895 left matters in the same condition as after the promulgation of the New Deed of Gift eight years previously; but the hearts of the stand-patters were gladdened by a "challenge" by cable:—

London, Sept. 20, 1895.

America's Cup Committee, New York.

I hereby challenge for the America's cup next year. The races to be sailed on conditions satisfactory to the committee.

(signed) Charles Day Rose,
39 Hill Street, Berkeley Square, London.

An acceptance of the "challenge" was promptly cabled before it was realized that, in his utter ignorance of the conditions governing the cup, Mr. Rose had challenged as an individual, instead of the challenge coming from a recognized yacht club. This blunder was remedied by the following letter under date of Sept. 28, 1895:—

J. V. S. Oddie, Esq.,
Seretary, New York Yacht Club.

Dear Sir:

I, on behalf of the Royal Victoria Yacht Club, and in the name of Charles Day Rose, a member of the club, challenge to sail a series of matches for the America's Cup in 1896 with the cutter, Distant Shore, load waterline 89 feet.

In the event of this challenge being accepted I should be obliged if you will kindly inform me what dates, courses and conditions the New York Yacht Club will propose to govern the races?

(signed) Percy Thelusson,
Secretary, Royal Victoria Yacht Club.

It will be noticed that Mr. Thelusson falls into the error of confusing the word match with race.

There came to the fore at once the question of the identity of Mr. Rose, as his name was unknown to yachtsmen; it was answered at some length in an article in *The Sun*; in brief, as follows. William Rose emigrated to Canada in the early part of the 19th century, his son, John, born in 1820, was a school teacher in the village of Athelstan, later studying law in Montreal; in 1869 he went to England, was knighted, and became a partner in the banking house of Morton, Bliss & Co., of New York, the English branch being known as Morton, Rose & Co. His son, Charles Day Rose, was born in Huntington County, P. Q., in 1847; as a boy and at McGill University he was prominent in athletics, he spent a part of his life in New York, and at the date in question he was a member of Morton, Rose & Co. He never had shown any interest in water sports, but was very prominent on the turf as a breeder and racing owner, one of his noted winners being named Distant Shore and another Penitent. Shortly before this he had entered yachting rather suddenly with the ownership of several small craft; just at this time he purchased Satanita, of 98 feet l.wl., the largest cutter ever built, and placed an order for a 52-rater, Penitent; his proposed challenger, to be designed by J. M. Soper, designer of Satanita, to be named Distant Shore.

The advent of Mr. Rose in yachting was deeply resented by the English yachting journals as a reflection on Lord Dunraven, and he was generally described as an "American". On the part of the Club, a special committee was appointed which drew up a set of very fair conditions for the match, setting the date of the first race for July 23, exactly ten months from the receipt of the challenge.

Following closely the publication of these conditions there came two cables:

Newmarket, Oct. 23.
Oddie,
Secretary, New York Yacht Club,
Owing to the general impression that my challenge might be construed as an expression of opinion on the result of the last race, I must regret having to ask you to withdraw my name.
(signed) Charles D. Rose.

Shamrock, the challenger, built by Thornycroft, was launched in June, 1899, and reached New York on August 18. © West & Son. Sir Thomas Lipton, her owner, in a typical pose. © M. Rosenfeld

Ryde, Oct. 23.
Secretary, New York Yacht Club,
Have received letter from Rose withdrawing challenge for Amerca's cup. Have called committee. Will mail you officially.
(signed) Thelusson.

Charles D. Rose, 39 Hill St., Berkeley Square, London,
Cable announcing withdrawal of your challenge received.
(signed) Oddie, Secretary.

Secretary, Royal Victoria Yacht Club, Ryde, England.
Your cable this date received.
(signed) Oddie, Secretary.

Thus the incident was closed, the only persons benefited by it being the shareholders of the Cable Company. Satanita was soon sold, the commission for the design of Distant Shore was not placed until 1889; when she was finally launched in 1901, she was immediately sold and began her career under a new name, Kariad. By way of epilogue, Lord Dunraven suggested that Defender should visit the Mediterranean to meet Valkyrie III in 1896. Another proposed challenger turned up in the person of Sir George Newnes, a wealthy publisher of pulp periodicals and fiction and a landlubber; while a third aspirant wrote from Australia that he would challenge with a yacht of local design to be named Western Australia. Again "quiet reigned in Warsaw" and on Madison Avenue.

The Long-Expected Happens

There had been rumors afloat for some time of a challenge from Sir Thomas Lipton, as well as from other non-yachtsmen; this rumor, however, proved true, as shown in the following cable:—

August 6, 1898.
New York Yacht Club, 67 Madison Avenue, N. Y.
I have to inform you that the Royal Ulster Yacht Club, on behalf of Sir Thomas Lipton, have the honor to challenge for the America's cup. Kindly say if this is agreeable to you? A small committee appointed by the club will shortly sail for New York with formal challenge, and will confer with you.
(signed) Hugh C. Kelly, Secretary,
Mt. Pottinger Road, Belfast.

The instant reply was:—

Hugh C. Kelly, Mt. Pottinger Road, Belfast.

I have the honor, on behalf of the New York Yacht Club, to acknowledge the receipt of cable of even date. Its purport is most agreeable, and will be considered as soon as meeting can be called. Your committee will be warmly welcomed.

(signed) Oddie, Secretary.

This was followed by another cable on August 11:—

Hugh C. Kelly, Mt. Pottinger Road, Belfast.

A challenge from your club will be most agreeable. Committee appointed with full power to act on challenge and arrange details. Challenge, to be binding and to carry precedence, must be accompanied by name of owner, and certificate, name, rig and dimensions of the challenging yacht as specified in Deed of Gift. Your committee will be warmly welcomed.

(signed) Oddie, Secretary.

The New York Yacht Club, having found the proposed challenge "most agreeable", appointed a special committee headed by the then Commodore J. Pierpont Morgan, who had just presented to the club the site at 37-39-41 West 44th Street on which the present club house stands, to confer with the visitors. *The Field* commented as follows in its issue of August 6:— "According to *The Times* of Thursday Sir T. Lipton, the tea merchant, proposes to challenge for the America Cup through the Royal Ulster Yacht Club. He does not appear to have had any extended experience in yacht racing; but, judging from the statement in *The Times,* he has summoned to his aid a whole army (query, navy?) of counsellors, including the Yacht Racing Association. Should the challenge be accepted it is said that Mr. W. Fife will be the designer and the yacht will be built at Belfast by Messrs. Harlan & Wolff. However, according to the terms of the cup deed of gift, the yacht must be actually built before the challenge is accepted, unless the New York Yacht Club will take everything on trust? Supposing this is not a 'fairy tale', it is to be regretted that it was made public before a definite and accredited challenge could be sent. To ask the New York Yacht Club if they will accept a challenge under the proposed scheme would be absurd, and the club would naturally decline to entertain it."

Thus entered on the scene the most remarkable of the many interesting characters who ornamented the pages of Cup history; born in poverty, with no advantages of education, by his own unaided efforts he made himself one of the great merchant princes of the world, possessed of unlimited wealth which he distributed with more generosity than discretion. The friend alike of prince and peasant, politicians, pork packers, prize fighters and publicans.

A New Yachtsman Is Made

Of Irish parentage, Thomas Johnstone Lipton was born in Glasgow on May 10, 1850. The son of a working man, at the age of ten he found a job as errand boy in a sta-

Above: Another view of Shamrock, and, below, the lines of Columbia, taken from the hull itself. © West & Son

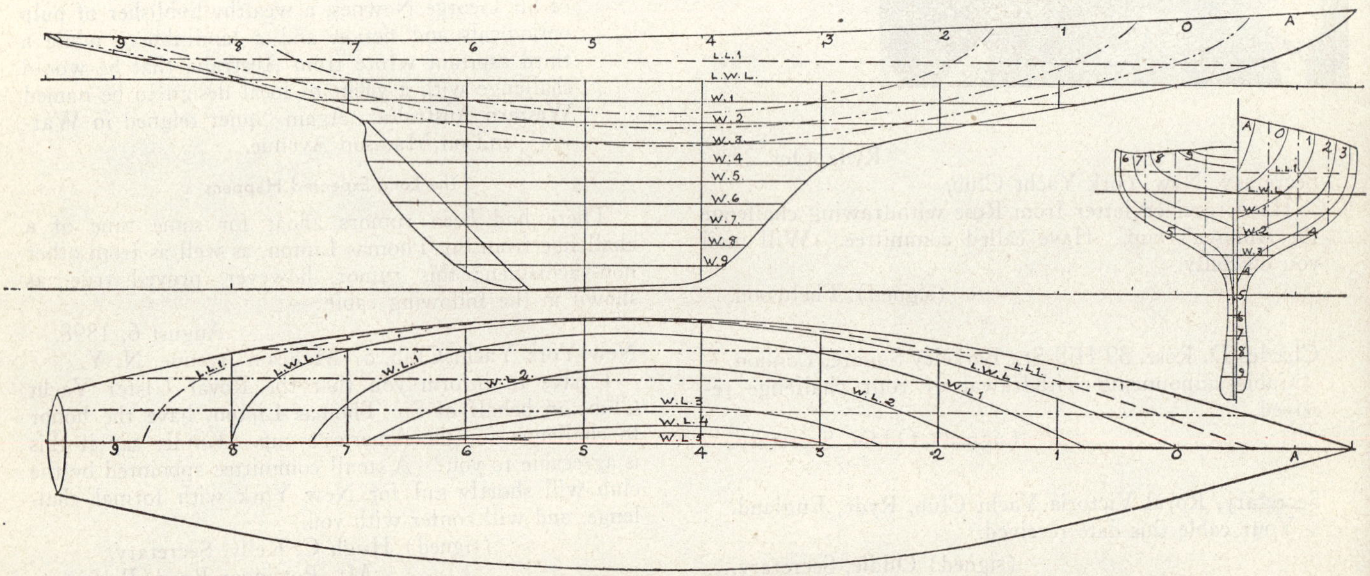

tioner's store at a half crown per week.

Later he earned four shillings per week cutting cloth patterns in a shirt-making shop; following this he earned eight shillings and his board as cabin boy on a small steamer plying between Glasgow and Belfast. By this time, 1865, he had saved enough money to pay his passage in the steerage aboard the Anchor Line steamer Devonia to New York, landing at Castle Garden with but thirty shillings in his pocket. His adventures in America included work on a tobacco plantation in Virginia, on a rice plantation in South Carolina, a job driving a horsecar in New Orleans, and finally as a grocery clerk in New York. Returning to Glasgow, he worked for a time in a little store which his father had established; on his 21st birthday he opened a little store of his own.

THE one store in Glasgow in time developed into a chain of stores throughout Britain and, as they expanded, to the ownership of tea, coffee and cocoa plantations in Ceylon, a packing house in Chicago, and another in South Omaha. His benefactions included a gift of 25,000 pounds to the poor of London on the occasion of Queen Victoria's Jubilee, another large sum for eating houses for the poor, still another for the India famine fund, and many others unrecorded. He was created a knight in 1898 and a baronet in 1901.

A man of few ideas, the predominating one was business, in all its branches; his principles being to buy for cash as close as possible to the source of supply; to sell for cash, giving full value for the price, to cultivate friendly relations with even casual customers, and to advertise freely and by the most extraordinary methods. Next to business, perhaps, came friendship; building up a vast circle of friends and entertaining them with lavish hospitality. He had no interest in sport, in art, in the stage, or music, and it was not until he was almost fifty that he was seized with the desire to—as he expressed it himself—"Lift the ould Mug with a green yacht named Shamrock." The reason given by him was characteristically Hibernian:—that "No Irishman has had a chance to compete for the Cup, though both English and Scotch have." Not only did the Earl of Dunraven claim descent from a line of Celtic kings preceding the Saxon invasion, but the fifth challenger, "Paddy" Henn, R.N., known to his intimates as the "Bird of Paradise" from his estate at Paradise Hill, Ennis, County Clare, was Irish to the backbone, and proud of it, as was J. Beavor Webb, designer of Genesta and Galatea.

In the minds of many Americans the leading motive in the mind of Sir Thomas was to advertise his tea; "Lipton Tea" being much more widely known than the bacon and ham which preceded it. While one of the most enterprising and inventive of advertisers, he was not guilty in this case. Though in no way offended by the publicity and business resulting from his yachting ventures, once seized with the idea of "lifting" the Cup, he pursued it with the same tenacity of purpose that marked all his other enterprises.

The Formal Challenge

ONCE having decided to challenge, Sir Thomas joined the Royal Ulster Yacht Club of Belfast and shortly after presented the Club with a 100-guinea cup; the first of scores of "Lipton cups" which he presented throughout his long career.

In its issue of August 11 *The Field* has the very caustic comment:—"The New York Yacht Club has telegraphed to the Royal Ulster Yacht Club that Sir Thomas Lipton's challenge is most agreeable to them. Probably it is, especially in the light of the fact that no other British club would have backed the challenge." At a meeting of the Council of the Yacht Racing Association on August 13 a letter was read from the Royal Ulster Yacht Club requesting the appointment of a committee to confer with a committee of the club on the details of the proposed match, but the Council refused to take action. On August 23 Charles Russell, the personal representative of Sir Thomas, arrived in New York and was personally escorted to the Fifth Avenue Hotel by two New York agents of the company; there he was called on by Secretary Oddie and Treasurer Hurst, and visited the Club House, later conferring with the Cup Committee. On September 2 there arrived in New York Vice Commodore R. G. Sharman Crawford, Honorary Secretary Hugh C. Kelly and H. G. MaGildowney, of the Royal Ulster Yacht Club, and Will Fife, Jr. After a meeting of the Cup Committee it was announced that the formal challenge, as below, had been tendered and accepted.

New York, Sept. 3.

J. V. S. Oddie, Esq., Secretary,
New York Yacht Club,
67 Madison Avenue, New York.

Dear Sir: We have the honor, on behalf of the Royal Ulster Yacht Club, and in the name of Sir Thomas Lipton, a member of the Club, to challenge to sail a series of matches with the yacht Shamrock against any one yacht or vessel constructed in the United States of America for the America's Cup, subject to the deed of gift, and subject to conditions to be agreed upon.

The following are the particulars of the challenging vessel; Owner, Sir Thomas Lipton; name of yacht, Shamrock; length of load waterline, 89.5 feet; rig, cutter.

We shall be much obliged if you will acknowledge the receipt of this challenge.

Yours truly,
(signed) R. G. Sharman Crawford, V.C.R.U.Y.C.,
Hugh M. MaGildowney,
Hugh C. Kelly, Hon. Secty, R.U.Y.C.

Here, at last, was a complete and unequivocal endorsement of the disputed New Deed, signed by the "bloody hand of Ulster." It will be noticed that the term "match" is again used as synonymous with "race", instead of applying to a set series of races; and that only one dimension, instead of the four specified in the Deed, is given.

AS a preliminary to his career in yachting Sir Thomas purchased a yachting cap; provided himself with a private signal, yellow field with green border and a green shamrock as device; and purchased one of the ten largest steam yachts not owned by Royalty, Ægusa, 1,242 tons, 252 feet l.w.l.; designed and built in 1896 by Scott & Co. of Greenock. He re-christened her Erin, but I have forgotten whether he re-painted her green.

This constituted him a yacht owner, but he never progressed to the rank of yachtsman; he paid, and paid liberally, for technical skill in designing, building, at the tiller and in other lines, but his personal activities were limited to entertaining on a magnificent scale aboard Erin. At the outset he announced that he had no knowledge whatever of the various disputed points, and it is doubtful if, even at the end, he knew anything of the history of the Cup or the many issues which came up in his attempts to "lift" it. The purchase of Erin opened a new world for him, greatly enlarging the circle of his friends and his opportunities for entertaining.

A New Advance in Yachting

THE tenth match for the America's Cup was marked by new extremes in elaborate construction, in multiplicity of outfit, in reckless expenditure, in foolish secrecy, and in failures in rig; in addition, it was proved that, though a draft of 20 feet was no disadvantage in racing over open courses, it involved danger and delay in frequent groundings in the ordinary operations of anchoring in harbors and in hauling out. The conditions of the match were more liberal than ever in the past, even those granted to Lord Dunraven.

The matter of a clear course was disposed of by a special act of Congress passed on May 19, 1896, as follows:

> In order to provide for the safety of passengers on excursion steamers, yachts, oarsmen, and all craft, whether as observers or participants, taking part in regattas, amateur or professional, that may hereafter be held on navigable waters, the Secretary of the Treasury be, and he hereby is, authorized and empowered, in his discretion, to detail revenue cutters to enforce such rules and regulations as may be adopted to insure the safety of passengers on said excursion steamers, yachts, oarsmen and all craft, whether as observers or participants, taking part in such regattas.

While the wording is not above criticism, grouping oarsmen, yachts, passengers, excursion steamers and "all craft" indiscriminately, the act answered its purpose completely and a patrol fleet of revenue cutters, torpedo boats, yachts and tugs maintained a clear course in all future races.

The defense began in October with the lengthening of the ways at the Bristol yard to 300 feet, with a depth of water of 20 feet, the installation of a more powerful wincn and the construction of a car of new design, of wood and steel and on rollers. At the same time Defender, at her mooring at New Rochelle, was cleaned by a diver; Captain Charles Barr, in the service of Charles A. Postley aboard Colonia, now a schooner, was loaned to Mr. Iselin for the season. Defender was sailed to Bristol under jury rig, hauled out and thoroughly overhauled as a trial yacht at the expense of Commodore J. Pierpont Morgan and C. Oliver Iselin, the owners of the new defender. On the other side, as a trial yacht for the challenger, Valkyrie III was docked at Greenock, her painted bottom cleared of a plenteous growth of mussels, and re-painted.

Work on the new boat began at once at Bristol, but the keel could not be cast until Defender was off the ways, on January 14, 1899; the casting coming off ten days later. The construction was the same as Defender, a cast brass keel plate in three sections, cast bronze stem and sternpost, Tobin bronze below the waterline and, in place of aluminum, nickel steel on the topsides; the ordinary in-and-out plating being used. A mast of Oregon pine was made, worked butt uppermost, and also one of steel, the former being stepped on launching. A steel mast was also built in the shop for Defender.

No particulars were given out officially, but some truths leaked out amid a mass of guesses, false reports and faked "lines." In April it was announced that the name chosen was Columbia, that of the schooner which had taken part in the defense in 1871. The new yacht was launched on June 10 and Captain Barr took command with a Deer Island crew. Defender was turned over to W. Butler Duncan, with Captain Urias Rhodes and "Lem" Miller as mate.

THE Fife yard at Fairlee being incapable of handling a metal job of such magnitude, the construction of the challenger was entrusted to J. I. Thornycroft & Co., of Millwall on Thames, noted as builders of torpedo boats. Working at such a distance the designer was seriously handicapped and the work progressed slowly; one cause of delay was the difficulty of boring holes in the lead keel. It will be remembered that this trouble was avoided by Herreshoff in the use of comparatively short lagscrews instead of long through bolts. Two skippers were engaged, Captain "Archie" Hogarth and Captain "Bob" Wringe, both noted for skill at the tiller. The long tiller with relieving tackles was retained on Shamrock, though Columbia was fitted with a wheel.

Launched on June 26, Shamrock was towed to the yard of J. G. Fay & Co., Southampton, for the final fit-out; she was not under sail until July 8, too late for more than a few informal sails against Britannia. She left the Clyde on August 3 with Erin as convoy and took a line from her for a part of the voyage, the two reaching Sandy Hook on August 18. As one ship after another came into New York from Scotland, duplicate, triplicate and even quadruple sets of spars, rigging and sails were unloaded; a big derrick barge being chartered to carry this equipment.

Meanwhile Columbia and Defender had sailed several informal races, the new boat leading. In one, on August 2, Columbia's mast doubled up half way above the deck, fortunately, with no injury to anyone aboard. The trial races were started on September 2, Columbia winning by over three minutes; on September 4 Columbia won by ten minutes; in a race for a special cup on the following day she won by over three minutes. First tried with the Oregon pine stick, the steel mast was stepped on August 24, her stability being materially improved by the lessened weight. In rounding up to their moorings off New Rochelle after a race at Larchmont on July 8 one of Columbia's shrouds fouled the end of Defender's boom, bending it almost to a right angle in the wake of the slings, so that it had to be sent to Bristol for repairs.

When Shamrock was rigged, the Lipton flotilla took up its station in the Horseshoe, just inside of Sandy Hook, a secure anchorage except in a blow from the northwest. The vessels were Erin, Shamrock, Nonawantuck, a large steamer from which the crew had been shifted from the Plymouth, a smaller steamer, which was still retained. The tug James A. Lawrence, the tug Adelaide, the derrick barge and two launches made a total of nine. In a northwest blow on September 11, with most of the fleet absent or without steam, the barge drifted down on Shamrock and a collision which might have been fatal to her was narrowly averted.

Shamrock made several trial sails against the watch; in one on September 13 her gaff buckled in the middle and was replaced by a shorter one. While Shamrock was docked at the Erie Basin, where Thistle and other yachts had been made ready, Columbia was docked in a new drydock recently completed at the Brooklyn Navy Yard. On October 2 the two were measured, with the following results:

	SHAMROCK	COLUMBIA
Length over all	128.00	131.00
Load waterline	87.69	89.66
Breadth	25.00	24.00
Draft	20.25	19.75
Mast deck to hounds	74.00	74.00
Topmast	58.06	64.50
Boom	107.00	106.00
Gaff	67.64	64.95
Spinnaker boom	79.46	73.35
Bowsprit end to boom end	189.13	181.62
Top of boom to topmast sheave	128.28	134.75
Sail area	13,135.45 sq. ft.	13,491.82 sq. ft.
Racing length	114.61	101.92

Columbia allows Shamrock 6 min. 31 sec.

Racing in Calm and Fog

THE first meeting, on October 3, failed to finish in time, as did the second and third. On October 10 they were kept at their moorings by fog, and on the 14th there was a flat calm. On the 16th the first race was sailed in a light breeze, Columbia winning by 10 minutes 8 seconds, corrected time. On the 17th there was a good working breeze, in which Columbia did the better work, but in less than a half hour from the start Shamrock, with her largest club topsail set, lost her topmast at the cap. On the 18th, with her new topmast on end, Shamrock took in some lead and was remeasured; losing 6 minutes 46 seconds in allowance. On October 19 they failed to finish. The following day there was a strong breeze, N. by E., calling for second club topsails. The start was made down wind, Shamrock showing the way over the line and holding her lead for an hour; Columbia sailing through her lee as they neared the turn and leading by 17 seconds. Shamrock held to a working topsail but Columbia's topmast was bare; Shamrock shifted to a small club topsail but in vain, the defender winning by 6 minutes 34 seconds. In addition to the buckling of her gaff, Shamrock had trouble with the bending of her boom in one race. Two facts were freely conceded: that Columbia was decidedly an improvement on Defender; and that she was materially faster than Shamrock.

The Why and Wherefore

THE ocean passage is an inevitable handicap to every challenger, even if towed; the time which should be devoted to leisurely completion and trial races at home is wasted on the passage, and much time is lost in stripping and refitting. In the cases of the sturdy old cutters, Genesta and Galatea, after crossing with masts on end all that was necessary was to heave out their bowsprits and bend racing sails. With the more modern rigs, however, the shipping of the racing rig took much more time. Shamrock was peculiarly unlucky owing to her late completion, the absence of home trials for working-up and the enormous outfit of spars and sails from which she had to choose. To make matters worse, her designer, who had been ill from the time of his arrival in New York, became much worse and saw nothing of her after the first day of measurement, being confined to his hotel during the races and finally carried aboard the steamer in a litter for his return trip. With such a complicated machine as he had created his presence was absolutely necessary for its final adjustment. All in all, the hull suffered from lack of opportunity for the development of such speed as lay latent in its lines; and, later, from conditions which prevented her from displaying her real speed.

After his defeat Sir Thomas was hailed as a hero; on October 23 he was entertained by Commodore Morgan at dinner at the Metropolitan Club, the party of fifty including the members of the Royal Ulster Yacht Club and the New York Yacht Club. The following day he was the guest of the Transportation Club and at the same time the crews of the two yachts were guests at the dinner of the Yacht Masters and Engineers Association in Brooklyn. On October 26 he was elected an honorary member of the New York Yacht Club, being proposed by Commodore Morgan, and on October 31 he was tendered a reception in the Club House. Shamrock, under ketch rig, left New York in tow of Erin on November 6, making the passage to Gourock in 15 days 7 hours. Sir Thomas estimated the cost of the experiment at between $400,000 and $500,000.

Before leaving New York aboard the steamer St. Louis of the American Line he was presented with a loving cup by his guests on Erin, and a popular subscription for another cup was started. On sailing he was accompanied to the pier by a procession of "distinguished citizens" headed by a brass band; he left with a promise of a second challenge in the near future.

TRADITIONS AND MEMORIES OF

Part Forty-Seven

AMERICAN YACHTING

By WILLIAM P. STEPHENS

TRUE to his promise, Sir Thomas was ready a year later with a second challenge:

Royal Ulster Yacht Club,
Mt. Pottinger Road,
Belfast, Ireland, Oct. 2, 1900.

J. V. S. Oddie, Esq.,
Secretary, New York Yacht Club,
New York.

Dear Sir: I am requested by Sir Thomas J. Lipton to forward you this challenge for the America cup; subject as to starts and courses and other details to the same conditions as upon the occasion of the last race, which were found so satisfactory.

The first race to be sailed on Tuesday, August 20, 1901.

The second race to be sailed on Thursday, August 22, 1901.

The third race to be sailed on Saturday, August 24, 1901.

Further races, if any, to be sailed upon the same days in the following week.

I, therefore, on behalf of the Royal Ulster Yacht Club, and in the name of Sir Thomas Lipton, rear commodore of the club, challenge to sail a series of match races with the yacht Shamrock II against any other yacht or vessel constructed in the United States of America for the America cup.

The following are the particulars of the challenging vessel: Owner, Sir Thomas Lipton. Name of yacht, Shamrock II. Length on load waterline, 89 ft. Rig, cutter.

The custom house measurement will follow as soon as the vessel can be measured for registration.

I shall be much obliged if you will cable the receipt of this challenge.

(signed) HUGH C. KELLY,
Honorable Secretary,
Royal Ulster Yacht Club.

Bowdoin B. Crowninshield and, below, Independence, designed by him in 1901 as a proposed Defender of the America's Cup

This challenge was promptly accepted and the negotiations went forward in true "After you, my dear Alphonse" style, all details being the same as in 1889 except for two requests by Sir Thomas: that no race should be started after 1 P.M., and that the time limit should be shortened from six to five and one-half hours. The first of these was granted and the second refused. Later on Sir Thomas requested that the one-gun start be used in place of the time start, that the yachts be measured in the graving dock of the Brooklyn Navy Yard, and that in the event of any unforeseen delay in the arrival of Shamrock II she be allowed three weeks for refitting. The first two were refused, the third was granted.

The Cup Committee appointed by the Club included Commodore Lewis Cass Ledyard, Vice Commodore August Belmont, Rear Commodore C. L. F. Robinson, Secretary, J. V. S. Oddie, S. Nicholson Kane, E. D. Morgan, E. M. Brown, J. Pierpont Morgan and C. Oliver Iselin. Though Columbia was still in perfect condition, an order was at once placed with the Herreshoffs for a new boat; the owning syndicate including Vice Commodore Belmont, Oliver H. Payne, Henry Walters, James Stillman and F. G. Bourne. Constitution, as she was christened when launched on May 6, was placed in the hands of W. Butler Duncan as manager and Captain Urias Rhodes as skipper.

Boston Comes to the Defense

After taking the lead in the defense for three successive years Boston had played no part in international racing for fourteen years; but, with another match assured, in the fall of 1900 a movement was begun toward the formation of a Boston syndicate. Without going into the many details it is enough to summarize that the task of providing a Boston representative was ultimately assumed by Thomas W. Lawson, a wealthy stock broker interested in copper. Mr. Lawson's attack of the racing fever seems to have been as sudden

© M. Rosenfeld

and violent as those of Lord Dunraven and Sir Thomas Lipton. After contenting himself with the steam yacht Random of 63 feet 6 inches l.w.l. which he purchased in 1898 and re-named My Gypsy he had built the steam yacht Dreamer, 148 feet 6 inches l.w.l., in 1899, and in 1900 we find him as the proposed owner of a Cup defender. Enlisting at first as a subscriber to the proposed syndicate, when certain obstacles were encountered in organization he very generously offered to carry the entire expense of Boston's defender. He not only was not a member of the New York Yacht Club, but his club affiliations were limited to joining the Hull-Massachusetts Yacht Club as a preliminary to his new career in yacht racing. His basic proposition in thus entering the field of international racing was that every American citizen, regardless of club affiliations, was possessed of the right to enter any vessel owned by him in the trial races; and, if successful, to defend the Cup. This proposition, which he claimed had the endorsement of no less an authority than General Paine, naturally did not meet the approval of the New York Yacht Club as responsible, during its holding of the trophy, for the management of the match. After a long controversy carried on in amicable correspondence with Commodore Ledyard the yacht was denied the privilege of entering the trial races.

Why Mr. Lawson was not a member of the New York Yacht Club, why he did not join it, and why he would not turn over the nominal ownership to a member for the trial races, are questions which do not pertain to this history. On his side it may be said today that he spent money most liberally in what he considered a righteous cause, and he set to shame the childish secrecy surrounding both challenger and defender and made public every technical detail as well as every item of cost of his yacht. In the end, to justify himself, he spent many thousand dollars in the publication of a large and elaborately illustrated "Lawson History of the America's Cup," the text by one of the leading yachting writers of the day, Winfield M. Thompson; the edition of three thousand copies being distributed free to yachtsmen and yacht clubs on both sides of the Atlantic. In addition to Mr. Thompson's very complete history, nearly a third of the volume is devoted to the exploitation of his thesis and his dispute with the Club by Mr. Lawson himself.

After the fact of the building of a Boston contestant had become known an attempt was made to form a second syndicate to build a purely American defender. The designer and builder was to be C. C. Hanley of Quincy, noted for his racing Cape catboats and later for very successful sloops of medium size. Mr. Hanley's proposition was to build a wooden hull of shoal draft but on modern lines, with a centerboard and all inside ballast; the plan, however, failed of fruition.

The Scow Invades the Cup Class

The number of designers qualified by experience to design for the Cup class was limited at best, and still more so when, for patriotic reasons, the choice was restricted to Boston. The most prominent of Boston designers was Bowdoin B. Crowninshield, a descendant of a family once close to the sea in connection with shipping from the port of Salem and trade with the Far East. Born in New York in 1867, the family returned to Boston in the following year and moved to Marblehead in 1874. The father, B. W. Crowninshield, was a yacht owner, and the boys,

Shamrock II, built in Scotland for Sir Thomas Lipton and challenger for the Cup. Below: Constitution, designed by N. G. Herreshoff for Cup defense

N. L. Stebbins

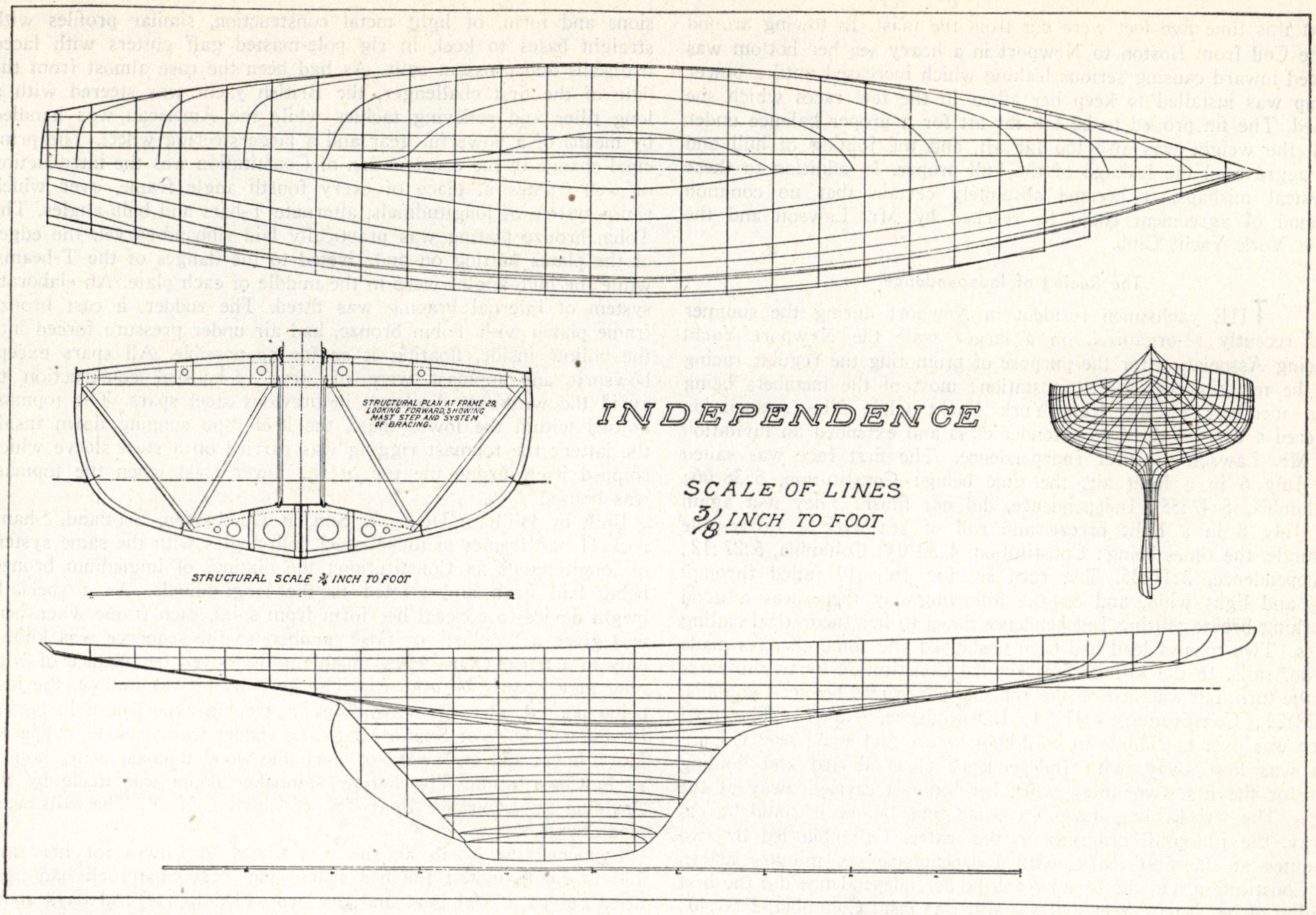

Lines of Independence, designed by B. B. Crowninshield for Thomas W. Lawson. From Lawson's History of the America's Cup (reproduction not to scale)

"Bowdy" and Frank, grew up in small craft—dories, catboats and small cabin yachts. After a year at the Massachusetts Institute of Technology Bowdoin entered Harvard, graduating in 1890. Engaged in various enterprises apart from salt water, in 1896 he entered the drafting room of J. R. Purdon and a year later set up his own office as a designer and yacht broker. In his designing he was very successful with scows, knockabouts and raceabouts up to 30 feet, and also turned out some larger yachts. His knowledge of yachts, his skill in tuning-up and at the tiller, and his racing experience, far as they went in general practice, were hardly such as to bridge the wide gap between a raceabout and a Cup defender, and in the selection of type an unfortunate choice was made in favor of the scow.

The second match for the Seawanhaka International Trophy for Small Yachts, to give it the official title, five years previously had proved the speed possibilities of the type, and also its serious limitations. Very high speeds had been obtained in centerboard boats with no fixed ballast which the crew could heel instantly to any desired angle; thus limiting the size to less than 30 feet l.w.l.; when it came to larger yachts with fixed ballast, inside or outside, the case was different, and it was much worse when there were added a fin and bulb which, once built into the hull, could not be altered. There was then, as had been proved in several large yachts, no known method of calculation by which the position of the fin could be determined beyond possibility of error. To add to the difficulties of the problem it was determined to cut the weight of construction to the minimum and to give her the largest sail plan ever seen over 90 feet of waterline. Whatever conditions may exist today, forty years ago the engineering of the hull construction and rig of a yacht of the Cup class had not progressed beyond the cut-and-try method; in no way approaching the certainty with which the strains and stresses of such a structure as, for instance, the Brooklyn Bridge might be calculated. This had been proven in the breakages of the Herreshoff Cup yachts in spite of long experience.

The work was pushed with all the force and energy characteristic of her owner; the designer's staff was greatly enlarged and the plans hurried, the contract for building was made with the Lawley Company. As this firm had other work in its own shops the actual construction was done by the Atlantic Works, in East Boston, under the personal supervision of George F. Lawley. The contract was signed on December 17, 1900, the price being $75,000, the yacht was launched on May 18, 1901, and had her first sail on June 3, with Captain Hank Haff in command. The construction included frames of nickel-steel, plating of bronze with an upper strake of steel, and a deck of aluminum. An elaborate system of struts was designed to take the strains between the floor system and deck. While a balance rudder was installed, there was also a rudder trunk of the normal type and provision for shipping the usual form of rudder if desired.

The physical troubles of Independence began with her first sail, her steering gear buckling from the strain of the balance rudder. This was condemned at once, but no drydock was available for her 20 feet draft; in this emergency the Government drydock of the Charlestown Navy Yard was placed at the disposal of Mr. Lawson and the ordinary rudder installed. On the next trial the new quadrant and pinion steering gear broke down and was replaced by a stronger one.

At this time five feet were cut from the mast. In towing around Cape Cod from Boston to Newport in a heavy sea her bottom was forced inward causing serious leaking which increased until a power pump was installed to keep her afloat in the few races which she sailed. The fin proved to be too far aft for a proper balance under sail, the weight was also too far aft, and the joining of hull and fin aggravated the leakage of the hull proper. In addition to these physical mishaps, it became absolutely certain that no common ground of agreement could be reached by Mr. Lawson and the New York Yacht Club.

The Racing of Independence

THE yachtsmen resident in Newport during the summer had recently re-organized on a larger scale the Newport Yacht Racing Association for the purpose of promoting the regular racing of the many yachts there on station; most of the members being also members of the New York Yacht Club. The Association offered a cup for the Cup defender class and extended an invitation to Mr. Lawson to enter Independence. The first race was sailed on July 6 in a light air, the time being: Constitution, 5:38:06; Columbia, 5:47:55; Independence, did not finish. They met again on July 8 in a light breeze and roll of sea over a thirty-mile triangle, the times being: Constitution, 4:59:04; Columbia, 5:27:12; Independence, 6:17:35. The race set for July 10 failed through fog and light wind, and on the following day there was a good working breeze putting Independence down to her theoretical sailing lines. Two tons of lead had been unshipped and some changes made in her sails. In the 15-mile beat she led Constitution by two minutes at the turn, but was last on the run, the final times being: Columbia, 4:28:22; Constitution, 4:32:59; Independence, 4:35:14. The final race was over a triangle in a 12-knot breeze and some sea; Columbia was first away, with Independence close aboard and holding her for the first two miles, when her topmast carried away at the cap. The wreck hung down for some time before it could be cut away, the jibtopsail dragging in the water. Columbia led by two minutes at the first mark, with Independence six minutes astern of Constitution. On the broad reach home Independence did the best sailing of her brief career, but she still was last: Columbia, 2:56:40; Constitution, 2:58:59; Independence, 3:07:24.

Sailing to New London, Independence was docked, patches were put on to stop the worst leaks, and a plate 11 feet long and 17 inches deep was riveted to flanges along the keel forward to give her more forefoot and remedy the lee helm; heavier struts were also installed between floors and deck. Her last races were off Newport on August 1 and 3; the first over the triangle in a light breeze and smooth sea. Constitution was at Bristol for repairs. After an even start to windward Columbia led at the first mark by 1 minute 9 seconds; almost before the wind Columbia gained 5 minutes 23 seconds; on the reach home Independence outsailed Columbia, but not enough to win, the times being: Columbia, 3:42:46; Independence, 3:47:40.

For the last race there was a breeze of 12 knots, which later increased to 18 knots, with sea smooth; the course being 10 miles to windward and return. Just at the start Independence was struck by a blast which laid her flat, immediately after she and Columbia were in contact through a foul on the part of the latter, though no protest was made. On the beat the hull twisted, the braces inside bending, the fore and after bodies were out of line, and the rudder stock bound, the three men on the wheel being unable to hold her on her course. Owing to her excessive heel her compass was off and she was steered to leeward of her course. At the first mark Columbia led by 3 minutes 12 seconds; on the second leg Independence gained 1 minute 37 seconds; on the last leg, still steering very badly, she made up all but 40 seconds of Columbia's lead, the times being: Columbia, 2:51:19; Independence, 2:52:28.

While her owner declared himself fully satisfied as to her speed, and needing only a few changes and repairs, it is doubtful whether, under any conditions, she could have been brought back to her original form, her hull made permanently tight, and her error of balance corrected. Just three months from the day of her trial sail she was placed out of commission, the hull was stripped and hauled on the beach and broken up. According to Mr. Lawson's detailed statement of expenditures the total cost of the experiment was $205,034.08. Mr. Crowninshield continued in business for some years before retiring, designing some successful yachts and the seven-masted schooner Thomas W. Lawson.

Type in 1901

THE three Cup yachts of 1901, Columbia, Constitution and Shamrock II, followed one general pattern, very similar in dimensions and form, of light metal construction, similar profiles with straight bases to keel, in rig pole-masted gaff cutters with laced mainsails and crosscut sails. As had been the case almost from the date of the first challenger, the British yacht was steered with a long tiller and relieving tackles while the American was handled by means of a powerful gear and a large steering wheel. The principal change in the construction of Constitution was the introduction of web frames in place of every fourth angle frame, over which ran a system of longitudinals, alternate T-bars and bulb-angles. The Tobin bronze plating was practically laid ribband-carvel, the edges of the plates butting on and riveted to the flanges of the T-beams, while the bulb-angles were in the middle of each plate. An elaborate system of internal bracing was fitted. The rudder, a cast bronze frame plated with Tobin bronze, had air under pressure forced into the hollow inside, floating it as far as possible. All spars except bowsprit and topmast were of steel, of special construction to avoid the weakness disclosed in previous steel spars. The topmast housed within the lower mast, the heel rope running down inside the latter; the topmast rigging was carried on a steel sleeve which shipped itself inside the top of the lower mast when the topmast was housed.

Built by William Denny & Son, at Dumbarton, Scotland, Shamrock II had frames of nickel-steel bulb-angles with the same system of longitudinals as Constitution; the plating, of immadium bronze, being laid flush and riveted to the longitudinals. As a specially bright device to conceal her form from spies, each frame when bent was given a "cooked" or false number, so the sequence was known only to a trusted few. How much this improved her chance of winning may readily be guessed. The keel or fin was hollow, the lead being poured later, thus avoiding the trouble experienced in boring for the keel bolts of Shamrock I. The rudder was of wood, coppered. Mast, boom and gaff were of steel, the wood topmast being housed as in Constitution. The hollow spinnaker boom was made by the Spalding-St. Lawrence Boat Co., at Clayton, N. Y. The sails were made by Ratsey.

Launched on April 30, she was towed to Cowes for her sails and to Southampton for her spars. The first Shamrock had been fitted out as a trial boat and the two sailed for several days about the Solent with no attempt at racing. On May 9 the gaff of Shamrock II folded up. On May 13 the two sailed a race in a good breeze, No. I winning from No. II by over three minutes on a 20-mile triangle. On May 20 they met again, No. II winning by 37 seconds; on the next day No. I won by 1 minute 24 seconds.

On May 22 Sir Thomas was honored by the presence on board of King Edward VII ("Tum Tum" or "His Nibs" to his intimates). The famous cutters, Samoena, Irex and Iverna were owned in succession by John Jameson, the maker of a celebrated brand of whiskey, and sailed by his cousin W. G. ("Willie") Jameson, for many years the leading Corinthian in Great Britain; he had charge of Shamrock II with Captain Edward Sycamore as the professional skipper. On this day while working about the line shortly before the start a sudden lone puff, such as capsized the great Mohawk in New York Bay in July 1876 and Grayling off the West Bank in 1883 struck the challenger, her mast doubling in the middle like a length of stovepipe, the topmast and all its gear under water. Captain Sycamore wiped her off smartly and the mast went over the side instead of aft, and no one was hurt.

Sir Thomas cabled at once for a postponement of six weeks or the substitution of No. I; a delay of one month being finally granted. The new mast was 158 feet 8 inches from heel to truck and in one piece, the first pole mast on a Cup yacht. Starting from Gourock on July 27 in tow of Erin and under the same jury rig as Shamrock I, she passed Sandy Hook on August 11 and was taken to Erie Basin.

The New Defender

DELIVERED on May 25, Constitution began her trial sails off Newport on June 4 with her designer at the wheel; the locust spreader broke and the topmast went at the cap, the lower mast folding up well above the middle. The mast was rebuilt and both upper and lower spreaders were replaced by heavier ones; later a heavier bobstay was shipped. The preliminary races in which Independence took part have been noted, the racing in the New York Y. C. began with the cruise; on the run from Glen Cove to Huntington on July 22, Constitution won by 4 minutes 18 seconds elapsed time. On the second run to Morris Cove she won by 5 minutes 16 seconds, and on the third to New London by 8 minutes 23 seconds.

These three races were sailed in light breezes and smooth water. On the final run to Newport in a 12-knot breeze and smooth water

Columbia won by 3 minutes 22 seconds, and in the Astor cup race over a 28-mile triangle in a strong breeze and some sea she won by 2 minutes 54 seconds elapsed and 4 minutes 28 seconds corrected time. Constitution went to Bristol for a new mast which, as stated by Mr. Duncan, would be five feet longer and the topmast five feet shorter in order to hold the gaff better, but the measurements as taken by John Hyslop on June 24 and again on August 23 show that this alteration was not made.

On August 10, 12 and 14, three special races of the Club were sailed off Newport, Constitution winning the first by 4 minutes 9 seconds, the second by 35 seconds, and in the third both being unable to finish. Five races were then sailed off Larchmont and Oyster Bay, Constitution winning two and Columbia three. The trial races started on August 31, the first 15 miles to windward in a 7-knot breeze and smooth water; Columbia leading by two minutes at the windward mark and 3 minutes 48 seconds over the course. In the second race over the triangle, in a light breeze and a calm at one time, Columbia led by 4 minutes 30 seconds at the second mark, the race being called later. In the last race Columbia was disqualified for fouling Constitution at the start, but no protest flag was set and she sailed the course; Constitution leading by 54 seconds elapsed and losing by 17 seconds corrected time. Following this race the committee disqualified Columbia for the foul at the start, but announced her selection as the defender of 1901.

Model or Men?

THE opinion of her designer that Constitution was the better boat never was shaken to the time of his death. She should have been, and it is quite possible that he was right. In considering the reasons for her failure we must go outside of the boat herself. As to the boats, Columbia had the great advantage of a full season of tuning-up and racing, the time of experiment and change was over, and her sails were fully worked into shape and superior to the newer and stiffer sails of Constitution. Both sets were made in the Bristol loft, but it was reported that the material obtainable in 1901 was inferior to that of 1899.

Turning now to the quarterdecks of the two yachts, C. Oliver Iselin learned his racing in a hard school; while still a student at Columbia in 1873 he bought the sandbagger Mary Emma, 23 feet over all, racing her until he replaced her by the 27-foot Dare Devil in 1877. There was no sentiment in the game of sandbag racing, the first thing was to win, the second to get the prize after you had won it. The actual work of sailing these wide, shoal over-rigged boats, with a capsize imminent every moment, was a game that hardened a man, and any young man who looked on it as pleasure for seven or eight years was well on his way to a broader career in yachting. Sailing aboard many notable yachts, Mr. Iselin built the 70-foot Titania and raced her in 1887; and later commanded Vigilant in 1893, Defender in 1895 and Columbia in 1899. His experience in tuning-up and racing these great yachts was such as few could equal.

Charles Barr was employed as a boy in a grocery store in Glasgow, and later had his first taste of sailing in a half-decked fishing boat, working in all weathers on the Clyde. After a season in the forecastle of the cutter Clara commanded by his elder brother John in 1884 he was the only one of the regular crew who made the passage to America, racing in her for two seasons. Settling in Marblehead, he studied navigation when unemployed and when one of the owners of Clara placed the order for the 40-foot Minerva, Charles was considered competent to navigate her from Fairlie to Boston; later making a reputation for her and for himself. Going from one yacht to a larger, he made a reputation as a racing skipper equal to those of men double his age. He knew the rules and his rights under them, and claimed all that was coming to him—and sometimes a little more. Handling Columbia in her second season as a man would a bicycle, turning her as on a pivot, he took chances with her that would have been dangerous in the extreme for the average good skipper; sometimes missing, as in the case just mentioned. He knew every one of his opponents as well as he knew his yacht. Such a combination aboard a tried yacht was hard to beat.

ONE of the spectators of the first race in 1870 was a boy of eight, the grand nephew and namesake of W. Butler Duncan who joined the New York Yacht Club in 1852 and owned the schooner Haze a few years later. His ancestry or his inborn love for the sea took the boy to Annapolis in later years and after graduation he served as signal officer aboard the old Vandalia before resigning to take up yachting as a lifetime diversion. As a member of the Seawanhaka Corinthian Y. C. he took a prominent part in the organization of the New York Naval Militia and as an officer of the 1st Battalion. He owned a number of yachts, racing them himself, and he was one of the quarterdeck crew of Vigilant, Defender and Columbia. While both experienced and skillful, he lacked the exceptional qualities necessary for the tuning-up and development of such a modern racing machine as Constitution.

Captain Urias Rhodes was born in Bay Shore, Long Island, on February 28, 1852, the son of Richard Rhodes, a captain of coasting vessels. His early experience was at sea. His long career in yachting was mainly in large schooners, Atlantic, Volunteer, Sea Fox, Lasca, Montauk, Ariel, Miranda, and the yawls Sybarita and Ailsa in American waters. He also commanded the auxiliary Hussar. After his retirement he lived in Bay Shore until his death on April 17, 1942, following three years of illness.

Shamrock II did her tuning-up alone, with no competitor. When finally docked, the green paint was scraped off her bronze topsides, the sheathing was removed from her rudder, it was planed down and new sheathing put on. The first race was set for September 26, the course 15 miles to windward in a 12-knot breeze; the patrol fleet maintained a clear course, with ample room about the line. With 14,000 square feet of sail over 90 feet waterline, a starting interval of two minutes, and Sycamore at the tiller of one yacht and Barr at the wheel of the other, it was Greek meet Greek. The fun began just before the starting gun, a collision being barely avoided; no protest flag was set, but each side claimed that the other was to blame. Columbia, to windward, led by twelve seconds; the wind was now light with soft spots, favoring alternately one and the other, Shamrock II at one time crossing Columbia's bow; but at the turn the defender led by 7 minutes 15 seconds. The race was finally called off with Columbia about one mile ahead. Two days later a start was made in a breeze of about 9 knots falling to 3; the start was won by Captain Sycamore, who crossed on Columbia's weather with a lead of two seconds. The fight to windward was close and hard, Shamrock II rounding with a lead of 41 seconds. On the run in the wind lightened materially and Columbia gained a little, finishing with a lead of 34 seconds, or 1 minute 20 seconds corrected time. The first trial over the triangle on October 1 failed for lack of wind, but Shamrock II was well in the lead in the middle of the second leg.

AT the suggestion of Sir Thomas it was arranged to sail the races every day unless one party objected. On October 3 over the triangle in a breeze of nearly 12 knots and freshening, with smooth water. Again Captain Sycamore won the start, but Captain Barr saved himself through the time start which was fought so bitterly for years by many American yachtsmen. On the reach of ten miles Columbia, still astern, gained 22 seconds; on the second leg she gained another 30 seconds; on the beat home in a strong breeze she passed Shamrock II, winning by 2 minutes 52 seconds elapsed, and 3 minutes 35 seconds corrected time. The wind held next day for what proved to be the final race, about 9 knots N.N.W., calling for a run on the first leg. This time both held back, crossing after the two-minute gun, Columbia a little ahead with spinnaker and big club topsail; Shamrock II led at the turn by 49 seconds. There was a hard fight home, Shamrock II holding her lead and finishing two seconds ahead, but losing by 41 seconds. It was computed that in the three races making up the match the 90 nautical miles were sailed in 12 hours, 18 minutes and 3 seconds; with a gain of 3 minutes 27 sec. for Columbia in actual and 5 minutes 56 seconds corrected time. It is evident that, what with the long series of races sailed by Columbia during the season, and the lack of trial races and the loss of time through breakdowns and the ocean passage, George Watson had turned out a very fast yacht; in the handling the honors were very even.

With Shamrock II laid up in Brooklyn, Sir Thomas proposed a new trial of the two in the following year, but he was informed that under the terms of the New Deed the Club had no power to accept a second challenge naming the same yacht unless a full year had elapsed, or a match had been sailed with some other vessel. Fond adieux were said by both parties and Sir Thomas sailed, this time without a brass band, with the promise of a third green challenger. Easy as it is to calculate times in such a contest, and also the cost to both sides, it is not so easy to evaluate the gain to yacht racing or to naval architecture.

American Yachting

Part Forty-Eight

By WILLIAM P. STEPHENS

TWO years having elapsed since the last match, and no English yacht club showing any disposition to challenge, Sir Thomas again entered the lists with a letter dated October 7, 1902 and identical, almost word for word, with that of October 2, 1900 as quoted in the previous chapter. The only important difference was that this letter was addressed to George A. Cormack, Esq., as Secretary. In the interim J. V. S. Oddie, who had been Secretary from 1889, had been taken ill, and Mr. Cormack offered to substitute for him temporarily. Unfortunately, Mr. Oddie's illness terminated fatally in 1902 and Mr. Cormack was elected to the office, serving until his death in 1938; the longest term of office in the Club's history.

The challenge was received on October 15 and at a special meeting on October 23 it was formally accepted and a Cup Committee appointed:—Commodore Lewis Cass Ledyard, Vice Commodore Frederick G. Bourne, Rear Commodore C. L. F. Robinson, Secretary George A. Cormack, E. D. Morgan, E. M. Brown, J. Pierpont Morgan, J. Malcolm Forbes, Archibald Rogers and W. Butler Duncan. Two sets of the conditions, identical with those of the previous match, were sent to Secretary Kelly; one set being signed by the committee of the Royal Ulster Yacht Club and returned to New York.

This time Sir Thomas swung back to Will Fife, with the Dennys of Dumbarton as the builders; and the indispensable stencil plate was dusted off for the naming of Shamrock III. The new yacht was just under 90 feet l.w.l., with an over-all length of 134 feet 4 inches and a breadth of about 23 feet; her draft being 19 feet. The hull, plated with nickel steel, was enameled white instead of green.

The new defender, of course ordered from the Herreshoffs, was paid for by a syndicate including Cornelius Vanderbilt, owner of the cutter Rainbow; Clement A. Griscom, owner of the steam yacht Alvina, 526 tons; P. A. B. Widener, steam yacht Josephine, 974 tons; W. B. Leeds, steam yacht Noma, 763 tons; J. J. Hill, steam yacht Wacouta, 803 tons; Henry Walters, steam yacht Narada, 490 tons; and Albert H. Gary, Wm. Rockefeller and Norma B. Ream, non-owners.

Captain Charles Barr, master of Reliance and earlier Cup yachts, whose skill helped to defeat successive challengers. Below: Lines of Reliance

© M. Rosenfeld

Again there was the tomfoolery of locked doors and soaped windows on both sides, with the added expense and loss of time inevitable when such methods are employed. It is self evident that the ultimate result would have been the same if the lines of both challenger and defender had been published as soon as each keel was cast and the frames bent; when this stage of construction is reached it is too late for either side to make any important change in the design. As far as the future is concerned, when it comes to docking and measuring each yacht is open to the scrutiny of the rival designer.

Reliance, as she was named, was discussed at some length by the writer at her debut on the basis of such information as was permitted to other than the select few, as follows. "It is typical of that uncertainty which constantly gives new zest to yachting that two of the great designers of the world have given radically different answers to the great problem involved in the twelfth match for the America's Cup. Of Mr. Herreshoff's answer it may be said confidently that she is not a scow, though more extreme than any of her older sisters; and it means much that the greatest of all designers, the inventor of the

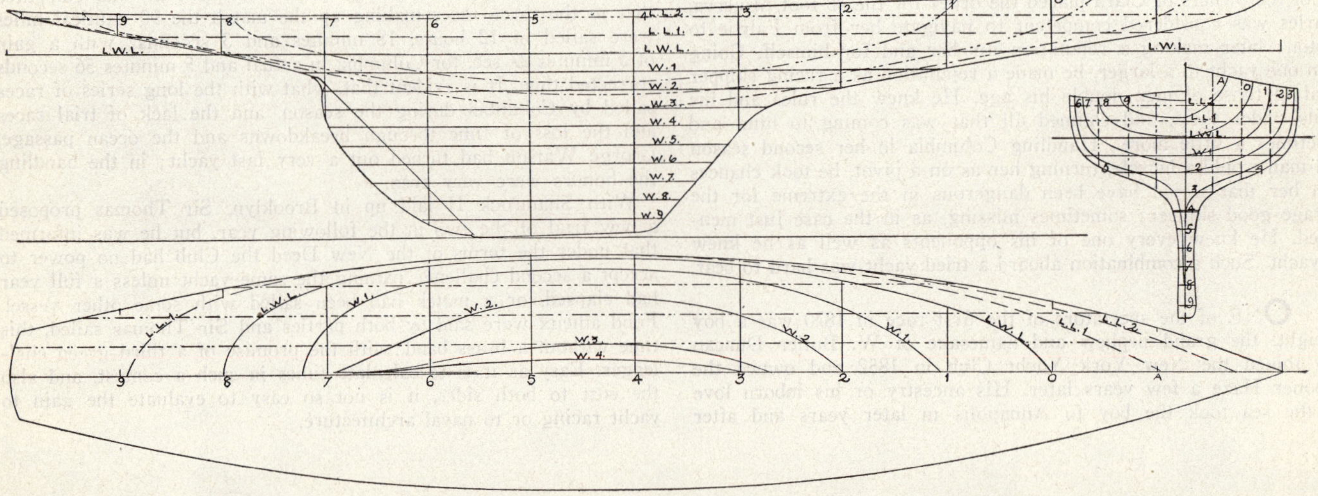

© M. Rosenfeld

Shamrock III, Sir Thomas Lipton's third challenger, which suffered defeat in 1903 as her predecessors did in 1899 and 1901

fin-keel type and, of course, fully informed as to the performances of the scow type in the smaller classes, has thus far declined to adopt either type for the defense of the America's Cup.

"In Reliance he has departed from the two older boats, Columbia and Constitution, by building a wider and shoaler body with a still thinner and finer fin; the flatter floor and fuller loadline being naturally worked out into longer overhangs. At the same time the old curves are retained. Except in some of the smaller fin-keels one looks in vain in Herreshoff's work in the past for the beautifully fair and flowing curves which have always characterized the work of Watson and Fife; the really artistic side of designing has evidently appealed but little to him, and if the slightest advantage was to be gained by a hard turn to the bilge or a sudden hollow at the tuck no consideration of mere external beauty was allowed to interfere. While some in experimenting in the direction of the scow type might be tempted to soften the curves for the mere sake of appearance, it is certain that such a consideration would have no weight with the designer of Reliance; and that the form is to a certain extent normal in its curvature is ample proof that in his opinion a more extreme type would be inferior in actual performance.

"Why Reliance is what she is must remain the secret of her taciturn designer; a man who thinks much and says little. At best we can only conjecture whether he selected this extreme form from the conviction that it represents a distinct advance in speed over the two older boats, or whether he merely availed himself of an opportunity to experiment. With Columbia and Constitution still available for Cup defense there was no possible reason for the construction of a third of identical type, and an experiment in a new line was almost a necessity. The most striking feature of the yacht as she is seen afloat is the excessive length of the forward overhang, nearly equal to that aft, making an over-all length of 140 feet; in addition, the freeboard is several inches less than in Constitution, so that the apparent length of hull is further increased. Not only are the ends long in being carried out to a fine point forward and a thin edge aft, but they are low, cutting the water at a small angle.

"The bulb is long, thin, and of very easy form, the depth at the fore end being about seven feet; the actual weight is, of course, unknown, but it is estimated at being about 100 tons. The midship section resembles Columbia rather than Constitution in having a marked straight to the floor, but it is much flatter than both of the older boats, with a sharper turn between fin and hull, while through the increased breadth the bilge has a very easy turn. The principal fore-and-aft lines, the bow-buttock lines and the diagonals, are exceptionally long and easy, and the form is one which will show an increased length when heeled.

"The construction, an evolution from that originated in Defender, and afterwards materially elaborated in Constitution, is distinctly original with Mr. Herreshoff. The first of the big Bristol boats, Navahoe, built in 1892-3, was of the ordinary steel construction, with a ballast-trough keel filled with molten lead: which, by the way, had to be cut out afterwards and re-cast and bolted outside. Both Colonia and Vigilant were of the same construction, with a flat plate keel and frames running from side to side; though their lead keels were cast independently and bolted outside at the start. The web frame system adopted in Constitution was followed; the plating of the hull is of Tobin bronze except the sheer strake, of nickel steel. Between this strake and the garboard are five strakes on each side, the thickness being but 6/40 inch as compared with 8/40 in Constitution. The joints are flush, being made on the T-bar stringers. The lead keel is entirely sheathed with light bronze, making one unbroken surface of this metal from the bottom of the keel to a foot above the water.

"This great hull is further stiffened by a system of diagonal braces of heavy steel tubing along each side, running from the deck at about the quarter breadth to the bilge, and riveted at both ends to the web frames. The weight of the great mast, and the tremendous downward thrust due to the shrouds call for special construction; a deep vertical keelson is worked for a length of 20 feet on each side of the mast, an extra web frame is added, and all frames are made deeper. The keelson and web frames carry a steel plate stiffened below by a cone of steel, the heel of the steel mast is bound by a ring of angle steel, and the flange of this ring is fastened by ⅝-inch bolts to the plate and the upper flange of the conical base. The chainplates are carried in to the base, and in addition, two struts built of steel plates run from the partners across and down to the bilge. The partners are formed of two rings of heavy angle steel, one above and one below the deck, these being tied by four vertical rods to the plate at the base.

"The spars and rigging are substantially the same as in Constitution; mast, boom and gaff of steel, bowsprit and topmast of wood, the latter housing within the mast. Two interesting changes are noticeable in the details, there is but one pair of spreaders instead of two, and there are two bobstays, of equal size, one just

Reliance, the Defender, built from Herreshoff designs, successfully defended the Cup in 1903, winning all three of the races completed and leading in those called off

inside the other, running from double eyes on the bobstay plate over the same martingale. All of the Herreshoff yachts are liberally supplied with capstans and winches for handling sheets and halyards, the main sheet capstans on the quarter deck being a special feature of the older Cup defenders. A new move has been made in Reliance in placing a number of winches below deck, both halyards and sheets being led below. By this arrangement the men are able to work more conveniently than on deck, a smaller number is necessary to handle any one line, and the power can be applied more evenly and smoothly.

"Just what the new defender represents in model it is impossible to say at the present time; it may be that the changes from the more conventional forms of Columbia and Constitution have been made from a conviction that they will result in greater speed under the conditions of a Cup match; but it is quite as probable that they represent a mere experiment in new lines whose value is as yet uncertain? In construction the yacht represents the designer's best work after years of experience in cutting down weight and at the same time strengthening every point which has shown the slightest sign of weakness. There is much in it to arouse admiration, but its true merit can only be demonstrated by actual tests; to criticise it fairly would require such full knowledge of all parts and such data of previous yachts as are possessed only by the designer."

Launchings a la Mode

The launching of Shamrock III on St. Patrick's Day, 1903, was a holiday for Glasgow and its suburb of Dumbarton, a special train carried several hundred guests, there was a popular turn-out of the entire countryside, bunting, brass bands, long speeches and feasting. Owing to the shoal water the yacht was slid overboard on camels, being christened by the Countess of Shaftsbury. The fitting-out was done quickly and by April 8 she was ready for her first trial. Shamrock II was still in New York (a short time later she was sold for junk and broken up) so Shamrock I was fitted out as the trial boat, under command of Captain Charles Bevis, while Captain "Bob" Wringe was in sole command of the new boat. The locale of the racing was Weymouth Bay, in the South of England, where clear deep-water courses were to be had.

Three days of sailing proved the new yacht to be materially faster than the old. On April 17 she was under way alone in a very strong breeze, Sir Thomas being on board; the upper eye of one of the shroud turnbuckles split, the mast went about seven feet above the deck, broke again where it hit the rail, and again near the masthead when the topmast struck the bottom of the Bay. One of the crew was drowned, Sir Thomas, Col. Crawford and Thomas W. Ratsey were slightly injured, and every part of the rig including the sails, with the exception of the boom, was ruined. She was towed to Gourock where a new rig was shipped and on May 7 she was under way again off that port.

The launching of Reliance on April 12 was also attended with much ceremony, more bunting, ribbons, flags, flowers and a brass band; Miss Nora Iselin christening the yacht. The trial races began on May 21 at the West end of Long Island Sound, continuing until the end of July and resulting in the selection of Reliance. Constitution did better than in her first season; Columbia, now in new hands, taking third place.

The invading flotilla left Gourock on May 28, Erin I having Shamrock III in tow, while Shamrock I was astern of Cruizer, an ocean tug specially purchased for the voyage. The personnel of the expedition included 156 men; 41 on each of the yachts, 59 aboard Erin I and Cruizer's crew of 15.

THE THIRD LIPTON CHALLENGE RESULTED IN A CONTEST BETWEEN RELIANCE AND SHAMROCK III, WHICH WAS EASILY WON BY RELIANCE, CAPTAIN CHAS. BARR

A New Measurer Holds the Tape

From Volunteer and Thistle in 1887 to Constitution and Shamrock II in 1901 every Cup candidate and contestant had been measured by the veteran John Hyslop; but he resigned in 1902 and a young designer, Charles D. Mower, was appointed. Both challenger and defender were berthed in the big graving dock of Erie Basin for a week of preparation; on Monday, August 17, the dock was flooded and the pair set afloat. A very large assemblage was present to view for the first time the results of months of secret work. Mr. Mower created a new precedent by going aloft in a bo's'un's chair on the spinnaker halyard to hold the upper end of the tape at the topmast sheave. Shamrock III was the first measured; of course, both designers were present and on the invitation of Mr. Fife, Mr. Herreshoff inspected Shamrock III on deck and below. The official figures were:

	Shamrock III	*Reliance*
Length, l.w.l.	89.78	89.66
Overhang Forward	21.30	27.63
Aft	23.34	26.40
Over all	134.42	143.69
Boom to Upper Sheave	144.83	149.68
Boom to Throat Halyard Sheave	72.52	77.68
Topmast	72.31	72.00
Base	187.53	201.76
Boom, including mast	106.13	117.47
Gaff	65.77	71.76
Spinaker Boom	81.40	83.75
Sail Area, square feet	14,154.23	16,159.45
Racing Length	104.39	108.39
Men on Board	56	64
Time for 30 Miles	1 min. 57 sec.	Allows

Through an oversight there was no anchor and chain aboard Shamrock III when the measurement of the waterline was taken. Mr. Fife on discovering the mistake reported it to the Cup Committee, but there was no opportunity for a re-measurement until Monday, August 24, after two races had been started. Shamrock III was docked then and re-measured, with so little difference that it did not affect the allowance as announced.

Racing in Calms and Fogs

THE rival fleets were anchored in the protecting arm of the Horseshoe on Sandy Hook, The William Fletcher, an old sidewheel passenger steamboat long familiar to New Yorkers, was chartered by Sir Thomas and on each day carried a party of 200 guests to be wined and dined aboard Erin I and to sing "He's a jolly good fellow."

The South Shore of Long Island and the East Shore of New Jersey line nearly at right angles, with the two guardians of the port, the Sandy Hook and the Scotland lightships about ten miles distant from each. The angle permits a 15-mile course E by N at one extremity of the arc, and S.S.W. ½ W. at the other; within this range is deep and open water for the windward-leeward and triangular courses of 30 miles.

The close work at the start which had marked the two previous matches was absent this year; Captain Barr knew that he had in Captain Wringe an opponent who was not easily bluffed, he did not know Reliance as he had known Columbia, and it would seem that he did not care to take the risks with this huge heavily canvassed machine which he felt safe in taking with the smaller craft. Whatever the reasons, while Barr was always working for the weather berth, the two yachts never came into dangerous proximity.

The first race was started in a very light breeze, the two sailing evenly at first, then came a rain squall; at the mark Reliance led by a long distance, but when it became evident that she could not finish in time, she hailed Shamrock III and it was agreed to abandon the race. On August 22 the wind was moderate from S.W., varying later in force and direction; in order to lay a true windward course it was necessary to shift the start five miles East. At the weather mark Reliance led by 3 minutes 15 seconds, and at the finish by 9 minutes elapsed time.

Monday was devoted to the re-measurement of Shamrock III; on Tuesday the pair started in a light but freshening breeze, the first leg to windward. Reliance led by 2 minutes 37 seconds at the first mark; 2 minutes 57 seconds at the second mark; and 3 minutes 16 seconds at the finish. On Thursday the wind was very light and the yachts failed to finish, Reliance leading by 12 minutes 31 seconds at the weather mark. On Saturday the yachts agreed not to start owing to a dense fog; on Monday with a light E.N.E. breeze and some sea they failed to finish, Reliance leading by 21 minutes 22 seconds at the weather mark.

Two more postponements followed through lack of wind, but a race was made on September 3 after a wait of an hour for a breeze, which came in light from the South but freshened. Reliance led by 11 minutes 7 seconds at the weather mark, increasing her lead down wind until both were lost in a dense fog when half way home. The Committee boat made a very short line so as to keep the Lightship in view; finally out of the fog loomed up Reliance, her elapsed time being 4 hours 28 minutes 6 seconds. When the fog lifted a half hour after Reliance finished Shamrock III was made out far from the finish line, which she had missed; she took a line from Cruizer and started for Sandy Hook.

From the Counter to the Quarterdeck

WHILE this race ended Charles Barr's connection with the Cup, he still had ahead a notable career in ocean racing and the handling of the largest schooners; in 1904 he had command of the Herreshoff schooner Ingomar, owned by Morton F. Plant; taking her across and winning 19 firsts out of 22 starts in European waters; in 1905 he commanded the three-masted schooner Atlantic, designed by William Gardner for Wilson Marshall, in the race from Sandy Hook to the Lizard for the German Emperor's Cup; crossing in 12 days 4 hours. Back in America he sailed the 70-footers Mineola II and Rainbow, and in 1908 he won a Lipton cup in a coastwise race in the 70-foot schooner Shamrock. In 1910 he commanded the Herreshoff schooner Westward, owned by Alexander Smith Cochran, taking her across the Atlantic and racing her successfully in British and German waters.

Born at Gourock, Scotland, in 1864, he died of a heart attack in Southampton, England, in 1911. In commenting on his death the London *Field* said: "We think that there can be no question that Charlie Barr stood first among the racing skippers of the world. He had great skill, judgment and nerve, he took the keenest and most intelligent interest in the accurate observance of sailing rules, and was himself careful to be obedient to them. In person he was dark, small and slight, with refined features, and he was of modest and unassuming demeanor. In fact, his manner, speech and appearance were that of a townsman of that part of Scotland in which he was born, and unlike that of a seafaring man. Whilst we know of no sailing master who was a stricter disciplinarian than Barr, nor one to be more promptly obeyed, his manner with his officers and crew was quiet and dignified, and the extraordinary amount of shouting that goes on aboard many English vessels was absent in the yachts under his command."

Unlike his elder brother, Captain John Barr, a powerfully built man with a heavy black beard who had years of experience in racing yachts, Charles began life as a grocer's clerk and had very little experience in yachts in his youth. After a season in the forecastle of the cutter Clara in 1884 under his brother, when that yacht was sent out to New York by a special hired crew Charles chose to sail in her forecastle for the seagoing experience. It is a matter of record that Clara passed Sandy Hook, the Narrows, and was abreast of the North River ferries before her captain realized that he was in New York.

From this point on he worked his way upward solely by his own efforts. Supplementing the eulogy of *The Field,* it may be said that with no benefit of technical education he made himself master of his profession, and by his inborn dignity he won the respect and esteem of the many men of wealth and position with whom he came in contact. Abstemious in the extreme in the use of liquor, his one dissipation was the big black cigar without which he was seldom seen.

Part Forty-Nine

TRADITIONS AND MEMORIES OF American Yachting

By WILLIAM P. STEPHENS

© M. Rosenfeld

Resolute, built by a syndicate to defend the cup in 1913, and which was successful in the 1920 series, after the war

THE long fight of a few against the forces of reaction and inaction ended about the beginning of the present century with the adoption in 1902 of a rule formulated by N. G. Herreshoff in which the two factors, load waterline and square root of sail area appeared above the line with the cube root of the displacement below the line as the divisor; thus barring the fin-keel and the scow types. An attempt in the same direction had already been made abroad in the adoption of the "Girth Rule," in which the girth in two forms, "chain girth" and "skin girth," was used in place of displacement. This rule was adopted for a time by the Yacht Racing Union of the Great Lakes, a local attempt at a national association. By slow degrees the New York Y. C. had abandoned its formula of a double tax on sail in favor of one in which the two factors were equal; the 40 percent allowance scale was changed to 50 percent, later to 60 percent and then to 80 percent, the latter proving too high and a return made to 60 percent, as in use today. The various forms of "anchor start" and "time starts" gave way to the present "one-gun start." These movements have been recorded in detail in the chapters on measurement and classification in these articles in book form.

In January 1906 there assembled in London, at the call of the Yacht Racing Association of Great Britain, the most notable conference of experts in the history of yachting. These included representatives of 16 European nations; racing men, naval architects and scientists. As early as May 1905 an invitation to send representatives was sent to the New York Y. C. to present the new Universal or Herreshoff Rule; and there is good reason for the belief that had this been done, in the absence of any other definite propositions at the outset it would have been adopted. Important as such a movement would have been in the advancement of national and international yachting, the reactionaries still held control; their motto being "no entangling alliances."

There was at the time a rather loose organization, "the Atlantic Coast Conference," and the invitation was submitted to this body by the New York Y. C. at a meeting on November 2, 1905, called primarily to consider a revision of the American racing rules. During the summer Henry Howard, of the New York and Eastern clubs, had visited Europe, receiving the assurance that American delegates were expected and would be welcomed. Two delegates were appointed at this meeting, Stuyvesant Wainwright of the New York Y. C. and Henry A. Morss of the Eastern Y. C. and the Corinthian Y. C. of Marblehead. The time was short, the appointments were not made until January 2, and the last steamer which would arrive before the opening of the Conference would leave New York on January 6. On January 4 a meeting of the Conference was called for the following day, what followed being described by Winfield M. Thompson.

"On this short notice only 11 delegates were present, friction was in the air and its cause was soon apparent; the New York Y. C., never in favor of sending delegates, now openly opposed it, questioned the authority of the appointment, and increased its own delegation from two to four. To influence the Conference an eminent sea-lawyer, Lewis Cass Ledyard, was introduced into the meeting as one of the Club's extra delegates. He eloquently opposed the sending of delegates along the line of a cable already sent, 'The Conference of American clubs feels compelled to the conclusion that they could not take part in the movement for an international rule without serious injury to the sport here, because it would practically amount to re-opening for our clubs the whole question of measurement which we have just succeeded, after years of effort, in settling. Your courteous invitation is highly appreciated and we much regret our inability to avail ourselves of it. Letter mailed you by the direction of the Conference explains fully.' "

One of his arguments was that a rule made by the London Conference might bar such a yacht as Reliance, whose type had already been barred by the adoption of the new Herreshoff Rule. The vote of the Conference was 7 to 6

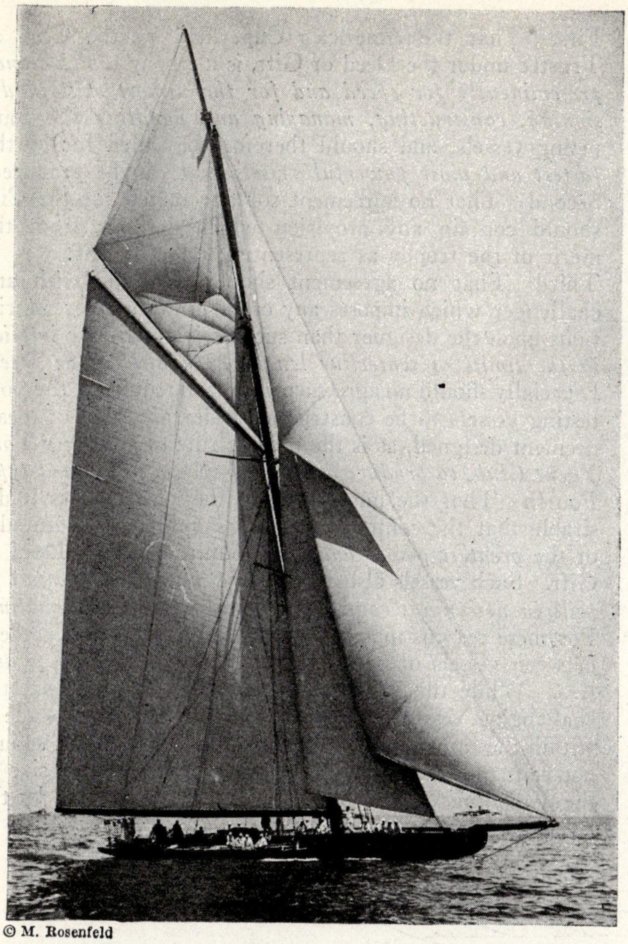

© M. Rosenfeld

Shamrock IV, Sir Thomas Lipton's challenger, designed by Charles E. Nicholson in 1913. Below: The lines of Resolute

against; Messrs. Wainwright and Morss cancelled their passages and unpacked their bags. The points in the letter were that it would not be courteous for Americans to attend the Conference merely to urge the adoption of their own rule; no other rule could be accepted by Americans; and, even if the Herreshoff Rule were adopted by the Conference, Americans could not bind themselves to abide by it.

The childish absurdity of this whole plea is evident when we remember that there was a general demand on the part of yachtsmen, including many members of the Club, for a rule which would bar such freaks as Reliance and Independence. In compliance with this demand the New York Y. C. requested the designer of Reliance to formulate such a rule; and adopted it as the legal rule of the Club. In spite of this, it repudiated the rule as inapplicable to the America's Cup matches.

The two rules, International and Universal, unchanged in principle in spite of changes in details, have stood the test of designing and racing for 37 years; the results are seen in the Meter classes, now well known on this side, and in our Rating classes, which, sad to say, have been allowed to disappear, except in the Cup Class, in recent years. Those familiar with the products of the two rules will recognize that, while both have largely attained the objects of their founders, some factors of the International Rule exert a cramping effect on the design, as shown in the comparison of a 6-Meter and a 25-Rater on Page 139 of the book.

"Once More into the Breach, Dear Friends."

The defeat of Shamrock III in 1903 left matters at a standstill, no real yachtsmen came forward to challenge, and in 1907 the redoubtable Sir Thomas returned to the attack. This time he changed his sponsors from the North to the South of Ireland, and the challenge came from the Royal Irish Y. C., a very old organization of Kingston, per cable:—

Dublin, September 13 1907

G. A. Cormack,
Secretary, New York Yacht Club, New York.

I have the pleasure to inform you that the Royal Irish Yacht Club, Kingstown, Ireland, on behalf of Sir Thomas Lipton, a member of the Club—(he had joined in the previous year)—, is today mailing you by steamer Umbria a challenge for the America's Cup, and would respectfully ask that on receipt of same the matter receive the earliest possible consideration.

(signed) Richard C. McMahon Smyth,
Honorary Secretary.

It would seem that in thus changing his sponsor Sir Thomas had found a technical advisor with some knowledge of yachting rules and usages, as the proposition put forth was both sportsmanlike and in accord with the advanced yachting practice of the day; to build to the established racing rule of the defending club. The challenge read as follows:

Royal Irish Yacht Club,
Kingstown, County Dublin, Ireland, Sept. 13 1907

G. A. Cormack, Esq.,
Secretary, New York Yacht Club, New York.

Dear Sir:

I am requested by Sir Thomas Lipton, Bart., K.C.V.O., to forward you this challenge for the America's Cup—subject to conditions to be mutually agreed upon—the winner of three out of five races to be entitled to the Cup. The first race to be sailed upon Thursday 20th August 1908, second race to be sailed on Saturday August 22d 1908, the third race to be sailed on Tuesday August 25th 1908; and further races, if any, to be sailed on each Thursday, Saturday and Tuesday until finished.

I therefore, on behalf of the Royal Irish Yacht Club, and in the name of Sir Thomas J. Lipton, a member of the Club, challenge to sail a series of matches for the America's Cup with the yacht Shamrock IV, to be built under Class J—68 foot rating—of the existing New York Yacht Club rules, which yacht shall conform to the regulations as to length of load waterline laid down in the Deed of Gift, against any one yacht constructed under the class above mentioned in the United States of America. The said series of matches to be sailed without time allowance.

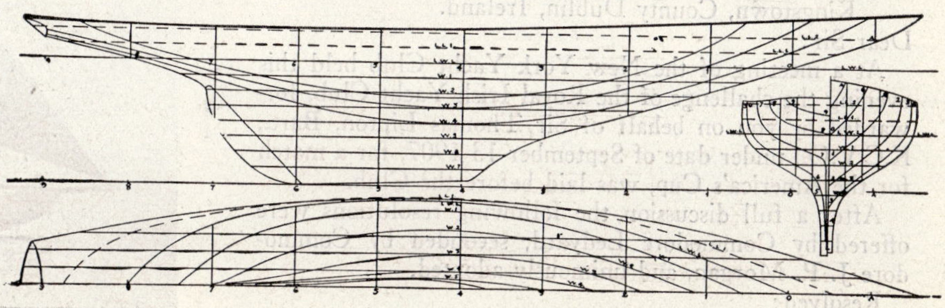

The following are the particulars of the challenging vessel, viz,

Owner, Sir Thomas Lipton, Bart, K.C.V.O.

Name of Yacht, Shamrock IV.

Rating to be not over 68 foot rating measurement by the existing New York Yacht Club rules.

Rig, Cutter.

The Custom House measurement will follow as soon as the vessel is measured for registration.

I shall esteem it a favor if you will kindly cable the receipt of this challenge.

(signed) Richard C. McMahon Smyth,
Honorary Secretary,
Royal Irish Yacht Club.

P. S. I cabled you today saying this letter was going to you per S.S. Umbria tomorrow.
(signed) R. C. McM. S.

To this Sir Thomas added a personal letter.

"In challenging with a yacht to be built under the existing rules of the New York Yacht Club I am animated solely by a desire to see the famous America's Cup competed for by a more wholesome and seaworthy type of boat than that which has been adopted in recent contests, and, in deciding upon Class J, I believe I am selecting a class which, while conforming to the limits of length prescribed in the Deed of Gift, will provide a more serviceable size of vessel."

Sir Thomas also requested permission to build two yachts, selecting the faster of the two after trial.

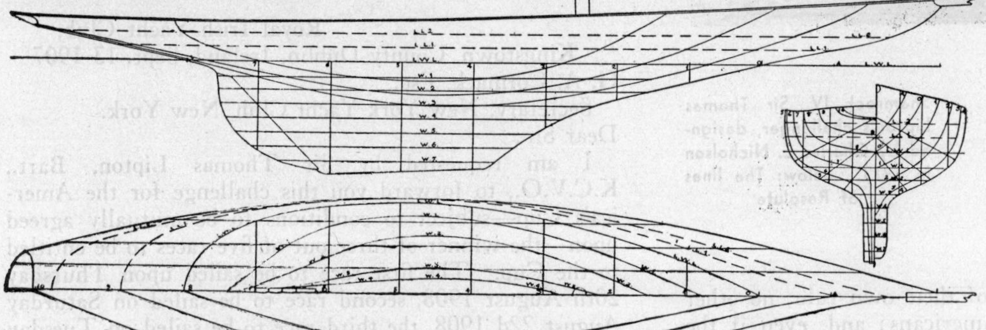

A special meeting of the Club was held on the evening of September 25 to consider and act upon the challenge. The following reply was cabled to the Secretary of the Royal Irish Yacht Club. The italics are ours.

Richard C. McMahon Smyth, Esq.,
Honorary Secretary, Royal Irish Yacht Club,
Kingstown, County Dublin, Ireland.

Dear Sir:

At a meeting of the New York Yacht Club held this evening the challenge of the Royal Irish Yacht Club, forwarded by you on behalf of Sir Thomas Lipton, Bart., K.C.V.O., under date of September 13 1907, for a match for the America's Cup, was laid before the Club.

After a full discussion the following resolutions were offered by Commodore Ledyard, seconded by Commodore J. P. Morgan, and unimously adopted.

Resolved:

First That the America's Cup, held by the Club as Trustee under the Deed of Gift, is a trophy *which stands pre-eminently for speed and for the utmost skill in designing, constructing, managing and handling* the competing vessels, and should therefore be sailed for by the *fastest and most powerful vessels* that can be produced.

Second That no agreement for any match for the Cup should contain any provision which detracts from the merit of the trophy as representing these objects.

Third That no agreement should be made with any challenger which imposes any other limitations or restrictions upon the designer than such as is *necessarily implied in the limits of waterline length expressed in the Deed.* Especially should no agreement be made requiring the contesting vessels to be constructed under any rule of measurement designed, as is the present rule of the *New York Yacht Club, to produce a vessel of special or limited type.*

Fourth That the importance of the event makes it desirable that the contesting vessels should be substantially of the *greatest power and size* permitted by the Deed of Gift. Such vessels also furnish the *most complete test of skill in designing, constructing, managing and handling.* For these reasons matches for the Cup should not be held between vessels of *comparatively insignificant power and size.* While the defending club cannot require that the challenging vessel be of any given size, so long as she is within the limits permitted by the Deed of Gift, it should not consent to any limitations upon the power or size of the defending vessel, other than such as is imposed by the Deed.

© M. Rosenfeld

The lines of Vanitie, and at right, the yacht which tried unsuccessfully to qualify as the defender in 1914 and again in 1920

Fifth The New York Yacht Club is prepared to accept a challenge in accordance with the Deed of Gift, and to enter again into mutual agreements with any challenger, similar to those which have governed matches for this Cup for many years past. It is also prepared to meet any qualified challenger in a series of races for this Cup, to be sailed boat for boat, without time allowance.

Sixth The challenge of the Royal Irish Yacht Club fails to conform to the provisions of the Deed of Gift, under which alone this Club can accept any challenge, in that it gives no dimensions of the challenging vessel, *and in that it imposes new and special conditions upon the type, size and power of the defending vessel.*

Moreover, it is of such a character that its acceptance would, in the judgment of this Club, *involve a complete abandonment of the objects for which the trust in respect to the America's Cup was constituted.*

Seventh That a Committee be therefore appointed by the Commodore, of which he shall be one, with instructions to decline on behalf of this Club the challenge of the Royal Irish Yacht Club, with an explanation of the reasons of this Club for its action.

The undersigned were appointed by the Commodore as the Committee mentioned in the resolutions, and in accordance with instructions therein contained, it is *with great regret* that we inform you that the New York Yacht Club declines your challenge.

We adopt this mode of communicating the result by cable in order that the action of the Club may reach you officially in advance of any information through any other channel.

Very Respectfully

Cornelius Vanderbilt, Commodore
Lewis Cass Ledyard
J. Pierpont Morgan
F. G. Bourne
C. Oliver Iselin
Edwin D. Morgan
Henry Walters
J. Rogers Maxwell

Committee

This communication was duly acknowledged by the Royal Irish Yacht Club; and, in spite of what was a decided kick in the pants, Sir Thomas acknowledged it with a very fair and sensible letter.

You cannot keep a good man down

Once again international racing was in the doldrums; and, as it eventually happened, destined to remain there for thirteen years. A break came, however, in 1913 in the form of the following cable:

London, February 28 1913

Cormack,
New York Yacht Club, N. Y.
Royal Ulster Yacht Club posted letter Wednesday Oceanic conveying challenge America's Cup under Deed of Gift on my behalf.
(signed) Lipton.

Had either side foreseen that this series of matches, begun in 1899 with Shamrock I, was to run until 1930 with Shamrock V, much time and money might have been saved by both sides by a series of printed forms for cables and letters expressing extreme appreciation, regard and regret, blank spaces for explanations and apologies, and on the one side spaces for demands and on the other for their rejection. In the case of this last challenge, as per cable just quoted, the correspondence ran from February 28 1913 to September 12, and in volume would cover a good part of this magazine. The high points of the long controversy were that Sir Thomas proposed to build Shamrock IV to a waterline of but 75 feet; this proposition was at first rejected, but finally accepted with a positive assertion of the Club's right (and possible intention) of defending with a yacht of 90 feet waterline.

The letter which followed Sir Thomas' cable and stated definitely that the new Shamrock IV would measure 75 feet on the waterline placed the leaders of American yachting, as sworn custodians of the Cup, in a most embarrasing position as "the slaves of Duty"; and the chorus rose:

"Duty, duty, must be done,
The fact is plain to everyone;
And, painful though the task may be,
To shirk it would be fiddle-de-dee."

Relying on recognized usage, the challengers persisted in the assumption that they would be met with a yacht of 75 feet waterline; while on their side the defenders insisted on not only their right but their duty, if it so pleased them, to defend with a 90-foot yacht. In spite of this disagreement, definite conditions were finally drawn up by the New York Y. C. similar to those of preceding matches, but with the start off the new Ambrose Channel Lightship and a time limit of 5½ hours; later changed to 6 hours.

For his fourth challenger Sir Thomas turned to a new designer, Charles E. Nicholson, of the very old firm of Camper & Nicholson of Gosport and Southampton; the designer of a number of very successful yachts. Having no experience in American waters, nor under the Universal Rule, Mr. Nicholson started by designing the yacht which he believed would best fit conditions as reported to him; turning out a very unconventional craft, big and powerful, with a large rig, and in no way such a beautiful hull as in his regular home practice. She was built by the firm of Camper & Nicholson, of composite construction with three skins, the outer of mahogany; and a deck of three-ply wood covered with canvas. The sheer was almost straight and of the same height at stem and transom, the short fore overhang had a blunt snubbed-in look, and the low after overhang ended in broad square transom. The topsides had a marked tumble-home, necessitating wide channels, open steel brackets. The lofty rig had a very short bowsprit carrying a single jib, later replaced by the double headrig. Thus rigged and fitted with a centerboard of the dagger type, she was termed by *The Field* a "sloop."

A Trio of Defenders

When it came to passing the hat for a new Herreshoff defender this honor was bestowed on Henry Walters, J. Pierpont Morgan, Cornelius Vanderbilt, Frederick J. Bourne, George F. Baker, Jr., and Arthur Curtiss James. Again a new and distinctive name was chosen (in contrast to the bewildering fleet of Valkyries and Shamrocks), Resolute, marking a high spot in the history of the Cup. With Robert W. Emmons as "managing owner" was Charles Francis Adams 2d, a racing man with thirty years experience in all classes of yachts from sandbaggers upward; the professional skipper was Captain Chris Christensen.

THE growing success of William Gardner in many racing classes led to an order for him from one of his clients, Alexander Smith Cochran; the result being a very beautiful yacht, Vanitie, built with bronze plating by George F. Lawley & Son. Several of the friends of George Owen, a graduate of the Herreshoff drafting room and later for many years Professor of Naval Architecture at the Massachusetts Institute of Technology, knowing of his work up to the medium size of racing yachts, organized a syndicate headed by George M. Pynchon and E. Walter Clark to build a third yacht, Defiance, of composite construction, by the Bath Iron Works. Entering into a much larger size of craft than in his previous experience, Mr. Owen turned out a beautiful and apparently fast hull, but with a very large and peculiar rig; a short base with great hoist, a single jib set to the stemhead, and a very small fore triangle. A short bowsprit was added later and many changes made in the whole rig.

Sailed mainly by Mr. Pynchon, Defiance was late in completion, many changes were made in ballasting and rig, and she was able to sail but a few races. At the end of June Mr. Pynchon notified the Committee that he had withdrawn the yacht as a competitor in the trial races.

As handled by Messrs. Adams and Emmons, Resolute proved very fast from the start, though many changes were found necessary, a second steel mast being shipped, ballast shifted, and the single jib was replaced by a jib and fore staysail. The professional skipper chosen for Vanitie, Cap'n Bill Dennis, was a schooner sailor, with no experience in single-stick craft or in working up a Cup yacht; at the end of June he resigned and was replaced by Cap'n Harry Haff, son of the veteran "Hank" Haff. When, at the end of July, there broke the news of the great World War I, all foreign yachting stopped instantly "for duration." When launched on May 26 Shamrock IV was placed in the hands of Sir William P. Burton, whose recent death is so widely mourned by yachtsmen; he brought with him his skipper in many yachts, Captain Alfred Turner. After trials against the 23-Meter Shamrock she sailed from Portsmouth on July 18 under a jury yawl rig. Taking the southern route, she put in to Bermuda as soon as the news of the war was received, later continuing to New York, where she was hauled out and securely housed over.

WHILE the majority of the races sailed in 1914 were won by Resolute, it was by a very small margin in time; the general opinion was that Vanitie not only was the larger and more powerful boat, but that she was the stronger, showing less signs of strain and leakage and fewer breakdowns than Resolute. Apart from the physical qualities of the two yachts, there was again the matter of concerted and consistent handling, in which the odds were most decidedly on the side of Resolute. The trials finished on August 6, the final news of the war coming a day later.

The Yachts Sail Again

THE war over and the earth being made safe for humanity, yachting gradually came into its own and Sir Thomas Lipton "bobbed up serenely" with a repetition of his original challenge under date of August 2 1919. The conditions, though newly printed, were practically the same as in the previous match; three races out of five, the start off the new Ambrose Channel Lightship (instead of the Sandy Hook Lightship), courses, 30 miles, a two-minute interval in starting. Resolute and Vanitie were in commission early, the latter now in the hands of George Nichols and C. Sherman Hoyt, and sailed a number of races on Long Island Sound and off Newport; Vanitie making a better showing than in 1914, but not enough to justify the Committee in selecting her.

The yachts were measured on July 12 by Prof. Harold W. Webb, of Columbia University, then Measurer of the Club, the figures being:

	Shamrock IV	Resolute
Sail area Mainmast	7,105.6	6,108.0
Fore triangle	3,353.8	2,757.0
	10,459.4	8,775.0
Length on waterline	75.0	74.97
Over all	110.38	106.34
Quarter Breadth Penalty	3.97	1.23
Length as per Rule	78.07	76.20
Displacement. Cubic feet	3,879.0	3,650.0
Measurement	93.8	83.5
Draft penalty	0.58	0.00
Rating	94.4	83.5
Allowance	7 min. 1 sec.	0.00

On July 13 Shamrock IV requested a re-measurement, as she had decided not to use her largest club topsail; on July 15 she requested another re-measurement, to cover a special canvas around the low mast and with edges laced to the luff of the mainsail to prevent a eddy of wind around the circular mast. On July 19 she decided use the largest club topsail, necessitating another re-measureme and on July 21 she was again re-measured, as she had decided use a smaller topmast and club topsail. The effects of these chang were negligible, the maximum measurement being 94.4 and t minimum 93.8; but they indicate a lack of thorough trials and perfect knowledge of the boat.

THE Cup races started on July 15 in a light and varia wind; Resolute drew the end of her wire throat halyard from drum and withdrew; thus giving Shamrock IV one race. Over t triangle on July 17 in a light and variable wind, the yachts fai to finish, Shamrock IV being becalmed at the first mark af Resolute had rounded. On July 20 in a light and variable wind terspersed with calms Shamrock IV led by over four minutes the first mark and 11 minutes at the second mark, winning by minutes 27 seconds elapsed time and 2 minutes 24 seconds correc time. On the next day, July 21, the wind was light, S by W, fre ening and then falling; Resolute won by 7 minutes, 1 second, exact amount of her allowance, the elapsed times being the same hours, 3 minutes, 6 seconds. Two days later, by request of Sha rock IV, they sailed the triangle in a S.S.W. wind varying fr four knots to fourteen, then after a rain squall dropping to 7 kn Resolute won by 9 minutes 58 seconds corrected time. On July the sea was rough with short high waves, the wind blowing fr 31 to 36¾ knots. When signaled by the Race Committee b yachts agreed to a postponement. On July 26 the race was star but was called off at 4:05 P.M. with Resolute leading about f miles from the outer mark. On July 27 the wind was S.S.W. S.W., from 4 to 8 knots; Resolute led by 4 minutes 10 seconds the weather mark and by 13 minutes 5 seconds elapsed and 19 m utes 45 seconds corrected time, finishing the match.

By way of additional statistics, it was officially calculated t the average speed to windward in the series was 5.08 knots Resolute and 4.99 for Shamrock IV; running, Resolute 7.42 kn Shamrock IV 7.29 knots; and reaching, Shamrock IV 6.37, Resol 6.25 knots. It is evident that the phrase "handsome is as hands does" might well be applied to Mr. Nicholson's effort; and that the odds of early completion, thorough trials and uniform and c sistent handling in both years were, as usual, on the side of defense.

A method of building hulls in inverted form was devised by the Herreshoff shops many years ago

TRADITIONS AND MEMORIES OF

AMERICAN YACHTING

THE HERRESHOFFS OF BRISTOL, Concluded

Part Fifty

By WILLIAM P. STEPHENS

THE debt of the world at large to American ingenuity and invention is a heavy one, including not only many novel ideas but many long known suggestions in crude form which have been brought to perfection and practical operation within the United States. Important as many have been—the work of Thomas A. Edison is but one example—two families stand out conspicuously through the variety and wide range of their work.

The Stevens family of Hoboken, remembered today mainly through their association with yachting, were pioneers in many lines of invention and development; notably the building of practicable steamboats and locomotives and the establishment of river routes and railroads. The Herreshoffs of Bristol, following the Stevens by about a generation, covered a still wider range of invention in the development of marine and stationary engines and boilers, in the construction of high-speed steam craft for both war and pleasure, in the invention and construction of many tools and machines and the development of methods for their own plants, in many lines of chemical research; and, as we have seen, in the development of almost every type of sailing yacht. In addition, in spite of the family handicap of blindness, members of the family have displayed exceptional ability as musicians and writers.

While many of the tools and processes perfected in the shops were based on outside ideas and experiments, a typical example of originality is found in the important advance in yacht building introduced by N. G. Herreshoff about 1880. In the conventional method of construction brought down from the earliest days of ship construction, the keel was laid down and on it were erected skeleton moulds, usually about seven in the length of the waterline. Around these moulds ribbands were run, and each half frame as bent was fitted to conform to the ribbands. When he assumed an active part in the building Captain Nat built a separate mould for every frame, at spacings of from 9 to 18 inches, according to the size of the yacht; the two members of the frame being bent on the mould and dogged fast; the moulds, at least treble in number over the old method, being set up on the keel and the planking begun. A few trials of this method led to a reversal of the process; the moulds were set up on the floor in inverted position and the keel laid *on top of them;* the planking following.

One advantage of this method was the ease of fitting the garboards, the workmen standing erect and working downward instead of crouching underneath and working upward. The laying of the broad strakes and the rest of the planking was similarly facilitated, the fastening was more easily done, and the "joining-off" and finishing the bottom, as well as the caulking where used, showed a still greater gain in convenience and ease of working. On my first visit to Bristol in 1885 I was greatly impressed by the half dozen steam yachts then building by this method; the moulds, as I distinctly remember, were of two thicknesses of inch boards, crossing diagonally, each mould of such depth that when set up on a level floor the upper side conformed to the curve of the keel. Why the moulds were made solid I do not know, perhaps to give a better base in bending, but this method was wasteful of lumber and was abandoned for the conventional form of skeleton mould. Two pieces of board were tacked together and the outline scribed from the floor, the pieces were cut out on a bandsaw, of course identical in outline, and formed together to make the mould. Experience proved that a frame 2 by 2 inches could be bent around this inch mould. In the steam yachts which were the chief product of the works for many years, the planking was double, fastened with brass screws; and, the hulls being comparatively narrow and shoal, the turning was a simple matter. When it came to building sailing yachts, wide and with deep keels, the problem became more difficult, but it was successfully carried out on hulls up to 65 feet over all.

Our history is necessarily limited to the two brothers, "John B." and "N. G." as they were colloquially known; the former was pre-eminently a mechanic and an inventor rather than a financier, and in its early days the company was at times in difficulty, but when the business which he started as a boy in selling vegetables which he had raised and twine from his home-made ropewalk developed into a great plant, he took over the business end, leaving to his younger brother the more practical side. At the

The Herreshoff plant at Bristol, R. I., as it was some years ago, with famous Cup Defenders on the docks

same time he kept up his contact with both design and construction, his delicate fingers handling a tool, passing over a model or inspecting hulls telling him more than most men learned through their eyes. Two of his most marked characteristics were great physical strength and a temper not always under perfect control. A hard worker from boyhood, he suffered a nervous break-down in the spring of 1915 and died in August of that year.

In spite of the size of the organization there was no one associated with it who was capable of taking his place; then in his 67th year, Captain Nat was unfitted for an entirely new line of work and, realizing this, made an effort to interest a number of the old patrons of the works in the organization of a new stock company. Prominent in this group were George Nichols, Harold S. Vanderbilt, Junius Morgan and Robert E. Todd of New York; Robert W. Emmons and Charles Francis Adams of Boston, and E. W. Clark of Philadelphia. During World War I the yard was engaged in navy work, but with no strong local management this entailed a loss rather than a profit. Following the War, yachting was slow in recovery and in 1924 it was decided to sell the plant. As no purchaser was found it was offered at auction on August 21 and 22. The property was first offered as a unit, there being no bidders, and then the real estate was offered in seven lots:—Lot No. One, the construction shops with waterfront piers, marine railway with its machinery and the launching ways; Lot No. Two, brick building 109 by 56 feet; Lot No. Three, six manufacturing buildings; Lot No. Four, building 48 by 36 feet; Lot No. Five, cottage and lot; Lot No. Six, building 96 by 47 feet, foundry 75 by 25 feet and cottage; Lot No. Seven, two-family house. Following the sale of these properties there was offered an enormous amount of material in the form of tools, machinery and stock.

In the marked absence of active bidding for any of the items there was something tragic in such an ending to an establishment that was not only nationally but internationally famous; the story is well told by that veteran scribe "Jeff" Davis, of *The Providence Journal.*

"At the sale Nat stood around watching the industry he had developed apparently being wrecked; I attended the auction and had one of the most disagreeable jobs of my life dealt out to me by the City Editor. The plant went on the rocks in 1924 and at that time Lipton was talking of another challenge; my City Editor ordered me to ask Nat if he would design a defender to meet the Lipton boat if the challenge were made. I told him something like this: 'I am ordered by my boss to ask you if you will design another boat for the defense of the America's Cup; I will not press you to answer, I hate to ask you, but I must.' The old man was on the verge of breaking down, but he smiled and walked slowly away.

"The plant was put up first as a whole and then auctioned off by lots; whichever way brought the biggest price was to be the sale. The prices at which the stuff went were criminal, a friend of mine bought the Emmons sloop Humma, minus lead, rig and bronze strapping, for $25.00 on the second bid; the first was made by a junk dealer who did not know whether Humma was a boat or a bottle of catsup. Other lots went at about the same comparative value, but the piece-by-piece plan brought several thousand dollars more than the best bid for the entire plant. Soon the trucks began carting the stuff away.

"It was my first meeting with R. F. Haffenreffer, who seemed to be just an interested observer, but I noticed

Tom Brigham bidding on some of the building, machinery, etc. He had a list in his hand, evidently of what would be needed to fit up a smaller plant, with a price against each article on which to bid; when that price was reached he stopped bidding. I knew that he was acting for someone, so I accosted Mr. Haffenreffer; at first he denied it, but finally he owned up. I asked him what he wanted with the plant, as he was not a yachtsman (Mr. Haffenreffer is a wealthy brewer, a resident of Fall River, but with a summer home in Bristol). I had this rather startling answer: 'The Herreshoff Manufacturing Company is more than a business, a place to build boats, it is a Bristol institution, and I am ashamed of the cheap —— in Bristol who will let it go to pieces.' He told me further that in Montana, where he had copper interests, the name 'Bristol' did not mean anything, but if you mentioned 'Herreshoff' the come-back would be 'Oh yes, that's where they build the America's Cup defenders.' Then I asked him what he would do with the plant if he got it. He said that he did not know, but he would work out some plan to keep it going; that if he could make it pay its way he would be satisfied, even though it never paid him a cent of profit.

After an interval the new Herreshoff Manufacturing Company was organized, with R. F. Haffenreffer as President and his son Carl W. Haffenreffer as General Manager. The only Herreshoff still associated with the company is A. Sidney DeWolf, a son of N. G., who remains as head of the Department of Engineering and Design.

A fixed rule of the original company from the start was that no yacht would be built from an outside design, and that no design would be furnished to be built outside; every Herreshoff vessel was a distinctive product of Bristol, R. I. Some care was necessary in the compilation of Lloyd's Register to keep out the alleged Herreshoff yachts which never had seen Bristol. Under the new management this policy was no longer necessary and would have been most impracticable; while continuing a very large line of standard craft from dinghies upward developed by the company, many large yachts of outside design have been built; notably the Cup defenders, Enterprise, Rainbow and Ranger, designed by W. Starling Burgess, and the Cup candidate, Weetamoe, designed by Clinton H. Crane.

* * * * * * * *

WHILE the past two decades have witnessed a sad decline in match sailing in individually designed yachts, this form of the sport being non-existent in America today, it is gratifying to note a great advance in two other lines. The growth of ocean racing, not so much in trans-Atlantic contests as in the races to Bermuda and the many long-distance races along the coast have brought into existence a sturdy, able and yet fast type in marked contrast to the later over-developed racing machines. Of perhaps even more importance is a smaller type of "single-hander," "tabloid cruiser" which appeals to the younger generation and those of moderate purses. This type originated in England almost a century ago when a few venturesome young men, with no experience and in the most crude forms of half-open fishing boats, sought their pleasure on the turbulent waters of the North Sea and the Channel. Mr. Stephens has long been familiar with this form of sport. Sixty years ago he was designing, building and sailing such miniature ships; his library contains almost all of the books on the sport. Having concluded the history of "The Herreshoffs of Bristol," he proposes to take up the story of the development of the small cruiser.—EDITOR.

TRADITIONS AND MEMORIES OF American Yachting

By WILLIAM P. STEPHENS

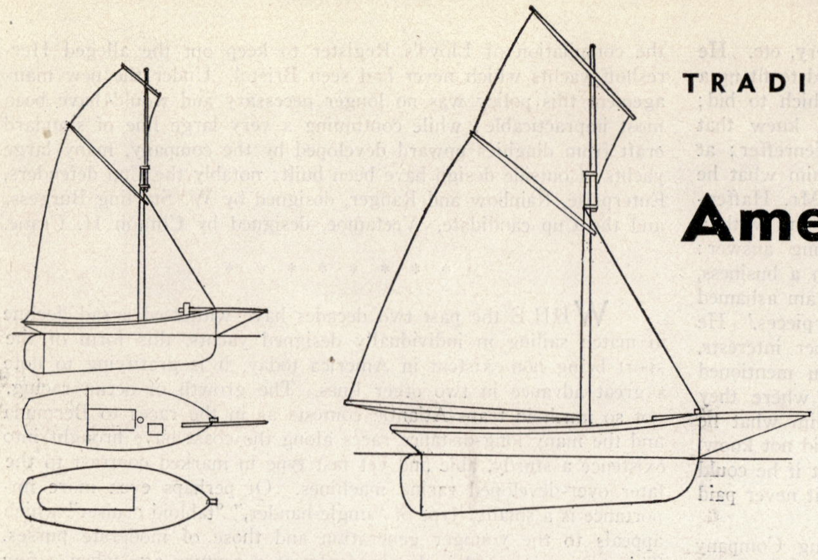

Left: Leo as originally built with large cockpit, and altered, with side decks. Loose-footed mainsail, no boom. Right: Sirius, loose-footed mainsail with boom

Part Fifty-one — THE DEVELOPMENT OF THE SMALL CRUISER

THE condition of American yachting today is the result of a long series of changes so numerous and far reaching that it is difficult to appraise the net result. One of the most notable, and the most to be regretted, is the disappearance of the old classes of individually designed and individually owned yachts of moderate cost in construction and running which furnished the backbone of racing for so many years, as in the 70-Ft. and 40-Ft. classes. Beginning with a challenge from a yacht of 81 feet l.w.l. in 1885, but greatly aggravated in recent years by the intrusion in yachting of a few men ignorant of the sport but with more money than brains, as told in recent chapters, the size and cost of racing yachts have increased a hundred fold, with lessening numbers and shorter lives.

The old regattas, such as those of the New York Y. C., the Seawanhaka Corinthian Y. C. and the Atlantic Y. C. in "Regatta Week" in June, followed by the Larchmont Y. C. on July 4, which brought out a host of non-yachtsmen through their appeal as a spectacle, have given place to a series of races over the Sound circuit under modern rules and capable management which have materially improved the first class racing. The great schooners which added so much to the old-time Regattas have disappeared, and with them the sensational ocean racing for high stakes.

On the other hand, there has been built up a fine class of smaller yachts specially designed for trans-Atlantic and other long-distance races. The perfection of the small and compact internal-combustion engine has given these yachts an efficient motive power in calms and at the same time has brought into existence a new and most useful class, the "Fifty-Fifty," in which speed and power under sailing rig and engine are nominally equal. At the low end of the scale are the innumerable number of classes of small racing boats appealing to juniors and novices: Snipes, Comets, Lightnings, Brutal Beasts, that are doing so much to keep alive the interest in yachting under war conditions.

One of the most notable additions to the modern fleet is in the class of sturdy and able yachts of small size specially adapted to the single-hand sailor and to crews of two or three, both for week-end work and for cruises: the Coastwise, Week-End and many other classes. How this fleet came into being will be told in this and following chapters.

The motives which impel a man to undertake solitary

Sailboat by Searle & Son, 16 feet 4 inches by 4 feet 8 inches breadth, and 8 inches draft. Left: Procyon

and dangerous voyages, even around the world, can be told only by individuals; and have been told by such navigators as Captain Joshua Slocum of Spray, Harry Pigeon of Islander, Alain Gerbault of Firecrest and W. A. Robinson of Svaap in the records of their voyages. Our story is not concerned with this phase of yachting, but rather with the use of the small yacht for pleasure sailing and recreation within the limits of ordi-

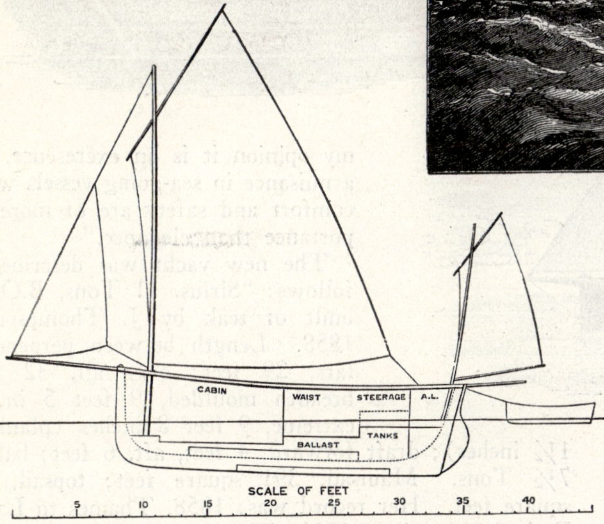

THE "PERSEUS."

nary business life. With all the charm of weekly competition within a well built-up racing class in which one's wits and skill are matched against competitors of equal ability, to many this form of sport does not appeal in comparison with the use, alone or in company of one or two friends, of a tabloid cruiser, possibly designed or even built by the owner.

A Rugged Individualist

Tracing the sport of single-hand sailing to its origin, we are led back nearly a century, to the year 1850, and to England. The first to make such voyages and to write of them was R. T. McMullen, who began his sailing in the year mentioned and ended it in June 1891 when his yacht, Perseus, was picked up by the crew of a French fishing boat some miles clear of the French coast, with her owner-skipper sitting dead at her tiller.

Very little is known of McMullen's personal history; the brief notices of his death did not give his age. He was described by Dixon Kemp, a personal friend, as "a staunch Conservative of the old type, a firm Protestant, and a devout believer in individual responsibility." He had a deep interest in civic affairs and published a number of pamphlets; he was bitterly opposed to Trade Unionism, even in the primitive form in which it existed in England almost a century ago. His writings, and what we know of his character, show him to be a man of strong determination, inflexible in pursuit of an object, with fixed convictions as to right and wrong. Most of his sailing was done from Greenhithe, on the South bank of the lower Thames. Mucking Creek, a few miles lower down, was his mooring for his 20-ton Orion. My old friend of the cutter days, the late Francis Peabody McGoun, as a boy of 15 visited England with his older cousin, Francis E. Peabody, the Boston yachtsman. They

Above: Kate off the Lizard. Left: Perseus. Below: The watch on deck

sailed down the Thames with George Wilson, the yacht outfitter, aboard his cutter Albertross, and found Orion in Mucking Creek. Her owner showed them over her; on the outside of every locker and drawer was a list of the contents. He would open a locker and tell what was in it, volunteering information, but if asked a question he became abrupt and testy. Later Frank wrote me, "I never felt quite sure that he enjoyed life at sea to anything like the degree possible for a less combative temperament." Every detail of work aboard his boats was performed with mechanical accuracy and according to routine, as a duty rather than a diversion. He cruised for so long, however, and learned so much, that even today his books are instructive as well as interesting.

His first craft, the cutter, Leo, was built to his order by J. Thompson of Rotherhithe, on the Thames, and is described as "2¾ Tons, Builder's Old Measurement, built of pine; length between perpendiculars, 18 feet; over all, 20 feet; breadth, moulded, 6 feet 1 inch; breadth, extreme, 6 feet 3 inches; draft forward, 2 feet 6 inches; aft, 4 feet; ballast, 23 cwt.; mainsail, 144 square feet; topsail, 67 square feet." Leo and the other yachts evidently carried a jib or foresail, but no mention is made of the area. As originally built she was half-decked with a large open cockpit, only 9 inches freeboard, and a 4-inch coaming with a movable washboard. Later

the side deck was carried aft to the transom and the cabin lengthened. She carried a bowsprit, set on one side of the stemhead so as to house, but the one headsail was tacked to the stemhead, her mainsail was loose-footed. Later a topmast and yard topsail were added, and a sail of his

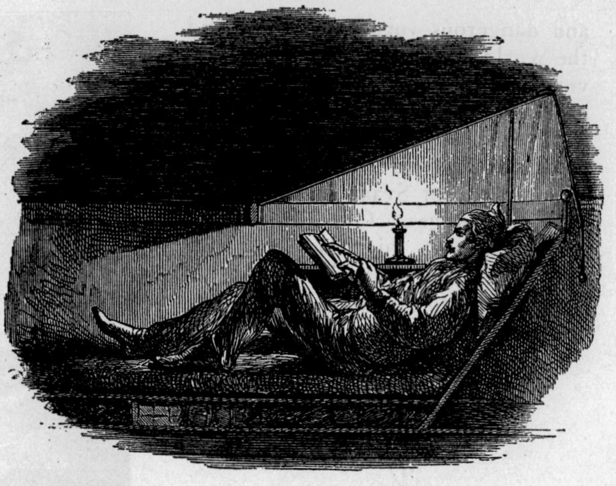

Below: The yawl Rob Roy. Right: The cabin with tarpaulin cover

own devising which was similar to that known a dozen years later as a "Sphynxer" or spinaker.

The first cruise began with all the mishaps attending the initial efforts of a novice; first grounding at low tide and filling, then her masthead fouling the bowsprit of a large vessel and almost filling her again. The first sails were made down Thames, with two companions, fouling a yacht at anchor; but the most serious disaster was of another sort. The outboard end of her main sheet was fitted with sisterhooks and a single block, the end and the block hooking into cringles. The hooks, unmoused, were in the clew cringle and the block in the first reef cringle when in thrashing about in a bad sea off the Nore Lightship the sister hooks came adrift, struck the skipper in the face, and one hook caught in the right eyelid, tearing it badly before he could release himself.

His companions never had handled a tiller, but by luck he had taken aboard two boatmen whose boat was towing astern; they took charge and sailed Leo into Gravesend. An examination by a surgeon next day showed that no injury had been done to the eyeball, but sailing was suspended for a month. He very soon decided that such companions as were available were of no real use, and resolutely continued to sail alone, gaining experience by one mishap after another. His record aboard Leo was: 1850, in the Thames, 600 geographical miles sailed; 1851, Thames, and to Ramsgate, 850 miles; 1852, as far as Dover, 1,450 miles; 1853, as far as Dungeness, 1,670 miles; 1854, 900 miles; 1855, Thames to S. E. coast and Hastings, 772 miles; 1856, to Isle of Wight, 1,200 miles; 1857, to Land's End, 1,380 miles; Total, 8,222 miles.

In 1858 Leo gave place to Sirius, described as "built to the same lines with two feet added to the bow; having experienced the great discomfort of riding at anchor in rough weather in a boat with a long counter, I had Sirius built with a round stern, which, although it was considered at the time as an ugly innovation in yacht building, has since become common. The long overhanging stern is undoubtedly more ornamental, and is useful in match-sailing yachts with long booms, but in my opinion it is an excresence, and a nuisance in sea-going vessels where comfort and safety are of more importance than elegance."

The new yacht was described as follows: "Sirius, 11 Tons, B.O.M., built of teak by J. Thompson in 1858. Length between perpendiculars, 29 feet; over all, 32 feet; breadth moulded, 9 feet 5 inches; extreme, 9 feet 8 inches (planking, 1½ inches); draft forward, 4 feet, aft, 6 feet; ballast, 7½ Tons. Mainsail, 391 square feet; topsail, 171 square feet. Her record was: 1858, Thames to Land's End, 1,816 miles; 1859, Thames and Isle of Wight, 1,163 miles; 1860, South Coast and to Harwich, 1,085 miles; 1861, Scilly Islands and Ireland, 1,750 miles; 1862, Thames and Isle of Wight, 1,467 miles; 1863, Round Great Britain, 2,640 miles; 1864, Thames and Isle of Wight, 1,752 miles; Total, 11,693 miles.

Following Sirius came Procyon (it will be noticed that McMullen chose original and distinctive names for his many yachts instead of the numbered stencils such as Tern, Pearl, Nautilus, Cherub so common among English yachts). This yawl, built in 1867 by Holloway of Whitestable, was 21 feet 6 inches over all; 7 feet 9 inches breadth; 3 feet draft; she had a cuddy forward and a large open cockpit; her iron centerplate weighed 2 cwt. Being lapstrake or "clincher-built," the lands amidship were filled in to avoid noise in rolling and pitching. In her fourth season she was lengthened 5 feet aft, and many miles were covered in her cruising.

The last of the fleet was Perseus, built by Holloway in 1890; 27 feet 2 inches over all; 7 feet 4 inches breadth;

The galley of Rob Roy was in the stern

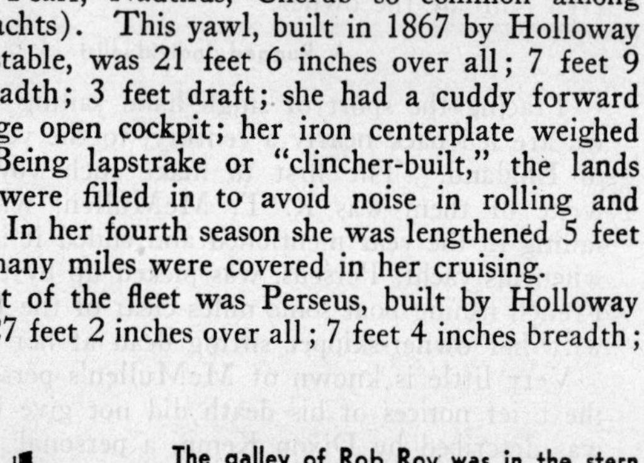

draft forward, 3 feet 3 inches, aft, 4 feet 6 inches. Least freeboard, 2 feet; ballast, lead on keel, 13 cwt., cast iron keelson, 20 cwt., kentledge, 32 cwt., total 3¼ tons. Tons B.O.M., 5½. She was sailed through the season until September 11 when she was laid up in Mucking Creek. Fitted out in June, 1891, she sailed from Greenhithe on the eighth, evidently bound for France; on June 13 a landing was made at Eastbourne to mail a letter; on the evening of June 15 the yacht was picked up by French fishermen, sailing herself with her skipper seated in the cockpit, his face turned to the sky. His death was placed by a doctor as probably on June 14. The boat was taken in to Beuzeval, about six miles West of Trouville, notified by the Vice Consul Mrs. McMullen and a brother arrived at Beuzeval on June 18 and the body was buried next day in the local cemetery after a ceremony in the local Protestant church.

WHILE most of his 41 years afloat were spent aboard these small yachts, McMullen is best known today through his ownership and handling of a larger craft, the 20-ton Orion, originally a cutter, but in 1873, lengthened 6 feet aft and converted to a yawl. This yacht was modelled and built by G. Inman, a yacht builder of

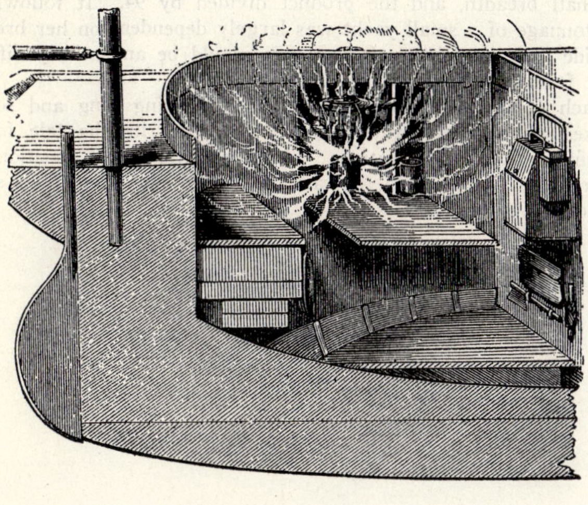

The galley arrangement of Kate

Lymington, in 1865; over all, 42 feet; breadth, 10 feet 5 inches; draft forward, 5 feet, aft, 7 feet. Ballast, 11¾ tons. Mainsail, 668 square feet; topsail, 294 square feet. It will be noted that all of the McMullen yachts had a decided amount of drag. With the many details which he gives there is no mention of headsails, and every one was altered after trial. The tonnage of Orion as launched was 16½ B.O.M. and after alterations 19½. She was sailed with a crew of two in the forecastle, Mrs. McMullen accompanying the skipper on many of his cruises.

Interesting as they are, these cruises in a large yacht do not fall within the scope of this history, but two must be noted. On a voyage to the French coast in 1877 the two paid hands were so complaining and nearly mutinous that they were set ashore at Cherbourg and their passage paid home by steamer; the resolute skipper, after days of laborious and well considered preparation, set sail alone and sailed across to Dover and then on to Greenlithe. On the occasion of the Jubilee of Queen Victoria in 1887 a race around Great Britain and Ireland was arranged by the Royal Thames Y. C. Not entering the race, McMullen started aboard Orion with a friend as "mate, masthead and bowsprit-end man" and two paid hands, completing the course of 1,745 miles, Dover to Dover, in 23 days.

The Poor Man's Yacht

NOT only the 11,000 who have joined the American Canoe Association since its organization in 1880 to this year of grace. but countless thousands the world over have reason to be thankful for the chance which brought into being what has been aptly called "the poor man's yacht", the canoe as it existed since 1865. How it came about is told in the words of its inventor, John Macgregor, M.A., a London barrister. "A smash in a railway carriage one day hurled me under the seat, entangled in broken telegraph wires. No worse came of it than a shake of those nerves which one needs for rifle shooting; but as the bull's eyes at a thousand yards were thereby made too few on the target, I turned in one night back again to my life on the water, and dreamed a new cruise and planned a new craft.

It was clear that no rowboat would serve on a land-water voyage of this sort, for in the wildest parts of the best rivers the channel is too narrow for oars. Now those very things which bother the pair-oar become cheery excitement to the voyager in a canoe; for, as he sits in his little bark, he looks forward and not backward, he sees all his course and the scenery besides. With one sweep of his paddle he can turn aside when only a foot from destruction. The canoe is also safer than the rowing boat because you sit so low in it, and never require to shift your place or lose hold of the paddle. But, it may well be asked of one who thus praises the paddle, has he travelled in other ways so as to know their pleasures? Has he climbed glaciers and volcanoes, dived into caves and catacombs, trotted in a Norway carriole, ambled on an Arab and galloped on Russian steppes? Does he know the charms of a Nile boat, or a Trinity eight, or a Yankee steamer, or a sail in the Aegean, or a mule in Spain. Yes, he has thoroughly enjoyed these and other modes of locomotion, fast and slow; and now, having used the canoe in Europe, Asia, Africa and America, he finds the pleasure of the paddle is the best of them all."

The new craft thus chosen was to be a civilized version of the Esquimau kayak, a frame of walrus bones covered with sealskin so sewn as to be watertight; completely decked with only an oval opening amidships for the crew of one, with a skin apron laced high under his arms. With his spear or harpoon lashed on deck, and his double-blade paddle, the Esquimau hunts the walrus and performs amazing evolutions in open water, even capsizing the canoe until his head hangs downward and righting her by coming up on the other side. Seeking the aid of Searle & Son, of Lambeth, a suburb of London, MacGregor described the kayak as best he could, leaving it to the builders, who specialized in racing shells and small sailing boats but were unfamiliar with the new craft, to produce in wood the image in his mind. The result was a canoe heavily built of oak, 15 feet long and 28 inches wide, in which the solitary voyager covered a thousand miles in the summer of 1865 in Belgium, France, Austria, Germany and Switzerland.

NEXT year, in an improved and slightly smaller canoe, he cruised on the Baltic and in Nórway, Sweden and Denmark. In the following year, 1867, a larger craft was planned to the owner's ideas by John Samuel White, the designer and builder of large vessels; the actual building being done by Forrest, of Limehouse, London, builder for the Royal National Lifeboat Institution. The boat was to be 18 feet over all, but at the suggestion of Mr. White she was built 21 feet; her lines are not shown and no other dimensions are given in the story of her cruise, the owner evidently considering such details of little importance. We are told that she was of 4 Tons, B.O.M., with an iron keel and 30 cwt. of pig iron inside. Fortunately the illustrations in the book give some idea of the size and arrangement.

Starting from London, a stop was made at Dover, then across the Channel to Boulogne, along the coast to Dieppe and Havre, up the Seine to Paris at the time of the Exposition. Down the Seine to Havre, the Channel was crossed at its widest point to the Isle of Wight and by slow degrees the return was made to London, the solitary but most interesting cruise filling the months of June, July and August.

The little yacht naturally obtained much publicity, which was increased by the publication of a third book, "The Voyage Alone in the Yawl, Rob Roy," in 1868. Following this came a summer of cruising in a third Rob Roy canoe in Palestine. These four books, all written in an interesting manner and describing practically new forms of sport afloat, made converts in many lands; it was a condensation of "A Thousand Miles in the Rob Roy Canoe," in *Harpers Magazine* in 1866 which guided me to MacGregor's books and thus exerted a powerful influence on my life. Their appeal was to two classes—men who felt that they could not afford a yacht of any size but might find an opportunity for sailing in small and comparatively inexpensive craft, and young men who found in the canoe a craft greatly superior to the ordinary rowing boat, either very heavily built or of the light "wager boat" type.

The Cruise of the Kate

ONE of the first to put the precepts of MacGregor into actual practice was Empson Edward Middleton, an Englishman who seems to have led a life of varied adverture. As a boy he threw the left knee out of its socket by a kick in football; as he recovered after three months he was shot in the same knee by a pistol bullet; later the knee failed him in a walking match in India against a native. A writer and a Latin scholar, when fifteen he made a voyage to Australia aboard a sailing ship, apparently as an apprentice. At the time of the Indian Mutiny he enlisted in Her Majesty's 51st Light Infantry, serving from 1858 to 1864 in the Punjab; he was gazetted as a lieutenant, but sold out after a dispute over pay and promotion.

What turned him to the sea again is told in his own words: "My wearied thoughts were wandering down the High Street of Southampton during the Christmas week of 1868, and conducted tired limbs to the excellent circulating library of Messrs. Gulch, where fading eyesight fell upon a work bearing the title, "The Voyage Alone in the Yawl Rob Roy." An instant sympathy with its contents created an exchange of matter, five shillings causing a deficiency of ballast on one pocket."

After reading the book an order was placed with the builders of Rob Roy for a similar craft, but with an iron keel of 6 Cwt., an iron keelson of 4 Cwt. and 11 Cwt. of iron cast to fit inside. Unfortunately, no lines of the yacht are shown, nor of her accommodation, but she evidently had a flush deck with a flat flush hatch sliding forward, and a small cockpit; the headroom must have been very limited.

While the yacht was under construction Lt. Middleton determined to make the circumnavigation of England; and as a preparation he hired a 17-foot boat with cutter rig and, with a boy as crew, made a dozen trips out of Southampton in the course of the winter. The yacht, named Kate after his sister, was not ready on time, and it was June 15 before she sailed from the Thames, going down Channel and up the West coast, calling on the Irish coast and visiting the Clyde, through the North Sea and back to the Thames at the end of September. In these four months he encountered all the adventures and misadventures which can befall a novice in an unknown boat, but came through them safely, telling his story in "The Cruise of the Kate, a Singlehand Voyage Around England." Like McMullen, his strong individualism would cause him to be classed as a "crank" in modern parlance.

THESE three pioneers in singlehand cruising have much in common; neither had any ancestral background of the sea, no realization of the dangers of the ocean in a very small boat, and of how to meet them, no knowledge of yacht designing and apparently no interest in the subject, no experience to guide in the selection and use of a boat; the sole equipment was an overwhelming impulse to sail. In ordering their craft they resorted to builders of boats of very different types, fishing boats, lifeboats or racing boats; they seem to have had no interest in design or dimensions, and they knew little more about their boats than the Builder's Old Measurement, which was the length along the rabbet less 3/5 of the extreme breadth, multiplied by this breadth and again by the half breadth, and the product divided by 94. It follows that the tonnage of a small yacht was largely dependent on her breadth; a wide and shoal boat of four tons would be an entirely different craft from a 4-tonner of moderate breadth.

Each of the three achieved his wish, making long and solitary cruises on turbulent waters and living to write the tale for the benefit of future generations; like the little insect mentioned in poetry, "he got there all the same"; though in reading their stories one often wonders how?

TRADITIONS AND MEMORIES OF **American Yachting**

Part Fifty-two

THE DEVELOPMENT OF THE SMALL CRUISER (Continued)

By WILLIAM P. STEPHENS

THE growth of canoeing was surprising, both in its speed and strength. MacGregor's first book was hardly in circulation before, on July 25, 1866, The Canoe Club was organized at the Star and Garter Inn, London, with the Prince of Wales as Commodore and Mr. MacGregor as Captain. In 1873, by virtue of a Royal warrant, the organization become the Royal Canoe Club. In 1867 the Cambridge University Branch was organized. followed by the Oxford University Branch in 1869, and the Trent Wanderers in the same year. In 1870 the Northern Branch was established on the Mersey; in 1872 came the Eastern Branch on the Humber and the Forth C. C. in Scotland, and in 1873 the Clyde C. C. A very large fleet of these craft was soon afloat and many cruises were made on the rivers of England and Scotland and, the canoes being transported by steamer, in Norway, Sweden, Denmark, Holland, Belgium, Germany and France. As a matter of course, the many who were unable to devote their time to long cruises started local racing in their home waters.

Prior to the invention of the Rob Roy canoe there were no small craft available for pleasure afloat, the existing types being the "wager boat," a lightly built racing shell; the wherry, with oars or one, two, or three pairs of sculls, for pleasure parties; and, for river fishing, the flat-battomed, square-ended punt. Outside of these were only the heavy and clumsily built fishing boats peculiar to different localities about the coast. In all this mixed fleet there was nothing to tempt a man to go afloat for mere pleasure.

The term "wherry," like the sister terms "punt" and "barge," is very elastic in its meaning. We find in the old song by Charles Dibdin:

> "Now farewell, my trim-built wherry,
> Oars and coat and badge farewell:*
> Never more at Chelsea ferry
> Shall your Thomas take a spell."

Such a wherry was similar to the noted Whitehall boats of New York Harbor, rowed by professional boatmen and carrying passengers; but the word is also in general use on English rivers as applied to boats carrying pleasure parties. Similar boats were used on the Seine for such gay parties as are shown in Renoir's famous painting, *"Le Dejeuner des Canotiers,"* the French *"canotier"* being a rowing man and not a canoeist.

The claims made by Captain MacGregor were fully substantiated as the new vehicle

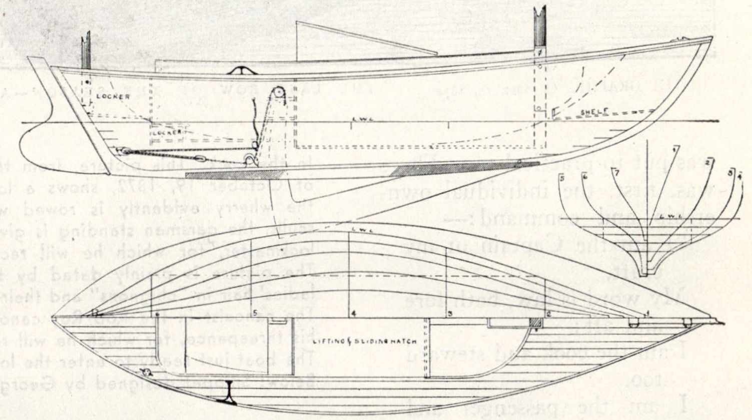

Albert Strange, 1856-1917, a portrait in 1913, Cherub II design for a Humber canoe-yawl, 1893, and at left a sketch of Cherub II, both by Albert Strange

*Doggett's coat and badge was a prize established by Thomas Doggett, an actor, in 1715, in commemoration of the coronation of George I; a red coat with a large silver badge on the arm bearing the white horse of Hanover as a device. It was to be rowed for annually by six young watermen not more than one year free of their apprenticeship.

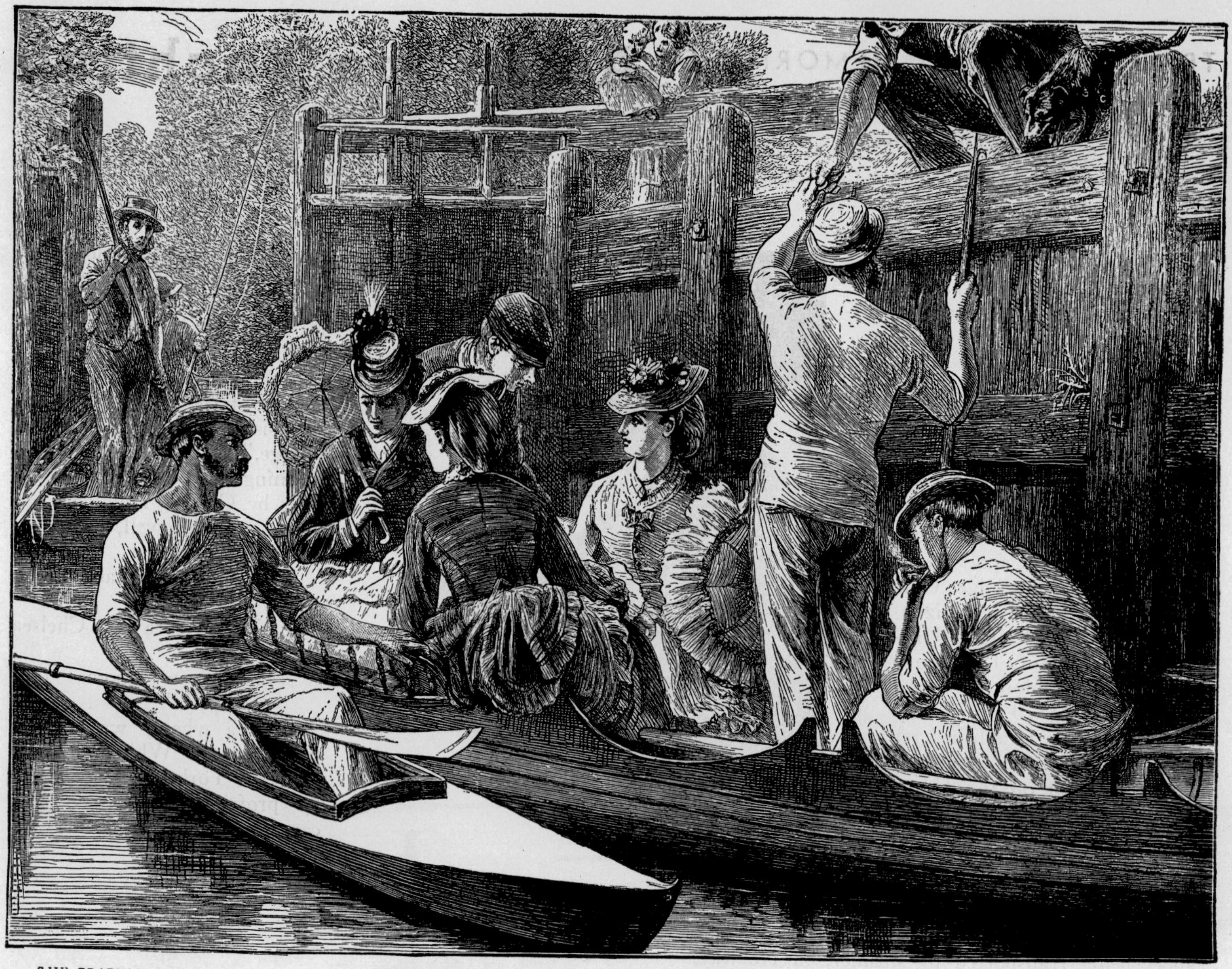

THE GRAPHIC, October 19, 1872 THE LAST ROW OF THE SEASON—A LOCK ON THE THAMES

was put to practical test. There was, first, the individual ownership and command:—

"I am the Captain of my craft,
My word is law, both fore and aft;
I am the cook and steward too,
I am the passenger and crew."

Even before its over-development for racing, the canoe was fast under the impulse of the double blade, and she was maneuverable to a high degree. The "crew," sitting upright instead of bending back and forth, faced in the direction in which he was going; in the best possible position for avoiding danger and viewing the new vistas opening to him as he explored unknown waters.

The Canoe-Yawl

Vast as were the possibilities of the canoe, proof was soon found that there was a limit to them, especially on estuaries such as that of the Humber at

In the Lock. This picture, from the London *Graphic* of October 19, 1872, shows a lock on the Thames, the wherry evidently is rowed with three pairs of sculls, the oarsman standing is giving sixpence to the lockmaster, for which he will receive a blue ticket. The picture is plainly dated by the dressing of the ladies' hair in "chignons" and their expansive "bustles." The canoeist in the Rob Roy canoe is waiting to pay his threepence, for which he will receive a red ticket. The boat just ready to enter the lock is a fishing punt. Below: Snippet designed by George F. Holmes in 1913

Hull and the Mersey at Liverpool. The former is described by John Taylor, a poet of the seventeenth century, a professional Thames waterman with a gift for verse, in "A very Merrie Wherrie-Ferry Voyage"; the log of a voyage from London to York begun with "Many farewells, cups and glasses."

"There (the Humber) the swifte ebbe tide ranne in such sort,
The winde at Easte, the waves brake thick and short
That in some doubts it me began to strike,
For in my life I ne'er had sene the like."

The rise and fall on the Humber ranges from 20 feet to 16 feet 3 inches; on the Mersey the range is from 26 feet to 20 feet 3 inches.

The Northern Branch severed its connection with the parent club in 1875 and reorganized under the name of the Mersey Canoe Club; the

sport being carried on very actively for some years both in cruising and racing in canoes of the Rob Roy and Nautilus types. As these craft were too fragile for the home waters they were gradually replaced by larger ones of similar model, as shown in the Mersey sailing canoe. The length was 17 feet; breadth, 4 feet 6 inches; depth from gunwale to garboard, 1 foot 8 inches; keel, 4 inches. With 100 pounds of lead or iron inside they carried 100 square feet of sail; the paddle being replaced by oars.

A young canoeist of Liverpool, Henry W. Eaton, of whom more anon, made what was considered a venturous voyage from the Isle of Man across the Irish Sea to the main land, a distance of some sixty miles, in 1875. His canoe, Kestrel, was similar to that shown, but only 15 feet long and 4 feet 1 inch in width. After careful planning of all details, including food for a week, the canoe was shipped by steamer from Liverpool to Douglas and launched on the evening of July 10 and the voyage begun at once. Calms, head winds, rough water and cross tides were encountered in the course of the ensuing forty hours before anchor was dropped in Llandudno Bay, the Captain much exhausted and very sleepy. Some miles of the trip were, perforce, made under sculls.

The next step in enlargement was the canoe-yawl, as now named, Vital Spark, designed and built by Samuel Bond of Birkenhead in 1882. She was 18 feet in length; 5 feet in breadth; and drew 2 feet 2 inches; with 4½ cwt of lead in her keel and the same amount cast to fit inside. Her sail area was originally 178 square feet. A duplicate of this craft was built by Lawley & Son in

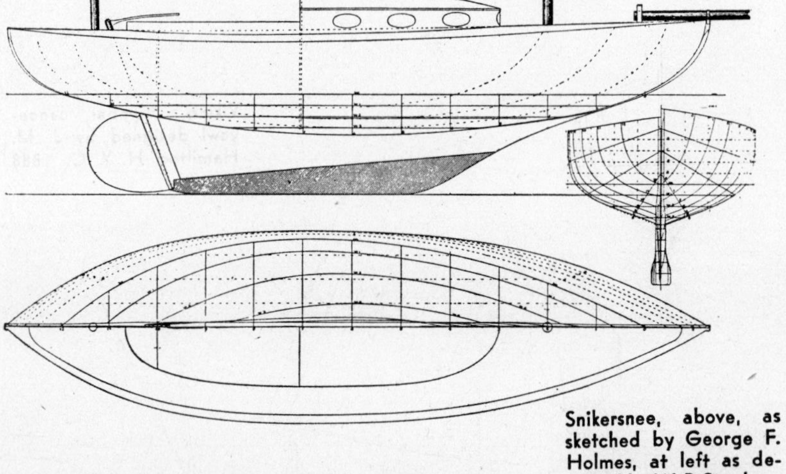

1884 for Sidney W. Burgess and was purchased by the writer in the following year and sailed under the name of Tomboy in New York waters.

The Humber Yawl Club

Interest in the canoe proper continued for some years in the Eastern Branch. Many cruises were made on the rivers and canals which joined Hull to the interior, and long cruises were made by fleets of canoes shipped across the North Sea. The dangers and difficulties of canoeing in the home waters eventually led to a lack of interest and the Eastern Branch died; but only to be revived in 1883 under the name of the Humber Yawl Club, devoted to a larger and abler type. This organization, still strong and vigorous, celebrates its sixtieth anniversary this year. The year book of the club, an unique publication in itself, showed a membership of 32 and a fleet of 30 in 1889, the first year of publication. The last book published, in 1940, shows a membership of over 200 and a fleet of 135 craft. The early boats were canoes not over 16 feet, and a few canoe-yawls up to 18 feet with a breadth of not over 5 feet. The fleet at the outbreak of the present war included a few large yachts, a number of motor cruisers, but mainly yawls, ketches and cutters from 25 to 30 feet in length and 8 to 10 feet breadth, with auxiliary power.

The location of the club is unusual, to the west is an extensive system of rivers suitable for cruising in centerboard craft, while easy steamer communication with the continent opens a still more extensive system of rivers, lakes and canals for the

Snikersnee, above, as sketched by George F. Holmes, at left as designed by W. P. Stephens for the year book of Humber Yawl Club, 1897. Below: Eel designed by Mr. Holmes in 1896

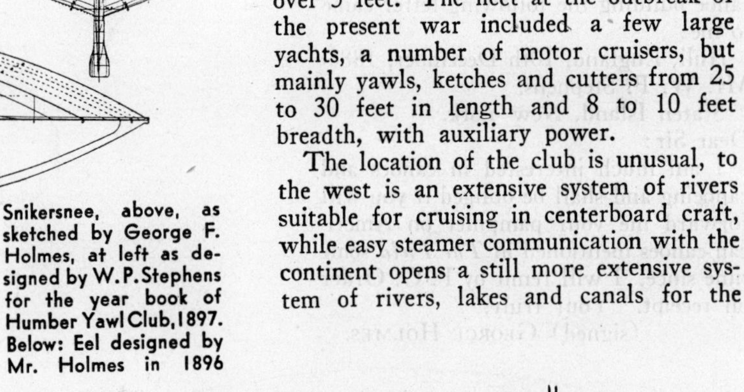

same shoal type. Once in the lower Humber there is rough water and the North Sea, calling for larger, abler and usually keel craft. The personnel of the club is also exceptional as shown by the 52 year books fully illustrated with pictures of yachts, views of home and foreign voyaging, and designs without number, all the

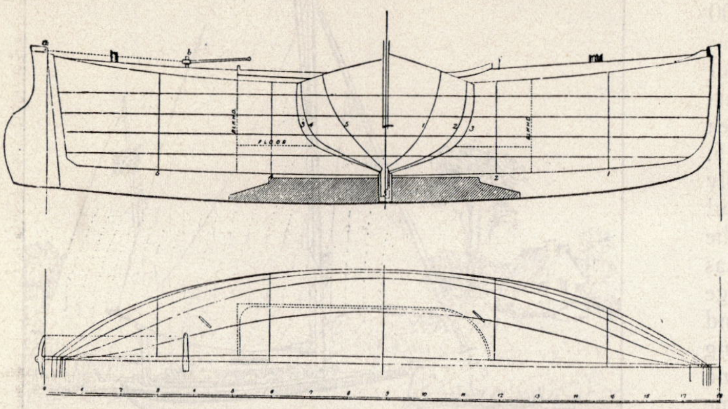

Vital Spark, Mersey canoe-yawl, 1886

work of the amateur artists and designers of the club. With the outbreak of the war, as in 1917, all activities of the club were suspended, many of the members entered service, and, at the request of the Admiralty, the club undertook the organization and manning of a fleet of motor boats. The Captain, Tom Martin, Jr., a lieutenant in the R.N.V.R., entered the anti-submarine patrol and after four years on the North Sea and about the Thames Estuary was recently in New York handling men, testing mine sweepers, and when last reported bound home in command of an American minesweeper.

George F. Holmes

WHILE still engaged in part in canoe building the following letter came to me:

Hull, England, 10th December, 1884.
Mr. W. P. Stephens,
Staten Island, New York.
Dear Sir:

I am much interested in canoes and canoeing and shall be obliged if you will forward me your pamphlet on American canoes mentioned in *The Field* some time since. I will remit by P. O. Order on receipt. Your truly,

(signed) GEORGE HOLMES.

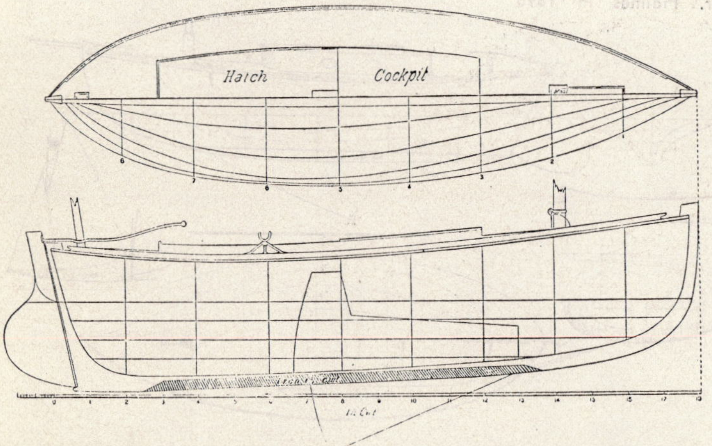

This letter started a correspondence which ended only with the death of Mr. Holmes in May, 1940; I have now two large file cases of letters in a full round hand as legible as print. Some of his many cruises were reproduced by process from written text of this kind. As for illustrations, the neatly made pen sketches closely interspersed through the text would make a book of boats comparable to that of H. C. Folkard. A lifelong resident of Hull, he was fortunate enough to have a business which afforded both the means and ample leisure for the gratification of his simple tastes, sailing, designing, sketching, etching and music. When afloat his sketchbook was ever close at hand; even at the tiller, in a light breeze it came out to catch some passing craft. I spent three delightful days with him in 1913 and no sooner was the hook down at Keadby, on the Upper Trent, than the sketchbook came out. As soon as his yacht was laid up, late in the year, the sketchbook came out again, the pencil sketches being reproduced in finished form on the metal plate for etching and printing. About Christmas time the annual crop came to me, twenty or thirty etchings, small or large; I have in all some 1,100 of them.

Apart from cruising in his own canoes and yachts, his wide friendship with owners of large craft took him to Ireland, Scotland and many English ports, all depicted in his sketchbooks. His designing began about the time that he helped to organize the club; at first, canoes, dinghies, odd little craft for a lake near his home; then

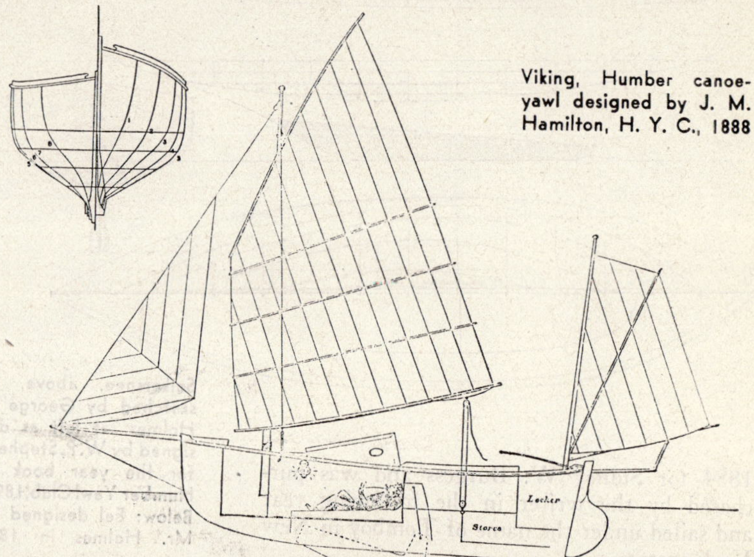

Viking, Humber canoe-yawl designed by J. M. Hamilton, H. Y. C., 1888

larger canoe-yawls and canoe-yachts. In 1896 he had built from his design the little Eel; selling her in 1913 to our mutual friend, Ernest H. Oliver, another etcher, and replacing her with the larger Snippet, which he owned at the time of his death. Eel, still sound and seaworthy after 48 years, was owned by Oliver when he died last year. Through my friendship with Holmes I became acquainted with other early members of the club. We had much in common in our interest in all types of small cruising craft, and I became a member in 1895. I still fly the white and red burgee when fortunate enough to get afloat.

THE dual objects of the club are well expressed in its motto, "Per Mare, Per Flumen." When, in 1895, I was asked to contribute a design to the year book my old cutter virus led me to select the keel rather than the centerboard type; though I have ever since regretted that, following the fashion of the day, I chose the fin-keel rather than the flowing S section.

The origin of the term "canoe-yawl" is very uncertain, it probably came about through the fact that the first of the type were yawl-rigged. As the size increased, with a deeper body, in many cases merging into a keel, with enclosed cabins, it seemed inadequate, and in *Forest & Stream* of July 7, 1892, I wrote: "Exact names and definitions are the exception rather than the rule in canoeing and yachting, there being very few terms which apply strictly to any one model or rig, or to both in combination. . . . It needs no proof that a vessel 20 to 24 feet long with a breadth of 5 to 6 feet and a ton of lead under her is not a canoe; while at the same time she may be a sloop, cutter or ketch in rig; but the same name, 'canoe-yawl' has stuck to her. . . . The need for some distinction between these two classes has been apparent for some time, and to meet it we suggest that the name 'canoe-yawl' be restricted to such boats as by their draft, model and ballasting may be beached and housed; while the other larger class may be called 'canoe-yachts.' . . . Such boats are increasing so rapidly that their recognition and limitation are only matters of time."

HAVING a good shop and a large collection of tools—all hand, as the wonderful electric saw which nipped off the ends of two fingers was not dreamed of—it occurred to me early in 1898 to build for myself from the design which I had made for the H. Y. C. book. I began with the mould loft equipment, a 16-foot straightedge, a square with arms 4 and 6 feet, and battens of clear spruce, 25 feet long and carefully tapering for sheer, waterlines, etc. The lines were laid down, moulds made and the work progressed by fits and starts, as occasion offered, down to September, 1903, when she was ready for launching. All the work had been done by myself alone, with the exception of the riveting of the shutters, a friend kindly holding on outside while I riveted on the inside.

Patterns were made for every piece of brass and bronze except the Merriam blocks: cap for bowsprit, gammon iron, clevis for bobstay, deckplate and caps for bitts, goosenecks and boom fittings, turnbuckles, mast slides, rudder cap, including core box, tiller yoke, gammon iron for boomkin. All turning and drilling was done on an old footlathe. The prices of wood are interesting today—real white pine, $55 per thousand; white cedar, $55; clear spruce, $25; teak 3 by 8 by 24 feet, $10.56; bronze castings, 33 cents per pound; iron keel, 2½ cents per pound; mainsail, mizzen and jib, with covers and tyers, $23. The total cost of materials, cushions, ground tackle and car for launching was $140.

While engaged in this work I had little else to do outside the editorship of two departments, the covering of the building of Columbia, Constitution and Reliance, and all trial and Cup races of 1899, 1901 and 1903, as well as the usual yacht and canoe races on the coast and the lakes.

Hindsight vs. Foresight

IN this work I made several mistakes which have worried me for the past forty years. The design was the first in which I attempted the "canoe stern," I was not designing for myself and I was feeling my way. If I had made the after overhang longer by two feet the appearance would have been greatly improved, there would have been no need for the mizzen boomkin, and I would have saved days in planking. What specially shames me, even now, is that when I came to building for myself I had a beautiful teak plank 24 feet long; instead of altering the design to make a more shapely overhang I deliberately cut 27 inches from each sheer strake.

Another serious mistake was in the rig; I had amply demonstrated in Ethelwynn and many other small yachts the superiority of the jib-headed pole-masted rig. I was, however, so impressed with the rig of Eel that I copied it, with all of its complication and weight. Not until two years ago did I change to the pole-masted rig. With a sail area of 338 square feet, three heavy battens in the mainsail and one in the mizzen, she was badly over-canvassed and with too much weight aloft. But most of my sailing, perforce, was done in Newark Bay, Staten Island Sound and the Kill von Kull, in very light winds.

The keel parallel to the waterline was another serious mistake. I was aiming at a draft of three feet. Had I raised the fore end of the keel three inches and lowered the after end as much, when she grounded it would have been on her heel in 3 feet 3 inches of water. Shifting weights forward would have lifted her off, or she might have been swung on her heel. As it is, when she grounds it is on the fore end of the keel and she will not turn to free herself. When beaching or hauling her this fore end of the keel hits the beach or ways and she is stuck, while a moderate drag to the keel would fit the average slope of the beach or car.

Carefully as I planned the keel, I did not allow enough for the fact that most of the weights would be well aft, the crew of one or two, the main storage spaces about the cockpit and the after end of the cabin. After testing her I cut off 15 inches from the after end of the keel, a weight of 90 pounds, using a wide-webbed hacksaw with blade inverted. First marking carefully a vertical line on each side of the keel, a hole was bored through the wood keel and the saw inserted. The sawing of the iron, about 7 inches by 3 to 5 inches, with a hard chill on top, took five hours; but I made a clean square cut, replacing the iron with an oak chock. The hull was very lightly constructed, too much on the canoe side, but I have no apologies to offer for the joiner work, of good teak and still standing well; the cabin roof, in three layers, was held together by 1,200 bronze screws and never has leaked.

Albert Strange

UNDER the date line, "Scarborough, England, Dec. 19, 1893," I received a letter from one known to me only by name; speaking in high terms of *Forest & Stream*. Every letter thus received was answered fully, though many of them were the reverse of commendatory. My reply in this case led to a close intimacy which ended only with the death of the correspondent 24 years later.

Albert Strange was born at Gravesend, at the mouth of the Thames, in 1856, and grew up as a boy sailing in such crude craft, mainly fishing boats, as were then available. Choosing art as his profession, he followed it with that thoroughness which characterized all of his work. He specialized in watercolor, land- and seascapes, but due probably to his modest disposition and his preoccupation with other pursuits he never received the full recognition which his talent merited.

Much of his life was spent in Scarborough, and when a School of Art was established there in 1883 he assumed the direction. He developed exceptional skill as an instructor in various lines, from the higher forms of art to textile and similar designing, many of his pupils attaining high rank in their special lines. Where he found a pupil interested in boats he added yacht designing to the regular curriculum. In the course of a busy life he still found time for designing, sailing and trout fishing.

I was attracted to him by our mutual interests in designing, in our advocacy of the canoe-stern, and music, of which he knew much while I know very little. In 1888 he had built from his own design the cutter Cherub, about 21 by 7, aboard which he did much cruising in open water.

In 1891 he joined the Humber Yawl Club and two years later he had built Cherub II, 20 feet by 5 feet 10 inches, of the local up-river type; followed in 1910 by Cherub III. By degrees he turned from his art to the drafting board and ultimately turned out 150 designs of all kinds from ketches and yawls up to 60 feet down to canoes and dinghies.

He knew the sea, what it liked and disliked, much of his personal sailing was done in small craft, and all of his yachts were noted for power, stability and sturdy construction. While the artistic side of his nature was evident in the lines of his yachts, of equal importance was the practical side; the thoroughness of construction shown in all of his specifications.

His family life, otherwise a happy one, was marred by illness, the loss of an only daughter by consumption, a son afflicted by the same disease, and a heart too weak for such an active body. A heart attack in 1912 curtailed his sailing, he was seriously affected by the first world war, and an attack of influenza in the spring of 1917 hastened his death from heart disease in July of this year, cutting short a series of articles on Yacht Design just begun in *The Yachting Monthly*. His long letters, though in a fine cramped hand very difficult to decipher, were always interesting, and fully illustrated with sketches of craft. His drafting was practically perfect, and his lettering on his designs equal to type. I learned much from our long and intimate correspondence (I spent only a few days with him personally), and as "Papa Strange" he was mourned by many canoeists and yachtsmen whom he had aided.

TRADITIONS AND MEMORIES OF

AMERICAN YACHTING

By WILLIAM P. STEPHENS

Part Fifty-three

THE DEVELOPMENT OF THE SMALL CRUISER (Continued)

THE many designs of Alfred Strange are in no sense dated; and, though thirty years old, are still perfectly adapted to their original purpose. They were made to meet the stern conditions of the sea, which knows no changes of fashion and imposes its own laws on men. While it would be possible today to fine the lines, to "streamline" them in order to gain speed, such a change could only spoil them for their designed use as single-handers for open water. Cherub III, designed for his personal use, was planned in 1910 with a square stern and no after overhang. Prior to building, however, the design was changed, giving her a canoe stern, of which form of overhang Strange was an early and earnest advocate. The details of the accommodation are very carefully worked out, giving a small stateroom for Mrs. Strange. The construction is in consonance with the purpose of the design, sturdy and durable. She was used by her owner for only two seasons, 1910-11, in the latter year making a long cruise in Scottish waters in company with Sheila II; owing to declining health she was sold in 1912. The details of the two are given in a table at the end of this article.

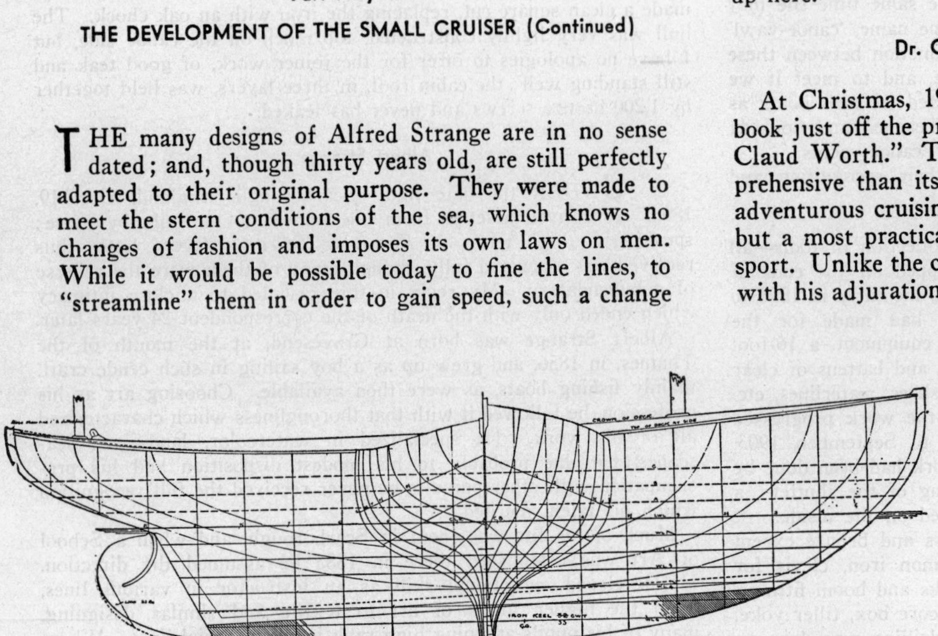

The one important change which time has wrought in the design of small cruising yachts is in the rig; the substitution of the pole-masted, jib-headed sail for the boom and gaff shown in Strange's plans. The fact seems to be generally accepted that this is an advance save in some special cases on the larger yachts. This, in turn, brings up another question:—for the past fifty years or more the yawl rig, with its "dandy" or small mizzen, had been universally recognized as the best for cruising yachts of small and medium sizes. Within a very few years past such hulls have been rigged with but one mast and two, or perhaps three, jib-headed sails; mainsail and jib or possibly jib and fore staysail. Important as it is, this question of the merits of the new rig is too big to be taken up here.

Dr. Claud Worth and His Books

At Christmas, 1910 I received from Albert Strange a book just off the press in London:—"Yacht Cruising, by Claud Worth." The work proved to be far more comprehensive than its title indicated; not only a record of adventurous cruising in small yachts from 1888 to 1910, but a most practical treatise on the technical side of the sport. Unlike the classic preachments of "Vanderdeckan," with his adjuration "Now, Mr. Tyro," the practical part of the book is leavened by narratives of personal experience in the small cutters of sixty years ago and more modern yachts. Eagerly read, page by page, item by item, it was then passed about among my friends, no less than forty having inscribed their names on the first blank page. The author was born some time in the sixties in

The lines and profile of Cherub III designed in 1910 by Albert Strange for his personal use

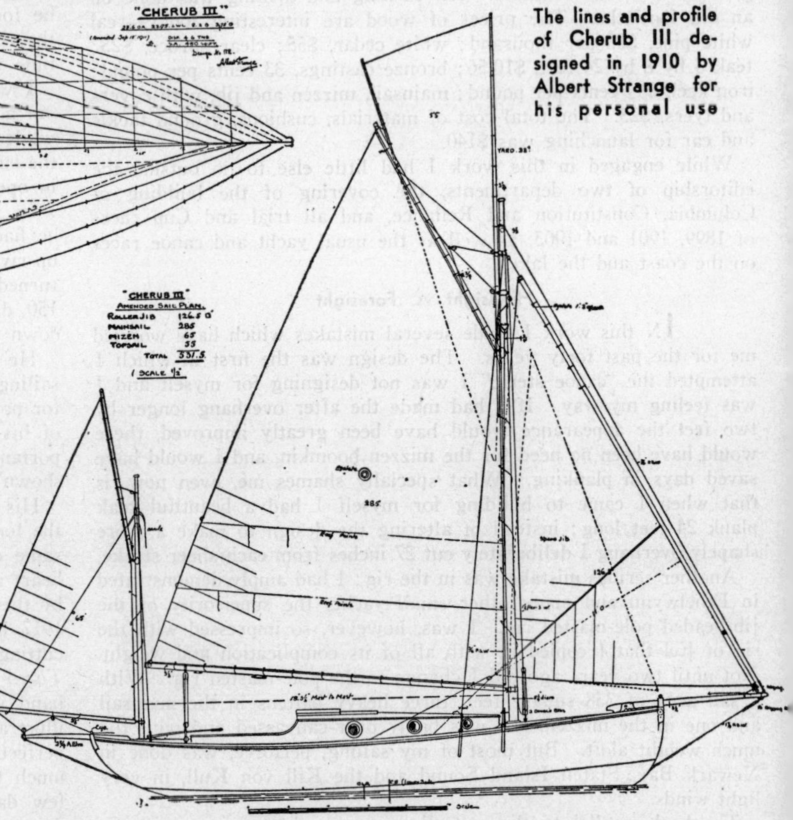

Lincolnshire, England, near "The Wash," the son of a country gentleman who rode to hounds and was interested in field sports but not in the sea.

Dr. Worth once told me that if he wanted a gun or a pony it was at once his, but if he said "Father, I have ten pounds and want another to buy a boat," the request was firmly refused. A boat was what the boy wanted, above all else, and such sailing as he did in his early years, with poaching fisherman or in a home-built craft, was without the parental knowledge or consent. His desire for a naval career was opposed by his father and he finally studied medicine and specialized in surgery; attaining high distinction as an ophthalmic surgeon. He was specially noted for his skill and delicacy of operation and for his tenderness with children who came under his knife. In spite of an over-arduous career in his profession, which obliged him to end his last years in quiet retirement, he always found time for cruising in many yachts and many waters; and, in addition, for a close study of the technical side of yachting. His writings covered such varied subjects as ground tackle, rigs and sails, sanitation, timber, standing and running rigging, spars and numerous other practical details.

The first book, "Yacht Cruising," which ran to a fourth edition, was supplemented by an authoritative work, "Yacht Navigation and Voyaging," treating of the theory and practice of navigation and also of cruising. One of his many yachts, Tern III, was originally designed by him, though his lines were checked and put into working form by Albert Strange; but the design of Tern IV was his personal work throughout. His knowledge of materials, construction and rigging would rival that of many professional builders. His excuse for the stencil habit was that the first Tern, purchased by him, was so satisfactory that "one good Tern deserved another"; hence the sequence to Tern IV. During the first World War he devoted much of his time to the eyes of soldiers and sailors, sacrificing his health in work of this kind; he wrote me:—"I go to bed tired and try to sleep, I dream that I am operating on an eye, my hand slips, and there is no more sleep for me that night."

A Long Life of Cruising

Just at the end of 1883 there came to Forest & Stream for review a modest little volume with the comprehensive title "Cruising in Small Yachts and Big Canoes, or notes from the logs of the Water Snake in Holland and on the South Coast, the logs of the Water Rat and Viper on the Thames and South Coast, with remarks on anchorages for small craft." The book was duly read and reviewed, and the review, with a copy of my new book, "Canoe and Boatbuilding for Amateurs" was sent to the author; thus beginning a correspondence which continued until his death forty-two years later.

Harry Fiennes Speed, born in 1857 in the North East corner of Kent near the mouth of the Thames, attended Brazenose College, Oxford, and as Captain of the Oxford Canoe Club made a cruise in a small canoe down Thames to Margate and back, 259 miles of river and coastal work in ten days. In 1878, with his brother and a fellow collegian, he made a cruise from the Thames through Holland and Belgium between August 10 and October 31 aboard Water Snake, a cutter 34 feet 6 inches over all; 8 feet breadth and 5 feet draft. In the following February he ordered from a local builder at Erith his first "Big Canoe" Water Rat.

Modelled by her builder, with plumb stem and sternpost, a flat floor and straight sides joined by a short turn of bilge, lapstrake with a six-inch keel, decked, with a small oval cockpit and yawl rig, she was crude in the extreme. With a length of 16 feet; breadth, 4 feet 1½ inches; draft of about a foot, she carried 180 square feet of

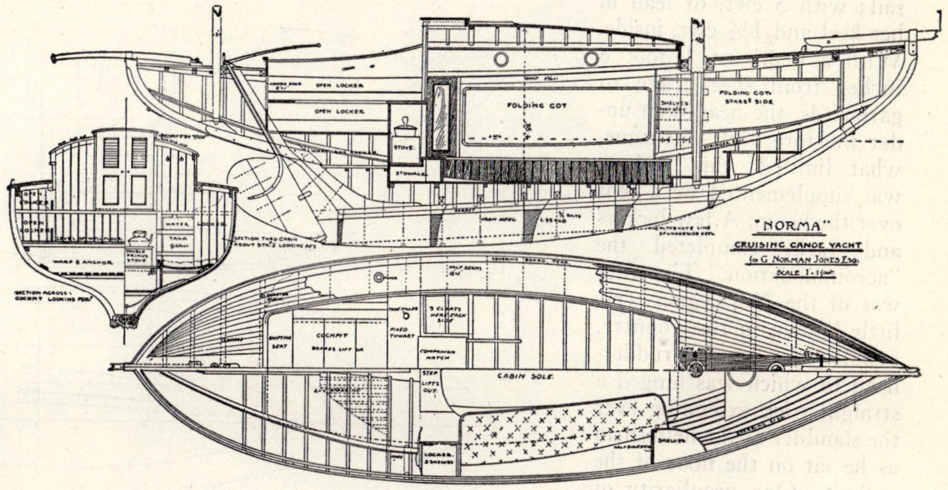

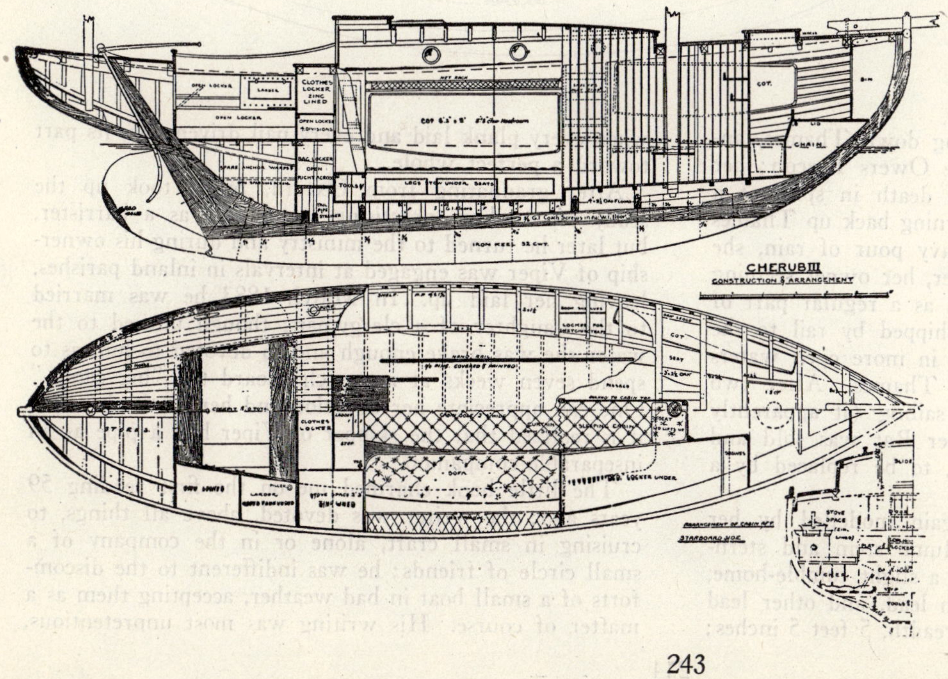

Carefully prepared construction drawings for Norma, and similar drawings for Cherub III made by Albert Strange in 1910

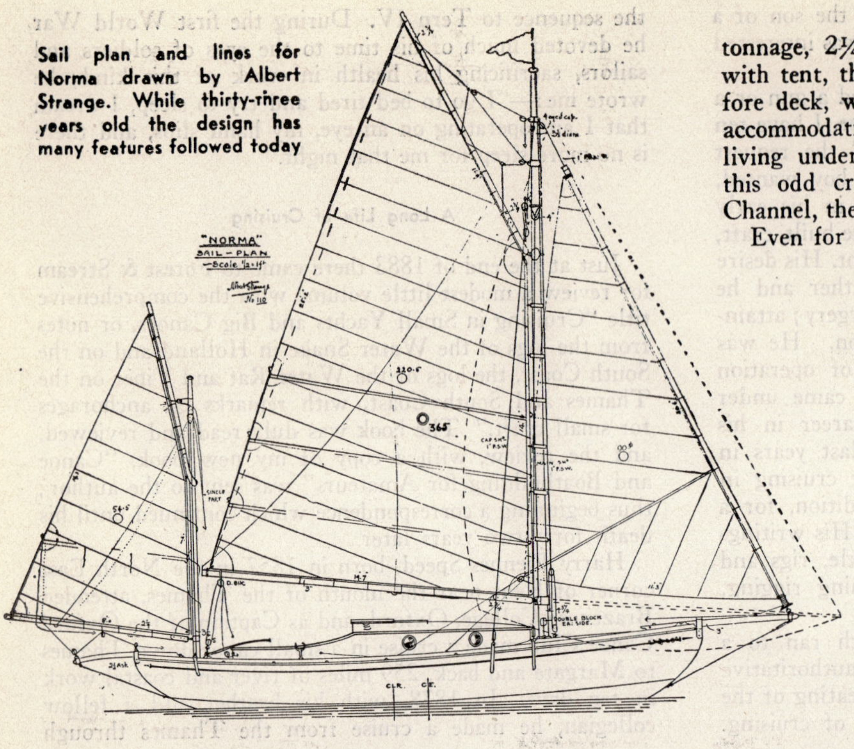

Sail plan and lines for Norma drawn by Albert Strange. While thirty-three years old the design has many features followed today

sail; with 3 cwt. of lead in her keel and 1½ cwt. inside. With a depth of 1 foot 8 inches from sheerstrake to garboards, the headroom under the fore deck was somewhat limited; this "cabin" was supplemented by a tent over the boom. A few lockers and racks completed the "accommodation." The tiller was of the Norwegian type, little known in this country, a half yoke on the rudderhead to which was hinged a straight stick extending over the shoulder of the helmsman as he sat on the floor of the cockpit. One peculiarity of this device is that a novice invariably puts the helm the wrong way in his first attempts.

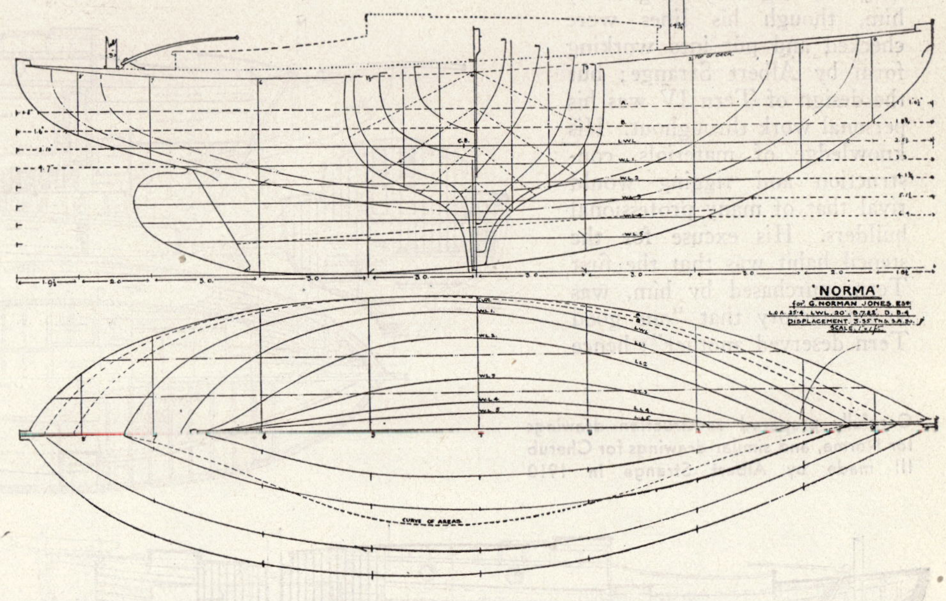

Launched in April of a wet spring, she started her cruising down Thames, anchoring for the first night off the Owers Beacon; her solitary owner nearly freezing to death in spite of a kerosene stove under his tent. Turning back up Thames with the river in flood and a heavy pour of rain, she was towed by wading in cold water, her owner seeming to consider days of this wet work as a regular part of the pleasure of cruising. Later, shipped by rail to the Solent, she continued her cruising in more open waters before ending the season on the Thames. After two seasons of this damp and dismal sailing (it apparently rained nearly all the time) Water Rat was sold and shipped to St. Petersburg, Russia, to be replaced by a larger "canoe."

The new boat, Viper, was again modelled by her builder, McWhirter of Erith; plumb stem and sternpost, flat floor, straight sides with a slight tumble-home, lapstrake, an oak keel loaded with lead, and other lead inside. Her length was 20 feet; breadth, 5 feet 5 inches; tonnage, 2¼ B.M. There was the same open cockpit with tent, the only approach to a cabin being under the fore deck, with 5 inches crown to the deckbeams. Her accommodation, in the words of her owner, was "like living under the dining table on the hearth rug." In this odd craft Speed cruised about the Thames, the Channel, the Wight and the Solent from 1881 until 1890.

Even for the man who cares only for sailing there is a fascination in watching the building of a boat or yacht; when one is also interested in the problems of design and construction there is a far greater charm. On this point Speed says:—"Week after week I used to come during the building of the ship; how interesting it is, to be sure, watching one's own boat gradually growing as, plank by plank, she approaches completion." If this is so in the case of a mere owner, it is still more true when one can claim not only the design but the actual construction; to see the first skeleton of moulds and ribbands grow into a solid form made up of fair and true curves in every direction, when every plank laid and every nail driven does its part toward a perfect whole.

After graduating from Oxford, Speed took up the study of the law, practising for a time as a barrister, but later he turned to the ministry and during his ownership of Viper was engaged at intervals in inland parishes, leaving her laid up. In March 1883 he was married to the daughter of a clergyman; though unused to the water she was brave enough and so devoted to him as to spend seven weeks at a stretch aboard the "big canoe." One can appreciate her devotion and her fortitude when it is realized that the skipper of Viper had a pipe as an inseparable companion.

The little book charmed me on the first reading 59 years ago; the writer was devoted, above all things, to cruising in small craft, alone or in the company of a small circle of friends; he was indifferent to the discomforts of a small boat in bad weather, accepting them as a matter of course. His writing was most unpretentious, but marked by a very keen sense of humor and a penchant for quizzical expressions. His brother, Laurence, was a professional artist, but his own sketches, which serve to illustrate the book, are crude in the extreme, and yet each expresses an idea. My library is always at the service of my friends, yet is still almost intact; but the review copy of this book, which I valued from old association, was loaned to a friend a few years ago who thinks that he in turn loaned it to a friend who forgot to return it.

As for penmanship, Speed was in the same class as Albert Strange and Dr. Worth, I could, with some difficulty, decipher most of the words of his letters, but had to guess at some from the context. However, my long correspondence with him was most enjoyable, he was almost as interested in handiwork as in sailing, and was a skilled amateur mechanic and engineer. When his duties to his congregation made dependence on wind and tide out of the question his interest in machinery led him to study a new type of launch engine recently introduced in England, the Lifu, a steam engine with a multitubular boiler using a liquid fuel. In 1903 Viper was displaced by a cabin launch, Pipefish, 41 feet over all; 8 feet 6 inches breadth; and of 11 tons, designed by her owner for work in open water.

In the interval between Viper and Pipefish there was a cruising cutter, Lerna, 4 tons, bought in 1891, aboard which he and Mrs. Speed cruised for nine seasons in English, Dutch and French waters; followed by Beaver, 6 tons, in which they made many long cruises in English and trans-Channel waters. In the spring of 1925 Pipefish had her usual fit-out, Mrs. Speed made a trip through the Engadine and the Tyrol, and on August 3 they started on an easy cruise about the Isle of Wight. In his last letter to me Speed spoke of ill health, but considered it as nothing alarming. They put in to Yarmouth to witness the regatta of the Solent Y. C., of which he was a member, in the afternoon Mrs. Speed rowed ashore to buy provisions and on her return found him lifeless on the floor. An autopsy disclosed that his death, which must have been instantaneous, was due to a heart attack.

A new edition of his book being called for in 1926, Mrs. Speed extended the original work by adding "Part II More Cruises," giving their many experiences between 1883 and 1925, with illustrations by Launcelot Speed. A very talented woman, with long experience in foreign travel in addition to the cruising just described, she has written "Snapshots on Life's Highway," incidents of her life as a young girl in Victorian England; "A Yachtswoman's Cruises" in the yachts already mentioned; and two volumes of travel, "Through Central France to the Pyrenees" and "A Scamper Tour to Rhodesia and South Africa with a Sketchbook." An amateur artist of more than ordinary ability, these books are illustrated by reproductions of her work with the brush in color and black. I am glad to be able to say that she is still one of my most valued correspondents.

Design as Dependent on Local Conditions

THE English yachtsman has much to be thankful for in the extent and variety of cruising waters which Nature has placed before him. Close at hand are many inland rivers, each with a charm of its own; the whole circumference of his "tight little island" is studded with small harbors at short intervals; Scotland and the sister island of Ireland offer a different variety of harbors and scenery. An open sea passage of from twenty to one hundred miles opens up the coasts of Norway, Sweden, Denmark, Holland, Germany, Belgium and France, with thousands of miles of cruising waters on the Baltic and the European canal systems. For craft as small as the canoe and canoe-yacht, a night aboard a steamer opens up all these inland waters for a cruise of a week, a month or a summer.

On the other side of the picture is the climate, with a shorter cruising season and far more rain (at least, in England); the tides, which average perhaps twenty feet (at Liverpool twenty-seven feet), as compared with about seven feet about New York and less at many points on our coast, giving rise to dangerous currents in many places; the formation of many harbors, two jutting points of rocks or two closely spaced pier heads.

Almost every English craft larger than a canoe was designed for a double purpose; much of its cruising would be on rivers where draft was limited, at the same time, when once clear of a harbor, the need was for a sturdy and able hull and moderate rig. The keel type shared honors or even out-numbered the centerboard or "drop-keel" type. On this side of the Atlantic not only the harbors but the whole coast line South of Boston called for a minimum of draft and made the centerboard type supreme for many years save in the case of some of the largest schooners; and even here the centerboard held its own. The crusade of the "Cutter-Cranks" some sixty years ago introduced the keel type as a formidable competitor of the centerboard in all classes. Due to this assimilation of ideas the single-hander of today enjoys the greatest possible freedom in the choice of type and of individuality in the choice of design.

Comparative Specifications for Cherub III and Sheila II

	Cherub III	Sheila II
Length, over all	28′ 6″	31′ 6″
waterline	23′ 0″	24′ 0″
Breadth, extreme	8′ 1″	8′ 6″
waterline	7′ 9″	8′ 0″
Draft	3′ 9″	4′11″
Displacement, long tons	4.6	5.1
Iron Keel, long tons	1.6	2.5
Freeboard, bow	3′ 6″	3′ 6″
least	2′ 3″	2′ 2″
stern	3′ 1″	2′ 6″
Mainmast from stem	7′ 7″	9′ 9″
diameter	5″	5″
deck to hounds	19′ 8″	20′ 0″
to truck	25′ 6″	26′ 9″
Mizzenmast from stem	26′ 6″	28′ 4″
diameter	3½″	3½″
deck to hounds	11′ 4″	11′ 8″
to truck	12′ 9″	14′ 0″
Bowsprit, outboard	5′ 0″	3′ 6″
Boomkim, outboard	3′ 6″	3′ 6″
Main Boom, length	18′ 3″	18′ 0″
diameter	3½″	3½″
Main Gaff, length	12′ 6″	13′ 6″
diameter	2¼″	2¼″
Mizzen Boom, length	8′ 6″	8′ 4″
diameter	2¼″	2¼″
Mizzen Gaff, length	8′ 6″	8′ 9″
diameter	2″	2″
Topmast Yards, length	15′ 0″	15′ 0″
diameter	2¼″	2¾″
length	7′ 9″	5′ 8″
diameter	2″	2″
Sails, sq. ft.		
Jib	126	120
Mainsail	285	283
Mizzen	65	72
Total	476	475
Topsail	55	58
C.L.R. from fore end, l.w.l.	13′ 6″	17′ 3″
C.E. from fore end, l.w.l.	12′ 3″	15′ 3″

Both yachts were fitted with storm jibs set from the stemhead.

TRADITIONS AND MEMORIES OF American

Part Fifty-four

THE DEVELOPMENT OF THE SMALL CRUISER

(Continued)

THE yawl, a rig almost unknown in America sixty years ago, was the favorite rig in British waters for craft under forty feet or so waterline, above which limit the ketch was preferred. It was used generally on fishing boats, on yachts, and, in particular, on the small craft with which this story is concerned. Its theoretical advantage was the division of sail into three elements, each small enough to be more easily handled than the mainsail of a cutter: headsails (jib or jib and fore staysail), mainsail and a small mizzen abaft the rudderpost. As additional advantages were the lessened weight of spars and the shorter main boom. As to handiness, the yawl would carry full sail in light weather, while reefing was dispensed with by lowering headsail and mizzen or stowing the mainsail and using the end sails.

How fully these theoretical advantages were realized depended on the shape of the lateral plane and the balancing of the various centers of the sails. In the case of fishing craft the mizzen was useful in laying to a net. In the larger racing classes the yawl had a fictitious advantage in the "allowance for rig"; racing with the cutters at 4/5 of her actual tonnage; the result being that many large cutters after their first few years of racing were thus converted by the shipping of a diminutive mizzen which was of little real use. The most famous of all the large yawls, originally designed for that rig, was Jullanar, of 100 feet l.w.l., designed and built by her owner, an amateur, in 1876.

Born on Staten Island, one of a family long associated with shipping, Charles P. Kunhardt entered the U. S. Naval Academy in 1866 and graduated in 1870, resigning from the navy in 1873 and entering the drafting room of the Cramp Shipyard in Philadelphia. Later he abandoned shipbuilding for writing and was associated with *The Nautical Gazette* of New York. In *The Aquatic Monthly* for April 1873, writing under the nom-de-plume of "Big Topmast," he argued for the small yacht and the pleasure of Corinthian sailing, accompanying the article by a design for a cruiser of 38 feet o.a.; 32 feet l.w.l.; 9 feet 6 inches breadth and 4 feet 6 inches draft; of course a keel cutter and a very attractive craft with a large angle of deadrise. A little later he was taking on all comers in the discussion of the eternal question of measurement, and also starting a series of articles on the method of designing as applied to yachts.

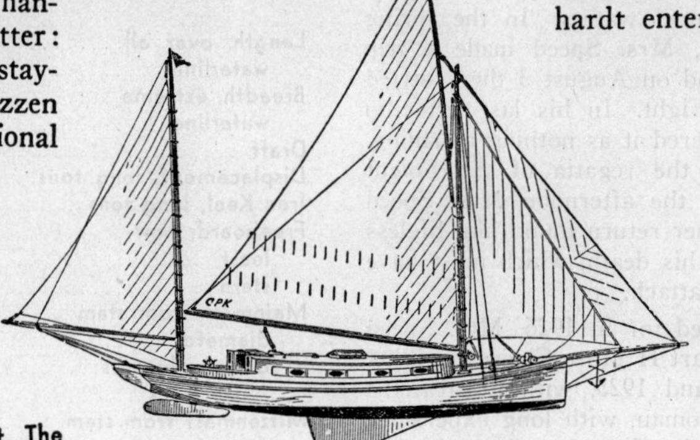

Above: Sketch by C. P. Kunhardt, The Stringpiece Critics. Right: The yawl Roslyn, and below, the sharpie Nonpariel designed and built by Thomas Clapham

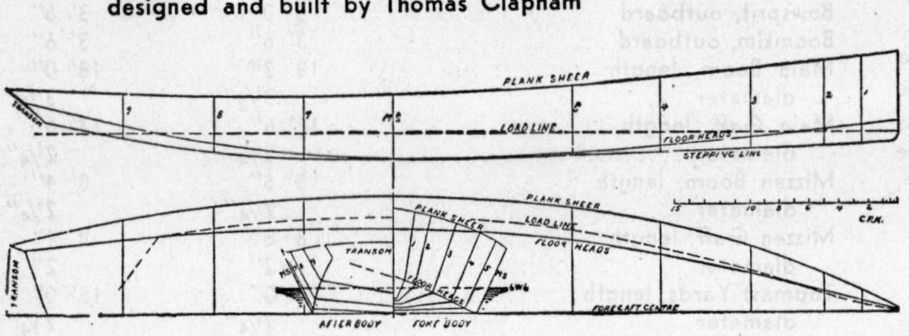

For some years he retained his nom-de-plume, most of the writers of that day being apparently too modest to sign their names. We find in this journal "Tom Cringle," writing from Boston, "Long Tom," "O. F. B.," "Mop Halyards," "Windward," "Spinnaker," "Podgers," "S. M. T.," "Ballast," "Binnacle," "Hard-a-Lee," "Nauticus," "Cuttyhunk," "Mast Rope" and "Canuck." The true names of nearly all of these are lost to fame, but we know that "O. F. B." was Otis F. Bradford, evidently familiar with New York yachting, though not prominent as a yacht owner. "S. M. T." was none other than Col. Stuart M. Taylor, U.S.A.,

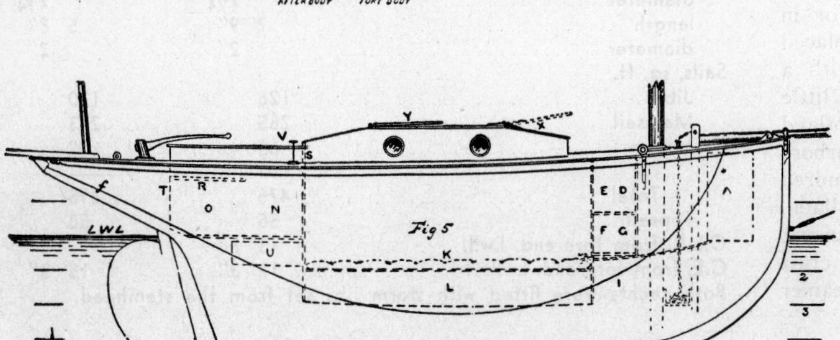

Left: Plan and lines of Deuce, designed and built by W. P. Stephens for E. M. Clarke of Providence in 1883

Yachting

By WILLIAM P. STEPHENS

a valiant scribe who, while the typewriter was unknown, thought nothing of reeling off ten or twelve pages of fine print; in even the most technical discussions he wrapped himself up in the folds of the American flag and proudly waved another in each hand, defying all foreign nations. "Podgers" was my old friend Captain Richard S. Ogden, U. S. A., a veteran of the Rebellion, equally well known in New York and San Francisco, a contributor on varied topics to *The New York Times* and to yachting publications. He was strongly anti-British and an enemy of the cutter, in spite of his personal friendship with Kunhardt and myself. He was at one time the proud owner of the Tulee Belle, one of the scow houseboats of San Francisco Bay.

Above: Deuce off Marblehead, 1886; crew, one boy and a dog

Kunhardt and His Crusades

Starting with a plea for a better knowledge of the principles of designing and abler yachts, a born crusader, he was quick to espouse the cause of a national organization of yachtsmen, as suggested in an editorial in *The Aquatic Monthly* as early as August 1872. Following this came a campaign for Corinthian helmsmen in the larger yachts and Corinthian crews in some of the races of these yachts. Later he advocated the British cutter, then a craft of about four beams to length and with nearly all her ballast inside. As the transfer of ballast from inside to a position below the wood keel progressed with increasing rapidity from about 1875 to 1880, with a consequent decrease of breadth and increase of depth and draft, resulting in the so-called "lead mines" of five, six and even seven beams, Kunhardt, then yachting editor of *Forest & Stream,* went from one extreme to a greater and was recognized as the leader of the so-called "Cutter-cranks"; fighting almost alone against older and more experienced yaching writers and the great body of American yachtsmen.

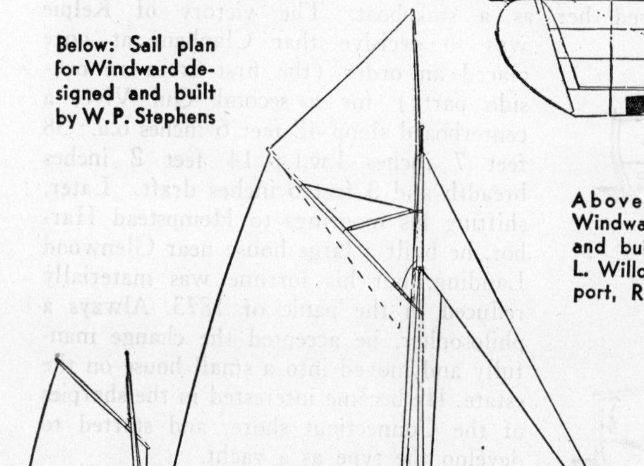

Below: Sail plan for Windward designed and built by W.P. Stephens

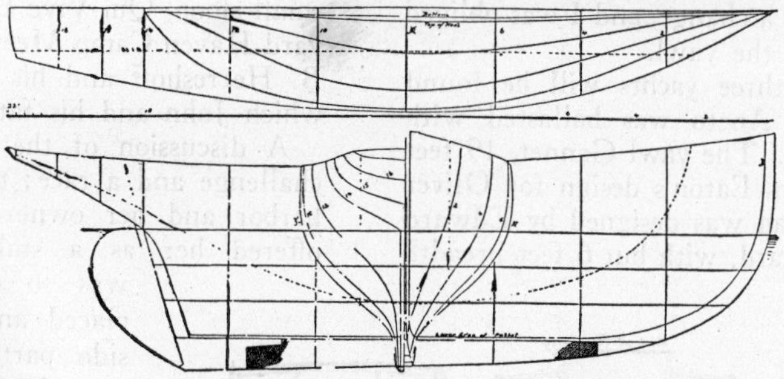

Above: Lines of Windward designed and built for Hugh L. Willoughby, Newport, R. I., in 1884

It was while thus fully engaged in 1882 that he began a new crusade for the introduction of the British yawl, at the same time extolling the joys of single-hand sailing and Corinthian yachting in the small classes. In a letter to *Forest & Stream* dated January 6, 1882, Franklin Beames, the owner of a small yacht, suggested the formation of a club devoted to the interests of cruising yachts too small to be recognized by the larger clubs; the many small clubs then about New York concerning themselves mainly with sandbag racing. This idea was promptly taken up and pushed by Kunhardt and met with some promise of success at the start, though it failed of realization. Very clever with his pencil, though making no pretensions as an artist, the yawl in its many aspects was fully illustrated and its merits detailed at length, finally receiving universal recognition as a most practical and useful rig.

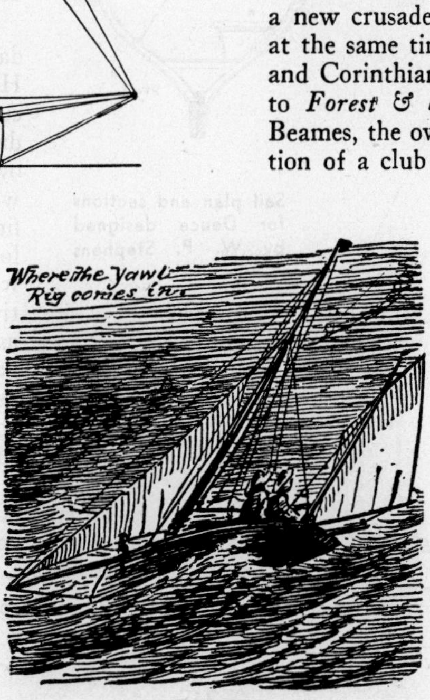
Where the Yawl Rig comes In

In the summer of 1882, when engaged in building canoes at West New Brighton, Staten Island, I was asked by my friend, Henry W. Eaton of the Seawanhaka Y. C., to build a yawl from his design. This was ultimately named Aneto, a transposition of the letters of his surname. In a yachting career of nearly half a century, including the ownership of a small fleet of yachts, Eaton never duplicated a name. At the same time, as an ardent proselyte of Kunhardt, I designed the smallest possible yawl which would give reasonable cruising accommodation for two of something less than Falstaffian dimensions. Deuce, as she was christened by her owner, E. M. Clarke of Providence, R. I., proved satisfactory to him and later found her way to Marblehead where she was sailed by a crew of two; a boy and a big mastiff. In 1884 I designed and built for my friend Hugh L. Willoughby the yawl Windward. When a boy of 19 in 1875 his father had built for him a centerboard sloop of 46 feet l.w.l., modelled and built by "Lon" Smith of Islip, Long Island, then locally famous. Through the kindly connivance of his father's friend, Samuel J. Colgate, owner of the schooner Idler, he was admitted to membership in the New York A. C. though still under his majority. I had already built for him a canoe named Windward, though I pleaded with him to name her Leeward for a change, and I was obliged to stencil the same name on the yawl.

The particulars of these three yachts will be found at the end of this article. Aneto was ballasted with lead, the other two with iron. The yawl Gannet, 19 feet l.w.l., was built in 1883 from Eaton's design for Oliver Adams; in 1884 the yawl Fad was designed by Edward Burgess for George A. Goddard, with but 6 feet breadth on 24 feet l.w.l., and many yachtsmen were quick to follow the new fashion.

Clapham and the Sharpie

The opening clause of this story calls for a slight correction; the correspondence resulting from Kunhardt's first articles brought out the complete history of the yawl in America, and then there were the Nonpareil sharpies of Thomas Clapham. Of English birth, born in 1839 and coming to America some time in the 50's, Clapham, a man of at least moderate fortune, scorned the attractions of the metropolis and settled on the Housatonic River. Always devoted to yachting, he owned a small sloop, Qui Vive I, in which he cruised to the Vineyard Haven Camp Meeting of 1863. There he met John B. Herreshoff and his brother Nat in a sloop, Kelpie, which John and his father had built for their own use.

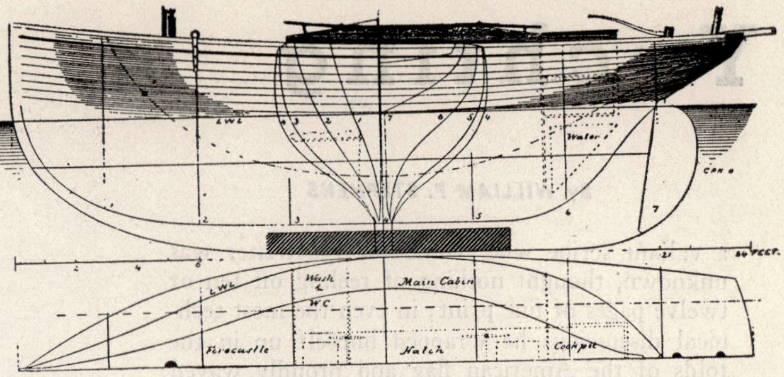

Aneto designed by Henry W. Eaton and built by W. P. Stephens in 1883

A discussion of the merits of their yachts led to a challenge and a race; the sloop Whitewings was in the harbor and her owner, Rutherfurd Stuyvesant, kindly offered her as a stakeboat. The victory of Kelpie was so decisive that Clapham at once placed an order (the first from an outside party) for a second Qui Vive, a centerboard sloop 42 feet 6 inches o.a.; 38 feet 7 inches l.w.l.; 14 feet 2 inches breadth and 3 feet 6 inches draft. Later, shifting his moorings to Hempstead Harbor, he built a large house near Glenwood Landing, but his fortune was materially reduced in the panic of 1873. Always a philosopher, he accepted the change manfully and moved into a small house on the estate. He became interested in the sharpies of the Connecticut shore, and started to develop the type as a yacht.

The oyster fishery which, from colonial days, was a leading industry about New Haven, was originally carried on in canoes cut from the trees which were then abundant. As these trees were cut off, the oystermen replaced them with a crude skiff with a flat bottom and pointed bow which finally developed into a craft some 40 feet long with centerboard and schooner rig without a headsail. Taking up this primitive craft, Clapham developed it further as a yacht, obtaining a patent on his Nonpareil model in which the forward ends of the garboards were turned up to improve the entrance and avoid the pounding incident to the flat bottom. Shifting the forward mast further aft and adding a jib with a small mizzen well aft he had a yawl rig. From the first small craft he built up an extensive business, his larger cabin sharpies running up to 60 feet and even higher, some being shipped to South America.

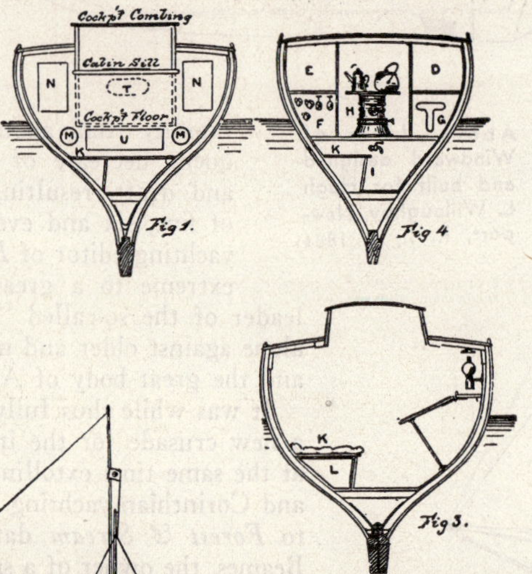

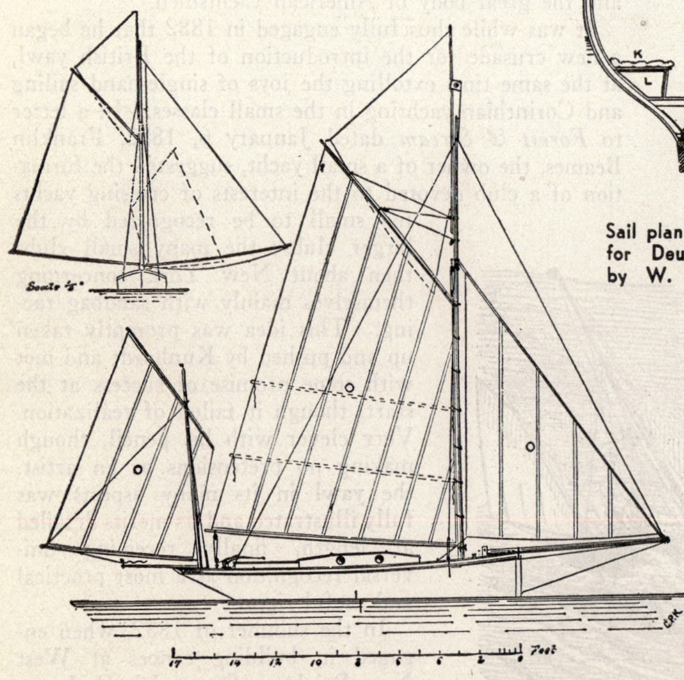

Sail plan and sections for Deuce designed by W. P. Stephens

The Clapham theory of design was simple in the extreme, its two leading principles being that a yacht should sail over the water and not through it; and that all fore-and-aft curves (bow-buttock lines) should be segments of circles of large diameter. His principal tool used in drafting was a flexible batten of white pine drawn into a bow by a string fast at both ends. This bow was used for all the fore-and-aft curves of the bottom and also for the deck line in the half-breadth plan. It was his custom to locate the center of lateral resistance by an inspection of the hull, and the center of effort by a mere eye study of his sail plan. An experienced and skillful sailor, he was able to show his yachts to the best possible advantage, and his ready pen and argumentative disposition made him capable of defending them against all hostile criticism.

The cutter crusade of Kunhardt offered every opportunity to advertise the sharpie; while repudiating all suggestion of such an intention, and claiming that all of his letters were purely a technical discussion of yacht design, he countered every claim for the deep yacht with a counter claim for his sharpie. In such qualities as seagoing ability, ease in a seaway, speed, weatherlines and even accommodation, the sharpie was superior to the cutter.

WITH such an adversary as Kunhardt it was Greek against Greek week by week throughout 1881, 2 and 3, and when I succeeded Kunhardt in the editorial chair I fell heir to all of his adversaries and all of his battles, including Clapham and his sharpies. He was a man of much personal charm, educated, a lover of art, and, as was the case with another opponent of the cutter, Captain Roland F. Coffin, we were good friends personally; but war is war, and some hard words were passed on both sides. Writing under date of August 14, 1883, Clapham said very frankly: "The cutter is all right when in her proper element, as is the sharpie in hers. *I had to make an issue about something in order to bring my boats to the front, or even to get them noticed at all.* I knew the cutter could never become popular here with the majority of so-called yachtsmen, the galoots don't want to go to sea, and you cannot educate them up to that notch." Ten years later, when such yachts as Vigilant, Defender and Columbia came from the Bristol yard, Clapham claimed that all were designed on the same principle as his Nonpareil sharpie.

While the sharpie was essentially a craft of light displacement and light draft, with a large centerboard, no skeg and a balanced rudder, all ballast being inside, at one time Clapham experimented with heavy iron centerplates and metal fins in order to increase the range of stability. In one case he actually did anticipate a very revolutionary development in yachting, the famous (or, as some would have, infamous) double-bilged or double-hulled Dominion designed by G. Herrick Duggan in 1898 for the defense of the Seawanhaka Cup. In the trial races of the challenging club off Oyster Bay there appeared a one-rater, Gold Bug, designed and built by Clapham for the late Clifford D. Mallory. With the deck and topsides of an ordinary yacht she had two projecting hulls or bilges with a tunnel between, the bottom of the main hull being about two inches clear of the water when at rest. The form was very crude, there was a large centerboard and a second centerboard in the rudder. Some comment was passed on this extraordinary nondescript, but her entry was accepted by the race committee as being a legitimate yacht, however, though entered, she did not start; my recollection is that she was ultimately converted to a sinkboat for ducking.

It must be said that Clapham did much to develop yachts of very light draft and to fit them with a simple, light and effective rig. In my many controversies with him I had the advantage, as I started in 1886 with a typewriter (he wrote a very good hand, using a purple pencil) and after a few trials I rigged up a spool of paper holding perhaps a hundred feet, on which I could write by the hour; some of my many opponents in those remote days objected to this as contrary to the rules of journalistic warfare.

The Yawl on the Pacific Coast

DUE to exceptional local conditions and several odd occurrences the yawl rig was established on the Pacific coast many years before it was known about New York and Boston. San Francisco Bay and San Pablo Bay with their tributary waters cover an area of some 500 square miles of inland sailing, with a stretch of 155 miles from North to South. The northwest trade wind, which blows almost every afternoon from April to October, averages 24 miles per hour, with much greater force at certain points. The average depth of these waters necessitates the centerboard type. Most of the early yachts were too small for the schooner rig, and the sloops imported from the Atlantic coast were over-rigged for the weather conditions.

One of my intimate friends in my canoeing days (by correspondence only, as we never met) was Will Brooks, a member of the San Francisco Y. C. and for a time diverted from yachting by the charms of the canoe. According to his story, his father-in-law, Edwin Moody, when a boy of 18 in 1846 in Maine, built a small yawl, Phantom, replacing her in 1849 by Chimera, of the same rig, 41 feet by 14 feet. She was shipped aboard a sailing vessel for San Francisco, but in a spell of bad weather was thrown overboard by the ship's captain and lost. In 1840 a small yawl was brought from England by C. H. Harrison, an Englishman who years later was commodore of the San Francisco Y. C. Owing to our navigation and tariff laws she was not permitted to be launched from the ship which brought her. In 1855 Harrison built a small yawl at San Francisco. About 1867 Brooks owned a small yacht, Petrel, rigged as a periagua, but after reading *The Cruise of the Yawl Rob Roy* shipped a yawl rig designed by Captain Moody. In 1869 he replaced her by a larger yawl of his own design, Sweetheart. In 1874 the yawl Enid was built for Charles Yale, long secretary of the San Francisco Y. C.; she was 30 feet o.a. and 10 feet in breadth.

In 1877 the yawl Frolic, 49 feet o.a.; 16 feet 3 inches breadth and 5 feet 6 inches draft, was built for Commodore Harrison; later two sloops, Sappho and Raven, were converted to yawls. A little later the sloop Startled Fawn, 45 feet 6 inches by 14 feet 8 inches, was changed, and in 1881 the yawl Chiquita was built. Two others were Emerald, built in 1868 as a sloop, and Fleta, 27 feet o.a., built in 1881. In practically all of these yawls the British lug mizzen was discarded in favor of the leg-o'-mutton sail known variously as driver, dandy or jigger.

The bugeye, a local type of fishing boat used on Chesapeake Bay, carried a variety of rigs, mainly schooner and ketch, but occasionally the yawl. None of these, the sharpie, the bugeye or the San Francisco yawl, exerted any influence in the introduction of the rig about New York and Boston; the credit is due solely to the foresight and fighting spirit of one man.

Particulars of Yachts Mentioned Earlier

	Aneto		*Deuce*		*Windward*	
Length, over all.....	24 feet		17 feet		22 feet	
Length, waterline ...	21		14		18	
Breadth, extreme ...	7		5		6	
waterline ...	6	9 inches	4	9 inches	5	9 inches
Draft	4	6	3	3	4	
Freeboard, bow	3		2	1	2	6
least	1	8	1	6	1	9
stern	2	1	1	9	2	
Displacement, long tons	4.75		1.6		3.35	
Keel, pounds	1850.0		750.0		1700.0	
Ballast, inside	2550.0		1000.0		2000.0	
Bowsprit, outboard ..	7 feet		5 feet		7 feet	6 inches
Mainmast, from stem.	5	3	3		4	6
deck to hounds	18		14	3	17	6
deck to truck	25		24	6	25	
Mizzenmast, from stem	5	3	3		4	6
deck to hounds	12	6	8		12	
deck to truck	14		9	6	13	
Main boom	16	6	12	4	15	
gaff	14		10		12	
Mizzen boom	8		7	6	9	
yard	6		7		6	9
Sails, square feet:						
Jib	105		58		105	
Mainsail ...	300		150		230	
Mizzen	47		48		61	
Total Sail Area....	470		256		376	

TRADITIONS AND MEMORIES OF

AMERICAN YACHTING

By WILLIAM P. STEPHENS

Part Fifty-five

THE DEVELOPMENT OF THE SMALL CRUISER

(Continued)

IF the Hibernianism may be permitted, the first yawl which I knew was a cutter; at least, when I first saw her she swung a small triangular "driver" or "dandy," but when I came to know her better and to sail aboard her she was rigged as a cutter. In the fall of 1879 I was informed that my services were no longer required in the shipyard where I had labored since March, so I returned to my home. I had heard that, through the liberality of one of its members, William Whitlock, the New York Canoe Club was housed for the first time in a home of its own on the northeast extremity of Staten Island, a point now occupied by a slip of the ferry from Manhattan. I visited the house, immediately adjacent to that of the Staten Island Rowing Club and sharing its runway and float, and inspected its fleet of canoes. The mooring of the iron sloop Mischief, launched that year, was a little offshore, and inside there lay a yacht such as I never had seen, a miniature yawl with all the curious and complicated rig of such a craft, brought from England in the previous year.

A Londoner by birth, Henry W. Eaton spent his early life in Liverpool and as a boy entered the service of the Liverpool & London & Globe Insurance Company; in 1878 he was sent out to a subordinate position in the New York office, retiring some forty years later as Resident Manager for the United States. His one diversion was yachting and he followed it most devotedly until the last few years of his life. A member of the Staten Island Rowing Club, when I joined the New York Canoe Club in 1880 we were neighbors, and soon became intimate; in that year I built for him Flirt, a catboat ten feet long by five feet breadth; she was housed in the Rowing Club by standing her on her broad transom, and launched for an evening sail when time or inclination made it undesirable to get the larger boat under way. In 1882 I built from Eaton's design the yawl Aneto, and throughout his life we worked together on many yachts.

When in 1893 he built the yawl Audax from a design by John Hyslop it was my task to get out the

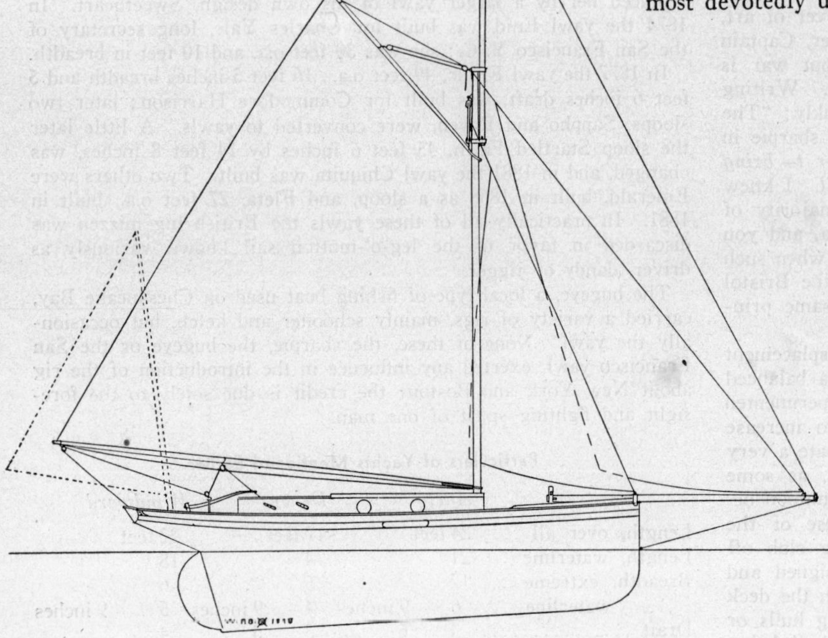

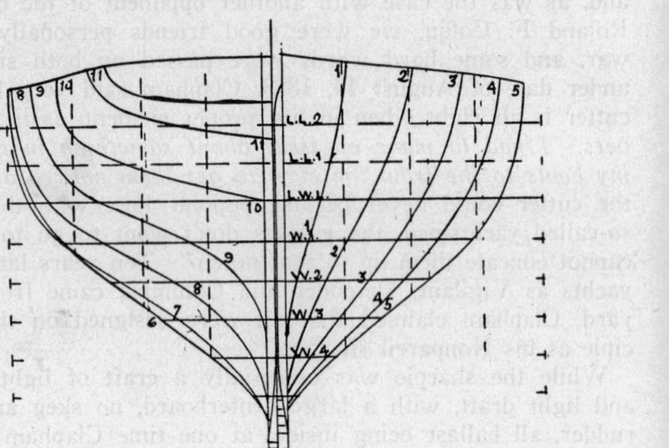

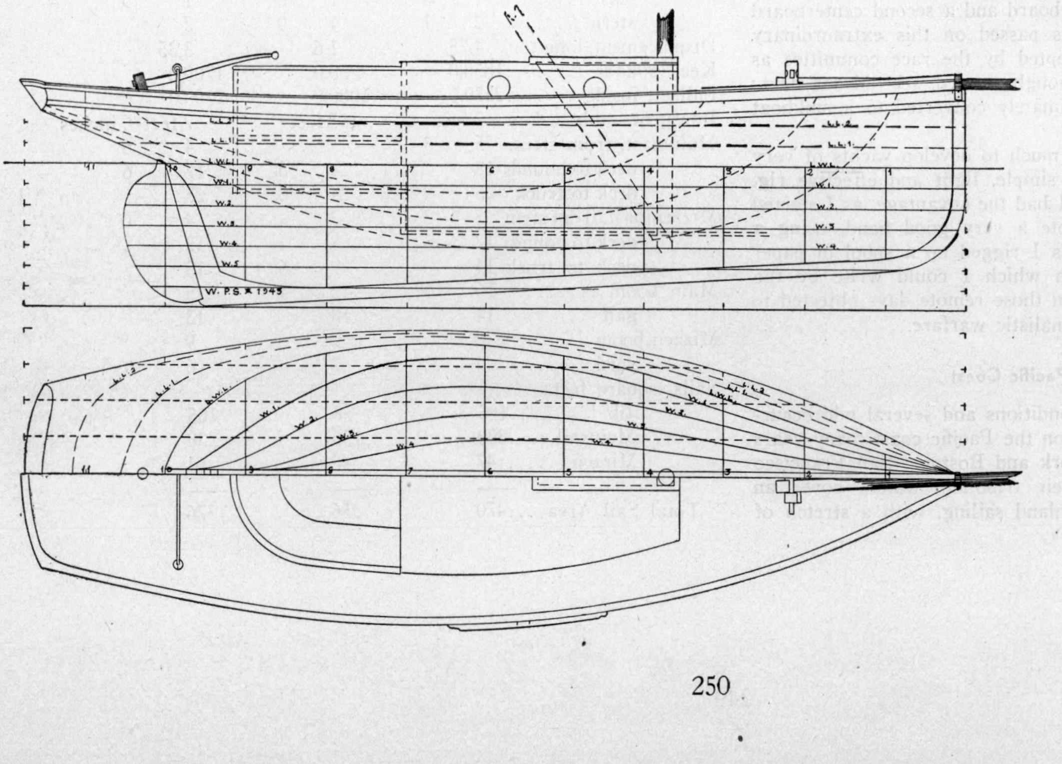

The profile, sail plan and lines for the interesting little English yawl Coquette built about 1868 and redrawn by Mr. Stephens

An old wet plate photograph of Coquette on the beach at the New York Canoe Club in Staten Island, 1879

specifications and superintend the building, when he gave up sail for power in 1910 I designed the raised-deck Florissa, 43 feet l.o.a.; 36 feet l.w.l.; later I made a trade for him for the 56-foot l.w.l. raised-deck Rampant, presumably the second of the type now known as "fifty-fifty," and when he found her too large we made a reverse trade for Florissa; in between these were other yachts purchased, altered and sold through our joint efforts.

Like so many who devoted themselves to yachting throughout life, Eaton began as a disciple of Captain John MacGregor in a narrow canoe, but after a short experience on the Mersey he changed, as told in Part 52, to a slightly larger craft, 15 by 4 feet 1 inch, in which he made a trip across the Irish Sea, 60 miles of open water. In 1878 his official duties took him to Weston super Mare, a little port in Somersetshire on the Bristol Channel. A young man, the owner of a small yacht, spent the summer here, he met another young man with nautical tastes who sailed with him, and also brought his fiance. At the end of the summer the owner of the yacht left suddenly, accompanied by the lady and leaving the yacht and sundry debts; the yacht was sold at marshal's sale and purchased by Eaton. When he was transferred to the New York office about this time he brought the yacht with him and found a home on Staten Island, then the most attractive suburb of New York, the home of the New York Y. C., the Seawanhaka C. Y. C., and many yacht, rowing and canoe clubs, all long since driven out by the advance of civilization. Joining the Rowing Club as the nearest to his home, he found a mooring near it for—

Coquette

The little craft is interesting from several points of view; in the first place, she is much more of a ship in form than those of McMullen, MacGregor and Middleton, she has a completely enclosed cabin, and a much superior rig. The form, with the straight keel, drag, V section and fine entrance, is suggestive of such old cutters as Mosquito and Volante; the finish, even to the square counter and trailboard, indicates the work of a skilled shipwright and not a mere boatbuilder. I had the same impression in looking over Commander E. G. Martin's Jolie Brise when she first visited us in 1926; she too was, in form and build, the work of a passing generation of shipwrights entirely apart from the

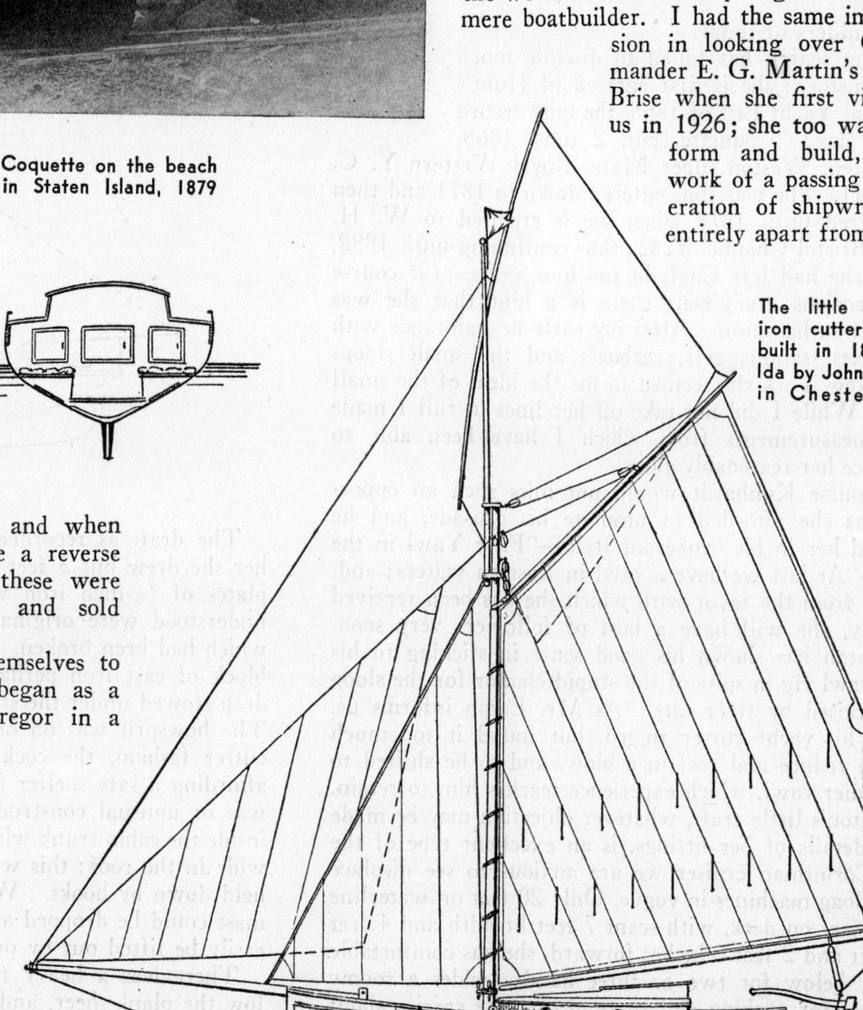

The little 18-foot iron cutter Elvira built in 1887 as Ida by John Roach in Chester, Pa.

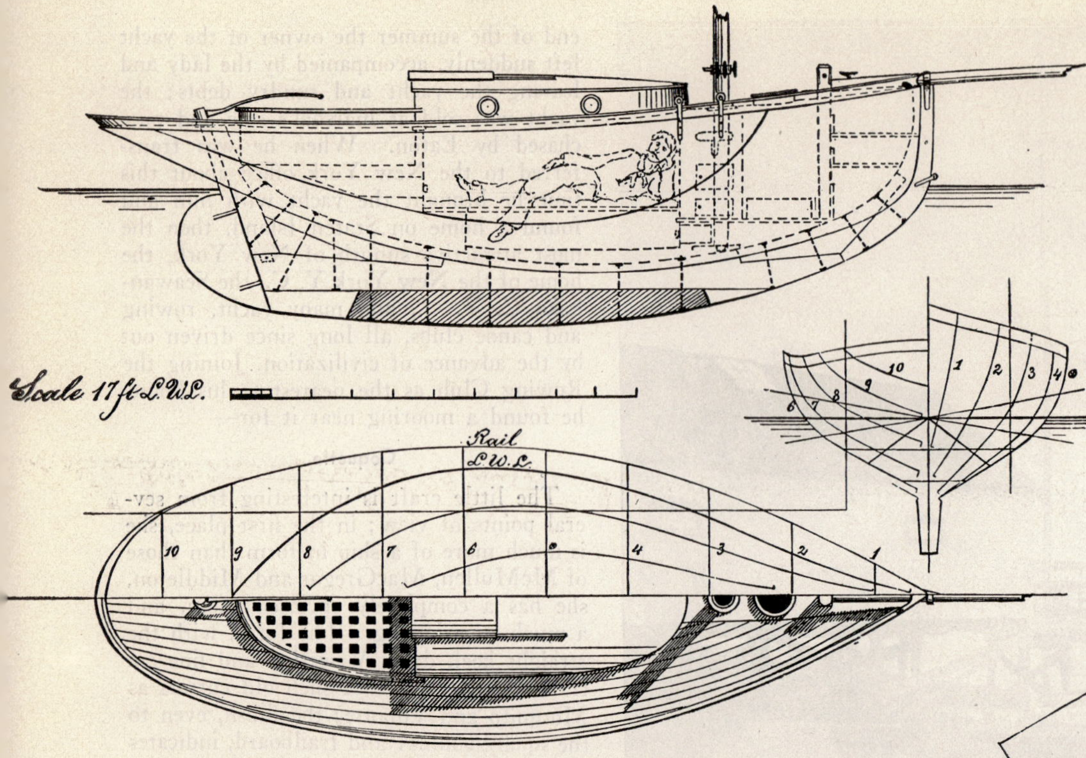

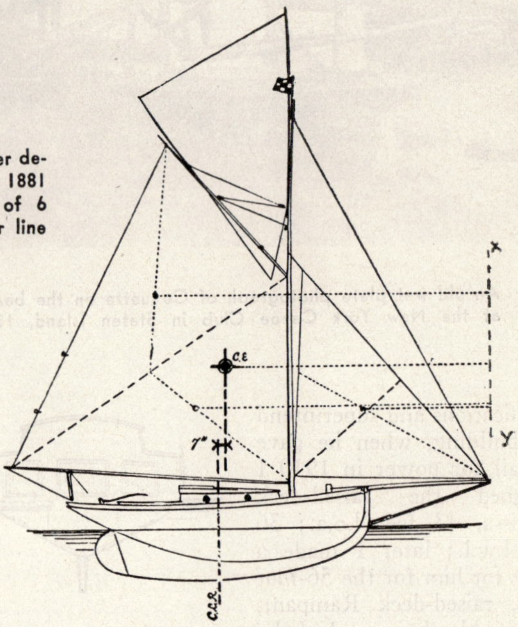

A single handed cruiser design by Kunhardt in 1881 which had a beam of 6 feet on 17 feet water line

yacht builders of today.

A long search has failed to disclose much of her history; she is first entered in Hunt's Universal Yacht List of 1868, the only record of that day; "Coquette, cut, 2 tons, 1868, H. Britten, Weston super Mare, Royal Western Y. C. (Ireland). She was thus entered down to 1871 and then disappeared until 1878 when she is credited to W. H. Eaton, Bristol Channel Y. C., thus continuing until 1882, though she had left England for four years. Of course no dimensions are given; there is a hint that she was built at Southampton. After my early acquaintance with sneakboxes, sandbaggers, catboats and the small sloops about New York she seemed to me the ideal of the small yacht. While I did not take off her lines in full I made many measurements from which I have been able to reproduce her reasonably close.

Of course Kunhardt would not miss such an opportunity as she afforded to promote his crusade, and he exploited her in his exuberant style—"First Yawl in the East"—"At last we have a yawl in Eastern waters; and, judging from the favor with which she has been received by many, she will have a host of followers very soon. Mr. Eaton has shown his good sense in sticking to his handy yawl rig in spite of the stupid clamor for the sloop or cat raised by river tars. As Mr. Eaton informs us, he had his yacht cutter rigged, but found it too much work to reduce and reef in a blow, and so he shifted to the handier yawl, which experience teaches him to retain. Mr. Eaton's little craft, whatever objection may be made to the details of her fittings, is an excellent type of the small Corinthian cruiser we are anxious to see displace the sandbag machines in vogue. Only 20 feet on waterline and 23 feet on deck, with scant 7 feet breadth and 4 feet draft aft and 2 feet 6 inches forward, she has comfortable stowage below for two or three hands besides a roomy forecastle for cooking and spare gear. She carries about 1½ tons of iron ballast, about half of which is on her keel. On deck her gangways and quarter are clear, the house being kept narrow and low so as not to interfere with working ship, while her cockpit is roomy enough for four. All this in a yacht which is only the length of a small catboat, and which can be built for less than $500.00. A little ship instead of a worthless sailing machine. A safe, handy, able little cruiser and not a man-trap of an open sandbag flinger."

The fact seems to be that she had a dual rig, two main booms and two mainsails, for either yawl or cutter rig; as Eaton's sailing was mainly about the Upper Bay of an evening and as far as Sandy Hook over the week-end, he must have chosen the cutter rig in 1880, and I knew her for some years later under it.

The draft as recorded was 4 feet, but when I knew her she drew but 3 feet 6 inches; in her bilge were two plates of ¼-inch iron with countersunk holes which I understood were originally made to patch an iron keel which had been broken. Part of her inside ballast was a block of cast iron perhaps a foot square and six inches deep stowed under the steps at the after end of the cabin. The bowsprit was on one side of the stemhead, in true cutter fashion, the cockpit was deep and non-draining, affording a safe shelter in bad weather. The tabernacle was of unusual construction, the mast was stepped just inside the cabin trunk with a long opening about six inches wide in the roof; this was covered by a removable hatch held down by hooks. When this hatch was removed the mast could be dropped aft to such an angle that it might easily be lifted out by one or two men on the cabin top.

There was a heavy rubbing-strip along each side below the plank-sheer, and just abaft the channels this was enlarged into a chock about two feet long with a mortice for a leg, two of which were carried in the bilge. When taking the ground for a scrub, or in case of accident, a tenon on each leg was shipped in its mortice to hold her upright. I think that each leg shipped in a piece of plank, perhaps eight inches square, to give it a bearing in soft ground. I cannot remember the amount of ballast, but it must have been heavy to carry the very long topmast. The housing of this topmast was a job in itself, even in still water; I think that it was on the eve of Decoration Day 1880 that I watched a man aloft for a long time, with another on deck handling the heel rope, preparing for a start for the Hook over the holiday. I still have a spare tiller, 3 feet 9 inches long. After Eaton sold her she was re-christened and her identity destroyed under the commonplace name of Teal, and I finally lost track of her.

A Single-Hand Cruiser

To help the good work Kunhardt, in the issues of February 17-24, 1881, presented a design of his own; down to the end of 1880 even the smaller of the racing cutters had hardly reached the proportion of five beams to length, and those of the cruising type were much wider. The proportion in this case—six feet breadth to seventeen feet l.w.l., was even less than three beams; five years later he would have made it less than five feet extreme breadth and almost five feet draft for the same l.w.l. At the same time he chose the sloop rig instead of cutter or yawl. The dimensions were:—

Length, over all	20 feet
waterline	17 feet
Breadth, extreme	7 feet
waterline	6 feet
Freeboard, least	1 foot 4 inches
Depth, deck to rabbet	3 feet 5 inches
Draft	3 feet 3 inches
Headroom	3 feet 10 inches
Displacement—long tons	2
Ballast—keel pounds	1000
inside pounds	500
Mainsail—square feet	261
Jib " "	87
Topsail " "	80
Total " "	328

For the benefit of those proposing to build, or even in the study of design, the various processes were described in detail:—the meaning of the plans, the nature and use of the curve of areas of displacement, then a new development in naval architecture, the scantlings, construction, fittings and equipment. In the lack of such works on design as are now readily available to the novice such articles as this did much to stimulate the interest in the small cruiser and the method of its production.

A Sheet-Iron Cruiser

ANOTHER interesting little craft, of which very little is known, was built at the shipyard of John Roach, in Chester, Pa. in 1887,, though I heard nothing of her when in the yard the following year. She is described as built of sheet-iron, lapstrake, and similar to a lifeboat, with air tanks in each end, but decked and with a cabin. Her original rig was two-masted, presumably schooner, but was later changed to cutter, as in the plan. Her framing included wood knees and wood clamps and stringers. Her dimensions were:—

Length, over all	18 feet
waterline	17 feet 6 inches
Breadth	6 feet 9 inches
Draft	2 feet 10 inches
Displacement—long tons	1.85
Ballast, keel—lead pounds	500
inside—iron pounds	1800
Sails, lower—square feet	275

Under her original name of Ida after a trial trip on Chesapeake Bay she started for Florida, with her owner and a boy as crew, calling at the St. Johns River and the Florida Keys, then at Brazos Santiago and back to the St. Johns River, then in 1879 up the coast to Newport. Under a new owner her original name, Ida, was changed to Elvira and she was rigged as shown.

Yacht Designing as a Profession

WHILE until compartively recent years the production of craft of all classes, but especially such as fishing boats, pilot boats and yachts, was in the hands of rule-o-thumb builders working from intuition, there were some who today would be fairly entitled to write N. A. after their name. Such builders as George Steers, Donald McKay and John W. Griffiths in this country and Michael Ratsey, John Harvey, Will Fife 2d., and Camper & Nicholson in Britain were familiar with the theory and practice of naval design, and employed it in their daily work as builders. The recognition of design as a profession, distinct from the craft of building, came about in yachting in the period of which we are writing. In 1875 our great American designer, A. Cary Smith, was busy in the old Studio Building, 51 West 10th Street (still standing) with yacht portraiture on large canvasses; with the designing of the iron sloop Mischief. In 1879 he abandoned his easel, pallet and brushes for the drafting board, splines and weights of the naval architect.

In Scotland young Will Fife, of the third generation, grounded in the craft of building in his father's yard, was studying the science of design preparatory to turning out many of the most beautiful as well as the fastest yachts of their day. Another young Scotchman, coming from private life, George Lenox Watson, was studying for the hardly recognized profession of yacht designing. A young house architect, J. Beaver Webb, was taking time from his chosen profession to sail the racing yachts of the old-time builders preparatory to making a name for himself as the designer of many fast sailing yachts and some of the largest steam yachts. Among those interested in this fascinating pursuit on the amateur side were Robert Center, Edward Burgess, Henry Bryant and a host of aspiring younger men.

An important factor in the promotion of the study of design was the writing of Dixon Kemp, originally a house architect by profession but tempted from this work by the fascination of sailing and later of yacht designing. His sailing and reporting of yacht races about Cowes, at first in an amateur way, led to his editorship of *The Field,* the authorship of the quarto volume "Yacht Designing" in 1875, and the later eight editions of "Yacht & Boat Sailing" and the three editions of "Yacht Architecture."

The genesis of amateur yacht design, however, may be traced back still further to Philip R. Marett, an Englishman who is far less known to his countrymen today than he deserves. In 1856 he began a series of articles in *Bell's Life in London,* a journal devoted to all forms of sport, the title when later published in book form being *Yachts and Yacht Building, being a Treatise on the Construction of Yachts and Matters relating to Yachting.* In his introduction he notes the imperfect knowledge of the theory of naval architecture on the part of most builders, the absence of full plans submitted to an owner before building, and the general indifference on the part of owners. As a remedy for such conditions he gives in detail the method of drafting, the calculations, and all operations necessary for the completion of the design.

As already told, it was the first edition of this book, purchased by Robert Center in London in 1867, which led to his design of the cutter Vindex and opened a new career for A. Cary Smith. The second edition, of 1872, came into my hands by chance at the time that my interest in boat building was first aroused, and I feel a deep sense of gratitude to the author. Fortunately for the aspiring amateur, we have progressed so far in the last three score and ten years that even a yachtsman who does not care to go so far as to design his own craft may readily familiarize himself with such basic principles of design as will enable him to select the yacht best suited to his needs and to handle her to the best possible advantage.

Part Fifty-six

TRADITIONS AND MEMORIES OF AMERICAN YACHTING

Sketch of an open Canadian Canoe, 16 to 18 feet, by H. K. Wicksteed. The use of oars in such canoes was exceptional. In running rapids the bow man rowed

By WILLIAM P. STEPHENS

THE DEVELOPMENT OF THE SMALL CRUISER

(Continued)

At its inception *Forest & Stream* set out to cover the whole field of outdoor sports, archery, athletics, baseball, cricket, croquet, dogs, fish, guns, horses, pedestrianism (then, in the days of Weston, a popular recreation with gentlemen), the turf; and, on the aquatic side, boating, canoeing, rowing and yachting. As the paper progressed its field became more restricted, the gun, in the field and over the traps (the manly sport of live-pigeon shooting not being prohibited by law), the dog, in the field and on the bench; fishing in all its forms, western life and exploration. The ownership of the paper was in the hands of landlubbers with a personal interest in these subjects, and what was left of the aquatic side—canoeing and yachting—received merely perfunctory recognition. With the installation of a permanent Yachting Editor in the person of C. P. Kunhardt there came a change, and within a few years his progressive and aggressive personality made the journal a recognized authority in yachting and a dangerous competitor to much older publication.

The crusade which Kunhardt inaugurated in the late seventies was most comprehensive in scope: first, non-capsizability, involving a material decrease in breadth from existing models with a corresponding increase in depth and draft, and ballast below the keel; second, for sailing outside of the North River, New York Bay and Long Island Sound, the cutter or yawl in place of the sloop rig; third, the yacht owner was urged to qualify himself to command his yacht, to handle the wheel, and also to study the art of designing to such an extent as would enable him to select the best possible craft for his special use. Going further, there was a call for Corinthian in place of professional crews whenever possible, for the use of small yachts in offshore cruising.

That such a campaign was necessary was proven by the immediate response and the heated controversy which followed; letters on both sides from "Grampus," "Corinthian," "Open Sea," "Podgers," "G. M," "T. C.," "Halliard," "Lubber," "Frisco" and "Bobstay," only a few being courageous enough to sign their names. In the issue of November 14, 1878, there appeared a letter on yacht measurement over the nom de plume of "Martin Gale," and this was followed on January 30, 1879, by a proposed design for a small cruiser. The little which is known of this writer is that his name was Maxwell Wrigley, he was a young relative of J. Rogers Maxwell, sailing in the Corinthian crew of the schooner Peerless, and that his writing ended suddenly with his death a year or so later. He evidently was keenly interested in

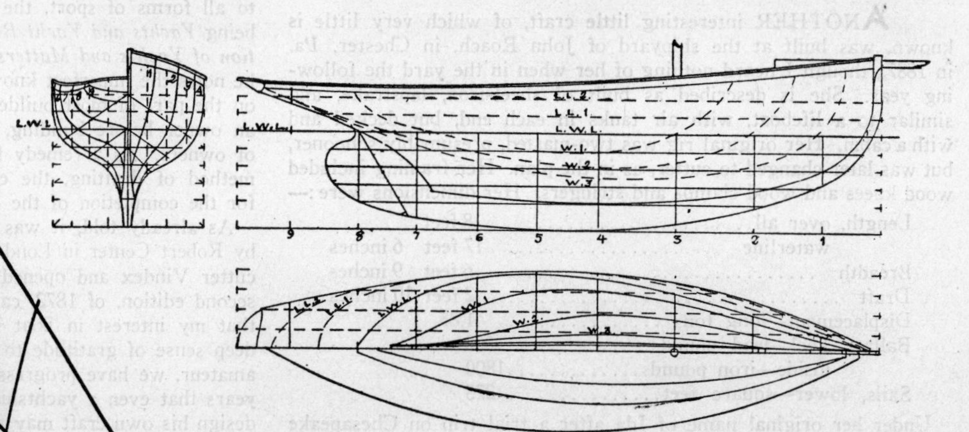

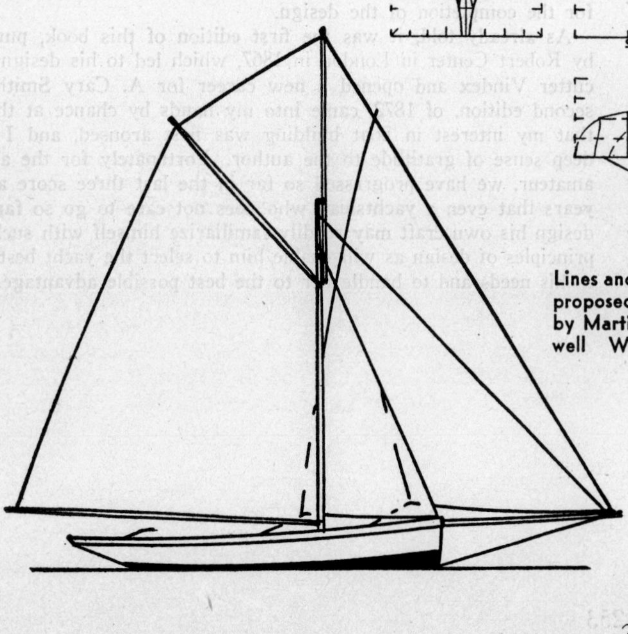

Lines and sail plan of a proposed small cruiser by Martin Dale (Maxwell Wrigley) 1878

yachting, and cognizant of existing conditions. The design speaks for itself in its moderate proportions, its fair and well balanced form, and—for an amateur—the character of the draftsmanship in those dark ages of yacht designing.

The design is described as suggested by the well known English Itchen boats; though this type, by the way, was characterized by a plumb square transom in place of an overhanging stern. The dimensions were:

Lines and sail plan of the keel cruising yawl Sylvia designed by Henry K. Wicksteed in 1888

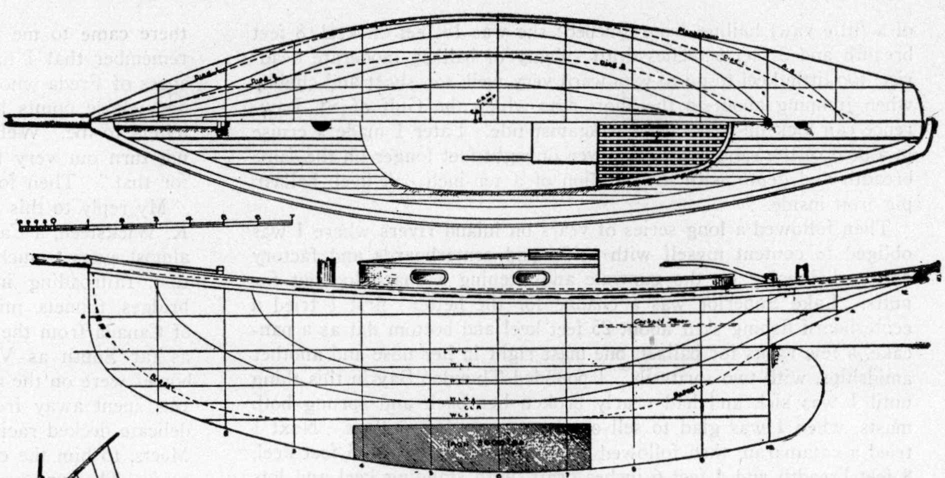

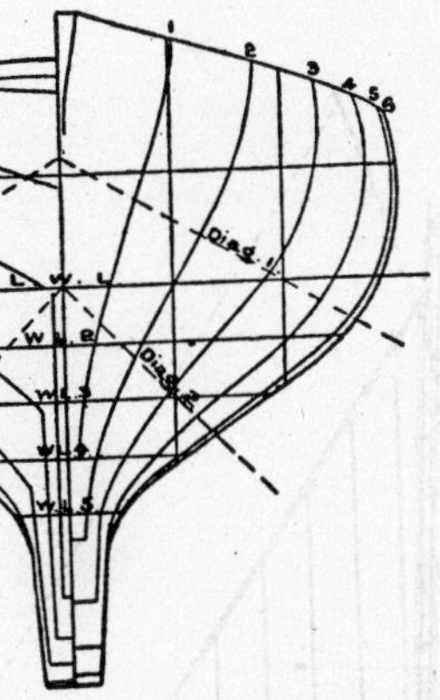

l.o.a., 37 feet; l.w.l., 30 feet; breadth, 9 feet; draft, 5 feet 6 inches. The displacement was 9 tons and the lead keel was of four tons. The first criticism came from "Grampus," to the effect that it was not possible to hang four tons of lead on the keel as shown, and that if it were she would bury herself every time she hit a heavy sea. A general comparison was also made as to width of floor, headroom, seagoing qualities, etc., as compared with the centerboard type. His reply proved that "Martin Gale" was fully capable of defending himself, explaining that the keel was sided eight inches at the rabbet and four inches on the bottom, and answering the other objections.

In connection with the current discussion another writer, "Open Sea," described his search for perfection and how it was completely realized in the building at Essex, Mass., of a yacht on the model of a fishing schooner which proved to be all that one could ask in speed, room, comfort, and ease in rough water. While "Open Sea" fails to give dimensions, he describes the mainmast as of 18 inches diameter at the heel, 12 inches at the head, and 73 feet 6 inches in length, so she must have been a craft of some size. The cost of hull and spars, built in the most perfect manner, was $2,800; of the yacht complete, $5,000; and she proved her speed in racing with other yachts. A diligent search of the yacht lists just prior to 1880 fails to disclose any large schooner recently built at Essex, so we are left in ignorance as to the identity of the writer. His statement as to speed was flatly contradicted by other writers and the long controversy brought out the following effusion:

Ode to my friend "Open Sea"

There was a young man of Swampscott,
Who built a fast fisherman's yacht.
She went such a pace, when she sailed in a race,
That she delighted all hands in Swampscott.

New York, April 18, 1879. (Signed) R. CENTER.

It is tantalizing today to realize that had I been as deeply interested in the matter then as I am today, I might have known the identities of all these writers; Bob Center could and would have told me.

Throughout the racing season the growing numbers of "regattas" as they really were, and the local races, were reported at length, as far as space permitted. Kunhardt was a ready and voluminous writer and could have filled every issue of the paper. It happened, however, that with no one else in the outfit interested in yachting, if there came a big live-pigeon match, a dog show or a line-casting tournament, yachting was given the deep six for the week, this continuing throughout my years. As soon as the season's winners were tabulated and the racing reviewed the controversy was renewed, continuing until well into the spring. Two points were finally settled, small cruisers were built in increasing numbers, and the practice of single-hand sailing was accepted as a matter of course. By degrees the main points at issue settled down to cutters vs. sloop, and Corinthian vs. professional.

When I succeeded Kunhardt in May, 1884, he gave me two items of advice, only one of which I followed. "If you hear anything, print it; if it is true it is news, if it is not true you can correct it next week, and that is news." "Reply to every letter which you receive." This latter injunction I followed rigidly, though still restricted to the pen for both correspondence and copy, and I rapidly built up a very extensive system of correspondence with yachtsmen and canoeists on both sides of the Atlantic. When I gave up the pen for the new typewriter, in 1886, the first thing I did was to build a foot pedal to operate the shift-key, then I rigged over the roller two standards, carrying a spool of paper and an empty spool. Thus equipped, I could write for a week without stopping to put a sheet in the machine. In the frequent controversies this placed my adversaries under a serious handicap in trying to reply with a pen to a yard or so of paper. The one disadvantage was that manifording was impossible, so that in referring today to old files my replies are missing.

Henry K. Wicksteed

Among the correspondents whom I inherited from Kunhardt was one "H. K. W.", who had written him from Port Arthur, Canada in March 1884 describing his experiences: "About six years ago (1878) I was skipper of a little yawl hailing from Quebec; she was 18 feet on keel, 8 feet breadth and 3 feet 6 inches draft; plenty of ballast, moderate deadrise, too little keel to go to windward very well, too short and chubby when jumping about in the short seas which the Gulf of St. Lawrence can kick up when wind is against tide. Later I made a cruise in a boat of the same type, but seven or eight feet longer on the same breadth and depth with the addition of a ten-inch oak keel, ballast, pig iron inside.

Then followed a long series of years on inland rivers where I was obliged to content myself with skiffs and centerboards and factory cotton, balancing on the gunwale and keeping a sharp lookout for puffs. Lake Superior was a change for the better; first I tried a centerboard fishing skiff about 25 feet keel and bottom flat as a pancake, a few rocks for ballast, one mast right in her nose and another amidships, with two spritsails. I pounded Thunder Bay in this thing until I was sick and had nearly broken her back and sprung both masts, when I was glad to sell out for twenty-five dollars. Next I tried a catamaran, then followed a good honest yawl of 25 feet keel, 8 feet breadth and 4 feet 6 inches draft, with standing keel and lots of ballast, built by a friend and myself."

"The next attempt was a rough and ready yawl 20 feet keel, 5 feet breadth and 4 feet 9 inches draft, with some ballast hitched on keel and any amount inside. This little hooker, with bottom coated with coal tar, bolt heads and rivets sticking out all over, ballast of blacksmith's scrap and sand, berthed three of us on a three-weeks cruise of 500 miles on Lake Superior; her faults were that she was too short, and 'jumped short' as the fishermen say, and her accommodation was rather meager. For the past two summers I have been

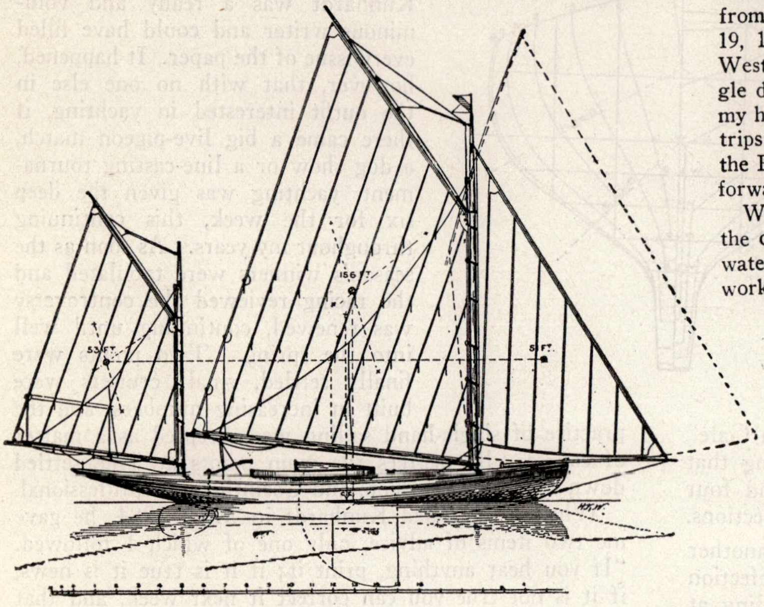

The centerboard cruising yawl Myra and her sail plan, designed in 1892 by Henry K. Wicksteed

knocking about the coast and incidentally have done a lot of boat traveling, long trips in every month from early in May to late in January, and have had a nerve-trying time in wretched flat-bottomed clinker-built boats. All this, and the prospect of more traveling next summer has moved me to design Freda, a narrow yawl or ketch-rigged yacht of 29 feet waterline, 6 feet 4 inches breadth, and 5,000 pounds on the keel." In May 1885 there came to me from Ottawa a letter from the same writer: "I remember that I had promised to send an account of the performances of Freda whose lines I sent to Mr. Kunhardt over a year ago, and whose points he was kind enough to discuss at length in two letters to me. Well, he was nearly right on every point; Freda did not turn out very fast, in fact she was too much of a compromise for that." Then followed a discussion of her good and bad points.

My reply to this letter disclosed that "H. K. W." stood for Henry K. Wicksteed, a Canadian, a civil engineer, and by practice covering almost every branch of that profession—original survey and exploration, railroading in original location, construction and operation, bridges, tunnels, mining. The locale of his life work covered most of Canada from the far North West to Labrador and extended even as far South as Venezuela and the Caribbean Sea. His various homes were on the north shore of Lake Ontario, but much of his life was spent away from them. As a canoeist he had no use for the delicate decked racing machines with which we visited the A. C. A. Meets, to him the canoe was one of the most important tools of his craft. The type was the open Canadian canoe of 16 to 18 feet, light enough to be packed on the head over a trail, with displacement to carry two men with their food and duffle on long trips, with buoyancy and maneuverability to negotiate swift currents and swirling rapids.

His long experience led him to designing such of these canoes as were best suited to his work. Yachting in small craft was his major passion, and when he came out of the woods after three or four months on small streams and rivers he had the lines of a new cruiser either in his head ready to transfer to the drafting board, or already completed for the builder. A characteristic letter came from Mattama, in the Hudson Bay territory, under date of October 19, 1893: "I have had a long three-months trip in the wilderness West of the Upper Ottawa, and I think that I have not passed a single day except one or two Sundays without having had a paddle in my hands." Again, from Toronto, January 3, 1918: "I have had four trips to Venezuela and have just returned from the West, out near the Rockies, where I have been operating a coal mine.—I am looking forward to the next job, which I think will be in Labrador.

Wicksteed's designing covered a wide range of small craft, from the canoes just mentioned up to sturdy keel yawls of 25 to 30 feet waterline. The designs here reproduced are merely samples of his work; in addition to the numerous small craft designed for his personal use he did outside work on larger craft, though never following designing as a profession. Myra was described as good for rough and tumble qualities in open water, she was too small for a permanent cabin; but in Vagabond, a somewhat later design, the dinghy was planned to form a roof over a part of the cockpit. Her dimensions were: l. o. a., 22 feet; l. w. l., 16 feet; breadth, 4 feet 9 inches; freeboard, bow, 1 foot 9 inches, least, 11 inches, stern, 1 foot 6 inches; displacement, 923 pounds, centerboard, 250 pounds; sail area, 260 square feet. The spinnaker was a lug sail set on a yard to give hoist and area. (*Continued on page* 260)

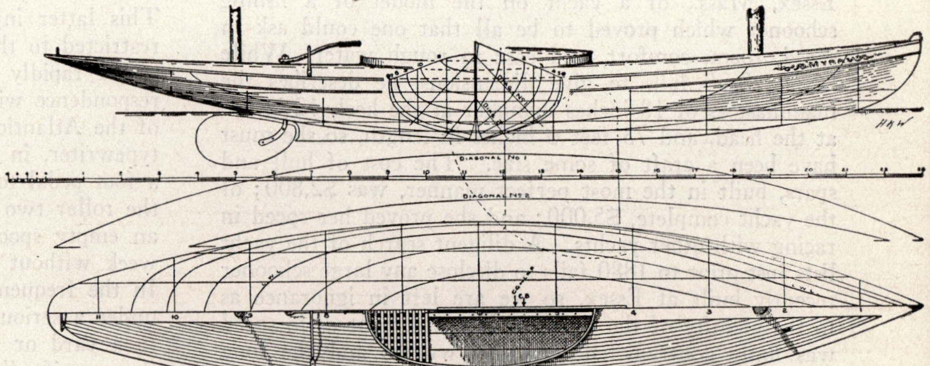

TRADITIONS AND MEMORIES OF

American Yachting

Part Fifty-Seven

By WILLIAM P. STEPHENS

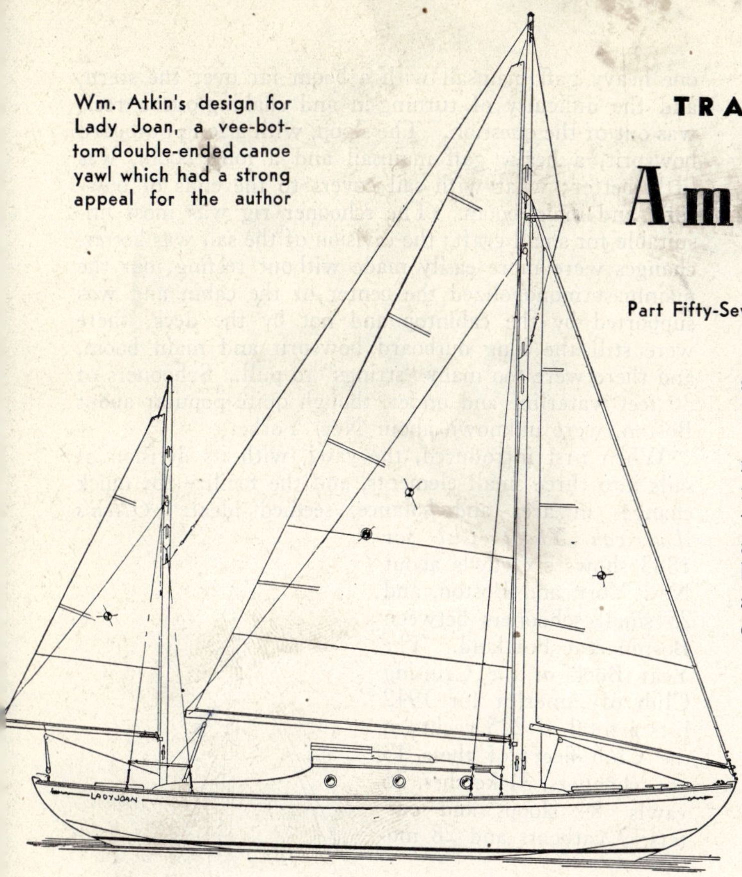

Wm. Atkin's design for Lady Joan, a vee-bottom double-ended canoe yawl which had a strong appeal for the author

THE DEVELOPMENT OF THE SINGLE-HAND CRUISER

IN considering the single-hander of tomorrow we may assume that whether of individual or one-design class, she will be designed to meet the requirements of her owner. Whatever may be achieved by the conversion of out-classed racing craft, such as the 6-meter, the chances are strongly against such a course. The two types of hull now most in use are the conventional yacht form and the Colin Archer or Norwegian. The former is the better known in this country and is well adapted to Long Island Sound and the Atlantic coast. An example of this type may be seen in Lady Joan, designed by William Atkin and illustrated in MoToR BoatinG for July 1942. Due to my first love, the canoe, I have always been interested in her sisters, the canoe-yawl and canoe-yacht, and this design appealed strongly to me, except for the fact that she was a V-bottom craft.

I confess to a prejudice against the V-bottom type, as I believe it to be inferior to the normal S-section type. It has one advantage in that anyone familiar with carpenter's tools and who can frame, sheath and shingle a house can build a very good V-bottom yacht, as was proved by Harry Pigeon in his Islander. In building a yacht of S section there are required a steambox, timber block, clamps and the whole outfit of a boatshop plus the skill acquired only by an apprenticeship to the trade. I have urged Mr. Atkin to give us another Lady Joan with the same sheer plan and sail plan but an S section, but thus far he has not done so.

For purposes of illustration I have made the attempt myself, as shown in the accompanying design. I am not fully satisfied with the result. Anyone desiring to build would go to the original designer who would turn out a better boat; but this serves to illustrate the difference between the normal and the Norwegian types. The characteristics of the former are an easy form of moderate draft, and overhangs both forward and aft. The advantage of the overhangs is a certain amount of lifting power in the ends, a long easy side when heeled, and the elimination of both bowsprit and boomkin. As to the restrictions on overhang so frequently urged, the plain fact is that while a moderate amount of overhang at each end is beneficial, and a great aid to appearance, if carried to excess it penalizes itself.

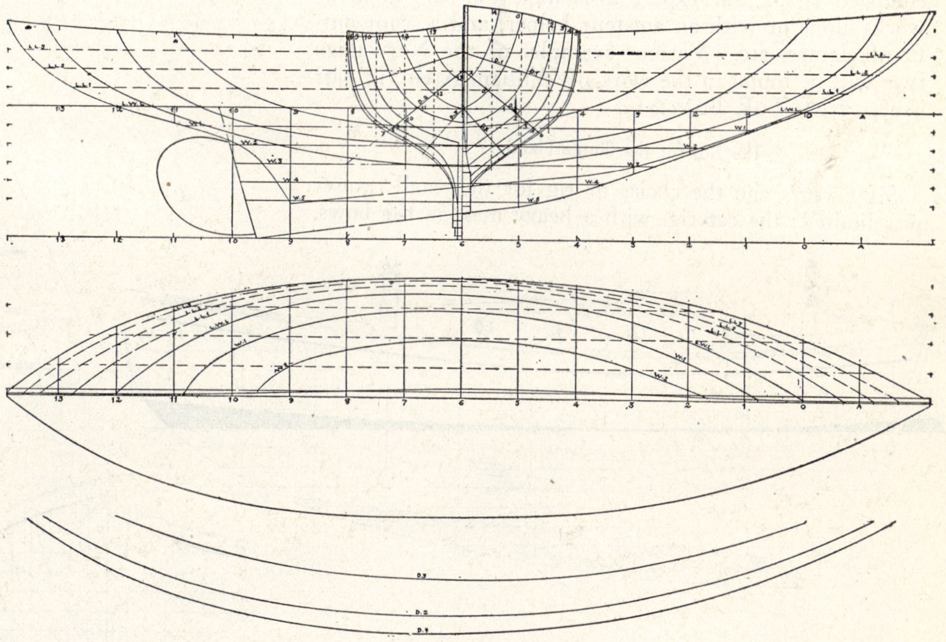

A set of lines for a similar boat of round bottom type worked up by the author for illustration

The Norwegian type is characterized by a full, round form with more breadth than the other, and very short overhangs. The added breadth, with the depth, give excellent accommodation in a small hull. The type is very popular in England and the Scandinavian nations, and seems well suited to the rough waters and short sharp seas. The leading proponent of the type is Dr. T. Harrison Butler, an Englishman, noted in private life as an expert ophthalmic surgeon, but among yachtsmen as a very clever amateur designer and a life-long cruiser in small craft. Many of his designs, all noted for symmetry of form as well as the careful detail in planning the interior, have been published in the English yachting journals. It must be admitted that his interior plans show about the maximum amount of accommodation, and in practicable shape, that can be compressed into a waterline length of 18 to 22 feet.

A good example of his work is seen in Zyklon, but what is still more interesting is the design of Prima, by his pupil and daughter, Miss Butler. All of his recent designs are made in conformity with the system of metacentric shelf balance devised by Admiral Alfred Turner, R. N. As one of his diversions is the reading, in the original Greek, of the descriptions of primitive Egyptian craft as recorded by Herodotus, many of Dr. Butler's yachts bear Greek names: Omicron, Omega, etc.

When it comes to the question of construction, partisans are found for both types; and this is important when we consider the amateur builder. There is a widely held idea that longer overhangs mean added cost; but this is not necessarily correct. The cost of material is negligible; the difference of say three or four feet in the upper strakes of the planking and in the decking. This may easily be more than offset by the lessened labor due to long flowing curves. On the side of the Norwegian type Dr. Butler urges the outboard rudder, readily accessible in case of damage; with the added cost of construction of the rudder trunk and the liability to dry-rot. There is an advantage here, but of no great amount, and against it we have the obvious difficulty of planking the full round form. With the professional builder this is a small matter; he has experience and practice, a fully equipped shop, and expert assistance, but the amateur works alone or with an amateur helper, and a scant outfit of clamps, etc. Various examples of the Norwegian type will be found in the work of William Atkin, in past issues of MoToR BoatinG.

The Rig for the Single-Hander?

Sixty years ago the choice of rig for the small cruiser was limited: the cat rig, with a heavy mast in the bows, one heavy gaff mainsail with a boom far over the stern, and the difficulty of turning-in and shaking-out a reef, was out of the question. The sloop, with a long outboard bowsprit, a heavy gaff mainsail and a long boom, was little better; what with sail covers to the ends of bowsprit and main boom. The schooner rig was most unsuitable for small craft; the division of the sail was better, changes were more easily made without reefing, but the mainmast monopolized the center of the cabin and was supported by the cabintop and not by the deck, there were still the long outboard bowsprit and main boom, and there were too many "strings" to pull. Schooners of 30 feet waterline and under, though quite popular about Boston, were unknown about New York.

When first introduced, the yawl, with its division of sails into three small elements, and the facility for quick changes in area and balance, seemed ideal. *Olsen's American Yacht List* for 1883 shows six yawls about New York and Boston, and 25 small schooners between Boston and Portland. The Year Book of the Cruising Club of America for 1942 lists a total of 225 yachts in the Club fleet; of these 43 are schooners, 31 ketches, 36 yawls, 84 sloops and cutters, 3 catboats and 28 mo-

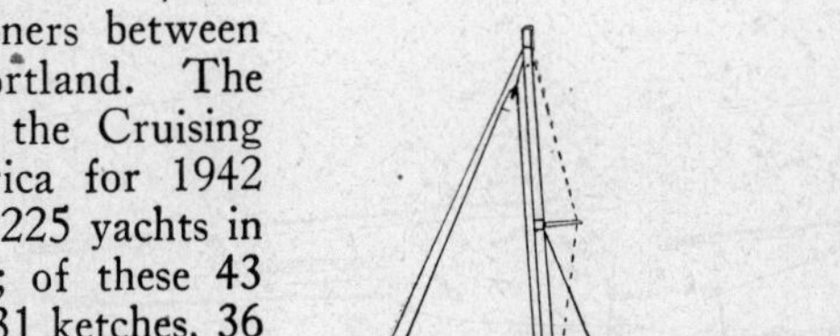

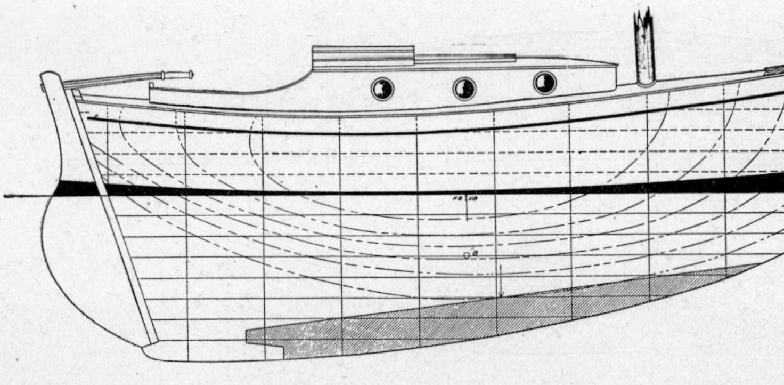

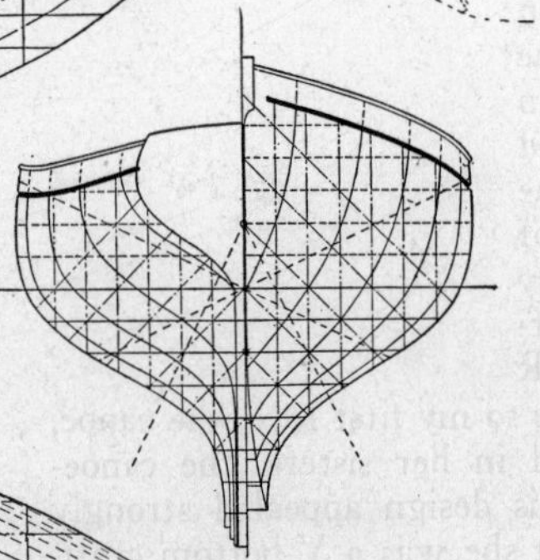

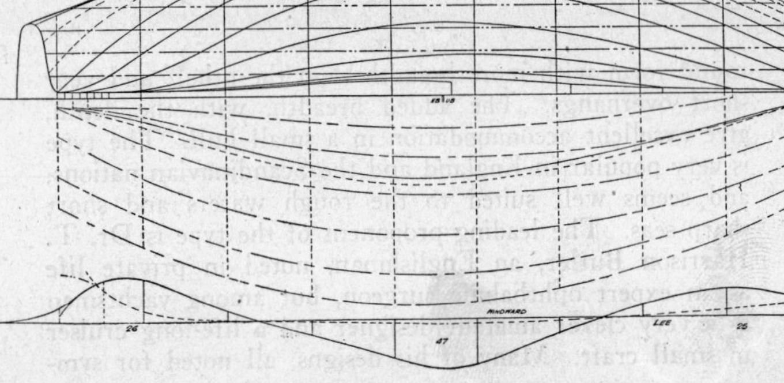

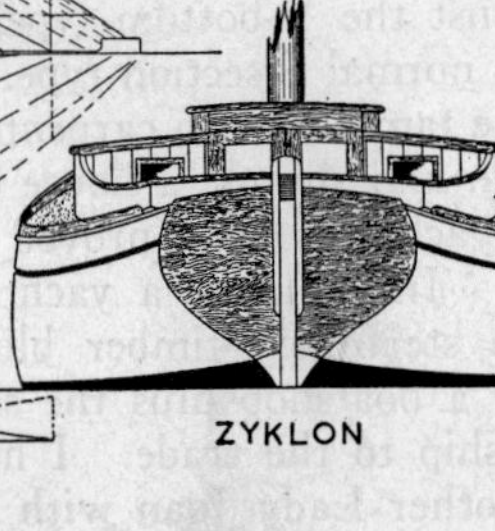

ZYKLON

Design for the little cutter Zyklon worked up by Dr. T. Harrison Butler, a strong proponent of the Norwegian type hull

tor boats, ranging in waterline from about 50 feet downward, a representative fleet of today. If the owners of the yawls would study and pass comment on Lt. Comdr. 'Griffiths' criticism it would throw light on an important question.

The radical change brought about in rigs by the introduction of the pole mast and jib-headed sails throws a new light on the question of the best rig for small cruising craft. This subject has been brought to the fore by an article in *The Yachting Monthly* for March 1943 by Lt. Comdr. Maurice Griffiths, R.N.V.R., for some years past the editor of that magazine and a practical designer and experienced cruiser. The article is too long to reprint in full, but may be summarized as follows: Although popularity in rigs has usually followed the fashion set by the racing classes and is known to move inevitably in cycles, there have always been a number of yachtsmen who have upheld the yawl as the ideal small cruiser's rig. For many years I, too, had this hankering to own a yawl; planned and built as a yawl, and not as a cutter converted. It was only after I had sailed several yawls belonging to friends that I was able at last to design and build my own two-sticker, hoping to benefit from the experience gained. The resulting observations on the rig for the small cruiser may infuriate or confirm, according to the reader's own views."

THE writer summarizes the advantages claimed and then proceeds to answer each. To condense his arguments we give together the pro and con of each point. (i) The rig is split up into handy sail areas—over a cutter's rig, the yawl's main boom is generally shorter and the mainsail better proportioned. (ii) Stowing the mizzen is simpler than tucking in the first reef in a cutter's mainsail.—In a small and short-handed cruiser this is true. If stowing the mizzen causes a lee helm, either the jib or the fore staysail must be stowed, and the skipper is faced with the problem whether (a) to jog along slowly under main and fore staysail only, or, in case the wind freshens more, (b) to reef the main and re-set mizzen and jib. (iii) In heavy weather, or for moving only a short distance, mizzen and jib or fore staysail make a convenient rig, and no reefing is required. —With a soldier's wind this may be granted, but few yawls can have their mizzens so well stopped and stayed as to set well when it is blowing very hard. The thoughtless skipper may get his vessel into serious trouble if he gets caught in broken water and shoals under his lee. Except for jogging along to leeward it is a fallacy to assume that the mizzen is a heavy-weather sail in a yawl. (iv) For lyin-to in a gale the mizzen, sheeted home, helps to keep the yacht's head to the seas.—Under jib and mizzen the two forces of backed jib and sheeted-in mizzen are at the far ends of the waterline, and very few yachts will heave-to satisfactorily with this rig. The mizzen and head sail are not the sails suitable for heaving-to in bad weather. (v) The mizzen mast enables extra canvas, e.g. mizzen staysail, to be set in light breezes. (vi) The mizzen mast and gear are extra handholds aft in bad weather.—The first is true, and with a lofty mizzen mast well stayed the yawl can carry a very useful mizzen staysail. The rigging around a yawl's stern is certainly an advantage for holding on when working on the after deck. The mizzen mast and its rigging become a distinct liability when canvas has to be shortened on a long turn to windward under reefed main and trysail. The weight of the mizzen mast and the windage of the stowed mizzen and its stays are not to be ignored if good windward performance is wanted.

This condensed summary gives only the leading points of Lt. Comdr. Griffith's article. He ends:—"My own conclusions on the rig after my trial yawl was eventually replaced in 1938 by a neat bobtailed Bermudian cutter, were that the yawl is usually improved for general purposes if converted to either (a) ketch, or (b) a short-boomed cutter." (a) Of course, applies only to yachts much larger than we have under consideration.

The Yawl, Yesterday and Tomorrow?

WERE we wrong in our earnest advocacy of the yawl rig sixty years ago? Most emphatically, No. We were confronted by a condition and not a theory; no other known rig was better suited to our purpose; and even if we concede today that Lt. Comdr. Griffiths has robbed us of all our talking points, the fact remains that the yawl has proved itself a practicable cruising rig. The next question is as to the future, and here we are confronted by another problem. The revolution brought about by the evolution of the pole-masted jib-headed rig, as told in MoToR BoatinG for November 1941 and on Pages 147-153 of this yarn in book form, bears directly on the rig of cruising yachts. For real sea-going in yachts of even medium size and upward the old two-part mast with its boom and gaff still holds its own. The old rig is not only less liable to a serious mishap, but it is much better adapted to repairs in case of an emergency. If a modern pole mast, presumably hollow, goes at the deck or higher there is not much to be done; but the annals of the sea are filled with records of total dismastings surmounted by the skill and ingenuity of the old race of sea dogs. While such a consideration as speed may act to retain the polemasted rig on many ocean racers, the old rig is likely to remain on the majority.

When it comes to the question of the small craft which we are considering, the new rig is small in area, light in weight, effective in driving power, and may be made safely strong for its purpose. In form it is reduced to four elements: Mast, boom, mainsail and jib; or jib and fore staysail; and there is no question of its speed and all-around efficiency. When reefing becomes necessary the problem is reduced to its simplest form; the mainsail is unshipped and stowed below and a trysail is set in its place; the jib, all inboard, is similarly and summarily disposed of and a storm jib set. No work outboard, no reefing, no making up of sails, no sail covers; if dry, the sails may be bagged at once and stowed below. In this modern rig the mast must be supported by the cabin top, but that is a mere matter of construction; it may also be an unwelcome guest below, so far as that goes. Today the question of rig is the first one demanding the attention of the proposed owner of a single-hander, and those interested are advised to study Lt. Comdr. Griffiths article before making a final decision.

As to the hull, not only MoToR BoatinG, but every yachting journal, home and foreign, has for some years past published designs, both amateur and professional; there are now a number of one-design classes to be had, and more are likely to follow when the time comes. It is not necessary to speculate on either form or construction, up-to-date, streamlined hulls of plastic or what you will; there is still much good left in honest woods put together by old conventional methods. With a growing interest in amateur design and also construction, there is no type of craft so well adapted to the amateur who will sail his yacht after he has built her.

Books on Small Yachts, Cruising and Canoeing

Orion, or How I Came to Sail Alone in a 19-Ton Yacht. R. T. McMullen. London 1878.

An Experimental Cruise, Single-handed, in the Procyon, 7-Ton Lugger. R. T. McMullen. London 1880.

Down Channel. R. T. McMullen. London 1893.

A Thousand Miles in the Rob Roy Canoe. John Macgregor, M. A. London 1866.

The Rob Roy on the Baltic. John Macgregor, M.A. London 1867.

The Voyage Alone in the Yawl Rob Roy. John Macgregor, M.A. London 1868.

The Rob Roy on the Jordan. John Macgregor, M.A. London 1870.

The Cruise of the Kate: A Single-handed Voyage Around England. Empson Edward Middleton, Author of the first two books of the Æneid of Virgil in Rhymed Verse. London 1870.

A Thousand-Mile Walk Across South America. N. H. Bishop. New York 1868.

Voyage of the Paper Canoe, from Quebec to the Gulf of Mexico. N. H. Bishop. New York 1878.

Four Months in a Sneakbox: A Boat Voyage of 2,600 Miles Down the Ohio and Mississippi Rivers and Along the Gulf of Mexico. N. H. Bishop. New York 1879.

Canoe Traveling: Log of a Cruise on the Baltic. Warrington Baden Powell. London 1871.

Cruises in Small Yachts and Large Canoes. Harry Fiennes Speed. London 1883.

More Cruises. New edition of above with additions. Maud Speed. London 1926.

A Yachtswoman's Cruises and Some Steamer Voyages. Maud Speed. London 1918.

Practical Canoeing by "Tiphys." London 1883.

Watery Wandering Mid Western Lochs. T. H. Holding. London 1886.

From the Adirondacks to the Gulf. C. A. Neide. New York 1885.

Canoe Mates. Kirk Munroe. New York 1893.

The Waterway to London. 1869.

Canoeing With Sail and Paddle. John D. Hayward, M.D. London 1893.

A Water Biography. Robert C. Leslie. London 1894.

Paddles and Politics Down the Danube. Poultney Bigelow. New York 1892.

Three in Norway, by Two of Them. London 1882.

Our Autumn Holiday on French Rivers. J. L. Molloy. Boston 1885.
Paddling in Florida. St. George Rathborne. New York 1889.
A Canoe Cruise in Danish Waters. Fred Good. Hull 1879.
Canoe Cruising and Camping. Perry D. Frazer. New York 1897.
Voyage of the Liberdade. Captain Joshua Slocum. Boston 1894.
An Inland Voyage. Robert Louis Stevenson.
Two Hundred Miles on the Delware River. J. Wallace Hoff. Trenton, N. J. 1893.
Up and Down the Merrimac. Pliny Steele Boyd. Boston 1879.
By Ocean, Firth and Channel, by "Diagonal White." London 1894.
A Thousand-Mile Cruise in Silver Cloud. London 1878.
Down West. H. V. Williams. London 1902.
The Riddle of the Sands. Erskine Childers. London 1903.
Yachting: How to Sail and Manage a Small Modern Yacht. Arthur E. Bullen and Geoffrey Prout. London 1827.
Single-handed Cruising. Francis B. Cooke. London 1919.
Cruising Chats. Francis B. Cooke. London 1932.
Week-End Yachting. Francis B. Cooke. London 1933.
Small Yacht Cruising. Francis B. Cooke. London 1937.
The Handyman's Yacht Book. C. E. Tyrrell Lewis. London 1930.
Ten Small Yachts. Maurice Griffiths. London 1933.
Sailing and Cruising. K. Adlard Coles. London 1937.
Cruising Is Fun. Brandt Aymar. 1941.
Down Channel in Vivette. E. Keble Chatterton. London 1910.
Through Holland in Vivette. E. Keble Chatterton. London 1913.
Log of the Blue Dragon. C. C. Lynam, M. A. London 1892-4.
Log of the Blue Dragon II in Orkney and Shetland. C. C. Lynam, M.A. London 1909.
To Norway and the North Cape in Blue Dragon II. C. C. Lynam, M.A. London 1913.
Our Wherry in Wendish Lands. H. M. Doughty. London.
Friesland Meres and Through the Netherlands. H. M. Doughty. London.
Summer in Broadland. H. M. Doughty. London.
Hotspur's Cruise in the Ægean. Alfred F. Loomis. New York 1931.
The Cruise of the Hippocampus. Alfred F. Loomis. New York.
Fair Winds in the Baltic. Alfred F. Loomis. New York.
From the Thames to the Netherlands. Charles Pears. London 1914.

THE DEVELOPMENT OF THE SMALL CRUISER

(Continued from page 256)

Sylvia was much more of a ship, designed for a long cruises on Lake Superior, several of these being published in *Forest & Stream.* Her dimensions were:

Freeboard:		
L. o. a.	25 feet	8 inches
L. w. l.	20	
Breadth	6	3
Bow	2	6
Least	1	6
Stern	1	9
Draft	3	9

Ballast, iron:	
Inside	500 pounds
Keel	3,000

Sail area:	
Mainsail	192 square feet
Jib	73
Foresail	60
Mizzen	57
Total	382
Topsail	64

Wicksteed's letters were always interesting, first there were the descriptions of his wanderings, then of yachts planned, building, or in actual use; discussions of form, stability, lateral resistance and rig; with personal notes about mutual friends. In spite of their age his designs are adaptable today, as each was carefully and deliberately planned to meet some specific conditions, usually of open water. Ultimately each was tested and the results carefully noted for the next craft. As to rig, much might be done in the light of more recent developments, but in form and construction the designs are basically correct.

F. C. Sumichrast of Halifax, a yachting enthusiast and member of numerous clubs, who contributed to the record of the early days with extensive articles

TRADITIONS AND MEMORIES OF American Yachting

Part Fifty-Eight

By WILLIAM P. STEPHENS

ASSOCIATION, CO-OPERATION AND UNION

THE necessity for union and co-operation in sport is so obvious that almost every form of sport has long had its national organization; in this country we had when rowing was popular the National Association of Amateur Oarsmen; later, when bicycling was new, about 1880, there was the League of American Wheelmen, with similar organizations for the advancement of archery, tennis and other land sports. In no other sport is a national association more essential than in yachting, with its many followers on coastal and inland waters and an elaborate and complicated tangle of sailing and measurement rules. The necessity for uniformity in such highly technical matters is beyond dispute, and yet it is only within the past few years that the end so long sought has been achieved.

The cause for this delay in a matter of such vital importance does not lie in any failure to realize its necessity, nor in efforts for its achievement; for more than seventy years we find men of advanced ideas struggling for their adoption. One of the early attempts is told in *The Aquatic Monthly* for August 1872 in the form of an editorial: "In another month or two, when the annual regattas and match races are over for the season, we will have abundant space to devote to yachting discussions respecting the vexed questions of time allowance, centerboard vs. keel, too much canvas and too little, heavy spars vs. light spars, and other questions which, today, notwithstanding the many folios written upon them in Great Britain and the United States, are probably as far from being settled as they were a score of years since.

"What progress have we made in adjusting a satisfactory or equitable scale of time allowance when the New York Yacht Club, the largest yachting organization in the country and one of the first in the world, changes its time allowances almost annually? Look at its last annual regatta when yachts withdrew from the line on the eve of a start, as was the case with Mr. James D. Smith's schooner Halcyon, her owner protesting against the unjust scale of time allowance adopted to govern the race; and, at this time, wagers are offered that the New York Yacht Club will never sail a second regatta with the time allowance of 1872.

"The only practical way, in our opinion, to arrive at any satisfactory basis is to call a convention of yacht owners of the United States, to be held in the city of New York, when, perhaps, the mooted points can be settled satisfactorily alike to the owners of large and small yachts; and standard rules adopted which will be readily acquiesced in by the yachting interests of the whole country. We are well aware that it is an exceedingly difficult matter to arrange, and that Great Britain has failed partially after attempting it at intervals for many years; yet we do not by any means despair of its accomplishment by an American yachting congress. At any rate, it is worth while to make the effort, and New York is the city to inaugurate the movement."

The incident alluded to occurred in the annual regatta of 1872; in 1871 the club abandoned the measurement of the load waterline parallelogram and adopted the "Cubic Contents Rule," the bulk below water computed by three sections; the rule proved unsatisfactory and the races of 1872 were sailed under a temporary rule, James D. Smith refusing to start Halcyon. In 1873 the "Cubic Contents Rule" was re-enacted with four instead of three sections measured.

Another far-sighted yachtsman, Lt. J. D. Jerrold Kelley, U.S.N., a member of the New York Y. C., wrote in 1884: "Should the present movement of the Boston Bay clubs result in the formation of a National Yachting Association, nothing but good can ensue for the sport; it is certain that there ought to be one general rule of measurement. . . . Are the New York yachtsmen willing to follow the course so manfully laid down by the earnest amateur sailors of Down-East waters?"

The First Step Forward

In May 1879 a small local club, the New Jersey Yacht Club issued a call to all yacht clubs, inviting each to appoint committees for the consideration of some plan looking toward the formation of a union or racing association of some kind. In its issue of June 5, *Forest & Stream* commented at length on the proposition: "We need some central authority through which yachtsmen as a class can be reached, an authority whose decisions and operations will be looked upon as the standard in all pertaining to the sport. . . . Let us have a yacht racing association representing all the clubs of the country, adopt one rule of classification, and time allowance and one set of sailing regulations. . . . Has not the time arrived when the close corporation system, the weakly and desultory efforts of individuals, the mere social aims of yacht racing, should give way to something more thorough, more manly, and more sportsmanlike and more dignified? Nothing short of the formation of a National Yacht Racing Association will rouse the sport from its worn-out rut and save racing." Again, under date of February 26, 1880, the subject was treated at length, with definite proposals outlining the full scope of operations.

In the early eighties the Hull (Mass.) Yacht Club was one of the most active clubs on the eastern coast, due largely to the work of one man, its secretary, Peleg Aborn. Like many others with limited opportunities for ownership and racing, his devotion to yachting took the form of work for his club and for the sport at large. It was due to him that in 1883 the club inaugurated a movement for a national association. A committee was appointed to study the subject and finally reported that it considered a national association impossible at the time, but recommended an association of eastern clubs.

In response to the call of the New Jersey Yacht Club, a preliminary meeting was held in October and a committee of three was appointed: W. H. Dilworth, E. W. Ketcham and Theo. H. Rogers. The object of the movement was to "initiate proceedings with a view to the organization of a body composed of delegates from the various yacht clubs of New York and vicinity. The committee has communicated with all the clubs of the country, and now asks that a call be issued bringing them together at as early a day as convenient. It has been decided to call together a convention at the Astor House on Monday, November 10, at 8:00 P. M."

The meeting was duly held, the clubs represented being the New Jersey, Hudson River, Columbia, Salem (Mass.), Manhattan, Empire and Jersey City. A committee of five was appointed to issue another call to all the yacht clubs of the United States. The objects set forth were to promote the general interests of yachting, to publish a record of clubs, of members and their yachts, and records of races, there being at this time no yacht register. No proposal was made for a standard rule of measurement, it was not proposed that the association should interfere with the local management of the clubs, each club to retain its own individuality of action, "and only when the common interests of the clubs required it would action be taken by the association."

While the larger clubs stood aloof and isolated, in fear of "foreign entanglements," on the part of small and inferior organizations, there was a general response from individuals. *Forest & Stream* had no paid contributors to its Yachting Department, but it had an enthusiastic body of volunteer correspondents. One of these was W. Lloyd Jeffries, of the Beverly (Mass.) Yacht Club, owner of a 19-foot Herreshoff catboat, Bluebell, and writing over that name as a *nom de plume;* throughout the season he sent in full reports of the races of the Beverly and other eastern clubs, and in the fall compiled a full list of races and winners.

Another enthusiast was F. C. Sumichrast, of Halifax, N. S., a member of the Royal Southern Yacht Club, the Y. R. A., the Yacht Club de France, the Nova Scotia Yacht Squadron and the Bay of Quinte Yacht Club. Though his ownership was limited to small cutters, his knowledge of yachting in all its phases was most extensive, and his interest led him to write without compensation. His private signal was a red cross on a white field and he wrote over the nom-de-plume of "Rouge Croix."

Clifford D. Mallory, organizer of the North American Yacht Racing Union. Photograph by Lazarnik from painting by James McBey

It is worth noting that all movements of this kind for the betterment of the sport came from men who, from lack of leisure or means, sailed small yachts or none at all; those whose financial interests were greatest had no interest in the general good of yachting. In *Forest & Stream* of July 10 "Rouge Croix" wrote: "The turf has its supreme tribunal, so has the rifle, so has rowing; so, in England, have cricket, football, fox-hunting and nearly every sport. Yacht racing would assuredly be vastly benefited by the establishment of a National Yacht Racing Association."

The weak point of this movement was that it worked from the bottom up, its promoters were members of the smaller New York clubs, owners of small yachts, but all Corinthian sailors and with a whole-hearted interest in the sport at large; but they were faced by the insurmountable obstacle of the "premier club" sentiment. When organized in 1875 the Yacht Racing Association of Great Britain side-stepped this situation by a proviso that: "The Association shall consist of former and present owners of racing yachts, and such other gentlemen interested in yacht racing as the Council may elect." Had the original movement taken the form of an organization of clubs it is a certainty that the Royal Yacht Squadron would have opposed it passively if not actively. In spite of the energetic efforts of its promoters, this movement failed and was soon forgotten.

The New York Yacht Racing Association

THE next move came in 1888, from the same quarter, the smaller New York clubs; in answer to a call about fifty yachtsmen met at the Gilsey House, in New York, on January 31, 1889, the clubs represented being the Albany, Columbia, Jersey City, Knickerbocker, Newark, Newark Bay, New Rochelle, New Jersey, Sing Sing, Tappan Zee, Williamsburgh, Yonkers, Yonkers Corinthian, and Staten Island Athletic Club, which, like the New York Athletic Club, had then an active yachting department. Among the leaders were Alanson J. Prime, then Commodore of the Yonkers Corinthian Yacht Club, long an advocate of a national association, and George E. Gartland, then Secretary of the New Jersey Yacht Club. He served his apprenticeship in yachting as a bilge-boy aboard the sandbaggers of the late seventies and forty years later was well known on Long Island Sound through his persistent racing of Robin Hood III of the Indian Harbor Yacht Club. Apart from his sailing, he was always active in behalf of his club and of yachting.

Commodore Prime in stating the object of the meeting urged the necessity of organization on the part of those clubs which regularly raced together, and suggested that only this subject should be considered, leaving the clubs free as to local rules and races. He specially urged that no action be taken on a common measurement rule. Unfortunately, his advice was not taken, and as each delegate was called he spoke for organization and then for his favorite rule: mean length, waterline plus 1/3 overhang, water line plus 1/5 overhang, or length and sail area.

Much time was wasted in this discussion, but it was finally settled by one old yachtsman who, generally liked and respected, was famous as one of the best handlers of every size of yacht from a sandbagger to a large schooner. When he took the floor for a speech which in simplicity and directness would have done honor to a congressman, he said: "What we want is a plain and simple rule, *with no plus in* it; who knows what *plus* is? I don't know what *plus* is. You take the length on deck and add it to the length on the waterline and divide by two, and you have a plain, simple rule *with no plus in it.* General applause: Question? All in favor say 'Aye,' contrary 'No'; the ayes have it." It is fifty-five years since I listened to this speech, and yet I can remember every inflection of the speaker's voice as I heard it. The obvious course at that time, if any action were to be taken, was on the question of measurement, was to adopt the length-and-sail area rule for the cabin yachts and the "rule with no plus in it" for the sandbag boats.

The constitution, modeled on that of the New England Y.R.A., was adopted, with the name New York Yacht Racing Association. The officers were: President, Alanson J. Prime; Vice President, Frederick T. Pangborn; Secretary, George Parkhill; Treasurer, Robert K. McMurray. One object of the Association was to hold an annual open regatta, and the first was sailed on Labor Day, September 1, 1889, with 81 starters. The second, in 1890, was preceded by a hard northwest blow which kept many yachts away from the rendezvous, 71 starting; the third followed a similar September gale, 75 starting. The Association also held an annual cruise. The interest in sandbag racing gradually declined, shifting ballast was prohibited and the boats, limited to fixed ballast, lost their speed, and new types were introduced. The "plain and simple rule" excluded the cabin yachts with overhangs and the organization died quietly about 1897.

The North American Yacht Racing Union

THE Yacht Racing Association of Long Island Sound, originally the Yacht Racing Union, was organized in 1895, largely through the efforts of the late Frank Bowne Jones, then a member of the crew of the sandbagger Phyllis, owned by his brother and sailing under the burgee of the Indian Harbor Yacht Club; he was also one of the founders of the Corinthian Mosquito Fleet, a contemporary club devoted to small boats. With him and others who had long visioned a national association was Æmilius Jarvis, a Canadian, born in 1860; after graduating from the College of Upper Canada he shipped before the mast for a time before entering the banking business. In yachting he was recognized as the best racing skipper of the Great Lakes. With his active participation in racing he was equally interested in union; being one of the organizers of the Lake Y.R.A. of Lake Ontario in 1884 and the Yacht Racing Union of the Great Lakes in 1896. The idea of a national union was fathered by him and Mr. Jones in the same year. With them was Oliver E. Cromwell, a member of the New York Yacht Club, son of Charles T. Cromwell, who joined that club in 1854 with his sloop Manursing, named after his home on an island off Rye.

Working with these gentlemen was President Louis M. Clark, of the Y.R.A. of Massachusetts, who visited New York on November 15, 1896, for a conference with other yachtsmen on the subject of a unification of rules; and, incidentally, the subject of a national organization. The feeling on the subject was so strong that three members of the New York Yacht Club, J. Rogers Maxwell, Clarence A. Postley and Edward N. Dickerson, requested that Commodore Brown would appoint a committee of that club to consider the following motion: "That a committee of five, one of whom shall be the Commodore, be appointed by the chair with power to call a convention of delegates from such yacht clubs in America as they may elect, for the purpose of considering the advisability of organizing a yacht racing league; the object of which league shall be to establish uniform co-operation on measurement, classification and racing rules; the promotion of yacht building; the encouragement and elevation of the sport, and the preservation of yachting history and racing records. And that this committee have power to enter this club in such league, said entrance to be complete and operative upon this club's ratification thereof by subsequent constitutional amendment."

The committee was very carefully selected, as in the case of all America's Cup Committees; the "Old Guard" of stand-patters and isolationists was represented by Commodore Edward M. Brown, Rear Commodore Lewis Cass Ledyard, ex-Commodore James D. Smith, ex-Commodore S. Nicholson Kane; with them were ex-Commodore Edwin D. Morgan, ex-Rear Commodore C. Oliver Iselin and Clarence A. Postley. The report, which is too long to quote in full, set forth that "The New York Yacht Club has never been purely a racing organization, if it had been it may well be doubted if it ever would have reached its present position. . . . If it should join a league such as is now proposed it must subject its classification and racing rules to the manipulation of others . . . in the opinion of your Committee it has everything to lose and nothing to gain in becoming a member of the proposed league." For over a half century the Club had conducted an annual regatta and an annual series of races on its cruises; for a quarter century it had conducted the great series of matches for the America's Cup; its position as the oldest and most prominent of American clubs was universally recognized; and the assumption that its rules might be set aside by some small clubs was sheer buncombe. Nothing was said of the general benefit to the sport through the co-operation of all elements of American yachting.

As usual in those days, *The New York Herald* came to the defense of the Club: "This league business is totally unnecessary; it cannot add to the prestige of the Club and it may involve it in so many outside complications as to be both inconvenient and unpleasant. The N.Y.Y.C. has been able to care for itself in the past and is likely to do so in the future. . . . It has a distinct antipathy to having its constitution tampered with; and for it to become a member of this proposed league there must be a change in that instrument. Most of the members appreciate that the difficulties to be overcome in forming such an association would be almost disheartening, but that might not be an insuperable objection if the N.Y.Y.C. were to derive any special benefit from the proposed league." Of course *The Boston Herald* played second fiddle to its New York associate.

AS the result of the November meeting a conference was called on May 1, 1897, at the Fifth Avenue Hotel, in New York, attended by representatives of the Y.R.A. of Massachusetts, the Y.R.U. of the Great Lakes, the Y.R.U. of Long Island Sound, the Lake Y.R.A., the Inter-Lake Y.R.A., the Lake Michigan Y.R.A., the Pacific Inter-Club Y.A., the Larchmont Yacht Club, the Atlantic Yacht Club, the Corinthian Yacht Club of Philadelphia, the New York Y.R.A., the Great South Bay Yacht Club, The Marine and Field Club, the New York Athletic Club and the Hempstead Bay Yacht Club. The personnel included Louis M. Clark of Boston, J. M. Macdonough of San Francisco, G. O. Richardson of Toledo, Æmilius Jarvis of Toronto, E. C. Berriman of Chicago, A. F. Bancroft of Philadelphia, and from New York, Oliver E. Cromwell, F. Bowne Jones, John F. Lovejoy, Stuyvesant Wainwright, E. Burton Hart, Charles T. Pierce, Oswald Sanderson, Frederick T. Adams, A. J. Prime and John R. Suydam. Nearly all were racing men, some were prominent as workers in various clubs; collectively they representesd the yachting sentiment of the nation from coast to coast.

Naturally the discussion covered a wide range of opinion, but the final conclusion was that a national organization be formed with a constitution, bylaws and sailing rules, but leaving to the future the questions of measurement and classification. In accordance with this sentiment a committee was appointed, N. D. Lawton, C. T. Pierce, L. M. Clark, J. M. Macdonough, A. J. Prime, Æmilius Jarvis and F. B. Jones, to report at a meeting in October. After adjournment the visitors were entertained at a mess dinner at the town house of the Seawanhaka Corinthian Y.C.

On October 30, 1897, a meeting was held lasting until 1 A. M., for a general discussion, Messrs. Cromwell and Stephens still serving as temporary officers. On the following day a meeting was held at the S.C.Y.C. house at which the formal articles of association were adopted; with the name, North American Yacht Racing Union. A Council was elected, E. W. Radder, Æmilius Jarvis, J. M. Macdonough, A. J. Prime, A. T. Bliss, F. B. Jones, G. H. Duggan, N. B. Lawton, Oswald Sanderson, E. H. Ambrose, Oliver E. Cromwell, A. F. Bancroft, Ralph E. Ellis, L. M. Clark and J. A. Mollenhauser. Mr. Clark was elected President, Mr. Jones Secretary and Mr. Lawton Treasurer. Those present represented 106 yacht clubs. On November 3, Messrs. Jarvis and Macdonough sailed for England, partly on business, but also to confer with British yachtsmen and to study the new rule of the Y.R.A.

Mr. Macdonough was called to the continent by business, but Mr. Jarvis visited all the yachting centers, calling on George L. Watson in Glasgow and Will Fife, Jr., in Fairlie and meeting all the other designers. He gathered a mass of data relating to the new rule, adopted by the Y. R. A. in 1895:—length plus breadth, plus 0.75 girth, plus 0.5 square foot of sail area, divided by two. This rule was designed to penalize the new fin-keel type such as Wenonah and Niagara. Mr. Jarvis examined many of the yachts designed to this rule and he gathered from their designers much data, including the midship sections of the most important yachts. At the second annual meeting, held in New York on October 1, 1898, this data was presented by Mr. Jarvis, with a detailed report of his visit and a strong argument for the adoption of the rule. This was done after a lengthy discussion including the examination of several other proposed and existing rules.

The new rule was put into operation on the Lakes, but in spite of the fact that it produced a normal type of keel yacht and was also fair to the centerboard type it was abandoned at the annual meeting on October 6, 1900, and the clubs were advised to use such rules as each preferred until another new rule could be found. In 1903 the New York Yacht Club adopted the "Universal Rule" formulated by N. G. Herreshoff and still in general use in this country. While still opposed to a national organization, the New York Yacht Club, in 1904, invited some of the larger clubs to participate in what was known as the Atlantic Coast Conference, for the general adoption of this rule; though a very loosely organized body, it functioned for a time.

The Union continued for several years, but with the passive opposition of the larger clubs it quietly passed out as its predecessors had done.

The Dream Becomes Reality

WITH a growing interest in yachting and yacht racing throughout the nation there were formed more local associations, these being consolidated into larger bodies, all tending toward one national body. In 1925 a positive step was taken by C. D. Mallory, a member of the New York and Indian Harbor clubs and a new conference was called resulting in the organization of the North American Yacht Racing Union now, in its 19th year, recognized as the governing body of American yachting. Clifford Day Mallory, son of Henry Rogers Mallory, was born in Brooklyn, N. Y. on May 26, 1881. The family, localized at Mystic, Connecticut, has been prominent in shipbuilding and ship management for several generations, an uncle, Charles Mallory, who joined the New York Yacht Club in 1873, built and raced a number of yachts. In 1898 young Clifford sailed an old freak built by Thomas Clapham in the trial races for the Seawanhaka Cup, and he continued as a yacht owner to the time of his death on April 7, 1941. In 1903 he raced the sloop Hanley, named after her builder, replacing her in 1906 by the New York Thirty, Banzai, racing her for three seasons. In 1910 he bought the knockabout Cliphora, racing her until she was replaced by the 21-foot Margaret; in 1917 he bought the 36-foot Joyant and the 21-foot Rani; in 1919 he owned Vayu II, re-naming her Remar. In 1920 he bought the auxiliary yawl Bonnie Dundee, the first of four auxiliary yachts of that name. In 1924 he bought the 50-foot Grayling, re-naming her Mystic and racing her for a season before replacing her by the 25-foot Barbara; in 1927 he started the class of 10-meter yachts with his Twilight, and in 1928 he built the 12-meter Tycoon, racing her for eight seasons. With continued ill health he gave up active racing, contenting himself with two small sloops and three sucessively larger cruising yachts each bearing the name of Bonnie Dundee.

During all these years he was managing an extensive steamship business, partly for the Government during the first World War; he was active in many yachting organizations, and yet found time to found the Union and to guide its growth as President for eleven years. At the annual meeting of the Union in February last its Secretary, Commodore George E. Roosevelt, of the New York Yacht Club, when his name was called as a delegate from the Cruising Club of America, requested that he be entered as representig the New York Yacht Club.

TRADITIONS AND MEMORIES OF

American Yachting

Part Fifty-nine

By

WILLIAM P. STEPHENS

THE decade from 1875 to 1885 was the most important period in American yachting; early in the seventies, a few yachtsmen inaugurated a crusade against the national type, the broad, shoal, easily capsizable centerboard sloop, with inside ballast. As this crusade progressed it assumed a more extreme form in the advocacy of the British cutter, a keel yacht with outside ballast, then of moderate breadth, but growing more narrow and deep each year. A fierce controversy ensued, breaking up friendships and dividing clubs. The end came in 1885 with the construction for the defense of the America's Cup of a compromise with a centerboard working through an outside lead keel and a cutter rig. The story of this historic battle of types, almost unknown to the present generation, will be told in full in this and succeeding chapters.

The production of water-borne craft throughout the ages has been governed by many diverse conditions—economical, mechanical, commercial, geographical; even the most ancient and crude give evidence of some underlying idea in the mind of the creator, some effort to meet special conditions. Among the smallest craft the kayak of the esquimaux is cleverly designed for the capture of the seal or walrus from whose bones and hide it is built; the birchbark canoe of the American Indian is another example of the economic side of construction. As we go up the scale we find that design is governed not alone by ultimate use, but by such material and skill as are available and by conditions of water and wind.

It is difficult to realize that little Holland, so powerless today, was in the seventeenth century one of the leading naval powers; foremost in discovery and colonization, and fighting the navies of Britain, France and Spain. Its main fleet of great warships was supplemented by another large

Above: The last of the Cutter-Cranks. From a pastel portrait of W. P. Stephens by Ruth Clark, Bayside, August, 1943. The term "Cutter-Crank" was first applied in derision to a small group of American yachtsmen who came forward in advocacy of the British cutter over sixty years ago. It was soon adopted by them as a mark of distinction

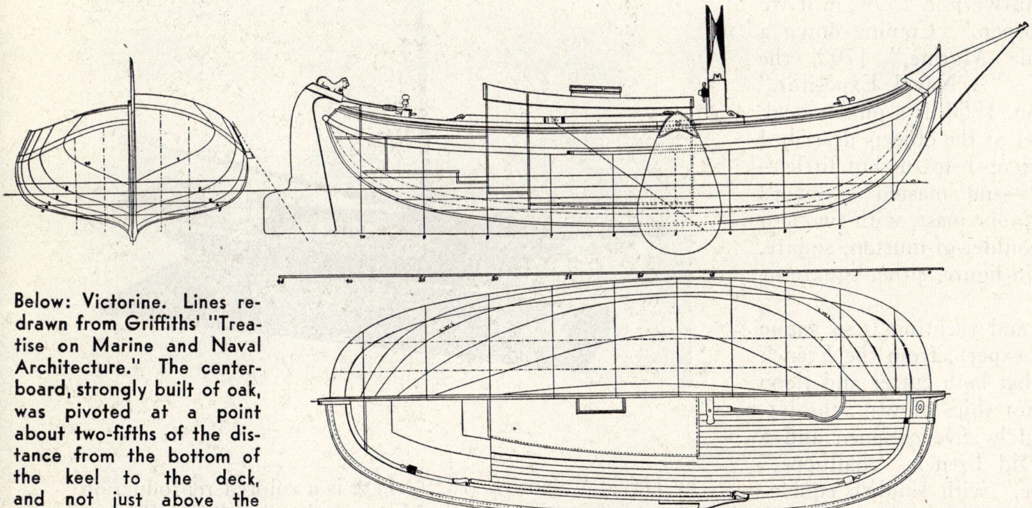

Above: Elizabeth, Dutch boier, built for pleasure sailing and racing. L.o.a., 36 ft. 1 in.; l.w.l., 32 ft. 10 ins.; breadth, 13 ft. 6 ins.; draft, 2 ft. 9 ins. This yacht, designed and built by M. L. Van Breen at Amsterdam in 1887, is in no way different from the boiers of the 17th Century; similar yachts over one hundred years old are still in use. Lines presented to W. P. Stephens by J. Jacob Classen, of Amsterdam

Below: Victorine. Lines redrawn from Griffiths' "Treatise on Marine and Naval Architecture." The centerboard, strongly built of oak, was pivoted at a point about two-fifths of the distance from the bottom of the keel to the deck, and not just above the keel, as in later yachts

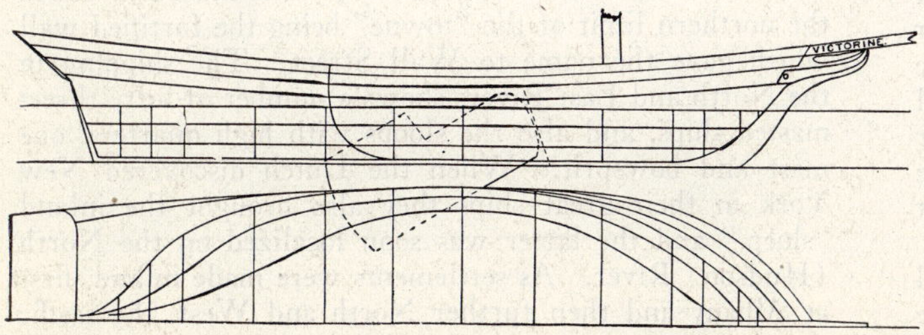

Illinois. North River Sloop 1818 from a model by Captain H. Percy Ashley

Victorine. North River Sloop 1848 from a model by Captain H. Percy Ashley

fleet exclusively for inland navigation. The local conditions which produced this fleet were a maze of narrow and shoal rivers and canals with cities and trees on their banks breaking the force of the sole driving power, the wind. To meet these conditions the craft were of shoal draft, while the rigs were lofty and narrow.

It is typical of Holland's prominence in maritime matters that one of the earliest marine dictionaries is in Dutch and Latin, published in Antwerp in 1599; in it we find the words "sloep" and "sloepen." Coming down a century to the "Dictionaire de Marine," 1702, the "sloep" is mentioned as Dutch. "A Naval Expositor," Thomas Riley Blanckley, London, 1750, is a quaint book with marginal engravings on steel of the objects described in the text. Its definition of a sloop helps us but little—"Sloops are sailed—canvassed?—and masted as men's fancies lead them, sometimes with one mast, with two and with three; with Bermudoes, shoulder-of-mutton, square, lugg and smack sails; they are; in figure, either square or round sterned."

The terminology of shipping and yachting is so vague and loose as to confuse even the expert; from the French dictionary mentioned we learn that both cutter and sloop were originally rowing tenders for ships of war; the latter being the smaller and rowed by five oarsmen and a coxswain. There is a term in Old French, "challuppe," in more modern form "chaloupe," with English equivalents, first "shalloop" and later "shallop," also a rowing boat. As sails were used on ship boats the meaning of both terms changed to apply to sailing craft of larger size, and in course of time to rig as well as hull. The "sloop-of-war" of the 18th century was a wooden hull mounting a number of guns and rigged as ship, brig or bark; in the war news of today we read of a new type of sloops, steel hulls with diesel engines recently built to hunt down submarines.

In modern yachting usage the terms cutter, sloop, yawl and cat are commonly understood as defining not the hull but the rig; in the period of which we are writing—from about 1844 to 1885—the term sloop was understood as applying to a wide, shoal centerboard yacht with one mast, bowsprit, mainsail and jib.

The Early Dutch Yachts

It is hardly necessary to recall today that Holland was the birthplace of yachting, the word "yacht," being of Dutch origin; or that the first yacht in England was Mary, presented to Charles II in 1661 by the Dutch. The "sloep" of the seventeenth century was a broad, shoal craft, very full in the bows, and rigged with a tall mast well forward, a short topmast, and a fixed bowsprit well steeved upward. Her mainsail, laced to a long boom, had a very short and often curved gaff; the single jib was set on a stay to the bowsprit end. The topsides of the hull tumbled in at a sharp angle, so that the leeboards pivoted to them were almost vertical when at a sailing angle. The main points of difference in rig of the cutter were that the mast, stepped further aft, was shorter, the topmast longer, the bowsprit was fitted to house, and there were two headsails, a jib set flying at the bowsprit end and a fore staysail set on a stay from stemhead to masthead.

In "The Manual of The City of New York," by David Valentine, 1859, there is a colored reproduction of a map in the British Museum showing "The Towne of Mannados, or New Amsterdam," as it existed in 1661; the northern limit of the "towne" being the fortified wall which gave the name to Wall Street. The shipping in the North and East Rivers shows a number of lofty three-masted ships, and also the sloops with high quarters, one mast and bowsprit. When the Dutch discovered New York in their great ships they also brought the inland "sloep," and the latter was soon localized on the North (Hudson) River. As settlements were made inland, first at Albany and then further North and West, the traffic on the river increased rapidly, and by the eighteenth century the "North River sloop" figured largely in American commerce.

The sloop Enterprise was built at Albany in 1780, her dimensions being length, 67 feet; breadth, 21 feet 6 inches; depth, 7 feet 10 inches. She carried passengers and freight on the river for five years and then was refitted at Brown's shipyard, foot of 8th Street, East River, for a voyage to China. The keel was deepened, a raised quarterdeck was added with sliding shutters to the windows. The mast and boom were shortened, a jib boom was shipped, but with no dolphin striker, a longer and stouter topmast was shipped with main, topsail and royal yards, two boats were lashed on deck. Captain Stewart Dean had a crew of seven men, two boys and a dog. She sailed to Canton, shipped a cargo of tea, and returned to New York within a year. The town turned out to witness the docking with a band to welcome her. The captain and crew were in uniform; whether the dog survived the voyage is not stated. Later in her history she carried stone from the Hudson to Connecticut and Massachusetts.

THE first sloops were keel craft, and thus barred from the upper Hudson by shoal water and mud banks covered by beds of weeds; the larger craft plied between Newburgh and New York, transferring freight to smaller sloops at the former port. One of the most famous of the big sloops was the Illinois, built at the foot of South Street, Newburgh, in 1818 by Timothy Wood; all the timber, including the mast of white pine, was cut on the river. She was of 140 tons; length, 83 feet 6 inches; breadth, 25 feet 9 inches; draft including keel, 9 feet. In those days a square topsail was carried, but no gaff topsail; green and red sidelights were unknown, there were no ratlines nor crosstrees. Iron stoves were unknown, the cooking being done in a brick oven with brick chimney through the deck, a copper trough filled with water protecting the woodwork. The 28-inch mast was 90 feet long, the boom 86 feet. As she was built to carry passengers the quarter deck extended almost to midships, with two staterooms and twenty berths and a large cabin, all finished in mahogany and other fine woods carved and gilded, rep curtains further ornamented the cabin. The forward hold was fitted for freight and in the fall she carried livestock for the New York slaughter houses, most of the meat for the city then coming from the vicinity of Catskill.

The sloop trade was affected first by the introduction of the steamboat and later by the construction of railroads. After the passenger trade fell off Illinois was rebuilt with a full flush deck and schooner rig and carried flagstones for pavements from Bigelow's quarry on the Hudson to the Eastern states. On July 2, 1878, when under command of Captain James Wilson, while lying-to in a fog off Captain's Island in Long Island Sound, she was run down and sunk by the steamer Massachusetts of the Stonington Line. The accident happened at 4 A. M., but within 30 hours she was on the ways at City Island and after repairs continued her voyage and delivered her cargo of bluestones. She was finally wrecked off Point Judith in 1893, ending a career of 75 years.

Leeboards and Centerboards

THE origin of the centerboard is shrouded in the mists of time; the idea probably came from the mind of some genius who, trying to go to windward in some sort of raft, pushed the blade of an oar, or a plank, down between the logs; it was, however, of very slow gestation. We know that in 1774 Captain John Schank, R.N., then in Boston, experimented with what he called a "sliding keel," a long and narrow plate or plank lowered and raised in a central trunk by means of screws or ropes at each end. Later he continued his experiments with three boards, each narrow and deep and sliding in its separate trunk. In 1811 three brothers, Jacocks, Henry and Joshua Swain, of Cape May, N. J., applied for a patent on a "leeboard through the bottom." In 1815 the sloop Advance was built by Henry Gesnor of Nyack, N. Y., with some form of centerboard.

The larger sloops plying as far as Newburgh were keel craft, but the smaller, from 50 to 60 feet in length, carried the Dutch leeboards. Writing in 1895 the late Francis B. Stevens informed me that: "About 70 years ago fully half of the North River sloops used leeboards instead of a centerboard. These sideboards were hung, one on each side of a vessel, on pintles, and were hauled up by a tackle. As one of them was always out of water, and as they were large and generally painted the same color that the Jerseymen of those days painted their barns (a red-brown) they were very conspicuous objects."

In a book, "Inventions and Devices," published in 1578, William Bourne describes a board raised and lowered in a well or trunk to prevent leeway. It is difficult to ascertain when the centerboard actually displaced the leeboard on the Hudson River, probably about 1830; but with it the larger sloops could make the trip between Albany and New York with no delay and labor in transfer. The passage one way took about 27 hours and the fare was $5.00. Leaving Albany on a certain day, cargo was discharged in New York on the following day, a new cargo was shipped, and the boat was back in her dock at Albany on the fourth day. Considering the beautiful scenery of the Hudson in those days, the trip must have been most interesting.

ONE of the most famous of the sloops was the Victorine, built in 1848 by John J. and Caleb H. Wilsie, at Piermont on the Hudson. Our American John W. Griffiths (1809-1882) was noted not only as a master shipbuilder but as a naval architect; in addition to much practical work in building he wrote with facility on both subjects. His "Treatise on Marine and Naval Architecture" (it is not clear how he discriminated between the two) was published in 1852; he was a contemporary of George Steers and evidently closely associated with him. He gives the lines of many important vessels, among them America, Sylva (Silvie), Mary Taylor, Moses H. Grinnell and Victorine. The numerous plates show white lines on a black background, many of them very crudely drawn. It is possible that they were the work of the author himself.

The form of Victorine is typical of her day and generation; the extreme "cod's-head-and-mackerel's-tail." The dimensions given are: length, 77 feet; waterline, 63 feet; breadth, 24 feet; draft, 5 feet. Her displacement was 110 tons, 93 Custom House tons. The mast is given as 77 feet, deck to hounds; topmast, 35 feet; bowsprit outboard, 23 feet 6 inches; boom, 75 feet; gaff, 34 feet 6 inches. Unfortunately there seems to be no sail plan in existence. Victorine was considered one of the fastest of the sloops; during the Rebellion she carried as freight the big Parrott guns cast at the West Point Foundry to the Brooklyn Navy Yard. Her career on the Hudson ended in 1890 when she was sold to the Standard Oil Company and converted to a lighter for carrying oil from Edgewater, N. J. In 1902 she was broken up at Staten Island, ending a career of 54 years. All of these sloops were very heavily built, to carry deck loads as well as cargoes below; Griffiths notes the extreme round of beam, over 12 inches in 26 feet. Due to the heavy construction they were long-lived, doing useful work, often as lighters, long after their career on the river; a number of them were finally beached and used as the foundations for piers.

With the type thus firmly implanted about New York it followed almost as a matter of course that it should exert a strong influence on the young yacht fleet of a century ago. The governing conditions were much the same; the first mooring ground was on the flats off Hoboken, the miles of flats about Manhattan, the Brooklyn, Staten Island and New Jersey shores offered safe and protected mooring grounds out of the track of commerce. While the keel type found favor at first with New York yachtsmen, it was soon displaced by an extreme type of centerboard sloop and even some of the larger schooners.

TRADITIONS AND MEMORIES OF AMERICAN YACHTING Part Sixty

By WILLIAM P. STEPHENS

Cutters, Cutter Cranks, and Corinthians (Part Two)

George Steers, 1820-1856, designer and builder of Maria, America and many other yachts. Below: Cygnet, schooner yacht, built by George Steers, 1844. Load waterline, 53 ft. 6 ins. General type of Revenue cutters, pilot boats and yachts from 1800 to 1845

ALL early records present a puzzle to the historian; the one detail usually given, tonnage, might mean Old Measurement, New Measurement, Custom House or displacement. It was not until 1872 that the New York Y. C. placed on record in its year book the length over all, the length on waterline, breadth, depth and draft. When length was recorded it might mean over-all, as now understood, between perpendiculars; from fore side of stem to after side of sternpost; from hood-ends forward to hood-ends aft; length on keel from scarph of stem to sternpost; or "as much of the keel as lies on the ground." Where length, breadth, and depth were given, very little attention was paid to length on waterline or to draft.

As to models, the old cut model was made to the outside of the frames (the inside of the planking), as that was the base from which the lines were laid down in the mould loft and the moulds made for getting out the frames. There was no indication of the stem and keel outside the rabbet, the skeg, sternpost and rudder; the positions of the centerboard and spars were seldom shown. It is a very difficult matter today to reconcile the discrepancies and contradictions which are found in records and models prior to 1870. In 1878 the Seawanhaka Y.C. incorporated in its "Sailing Regulations" the following proviso: "Every yacht winning a prize in any regatta of the Club shall deposit with the Secretary her lines accurately taken off and drawn on paper by the Measurer of the Club; or approved and certified to by him." This requirement was objected to by some of the modellers who considered it an infringement on what they claimed was a trade secret; but its rigid enforcement resulted in the preservation of many valuable lines which would otherwise have been lost.

What is nominally the first though actually the second of "Manning's Yacht Lists," for 1875, includes a very complete article on "Measurements" by A. Cary Smith: "The length over all is taken from where the planksheer intersects the stem — called the wood-ends — to the after edge of the planksheer at the middle of the stern. The length for tonnage is from the wood-ends to the after side of the sternpost on deck; the depth of hold is the distance from the top of the deck beam at the forward end of the cabin to the ceiling at the side of the keelson. O.M. is the Old Custom House Measurement: "From the length on deck from the wood-ends to the after side of the sternpost subtract 3/5 of the breadth, multiply the remainder by the breadth and this product by the depth, divide by 95 and the quotient is the tonnage."

In an accompanying article on time allowance Oscar F. Burton writes: "The New York Yacht Club, in their endeavors to originate some new style of measurement, has so befogged the question that the Club itself, despairing of attaining the object sought for, let measurement and allowance of time go by the run, and sailed their annual regatta last season (1874) without any allowance of time." In this matter the New York Y.C. was no worse off than the other clubs of the day. Due to such conditions, almost all records, lines and even models prior to about 1875 must be accepted as merely representative and in no way authoritative.

The First Yachtsmen and Their Yachts

The use of small vessels for pleasure sailing in America began with sporadic and isolated efforts on the part of a few individuals. There was lacking the coherency, the co-operation and the competition engendered by union in a club. Some of the first yachts were fishing vessels or pilot boats bought and re-fitted for comfort rather than business. Such as were built as yachts followed the same types; the yacht builder as a specialist was unknown, and building was in the hands of small local builders or of yards specializing in large ships. The pilot boat as a type

had much in common with the yacht: she carried no cargo, she had to keep the sea in all weathers, and she had to be fast. The fisherman complied in a lesser degree with the same requirements.

Such craft as were not converted but were modelled and built as yachts followed very closely the revenue cutters and pilots boats of the beginning of the 19th Century: keel craft, deep at the heel of a vertical or slightly raking sternpost, a long straight keel with light draft forward, a plumb or

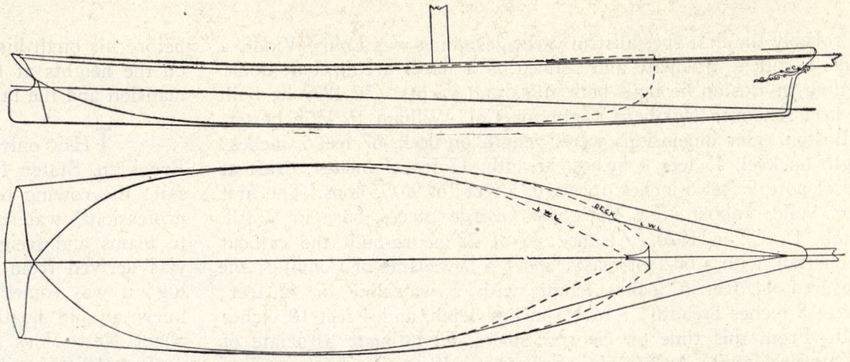

Study of Maria by T. R. Hedengren. The broken lines represent the original deck and load waterline, but with 12 feet of middle body added in 1849. The full lines represent the final alteration to the hull in 1858, with a new and longer forebody, the load waterline a curve of versed sines. The mast is shown in its original position. The rig was changed to schooner in 1861

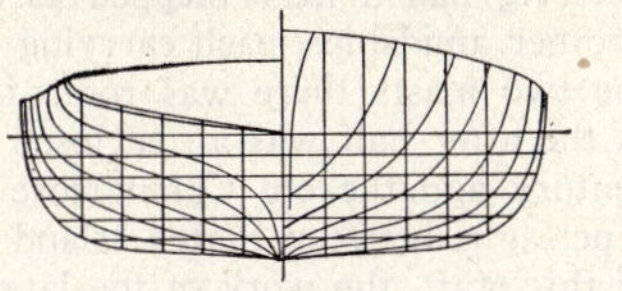

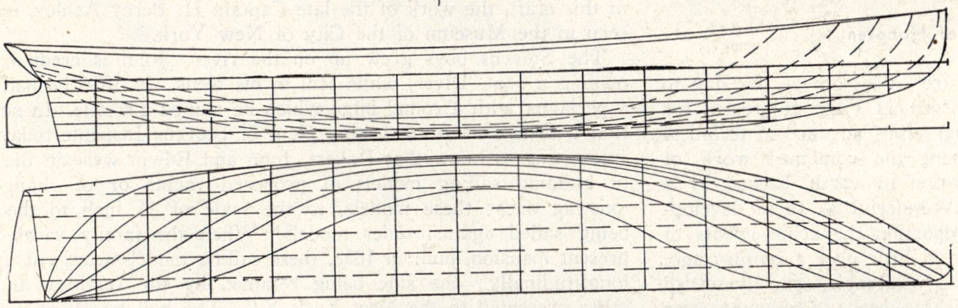

Maria sloop yacht. Designed by Robert L. Stevens, built 1846. Lines taken from sailing test model lengthened 12 feet from original dimensions

short clipper stem and a short V transom. The "dead flat" or midship section was well forward of the middle of the waterline, of deep V form, and the blunt "cod's-head" entrance was supplemented by a long, easy "mackerel's-tail" run. The schooner yacht Cygnet, designed by George Steers in 1844, is representative of the type. It was not until about 1850 that the centerboard came into common use, modifying the form of hull.

The lives of these yachts followed a regular course: bought as fishing or pilot boats, or built like them, they were used for a few years as yachts and then sold for one of two reasons. Either they proved failures as yachts or they made a reputation which led to their purchase by pilots.

Prior to 1844 there were not more than twenty vessels about New York and Boston which could be classed as yachts. At the beginning of the 19th Century we find a yacht, the Jefferson, built in 1801 for George Crowninshield of Boston; her dimensions are given as length 35 feet 10 inches; breadth, 12 feet 4 inches; depth 6 feet; 22 15/95 tons. Captain Crowninshield used her as a privateer in the War of 1812 and sold her in 1815 for use as a fisherman.

John Cox Stevens, 1785-1857, first commodore of the New York Yacht Club, 1844-1854

In 1816 he had built the extraordinary craft known as Cleopatra's Barge; familiar to modern readers through various descriptive articles. Hornet, said to be a yacht, was built in Baltimore in 1819 and re-built later by George Steers under the name of Sport. A centerboard yacht, Teaser, was built in 1821 for George B. Rollins of New York, a charter member of the New York Y.C.; in 1824 he replaced her with the yacht Undine. A keel schooner, Dream, was built by Webb & Allen of New York, in 1832; length, 47 feet; breadth, 13 feet 6 inches; draft, 7 feet 6 inches. A yacht of the same name, said to have been built in Baltimore, 46 feet length, 30 tons, was owned in Boston about the same time by Thomas H. Perkins, Jr. He sold her to a syndicate of which he was a member, the Dream Club; she is reported to have been sold later to George L. Schuyler, of New York. The keel schooner Sylph was built by Wetmore & Holbrook, of Boston, under the supervision of Robert Bennett Forbes, for John P. Cushing; she was 72 feet in length; 18 feet 4 inches in breadth and drew 7 feet 4 inches.

The home of that noted seaman, yachtsman and historian, Captain Arthur H. Clark, was at Nahant, on Boston Harbor. His father, Benjamin Cutler Clark, after using a half-decked boat, built a yacht of 12 tons, Mermaid, in 1832, replacing her two years later with the schooner Raven, 12 tons.

Probably the first specialist in yacht designing was Louis Winde, a Dane, a college graduate and trained as a naval architect at home. Settling in Boston he built both ships and yachts. In 1839 he built the keel schooner Northern Light for Col. William P. Winchester, of Boston. Her dimensions were: length on deck, 67 feet 7 inches; length on keel, 45 feet 4 inches, breadth, 17 feet 4 inches; draft at heel of post, 9 feet 6 inches, forward, 5 feet; 69 90/95 tons. The first yacht builder about New York was George Steers, born in Washington, D. C., in 1820. At the age of 22 he re-built the catboat Manhattan, with a 60-foot mast; under a new name of Coquille; she measured 44 feet 6 inches length with a waterline of 42 feet; 14 feet 8 inches breadth; 5 feet 3 inches depth, and 4 feet 10 inches draft. From this time on George Steers, an intimate associate of the Stevens family, built many yachts as well as pilot boats, sailing and steam vessels and war ships. Petrel, a centerboard sloop, was built in 1840, and Lancet, a keel sloop, in 1842; the latter had a length of 44 feet; breadth 12 feet 6 inches; depth, 7 feet; draft, 8 feet 6 inches. Meagre as these details are, they serve to give a good idea of American yachts as they were prior to the organization of the New York Y.C.

The Stevens Family of Hoboken

IN this age of wonders we are called on day by day to study some new discovery for the betterment (just at present for the destruction) of mankind; some marvelous advance in technical development. These advances represent the combined work of scientists and technicians of every nation on earth, backed by a century of discovery and invention. Wonderful as these developments are, they hardly surpass in proportion the achievements of a single family, a father and four sons, a little over a century ago. At a time when most of America was a wilderness, sparsely settled along the East coast and with no practicable means of communication and transportation, this family furthered the development of the steam engine, the construction of the first railroad, and the building and running of the first steamboats in American waters. Even a brief catalogue of their work would be too long for a story devoted to yachting.

In 1699 there landed in New York an English boy of seventeen, sent out by his father as an apprentice for seven years to one Barna Cosans, an official of some standing in the colony. The boy prospered, his work brought him in contact with land, and he bought with good judgement. He settled in Perth Amboy, married in 1714, and a son born in 1716 was named after him, John Stevens. In early life the second John engaged in commerce, sailing his own vessels to England and the West Indies; but not neglecting land ownership. His son, the third John, was born in 1749 in New York. Coming to his majority in the troublous days preceding the Revolution, he sided with the colonists and won his title of colonel in the Continental Army. The family was now established in a house at No. 7 Broadway. In 1782 he married Rachael Cox, and their son, John Cox Stevens, was born in 1785 in this house. Following John came Robert Livingston Stevens, 1787; James Alexander in 1790; Richard in 1792; Francis Bowne in 1793; Edwin Alexander in 1795; Elizabeth Juliana in 1797; Mary in 1799; Harriet in 1801, Esther Cox in 1804 and Catharine Sophia Van Cortland Stevens in 1806.

The second son, Robert, was the intimate associate of his father in many lines of technical work: experiments with the steam engine and coil boiler, with steam craft including the marine engine and screw propeller, and with the locomotive. Together they built the Camden & Amboy Railroad, importing the engine John Bull from England. The T rail, now in use the world over, was the invention of Robert; designed in the course of a voyage to England to make a contract for rails for the new road. In all of this work they were in regular correspondence with the leading minds of Great Britain, inventors and scientists. The youngest of the six boys, Edwin, while a man of many interests, stands out less prominently than Robert and John. While participating in some of his father's work he seems to have looked well after the family fortunes, building up the Hoboken estate to a point which enabled him, after spending a fortune on the experimental Stevens Battery, an ironclad still uncompleted at the end of the Rebellion, to have established a permanent monument in the endowment of Stevens Institute.

John Cox Stevens was the sportsman of the family. He seems to have had little interest in the civic and mechanical work of his father and Robert, but he was a leader in all forms of sport. He introduced cricket in America, he was a patron and participant in such sports as walking, running, hunting, horse racing and yachting. The year before his birth his father had purchased for $18,340 a tract of land on the heights at Hoboken, just opposite the city. Here he built a mansion and the family gradually transferred from the city home.

THE only means of communication between Manhattan, Brooklyn, Staten Island and New Jersey was by means of oars or sail; the rowing boats were mainly the Whitehall boats rowed by professional watermen and carrying the foot traffic. When it came to teams and freight the local craft was the periagua. This term was derived from the indian Pirogue, a canoe cut from the solid log; it was sometimes spelled "pittyaguer" and many years ago I knew an old boatbuilder who spoke of "perrygimlets." As used about New York the periagua was a flat-bottomed craft of light draft and fitted with leeboards; about 60 feet long and 20 feet wide. The rig had a mast stepped as close to the bow as possible, with another amidships, each carrying a boom-and-gaff mainsail. Between the two masts there was room for two carriages and their teams; in the after half was an enclosed cabin for passengers. Well over a century ago the old Commodore Vanderbilt as a boy was running a periagua between Staten Island and Manhattan. A very fine model of this craft, the work of the late Captain H. Percy Ashley, may be seen in the Museum of the City of New York.

The Stevens boys grew up on the river. John is credited with owning a boat, Diver, while still in his teens. In 1816 he had built a periagua with a round bilge which he named Trouble. In connection with the elaborate testing plant of Stevens Institute today it is interesting to know that Robert, John and Edwin were in the habit of building sailing models of proposed yachts or of changes in existing ones; these models, to the scale of ½ inch to the foot, being sailed against older models. When the family vacated the present mansion, built in 1852, these sailing models were cut in half longtitudinally; one side being retained by the Institute and the other presented to the New York Y.C. The half model of Trouble shows her to have been 63 feet 6 inches over all; 55 feet 9 inches waterline; 21 feet 9 inches breadth and 5 feet 6 inches draft. It is said that a favorite amusement of John was to race Trouble against the working sloops. In 1820 Trouble was replaced by a catamaran, Double Trouble, of whose brief life little is known.

In 1832 the keel schooner Wave was built by Bell & Brown, shipbuilders, of New York, for Mr. Stevens: l.o.a., 92 feet 3 inches; l.w.l., 65 feet; breadth, 22 feet; draft, 8 feet. His next yacht, the schooner Onkahye, was designed by Robert and built by William Capes at Hoboken in 1839. At this time Robert was president of the Camden & Amboy Railroad and Edwin was living near the Delaware River. Models of Wave and of the new yacht were sailed on the river and the Delaware and Raritan Canal. Onkahye was of most unusual form; the main body of the hull was shallow, but extending down in the form of a thick fin with a cast iron trough at the bottom; a centerboard working through the fin. Experiments were made with both iron and lead ballast in the trough keel. Her dimensions were: l.o.a., 95 feet 3 inches; l.w.l., 91 feet 8 inches; breadth, 23 feet 10 inches; draft, 10 feet 2 inches. She was considered fast in heavy weather but slow in light; in 1843 she was sold to the U. S. Government and finally lost off Caicos Reef in 1948.

From Working Sloop to Yacht

THE working sloops of the North River had engaged the attention of Robert and he is credited with the design of one, Dart. In 1845 the three brothers planned a new yacht following closely the conventional sloop model, as in Victorine. We may well believe that, as claimed, she was the product of Robert's inventive brain, as she was emphatically an enginer's yacht. Our knowledge of her today is very incomplete, as there seems to be no original model. There are in the New York Y. C. three models; two, the halves of the test models mentioned, the third the conventional half block model. The last is the most complete, handsomely finished with black topsides and mahogany lifts below water, the waterlines shown by holly veneer. Mast, bowsprit, centerboard and rudder are shown.

Out of a mass of incomplete data and conflicting statements this much may be boiled down as fact. The lines here shown were taken off in 1905 from what is said to be the original model; they show the very full bow and fine run. Launched in 1846, she was sailed for three seasons and then cut in half and twelve feet of middle body inserted; apparently the cut was made just abaft the centerboard trunk. The figures recorded as original are: l.o.a., 94 feet 9 inches (we do not know how this was taken), waterline, 8 feet; breadth, 26 feet 6 inches; depth, 8 feet 3 inches; draft, 5 feet 2 inches.

If the insertion represents the original form with 12 feet added, the original length must have been about 84 feet.

Looking at the lines and dimensions of Victorine suggest that Maria was at first practically an enlargement of her. The second alteration, as shown in the second model, was made in 1850, an entirely new and finer bow on the same waterline, but with a little more fore rake to the stem, giving an over-all length of 97 feet. The third alteration, made in 1858, was in the form of another new fore body; the waterlines being the curve of versed sines advocated by Scott Russell. After this change the l.o.a. is given in various figures from 115 to 122 feet with a waterline of 107 feet, more or less.

Perhaps the most reliable record is to be found in the year books of the Club. Though owned jointly by John, Edwin and Robert, while John was Commodore she was entered under his ownership, with a tonnage of 160. In 1851 the tonnage had grown to 170, and in 1857 to 216. As to the new hollow bow, we know that Robert was in correspondence some years previously with John Scott Russell in relation to the design of steam vessels, and it seems reasonable to assume that the new bow of Maria, with the models of Mary Taylor and America and the lengthening of older yachts came from a knowledge of Scott Russell's theory communicated to George Steers. By 1861, when she was re-rigged as a schooner, her tonnage had increased to 231. Named after the wife of Commodore Stevens, and painted black, she was nicknamed "Black Maria" at home and is seriously described under that name in English publications. The late T. R. Hedengren, a Finnish engineer, naval architect and yachtsman, was fascinated by everything relating to the yachts of the Stevens and Steers; he worked out a study of the original deck plan and load waterline, including the 12 feet added length, as shown in the broken lines; and also the deck and waterline after the final lengthening.

Ancient Practice vs. Modern Improvements

THE builder of Maria was William Capes, at the foot of Second Street, Hoboken. She was built of wood, with the heavy construction of the working sloops; but luxuriously fitted below. One peculiarity was the housing of her bowsprit under instead of above the deck. Her centerboard, in a trunk immediately abaft the mast, was 24 feet long, and not pivoted on a pin but suspended by chains at each end. The weight of the "board" was 7 tons, the first one being of cast iron; others of wood weighted.

The lifting mechanism, as described to me many years ago by an old shipwright, included a horizontal shaft for the full length of the trunk with a barrel at each end carrying a chain; the forward barrel being the smaller, the after end of the board dropped to a greater depth, 15 feet, with but 13 feet forward. The shaft was operated by two winches, each requiring four men, with an extra man to handle the pawl. Spiral springs were fitted to take a part of the weight. Steered with a 12-foot tiller, she was hard to handle and when the final lengthening was done in 1858 a second centerboard was added 10 feet forward of the sternpost, 8 feet long and with a drop of 5 feet.

At the same time outside ballast was added by an unusual operation. A mould was built under the bottom for a length of twenty feet, leaving a space five inches deep at the rabbet tapering out to a shim edge at the turn of the bilge. Melted lead was poured into this space through holes in the bottom planking; when the lead had been smoothed off it was covered with copper in the usual way.

The rig was that of the working sloops, a huge mainsail and jib, a gaff topsail being seldom used. The mast was 92 feet, deck to hounds, 32 inches diameter at the deck and 23 inches at the hounds. It was bored out hollow; 12 inches diameter for the first 20 feet, 10 inches for the second 20 feet, and 7 inches to the hounds. It was "stream-lined" by triangular oak battens on both forward and after sides. In 1816 a mast track and slides were fitted on Trouble and later on Onkahye. The track on Maria was of channel iron with four-wheeled trolleys of brass to which the luff was lashed.

The bowsprit was 27 feet outboard and hollow. The boom, 92 feet long, was 31 inches in diameter in the middle and 26 inches in the slings. It was built like a barrel, with staves of white pine 2½ by 2½ inches, dowelled to prevent slipping, and hooped with iron bands. It was trussed inside by iron rods and also by outside rods over wiskers three feet long. The hollow gaff was 50 feet long (some say 60) and 9 inches diameter; the hollow club on the foot of the jib was 70 feet long. The main sheet horse was fitted with rubber compressors; the sails were crosscut, in modern fashion.

The area of the mainsail is given as 5,790 square feet; of the jib, 2,100; a total of 7,890 square feet. While these figures are on record they cannot be relied on, as dates are not given and many changes in the spars were made with the various alterations in the hull. When re-rigged as a schooner the sail area is given as 12,000 square feet. Under the rules of the Club she was allowed a crew of 55 as a sloop and 39 as a schooner; she was obliged to carry one 12-foot boat.

After the death of John C. Stevens on June 10, 1857, a year after the death of Robert, Edwin succeeded as Commodore down to 1869; on his death Maria was sold to a Captain Buckalew who re-named her Maud and used her for carrying fruit from Honduras to New York. She sailed from New York on July 15, 1870, returned in September and sailed on what was destined to be her last voyage. She never was heard from and the presumption is that she was lost in a heavy gale which swept the coast on October 6. Her racing career was uneven. She outclassed in size all of her competitors; she was raced under varying systems of measurement, most of them very defective; she showed bursts of speed under favorable conditions. In the very inconclusive trials with the new America before the latter's departure for England she was easily superior. She is most notable as an example of the ingenuity of one of the first of America's great engineers.

TRADITIONS AND MEMORIES OF

American Yachting

By WILLIAM P. STEPHENS

Part Sixty-one

Cutters, Cutter Cranks, and Corinthians (Part Three)

IN studying this interesting period we are confronted by the old problem—the egg or the chicken? Was the New York Yacht Club founded by a small number of enthusiasts in order to promote the development of yachting; or was it the spontaneous outgrowth of an interest in a new sport? In considering the former proposition we must remember that the Stevens brothers had long been interested in water sports, especially in sailing; that as early as 1830 John and Robert had been the leaders in the New York Boat Club of 100 members, presumably a rowing club; and that in 1840 John had organized the Hoboken Model Yacht Club, devoted not to the sailing of model yachts but of sailing boats.

What we do know is that in 1844 John C. Stevens had built by William Capes from the design of George Steers the schooner Gimcrack; 51 feet over all; 49 feet 6 inches waterline; 13 feet 6 inches breadth; 7 feet draft; 33 tons, O.M. On Tuesday, July 30, of that year Gimcrack anchored off the Battery in New York with her owner and a few friends aboard and the New York Yacht Club was formally organized. On the following Monday the fleet started on the first cruise, to Newport. The yachts represented at this initial meeting were: Cygnet, 45 tons, William Edgar; Dream, 28 tons, George L. Schuyler; Gimcrack, 33 tons, John C. Stevens; Lancet, 22 tons, James Rogers; La Coquille, 38 tons, John C. Jay; Minna, 30 tons, James M. Waterbury; Mist, 40 tons, Louis A. Depau; Petrel, 15 tons, George B. Rollins; Spray, 37 tons, Hamilton Wilkes. All were keel yachts of the general type of Cygnet and this type retained its prominence for some years.

New York—The Home of Aquatic Sports

All physical conditions about the port of New York were favorable to the growth of water sports; yachting in both small and large craft, rowing, canoeing; this development, now practically extinct, reached its climax about 1890. The island of Manhattan offered the fewest facilities; the East River, with its swift tides and rocky shores, was out of the question; the North River front abreast the populated part of the island was lined by piers; where these ceased it was open country with the waterfront practically inaccessible, the upper shores were rocky and steep.

The only sport which found a foothold was rowing; the Harlem River, with a moderate current and no traffic, affording a good racing course, with cheap land for the many boathouses which lined its banks. Across the Hudson along the New Jersey shore from Hoboken to Constable's Hook were great areas of shoal water out of the way of traffic, such piers as existed down to fifty years

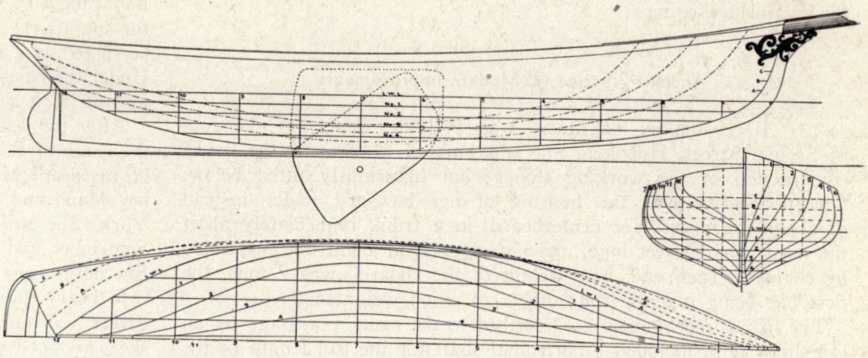

Julia, centerboard sloop by George Steers, 1854. L.o.a., 81 feet; l.w.l., 71 feet 2 inches; breadth, 20 feet; depth, 6 feet 6 inches; draft 6 feet 3 inches; 83 tons, O.M.; sail area, 3,407 square feet

ago were short and of little hindrance, the waters were clear and clean. With the New York Y.C. established at Hoboken many smaller clubs grew up further South. The Kill von Kull, a strait between New Jersey and Staten Island, was little troubled by traffic, there were few piers, and prosperous rowing clubs were berthed on both shores. The South Shore of Staten Island had few piers, several basins, and acres of flats available for yachts of light draft; from 1870 to 1890 it was the center of New York yachting. The other shores of the island offered many protected harbors and mooring grounds for the smaller yachts.

The Brooklyn shore, from Red Hook to Coney Island, a distance of about six miles, had few piers, the protected flats of Gowanus Bay—

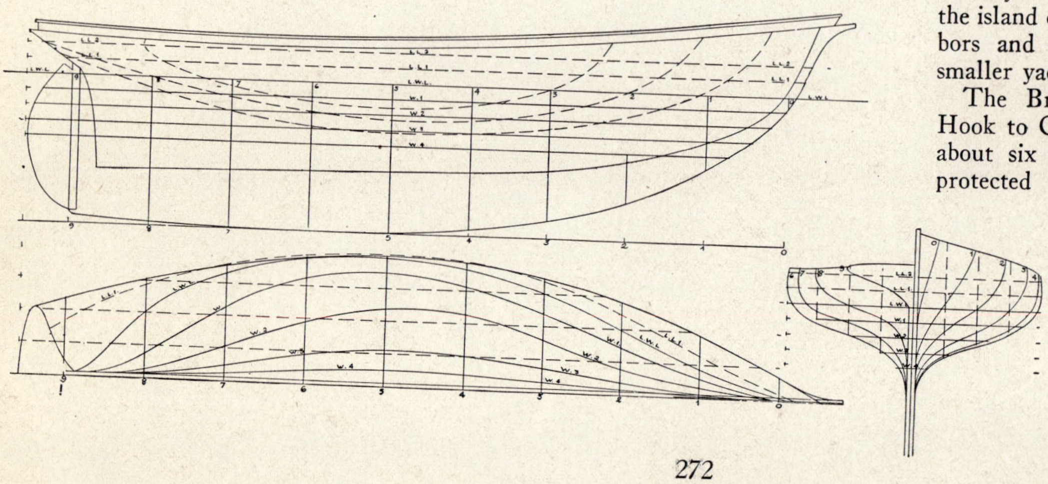

Keel sloop, presumably by George Steers. L.o.a., 41 feet 6 inches; l.w.l., 38 feet; breadth, 13 feet; draft, 7 feet 2 inches

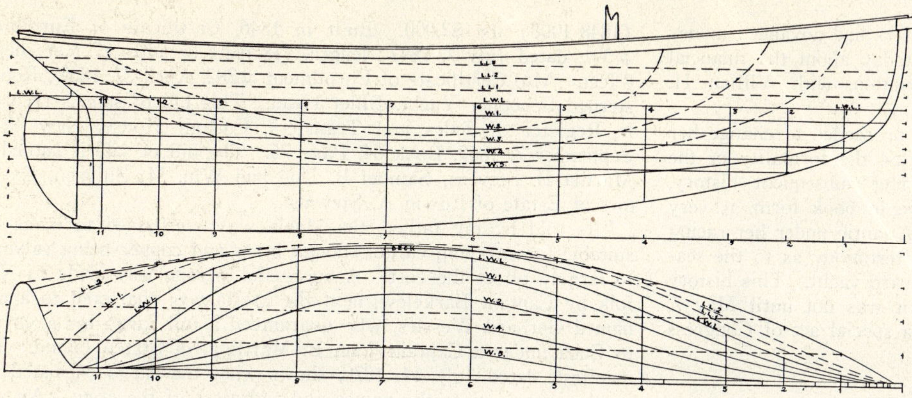

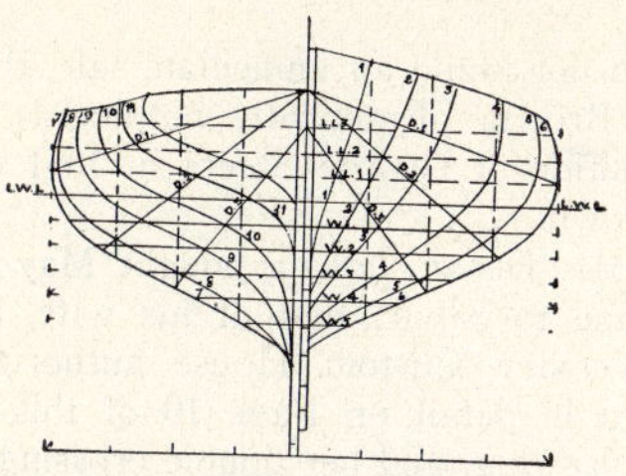

Left: L'Esperance, keel sloop designed and built by George Steers, 1853. L.o.a., 42 feet; l.w.l., 38 feet; breadth, 12 feet 4 inches; draft, 6 feet

Right: May Flower—Silvie. Centerboard sloop by George Steers, 1851. L.o.a., 80 feet; l.w.l., 68 feet; breadth, 24 feet 6 inches; depth, 6 feet 9 inches; draft, 6 feet; 105 4/95 tons, O.M.

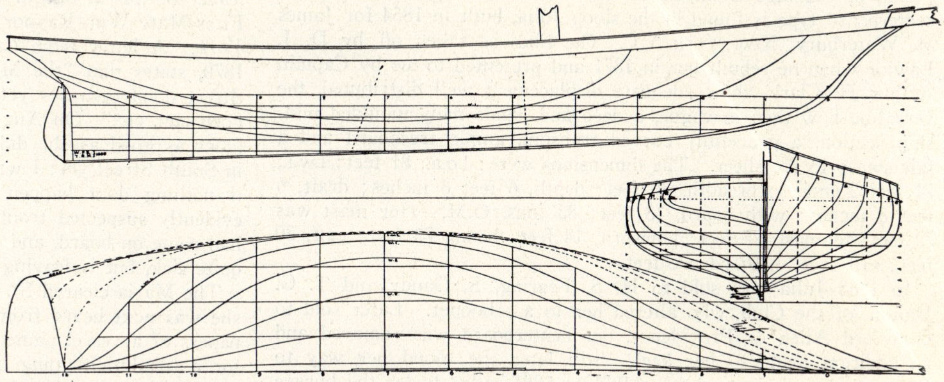

that classic locality known in local parlance as "Foot-o'-Court Street," the hospitable shores of Bay Ridge and Gravesend Bay were lined with waterside pubs, yacht, boat and canoe clubhouses, boat shops and basins. Craft of light draft found a safe refuge everywhere on this shore, while the great yachts of the New York, Brooklyn, Seawanhaka and Atlantic clubs anchored off the Staten Island and Bay Ridge shores well inside the stream of harbor traffic. Bridges there were none; about 1865 the Central Railroad of New Jersey built a low pile drawbridge across the mouth of Newark Bay, but there was very little yachting above this point. In 1885 the construction of the Staten Island Railroad along the North Shore killed all water sports on the Kill von Kull.

Today all of this waterfront is not only valuable for commercial use, but it is studded with long piers increasing the force of the tides, the water is foul with sludge acid, coal tar and rotten débris, and boating and bathing are banished. Many of these changes are unavoidable in the growth of a great port, but such improvements as the girdling of all shores by automobile speedways have been carried out in a spirit of avowed hostility to all those forms of water sports which once made New York famous.

The Centerboard Displaces the Keel

It was natural that as the interest in yachting became more general there should be a change from the keel to the centerboard type. Many new converts had not the time for long cruises but used their yachts more or less for local sailing and racing and week-end cruises. In default of deep natural harbors and of artificial basins they found cheap and accessible moorings on the flats of Hoboken or Gowanus or inside the line of traffic on other shores.

Prominent in this new development was George Steers, and there are several reasons why he stands out so conspicuously from his contemporaries and his successors. He evidently was a man of initial ability and original ideas, at the same time receptive to the ideas of others. Due to his work from boyhood under his father he was familiar with the theory of design and also the practical work of the mould loft and shipyard; his association with the Stevens brothers served to enlarge his field of knowledge. Unlike some of the older shipbuilders engaged in yacht work, he had sailed boats and was as deeply interested in yachts as in ships. In the course of his brief life, only 36 years, he built famous pilot boats and yachts, packet ships, the screw frigate Niagara for the United States Navy and the Collins Line steamship Adriatic.

An example of his work in the smaller yachts is found in the keel sloop L'Esperance, built in 1853 for Woodbury Langdon, later sold to Providence and Boston. After many years as a yacht at the latter port she was used as a party boat, and ended her days, after a half century, as an auxiliary fishing boat at Portland, Me. The sister design cannot be identified by name, but is evidently the work of Steers; both show the characteristic form of that era; the forward waterlines curves of versed sines, a strong tumble-home to the topsides amidships carried out into a well shaped V transom.

May Flower—Silvie

One of the early Steers centerboard yachts, known in history as Silvie, as experience proved was an able as well as a fast vessel. From such meager facts as are on record today she was apparently built on speculation by William H. Brown and George Steers, side by side with the keel of America in 1851. Her enrollment is under the name of May Flower, as built by Brown, under date of August 21, 1851, just one day before her sister America won the historic race at Cowes. No one, however, rushed forward to purchase her, and on April 24, 1852, she was transferred, still under her original name, to George L. Schuyler and his brother Robert. On June 24 she was transferred to a relative, Mortimer Livingston, who in turn transferred her to Louis A. Depau, all being members of the New York Y.C. While Mr. Depau bought the yacht for his personal use, the reasons for the previous sales are unknown. It is possible that, as the yacht had not found an immediate sale, the Schuylers had advanced money to Brown. Practically nothing is known today about the financial position of George Steers in 1851 or his relations with William H. Brown.

Mr. Depau, having bought May Flower, proceeded to change her name to Silvie, that of his wife, but omitted the formality of the necessary Custom House authorization. Her subsequent history, told in detail on Page 10 of this narrative in book form, is very interesting, and her double crossing of the Atlantic under her racing spars, with her racing abroad, gives ample testimony as to the seagoing ability of a properly designed centerboard yacht. This history was made under the name of Silvie, and it was not until May 7, 1867, that the change was legalized under a special act of Congress passed February 25, 1867.

Julia and Her Many Changes

One of the best examples of the work of George Steers in the centerboard type is found in the sloop Julia, built in 1854 for James M. Waterbury, New York Y.C. The lines as taken off by D. J. Lawlor when he rebuilt her in 1871 and presented to me by Captain Arthur H. Clark, show adequate displacement well distributed, the very fine bow then in vogue, a deep and handsomely moulded midship section, a gracefully curved transom, ample freeboard and a fair sweep to the sheer. The dimensions were: l.o.a., 81 feet; l.w.l., 71 feet 2 inches; breadth, 20 feet; depth, 6 feet 6 inches; draft, 6 feet 3 inches; with board, 13 feet; 83 tons, O.M. Her mast was 72 feet; topmast, 27 feet; bowsprit, 14 feet; boom, 73 feet; gaff, 30 feet; sail area, 3,407 square feet.

In 1863 Julia was sold to H. S. Fearing, S. Gandy and T. G. Dalton, of the Club, who altered her to a schooner. Later sold to Crawford Allen of Providence, her centerboard was removed and an addition made to her keel. Still later she found her way to Boston, was rebuilt, and from 1871 to 1881 sailed under the burgee of the Eastern Y.C. In the latter year there was a revival of the 70-foot Class of sloops in New York due to the challenge of the Canadian sloop Atalanta for the America's Cup. Julia was bought by Vice Commodore James D. Smith, New York Y.C., and every effort was made to restore her to her original condition as a centerboard sloop. Her mast was lengthened 1 foot 6 inches; topmast lengthened 8 feet 4 inches. The result was not satisfactory and in 1883, as the flagship of Commodore Brown, she came out under schooner rig and a new name, Nirvana.

The Loss of Maria

The account of the loss of Maria, as given in MoToR BoatinG for June, has long been accepted as correct; though there have been afloat vague rumors of barratry, slave-running and even murder. A letter dated May 11 from Charles S. Barkelew of Pasadena, California, gives a story so complete in detail and so backed by documentary evidence that it must be accepted as correct.

Mr. Barkelew writes: "My grandfather Charles Smith Barkelew (1818-1896), was in the employ of Mr. Edwin A. Stevens and the Stevens Estate from about 1858 until he retired in 1885. I believe that his first employment by Mr. Stevens was as skipper of Maria. I have from an old uncle all the manuscripts pertaining to the loss and attempt at recovery of Maria. One document is the original bill of sale, dated May 12, 1869, to my father, Charles H. Barkelew (1848-1908) for $2,000. Built in 1846, Certificate of Enrollment #591, dated July 7, 1847; length, 118 feet; breadth, 27 feet; depth, 8 feet. Also Certificate of Enrollment #282, April 27, 1869; Round-sterned Schooner Yacht, Billet Head. This bill of sale is recorded in Register of Sales and Transfers, Custom House, New York, September 7, 1869, Book 64, Page 75. The bill of sale is signed by Martha B. Stevens, Samuel B. Dod and Wm. M. Shippen, Executors of Estate of Edwin A. Stevens.

"As told by my father, the Maria was overhauled to make her suitable for carrying cargo, enough brass and copper being salvaged to largely offset the cost. A successful voyage was made to Norfolk by Captain Barkelew, next the Maria was chartered to a man named Gerhard Wessles, who guaranteed a full cargo for a voyage to Cuba under a Captain John B. Martling, of Staten Island. The manifest, dated July 14, 1870, shows what the cargo consisted of; another paper gives the names and addresses of the crew. An affidavit by Second Mate Wm. Burden states that he was permitted to leave the vessel out in the harbor after having been informed by First Mate Wm. Raynor that it was *not designed to return to New York.* A letter from Captain Martling dated Truxillo, August 7, 1870, states that "the Maria is all right and that house on South Street don't own her yet and I don't think that they will; I had a good run, etc." On August 20 a letter from Aspinwall states: "She looks as good as she did when I left New York and is not owned in South Street yet; I will leave for home in about eight or ten days if nothing dont happen to me on the vesal." Captain Martling evidently suspected trouble; another letter states that many people had come on board, and on September 10 he states that he had been quite sick, but is leaving Porto Bello next day for home.

The Maria cleared St. Andrews for New York but did not arrive; she was next heard from in Spain, where she had entered with the papers of a vessel named Maria Ampero; she had a cargo of arms for a revolution going on in Spain at that time. The real Maria Amparo had met the Maria somewhere with a cargo of flour which was stowed over the arms. Examination showed that the name "Maria" had been painted over, but it could still be read at a place in the cockpit. In order to hold the vessel it was necessary to deposit $4,000; which, as notes show, was borrowed from S. B. Dod. There are numerous other letters and documents. Before Captain Barkelew's arrival in Spain dishonest officials had allowed the Maria to slip away; after some trouble in recovering the deposit it was decided to abandon the search. Between the time that she disappeared and the time she turned up in Spain it was believed that she had been engaged in the slave trade. Whether more might be learned at this late date to complete and verify this strange story is doubtful; even if possible it would involve much time and labor.

Only One Dream

Mention was made in the May issue of two yachts named Dream of about the same size and age; a further investigation shows that there was but one. Dream was built by Webb & Allen in New York, it is stated in 1832, but her enrollment is dated July 5, 1833; she was built for Henry Bohler, a schooner of 28 68/95 tons, O. M.; length, 46 feet 4 inches; breadth, 14 feet 5 inches; depth, 5 feet; draft, 7 feet 6 inches. Under date of August 29, 1834, she was enrolled at the Boston Custom House under the ownership of Thomas H. Perkins, Jr.; in 1841 she was sold to George L. Schuyler of New York.

TRADITIONS AND MEMORIES OF AMERICAN YACHTING

Part Sixty-two

By WILLIAM P. STEPHENS

Pocahontas, last of the American sloops; built in 1881 for the defense of the America's Cup. Long mast, well forward, short masthead and short topmast, long boom, single headsail (jib) set on stay

Cutters, Cutter Cranks, and Corinthians (Part Four)

AS, with the growing popularity of yachting, the number of builders increased, the larger yachts were built by men trained in the profession of ship modeling and building. The schooners Fleetwing, Fleur de Lis, Phantom, Rambler, Alarm, Viking, Columbia and Mohawk were built by Joseph B. Vandeusen, at 16th Street on the East River; David Carll at City Island, a builder of the great centerboard schooners used in coastal trade, also built Ambassadress, Vesta, Calypso, Resolute and Atalanta. C. & R. Poillon in Brooklyn, specializing in ship repairs and the building of pilot boats, built the schooner yachts Meteor, Sappho, Dreadnaught, Peerless, Viking, Ariel, Clio and the sloop Coming (the latter modeled by Captain Bob Fish). The designing for the firm was done by its superintendent, William Townsend; later it built Norna and Coronet. Other ship builders about New York and the Sound had their share of yacht work.

The demand for yachts of smaller size was met by a new class of builders, men with no benefit of shipyard training who drifted into yacht building through one chance or another. One wanted a boat, so built her, following with a second and a third until launched professionally. Pat McGiehan was a carpenter who thus started yacht building; Jake Schmidt was hatter by trade, sailing sandbag boats as a diversion and then building them; Captain "Phip" Elsworth was a partner of his brother, Captain Joe, in the oyster business, but developed exceptional ability in modeling and turned out many fast yachts from the schooner Montauk down to cabin boats of twenty feet. All of these men worked by rule-o'thumb, carving the half model from a block of sotf white pine; they knew nothing of the calculation of displacement or the various centers, but worked solely by intuition and a sense of form. They made many mistakes, but these were offset by noted successes, and they held their own for many years against the new school of designers on paper.

A very able plea for the block model as compared with the paper design is found on pages 54-55 of this history in book form; but opposed to it is the record of alterations and rebuilding, often begun immediately after the first trial under sail. When we consider the care and study devoted today to the questions of trim, ballasting, and the adjustment of centers—to say nothing of the recent tank tests of models—we are led to wonder why even more alterations were not found necessary.

As building became more general from about 1850, the keel type was greatly outnumbered by the centerboard. This was due partly to the local conditions previously noted, to the superior speed of some of the centerboard yachts, and largely to the theory of design then prevalent; the belief that more work was required to move water at a depth than at the surface; or, in practice, that it was easier to propel a board lying flat on the water than if held upright on edge by a strip of metal attached to its bottom. Under these conditions the standard of design deteriorated very rapidly; breadth was increased, depth of hold and draft were decreased, and little consideration was given to other qualities than speed in light weather. As most of the cruising and racing was done within the protecting arms of Sandy Hook and Coney Island to the South and Montauk Point and New London to the East, the deterioration was accepted as a matter of course.

At the same time the standard of construction was similarly lowered; some of the best modelers had no practical knowledge of building; the form itself, a long wide girder of little depth, was necessarily weak; the central section was amply strengthened by a deep truss—the centerboard trunk—but there was a hinge joint at each end of this trunk. Soft wood was largely used, with iron nails or spikes, and the disposition of the members was faulty. There is one yacht which stands out prominently as the embodiment of both the good and the bad in the American sloop between 1850 and 1880.

Schemer in race of July 4, 1885. Typical American sloop of medium size; mast well forward, short topmast, long boom, long cabin trunk

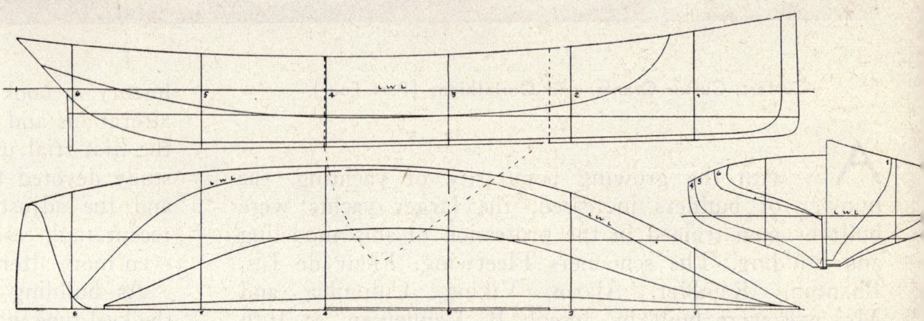

Schemer. Lines taken off by A. Cary Smith, November 12, 1880. Winner in Seawanhaka Regatta of June 12, 1880. Dimensions from lines: Length on deck, 39 feet, 4 inches; l.w.l., 37 feet, 4 inches; breadth, 14 feet, 2 inches; draft, 3 feet; with board, 8 feet. The breadth as published in club books was 14 feet, 6 inches

Gracie

This notable yacht made her debut in the fall regatta of the New York Y. C. of 1868—she was launched in June—for prizes given by Vice Commodore James Gordon Bennett, Jr. In 1909 she was sold, to be converted to a twin-screw freight boat plying between Milton Point on the Sound and New York. Throughout her active career of 42 seasons she carried the same name and rig, that of the American sloop, save that about 1885 she discarded her big jib and shipped a jib and fore staysail, making her nominally a cutter.

Gracie was built in the yard of James E. Smith at Nyack on the Hudson, from a model cut by Abraham A. Schank, who goes down in history as the owner of a paint store in Nyack and a painter of yacht portraits. Her builder was A. G. Jolemus, also of Nyack, of whom little is known except that he also collaborated with Schank in the building of the big schooner Tidal Wave, known from her great breadth and fine ends as "the snake with a toad in her Belly." Both of these yachts were built for William Voorhis of Nyack, a member of the New York Yacht Club.

The first dimensions on record are:—length for tonnage, 58 feet 3 inches; breadth, 16 feet 3 inches (obviously an error); depth, 4 feet 8 inches. In 1868 she was altered by J. E. Smith, and again in 1874 and 1877. By 1872 she had grown to 65 feet over all; 58 feet 6 inches waterline; 18 feet 9 inches breadth; 6 feet 6 inches depth; and 5 feet 6 inches draft. By 1875 her over all length had increased to 72 feet 6 inches; her waterline to 65 feet; breadth to 21 feet 3 inches and draft to 6 feet 3 inches. In 1878 she was rebuilt by David Carll at City Island:—length over all, 79 feet 10 inches; waterline, 69 feet 9 inches (this was printed for years as 60 feet 9 inches); breadth, 21 feet 6 inches; depth, 6 feet 8 inches; draft, 6 feet 6 inches.

In 1880 she was sold to Joseph P. Earle and Charles R. Flint, two young men who had just joined the New York Y.C., and for the next 19 years she sailed under the blue and white diagonal stripes of Mr. Earle. For much of this time she was under the professional command of Captain Sam Gibson, and most of her Corinthian races were sailed with J. Frederick Tams at the wheel. In the Cup match of 1881, after being defeated by Mischief in the trial races, she was widely criticised for sailing over the course as an outside boat against Atalanta and Mischief.

Wide and shoal, with the flimsy construction of the day, by 1886 she had developed a hinge-joint at each end of her centerboard trunk, with other weaknesses, so she was placed in the hands of Henry Piepgrass, at Pottery Beach, Long Island City, where I saw her. The rebuilding, under the personal supervision of Mr. Tams, was described as follows:—"Her sides will be raised one foot amidships, reducing the sheer, as the height at bow will remain unchanged and the height aft will be increased but little. The stern will be narrowed in and altered in shape to conform more nearly with modern ideas; and a new deck and cabin house will be added. Sister keelsons will be worked along the keel, jogged down over the heels of the floor timbers, as this part of the boat has been weak ever since the alterations to her centerboard trunk. The new trunk, a large one put in a few years since, will be cut down two feet on the after end. The interior will be refitted throughout.

In these days when owners change so quickly and the racing life of a yacht is limited to a few seasons, it speaks well for the spirit of the owners of Gracie that they were willing to spend a very considerable sum in attempting to bring the old boat up to modern form. After the alterations her dimensions were given as 79 feet 10 inches over all; 72 feet 2 inches waterline; 21 feet 6 inches breadth; 8 feet depth; 6 feet 6 inches draft. Later her waterline was reduced to 69 feet 4 inches to bring her into the limit of the 70-foot waterline class. Without going into her record in detail it is safe to say that Gracie made more starts and won more prizes than any other American sloop; during the battle of the cutters she held the van of the home fleet. In addition to the unique record of 42 years without change of name or rig she never had a capsize.

Schemer

A NOTABLE sloop in a smaller class was Schemer, of whose origin little is known save that she was built by Isaac P. Wilkens of Jersey City, N. J., in 1871; a builder whose name is otherwise unknown in yachting history. Her record, in brief, is first as an open or half-decked boat, rebuilt with a trunk cabin in 1873; again rebuilt in 1882 and 1886, a new stern in 1892 and lengthened in 1901. Her dimensions after the first rebuilding were: over all, 39 feet 4 inches; waterline, 37 feet 2 inches; breadth, 14 feet 6 inches; depth, 4 feet 6 inches; draft, 3 feet; with board, 8 feet. From 1876 to 1880 she was owned by C. Smith Lee of the Seawanhaka Y. C., a young Corinthian who raced her regularly; from 1881 to 1890, with the exception of two seasons, she was owned and raced by another keen racing man, William S. Alley, of the Larchmont Y. C.; in 1891 she was sold to Philadelphia and raced there, ending her career about New York in 1905; at least a quarter century of hard and, in the main, successful racing. It is difficult to conceive of anything more crude in hull and rig, to say nothing of construction, equipment and sails, and yet Schemer stands out as representative of her era. Like Gracie, she sailed throughout without a change of name, and she never capsized.

Only a little less crude in form was Wave, of the same class:—length over all, 41 feet 3 inches; waterline, 38 feet 9 inches; breadth, 14 feet 11 inches; depth, 4 feet 3 inches; draft, 4 feet. The record gives her builder as John Gorman, Brooklyn, 1878, another unknown; possibly the Cornelius Gorman who was later a partner of Dick Wallin. From 1880 to 1886 she was owned by Dr. John C. Barron, a keen racing man who later owned larger yachts. As we shall hear more of Schemer and Wave later it is interesting to note the comment of an expert, Captain Roland F. Coffin, one of the most vigorous partisans of the sloop:—"There can be no doubt that the two sloops selected as the champions of the club were as good as any in the club. It is equally certain that they were brought to the line in a miserably slipshod condition. Captain Ira Smith, who sailed Schemer, when his attention was called to the miserably setting topsail on his yacht—an old one borrowed for the occasion—shrugged his shoulders and said:— 'Oh, it's good enough; anything will beat that thing.'"

Luxury vs. Safety

AS yachting became more fashionable as well as more popular a new factor appeared, one which has just reached its fruition in the modern diesel-driven "floating palaces" which, if not sunk, are now justifying their creation by their work in the war. The main idea was to beat all creation, something not necessarily faster, safer or more seaworthy, but bigger, more costly and more elegant in appointment. In 1875 there was launched at the yard of Joseph B. Vandeusen in Williamsburgh the schooner Mohawk: 141 feet over all; 126 feet 6 inches waterline; 30 feet 4 inches breadth; 9 feet 4 inches depth; and 6 feet 6 inches draft; with centerboard down she drew 31 feet 6 inches. The main truck was 140 feet above the water and from the point of the flying jib-boom to the end of the main boom was 235 feet; her sail area was given as 32,000 square feet. Her main saloon was 28 feet square, with fireplace, bookcase and sideboard; "the furniture was of the most costly kind and the decorations superb." Her ballast was laid in loose under the floor, and the furniture was not fastened down. Her owner, William T. Garner, then 35 years old, was a very wealthy man, the owner of the Harmony print mills in Cohoes, N. Y., and of other mills. He joined the New York Y. C. in 1871 and had owned two smaller yachts before building Mohawk. He placed the order with one of the leading builders of large schooners.

Two years later another large schooner, Ambassadress, was built for William Astor; his friends jocularly called her "The Astor House" after the once famous hotel. She was modelled and built by David Carll at City Island; in addition to a number of large yachts Carll was noted for his large centerboard coasting schooners. She was 146 feet 2 inches over all; 130 feet 6 inches waterline; 28 feet 2 inches breadth; 12 feet 3 inches depth, and 11 feet draft; her centerboard was 26 feet 3 inches by 13 feet 8 inches. The height of the main truck was 142 feet; from the point of the jib boom to the end of the main boom was 235 feet. The sail area was 21,125 square feet in the ordinary rig, with 10,010 square feet in the balloon sails.

"The main saloon is reached by a broad mahogany stairway, and is one of the most elegant apartments that can possibly be provided on shipboard. Its dimensions are 22 by 24 feet and it is furnished in walnut, maple, mahogany and cherry; furniture of a very elaborate description in the way of sofas, lounges, chairs, sideboard, etc., in blue upholstery adorn the room. The carpet is Wilton; the mainmast from floor to ceiling is panelled with mirrors; the smoking room, aft of the saloon, is 11 by 17 feet, finished in maple and oak." Then follows detailed descriptions of the other apartments:—"The judgment exhibited in the furnishing of this fine craft is most excellent, nothing violating the standard of good taste; the ornamentation, upholstery, furniture and carpeting all blending in proper contrast and effect."

What is much more important is the construction:—the keel is composed of three pieces of Ohio white oak joined together with scarfs eight feet long; it is two feet deep and one foot thick, and is shod with a 2-inch shoe. Her stem is of Connecticut white oak, sided 10 inches and moulded 20 inches. The keelson is what is termed a double patent trunk, constructed of logs 57 feet long and 12 inches thick; the two lower logs are continued out fore and aft to the siding of the stem and sternpost, with an Ohio oak side keelson of 12 by 14 inches. There is also a side keelson 10 by 10 inches on each side of these keelson logs that extends both forward and aft to the siding.

The frame was of live oak, white oak, hackmatack, chestnut and Long Island locust; the floors being of white oak sided 8 to 12 inches and moulded from 11 inches at the keel to 5½ inches at the heads; the frames were spaced 24 inches, the tops being locust stanchions 30 inches above the deck. The ceiling was of yellow pine, 3 inches from keelson to floor heads and 4 inches upward to the clamps. The deck beams were sided from 10 to 12 inches and moulded from 8 inches at the center to 7 inches at the ends, of yellow pine. The planking, of Ohio oak, was 3 inches to the wales, above that, 4 inches; the white pine planksheer was 8 inches thick and 20 inches wide; the deck of white pine 3⅛ by 3½ inches; the rail was of Ohio oak, 4 by 12 inches. This construction, so different from most other American yachts, was the same as that of a cargo-carrying schooner intended to run the beach in winter and summer and in all weathers.

The Sloop as She Was

THE most extreme type of racing yacht known in America was the "sandbagger" or "jib-and-mainsail boat" so popular about New York down to about 1890. The origin of the type is unknown, but it was evidently an outgrowth of the shoal wide catboat dating back beyond the fifties. Under a sloop rig, with a crew of trained experts to handle its deck load of sandbags, it came as a part of the revival of yachting after the Rebellion. Perhaps the most famous of all, Bella, better known as Susie S., was built by Pat McGiehan in 1869. The type was found everywhere about the waters of New York, New Jersey and the Hudson River; every longshore pub had its fleet, racing weekly, and the matches of the more prominent boats, for big stakes, attracted as much public attention as a prize fight.

Throughout this period each club was a law unto itself in the subjects of classification and measurement; not only did yachts race under different rules in the various regattas, but in different classes. Among the cabin yachts were many of 20 to 30 feet waterline used for both cruising and racing; some of these, such as the work of Captain "Phip" Elsworth, John Mumm, Dick Wallin and Sammy Ayers, were fairly able boats, but they were not as fast as those of poorer model. Another popular size was of about 35 feet waterline; the next larger was about 45 feet; the largest sloops ran from 60 to 70 feet. As a rule the prizes went to the most extreme and least able; the "flat-irons" and "skimming dishes." The following table shows the dimensions and proportions of some of the more prominent yachts. From about 1880 onward there was an increasing movement to build into certain classes such as were ultimately the 46, 53, 61 and 70-foot classes of sloops.

							B	L.W.L.
YACHT	BUILT	L.O.A.	LWL	BREADTH	DEPTH	DRAFT	LWL	DEPTH
Julia	1853	81-8	71-0	20-2	6-8	6-4	.285	10.7
Haswell	1858	63-0	58-0	18-6	5-6	4-6	.319	10.5
Gracie	1868	...	58-3	...	6-6	4-8	...	9.0
as altered	1886	82-6	69-9	21-6	8-0	6-6	.308	8.7
Bella	a 1869	27-3	27-3	11-0	3-6	1-9	.403	7.7
Coming	1869	62-0	57-0	20-3	5-5	5-0	.357	10.5
Tidal Wave sch.	1870	120-0	100-0	25-0	8-6	8-4	.250	11.8
Schemer	1871	39-1	36-4	14-6	4-6	3-0	.400	8.7
Vision	1872	66-0	52-4	20-9	5-11	5-9	.397	8.8
Arrow	1874	66-6	61-8	20-2	6-6	5-6	.327	9.5
Fanny	1876	72-0	66-0	21-9	6-9	5-0	.329	9.8
Niantic	b 1876	69-5	60-6	19-2	6-0	5-5	.317	10.1
Amb'ss'dress sch.	1877	146-1	130-5	28-2	12-3	11-0	.216	10.7
Pocahontas	1881	72-0	68-0	21-0	7-4	6-7	.309	9.4
Grayling sch.	1883	91-0	81-0	23-0	8-3	5-9	.284	9.1

a—Half-decked sandbag boat. Later known as Susie S. and Albertine Depth assumed. b—Better known as Hildegard.

Harsh Words from a Friend

THE most severe indictment of American yachts was that penned by the Reverend George H. Hepworth of New York, an enthusiastic yachtsman, hunter and fisherman; who in 1875 made a cruise from Boston to Gaspe, New Brunswick, and back to New York aboard his schooner Nettie, a keel boat of 67 feet 7 inches waterline and 8 feet draft built by Samuel Hart at Northport, Long Island, in 1861. The cruise was made in 1875 and described in a book, "Starboard and Port," published in the following year. The yachting scenes in gilt frames now in the bar of the New York Y. C. were painted for the cabin of this yacht when she was owned by E. M. Padelford in 1881 under the name of Nokomis. In preparation for the cruise Nettie's masts were cut down and her main boom shortened:—"The sticks were preposterously long and made her roll badly in a heavy swell, while the main boom ran outboard so far that when the wind was on the quarter the end of it dipped as she swayed and threatened to carry away the mainmast."

The opening chapter of the book is devoted to a severe criticism of American yachting and American yachts:—"It seems to me that yachting in America has hardly reached the dignity it possesses in England; we Americans play on the water while the English live on it. It is, with us, the sport of an afternoon, and consists, in its most extended expression, of a trip along the shore of Long Island. Our craft seldom venture on long voyages, and would do themselves little credit in a North East gale. They have generally very graceful lines, great breadth of beam, which makes them roomy and comfortable under deck; but are often so loaded with spars and canvas that they are unfit for rough outside work. The main boom runs outboard as though the mast had fallen over the stern; our topmasts, too, run up to such an incredible height that when the boat begins to roll in a seaway it seems as though she would never stop until she had jerked out her spars.

"I am ready to admit that our American yachts are the most graceful pieces of marine architecture in existence; nothing can exceed the beauty of a regatta off Sandy Hook in a six or eight knot breeze. It is an infinite pity, however, that their mission ends when the wind increases; and, that before the stiff breeze which the fisherman or pilot boat only laughs at, they creep under a lee for safety.

"The truth is, they are built to look at and not to last; that part of the hull which is seen is looked after carefully, but that part which is under the water is left to neglect; the average yacht is hermetically sealed by the builder, and ventilation is regarded as entirely unnecessary. The Gloucester fisherman pickles his vessel and leaves air holes in every corner, he fills the space between the plank and the ceiling with salt clear up to the deck; and as a consequence his craft when fifteen or twenty years old is as solid as when she came off the stocks. Our yachtsmen forget that a boat is like the human lungs, she must have air or she will surely rot; a well known shipbuilder told me the other day that most of our yachts which are more than five years old have passed their usefulness; they are likely to be pricked both at the stem and in the run, the two places which it is most difficult to ventilate.

The truth is that we are consumed by a madness for speed, and everything is sacrificed to that quality—Long Island Sound is the disease of which we are dying, to it we are indebted for that evil invention, the centerboard; it has taught us to dread Cape Cod. . . . I have a strong conviction that yachting may be made, and will yet become, a very much more important matter than it is at present. . . . Just now our yacht owners leave their business at three o'clock in the afternoon, take a turn around the South West Spit or possibly a run out to the Lightship, and that is all. Their yachts, like their carriages, are governed by a hired man. . . . The ideal model is in the future, the English yacht is narrow and deep, the American wide and flat; it is not impossible to combine the best qualities of both styles, and then we shall leave the Sound and take to deep water." This is but an abstract of a long and severe diatribe which, however, contained much solid truth.

The Last Sloop

THE fourth challenge for the America's Cup came from fresh water, Lake Ontario, and from a typical American sloop, although modelled and built by a Canadian; in fact Captain Cuthbert was accused of having deliberately pirated the lines of yachts from New York imported to Lake Ontario. The sloop Arrow, modelled and built by David Kirby of Rye, N. Y., in 1874, was considered one of the best of her class in this era, but in her third season she was sold away from New York and did not return to the Club until 1884, when she was purchased by Vice Commodore William P. Douglass.

Though there were then available for the defense Gracie, Mischief, Hildegard, Fanny and Vision, the flag officers formed a syndicate to build, and the order was placed with Kirby. The new yacht, Pocahontas, was late in completion, she started in the trial races with no tuning-up and in very poor condition, and was badly defeated by both Mischief and Gracie, the former being chosen. Her failure was a very severe blow to her builder and he put out a strong protest against the manner in which the tuning-up and trials were conducted. By the time of the next challenge, four years later, the American sloop was a thing of the past.

The condition of the New York fleet after thirty years of development may be judged from this general survey; in the size and the number of yachts it stood as the representative of our national progress. East of Cape Cod the yacht fleet was made up of a very large number of comparatively small craft; owing to local conditions, the proximity of Boston to the open sea and the many excellent harbors on the Massachusetts and Maine coasts, there was a much larger proportion of keel yachts, while the centerboard models were decidedly deeper and abler than those of New York Bay and Long Island Sound.

Traditions and Memories of

American Yachting

Part Sixty-three

By WILLIAM P. STEPHENS

Cutters, Cutter Cranks, and Corinthians (Part Five)

SEVERE as was his indictment of the American sloop, Dr. Hepworth omitted the principal count—the liability to capsize. In the case of small racing boats this was a matter of small moment, every man who shipped aboard a sandbagger knew that at any moment his life might depend on his ability to swim; in the case of the Hiker of the Delaware River (an extreme example of the same type) the accepted usage was that in the event of the wind falling light the skipper might order any of his crew to "light ship" by diving overboard and making his way to shore as best he might. With cabin yachts, both cruising and racing, the matter was more serious; as those, often ladies or landsmen, going afloat for pleasure, were not prepared for an involuntary bath. The capsizing of the smaller and middle size yachts was so common as to attract but little notice, and size was no guarantee of safety. Fatal disasters to both pleasure parties and experienced yachtsmen were almost as numerous and as commonplace as the crashes of air planes are today.

The most notable of these disasters was that of Mohawk, on July 20, 1876. The yacht was off the New York Y. C. Station at Stapleton, Staten Island, on a clear summer day, ready for an afternoon sail with a party, Mrs. and Mr. Garner (her owner), Miss Adele Hunter, Miss Edith Sybil May, Col. Schuyler Crosby and Messrs. Gardner Howland, Louis B. Montant and Frost Thorne. Both mainsail, foresail and topsails were set and the crew was just ready to weigh the anchor when a puff from the Staten Island hills struck her; held by her cable she went by the bow and capsized. Boats from the anchored fleet came to the rescue and picked up the captain, crew and some of the guests, but Mr. and Mrs. Garner, Miss May, Frost Thorne and a cabin boy were drowned. Mr. Garner went into the cabin to save his wife, but both were carried to leeward under the heavy furniture and loose ballast.

Just two years previously the schooner Josephine, 87 feet 6 inches waterline, owned by Lloyd Phoenix, capsized under similar conditions in the Upper Bay while a party of guests were watching a sandbag race; all hands being saved. On June 15, 1888 the schooner Agnes, 53 feet waterline, while at anchor at night off Tompkinsville with sails stowed, quietly rolled over, three out of her crew of four being drowned in their bunks. Her owner, J. Norton Winslow, explained to me very carefully that she did not "capsize" but only "cut under." On May 15, 1883, the schooner Grayling, 81 feet waterline, left the Atlantic Basin, Bay Ridge, for her trial sail, just off the ways at Mumm's Yard; a couple of hours later she was under water, only her mastheads showing, off the West Bank on a clear spring day. A very serious disaster was the capsize of the yacht Venitzia in Long Island Sound in 1890, drowning her owner and his family.

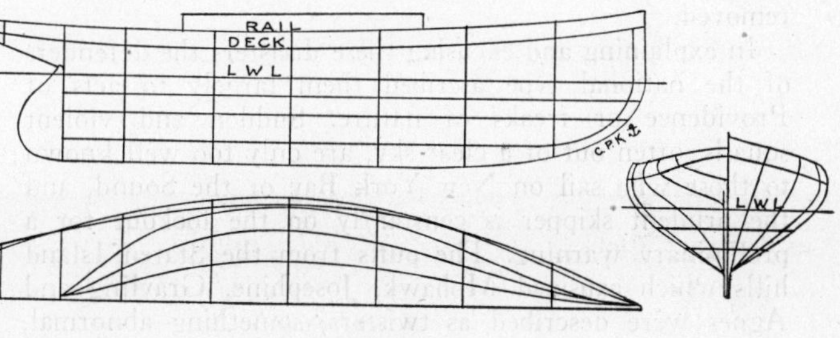

Design for Sea-Going Sloop Yacht by C. P. Kunhardt, 1873. Length over all, 38 feet; waterline, 32 feet; breadth, 9 feet 8 inches; draft 4 feet 6 inches

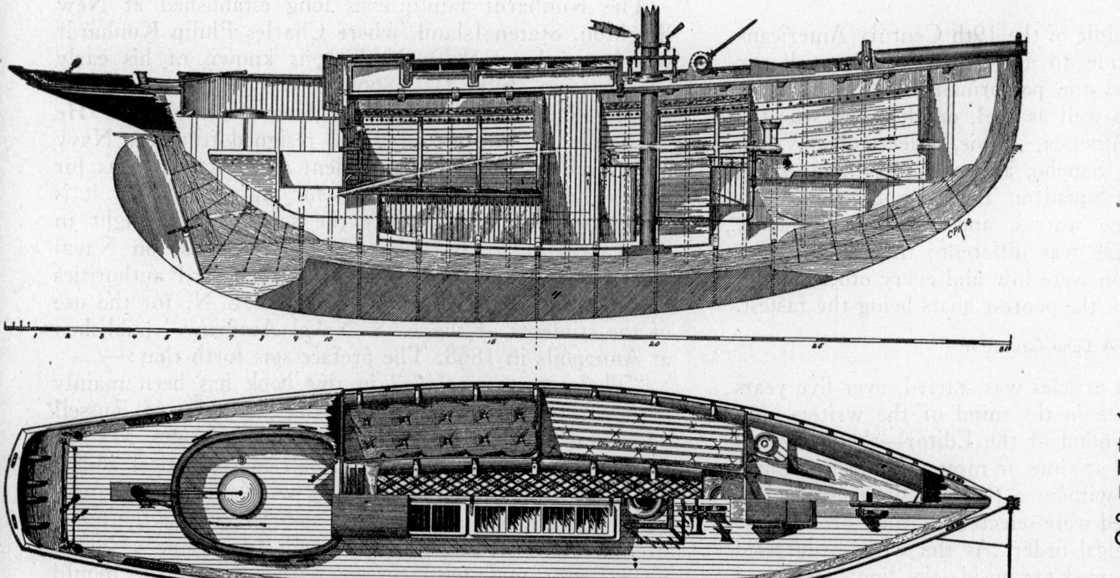

Yolande, cutter, built for M. Roosevelt Schuyler from his own design, 1880. Arrangement and details as drawn by C. P. Kunhardt

Coot, South Bay catboat, aboard which C. P. Kunhardt cruised from New York to Beaufort, N. C., and return, 1600 miles, between November, 1885, and July, 1886

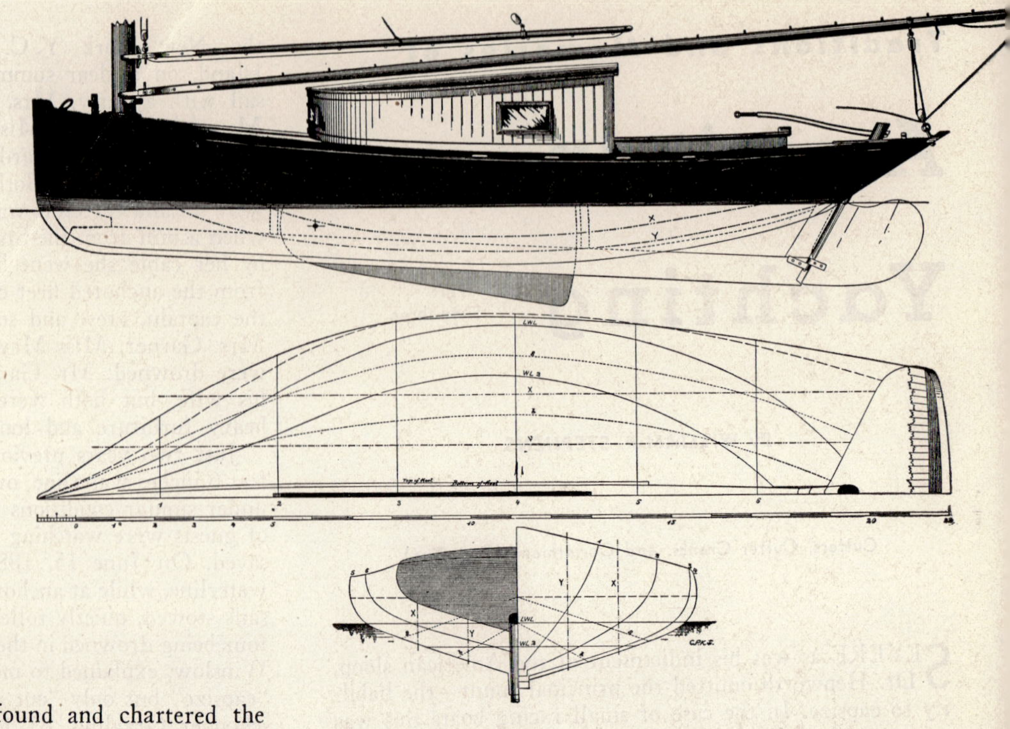

Still another disaster, in which the principal was not a skimming dish but a sturdy centerboard working schooner, occurred off Sandy Hook on July 30, 1886, resulting in the drowning of seven persons. The vessel, the Sarah Craig, 25 tons, hailed from Patchogue, Long Island, and plied about the coast carrying cargo; she had brought a load of watermelons from Edenton, N. C., to Philadelphia. A party of Philadelphians, an elderly lady with her two daughters and three friends, and four young men, had planned a cruise to New York and by chance found and chartered the Craig. They took with them two colored servants and their own bedding and stores. After calling at Cape May and Atlantic City the yacht was off Sandy Hook about 7 P. M. when a sudden and violent squall from S. W. hit her. Her foresail had been stowed, an effort was made to lower the jib, but it jammed and she capsized. The hull floated on its beam-ends, the six ladies and one man were trapped in the cabin where they lived for some time. Tugs came to the rescue but too late; after the hulk was towed into Sandy Hook Bay seven bodies were removed.

In explaining and excusing these disasters the defenders of the national type ascribed them largely to acts of Providence or freaks of nature. Sudden and violent squalls, often out of a clear sky, are only too well known to those who sail on New York Bay or the Sound, and the prudent skipper is constantly on the lookout for a preliminary warning. The puffs from the Staten Island hills which capsized Mohawk, Josephine, Grayling and Agnes were described as twisters, something abnormal, much as every big snowstorm since 1888 is described as a blizzard.

Throughout the middle of the 19th Century Americans could point with pride to their packet ships, clipper ships, pilot boats, and the performance of their larger yachts, centerboard as well as keel, on the open sea; the ocean passages of America, Silvie, Fleetwing, Vesta, Henrietta, Dauntless, Sappho, and even the little Alice; with the Royal Yacht Squadron Trophy and other prizes won abroad. In home waters, and the cruising-racing fleet, however, the case was different; the standards of design and construction were low and every other quality was sacrificed to speed, the poorest boats being the fastest.

A Lone Crusader

When this series of articles was started, over five years ago, there was no idea in the mind of the writer—and probably none in the mind of the Editor—that it would run for such a length of time or meet with such popular favor. It was started without a thoroughly digested plan, and the subjects treated were selected for their prominence and not in chronological order. As the work progressed the original idea expanded far ouside the limits indicated in the title, including much about foreign as well as American yachting. This lack of a comprehensive plan at the start has necessarily led to repetition. The period now under consideration, the battle between the sloop and the cutter, marks a revolution in the whole course of American yachting, very little of it is known to the yachtsmen of today, but the story is one which should be set forth in full detail. This leads us back to a character already mentioned, Charles P. Kunhardt, the original Cutter-Crank.

As a rugged individualist, a man of original ideas and strong convictions which he was not afraid to expound and defend, Kunhardt deserved the derisive appelation of crank. One of his peculiarities was his refusal to accept even ordinary courtesies and amenities under the idea that they might place him under obligations which he might not be able to fulfill. This was the case not only with strangers but with his associates on *Forest & Stream,* with whom his relations were most cordial. Of himself he said nothing; and intimate as I was with him for years, I knew nothing of his private life, or where he lived.

The Kunhardt family was long established at New Brighton, Staten Island, where Charles Philip Kunhardt was born about 1850. Nothing is known of his early life, but on July 31, 1866 he was appointed to the United States Naval Academy from Pennsylvania. He graduated on June 7, 1870 and resigned from the Navy on March 22, 1873. It is evident that his taste was for naval architecture rather than for sea service, but it is a question as to how fully the science was taught in those days. The textbook was:—"A Treatise on Naval Architecture compiled from various standard authorities by Lt. Commander R. W. Meade, U. S. N. for the use of the students of the U. S. Naval Academy," published at Annapoils in 1868. The preface sets forth that:—

"The matter contained in this book has been mainly gathered from such standard works as those of Russell and Knowles, with some assistance from Creuze, Marett, and Peake. A Naval Officer of fair mathematical ability can readily make himself familiar with all essential principles governing the design of a ship, as well as the mode of making the calculations; though to become a Naval Constructor may need the apprenticeship of the mould loft and shipyard. In fact, there is no more mystery about the subject of Naval Construction than there is about

Maggie, cutter, 15 tons.
Sketch by C. P. Kunhardt, 1882

the subject of Steam Engineering; and any intelligent officer may easily make himself perfectly conversant with both; while the importance of acquiring such knowledge is self-evident. In accordance with these views the first portion of this work, entitled 'Naval Architecture,' has been put together for the use of the students at the U. S. Naval Academy. A short treatise on 'Ship-building' will be added in the next edition."

The work is quite complete, carefully written, the selections made with judgment, and seems well adapted for its purpose.

No record is available of Kunhardt's three years of sea service, but in *The Aquatic Monthly,* Vol. 1, No. 7, December 1872 there is a letter from New Bedford over the nom-de-plume of "Big Topmast," over which name he continued to write for some years, though his identity was known. In commenting on it the editor says:—"Big Topmast", who wears with pride and credit the U.S.N. buttons, and who first saw our publication in a far-distant land while performing faithful duty on board a gallant cruiser of Uncle Sam's, and who straightway sent us one of his ever-welcome missives." The letter comments as follows on a criticism of the American yacht by Captain B. S. Osbon, editor of *The Nautical Gazette:*—

"It is undoubtedly with regret that every person connected with the briny must confess to himself the fact that our yachts, with but few exceptions, are simply objects of speed and beauty—there is no demand for strong, healthy and trustworthy craft, but a great demand for fancy work, gewgaw and gimcrack cabin work; all gilt and velvet, nice marble mantelpieces, silver sets, and, in short, all manner of luxurious but nautically useless trash.—A *Herald* reporter would delight in filling a column or so with delicious nonsense about her cabin and stateroom fittings, but that is not what delights the true amateur seaman, though it may be good to carry home to the girls—How was it with the crack Gracie in her trial with Vision? To be sure, it was blowing fresh, but is it expecting too much of a yacht to hold together in a reefing breeze? Flying jib tack parts, clew tears out, then one reefband rips, still another, next the jib outrigger and jib sheets carry away, a few men overboard, that's all, and the race is finished. The owner of Gracie publishes his misfortunes and that partly accounts for the loss of the race, being willing that all should know her unfitness to sail in a close-reef breeze rather than to sacrifice her reputation for speed.—In the Madeline and Rambler race Madeline tears her mainsail a few times, parts all her head sheets, splits her fore staysail and tears things generally; and she is certainly one of the best and strongest of our yachts.—Give our sporting craft good bulwarks, higher than at present; topmasts twice the size of those homely flagpoles now in use, with corresponding jacks, heavier canvas, gear and outfit generally; give them better ground tackle, larger and stronger boats and davits, stronger steering gear, fit them out with good binnacles, and my heart will be joyful."

This was the opening gun in what then seemed a hopeless crusade on the part of one unknown individual against a long-established national institution.

The next letter was from Chester, Pa., dated December 9, 1872, dealing with measurement; in it he touches on a new subject: "A Yachting Congress—I hope and pray for one; it would be a great boon to the yachting fraternity and do much toward promoting good will and *sprit de corps* among the brotherhood of amateur barnacles. Won't some influential yachtsman start the matter?" In the issue of April 1873 (Kunhardt resigned from the Navy on March 22) he took up two new subjects; the small cruising yacht and Corinthian sailing. A design was presented for a cutter of 32 feet waterline; at this time and for some years later he favored the pegtop section of America with a compromise between the less extreme American and British types. In May he wrote at length on the subject of designing, with diagrams and calculations. In June he contributed sixteen pages, a matter of some 10,000 words, in answer to a letter of O.F.B. on measurement; following in July with twelve pages on design, advocating a breadth of one-fourth the waterline and a depth of one-half the breadth. The September issue contained only nine pages, mainly on measurement, but in October, writing from Philadelphia on "Spars and Canvas," he covered fourteen pages. An article on "How to Design a Yacht" in the November issue ran to sixteen pages, with the lines and sail plan of a cutter of forty feet waterline.

In January 1875 he discussed "Small Sea-Going Yachts," with diagrams illustrating stability, in June he followed with an article on "Rigs" and in September a description of experimental tests of stability. Similar letters from other correspondents ran to great lengths and were, apparently, voluntary contributions. The star writer of the day, "S.M.T.," Col. Stuart M. Taylor, U.S.A., in March 1873 contributed no less than 17,000 words in small type in a reply to "Devoted Yachtsman." As the only magazine treating of yachting *The Aquatic Monthly* had a wide circulation and an able corps of contributors, including men like Robert B. Forbes and J. W. Norcross. The discussion, largely provoked by Kunhardt, his descriptive articles, and his advocacy of the study of design, were important factors in arousing new interest on the part of yachtsmen. After leaving the Navy he was employed for a time in the drafting room of the Cramp Shipyard in Philadelphia, meanwhile continuing his writings. Some of his co-contributors agreed with him wholly or in part, but many opposed his novel ideas and strenuous method of expressing them. Even a fighter, in June 1874 he threw down the glove to his adversaries: "Where are Windward, Blue Peter, Binnacle, Long

Tom, A. A., Blue Jacket, Mop Halliards and others; surely some of them must be alive and kicking?"

His Articles of Faith

For the first five years of its existence the Yachting Department of *Forest & Stream* was conducted on the scissors and pastepot plan; in the latter part of 1877 there began a series of articles on the construction of boats, yachts and launches by an anonymous writer who signed himself "Nauticus," the articles were well written in a simple way suited to the wants of the amateur. The following, from the issue of February 7, 1878, is typical of the expert advice handed out editorially:—"Boat and Yacht Building:—In reply to the queries of several correspondents, our regular correspondent on marine architecture writes:—'I would say that the *load line* is shaped according to the judgment or fancy of the designer; the curve of the stem is also a matter of fancy. The paper on drawing, published November 1, contains *all* that is required to learn the art, and I would reiterate the advice there given—The quickest way to learn boat drawing is to draw or copy drawings, continue the practice until every point and line and their meanings is indelibly fixed in the mind. No one may expect to master the subject by simply reading it over—It requires *study* and *practice*."

In May Kunhardt signed on, and the result was at once evident; in answer to "Lubber" as to a change of rig for his sloop, under the caption "The Sloop's Unhandiness," he was advised to change her to a yawl. The June regattas were reported in full to the extent of two and one half pages in the issue of June 20 and this work continued through the racing season, ending with a summary and review. In the dead season when news is scarce he returned to the battle in the issue of October 10 with an article:—"Can the Cutter Cruise?"; a week later, "Is the Sloop Seaworthy?" and an article on Corinthian cruising; and on October 31 a long review of "The Yawl in America."

Prior to the introduction of outside ballast early in the seventies the English cutter was a very fine craft for other than very shoal water, the proportion of length was about four and one half breadths, with good depth of body. Kunhardt's ideal at this time was an adaptation of this type to American conditions. After several years of timid experiment with outside lead the British designers awakened to the evil possibilities of the Thames Tonnage Rule, all lead was placed outside under a very wide wood keel, and with stability thus assured the ratio of breadth to length was reduced season by season. The "five-beam" cutter of 1883 was displaced by the "six-beam" in 1884, and this by the "seven-beam" in 1886; such freaks as Evolution and Oona going much further. As Kunhardt's crusade progressed his ideas grew more and more narrow until he exalted the "seven-beam" cutter as the acme of yacht architecture.

As his criticism of American ideas became more severe a small number of American yachtsmen fell into line, but they counted for little against the enemies of the cutter. This contingent was led by two old men who had commanded big ships, but on retirement had taken to writing. Both, in addition to their experience at sea, had been noted for years as competent yachting reporters. Captain Roland F. Coffin, who wrote on a variety of subjects as well as on yachting for *The New York World,* also contributed for many years to *The Spirit of The Times,* a weekly largely devoted to the turf. Captain Cornelius McKay, son of the great shipbuilder, Donald McKay, had a technical education in his father's shipyard and at this period wrote on yaching for *The Evening Telegram.* In the seventies and eighties the New York dailies devoted far more space to yaching than in recent years; some of the writers were well qualified, but others were mere scribblers who filled space. Captain Coffin and Captain McKay had a wide acquaintance with owners, builders and skippers, they made frequent rounds of the building and storage yards, often writing a couple of columns of reliable news.

Writing of Captain Coffin in August 1875 Kunhardt says:—"It is only due to the able and experienced correspondent of *The New York World,* Capt. R. F. Coffin, to make an honorable exception of his name to the class of shiftless writers who regularly parade their unfitness for their allotted tasks—*The World's* reports are a credit to itself and our yachting fleet." The reader will please note carefully this well-deserved commendation in view of subsequent events.

His Search for Fortune

A FATALIST with a supreme belief that some day he would make his pile, Kunhardt was interested in mining as a means to this end; with no family ties to hinder, whenever civilization irked him he wandered off on some wild-goose chase which ended nowhere. No one knows how many of these expeditions he made before settling down to the work on *Forest & Stream* which kept him engaged for five years, but in March 1883 he resigned and started for Nicaragua to mine gold. His successor, John Harvey, of an old family of yacht builders, was a master of yacht construction and the designer of many successful yachts; but, as an old conservative Englishman, he was in every way unfitted for this new work. A foolish reply to an inquiry concerning canoes brought out much criticism, and as a result I was asked to start a department on canoeing, beginning May 22, 1883.

The schooner Grayling had been severely criticised by Kunhardt while on the stocks, as already stated she capsized on May 15, and on May 17 Kunhardt returned to New York, his mining scheme having also capsized. He resumed his old position with a scathing article on "The Death-Trap Grayling." Again the battle was on, the fascination of the fray kept him interested for a year, and then, in the middle of May 1884, he made another pier-head jump, this time to the newly discovered Leadville region of Colorado. A novice in yacht reporting, this time the editorial mantle was unexpectedly draped over my shoulders, with the Atlantic Y. C. regatta on June 10, followed by the New York Y. C. on June 12, the Seawanhaka C. Y. C. regatta on June 14 and the N. Y. Y. C. race around Long Island starting on June 16.

This time he struck it rich, a letter dated Leadville, Col., Sept. 17, 1884 began:—"Struck her BIG:—Shirt in rags on my back, soles off my boots and walking on the uppers, nothing to eat except an old end of 'sow-belly' and a few rotten potatoes; starvation staring me in the face. In the eleventh hour and fifty-ninth minute struck from barren line into a heavy body of high-grade ore running up to $420 per ton. Average of 8 feet thick is $62 per ton. Have sent an engine up to the mine today and in two or three days will have forty men at work sending the stuff up a 170-foot shaft as fast as the engine can hoist—Bully for Bedouin, the cutters will come out on top, put your last penny on that and write in *F. & S.* with a stiff backbone. Keep up the boom, don't let her drop, go for *The Herald's* partiality for Montauk vs Bedouin. Hurrah. Bully for the Cutters, Bully for the mine, Bulliest of all for C. P. K., at last." A month later he had sold this Golconda and was in Santa Fe, New Mexico, placer mining.

After the failure of each successive venture he turned up in New York, as optimistic as ever; at the end of 1884 he started the book "Small Yachts," which is still a standard work; he also wrote a book on the steam launch, then coming into more general use. Again the wanderlust seized him and he determined on a cruise to Florida; with the inconsistency which was one of his characteristics he chose for the cruise a small centerboard catboat, defending his choice with his usual verbal agility. The best that can be said of Coot is that her form was good for the type; with but 20 feet waterline she had a small "summer cabin," a light roof supported on posts over a part of the cockpit, the open space between coaming and roof being closed by curtains. The curtains were replaced by staved up sides with windows, this and many other necessary changes delaying the start, from Port Morris, a suburb of New York, until the end of November. Sailing alone in this little craft, with no means of adequately heating the "saloon" in which he wrote, cooked and slept, he made his way slowly down the coast, often in serious danger, finally fetching up at Beaufort, N. C. where he wintered, making his way North and dropping anchor off my shop at West Brighton, Staten Island, on July 24, 1886. The cruise was published serially in *Forest & Stream,* but not in book form.

The End of the Search

WHEN in the latter part of 1888 the island of San Domingo was enjoying one of those revolutions once so popular in the West Indies a firm of shipping merchants in New York was commissioned to buy a vessel and convert her to a man-of-war for the service of one of the factions. This task was committed to Kunhardt and he finally found an iron steamship, Madrid, of 861 tons, built in Dumbarton in 1857 and said to have been re-built with new engines in 1886. She was purchased and placed in the hands of Handren & Robbins, Brooklyn, the hull plated in part with heavy iron and the wooden deck work sheathed in iron, some guns being installed, all under Kunhardt's superintendence. Finally re-christened Conserva, she left New York in February 1889 but was overtaken by a U. S. Marshall and brought back. After various legal disputes and trouble with the crew she sailed again in the middle of March with an American captain, a mixed crew, and Kunhardt as purser,

(*Continued on page* 286)

The cutter Arrow built in 1822 was of lapstrake construction and about 70 feet long.

Part Sixty-four

Traditions and Memories of

AMERICAN YACHTING

By WILLIAM P. STEPHENS

Cutters, Cutter Cranks, and Corinthians (Part Six)

We have traced the American sloop to her Dutch progenitor, the *sloepe* with her leeboards, a product of local conditions, shoal narrow waterways; but in the 17th Century Holland was a great maritime power; its vessels engaged in commerce, exploration and war on the waters of the world. In spite of many notable voyages made by the typical Dutch *sloepe,* she was in no way fitted for the open sea. Supplementing the large square-rigged ships which composed the main Dutch navy were many smaller craft known as cutters. The term cutter is as elastic as most others in nautical terminology, in some cases applying to the second in size of the series of ship's boats: long-boat or launch, cutter or pinnace, life-boat and gig. In our story it refers in a limited way to the rig, and in a broader and more popular sense to this rig and a certain type of hull.

The cutter rig as distinguished from the sloop had a much shorter mast stepped more nearly amidship; to this was added a long topmast so fitted as to be readily lowered or "housed" while under way; the ordinary topmast of the sloop could not be lowered through the caps. In June 1872 *The New York Herald* noted that "the Vision has been fitted with the English plan of striking her topmast when under way." Similarly, the bowsprit was fitted to house, the fixed bobstay and bowsprit shrouds of the sloop being replaced by tackles by means of which it might be drawn in and fully secured. The boom-and-gaff mainsail was much shorter in the hoist than that of the sloop, and its foot was not laced to the boom but made fast only at the tack and clew. The topsails were much larger than those in the sloop, and the ordinary "working topsail" was supplemented by two sizes of yard topsails, the upper yard crossing the topmast in the manner of a lugsail. The bowsprit carried a jib "set flying," the tack hauled out to the bowsprit end and the head hoisted above the hounds. In addition to the shrouds, the mast was supported by a fore stay set up permanently from the stemhead to the hounds, a foresail being hanked to this stay.

With the sloop rig there was nothing to do in bad weather but to make the best of it; the topsail was taken in, one or more reefs tied in the mainsail and jib or the jib "bobbed," the whole weight and windage of the rig remaining aloft. With the cutter rig, after reefing, the mainsail might be stowed and a storm trysail set, jibs taken in, and, if necessary, a smaller foresail set. With the topmast housed, or lowered entirely on deck, and the bowsprit run in, the weight and windage aloft were materially lessened and the pitching weights lessened.

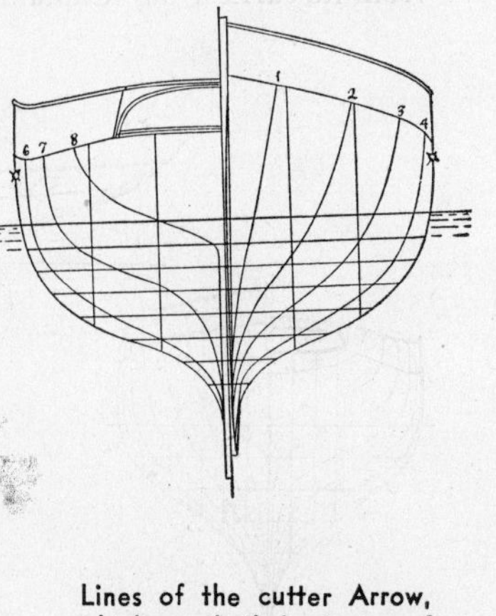

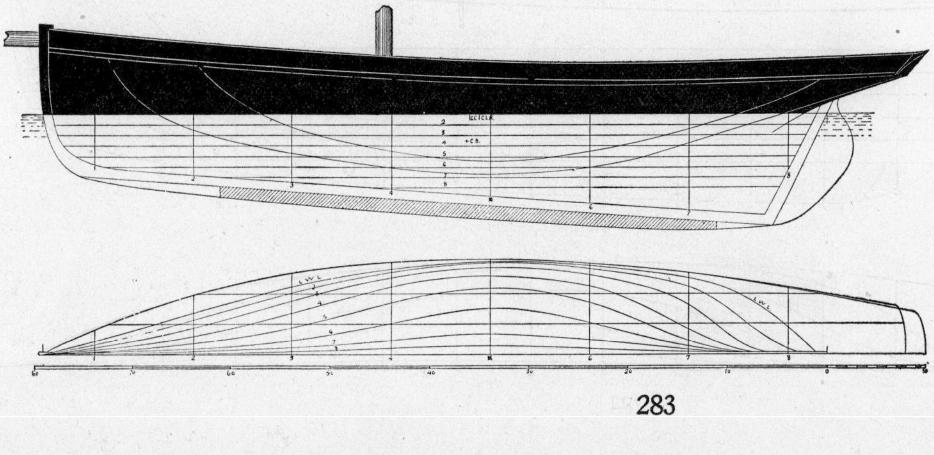

Lines of the cutter Arrow, which was built by Inman of Lymington for Joseph Weld

The lapstrake cutter Pearl, 92 feet long, built in 1820 for the Marquis of Angelsey by the brothers Sainty

The Primitive Cutter

In hull the Dutch cutters were of less breadth than the *sloepes* of equal tonnage, much deeper in body, and the lee-boards were discarded in favor of a deep keel. When the change of rig came about is not known; that reliable antiquarian, Captain Arthur H. Clark, credits the origin of the sloop rig to Holland, the cutter rig to France and England, the ketch and lugger to France, and the schooner to the United States. There is no evidence of the cutter rig in England prior to 1761, in which year the cutter Swift was captured from the French. Charnock described her as of 83 tons, 53 feet 10 inches on gun deck; 40 feet 5 inches on keel; 9 feet 8 inches breadth and 8 feet 5 inches depth; she mounted ten guns and carried a crew of thirty men. By way of definition, Falconer describes a cutter as "a small vessel commonly navigated in the channel of England; it is furnished with one mast and is rigged as a sloop. Many of these vessels are used in illicit trade and others are employed by the government to seize them; the latter are either under the direction of the Admiralty or Custom House."

The size, handiness and speed of these early cutters made them suitable for a variety of uses; for instance, privateering. This sport, more or less allied to piracy, was popular with the gentlemen mariners of both France and England in the days before yachting was known and when pleasure sailing on the high seas was unsafe. Another use was smuggling, a very fashionable pursuit; the cutter was fast, seaworthy, of fair carrying capacity for such cargoes as French brandy, Holland gin, Portuguese and Spanish wines, silk and tobacco; she called for a small crew when it came to a division of the profits. To chase the smugglers there was nothing better than the same type of craft, faster on the wind than the larger warships with square rigs. Under the competition thus engendered in these rival services the cutter developed rapidly.

In tracing the history of yachting from its earliest day Captain Clark deals first with the preliminary period from about 1600 to the beginning of the 19th Century. Most of the "yachts" of this period were official craft, used by royalty, officers of the government, in revenue service; and comparatively few for the pleasure of individuals; they were largely the product of the national dockyards. The building and use of yachts by individuals, and the racing of yachts, began about 1812-15 just prior to the organization of the Royal Yacht Squadron. At this period there came into existence a new class of yacht builders, the Ratseys, the Whites, Nicholsons, Steeles, Inmans, Fifes and others of less note. Most of the building centered about the Isle of Wight, but when Lord Uxbridge, later the Marquis of Angelsey, a man whose motto was "I want what I want when I want it," decided that he must have a yacht to outsail the more westerly craft, he sought out an unknown builder.

Philip Sainty, a Smuggler-Builder

The Essex coast of England was noted for its hardy sailor men. Even down to today its skippers and crews, Pittucks, Harlows, Carters, Cranfields, Downs, are found aboard many of the fastest racing yachts and in the off-season they fish the North Sea. The opposite nation of Holland was noted for the quality of its gin, and there was much less work in smuggling than in fishing. Early in the 19th Century a citizen of Colchester, one John Philip Sainty, was carrying on a profitable business in

Lines of Vanguard, last of the designer-shipwright built vessels, built by Michael Ratsey of Cowes

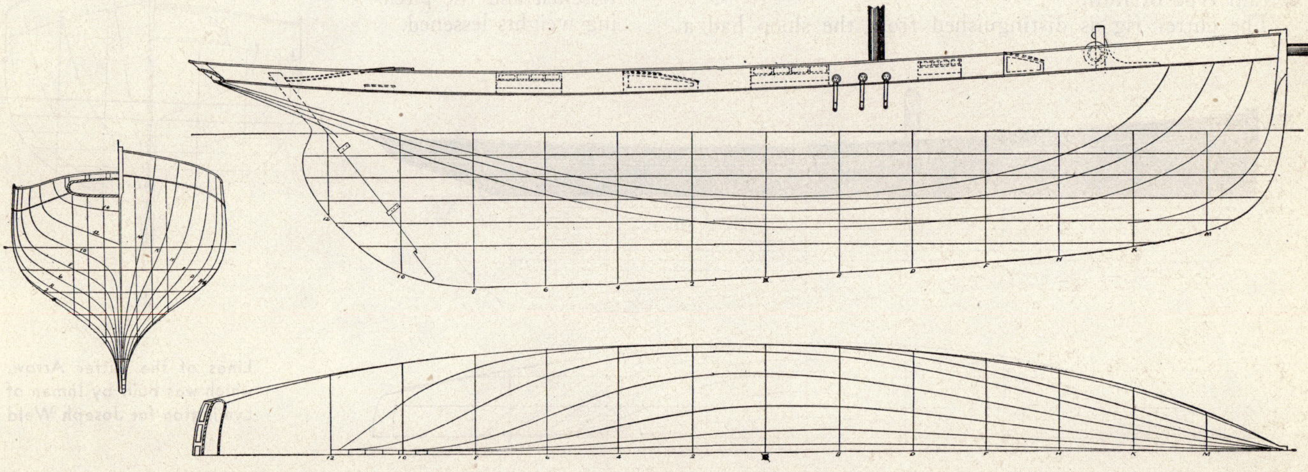

smuggling in vessels which he built for himself. They were lapstrake, of light construction, rigged as luggers, and designed for speed rather than a long life. The tradition is that after outstailing the revenue cutters, in a successful run the vessel was broken up for her copper fastenings and a still faster one built.

About 1812 Lord Uxbridge sought out Sainty, who built a cutter, Emerald, which proved fast; when he joined the Duke of Wellington on the Peninsular he presented Emerald to the Prince of Wales. After his return from the war with but one leg—he lost one at Waterloo—he was created Marquis of Angelsey, the title under which he is known in yachting history. Desiring another yacht, he went to Colchester and found that Sainty was in Chelmsford gaol, in company with his son John and his brother Robert. How they got there is another story.

There had been in Colchester a man, Brown, by trade a whip-maker, who was caught passing counterfeit guineas, but escaped to Holland. On one of his trips Sainty met his friend Brown, and through his "pull" with certain personages secured his release and brought him back to Colchester; whereupon Brown sought to turn an honest penny by betraying Sainty to the authorities and telling of the double sides in his vessel and his caches of gin ashore. It is said that when told of Sainty's predicament the Marquis swore that "if he were in hell he would get him out."

It would seem that the course of Justice ran much the same "in good King George's glorious days" as in modern times when each Christmas season is celebrated by a general jail delivery of criminals, on pardon or parole, by our humanitarian governors. The "pull" of the Marquis with the Prince Regent was strong enough to win a pardon for "John Sainty." When it came into the hands of John Philip, Sr., he turned it over to son John, Jr., and the prison doors opened for him. The Marquis apparently saw the point of the joke and took another "pull" which freed the father. He was then told that Brother Robert was absolutely indispensable for the construction of the proposed yacht; and he, too, was freed.

THE trio set to work upon the banks of the Colne about a mile outside of Colchester and built a cutter, of lapstrake construction, 92 feet 1 inch length for tonnage; 22 feet 1 inch breadth; 12 feet depth; of 130 tons. Pearl, as she was named, was evidently satisfactory to the Marquis, as he owned her from 1820, the year in which she was launched, until his death in 1853. After passing through various hands she was purchased in 1885 by my canoeing associate Lt. Warrington Baden-Powell, R.N.V.R., who owned her until 1902 when she was sold to be broken up, a career of 81 years. By way of odd coincidence, for many years the late E. B. Tredwen and Lt. Baden-Powell were rivals in canoe racing, each bringing out a new canoe every year. While all of Baden-Powell's canoes were named Nautilus, those of Tredwen, even down to his final "barge-yacht," were named Pearl.

A pension of 100 pounds per year was settled on Sainty by the Marquis on condition that he built no more yachts, but he did build a number: Swallow, Arundel, Gipsy, Gazelle, Corsair, Ruby and others. Sainty died in 1844 at the age of 93; in his last years he was aided by the Marquis of Angelsey, the Duke of Norfolk and others of his clients.

Active for many years in pursuit of Sainty was Post Captain Edward Martin, R.N., in command of a revenue cutter, another notable Wivenhoe man; he was married four times and had a family of 28 children. The eldest daughter married one Thomas Harvey, who succeeded Philip Sainty in his yard, now at Wivenhoe, and built a number of fast yachts. In 1857 his son, John Harvey, joined him in the management of the yard and succeeded him about 1865. Lord Alfred Paget, son of the Marquis of Angelsey, continued a patron of the yard; the Harveys building for him the cutters Resolute, Snowdrop I, Snowdrop II, Cecile, Water Lily, Xantha, and the steam yacht Xantha. For over a quarter of a century under John Harvey, Wivenhoe was an active competitor of Cowes, Gosport and Fairlie in building the fastest of the large cutters; in its later years it turned out two of the most notable schooners, Sea Belle and Miranda; the latter known from her rig and her ability to windward as "the two-masted cutter."

The "Old Arrow"

CONTEMPORARY with Pearl, and even more famous in racing, was the cutter Arrow, built in 1822. Her first owner, Joseph Weld, was, like the Marquis of Angelsey, one of the founders of the Royal Yacht Squadron; like the Marquis, he had ideas of his own, and he chose as a builder, Inman of Lymington, to carry them out. He is said to have based his model on a fast smuggler, and, like Pearl, she was of lapstrake construction, about 70 feet in length and of 85 tons. She proved successful from the start; in 1825 she sailed a match with Pearl for 500 pounds. In accepting Mr. Weld's challenge the owner of Pearl is said to have remarked: "If the Pearl should be beaten I will burn her as soon as we get back." However, she won and the cremation was postponed.

Mr. Weld sold Arrow in 1828 and continued his experiments with Lulworth in that year, Alarm in 1830, Meteor in 1856 and a second Lulworth in 1857. After passing through the hands of two other owners Arrow was sold to be broken up in 1845; it is probable that the lightly built lapstrake hull had been strained by continuous hard racing. How she started a new career is told by Thomas Chamberlayne, another member of the Squadron. "I bought the Arrow when she was lying on the banks of the river Itchen, full of mud and water and waiting to be broken up for firewood; it was December 1846 and I gave 116 pounds for her. Her length was then 61 feet 9½ inches; breadth, 18 feet 5¼ inches; and depth of hold 8 feet 8 inches. My wish was to get her midship section to build from, knowing how celebrated she had been in her former days. I built from the old moulds, and, out of respect for my esteemed friend, Mr. Weld, her original constructor, called her after the old vessel, "The Arrow." I have since altered her on several occasions, bringing her up to 84 tons, then to 117."

Such men as Angelsey, Weld and Chamberlayne were not out for bargains by building in one-design classes and thus saving the designer's fee, they spent their money freely in backing the builder which each chose as the best to realize his ideas; many of their experiments were costly failures, yet all served to further the improvement of yachts.

The Secrets of Yacht Designing

THE sentiment of the day, 1874, in matters both technical and ethical, are shown in a later letter in answer to a request by Dixon Kemp for the lines in order to compare them with other yachts. "I have invariably refused all applications to take and make drawings of the lines of my vessels, never having myself looked at or examined the lines of one single yacht for the purpose of their adaptation to my own designs in any one particular. My only guide in the construction of my vessels has been the endeavor to perfect a form that would offer the least possible resistance to the element it is intended to pass through; and, when going through the water, I never miss an opportunity of observing where the water, by coming in contact with the vessel, is broken up. I note this particular spot and, in laying the vessel up, endeavour to remedy the evil as it shows friction and, consequently, resistance. In building on the above plan, of course, I never for a moment lose sight of the *sine qua non,* namely, power to stand up under a heavy press of canvas, and to keep those on deck as dry and comfortable as possible.

"I must now, however, assure you that it affords me very great pleasure to waive in your favor my objections to the lines of my vessel being taken; and when I do this I consider that I but poorly pay the debt we all owe you." As the result of this "generous concession" the lines were taken off by Mr. Kemp and a copy given to the owner; but, when in 1875, Mr. Kemp asked permission to publish the lines in *The Field,* he was again rebuffed as follows: "My dear Sir—In reply to your letter requesting to be allowed to publish the lines of my vessel, The Arrow, I do assure you in all sincerity that nothing gives greater pain than to find myself compelled at any time to refuse to comply with the wishes of a friend, and more particularly so in the present instance when that friend's intent is merely to benefit other yachtsmen by the publication which he proposes, but I shall feel greatly obliged by your kindly omitting from your list my vessel. Her lines are wholly my own ideas, copied from no vessel—not even the bow from 'Il Americo' as so often said (it was not likely I should adopt the bow of a vessel I beat). Your list consists of vessels built by public builders, so your publishing their lines is an act of kindness to them and a public benefit to the yachting community.

Yours very truly,
(Signed) THOS. CHAMBERLAYNE."

It will be noticed that in this example of fine old crusted conservatism the writer always speaks of his yacht as a "vessel," and that he uses the definite article before the name. As to the "act of kindness" to the "public builders," many at that date shared his ideas as to the sanctity of the lines of their yachts.

It was not until after Mr. Chamberlayne's death that his son permitted the lines as here shown to be published in *The Field,* March 1879, her dimensions then being: l.o.a., 90 feet 2 inches; l.w.l., 79 feet 2 inches; breadth, 18 feet 4 inches; depth, 8 feet 2 inches; draft, 11 feet 6 inches; displacement, 106 tons; ballast, 40 tons (on keel, 13.7 tons); area of lower sails, 4,680 square feet. By this time she had been repeatedly rebuilt, the length for tonnage had grown from the original 61.75 to 81.4, showing a lengthening of 20 feet; in fact, nothing was left of the original Arrow but her midship section. At this date, which ended her racing career of 58 years, she was described among a fleet of more modern yachts as being "the most formidable cutter afloat."

Development Under Inside Ballast

THE revenue cutters of the 18th Century were very crude in form, broad, with a midship section only a third of the length from the stem; by the early part of the 19th Century the form had improved, the excessive breadth was reduced, but the cod's-head entrance was retained with the midship section still well forward of the middle. Except for the rig, they shared the general characteristics of the vessels described on page 52 of MoToR BoatinG for June. By the middle of the century a further improvement in form might be noted, as shown in Cygnet, of 1846. From this time on, keen competition between a dozen British builders wrought further improvement, and as long as the use of inside ballast continued the British cutter was far in advance of American models. There is little fault to be found with either the proportions or lines of the cutter Vanguard, 60 tons, designed and built by Michael Ratsey in 1866.

The ballast of such yachts as Pearl consisted of stones from the beach or rough kentledge—grate bars or cannon balls—later the iron was cast to fit between the floors as low as possible; still later this iron was displaced by lead cast to fit. That ancient mariner, "Vanderdecken," writing in 1853, discusses at length the subject of ballast. He suggests as preferable but impracticable bar iron with a specific gravity of 7.700 as compared with cast iron at 7.264, quoting the extra speed of a vessel carrying a cargo of bar iron as compared with iron in other forms. He quotes prices: scrap, 1 pound to 2 pounds 10 shillings; pig iron, 3 pounds 10 shillings to 4 pounds; cast limber pieces, 6 pounds per ton. He is insistent as to the distribution; no ballast outside the middle third of the length; cast iron plates for the cabin floor, ballast stowed in the wings or lockers, a ballast box under the cabin table; the desirability of ballast on springs, but the impracticability of shavings, cork or rubber under iron. He speaks with approval of the prohibition of shifting ballast in 1856; prior to that date shot bags were piled on the lockers or on special ballast shelves back of the lockers, to be shifted on every tack. In the wooden yachts of the late sixties the ratio of ballast to displacement was as low as 33 per cent, in the extreme narrow cutters of 15 years later it was as high as 70 per cent.

The origin of the outside metal keel is unknown, but George L. Watson mentions the yacht Wave, built by Robert Steele of Greenock in 1834, as fitted with an iron keel. The transfer of ballast from inside to outside the hull began early in the seventies; in 1871 four tons of lead were cast under the keel of the schooner Dreadnaught in New York, and six tons under the Dauntless; and Magic replaced her inside iron by lead centered more nearly amidship. In the same year the English schooner Cetonia sent her loose iron ashore and replaced it by moulded lead inside. The cutter Arethusa was only one of many at this time experimenting with lead padding on both sides of a narrow wooden keel, at the same time shipping lead instead of iron inside. Lead could not be carried on such a keel as that in Vanguard, and in 1872 in building the 5-ton cutter Hilda John Inglish of Glasgow made the wood keel of three times the usual breadth. The builders were very reluctant to trust even a moderate weight of lead secured to the keel by bolts, and even used dovetail plates on the sides for additional security.

In building the schooner Sea Belle, 142 tons, in 1874 John Harvey devised an elaborate system of internal ballasting, the floors being iron angles bent to shape, with lead cast around them to fill out the full form of a floor knee; the stringers had centers of angle bars similarly encased in lead. In building the schooner Miranda, 135 tons, two years later, the moulded lead blocks were hung by iron straps from stringers so as to distribute the weight over the bottom structure. With the general adoption of the wide wood keel built up of several pieces and carrying a large mass of lead beneath it, breadth was no longer necessary for stability, the evil dormant in the Thames Tonnage Rule came to life, and year by year the cutter became narrower and deeper.

A MARKED departure from the first crude models is seen in Vanguard, 60 tons, built 20 years later by Michael Ratsey of Cowes. Her dimensions were: l.o.a., 74 feet 8 inches; l.w.l., 65 feet; breadth, 14 feet 8 inches; depth, 11 feet 1 inch; draft, 10 feet 5 inches. The V section had given place to a fairly swept S curve from planksheer to bottom of keel, the midship section was more nearly amidships, and the entrance was fine and the run filled in. As to unity and fairness of form, Vanguard shows up in marked contrast to the many American sloops of even later date whose lines have been shown in preceding pages. With the siding of the keel but little greater than that of the stem and sternpost all ballast was necessarily inside.

Vanguard marks the end of the era of the designer-shipwright; men trained in generations of shipbuilding but adapting their methods to the lighter work called for in the yacht. Her stem head is carried up above the rail as a support to the bowsprit which ran out on the port side and was set at a slight angle so that the heel would clear the mast when fully housed. There was a high bulwark on locust stanchions and capped by a rail of elm or teak such as Kunardt sighed for. The transom was of elaborate construction, open under the rail; the art and skill of the ship carver were called on for elaborately wrought carved and gilded trail-boards and rope mouldings. A dozen years later young Will Fife III and George Lennox Watson were designing yachts with a mere footrail in place of the bulwarks and a counter fined down to a knife-edge in place of the deep-framed transom.

CUTTERS, CUTTER-CRANKS, AND CORINTHIANS

(*Continued from page 282*)

to make delivery. She was never heard from, incoming steamers for days reported a heavy storm off the Virginia coast, and several reported passing through two groups of wreckage indicating the sinking of two vessels. A life raft with two bodies was picked up and also two lifeboats, one with the name, Conserva. The most plausible conclusion was that she was sunk in collision with another vessel. The fee which Kunhardt was to receive would have been a fortune to one of his simple tastes and would have justified his belief that he would "make his pile."

While making no claims as an artist, Kunhardt was, nevertheless, very skillful with the pen, and possessed of an artistic sense which was of great help in his work. All of his designs were supplemented by artistic shading and coloring which not only pleased the eye but made them better understood. His figure drawing was very crude, but when it came to the work which he loved best, the exaltation of the narrow cutter at her normal sailing angle of about 35 degrees, his portrayal was really artistic. A good example of the work is seen in the drawing of the cutter Yolande, in the careful shading and the minute detail. Some of us might surpass his work in the actual lines drawn along a batten with a rightline pen, but he stood alone among naval architects in the line of artistic delineation.

Beyond question Kunhardt was a fanatic, an extremist, making claims which he could not substantiate, often using language which was other than parliamentary; but no milder methods could have accomplished the immense task which he assumed voluntarily. The battle of the sloop and cutter was War, in every meaning of the word, and it was not carried on by either side with that calm appeal to reason and observance of all amenities which is so characteristic of a 20th Century political convention. He took and gave hard blows in a cause which he honestly believed to be right.

Traditions and Memories of

American Yachting

By WILLIAM P. STEPHENS

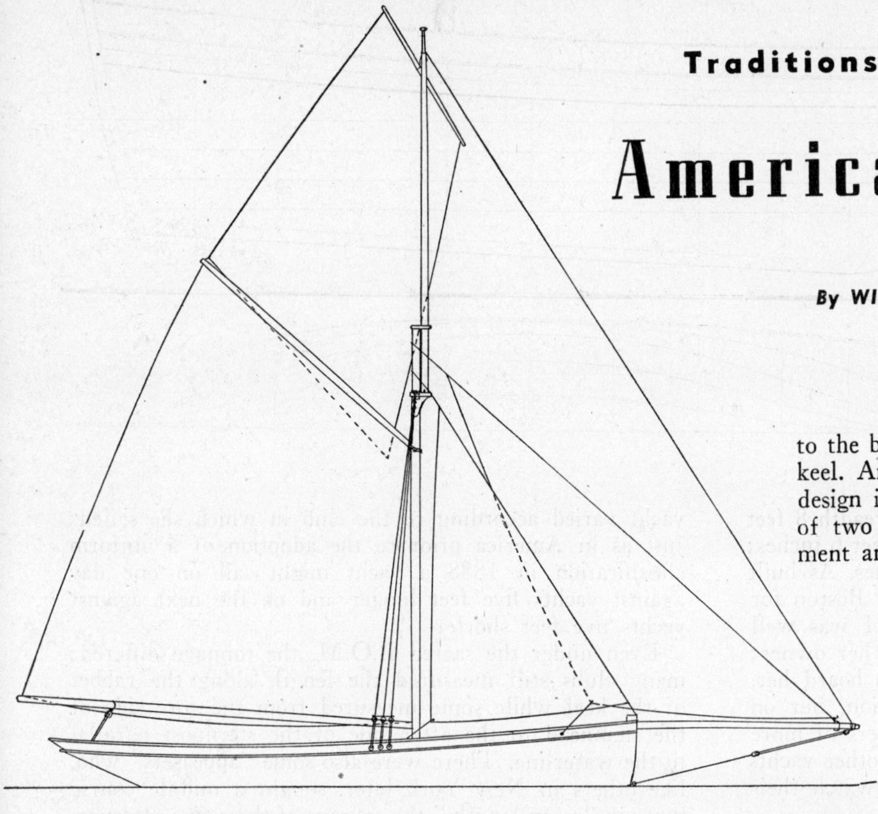

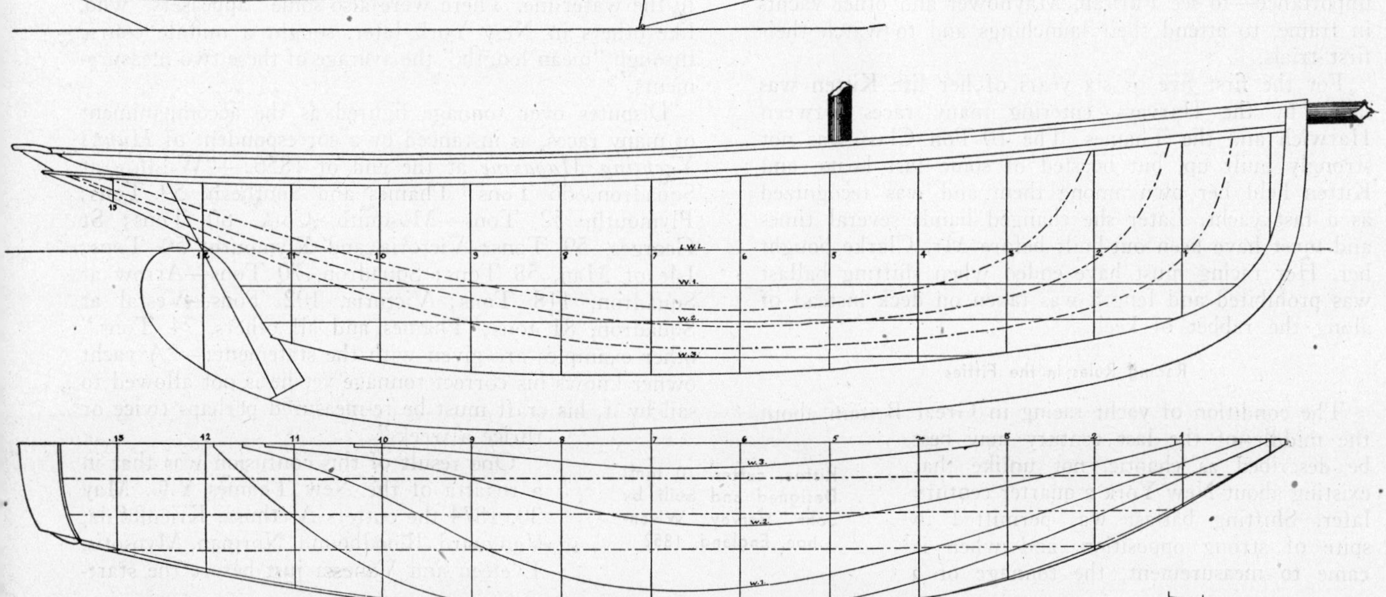

Part Sixty-five

Cutters, Cutter-Cranks and Corinthians (Part Seven)

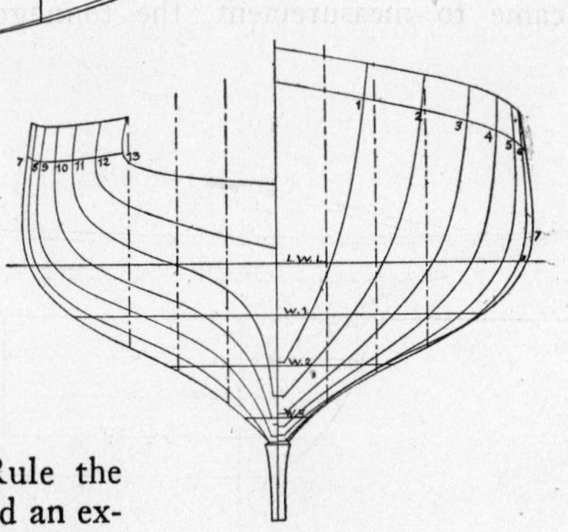

Valiant, cutter. Designed and built by Henry Piepgrass, New York, 1879. Sail plan of Valiant above

THE introduction of the British cutter to American waters was, as far as is known, a matter of chance, and not of deliberate planning. About 1870 the cutter Kitten, 10 tons, was purchased in England and brought to Boston by George F. Clarke. It is a question whether Mr. Clarke was an Englishman migrating to America and bringing his yacht, or a Bostonian with an interest in an unknown type of craft. The known facts are that he brought Kitten to Boston, re-named her Saxon, and entered her in the Dorchester Y.C. and later in the Eastern Y.C.

Kitten was designed by John Harvey, at Wivenhoe on the Colne, in 1852. Her lines, published in Dixon Kemp's "Yacht Designing" in 1876, were shown in a very peculiar manner, the 16 stations of the body plan, oddly spaced according to the frames, were perpendicular not to the base line nor the waterline but to the raking keel. An attempt has been made to reproduce the design in modern style. The design was the victim of two very bad rules:—Builders' Old Measurement and a rule permitting shifting ballast; or, at least, no rule prohibiting it. Under the B.O.M., as described in this story in book form, Page 99, length was measured from a perpendicular dropped from the foreside of the stemhead, along the rabbet of keel, to the after side of the sternpost. In order to take the utmost advantage of this Rule the yachts of that day had an excessive rake to the sternpost. A material proportion of the ballast, all inside, was in the form of shot bags. When on the wind they were shifted from the cabin floor to the weather locker, or to a special ballast shelf built over the locker. The result, as shown, was a long narrow hull with limited room below, both in breadth and headroom, a very narrow floor, and very little space between the fronts of the lockers.

The dimensions of Kitten were:—l.o.a. 43 feet; l.w.l.

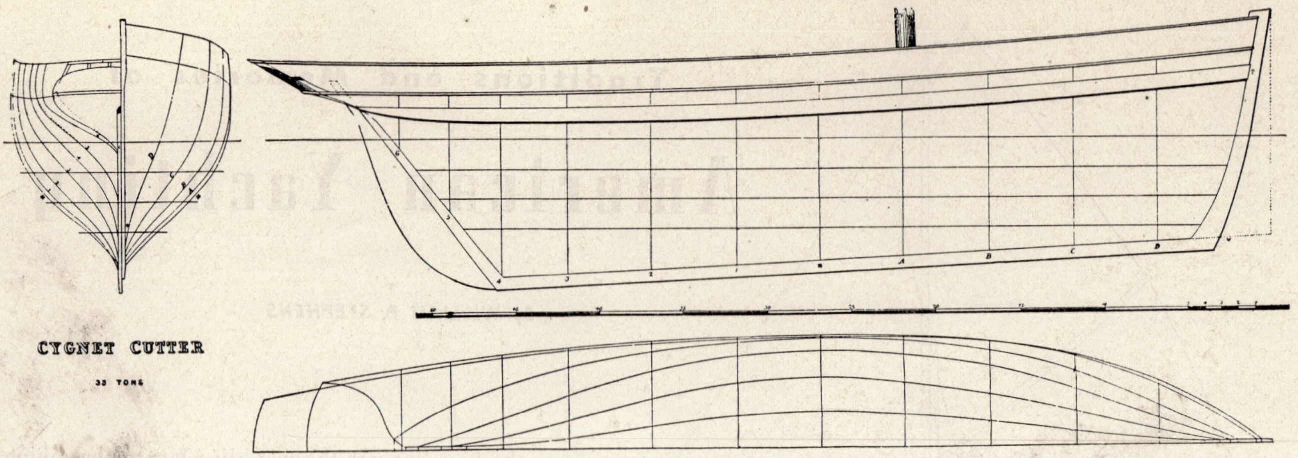

Cygnet, cutter, 35 tons. Designed and built by Wanhill of Poole, England, 1846

37 feet 4 inches; breadth 8 feet 9 inches; depth 5 feet 6 inches; draft 6 feet 8 inches. As built she measured 10 tons. I remember her about Boston for many years under the name of Saxon and I was well acquainted with Eben B. Clarke, the son of her owner; I wish now that I had taken a half day to board her, take measurements and study her construction, but on my hurried visits to Boston there were matters of more importance—to see Puritan, Mayflower and other yachts in frame, to attend their launchings and to watch their first trials.

For the first five or six years of her life Kitten was sailed by the Harveys, entering many races between Harwich and the Thames. The 10-Ton Class was not strongly built up, but boasted of some fast boats, and Kitten held her own among them and was recognized as a fast yacht. Later she changed hands several times and must have been out-built before Mr. Clarke bought her. Her racing must have ended when shifting ballast was prohibited and length was taken on deck instead of along the rabbet of keel.

Racing Rules in the Fifties

The condition of yacht racing in Great Britain about the middle of the last century may best be described as chaotic, not unlike that existing about New York a quarter century later. Shifting ballast was permitted in spite of strong opposition, and when it came to measurement, the tonnage of a yacht varied according to the club in which she sailed; just as in America prior to the adoption of a uniform classification in 1888 a yacht might sail on one day against yachts five feet longer and on the next against yachts five feet shorter.

Even under the sacred B.O.M. the tonnage differed; many clubs still measured the length along the rabbet of the keel while some measured from the fore side of the stemhead to the after side of the sternpost parallel to the waterline. There were also some "appeasers" who, like others in New York later, sought a middle course through "mean length," the average of these two measurements.

Disputes over tonnage figured as the accompaniment of many races, as instanced by a correspondent of *Hunt's Yachting Magazine* at the end of 1856:—"Wildfire at Squadron, 66 Tons; Thames and Southern, 59 Tons; Plymouth, 52 Tons—Mosquito, Cork, 60 Tons; St Georges, 59 Tons; Victoria and Plymouth, 50 Tons; Isle of Man, 58 Tons; Squadron, 70 Tons—Arrow at Squadron, 118 Tons; Victoria, 102 Tons—Vestal at Squadron, 81 tons; Thames and all others, 74 Tons." other examples are given with the statement:—"A yacht owner knows his correct tonnage yet he is not allowed to sail by it, his craft must be re-measured perhaps twice or thrice a week."

One result of this confusion was that in a regatta of the New Thames Y.C. May 30, 1874 the cutters Arethusa, Kriemhilda, Vanguard, Bloodhound, Norman, Myosotis, Eveleen and Vanessa just before the start-

Kitten, cutter, 10 tons. Designed and built by John Harvey, Wivenhoe, England, 1852

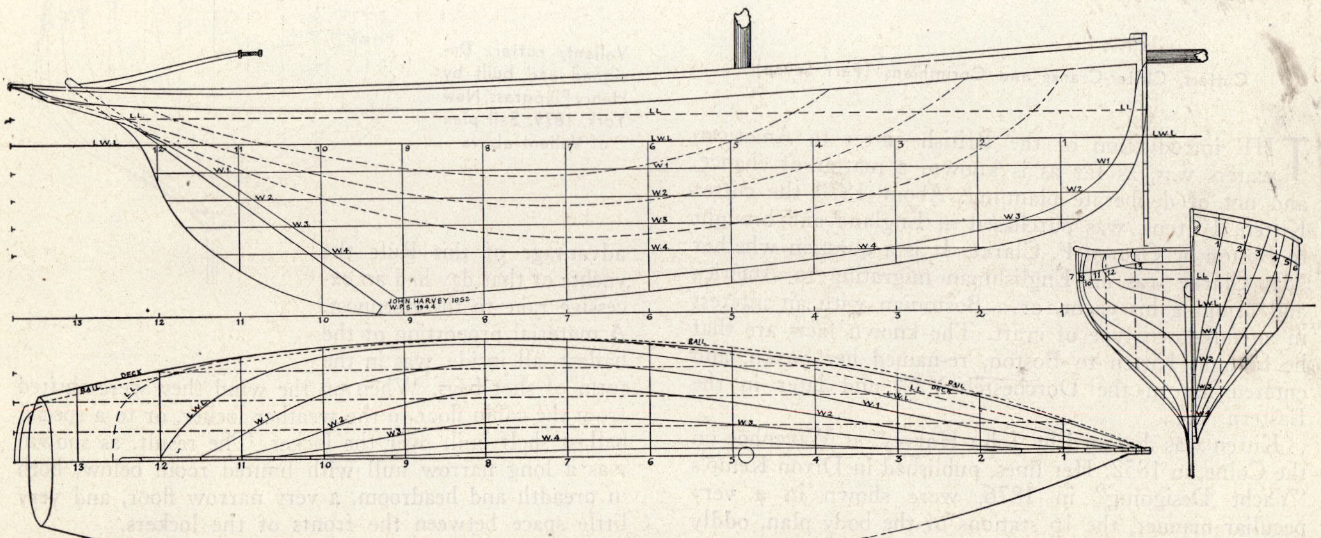

ing gun hauled down their racing flags and ran up the burgee of the Royal Thames Y. C., whose measurement they preferred to that of the New Thames, refusing to start. A similar strike occurred, as told in MoToR BoatinG for April, in the New York Y. C. on the occasion of the annual regatta of 1872, when James D. Smith withdrew his schooner Halcyon just before the start in protest against an experimental rule temporarily adopted.

The pleasures of ballast shifting are pictured by other contributors to *Hunt's*:—"*NO Shifting Ballast* and you'll see what a noble class of yachts will enter the racing; the long, lean-ribbed clipper, shifting ballast, is sent around to carry off prizes and to enlighten a club audience as to what a wonderful boat the Greased Flash is, how she scuds along under a close-reefed trysail, lies to in unheard-of hurricanes, and never as much as a damp plank on deck. Descend in the scale of society, don the rough jacket, rugged trousers and tarpaulin hat, and scruple not to rub shoulders with the hardy tars who have sailed the Greased Flash through the aforesaid terrific weather, and mayhap, you may chance to hear some untutored son of Neptune, with more of truth than refinement, exclaim, "I wish I had never slung a hammock in the ——— hooker, it's worse nor slavedriving in Yankee land." ——— "We have sailed and served our time in such craft since we were the height of a carpenter's rule, and many a hard-sailed match have we put in at the aforesaid Shot Bags in company with three other good men and true, and the deuce a thing did we do but watch the word from the deck, and then 'twas 'Heave, heave with a will' and three or four tons of good shot would be hurled from locker to locker in less time than we take to write it. Imagine what a fine school for learning the art of cutter sailing; four hardy fellows as ever tailed on to a fall contributing by their exertions below the chief element of success." These ballast-shifters seem to have had the same opportunities for enjoying fresh air and a view of sea and sky and yachts as the "bilge-boy" of a New York sandbagger, low in the bilge, with his scoop and pail, and ducking his head still lower as the sandbags came hurtling over.

As to the modus operandi, we quote another anonymous correspondent of *Hunt's* replying to a charge of injury to cabin fittings:—"If the cabin is properly arranged for the purpose, no damage whatever is likely to occur; but when a man starts his yacht in a race and allows ballast to be trimmed into his lockers without removing any part of his cherished fancy work, he must expect to see it more or less chipped, as a shot bag is not exactly calculated to put a lustre on French polish. In a yacht properly fitted for trimming operations the sofa lockers were made of a strong plank about 1½ inches thick, securely kneed to the vessel's side. The ornamental front of these lockers was fastened to them by means of large brass thumb screws from the inside. The buffets fitted on the locker boards and were fastened to them and to the vessel's sides with screws. By this arrangement all the fancy work could be removed in a few minutes, and the shot bags thrown from locker to locker without damage to the elegant paint of the cabin.

"In a vessel which can stay quickly four men are supposed to trim a ton and a half of shot; but I never knew more than half this weight to be thrown over before the vessel was round; the consequence is that she falls over, stays sluggishly, and hangs some time before she gets good way again. The last twenty bags or so are terribly heavy and go over but slowly, consequently when working very short tacks the vessel does not acquire her full speed before 'Bout Ho, over with the ballast' is the cry; once more she turns sluggishly, falls over, and just steadies herself in time to go through the same ceremony. If, instead of 30 cwt, half a ton only were shifted and the remaining ton placed amidships, the vessel will work quicker and sail better." Thus were the pleasures of racing depicted by one who knew almost a century ago.

Discussion and Dissension

It is evident that the art of "writing to the paper" flourished in the fifties as in the eighties, most of the writers being too modest to sign their names. The origin of the measurement discussion is lost in the mists of history, at the time that *Hunt's* was started—1852—it was under full headway, and it continued in *Hunt's, Bell's Life, Land and Water, The Field* and other publications for a generation; marked by the same verbosity and vituperation as later characterized the fight in America. Down to 1880 few ventured to question the sanctity, sanity and scientific basis of the proposition that the depth of hold of a yacht must be equivalent to one half of the breadth. In 1853 that spirited yachtsman, George Holland Ackers, who ten years before had made public "Ackers Scale" for time allowance, and who invented a yacht signal code, suggested length as the basis of measurement; and a little later Philip R. Marett proposed sail area. It was not until 1880 that these two factors, in combination, were recognized; and not until 1886, following the successive defeats of Genesta and Galatea at New York, that the Thames Rule was finally given the deep six.

In 1878 Dixon Kemp, who certainly was qualified to pose as an authority, read before the Institute of Naval Architects a paper entitled "On Depth as Factor in the Computation of Yacht Tonnage," treating the subject from both a historical and scientific basis. He stated that:—"The Thames Rule fairly estimates the value of yachts that are not of very extreme types for competitive sailing, as it is a rough expression of their sail-carrying power; all yachts built under it being practically proportional in depth and having a similar disposition of their weights. The objections to the Rule are:—(1) That in consequence of the value for competitive sailing being made dependent on beam and length, to the total exclusion of depth, an inducement exists to attempt a possible evasion of the Rule by decreasing beam and compensating for it by an increase of depth. (2) That the effect of the Rule is to produce one type of vessel—that is, a narrow and deep one."

Though the movement for the transfer of the ballast from the hold to a point beneath the keel had already started, Mr. Kemp did not look far into the future; only a half dozen years later most of the ballast was in this position and a complete revolution in yacht form was accomplished. Going into figures to demonstrate that the depth is equal to half the breadth both in theory and practice, with comparisons of the British Seabelle and the American Columbia of similar length and displacement but different form, his conclusion was that there was no need of any change from the Thames Rule. As to the second objection, while he admitted that the tendency was to produce one type only, he claimed that this type was the best possible for sea-going qualities. Another point, which would not appeal to American yachtsmen, was that for many years the cost of building had been based on so much per ton under the Rule; the rate, of course, varying from time to time as construction became more complicated and costly.

The progress in cutter design is shown in Cygnet, 35 tons, built by the Wanhill brothers of Poole in 1846, the Harvey Kitten, 10 tons, 1852, and the Ratsey Vanguard, 65 tons, 1865. Cygnet has the pegtop or V section with a long straight keel parallel to the waterline and a deep forefoot, with a very marked cod's-head entrance. Kitten shows a raking keel, and a moderate forefoot, with a more even balance in fullness of entrance and run; Vanguard has a sweetly swept curve from planksheer to the bottom of keel, a moderate rake to both keel and sternpost, a well-rounded forefoot, and an easy entrance and clean run.

A Danish Cutter

An interesting example of another variety of the cutter type is found in Valiant, built as recently as 1879 but belonging to an earlier era. She was designed and built by Henry Piepgrass at Pottery Beach, Greenpoint, a section of the Brooklyn waterfront which it might be difficult to locate by name today. Piepgrass was a Dane who had followed the sea and finally fetched up in New York, where he built many yachts. Like his compatriot, Louis Winde, he had profited by that technical instruction in naval architecture and designing which seems to have been common in the Scandinavian nations as far back as the sixties, though not known in the States until twenty or more years later. He was a skilled mechanic, an expert draftsman, and a qualified naval architect.

Valiant was designed and built for W. Gordon Diedricksen, a young man of Danish origin then living at New Brighton, Staten Island. She is a cutter in all respects in spite of her breadth; her dimensions being:—l.o.a. 30 feet; l.w.l. 25 feet 4 inches; breadth 8 feet 4 inches; draft 4 feet. She displaced 6 tons and carried 4 tons of iron moulded to fit between the floors. She had a trunk cabin 9 inches at side and with 4 inches crown, I knew her well and now that it is too late I regret that I did not note more of her details. Teak, which Piepgrass wanted for her rails, was then unknown and unappreciated in New York. He found a ship from the East Indies with teak yards, bought them and replaced them with spruce or hard pine and ripped them up for rails. I understood that the teak which he used for planking and other members of the cutters he built a few years later was obtained in the same way.

(*Continued on page 293*)

Traditions and Memories of

AMERICAN YACHTING

Part Sixty-six

By *WILLIAM P. STEPHENS*

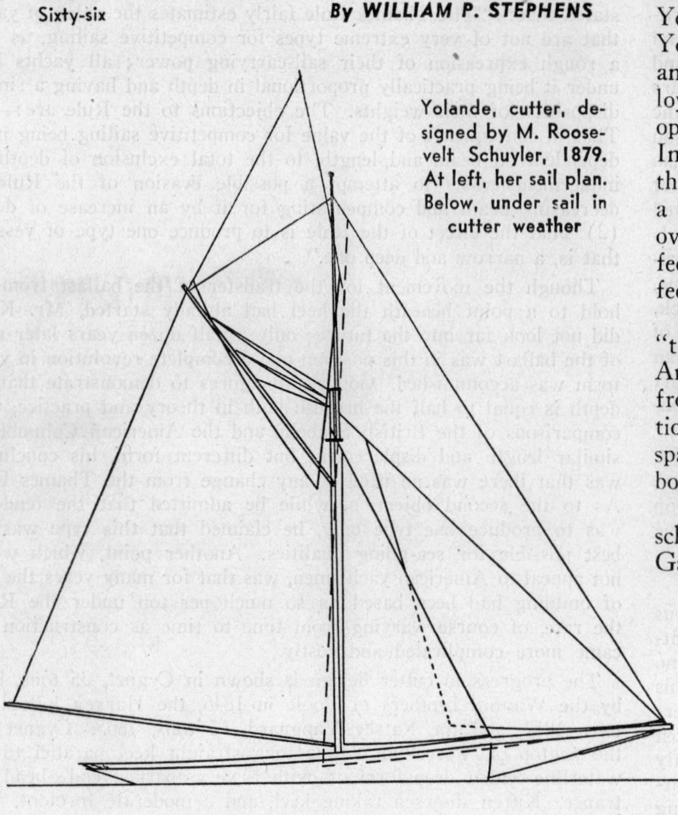

Yolande, cutter, designed by M. Roosevelt Schuyler, 1879. At left, her sail plan. Below, under sail in cutter weather

Cutters, Cutter Cranks, and Corinthians (Part Eight)

THE designing and building of the cutter Vindex in 1871 has already been told in detail. Robert Center, of an old New York family and son of a yachtsman, was born in 1840 and with his brother Henry joined the New York Y. C. on May 15, 1862. His first yacht was a small sloop, Ariel, followed by the larger Bonita, 46 tons, built by D. O. Richmond in 1860. On one of his visits to Europe he picked up Marett's book, so frequently mentioned in this story, and from it perfected himself in designing. There was no thought of propaganda in the building of Vindex. Thoroughly familiar with the national centerboard type, and also with the cutter, he selected the latter as better suited for his purposes of sailing with the New York fleet and cruising on the Atlantic coast.

In 1877 he designed another cutter, Volante, for his nephews, Thomas Hitchcock, Jr. and Francis R. Hitchcock. Built of wood, by John Mumm, she was 45 feet over all, 40 feet waterline, 12 feet breadth, 5 feet 10 inches depth, and 6 feet 11 inches draft, with full cutter rig. Both yachts made a creditable showing in the regular races and on club cruises, and Vindex also made a reputation in coastal cruising.

Shortly after the end of the Rebellion a young Englishman, Frank W. J. Hurst, who had been purser of an English blockade runner during the war, settled in New York, marrried an American wife, and joined the New York Y. C. in 1874. He was elected treasurer in 1886 and held the office until his death in 1902. He was a loyal member of the club, and one of the most staunch opponents of all attempts of the British to "lift" the cup. In 1875 he had built by W. L. Force of Keyport, N. J., the yacht Active, listed in the club as a cutter. She was a centerboard boat, with inside ballast, 55 feet 6 inches over all, 50 feet waterline, 16 feet 6 inches breadth, 5 feet 6 inches depth, 4 feet 6 inches draft, and drew 11 feet 6 inches with board down.

In describing Active *The Aquatic Monthly* stated that "the stern will have an English overhang" with "an American rig." It adds:—"Mr. Smith made drawings from a model furnished by Mr. Force" including calculations and sail plan; "the object of this is to have the spars, rigging, sails, and everything ready to put on the boat when it is launched."

This idea of combining the methods of the old and new schools came up again in 1886 when the match with Galatea was in preparation. Edward A. Willard, an experienced yachtsman, had the sloop Eclipse, 49 feet waterline, built by "Neef" Willis in 1881, the largest yacht turned out by this noted builder of sandbag boats. In the fall of 1886 he had Willis cut a model for a sloop of 86 feet waterline which he proposed to take to Edward Burgess as the basis of a design for a Cup defender. As it happened, the plan never progressed beyond the model and

selection of the name, Cavalier.

Active steered with a wheel; in 1878 Mr. Hurst had a handsomely carved and mounted tiller sent out from England, but it would not hold her and the wheel was retained. The cutter Petrel, previously described, built in 1876 from the design of her owner, John Hyslop, was a keel yacht with outside lead, a combination of British and American ideas.

In 1878 Charles Stillman, son of an old yachtsman, James Stillman, for years owner of the schooner Wanderer, had built by Piepgrass the cutter Muriel, 45 feet 6 inches over all; 40 feet 6 inches waterline, 9 feet 2 inches breadth, 6 feet 3 inches depth, 7 feet 9 inches draft. She started with 6 tons of lead on her keel, but in 1879 1½ tons was shifted from inside to the keel. She had the full cutter rig. The origin of the design is a matter of doubt; it was ascribed both to Cary Smith and John Harvey, but a more plausible story is that it was enlarged from the design of the 10-tonner Lily, designed by Alexander Richardson in 1875 and published in the following year in Dixon Kemp's *Yacht Designing*. An English skipper, Captain Harlow, who had made a reputation with the schooner Egeria, was brought over to sail her.

While *The Spirit of The Times* had a competent yachting writer in Captain Coffin, it was devoted almost entirely to the interests of the turf; its owner-editor was much more concerned with the performance of Maud S. than of Susie S., and of the four-legged Parole than of Jake Schmidt's masterpiece. Through the winter of 1879-80 it carried in its yachting columns but little more than cut-and-paste items; but, whether spurred by Kunhardt or sensing the growing interest in cutters, is started up with the coming of the yachting season and on May 1, 1880, commented as follows on Muriel:—"'Tis hard to tell which is the most senseless, the carrying of 1½ tons of sandbags on the weather gunwale, as in the Dodo, or the dragging of 3 tons of lead or more in the keel? It would seem that a compromise between the two styles of model, the English and the American, was something just now much to be desired?" It is hard to understand this crack at the new sloop, Mischief, except that she represented "science" as opposed to "rule-o'thumb": "It is said that the owner of the sloop Mischief declines to enter her for the regatta of Thursday next; he thinks that June zephyrs are more suited to the Mischief than September breezes, and possibly he is right? The Gracie, Fanny, Hildegard and Vision, however, will be entered."

The occasion was a special race for cups of $500 value presented by James Gordon Bennett, Jr., the course being around the Scotland Lightship. Though the weather was light only three schooners and three sloops started. Gracie won on allowance from Mischief, Fanny withdrawing. As a matter of fact, Mischief with a sturdy iron hull and new rig in her second season was better able to face a blow than any of the older wooden boats.

Apropos of the building of a sloop of the ordinary Bay Ridge run with 16 feet 6 inches breadth on 40 feet waterline *The Spirit* commented:—"Those gentlemen who have lost their heads over the English cutter craze will do well to inspect this yacht, see how much room

M. Roosevelt Schuyler, leader of the Cutter Cult, with Will Fife III at Seawanhaka Cup match, 1922

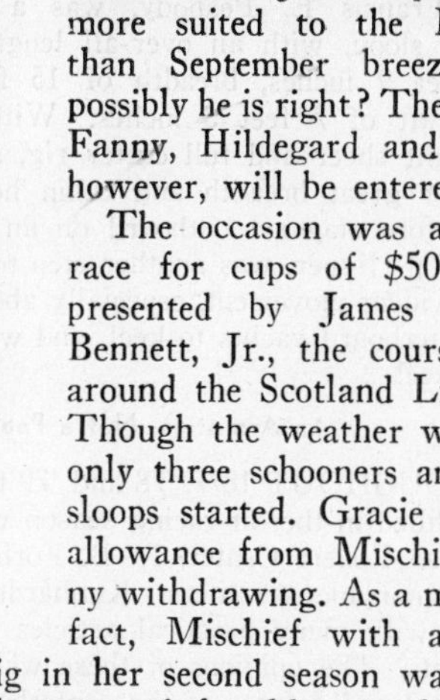

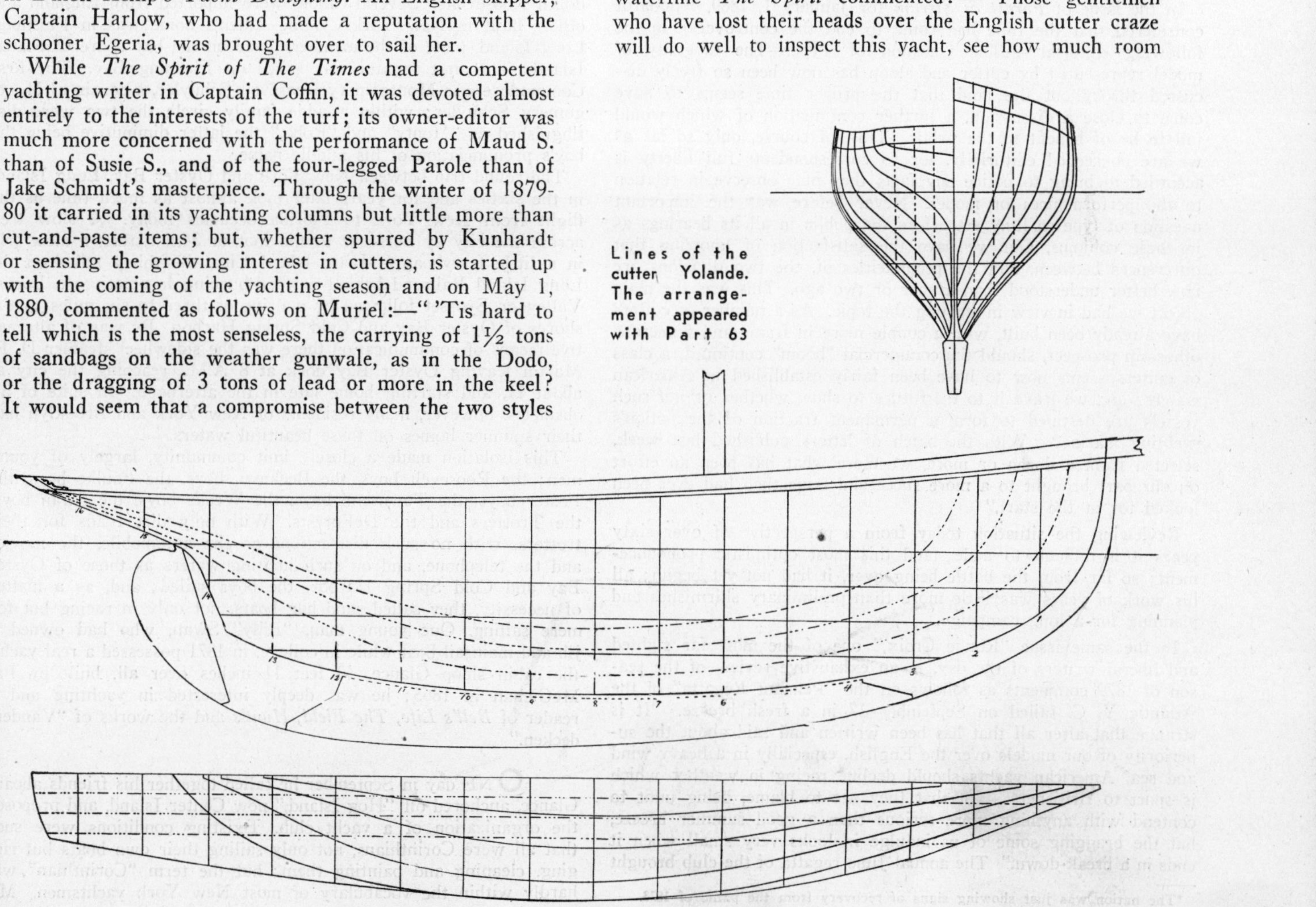

Lines of the cutter Yolande. The arrangement appeared with Part 63

there is on board of her; and, as it is quite certain that she will outsail any cutter of equal length and has been built at much less cost, the probability is that their enthusiasm in favor of the cutter model will be somewhat checked." So far as the records show, this particular yacht never outsailed anything.

The long existing popularity of the keel type in sizes from 20 to 40 feet waterline East of Cape Cod makes it difficult to trace the growth of the cutter sentiment about Boston. The average keel sloop had a deep wooden keel, often with an iron shoe, great breadth and draft, though with a limited depth of hold. From her general dimensions she might well have passed for a cutter save for her rig.

The "cutter" Enterprise, designed and built in 1878 by D. J. Lawlor for Francis E. Peabody, was a step beyond the conventional keel sloop, with an over-all length of 50 feet, a waterline of 43 feet 9 inches, breadth of 15 feet 8 inches, depth of 6 feet and draft of 7 feet 3 inches. With plumb stem, circular counter, straight sheer and full cutter rig, she looked true to type in spite of her great breadth and cabin house. The double head rig, with the fore stay set outboard on an American bowsprit, as in the keel sloop Hesper, was another step toward the cutter. There was also an evident movement, especially about Boston, for the conversion of centerboard yachts to keel, and with some weight of iron in the wood keel.

An Armistice, Not a Peace

THROUGHOUT 1877, '78 and '79 the columns of *Forest & Stream* were filled in the off-racing season with letters, some signed by such men as Robert Center, R. B. Forbes and A. Cary Smith, but more by anonymous writers. Kunhardt meanwhile contributed his comments with many practical articles on design, stability and kindred subjects. The opinions of these writers ranged from patriotic and impassioned defense of the centerboard sloop through various compromises and on to the open advocacy of the cutter. There was at the time a growing interest in amateur design, John L. Frisbie of Boston being a leader in this work.

In the issue of *Forest & Stream* for January 1, 1880, Kunhardt considered that the time had come to end the controversy in the following editorial:—"The Question of Type.—The diversity of model represented by cutter and sloop has now been so freely discussed throughout the land that the proper time seems to have come to close a discussion, a further continuation of which would fail to be of benefit to the public. This, of course, only so far as we are concerned editorially, for to correspondents full liberty is accorded to bring to notice any facts they may observe in relation to the performances of model. Never before was the important question of type so fully set before the public in all its bearings as in these columns, and we have the satisfaction of knowing that differences between, and the peculiarities of, the two divisions are now better understood than a year or two ago. This was the main object we had in view in starting the topic. As a number of cutters have already been built, with a couple more in frame and numerous others in prospect, should the commercial "boom" continue*, a class of cutters seems now to have been fairly established in American waters; and we leave it to the future to show whether or not such vessels are destined to form a permanent fraction of the nation's yachting marine? With the batch of letters published last week, selected from a dozen or more, we close what has been an effort on our part brought to a more successful issue than had ever been looked for at the start."

Reviewing the situation today from a perspective of over sixty years it is difficult to understand this most optimistic pronouncement; so far from the battle being over, it had not yet begun; all his work of years was little more than preliminary skirmishes and planning for a long campaign.

In the same issue "Rouge Croix," one of the most far sighted and liberal writers of the day, in an exhaustive review of the season of 1879 comments as follows on the "Pennant Regatta" of the Atlantic Y. C. sailed on September 17 in a fresh breeze. "It is strange that after all that has been written and said about the superiority of our models over the English, especially in a heavy wind and sea, American yachts should decline racing in weather which is sport to Britishers. Not that they are to blame, being unfit to contend with anything more serious than a good summer breeze, but the bragging some of us indulge in looks very small when it ends in a break-down." The annual June regatta of the club brought out a fleet of 19, but on this occasion the only starters were the schooners Peerless and Agnes, Dolphin a big husky sloop in the first class, Genia and Lizzie L. in the second class, and the sandbag catboat Wind. All were reefed, Agnes sprung her foremast and withdrew, Genia withdrew and Wind capsized, leaving only Peerless, Dolphin and Lizzie L. to finish.

The review continues: "At present it is extremely difficult to trace the records of yachts owing to the general absence of owners' and builders' names, of lengths, and the awful multiplicity of classes. It would greatly facilitate matters if we had an 'American Yacht List' published annually, containing full particulars of each yacht such as name, name of owner, club belonging to, rig, tonnage, length on waterline, beam, name of builder. The names of yachts to be arranged alphabetically, and a number placed opposite each by which reference could be made to it. If the proposed Yacht Racing Association succeeds, the 'List' might be issued under its authority." The first ventures for an "American Yacht List," between 1872 and 1875, had failed for lack of support, in 1881 Niels Olsen resumed the publication of his 'List' in the once familiar oblong form, and the publication of an annual "List" under various auspices has continued down to the temporary suspension of "Lloyd's" in 1943.

From Canoes to Corinthians

THE growing interest in small craft found expression at the beginning of 1872 in the organization of the New York Canoe Club, introducing to America the modern English adaptation of the oldest and most primitive craft. The leader in this enterprise was William L. Alden, an editorial writer on *The New York Times* and also known as "the funny man of *The Times*" from a series of broadly humorous articles. With him were associated G. Livingston Morse, publisher of *The New York Observer;* Montgomery Schuyler associated with *The New York World* (I believe the three were related); Col. Charles Ledyard Norton, a writer, Dr. J. S. Mosher of the Quarantine Station and Dr. J. H. Kidder of the Marine Hospital, both on Staten Island. Others were Captain S. Grosvenor Porter of the S. S. Alaska; Homer Martin, an artist, and a half dozen Roosevelts. Several canoes were imported from England and others built in New York. While Alden's home was in Flushing, Long Island, most of the members lived on the bay shore of Staten Island. The first regatta was sailed on Flushing Bay. The first Commodore was Montgomery Roosevelt Schuyler, a cousin of Montgomery Schuyler; within a wide family circle the two were distinguished as "Monty" and "Robo," the latter diminutive being the boy's pronunciation of his middle name.

The round trip between New York and Oyster Bay, Long Island, in the sixties and for years later took almost as much time as the flight from New York to Florida occupies today. A slow trek across the city by horsecar to the foot of 34th Street, a slow trip in a little ferryboat to Long Island City, the thirty miles on the Long Island Railroad behind a wood-burning locomotive to Locust Valley or Syosset followed by a drive of three to six miles to the shores of Oyster Bay and Cold Spring Harbor. By way of alternative means of communication there was the sidewheel steamer D. R. Martin leaving Oyster Bay dock at 8 A.M., reaching the city at about 11, and starting home late in the afternoon. In spite of all obstacles, however, many residents of New York and Brooklyn had their summer homes on these beautiful waters.

This isolation made a closely knit community, largely of young men; the Roosevelt boys, the Beekman boys, the Foulke boys, the Foster boys, the Townsend boys, the Weeks boys, the Swan boys, the Trotters and the DeForests. With only dirt roads for their trotters, with no such distractions as the automobile, the movies and the telephone, and on such inviting waters as those of Oyster Bay and Cold Spring Harbor, the boys sailed; and, as a matter of necessity, they sailed sand bag boats, not only in racing but for mere sailing. One young man, "Billy" Swan, who had owned a jib-and-mainsail boat while in college, in 1871 possessed a real yacht, the cabin sloop Glance, 40 feet 11 inches over all, built by Pat McGiehan in 1865; he was deeply interested in yachting and a reader of *Bell's Life, The Field, Hunt's* and the works of "Vanderdecken."

ONE day in September he called together his friends aboard Glance, anchored off "Hog Island," now Center Island, and proposed the organization of a yacht club. Existing conditions were such that all were Corinthians, not only sailing their own boats but rigging, cleaning and painting them; but the term "Corinthian" was hardly within the vocabulary of most New York yachtsmen. Mr.

*The nation was just showing signs of recovery from the panic of 1873.

Swan's reading had impressed on him the growth of Corinthianism in Britain, and in proposing a club he stated as its objects:—"First, In becoming proficient in navigation. Second, In the personal management, control and handling of yachts. Third, In all other matters pertaining to seamanship." The name chosen for the new club, "Seawanhaka," is found in an old Indian deed in the form of "Seawanhaky."

Though the "yachts" of the club with two exceptions were built to carry sandbags, the universal custom of the day, the following restrictions were made part of the Sailing Regulations:—"Sec. 1. No yacht contending for a prize, after having taken her position, will be permitted to start water or ballast. Sec. 2. No yacht can carry shifting ballast. Sec. 3. No booming-out of ballast allowed in a race. Sec. 4. All yachts must bring home the same ballast with which they started." As the local fleet of some twenty yachts were boats from 20 to 30 feet, built by Smedley, Kirby and Willis, they must have carried sandbags, and presumably these restrictions necessitated a reduction of sail.

The social connections of the members in town during the winter brought them into contact with many yachtsmen, and the Corinthian idea met with immediate favor. By 1874 the Seawanhaka fleet included the schooners Alarm, Foam, Halcyon, Idler, Palmer, Peerless and Restless, and the sloops Vindex, Vision, Coming, Madcap and other large yachts. The first accessions to membership from outside the little circle at Oyster Bay came, however, from the ranks of the New York Canoe Club; devotees of "the poor man's yacht," a craft 14 feet long and 26 to 28 inches breadth, turning to yachting on a larger scale. Among these were Commodore M. Roosevelt Schuyler, James A. Roosevelt, John E. Roosevelt, Alfred Roosevelt, Cornelius Roosevelt, J. H. Mosher and Louis P. Bayard.

A New Richmond in the Field

FAMOUS from pre-Revolutionary days, the Schuylers, Livingstons, Morses, Roosevelts, and Montgomerys dwelt in central New York State. In the forties of the last century the Reverend Montgomery Schuyler had charge of an Episcopal Church in Skaneateles, near Syracuse, his wife Lydia Eliza being the daughter of Nicholas J. Roosevelt, of the same city. A son born on February 18, 1847, was christened Montgomery Roosevelt Schuyler; the child's efforts to pronounce his middle name went no further than "Robo," at first a pet name within the family circle, but later familiar to yachtsmen the world over. In September the boy was admitted to the U. S. Naval College at Newport, where he had as classmates S. Nicholson Kane, J. J. Hunker, John C. Soley and Daniel Edgar, all yachtsmen in later life.

The young midshipman completed a two-year course in his first year and was third in the Advanced Class of 53 members when ill health forced him to discontinue his studies. On returning in the following year he was placed at the foot of the Second Class, and in October 1865 he resigned. Following a cruise around the world in a vessel commanded by Captain Louis F. Timmerman, later one of his associates in the Canoe Club, he came to New York about 1870 and took up a business career, but not to an extent which would interfere with his yachting.

An early convert to Kunhardt's doctrines, he became one of the most earnest propagandists of the cutter; while Kunhardt was pressing his fight in print "Robo" was sailing in Corinthian crews and preaching cutter doctrine in both the Seawanhaka and New York Yacht Clubs as well as the Larchmont Y. C. which he joined in 1881 shortly after its organization. He was soon widely known and, as Kunhardt withdrew from editorial work, was recognized as the head of a small but active clique known derisively as "Cutter-Cranks." Perfecting himself in the methods of yacht designing, in the fall of 1879 he completed the design here shown, the cutter Yolande. Her particulars were:—

Length, on deck	31 feet
Length, Waterline	27 feet 5 inches
Breadth	7 feet
Draft	5 feet 7 inches
Area of Midship section	14.78 sq. feet
Area, Loadwater plane	121.00 sq. feet
Area, Lateral plane	118.00 sq. feet
Abaft middle of L. W. L.	
Midship section	1.3 feet
Center of Gravity	1.0 feet
Center of Gravity below L. W. L	1.4 feet
Metacenter above C. B	1.5 feet
Displacement	7 tons
Ballast, Lead Keel	4.29 tons
Ratio of ballast to displacement	.60
Sail Area	
Mainsail	479 sq. ft.
Foresail	115 sq. ft.
Jib	171 sq. ft.
Total	765 sq. ft.

BUILT by Piepgrass, the construction was carefully planned for strength in spite of the proportion of lead in the keel. Sailed hard in both racing and cruising for 25 years, the transom of Yolande is preserved in the house of the Knickerbocker Y. C. at Port Washington. The interior, as shown in MoToR BoatinG for September, was planned by her owner to give a maximum of convenience in very small space. The headroom under the skylight was 5 feet 10 inches, the floor was but 18 inches wide but there were transoms and folding berths for four, with a paid hand forward and plenty of lockers. At the same time Schuyler designed for a friend a smaller cutter, Leila, 22 feet over all; 18 feet 4 inches waterline, 6 feet breadth and 3 feet 9 inches draft.

With the rapid growth of membership and fleet the ties of Seawanhaka to its birthplace were gradually weakened. Most of its yachts had permanent moorings off Staten Island, the home of many members. The club races were started off Stapleton and the club meetings were held at Delmonico's in New York. In 1880 William A. W. Stewart was elected Commodore, with the sloop Regina as flagship, Schuyler being Vice Commodore. A special committee was appointed to consider the question of a station on the water. As the result an arrangement was made to lease a shore site in Manning's Yacht Basin at Edgewater, Staten Island, with the privilege of building a club house. Under the active management of Commodore Stewart a building company was formed within the club to finance the house and lease it to the club, and a convenient two-story house was built.

While the weekly assaults of Kunhardt continued in 1880, the building of Yolande and the placing of orders for several large cutters under the aggressive campaign of Schuyler afloat forced the advocates of the sloop to a war on two fronts.

CUTTERS, CUTTER-CRANKS AND CORINTHIANS

(*Continued from page* 289)

The centerboard type is so nearly universal on all the Lakes (the three Cup challengers from Canada were all centerboard) that I almost overlooked a cutter which antedates Kitten; Rivet, long of the Royal Canadian Y. C. fleet at Toronto. This yacht, appropriately named, as she was of iron, was built by Symonds of Glasgow in the fifties and brought to Montreal, later hailing from Toronto. She was about 45 feet over all; 40 feet waterline; 9 feet 3 inches breadth; 5 feet depth and 8 feet draft, 17 Tons. She had the raking sternpost and keel and the square forefoot of the era, with a short square transom. She raced in her early days as a cutter, a schooner, a sloop and later as a cutter; as I remember her in the eighties she was notable mainly from the many bumps and dents in her ancient sides. In 1890 she was stripped of her rig and demoted to a steam ferryboat at Hamilton, Ontario, and was last reported hauled out in Toronto for breaking up about 1912. The Royal Nova Scotia Yacht Squadron of Halifax was organized in 1875. There may have been a few imported cutters in its fleet, but no records are available.

A

Sailing Match

WILL TAKE PLACE ON

MONDAY the 31st Day of JULY, 1815,

BY

Gentlemen's Pleasure Boats,

UNDER TWENTY TONS,

From Blackwall to Gravesend and back, for a

SILVER CUP and COVER

GIVEN BY AMATEURS.

The BOATS to start from a Boat moored off the Artichoke Tavern, Blackwall, at Nine o'Clock in the Morning precisely, sail round His Majesty's Receiving-Ship, Gravesend, and return to the Boat moored off the Artichoke Tavern, where the CUP and COVER will be presented in the Evening to the Winner.

Each Boat will be distinguished by a St. George's Broad Pennant, *viz*, a red Cross on a white Ground at her Peak, marked with red Spots or Balls to correspond with the following List.

LIST OF BOATS.

Spots.	Boats Names.	Place.	Owners.	Tonnage.
1	Betsey,	Blackwall,	Samuel Grainger,	XVII.
2	Produce,	Strand Lane,	Wm. Nettlefold,	IX.
3	Mermaid,	Paul's Wharf,	Geo. Gunston,	VII.
4	Atlanta,	Dowgate,	B. Spedding,	VII.
5	Syren,	Hungerford,	Wm. Thompson,	VIII.
6	Mercury,	Stangate,	John Astley,	IX.
7	Ludlow,	Wandsworth,	A. Lyon,	[illegible]
8	Spitfire,	Chelsea,	Tho. Bettesworth,	[illegible]

W. Hildyard, Printer, Poppin's Court, Fleet Street.

Traditions and Memories of

AMERICAN YACHTING

By WILLIAM P. STEPHENS

Part Sixty-seven

Cutters, Cutter-Cranks and Corinthians (Part Nine)

As a *casus belli* for vocal argument and written discussion the first place in yachting belongs to the subject of Measurement, but there can be no question in awarding the second place to that of Corinthianism. Though no longer a matter of dispute, the term Corinthian created a turmoil among American yachtsmen some three score and ten years ago. If we seek a dictionary definition we find in Webster: "A fashionable man about town, especially a man of means, given to sport, who drives his own horses, sails his own yacht, or the like.' At the same time Corinthianism has a supplementary definition: "(U. S.) Amateur yachting."

This definition would not help us much in deciding the many disputes and protests which have arisen, so we may turn to Dixon Kemp in his *Manual of Yacht and Boat Sailing*, 1878: "A term in yacht parlance synonymous with amateur. The term Corinthian half a century ago was commonly applied to the aristocratic patrons of sports, some of which, such as pugilism, are not now in fashion (?). A Corinthian sailor has never been defined. The Royal Alfred Yacht Club enjoins that in all matches the amateur element shall consist of 'members of the Club; their sons, or members of a Royal, foreign, or recognized yacht club, or naval officers.' Anyone not being a mechanic or menial is generally recognized as a qualified amateur."

This being far from conclusive, we turn to *Roget's Thesaurus* and find the synonyms: "Connoisseur, critic, virtuoso, diletante, purist, etc." Foiled again, we must go back to the early Christian era, when Paul wrote his first and second Epistles to the Corinthians. These seem to be directed mainly at matters of faith, though not entirely ignoring the matter of morals. It is an historic fact that the citizens of Corintha had in general an unsavory reputation which was the origin of the term. As meanings change with time we find Shakespeare writing of "A Corinthian and a man of mettle"; while Thackeray says: "Corinthian, it appears, was a phrase applied to men of fashion and *ton* in Plancus's time; they were the brilliant predecessors of the swell of the present period." The British have always been a sporting nation and there was a period about a century and a half ago when all classes, from duke to costermonger, met on a common ground of fraternity in attendance on such sports as bull and bear-baiting, badger drawing, "the manly art" (with bare fists), cock-fighting, dog-fighting and burring—Welsh miners in heavy boots kicking at each others' shins.

Turning now to yachting, in his comprehensive volume *Yachts and Yachting* "Vanderdecken" (William Cooper) writes of the Corinthian: "Many, I have no doubt, may laugh at the idea of any man wealthy enough to keep a large yacht taking so much trouble when he can get all these things done for him; and perhaps think they were lowering themselves by

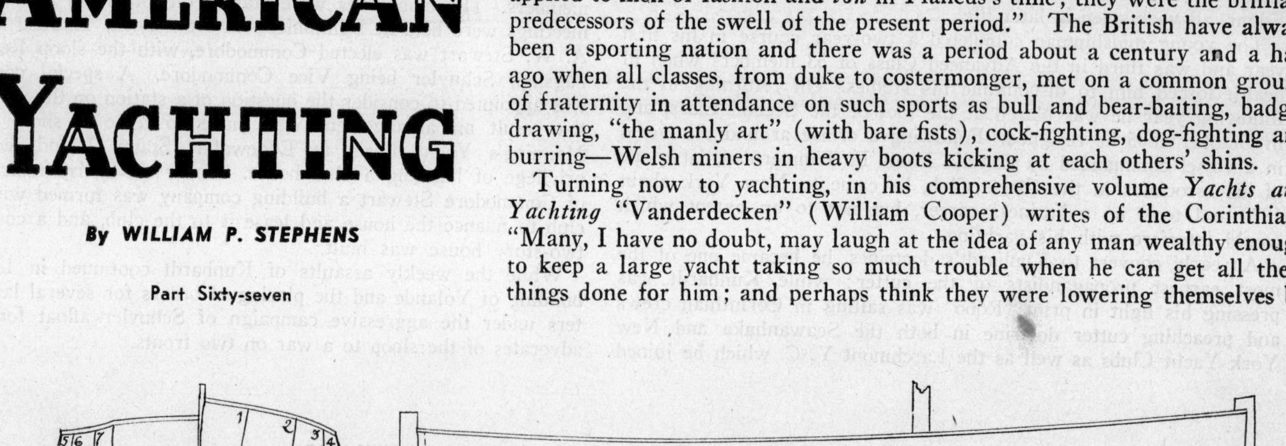

Above: An early program for a Corinthian Race, 1815. Right: "Itchen Boat" Wild Rose, on which the design of Moya was based. Designed by W. Shergold, 1872. L.o.a., 25'; l.w.l., 24'8"; breadth, 8'10"; draft, 4'2". Lines from "Yacht and Boat Building, 1878"

"Itchen Boat" Daisy, 25 Foot Class, designed by J. M. Soper, 1882. L.o.a., 32'; l.w.l., 25'; breadth, 8'8"; draft, 5'9". Displacement, 7.86 tons.

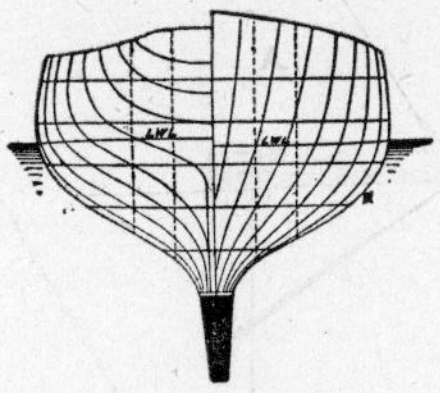

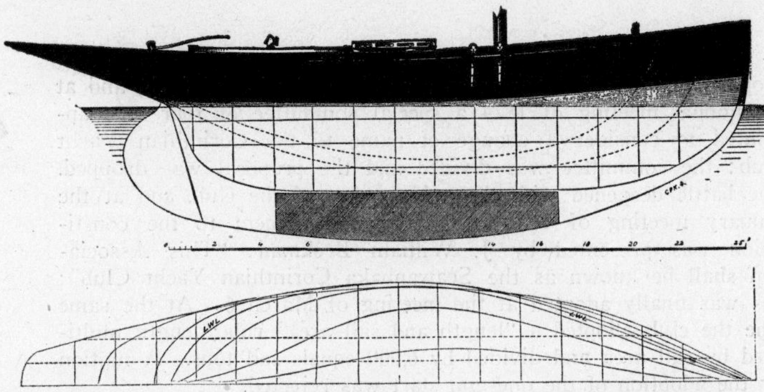

Lead keel, 4.38 tons. Sail area (lower sails), 862 square feet. Daisy, Sail Plan. Fore stay carried out on bowsprit

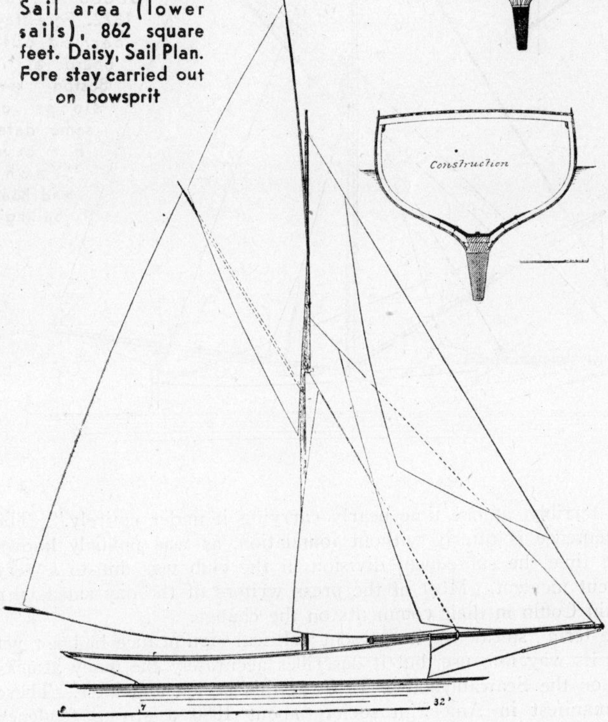

"Itchen Boat" Keepsake, 30 Foot Class. Designed by C. P. Clayton, 1882. L.o.a., 40'8"; l.w.l., 30'; breadth, 9'7"; draft, 7'2". Displacement, 13.7 tons; lead keel, 7.8 tons

tailing on to the same end of a rope as a foremast jack; but, as I presume to offer my lucubrations only to those who propose to become thorough good practical yachtsmen and seamen, and not mere passengers aboard their vessels, I can only say there is no royal road for becoming proficient in this, no more than in any other active pursuit that a man wishes to excel in. As to any unpleasant position that a thirst for nautical information may lead to by undue familiarity with the crew in mixing in and working amongst them, I do not think that any such thing is likely of occurrence." The first sentence quoted above recalls a criticism passed on one of the first Corinthian races of the Seawanhaka Yacht Club, to the effect that the writer could not understand how a gentleman could demean himself by performing work which he paid his servants to do.

The Corinthian in Yachting

The principle of Corinthian or amateur handling of yachts seems to have made its way into British yachting at an early date, and to have been accepted without opposition. Yacht racing in England began with the Cumberland Fleet of small cutters on the Thames in 1775, the races being promoted by the proprietors of Vauxhall Gardens, an amusement park similar to the Elysian Fields in Hoboken at the period of the organization of the New York Yacht Club (1844). The yachts, necessarily, were of small size, but from this club and its races sprung the Royal Thames Yacht Club. In a race on June 27, 1791, nine yachts of from four to six tons started, each flying a broad pennant with the red cross of St. George on a white field. Before the start numbers were drawn, and the identity of each yacht was shown by the number of black discs on her pennant. It seems certain that the sailing was Corinthian, and this is confirmed by the circular of a "Sailing Match by Gentlemen's Pleasure Boats; 31st day of July, 1815, from Blackwall to Gravesend and back, for a Silver Cup and Cover given by Amateurs." From this beginning Corinthian sailing was accepted without opposition in the larger clubs.

We have seen how Kunhardt, from his first writings in 1872, upheld the Corinthian principle; in this he was seconded by his erstwhile friend Captain Coffin, who wrote in *The Spirit of The Times* of April 29, 1876: "Corinthian Racing:—There is a prospect this season of a series of races conducted on the Corinthian principle, and it is to be hoped that the suggestion will be carried out, as nothing that could be done would be more beneficial to yachting interests. Corinthian yacht racing builds up a class of sailors that are invaluable on board a yacht, and also enables many gentlemen to own a yacht that could not afford an expensive crew. Schooners of 100 tons and under and sloops of 60 tons and under can be easily and efficiently handled by a Corinthian crew. It is only necessary to allude to the Vision, as that fast sloop has been handled and sailed for the past two years in all her regattas and matches by an amateur crew. A suggestion has been made to sail a Corinthian race once a week or once a fortnight throughout the season."

Having started as a Corinthian organization, the Seawanhaka Yacht Club, meeting with some opposition,

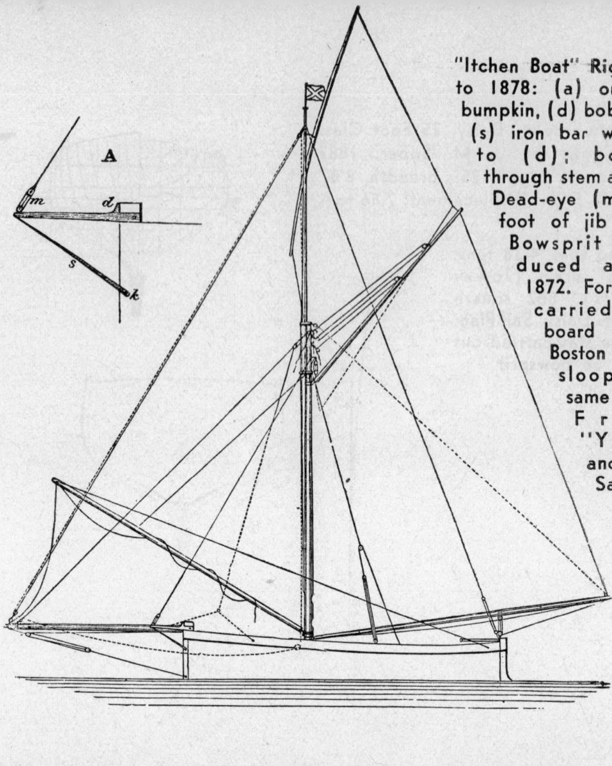

"Itchen Boat" Rig prior to 1878: (a) original bumpkin, (d) bob stay, (s) iron bar welded to (d); bolted through stem at (k). Dead-eye (m) on foot of jib stay. Bowsprit introduced about 1872. Fore stay carried outboard as in Boston keel sloops of same date. From "Yacht and Boat Sailing"

proposed to change its name as a public profession of faith, and at the annual meeting of 1874 a special committee of four was appointed to consider a change of name to the Corinthian Yacht Club; the committee was divided and the proposal was dropped. The battle deepened with the enlargement of the club, and at the January meeting of 1882 a proposed amendment to the constitution was presented by J. William Beekman: "This Association shall be known as the Seawanhaka Corinthian Yacht Club"; this was finally adopted at the meeting of March 6. At the same time the club adopted a "length and sail area" rule; length multiplied by sail area and divided by 6,000 equals sail tons. A motion for the adoption of the one-gun start was rejected.

This movement found Captain Coffin on the other tack; going ahead a few years, he wrote in *Outing* for June, 1886: "There has been some little boasting on the part of the Seawanhaka club over a claim that they were the first to introduce 'Corinthian' racing; and so fearful have the members been that their superiority in this respect would be lost sight of in the now almost general adoption of this method, either in whole or in part, that some years ago they tacked the word 'Corinthian' on to their originally beautiful Indian name of 'Seawanhaka,' making a clumsy and cumbersome title out of their first extremely appropriate name; and I suppose few, if any, of these young gentlemen are aware that on the 6th day of October 1846, the New York Yacht Club sailed a match for a cup subscribed for by members, the rule being—I quote literally—'none but club members allowed to sail or handle the boats, but each may carry a pilot.' They could not even have their sailing master except as pilot, which is further on the 'Corinthian' line than the Seawanhakas have ever gone."

To this he added later, in his history of American yachting: "The idea was, as stated by the advocate of the change, that this Club having been the first to introduce Corinthian yachting, ought to have something in its name to call attention to the fact; that so many clubs were now adopting the Corinthian system, the glory of its introduction would be lost to the Seawanhakas if they did not, in some way, label themselves as 'the only true and original Jacobs.' It was a snobbish reason for an ugly suffix, and it weighted the club down terribly, at one time nearly carrying it under entirely." The last sentence is utterly without foundation, as was publicly known at the time the subsequent division in the club was due to a very different incident. Most of the press writers of the day sided with Captain Coffin in their comments on the change.

The term "smear" in its present political significance had not yet found its way into use, but it describes accurately the many attacks made on the Seawanhaka C. Y. C. at this period and later. There was manifest in American society about 1880 a strong tendency toward what was termed "Anglo-Mania," the aping of English fashions and usages. Cuffs were introduced on American "pants" because it rained in London; creases were pressed in the same garments through an accident, an English visitor to New York invited to a social function just after he had landed, donned his "pants" as he took them from his trunk with creases still in them. There was an invasion of English music hall songs, chiefly featured by Harry Lingard, silly but with catchy tunes; "Captain Jinks of the Horse Marines," "Champagne Charley", and one, "The Queer Things You See and the Queer Things You Do, Are English, You Know, Quite English, You Know." Where technical arguments failed, resort was had to ridicule to combat both the Corinthian and the cutter movements.

One provision of the Seawanhaka "Sailing Regulations" aroused as much opposition in certain quarters as that calling for the deposit of the lines of a winning yacht before the prize could be delivered.

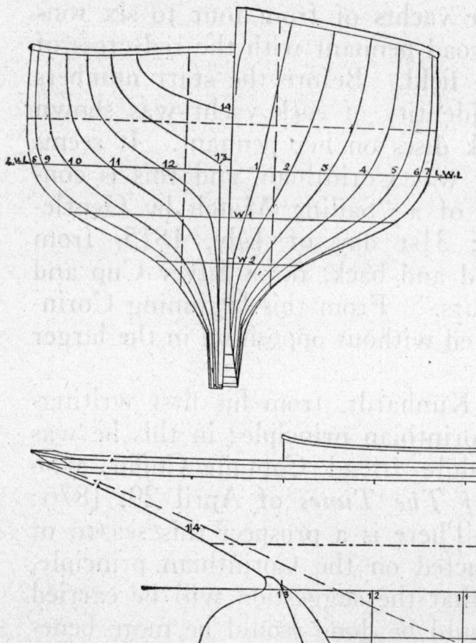

Moya cutter, designed by A. Cary Smith for Edward Burgess, 1881. L.o.a., 32'; l.w.l., 26'4"; breadth, 9'1"; draft, 4'8"

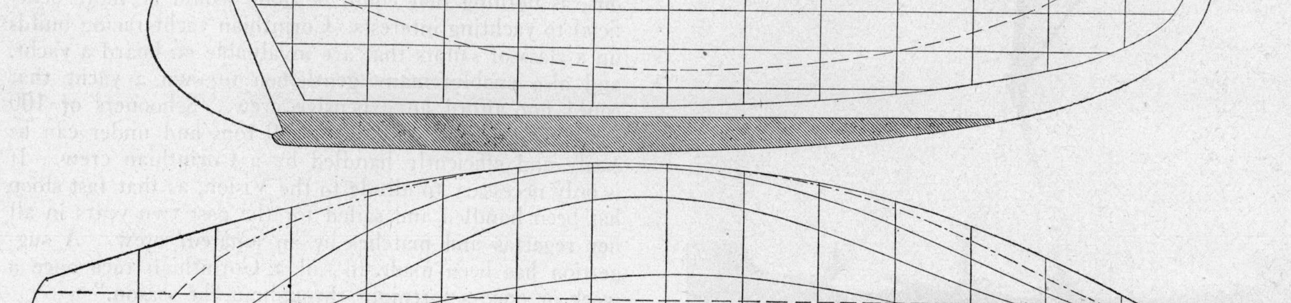

Rule VII read: "Every yacht, before starting in a Corinthian Race, must have filed with the Regatta Committee a list of the names comprising her crew, with the occupation and address of each." There was much amusement over one such entry list in which some of the crew who were openly knon to be employed on the water were described as "agriculturists"; the entry was not accepted. These entry lists, beginning in 1874, are interesting reading today, containing the names of many who, young then, were conspicuous in yachting for many years in later life.

The race of the New York Yacht Club mentioned by Captain Coffin was sailed on October 6, 1846, the condition being: "Only members to sail and handle their own yachts." The course was from off the Club House, Elysian Fields, up the Hudson and turning a mark off Fort Washington, down to a mark in the Narrows and return; forty miles. The yachts were: Maria, Commodore Stevens; Siren, William E. Miller; Cygnet, D. L. Suydam; Spray, Hamilton Weeks; La Coquille, John C. Jay; Lancet, George B. Rollins. As a matter of course, Maria, 160 tons, won by an hour from Siren, 72 tons, the others finishing in the order given. While the race seems to have been a success, no attempt was made to repeat it.

Edward Burgess—From Centerboard to Keel

THE interest in the smaller sizes of yachts other than sandbaggers was far keener about Boston than New York; local conditions fostering many small clubs within the broad limits of Boston Harbor. The two families which were most prominent in yachting were the "Adams boys" and the "Burgess boys." Both families were wealthy, with summer homes on the water; the Adams at Quincy and the Burgesses at Beverly; both began their yachting in the seventies in small Herreshoff catboats. It was not until 1884 that the Adams boys could boast of a real yacht, the keel sloop Cricket, built by Wood Brothers; she was followed in 1887 by the noted Papoose, and since by enough yachts to fill up a Yacht Register. The Burgess boys, Edward, Arthur, Franklin, Sidney and Walter, began with catboats from 12 to 16 feet, sailing regularly in the races of the Beverly and other clubs.

Born at Sandwich, on Cape Cod, on June 30, 1848, Edward began his sailing off Sandwich and Beverly. He graduated from Harvard in 1871 and for some years followed a bent for natural history, specializing in entomology. For a year he was instructor in the Bessey Institute, resigning to become Secretary of the Boston Society of Natural History. Beginning in small catboats, by 1874 he had progressed to the ownership of a yacht, the centerboard sloop Nimbus, built by J. B. Herreshoff in 1868, 37 feet over all; 33 feet 6 inches waterline; 12 feet 6 inches breadth and 4 feet draft; with board, 10 feet 6 inches. Deeply interested in all pertaining to yachting, he almost committed to memory the first edition of *Yacht and Boat Sailing* (1878). The summer of 1883 was spent with Mrs. Burgess on the South coast of England, where he saw much of yachting and made the acquaintance of Dixon Kemp.

In 1881 Mr. Burgess placed in the hands of A. Cary Smith the lines of an "Itchen Boat," from Kemp's book, and from this design with some modifications including the addition of a counter had Moya built by Lawley. In 1882 he sent to Mr. Kemp for a design for his friend, J. Malcolm Forbes, a modification of an "Itchen Boat," built by Lawley under the name of Lapwing: l.o.a. 45 feet; l.w.l. 35 feet; breadth 10 feet; draft 7 feet. In the following year he had built for himself the cutter Butterfly, designed by J. Beavor Webb: l.o.a. 39 feet; l.w.l. 32 feet 6 inches; breadth 8 feet 6 inches; draft 6 feet 9 inches; lead keel 8 tons. The failure of his father in 1883 made it necessary that Edward should enter business, and with his brother Sidney he started a yacht agency under the name of Burgess Brothers, representing A. Cary Smith in Boston. The first effort of the new firm was the design for the cutter Rondina, built for Dr. W. F. Whitney. in 1884; l.o.a. 38 feet; l.w.l. 30 feet 6 inches; breadth 8 feet; draft 6 feet 9 inches; the proportions being similar to his Butterfly. The proportion of length to breadth in these two yachts, 3.8, was as far as Burgess went toward the narrow cutter.

The "Itchen Boat"

THE "Itchen Boat," so called, was an anomaly in British yachting, free from all influence of the Tonnage Rule. Starting well over a century ago as a small working boat used by the fishermen of Itchen Ferry on the little river flowing by Southampton, it ended as an over-developed racing yacht. The first boats, used in the twenties of the preceding century, were small sailing craft; by 1852 they had developed to a length of about 18 feet, a breadth of 7 to 8 feet, and a couple of feet of draft; even in those days they were noted for the fair sweep of the midship section and the generally artistic lines in spite of a plumb stem and transsom. The original rig carried a high, narrow, gaff mainsail, loose on the foot, with main sheet on a horse across the transom, and a high jib set from the stem head. Open, with only a cuddy, they were used for fishing, but they were raced by their owners both for pleasure and business. The rig was enlarged about 1852 by the addition of an iron bumpkin to carry a larger jib. The lines were gradually refined, and about the same time an iron shoe of two to three hundredweight was added.

About 1870 the type was taken up by the yachtsmen of the Solent for racing on a measurement of waterline with no limit on sail. It developed rapidly in classes of 21 feet, 25 feet, and 30 feet, and competition both in out-building and racing became very keen, the leading local designers competing. The first counters were added in 1876; by 1880 clipper stems had been introduced, and professional designers were outdoing each other in displacement, draft, and sail area, all characteristics of the original "Boats" being lost. The craft thus developed were costly and in many respects undesirable, and the type disappeared with the adoption of the Rating Rule in 1886.

In its later years the "Itchen Boat" was quite similar to the Boston keel sloops of the seventies, the product of a "Mean Length" rule; with a foot or more less breadth and more draft, more displacement and metal keel, and an excessive sail plan for the length. Both richly deserved the designation of "brute" in its yachting sense; the extreme of breadth, draft, displacement, ballast, and sail on a fixed length.

In the decade immediately following the end of the Rebellion there was a marked increase in the interest in yachting, especially on the part of the younger men; this interest was by no means limited to actual sailing, but to the study of types and models. To the young man accustomed to the "all deadrise and no bilge" of the sandbagger, and the straight flat or V floor, hard bilge and plumb topsides of the average large sloop, the lines of British yachts as shown in *Yacht Designing* (1876) and *Yacht and Boat Sailing* (1878), a fair symmetrical reverse curve from lower edge of keel to planksheer, came as a revelation. Edward Burgess was only one of many who succumbed to the fascination of such lines; I do not know how many hundreds of midship section I was sketching a few years later.

As the ranks of yachtsmen divided under the assaults of the Cutter-Cranks Mr. Burgess frankly aligned himself on the side of the cutter and the keel, but he never went beyond the very moderate proportion of four beams, as in Lapwing and Rondina. Sidney ultimately went to live in England and Edward continued the business alone, doing very little until the challenge of Genesta came in the winter of 1884.

Traditions and Memories of

AMERICAN YACHTING

Part Sixty-eight

By WILLIAM P. STEPHENS

Cutters, Cutter Cranks, and Corinthians (Part Ten)

TRIALS between small yachts of different nations have been few in number and have proved very little, the reasons being the difference in weather and water conditions, the resultant difference in types, and the lack of a system of measurement not obviously unfair to one side or the other. The trials between British and American craft seem to have begun in 1853 with the shipping of two centerboard boats from New York to England. In 1852 Earl Mount Charles, later third Marquis of Connyngham, being in New York visited the boat shop of Captain Bob Fish and was so pleased with a catboat that he purchased her and shipped her to London. One story is that the boat was presented to him by William Butler Duncan. The Earl was the son of the second Marquis, who, joining the Royal Yacht Squadron in 1840, owned 18 yachts, mainly of large tonnage, down to his death in 1876.

Una, as she was named, was a typical New York catboat, 16 feet 6 inches long, 6 feet 6 inches breadth, and 9 inches draft. During the summer she was sailed on the Serpentine, a narrow piece of water between Hyde Park and Kensington Gardens; in the following year she was shipped by rail to Southampton and sailed to Cowes. With a centerboard and a small mainsail set with a single halyard for throat and peak, she represented the extreme of simplicity and maneuverability as compared

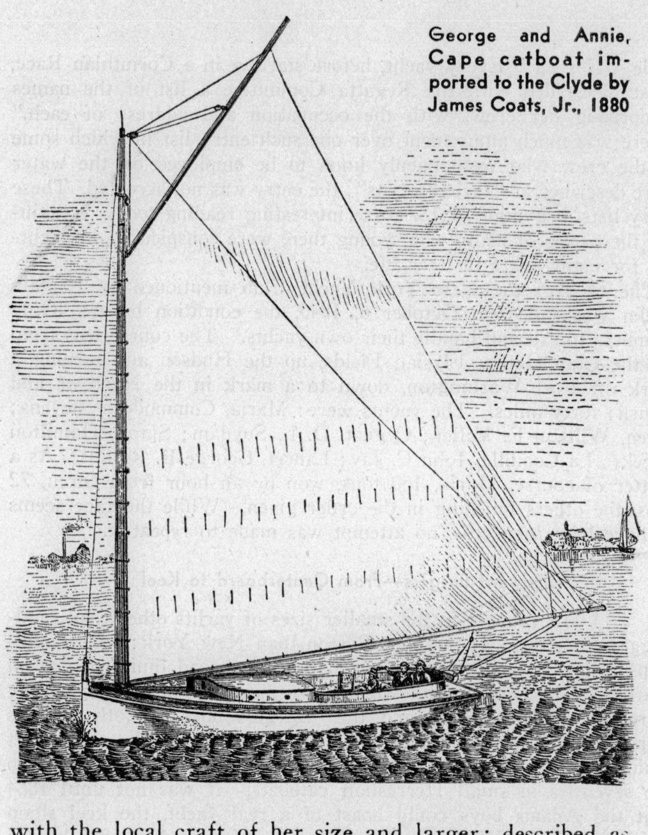

George and Annie, Cape catboat imported to the Clyde by James Coats, Jr., 1880

with the local craft of her size and larger; described as "nothing more handy under canvas than a waterman's skiff with three sails or an Itchen boat with two; or less unhandy than a boat with one sail—a dipping lug." There is no record of her racing, but her speed and handiness in smooth water and moderate breezes made her popular and gave the name to the type, in use in England down to the present day as "una boat."

In 1852 Robert Minturn Grinnell, a member of an old New York family prominent in the New York Y. C., which he joined in 1851, shipped to England aboard the clipper ship New World, owned by his firm of Grinnell, Minturn & Co., a small yacht named Truant. As his business kept him in England for some years he joined several clubs and raced Truant regularly. After such a lapse of time it is impossible to find a complete record of all races, but the brief summary shows that she was very successful. The only dimensions recorded are 20 feet 6 inches waterline and 14 inches draft; her breadth seems to have been a little over 7 feet. She was half-decked, with the usual cockpit, carried a large mainsail with a short gaff, a large jib with foot laced to a club which was tacked at about 1/5 of its length to a short bowsprit, and a small gaff topsail set on a vertical yard. As no comment was made on sandbags visible on deck, it is probable that none were car-

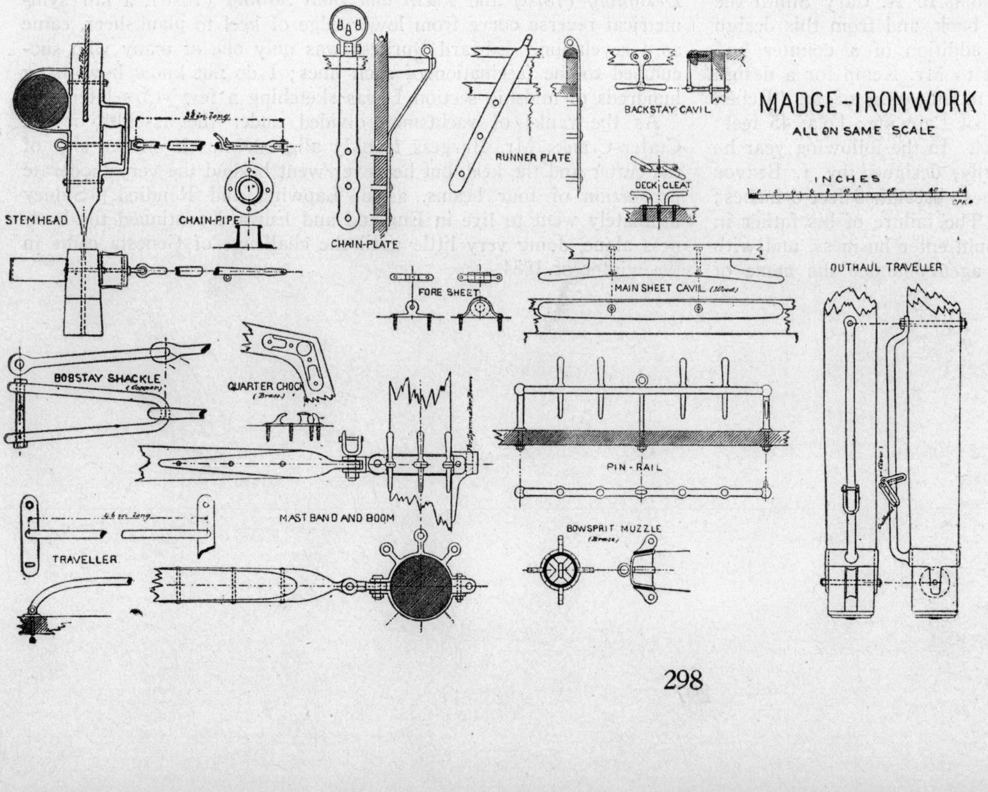

Iron work for Madge, drawn by C. P. Kunhardt

ried; but stories were told of her crew carrying their pockets filled with shot, and she may have used shotbags below, as was then the general practice.

Truant was built by Fish & Morton in 1852, of the type most popular in those days. Captain Bob Fish started as a boatbuilder in a shop on Front Street, New York, in 1840 moving to Water Street, where he maintained an office for many years. In 1850 he started a boatshop in Pamrapo, New Jersey, within the borders of what has been for many years the city of Bayonne. Near him was the boatshop of Pat McGiehan, the wharves of the Elsworth oyster fleet, while for more than half his life A. Cary Smith had a home a little further north. Nothing could be more depressing than a view of this once historic shrine of yachting as it exists today. About this time Captain Fish had as a partner C. F. Morton, a member of the New York Y. C. residing at Newburgh on the Hudson. In 1855 the firm built a sharpie, Luckey, 55 feet over all, and Mr. Morton used her for visits to New York, anchoring off Pamrapo.

From Liverpool, Truant was shipped, presumably by rail, to London. Later she visited Lake Windermere, Liverpool and Dublin, sailing across the Irish Sea on her trips back and forth to races on the Mersey and in Cork Harbor. As there were then no motor cars and trailers, much of her land transit must have been by means of "wains" or "lorries." Her first race seems to have been under the Prince of Wales Y. C., on May 18, 1853, the summary being:

	Tons	Class	Finish
Truant	5	2d	6-14-00
Julia	7	1st	6-37-00
Idas	6	2d	6-56-00
Britannia	7	1st	7-14-00
Albatross	7	1st	7-30-00
Calliope	3	3d	7-30-00
Demon	3	3d	D.N.F.

The start was off Blackwall, the course being a beat down the Thames against a fresh breeze and a run home. We can judge her competitors from a portrait of Idas, built in 1850, a sturdy little cutter 22 feet 6 inches long by 7 feet 10 inches breadth, of course a keel, possibly clinker-built, and fully rigged with topmast, running bowsprit, and a square-headed topsail. She had a record of a cruise of twenty days from Blackwall to Boulogne and

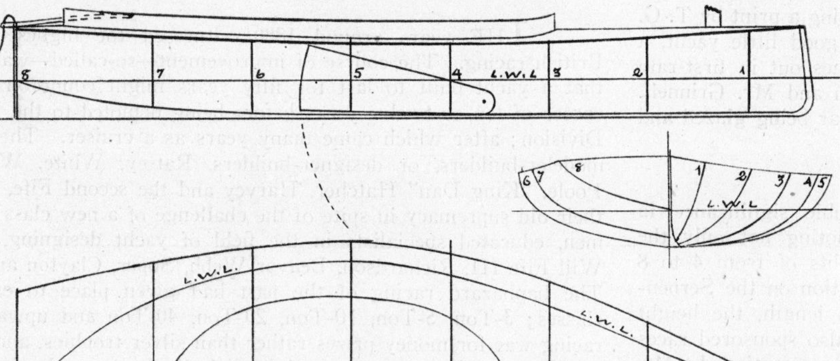

Una, Catboat built by Captain Bob Fish, 1852. First of the type in British waters and sponsor for English name for a catboat

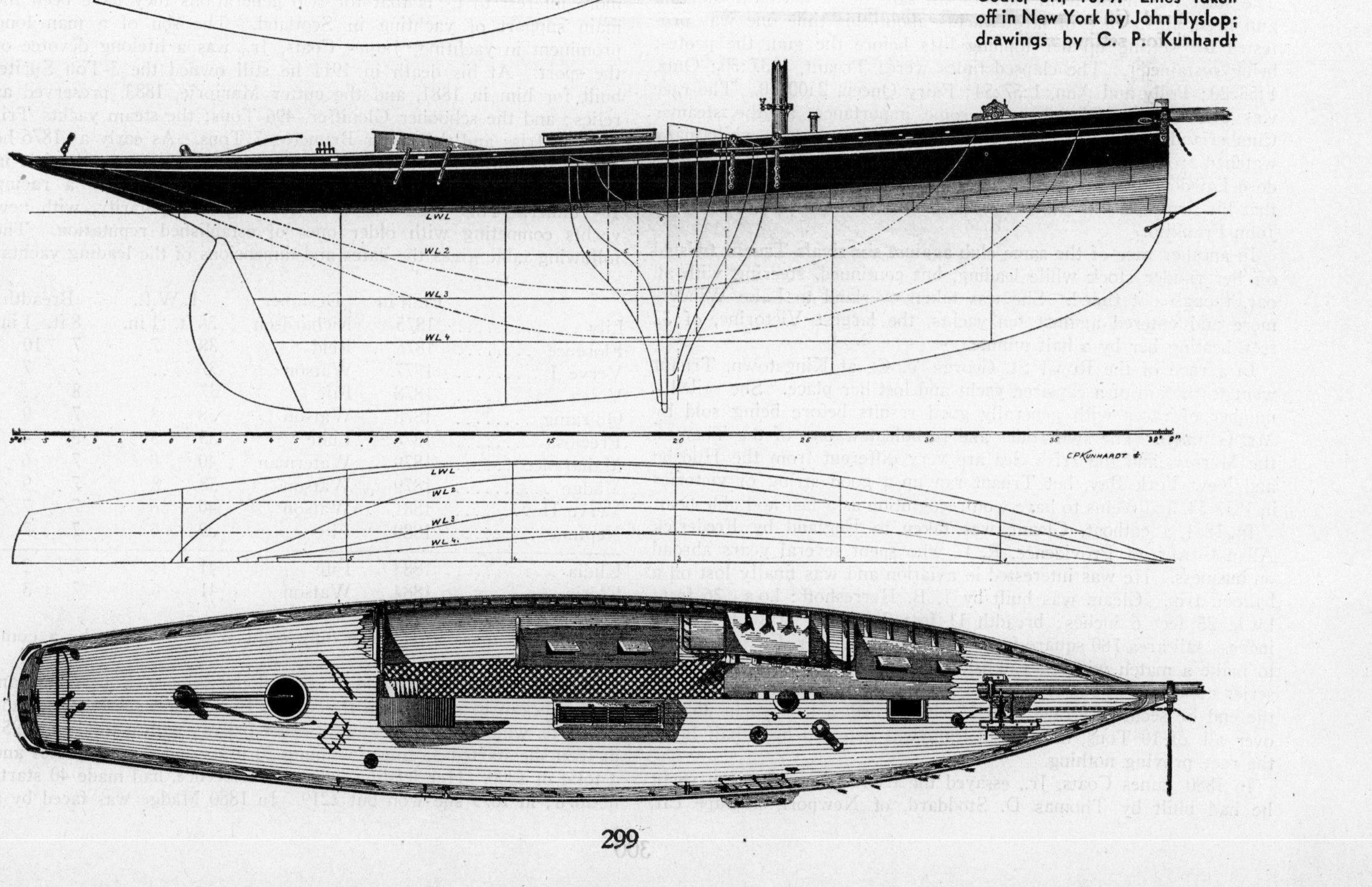

Madge, ten-ton cutter designed by George L. Watson for James Coats, Jr., 1879. Lines taken off in New York by John Hyslop; drawings by C. P. Kunhardt

back, proving that she was no light racing machine; the others were similar.

The comment of *Hunt's* on this race was: "Great anxiety was manifested to witness the start, owing to Truant being a Yankee clipper, the first that has ever sailed on the river Thames; and to her being fitted, not with a fair fixed keel, but with a centerboard or sliding keel; a dodge which enabled her to butter her toast on both sides, using the keel when beating and hauling it inboard when running." The race is summed up by *Hunt's:* "This time the Truant won, but we may just as well call her a yacht as term a match-cart a comfortable family carriage. If Englishmen be content to build for mere speed, they're not the sensible boys we take them for."

For the information of our readers we quote as follows from the *Manual of British Rural Sports,* published in London in 1856, a copy presented to me by N. H. Bishop in 1888: "Match-Carts and Harness. The carts and harness for these feats are very light; some of the former, with five-foot wheels, being little over 100 pounds. The American carts far excel the English in all points, and in their lightest pattern the driver actually sits partly by the side of the horse." The reference evidently is to the American trotting sulky, in which the driver sits almost over the horse's rump.

We learn from the same volume that: "The American yacht, the Black Maria, embodies all the latest improvements of our clever rivals in naval architecture." Later on, in reviewing a print by T. G. Dutton, Truant is described by *Hunt's* as: "A good little yacht, a good likeness, a good picture. The Truant comes out in first-rate company and style, and does honor to Mr. Fish and Mr. Grinnell. Buy a print, we say, to all yachtsmen; it will bear being glazed and framed and hung in a conspicuous position."

THE term "model yacht" had a double significance in England, some of the model-yacht clubs promoting not only the racing of small sailing models, but also of yachts of from 4 to 8 tons. The London Model Yacht Club had a station on the Serpentine where it sailed models not over 6 feet in length, the height from bottom of keel to truck being 13 feet; it also sponsored races on the Lower Thames for such yachts as those just mentioned. Mr. Grinnell was a member of the Birkenhead Model Yacht Club and at one time raced two models, the sloop Una and the schooner America; he also sailed Truant in the races of the Club for small yachts.

In one race of the Club, Truant at 3½ Tons, sailed against Polly and Ann (schr), 5 Tons, Quiz, 3 Tons, and Fairy Queen, 2 Tons. The start was made from anchors, all sails down until the starting gun fired (in a race of large yachts about this time one was protested for setting up her topping lifts before the gun, the protest being sustained). The elapsed times were: Truant, 1:37:30; Quiz, 1;53:20; Polly and Ann, 1:57:54; Fairy Queen, 2:00:30. The race was evidently considered as of some importance, as the steamer Cumberland, with a band of music, carried a large party, while many watched from the shores. Mr. Grinnell was presented by Commodore Laird with two silver goblets, special mention made of the fact that his firm had sent two ships to the Arctic in the search for Sir John Franklin.

In another race of the same club against six rivals Truant twisted off her rudder stock while leading, but continued, steering with an oar, though not timed. She was taken overland to Lake Windermere and entered against ten yachts, the largest Victorine, of 32 feet, beating her by a half minute.

In a race of the Royal St. George Y. C., at Kingstown, Truant went to the aid of a capsized yacht and lost her place. She sailed a number of races with generally good results before being sold by Mr. Grinnell. The swift tides and turbulent waters of the Thames, the Mersey, and the Irish Sea are very different from the Hudson and New York Bay, but Truant ran up a good string of victories in 1853-54, and seems to have won recognition as a fast and able boat.

In 1881 a catboat, Gleam, was taken to England by Frederick Allen Gower, of Providence, R. I., who spent several years abroad on business. He was interested in aviation and was finally lost on a balloon trip. Gleam was built by J. B. Herreshoff: l.o.a., 26 feet; l.w.l., 25 feet 6 inches; breadth 11 feet 2 inches; draft 1 foot 11 inches; sail area 780 square feet; 10 Tons, T.M. Mr. Gower's desire to make a match with an English yacht only served to bring out a series of letters in *The Field* over the question of measurement. In the end he secured a race with Mocking Bird, a keel yacht 36 feet over all, of 10 Tons, in which Gleam was defeated by a half hour, the race proving nothing.

In 1880 James Coats, Jr., essayed the trial of an American yacht he had built by Thomas D. Stoddard, of Newport, a Cape cat. George and Annie. Her dimensions were: l.o.a., 26 feet; l.w.l., 26 feet; breadth 11 feet; she carried a 34-foot boom and 19-foot gaff. A skilled local skipper, Josiah Albro, Jr., went along to sail her. She was shipped from New York to Glasgow aboard the Anchor Line steamer Devonia on April 24 and was soon sailing on the Clyde. She was under way on the occasion of the Royal Clyde Y. C. regatta, but apparently not racing.

Though several races were sailed, a diligent search of the pages of *Hunt's* and *The Field* fails to disclose any record, so it would seem that little came of the experiment. Her nearest competitors would have been the 22-foot Class of Clyde lugsail boats, plumb stem and transom, 7 feet breadth, 3 feet 2 inches draft, lapstrake, ballasted with lead inside and shotbags on a shelf, and over-rigged for racing with a large standing lug and a big jib. Such a test, if made, would have afforded no useful data. There are no records of small craft other than canoes being imported from England for racing on this side. When two English canoes came to New York in 1886 the first three or four days of preliminary sailing about New York Bay proved that ten years of intensive effort in designing and racing expensive canoes of great displacement and complicated rig had been absolutely wasted.

The Peak of British Yacht Racing

THE years around 1880 witnessed the highest point of British racing. The course of improvement—so-called—was so slow that a yacht built to last for fifty years might count on a racing career of ten or twelve years before being demoted to the Handicap Division; after which came many years as a cruiser. The old-time modeler-builders, or designer-builders, Ratsey, White, Wanhill of Poole, "King Dan" Hatcher, Harvey and the second Fife, still held their old supremacy in spite of the challenge of a new class of young men, educated specialists in the field of yacht designing, Watson, Will Fife III, Richardson, Beavor-Webb, Soper, Clayton and others. The haphazard racing of the past had given place to established classes; 3-Ton, 5-Ton, 10-Ton, 20-Ton, 40-Ton and upward. The racing was for money prizes rather than silver trophies, and supremacy in any class meant a substantial dividend on the investment. Of the classes which flourished at this period the 10-Ton was one of the most popular, both on the South Coast and on the Clyde.

The names of Coats and Clark are known in every part of the world where thread and needles are used, as both families have long been prominent in the manufacture of sewing cotton. What is of more interest to us is that for two generations they have been the main support of yachting in Scotland. The son of a man long prominent in yachting, James Coats, Jr., was a lifelong devotee of the sport. At his death in 1911 he still owned the 3-Ton Sprite, built for him in 1881, and the cutter Marjorie, 1883, preserved as relics; and the schooner Gleniffer, 496 Tons; the steam yachts Triton and Iris; and the cutter Brunette, 7 Tons. As early as 1876 he owned the cutter Diana, 40 Tons, with a small steam yacht, but in 1878 he placed an order with George L. Watson for a racing 10-Tonner. This class was then growing in popularity, with new yachts competing with older ones of established reputation. The following table gives the dates and dimensions of the leading yachts:

	Built in	Designer	L.W.L.		Breadth	
Lily	1875	Richardson	36 ft.	1 in.	8 ft.	1 in.
Florence	1876	Reid	38	7	7	10
Verve I	1877	Watson	37	..	7	7
Volga	1878	Fife	37	..	8	..
Quiraing	1878	Watson	38	8	7	9
Preciosa	1878	Luke	35	3	8	4
Maharanee	1879	Waterman	40	8	7	6
Madge	1879	Watson	38	8	7	9
Verve II	1881	Watson	40	6	7	7
Neptune	1880	Fife	39	6	7	7
Ulidia	1883	Fife	41	11	7	2
Ulerin	1884	Watson	41	6	7	3

The change in proportions in only eight years is shown by a comparison of Lily with Ulidia.

In the hands of a very clever professional skipper, Robert Duncan, Madge began to score from the start. In her first season she made 24 starts, winning 22 firsts and 2 other prizes; with a total of £395; in 1880 she started 35 times, winning 20 firsts and 2 other prizes and a total of £300. Her leading opponent, Florence, had made 40 starts in 1878; in 1879 she won but £219. In 1880 Madge was faced by a new rival, Neptune; in her third season she was completely eclipsed by Neptune, taking only £47 to the £260 of the other.

James Coats was a man of sentiment and spirit. As already noted, he kept one of his first small yachts and his cutter Marjorie until his death, or 25 years after her racing career ended. A characteristic incident was his promotion of a race in 1901 between the yawl Sybarita, owned by his friend Whitaker Wright, and the cutter Kariad, owned by Kenneth M. Clark. This race stands out as one of the most noted ever sailed on the Clyde, a course of 76 miles, one-half to windward, sailed in a northwest gale in 6 hours 13 minutes, or a rate of 12 knots. There had been some rivalry between the two Watson yachts, and Mr. Coats, believing that Sybarita was the faster, backed her for 500 guineas. Had Kariad won he would have received nothing, but had she lost he would have paid the stake. Though by no means a young man, and a sufferer from rheumatics, Mr. Coats followed the race aboard Gleniffer, watching the yachts from the companionway.

In the ordinary course of events Madge would have been sold, probably for conversion to a cruising yawl, but such a fate did not suit the ideals of her owner, and he determined to send her to America for a trial against the native sloops. She was shipped aboard the Anchor Line steamer Devonia, consigned to the Auchincloss brothers, the American agents of the Coats Company, and arrived in New York on August 16, 1881. She was lowered over the side, promptly rigged by Captain Duncan, and took up her mooring close to that of Mischief, just off the northeast point of Staten Island. I can still remember the thrill with which I boarded her from my canoe, putting out from the house of the New York Canoe Club, just after my return from the second Meet of the American Canoe Association; my feet on the deck of a real cutter. Kunhardt's comment on her arrival proves that he was not yet fully inoculated with the virus of narrow beam: "In point of beam she has been unreasonably squeezed by the English Rule." In sending out Madge, Mr. Coats had no definite plan of campaign, but left all details to a friend, a Scotch yachtsman, W. Lindsay Blatch, then living in New York and a member of the New York Y. C.

From the Past to the Future

WE Americans have much to be proud of in the fact that we have held the foremost yachting trophy of the world through 93 years, winning 16 matches and 41 individual races. At the same time this is by no means conclusive proof that we hold a monopoly of talent in the designing, construction and handling of yachts. With the resumption of international racing—let us hope, in the not too far distant future—it may be that our luck will change. In view of such a possible contingency it is only prudent to study the contests of the past.

Looking first at the defense, it has been from the outset organized and continuous, in the hands of one permanent organization with ample means, a more or less continuing body of officers and committees, and a large fleet available for defense. Not only has the racing been in home waters and under conditions which have fostered a type suited to them, and under a home rule, but the element of time has proved a serious handicap to the challenger.

In marked contrast, the challenger has been an individual, obliged to rely on his personal efforts in planning, financing and building; the most aid that he has had has been the endorsement of a club. The endorsing club has, at times, backed the challenger in discussions and disputes; but, broadly, it is a case of an individual against an organization. Down to comparatively recent years the challenger has been tied to a type distinctly unsuited to the waters in which the match must be sailed, and he was compelled to design to a rule which handicapped his home fleet.

The greatest obstacle, however, is the matter of time. We may assume that both challenger and defender are in the water by June, though this has seldom been the case. The defender, sailing in home waters, first breaks a few spars, has them replaced and then goes to the builder's yard for changes in ballast, etc., while her sails go to the loft for re-cutting. By July she is ready to sail with the existing fleet and possibly one or more rival defenders; this racing going on continuously, with less or more returns to the yard, down to the start of the trial races. By this time she has been strengthened, worked up to form, and her weak and strong points discovered.

Starting at the same date, the challenger has her period of trial and repair, followed by a brief series of trials against the home fleet, reports of her phenomenal speed being cabled to the ends of the earth. Then, in the middle of the season, she is stripped, fitted with a jury rig, and starts out on an ocean passage of 3,000 miles, for which she is quite possibly unfitted in model and build. Until recent years it was a matter of a month from the time her home trials ended until she was in New York, to be re-rigged and restored to racing form. When this was done she sailed about with no competitor to measure and improve her form. The recently accorded privilege of towing, and the bringing of a sister yacht as a "trial horse" have done something to lessen this handicap, but only to a degree. Assuming that her crew are acclimated and that she seems in proper form, she is still at a disadvantage as compared with the defender.

"Of All Sad Words of Tongue or Pen"

HAD there been on the part of the Royal Yacht Squadron or of any body of British yachtsmen a deliberate effort to retrieve the trophy lost in 1851, there would have been a study of the development of yacht racing in America as compared with that at home, and a time would have been selected when the defense was weakest and the offense strongest. This opportunity came about the period which we now have under observation, with the sloop fleet composed of old yachts, of obsolete model and weak in hull and rig, accompanied by a deterioration in personnel. Contemporary with these conditions, the modern racing cutter had reached the highest point of its development at the moderate proportion of five beams to length, as in the Watson May, 64 by 12; the Fife Annasona, 64.27 by 11.85; the Watson Marjorie, 75.35 by 14.50. The lines of May, as shown on page 72 of this story in book form, represent the highest point of cutter development in both form and construction. The round of the British coast, through June, July and August, making passages under racing rig regardless of weather, and sailing thirty or more races, had built up a strong personnel of professional racing men.

The confidence of American yachtsmen in the tried and true veterans of the 70-Foot Class, Gracie, Fanny, Arrow, Hildegard, Vision and Mischief, was unbounded. If these yachts could defeat a Canadian sloop, they most certainly could take care of a British cutter. A challenge in behalf of May or Annasona in the fall of 1881 would have been met without a thought of building a new defender. To quote again that unimpeachable authority, Captain Coffin: "It was also in the early part of this year (1883) that the cutter Marjorie, since so celebrated, was launched at Greenock, and it was rumored that she was to come here for the America's Cup. In the light of subsequent history I think that there is good reason for saying that if she had then come she would have carried it home with her. We had not much opinion of the speed of cutters at that time, and I don't think, after the experience of Pocahontas, that anything would have been provided to sail against Marjorie except Mischief, Gracie or Fanny."

As both May and Annasona were well under the limit of 70-Foot l.w.l., there would have been no thought of a longer yacht, the 70-Foot Class would have held its first place, and yachting would have been spared the ephemeral and expensive "Jay-boat." When in 1884 there came a challenge from a cutter of 81 feet waterline it spelled the doom of the old class. Past experience has proved that the old rules and special provisions were very far from perfect even in their day; when the time comes to consider new rules and conditions they must be framed in the light of 1951 rather than 1851.

TRADITIONS AND MEMORIES OF American Yachting

Part Sixty-nine

By

WILLIAM P. STEPHENS

●

Cutters, Cutter-Cranks and Corinthians, Part II

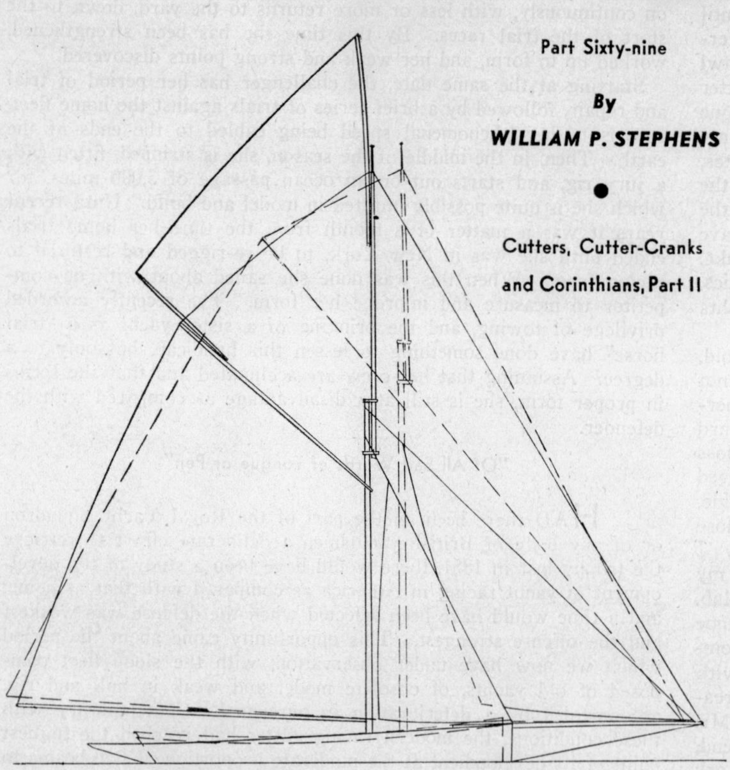

Madge Sail plan. Schemer shown by broken lines

THE visit of Madge, though accidental and unpremeditated, came at the right moment; the discussion, vocal and written, had passed the limit of polite controversy and degenerated into an exchange of billingsgate; now the issue was shifted to the racing courses. Opposing Kunhardt were Captain Coffin, writing in the daily *World* and the weekly *Spirit of The Times*; Captain Cornelius McKay, writing in *The Herald* and later in *The Telegram*; and B. S. Osbon, owner and editor of *The Nautical Gazette,* with other writers on *The Sun, The Times* and Boston dailies. At one time Kunhardt had been associated with *The Nautical Gazette*, but now they were sworn enemies. While on his part Kunhardt was capable of discussing the question on its technical merits, he was not content with this, but showered ridicule and invective on his opponents, who retorted in similar style. The other side paid little attention to technical argument, but went back to the Battle of Bunker Hill, the Declaration of Independence, and allied items of history.

In *The Spirit* of June 11, 1881, we read: "The cutter-craze still continues. Mr. Morgan, the owner of the schooner Wanderer, has given Mr. A. Cary Smith an order for a boat—or 'ship' as Rear Commodore Schuyler loves to call them—about the length of Muriel but with one and one half feet less beam. Every little helps, the next man will see that and go one and one half foot better. Why on earth anybody should desire to build a wedge in this country only a Fitz-Noodle (Kunhardt) can tell?" A little later: "I don't care for news, you know, says Fitz-Noodle, I'm a writah, not a reportah." Commenting on the small number of starters in the Atlantic Y.C. regatta of June 14, *The Spirit* said: Of course the advocates of the wedges or cutters (one hardly knows what to call them since it has been gravely stated by one high authority that the term 'cutter' applies only to the rig and not to the model) will raise an exultant shout over this failure to start."

In September, just prior to the races, *The Nautical Gazette* predicted: "If report be true the Scotch racing cutter Madge will get a bellyfull of racing from our yachtsmen before the season closes." In *The Spirit* of September 10 we find the following prediction: "The honest fight which *The Spirit* has made against the importation of the plank-on-edge principle in the modeling of American yachts seems likely to be crowned with entire success. In a recent publication we notice that one of the staunchest advocates of the latest British style speaks of boats of five and six beams as extravaganzas, which they certainly are; and calls yachts of three and three and one half beams 'healthy craft,' and is right again. Until something has been found to beat them we shall still insist that the beamy centerboard is the best type of boat for speed in the ordinary yachting waters, and by that we mean the New York Yacht Club's course here and the inland route from New York to Martha's Vineyard. We have not seen Madge, but we learn that she has been beaten by everything that has encountered her since she came here."

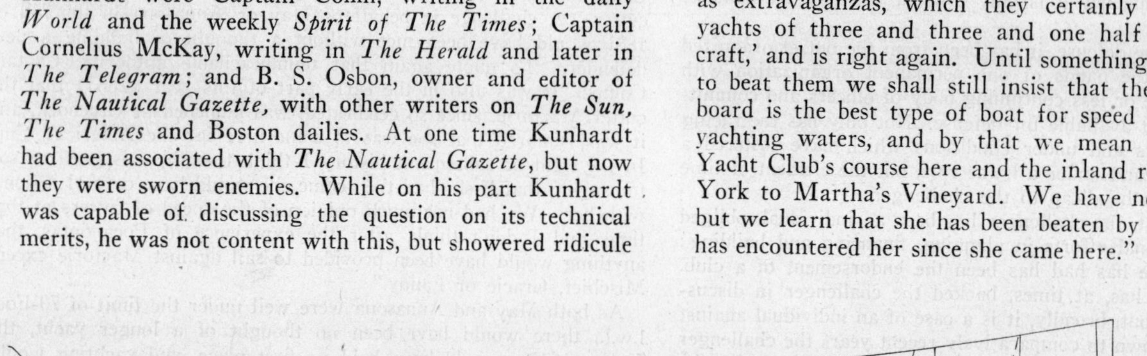

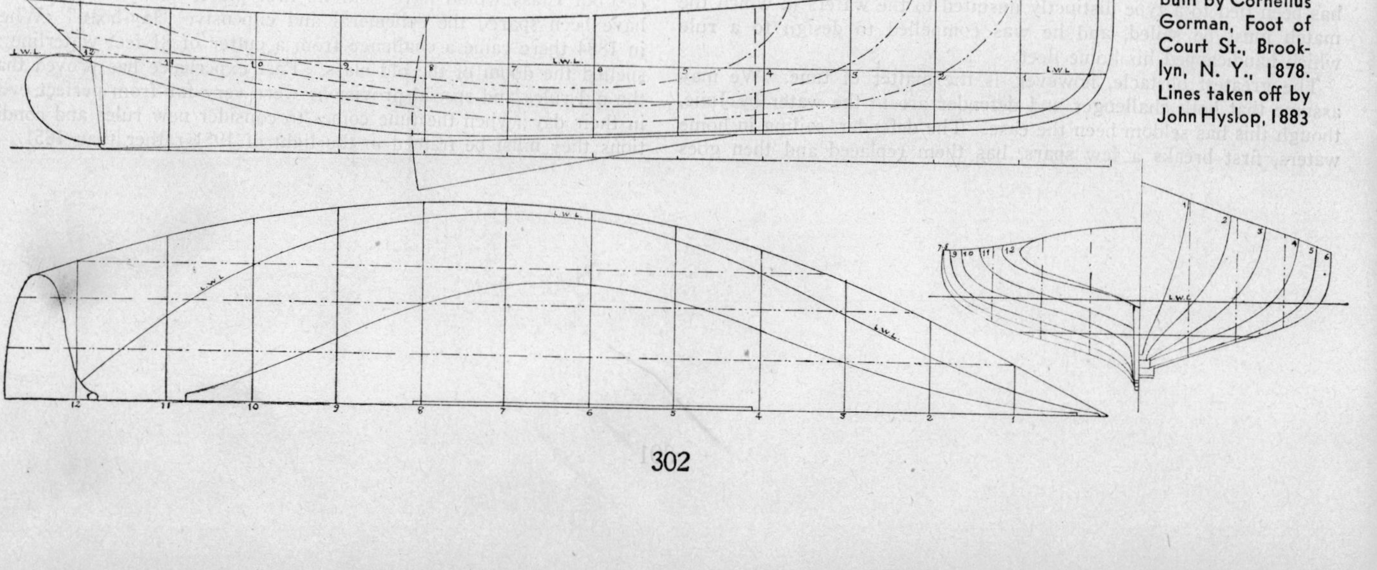

Wave, sloop. Modeled and built by Cornelius Gorman, Foot of Court St., Brooklyn, N. Y., 1878. Lines taken off by John Hyslop, 1883

Diplomacy and Tactics in Yacht Racing

Wave, Madge and Schemer. From The Spirit of The Times, October 15, 1881. "Engraving on wood," as employed for newspaper illustration prior to the introduction of photo-lithography. Below: Madge abandoned in a swamp at Charlotte, (Rochester, N.Y.), in 1905. Her greenheart keelson and teak members were still sound

The position of Captain Duncan was a delicate one, three thousand miles away from his owner, and relying only on his own judgment. Once under way, he sailed about the bay every day, accepting the implied challenges of the sloops which came out to meet him; while Madge was to all appearances in racing form, her head sheets were always off an inch or two, and her topsail yards in their chocks on deck. As the result of these informal brushes the boat sharps of Gowanus Bay formed an opinion which was well expressed by Captain Ira Smith on the morning of the first race. When his attention was called to the miserably fitting topsail on Schemer, an old one borrowed for the race, he shrugged his shoulders and said: "Oh, it's good enough, anything will beat that thing." Just by way of diversion, while waiting for the first race, let us turn again to *The Spirit of The Times*, this time of the date of October 11, 1851, in which is reported the speech made by Commodore Stevens at the dinner given him on his return from England.

"You may, perhaps, observe that my hair is somewhat grayer than when I last met you; I'll tell you how it happened. In coming from Havre we were obliged to anchor some five or six miles from Cowes. At nine o'clock a gentle breeze sprang up, and with it came gliding down Lavrock, one of the newest and fastest cutters of her class. The Lavrock stuck to us, sometimes lying to and sometimes tacking round us, evidently showing no intention of quitting us. We were loaded with extra sails, with beef and pork, and bread enough for an East India voyage, and were some five or six inches too deep in the water. We got up sails with a heavy heart—the wind had increased to a five or six knot breeze, and after waiting until we were ashamed to wait longer we let her get about 200 yards ahead and then started in her wake.

"I have seen and been engaged in many exciting trials at sea and on shore. I made the match with Eclipse against Sir Henry (a horse from the South), and had heavy sums both for myself and my friends depending on the result. I saw Eclipse lose the first heat and four fifths of the second without feeling one hundredth part of the responsibility, and without suffering one hundredthu part of the fear and dread I felt at the thought of being beaten by the Lavrock in this eventful trial. During the first five minutes not a sound was heard save, perhaps, the beating of our anxious hearts or the slight ripple of the water upon our sword-like stem. The captain (Old Dick Brown) was crouched down upon the floor of the cockpit, his seemingly unconscious hand upon the tiller, with his stern, unaltering gaze upon the vessel ahead. The men were motionless as statues, with their eager eyes fastened upon the Lavrock with a fixedness and intensity that seemed almost unnatural. It could not last long. We worked quickly and surely to windward of her wake; the crisis was past and some dozens of deep-drawn sighs proved that the agony was over."

The Lavrock's report of this impromptu brush spread through Cowes immediately on her arrival and ended all chances of matches with the British fleet. Later on one yachtsman, and one only, accepted Commodore Steven's challenge and sailed against the Yankee.

This was Tactical Error No. 1 in international racing; there have been others. Those yachtsmen of today who can spare the time from war, political and baseball reports are advised to read the long and interesting speech of which this is only a brief extract.

From the Narrows to the Sea

When it came to making matches Mr. Blatch had no trouble, and five yachts were soon signed up. In the course of a generation the New York Yacht Club had moved from its birthplace off Hoboken to Stapleton, Staten Island, on the Upper Bay. The Seawanhaka Yacht Club had left its birthplace and had a station nearby at Tompkinsville, and across on the Bay Ridge shore were two strong clubs, the Brooklyn and the Atlantic. Long Island Sound was almost as far in the future as Hoboken was in the past, the metropolitan yacht fleet moored and started its races in the center of the Upper Bay. The Seawanhaka course was from off Fort Wadsworth, just inside the Narrows, past Buoy 10 and down the ship channel, around South West Spit, out past Sandy Hook, and around the Sandy Hook Lightship; which, prior to the dredging of Ambrose Channel, was about six miles due East of the point of the Hook; the length of the course was 32 nautical miles.

The measurement rule in use by the Seawanhaka Y.C. in 1881 was no better and no worse than others of the variety of empirical rules then in use. The "mean length" was multiplied by the extreme breadth, but what this proved as to the "size" of a vessel was an open question. The overhang of Madge was 6.51 feet, for which she was taxed 3.25 feet; the overhang of Schemer was 2.64 feet, for which she was taxed 1.32 feet; that of Wave was 2.80 feet, with a tax on 1.40 feet. While this was unfair to Madge, the breadth factor was equally unfair to the two sloops. The first attempt at a sane measurement rule was made by the Seawanhaka Y.C. in 1882 in the introduction of sail area as a co-factor with length. This rule, amended in 1883 and later generally adopted, worked satisfactorily as applied to both sloops and cutters down to 1891, when the introduction of a weighted lever in place of displacement made it useless. Under this Seawanhaka Rule the measurements of the three would have been: Madge, 43.76; Schemer, 42.27; Wave, 42.71; rating them, as events proved, practically on an equality. In 1881 the question of the one-gun start was being mildly discussed as an improvement on the crude methods then followed, it was condemned by Captain Coffin as too dangerous, involving risk of collision. In this series of races an interval of ten minutes was used, each yacht being timed as she crossed the line.

THREE races were arranged by Mr. Blatch and the Seawanhaka Y.C., one with Schemer, one with Wave, and one with an un-named yacht, to be sailed on September 20, 21 and 22; but the complete list of contestants is as below.

Yacht	Owner	Captain
Madge	James Coats, Jr.	Robert Duncan
Schemer	W. S. Alley	Ira Smith
Wave	Dr. J. C. Barron	Michael Wallin
Mistral	Edward Fox	John Prior
Paloma	C. H. Leland	
Shadow	Dr. John Bryant	Aubrey Crocker

Yacht	L.O.A.	Over hang	L.W.L.	Beam	Depth	Draft
Madge	45.91	6.51	39.40	7.75	6.2	7.83
Schemer	39.48	2.64	36.84	14.50	3.8	3.10
Wave	41.52	2.88	38.64	14.96	4.25	4.00
Mistral	39.50	2.84	36.66	14.94	4.33	3.92
Paloma	41.00	3.00	38.00	14.00	4.66	4.00
Shadow	37.08	2.91	34.17	14.25	...	5.33

The lines and portrait of Schemer were given in MoToR BoatinG for August, 1944; William S. and A. Bryan Alley were sandbag sailors, both charter members of the Larchmont Y.C. organized a year previously; "Bill" had bought Schemer and "Bry" was still racing Cruiser, one of the fastest of the 21-foot class. Wave was the last yacht built for the veteran John H. Dimon, who joined the Brooklyn Y.C. in 1858, its second year, then owning Arago, 30 tons, and Laura, a 26-foot sandbagger; he continued to build and race yachts down to the building of Wave, in 1878, by Cornelius Gorman at Gowanus, selling her to Dr. Barron in 1880. For some years after that he was a familiar figure among the boat yards and yacht clubs of Bay Ridge. Dr. Barron was a spirited and enthusiastic racing man. In 1884 he replaced Wave with the compromise keel-centerboard sloop Athlon, modelled and built by John Mumm; later he owned and raced the cutter Clara.

MISTRAL was modeled and built in 1878 by D. O. Richmond of Stonington; in model she was deeper and abler than the Gowanus boats. Paloma, originally named Blanche, was built by Albertson Bros. in Philadelphia in 1871; as it happened she did not race. Shadow was illustrated and described in MoToR BoatinG for September, 1942, but her regular rig was that shown in the photo, a single big jib, and not the "morfydyte" cutter shown in the sail plan, a rig then popular about Boston. Shadow's owners for many years were Dr. John Bryant and his brother Henry, experienced racing men; throughout their ownership she was sailed by "Capt'n Aub" Crocker. Captain Crocker was selected by General Paine to sail Puritan in her races with Genesta. In dimensions and model Shadow had nothing in common with the New York sloops of her size.

Among the leading professional skippers of the day were the veterans, "Capt'n 'Than" Clock, "Capt'n Hank" Haff, "Capt'n Jim" Berry, "Capt'n Lou" Tonns and "Capt'n Sam" Gibson; apart from these was a class of semi-professionals, "boat-handlers," who were called on to supplant the regular skipper at the wheel of a cabin yacht, or to take the stick of a sandbagger, in the more important races. In this class head and shoulders above all others in his knowledge of wind, weather and tides, his judgment, and his skill at the wheel was "Capt'n Joe" Elsworth, the patriarch of a web-footed tribe of Elsworths and Van Buskirks, interrelated, which inhabited the Bayonne-Pamrapo shore. The family business was oystering, and Elsworth oysters, no longer from Raritan Bay but from Greenport, L. I., are still esteemed by New York's gourmands. With "Capt'n Joe" were his brothers, "Capt'n Bill," "Capt'n Bob" and "Watty." The best "boat-handler" of the sandbaggers was "Capt'n Ira" Smith, a pilot in the Brooklyn ferry service, always called on in the matches for big money. When he bought Bella, the fastest of the 27-foot Class, he changed the name to Susie S. after his daughter. Jake Schmidt, though best known as a builder, was a skillful sailer of his own boats.

Like Lambs to the Slaughter

AFTER several changes of plan the first race was started on Tuesday, September 27, the prize being a cup costing $100 given by the club. The Regatta Committee of the club had a tug to follow the course. With Captain Duncan and his two men were Niels Olsen, the Superintendent of the New York Y.C., a hardy Norse sailor, Mr. Blatch and Rear Commodore Schuyler representing the club. Mr. Alley was not able to sail aboard Schemer, but Captain Ira Smith was in command, with John M. Sawyer as mate and "Capt'n Jimmy" Smith, long in the employ of J. Roger Maxwell on many yachts. The day was clear, with a light SE wind inside the Narrows; the tide being against the yachts going and returning. Madge sailed down from the Seawanhaka Basin and Schemer came across from Bay Ridge; the sloop carried the borrowed sail just mentioned while the cutter swung her big yard topsail. Schemer crossed on the gun at 10:40 and Madge 40 seconds later. Beating down to Buoy 10 Madge gained 57 seconds, when they reached the bar Schemer housed her topmast, and Madge lowered her club topsail, both pitching. Madge rounded the Lightship at 1:41:18 with a lead of 5 minutes 35 seconds. Once inside the Hook Schemer sent up her topmast and set her topsail; from Buoy 10 they ran under spinnakers. The finish was timed: Madge, 3:58:05; Schemer, 4:03:06, a difference of 5 minutes 1 second elapsed time.

The conditions were the same for the second race on September 28, with Wave. The wind was light south, outside it was southwest and variable. Wave led over the line at 10:37:43, Madge following at 10:38:09, both carrying working topsails. Wave gained for a time, but her skipper broke tacks and worked her out of the wind, which shifted to the westward and gave Madge the advantage; at Buoy 10 she led by 10 minutes 23 seconds. On the reach out to the Lightship Wave cut the lead down to 6 minutes 51 seconds; they were even on the beat in to Buoy 10, but in the final run Madge gained nearly five minutes, the finish being timed: Madge, 5:45:59; Wave, 5:56:39. Madge won by 11 minutes, 51 seconds, elapsed time.

The third race on September 29 was a private match for $250 per side in answer to a challenge from Edward Fox, owner of Mistral. Nothing is known about Mr. Fox save that he bought Mistral in the previous year and sold her at the end of this season. His name does not appear in any yacht register or club book, and this was his only appearance in yachting history. It is possible that he was the Englishman who published the first yacht register in 1872. The race was over the New York Y.C. course, from off the club station, around the Lightship and finishing off Buoy 15. The wind was strong from ESE and the start was made after half flood. Under the club rule Madge would have received 32 seconds, but this was waived. The skipper of the yawl Caprice held the wheel on Mistral. The tug used on the first two days was replaced by the larger Luckenback, carrying a large party, some of whom paid tribute to Neptune in crossing the bar.

MISTRAL crossed close to the tug 35 seconds after the gun, but Madge, 10 seconds later, was on her weather. Both carried working topsails but were glad to douse them before they were clear of the Narrows. Madge gained steadily; at 11:35 Mistral turned in two reefs and soon after Madge lowered her foresail. Nearing Buoy 10 Madge housed her topmast, the times at this mark being: Madge, 12:06:51; Mistral, 12:16:35. As they neared the Hook Madge turned in one reef; a little later Mistral set a staysail in place of her big jib, but the stay parted and she was obliged to re-set her jib. In crossing the bar Madge justified the opprobrious epithets freely bestowed by her opponents: "half-tide rock," "diving-bell" and "submarine." When Madge turned the Lightship at 2:37:23 Mistral was a mile and a half to leeward; shortly after her jib blew into ribbons and she turned for home with her crew bailing with buckets. Madge passed Buoy 10 at 4:06:40 and was off Buoy 15 at 4:59:59, her elapsed time being 6:14:35.

The fourth race, on September 30, was again with Schemer, under the same conditions as the first; the wind was light SSE, freshening through the race. Schemer started with a balloon jib topsail; Madge had her club topsail aloft. Schemer crossed on the gun, but Madge held back until the last gun. Outside the Narrows Madge shifted to working topsail at 12:50; at Buoy 10 Schemer was timed: 1:14:56, Madge, 1:23:56. Schemer turned the Lightship at 2:39:45 and Madge at 2:45:47. The finish was timed: Schemer, 4:55:33; Madge, 5:01:01; or a lead of 5 minutes 6 seconds elapsed time.

The fifth race, on October 1, was again with Schemer, for a stake of $75. Madge was ready to sail but Captain Smith sailed over from Bay Ridge in the sloop Dream and reported to the committee that his yacht had sprung her rudderstock and was unable to sail. On the advice of Commodore Stewart, Mr. Blatch ordered Madge to sail over the course, which she did in company with the cutter Oriva. Mr. Alley sent his check for $75 to Mr. Blatch, but it was returned to him. A match had been made with Paloma for October 4, but was cancelled on account of a death in the family of her owner. On the following day Madge and Wave were to meet again. Madge was ready at the start with topmast housed when it was announced that Wave, out for cleaning, could not be launched on account of the heavy sea on the Brooklyn shore. Another proposed race with Elephant fell through, and on October 8 Madge sailed for Newport to meet the renowned Shadow.

Shadow and Madge

AS told in the chapter, "East of the Cape," the sloops of about forty feet and under about Boston were deeper in body, more able, and of better build than the average of New York. The work of "Old George" Lawley, "Billy" Smith, "Mel" Wood and the Pierce Brothers was of a high quality for the day. The Herreshoffs always led in original and sound construction. Throughout a racing career of almost a quarter century Shadow was recognized as the fastest sloop of her class. For most of this time she was under the ownership of the Bryant brothers, with "Capt'n Aub" Crocker to care for and sail her. She had her own railway and house on her owner's beach at Cohasset and was kept in perfect racing condition. Her record under the Bryant ownership from 1877 to 1881 was said to be 49 starts, 39 firsts, 7 seconds and 3 thirds.

The measurement rule of the Eastern Y.C. was another of the weird formulas then fashionable: one fourth of the overhang being added to the waterline to give the "length," and two-thirds of this "length" being added to the extreme breadth. The match was to include two races, the first ten miles to windward and return with no time allowance, the second a triangle of ten-mile sides under the Eastern Y.C. rule, by which Shadow allowed 3 minutes 4 seconds. The match aroused much interest and a number of yachts were present, while the passenger steamer Day Star carried a large party over the course. N. G. Herreshoff, the designer of Shadow, covered the course on both days in a 32-foot steam launch. The committee included three members of the Eastern Y.C. Regatta Committee, Henry B. Jackson, George A. Goddard and Francis W. Lawrence. The party aboard Shadow included Dr. Bryant, Henry Bryant, Joseph S. Fay, J. P. Hawes and Henry G. Hawes, with Captain Crocker. With Captain Duncan and his two men aboard Madge were Gouverneur Kortright, of the New York Y.C., owner of the sloop Wizard, and Josiah Albro, the Newport boatman who had taken George and Annie to Scotland; both were unfamiliar with the complicated gear of a cutter. Both yachts were docked at Newport for cleaning.

On October 14 the wind was ENE moderate, and the course was laid SSW from Brenton's Reef Lightship, the committee boat being anchored to the eastward. Shadow started out of Newport Harbor with a single reef, but cast it out before the start; she swung a club topsail while Madge set her working topsail. There was the usual ten-minute interval, Shadow going over at 11:11:20 and Madge following at 11:12:09; both with booms to port. Shadow had trouble with her spinnaker, the stops failing to break, and lost some time, Madge taking the lead and holding it until they jibed on nearing the mark, there now being some sea running. Shadow's spinnaker was handled smartly at the turn, but the green crew on Madge bungled badly. She was obliged to run off to clear the sail, and the spinnaker boom was topped up with a run, carrying away the starboard spreader. The turn was timed: Shadow, 12:16:31; Madge, 12:17:31. On the beat in, the wind varied in force and direction and topsails were shifted. The big club topsail of Madge was never properly hoisted, and she could carry it only on the port tack. One or the other profited at times by slight shifts of wind, but Shadow continued to gain, finishing at 2:43:17 with a lead of 22 minutes 42 seconds on Madge.

THE second race was sailed on October 15 over a triangular course estimated at 30 miles, the first leg S by E ½-E, the second W by N, and the third NE by E. The wind through the night had been fresh SSE, kicking up a good sea outside. Shadow sailed to the start with a reef in both mainsail and jib; Madge was towed out by the committee boat with a single reef in her mainsail and working topsail. The start was given at 11:20, Shadow crossing at 11:23:50 and Madge at 11:26:49. They beat out evenly to the first mark, Madge having a lead of 45 seconds, or a gain for Shadow of 2 minutes 14 seconds in the ten miles. On the reach to the second mark Shadow shook out her reef, Madge gained 6 minutes 30 seconds, and on the run Shadow sprung her spinnaker boom and set a shorter one, losing 26 seconds. The finish was timed: Madge, 3:43:05; Shadow, 3:49:09. Madge won by 9 minutes 3 seconds elapsed time and 12 minutes 7 seconds corrected time.

The failure of Wave to meet Madge on October 5 owing to difficulty in launching brought some hostile criticism on Dr. Barron. That it was most unjust was proved on October 17 when, at 6 A.M., coming from New York, Wave sailed up beside Madge and proposed a start at 11 A.M. After some discussion this was agreed to and hurried arrangements were made to lay out a course and find a committee. A Newport partyboat man, Tom Shea, well known to all yachtsmen in his day, was found to handle Wave, and Josiah Albro again sailed aboard Madge. The course was an estimated triangle of thirty miles, the wind ESE and fresh. Wave crossed at 11:43:45 and Madge at 11:45:27; at the end of the ten-mile beat they were timed: Madge 1:05:12; Wave, 1:10:56. On the reach Wave picked up 2 minutes 9 seconds, and on the run she added 2 minutes 8 seconds, losing by an even 2 minutes elapsed time.

The Post-mortem

THE joyous chortlings of Kunhardt may be left to the imagination of the reader, but the comments of the other side are interesting. In the reports day by day in many papers the superior speed and weatherliness of the cutter, as well as her condition and handling, were freely recognized; but at the conclusion of the series the press took a new tack. It was declared that American gentlemen desired comfortable yachts for the pleasure of themselves and their friends, merely racing them ocasionally. Madge, on the other hand, was a mere shell of a racing machine, with no internal room or fittings. As to condition and handling, while a British yacht made a business of thirty to forty races in a season, our racing was merely incidental, and did not call for new sails and skilled handling. The owners of the larger yachts of the New York Y.C. were called on to substantiate these statements, among them being "the prominent yachtsman who does not desire his name to be mentioned."

Apart from the professional scribes like Captain Coffin, Captain McKay and B. S. Osbon, an active discussion in print brought out the usual anonymous writers. My old friend Podgers, waving the American flag, declared that no cutters were wanted in this free country, and that the America, now in her thirtieth year, was superior to all the more recent schooners. The irrepressible Clapham put in his oar, sniping at both sides and proclaiming that his patent Nonpariel sharpie surpassed in speed, accommodation and general good qualities both the shoal sloop and the deep cutter. In the quasi-scientific discussions every known rule of measurement was called on to prove one thing or the other.

Sailed so late in the season, in all the races there were shifts of wind and calms favoring one yacht or the other; as the reporting was entirely on a partisan basis much was made of these incidents, but they practically offset one another and had no material effect on the final result: that Madge won six out of the seven races, and on elapsed time.

After her race with Wave, Madge was laid up at Newport and Captain Duncan and his crew returned home; for a couple of years she was used by the Auchincloss brothers but not raced, she was later owned by E. W. Sheldon of New York who, in 1889, sold her to George P. Goulding of Rochester, who took her to Lake Ontario. Here she was in company with her older sister, Verve I ("Toronto Verve") and her younger Verve II, ("Chicago Verve"); racing with both. About 1899 I made the round of Ontario with the L.Y.R.A. fleet and at Charlotte, the port of Rochester and the home of the Rochester Y.C., there lay in a swamp all that was left of Madge, a mere skeleton. My friend AEmilius Jarvis was in the fleet with his cutter Merrythought. He found Captain Goulding and bought from him all the spars and gear, taking the stuff to Toronto and setting up the mast as a flagpole on his property. The tiller was presented to the New York Yacht Club. The abandoned hull had been well stripped, but the greenheart keelson was still sound, as were the oak frames. The rudder, unshipped, lay in the swamp. I borrowed a saw from Henry Stanton's boatshop and sawed off about seven feet of the stock, shipping it to my home in Bayonne. It is still one of my sacred relics, in company with the rudder stock and bronze cap of Papoose.

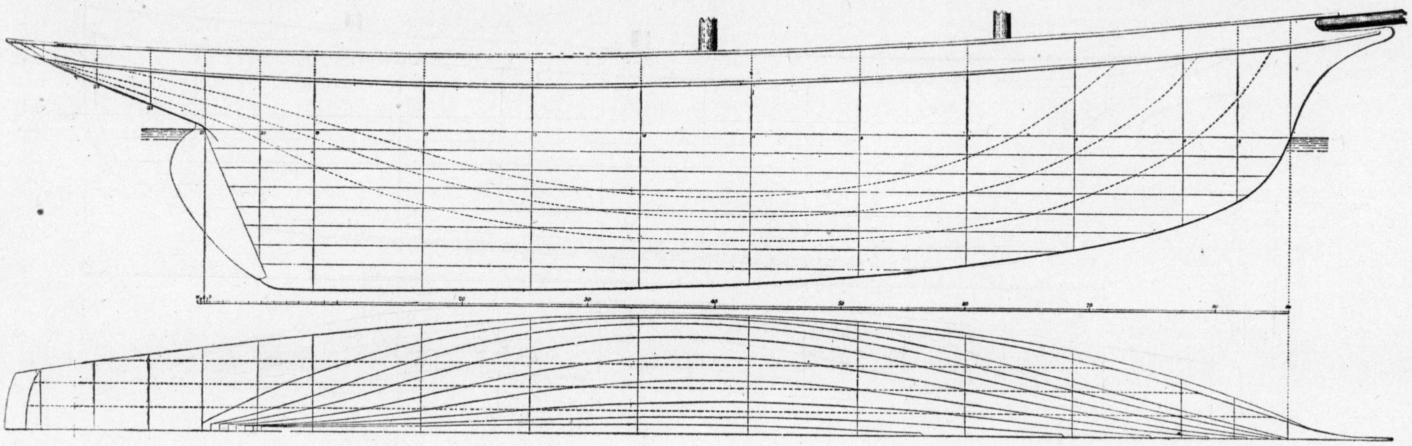

Traditions and Memories of

AMERICAN YACHTING

Part Seventy

Cutters, Cutter Cranks, and Corinthians
(Part Twelve)

By WILLIAM P. STEPHENS

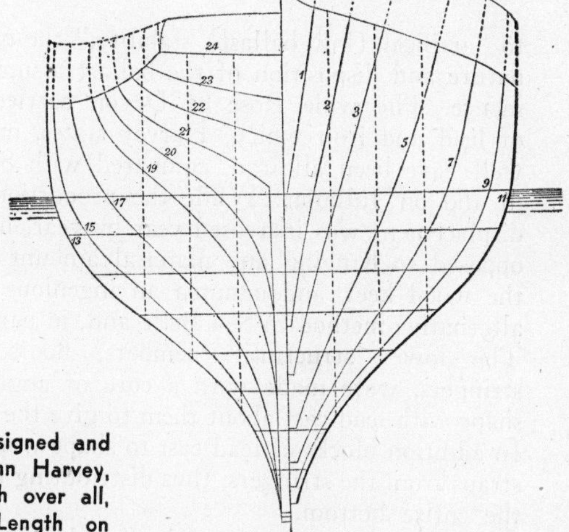

Miranda, designed and built by John Harvey, 1876. Length over all, 112 feet. Length on waterline, 86 feet 5 inches. Breadth, 18 feet 11 inches. Draft, 13 feet. Displacement, 160 tons. Sail area, 7,700 square feet. Ballast, 78 tons. Lead keel, 30 tons. From *Yacht Architecture,* by Dixon Kemp

BRIEF mention was made in part 64 of this series of the little town of Wivenhoe, on the river Colne, in Essex, and of the origin of its fame as a center of yacht building. Much more might be said of a region so rich in traditions, but we are concerned more immediately with the family which made it noted in yachting history. The romantic career of Philip John Sainty, smuggler and yacht builder, ended with his death in 1844 at the age of 94. Some years previously his yard had been taken over by Thomas Harvey, of a family presumably of French origin but long resident in Essex. He continued the management of this yard, and for a time another in Ipswich, until 1862, when he retired, turning the yard over to his son John. The latter died on May 6, 1901; it is a sad commentary on the evanescence of human fame that no obituary is to be found in any of the yachting journals of that date, and the date of his birth, which must have been about 1820-25, is unrecorded.

The boyhood of John was spent about his father's yard, and he was set to work at an early age, probably in the mould loft and the drafting room. Whether he was trained in the use of the tools of ship building is uncertain. Naval architecture as a profession was hardly recognized, and no instruction was available for a young man. There is no record of the manner in which he qualified himself for the initials, M.I.N.A. (Member of the Institution of Naval Architects) which he was always proud to append to his signature. In 1857 he was taken into the firm as a partner and in 1862 he became sole owner. The output for a period of a half century included some of the most famous of British yachts, with commercial and Government craft. In person John Harvey was of medium height, sturdily built, with square shoulders, positive in his beliefs, and determined in action. His life was marked by a pride in his work, by a deep interest in yachting as a sport, and by his efforts for the advancement of design and construction.

Two noted yachts, the cutters Volante and Kitten, have recently been described in this history; both belonged to the era of ballast-shifting which ended in 1856. Of light displacement and peg-top form, they were preceded, and followed, by many racing cutters, but the fame of the yard rests today mainly on the schooners Rose of Devon, Sea Belle and Miranda. The first, built in 1869, of 140 tons, and in 1871 converted to a yawl, was of light displacement and considerable breadth, almost four beams; Sea Belle, 1874, 142 tons, and Miranda, 1876, 143 tons, were progressively of greater displacement.

The use of a double, instead of a single, skin was quite general at the time of the construction of Sea Belle and Miranda, but with iron or steel frames. Harvey would not trust the insulation of the fastenings but used wood frames throughout, two steamed and bent frames between each pair of grown frames. When Miranda was classed by Lloyd's in 1880, her fourth year, she was given A.1. 14 years; in her 16th year her class was continued for 9 years, and for a second time for 9 years. She was broken up in 1910 after a life of 34 years, while Jullanar, of the same construction, was broken up after 30 years.

For the Good of the Sport

As yachts became narrower and deeper and what Harvey called "natural (breadth) stability" gave place

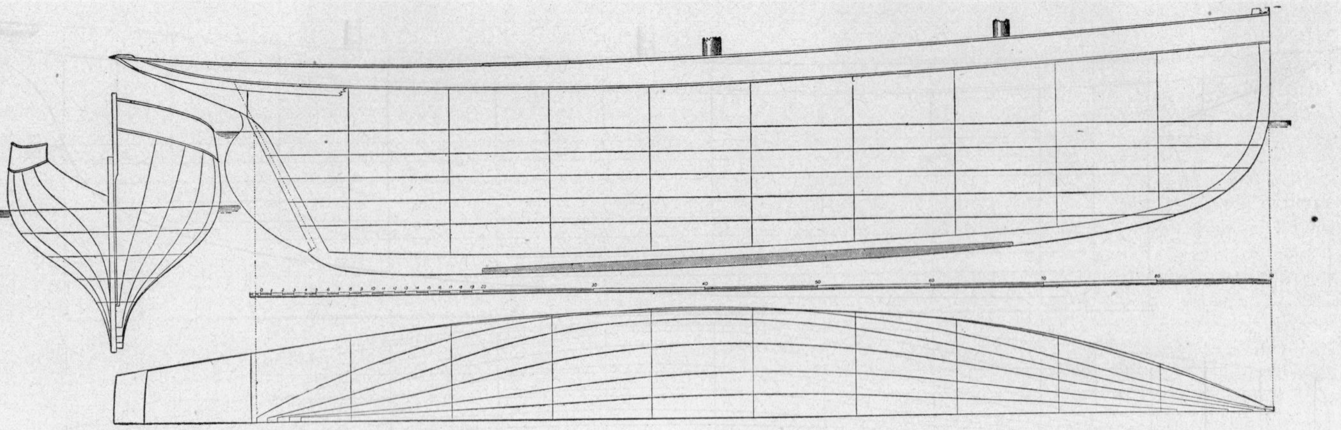

Sea Belle, designed and built by John Harvey, 1874. Length over all, 103 feet 9 inches. Length on waterline, 90 feet 6 inches. Breadth, 19 feet. Draft, 12 feet. Displacement, 155 tons. Sail area, 6,880 square feet. Ballast, 73 tons. Lead keel, 6.4 tons. From *Yacht Architecture*, by Dixon Kemp

to "artifical (low ballast) stability," the questions of the nature and disposition of the ballast assumed new prominence. The wide Rose of Devon carried but 57 tons of lead and iron which, Harvey states, might almost as well have been all iron, compared with 81 tons of lead in and on Jullanar. While the proportion of ballast to displacement was increased year by year, he was strongly opposed to hanging any material amount of lead below the wood keel, and adopted an ingenious and expensive alternative method in Sea Belle and, in part, in Miranda. The lower structural members, floors, keelson and stringers, were made with a core of angle iron bent to shape with lead cast about them to give the form required. In addition blocks of lead cast to shape were hung by iron straps from the stringers, thus distributing the weight over the entire bottom.

Another innovation was the "shadow sail," introduced in 1874 in conjunction with his partner, George Pryer. This sail, designed to replace the spinnaker, was of very light texture, set on a gaff attached to the mast on the fore side of the hounds by a universal joint which permitted it to be swung from side to side, the "shadow" boom being similarly fitted, a "shadow" working topsail could also be set over the mainsail. Various halyards, guys, vangs, and braces were necessary, the rig was complicated and slow in handling, and it proved weak in a breeze. It was tried on Sea Belle and then abandoned as impracticable.

In 1876 Harvey started a movement for what he called a "Yachting Lloyd's," an organization of yachtsmen which would formulate rules for the regulation of construction and also undertake the publication of a yacht register, copying the work of Lloyd's in shipping. As the result of his work, seconded by Dixon Kemp and others, Lloyd's was induced to extend its powerful machinery to include the classification and survey of yachts. Rules for construction were drawn up in 1877 and in the

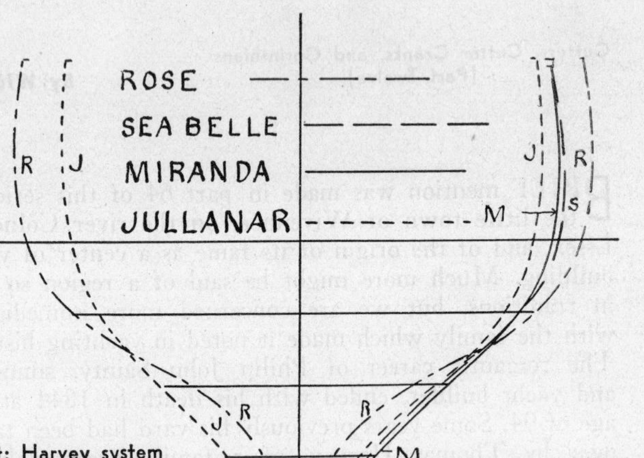

Left: Harvey system of adjusting fineness of fore and aft bodies. Miranda, solid line; Sea Belle, broken line. Above: Midship sections of Miranda, Sea Belle, Rose of Devon and Jullanar

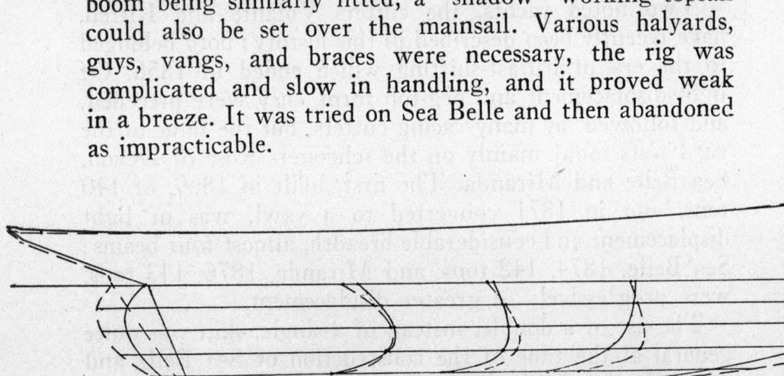

Below: Sea Belle. Keel construction, Harvey double-skin, with heavy single garboards. Lead keel, 6.4 tons, cast in five sections, and partly secured by dovetail plates let into lead and wood keels. Lead floors and keelson, 24 tons. Lead blocks suspended from keelson and stringers, 36 tons. Loose lead, 5 tons. Cast iron step for mainmast, cannon balls and other iron, 2.5 tons

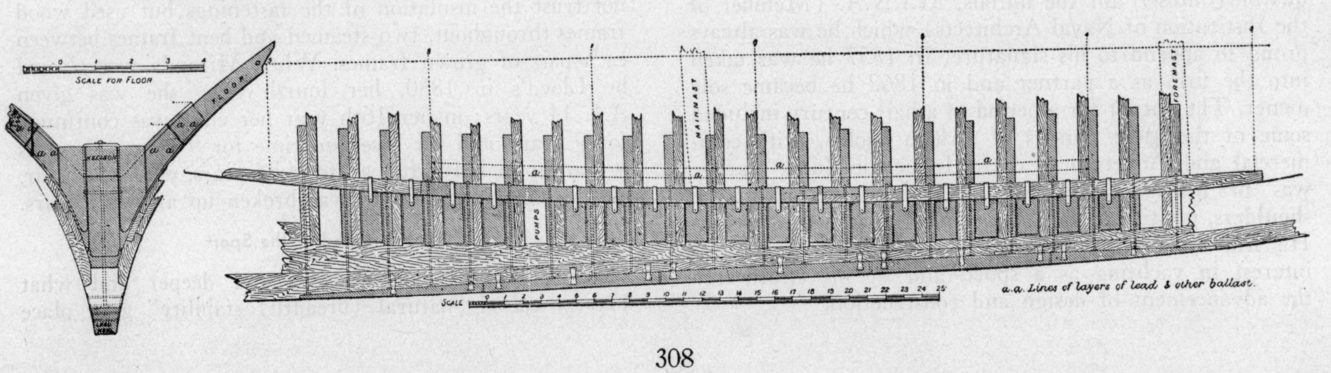

following year the first *Lloyd's Yacht Register* was published. This service to yachting, establishing a new and higher standard of construction and a guarantee of condition, received no recognition.

A Unique Theory of Design

In a paper presented before the Institution of Naval Architects in London on April 12, 1878, Harvey set forth a theory of design which was, at least, original and unique. In the opening of the paper he mentions that he once started to write a history of yachting, the first and only chapter appearing in *Once A Week* of April 1868. The name of this magazine brought back memories of certain octavo volumes in blue cloth which I had read as a boy, and a search of my library revealed in a remote corner three volumes; blue, as I had pictured them, but too late, 1870-71. The magazine purported to be "A miscellany of entertaining literature," with serial novels and general matter, the last place in which one would look for an article on yachting.

The Institution paper contains much interesting data on four yachts, Rose of Devon, Sea Belle, Miranda and Jullanar. As far as the many novel and striking features of this great yawl are concerned—the proportion of length to breadth, the absence of forefoot, the canoe stern and immersed counter, and the forward position of the sternpost, as well as the actual building on his own property, the credit must go to her amateur owner, E. H. Bentall, but he called on his neighbor John Harvey for all calculations of centers, weights and other elements, as well as for the plan of construction.

HARVEY'S theory of design is somewhat difficult to explain:—the center of gravity of each successive waterline plane, including and below the L.W.L., is calculated and plotted on the sheer plan, a curved line being drawn through all these centers. The fore body and the after body are treated in the same way, the center of each half waterline plane being spotted and a curved line drawn through the spots. For the best performance on the wind, which Harvey considered of first importance, the forward curve of both fore and after bodies should be at the maximum, in other words, filling out the entrance and fining the run; for instance, as compared with the normal curve of areas. If I have not made myself entirely clear to the reader it may be because I do not fully understand it myself, and the discussion before the Institution seems to have left the speakers equally in the dark. Harvey believed, however, that it was due to this method that progressive improvement was found in Sea Belle and Miranda over Rose of Devon. According to the diagram, the fuller curve of Sea Belle's fore body should indicate superiority to windward as compared with better all around qualities in Miranda. I do not know whether this was proved in their sailing, nor whether this method was applied in designing the American cutters.

The paper was illustrated by a model of Miranda and an artistically drawn sheer section, which I now have, one inch to the foot, on linen-backed paper 10 feet 6 inches long, showing the cabin arrangement and the suspension of the ballast blocks. A water heater was installed under the cabin floor, piped to radiators in the saloon and cabins, and a suplementary compartment for some of the crew was also in the hold, warmed by water pipes. Miranda's winnings in 1877 were 540 pounds; in 1879, 431 pounds; in 1880, 800 pounds; in 1881, 475 pounds. From 1880 on she raced mainly against the larger cutters and yawls, the schooner class being virtually extinct. In 1882 she was placed in Watson's hands for an alteration to her lead keel and the reduction of her spars.

The Wivenhoe yard seems to have prospered for years, but when in 1872 it was destroyed by fire, in order to rebuild it was found necessary to reorganize as "The John Harvey Yacht and Shipbuilding Company, Limited," with a board of directors. Under the new organization Harvey's strong individuality was hampered; though the fashion in yachting brought in large schooners instead of smaller cutters, and the succeeding years brought success through Sea Belle and Miranda—named the "two-masted cutter" on account of the forward positions of her masts—the business fell off, the last yacht built, in 1881, being the yawl Chloris, 110 tons, for W. S. Gilbert of "Pinafore" fame.

In the Harvey Home

A MAN of domestic tastes, and devoted to his family, John Harvey's home life was saddened by two unfortunate events; the death of his wife, and the rebellion of his oldest son. Mrs. Harvey was a woman of artistic tastes, transmitted to the eldest living son; the three youngest children died in infancy. Always delicate, she died leaving four young children, the eldest, John Martin, being named in part from his paternal grandmother's family of Revenue officers, one of whom was killed in a fight with smugglers. Young Martin was destined by his father as his successor in the yard; and his early schooling was planned as a preparation for a course in the School of Naval Architecture in place of the hard road which his father had to follow to the same end. The boy, however, was of a different disposition; possessed, as his later work in portraiture shows, of a natural talent as an artist which he never fully developed. He was fond of poetry and romance, reading Telemaque in the French when he was supposed to be figuring C.B., C.L.R. and M.G., and attempting to write poetry and plays. The maternal grandfather was a follower of Swedenborg and the family was brought up in that gloomy belief; as distasteful to the boy as the mechanical work of the yard. In his autobiography he tells of "the lugubrious Sundays, then all the blinds are decently pulled down, the piano and bookcases locked up, no books allowed except the Bible and a volume of Swedenborg; even whistling is an irreligious outrage. After breakfast a passage from Swedenborg's *Arcana Celestia* is read aloud and then off to church in a gloomy, purposeful procession."

While at school the boy took prizes in drawing but proved very dull at mathematics. In 1878, at the age of fifteen, he was formally indentured as an apprentice to the John Harvey Yacht and Shipbuilding Company, Limited, with a weekly wage of twelve shillings and sixpence. The yard gate was closed at 6:30, necessitating a turnout at 5:30 A.M. At this same time I, in America, was "passing in my check" in a shipyard at 7 A.M. for a wage of just twice that sum, but I was paying $4.50 per week for lodging and board while Martin lived in his home.

THE first work, in the mould loft and the drafting room, was as distasteful to him as they would have been congenial to me. Finally he determined to run away, planning with a fellow apprentice to take up a section in Manitoba and become pioneer farmers. Matters went from bad to worse until father and son were no longer speaking, but finally the elder realized the futility of the quarrel, recognizing a will as strong as his own, and asked the boy whether he would like to be an actor. Following the advice of a family friend, W. S. Gilbert, Martin was placed under the tuition of an old actor and ultimately entered the company of Sir Henry Irving as a "supe," in non-speaking parts and working slowly upward until he finally succeeded Irving as the first actor in England and, in 1921, was knighted as Sir John Martin-Harvey. After several years of retirement he died on May 15, 1944, at the age of 81. His sister, a beautiful young girl when I knew her about 1882-3, finally went on the stage through chance and made a name for herself.

To return to the father, the popularity of the big schooners declined about 1880—Miranda is credited with having killed the class. At the same time a new type and class came into fashion, large cutters with all ballast on the keel and designed by a new generation of professional designers, Watson, Fife and Richardson. There was no longer a demand for the classes of yachts for which the Wivenhoe yard had been famous and it quietly folded up. At the same time there was a new demand for cutters in America, and John Harvey left England for New York.

Leaving until the next part the history of the Harvey cutters in New York, we may follow his personal history to the end. The introduction of a new compromise type in 1885 ended the demand for cutters; in 1883 for a short period on the occasion of one of Kunhardt's mining ventures, Harvey took his place on Forest & Stream, but he was in every way unfitted for such work. About 1889-90 he was associated with William Gardner, just beginning his career as a yacht designer; in 1898 he returned to London. Knowing that Harvey's finances were none of the best, George L. Watson, in a characteristically generous letter, sent out an appeal to yachtsmen for a testimonial fund for the purchase of a life annuity. He recalled Harvey's part in the establishment of the *Yacht Register,* his perfection of the system of double-skin planking, his noted yachts, concluding:—"After a life of labor here and in America Mr. Harvey returns to his native land to enjoy the afternoon of his life among his own kinsfolk, but, unlike some of us who have had more luck, if, possibly, no more ability, he is unable to look forward to a leisured old age undisturbed by pecuniary

(*Continued on page* 313)

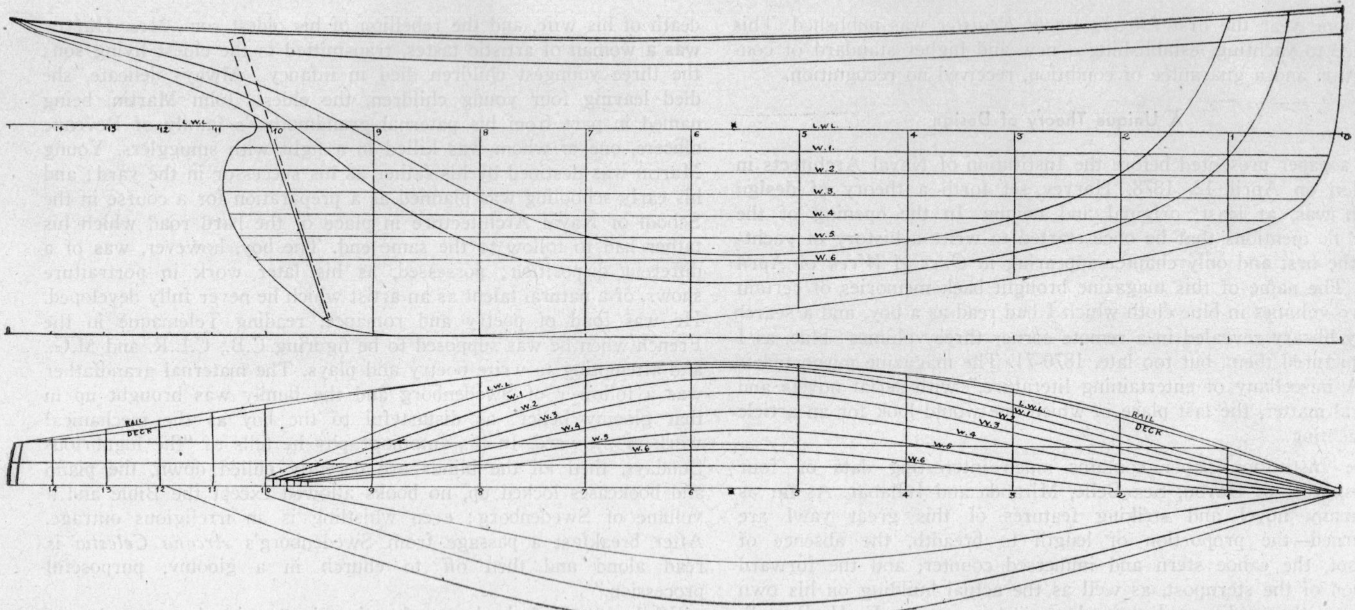

TRADITIONS AND MEMORIES OF

AMERICAN YACHTING

Part Seventy-one

By

WILLIAM P. STEPHENS

Cutters, Cutter-Cranks and Corinthians, Part 13

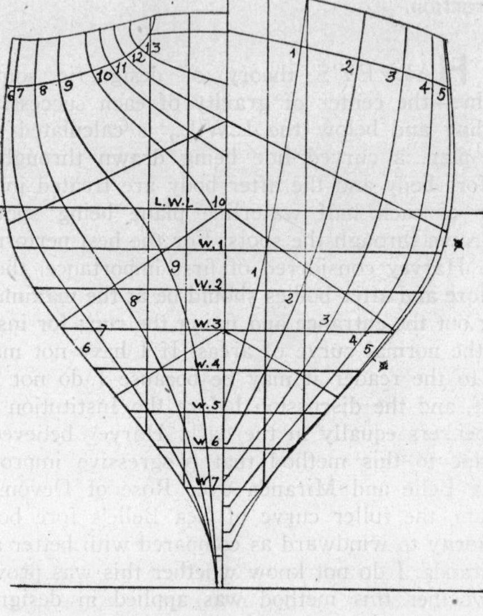

Above: Lines of Oriva, cutter 50 feet L.W.L. Designed by John Harvey for C. Smith Lee, 1881. Below: Sections for Bedouin

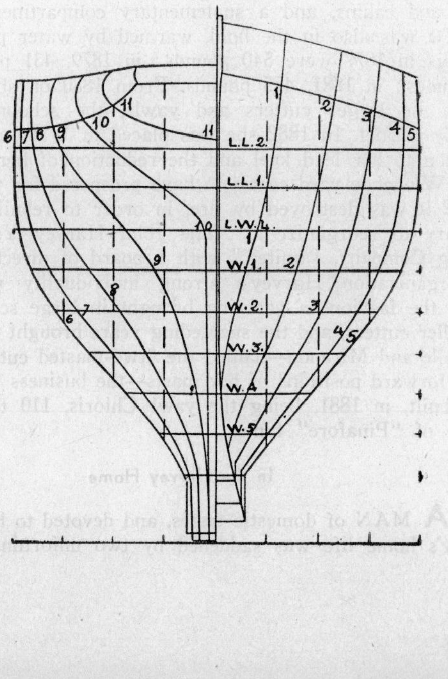

THROUGHOUT his long career in England John Harvey's work was limited to the designing and building of yachts of light or moderate displacement, and with all ballast inside the hull. In starting a new career in America he had to meet a demand for yachts of limited breadth, great depth and displacement, and with most of the ballast beneath the wood keel. In this new line of work his slogan was:— "If you want them to go you must give them the guts." If we interpret "guts" as displacement this was in accord with the most extreme ideas, but Harvey placed the "guts" in the wrong place, about the garboards. Unlike the S section employed by other designers, and by himself in earlier yachts, the half section of his cutters was almost an arc of a circle, and might have been swept with compasses.

Harvey's work in America included five cutters:— Oriva, 50 feet, 1881; Bedouin, 70 feet, 1882; Wenonah, 60 feet, 1882; Ileen, 65 feet, 1883; and Surf, 35 feet, 1883. In addition he designed one steam yacht, Wanda, 127 feet waterline, in 1885. In designing the cutters no consideration was given to rules, as they would be called on to sail under any one of a half dozen different rules; though nearly all of these penalized overhang, the yachts were given the conventional long cutter counter. As to breadth, while the designer was free from the vice-like influence of the Thames Rule, conditions demanded that the breadth be kept down in accordance with the ideas of the cutter-cranks. The lines of Oriva and Bedouin speak for themselves. Many designs of cutters of various periods and proportions have appeared in the course of this history and the reader may form his own judgment by comparison. It is enough to say that the midship sections are unlike those of all other Harvey yachts.

On her debut in the Seawanhaka Y. C. cruise of 1881 Oriva was criticized by Kunhardt:— "The new 'thirty,' Oriva, though sailing

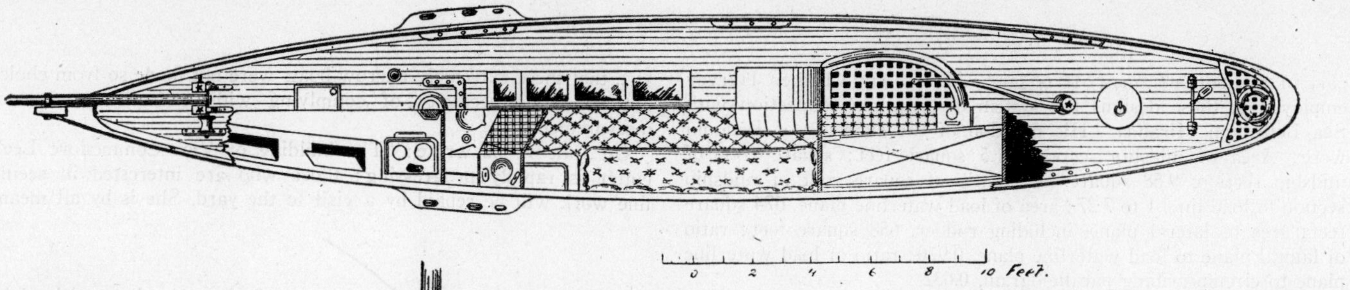

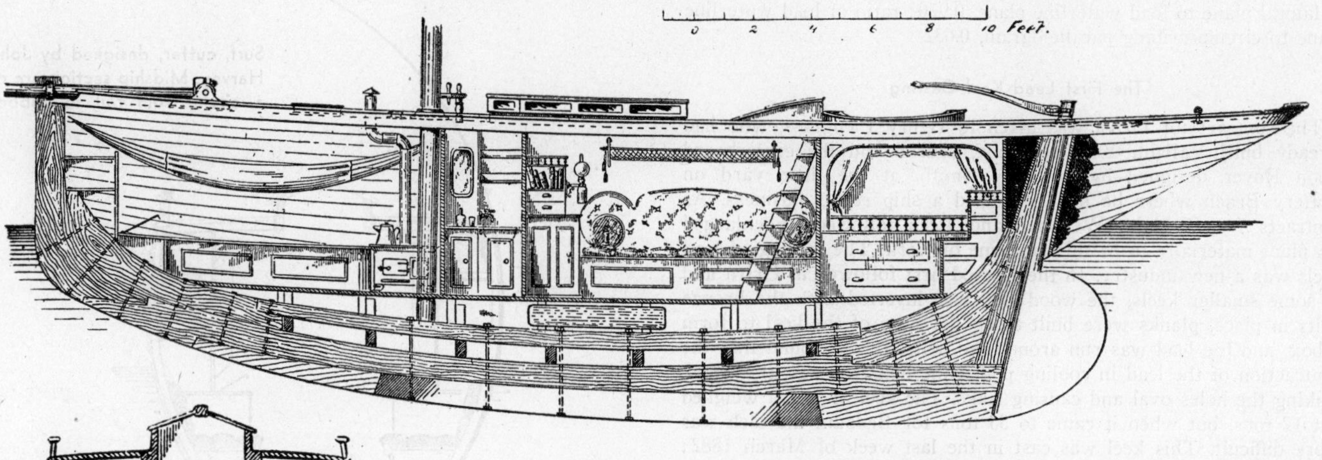

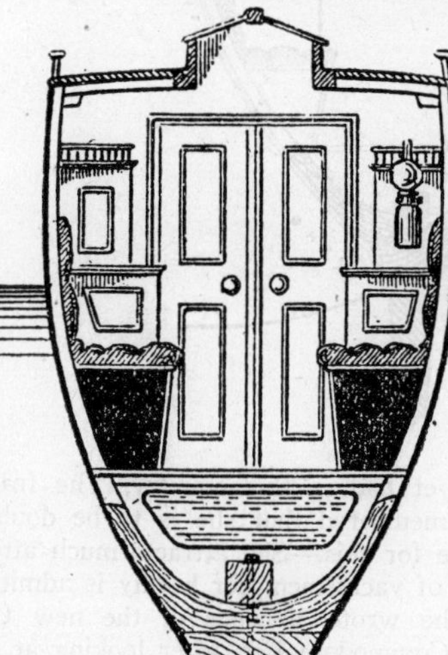

fairly well, failed to exhibit marked speed. Her trim has not yet been got. We doubt, however, whether Oriva will ever sail fast. Her model is very peculiar, to say the least, and looks to us much like an experiment of Harvey's at the expense of Oriva's enterprising owner. There was a marked absence of fairness to the design; and, to our mind, the ends did not belong to the middle body, and the hogging of her section lines was over-done. Still, Oriva is a stylish and useful craft and may yet give a good account of herself in spite of her somewhat violent departure from the orthodox."

The designs are, to say the least, peculiar; the midship sections, the long straight load line of the fore body and almost as straight aft, and the hard curves of the buttock lines, with the hollowing in of the deck line in the half breadth plan abaft the sternpost. The only lines of Bedouin which I have were drawn by Harvey, to a scale of ¼ inch, in faint red, green and blue inks, and with the diagonals superimposed on the waterlines of the half-breadth plan. Tracing was out of the question and the only thing was to plot the lines anew on a scale of ⅜ inch by means of proportional dividers. I confess that the result was not entirely satisfactory as to the after

Above: Proposed Six-Beam cutter. Designed by C. P. Kunhardt, 1882. L.O.A., 42 feet 5 inches, L.W.L. 36 feet, breadth 6 feet, draft 6 feet 6 inches, ballast 8 tons, inside lead 3 tons, lead keel 5 tons, sail area, lower sails 1050 sq. ft.

Below: Bedouin, cutter, 70 feet L. W. L. Designed by John Harvey for Archibald Rogers, 1882

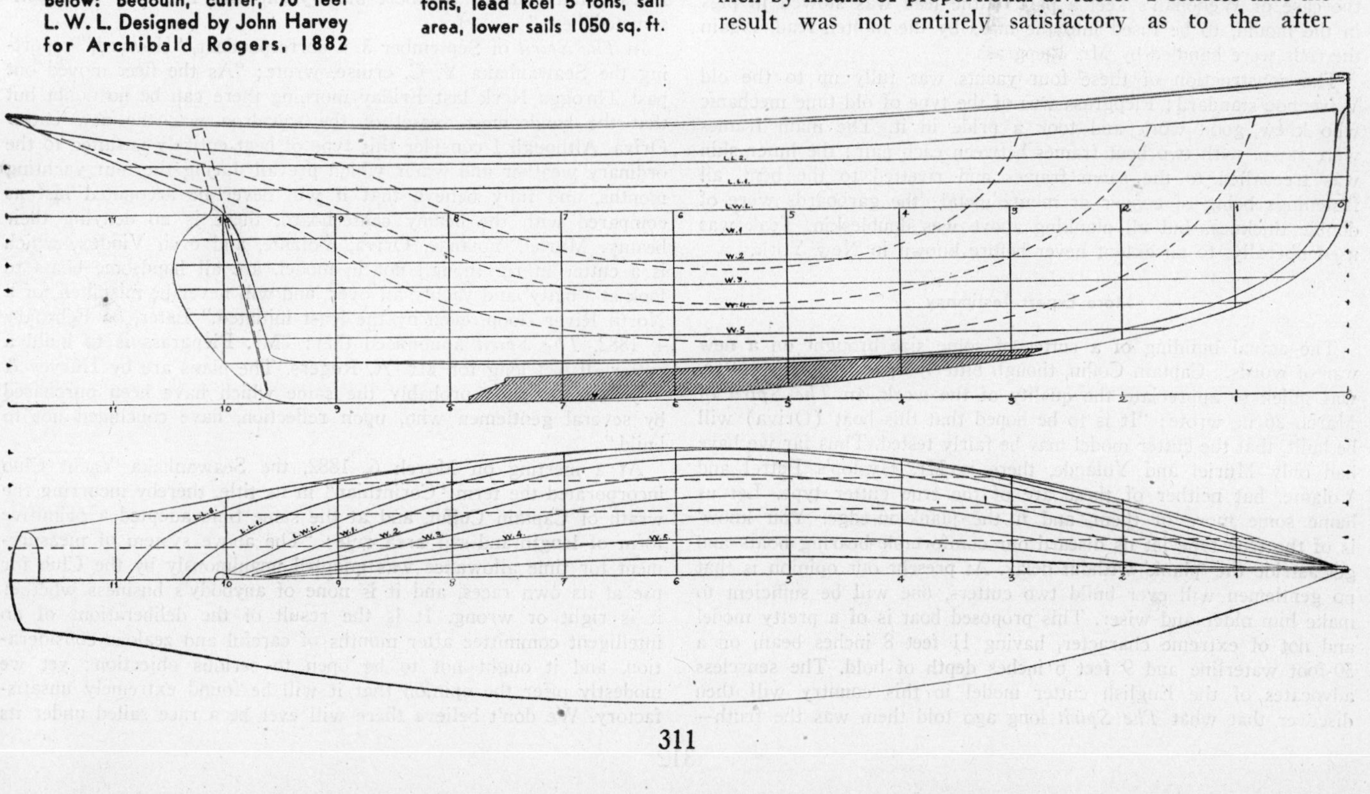

part of the buttock lines. It is impossible to say whether Harvey employed in these designs the system described in connection with Sea Belle and Miranda. His notation of the elements of Bedouin were: Area of midship section, 91.5 square feet; square root of midship section, 9.58 square feet; ratio of square root of midship section to load line, 1 to 7.27; area of load waterline plane, 674 square feet; area of lateral plane, including rudder, 658 square feet; ratio of lateral plane to load waterline plane, 0.970; ratio of load waterline plane to circumscribing parallelogram, 0.632.

The First Lead Keel Casting

The contract for Oriva was given to Henry Piepgrass, who had already built Valiant, Yolande, Leila, Muriel and the centerboard sloop Rover designed by A. Cary Smith, at the little yard on Pottery Beach where he had conducted a ship repair business. As contracts for Bedouin, Wenonah and Ileen followed he enlarged his plant materially to fit this new line of work. The casting of lead keels was a new industry. In the method first followed in Oriva and in some smaller keels, the wood keel was inverted with the bronze bolts in place, planks were built along the sides of the keel to form a box, and the lead was run around the bolts. It was found that the contraction of the lead in cooling pulled the bolts through the wood, making the holes oval and causing leaks. The keel of Oriva weighed but 12 tons, but when it came to 33 tons for Bedouin the task was more difficult. This keel was cast in the last week of March 1882; the planks spiked on each side to form the box were curved on top, as the lines show. As the middle was higher than the ends short pieces of plank were laid beside the keel, and as soon as the lead began to flow over the edge a plank was spiked down. Two large melting pots were set alongside the keel, each with a 3/8-inch hole stopped by an iron bar ten feet long.

The fires were started at midnight to avoid the attendance of a large crowd and by 7 A.M. the lead pigs were fluid in the pots. Piepgrass, a big powerful man, handled the iron bars, withdrawing one and letting the lead flow into the mould, then the other; fresh pigs being added from time to time to cool the lead to such a point that it would just flow without scorching the wood. When the mould was filled the entire top had been closed by the pieces of plank. After the lead had cooled the holes for the bolts were bored through the lead and wood, the bolts driven, and the lead and wood turned rightside up on the building blocks.

When the 21-ton keel for Wenonah was poured six weeks later a different procedure was followed; a plate iron tank about 8 feet long, 2 feet wide and 2½ feet deep was built and set permanently in brickwork, with a 3/8 hole at each end and cast iron troughs leading to the mould. I have not seen this tank for many years, but no doubt it is still around the Jacobs yard at City Island. In the case of Wenonah's keel a part of the lead was stowed in pigs in the mould, to be fused into the mass by the molten lead. Again the rods were handled by Mr. Piepgrass.

The construction of these four yachts was fully up to the old Wivenhoe standard; Piepgrass was of the type of old-time mechanic who knew good work and took a pride in it. The main frames were sawn, with two bent frames between each pair; the inner skin was treenailed to the sawn frames and rivetted to the bent, all fastenings being of copper or muntz metal; the garboards were of double thickness but all planking above was doubleskin. Teak was used liberally, to an extent never before known in New York.

More Expert Testimony

The actual building of a cutter of some size brought on a new war of words. Captain Coffin, though bitterly opposed to the cutter, was quick to appreciate the quality of the work. In *The Spirit* of March 26 he wrote: "It is to be hoped that this boat (Oriva) will be built, that the cutter model may be fairly tested. Thus far we have had only Muriel and Yolande, there is Mr. Hyslop's Petrel and Volante, but neither of these are of the true cutter type. Let us hame some more of them, and if the plank-on-edge, You know' is of the true type let us discard our comfortable-bearing boats and get astride the 'plank' without delay. At present our opinion is that no gentlemen will ever build two cutters, one will be sufficient to make him older and wiser. This proposed boat is of a pretty model and not of extreme character, having 11 feet 8 inches beam on a 50-foot waterline and 9 feet 6 inches depth of hold. The senseless advocates of the English cutter model in this country will then discover that what *The Spirit* long ago told them was the truth—viz., that these extremely narrow boats were not made so from choice but from the necessity of complying with a foolish system of measurement."

On June 11 he wrote: "The building of Vice Commodore Lee's cutter is rapidly progressing; those who are interested in seeing fine work will be repaid by a visit to the yard. She is by all means the best built boat we have yet had in this country. The frame looks light, but it must be remembered that she is to be double-planked, which will compensate for this.—She attracts much attention and is visited by numbers of yachtsmen, her beauty is admitted by everyone." A little later he wrote, apropos of the new Cup candidate, Pocahontas; "Vice Commodore Lee, after looking at the new sloop that is being built at Rye, is reported to have said: 'She is nothing but a big sailboat.' He is correct, that is just what she (Pocahontas) is, and the Commodore's cutter now building in Brooklyn is a big boat that will not sail." Again, "Commodore Lee's cutter will be the best built yacht that has ever been constructed here."

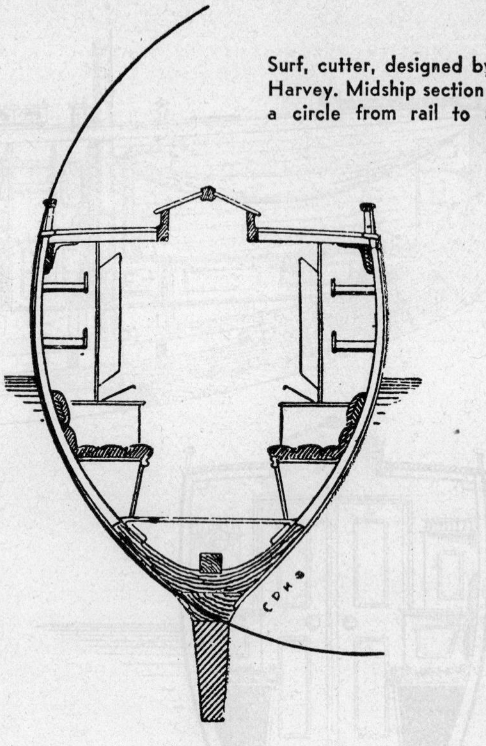

Surf, cutter, designed by John Harvey. Midship section arc of a circle from rail to rabbet

In *The Spirit* of September 3, a correspondent, "Howard," reporting the Seawanhaka Y. C. cruise, wrote: "As the fleet moved out past Throggs Neck last Friday morning there can be no doubt but that the handsomest vessel of the squadron was the new cutter Oriva. Although I consider this type of boat entirely unsuited to the ordinary weather and water which prevail during the four yachting months, and fully believe that it will never be accounted fast as compared with the beamy centerboard, there is no denying their beauty. Muriel, Yolande, Oriva, Volante, and even Vindex, which is a cutter in rig though not in model, are all handsome boats to look at; 'natty' and yachty all over, and will never be mistaken for a North River sloop, even by the least initiated." Later, on February 4, 1882, *The Spirit* announced that: "Mr. Piepgrass is to build a cutter 70 feet long for Mr. A. Rogers. The plans are by Harvey & Pryer of London; probably the same which have been purchased by several gentlemen who, upon reflection, have concluded not to build."

At a meeting on March 6, 1882, the Seawanhaka Yacht Club incorporated the term "Corinthian" in its title, thereby incurring the wrath of Captain Coffin, and at the same time adopted a primitive form of length-and-sail area rule: "The above system of measurement for time allowance was adopted unanimously by the Club for use at its own races, and it is none of anybody's business whether it is right or wrong. It is the result of the deliberations of an intelligent committee after months of careful and zealous consideration, and it ought not to be open to serious objection; yet we modestly offer the opinion that it will be found extremely unsatisfactory. We don't believe there will ever be a race sailed under its provisions." In the following year the same factors in more practical form were incorporated in the "Seawanhaka Rule" as it was known for many years. At this meeting Commodore Lee proposed the adoption of the "one-gun start," but it was not adopted. Concurrent with the cutter issue, all hands were still quarreling over measurement; Captain Coffin for "Mean-length" and Kunhardt for "Cubic-contents"; and at the same time over the different methods of starting.

The order for Oriva was placed by Cornelius Smith Lee, a young yachtsman who had begun his sailing in the 21-foot sandbagger Cruiser, racing her for several years and replacing her in 1876 with the sloop Schemer. He joined the Seawanhaka Y. C. in 1873 and raced both of those shoal yachts successfully until, in 1880, he saw the error of his ways and joined the cutter cult. His experience in the two centerboard yachts had taught little of the handling of a cutter, but he started in to sail Oriva himself, never employing a professional captain. In her first session she did little; her sails, made by Sawyer, were of American cotton and the loose foot of the mainsail stretched badly; in 1882 hemp canvas was imported for her. As a matter of course her hull was coppered, and before launching the copper was coated with an oil supposed to give a better surface, but it proved thick and sticky.

The owner of Bedouin, Archibald Rogers—1852-1928—had an estate at Hyde Park on the Hudson; with ample means he devoted himself to sport, big game in the West, fox hunting, polo and ice yachting; it was not until he joined the Seawanhaka Y. C. in 1881 that he became interested in sailing. He soon succumbed to the wiles of "Robo" and placed the order for Bedouin. A competent skipper was picked for him by Harvey, Captain George Pittuck, a Colne man. Mr. Rogers continued in yachting throughout his life, building the 46-foot Wasp in 1892 and being in command of the Cup candidate Colonia in the following year. Wenonah was ordered by James Stillman, an experienced yachtsman who had joined the New York Y. C. in 1874 and the Seawanhaka Y. C. in the following year, owning the schooner Wanderer; he had already built the cutter Muriel for his son.

The American Cutter Fleet, 1881-1885

Yacht		Designer	L.O.A.	L.W.L.	Breadth	Depth	Draft	Sail Area
Yalkyr	1881	A. C. Smith	54-6	46-6	15-0	7-10	6-3	....
Oriva	1881	Harvey	62-3	50-0	11-8	9-6	9-6	3,330
Maggie	1882	Hatcher	51-4	44-3	8-8	8-0	8-6	2,619
Bedouin	1882	Harvey	83-10	70-0	15-8	12-6	11-6	5,196
Wenonah	1882	Harvey	72-0	60-0	14-0	10-0	10-0	....
Ileen	1883	Harvey	79-9	65-3	11-4	11-8	11-0	4,502
Surf	1883	Harvey	43-0	35-4	7-8	7-0	7-6	....
Huron	1883	Gray	63-0	56-6	15-9	9-3	8-0	....
	1885		73-5	63-6	15-9	....	10-6	5,172
Thetis	1884	Bryant	72-0	64-0	19-0	9-6	8-3	....
Stranger	1885	Richardson	79-0	65-2	13-6	9-0	10-6	5,129
Clara	1885	Fife	63-0	53-0	9-1	8-6	10-0	3,483

The dates given mark the first racing in American waters.

One of the most active and enthusiastic of the cutter-cranks was Edward M. Padelford—1857-1921—born in Savannah, Georgia; educated in Europe, and coming to New York with his brother Arthur in 1881. Throughout his life his first interest was in cruising, though he sailed in many races in home and foreign waters. Joining the New York and Seawanhaka clubs, he bought the schooner Nokomis and cruised aboard her for a season, then built the cutter Mona, 36 feet 6 inches waterline by 8 feet breadth, in which he cruised between Boston and Norfolk with but one paid hand. In 1883 Ileen was built for Arthur Padelford and used by the brothers in both racing and cruising about the coast. The professional skipper aboard Ileen was the noted "Tommy Dutch" Diaper of the Itchen family of racing men. When first introduced to Lieutenant Henn the latter apologized but said that he did not quite catch the name "Was it Paddlebox?" and the nickname stuck.

The cutter Surf was built for cruising by two young members of the Knickerbocker Y. C., Theodore C. Zerega and R. W. Rathborne, both sandbag sailors, though the latter was also noted as an oarsman and all-around athlete. They fell victims to Kunhardt's arguments and ordered the yacht as a cruiser. Huron was designed by her owner, William Gray, an amateur, and built by "Billy" Smith at City Point, Boston. As she proved unsuccessful her owner had her taken apart and entirely rebuilt in 1885, with an added length of 10 feet. Valkyr, designed by Cary Smith, and Thetis, designed by her amateur owner, Henry Bryant, and strongly built by "Billy" Smith, call for more extended notice later. The comments of Captain Coffin have been quoted so freely for several reasons; he was generally recognized as the most competent yachting writer of his day, the best known and most respected; he took his position as the most determined opponent of the cutter, and all the other writers of the daily press as well as those who wrote for such other publications as paid any attention to yachting tuned their pipes to his lay.

As true propagandists the cutter-cranks had two aims: the introduction of the narrow British cutter and the advancement of Corinthian yachting. As events proved, the two were antagonistic and each injured the other. In the first place, the number of qualified Corinthians was limited, and of these the majority had learned their lessons by tossing sandbags or paddling and sailing canoes. As a class they were all at sea in handling the novel and complicated gear of a cutter. Many yachts were unable to start in the increasing number of Corinthian races through lack of crews; and when the first cutters sailed in open regattas they were handicapped by their Corinthian crews opposed to professionals. As a matter of faith some of the cutters carried their Corinthian crews in races where professionals were allowed. A typical crew list is that of the Seawanhaka Corinthian regatta of June 17, 1882; though none are alive today there are many names still familiar in yachting as owners of large yachts. The fleet of 14 yachts called for a total of 109 Corinthians, some of whom are listed below.

Clytie, Schooner, Anson Phelps Stokes. Captain, Charles H. Stebbins; Mate, Henry W. Eaton. Crew: John E. Roosevelt, W. Gordon Diedricksen, John W. Edwards, William Krebs, Matthias Nichol, Gouveneur Kortright, E. G. Cruger, A. J. Maginn, Charles D. Ingersoll, Anson Phelps Stokes, Herman Clark, William Gardner, Frederick Corwin, Oliver Johnson.

Albatross, Schooner, Edward W. Humphreys. Captain, J. Frederick Tams; Mate, J. Leland Hoppock. Crew: W. Emlen Roosevelt, Ferdinand Yznaga, William M. Wright, David Crocker, William B. Parsons, Harry Sampson, Sidney Chubb, J. William Beekmann, Henry P. Egleston, Henry C. Meigs, A. Duane, Jules A. Montant.

Gracie, Sloop. Charles R. Flint, Joseph P. Earle. Captain, J. Rogers Maxwell; Mate, J. Norton Winslow. Crew: Thomas J. Pratt, Joseph Lyman, Oliver Adams, William D. Steele, Orville Lowell, F. A. Soule, Wallace Soule, Charles B. Warner, Newbury D. Lawton, W. C. Sanger, Edmund Randolph, James L. Smith.

Fanny, Sloop. E. Harold Ferris. Captain, W. A. W. Stewart; Mate, M. Roosevelt Schuyler. Crew: David Paton, Charles E. Jenkins, Charles Catset, George C. Clark, William Whitlock, Cyrus L. W. Eidlitz, G. Ayre.

Valkyr, Cutter. Dr. B. F. Dawson. Captain, A. Cary Smith; Mate, Charles G. Peters. Crew: Robert Center, W. H. Calhoun, Charles H. Leland, R. W. Rathborne, W. M. Donald, George L. Rives, John F. Lovejoy, John P. Kingsford, D. S. Stone.

CUTTERS, CUTTER-CRANKS AND CORINTHIANS

(*Continued from page 309*)

anxieties"; his own contribution was fifty guineas. By way of coincidence, a similar movement was under way at this time for a fund for Dixon Kemp, Harvey's old friend and co-worker, who had retired two years previously from the editorship of *The Field* on account of illness and who died a year later.

After two years of retirement the end came on May 6, 1901; a strong character, honest, and with the highest ideals in his work, I look back with kindly recollection to my friendship with him, mingled with regret that his life was marked by many trials and small reward in the end.

Part 72

CUTTERS, CUTTERCRANKS AND CORINTHIANS

CHAPTER 14

THE early races of the rival types were of a haphazard nature and more or less inconclusive; the then existing rules favored one type or the other, the same may be said of the extremes of weather, and the yachts differed greatly in "size" by whatever standard they were appraised. There is apparent an increased interest in yacht racing in the second half of the seventies, as evidenced by the building of more of the smaller yachts as the racing of the great schooners was diminishing. A similar movement is seen in British yachting of the same period with the death of schooner racing, the passing, due to age, of many of the most famous of the large cutters and a rapid growth of the fleet of 20 Tons and under.

While classification was still in a backward state, the Yacht Racing Association ventured so far as to recommend that yachts should be built to the limits of 5, 10, 15, 20, 40, 60 and 80 tons, but it was not until the adoption of the International Rule in 1920 that class limits were made imperative and not merely suggestive. In the sixties there were classes of 12 and 15 tons, both popular; but by 1880, in the period of the rapid development of the narrow cutter, the classes were: 3, 5, 10, 20, 40 and 60 tons. Though small in numbers, the 15 Ton Class was noted for some very fast yachts; ultimately displaced by the 10 and 20 Ton classes.

If any one yacht may be selected as the best of this class over a term of years it is Maggie, the work of one of the last of the designer-builders, Hatcher of Southampton, whose many successful cutters won him the soubriquet of "King Dan." Her dimensions were: l.o.a., 51 feet 4 inches; l.w.l., 44 feet 3 inches; breadth, 8 feet 10 inches; depth, 7 feet 11 inches; draft, 8 feet 6 inches. King Dan's objection to lead below the keel has been mentioned in connection with the building of Freda, in Maggie he placed five tons, just one third of her lead, below the keel. She raced for two seasons under her original owner, L. Wheeler, winning 15 firsts and 2 seconds in 20 starts in

TRADITIONS AND MEMORIES OF

American Yachting

By W. P. STEPHENS

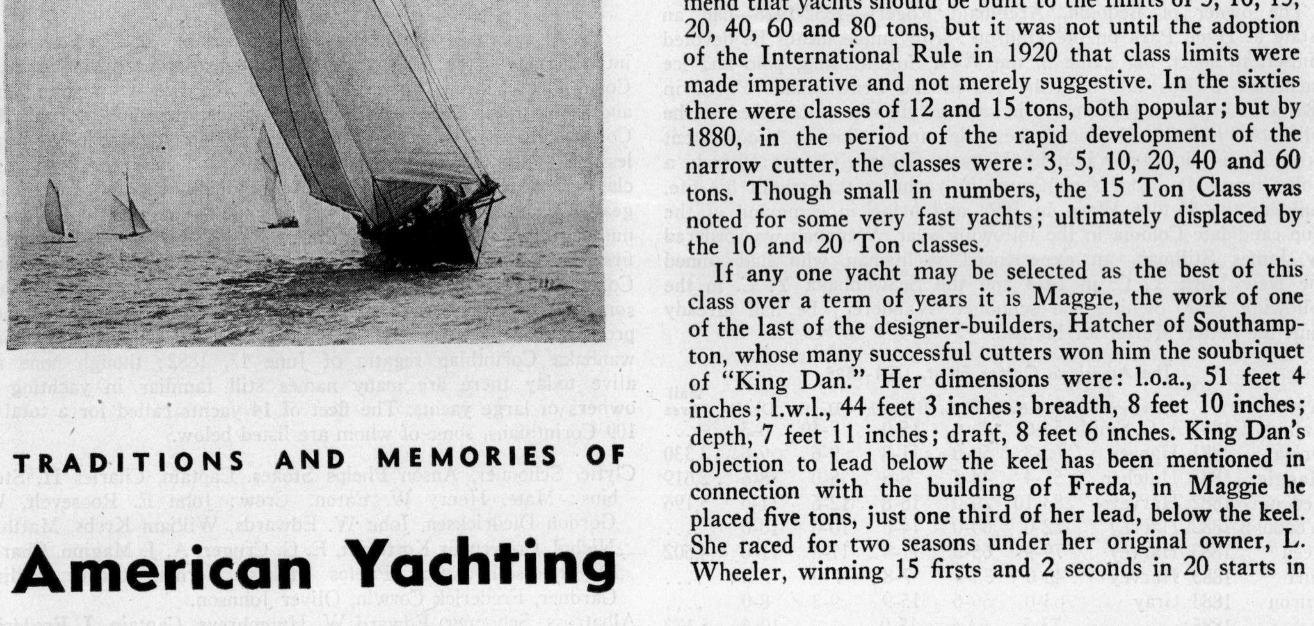

Above: The cutter Bedouin under sail. Below: Cutter sketches by C. P. Kunhardt

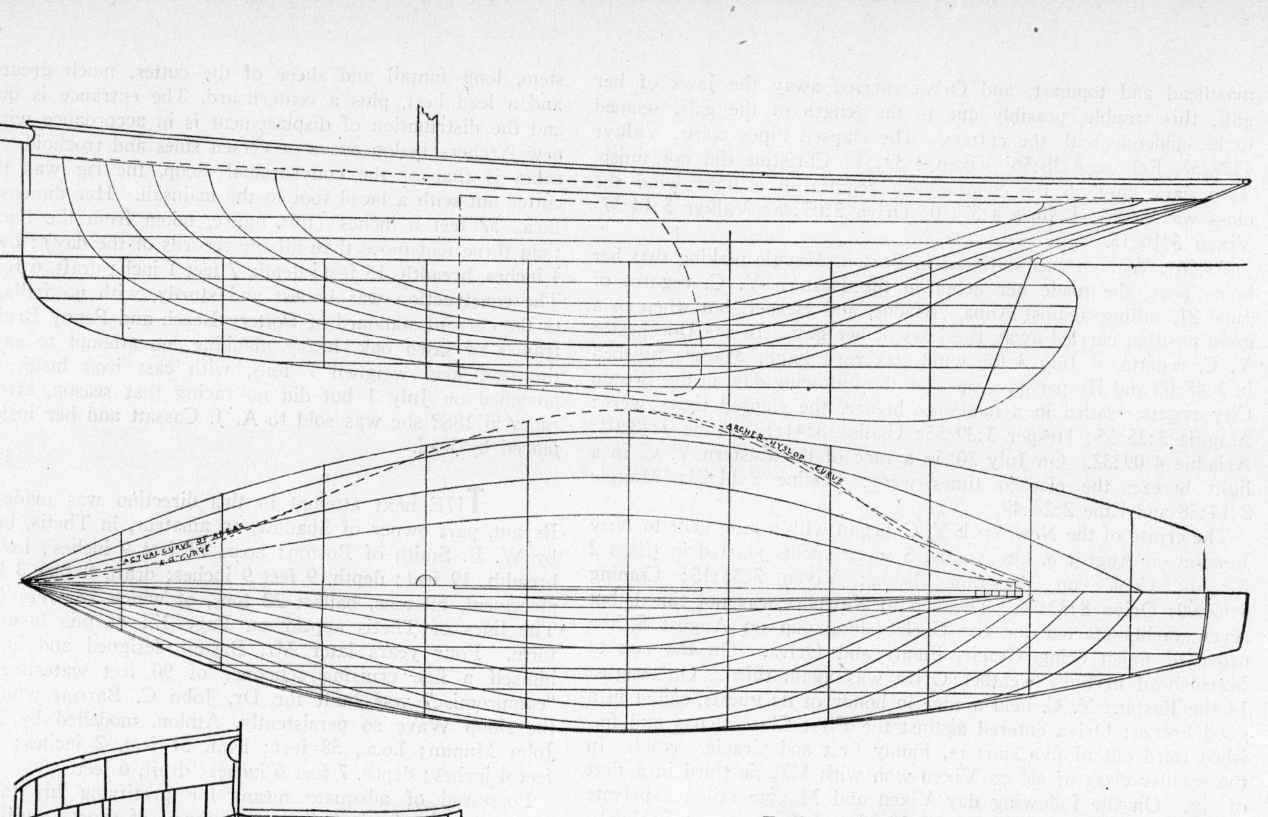

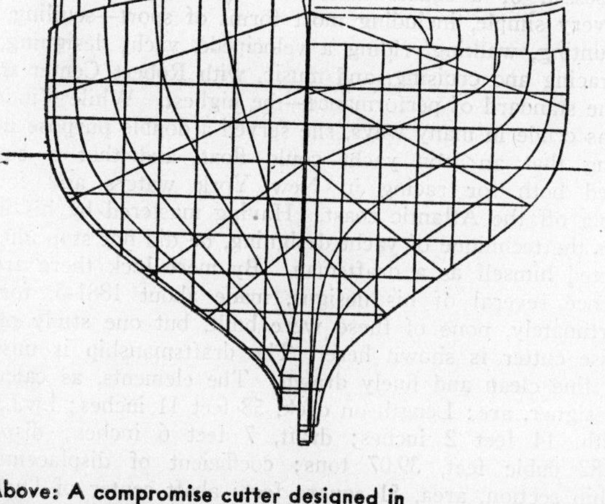

Above: A compromise cutter designed in 1881 by Robert Center. Right: Lines of Valkyr, first of a compromise type designed by A. Cary Smith and built in 1881

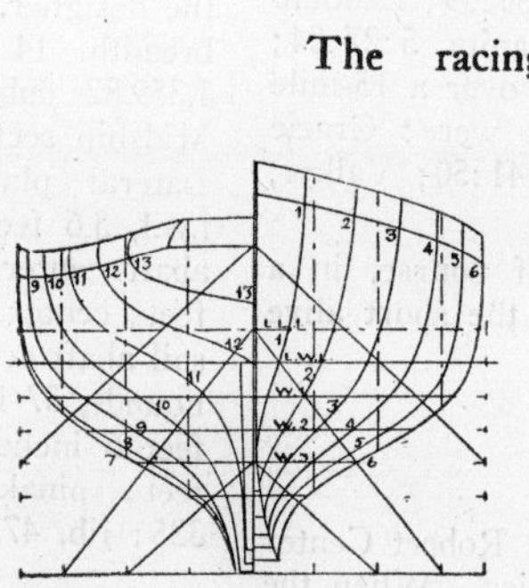

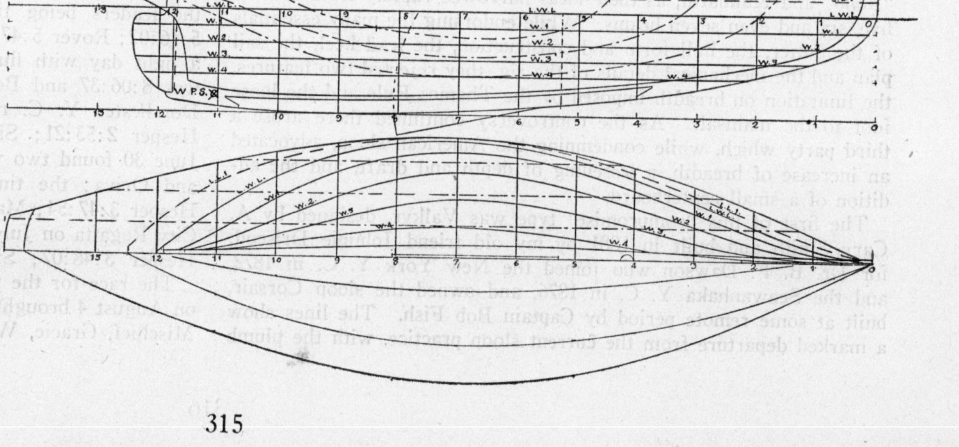

1878 and 11 firsts and 2 seconds in 18 starts in 1879. In these races, as in all others in England, she fitted in badly between the growing 10 and 20 Ton classes of narrower yachts with more outside lead; winning or losing on time allowance. In 1880 she was purchased by Francis Taylor, who raced her through that season, laying her up after only six starts in 1881 when he bought the 20 Ton Freda. Maggie's record for the four years was 85 starts, 39 first prizes and 10 seconds, with a total of £846 prize money. George H. Warren, the son of the owner of the Warren Line of steamships, was sent to Boston in 1881 as the agent of the Line, and he bought Maggie. In April 1882 she arrived in Boston aboard the steamship Kansas, in the charge of Captain Harry Randall, an experienced racing skipper. The yachts which were to meet her were:

	Built	L.w.l.	Breadth	Depth	Draft
Anna	1868	39-1	13-6	4-7	3-6
Ariadne	1872	52-6	17-11	5-2	4-9
Hesper	1880	44-7	15-5	6-7	5-3
Undine	1866	50-0	17-6	5-4	5-6
Maggie	1878	44-11	8-10	8-0	8-6

Ana was a Kirby boat, rebuilt and lengthened at various times; Undine, built by Mc Garrick in Brooklyn, had been similarly improved in the course of 16 years; Hesper, a keel boat designed by A. Cary Smith, was of heavy construction and ballasted with iron.

Yacht Racing in 1882

The racing season opened with the regattas of the three leading New York clubs; Atlantic, New York, and Seawanhaka; no cutters started in the Atlantic regatta. That of the New York Y. C. was sailed on June 15 in a strong S.W. wind over the outside course, topmasts being housed on the sloops in crossing the bar. The starters in Class 2 were the new keel sloop Mystery, Criva, and Valkyr. Mystery lost her bowsprit, masthead and topmast, and Oriva carried away the jaws of her gaff, this trouble, possibly due to the length of the gaff, seemed to be epidemic with the cutters. The elapsed times were: Valkyr 4:29:57, Eclipse 4:38:56, Vixen 4:39:51; Christine did not finish. Two days later in the Seawanhaka regatta in a light wind the class was timed: Eclipse 4:57:10; Oriva 5:05:48; Valkyr 5:14:57- Vixen 5:16:15.

As Mr. Warren was stationed in Boston, Maggie making that her home port, she made her debut in the Eastern Y. C. regatta of June 21, sailing against Anna, Ariadne, and Hesper, but when in a good position carried away the jaws of her gaff. In the Dorchester Y. C. regatta of July 3 the wind was very light; Maggie finished in 3:48:08 and Hesper gave up. On the following day, in the Boston City regatta, sailed in a moderate breeze, the elapsed times were: Maggie 3:35:55; Hesper 3:39:55; Undine 3:44:12; Anna 3:48:03; Ariadne 4:09:32. On July 20, in a race of the Eastern Y. C. in a light breeze, the elapsed times were: Undine 2:14:23; Maggie 2:14:58 and Effie 2:24:49.

The cruise of the New York Y. C. began with a long drift to New London on August 3. On August 5 seven yachts started in Class 2 for the Cook cup, the times being: Vixen 7:35:15; Coming 8:07:00; Oriva 8:32:24. The run to Newport was not timed, but seven yachts started for the Goelet sloop cup on August 8, the order of finish being Gracie, Fanny and Oriva. On the run to Marblehead in fluky weather Oriva was again third. On August 14 the Eastern Y. C. held a race in honor of its guests, sailed in a good breeze; Oriva entered against the First Class sloops and finished third out of five starters, Fanny first and Gracie second. In the smaller class of sloops Vixen won with Maggie third in a fleet of six. On the following day Vixen and Maggie sailed a private match, the sloop being timed at 5:13:00 and the cutter at 5:32:00.

The Seawanhaka Y. C. held a series of races for sloops and cutters in October, the first on the 24th, from off Fort Wadsworth around Sandy Hook Lightship and return to Buoy 15, 32 miles. Professional helmsmen and crews were allowed. The wind was from N to N E and back to N, fresh to moderate. Bedouin, sailing her first race, was steered by Captain Pittuck, and Gracie by Captain Frank Baker. In Class 2 Valkyr was steered by Captain Harlow, of Wenonah; Fanita by Captain John Van Buskirk, and Oriva by Mr. Lee. When nearing the Lightship a crack developed in Gracie's quadrant, but she sailed the course. The elapsed times were: Bedouin 3:37:09; Gracie 3:53:48; Valkyr and Oriva, 4:08:29; Fanita, 4:14:30. In the second race, October 26, the start was from Buoy 5, outside Sandy Hook, 18 miles to leeward and return, in a light to fresh S W wind. The times were: Gracie 4:59:59; Bedouin 5:12:00. In the second class, Oriva 5:22:00; Fanita 5:27:04; Valkyr 5:41:10. The final race, two days later, was over a 15-mile triangle, two rounds, in a light breeze. The times were: Gracie 4:20:25; Bedouin 4:24:03; Oriva 4:39:45; Fanita 4:41:50; Valkyr, disabled.

The results of the season's races, interpreted, of course, in a strictly partisan spirit by both sides, served to keep the sport alive through what is normally the dead season.

The "Compromise Cutter"

AS the builder and master of Vindex in 1871 Robert Center stands as the first proponent of the cutter in America. When the crusade began a few years later he naturally enrolled under the banner of the Cutter-Cranks, and with him were A. Cary Smith, Edward Burgess and John Hyslop. All of them, however, while advocating the cutter hull and rig, stopped short at the figure of four beams, and refused to follow the high priests of the cult, "Robo" and Kunhardt, as their ideas narrowed rapidly from four to five, six and even seven beams. While endorsing the many essentials of the cutter, the hull form and construction, the lead keel, the sail plan and the mechanical details of the rig, they rejected two features, the limitation on breadth imposed by the Thames Rule and the loose foot to the mainsail. As the controversy continued there arose a third party which, while condemning the American sloop, advocated an increase of breadth, a lessening of depth and draft, and the addition of a small centerboard.

The first of this "compromise" type was Valkyr, designed by A. Cary Smith and built in 1881 by my old friend Johnnie Driscoll, for Dr. B. F. Dawson who joined the New York Y. C. in 1872, and the Seawanhaka Y. C. in 1876, and owned the sloop Corsair, built at some remote period by Captain Bob Fish. The lines show a marked departure from the current sloop practice, with the plumb stem, long fantail and sheer of the cutter, much greater breadth and a lead keel, plus a centerboard. The entrance is quite hollow and the distribution of displacement is in accordance with the then new Archer-Hyslop curve of versed sines and trochoid. The trunk cabin is that of the conventional sloop, the rig was that of the cutter but with a laced foot to the mainsail. Her dimensions were: l.o.a., 57 feet 6 inches (this figure, taken from the lines, is more than three feet more than all the records of the day); l.w.l., 47 feet 4 inches, breadth, 15 feet; depth, 7 feet 1 inch; draft, 6 feet 8 inches. The construction was honest and sturdy, with no frills, according to the current standard of Pottery Beach and Penny Bridge; double frames of sawn oak, heavy planking, no attempt to save weight; the lead keel weighed 7 tons, with cast iron inside. She was launched on July 1 but did no racing that season, after her first races in 1882 she was sold to A. J. Cassatt and her inside iron replaced by lead.

THE next attempt in this direction was made by Henry Bryant, part owner of Shadow, an amateur, in Thetis, built in 1884 by W. B. Smith of Boston; l.o.a., 71 feet 9 inches; l.w.l., 64 feet; breadth, 19 feet; depth, 9 feet 9 inches; draft, 8 feet 3 inches; displacement, 59 tons, ballast 22 tons, of which 18 were in the keel. The lines of Thetis appear on Page 171 of this history in book form. Four years later Mr. Bryant designed and had built for himself a fine cruising schooner of 90 feet waterline. Another "compromise" was built for Dr. John C. Barron who had raced the sloop Wave so persistently, Athlon, modelled by her builder, John Mumm; l.o.a., 58 feet; l.w.l. 51 feet, 2 inches; breadth, 17 feet 4 inches; depth, 7 feet 6 inches; draft, 6 feet.

Possessed of adequate means for gratifying his tastes, which were very simple, including most forms of sport—sculling, driving, fox hunting, walking, riding a velocipede, yacht designing, sailing, both racing and cruising, and music, with Robert Center there was but one standard of performance—the highest. While Vindex, Page 82, was crude in many ways, she served a double purpose in demonstrating that an iron yacht could float, and that a cutter was adapted both for racing in New York waters and for winter cruising off the Atlantic coast. Having mastered by his individual efforts the technique of yacht designing, he did not stop until he had perfected himself as a draftsman. By mere luck there are still in existence several of his designs, made about 1881-3, for cutters. Unfortunately, none of these were built, but one study of a compromise cutter is shown here. The draftsmanship is unsurpassed, every line clean and finely drawn. The elements, as calculated by the designer, are: Length on deck, 58 feet 11 inches; l.w.l., 50 feet; breadth, 14 feet 2 inches; draft, 7 feet 6 inches; displacement, 1,359.82 cubic feet, 39.07 tons; coefficient of displacement, 0.34. Midship section, area, 51 square feet; abaft center of l.w.l., 5 feet. Lateral plane, area, 297 square feet; center abaft center of l.w.l, 3.6 feet. Centerboard, immersed area, 54 square feet; center abaft center of l.w.l. 3 feet. Load water plane, area, 463 square feet; center abaft center of l.w.l., 2.3 feet. Center of effort of lower sail abaft center of l.w.l., 3.1 feet. Mast: from stem, 20 feet; deck to hounds, 37 feet 11 inches; masthead, 7 feet 10 inches. Top mast, 35 feet 6 inches; bowsprit, 24 feet 6 inches; boom, 47 feet; gaff, 34 feet; spinaker boom, 34 feet. Mainsail 1,550 square feet; foresail, 325; jib, 477.

Yacht Racing in 1883

THE New York Y. C. Regatta on June 21 found four of Class 1 at the starting line in a day of squalls and calms; the times were: Gracie 5:31:12; Fanny 5:21:20; Bedouin 5:37:15; Mischief 5:39:05. In Class 2 eight yachts started and two were disabled, the leaders being timed: Vixen 5:43:20; Fanita 5:44:15; Oriva 5:46:02; Rover 5:47:41. In the Seawanhaka regatta two days later, a light day with fluky winds, Fanny's time was 8:03:23; Gracie's was 8:06:37 and Bedouin's 9:10:03. Turning now to Boston, the Dorchester Y. C. race of June 18 was timed: Maggie 2:51:42; Hesper 2:53:21; Siren 3:10:00. The Eastern Y. C. Regatta on June 30 found two visitors, the new Wenonah sailing her first race and Oriva; the times were: Wenonah 3:22:30; Oriva 3:35:06; Hesper 3:47:54; Maggie 3:38:08; Dream not timed. In the Boston City Regatta on July 4 in a light breeze Maggie was timed 3:48:03; Hesper 3:48:07; Siren 3:53:55.

The race for the Goelet sloop cup on the New York Y. C. cruise on August 4 brought out nine starters, the order of the leaders being Mischief, Gracie, Wenonah; Bedouin sprung her boom, Julia drew

(*Continued on page 320*)

TRADITIONS AND MEMORIES OF

American Yachting

CUTTERS, CUTTER CRANKS AND CORINTHIANS **Part 73** ***By WM. P. STEPHENS***

CHAPTER 15

THE design of the "compromise" (centerboard) cutter, shown in the previous issue, is one of several studies by Robert Center which, preserved by mere chance, came to light only recently. These show the development of what may be called the American cutter. Center's first yacht was a centerboard sloop, Ariel; when he joined the New York Y. C. in 1862 he bought another centerboard sloop, Bonita, built by D. O. Richmond in 1860, 60 feet l.o.a.; 55 feet l.w.l.; 19 feet 6 inches breadth and 4 feet 2 inches draft; using her until 1869 in both racing and cruising and replacing her in 1871 with the iron cutter Vindex. In visiting England in 1867 as a guest aboard Fleetwing he became familiar with the cutter in her native environment. After collaborating with Cary Smith in the designing of Vindex he took up the study of designing and in 1876 made the design for the cutter Volante, for his nephews, Thomas Hitchcock, Jr., and F. B. Hitchcock.

The inspiration for this work came from the new book *Yacht Designing* by Dixon Kemp, 1875. Center had the single large quarto volume in blue cloth taken apart and rebound in two volumes, one of the text and the other of the plates mounted on canvas; after his death the books were presented to me by his mother. The system of designing laid down by Kemp was followed; and, while no design was copied, Volante had the general characteristics of the cutters of the seventies:—plumb stem, high bulwarks, tumble-home to topsides, and square counter. Her dimensions were:—l.o.a., 45 feet 9 inches; l.w.l., 40 feet; breadth, 12 feet 1 inch; depth, 5 feet 10 inches; draft, 6 feet 11 inches; displacement, 20.8 tons; ballast, 9.37 tons, including 2.32 tons in lead keel. The keel was sided 10 inches, moulded 12 inches, sawn frames doubled, oak garboards; Georgia pine planking; oak wales 1⅜ inches. The mast was 39 feet, 9 inches deck to hounds; topmast, 22 feet; bowsprit, 17 feet; boom, 33 feet 6 inches; gaff, 20 feet. A trunk cabin 14 inches high at the sides gave a headroom of 6 feet 1 inch.

This design, crude in many ways, represents Center's first attempt in a new art; it lacks the fairness noticeable in his later studies, and it would seem that he was working with poor battens. The lines, in black, red, and blue, are very fine; two diagonals are shown and also the immersed and emersed waterline at 20 degrees. There are two dotted lines, A,A, in the body plan which I do not understand, and a dotted line B, in the half-breadth plan which is a mystery. Volante, launched in May, 1877, was built by John Mumm according to the established standards of Gowanus Bay; she was designed for cruising, but sailed in some races. None of these designs are dated, but the second was probably made about 1880; the dimensions were:—l.o.a., 59 feet 4 inches; l.w.l., 50 feet; breadth, 13 feet 6 inches; draft, 8 feet.

The design of the "compromise" cutter shown in the previous chapter probably dates from about 1881-2; the last design here

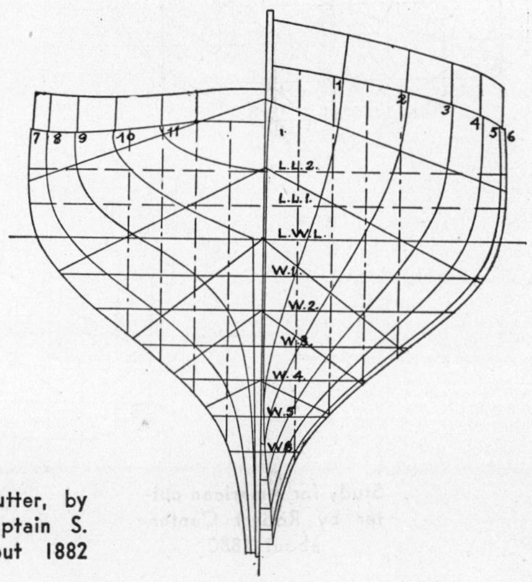

Design for American cutter, by Robert Center, for Captain S. Grosvenor Porter. About 1882

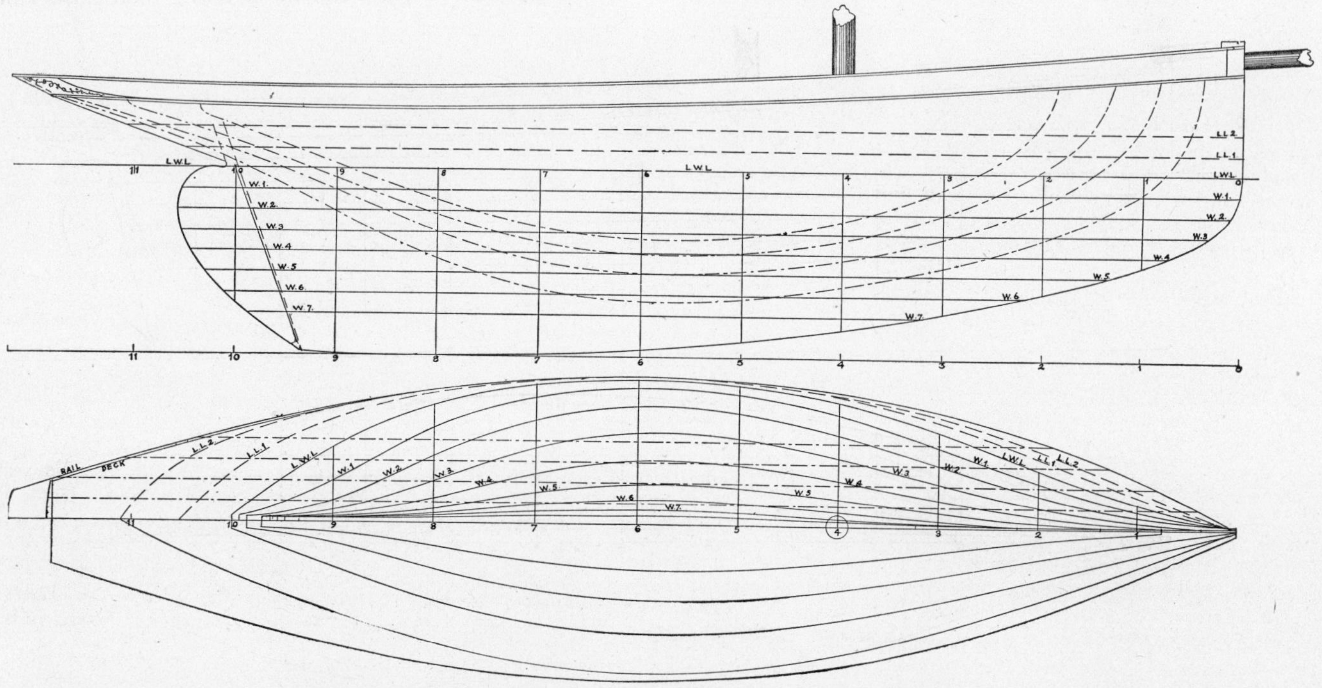

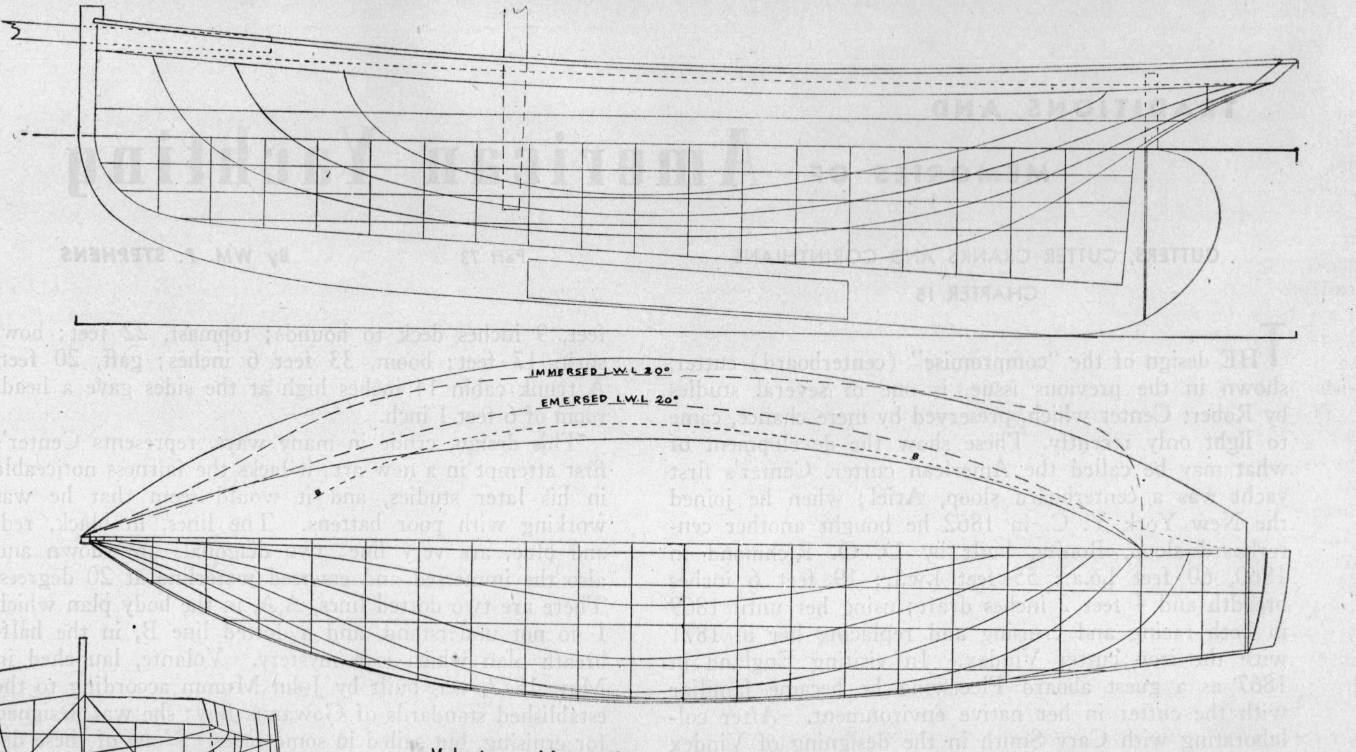

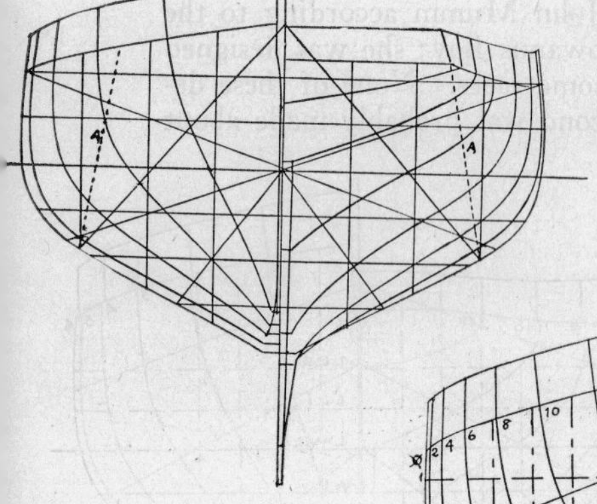

Volante, cruising cutter, designed by Robert Center, 1876

shown, made for Captain S. Grosvenor Porter, is of a little later date and shows a higher degree of workmanship; the form fair, beautiful and powerful; on a waterline of 50 feet, the same as that of Oriva, she had a breadth of 14 feet 4 inches with a draft of 9 feet; the over-all length being 61 feet 2 inches. Unfortunately, she was not built, but the reader who cares to compare her with Bedouin and Oriva can form his own conclusions had she been matched with them. In approaching the problem of a cutter for America, Center had a great advantage over Harvey in spite of the latter's professional skill and long experience in construction. Center was not only familiar with the cutter, but with the sloop in all its forms, and with all conditions of American yachting; he had no inhibitions as to rules and was uninfluenced by the craze for narrow beam.

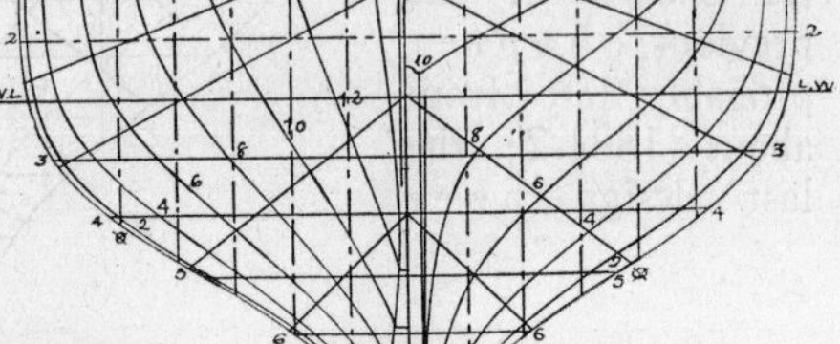

Study for American cutter by Robert Center, about 1880

Early Methods in Designing

When the yacht designer came into his own as the rival of the old builder there was even less system in the arrangement of parts and the lettering than exists among

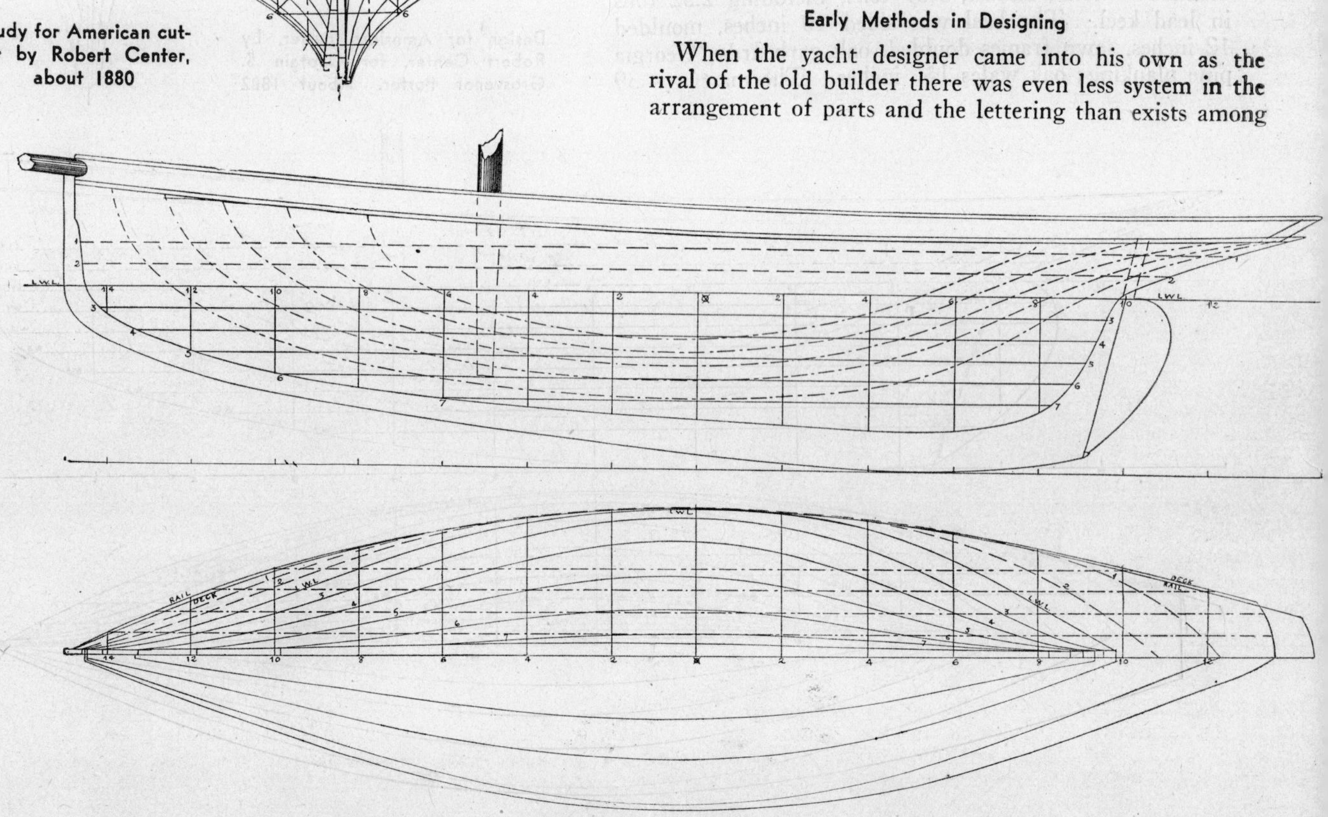

professional designers today. In all of these designs the port side is shown, the bow facing to the left; the half-breadth plan, also of the port side, is immediately above the sheer plan, with the diagonals above its centerline. It is in one sense immaterial whether the bow faces to right or left, but many persons today are interested in the comparison of designs; the majority face to the right, and uniformity in this respect is desirable. Until the designing of a yacht was recognized as a distinct function entirely apart from the construction, all lines were drawn with a view to easy reproduction on the mould loft floor, the stations being located to correspond with the locations of the frames. In the design of Volante the first and last stations are spaced three feet from the ends, all others being spaced two feet.

The practice of the old shipbuilders was, in order to avoid confusion, to mark all frames from the midship section (dead-flat) forward with letters, and those aft with figures. In the second drawing all stations are numbered; forward of the midship section from 2 to 14 and aft from 2 to 10, all uneven numbers being omitted. This would make the frame spacing two feet. The load waterline is marked properly, l.w.l., but the first level line above is numbered 2 and the next above 1, the numbering being continued below the l.w.l., 3, 4, 5, etc.

When, in the early eighties, the work of the drafting room was finally divorced from that of the mould loft and yard, the custom came in of dividing the load waterline into equal parts, 6, 8, or 10; thus facilitating computations but leaving it to the loftsman to mark the frames. Even then no one system was adopted in the arrangement of the three plans; and the lettering and numbering of the various stations, waterline, diagonals and buttock lines were left to the taste of the individual designer. In the designing of Volante no curve of areas was used, as the theory of Colin Archer was just being made public in England, and none is shown in the second design, but in the two later ones the theoretical curve of areas is drawn in red and the actual areas of the design in blue.

The designs of all of these old cutters presents a problem to the draftsman; looking at the midship section in the body plan it will be noticed that the greatest breadth is a little above the water, with a tumble-home to the deck. Here, and for some distance forward and abaft the midship section, are five lines which almost overlay: the load water line, two level-lines, the half-breadth at deck and the half-breadth at the rail. Toward the bow the bulwark flares outboard while toward the transom it tumbles in. The only way in which these lines can be shown is by drawing them very fine and in different colors. In all of Center's drawings the lines are drawn in black, red, blue and green ink, and so fine as to be rarely discernable even through very thin tracing paper; to trace them all distinctly in black for reproduction is impossible. It also happens that the many small set curves needed in the body plan and toward the ends were just a little different from mine of a later date. Such unfairness as is evident in the reproduction of the designs must be laid to these conditions, and not to Center's perfect draftsmanship.

The Day Dawns for the Cutter

TURNING now to the sailing season of 1884, the opening was the annual regatta of the Atlantic Y. C. on June 10. Bay Ridge, on the Long Island shore, was still faithful to the sloop, while the enemy was posted along the Staten Island shore on the west side of the Upper Bay; no cutters started in this race, in a light S.W. wind. The annual regatta of the New York Y. C. on June 12 brought out a fleet of seven schooners, eight sloops, five cutters and the "compromise" Athlon. The building of a cutter was usually well advertised in advance, but the entry list on this day showed one unannounced and unknown, Isis, in Class 2, owed by A. Cass Canfield. A man of independent means, born in Detroit, Michigan in 1853, Canfield graduated from Princeton in 1874 and from the School of Mines of Columbia in 1877. In 1883 he made his home in New York, buying an old centerboard sloop, Rosalie, and joining the Seawanhaka C.Y.C. as a novice in June of that year. He became interested in the cutter controversey and took up the study of designing, his first work being Isis, l.o.a., 62 feet 9 inches; l.w.l., 51 feet, breadth, 13 feet and draft 9 feet, with 16 tons of lead under her keel.

Being unfamiliar with New York yachting he took the design to C. & R. Poillon, who had a well deserved reputation as builders, but of the largest schooner yachts, coasting schooners and pilot boats. Isis was so loaded down with a bulk of heavy oak and yellow pine that the merits of her design were never tested; her form was fair and her bulk well distributed. Joining the New York Y.C. in 1884, Mr. Canfield held a prominent place in yachting for many years; after Priscilla proved a failure as a Cup contestant he bought her and made many improvements, and in 1888 he had built from his own design the 90-foot schooner Sea Fox, an iron vessel which, after a long and successful career in racing followed by years at sea as a cargo carrier, is still sound and seaworthy in her 58th year.

The weather on June 12 was light and fluky, Ileen sailing her first race led the fleet for a time, turning the Sandy Hook Lightship in company with the schooner Montauk only three minutes astern of the leader, Mischief. The race finally failed to finish within the limit of eight hours. The race was re-sailed next day, starting in a drizzle and light wind which freshened until reefs were turned in and topmasts housed or carried away; the Race Committee and guests aboard the big tug Luckenbach had a very unpleasant time in crossing the bar. Six of the Thursday starters were missing, Crusader, Triton, Whileaway, Isis and Espirito; outside the Hook Mischief sheared off two chainplates, Clio parted her bobstay and a bowsprit shroud, Fanita, Athlon and Estelle started for home. Ileen was third at the Lightship, astern of the big schooners Montauk and Grayling; at the finish Fanny's corrected time was 5:47:27; Gracie's 4:49:08; Ileen's 4:52:25 and Hildegard's 4:56:30. Wenonah carried away her port shrouds on the way home. In the second class Eclipse and Fanita withdrew and Oriva beat Vixen by over three minutes.

THERE was a poor turnout next day for the Seawanhaka regatta; the schooners Ray and Clytie, Gracie and Athlon in the first class sloops, Oriva and Isis in the second class, and Petrel and Amazon in the fourth class. Topmasts were housed and reefs turned in for the long beat to the Sandy Hook Lightship; Oriva turned at 3:06, leading Gracie by one minute, but in the long run home the sloop's twenty feet of extra length told and she finished nine minutes ahead of the cutter. Petrel made the course, turning Buoy 5 off the point of the Hook, but Amazon was disabled and withdrew.

The race around Long Island, 240 miles, on the following Monday, proved a mere drift, calms varied by light winds. Fanny covered the course in 43 hours, 37 minutes, 10 seconds, the other times being: Gracie, 44:10:47; Hildegard, 45:53:59; Ileen, 46:14:25; Wenonah, 47:56:02. In the second class Vixen's time was 46:04:59; Athlon, 46:28:27; Oriva, 47:06:32. The time of Grayling, the winning schooner, was identical with that of Fanny.

On the occasion of the Eastern Y.C. regatta on June 27 three cutters, Bedouin, Wenonah and Ileen, visited Marblehead, meeting the old sloops Addie, Huron and Hesper. The wind was E.N.E., all carried club topsails, and the water was smooth. The times for the 21-mile course were: Bedouin, 3:39:07; Wenonah, 3:57:07; Huron, 4:08:21; Ileen, 4:10:25; Hesper, 4:51:38. In the second class Maggie did no better than third, astern of Shadow and Hera. In this race the flagship, Fortuna, sailed over; Commodore Hovey offered the prize, $250, for a race of schooners and a similar one for sloops to be sailed for on a visit of the Eastern Y.C. fleet to New Bedford on July 20; Maggie, Huron, Hesper and Windward sailing down from Marblehead while Bedouin and the sloop Rover came from New York. The course was a triangle of 27 miles; the wind, light at the start, freshened from S.S.W. The corrected times were: Bedouin, 4:28:36; Maggie, 4:33:10; Huron, 4:34:37; Hesper, 4:44:01; Windward, 4:56:32; Rover, 5:24:02. On the following day the fleet ran to Newport in a strong S.E. breeze, but was not timed. Two days later the fleet raced to Newport for another prize offered by Commodore Hovey, Bedouin winning.

THE pre-arranged program for the cruise of the New York Y.C. was completely upset by bad weather, and it was not until August 8 that the racing began with the annual contest for the Goelet cups off Newport, a light weather race over the Block Island course of 45 miles. The starters for the sloop cup were: Gracie, Bedouin, Ileen, Mischief, Wenonah, Whileaway, Athlon, Isis, and Eclipse. The only yachts timed at the second mark were: Bedouin, 7:40:20; Ileen, 7:54:40; Wenonah, 8:21:40; Athlon, 8:53:00. The only times taken at the finish were: Bedouin, 9:33:20; Ileen, 9:49:00; Wenonah, 10:22:12; Athlon, 11:15:25. Only two schooners, Grayling and Varuna, out of 14 starters, were timed. There was a fresh N.E. breeze and some sea next day for the run to Oak Bluffs, the elapsed times being: Bedouin, 6:30:50; Mischief, 7:09:04; Ileen.

7:12:32; Wenonah, 7:40:56; Athlon, 8:14:53. The allowances for the run back to Newport on Monday were based on the performances of the yachts on Saturday, thus penalizing the winners.

Rain on Sunday and on Monday morning was followed by clearing and a light wind astern, the elapsed times being: Mischief, 5:32:16; Athlon, 5:39:11; Vixen, 5:40:53; Ileen, 5:43:33; Wenonah, 5:46:10; Bedouin, 5:56:48; Windward, not timed. The final race was for four cups, $250 each, two classes of schooners and two of sloops, with a $250 cup for the first yacht on corrected time. The wind was light from S.E. and E. and the corrected times were: Mischief, 8:42:10; Bedouin, 8:42:11; Ileen, 8:50:00; Montauk, 8:59:49; Oriva, 9:11:04; Vixen, 9:24:09; Fortuna, 9:33:31; Athlon, 9:38:42; Varuna, 9:55:21; Regina and Hesper, not timed, Dauntless and Social did not finish. Mischief, the old "Iron pot," scored a well deserved victory over the modern Bedouin; Ileen won third place. Of the old sloops only Vixen held on to battle with her chosen enemy, Oriva; while such flyers as Fanny, Gracie, Hildegard and Vision had business elsewhere.

Again Commodore Hovey came forward with two more prizes, $300 for first class sloops and $200 for the second class; the race being sailed on September 6 from Marblehead around Half-Way Rock, Harding's Bell Buoy and Egg Rock, 28 miles. The wind was light SW when it was not a flat calm. The New York fleet was represented by Ileen, Oriva, Valkyr and Isis. The elapsed times were: Ileen, 4:47:31; Oriva, 5:05:21; Huron, 5:08:13; Maggie, 5:18:42; Valkyr, 5:36:41; Shadow, 5:49:53; Isis, 6:17:00. Ileen won in her class and Oriva in hers.

THE season of 1884 ended with two races by the Seawanhaka C.Y.C., the first on October 15 starting from Buoy No. 3 in Gedney's Channel 20 miles out and back for the first and 10 miles for the third class. None of the large sloops cared to enter, though some were still in commission; Oriva had been laid up in the Seawanhaka Basin, but as soon as the races were announced Mr. Lee had her put in commission solely for these races, laying her up again after the second race. With a light NW wind the course was laid down the Jersey beach; before the start Mona carried away the jaws of her gaff, leaving only Bedouin, Athlon, Oriva, Surf and Happy Thought, the latter a husky mongrel cutter from New Haven. Oriva having no class competitor went up into first class at a nominal measurement of 55 feet. The final times showed a victory for Bedouin over Oriva by one second, with Athlon nine minutes later by corrected time. Happy Thought defeated the narrow Surf by less than three minutes.

On the following day the regular club course was sailed, from off Fort Wadsworth down the Ship Channel and out past Sandy Hook, rounding the Sandy Hook Lightship and returning to finish off Buoy 15; the Fourth Class turning Buoy No. 5. The entries included the cutters Bedouin, Oriva, Mona, Daisy, Yolande and Petrel and the sloops Penguin, Annie, Wacondah, Aria, Sara and Stranger, with the semi-cutters Athlon and Happy Thought. This time there was wind and sea enough to cause some of the party on the big committee tug Luckenbach to lose their luncheons while crossing the bar; as the full force of the wind was felt outside the Narrows one and then two reefs were turned in, topmasts came down, and the fleet began to disintegrate. Some like Athlon and Happy Thought, were disabled and others found the weather neither "suitin' nor fittin'" to use a phrase current in those days. The finish was timed: Bedouin, 4:37:31; Oriva, 5:02:43; Mona, 5:11:54; in Class Four, Daisy, 4:54:00; Yolande, 5:07:28. The net result was: started, cutters 5; sloops 8; finished, cutters 5; sloops, none. The cutter Petrel came to the line late and withdrew after starting a hopeless stern chase.

Bedouin's record for the season was 9 starts, 8 firsts and a total of $2,225 in prizes. The largest and most famous of the sloops made comparatively few starts; leaving the field to their rivals. Mr. Lawrence showed a very determined spirit in sailing it out with his thirteen year old Vixen against Oriva. There was comparatively little of what was called "cuttah weather" throughout the season, but Ileen showed some very fast bursts of speeds in light weather. Athlon was not a fast yacht, but Dr. Barron raced her boldly and persistently through the whole season; not only about New York Bay but in the East.

CUTTERS, CUTTER-CRANKS AND CORINTHIANS

(Continued from page 316)

a splice in her forestay and Arrow lost a man from her bowsprit and withdrew. Vixen beat Maggie by 3 minutes 30 seconds corrected time. The fleet again visited Marblehead and on August 10 in a light to moderate breeze Wenonah was timed 4:21:25; Mischief 4:21:26; Gracie 4:28:28; Julia 4:49:51. Julia, the Steers sloop of 1854, had been resurrected and after many changes, from centerboard to keel and back to centerboard, from sloop to schooner and back to sloop, she was looked to as a proof that no advance had been made in yacht designing in thirty years. In the same race Vixen was first, Rover second, while Maggie failed to finish. In the open race of the Beverly Y. C. on August 18 in a variable breeze Wenonah was timed at 5:02:46; Alice (a keel sloop built in 1866) at 5:21:27; Huron at 5:21:29. On August 25 in the Hull Y. C. open race sailed in a good breeze Maggie was timed 2:52:28; Wave (of New York) 3:13:30; Anna 3:24:47; Siren 3:32:28.

On September 29 the Seawanhaka C.Y.C. sailed a race over the Club course from off Fort Wadsworth around Sandy Hook Lightship in a light NE breeze, Oriva turning the Lightship at 4:58:24 followed by Vixen at 5:17:20 and finishing at 7:58:10 with Vixen at 8:36:10. On October 16 the same Club held its fall regatta starting from Buoy 5½ and sailing 20 miles to windward and return in a strong N E wind which fell in the second half. The elapsed time of Bedouin was 5:19:25; Gracie 5:37:00. On October 18 the two sailed a match for a $300 cup and the Bennett cup, over the same course, the S E wind being moderate to fresh. Bedouin was timed at 7:16:12 elapsed, and Gracie at 7:29:25. On October 20 the course was a triangle of 14½ miles, Gracie was sailed by J. F. Tams, Bedouin and Oriva by their owners; the latter being permitted to enter at the lower limit of Class 1, 55 feet. The wind was W N W, light to fresh. In the latter part of the race Bedouin's mainsail stretched badly on the leech. The elapsed times were: Gracie, 3:05:10; Bedouin, 3:07:35; Oriva, 3:43:50.

THIS summary, though necessarily condensed and rough, will give an idea of racing as it was sixty odd years ago; the entries in many classes were much smaller than they should have been; the lack of uniform classes and measurement rules brought together yachts varying greatly in size, making accurate comparisons impossible. It will be noticed that there was a general absence of what was described by the opposition as "cutter weather." Opposed to such hardened veterans as Gracie, Fanny, Hildegard, Vision, Vixen and Active were four or five yachts of experimental type in their first or second season.

Even if over estimated by their proponents, the performances of the cutters were such as to confuse their adversaries, as shown in the following comments by the same writer from *The New York World.*

August 9, 1882

"The race for the cups offered by Mr. Ogden Goelet was sailed here today and was an extremely successful affair. The cutter Oriva has covered herself with glory and has proved conclusively that the cutter model has the most speed. The result of this race will work an entire revolution in American yacht models, the advocates of the broad and shallow centerboards being obliged to admit that the day for such models has passed."

August 25, 1883

"The superiority claimed for vessels of what have been termed the cutter type is a myth. The old-fashioned centerboard craft can more than hold her own. I feel more confident than ever that if ever Marjorie, Samoena or Wendur should come it will be the easiest thing in the world to build a centerboard sloop that shall beat her. The cutter furore is over."

Date Due